DogFriendly.com's

# California and Nevada Dog Travel Guide

by
Len Kain
DogFriendly.com, Inc.

DogFriendly.com's California and Nevada Dog Travel Guide
by Len Kain

DogFriendly.com, Inc.
PO Box 1017 Anchor Point AK 99556
1-833-475-2275
email: email@dogfriendly.com
http://www.dogfriendly.com

PLEASE NOTE
Although the author and publisher have tried to make the information as accurate as possible,  they do not assume, and hereby disclaim, any liability for any loss or damage caused by errors, omissions, misleading information or potential travel problems caused by this book, even if such errors or omissions result from negligence, accident or any other cause.

CHECK AHEAD
We remind you, as always, to call ahead and confirm that the applicable establishment is still "dog-friendly" and that it will accommodate your pet.

DOGS OF ALL SIZES
If your dog is over 75-80 pounds, then please call the individual establishment to make sure that they allow your dog. Please be aware that establishments and local governments may also not allow particular breeds.

OTHER PARTIES DESCRIPTIONS
This book is a work for hire. Some of the descriptions have been provided  to us by our web site advertisers, paid researchers or other parties. Part of the introductions and descriptions were contributed to by former DogFriendly.com president Tara Kain.

ISBN - 9780999546345
Printed in the United States of America

# TABLE OF CONTENTS

## Introduction

DogFriendly.com's guides have helped millions of dog lovers plan vacations and trips with their dogs. The ultimate in Dog Travel Guides, our California and Nevada Dog Travel Guide includes dog-friendly lodging and attractions such as tours, historical places and more. Also included are restaurants with outdoor patio dining where your dog is welcome, national parks, information about the airlines, subways, buses and other transportation systems that permit dogs and emergency veterinarians just in case. The guide gives detailed pet policies for most places, including how many dogs may be allowed per room, weight limits, fees and other useful information. In many cases, toll-free numbers and websites are given. Also very importantly, our lodging guide focuses on those places that allow dogs of all sizes and do not restrict dogs to smoking rooms only. Not included in this guide are places that allow, for example, only dogs up to ten pounds or require that your dog be carried or in a carrier while on the premises. Also, we do not think that places that require dog owners to stay in smoking rooms are dog-friendly and we do not include them. Accommodations in this book have been called by DogFriendly.com to verify pet policies although these policies do change often. Thank you for selecting our pet travel guide and we hope you spend less time researching and more time actually going places with your dog. Enjoy your dog-friendly travels!

## About Author Len Kain

Len Kain began traveling with his dog when he was young. His family traveled with a camping trailer and brought along their standard poodle, Ricky. On trips, he found places and attractions that welcomed his best friend. When Len grew up and got his own dog, he continued the tradition of bringing his dog on trips with him. Len and his family have traveled over 200,000 miles across the country on road trips. Today he continues to travel and find fun and exciting dog-friendly places.

Currently, Len serves as DogFriendly.com's President. Len has been quoted numerous times in print, on radio and television about issues relating to traveling with dogs. Prior to joining DogFriendly.com Len served in various executive and management positions in several Silicon Valley and Internet Companies. Len holds a Bachelor of Engineering degree from Stevens Tech in New Jersey, a Master of Science degree from Stanford University and an MBA from the University of Phoenix. Len resides in Anchor Point, Alaska.

## Your Comments and Feedback

We value and appreciate your feedback and comments. If you want to recommend a dog-friendly place or establishment, let us know. If you find a place that is no longer dog-friendly, allows small dogs only or allows dogs in smoking rooms only, please let us know. You can contact us using the following information.

Mailing Address and Contact Information:
DogFriendly.com, Inc.
PO Box 1017 Anchor Point, AK 99556 USA
Toll free phone: 1-833-475-2275
email: email@ dogfriendly.com
http://www.dogfriendly.com

# How To Use This Guide

## General Guidelines

1. Please only travel with a well-behaved dog that is comfortable around other people and especially children. Dogs should also be potty trained and not bark excessively.

2. Always keep your dog leashed unless management specifically tells you otherwise.

3. Establishments listed in this book should allow well-behaved dogs of ALL sizes (at least up to 75 pounds) and in non-smoking rooms. If your dog is over 75-80 pounds, then please call the individual establishment to make sure they will allow your dog. We have listed some establishments which only allow dogs up to 50 pounds, but we try our best to make a note in the comments about the restrictions. All restaurants and attractions we list should allow dogs of all sizes.

4. Accommodations listed do not allow dogs to be left alone in the room unless specified by hotel management. If the establishment does not allow pets to be left alone, try hiring a local pet sitter to watch your dog in the room.

5. All restaurants listed as dog-friendly refer to outdoor seating only. While dogs are not permitted to sit in a chair at a restaurant's outdoor dining table, they should be allowed to sit or lay next to your table. We do not list outdoor restaurants that require your dog to be tied outside of a fenced area (with you at the dining table on one side and your dog on the other side of the fence). In our opinion, those are not truly dog-friendly restaurants. Restaurants listed may have seasonal outdoor seating.

6. Pet policies and management change often, especially within the lodging and restaurant industries. Please always call ahead to make sure an establishment still exists and is still dog-friendly.

## Preparation for a Road Trip

### A Month Before

If you don't already have one, get a pet identification tag for your dog. It should have your dog's name, your name and phone number. Consider using a cell phone number, a home number and, if possible, the number of where you will be staying.

Get a first aid kit for your dog. It comes in very handy if you need to remove any ticks. The kits are usually available at a pet store, a veterinary office or on the Internet.

If you do not already have a dog harness for riding the car, consider purchasing one for your dog's and your own safety. A loose dog in the car can fly into the windshield, out of the car, or into you and injure you or cause you to lose control of the car. Dog harnesses are usually sold at pet stores or on the Internet.

Make a trip to the vet if necessary for the following:

- A current rabies tag for your dog's collar. Also get paperwork with proof of the rabies vaccine.
- Dogs can possibly get heartworm from mosquitoes in the mountains, rural areas or on hikes. Research or talk to your vet and ask him or her if the area you are traveling to has a high risk of heartworm disease. The vet may suggest placing your dog on a monthly heartworm preventative medicine.
- Consider using some type of flea preventative for your dog, preferably a natural remedy. This is out of courtesy for the dog-friendly hotels plus for the comfort of your pooch.
- Make sure your dog is in good health.

### Several Days Before

Make sure you have enough dog food for the duration of the trip.

If your dog is on any medication, remember to bring it along.

Some dog owners will also purchase bottled water for the trip, because some dogs can get sick from drinking water they are not used to. Talk to your vet for more information.

### The Day Before

Do not forget to review DogFriendly.com's Etiquette for the Traveling Dog!

### Road Trip Day

Remember to pack all of your dog's necessities: food, water, dog dishes, leash, snacks and goodies, several favorite toys, brush, towels for dirty paws, plastic bags for cleaning up after your dog, doggie first aid kit, possibly dog booties if you are venturing to an especially cold or hot region, and bring any medicine your dog might be taking.

Before you head out, put on that doggie seat belt harness.

*On The Road*

Keep it cool and well ventilated in the car for your dog.

Stop at least every 2-3 hours so your dog can relieve him or herself. Also offer him or her water during the stops.

Never leave your pet alone in a parked car - even in the shade with the window cracked open. According to the Los Angeles SPCA, on a hot day, a car can heat up to 160 degrees in minutes, potentially causing your pet (or child) heat stroke, brain damage, and even death.

If your dog needs medical attention during your trip, check the yellow pages phone book in the area and look under Veterinarians. If you do not see an emergency vet listed, call any local vet even   during the evening hours and they can usually inform you of the closest emergency vet.

## Etiquette for the Traveling Dog

So you have found the perfect getaway spot that allows dogs, but maybe you have never traveled with your dog. Or maybe you are a seasoned dog traveler. But do you know all of your doggie etiquette? Basic courtesy rules, like your dog should be leashed unless a place specifically allows your dog to be leash-free. And do you ask for a paper bowl or cup for your thirsty pooch at an outdoor restaurant instead of letting him or her drink from your water glass?

There are many do's and don'ts when traveling with your best friend. We encourage all dog owners to follow a basic code of doggie etiquette, so places will continue to allow and welcome our best friends. Unfortunately all it takes is one bad experience for an establishment to stop allowing dogs. Let's all try to be on our best behavior to keep and, heck, even encourage new places to allow our pooches.

*Everywhere...*

- Well-Behaved Dogs. Only travel or go around town with a well-behaved dog that is friendly to people and especially children. If your dog is not comfortable around other people, you might consider taking your dog to obedience classes or hiring a professional trainer. Your well-behaved dog should also be potty trained and not bark excessively in a hotel or other lodging room. We believe that dogs should be kept on leash. If a dog is on leash, he or she is easier to bring under control. Also, many establishments require that dogs be on leash and many people around you will feel more comfortable as well. And last, please never leave your dog alone in a hotel or other lodging room unless you have the approval from the establishment's management.

- Leashed Dogs. Please always keep your dog leashed, unless management specifically states otherwise. Most establishments (including lodging, outdoor restaurants, attractions, parks, beaches, stores and festivals) require that your dog be on leash. Plus most cities and counties have an official leash law that requires pets to be leashed at all times when not on your property. Keeping your dog on leash will also prevent any unwanted contact with other people that are afraid of dogs, people that do not appreciate strange dogs coming up to them, and even other dog owners who have a leashed dog. Even when on leash, do not let your pooch visit with other people or dogs unless welcomed. Keeping dogs on leash will also protect  them from running into traffic, running away, or getting injured by wildlife or other dogs. Even the most well-behaved and trained dogs can be startled by something, especially in a new environment.

- Be Considerate. Always clean up after your dog. Pet stores sell pooper scooper bags. You can also buy sandwich bags from your local grocery store. They work quite well and are cheap!

*At Hotels or Other Types of Lodging...*

- Unless it is obvious, ask the hotel clerk if dogs are allowed in the hotel lobby. Also, because of health codes, dogs are usually not allowed into a lobby area while it is being used for serving food like continental breakfast. Dogs may be allowed into the area once there is no food being served, but check with management first.

- Never leave your dog alone in the hotel room without the permission of management. The number one reason hotel management does not allow dogs is because some people leave them in the room alone. Some dogs, no matter how well-trained, can cause damage, bark continuously or scare the housekeepers. Unless the hotel management allows it, please make sure your dog is never left alone in the room. If you need to leave your dog in the room, consider hiring a local pet sitter.

- While you are in the room with your dog, place the Do Not Disturb sign on the door or keep the deadbolt locked. Many housekeepers have been surprised or scared by dogs when entering a room.

- In general, do not let your pet on the bed or chairs, especially if your dog sheds easily and might leave pet hair on the furniture. Some very pet-friendly accommodations will actually give you a sheet to lay over the bed so your pet can join you. If your pet cannot resist coming hopping onto the furniture with you, bring your own sheet.

- When your dog needs to go to the bathroom, take him or her away from the hotel rooms and the bushes located right next to the rooms. Try to find some dirt or bushes near the parking lot. Some hotels have a designated pet walk area.

*At Outdoor Restaurants...*

- Tie your dog to your chair, not the table (unless the table is secured to the ground). If your dog decides to get up and move away from the table, he or she will not take the entire table.

- If you want to give your dog some water, please ask the waiter/waitress to bring a paper cup or bowl of water for your dog. Do not use your own water glass. Many restaurants and even other guests frown upon this.

- Your pooch should lay or sit next to your table. At restaurants, dogs are not allowed to sit on the chairs or tables, or eat off the tables. This type of activity could make a restaurant owner or manager ban dogs. And do not let your pooch beg from other customers. Unfortunately, not everyone loves dogs!

- About Restaurant Laws regarding dogs at restaurants
State health codes in the United States prohibit all animals except for service animals inside indoor sections of restaurants. In recent years some health departments have begun banning dogs from some outdoor restaurant areas. It is complicated to determine where dogs are and are not allowed outdoors because most State laws are vague. They state something such as "Animals are not allowed on the premises of a food establishment". These laws also define animals to include "birds, vermin and insects" which are always present at outdoor restaurants. Various health departments have various interpretations of where the premises start and stop. Some allow dogs at outdoor areas where food is served, some allow dogs at outdoor areas only where you bring your own food to the table. Some will allow special pet-friendly areas or will allow dogs on the outside of the outer most tables. Any city or county can issue a variance to State law if it wants to allow dogs into outdoor (or indoor) restaurants. This can be done in two ways, directly by the local health department or through a vote of the local government. If a restaurant that you are visiting with your dog cites some curious requirement it is probably due to the health code. Please also understand that in all places the owner of a restaurant has the choice to not allow dogs with the exception of service dogs. Nationally, Austin, Dallas, Orlando, Chicago, Denver and Alexandria forced law changes to allow dogs at outdoor restaurants when their health departments went too far in banning dogs from outdoor seats. Dogs are now allowed in outdoor areas in these cities through variances (or in Orlando's case) changing Florida state law. For up to date information please see http://www.dogfriendly.com/dining . The laws are in a state of flux at the moment so please understand that they may change.

*At Retail Stores...*

- Keep a close eye on your dog and make sure he or she does not go to the bathroom in the store. Store owners that allow dogs inside assume that responsible dog owners will be entering their store. Before entering a dog-friendly store, visit your local pet store first. They are by far the most forgiving. If your dog does not go to the bathroom there, then you are off to a great start! If your dog does make a mistake in any store, clean it up. Ask the store clerk for paper towels or something similar so you can clean up any mess.

- In most states dogs are allowed in stores, shops and other private buildings with the exception of grocery stores and restaurants. The decision to allow dogs is the business owner's and you can always ask if you may bring your dog inside. Also in most states packaged foods (bottled sodas, waters, bags of cookies or boxes of snacks) does not cause a store to be classified as a grocery. Even pet stores do sell these items . In many states, drinks such as coffee, tea and water are also allowed. You can order food from a restaurant to a pet-friendly establishment (so long as the establishment is not also the restaurant with the kitchen) in most areas.


*At Festivals and Outdoor Events...*

Make sure your dog has relieved himself or herself before entering a festival or event area. The number one reason that most festival coordinators do not allow dogs is because some dogs go to the bathroom on a vendor's booth or in areas where people might sit.

## Breed Specific Laws and the Effect of These Laws on Travel With Dogs

There has been a trend in cities, counties, states and provinces towards what is known as Breed-Specific Laws (BSL) in which a municipality bans or restricts the freedoms of dog owners with specific breeds of dogs. These laws vary from place to place and are effecting a greater number of dog owners every year. Most people may think that these laws effect only the "Pit Bull" but this is not always the case. Although the majority of dogs effected are pit-bulls other breeds of dogs as well as mixed breeds that include targeted breeds are also named in the various laws in North America. These laws range from registration requirements and leash or muzzle requirements to extreme laws in which the breed is banned from the municipality outright. Some places may even be permitted to confiscate a visitor's dog who unknowingly enters the region with a banned breed.

As of August 29, 2005 the province of Ontario, Canada (including Toronto, Niagara Falls, and Ottawa) passed a very broad breed-specific law banning Pit Bulls and "similar" dogs from the province. The law allows for confiscation of visiting dogs as well as dogs living in Ontario. It is extremely important that people visiting Ontario make sure that they are able to prove that their dog is not a Pit Bull with other documentation. Various cities throughout the U.S. and Canada have muzzle requirements for Pit Bulls and other restrictions on targeted breeds as well. Breed-specific laws do get repealed as well. In October, 2005 the city of Vancouver, BC removed its requirement that Pit Bulls be muzzled in public and now only requires dogs with a known history of aggressiveness to be muzzled.

The breed specific laws usually effect pit bull type dogs but are often vaguely written and may also effect mixed breed dogs that resemble the targeted breeds. These laws are always changing and can be passed by cities, counties and even states and provinces. We recommend that travelers with dogs check into whether they are effected by such laws. You may check www.DogFriendly.com/bsl for links to further information on BSL.

DogFriendly.com does not support breed-specific laws. Most people who take their dogs out in public are responsible and those that choose to train a dog to be viscous will simply choose another breed, causing other breeds to be banned or regulated in the future.

## Customs Information for Traveling Between the United States and Canada

If you will be traveling between the United States and Canada, identification for Customs and Immigration is required. U.S. and Canadian citizens traveling across the border need the following:

*People*

- A passport or passport card is now required to move between the U.S. and Canada. Children also need a passport of their own now.

*Dogs*

- Dogs must be free of evidence of diseases communicable to humans when possibly examined at the port of entry.

- Valid rabies vaccination certificate (including an expiration date usually up to 3 years from the actual vaccine date and a veterinarian's signature). If no expiration date is specified on the certificate, then the certificate is acceptable if the date of the vaccination is not more than 12 months before the date of arrival. The certificate must show that the dog had the rabies vaccine at least 30 days prior to entry.

- Young puppies must be confined at a place of the owner's choosing until they are three months old, then they must be vaccinated. They must remain in confinement for 30 days after the vaccination.

## Chain Hotel Websites

| | | |
|---|---|---|
| Best Western: bestwestern.com | Candlewood Suites: ichotelsgroup.com | Clarion: choicehotels.com |
| Comfort Inn: choicehotels.com | Days Inn: daysinn.com | Drury Inn: druryhotels.com |
| Extended Stay: extendedstayhotels.com | Hilton: hilton.com | Holiday Inn: ichotelsgroup.com |
| Howard Johnson: hojo.com | Kimpton Group: kimptonhotels.com | La Quinta: lq.com |
| Loews Hotels: loewshotels.com | Marriott: marriott.com | Motel 6: motel6.com |
| Quality Inn: www.choicehotels.com | Red Roof Inn: redroof.com | Residence Inn: residenceinn.com |
| Sheraton: starwoodhotels.com | Sleep Inn: choicehotels.com | Staybridge Suites: ichotelsgroup.com |
| Super 8: super8.com | Townplace Suites: towneplaceSuites.com | Westin: starwoodhotels.com |

## Traveling with a Dog By Air

Many commercial airlines allow dogs to be transported with the traveling public. Small dogs, usually no more than 15 to 20 pounds and with shorter legs, may travel in a carrier in the cabin with you. They must usually be kept under the seat. Any larger dogs must travel in a kennel in the cargo hold. It can be difficult for dogs to travel in the cargo hold of airplanes. Most airlines restrict cargo hold pet transportation during very hot and cold periods. Most require that you notify them when making reservations about the pet as they limit the number of pets allowed on each plane and the size of the carriers may vary depending on what type of plane is being used. There are no commercial airlines that we are aware of today that will allow dogs larger than those that fit in a carrier under a seat to fly in the cabin. Service animals are allowed in the cabin and are harnessed during takeoff and landing. The FAA is now tracking pet injury and death information from airline cargo section pet travel. Their monthly reports are at the website airconsumer.ost.dot.gov/reports. In the past we have been more concerned with larger dogs in the cargo hold of airplanes. However, with the newer jets, it is becoming safer and more common, although incidents can happen.

*Charters and Shared Charters:*

A charter airline flight is a flight reserved by an individual, a company or a small party or club to transport in smaller jets or other small aircraft their group on a schedule and route selected by them. This option is always available to people traveling with dogs but is very expensive. A charter is a flight reserved by you. A shared charter is when you "hitch" a ride on a charter set up by another party. This is still quite expensive, but less so than a solo charter. Many charter aircraft will allow your dog of all sizes on board.

*Commercial Airlines:*

| Airline | Cabin – Small Dogs Allowed | Cargo – Dogs Allowed | Phone | Fees (US) (each way) | General Information (For more updated information see: dogfriendly.com/airlines |
|---|---|---|---|---|---|
| Air Canada | Yes | Yes | 888-247-2262 (US) | $50 to $60 each way (cabin) - $105 to $120 each way (cargo) - North America more elsewhere | Pets are allowed on domestic Canadian/North American flights; Health Cert rqd plus some shots |
| Alaska Air | Yes | Yes | 800-252-7522 | $100 each way (cabin), $100 each way (cargo) | Pets not allowed as Chked Bags during winter months; Health Cert within 30 days; |
| American | Yes | Yes | 800-433-7300 | $125 each way (cabin), $200 each way (cargo) | Dogs, including the kennel, can weigh no more than 100 pounds for the cargo area. Dogs are not allowed in the cabin for International flights. |
| Delta | Yes | Yes | 800-221-1212 | $125 each way (cabin), $200 each way domestic $ more each way Int'l (cargo) | Only a limited # of pets allowed per flight, so check ahead. There is no cert required for domestic flights. |
| Frontier | Yes | No | 800-432-1359 | $75 each way small/ medium kennels, | Dogs may not be transported in cargo. |
| Jet Blue | Yes | No | 800-538-2583 | $100 each way (cabin only) | 4 pets allowed per flight; 20 lbs or less (with kennel) in cabin |
| Southwest | Yes | No | 800-IFLY-SWA | $95 each way (cabin only) | Dogs in cabin must fit in a carrier under the seat. Reservations with pets must be made by phone. |
| United | Yes | Yes | 800-241-6522 | $125 each way (cabin), $169 to $210 each way (cargo) | 800-825-3788 to ship unaccompanied pets; Pets must be booked within 7 days of flight; 30 day health certificate; Short nosed dogs not allowed in summer |
| Virgin America | Yes | No | 877-359-8474 | $100 each way | Pets can only be booked in the Main Cabin (Coach) and can not weigh over 20 pounds. |

## Traveling with a Pet On Amtrak

Dogs and cats up to 20 pounds are now allowed to travel with you on certain United States Amtrak routes. There are certain restrictions, however. Only certain train routes allow pets. Pet travel is restricted to routes under 7 hours long. There is a maximum of five pets per train and it is first come first serve with regard to buying pet tickets. So you should make your reservation as soon as possible. A passenger may only take one pet. There is a $25 pet fee for each travel segment. In the event of a service disruption, Amtrak will try to make accommodations at a pet-friendly hotel but will not guarantee that they can. The dog must remain in a pet carrier at all times on the train. The pet carrier counts as one of your pieces of baggage allowed.

At check-in at the station you must arrive 30 minutes before departure to allow the staff to verify eligibility of your pet. They will verify the size and weight, see that the pet is not distruptive such as non-stop barking or growling and have you sign a pet document. The pet must be at least 8 weeks old. You will need to certify that your pet is up to date on vaccinations.

Pets may not be shipped on Amtrak or checked as baggage. They must travel with a person.

Here are the routes that pets are allowed on at this time. You should check at www.amtrak.com/pets for updates as your trip approaches.

Northeast Routes:
Acela Express (Weekends and Holidays Only), Adirondack (excluding Canada), Downeaster, Empire Service, Ethan Allen Express, Maple Leaf (excluding Canada), Northeast Regional, Vermonter

Eastern Routes:
Capitol Limited, Carolinian, Cardinal, Crescent, Lake Shore Limited, Piedmont, Palmetto, Silver Star, Silver Meteor

Midwest Routes:
California Zephyr, Capitol Limited, Cardinal, City of New Orleans, Empire Builder, Heartland Flyer, Hiawatha, Hossier State, Carl Sandburg, Illinois Zephyr, Illini, Saluki, Pere Marquette, Wolverine, Blue Water, Lake Shore Limited, Missouri River Runner, Southwest Chief, Texas Eagle

Western Routes:
Amtrak Cascades (excluding Canada), California Zephyr, Coast Starlight, Southwest Chief, Sunset Limited, Texas Eagle

To make reservations call 1-800-USA-RAIL or visit a staffed station. At this time, you cannot make your pet reservations online. Service animals are allowed on all trains and routes for no fee.


VIA Rail in Canada

In Canada, dogs of all sizes are allowed to be taken as baggage on the VIA trains that serve the entire country. They are not allowed in passenger cars regardless of their size. So the train must offer baggage service for you to take your dog. Since the baggage cars are not air-conditioned pets are not allowed between June 1 and September 22. The fee for taking a dog in a carrier is between $30 and $50.

You are allowed to take your pet on longer train routes in Canada – including cross country. It will be your responsibility to take your pet out at station stops for a quick bathroom break and to feed and give water to your pet. You can access the pet at the stations and many of the stops are 5 – 15 minutes long allowing you time for this. It appears that you should have no more than about 5 hours between stops on normal schedules.

For reservations and to check if a route allows pets call VIA Rail at 888-842-7245. For more online information see www.viarail.ca/en/travel-info/baggage/travelling-with-pets


Intercity Buses

Unfortunately, Greyhound and all intercity bus routes and lines in the United States do not allow any pets of any size. Only service dogs are allowed. This policy has been in place for years.

# Special Considerations for California and Nevada with your Dogs

Each region of the country and the world has different considerations that should be considered with regards to traveling with your dog. California and Nevada is often very hot in the summer and has long stretches of highway with minimal stops. There is desert that is quite hot, fleas and parasites to consider and rattlesnakes live throughout the state.

Heat

The Southwest can be hotter than 110 degrees during summer months for days at a time. Dogs can dehydrate quickly and they perspire only through their tongues. Their heavy fur coats also mean that they will not be able to handle heat as well as humans. Dogs should not go on long hikes during these periods. They must have water with them and snacks. And we recommend dog boots for hot temperatures so that the dog does not burn their paws – which is easy for them to do. If you groom your dog it is best that for summer in the Southwest that their hair is kept short.

Parasites

The Southwest, because of its heat and mild winters, has a lot of ticks, fleas, and parasitic worms that affect dogs. Dogs should be up to date on their heartworm and other parasite medications. If your dog gets unexpected diarrhea that can be an indication of parasites.

Rattlesnakes

Rattlesnakes are found all over the region and can be a threat to you and your dog. Rattlesnakes will usually hide in a cool place such as under a rock when temperatures are real high. They will hibernate when temperatures are low. When temperatures are in the 50s through 70s and at night they are most active. You will probably not have trouble with rattlesnakes if your dog is kept leashed. However, if your loose dog approaches rattlesnakes in an aggressive manner the snake will strike.

Snow

The mountains of California get significant snow during the Winter months. Dogs can get frostbite on their paws and need to stay out in the snow for limited time only. In addition, dogs can wear boots on their paws.

Travel to and from Mexico

There are certain requirements to bring your dog into Mexico from the United States and to return from Mexico to the United States.

Going to Mexico from the U.S.

Visitors are allowed to bring up to 2 dogs into the country. A Health Certificate, issued not more than 72 hours before the animal enters Mexico, must be obtained (in duplicate) by a licensed veterinarian or other official authority with the name, address of pet's owner, the animal's stats (breed, sex, age), and confirmation of a clean bill of health. Proof of inoculations against rabies and distemper at least 15 days before arriving in Mexico is also required.

Exit permits from Mexico for pets may also be required and can be obtained via SAGAPRA at: http://www.sagarpa.gob.mx/english/Pages/Introduction.aspx; this is a free service.

To return to the U.S. with your dog you should have a Health Certificate no more than 10 days old and proof of vaccination.

Official U.S. Government information on entry/exit of pets to Mexico can be found at: https://www.aphis.usda.gov/aphis/pet-travel/by-country/pettravel-mexico

Chapter 1

# Top Dog-Friendly Destinations in California and Nevada

# California

## Anaheim/Disneyland

Anaheim is to the West Coast what Orlando is to the East Coast. The vacation hub known for the major theme parks is, however, really part of Los Angeles as there is no separation between the cities 40 miles apart. If there were no signs you would not be able to tell where one city begins and another ends. Anaheim is in Orange County with a population of 3 million people. Dogs are not allowed in the Anaheim theme parks but they do have day kennels to board dogs in while you attend. More dog-friendly destinations are nearby Orange County cities Huntington Beach and Newport Beach.

Many people go to Anaheim to visit Disneyland. While dogs are not allowed into Disneyland, except for service dogs, there is an air-conditioned and supervised kennel at the park. It is located outside of the main entrance and dogs must be picked up at the end of the day. There are no overnight stays. There are many dog-friendly hotels in the area around Disneyland. The Sheraton Anaheim Hotel is designed like a castle and welcomes dogs to stay with you in the rooms. There are 13 acres of gardens at the hotel. The Sheraton Park Hotel allows dogs up to around 40 pounds. The Anaheim Marriott Suites (1 mile from Disneyland),the La Quinta Anaheim near Disneyland and the Residence Inn Anaheim Maingate all allow dogs as well. If you want to stay closer to the beach communities then the Hilton Orange County in Costa Mesa or the La Quinta Orange County at John Wayne Airport are dog-friendly choices. If you want to camp in a motorhome or travel trailer then the Canyon RV Park on the Santa Ana River is 14 miles from Disneyland and the Newport Dunes RV Park is a waterfront resort campground minutes from the dog-friendly Fashion Island Mall.

The Park Bench Cafe Huntington Beach, CA

Dog-friendly restaurants abound in Southern California. There are even a few restaurants that have a special dog menu just for your pup. The Lazy Dog Cafe is a chain of restaurants in Southern California that are famously dog-friendly. This Sports Bar chain has TVs on the patio and special dog menus and water bowls. There are two locations near Anaheim at 1623 West Katella Avenue in neighboring Orange and at 16310 Beach Blvd in Westminster. In Huntington Beach there is the original restaurant with dog menus probably in the country, the

Park Bench Cafe. This breakfast and lunch restaurant is located in Huntington Central Park and has a multitude of outdoor tables and a big doggie menu. Many of the Johnny Rockets hamburger restaurants in the area are also dog-friendly and some have dog menus also. There are a few dog-friendly restaurants for all budgets and tastes at the dog-friendly Fashion Island Mall in Newport Beach. This upscale open-air mall is very dog-friendly and has many dog-friendly stores and patio restaurants to choose from. See DogFriendly.com's directory for more choices in dog-friendly dining near Anaheim and in the beach areas.

Huntington Beach is very dog-friendly. For dog-friendly dining there is the original doggy menu, the Park Bench Cafe. Huntington Dog Beach is one of the premier dog beaches in America. This one mile stretch of off-leash dog beach is a great beach for you to take your dog to. Newport and Balboa Beaches in Newport Beach and Corona Del Mar State Beach in Corona Del Mar allow leashed dogs only before 9 am and after 5 pm. These beaches are located along Balboa Blvd. There are also a number of off-leash and fenced dog parks in the area.

Huntington Dog Beach

Want to take your dog with you on a boat tour of Newport Beach? The Fun Zone Boat Tours at 6000 Edgewater Place offers a 1 hour harbor tour of the homes of the rich and famous and two hour whale watching tours. They welcome your well-behaved, leashed dog. You can also rent power boats at Boat Rentals of America's boat rental locations in Southern California.

Nearby places to visit with your dog while in the Anaheim area include San Diego, Los Angeles, Temecula and Big Bear Lake.

## Big Bear Lake

Big Bear Lake sits in the mountains only a two hour drive from Los Angeles. But it could be a world away. A mountain resort with heavy winter snow and summer hiking and camping Big Bear is a year round resort area. The actual population of Big Bear is 5,000 people, however, over 100,000 may be here on some weekends per year. Big Bear Lake is located at 6,752 foot elevation which explains it winter snow and mild summers. Big Bear City is the center of commerce on Big Bear Lake but many of the resorts and activities are surrounding the lake at other areas. The Big Bear area is quite dog-friendly and can make for a great dog-friendly escape from Los Angeles.

Most of the dog-friendly lodging in the Big Bear area consists of small hotels, B&Bs and vacation rentals. Pine Knot Guest Ranch offers you and your pet 2 acres of off-leash area and a five minute walk to the village. They also offer in-room Jacuzzis and fireplaces in their cabins. Also pet-friendly are the Best Western Plus Big Bear Chateau, the Robin Hood Resort, Eagle's Nest Lodge and Majestic Moose Lodge. Pet-friendly vacation rentals can be arranged through Gold Rush Resort Rentals, Big Bear Cabins California and Access Big Bear Cabin Rentals. There are also other dog-friendly choices in the area. If you are camping in Big Bear in an RV, motorhome or travel trailer then you can stay with your dog at the Big Bear Shores RV Resort & Yacht Club or Holloway's RV Park. For dry camping with small tent campers, tents or backpacking the National Forests in the area have many campgrounds. Hanna Flat Campground, Serrano Campground and Pineknot Campground are some of these. Dogs are allowed in most parts of the National Forests in the area and in the camping areas.

For Winter cross-country skiing, snowshoeing or skijoring with your dog you can rent showshoes, skiing equipment or other items at Big Bear Bikes/Snowshoes at 41810 Big Bear Blvd (909-866-2224). You can cross country ski in many areas of the National Forests but for a well maintained trail you can visit the Forest Trail off Mill Creek Road. The rental shop can give you other suggestions for trails. For Summer activities you can rent boats which allow your dog to join you at Pine Knot Landing at 400 Pine Knot Avenue. This dog-friendly company rents pontoon boats and other boats. They have a paddleboat tour that will allow well-behaved leashed dogs or carried dogs if they are not too crowded and it is not a busy holiday weekend. There are other dog-friendly boat rentals at Big Bear Marina and Pleasure Point Landing. For electric boat tours of the lake try Captain John's Fawn Harbor and Marina at 39368 North Shore Drive which welcomes well-behaved, leashed dogs on its tours. Dogs are allowed on the Bear Valley Stage Lines horse drawn carriages at the village. Want to visit a ghost town? Belleville Ghost Town on Holcomb Valley Road is at the end of a moderate 2 mile long dirt road. Dogs are welcome to explore. As with all hiking in the area, be aware that there are many rattlesnakes around. For that reason, please keep dogs leashed at all times.

When in Big Bear many of the restaurants have seasonal patio seating in the summer that welcome leashed dogs. BLT's Restaurant at 41799 Big Bear Blvd offers a doggy menu for you dog where they can choose a hamburger patty, chicken fingers or more. Also with dog-friendly patios are Big Bear Mountain Brewery and Village Pizza. For a list of seasonal dog-friendly restaurants see DogFriendly.com's directory.

Some good dog-friendly hikes in the area include the Woodland Trail and Nature Walk, Hanna Flat Trail and Alpine Pedal Path. The Woodland Trail is a 1.5 mile self-guided nature hike. The Hanna Flat Trail is 9 mile moderate rated trail in the San Bernardino National Forest. The Alpine Pedal Path is a paved 4.5 mile round trip along the lake. There are many other dog-friendly hiking trails in the forests of the area. Rangers can give you more information. Please be aware of rattlesnakes during the summer months. In the Winter, snowshoeing, cross country skiing and skijoring can be done on most of the forest trails.

Nearby Big Bear Lake is Lake Arrowhead which is also a mountain resort with dog-friendly activities and lodging.

Woodland Trail and Nature Walk

# Carmel

You can be certain of few things always being true. One of those things is that Carmel California will rank at or very near the top of any national pet-friendly city list. It has been in DogFriendly.com's Top 3 resort cities to visit with a dog every year, and has held the number one spot about half the time. Carmel is made for a vacation with a dog. It is not too hot, with moderate summertime temperatures and the ocean fog cooling things off. It is not too cold in winter, so you can do the outdoor activities that make up much of a great dog-friendly vacation. But if weather was the only factor, there could be lots of other places like Carmel. There are not.

If you are looking for a big four star resort hotel, Carmel is not the place. There are some in neighboring Monterey which is an easy drive to Carmel, but the treasure of Carmel is the small inns and B&Bs, many of which are extremely dog-friendly. The town is small, and easy to walk. You will need your car for some of the attractions, however. You will want your car for the famous Seventeen Mile Drive which takes you to and past the world renowned Pebble Beach Golf Course and some of the most beautiful coastline anywhere. You may also want to take short car excursions to the beautiful Carmel Valley, Big Sur and the relatively larger city of Monterey which is also dog-friendly to the north.

In town, you can park your car at your B&B and do most of your touring, shopping and, of course, dining by foot. Perhaps the biggest jewel for the traveler with a dog in Carmel is the Carmel City Beach. This is the main city beach and it allows dogs, and in fact, it allows dogs off-leash. Usually, you need to choose the best beach for people or the best beach for dogs. Not in Carmel as they are one and the same. For other attractions, take in a walking tour of town, visit the doggy happy hour at Cypress Inn, or shop to your heart's content. Many stores in town will welcome your leashed dogs, and you can shop in the Carmel Plaza, Crossroads Shopping Center or the Carmel Village Shopping Area.

Carmel City Beach

When it comes to dining with your dog, Carmel really shines. For a doggy menu along with a "people menu" try the Forge in the Forest. It's like sitting in a garden. One of our favorite restaurants in Carmel is PortaBella which will bring your dog water in a champagne bucket and has a very well covered and heated patio that will serve you and your dog well in any weather. Other favorites for the four-legged crowd are Anton and Michel's and the western themed Hog's Breath Inn of Clint Eastwood fame.

Carmel is just a few hours from anywhere in the San Francisco Bay Area, about six hours from Los Angeles and in a world of it's own for the vacationing pooch.

## Lake Tahoe

Lake Tahoe is a beautiful Alpine Lake that sits at just over 6,000 foot altitude in the Sierra Nevada Mountains of California and Nevada. The lake is a year round recreational destination with skiing in Winter and water sports, hiking and camping in Summer. The lake stradles the California and Nevada border, and in

Stateline Nevada there are casino hotels. The road that circles Lake Tahoe is the main street here, it is Highway 50 on the South and East and Highway 89 on the West side of the Lake. It is about 70 miles on the road to circle the lake. Lake Tahoe is a truly dog-friendly destination year round. Dogs like the colder Winter temperatures perhaps more than their people do. The higher altitude keeps the temperatures from rising too high in the summer. Many businesses in the Tahoe area are very pet-friendly.

Lodging in the Tahoe area is very pet-friendly with the best lodging smaller B&Bs and Vacation Rentals. For pet-friendly rentals in South Tahoe you can try Tahoe Keys Resorts and Holly's Place. In the Northern and western parts of the lake you can look up Tahoe Moon Properties, Tahoma Meadows, Waters of Tahoe and Tahoe Time Vacation Rentals. There are also many other vacation rental companies in the Tahoe Basin. For Dog-friendly hotels in South Tahoe there are the 3 Peaks Resort, the Super 8 and Inn at Heavenly. If you desire a pet-friendly hotel casino room in Stateline Nevada then Harvey's Lake Tahoe has a number of dog-friendly rooms.

Camping during the Summer is a pastime at Tahoe. If you are traveling here with an RV then there is the Zephyr Cover RV Park and Campground. From this campground you can walk to the dog-friendly North Beach at Zephyr Cove Resort. Other campgrounds are the KOA at the west entrance to the Tahoe Basin on Highway 50 and the Encore Tahoe RV Resort. There are a number of dry campgrounds for tent camping and small RV camping at the many State Parks in the area. Emerald Bay State Park and D. L. Bliss State Park are two of these. Since Winter weather is rather harsh at this altitude in the Sierras camping is pretty much a Summer only adventure for most.

Squaw Village

Summer attractions for people with pets at Tahoe include boat rentals, sport fishing and hiking. Tahoe Keys Boat Rentals will rent you a pontoon or motor boat. You can go fishing with some of the South Tahoe charter fishing outfits. Even your dog can go. There are raft rentals on the Truckee River in Tahoe City. There are a lot of seasonal patio dining restaurants that are available to you and your pup.

Winter attractions are predominantly cross country skiing and skijoring with your dog. You can cross country ski with your dog at Hope Valley, Blackwood Canyon, Fallen Leaf, Page Meadown and at the Tahoe Cross Country Ski Area in Tahoe City.

Year round attractions in the Tahoe Basin include a visit to the Village at Squaw Valley. This European Alpine Village at the foot of the world-famous Squaw Valley Ski Resort is especially appealing to travelers with dogs during the Summer. Then, you and your dog can hop the gondola to the top of Squaw for a meal and to explore the world from above 10,000 feet. During the ski season dogs are not allowed on the gondola. The village has an annual "Bark Festival", has outdoor movies during the summer for you and your pup, and has a lot of patio dining and dog-friendly restaurants and stores. Also in the Tahoe area there are dog-friendly Wedding Chapels if you want your dog to be present when you tie the knot.

Nearby dog-friendly attractions to Lake Tahoe include Virginia City Nevada, Yosemite National Park and Reno Nevada.

## Los Angeles/Hollywood

Los Angeles, the City of Angels, is also a city for dogs. This city is huge, with nearly 4 million residents spread over an area that stretches nearly 80 miles from end to end. Los Angeles is the center of the entertainment industry, with Hollywood and Beverly Hills a major tourist draw. There are many miles of beach, but not much of the beaches are dog-friendly. Los Angeles is built in a basin surrounded by mountains. While the close in mountains do not get winter snow, mountains further inland most certainly do. The Los Angeles hills serve to separate areas of the city with natural boundaries, also making it time consuming to drive between these areas. However, they come with benefits such as some excellent observation points overlooking the city, hiking trails and some off-leash dog areas. Most visitors to Los Angeles focus on the Hollywood and West Los Angeles areas, however, since Los Angeles is so big we have divided the city into six different regions. These do not include neighboring Orange County, home of Disneyland, Knotts Berry Farm, Anaheim, Newport Beach and more.

Los Angeles has many luxury pet-friendly hotels. The Sofitel at Beverly Hills is very dog-friendly. An extremely interesting choice of hotel is the Chateau Marmont Hotel at 8221 Sunset Boulevard. This hotel is modeled after a royal residence in France and is, in essence, a castle. Dogs up to 100 pounds are allowed. There is a beautiful garden patio restaurant as well. Another extremely dog-friendly hotel is the Loews Santa Monica Beach Hotel. This hotel, like most Loews hotels, offers a variety of dog amenities, such as doggie room service, beds, treats, water dishes and patio dining. They will also arrange for pet sitters as needed. In addition to these top of the line dog-friendly hotels Los Angeles offers hotels that allow dogs from all of the major chains. If you are looking to stay for a long time, then you might consider an extended stay hotel such as Residence Inn, Candlewood Suites or Extended Stay America. There are also dog-friendly vacation rentals in the Hollywood and beach areas.

A great area to spend some time if traveling to Los Angeles with a dog is in the Griffith Park area. Griffith Park is a large city park with many hiking trails that are open to leashed dogs. From the Griffith Observatory you get a panoramic and famous view of the city. The Travel Town Museum allows your well-behaved, leashed or carried dog to visit with you. Another attraction for tourists are to follow the Hollywood Walk of Fame on the sidewalks in Hollywood. Your dog can look up their favorite movie star (Does Lassie have a star?). You can buy the tourist maps of the Hollywood Star's homes and walk the sidewalks or drive the self-guided tours. If they are not too busy, some of the tour vans will allow smaller dogs to ride. Another great place to visit is the Will Rogers State Historical Park. This was Will Rogers personal home and ranch. It has been maintained to show how the Rogers' family lived and the ranch has been maintained. There are also equestrian events here. If you want to visit Universal Studios, although your dog is not allowed on the tour, there is an air conditioned kennel at Universal. In the San Fernando Valley, there is the Dog's Gallery, a dog-friendly art gallery. Los Encinos State Historic Park is a five acre historical site where dogs can walk the grounds. For movie buffs, you and your dog can walk around Paramount Ranch in Agoura Hills. Paramount Ranch is part of the Santa Monica National Rec Area and is a Western Town movie set that has been used in hundreds of movies. The trails are easy and mostly less than one mile in length.

Runyon Canyon

Many people come to Los Angeles for the beach. Unfortunately for dogs, the vast majority of Los Angeles beaches do not allow dogs. However, Long Beach is a dog-friendly haven and has the Long Beach Dog Beach Zone between Roycroft and Argonne Avenues. This is a 3 acre off-leash dog beach. While in Long Beach you and your dog can dine at the patio at Stefano's Restaurant. This eatery serves Italian food and dog treats and water as well. Also in Long Beach there are other dog-friendly restaurants, two off-leash dog parks and from here you and your dog can take the ferry to Catalina Island. A muzzle may be required on the ferries to Catalina. The only other Los Angeles County beach that allows dogs is Leo Carrillo State Beach which is up the Pacific Coast Highway in Malibu. Dogs must be leashed on this beach.

For dog-friendly dining in Los Angeles there are a lot of choices. One of the best is the Lazy Dog Cafe in Torrance. There are also some other locations in the Southland (Southern California). The Lazy Dog Cafe, at 3525 Carson Street, offers a heated outdoor patio and a dog menu and water for your dog. They have a complete menu for people and a good selection of wines and brews. There are also Lazy Dog Cafe's at 278 Los Cerritos Center Cerritos and 1440 Plaza Drive in West Covina. For hamburger lovers, Johnny Rockets locations in Southern California are usually very dog-friendly and may also have a dog menu. There are many other choices in various parts of the city.

There is probably no higher end shopping than Rodeo Drive in Beverly Hills and you will see a variety of dogs there. Small dogs are allowed almost everywhere but large dogs on leash are welcome in many stores as well. There are water bowls outside many stores. Also good places to shop with a dog are Sunset Plaza in West Hollywood, The Grove Shopping Center and the Westfield Century City. In Pasadena, there is the Old Town area and in Glendale there is the Americana at Brand Shopping Center. In the Simi Valley there is the Town Center Mall.

For dog play, Los Angeles has many off-leash dog parks in various areas of the city. These are fenced areas where dogs can play by themselves or with other dogs. There often are two separate areas so that small dogs don't have to be in with the larger dogs. Two of the nicest off-leash dog parks are in the Hollywood Hills. One is Laurel Canyon Park at 8260 Mulholland Drive. The next is Runyon Canyon Park which is an off-leash trail with panoramic views of Los Angeles. This is an excellent place for your dog to run off-leash, or stay with you on leash if you prefer.

Los Angeles has good weather all year round which makes it an ideal getaway for you and your dog at any time of year. You will need a car in Los Angeles, there is no other practical way to get around. Nearby trips from Los Angeles include Santa Barbara, San Diego, Big Bear Lake and Orange County.

# Mendocino

Although located on the North Coast of California, Mendocino looks more like a New England fishing village along the Pacific Ocean. The town of 1200 people on a rocky bluff of the Pacific was founded in 1852 by settlers from New England

and the town has retained that New England look. Previously serving as a fishing village today Mendocino has a large number of artists, B&Bs and crafters. The more commercial fishing operations have moved to Fort Bragg fifteen minutes up the Pacific Coast Highway (Highway 1). Tourism is a major industry in Mendocino which is a three hour drive from San Francisco and Sacramento and four hours from San Jose. Many people arrive at Mendocino by car while driving the scenic and winding Pacific Coast Highway (Highway 1).

Mendocino is the tourist center of the region, although you will find Fort Bragg an interesting destination as well. There are a number of especially dog-friendly hotels and B&Bs in Mendocino. Stanford Inn is nestled on a hillside with its own organic gardens, a dog-friendly organic patio restaurant called the Raven and pet-friendly room packages. Little River Inn offers pet-friendly lodging and breakfast and dinner in Ole's Whale Watch Bar. The Cottages at Little River Cove offers pet beds, treats and a "Pet Package". And the Inn at Schoolhouse Creek offers 8 acres of ocean view comfort for you and your pet. Smaller B&Bs include MacCallum House, Mendocino Seaside Cottages and for people looking for pet-friendly vacation rentals there is Mendocino Preferred Vacation Rentals. In Fort Bragg there is The Rendezvous Inn and Restaurant, Tradewinds Lodge and the Emerald Dolphin Inn & Mini Golf, which offers a special dog package known as the "Dyno Doggie Bag".

People who arrive with dogs via Motorhome or Travel Trailer can stay at Casper Beach RV Park and Campground in Mendocino or Pomo RV Park and Campground in Fort Bragg. Fort Bragg's Dolphin Isle Marina offers 85 full hookup sites, access to the marina and the Noyo River and a deli with outdoor patio dining for you and your dog. If you are tent camping try Van Damme State Park in Little River or Navarro River Redwoods State Park.

Mendo Burgers

While in Mendocino you can find a number of dog-friendly attractions. You can canoe with your dog at Catch a Canoe Rentals next to Stanford Inn in Mendocino. The Mendocino Coast Botanical Gardens is pet-friendly and you can walk your leashed dog through  the only botanical garden in the U.S. directly on the ocean. Dogs are allowed on some of the boat tours by Fort Bragg's charter fleets, which offer sightseeing, fishing and individual charters. However, what most visitors with or without dogs do in Mendocino is browse the quaint maritime town. You can walk the streets and visit the art galleries, shops, and stores. Along the scenic Pacific Bluff there are small and level trails between the town and the ocean. There are a number of very dog-friendly restaurants for you to dine at in town and most of the town is dog-friendly. For great burgers try Mendo Burgers. For great all around organic dining in a pleasant setting there is the Mendocino Cafe. The Raven Restaurant at the Stanford Inn is a bit out of town but serves organic food on it's dog-friendly outdoor patio. In Fort Bragg for seafood visit Silver's at the Wharf.

For beach access with a dog there are a number of choices. For an off-leash beach visit Noyo Beach Off-leash Dog Beach in Fort Bragg. Leashed dogs can visit Caspar Beach for miles north of Mendocino, Big River Beach just south of Mendocino and  Van Damme State Beach 2 miles south of town.

When on the North Coast of California you may also consider visiting  the Redwood National and State Parks region and the Trees of Mystery, a very dog-friendly attraction. Also, you may want to drive the Avenue of the Giants.  If driving the Pacific Coast Highway from San Francisco there a many interesting stops including Bodega Bay , Point Reyes National Seashore and Muir Beach. For other sights in that area, see the DogFriendly.com guide to Marin County and the North Bay.

## Monterey

Monterey Recreation Trail

Monterey California is one of the most pet-friendly destinations there is. Coupled with nearby Carmel, this place is not to be beat as a dog-friendly vacation haven. Carmel provides the quaint village, one of the nation's best dog-friendly beaches and Monterey provides long ocean beaches, walking trails, larger hotels and more selection in city amenities. Monterey, named for the Count of Monterrey, was first explored by Europeans in 1602.

It served as the Spanish Colonial capital of California until the gold rush when the capital moved to San Francisco temporarily. It is primarily a fishing town. To see it's Spanish heritage you can walk in the center of town at the Monterey State Historic Park. Unlike Carmel, there are many chain hotels in Monterey, many of them are pet-friendly hotels. From the large Hyatt Regency, the Best Western Plus Victorian Inn and the Best Western Plus Beach Resort to smaller hotels like Monterey Fireside Lodge or Old Monterey Inn there are a number of pet-friendly choices. The Marina Dunes RV Park, a stone's throw from the beach, is a great RV park for people with motor homes or travel trailers.

Dogs love the Monterey Recreation Trail, which provides beautiful scenery with beach and shopping on either side of you. The trail extends for miles along the bay. Monterey State Beach, which extends from town to a number of miles north of town is pet-friendly, but dogs must be on leash. You can shop with your dog at Del Monte Shopping Center and at the shops and stores downtown and at the wharf.

Monterey State Beach

There are a lot of dog-friendly restaurants in Monterey. Abalonetti Seafood, Cafe Fina and Domenico's on Fisherman's Wharf all have a special dog menu and water for your dog. There are many other dog-friendly restaurants in town as well. A number of the boat harbor and whale watching tours and even fishing trips may take your dog on some of their cruises out of Fisherman's Wharf. The Ag Venture

Tours will allow dogs on the van tours of nearby agricultural regions.

Nearby dog-friendly trips from Monterey include next door Carmel, Santa Cruz, and the Bay Area.

## Napa Valley/Sonoma Valley Wine Country

Napa Valley and Sonoma Valley encompass the area known as "Wine Country" in California. The California wine industry was launched in the Sonoma Valley in 1823 when grapes were first planted. In 1857 Hungarian Count Agoston Haraszthy created the first big vineyards here. He is now known as the "Father of California Wine". An interesting historical fact is that in Sonoma a band of farmers captured the controlling Mexican General in 1846 and declared California an independent republic. 25 days later the United States annexed California. Napa Valley now boasts over 250 wineries and Sonoma Valley adds scores more. Many of the wineries in both valleys are dog-friendly and some have dog mascots and dogs that greet visitors and visiting dogs.

Calistoga California's Old Faithful Geyser

In Napa Valley you have a choice of pet-friendly small inns, B&Bs and vacation rentals. The Inn on First in Napa is a circa 1900 mansion which presents your dog with a doggy welcome basket on check in. The Beazley House B&B also in Napa provides a doggy welcome basket as well. Also pet-friendly is the Chanric Inn in Calistoga and the Harvest Inn in St. Helena. If you are seeking a larger brand name hotel then the Westin Verasa Napa Valley allows small and medium sized dogs up to around 40 pounds. In Sonoma Valley dog-friendly hotels include the Dawn Ranch Lodge in Guerneville. Doggy beds, bowls and treats are provided. In Sonoma there are a number of hotels from many of the major hotel chains. The Hilton Sonoma Wine Country is a good choice here. There are also a large number of vacation rentals that welcome your dog including Russian River

Getaways and Russian River Vacation Homes in Guerneville, a Napa Valley Hideaway in Napa and other vacation rentals to choose from. If you prefer to camp there is an RV Park at the Napa County Fairgrounds in Calistoga and you can camp in the Putah Creek Resort in Napa. In Sonoma Valley is the Cloverdale KOA or the Casini Ranch Family Campground.

Napa Valley boasts dog-friendly attractions and, of course, dog-friendly wineries. A great dog-friendly attraction is the Old Faithful Geyser in Calistoga where you can see up close a geyser similar to the one at Yellowstone. The Petrified Forest has a 1/2 mile round trip walking tour for you and your dog. Then there are the wineries. If you want a tour, consider taking Small Lot Wine Tours, whose guides drive your car or in your car to some excellent and not as well known wineries or wherever you would like them to show you. If you want to do the wineries yourself then there are many dog-friendly wineries in Napa Valley. Chateau Montelena, Beringer Vineyards and V. Sattui Winery are some of the dog-friendly wineries but for many more see DogFriendly.com's directory. There are many dog-friendly restaurants in Napa Valley. One of the most dog-friendly is the Rutherford Grill in Rutherford. They will bring treats to your dog. The Canine Commons Dog Park and the Shurtleff Park Dog Park in Napa are two fenced off-leash dog parks.

In Sonoma Valley there are also a number of dog-friendly attractions as well as dog-friendly wineries. Take your dog canoeing with Russian River Adventures Canoe Rentals in Healdsburg. Jack London State Historic Park in Glen Ellen is a memorial to writer Jack London including the cottage residence where he lived. As in Napa Valley the Small Lot Wine Tours offer you guided tours to various wineries. There are many dog-friendly wineries in Sonoma Valley as well. See DogFriendly.com's guide for a complete listing. There are many dog-friendly restaurants in Sonoma Valley. The Garden Court Cafe & Bakery offers a special doggy menu for your dog's eating enjoyment as well as a selection of great food for people. The Roadhouse Restaurant at the pet-friendly Dawn Ranch Lodge offers a variety of local wines and contemporary California cuisine. Dogs are welcome on the deck. There are a number of dog-friendly beaches including Cloverdale River Park on the Russian River, Healdsburg Memorial Beach on the Russian River and access to the coast at Sea Ranch.

When visiting Wine Country you are near a large number of dog-friendly areas including San Francisco, Mendocino, Gold Country and Sacramento.

## Sacramento

The state capital of California, Sacramento, is a bustling city of 500,000 people with a metro area population of 2 million. The city was founded in 1839 by John Sutter and grew in prominence due to the gold rush. Many of the older buildings are preserved at the Old Sacramento Historic Area along the Sacramento River. Sacramento sits in the middle of the Central Valley of California about 30 miles west of the Sierra Nevada foothills and about 90 miles from San Francisco. The winters are wet and the summers are very dry and very hot, with high temperatures often at or near 100 degrees. Sacramento has a lot of dog-friendly attractions and things to do both in the city and within a few hours drive where you can take a day trip and return to your accommodation in town.

There are many dog-friendly hotels in Sacramento. Downtown there is the Sheraton Grand Sacramento Hotel next to the State Capitol and near all of the government buildings and the dog-friendly Downtown Plaza Shopping Center. There is the Hilton Sacramento Arden West next to Arden Fair Mall (which is not dog-friendly). If you want to stay in historic downtown Folsom the Lake Natoma Inn would be a great choice. This hotel overlooks Lake Natoma and is on the 20 mile American River Trail. There are also many other pet-friendly hotels in various parts of Sacramento, Folsom, Rancho Cordova and Roseville. If you are planning to camp while in the Sacramento area there is the Sacramento Metropolitan KOA just west of the city and a KOA about 30 miles east of town on Highway 50 near Placerville. Cal Expo, the State Fairgrounds, also has an RV Park if you are attended an event at the fairgrounds. Small dogs that can be carried in a carrier are allowed on the RT buses and light rail.

Old Sacramento

While in Sacramento any dog should be taken to Old Sacramento Historic Area along the river in downtown. This dog-friendly area has shops, patio dining and historic buildings from the 1860s. The Top Hand Ranch Carriage Rides that leave from here will take your dog on their shorter tours of Old Sacramento or there longer tours that go past the State Capitol and government center. You can also take a self-guided walking tour of Capitol Park which surrounds the California State Capitol. If you would like to wine taste in Sacramento the Scibner Bend Vineyards are located at 9051 River Road. There is lots more wine tasting about 1 hour out of town in El Dorado and Amador Counties. This area has developed into a second Napa Valley. Shopping in Sacramento with your pet is excellent, with the Downtown Plaza Shopping Center for downtown shopping and in Folsom the new Palladio offers a European style outdoor shopping environment with upscale stores and patio dining. Day trips from Sacramento include a trip to Napa Valley about 2 hours away and, in the fall, a trip to Apple Hill just past Placerville to visit the apple farms in season.

Sacramento has a lot of dog-friendly dining in most parts of town. It should be easy to find an outdoor patio which will welcome your dog. Downtown Plaza has the River City Brewing Company and Johnny Rockets. Folsom's Palladio has a number of excellent patio restaurants as well. Try Panera Bread, San Francisco Sourdough, or Freebirds World Burrito.

For exercise for you and your dog, there is the American River Parkway which weaves its way for 32 miles from downtown to Folsom Lake. This is a bike and hiking trail. Please keep your dog on leash on the trail. Folsom Lake State Rec Area surrounds Folsom Lake and the Folsom Dam. Gibson Ranch Park is predominantly an equestrian park but leashed dogs can share the trails with the horses. William Land Park, south of downtown, houses the Sacramento Zoo (dogs not allowed in the zoo) and lots of room to walk. A good place to walk is also Old Sacramento as well as Old Town Folsom. Sacramento has quite a few off-leash dog parks located in each part of town and there seem to be more each year. Most have fencing, water, benches and clean up stations and many have separate areas for small dogs.

Nearby trips to Sacramento include the San Francisco Bay Area, Gold Country, Napa Valley, Lake Tahoe and Reno.

American River Parkway

# San Diego

Nearly everyone agrees that San Diego has the perfect weather in the country. Never too cold, never too hot, always just right. And with only a minimal amount of rain every year, San Diego suits a person vacationing with a dog or dogs very well. But the weather in the San Diego area can vary quite a bit. As you move inland from the ocean summer temperatures reach above one hundred degrees F often. But in the central area of San Diego, it will usually remain in the seventies or lower. San Diego is a big city with big city traffic. So you will probably need to drive a car to take your pet where you want to go. Depending on the time of day this can be difficult. Small dogs that can fit into a carrier are allowed on the cities buses and light rail. You will have to carry the dog and the carrier. Another way to transport a pet in San Diego is with the San Diego Pet Driver. These pet taxis will take people with pets around town and to the airport and will also pet sit and walk pets at locations in the city.

Hiking at San Diego Bay

Accommodations in San Diego for visiting pet people range from luxurious pet-friendly hotels such as the Loews Coronado Bay Resort, which hosts an annual dog surfing event, and the Palomar San Diego to very pet friendly chain hotels and motels in all price ranges and a large selection of pet-friendly vacation rentals in Pacific Beach, downtown and elsewhere. The main attractions of the city for tourists usually include Balboa Park and the world-famous San Diego Zoo, Sea World, the cities beaches, La Jolla, and a trip or trips to nearby sites such as Tijuana, Mexico and mountain towns such as Julian. Despite the fact that the San Diego Zoo is home to a large number of animals, or perhaps because of it, dogs are not allowed in the zoo. To visit the zoo, if you have two adults with you, you may have to split your time with the dogs or utilize a pet sitter or day kennel in the city. Both the Loews Coronado and the Palomar will provide a pet sitter with prior arrangement. Some of the vacation rentals may as well. Or you can arrange your own. Balboa Park is dog-friendly and has an off-leash dog run as well. Sea World has day kennels on the premises. La Jolla's quaint shopping streets are very dog-friendly with lots of patio dining for you and your pet. And the beaches, oh the dog-friendly beaches around San Diego are every dog's dream.

The San Diego Dog Beach is a large off-leash dog beach on the north end of Ocean Beach. It is a 24 hour beach for dogs and is one of the nation's best off-leash beaches. Also off-leash is Coronado's Dog Beach. A number of other beaches serving San Diego allow dogs, which must be leashed. Most of Fiesta Island is also open to off-leash dog play.

Balboa Dog Park

Shopping, dining and entertainment in San Diego rivals that of most large cities for people and exceeds all expectations for dogs. Where else can you find a shopping center with a built in dog park? In San Diego there are two - Otay Ranch Town Center in Chula Vista and Westfield UTC Mall on La Jolla Village Drive. Leashed dogs will find many accommodating stores at these centers as well as the Horton Plaza downtown. Dining with a dog in San Diego is a pleasure with a number of restaurants offering dog menus. The best of these are probably The Wine Pub for the 21 and older crowd and Terra American Bistro and the Lazy Dog Cafe for families. All areas of the city have dog-friendly dining where your leashed dog can accompany you to the outdoor tables. And in San Diego is is rare for the weather to hinder outdoor dining. Other activities that you can do with your pet are Kayaking, Hiking though many city and hilly parks, carriage rides and boat rentals. Once a year, you can take your dog to a San Diego Padres baseball game at Petco Park.

In the mountain town of Julian, about 45 minutes by car from San Diego, you can dine with your dog, walk the town, visit Cuyamaca Ranch State Park and William Heise County park or camp. If you love to stay at a vacation rental there are a number of pet-friendly vacation rentals in Julian as well. To take a pet across to Tijuana Mexico may require some advance planning. But you can walk across the border, shop a bit in the first few miles of Mexico and walk back across to avoid getting car insurance to drive into Mexico. Another short out of town destination for many tourists would be Legoland in Carlsbad 30 minutes to the north of San Diego. Legoland provides kennels for your dog while you attend the amusement park.

San Diego, by virtue of it's outdoor qualities and it's overall pet-friendliness, ranks high for the traveling pet and their families.

## San Francisco

San Francisco has a population of 805,000 in only 47 square miles. This makes it the second most densely populated city in the U.S. after New York. This is good for people visiting with dogs as it makes the city very walk-able. To walk from anywhere to anywhere else in San Francisco you would not have to walk more than 7 miles. Most of the visitor areas are within three miles of each other, however. San Francisco is very scenic and has many hills some of which are quite steep with sidewalks made as stairs. There is a lot to do for a visitor with a dog in the City by the Bay.

San Francisco's Baker Beach

San Francisco is a city of neighborhoods where you can easily walk to where you want to go. To get around town between neighborhoods you can drive (although parking can be expensive), take the famous cable cars or the MUNI buses or subways. Dogs are allowed on all of these, although they may require that you muzzle your dog. You should have a muzzle with you when using the public transportation with a dog. BART, the larger subway trains that connect San Francisco with the airport, Oakland, Berkeley and the East Bay only allow dogs small enough to be carried. Since most tourists to San Francisco want a cable car ride, that is the choice we would take if one is available.

One neighborhood where tourists inevitably end up is the Fisherman's Wharf area. There are little shops, patio dining and all kinds of tourist attractions here. Dogs will enjoy walking the area with you and can go in some shops and patio restaurants. Also nearby here is Ghirardelli Square, famous for chocolate and ice cream. The Ghirardelli Square Shopping Center also has a number of stores that welcome your dog and dogs are allowed in the common areas. Usually, there will be all kinds of street entertainment in this area as well as carriage rides. Next door is the Italian neighborhood with shops and restaurants.

You can visit San Francisco's famous Chinatown with your dog although it is a somewhat crowded area to walk. Also, there are very limited options for outdoor dining so you may need to get food to go here. Other activities in San Francisco for you and your dog are to walk the most crooked street in the world on Lombard St, view the city from the hill at Coit Tower, walk the 3.5 mile Barbary Coast Trail or drive the 49 Mile Scenic Drive where you can follow the signs. The 49 Mile Drive will visit most of the major sights in the city. Once or twice each year you can take your dog to a San Francisco Giants baseball game at AT&T Park but during every game there is a viewing gate where you can catch a few plays. There is also usually an annual Bark and Wine Ball where people and dogs can party it up.

San Francisco has many dog-friendly restaurants. Rogue Ales Public House has a dog menu as well as food and drink for the people in your party. Cuisine choices at dog-friendly restaurants range from organic and natural foods to hamburgers, smoothies, fish and steak. One of our favorites is ice cream at Ghirardelli Square. For dog-friendly shopping there are many choices including the world famous Union Square district especially around Christmas, Westfield San Francisco Center and Ghirardelli Square.

San Francisco has more off-leash areas for dogs than almost any city in North America. New York and Calgary may have more, but there are a lot in San Francisco. There are over twenty off-leash dog parks in San Francisco. For a large city, there are a lot of dog-friendly beaches as well. Baker Beach in the shadow of the Golden Gate Bridge, Fort Funston and Burton Beach and Ocean Beach are all dog-friendly.

Pet-friendly hotels are mostly high-end, expensive hotels in San Francisco downtown and tourist areas. For a real bargain, you will have to stay in the suburbs. If you want especially dog-friendly accommodations try the Palomar, Argonaut , Serrano , Sir Francis Drake, Sheraton Fisherman's Wharf or the Hilton San Francisco. If you have an RV, the only place near town is the Candlestick RV Park near the stadium.

There are many nearby places to go for dog-friendly road trips from San Francisco. Day trips can include Napa Valley, Marin and Sonoma Counties just north of the Golden Gate Bridge. There is also Oakland, San Jose & Silicon Valley and Berkeley. For overnight trips, three hours north is Mendocino and four hours east is Lake Tahoe. Three hours south are Monterey and Carmel and two hours south is Santa Cruz.

## San Jose/Silicon Valley

San Jose was one of the original Spanish settlements in California and was founded in 1777 by Felipe de Neve. It is now the state's third largest city and is best known as the center of Silicon Valley and the computer hardware and software industries. In addition to San Jose, the Silicon Valley area consists of Palo Alto and Stanford University, Santa Clara, Mountain View and Sunnyvale and the peninsula cities of San Mateo, Redwood City and San Carlos. The area has a number of very dog-friendly pockets where shops, restaurants and parks welcome your four legged friend.

Dog-friendly hotels are not hard to find in San Jose and Silicon Valley. The Cypress Hotel at 10050 South De Anza Blvd in Cupertino is perhaps the most dog-friendly with special doggie packages and pet sitting available. The upscale Fairmont Hotel in downtown San Jose is also pet-friendly. The Best Western Plus Brookside Inn in Milpitas offers good value as does the La Quinta San Jose. In Palo Alto small to medium sized dogs are allowed at the Sheraton Palo Alto and the Westin Palo Alto. There are also a number of dog-friendly hotels in the area around the San Francisco Airport in the northern part of San Mateo County. In Half Moon Bay along the coast the Half Moon Bay Inn at 401 Main Street offers pet-friendly lodging.

Santana Row

For dog-friendly shopping and dining there are a number of excellent options in the San Jose area. The upscale Santana Row Shopping Center, at Highway 880 and Interstate 280, has a large number of dog-friendly shops as well as patio dining. Los Gatos, a community that sits against the Santa Cruz Mountains, is a great area to walk around with your dog. You can shop and dine here as well as hike the Los Gatos Creek Reservoir Trail to the Lexington Reservoir or walk the paved Los Gatos Creek Trail towards Campbell. Campbell and Saratoga, both nearby to Los Gatos, are also dog-friendly. Palo Alto's downtown has a quaint shopping area to walk around and is very pet-friendly as well. Stanford Shopping Center, just north of the Stanford Campus, offers an excellent open-air dog-friendly shopping location.

Dog-Friendly restaurants in the area are not hard to find. La Fondue, in Saratoga, not only welcomes dogs but offers complimentary filet mignon for their canine guests. They have two patios with doggie tie down areas. In Redwood City, the Redwood Creek Grill offers a doggie menu as well. Steak Out, in Mountain View at 383 Castro Street, is a burger and beer garden with a large dog-friendly outdoor area and a visiting dog named Stout. There are other pet-friendly patio restaurants in Palo Alto, Santana Row, and most other areas of town.

For dog-friendly parks where you can jog, hike or hang out with your dog there are a number of options. The Stanford University campus offers a large amount of grassy areas as do the hills above the campus in what is known as the "Dish Loop" to the large antennas on the hill. The Palo Alto Baylands Preserve is against the bay and offers trails as well. Closer to San Jose there are the Los Gatos Creek Trail between Campbell and Los Gatos, the Guadalupe River Park & Gardens downtown, Ed Levin County Park on the east hills in Milpitas and Fremont Older Preserve in Cupertino. There are also many fenced off-leash dog parks in San Jose, Palo Alto and many of the cities that make up the area. There are a number of dog-friendly beaches in the Half Moon Bay and Pescadero area, about a 1/2 hour drive from Palo Alto and in the Santa Cruz area about a 40 minute drive from San Jose. William Street Park in San Jose hosts a huge "Bark in the Park" event each September with over 10,000 dogs and people attending.

Nearby pet-friendly trips from San Jose include dog-friendly Carmel and Monterey, San Francisco, Napa Valley and very close by, Santa Cruz.

## San Luis Obispo/Cambria

San Luis Obispo is located about half way between San Francisco and Los Angeles on Highway 101 or the Pacific Coast Highway (Highway 1). It is a region that would be a farming region except for the fact that there are a lot of tourists. San Luis Obispo is also home to Cal Poly University. The town's population is 44,000. There are also a number of other interesting communities around San Luis Obispo. Cambria, near Hearst Castle, is a well-known and dog-friendly destination. Also well-known and dog-friendly are Pismo Beach, Morro Bay and Paso Robles which lies on Highway 101 to the north of San Luis Obispo. You and your dog can find a lot to do in this region.

The most well-known hotel in San Luis Obispo is the Madonna Inn, known for it's multiple theme rooms. This hotel is not dog-friendly, unfortunately. There are other dog-friendly hotels. However, the Best Western El Rancho hotel is and offers a nice base of operations if visiting San Luis Obispo. For dog-friendly delight the Cambria Shores Inn in Cambria and the Las Serena Inn in Morro Bay will welcome your dog to their establishments. Also pet-friendly are the Cayucos Beach Inn in Cayucos, the SeaCrest OceanFront Hotel in Pismo Beach  and the Morro Bay Sandpiper Inn. If you are looking for a dog-friendly vacation rental then try the Big Red House in Cambria or Central Coast Getaways for homes in the area. If you are camping in a Motorhome or travel trailer then consider the Pacific Dunes RV Resort of the Pismo Coast Village RV Park located right on the dog-friendly and car-friendly Pismo State Beach.

You can take your dog to a number of area vineyards or wineries if you would like to do wine tasting. The Changala Winery, Chumeia Vineyards, Tablas Creek Vineyard and Venteaux Vineyards are dog-friendly. Other attractions to take your dog to include the San Luis Obispo Botanical Garden and Lake Lopez Boat Rentals. There are a number of dog-friendly beaches in the area. Pismo Beach State Beach, the Cambria beaches, Cayucos State Beach and the Oceano Dunes State Vehicular Rec Area are some of the dog-friendly beaches. If you want to shop with your dog you can find dog-friendly stores and patio restaurants at the downtown shops in San Luis Obispo and Cambria and the Pismo Beach Premium Outlets.

San Luis Obispo

Dog-Friendly restaurants are available throughout the San Luis Obispo region. Tognazzini's Dockside Too in Morro Bay specializes in seafood and is located right on the water. Big Bubba's BBQ and Good Ol' Burgers of Paso Robles have dog-friendly patios. There are also quite a few additional dog-friendly restaurants in Paso Robles, San Luis Obispo and Pismo Beach. See DogFriendly.com's directory for additional choices.

For off-leash fun there are a number of off-leash dog parks in the San Luis Obispo area. Heimann Dog Park in Atascadero, Cambria Dog Park in Cambria and Nipomo Park Off-Leash Area are some of these dog parks. There is also hiking with leashed dogs at Lake Lopez Rec Area, santa Margarita Lake Regional Park and Lake Nacimiento in Paso Robles.

Visitors with dogs to San Luis Obispo might consider a one hour trip south on Highway 101 to Solvang, a transplanted Dutch Village with delicious foods, neat shops and a great walking village.

## Santa Barbara

Santa Barbara, the Queen of the California Missions, was founded in 1786. The current Mission was built in 1812 after an earthquake destroyed the last one. There was a large earthquake in 1925 and the entire center of town had to be rebuilt. It is now almost entirely a Mediterranean architecture. Santa Barbara has been a paradox for dog lovers. Most locals think it is dog-friendly, while visitors have their doubts. Due to a political "situation" Santa Barbara for many years was the main holdout in California about allowing dogs on outdoor patios. Recently this problem has been relaxed and dogs can find patio dining here as well as in the rest of the state. In addition, the beaches of Santa Barbara are not as pet-friendly as those south of here in Ventura County, but they are more pet-friendly than the beaches of Los Angeles 90 miles to the south. Today, Santa Barbara is dog-friendly in most respects.

Santa Barbara is home to many dog-friendly resorts and hotels. The San Ysidro Ranch is an upscale resort. The good news for dog lovers is this place is very dog-friendly. The bad news is it can cost $600 per night. They do have a Privileged Pet Program and even dog massages. For a more moderate but still high budget hotel with dog-friendly perks and doggy room service try the Fess Parker Doubletree Resort located right in town. The Best Western Beachside Inn, the Blue Sands Motel and the Secret Garden Inn and Cottages are also dog-friendly. For someone looking for a pet-friendly suite hotel for a long stay there is an Extended Stay America. Santa Barbara has a large number of pet-friendly vacation rentals as well.

Santa Barbara Botanical Gardens

In Santa Barbara you can find a number of dog-friendly attractions. Explore Chumach Painted Cave State Historic Park and see Chumash Native drawings from the 1600s. Leashed dogs are welcome. You can tour the Santa Barbara Botanical Garden with your dog as well. Or explore the Stearns Wharf which is California's oldest working wharf. There are shops and patios for food available to you and some of the stores will allow your dogs. If shopping is your thing, then explore the downtown State Street Shopping Area with your dog. There are a number of pet-friendly stores here including the world headquarters of Big Dog Sportswear, a famously dog-friendly chain. You can also shop with your dog at the La Cumbre Plaza Shopping Area.

Today it is easy to find dog-friendly restaurants in Santa Barbara. This was not always the case as the city health department parted ways with the Santa Maria Branch of the health department and with most of the state and stopped dogs from sitting on patios at restaurants in town. Now finding dog-friendly patios is not such a challenge. The Brewhouse Restaurant at 229 West Montecito Street has handcrafted brews and a menu of comfort foods for you - and a menu for your dog as well. Another extremely dog-friendly restaurant is the Summerland Beach Cafe in Summerland just south of Santa Barbara. This restaurant is set in a Victorian house with a large outdoor dining area. Summerland Beach, right across from the restaurant, is a dog-friendly beach as well.

There are a number of dog-friendly beaches in the area. Summerland Beach, 8 miles south of town, is one. Leashed dogs are allowed in Rincon Park and Beach on Bates Road in Santa Barbara, Arroyo Burro Beach and Goleta Beach County Park. There are a number of off-leash dog parks in and around Santa Barbara. The Douglas Family Preserve is an entire park where off-leash dogs are allowed.

Nearby Santa Barbara are Ventura and Ojai, the quaint Dutch town of Solvang and San Luis Obispo and Cambria.

# Yosemite National Park

Yosemite National Park, with its sheer granite cliffs and natural beauty, is one of America's most visited National Parks. Although dogs are not allowed on the back country trails, they are allowed on the paved trails that make up most of the Yosemite Valley. This is the area that most visitors to the park visit and spend most of their time. There are also other dog-friendly attractions in the area surrounding the park. So it makes for a great dog-friendly vacation.

There are many dog-friendly hotels and lodging in the Yosemite area. They are either outside the South gate to the park at Fish Camp or Oakhurst or west of the park in Groveland and Mariposa. A great place to stay for your visit to Yosemite with your dog is the Tenaya Lodge in Fish Camp. This upscale lodge allows dogs up to 55 pounds (ask about larger dogs) and offers dog-sitting and walking services. Also in Fish Camp is the Narrow Gauge Inn near the dog-friendly Sugar Pine railroad rides. In Oakhurst is the Best Western Yosemite Gateway Inn. To the north and west of the park is the Groveland Hotel, a historic building in it's own right and the Best Wester Plus Yosemite Way Station Motel. For vacation rentals near the park there is Yosemite's SierraScape Vacation Rentals in Mariposa among other choices.

Yosemite Valley

Many people coming to Yosemite plan on camping. If you do, there are many options for dog-friendly camping. Many of the Yosemite Park campgrounds allow dogs. Dogs are allowed at the Bridalveil Creek, Crane Flat, Hodgdon Meadow, Tuolumne Meadows, Upper Pines, Wawona, White Wolf and Yosemite Creek Campgrounds. They are not allowed at other campgrounds in the park. If you are looking for a private RV Park outside of the park then there is the Yosemite/Mariposa KOA and the Yosemite Pines RV Resort in Groveland.

The main attraction that draws people to the region is, of course, Yosemite National Park. It is one of the most popular National Parks and is known for its granite cliffs, tall waterfalls and giant sequoia groves. People with dogs can get to see most of the sites in the Yosemite Valley. If you are into the big hikes up from the valley floor to the tops of the waterfalls or Half Dome, you will need to leave your dog behind. But if, like 95 percent of tourists, you keep your feet on the valley floor then you can take your leashed dog on many of the trails which are often paved. The lodges and shuttle buses in the park do not allow dogs. There are short hikes on paved trails where you can take your dog such as Bridalveil Falls. Many of the roads through Yosemite Valley have paved sidewalks and your dog is welcome there. For dining, there are ample restaurants and snack bars where you can get food inside and bring it outside to eat with your dog. Outside of the park you can take your dog on the Yosemite Mountain Sugar Pine Railroad which is a one hour steam engine ride. It is located in Fish Camp just south of the park gate. You and your dog can also rent boats at the Millers Landing Resort on Bass Lake. Some dog-friendly hikes in the area include The Way of the Mono Tail at Bass Lake and the Shadow of the Giants Trail in Oakhurst.

Sugar Pine Railroad

On the east side of the Sierra Mountains and south of the East Entrance to the park is Mammoth California. Lake Tahoe is a few hours to the north.

# Nevada

## Las Vegas

Las Vegas is one of the most visited destinations in the country. Business conventions, gambling, entertainment, and in recent years even kid's activities has made Las Vegas a spot that many visitors frequent each year. The largest city in Nevada, Las Vegas grew as a gambling center and as the years went by, other entertainment was added. When DogFriendly.com was started in 1998 we had a hard time finding any hotels in the city that would accept dogs. The ones that did were usually small hotels far from the Strip and without casinos. No more. Now, you and your dog can stay on the Strip in some of the fanciest casino hotels in Las Vegas.

Red Rock Canyon National Area

Pet-friendly hotel casinos in Las Vegas include Caesars Palace, Paris, Planet Hollywood, Harrahs, Flamingo, Bally's, Rio and The Quad. These are all run by Caesars and are participants in their "PetStay" Casino program. Two dogs up to 50 pounds each are allowed under this program per room. No other types of pets are allowed. They will also provide you information about dog walking and pet sitting. Also dog-friendly is the Vdara Hotel & Spa, which is smoke free and casino free. They have a room service menu for dogs and there is a dog park nearby. Mandalay Bay is also dog-friendly. The Westin Lake Las Vegas Resort & Spa is not on the Strip but is on Lake Las Vegas in Henderson and is very dog-friendly. Other Casino Hotels allow smaller dogs, such as the Trump International and the Cosmopolitan of Las Vegas. For extended stay visitors you can use the Residence Inn Hughes Center near the Strip of other pet-friendly extended stay hotels around Las Vegas and Henderson. If you need to leave your dog for a while during the day or overnight while in Las Vegas there are a few Petsmart Pet Hotels, a Camp Bow Wow and other day and night kennels in town. The pet-friendly hotels can often find you a pet-sitter as well.

If you are planning to camp in the Las Vegas area then you can park your motorhome or Travel Trailer at the KOA at Circus Circus. Behind the Circus Circus Casino, you can walk to the casino and many other casinos on the Strip. There is also the Oasis Las Vegas RV Resort located just south of the city. If you prefer tent camping then you may want to stay out of town at Red Rock Campground at Red Rock National Rec Area which has beautiful dog-friendly hiking as well. Also available for camping is Lake Mead National Rec Area in Boulder City.

Old Las Vegas Mormon Fort

We used to take our dog on a walk on the Strip to see all of the latest casinos, sites and such. You can still do this but the city has now banned dogs from the Strip sidewalk from Noon to 5 am so you will need to take this sightseeing walk in the morning. If you are staying with your dog on the Strip you can go out the back doors of the casinos at any time. For history buffs, you can visit Old Las Vegas Mormon Fort in downtown Las Vegas. You may also visit Historic Spring Mountain Ranch with your dog. Howard Hughes, among other celebrities, used to own this property. Dogs are allowed on the outside grounds. For shopping with your dog in Las Vegas, you can visit the District at Green Valley Ranch in Henderson. This upscale outdoor shopping area has a number of dog-friendly stores and restaurants with outdoor patios. The Town Square in Las Vegas is also dog-friendly as are many stores scattered throughout the city. There are many dog-friendly restaurants throughout the city for you and your dog to eat at. Dogs like the outdoors and there is much for a dog to do outdoors in the Las Vegas area. Keep in mind that summer temperatures often reach beyond 110 degrees and this is too hot for a dog to do much activity. Early morning or late evening may work in the summer. However, a fall, winter or early spring trip to Vegas allows for much dog-friendly hiking and activity. Red Rock Canyon National Area is about 15 miles west of Las Vegas and has many beautiful but hilly dog-friendly trails. Spring Mountain, 35 miles Northwest of Las Vegas includes hikes to Mt. Charleston and other hikes. Temperatures here are often much cooler than in Las Vegas below so your dog may appreciate this. One nice trail is the Mary Jane Falls Trail. Lake Mead National Rec Area covers 1.5 million acres and leashed dogs are allowed. In town, there is Desert Breeze County Park. There are also many fenced dog parks in Las Vegas where your dog can romp and play with other dogs. The Dog Fancier's Park is a 12 acre park to allow people to train their dogs off-leash.

Chapter 2

# Dog-Friendly California and Nevada

## A guide to everything dog-friendly

# California Listings

## Adelanto

### Dog-Friendly Hotels
**California Inn Hotel And Suites**
11628 Bartlett Avenue
Adelanto CA
760-246-8777 (800-329-7466)
Dogs are welcome at this hotel.

## Agua Dulce

### Dog-Friendly Parks
**Vasquez Rocks Natural Area Park**
10700 W Escandido Canyon Road
Agua Dulce CA
661-268-0840
This high desert, 745 acre park offers unique towering rock formations, "Birds of Prey" presentations that begin each October, Star Group parties, and various recreational opportunities. The park features a history trail tour of the Tatavian Indians and Spanish settlers, a seasonal stream, and hiking trails. Dogs are allowed throughout the park and on the trails. Dogs must be on leash and please clean up after them.

## Alpine

### Other Organizations
**Alpine Stagecoach Lions Club**

2707 Alpine Blvd
Alpine CA
619.445.6201
alpinelions.org
Alpine Stagecoach Lions Club is part of Lions International a volunteer service organization. We help the visually impaired,
assist the hearing impaired, provide diabetes awareness, help meet the needs of our community and our club's goal is to raise money to sponsor assistance dogs for special needs individuals.

## Alturas - Modoc National Forest

### Dog-Friendly Hotels
**Super 8 Alturas**
511 N Main Street
Alturas CA
530-233-3545 (800-800-8000)
Dogs are welcome at this hotel.

**Trailside Inn**
343 N Main St
Alturas CA
530-233-4111
Pets may be accepted. Please contact the hotel directly for full details.

### Dog-Friendly Attractions
**Surprise Valley Back Country Byway**
Highway 299
Cedarville CA
530-279-6101
ca.blm.gov/surprise/valley.html
If you are up for some adventure, try this 93 mile driving tour which traverses by many points of interest in the Great Basin Desert. The loop begins and ends in Cedarville and takes a minimum of three hours and longer if you make any stops. The Bureau of Land Management offers a 32 page self-guided Byway Tour Guide which tells about the historic and prehistoric stories of Surprise Valley. It includes details about fossils and wildlife. The byway is paved in California and is a gravel road in Nevada which can be passable by all vehicles when the road is dry. Dogs on leash are allowed. Please clean up
after your dog. Contact the following BLM office for a map and more details: BLM, Surprise Field Office, 602 Cressler Street, Cedarville, CA 96104, 530-279-6101. The office is open Monday through Friday.

### Dog-Friendly Parks
**Modoc National Forest**
800 West 12th Street
Alturas CA
530-233-5811
fs.usda.gov/modoc/
This national forest covers over 1.9 million acres of land which ranges in elevation from 4,300 to 9,934 feet. Please see our listings in this region for dog-friendly hikes and/or campgrounds.

**Blue Lake National Recreation Trail**
Forest Service Road 64
Likely CA
530-233-5811
This 1.5 mile one way trail is located at Blue Lake, in the Modoc National Forest, at an elevation of 6,000 feet. At least 90 percent of the trail is shaded by white fir and massive ponderosa pine trees. The trailhead begins at the Blue Lake Campground and ends at the boat ramp. Dogs on leash are allowed at the campgrounds, on the trail and in the water. Please clean up after your pets. The trail is located is 16 miles from the small town of Likely. From Highway 395 go east on Forest Service Road 64. At about 10 miles you will come to a road junction. Stay on Forest Service Road 64 for the remaining 6 miles.

**Clear Lake Trail**
Mill Creek Rd.
Likely CA
530-233-5811
This trail is located in the Modoc National Forest at an elevation of 5,700 feet. At .5 miles into the trail, you will reach Mills Creek Falls. Beyond that the trail serves as a major entry way to the trails of the South Warner

Wilderness. Dogs on leash are allowed on the trail and in the water. Please clean up after your pets. To get there from the town of Likely, go 9 miles east on Co. Rd. #64. Then go northeast on West Warner Road for 2.5 miles. Go east on Mill Creek access road for 2 more miles. The trailhead is located in the Mill Creek Falls Campground.

## Anaheim Resort Area

## Dog-Friendly Hotels

**Clarion Hotel Anaheim Resort**
616 Convention Way
Anaheim CA
714-750-3131 (877-424-6423)
Clarion Hotel Anaheim Resort is only 1 block from the Disneyland Resort and less than an 1/8 of a mile from the

**Four Points By Sheraton Anaheim**
1221 South Harbor Blvd
Anaheim CA
714-758-0900 (888-625-5144)
Hotel Menage welcomes two pets up to 60 lbs for an additional fee of $25 per pet, per night. Pets are only allowed on the first floor.

**Hotel Indigo Anaheim Maingate**
435 West Katella
Anaheim CA
714-772-7755 (877-698-9593)
Dogs of all sizes are allowed.

**Sheraton Park Hotel At The Anaheim Resort**
1855 South Harbor Boulevard
Anaheim CA
714-750-1811 (888-625-5144)
Conveniently located within walking distance to Disneyland, this resort hotel also features a lush tropical setting, numerous in-house amenities, and easy access to the Anaheim Convention Center and the Anaheim GardenWalk. One dog up to 40 pounds is allowed on

the ground floor for an additional 1 time pet fee of $50;there is a pet waiver to sign at check in.

**Hyatt House Cypress/anaheim**
5905 Corporate Avenue
Cypress CA
714-828-4000
COMMENTS

**Fullerton Marriott At California State University**
2701 East Nutwood Avenue
Fullerton CA
714-738-7800
Dogs of all sizes are allowed. There is a $35 one time pet fee.

**Anaheim Marriott Suites**
12015 Harbor Boulevard
Garden Grove CA
714-750-1000
Dogs of all sizes are allowed. There is a $35 per pet per night pet fee.

**Sheraton Garden Grove-Anaheim South**
12221 Harbor Boulevard
Garden Grove CA
714-703-8400 (888-625-5144)
Setting only a mile from the Anaheim Convention Center and a mile and a half from Disneyland, this upscale hotel sits central to many of the areas star attractions and recreational venues. This newly built hotel also features a number of amenities for all level of travelers. One dog up to 60 pounds is allowed for a $150 one time pet fee.

**Doubletree Hotel Anaheim/Orange County**
100 The City Drive
Orange CA
714-634-4500 (800-222-TREE (8733))
Only a few minutes from Disneyland and the Anaheim Convention Center, this upscale hotel offers a number of on site amenities for all level of travelers, plus a convenient location to business, shopping, dining, and recreation areas.

Dogs up to 75 pounds are allowed for an additional one time pet fee of $75 per room.

**La Quinta Inn & Suites Orange County - Santa Ana**
2721 Hotel Terrace
Santa Ana CA
714-540-1111 (800-531-5900)
Dogs up to 75 pounds are allowed. There are no additional pet fees. Dogs must be leashed, cleaned up after, and removed for housekeeping.

**Red Roof Inn - Santa Ana**
2600 North Main Street
Santa Ana CA
714-542-0311 (800-RED-ROOF)

One well-behaved family pet per room. Guest must notify front desk upon arrival. Guest is liable for any damages. In consideration of all guests, pets must never be left unattended in the guest rooms.

## Pet-Friendly Extended Stay Hotels

**Extended Stay America - Orange County - Anaheim Convention Cente**
1742 S. Clementine St
Anaheim CA
714-502-9988 (800-804-3724)
One dog is allowed per suite. There is a $25 per night additional pet fee up to $150 for an entire stay.

**Extended Stay America - Orange County - Anaheim Hills**
1031 N. Pacificenter Drive
Anaheim CA
714-630-4006 (800-804-3724)
One dog is allowed per suite. There is a $25 per night additional pet fee up to $150 for an entire stay.

**Residence Inn Anaheim Maingate**
1700 South Clementine Street
Anaheim CA
714-533-3555
Dogs of all sizes are allowed. There is a $100 one time

additional pet fee.

## Staybridge Suites Anaheim Resort Area
1855 South Manchester Avenue

Anaheim CA
714-748-7700 (877-270-6405)
Dogs up to 80 pounds are allowed. Pets allowed with an additional pet fee. Up to $75 for 1-6 nights and up to $150 for 7+ nights. A pet agreement must be signed at check-in.

## Towneplace Suites By Marriott Anaheim Maingate Angel Stadium
1730 South State College Boulevard
Anaheim CA
714-939-9700
Dogs up to 25 pounds are allowed. There is a $100 one time pet fee.

## Extended Stay America - Orange County - Cypress
5990 Corporate Avenue
Cypress CA
714-761-2766 (800-804-3724)
One dog is allowed per suite. There is a $25 per night additional pet fee up to $150 for an entire stay.

## Candlewood Suites Anaheim South
12901 Garden Grove Blvd
Garden Grove CA
714-539-4200 (877-270-6405)
Dogs up to 80 pounds are allowed. Pets allowed with an additional pet fee. Up to $75 for 1-6 nights and up to $150 for 7+ nights. A pet agreement must be signed at check-in.

## Residence Inn Garden Grove
11931 Harbor Boulevard
Garden Grove CA
714-591-4000
Dogs of all sizes are allowed. There is a $100 one time additional pet fee.

## Residence Inn Cypress Los Alamitos
4931 Katella Avenue
Los Alamitos CA
714-484-5700

Dogs of all sizes are allowed. There is a $100 one time additional pet fee.

## Extended Stay America Orange County - Katella Ave.
1635 West Katella Avenue
Orange CA
714-639-8608 (800-804-3724)
One dog is allowed per suite. There is a $25 per night additional pet fee up to $150 for an entire stay.

## Candlewood Suites Orange County
2600 South Red Hill Avenue
Santa Ana CA
949-250-0404 (877-270-6405)
Dogs of all sizes are allowed. Pets allowed with an additional pet fee. Up to $75 for 1-6 nights and up to $150 for 7+ nights. A pet agreement must be signed at check-in.

# Dog-Friendly Attractions
## Disneyland Kennel
1313 Harbor Blvd
Anaheim CA
714-781-4565
Disneyland is really more of an attraction for people, but we thought we would mention it because of their kennel. The great folks at Disneyland offer a day kennel for your pup while the rest of the family enjoys the theme park. There is a full time attendant at the kennels and the kennel hours are the same as the park hours. The cost is $20 for the whole day and you can come and walk your dog or just say hi as many times as you want. Just be sure to get your hand stamped for in/out park privileges. The cast members (Disneyland employees) suggest that you might want to bring a favorite blanket for your pup to lay on if he or she is used to that. The kennel is located to the right of the main Disneyland entrance/ticket booths. Please note the following special information: When driving to Disneyland, follow the signs to the main parking lot. At the

parking garage toll booth, tell the attendant that you have a dog and would like to use the RV/Oversize parking lot so you can be within closer walking distance to the kennels. From this parking lot, you can either walk to the main entrance of Disneyland (about 10-15 minutes) or take the parking lot tram from the parking lot to the entrance. Dogs are allowed on the parking lot tram, just make sure they are in the middle of the seat so they won't fall out during the ride. Once you arrive at Disneyland, make sure you walk your dog straight to the kennels. Dogs are not allowed in Downtown Disney and the security guards will remind you of this. If you are approached by a guard, just ask where the kennels are and they will point you in the right direction. Since August 28, 2006 dogs boarded at the Disneyland Kennel are required to show proof of rabies and distemper vaccines from the dogs vet. This is due to an Orange County requirement placed on kennels in the county.

# Outdoor Restaurants
## Chipotle
8182 E Santa Ana Canyon Road
Anaheim CA
714-283-3092
chipotle.com
Specializing in organic, natural and unprocessed food, this Mexican Eatery offers fajita burritos, tacos, salads, and salsas. Dogs are allowed at the outdoor tables but you will need to order your food inside the restaurant and dogs must remain outside.

## Coffee Bean & Tea Leaf
2002 E Lincoln Blvd
Anaheim CA
714-772-4861
coffeebean.com
The coffee here is sourced globally from family coffee farms to procure only the top of 1% of Arabica beans. They offer 30+

varieties of coffee;the beans are roasted in small batches daily for freshness, and they also offer 20 varieties of teas that are hand-blended by their tea master. Additionally, they offer a variety of tasty sweets, powders, extracts, sauces, gifts, and cards. Leashed, well mannered dogs are allowed at their outside dining area.

## Johnny Rockets
321 W Katella Avenue #320
Anaheim CA
714-491-1800
johnnyrockets.com/
All the American favorites can be found here: A fun retro, all-American decor and atmosphere, juicy burgers, specialty sandwiches, crispy fries, hand-dipped malts and shakes (dark chocolate ones too), fresh baked apple pies, tasty vegetarian choices, and something for all ages. Leashed, friendly dogs are allowed at their outside dining area.

## Rubios Baja Grill
520 N Euclid St
Anaheim CA
714-999-1525
rubios.com/
Sustainable and innovatively prepared seafood is the specialty of this eatery. They also offer a full day's menu and many made-from-scratch foods highlighting Mexican and Southern California cuisines. Leashed, well mannered dogs are allowed at their outside dining area.

## Subway Sandwiches
514 N Euclid Street
Anaheim CA
714-535-3444
This eatery specializes in made-to-order fresh, baked bread sandwiches with a variety of accompaniments to round out your meals. They also provide a kid's menu and catering services. Leashed dogs are allowed at the outer tables.

## Chipotle
501 N State College

Fullerton CA
714-525-2121
chipotle.com
Specializing in organic, natural and unprocessed food, this Mexican Eatery offers fajita burritos, tacos, salads, and salsas. Dogs are allowed at the outdoor tables but you will need to order your food inside the restaurant and dogs must remain outside.

## Coffee Bean & Tea Leaf
205 Orangefair Avenue, Space 11A
Fullerton CA
714-447-4160
coffeebean.com
The coffee here is sourced globally from family coffee farms to procure only the top of 1% of Arabica beans. They offer 30+ varieties of coffee;the beans are roasted in small batches daily for freshness, and they also offer 20 varieties of teas that are hand-blended by their tea master. Additionally, they offer a variety of tasty sweets, powders, extracts, sauces, gifts, and cards. Leashed, well mannered dogs are allowed at their outside dining area.

## Tropical Smoothie Cafe
229 E. Common Wealth Avenue
Fullerton CA
714-680-3008
tropicalsmoothie.com
Offerings from this health-minded cafe include all natural real fruit Super Fruit, Simply Indulgent, Super Charged, and Low Fat Smoothies;plus a selection of Coffee Smoothies. They also serve up freshly prepared signature wraps, flatbread and bistro sandwiches, garden fresh salads, all natural gourmet cheeses and meats, artisanal breads, vegan/vegetarian choices, and catering services. They are open for breakfast, lunch, and dinner. Leashed, well mannered dogs are allowed at their outside seating area.

## Byblos Mediterranean Cafe
129 W Chapman Ave
Orange CA
714-538-7180
Dogs are welcome at the outside tables of this eatery.

## Chipotle
2202 N Tustin Avenue
Orange CA
714-283-5010
chipotle.com
Specializing in organic, natural and unprocessed food, this Mexican Eatery offers fajita burritos, tacos, salads, and salsas. Dogs are allowed at the outdoor tables but you will need to order your food inside the restaurant and dogs must remain outside.

## Jamba Juice
20 City Blvd W K #5
Orange CA
714-769-3151
jambajuice.com
All natural and organic ingredients, no high-fructose corn syrup, 0 grams trans fat, no artificial preservatives, a healthy helping of antioxidants, vitamins, and minerals, and fresh whole fruit and fruit juices set the base for these tasty and healthy beverages. Their organic Hot Blends provides a new spin on coffee, green or chai tea, and hot chocolate;plus they offer probiotic fruit and yogurt Blends. Additionally, they feature organic steel-cut oatmeal prepared fresh every morning, all natural salads, wraps, sandwiches, and grab n' go specialties. They also offer healthy community support through fundraisers, special sales, and school lunch programs. Leashed, well mannered dogs are allowed at their outside dining area.

## Johnny Rockets
20 City Blvd
Orange CA
714-385-0086
johnnyrockets.com/
All the American favorites can be found here: A fun retro, all-American decor and atmosphere, juicy burgers,

specialty sandwiches, crispy fries, hand-dipped malts and shakes (dark chocolate ones too), fresh baked apple pies, tasty vegetarian choices, and something for all ages. Leashed, friendly dogs are allowed at their outside dining area.

**Krispy Kreme Doughnuts**
330 The City Dr S
Orange CA
714-769-4330
krispykreme.com/home
This donut shop allows well mannered dogs at their patio seating;owner's must clean up after their pets.

**Lazy Dog Restaurant & Bar**
1623 West Katella Ave.
Orange CA
714-769-7020
lazydogrestaurants.com/dogs/info
Known for it's dog-friendly patio, the Lazy Dog offers your dog a complimentary bowl of water, and a menu consisting of grilled hamburger patty, chicken breast or brown rice. They just ask that you respect their common sense rules while your dog is dining there. This is as dog-friendly as dining gets. For the humans in your party there is hamburger, steak, salads and some great desserts.

**The Coffee Bean & Tea Leaf**
2202 N. Tustin Street, Suite C
Orange CA
714-283-0088
coffeebean.com
The coffee here is sourced globally from family coffee farms to procure only the top of 1% of Arabica beans. They offer 30+ varieties of coffee;the beans are roasted in small batches daily for freshness, and they also offer 20 varieties of teas that are hand-blended by their tea master. Additionally, they offer a variety of tasty sweets, powders, extracts, sauces, gifts, and cards. Leashed, well mannered dogs are allowed at their outside dining area.

**The Loving Hut**

237 S Tustin Street
Orange CA
714-464-0544
lovinghut.us/orange/
A quick-service 100% vegan eatery, guests will find a full menu of affordable, freshly prepared gourmet cuisine made with the finest and freshest quality ingredients available. They offer organic coffee and tea, specialize in traditional, regional, and Chinese vegan cuisines, and in providing foods that are gluten free with no GMOs, milk or eggs. Services include dine-in, take-out, frozen and dried food sales, and catering. Leashed, well mannered dogs are allowed at their outside dining area.

**Two's Company**
22 Plaza Square
Orange CA
714-771-7633
twoscompanycafe.com/
This café is open daily from 8:30 am until 6:30 pm. Leashed dogs are allowed at their outside dining area.

**Chipotle**
3705 S Bristol Street
Santa Ana CA
714-754-7380
chipotle.com
Specializing in organic, natural and unprocessed food, this Mexican Eatery offers fajita burritos, tacos, salads, and salsas. Dogs are allowed at the outdoor tables but you will need to order your food inside the restaurant and dogs must remain outside.

**The Coffee Bean & Tea Leaf**
2264 17th Street
Santa Ana CA
714-542-5307
coffeebean.com
The coffee here is sourced globally from family coffee farms to procure only the top of 1% of Arabica beans. They offer 30+ varieties of coffee;the beans are roasted in small batches daily for freshness, and they also offer 20 varieties of teas that are hand-blended

by their tea master. Additionally, they offer a variety of tasty sweets, powders, extracts, sauces, gifts, and cards. Leashed, well mannered dogs are allowed at their outside dining area.

**The Coffee Bean & Tea Leaf**
2783 N Main Street
Santa Ana CA
714-667-7840
coffeebean.com
The coffee here is sourced globally from family coffee farms to procure only the top of 1% of Arabica beans. They offer 30+ varieties of coffee;the beans are roasted in small batches daily for freshness, and they also offer 20 varieties of teas that are hand-blended by their tea master. Additionally, they offer a variety of tasty sweets, powders, extracts, sauces, gifts, and cards. Leashed, well mannered dogs are allowed at their outside dining area.

**Z Pizza**
3941 South Bristol
Santa Ana CA
714-437-1111
zpizza.com
Specializing in organically and international inspired pizzas, this pizzeria cooks their pizzas on hot bricks in a fire baked oven. They feature a 100% certified organic gluten free wheat crust, homemade organic sauces and ingredients, fresh produce, and additive-free meats. They also offer gourmet salads, sandwiches, and catering services. Leashed, well mannered dogs are allowed at their outside tables.

**Rubio's**
7063 Katella Ave
Stanton CA
714-827-6495
rubios.com
Rubio's offers a variety of mexican food, seafood, chicken, salad, and more. Leashed, well behaved dogs are allowed on the outdoor patio.

**Chipotle**
13348 Newport Avenue

Tustin CA
714-665-6730
chipotle.com
Specializing in organic, natural and unprocessed food, this Mexican Eatery offers fajita burritos, tacos, salads, and salsas. Dogs are allowed at the outdoor tables but you will need to order your food inside the restaurant and dogs must remain outside.

**Jamba Juice**
2937 E Camino Real #B
Tustin CA
714-505-2582
jambajuice.com
All natural and organic ingredients, no high-fructose corn syrup, 0 grams trans fat, no artificial preservatives, a healthy helping of antioxidants, vitamins, and minerals, and fresh whole fruit and fruit juices set the base for these tasty and healthy beverages. Their organic Hot Blends provides a new spin on coffee, green or chai tea, and hot chocolate;plus they offer probiotic fruit and yogurt Blends. Additionally, they feature organic steel-cut oatmeal prepared fresh every morning, all natural salads, wraps, sandwiches, and grab n' go specialties. They also offer healthy community support through fundraisers, special sales, and school lunch programs. Leashed, well mannered dogs are allowed at their outside dining area.

**Tustin Brewing Company**
13011 Newport Avenue
Tustin CA
714-665-2337
tustinbrewery.com
In addition to an impressive selection of brews, wines and spirits, this lively gathering place serves up some great appetizers, fresh salads, specialty sandwiches, pastas, signature dishes, wood fired pizzas, and house-made desserts. Leashed, well mannered dogs are welcome at their outside tables.

**Whole Foods Market**

14945 Holt Ave.
Tustin CA
714-731-3400
wholefoods.com/
This natural food supermarket offers natural and organic foods. Order some food from their deli without your dog and bring it to an outdoor table where your well-behaved leashed dog is welcome.

**Z Pizza**
12932 Newport Avenue
Tustin CA
714-734-9749
zpizza.com
Specializing in organically and international inspired pizzas, this pizzeria cooks their pizzas on hot bricks in a fire baked oven. They feature a 100% certified organic gluten free wheat crust, homemade organic sauces and ingredients, fresh produce, and additive-free meats. They also offer gourmet salads, sandwiches, and catering services. Leashed, well mannered dogs are allowed at their outside tables.

**Lazy Dog Restaurant & Bar**
16310 Beach Blvd
Westminster CA
714-500-1140
lazydogrestaurants.com/dogs/info
Known for it's dog-friendly patio, the Lazy Dog offers your dog a complimentary bowl of water, and a menu consisting of grilled hamburger patty, chicken breast or brown rice. They just ask that you respect their common sense rules while your dog is dining there. This is as dog-friendly as dining gets. For the humans in your party there is hamburger, steak, salads and some great desserts.

# Pet-Friendly Stores
**Petco Pet Store - Anaheim**
430 North Euclid St.
Anaheim CA
714-635-1714
Your licensed and well-

behaved leashed dog is allowed in the store.

**Petco Pet Store - Anaheim Hills**
8092 East Santa Ana Canyon Road
Anaheim CA
714-998-6833
Your licensed and well-behaved leashed dog is allowed in the store.

**PetSmart Pet Store**
8321 La Palma Ave
Buena Park CA
714-739-2100
Your licensed and well-behaved leashed dog is allowed in the store.

**Petco Pet Store - Buena Park**
6020 Ball Road
Buena Park CA
714-828-4600
Your licensed and well-behaved leashed dog is allowed in the store.

**PetSmart Pet Store**
1411 S Harbor Blvd
Fullerton CA
714-992-5116
Your licensed and well-behaved leashed dog is allowed in the store.

**Barnes and Noble Bookstore**
791 S Main Street
Orange CA
714-558-0028
Well-behaved, leashed dogs may accompany shoppers in the bookstore or at the outdoor tables at the coffee shop.

**Petco Pet Store - Orange**
1824 East Katella Ave.
Orange CA
714-289-1400
Your licensed and well-behaved leashed dog is allowed in the store.

**PetSmart Pet Store**
2140 E 17th St
Santa Ana CA
714-480-0620
Your licensed and well-behaved leashed dog is allowed in the store.

**Petco Pet Store - Santa Ana**
3327 South Bristol St.
Santa Ana CA
714-979-3802
Your licensed and well-behaved leashed dog is allowed in the store.

**Petco Pet Store - Tustin**
13942 Newport Ave.
Tustin CA
714-669-9030
Your licensed and well-behaved leashed dog is allowed in the store.

**Petco Pet Store - Westminster**

6761 Westminster Blvd
Westminster CA
714-799-4558
Your licensed and well-behaved leashed dog is allowed in the store.

## Off-Leash Dog Parks
**Bellis Park Dog Park**
7171 8th Street
Buena Park CA
714-236-3860
There is an acre of fenced, doggy play area at this off leash park with benches, trees, and plenty of grass. Dogs must be sociable, current on all vaccinations and license, and under their owner's control at all times. Dogs must be leashed when not in designated off-lead areas.

**Fullerton Pooch Park**
S Basque Avenue
Fullerton CA
714-738-6575
Located next to the library, this off leash area offers 2 sections; one for larger dogs, and one for small dogs. Water is available in the off lead area. Dogs must be sociable, current on all vaccinations, and under their owner's control at all times. Dogs must be leashed when not in designated off-lead areas.

**Fullerton Pooch Park**
201 S Basque Ave
Fullerton CA
714-738-6575

The Fullerton Pooch Park, located in Fullerton, California was established in June 2007 and became a permanent City of Fullerton park facility in 2009 .There is a small dog area for pooches under 25lbs as well as a large dog area for big and active pooches. Pooch Park also features a third "wood chip" area that is open to all dogs. All pooches and their owners are welcome provided everyone follows the rules and regulations. The park is closed for routine maintenance every Wednesday.

**Garden Grove Dog Park**
13601 Deodara Dr
Garden Grove CA
714-741-5000
The Garden Grove Dog Park features separate play areas for large and small dogs. It also has a leash/unleash area, benches, and doggie waste bag stations. The hours of operation are dawn to dusk, 7 days a week. The park is free of charge.

**Yorba Dog Park**
190 S Yorba Street
Orange CA
714-633-2980
orangedogpark.com/
There is a separate small dog section at this park, and until there are benches installed, lawn chairs may be brought into the park and set along the fence that separates the big dog/small dog areas. Chairs must be taken out each night. The park is closed for maintenance on Wednesdays.

## Dog-Friendly Parks
**Santa Ana River Path**
E. La Palma Ave.
Anaheim CA

This path stretches for about 20 miles each way. The trail parallels the Santa Ana River. In most spots, there are two sets of trails, one for bikes and one for horses. Dogs are allowed on either trail (paved

and dirt). Parking is available at the Yorba Regional Park which is located on E. La Palma Avenue between the Imperial Hwy (Hwy 90) and S. Weir Canyon Rd. There is a minimal fee for parking.

**Yorba Regional Park**
E. La Palma Ave.
Anaheim CA
714-970-1460
ocparks.com/parks/yorba
This regional park has 175 acres with several streams and four lakes. There are also over 400 picnic tables and over 200 barbecue stoves. If you want an longer walk or jog, the park is adjacent to the twenty mile long Santa Ana River Bike Path and Trail. The park is located on E. La Palma Avenue between the Imperial Hwy (Hwy 90) and S. Weir Canyon Rd. There is a minimal fee for parking.

**Irvine Regional Park**
1 Irvine Park Rd
Orange CA
714-633-8074
ocparks.com/parks/irvine/
Located in the foothills, this is California's oldest regional park. With over 470 acres, this park has a variety of Oak and Sycamore groves, streams, a pond, a paved trail, picnic tables and barbecues. There are also several historical sites and plaques located throughout the park. Maps are available from the park ranger at the main entrance. Because this park is also a wilderness area with mountain lions, park rules state that minors must be under adult supervision at all times. Dogs must be leashed. There is a minimal parking fee.

**Peters Canyon Regional Park**
Canyon View Ave
Orange CA
714-973-6611
ocparks.com/parks/peters
This park has over 350 acres of coastal sage scrub, woodlands, a freshwater marsh, and a 55 acre reservoir. They have a variety of dirt paths and trails (approx. 2-3 miles) which are

frequented by hikers, mountain bikers, equestrians and of course, leashed dogs. All trails are closed for three days following rainfall. To get there from Hwy 5 or Hwy 405, take the Jamboree Road exit north. Then turn left at Canyon View Ave. Proceed 1/4 mile to the park entrance and parking lot. Maps should be available at a stand near the parking lot.

**Centennial Regional Park**
3000 W Edinger Avenue
Santa Ana CA
714-571-4200
This large, day-use park features a 10 acre lake stocked with fish and an historic trail that follows the original path of the Santa Ana River. There are picnic areas, restrooms, and several multi-use trails. Dogs are allowed throughout the park and on the trails. Dogs must be well behaved, leashed, and cleaned up after at all times.

**Airports**
**John Wayne Airport (SNA)**

Santa Ana CA

The Pet Relief Area can be found on the lower level outside of Terminal A near the entrance to Parking Structure A1. Owners are asked to clean up after their animals, using the waste disposal bags and receptacle provided. There is a map of the pet relief areas at this link.

**Emergency Veterinarians**
**Yorba Regional Animal Hospital**
8290 E. Crystal Drive
Anaheim CA
714-921-8700
yorbaregionalvets.com
This hospital has regular vet services and is fully staffed for walk-in emergencies 24 hours a day.

**Orange County Emergency Pet Hospital**

12750 Garden Grove Blvd
Garden Grove CA
714-537-3032
Monday - Friday 6pm to 8am, Noon Saturday to 8 am Monday.

## Anderson

**Dog-Friendly Hotels**
**Baymont Inn & Suites Anderson**
2040 Factory Outlets Drive
Anderson CA
530-365-6100
Dogs of all sizes are allowed. There is a $15 one time pet fee.

**Best Western Anderson Inn**
2688 Gateway Drive
Anderson CA
530-365-2753 (800-780-7234)
Dogs up to 80 pounds are allowed. There is a $20 per day pet fee up to $100 for the week. Up to two dogs are allowed per room.

## Arcata

**Dog-Friendly Hotels**
**Best Western Arcata Inn**
4827 Valley West Blvd.
Arcata CA
707-826-0313 (800-780-7234)
Dogs up to 80 pounds are allowed. There is a $20 per day pet fee up to $100 for the week. Up to two dogs are allowed per room.

**Ramada Arcata**
3535 Janes Road
Arcata CA
707-822-0409 (877-424-6423)
Located in a quiet country setting on the Redwood Coast area of Northern California. Outdoor pool and hot tub.

Dogs of all sizes are allowed. Dogs are allowed for a pet fee

of $10.00 per pet per night. Two dogs are allowed per room.

**Red Roof Inn Arcata**
4975 Valley West Boulevard
Arcata CA
707-822-4861 (800-329-7466)
Dogs of all sizes are allowed. Dogs are allowed for a pet fee.

**Super 8 Arcata**
4887 Valley West Boulevard
Arcata CA
707-822-8888 (800-800-8000)
Dogs are welcome at this hotel.

**Dog-Friendly Beaches**
**Mad River Beach County Park**
Mad River Road
Arcata CA
707-445-7651
Enjoy walking or jogging for several miles on this beach. Dogs on leash are allowed. The park is located about 4-5 miles north of Arcata. To get there, take Highway 101 and exit Giuntoli Lane. Then go north onto Heindon Rd. Turn left onto Miller Rd. Turn right on Mad River Road and follow it to the park.

**Clam Beach County Park**
Highway 101
McKinleyville CA
707-445-7651
This beach is popular for fishing, swimming, picnicking and beach-combing. Of course, there are also plenty of clams. Dogs on leash are allowed on the beach and at the campgrounds. There are no day use fees. The park is located off Highway 101, about eight miles north of Arcata.

**Dog-Friendly Parks**
**Arcata Community Forest**
11th and 14th Streets
Arcata CA
707-822-3619
Leashed dogs are allowed on this 600+ acre park which offers 18 trails. The trails range from 1/10 of a mile to almost 2 miles long. The park is located on the

east side of the City of Arcata, accessible from Redwood Park located at the east ends of 11th and 14th Streets; on the southern side from Fickle Hill Road, which begins at the east end of 11th and 7th Streets at Bayside Road; and from the east end of California Street which connects with L.K. Wood Blvd. north of Humboldt State University.

## Arrowbear

### Dog-Friendly Parks
**Crab Creek Trail and Fisherman's Camp**
off Green Valley Road
Arrowbear CA
909-337-2444
This 2.5 mile moderate rated trail is located in the San Bernardino National Forest. On the trail, you may have to cross Deep Creek. Do not attempt to cross the creek when the water is high as it is too dangerous. Pets are allowed but must be on a 6 foot or less leash. Please clean up after them. The trailhead is located at Forest Road 3N34, west of the Crab Flats Campground. To get there take 330 north and go through Running Springs and Arrowbear to Green Valley Road. Turn left and go about 4 miles to the Crab Flats Campground sign at Forestry (dirt road). Turn left and go about 4.5 miles.

### Crab Flats Trail
off Green Valley Road
Arrowbear CA
909-337-2444
This 1.3 mile long moderate rated trail is located in the San Bernardino National Forest. The trail descends and joins up with the Pacific Crest Trail west of the Holocomb Crossing Trail Camp. Pets are allowed but must be on a 6 foot or less leash. Please clean up after them. The trailhead is located at Forest Road 3N34, west of the

Crab Flats Campground. To get there take 330 north and go through Running Springs and Arrowbear to Green Valley Road. Turn left and go about 4 miles to the Crab Flats Campground sign at Forestry (dirt road). Turn left and go about 4.5 miles.

### Pacific Crest National Scenic Trail
off Green Valley Road
Arrowbear CA
909-337-2444
lakearrowhead.com/hiking.html

The 40 mile one way moderate rated trail is located in the San Bernardino National Forest. Pets are allowed but must be on a 6 foot or less leash. Please clean up after them. One entry point to this trail is at Forest Road 3N16, which is near the Crab Flats Campground. To get there take 330 north and go through Running Springs and Arrowbear to Green Valley Road. Turn left and go about 4 miles to the Crab Flats Campground sign at Forestry (dirt road). Turn left and go about 4.5 miles.

## Atwater

### Pet-Friendly Stores
**Tractor Supply Company**
1700 Bell Lane
Atwater CA
209-357-7351
tractorsupply.com
Some offerings of this comprehensive farm store includes agriculture, farming and ranching supplies; outdoor power equipment with all the necessities; hundreds of thousands of parts and accessories accessible for yard and garden; metal working and welding supplies; tools for auto and home; a wide range of livestock/farm feed and needs; and a variety of foods and

care/play/groom items for household pets. Additionally, they provide trailer and towing supplies, vehicle maintenance accessories, clothing, work wear, foot wear, gifts, home improvement items, a lot of "know-how" and much more. Leashed, friendly dogs are welcome in the store.

## Auburn - Gold Country North

### Dog-Friendly Hotels
**Best Western Golden Key**
13450 Lincoln Way
Auburn CA
530-885-8611 (800-780-7234)
Dogs up to 80 pounds are allowed. There is a $15 per day pet fee up to $100 for the week. Up to two dogs are allowed per room.

**Holiday Inn Auburn**
120 Grass Valley Highway
Auburn CA
530-887-8787 (877-270-6405)
Dogs up to 40 pounds are allowed. Dogs are allowed for a pet fee of $30.00 per pet per stay.

**Rodeway Inn Auburn-Foresthill**
13490 Lincoln Way
Auburn CA
530-885-7025 (877-424-6423)
The Quality Inn is in the historical town of Auburn in the heart of the gold country. We are minutes from the American River.

Dogs up to 10 pounds are allowed. Dogs are allowed for a pet fee of $15.00 per pet per night. Two dogs are allowed per room.

**Super 8 Auburn**
140 East Hillcrest Drive
Auburn CA
530-888-8808 (800-800-8000)
Dogs are welcome at this hotel.

**Best Western Gold Country Inn**
972 Sutton Way
Grass Valley CA
530-273-1393 (800-780-7234)
Dogs up to 80 pounds are allowed. There is a $20 per day pet fee up to $100 for the week. Up to two dogs are allowed per room.

**Gold Miners Inn An Ascend Hotel Collection Member**
121 Bank Street
Grass Valley CA
530-477-1700 (877-698-9593)
Dogs of all sizes are allowed. Dogs are allowed for a pet fee of $50 per pet per stay.

**Grass Valley Courtyard Suites**

210 North Auburn Street
Grass Valley CA
530-272-7696
gvcourtyardsuites.com/
they have provided a doggy station with a scooper and receptacles.

# Dog-Friendly Attractions
**Empire Mine State Historic Park**
10791 East Empire Street
Grass Valley CA
530-273-8522
This park is home to one of the oldest, largest, deepest, longest, and richest gold mines in California. The park consists of over 800 acres and has eight miles of trails. Dogs on leash are allowed in the park and on the trails.

**Nevada City Horse & Carriage**
downtown Nevada City
Nevada City CA
530-265-9646
Well-behaved dogs are allowed to ride in this horse and carriage with their family.

# Outdoor Restaurants
**Bootleggers Tavern and Grill**
210 Washington St
Auburn CA

530-889-2229
bootleggersauburn.com/
This restaurant is located in historic Auburn in the original City Hall which was built in 1870. Leashed dogs are welcome at the outdoor tables during the summer.

**Ikeda's**
13500 Lincoln Way
Auburn CA
530-885-4243
ikedas.com/auburn.htm
Award winning hamburgers, homemade soups and fair, a country market with local grown fruits and vegetables, and a bakery for fresh goods are all to be found at this restaurant. There is outdoor seating, just order and pick up your food inside. Dogs are allowed on the patio. They must be attended to at all times, well behaved, and leashed.

**La Bou**
2150 Grass Valley Hwy
Auburn CA
530-823-2303
labou.com/
This café and bakery specializes in gourmet made from scratch soup, pastries, and breakfast items. Leashed dogs are allowed at their outside seating area.

**Max's**
11960 Heritage Oak Place
Auburn CA
530-823-6297
eatatmaxs.com/
A deli and catering company, this eatery specializes in hearty sandwiches, tasty accompaniments, and specialty coffees;there is also free WiFi with purchase. There is outside dining, and dogs are allowed at the outer tables;they must be leashed and under owner's control/care.

**Tio Pepe's**
216 Washington Street
Auburn CA
530-888-6445
tiopepemex.com/
Dogs are allowed at the outdoor tables.

**Bubba's Bagels**
11943 Nevada City Hwy
Grass Valley CA
530-272-8590
This bagelery is open Monday to Friday from 6 am until 3 pm and on Saturday and Sunday from 7 am until 3 pm. Dogs are allowed at the outdoor table.

**Cousin Jack Pasty Company**
100 S Auburn St
Grass Valley CA
530-272-9230
cousinjackspasty.com/
Well mannered, leashed dogs are allowed at the covered outdoor tables. The restaurant is in downtown Grass Valley and offers homemade pasty pastries crafted from local and organic ingredients.

**Broad Street Bistro**
426 Broad St
Nevada City CA
530-265-4204
broadstreetbistro.com/
Dogs are not allowed on the patio, but there is one table near the back door. There is a water bowl for your dog next to this table.

**California Organics**
135 Argall Way
Nevada City CA
530-265-9392
This market and café features healthy, organic, foods for breakfast, lunch, and dinner dining. They offer patio dining where your pet may join you. Dogs must be attended to at all times, well behaved, and leashed.

**New Moon Cafe**
203 York Street
Nevada City CA
530-265-6399
thenewmooncafe.com/#
This café offers sophisticated dining with a small town atmosphere, variety in their season-changing menu, and natural/organic foods that are prepared fresh daily, including the breads and deserts. Your pet is welcome to join you at the outside tables. Dogs must be

attended to at all times, well behaved, and leashed.

## Off-Leash Dog Parks
### Ashley Memorial Dog Park
Auburn Ravine Road (back of Ashford Park)
Auburn CA
530-887-9993
A fairly new park, there will be more amenities/events to be added as time goes by. At present there are 2 sections for large and small dogs, water features, agility play areas, picnic areas, and lots of shade trees. Dogs must be sociable, current on all vaccinations and license, and under their owner's control at all times. Dogs must be leashed when not in designated off-lead areas.

### Condon Park Dog Park
660 Minnie Street
Grass Valley CA
530-273-9268
Tall shade trees, benches, and lots of play room are offered at this off leash doggy play area. Dogs must be healthy, sociable, current on all vaccinations and license with tags on collar, and under their owner's control at all times. Owners must clean up after their pets, and keep them leashed when not in designated off-lead areas.

### Grass Valley Dog Park
660 Minnie Street
Grass Valley CA
530-273-9268
dogsrunfree.net/
Located at Condon Park, this fenced doggy playground offers shade trees, benches, and waste disposal stations. The park is open daily from sunup to sunset. Dogs must be healthy, sociable, current on all vaccinations and license with tags on collar, and under their owner's control at all times. Owners must clean up after their pets, and keep them on no more than a 6 foot leash when not in designated off-lead areas.

## Dog-Friendly Parks
### Auburn State Recreation Area
Highway 49 or Auburn-Foresthill Rd.
Auburn CA
530-885-4527
Dogs on leash are allowed everywhere except at Lake Clementine. Located in the heart of the gold country, this recreation area covers over 35,000 acres along 40 miles of the North and Middle Forks of the American River. Major recreational uses include hiking, swimming, boating, fishing, camping, mountain biking, gold panning and off-highway motorcycle riding. One of the more popular trails is the Western States National Recreation Trail. It hosts the Tevis Cup Endurance Ride and Western States100 Endurance Run each summer. The park is located south of Interstate 80, stretching from Auburn to Colfax. The main access is from Auburn, either on Highway 49 or the Auburn-Foresthill Road.

### Stevens Trail
North Canyon Way
Colfax CA
916-985-4474
mvtrails.org/stevens.htm
This 4.5 mile trail is a popular year-round hiking, mountain biking and horseback riding trail which follows the northwestern slope of the North Fork of the American River. The trail offers a gentle slope that is suitable for novice hikers. Along the trail you can enjoy great views of the river, pass by several mine shafts, and see the China Wall built by Chinese laborers during the Gold Rush era in the 1850s. Please stay away from the mines because they are extremely dangerous and unstable. In April and May there should be a nice wildflower display. Leashed dogs are welcome. Please clean up after your dog. To get

there from Sacramento, head east on Highway 80 towards Colfax. Take the North Canyon Way exit. Take this road past the Colfax cemetery to the trailhead. On weekends and in high use season, parking may be very limited.

### North Yuba Trail
Highway 49
Downieville CA
530-288-3231
This 7.5 mile moderate rated trail is located in the Tahoe National Forest. Pets must be either leashed or off-leash but under direct voice control. Please clean up after your pets. The trail is located on Highway 49, 7.5 miles west of Downieville at the Rocky Rest Campground.

### Big Trees Nature Trail (Loop)
Mosquito Ridge Road
Foresthill CA
530-367-2224
This .5 mile easy trail is located in the Tahoe National Forest and is a popular interpretive trail. The trail is accessible when the road is open, generally from late May to early November. Pets on leash are allowed and please clean up after them. To get there from Foresthill, take Mosquito Ridge Road 24 miles to Road 16.

### French Meadows Reservoir
Mosquito Ridge Road
Foresthill CA
530-367-2224
Activities at this reservoir include fishing, boating, swimming, picnicking, hiking, and viewing scenery. Dogs are allowed in the water. Pets must be either leashed or off-leash but under direct voice control. Please clean up after your pets. The reservoir is located in the Tahoe National Forest, 36 miles east of Foresthill on Mosquito Ridge Road.

### Little Bald Mountain Trail
Foresthill Divide Road
Foresthill CA
530-367-2224
This trail is located in the Tahoe

National Forest and is a 3.39 mile moderate rated trail. The trail is open from May to November, weather permitting. Pets must be either leashed or off-leash but under direct voice control. Please clean up after your pets. To get there, go 28 miles from Foresthill on Foresthill Divide Road to Robinson Flat and park in the day use area.

## Sugar Pine Trail
Foresthill Divide Road
Foresthill CA
530-367-2224
This popular 3.5 mile easy trail goes around Sugar Pine Reservoir. Dogs are allowed on the trail and in the water on non-designated swim beaches. Pets must be either leashed or off-leash but under direct voice control. Please clean up after your pets. The primary season for this trail is usually from May to October. This trail is located in the Tahoe National Forest. To get there from Foresthill, go 18 miles northeast on Foresthill Divide Road.

## Salmon Lakes Trail
Road 38
Nevada City CA
530-265-4531
This 2 mile easy rated trail is located in the Tahoe National Park. It used by hikers, mountain bikers and equestrians. Pets must be leashed in the campground and please clean up after them. To get there from I-80 at Yuba Gap, go south for .3 miles and turn right toward Lodgepole Campground. After 1.1 miles, turn right on Road 19 (unpaved). After 2 miles turn left on Road 38. The trailhead is 2 miles ahead and .5 miles past Huysink Lake.

## South Yuba Trail
North Bloomfield Road
Nevada City CA
916-985-4474
This 12 mile trail is popular with hikers, runners, mountain bikers and horseback riders. The trail offers pine tree covered

canyons, gentle slopes and open meadows. Along the trail you will see historic flumes and waterworks. Leashed dogs are welcome. Please clean up after your dog. The South Yuba River Recreation Area is located about 10 miles northeast of Nevada City. From Nevada City, take Highway 49 north to North Bloomfield Road. Drive 10 miles to the South Yuba Recreation Area. From the one lane bridge at Edwards Crossing, go about 1.5 miles on a dirt/gravel road to the campground and trailhead. Trailers and motorhomes should take Highway 49 and then turn right at the junction of Tyler Foote Road. At the intersection of Grizzly Hill Road turn right and proceed to North Bloomfield Road.

## Tahoe National Forest
631 Coyote Street
Nevada City CA
530-265-4531
fs.usda.gov/tahoe
This national forest includes the Lake Tahoe Basin Management Area. Elevations range from 1,500 feet up to 9,400 feet. Please see our listings in the Gold Country and Sierra Nevada region for dog-friendly hikes and/or campgrounds.

## Other Organizations
### Ashley Memorial Dog Park Foundation
565 Riverview Drive
Auburn CA
530-889-2486
ashleydogpark.com
The Auburn Area Recreational Park District has no funding to build or maintain the dog park. The Ashley Memorial Dog Park is being built by volunteers and dedicated dog enthusiasts for the community of Auburn.

# Avenue Of The Giants

## Dog-Friendly Hotels
### Best Western Plus Humboldt House Inn
701 Redwood Drive
Garberville CA
707-923-2771 (800-780-7234)
Dogs up to 80 pounds are allowed. There is a $15 per day pet fee up to $100 for the week. Up to two dogs are allowed per room.

## Dog-Friendly Attractions
### One Log House
705 US Hwy 101
Garberville CA
707-247-3717
This espresso and gift shop hosts the One Log House, a house built inside of a single 13 foot diameter redwood tree. You can get an espresso to drink outside with your pet after viewing the home.

### Avenue of the Giants
Highway 101
Phillipsville CA
707-722-4291
This 33 mile drive offers spectacular views of redwoods and some very unique redwood trees, including some of the biggest trees in the world. You and your pooch might be able to drive your car through a redwood tree or two (depending on the size of your car). There is a fee to drive through some of the trees. The auto tour can be taken from the northbound or southbound direction. Allow about 1-2 hours, depending on stops and any traffic. From the north start at the Pepperwood/Jordan Creek exit off Highway 101 and from the south, start at the Phillipsville exit off Highway 101. The auto tour map can be picked up at either entrance. Dogs are not allowed on the trails in the state park, but they are allowed on fire roads and access roads in

the Humboldt Redwoods State Park. One of the access points to the fire roads is at Albee Creek Campground.

## Dog-Friendly Parks
**Benbow State Recreation Area**
1600 Highway 101
Garberville CA
707-923-3238
Leashed dogs are allowed. The park consists of about 1,200 acres with campsites and a large day-use picnic area. Hiking, picnicking and camping are popular summer time activities, while salmon and steelhead fishing are popular in the winter.

**Humboldt Redwoods State Park**
Avenue of the Giants
Weott CA
707-946-2409
This park is located along the scenic Avenue of the Giants. While dogs are not allowed on the trails, they are allowed in the campgrounds and on miles of fire roads and access roads. These paths are used mainly for mountain biking, but dogs are allowed too. There are both steep and gently sloping fire roads. Some of the fire roads are located next to the Albee Creek Campground. Pets on leash are allowed and please clean up after them. The park is located along the Avenue of the Giants, about 45 miles south of Eureka and 20 miles north of Garberville.

## Avila Beach

## Outdoor Restaurants
**The Customs House**
404 Front Street
Avila Beach CA
805-595-7555
oldcustomhouse.com
This popular beach-side eatery

has meats, seafood, and produce delivered fresh every day, and offer a full menu of freshly prepared regional and seasonal cuisine. They also feature specialty cocktails, an extensive wine list, and a venue for special events. Leashed dogs are welcome at their outside dining area.

## Dog-Friendly Beaches
**Avila Beach**
off Avila Beach Drive
Avila Beach CA
805-595-5400
This beach is about a 1/2 mile long. Dogs are not allowed between 10am and 5pm and must be leashed.

**Olde Port Beach**
off Avila Beach Drive
Avila Beach CA
805-595-5400
This beach is about a 1/4 mile long. Dogs are not allowed between 10am and 5pm and must be leashed.

## Baker

## Dog-Friendly Parks
**Mohave National Preserve**
72157 Baker Road
Baker CA
760-255-8800
nps.gov/moja/
Located in the heart of the Mohave Desert, this 1.6 million acre park offers rose-colored sand dunes, volcanic cinder cones and Joshua tree forests. The park offers hundreds of miles of dirt roads to explore the land in your own 4 wheel drive vehicle. There are many hiking opportunities including the Teutonia Peak Hike. This trail lets you explore a dense Joshua tree forest on the way to a peak on Cima Dome. The 4 mile roundtrip trail is located 10.5 miles south of I-15 on Cima Road. Dogs are allowed

on trails and in the campgrounds. They must be leashed except dogs that are being used for hunting. Please clean up after your pet. For more park details and information, including maps, visit the Baker Desert Information Center in Baker. They are open all year from 9am to 5pm.

## Bakersfield

## Dog-Friendly Hotels
**Americas Best Value Inn And Suites Bakersfield Central**
830 Wible Road
Bakersfield CA
661-831-1922
Does not wish to have information made available

**Best Economy Inn & Suites**
5200 Olive Tree Court
Bakersfield CA
(877-424-6423)
The Econo Lodge hotel is conveniently located off the 99 freeway and just three miles from Meadows Field Airport.

**Best Western Heritage Inn**
253 Trask Street
Bakersfield CA
661-764-6268 (800-780-7234)
Pets may be accepted. Please contact the hotel directly for full details.

**Best Western Plus Hill House**
700 Truxtun Avenue
Bakersfield CA
661-327-4064 (800-780-7234)
Dogs are allowed. There is a $10 per pet per night pet fee. Up to four dogs are allowed per room.

**Hotel Rosedale**
2400 Camino Del Rio Court
Bakersfield CA
661-327-0681
Dogs up to 80 pounds are allowed for a $20 per night per pet additional fee. There is a $15 pet fee for R&R members,

and the R&R program is free to sign up.

## Howard Johnson Express Inn - Bakersfield
2700 White Lane
Bakersfield CA
661-396-1425 (800-446-4656)
Dogs of all sizes are allowed. There is a pet of $5 per pet per night.

## La Quinta Inn Bakersfield South
3232 Riverside Drive
Bakersfield CA
661-325-7400 (800-531-5900)
Dogs of all sizes are allowed. There are no additional pet fees. Dogs must be housebroken, well behaved, leashed, and cleaned up after.

## Red Lion Hotel Bakersfield
2620 Buck Owens Blvd.
Bakersfield CA
661-327-9651
Dogs up to 80 pounds are allowed. There is a $10 per day pet fee up to $100 for the week. Up to two dogs are allowed per room.

## Sleep Inn And Suites
6257 Knudsen Drive
Bakersfield CA
661-399-2100 (877-424-6423)
Located in the southern end of the San Joaquin Valley, just minutes from Kern County Airport.

## Super 8 Bakersfield/central
901 Real Road
Bakersfield CA
661-322-1012 (800-800-8000)
Dogs are welcome at this hotel.

## Travelodge Motel Bakersfield
1011 Oak St
Bakersfield CA
661-325-0772
Dogs up to 50 pounds are allowed. There is a pet fee of $10 per pet per night.

## Vagabond Inn Buttonwillow I-5
200 Trask Street
Bakersfield CA
661-764-5221 (877-424-6423)

The Rodeway Inn Near I-5 is conveniently located minutes from Buena Vista Lake, Elk Reserve, Buck Owens Crystal Palace, and Cal

Dogs of all sizes are allowed. Dogs are allowed for a pet fee of $5.00 per pet per night.

# Pet-Friendly Extended Stay Hotels
## Extended Stay America - Bakersfield - California Avenue
3318 California Ave.
Bakersfield CA
661-322-6888 (800-804-3724)
One dog is allowed per suite. There is a $25 per night additional pet fee up to $150 for an entire stay.

## Residence Inn Bakersfield
4241 Chester Lane
Bakersfield CA
661-321-9800
Dogs of all sizes are allowed. There is a $100 one time additional pet fee.

# Outdoor Restaurants
## Baja Fresh Mexican Grill
9660 Hageman Rd.
Bakersfield CA
661-587-8700
bajafresh.com
This Mexican restaurant is open for lunch and dinner. They use fresh ingredients and making their salsa and beans daily. Some of the items on their menu include Enchiladas, Burritos, Tacos Salads, Quesadillas, Nachos, Chicken, Steak and more. Well-behaved leashed dogs are allowed at the outdoor tables.

## Baja Fresh Mexican Grill
9000 Ming Ave.
Bakersfield CA
661-665-2252
bajafresh.com
This Mexican restaurant is open for lunch and dinner. They use fresh ingredients and

making their salsa and beans daily. Some of the items on their menu include Enchiladas, Burritos, Tacos Salads, Quesadillas, Nachos, Chicken, Steak and more. Well-behaved leashed dogs are allowed at the outdoor tables.

## Black Angus
3601 Rosedale Highway
Bakersfield CA
661-324-0814
blackangus.com/
Steaks are the specialty here with numerous signature food and beverages choices as well. Leashed, well mannered dogs are allowed at their outside bar patio.

## Cafe Med
4809 Stockdale Hwy
Bakersfield CA
661-834-4433
cafemedrestaurant.com/
Dogs are allowed at the outdoor tables.

## Chipotle
4950 Stockdale H
Bakersfield CA
661-335-0400
chipotle.com
Specializing in organic, natural and unprocessed food, this Mexican Eatery offers fajita burritos, tacos, salads, and salsas. Dogs are allowed at the outdoor tables but you will need to order your food inside the restaurant and dogs must remain outside.

## Filling Station
1830 24th Street
Bakersfield CA
661-323-5120
This is a drive-thru and walk-thru coffee and tea outlet. During spring and summer they have outdoor seats as well. They are open Monday to Friday from 5:30 am until 8 pm;Saturday from 6:30 am until 8 pm, and from 7:30 am until 8 pm on Sunday. Leashed, well mannered dogs that are hound and human friendly are welcome at their outside table.

## Jamba Juice

5180 Stockdale Hwy #AB
Bakersfield CA
661-322-6722
jambajuice.com/
Dogs are allowed at the outdoor tables.

**Jamba Juice**
9360 Rosedale H/H 58
Bakersfield CA
661-829-1830
jambajuice.com
All natural and organic ingredients, no high-fructose corn syrup, 0 grams trans fat, no artificial preservatives, a healthy helping of antioxidants, vitamins, and minerals, and fresh whole fruit and fruit juices set the base for these tasty and healthy beverages. Their organic Hot Blends provides a new spin on coffee, green or chai tea, and hot chocolate;plus they offer probiotic fruit and yogurt Blends. Additionally, they feature all natural salads, wraps, sandwiches, and grab n go specialties. They also offer healthy community support through fundraisers, special sales, and school lunch programs. Leashed, well mannered dogs are allowed at their outside dining area.

**Los Hermanos**
3501 Union Ave
Bakersfield CA
661-328-1678
Specializing in Mexican cuisine, this eatery is open daily from 9 am until 9: 30 pm. Dogs are allowed at the outdoor tables.

**Los Hermanos**
8200 Stockdale Hwy #N
Bakersfield CA
661-835-7294
Dogs are allowed at the outdoor tables. They are open Monday to Saturday from 10:30 am until 9:30 pm and on Sunday from 10 am until 9 pm.

**Patio Mexican Grill**
13001 Stockdale Hwy
Bakersfield CA
661-587-6280
This Mexican café is open on Monday from 5 pm until 9 pm;Tuesday to Friday from 11

am until 3 pm and from 5 pm until 9 pm, and on Saturday and Sunday from 11 am until 9 pm. Dogs are allowed at the outdoor tables.

**Rosemary's Family Creamery**

2733 F Street
Bakersfield CA
661-395-0555
Dogs are allowed at the outdoor tables. They have outdoor tables in the spring and summer months only;they are open daily from 11 am and usually close at 10 pm weekdays and 11 pm Friday and Saturdays.

**Sequoia Sandwich Company**
1231 18th Street
Bakersfield CA
661-323-2500
sequoiasandwich.com/v3/
Dogs are allowed at the outdoor tables.

**Sonic Drive In**
1402 23rd Street
Bakersfield CA
661-324-9100
sonicdrivein.com/home.jsp#/home
Burgers and all American favorites are on the menu of this eatery. Leashed dogs are allowed at their outside tables.

**Sonic Drive-In**
13015 Stockdale Hwy
Bakersfield CA
661-587-9400
Dogs are allowed at the outdoor tables.

**Sub Station**
5464 California Ave
Bakersfield CA
661-323-2400
Sub sandwiches are the specialty here. They are open 10:30 am until 7 pm;Saturday from 7 am until 4 pm and they are closed on Sunday. Leashed dogs are allowed at their outside tables.

**Subway**
8346 East Brundage Lane
Bakersfield CA
661-366-3300

This eatery specializes in made-to-order fresh, baked bread sandwiches with a variety of accompaniments to round out your meals. They also provide a kid's menu and catering services. Leashed dogs are allowed at the outer tables.

**The Gourmet Shoppe**
4801 Stockdale Hwy
Bakersfield CA
661-834-5522
Dogs are allowed at the outdoor tables.

# Pet-Friendly Stores
**Camping World**
5500 Wible Road
Bakersfield CA
661-833-9797
campingworld.com/
This comprehensive RV and outdoor store carries a wide variety of RV, boat, bike, and outdoor cooking accessories; all kinds of camping gear; RV screens, shades, and patio decorations; racing/tailgating gear, and all items for RV maintenance. They also carry RV towing supplies, electronics, and interior decorating items as well as pet supplies, RV directories/books, and games. Plus, they offer a tips and advice service, RV sales, rentals, and RV technicians to take care of any installations and repairs. They also welcome your canine companion in the store; they must be friendly and leashed.

**PetSmart Pet Store**
2661 Oswell St
Bakersfield CA
661-873-1092
Your licensed and well-behaved leashed dog is allowed in the store.

**PetSmart Pet Store**
4100 Ming Ave
Bakersfield CA
661-834-1044
Your licensed and well-behaved leashed dog is allowed in the store.

**Petco Pet Store - Bakersfield**
8220 Rosedale Hwy
Bakersfield CA
661-587-1097
Your licensed and well-behaved leashed dog is allowed in the store.

**Petco Pet Store - Bakersfield - Southwest**
5151 Gosford Road
Bakersfield CA
661-664-6874
Your licensed and well-behaved leashed dog is allowed in the store.

**Tractor Supply Company**
2749 Calloway Drive
Bakersfield CA
661-589-1504
tractorsupply.com
Some offerings of this comprehensive farm store includes agriculture, farming and ranching supplies; outdoor power equipment with all the necessities; hundreds of thousands of parts and accessories accessible for yard and garden; metal working and welding supplies; tools for auto and home; a wide range of livestock/farm feed and needs; and a variety of foods and care/play/groom items for household pets. Additionally, they provide trailer and towing supplies, vehicle maintenance accessories, clothing, work wear, foot wear, gifts, home improvement items, a lot of "know-how" and much more. Leashed, friendly dogs are welcome in the store.

## Off-Leash Dog Parks
**Centennial Park Off-Leash Dog Park**
On Montclair north of Stockdale Hwy
Bakersfield CA
661-326-3866
Centennial Park off-leash dog park, close to Highway 99, is a fenced in dog park that is easily accessible to locals and travelers alike. From Highway 99, take the Stockdale Hwy exit west and turn right onto

Montclair. The park is on the right.

**Kroll Park Off-Leash Dog Park**
Kroll Way and Montalvo Dr
Bakersfield CA
661-326-3866
This large, fenced off-leash dog park is located near Stockdale Hwy and Gosford on the west side of Bakersfield. To get there from Highway 99, take Stockdale Hwy west to Gosford, turn left and then turn left onto Kroll Way.

**University Park Off-Leash Dog Park**
University Ave east of Columbus
Bakersfield CA
661-326-3866
This fenced, off-leash dog park is located in University Park. The park is located on University Ave east of Columbus Street and between Camden and Mission Hills.

**Wilson Park Off-Leash Dog Park**
Wilson Road and Hughes Lane

Bakersfield CA
661-326-3866
This fenced off-leash dog park is located in Wilson Park south of central Bakersfield. The park is located on Wilson Road at Hughes Lane. Wilson Road is one major block south of Ming Ave. You can exit and Ming Avenue from Highway 99 and take the access roads to Wilson.

## Dog-Friendly Parks
**Beach Park**
Oak Street and Rosedale Hwy
Bakersfield CA

This city park is a good park to take your dog while in Bakersfield. The Kern River Parkway paved exercise trail passes through here and there are picnic tables and open areas. Dogs must be on leash in the park and on the Kern

River Parkway trail.

**Hart Park**
Harrell Highway
Bakersfield CA
661-868-7000
Hart Park is 8 miles northeast of Bakersfield on Alfred Harrell Highway. It is on 370 acres along the Kern River. There are hiking trails and fishing. Pets are allowed but must always be on leash.

**Kern River County Park**
Lake Ming Road
Bakersfield CA
661-868-7000
This park consists of over 1,000 acres and includes a river, a lake, campgrounds and picnic areas. Hills surround the lake, and the Greenhorn Mountains stretch along the eastern horizon. Please note that Kern River currents are very strong at times and can be extremely dangerous. Do not leave children or dogs unattended at the river. The park is located about10 miles northeast of Bakersfield, off the Alfred Harrell Highway on the Lake Ming Road exit. Dogs must be on leash.

**Kern River Parkway**
Oak Street and Rosedale Hwy
Bakersfield CA

The Kern River Parkway trail is a paved biking, walking and running trail along the Kern River. It can be entered at many points, including Beach Park at the address listed here. The trail is about 12 miles long. Dogs on leash are permitted.

**The Bluffs - Panorama Park**
Panorama Drive
Bakersfield CA

This walking and jogging trail overlooks the oil wells in the valley below. It stretches a number of miles from Bakersfield along Panorama Drive towards Lake Ming and Hart Park. There is also an exercise trail. Dogs on leash are permitted.

## Emergency Veterinarians
**BakersvilleVeterinary Hospital**

8610 Harris Road
Bakersfield CA
661-327-4444
bakersfieldvet.com/
Offering a variety of services for small and large pets, this veterinary hospital offers 24 hour state-of-the-art emergency care, a large dog play area, and luxury boarding facilities. Their emergency hours and fees begin at 6 pm and end at 8 am Monday thru Friday.

**Kern Animal Emergency Clinic**
4300 Easton Dr #1
Bakersfield CA
661-322-6019
Monday - Friday 5:30 pm to 8 am, Noon Saturday to 8 am Monday.

## Balboa

### Outdoor Restaurants
**Ruby's Diner**
#1 Balboa Pier
Balboa CA
949-675-7829
rubys.com
Ruby's Diner serves breakfast, lunch, and dinner. Well-behaved, leashed dogs are welcome at the outdoor seats.

## Banning

### Dog-Friendly Hotels
**Days Inn Banning**
2320 W. Ramsey St.
Banning CA
951-849-0092 (800-329-7466)
Dogs of all sizes are allowed. Dogs are allowed for a pet fee of $10.00 per pet per night.

**Quality Inn Banning I-10**

1690 West Ramsey Rd
Banning CA
951-849-8888 (877-424-6423)
Dogs are welcome at this hotel.

**Travelodge Banning**
1700 West Ramsey Street
Banning CA
951-849-1000
Dogs of all sizes are allowed. There is a pet fee of $10 per pet per night.

## Barstow

### Dog-Friendly Hotels
**Baymont Inn And Suites Barstow Historic Route 66**
1861 W. Main St.
Barstow CA
760-256-1300 (877-698-9593)
Dogs of all sizes are allowed. Dogs are allowed for a pet fee of $25.00 per pet per night.

**Best Western Desert Villa Inn**

1984 East Main Street
Barstow CA
760-256-1781 (800-780-7234)
Dogs are allowed. There is a $15 per pet per night pet fee.

**Comfort Suites Barstow**
2571 Fisher Blvd.
Barstow CA
760-253-3600 (877-424-6423)
Walking distance to Tanger and Barstow outlets. Near Calico Ghost Town, Historical Route 66, Afton Canyon and Desert Discovery Center.

Dogs up to 40 pounds are allowed. Dogs are allowed for a pet fee of $25.00 per pet per night. Two dogs are allowed per room.

**Days Inn South Lenwood**
2551 Commerce Parkway
Barstow CA
760-253-2121 (800-329-7466)
Dogs are welcome at this hotel.

**Econo Lodge On Historic Route 66**
1230 E Main St
Barstow CA
760-256-2133 (877-424-6423)
Located on historic Route 66, the Econo Lodge Barstow is close to Marine Corps Logistic Base, BNSF Railway.

Dogs of all sizes are allowed. Dogs are allowed for a pet fee of $10.00 per pet per night.

**Hampton Inn & Suites Barstow**
2710 Lenwood Road
Barstow CA
760-253-2600
Dogs of all sizes are allowed. There is no pet fee.

**Holiday Inn Express Hotel & Suites Barstow**
2700 Lenwood Road
Barstow CA
760-253-9200 (877-270-6405)
Dogs of all sizes are allowed.

**Quality Inn On Historic Route 66**
1520 E. Main St.
Barstow CA
760-256-6891 (877-424-6423)
Facilities such as large courtyard, pool, barbecue island and pits, outdoor fireplace, Gazebo, Putting green in Desert oasis.

Dogs up to 45 pounds are allowed.

**Ramada Barstow**
1511 East Main Street
Barstow CA
760-256-5673
Dogs up to 75 pounds are allowed. There is a $20 one time pet fee.

**Super 8 Barstow**
170 Coolwater Lane
Barstow CA
760-256-8443 (800-800-8000)
Dogs of all sizes are allowed. Dogs are allowed for a pet fee of $10 per pet per night.

**Travelodge Barstow**
1630 E Main St

Barstow CA
760-256-8931
Dogs up to 70 pounds are allowed. There is a pet fee of $8 per day and a $20 refundable deposit.

## Dog-Friendly Attractions
### Calico Early Man Site
Minneola Road
Barstow CA
760-252-6000
ca.blm.gov/barstow/calico.html
In 1942 amateur archaeologists discovered what they believed to be primitive stone tools at this site. Archaeologists have classified the site as a possible stone tool workshop, quarry and camp site for early nomadic hunters and gatherers. It is estimated that the soil at this site may date back to over 200,000 years. The site is open on Wednesday from 12:30pm to 4:30pm and Thursday through Sunday from 9am to 4:30pm. Guided tours are available on Wednesday at 1:30pm and 3:30pm, and on Thursday through Sunday at 9:30am, 11:30am, 1:30pm and 3:30pm. There is a $5 fee per person and less for children and seniors. Well-behaved leashed dogs are allowed. Please clean up after your dog.

### Route 66 Mother Road Museum
681 North First Ave
Barstow CA
760-255-1890
barstow66museum.itgo.com/
The museum offers a collection of historic photographs and artifacts related to Route 66 and the Mojave Desert Communities. Displays include the development of the U.S. Route 66 from early pioneer trails and railroads to automotive history, businesses and sites. Well-behaved, leashed dogs are welcome. The museum is open Friday through Sunday from 11am-4pm. Admission is free. The museum is located in the historic Casa del Desierto Harvey House.

### Calico Ghost Town
PO Box 638
Yermo CA
760-254-2122
Dogs are allowed at this old ghost town but not inside the restaurants. Founded in March 1881, it grew to a population of 1,200 with 22 saloons and more than 500 mines. Calico became one of the richest mining towns in California, producing $86 million in silver, $45 million in borax and gold. After 1907, when silver prices dropped and borax mining moved to Death Valley, Calico became a ghost town. Today, Calico is one of the few remaining original mining towns of the western United States. It was preserved by Walter Knott (founder of Knott's Berry Farm and a relative of the owner of Calico's Silver King mine). Mr. Knott donated Calico Ghost Town to the County of San Bernardino in 1966, and it remains alive and well as a 480-acre County Regional Park. Live events like gunfights and living history reenactments are common at the park. Take a self-guided town tour or go for a hike on one of their trails. You and your pooch can also take a guided walking tour (Mon-Fri) with Calico's historian who will examine the history of the miners, the famous 20-mule team and a U.S. Postal Mail dog named Dorsey. The park also offer many festivals throughout the year. Camping and RV hookups are available here. The park is located 8 miles north of Barstow and 3 miles east of Interstate 15.

## Outdoor Restaurants
### Baja Fresh Mexican Grill
2854 Lenwood Rd
Barstow CA
760-253-2505
bajafresh.com
This Mexican restaurant is open for lunch and dinner. They use fresh ingredients and making their salsa and beans

daily. Some of the items on their menu include Enchiladas, Burritos, Tacos Salads, Quesadillas, Nachos, Chicken, Steak and more. Well-behaved leashed dogs are allowed at the outdoor tables.

### El Pollo Loco
2820 Lenwood Road
Barstow CA
760-253-5222
elpolloloco.com/home.html
Favored for their all natural, specially marinated flame broiled chicken, El Pollo Loco - meaning The Crazy Chicken in Spanish, also serves up a variety of other fresh signature entrees, appetizers, healthy sides, and more. Leashed, friendly dogs are allowed at their outside tables.

## Pet-Friendly Stores
### Barstow Outlets.
2552 Mercantile Way
Barstow CA
760-253-7342
barstowoutlet.com/
This outlet center offers almost 2 dozen shops and services. The complex is open from 10 am until 8 pm. Dogs are allowed in the common areas of the mall; it is up to individual stores whether they allow a dog inside. Dogs must be well behaved, leashed, and under their owner's control at all times.

## Dog-Friendly Parks
### Mojave National Preserve
2701 Barstow Road
Barstow CA
760-252-6100
nps.gov/moja/index.htm
Dogs on leash are allowed in the park. This park features nearby camping, auto touring, hiking, climbing, and more.

### Rainbow Basin Natural Area
Fossil Bed Road
Barstow CA
760-252-6060
This park offers a diverse landscape of hills, canyons,

washes, multi-colored rock walls, and mesas that are ever changing in color and light. The park has geological and paleontological importance, an auto tour of an Area of Critical Environmental Concern, and a variety of recreational activities to pursue. Dogs are allowed throughout the park and on the trails. Dogs must be under their owner's immediate control, leashed, and cleaned up after at all times.

## Beaumont

### Dog-Friendly Hotels
**Rodeway Inn Beaumont**
1265 E. 6th Street
Beaumont CA
951-845-1436 (877-424-6423)
The hotel is close to the outlet mall and all rooms have micro-fridge, free internet and iron and board.

Dogs up to 50 pounds are allowed. Dogs are allowed for a pet fee of $10.00 per pet per night. Two dogs are allowed per room.

## Big Bear Lake

### Dog-Friendly Hotels
**Best Western Big Bear Chateau**
42200 Moonridge Road
Big Bear Lake CA
909-866-6666 (800-780-7234)
Dogs are allowed in pet friendly rooms. There is a $30 per pet per stay pet fee.

**Timberline Lodge**
39921 Big Bear Blvd
Big Bear Lake CA
909-866-4141 (800-803-4111)
thetimberlinelodge.com/
Timberline Lodge offers accommodation in Big Bear Lake. It features an outdoor

seasonal pool.
All cabins offer a microwave a coffee machine and a refrigerator. as well as a TV with satellite channels HBO and Cinemax.
Timberline Lodge is located close to the Big Bear Lake Village restaurants galleries movie theater and unique gift shops. The lake and marinas are nearby.

**Quail Cove Lakeside Lodge**
39117 Northshore Dr. P.o.box 517
Fawnskin CA
800-595-2683
quailcove.com/
Located in Fawnskin Quail Cove Lakeside Lodge offers accommodation in a wooded and secluded area on the quiet side of Big Bear Lake. The city of Big Bear Lake and ski slopes are just 10 minutes drive away. Guests can enjoy private barbecue facilities.
All of the cabins at the lodge feature fully equipped kitchens full bathrooms with toiletries and wood burning fireplaces along with flat screen TVs and DVD players.
Guests have access to a central courtyard with a fire pit for roasting treats. Horseshoes and a Bocce Ball court are available for guest enjoyment. Fontana is 49 km from Quail Cove Lakeside Lodge. Lake Arrowhead is 22 km from the property. The nearest airport is LA/Ontario International Airport 64 km from Quail Cove Lakeside Lodge.

### Dog-Friendly Attractions
**Bear Valley Stage Lines**
Village Drive and Pine Knot Avenue
Big Bear Lake CA
909-584-2277
stagelines.com/
This company offers horse drawn carriage rides of the Village, and for special occasions/events they will travel anywhere in the Los Angeles metropolitan area.

Dogs are allowed to come along for the ride for no additional fee if they are trained and well behaved. Dogs must be leashed and cleaned up after.

**Belleville Ghost Town**
Holcomb Valley Road
Big Bear Lake CA

Belleville Ghost Town, located in Holcomb Valley, is one of the old Southern California ghost towns. To get there, you'll take a dirt road, but it is rated a 2 wheel drive road meaning you don't necessarily need a 4WD. At the ghost town, you'll find the old saloon, mining equipment, hanging tree, mines, graves and foundations. This ghost town is located within a National Forest which means you and your pup are welcome to walk or hike on almost any of the trails (the Pacific Crest Trail is the exception). To get there from the northeast corner of Big Bear Lake, take Hwy 38 east and turn left onto Van Dusen Canyon Road. Once on this road, you'll travel about 4-5 miles on a dirt road. When the road ends (there is a campground to the left), turn right on Holcomb Valley Road. The ghost town of Belleville will be approx. less than 1 mile on the right. Go during the late spring through fall when there is no snow.

**Big Bear Marina**
500 Paine Road
Big Bear Lake CA
909-866-3218
bigbearmarina.com/
At Big Bear Marina you can rent fishing boats for a fishing trip on the lake. Dogs are only allowed on the fishing boats, not the other types of boats rented here.

**Holloway's Marina**
398 Edgemoor Road
Big Bear Lake CA
909-866-5706 (800-448-5335)
bigbearboating.com/
Here you and your pup can rent a covered pontoon boat or a fishing boat for a morning, afternoon, or day on the lake.

**Pine Knot Landing-Boat Rentals & Paddleboat**
400 Pine Knot Ave.
Big Bear Lake CA
909-866-7766
pineknotmarina.com/
Rent a boat with your pup in beautiful Big Bear Lake. You'll drive your own gas powered pontoon boat which goes up to 15 miles per hour. These are nice boats which have a covering and a good amount of room for your dog to walk around. Remember to bring along some water. If you've never driven a boat, don't worry. The people working there say if you know how to drive a car, you'll be fine. Rent a boat by the hour or day. The rate for 3 hours is about $200. Prices are subject to change. The boat rental company is at Pine Knot Landing which is located at the end of Pine Knot Ave- near Hwy 18 (Big Bear Blvd.) Dogs are allowed on the Paddleboat tours that dock here as well with some restrictions. Pet dogs, other than assistance dogs, are not allowed on holiday or special cruises. They also may not be allowed if it is too crowded at the captain's discretion. They need to be well-behaved and quiet.

**Pleasure Point Landing**
603 Landlock Landing Rd
Big Bear Lake CA
909-866-2455
You can rent boats here for boating on Big Bear Lake.

**Captain John's Fawn Harbor and Marina**
39368 North Shore Drive
Fawnskin CA
909-866-6478
fawnharbor.com
This marina offers lake tours of Big Bear Lake as well as boat rentals. The tours are on a quiet electric boat, the Serena. Well-behaved, leashed dogs are allowed on the boats. Thanks to a reader for recommending this dog-friendly marina.

## Outdoor Restaurants
**Alpine High Country Cafe**
41546 Big Bear Blvd
Big Bear Lake CA
909-866-1959
They have a few outdoor tables and leashed dogs are allowed to join you.

**BLT's Restaurant**
41799 Big Bear Blvd
Big Bear Lake CA
909-866-6659
BLT's Restaurant in Big Bear, located on Big Bear Blvd, allows leashed dogs on their outdoor patio. They even offer a doggy menu, which includes free kibble and water. Dogs can order a large hot dog, a hamburger patty, chicken fingers, and more! They serve breakfast, lunch, and dinner seven days a week.

**Big Bear Mountain Brewery**
40260 Big Bear Blvd
Big Bear Lake CA
909-866-2337
mountainbrewery.com/
Dogs are allowed at the outdoor tables.

**Jasper's Smokehouse and Steaks**
607 Pine Knot Avenue
Big Bear Lake CA
909-866-2434
jasperssmokehouse.com/
A real wood-fired barbecue brings out the flavor of the meats at this restaurant, and that is only the beginning of a number of tasty items on their sizable menu. Outdoor seating is available. Well mannered dogs are allowed at the outer tables.

**Nottingham's Restaurant and Tavern**
40797 Lakeview Drive
Big Bear Lake CA
909-866-4644
nottinghams.info/
In addition to dining on great California cuisine, guests will be surrounded by unique antiques and entertained by the rich history of these historic surroundings. They offer 5 distinct dining areas, including a courtyard with a water fountain that seats 20. Leashed, well mannered dogs are welcome at their outside dining area.

**Village Pizza**
40568 Village Dr
Big Bear Lake CA
909-866-8505
This pizza place is within walking distance to Big Bear Village. Dogs are allowed at their outside tables.

## Pet-Friendly Stores
**Big Bear RV Rentals**
1356 E Country Club Dr
Big Bear City CA
909-833-1516
bigbearrvrentals.com
This company rents RV and campers in the Big Bear area. Dogs are welcome to camp with you in the rented vehicles.

## Dog-Friendly Beaches
**Big Bear Lake Beaches**
Hwy 38
Big Bear Lake CA

There are various beaches along the lake on Hwy 38. You can get to any of the beaches via the Alpine Pedal Path. To get there, (going away from the village), take the Stanfield Cutoff to the other side of the lake and turn left onto Hwy 38. In about 1/4 - 1/2 mile, parking will be on the left.

## Dog-Friendly Parks
**Alpine Pedal Path**
Hwy 38
Big Bear Lake CA

This path is mostly paved and is about a 4-5 mile round trip. Throughout most of the path, there are various access points to the lake and various beaches. The beginning of the path is located off of the Stanfield Cutoff (bridge over Big Bear Lake, close to the village). For easier access, (going away from the village), take the Stanfield Cutoff to the other side of the lake and turn left onto Hwy 38. In about 1/4 - 1/2 mile, parking will be on the left.

## Cougar Crest Trail
Highway 38
Big Bear Lake CA
909-866-3437
Within the San Bernardino National Forest this trail is well known to visitors and residents alike. Leashed dogs are allowed throughout the San Bernardino Forest Trails in Big Bear. The trailhead is located on Highway 38 west of Big Bear. There is parking at the trailhead. The trail heads two miles up and connects to the Pacific Crest Trail on which you can extend your hike significantly should you desire. The trail offers spectacular views of the lake valley. The Cougar Crest Trail is strenuous and please bring enough water for dogs and people.

## Grout Bay Trail
Hwy 38
Big Bear Lake CA
909-866-3437
This hiking trail is about 3-5 miles each way and is rated easy to moderate. To get there from the village, head west on Hwy 18. Take Hwy 38 to the right, towards the northwest corner of the lake. The trail begins by the Grout Bay Picnic Area.

## Meadow Park
41220 Park Ave
Big Bear Lake CA
909-866-9700
Located on Big Bear Lake, Meadow Park is a large 16.25 acre park featuring playground equipment, tennis courts, volleyball court, horseshoe pits, 2 lighted ball fields, play lot, group picnic pavilion, group picnic grove, picnic tables, barbecues, and restrooms. For your pooch, there is a dog park located inside the park.

## Pine Knot Trail

Tulip Lane
Big Bear Lake CA
909-866-3437
This hiking trail is about 3 miles each way and is rated moderate to difficult. To get there from the village, head west on Hwy 18 and turn left onto Tulip Lane. The trail begins by the Alpine Glen Picnic Area. Remember, to park here, you'll need a Forest Day Pass. Check with your hotel or some of the stores in the village for info on where to purchase this pass.

## Woodland Trail / Nature Walk
Hwy 38
Big Bear Lake CA
909-866-3437
This is a nature trail with about 20 informational stops. Pick up one of the maps and follow the self-guided 1.5 mile nature walk. This is rated as an easy loop. To get there, (going away from the village), take the Stanfield Cutoff to the other side of the lake and turn left onto Hwy 38. In about 1/2 mile, parking will be on the right.

## Hanna Flat Trail
Rim of the World Drive
Fawnskin CA
909-337-2444
This 9 mile round trip moderate rated trail is located in the San Bernardino National Forest. Pets on leash are allowed and please clean up after them. This trail is closed every year from November 1 to April 1 due to the bald eagle wintering habitat. To get there take Highway 18 to Big Bear Lake Dam. Go straight, do not cross over the dam. Highway 18 becomes Highway 38. Go the Fawnskin Fire Station and turn left onto the Rim of the World Drive. Go about 2.5 miles on a dirt road to the campsite and trailhead.

## Emergency Veterinarians
**Bear City Animal Hospital**
214 Big Bear Blvd W

Big Bear City CA
909-585-7808
Monday - Friday 7:30 am - 6 pm. Closed Weekends.

### VCA Lakeside Animal Hospital

42160 N Shore Dr
Big Bear City CA
909-866-2021
Monday - Saturday 8 am - 6 pm. Sunday 9 am - 5 pm.

## Big Pine

## Dog-Friendly Hotels
**Bristlecone Motel**
101 North Main Street
Big Pine CA
760-938-2067
Located just off US 395 less than 20 minutes drive from Bishop this motel features a gas station and convenience store on site. Rooms include free Wi-Fi.
A TV is available in each room at the Bristlecone Motel. A microwave and small fridge are provided.
A hardware store and sporting goods store are featured on site at the Motel Bristlecone. Token operated showers are available for campers and travelers. Death Valley is 1 hour and 20 minutes drive away.

## Dog-Friendly Parks
**Big Pine Canyon Trails**
Glacier Lodge Road
Big Pine CA
760-873-2500
These trails start and an elevation of 7,800 feet and go up to 12,400 feet. There are about 15 miles of trails. The trails lead into the dog-friendly John Muir Wilderness. One of the closest lakes, Willow Lake, is a 4 mile hike from the trailhead. At the campgrounds pets must be on a 6 foot or less leash. While hiking on the trails, pets must be on leash or under

voice command at all times. Dogs are also allowed in the lake. Please clean up after your pets. This trail is located in the Inyo National Forest. To get there from Highway 395, exit in Big Pine and go 11 miles west on Glacier Lodge Road.

**John Muir Wilderness**
Glacier Lodge Road
Big Pine CA
760-873-2500
The wilderness trails are located in the Inyo National Forest and can be accessed from many points, including the Big Pine Canyon Trails near Big Pine. See our listing for Big Pine Creek Canyon Trail. From these trailheads, there are about 9 miles of hiking trails and several campgrounds. To get there from Highway 395, exit in Big Pine and go 11 miles west on Glacier Lodge Road.

## Big Sur

## Outdoor Restaurants
**Big Sur Coast Gallery & Cafe**
49901 H 1
Big Sur CA
831-667-2301
This cafe is located at what is considered the largest gallery of American crafts in the country with some 250+ artist and craftsmen. They are open daily from 9 am until 5 pm. Leashed, friendly dogs are allowed at their outside dining area.

## Dog-Friendly Beaches
**Pfieffer Beach**
Sycamore Road
Big Sur CA
805-968-6640
Dogs on leash are allowed at this day use beach which is located in the Los Padres National Forest. The beach is located in Big Sur, south of the Big Sur Ranger Station. From Big Sur, start heading south on

Highway 1 and look carefully for Sycamore Road. Take Sycamore Road just over 2 miles to the beach. There is a $5 entrance fee per car.

## Dog-Friendly Parks
**Los Padres National Forest**
Big Sur Station #1
Big Sur CA
831-385-5434
fs.usda.gov/lpnf/
While dogs are not allowed in the state park in Big Sur, they are welcome in the adjacent Los Padres National Forest. Dogs should be on leash. One of the most popular trails is the Pine Ridge Trail. This trail is miles long and goes through the Los Padres National Forest to the dog-friendly Ventana Wilderness. To get there, take Highway 1 south, about 25-30 miles south of Carmel. Park at the Big Sur Station for a minimal fee. From the Big Sur Station in Big Sur, you can head out onto the Pine Ridge Trail. The Los Padres National Forest actually stretches over 200 miles from the Carmel Valley all the way down to Los Angeles County. For maps and more information about the trails, contact the Monterey Ranger District at 831-385-5434 or at the Forest Headquarters in Goleta at 805-968-6640.

## Bishop

## Dog-Friendly Hotels
**Best Western Bishop Lodge**
1025 North Main Street
Bishop CA
760-873-3543 (800-780-7234)
Dogs are allowed. There is a $20 per pet per night pet fee. Up to two dogs are allowed per room.

**Cielo Hotel An Ascend Hotel Collection Member**

651 N. Main St
Bishop CA
760-873-6380 (800-531-5900)
Dogs up to 50 pounds are allowed for no additional fee; there is a pet policy to sign at check-in. A contact number must be left with the front desk when a pet is left alone in the room.

**Comfort Inn Bishop**
805 N. Main St.
Bishop CA
760-873-4284 (877-424-6423)
Hotel is surrounded by the High Sierra Mountains with a Swiss Village atmosphere.

Dogs of all sizes are allowed. Dogs are allowed for a pet fee of $15.00 per pet per night. Two dogs are allowed per room.

**Days Inn Bishop**
724 West Line Street
Bishop CA
760-872-1095 (800-329-7466)
Dogs of all sizes are allowed. Dogs are allowed for a pet fee of $10 per pet per night.

**Holiday Inn Express Hotel And Suites Bishop**
636 North Main Street
Bishop CA
760-872-2423 (877-270-6405)
Dogs of all sizes are allowed. Dogs are allowed for a pet fee of $25.00 per pet per night.

**Red Roof Inn Bishop**
150 E. Elm St.
Bishop CA
760-873-3564 (877-424-6423)
At the Rodeway Inn we are conveniently located in downtown Bishop while still off of the main road. We are walking distance from

Dogs up to 100 pounds are allowed. Dogs are allowed for a pet fee of $5.00 per pet per night. Two dogs are allowed per room.

**Super 8 Bishop**
535 South Main Street
Bishop CA
760-872-1386 (800-800-8000)
Dogs are welcome at this hotel.

## Travelodge Bishop
155 East Elm Street
Bishop CA
760-872-1771
Dogs of all sizes are allowed.
There is a pet fee of $15 per pet
per night.

## Vagabond Inn Bishop
1030 North Main Street
Bishop CA
760-873-6351
Free high-speed internet a pool
and fairgrounds adjacency are
perks that please at the
Vagabond Inn Bishop. The 80-
room Vagabond offers comfort
and convenience for active
vacationers. Rooms have
microwaves mini-fridges
coffeemakers cable TV with
HBO and free local calls.
Lounge in the seasonal outdoor
pool and hot tub let Spot loose
in the dog playground use the
facilities for cleaning and
freezing fish or grill fresh trout
in the barbecue area. The inn
also provides a complimentary
continental breakfast and free
weekday newspapers. The
Vagabond inn is adjacent to the
Tri County Fairgrounds host of
Bishop's annual "Mule Days"
celebration and a five-minute
walk from Bishop City Park. A
24-hour restaurant is next door.
The Owens Valley Paiute
Shoshone Cultural Center
featuring local indigenous art is
less than a mile and a half. The
Ancient Bristlecone Pine Forest
home to the world's oldest tree
is 38 miles away and fishing on
Lake Crowley is a half-hour
drive. Daily round-trip flights to
Los Angeles leave from
Mammoth Yosemite Airport 37
miles northwest.

## Dog-Friendly Attractions
### Bristlecone Pine Forest
White Mountain Rd
Bishop CA
760-873-2500
This forest, located in the Inyo
National Forest, is home to the
world's oldest known trees. They
are the ancient bristlecone

pines. Some of these trees
were growing when the
Egyptians built the pyramids
over four thousand years ago.
At the Schulman Grove
Visitor's Center, there are
picnic areas, restrooms,
outdoor exhibits and two self-
guided nature trails. You can
also get information on hiking
trails in the area from the
visitor's center. Open daily from
Memorial Day through October,
weather permitting. July
through September are usually
the best months for hiking in
the White Mountains. Dogs are
allowed on leash. Driving time
from Big Pine to Schulman
Grove is approximately 45
minutes on paved roads. Take
Highway 168 east 12 miles
from Big Pine to White Mtn
Road. Turn left and drive ten
miles to the Schulman Grove
Visitor Center. The Bristlecone
Pines can be viewed from the
parking area of the visitor
center and along three nature
trails.

## Outdoor Restaurants
### Pizza Factory
970 N Main Street/H 6/395
Bishop CA
760-872-8888
pizzafactory.com/locations.html

In addition to freshly
handcrafted pizzas with fresh
ingredients and their signature
dough, this eatery also offer a
variety of wraps, pastas,
calzones, subs, and salads.
Dogs are allowed at their outer
tables;they must be leashed
and well mannered.

## Off-Leash Dog Parks
### Bishop Dog Park
690 N Main Street /H 395
Bishop CA

There are separate sections for
large and small dogs at this
newly opened doggy play area.
It is located in the back of the
city's Bishop Park. Future

improvements planned include
agility equipment, benches, a
pond, and green salt grass.
Dogs must be healthy, sociable,
current on all vaccinations and
license with tags on collar, and
under their owner's control at all
times. Owners must clean up
after their pets, and keep them
leashed when not in designated
off-lead areas.

## Dog-Friendly Parks
### Hilton Lakes Trail
Rock Creek Canyon Rd.
Bishop CA
760-873-2500
This trail is located in the Inyo
National Forest. It starts at an
elevation of 9,600 feet and goes
up to 10,720 feet over 5.25
miles. From the trailhead you
can hike to several lakes. At the
campgrounds pets must be on a
6 foot or less leash. While hiking
on the trails, pets must be on
leash or under voice command
at all times. Please clean up
after your pets. To get there
from Highway 395, exit at Tom's
Place. Go up Rock Creek
Canyon Road. The trail starts
before the Rock Creek Pack
Station on the road to Mosquito
Flat.

### Inyo National Forest
351 Pacu Lane, Suite 200
Bishop CA
760-873-2400
fs.usda.gov/inyo
This national forest covers
thousands of acres of land
ranging in elevations up to
14,246 feet in the White
Mountain Range which is
located near Mt. Whitney.
Please see our listings in the
Sierra Nevada region for dog-
friendly hikes and/or
campgrounds.

### Inyo National Forest
351 Pacu Lane
Bishop CA
760-873-2400
fs.usda.gov/inyo
Dogs are allowed on all trails in
the Inyo National Forest except if
restricted due to a sheep habitat

area. But they are allowed on the vast majority of trails. Up to two dogs are allowed to stay in each campground site in the forest. Dogs should be on a six foot leash in the forest.

**Little Lakes Trail**
Rock Creek Canyon Rd.
Bishop CA
760-873-2500
This trail is located in the Inyo National Forest. It starts at an elevation of 10,300 feet and the first 1.5 miles of the trail goes up to 10,440 to Heart Lake. From there you can go several more miles up to elevations around 11,000 feet. At the campgrounds pets must be on a 6 foot or less leash. While hiking on the trails, pets must be on leash or under voice command at all times. Please clean up after your pets. To get there from Highway 395, exit at Tom's Place. Go up Rock Creek Canyon Road to the end, about 10 miles to the Mosquito Flat parking.

**Emergency Veterinarians**
**Bishop Veterinary Hospital**
1650 N. Sierra Highway
Bishop CA
760-873-5801
Weekdays 9 - noon, 2 - 5 pm. Saturday 9 - noon by appt. Emergency doctor on call 24 hours.

## Blythe

**Dog-Friendly Hotels**
**Knights Inn Blythe**
1127 East Hobsonway
Blythe CA
760-922-4126 (800-843-5644)
Dogs of all sizes are allowed. Dogs are allowed for a pet fee of $5.00 per pet per night.

**M-star Inn And Suites Blythe**
9232 E Hobsonway
Blythe CA

760-922-3334 (877-424-6423)
The newly renovated Rodeway Inn is conveniently located a few miles awaw from the Colorado River and the Fairgrounds.

**Super 8 Blythe**
550 West Donlon Street
Blythe CA
760-922-8881 (800-800-8000)
Dogs are welcome at this hotel.

## Boonville

**Dog-Friendly Attractions**
**Anderson Valley Brewing Company**
17700 H 253
Boonville CA
707-895-BEER (895-2337)
avbc.com
Home to various events and activities throughout the year, this top-award winning brewery features carefully crafted ales of the highest caliber. They also have an 18 hole Disc Golf Course right on the grounds, and a gift shop and visitor center. Dogs are welcome around the grounds and on the course; they are not allowed in the buildings. Dogs must be well mannered, leashed, and cleaned up after.

**Boont Berry Farm**
13980 H 128
Boonville CA
707-895-3441
This organic farm and store has even been seen on TV as a "Pet Friendly Place" and welcome their four-legged visitors. Dogs are allowed around the farm and store areas. They must be friendly, leashed and cleaned up after at all times.

**Outdoor Restaurants**
**Boonville Hotel/Table 128**
14050 H 128

Boonville CA
707-895-2210
boonvillehotel.com/eat.php
With an emphasis on using local fresh produce and products when available - and from their garden when in season, this modern day roadhouse offers a seasonally inspired menu, an international and domestic wine list, and alfresco dining. Leashed, well mannered dogs are welcome at their outside tables.

**Mosswood Market Cafe**
14111 H 128 Suite A
Boonville CA
707-895-3635
mosswoodmarket.com
This coffee and espresso shop also offers bakery delights and artisanal breads for take home. Leashed dogs are allowed at the outside seating area.

**Dog-Friendly Wineries and Vineyards**
**Foursight Wines**
14475 H 128
Boonville CA
707-895-2889
foursightwines.com/
This small family owned and operated winery specializes in Pinot Noir and Anderson Valley Sauvignon Blanc. Well mannered hound and human-friendly leashed dogs are allowed on the grounds and in the tasting room.

**Zina Hyde Cunningham Winery**
14077 H 128
Boonville CA
707-895-9462
zinawinery.com/
Some of the specialties of this scenic winery include a Bordeaux Cepage blend, Carignane, Sauvignon Blanc, Zinfandel, and Petite Sirah. Dogs are allowed around the property, but not in the tasting room. Dogs must be well behaved, and leashed and cleaned up after.

## Borrego Springs

### Outdoor Restaurants
**The Red Ocotillo**
818 Palm Canyon Drive
Borrego Springs CA
760-767-7400
thepalmsatindianhead.com/
Look for the Quonset hut with an 'EAT' neon sign, and you've found this retro-theme breakfast and lunch café (breakfast served all day). There is free WiFi and outside seating available. Dogs are allowed at the outer tables;they must be leashed and under

### Dog-Friendly Parks
**Anza-Borrego Desert State Park**
Highway 78
Borrego Springs CA
760-767-5311
Dogs are not allowed on any trails. They are allowed in day use areas and on over 500 miles of dirt roads. The roads can be used by cars but there is usually not too much traffic. Pets must be leashed and please clean up after them. The park is located about a 2 hour drive from San Diego, Riverside and Palm Springs off Highways S22 and 78.

## Bridgeport

### Dog-Friendly Hotels
**Walker River Lodge**
100 Main Street
Bridgeport CA
760-932-7021
Featuring a seasonal outdoor pool and hot tub this Bridgeport lodge is 45 miles from the Eastern Gate at Yosemite National Park. Free Wi-Fi is offered in all rooms. Twin Lakes is 15 miles away.
The air-conditioned rooms provide an alarm clock and an

en suite bathroom. Select suites feature a fully equipped kitchen and log cabin furnishings.
Mono Lake Park is 30 miles away. South Lake Tahoe is 85 miles away from Walker River Lodge. Bodie State Park is 20 miles away.

### Dog-Friendly Attractions
**Bodie State Historic Park**
State Route 270
Bridgeport CA
760-647-6445
This park is a ghost town. It looks much the same today as it did 50 years ago. Bodie is now listed as one of the worlds 100 most endangered sites by the World Monuments Watch. A self guided brochure describing a brief history of each building is available at the park. Dogs are welcome but must be on a leash at all times. From Highway 395 seven miles south of Bridgeport, take State Route 270. Go east 10 miles to the end of the pavement and continue 3 miles on an unsurfaced road to Bodie. The last 3 miles can at times be rough. Reduced speeds are necessary.

## Burney

### Dog-Friendly Parks
**McArthur-Burney Falls Memorial State Park**
24898 H 89
Burney CA
530-335-2777 (800-444-PARK (7275))
Formed from volcanic activity, this park also has a rich natural and cultural history, and the park's showcase is the beautiful 129 foot Burney Falls flowing from springs at 100 million gallons a day. There is a variety of land and water recreation and activities to pursue, exhibits, and the park

now has Wi-Fi service. Dogs of all sizes are allowed for no additional fee. Dogs are not allowed on the trails or on the beach. Dogs must be under their owners control at all times, and be leashed and cleaned up after.

## Buttonwillow

### Dog-Friendly Hotels
**Motel 6 Buttonwillow Central**
20645 Tracy Avenue
Buttonwillow CA
661-764-5121 (800-RED-ROOF)

One well-behaved family pet per room. Guest must notify front desk upon arrival. Guest is liable for any damages. In consideration of all guests, pets must never be left unattended in the guest rooms.

**Rodeway Inn I-5 At Rt. 58**
20688 Tracy Avenue
Buttonwillow CA
661-764-5207 (877-424-6423)
EconoLodge Inn and Suites is conveniently located near the I-5. We offer an outdoor swimming pool, guest laundry and cont breakfast.

Dogs up to 100 pounds are allowed. Dogs are allowed for a pet fee of $5, per pet per stay. Two dogs are allowed per room.

**Super 8 Buttonwillow**
20681 Tracy Avenue
Buttonwillow CA
661-764-5117 (800-800-8000)
Dogs of all sizes are allowed. Dogs are allowed for a pet fee.

## CA

### Dog-Friendly Hotels
**Motel 6 San Bernardino South**

111 West Redlands Boulevard
CA CA

Free parking and local calls plus easy access to I-10 and I-215 at budget-friendly rates add up to big savings at the Motel 6 San Bernardino South. The two-story Motel 6 houses 120 rooms featuring cable TV and free local calls. Wi-Fi is also available for a small fee. Cool off year-round in the outdoor pool and tidy up travel clothing in the on-site coin-operated guest laundry. Pets are permitted for an additional fee with restrictions. Parking is free. Situated off I-10 and I-215 the Motel 6 is 10 minutes south of downtown San Bernardino and less than one mile from the Santa Ana River. In less than a three-mile drive north guests discover retail fun at Inland Mall and top events held at the National Orange Show Events Center. Fights land 19 miles west at LA/Ontario International Airport.

## Campo

### Dog-Friendly Parks
**Lake Morena County Park**
2550 Lake Moreno Drive
Campo CA
858-565-3600
This park of just over 3,200 acres has the distinction because of it's location to have the characteristics of desert, coastal and mountain habitats. It is home to a vast variety of plants, birds, and wildlife. There is a good variety of land and water recreation, many hiking trails including a piece of the Pacific Crest Trail, and they also provide boat rentals; dogs are allowed on the boats. Dogs of all sizes are allowed for camping for an additional fee of $1 per night per pet. Dogs must be leashed and cleaned up after at all times. They are allowed throughout the park and on the trails; they are not allowed at the

cabins.

## Camptonville

### Dog-Friendly Parks
**Rebel Ridge Trail**
Marysville Road
Camptonville CA
530-288-3231
go-nevada.com/Rebel-Ridge-Trail/
This 1.6 mile moderate rated trail is open all year. Pets must be either leashed or off-leash but under direct voice control. Please clean up after your pets. It is located in the Tahoe National Forest, on Marysville Road, .6 miles west of Highway 49.

## Cardiff By The Sea

### Dog-Friendly Hotels
**Holiday Inn Express Encinitas-cardiff Beach Area**
1661 Villa Cardiff Drive
Cardiff By The Sea CA
760-944-0427 (877-270-6405)
Dogs up to 50 pounds are allowed. Dogs are allowed for a pet fee of $50 per pet per stay.

## Cardiff by the Sea

### Pet-Friendly Stores
**Patagonia**
2185 San Elijo Avenue
Cardiff by the Sea CA
760-634-9886
patagonia.com/us/home
With a commitment to the four R's: reduce, repair, reuse, and recycle, this LEED certified company has implemented many eco-friendly initiatives throughout the company; plus, they offer environmental

support thru a number of venues - including grants, internships, and alliances. Some products carried include family apparel, sports apparel, travel gear, video/music, and gift items. Leashed friendly dogs are welcome in the store.

## Carmel

### Dog-Friendly Hotels
**Hofsas House Hotel**
4th Ave And San Carlos Street
Carmel CA
831-624-2745
There is a $15 per day additional pet fee. The hotel is located between 3rd Ave and 4th Ave in Carmel. Thanks to one of our readers for recommending this hotel.

**Hofsas House Hotel**
4th Ave And San Carlos Street
Carmel CA
831-624-4862 (800-634-1300)
fireplaceinncarmel.com/
the fee for 1 large dog is $40 per night. If there are 2 pets the fee is $40 per night. Aggressive breed dogs are not allowed. Dogs may not be left alone in the rooms, and they must be leashed and cleaned up after.

**Carmel Valley Lodge**
8 Ford Road
Carmel Valley CA
831-659-2261 (800-641-4646)
Your dog will feel welcome at this country retreat. Pet amenities include heart-shaped, organic homemade dog biscuits and a pawtographed picture of Lucky the Lodge Dog. Dogs must be on leash, but for your convenience, there are doggy-hitches at the front door of every unit that has a patio or deck and at the pool. There are 31 units which range from standard rooms to two bedroom cottages. A great community park is located across the street and several restaurants with outdoor seating are within a 5 minute

walk. Drive about 15 minutes from the lodge and you'll be in downtown Carmel or at one of the dog-friendly beaches. Dogs are an extra $10 per day and up to two dogs per room. There is no charge for childen under 16. The lodge is located in Carmel Valley. From Carmel, head south on Hwy 1. Turn left on Carmel Valley Rd., drive about 11-12 miles and the lodge will be located at Ford Rd.

## Accommodations
### Carmel Country Inn
Dolores Street & Third Avenue
Carmel CA
831-625-3263 (800-215-6343)
carmelcountryinn.com
This dog-friendly bed and breakfast has 12 rooms and allows dogs in several of these rooms. It's close to many downtown outdoor dog-friendly restaurants (see Restaurants). A 20-25 minute walk will take you to the dog-friendly Carmel City Beach. There is a $20 per night per pet charge.

### Carmel Mission Inn
3665 Rio Rd.
Carmel CA
831-624-1841 (800-348-9090)
Dogs up to 100 pounds are allowed. There is a $35 one time additional pet fee.

### Carmel Valley Ranch
One Old Ranch Road
Carmel CA
831-625-9500
carmelvalleyranch.com
This resort is on 500 acres in Carmel Valley and includes a plush doggie bed, bowls and clean up bags. There is a one time $150 dog fee. There is also a doggy menu.

### Happy Landing Inn
Monte Verde at 6th
Carmel CA
831-624-7917 (800-297-6250)
carmelhappylanding.com
This dog-friendly B&B is located six blocks from the Carmel leash free beach and in the middle of Carmel-By-The-Sea.

Pets of all sizes are allowed. There is a $20 per day pet fee for one pet and $30 per day for two pets.

### Carmel Green Lantern Inn
Casanova & 7th Avenue
Carmel by The Sea CA
831-624-4392 (888-414-4392)
greenlanterninn.com
There is a $35 pet fee. 2 dogs up to 50 pounds are allowed.

### Tradewinds Carmel
Mission Street at 3rd Avenue
Carmel-by-the-Sea CA
831-624-2776
tradewindscarmel.com
This motel allows dogs in several of their rooms. They are a non-smoking inn. It's located about 3-4 blocks north of Ocean Ave and close to many outdoor dog-friendly restaurants in downtown Carmel. A 20-25 minute walk will take you to the dog-friendly Carmel City beach. There is a $25 per day pet charge.

## Dog Businesses
### The Raw Connection
26200 Carmel Rancho Blvd
Carmel CA
831-626-7555
therawconnection.com/
The Raw Connection is your source for quality raw food diets, supplements, and natural treats for dogs and cats on the Monterey Peninsula. They not only sell natural & raw food and treats, they also have many seminars and on-site classes for you and your dog.

## Dog-Friendly Attractions
### Carmel Walks-Walking Tours

Lincoln and Ocean Streets
Carmel CA
831-642-2700
carmelwalks.com
Discover the special charms and secrets of Carmel on this two hour guided walking tour. Walk through award-winning gardens, by enchanting

fairytale cottages and learn the homes, haunts, and history of famous artists, writers, and movie stars. Your leashed dog is welcome to join you. Tours are offered every Saturday at 10am and 2pm. Tuesday thru Friday, the tours are at 10am. The cost is $25 per person and dogs get the tour for free. Prices are subject to change. Reservations are required.

### Seventeen Mile Drive
Seventeen Mile Drive
Carmel CA

This toll road costs $8 and allows you to access a very scenic section of coastline, walking trails and beaches. Dogs are allowed all along 17 mile drive on leash.

## Outdoor Restaurants
### Allegro Gourmet Pizzeria
3770 The Barnyard
Carmel CA
831-626-5454
allegrogourmetpizzeria.com/
Although the specialty is gourmet pizzas, this Italian eatery also serves up a variety of salads, starters, pasta, paninis, wines/brews, and desserts. Leashed, well mannered dogs are allowed at this pizzeria.

### Anton and Michel
Mission Street and 7th Avenue
Carmel CA
831-624-2406
This fine dining eatery is considered one of the areas most beautiful and romantic restaurants and they offer an innovative continental cuisine combined with traditional fare giving an emphasis on light and flavorful sauces. Leashed, well mannered dogs are welcome at their outside dining area.

### Casanova Restaurant
Mission & 5th
Carmel CA
831-625-0501
casanovarestaurant.com/
This dog-friendly restaurant has

several outdoor tables in the front with heaters. It's located in downtown near several hotels and within a 20-25 minute walk to the dog-friendly beach. Leashed dogs are allowed at the front and the back downstairs patios.

## Forge in the Forest
5th and Junipero, SW Corner
Carmel CA
831-624-2233
forgeintheforest.com/
Dogs are allowed to dine in this elegantly designed outdoor patio. Dogs are only allowed at certain tables on the upper patio.

## Hog's Breath Inn
San Carlos St and 5th Ave
Carmel CA
831-625-1044
hogsbreathinn.net/
Daily made soups, fresh salads, American and regional favorites, sandwiches and burgers, a pub menu, fine wines and brews, and more are offered at this old west themed eatery. Leashed, well mannered dogs are allowed at their outside dining area.

## Nico's
San Carlos St and Ocean Ave
Carmel CA
831-624-6545
This restaurant serves Mediterrian food and fine wines. Dogs are allowed at the outdoor tables.

## PortaBella
Ocean Ave
Carmel CA
831-624-4395
portabellacarmel.com
Dogs... come here to be treated first class. Your waiter will bring your pup water in a champagne bucket. They have several outdoor tables with heaters. It's located in downtown near several hotels and within a 15-20 minute walk to the beach.

## R. G. Burgers
201 Crossroads Shopping Village
Carmel CA
831-626-8054

realgoodburgers.com/
The 'R' and 'G' in this eatery's name stands for Real Good;they offer appetizers, soups and salads, specialty sandwiches, all beef hot dogs, and quality burgers of ground beef, bison, or turkey, chicken breast, and vegetarian falafel. Leashed well mannered dogs are allowed at their outside tables.

## The Forge In the Forest
Fifth and Junipero Avenues
Carmel CA
831-624-2233
forgeintheforest.com/
Diners will find an extensive menu of American and International cuisine that also includes vegetarian and low carb choices, a full service bar, and a variety of California-grown fine wines. This dog friendly restaurant offers a special doggy menu and a pet friendly patio. Dogs must be leashed and well mannered.

## Cachagua General Store
18840 Cachagua Rd
Carmel Valley CA
831-659-1857
cachaguastore.blogspot.com/
The Cachagua General Store is located in the mountains, 25 miles from the Carmel coast. It is a spanish/new american restaurant that serves breakfast, dinner, and drinks as well as operating as a general store. Well-behaved, leashed dogs are welcome to come with you.

## Cafe Stravaganza
241 The Crossroads
Carmel Valley CA
831-625-3733
facebook.com/CafeStravaganza
Located in the Crossroads Shopping Center in Carmel Valley, this restaurant offers dog-friendly outdoor dining. A pet store is nearby.

## Plaza Linda
9 Del Fino Pl
Carmel Valley CA
831-659-4229

plazalinda.com/fram.asp
This dog-friendly restaurant has a sign out front that says so. Sit on the front patio.

## The Corkscrew Cafe
55 W Carmel Valley Rd
Carmel Valley CA
831-659-8888
corkscrewcafe.com/
Their daily menu reflects the use of fresh herbs and seasonal produce from their large gardens, paired with local fish and meats. Dogs are allowed at the outdoor tables.

## Carmel Belle
SW Corner of San Carlos and Ocean
Carmel-by-the-Sea CA
831-624-1600
carmelbelle.com/
This breakfast and lunch eatery features healthy California Coastal cuisine. Besides offering a seasonally inspired menu, they also offer local organic eggs/dairy/fresh roasted coffees, free range poultry, naturally raised meats, daily homemade soup, specialty salads, vegetarian choices, California wines, and alfresco dining. Leashed, well mannered dogs are allowed at their outside tables.

## Flaherty's Seafood Grill & Oyster Bar
6th Avenue between San Carlos & Dolores
Carmel-by-the-Sea CA
Oyster Bar 831-624-0311 /
Seafood Grill 831-625-1500
flahertysseafood.com/
Sustainability, fresh caught fish and seafooddelivered daily (sometimes 2 or 3 times), and prepared to the highest standards for freshness and flavor is the specialty of these eateries. They sit side by side and are under the direction of the their longtime chef;plus, they offer daily specials, a list of fine wines, a kid's menu, and a gluten-free menu in addition to their regular menus. Leashed, well mannered dogs are allowed at their outside dining area.

**Village Corner Mediterranean Bistro**
Dolores & 6th Avenue
Carmel-by-the-Sea CA
831-624-3588
Specializing in Californian and Mediterranean dishes, they also offer a beautiful, floral outside dining area. Dogs are allowed at the outer tables;they must be leashed and under their owner's control at all times.

## Pet-Friendly Shopping Centers
**Carmel Village Shopping Area**

Ocean Ave
Carmel CA

This shopping expedition is more of a window shopping adventure, however there are some dog-friendly stores throughout this popular and quaint village. Just ask a store clerk before entering into a store with your pooch. We do know that the Galerie Blue Dog (Blue Dog Gallery) located at 6th Ave. and Lincoln St. is dog-friendly. There are also many dog-friendly restaurants throughout the village (see Restaurants).

**Crossroads Shopping Center**
Cabrillo Hwy (Hwy 1)
Carmel Valley CA

This is an outdoor shopping mall with many dog-friendly outdoor restaurants and a pet store. While your dog cannot go into the shops, he or she is more than welcome inside the pet store.

**Carmel Plaza**
Ocean Avenue and Mission Street
Carmel-by-the-Sea CA
831-624-1385
carmelplaza.com/
Offering more than 35 shops and eateries, this open air, dog friendly mall even has a designated drinking fountain for dogs, many of the stores will allow pets inside, and canine

visitors get 'treats' as well. Dogs must be leashed and well mannered.

## Pet-Friendly Stores
**Blue Dog Gallery**
6th Ave. and Lincoln St.
Carmel CA
831-626-4444
First created in 1984, Blue Dog is based on the mythical "loup garou," a French-Cajun ghost dog, and Tiffany, Rodrique's own pooch who had passed away a few years prior to the notoriety. Blue Dog represents a dog who is between heaven and earth. Ask about the story behind Blue Dog when you visit this gallery. The painter, Rodrique, is an internationally acclaimed painter. Blue Dog will probably look familiar to you because Absolut Vodka and other companies have used it for their marketing campaigns. This gallery usually has some cookies and treats for visiting pooches. Thanks to one of our readers who writes: "A most wonderful place, I called asking for information after Rodrigue did a picture for Neiman Marcus . . . the lady with whom I spoke sent us information plus dog biscuits for our corgi.."

**Diggidy Dog**
Ocean Ave
Carmel CA
831-625-1585
diggidydog.com/
The Diggidy Dog is a dog & cat boutique located in Carmel, California. They sell collars & leashes, harnesses, toys, treats, pet apparel, bowls, beds, car travel supplies, grooming supplies, and much more.

**Pet Food Express**
300 Crossroads Blvd
Carmel CA
831-622-9999
One of the country's leading pet retailers, this comprehensive pet store offers a number of other stores,

quality foods/treats, a wide variety of pet supplies, breed-specific items, pet care products, apparel, health items, hound and human accessories, and much more. Some of the services they offer include working with local SPCAs and rescue groups helping tens of thousands of homeless pets find new homes (they do not sell animals as pets), providing low cost vaccination clinics, dog training classes, and self-service pet washes. All leashed, friendly pets are welcome.

**Yellow Dog Gallery**
Dolores & 5th Ave
Carmel CA
831-624-3238
yellowdoggallery.com/index.html

This contemporary art gallery has a large number of dog works and allows your dog to visit with you.

**Anthropologie**
93921 Ocean at Mission St, #213
Carmel by the Sea CA
831-624-2129
Items of distinction can be found for all ages and in all departments of this unique shop. Carefully selected to add to the enjoyment of the shopping experience, they carry fine clothing, amazing accessories, jewelry, hobby and leisure items, and a full line of bright and useful items for the home, garden, and office. Leashed, well behaved dogs are allowed in the store.

## Dog-Friendly Wineries and Vineyards
**Taste Mogan**
204 Crossroads Blvd
Carmel CA
831-626-3700
This certified organic vineyard offers a variety of fine handcrafted wines reflecting the Santa Lucia Highlands and Monterey appellations. They also have various events so be

sure to check their calendar for special activities. Leashed, well mannered dogs are welcome in the tasting room.

## Dog-Friendly Beaches
### Carmel City Beach
Ocean Avenue
Carmel CA
831-624-9423
This beach is within walking distance (about 7 blocks) from the quaint village of Carmel. There are a couple of hotels and several restaurants that are within walking distance of the beach. Your pooch is allowed to run off-leash as long as he or she is under voice control. To get there, take the Ocean Avenue exit from Hwy 1 and follow Ocean Ave to the end.

### Carmel River State Beach
Carmelo Street
Carmel CA
831-624-9423
This beach is just south of Carmel. It has approximately a mile of beach and leashes are required. It's located on Carmelo Street.

### Garrapata State Park
Highway 1
Carmel CA
831-649-2836
There are two miles of beach front at this park. Dogs are allowed but must be on a 6 foot or less leash and people need to clean up after their pets. The beach is on Highway 1, about 6 1/2 miles south of Rio Road in Carmel. It is about 18 miles north of Big Sur.

## Dog-Friendly Parks
### Garland Ranch Regional Park
Carmel Valley Rd.
Carmel Valley CA
831-659-4488
This 4,500 acre regional park offers about 5 to 6 miles of dirt single-track and fire road trails. The trail offers a variety of landscapes, with elevations ranging from 200 to 2000 feet. If

you are looking for some exercise in addition to the beaches, this is the spot. Dogs must be on a 7 foot or less leash. They can also be under direct voice control which is defined by park management as you having close visual contact of your dog, not letting them run far ahead or behind you, and having a dog that listens to your commands. Dogs are not allowed to bother any wildlife, other people or other dogs. People who violate this regulation may be citied and lose access priviledges. Please also clean up after your pet. The park is located 8.6 miles east of Highway 1 on Carmel Valley Road.

## Veterinarians
### Animal Hospital At-Crossroads
3 Crossroads Blvd
Carmel CA
831-624-0131
carmelvet.com/
The Animal Hospital at the Crossroads in Carmel, California, is a full service facility providing diagnostics, care and treatment in all areas of modern small animal medicine, dentistry and surgery. Their goal at the animal hospital is to provide quality, dependable and conscientious care for all of their patients. Their regular office hours are:Monday through Friday 8:00 a.m. to 6:00 p.m. Saturday 8:00 a.m. to 4:00 p.m. Sunday 10:00 a.m. to 12:00 p.m. and 1:00 p.m. to 4:00 p.m. They do have a full service staff 7 days a week for those clients needing boarding services for their pets.

## Emergency Veterinarians
### Monterey Peninsula - Salinas Emergency Vet
2 Harris Court Suite A1
Monterey CA
831-373-7374
Monday - Thursday 5:30 pm to

8 am. Friday 5:30 pm to Monday 8 am.

## Carson

## Pet-Friendly Extended Stay Hotels
**Extended Stay America - Los Angeles - Carson**
401 E. Albertoni St.
Carson CA
310-323-2080 (800-804-3724)
One dog is allowed per suite. There is a $25 per night additional pet fee up to $150 for an entire stay.

## Castaic

## Dog-Friendly Hotels
**Rodeway Inn Magic Mountain Area**
31558 Castaic Road
Castaic CA
661-295-1100 (877-424-6423)
The Rodeway Inn Magic Mountain Area is conveniently located just five minutes from Six Flags Magic Mountain. Free breakfast.

Dogs up to 25 pounds are allowed. Dogs are allowed for a pet fee of $10.00 per pet per night.

## Cherry Valley

## Dog-Friendly Parks
**Bogart Park**
9600 Cherry Avenue
Cherry Valley CA
951-845-3818
Located on the foothills of San Gorgonio Bogart Park, this 400 acre park offers a number of recreational pursuits, a scenic fishing pond, great mountain

views, multi-use trails, and acres and acres of lush greenery. Dogs are allowed throughout the park, on the trails, and in the campground for an additional fee of $1 per day per pet. Dogs must be kept on no more than a 6 foot leash, not be left unattended, cleaned up after promptly, and under their owner's control at all times.

# Chico

## Dog-Friendly Hotels
**Oxford Suites Chico**
2035 Business Lane
Chico CA
530-899-9090 (800-870-7848)
Exceptional has never been so affordable. Featuring 184 suites Oxford Suites Chico offers every comfort starting with our premium bedding and comfortable mattresses. Suites also include helpful amenities like a writing desk sofa satellite TV and in-room DVD player. Complimentary amenities include Full Hot Breakfast Buffet for 2 adults Evening Reception excluding Sundays High Speed Wireless Internet Access and Parking. 100 percent Non-Smoking Hotel

**Ramada Plaza Chico**
685 Manzanita Ct
Chico CA
530-345-2491 (877-698-9593)
Dogs of all sizes are allowed. Dogs are allowed for a pet fee of $30.00 per pet per stay.

**Super 8 Motel - Chico**
655 Manzanita Ct.
Chico CA
530-345-2533 (800-800-8000)
Dogs of all sizes are allowed. Dogs are allowed for a pet fee of $10.00 per pet per night.

**Best Western Paradise Hotel**
5475 Clark Road
Paradise CA
530-876-0191 (800-780-7234)
Quite country location,

beautifully appointed guest rooms, excellent customer service, award winning hotel. Numerous antique shops.

Dogs of all sizes are allowed. Dogs are allowed for a pet fee of $10.00/ per pet per night.

# Pet-Friendly Extended Stay Hotels
## Residence Inn By Marriott Chico
2485 Carmichael Drive
Chico CA
530-894-5500
Dogs of all sizes are allowed. There is a $100 one time additional pet fee.

# Outdoor Restaurants
**Baja Fresh Mexican Grill**
2072 E. 20th St.
Chico CA
530-896-1077
bajafresh.com
This Mexican restaurant is open for lunch and dinner. They use fresh ingredients and making their salsa and beans daily. Some of the items on their menu include Enchiladas, Burritos, Tacos Salads, Quesadillas, Nachos, Chicken, Steak and more. Well-behaved leashed dogs are allowed at the outdoor tables.

**Bellachinos**
800 Bruce Road
Chico CA
530-892-2244
This restaurant welcomes leashed dogs on their outdoor patio which has music and a fountain.

**Cal Java**
2485 Notre Dame Blvd.
Chico CA
530-893-2662
caljavachico.com/
Leashed dogs are welcome at their outdoor tables.

**Celestino's Pasta and Pizza**
1354 East Ave

Chico CA
530-345-7700
Well-behaved leashed dogs are allowed at the outdoor seating area.

**Chipotle**
620 Mangrove Avenue
Chico CA
530-343-8707
chipotle.com
Specializing in organic, natural and unprocessed food, this Mexican Eatery offers fajita burritos, tacos, salads, and salsas. Dogs are allowed at the outdoor tables but you will need to order your food inside the restaurant and dogs must remain outside.

**El Patron**
1354 East Ave
Chico CA
530-343-9779
El Patron serves Mexican food. Well-behaved, leashed dogs are allowed at the outdoor seats.

**Jamba Juice**
201 Broadway Street
Chico CA
530-345-5355
jambajuice.com
All natural and organic ingredients, no high-fructose corn syrup, 0 grams trans fat, no artificial preservatives, a healthy helping of antioxidants, vitamins, and minerals, and fresh whole fruit and fruit juices set the base for these tasty and healthy beverages. Their organic Hot Blends provides a new spin on coffee, green or chai tea, and hot chocolate;plus they offer probiotic fruit and yogurt Blends. Additionally, they feature organic steel-cut oatmeal prepared fresh every morning, all natural salads, wraps, sandwiches, and grab n' go specialties. They also offer healthy community support through fundraisers, special sales, and school lunch programs. Leashed, well mannered dogs are allowed at their outside dining area.

**S & S Organic Produce and Natural Foods**

1924 Mangrove Avenue
Chico CA
530-343-4930
ssproduce.com/
This natural food store has an onsite deli. Well-behaved leashed dog are allowed at the outdoor tables.

**Shubert's Ice Cream**
178 E 7th Street
Chico CA
530-342-7163
shuberts.com/
This ice cream shop allows pets at their outdoor tables. They will even give ice cream to your pet.

**Spiteri's Delicatessen**
971 East Avenue
Chico CA
530-891-4797
Well-behaved leashed dogs are allowed at the outdoor seating area. They are open Monday to Saturday from 9 am until 6:30 pm.

**Pet-Friendly Stores**
**Petco Pet Store - Chico**
2005 Dr. Martin Luther King Hwy

Chico CA
530-899-1422
Your licensed and well-behaved leashed dog is allowed in the store.

**Off-Leash Dog Parks**
**DeGarmo Dog Park**
Leora Court
Chico CA

This off leash doggy play area is located at DeGarmo Park, and they are open daily from 7 am until dusk except on Wednesdays from 7 am until 10 am when they close for maintenance. Dogs must be healthy, sociable, current on all vaccinations and license with tags on collar, and under owner's control/care at all times. Owners must clean up after their pets, and keep them leashed when not in designated off-lead areas.

**Lower Bidwell Park Off-Leash Hours**
Various Entrances
Chico CA
530-891-4671
Setting along both sides of the Big Chico Creek Canyon, this spectacular 3,618 acre park offers numerous recreational, cultural, and educational opportunities. Bidwell Park has 2 basic sections; the Upper Bidwell Park and Lower Bidwell Park. Dogs can be off leash in Lower Bidwell Park from 5:30 am until 8:30 am only. Dogs may be off leash if under voice control at anytime along the north side of Upper Park Road. Dogs are not allowed at the swimming holes in Upper Lake or in the 1 Mile or 5 Mile swimming areas. Dogs must be leashed when in not in designated off leash areas.

**Dog-Friendly Parks**
**Bidwell Park**
Highway 99
Chico CA
530-895-4972
bidwellpark.org/
This park exceeds 3,600 acres, making it the third largest municipal park in the United States. The park is comprised of three major sections: Lower Park, Middle Park and Upper Park. Lower Park has children's playgrounds, natural swimming areas, and vehicle-free roads for runners, cyclists, rollerbladers and walkers. Middle Park features ball-playing fields, picnic areas, the "World of Trees" walk, which is accessible to the physically challenged, and the park's environmental and informational headquarters. Upper Park remains relatively untouched with majestic canyons overlooking Big Chico Creek, which contains some of the most spectacular swimming areas in Northern California. Dogs on leash are allowed. Please clean up after them.

**Other Organizations**
**Chico Elks Lodge**
1705 Manzanita Court
Chico CA
530 521-2334
chicoelks.com
This is the 4th Annual Dog Parade Contest & Chili Cook-Off. The Elks is a non profit org. The proceeds go to local and national children's charities. We have 150 to 200 dogs in this contest. It is very exciting. The Chili Cook-Off is fabulous with local restaurants competing. Everyone is invited. This year we will have barrel roasted Santa Maria style tri tip sandwiches and wine tasting with your dog.

## Chowchilla

**Dog-Friendly Hotels**
**Days Inn Chowchilla Gateway To Yosemite**
220 East Robertson Blvd
Chowchilla CA
559-665-4821 (800-329-7466)
Dogs are welcome at this hotel.

## Clear Lake

**Dog-Friendly Hotels**
**Super 8 Upper Lake**
450 East Highway 20
Upper Lake CA
707-275-0888 (800-800-8000)
Dogs of all sizes are allowed. Dogs are allowed for a nightly pet fee.

**Accommodations**
**Clear Lake Cottages & Marina**
13885 Lakeshore Drive
Clearlake CA
707-995-5253
clearlakecottagesandmarina.com

Dogs are welcomed ath these cottages with pet beds, treats and water bowls.

## Outdoor Restaurants
### Vigilance Winery
13888 Point Lakeview Road
Lower Lake CA
707-994-9656
vigilancewinery.com/
Sauvignon Blanc, Cabernets, Petite Sirah, and Cimarron a just a few of the fine wines produced at this sustainably farmed vineyard. They also feature a scenic picnic area, hiking trails, horseshoes, and bocce ball. They are open daily from 11 am until 5 pm. Hound and human friendly dogs are welcome at the vineyard. They must be leashed and under their owner's control.

### Blue Wing Saloon and Cafe
9520 Main Street
Upper Lake CA
707-275-2233
bluewingsaloon.com/
An eclectic blend of comfort foods and California cuisine is offered at this restaurant. They also offer a special Mexican food menu for Fiesta Tuesdays, ongoing weekly specials, a full bar, live music and entertainment on select days, a tasty brunch on Sunday's, and garden patio dining. Leashed, well mannered dogs are welcome at their outside tables.

## Dog-Friendly Parks
### Clear Lake State Park
Soda Bay Road
Kelseyville CA
707-279-4293
While dogs are not allowed on the trails or the swimming beaches at this park, they are allowed in the campgrounds and in the water at non-designated swim areas. One of the non-designated swim beaches is located between campgrounds 57 and 58. Pets must be on leash and please clean up after them. The park is located is 3.5

miles northeast of Kelseyville.

### Mendocino National Forest
10025 Elk Mountain Road
Upper Lake CA
707-275-2361
fs.usda.gov/mendocino
This forest consists of one million acres of mountains and canyons and offers a variety of recreational opportunities like camping, hiking, backpacking, boating, fishing, hunting, nature study, photography, and off highway vehicle travel. Elevations in the forest range from 750 feet to 8092 feet with an average elevation of about 4000 feet. For a map of hiking trails, please visit the Visitor Center at 10025 Elk Mountain Road in the town of Upper Lake.

### Sunset Nature Trail Loop
County Road 301/Forest Road M1
Upper Lake CA
530-934-3316
This self-guided interpretive trail is an easy .5 mile one way hike. Elevation begins at 1,800 feet and has a 100 foot climb. The trail is located in the Mendocino National Forest, adjacent to a campground. Pets on leash are allowed. Please clean up after your pets. To get there from Upper Lake, take County Road 301 north for 31 miles. The trail begins at the Sunset Campground.

## Rescue Organizations
### Lake County Animal Services

PO Box 662
Lakeport CA
707-549-3507
lakecountyanimalservices.org
We are a registered 501(c)3 (non profit) association composed of a group of public and private citizens who have come together with the sole objective of saving lives. While working closely with Lakeport Animal Control in an ongoing effort to lower the overall

number of companion animals put to sleep, we welcome the participation of individuals who share our common goals. These common goals include putting aside personal differences and focusing only on the job at hand: saving lives.

## Coalinga

## Dog-Friendly Hotels
### Best Western Big Country Inn
25020 West Dorris Avenue
Coalinga CA
559-935-0866 (800-780-7234)
Dogs up to 50 pounds are allowed. There is a $20 per pet per night pet fee.

### Coalinga Travelodge
25278 West Dorris Avenue
Coalinga CA
559-935-2063
Dogs up to 50 pounds are allowed. There is a pet fee of $10 per pet per night.

## Colusa

## Dog-Friendly Parks
### Colusa National Wildlife Refuge
H 20 at Ohair Road
Colusa CA
530-934-2801
fws.gov/refuge/colusa/
This 4,507 acre refuge consists mostly of seasonal wetlands, uplands, restored/maintained habitats for migratory birds and endangered species, and the preservation/maintenance of as much of the indigenous flora and fauna as possible. The area is popular for wildlife viewing, nature photography, hiking, and hunting. There is a 3 mile graveled auto tour that wanders through freshwater wetlands, a 1 mile Discovery Trail walk along dense riparian marshes, and it is home to more than 200,000

ducks and 50,000 geese every winter. Dogs are allowed and they may go just about anywhere their human companions can go. Dogs must be kept under control, leashed, and cleaned up after at all times.

## Corning

### Dog-Friendly Hotels
**Best Western Plus Corning Inn**
910 Highway 99 W
Corning CA
530-824-5200 (800-780-7234)
Dogs up to 80 pounds are allowed. There is a $10 per day pet fee up to $100 for the week. Up to two dogs are allowed per room.

**Econo Lodge Inn & Suites Corning**
3475 Highway 99 West
Corning CA
530-824-2000 (800-329-7466)
Dogs are welcome at this hotel.

**Holiday Inn Express Corning**
3350 Sunrise Way
Corning CA
530-824-6400 (877-270-6405)
Dogs of all sizes are allowed. Dogs are allowed for a nightly pet fee.

## Crescent City

### Dog-Friendly Hotels
**Quality Inn & Suites Redwood Coast**
100 Walton Street
Crescent City CA
707-464-3885 (877-424-6423)
Free high-speed Internet access. Hotel is located at the gateway to the redwood forest and offers large rooms, some with ocean views.

**Super 8 Crescent City**

685 Redwood Highway
Crescent City CA
707-464-4111 (800-800-8000)
Small dogs are allowed. Dogs are allowed for a pet fee of $10.00 per pet per night.

### Outdoor Restaurants
**Los Compadres Mexican Food**
457 Highway 101
Crescent City CA
707-464-7871
Well-behaved leashed dogs are allowed at the outdoor seating area. They are open daily from 11 am until 9 pm.

### Dog-Friendly Beaches
**Beachfront Park**
Front Street
Crescent City CA
707-464-9507
Dogs are allowed at park and the beach, but must be leashed. Please clean up after your pets. To get there, take Highway 101 to Front Street. Follow Front Street to the park.

**Crescent Beach**
Enderts Beach Road
Crescent City CA
707-464-6101
While dogs are not allowed on any trails in Redwood National Park, they are allowed on a couple of beaches, including Crescent Beach. Enjoy beach combing or bird watching at this beach. Pets are also allowed at road accessible picnic areas and campgrounds. Dogs must be on a 6 foot or less leash and people need to pick up after their pets. The beach is located off Highway 101, about 3 to 4 miles south of Crescent City. Exit Enderts Beach Road and head south.

### Dog-Friendly Parks
**Myrtle Creek Trail**
Highway 199
Gasquet CA

707-442-1721
This trail is located in the Smith River National Recreation Area and is part of the Six Rivers National Forest. The trail is an easy 1 mile interpretive hiking path. The elevations range from 250 to 500 feet. From this trail you can also access the Smith River. Pets on leash are allowed and please clean up after them. The trail is located 8 miles west of Gasquet at Milepost 7.0. Park on the south (river) side of the highway. Use caution when crossing Highway 199 to reach the trailhead.

## Davis

### Dog-Friendly Hotels
**Best Western University Lodge**
123 B Street
Davis CA
530-756-7890 (800-780-7234)
Dogs up to 80 pounds are allowed. There is a $10 per day pet fee up to $100 for the week. Up to two dogs are allowed per room.

**Econo Lodge Davis**
221 D Street
Davis CA
530-756-1040 (877-424-6423)
2 blocks to UC Davis campus. Quiet location in center of quaint college town. Restaurants, movie theater short walk.

Dogs of all sizes are allowed. Dogs are allowed for a pet fee of $5.00 per pet per night.

**La Quinta Inn & Suites Davis**
1771 Research Park Drive
Davis CA
530-758-2600 (800-531-5900)
Dogs of all sizes are allowed. Dogs may not be left alone in the room.

### Outdoor Restaurants
**Ali Baba Middle Eastern**

**Restaurant**
220 3rd Street
Davis CA
530-758-2251
daviswiki.org/Ali_Baba
This restaurant serves Middle Eastern food. Leashed dogs are allowed at the outdoor tables.

**Cafe Bernardo Davis**
234 D Street
Davis CA
530-750-5101
With the ambiance of a traditional European cafe, this gathering place puts an emphasis on sustainable and locally sourced ingredients. The menu changes seasonally;breads are made fresh every day;they offer a full bar, and their foods are all prepared in their certified green kitchen. Some of their offerings include sandwiches, pizzettas, burgers, fresh caught fish, and steaks. Leashed, well mannered dogs are welcome at their outside tables.

**Chipotle**
227 E Street
Davis CA
530-758-3599
chipotle.com
Specializing in organic, natural and unprocessed food, this Mexican Eatery offers fajita burritos, tacos, salads, and salsas. Dogs are allowed at the outdoor tables but you will need to order your food inside the restaurant and dogs must remain outside.

**Davis Food Co-op**
620 G Street
Davis CA
530-758-2667
daviscoop.com/index.html
This co-op offers over 750 items in bulk and 40 different varieties of organic produce, a deli, and more. There are tables on the side of the market where your well behaved, leashed dog may join you. There are also tie-ups if needed.

**Dos Coyotes**
1411 W Covell Blvd
Davis CA

530-753-0922
doscoyotes.net/home.html
Fresh local produce, all natural cheeses, a seasonally evolving menu, freshly made guacamole, salsas and marinades, several vegetarian choices, daily specials, and alfresco dining are just some of the offerings of this Mexican eatery. No animal products are used in their foods and they also offer catering services. Leashed, friendly dogs are allowed at their outside dining area.

**Dos Coyotes**
2191 Cowell Blvd
Davis CA
530-758-1400
doscoyotes.net/home.html
Fresh local produce, all natural cheeses, a seasonally evolving menu, freshly made guacamole, salsas and marinades, several vegetarian choices, daily specials, and alfresco dining are just some of the offerings of this Mexican eatery. No animal products are used in their foods and they also offer catering services. Leashed, friendly dogs are allowed at their outside dining area.

**Jamba Juice**
500 1st Street #3
Davis CA
530-757-8499
jambajuice.com
All natural and organic ingredients, no high-fructose corn syrup, 0 grams trans fat, no artificial preservatives, a healthy helping of antioxidants, vitamins, and minerals, and fresh whole fruit and fruit juices set the base for these tasty and healthy beverages. Their organic Hot Blends provides a new spin on coffee, green or chai tea, and hot chocolate;plus they offer probiotic fruit and yogurt Blends. Additionally, they feature all natural salads, wraps, sandwiches, and grab n go specialties. They also offer healthy community support through fundraisers, special

sales, and school lunch programs. Leashed, well mannered dogs are allowed at their outside dining area.

**Mishka's**
514 2nd Street
Davis CA
530-759-0811
mishkascafe.com/
This coffee bar serve only Organic Fair Trade Coffee and places an importance on Green and sustainable. Leashed dogs are allowed at the outside seating area.

**Posh Bagels**
206 F Street
Davis CA
530-753-6770
This bagel shop is in downtown Davis. Dogs are allowed at the outdoor tables.

**Redrum Burger**
978 Olive Drive
Davis CA
530-756-2142
This burger place is a local favorite in this college town (the original name was Murder Burger and the new name is Redrum Burger). They serve regular hamburgers and ostrich burgers, chicken sandwiches, shakes and more. You can order with your pup from

**Steve's Place Pizza, Pasta & Grill**
314 F Street
Davis CA
530-758-2800
theoriginalsteves.com/
Steve's Place has a nice outdoor seating area for you and your leashed dog.

**Subway**
4748 Chiles Rd
Davis CA
530-753-2141
This eatery specializes in made-to-order fresh, baked bread sandwiches with a variety of accompaniments to round out your meals. They also provide a kid's menu and catering services. Leashed dogs are allowed at the outer tables.

## Sudwerk
2001 2nd Street
Davis CA
530-758-8700
sudwerk.com/
In addition to sharing good food and hand-crafted brews, this brewery and restaurant will also share tours of their beer making process. Patio dining is available with plenty of shade and trees. Dogs are allowed on one half of the patio unless it is an extremely busy night;they must be leashed and well mannered.

## Pet-Friendly Stores
### Outdoor Davis
623 2nd St
Davis CA
530-757-2997
facebook.com/OutdoorDavis
Outdoor Davis is a outdoor sports shop dedicated to items for outdoor activities such as hiking and backpacking and living for all seasons. They carry clothing/gear for kids, teens, and adults. Outdoor Davis has a water bowl outdoor their store for thirsty pooches and allows well-behaved dogs inside the store.

### Petco Pet Store - Davis
1341-B West Covell Blvd
Davis CA
530-750-0111
Your licensed and well-behaved leashed dog is allowed in the store.

### The Cultured Canine
231 G Street #3
Davis CA
530-753-3470
Well-behaved dogs are allowed inside this gift store.

## Off-Leash Dog Parks
### Toad Hollow Dog Park
1919 Second Street
Davis CA
530-757-5656
Toad Hollow Dog Park is located in Davis on Second Street between L Street and the Pole Line Road bridge. The fenced park is large (about 2 1/2 acres). The dog park will be closed during periods of heavy rains. The dog park is run by the Davis Parks & Community Services Department.

## Dog-Friendly Parks
### Community Park
1405 F Street
Davis CA

Dogs on leash are permitted in this and most parks in Davis. The park is 28 acres in size.

## Veterinarians
### UC Davis Medical Teaching Hospital
One Shields Avenue
Davis CA
530-752-1393
vmth.ucdavis.edu
This large teaching veterinary hospital offers small animal emergency and specialized care. They also have a large animal hospital for horses and other larger animals.

## Death Valley

## Outdoor Restaurants
### Panamint Springs Resort
40440 H 190
Death Valley CA
775-482-7680
panamintsprings.com/
This restaurant serves a variety of tasty homemade food. Leashed dogs are allowed at the outdoor tables.

## Dog-Friendly Parks
### Death Valley National Park
Highway 190
Death Valley CA
760-786-2331
nps.gov/deva
Death Valley is one of the hottest places on Earth, with summer temperatures averaging well over 100 degrees Fahrenheit. It is also the lowest point on the Western Hemisphere at 282 feet below sea level. Average rainfall here sets yet another record. With an average of only 1.96 inches per year, this valley is the driest place in North America. Because of the high summer heat, the best time to visit the park is during the winter. Even though dogs are not allowed on any trails, you will still be able to see the majority of the sights and attractions from your car. There are several scenic drives that are popular with all visitors, with or without dogs. Dante's View is a 52 mile round trip drive that takes about 2 hours or longer. Some parts of the road are graded dirt roads and no trailers or RVs are allowed. On this drive you will view scenic mudstone hills which are made of 7 to 9 million year old lakebed sediments. You will also get a great view from the top of Dantes View. Another scenic drive is called Badwater. It is located about 18 miles from the Visitor Center and can take about 1.5 to 2 hours or longer. On this drive you will view the Devil's Golf Course where there are almost pure table salt crystals from an ancient lake. You will also drive to Badwater which is the lowest point in the Western Hemisphere at 282 feet below sea level. Dogs are allowed at view points which are about 200 yards or less from roads or parking lots. Pets must be leashed and attended at all times. Please clean up after your pets. While dogs are not allowed on any trails in the park, they can walk along roads. Pets are allowed up to a few hundred yards from the paved and dirt roads. Stop at the Furnance Creek Visitor Center to pick up a brochure and more information. The visitor center is located on Highway 190, north of the lowest point.

## Delano

### Dog-Friendly Hotels
**Best Western Liberty Inn**
14394 County Line Road
Delano CA
661-725-0976 (800-780-7234)
Dogs up to 80 pounds are
allowed. There is a $20 per day
pet fee up to $100 for the week.
Up to two dogs are allowed per
room.

**Rodeway Inn Delano**
2211 Girard Street
Delano CA
661-725-1022 (877-424-6423)
Hotel is 35 miles North of
Bakersfield in the heart of
agriculture county. FREE
continental breakfast.

Dogs of all sizes are allowed.
Dogs are allowed for a pet fee of
$10.00 per pet per night.

## Dinuba

### Dog-Friendly Hotels
**Holiday Inn Express Hotel &
Suites Dinuba West**
375 S. Alta Ave.
Dinuba CA
559-595-1500 (877-270-6405)
Dogs of all sizes are allowed.
Dogs are allowed for a pet fee of
$50.00 per pet per night.

## Dixon

### Dog-Friendly Hotels
**Best Western Plus Inn Dixon**
1345 Commercial Way
Dixon CA
707-678-1400 (800-780-7234)
Dogs up to 80 pounds are
allowed. There is a $15 per day
pet fee up to $100 for the week.
Up to two dogs are allowed per
room.

## El Centro

### Dog-Friendly Hotels
**Comfort Inn & Suites El
Centro**
2354 South 4th Street
El Centro CA
760-335-3502 (877-424-6423)
El Centro Comfort Inn and
Suites convenient to Mexicali
and Calexico. Nearby golfing,
shopping, restaurants and
lounges.

Dogs up to 25 pounds are
allowed.

**El Centro Inn & Suites**
455 Wake Avenue
El Centro CA
760-352-6620 (877-424-6423)
Our hotel is in walking distance
to
business,shopping,restaurants.
Near Imperial Valley Mall.

Dogs up to 20 pounds are
allowed. Dogs are allowed for a
pet fee of $5.00 per pet per
night. Two dogs are allowed
per room.

**Value Inn & Suites**
2030 Cottonwood Circle
El Centro CA
760-353-7750 (800-843-5644)
Dogs of all sizes are allowed.
Dogs are allowed for a nightly
pet fee.

### Pet-Friendly Extended
Stay Hotels
**Towneplace Suites By
Marriott El Centro**
3003 South Dogwood Avenue
El Centro CA
760-370-3800
Dogs of all sizes are allowed.
There is a $75 one time pet
fee.

### Dog-Friendly Attractions

**Tumco Historic Townsite**
Ogilby Road
El Centro CA
760-337-4400
Located in the mountains east
of El Centro, is an abandoned
gold mine town called Tumco.
Today a few buildings and mine
shafts remain. The mine shafts
have very steep drop offs and
are dangerous, so make sure
you and your pooch stay clear of
them. Also be aware of
rattlesnakes in the area. It is
best to visit during the fall,
winter or spring months when it
is not too hot. The remote site is
managed by the Bureau of Land
Management. Dogs must be on
leash and please clean up after
your dogs. To get there from
Highway 8, east of El Centro,
take Highway S34 North.

## Eureka

### Dog-Friendly Hotels
**Carter House Inns**
301 L Street
Eureka CA
707-444-8062 (800-404-1390)
carterhouse.com
The most fanciful B&Bs along
the Redwood Coast the historic
Carter House Inns feature
stunning non-smoking rooms
decked out in antiques a world-
class restaurant organic
breakfast and free Wi-Fi within a
hour's drive of the magnificent
Redwood National Park. The
three-story Victorian Carter
House Inns house 32 non-
smoking rooms with canopy
beds free Wi-Fi cable TV and
coffeemakers. Guests receive a
free hot organic breakfast each
morning and a glass of wine
with appetizers in the evenings.
The on-site restaurant sources
much of its produce from the
garden on the property. Guests
can assist in the harvest of the
garden or try the horticulture
and cooking classes. Guests
can book a massage treatment
for an extra fee. Pets are

allowed and parking is free. Three blocks from Humboldt Bay in Old Town Eureka the Carter House Inns are close to many shops galleries and restaurants. The Morris Graves Museum of Art is a half-mile from the inn. Sequoia Park and Zoo is less than three miles away. Redwood National Park with the tallest trees on the planet is 40 miles away. Arcata Airport is 16 miles from the inn and San Francisco International Airport is 284 miles south.

**Discovery Inn - Eureka**
2832 Broadway Street
Eureka CA
707-441-8442
Along Highway 101 and across from the Humboldt Bay the Discovery Inn Eureka features rooms with free Wi-Fi and cable TV for an attractive price. The two-story Discovery Inn Eureka features 45 rooms with free Wi-Fi. Rooms include a microwave coffeemaker cable TV and work desk; non-smoking rooms are available. The hotel offers fax/copier services laundry facilities and free parking. Pets are allowed. On Highway 101 a block from the bay and less than a mile from Bayshore Mill the Discovery Inn Eureka is close to Eureka's Old Town which is full of fun restaurants galleries historic buildings and museums. Sequoia Park Zoo and Redwood Discovery Museum are within three miles of the hotel. Arcata with its university redwood park and amazing restaurants is 10 miles away. Redwood National Park is a-40 mile drive. Arcata Airport is 17 miles away and San Francisco International Airport is 283 miles from the property.

**Laguna Inn**
1630 4th St
Eureka CA
707-443-8041 (877-424-6423)
Set on the incomparable northern California coast. Eureka's charming downtown is perfect base for exploring

Dogs up to 30 pounds are

allowed. Dogs are allowed for a pet fee of $8.00 per pet per night.

**Quality Inn Eureka**
1209 Fourth Street
Eureka CA
707-443-1601 (877-424-6423)
Walking distance to Old Town Shops and restaurants. 2 blocks from Humboldt Bay.

Dogs up to 50 pounds are allowed. Dogs are allowed for a pet fee of $10.00 per pet per stay. Two dogs are allowed per room.

# Outdoor Restaurants
## Mad River Brewing Company

195 Taylor Way
Blue Lake CA
707-668-4151
madriverbrewing.com/
Some of the offerings of this brewing company include a selection of signature brews, live music in the tasting room on select nights, keg sales, tours, and a beautiful beer garden. Leashed, well mannered dogs are welcome at their outside tables, and, with a location next to the Mad River, they may also enjoy a walk along the trails and levee.

**Hana Sushi Restaurant**
2120 4th Street
Eureka CA
707-444-3318
Well-behaved dogs are welcome this Japanese restaurant's outdoor seating area. Dogs need to be leashed.

**Los Bagels**
403 Second Street
Eureka CA
707-442-8525
losbagels.com
This bakery offers a variety of breads, bagels and pastries. It is located in Eureka's historic Old Town. Well-behaved, leashed dogs are allowed at the outside tables.

**Starbucks Coffee**
1117 Myrtle Avenue
Eureka CA
707-445-2672
starbucks.com/
Fuel up with some coffee and pastries at Starbucks. Well-behaved, leashed dogs are allowed at the outside tables.

# Pet-Friendly Stores
**Petco Pet Store - Eureka**
3300 Broadway St.
Eureka CA
707-445-1256
Your licensed and well-behaved leashed dog is allowed in the store.

**Restoration Hardware**
417 Second Street
Eureka CA
707-443-3152
Utilizing the finest of products, this store features a large selection of home restoration products. Your leashed, well behaved dog is welcome to join you in the store. They must be housebroken and under their owner's control at all times.

# Dog-Friendly Beaches
**Samoa Dunes Recreation Area**
New Navy Base Road
Samoa CA
707-825-2300
The Bureau of Land Management oversees this 300 acre sand dune park. It is a popular spot for off-highway vehicles which can use about 140 of the park's acres. Dogs are allowed on leash or off-leash but under voice control. Even if your dog runs off-leash, the park service requests that you still bring a leash just in case. To get there, take Highway 255 and turn south on New Navy Base Road. Go about four miles to the parking area.

# Dog-Friendly Parks

## Fort Humboldt State Historic Park
3431 Fort Avenue
Eureka CA
707-445-6567
This old military post was established in 1853 to assist in resolving conflicts between Native Americans and settlers who were searching for gold. Dogs are not allowed inside any buildings but they can walk through the outdoor exhibits and view historic logging equipment. There is also a grassy bluff area where you can walk your dog. Pets must be on leash and please clean up after them. The park is located south of Eureka off Highway 101. Go east on Highland Avenue for one block.

## Six Rivers National Forest
1330 Bayshore Way
Eureka CA
707-442-1721
fs.usda.gov/srnf
This national forest covers almost 1 million acres of land which ranges in elevation from sea level to almost 7,000 feet. Please see our listings in this region for dog-friendly hikes and/or campgrounds.

## Fillmore

### Dog-Friendly Hotels
**Best Western La Posada Motel**
827 W Ventura Street
Fillmore CA
805-524-0440 (800-780-7234)
Dogs are allowed, no restrictions. There is a $15.00 one day charge per dog.

## Fortuna

### Dog-Friendly Hotels
**Best Western Country Inn Fortuna**
2025 Riverwalk Drive
Fortuna CA
707-725-6822 (800-780-7234)
Dogs up to 80 pounds are allowed. There is a $20 per day pet fee up to $100 for the week. Up to two dogs are allowed per room.

### The Redwood Fortuna Riverwalk Hotel
1859 Alamar Way
Fortuna CA
707-725-5500 (877-698-9593)
Dogs of all sizes are allowed. Dogs are allowed for a pet fee of $20.00 per pet per night.

### Dog-Friendly Attractions
**Fortuna Depot Museum**
3 Park St
Fortuna CA
707-725-7645
The museum contains the history of the Eel River Valley. Museum collections include memorabilia from railroad, farm and war eras. There is also a doll collection. Well-behaved, leashed dogs are allowed, just keep them right next to you.

### Outdoor Restaurants
**Shotz Coffee**
1665 Main Street
Fortuna CA
707-725-8000
This coffee shop offers a table and bench outside where guests may sit with their pet. Dogs must be under owner's control at all times and leashed.

## Fowler

### Dog-Friendly Hotels
**La Quinta Inn & Suites Fowler**
190 North 10th Street
Fowler CA
559-834-6300 (800-531-5900)
Dogs of all sizes are allowed. Dogs may not be left alone in the room.

## Fresno

### Dog-Friendly Hotels
**Hampton Inn & Suites Clovis**
855 Gettysburg Avenue
Clovis CA
559-348-0000
Dogs up to 40 pounds are allowed. There is a $50 one time pet fee.

**Best Western Village Inn**
3110 North Blackstone Avenue
Fresno CA
559-226-2110 (800-780-7234)
Dogs up to 80 pounds are allowed. There is a $20 per day pet fee up to $100 for the week. Up to two dogs are allowed per room.

**Days Inn Fresno South**
2640 South 2nd Street
Fresno CA
559-237-6644 (800-329-7466)
Dogs are welcome at this hotel.

**Executive Inn Fresno**
1087 North Parkway Drive
Fresno CA
559-268-0741 (800-800-8000)
Dogs of all sizes are allowed. Dogs are allowed for a pet fee of $10 per pet per stay.

**Fresno-days Inn**
1101 N Parkway Drive
Fresno CA
559-268-6211 (800-329-7466)
Dogs of all sizes are allowed. Dogs are allowed for a pet fee of $10.00 per pet per night.

**La Quinta Inn & Suites Fresno Northwest**
5077 North Cornelia Avenue
Fresno CA
559-275-3700 (800-531-5900)
Dogs of all sizes are allowed. Dogs may not be left alone in the room.

**La Quinta Inn & Suites Fresno Riverpark**
330 E. Fir Avenue

Fresno CA
559-449-0928 (800-531-5900)
Dogs up to 50 pounds are allowed for no additional pet fee. There is a pet policy to sign at check in, and dogs may not be left alone in the room. Dogs are not allowed in food service areas.

### La Quinta Inn Fresno Yosemite
2926 Tulare
Fresno CA
559-442-1110 (800-531-5900)
Dogs of all sizes are allowed. There are no additional pet fees, and there is a pet waiver to sign at check in. Dogs must be leashed and cleaned up after.

### Motel 6 Fresno - Belmont Ave
445 N Parkway Drive
Fresno CA
559-485-5019 (877-424-6423)
Easy access to Hwy 99 and Hwy 41. 6 mi. from Fresno Air Terminal and 3 miles to the Convention Center.

### Parkway Inn
959 North Parkway Drive
Fresno CA
559-445-0322 (877-424-6423)
Rodeway Inn is conveniently located right off the 99 Freeway in Fresno, CA.

Dogs of all sizes are allowed. Dogs are allowed for a pet fee of $15.00 per pet per night. Two dogs are allowed per room.

### Ramada Fresno Northwest
5046 North Barcus Avenue
Fresno CA
559-277-5700
Dogs of all sizes are allowed. There is a $20 one time pet fee.

### Travelodge Fresno Convention Centre Area
2127 Inyo Street
Fresno CA
559-268-0621 (800-800-8000)
Dogs of all sizes are allowed. Dogs are allowed for a pet fee.

### University Inn Fresno
2655 East Shaw Avenue
Fresno CA
559-294-0224

Across the street from California State University-Fresno the pet-friendly University Inn Fresno provides free daily continental breakfast and Wi-Fi as well as an outdoor pool. The two-story University Inn has 105 budget rooms each with free Wi-Fi and cable TV. Guests can order room service or enjoy free continental breakfast then soak in the outdoor pool and hot tub. Non-smoking rooms are available. Pets are allowed for an additional charge. Parking is free. One block from Highway 168 and eight miles from Highway 99 the University Inn is across the street from California State University-Fresno and its concert and sports venue the Save Mart Center. The shops and restaurants of downtown Fresno are seven miles away and Sierra National Forest is a 33-mile drive. Fresno Yosemite International Airport is five miles from the hotel.

# Pet-Friendly Extended Stay Hotels

### Homewood Suites By Hilton Fresno Airport-clovis Ca
835 Gettysburg Ave
Clovis CA
559-292-4004
This upscale all suite hotel offers large, comfortable suites for longer stays and/or temporary housing needs;plus numerous on site amenities for all level of travelers and a convenient location to local sites of interest. Dogs are allowed for an additional one time pet fee of $75 per room.

### Extended Stay America - Fresno - North
7135 North Fresno Street
Fresno CA
559-438-7105 (800-804-3724)
One dog is allowed per suite. There is a $25 per night additional pet fee up to $150 for an entire stay.

### Residence Inn Fresno
5322 N Diana Ave
Fresno CA
559-222-8900
Dogs of all sizes are allowed. There is a $100 one time additional pet fee.

### Towneplace Suites By Marriott Fresno
7127 Fresno Street
Fresno CA
559-435-4600
Dogs of all sizes are allowed. There is a $100 one time pet fee. They are not allowed in room unattended or in lobby during breakfast.

# Outdoor Restaurants

### Chipotle
1210 Shaw Avenue
Clovis CA
559-298-4708
chipotle.com
Specializing in organic, natural and unprocessed food, this Mexican Eatery offers fajita burritos, tacos, salads, and salsas. Dogs are allowed at the outdoor tables but you will need to order your food inside the restaurant and dogs must remain outside.

### Jamba Juice
775 W Herndon Avenue, Suite 100
Clovis CA
559-325-8974
jambajuice.com
All natural and organic ingredients, no high-fructose corn syrup, 0 grams trans fat, no artificial preservatives, a healthy helping of antioxidants, vitamins, and minerals, and fresh whole fruit and fruit juices set the base for these tasty and healthy beverages. Their organic Hot Blends provides a new spin on coffee, green or chai tea, and hot chocolate;plus they offer probiotic fruit and yogurt Blends. Additionally, they feature all natural salads, wraps, sandwiches, and grab n go specialties. They also offer healthy community support through fundraisers, special

sales, and school lunch programs. Leashed, well mannered dogs are allowed at their outside dining area.

**Baja Fresh Mexican Grill**
7675 N. Blackstone
Fresno CA
559-431-8811
bajafresh.com
This Mexican restaurant is open for lunch and dinner. They use fresh ingredients and making their salsa and beans daily. Some of the items on their menu include Enchiladas, Burritos, Tacos Salads, Quesadillas, Nachos, Chicken, Steak and more. Well-behaved leashed dogs are allowed at the outdoor tables.

**Chipotle**
5128 North Palm Ave
Fresno CA
559-225-1166
chipotle.com
Specializing in organic, natural and unprocessed food, this Mexican Eatery offers fajita burritos, tacos, salads, and salsas. Dogs are allowed at the outdoor tables but you will need to order your food inside the restaurant and dogs must remain outside.

**Dai Bai Dang Restaurant**
7736 N Blackstone Ave
Fresno CA
559-448-8894
daibaidang.com/
Asian cuisine is the specialty here;they also feature a full bar and outdoor dining. Leashed dogs are allowed at the outdoor tables.

**Jamba Juice**
3696 W Shaw Avenue
Fresno CA
559-271-7493
jambajuice.com
All natural and organic ingredients, no high-fructose corn syrup, 0 grams trans fat, no artificial preservatives, a healthy helping of antioxidants, vitamins, and minerals, and fresh whole fruit and fruit juices set the base for these tasty and healthy beverages. Their organic Hot

Blends provides a new spin on coffee, green or chai tea, and hot chocolate;plus they offer probiotic fruit and yogurt Blends. Additionally, they feature all natural salads, wraps, sandwiches, and grab n go specialties. They also offer healthy community support through fundraisers, special sales, and school lunch programs. Leashed, well mannered dogs are allowed at their outside dining area.

**Jamba Juice**
1512 E Champlain Drive, #101
Fresno CA
559-433-6970
jambajuice.com
All natural and organic ingredients, no high-fructose corn syrup, 0 grams trans fat, no artificial preservatives, a healthy helping of antioxidants, vitamins, and minerals, and fresh whole fruit and fruit juices set the base for these tasty and healthy beverages. Their organic Hot Blends provides a new spin on coffee, green or chai tea, and hot chocolate;plus they offer probiotic fruit and yogurt Blends. Additionally, they feature all natural salads, wraps, sandwiches, and grab n go specialties. They also offer healthy community support through fundraisers, special sales, and school lunch programs. Leashed, well mannered dogs are allowed at their outside dining area.

**Jamba Juice**
190 Paseo del Centro
Fresno CA
559-261-2619
jambajuice.com
All natural and organic ingredients, no high-fructose corn syrup, 0 grams trans fat, no artificial preservatives, a healthy helping of antioxidants, vitamins, and minerals, and fresh whole fruit and fruit juices set the base for these tasty and healthy beverages. Their organic Hot Blends provides a new spin on coffee, green or chai tea, and hot

chocolate;plus they offer probiotic fruit and yogurt Blends. Additionally, they feature all natural salads, wraps, sandwiches, and grab n go specialties. They also offer healthy community support through fundraisers, special sales, and school lunch programs. Leashed, well mannered dogs are allowed at their outside dining area.

**Jamba Juice**
570 S Clovis Avenue, Suite 105
Fresno CA
559-456-0518
jambajuice.com
All natural and organic ingredients, no high-fructose corn syrup, 0 grams trans fat, no artificial preservatives, a healthy helping of antioxidants, vitamins, and minerals, and fresh whole fruit and fruit juices set the base for these tasty and healthy beverages. Their organic Hot Blends provides a new spin on coffee, green or chai tea, and hot chocolate;plus they offer probiotic fruit and yogurt Blends. Additionally, they feature all natural salads, wraps, sandwiches, and grab n go specialties. They also offer healthy community support through fundraisers, special sales, and school lunch programs. Leashed, well mannered dogs are allowed at their outside dining area.

**Revue News**
620 E. Olive Avenue
Fresno CA
559-499-1844
This news stand also serves coffee and pastries. They are open from 8am-10pm and allow dogs at the outdoor tables. It is located on Olive Avenue between N. Blackstone Avenue and N. Palm Avenue.

**TGI Fridays**
1077 E. Herndon Avenue
Fresno CA
559-435-8443
tgifridays.com/
This casual dining restaurant chain allows well-behaved leashed dogs at the outdoor

tables. Please do not feed your pet from the table. Thanks to one of our readers for recommending this restaurant.

**The Loving Hut**
1495 N Van Ness Avenue
Fresno CA
559-237-4052
lovinghut.us/fresno_01/
A quick-service 100% vegan eatery, guests will find a full menu of affordable, freshly prepared gourmet cuisine made with the finest and freshest quality ingredients available. They offer organic coffee and tea, specialize in traditional, regional, and Chinese vegan cuisines, and in providing foods that are gluten free with no GMOs, milk or eggs. Services include dine-in, take-out, frozen and dried food sales, and catering. Leashed, well mannered dogs are welcome at their outside dining area.

**Whole Foods Market**
650 West Shaw Avenue
Fresno CA
559-241-0300
wholefoods.com/
This natural food supermarket offers natural and organic foods. Order some food from their deli without your dog and bring it to an outdoor table where your well-behaved leashed dog is welcome.

**Jamba Juice**
775 Bethel Avenue, Suite 108
Sanger CA
559-876-3026
jambajuice.com
All natural and organic ingredients, no high-fructose corn syrup, 0 grams trans fat, no artificial preservatives, a healthy helping of antioxidants, vitamins, and minerals, and fresh whole fruit and fruit juices set the base for these tasty and healthy beverages. Their organic Hot Blends provides a new spin on coffee, green or chai tea, and hot chocolate;plus they offer probiotic fruit and yogurt Blends. Additionally, they feature all natural salads, wraps, sandwiches, and grab n go

specialties. They also offer healthy community support through fundraisers, special sales, and school lunch programs. Leashed, well mannered dogs are allowed at their outside dining area.

# Pet-Friendly Stores
**PetSmart Pet Store**
470 Shaw Ave
Clovis CA
559-297-9514
Your licensed and well-behaved leashed dog is allowed in the store.

**Tractor Supply Company**
1630 Herndon Avenue
Clovis CA
559-298-1496
tractorsupply.com
Some offerings of this comprehensive farm store includes agriculture, farming and ranching supplies; outdoor power equipment with all the necessities; hundreds of thousands of parts and accessories accessible for yard and garden; metal working and welding supplies; tools for auto and home; a wide range of livestock/farm feed and needs; and a variety of foods and care/play/groom items for household pets. Additionally, they provide trailer and towing supplies, vehicle maintenance accessories, clothing, work wear, foot wear, gifts, home improvement items, a lot of "know-how" and much more. Leashed, friendly dogs are welcome in the store.

**Anthropologie**
639 E. Shaw Avenue, #115
Fresno CA
559-241-0088
Items of distinction can be found for all ages and in all departments of this unique shop. Carefully selected to add to the enjoyment of the shopping experience, they carry fine clothing, amazing accessories, jewelry, hobby and leisure items, and a full line of bright and useful items

for the home, garden, and office. Leashed, well behaved dogs are allowed in the store.

**Camping World**
3633 S Maple Avenue
Fresno CA
559-494-0187
campingworld.com/
This comprehensive RV and outdoor store carries a wide variety of RV, boat, bike, and outdoor cooking accessories; all kinds of camping gear; RV screens, shades, and patio decorations; racing/tailgating gear, and all items for RV maintenance. They also carry RV towing supplies, electronics, and interior decorating items as well as pet supplies, RV directories/books, and games. Plus, they offer a tips and advice service, RV sales, rentals, and RV technicians to take care of any installations and repairs. They also welcome your canine companion in the store; they must be friendly and leashed.

**PetSmart Pet Store**
3220 W Shaw Ave
Fresno CA
559-277-2220
Your licensed and well-behaved leashed dog is allowed in the store.

**Petco Pet Store - Fresno**
4144 North Blackstone Ave.
Fresno CA
559-226-4941
Your licensed and well-behaved leashed dog is allowed in the store.

**Urban Outfitters**
639 E Shaw Avenue, #179
Fresno CA
559-241-0526
In addition to a large inventory of indoor and outdoor apparel for men and women, this major department store also carries vintage wear, designer brands, and a variety of accessories for all types of active lifestyles. They also carry shoes, furnishings, home decor, cameras, electronics, novelty items and more. Leashed, well

mannered dogs are allowed in the store.

## Off-Leash Dog Parks
### Basin AH1 Dog Park and Pond

4257 W. Alamos
Fresno CA
559-621-2900
This is a seasonal dog park which offers a wading pool for dogs to use during the summer. The park is open from May through November from 7 am to 10 pm daily. The dog park is located at 4257 W. Alamos at El Capitan. To get to the dog park from Highway 99, exit at Shaw Avenue and head east. In about a mile turn right on El Capitan.

### Woodward Park Dog Park
E. Audubon Drive
Fresno CA
559-621-2900
Thanks to one of our readers who writes "Woodward Park now has a wonderful, enclosed area built specifically for dogs to play off-leash. It is located inside the park area and contains toys, water bowls and plastic bags."

## Dog-Friendly Parks
### Sierra National Forest
1600 Tollhouse Road
Clovis CA
559-297-0706
fs.usda.gov/sierra/
The dog-friendly Sierra National Forest, just south of Yosemite, consists of 1.3 million acres. Your leashed dog is allowed in this forest and on over 1,000 miles of trails. Just make sure you stay within the Sierra National Forest and do not accidentally cross over to the bordering National Parks which don't allow dogs on hiking trails. The Sierra National Forest trails offer gentle meadows, pristine lakes and streams, and rugged passes in the forest's five wilderness areas. A Wilderness Visitor Permit is required if you plan on hiking into one of the five wilderness areas. In the Sierra National Forest, one of the more popular trails is the Lewis Creek National Recreation Trail. This 3.7 mile hike makes a great day hike as it offers scenic views of waterfalls like the Corlieu and Red Rock Falls. The trail gains 880 feet in elevation from south to north. There are three trailheads along the Lewis Creek Trail. From Oakhurst, take Highway 41 north towards Yosemite National Park. The southernmost trailhead, located 7 miles from Oakhurst, is about 0.5 mile off the highway along the Cedar Valley Road. The middle trailhead is about 3 miles further along Highway 41, at a large turnout just beyond the snow chain station. The northernmost trailhead is just off Highway 41 along the Sugar Pine Road, 500 feet past the bridge on the south side of the road.

### Kearny Park
7160 W. Kearney Blvd
Fresno CA
559-441-0862
This park consists of over 220 green acres with a variety of trees and plants. The park features several playgrounds, picnic tables, soccer fields, and the Kearny Mansion Museum. The Kearney Mansion was the home of M. Theo Kearney. It was constructed in the early 1900s. Kearny was a key Fresno land developer and agricultural leader. He was known as the "Raisin King of California" and formed the California Raisin Growers' Association. When he passed away in 1906, he donated his entire 5000 acre estate to the University of California. Thus 220 acres were developed into Kearny Park. Dogs on leash are allowed at the park, but not in the museum. The park is located about 7 miles west of Fresno off Kearny Road.

### Roeding Park
W. Olive Avenue
Fresno CA
559-498-1551
This large city park has public tennis courts, an exercise course, barbecue and picnic areas, and playgrounds. Leashed dogs are allowed. There is a minimal fee for parking. The park entrance is on W. Olive Avenue by Hwy 99.

### Woodward Park
E. Audubon Drive
Fresno CA

Leashed dogs are allowed at this regional park. There are over 280 acres for you and your pup to explore. This park has some small hills, lakes and streams. There is also a fenced off-leash area in the park. It is located on the north side of Fresno, near Hwy 41. Take Hwy 41, exit N. Friant Rd to the right. Turn left onto Audubon and the park will be on the right.

## Day Kennels
### PetsHotel by PetsMart Day Kennel
615 W. Hearndon Ave.
Clovis CA

petsmart.com/PETsHOTEL/
This PetSmart pet store offers day care and day camp only. You may drop off and pick up your dog at any time they are open. Their hours are 7 am - 9 pm M-F, Sunday 8 am - 7 pm. Dogs are required to have proof of current rabies, DPP and bordatella vaccinations.

## Emergency Veterinarians
### Fresno Veterinary Specialty and Emergency Center
6606 N Blackstone Ave
Fresno CA
559-451-0800
The Fresno Veterinary Specialty and Emergency Center is open 24 hours a day, 7 days a week.

### Veterinary Emergency Services
1639 N Fresno St

Fresno CA
559-486-0520
Open 24 hours.

## Rescue Organizations
### Fresno Bully Rescue
8547 W. Herndon Avenue
Fresno CA
5598035214
fresnobullyrescue.org
Fresno Bully Rescue (FBR) is a volunteer-based, non-profit, no-kill center and sanctuary dedicated to rescuing bully breed dogs (i.e. American Pit Bull Terriers, American Staffordshire Terriers, American Bull Dogs, Bull Terriers, etc.). We provide a healthy and loving temporary home while we look for forever homes for our bullies. We are a 501( c) (3) public charity and all donations to our facility are tax deductible. We are unique in the fact we do have a center that houses nearly 40 dogs and strives to better their quality of life and not keep them in a kennel environment 24/7. All of our dogs get out for walks with our volunteers or play/yard/swim time daily. Besides rescuing and adopting, FBR is also committed to providing educational services in the community, micro-chipping, and promoting spaying and neutering and responsible ownership of the bully breeds. In addition, FBR is committed to advocating for the bully breeds by providing educational outreach to the high risk communities about the illegal practice of dog fighting, as well as providing mental & physical rehabilitation and training to our bully residents while in our care. Fresno Bully Rescue also is available to provide guidance and assistance to forever families of our dogs during the transition to their forever home.

## Service Dog Organizations

### Service Dogs for Self-Reliance
P.O. Box 9700
Fresno CA
(559) 271-0205
servicedogsforselfreliance.org
Service Dogs for Self-Reliance trains assistance dogs for people with disabilities other than blindness or deafness. We specialize in training service dogs, home help-mates, and social therapy dogs, for children and adults with disabilities.

## Other Organizations
### Missing Pet Partnership
P.O. Box 2457
Clovis CA
559-292-4385
lostapet.org
Missing Pet Partnership is a national, nonprofit organization based in Fresno providing lost pet behavior and recovery training for animal shelters, humane societies, rescue groups and animal welfare organizations. According to the American Animal Hospital Association's 1995 Pet Owner's Survey, nearly 30% of pet owners in our nation have lost, and never again found, a missing pet. There is a science to finding lost pets, and it is based on a combination of law enforcement techniques used to find lost people and research into the behavior of lost pets. Through educational programs for staff and volunteers of animal welfare organizations, we can alleviate the suffering of lost pets and their owners. We can also have a significant effect on pet overpopulation by returning lost dogs and cats to their owner so they never become strays, and never end up in overcrowded shelters facing an uncertain fate.

## Garberville

## Dog-Friendly Hotels
### Dean Creek Resort
4112 Redwood Drive
Redway CA
707-923-2555 (877-923-2555)
Offering an outdoor pool and a childrens playground Dean Creek Resort is located in Redway. Free WiFi is available in public areas. The Avenue of the Giants is just 5 km away. River access is available on site. A TV is provided in each air-conditioned accommodation at Redway Dean Creek Resort. A microwave is provided. All accommodations feature an en-suite bathroom with a shower. Bed linens are provided. A variety of activities including table tennis mini golf and hiking area available on site. Guests can relax in the hot tub. barbecue facilities are available. Humboldt Redwoods State Park is 35 km away.

## Gardena

## Pet-Friendly Extended Stay Hotels
### Extended Stay America - Los Angeles - South
18602 South Vermont Avenue
Gardena CA
310-515-5139 (800-804-3724)
One dog is allowed per suite. There is a $25 per night additional pet fee up to $150 for an entire stay.

## Gilroy

## Dog-Friendly Hotels
### Best Western Plus Forest Park Inn
375 Leavesley Road
Gilroy CA
408-848-5144 (800-780-7234)
Dogs up to 80 pounds are allowed. There is a $20 per day pet fee up to $100 for the week.

Up to two dogs are allowed per room.

**Quality Inn & Suites**
8430 Murray Ave
Gilroy CA
408-847-5500 (877-424-6423)
Quality Inn & Suites

Dogs of all sizes are allowed. Dogs are allowed for a pet fee of $10.00 per pet per night. Two dogs are allowed per room.

**Dog-Friendly Attractions**
**Bonfante Gardens Family Theme Park Kennel**
3050 Hecker Pass H/H 152
Gilroy CA
408-840-7100
bonfantegardens.com/
The park, designed to educate guests and to foster a greater appreciation of horticulture, features over forty rides, attractions, educational exhibits, majestic gardens, an event plaza, a unique kid's splash garden, a variety of interactive educational and performance experiences for youth, and more. All the rides and attractions are built around a beautifully designed landscape featuring many different varieties of trees, flowers, water elements and rock formations. However, the real attraction here is the one of a kind Circus Trees that were rescued and moved to this park. Using intricate grafting techniques, these amazing trees were coiled, scalloped, woven, and spiral shaped from Sycamore, Box Elder, Ash, and Spanish Cork trees. Dogs are not allowed in the park; however, there is a free kennel at the entrance with a latch gate. The kennel space is limited, only dog owners are allowed in this area, and they must provide the pet's food and water. The kennel is open Monday through Thursday from 10 am to 6 pm, and on Friday from 10 am to 7 pm. Park hours vary depending on the season.

**Pet-Friendly Stores**
**PetSmart Pet Store**
6755 Camini Arroyo
Gilroy CA
408-848-1383
Your licensed and well-behaved leashed dog is allowed in the store.

**Petco Pet Store - Gilroy**
8767 San Ysidro Ave.
Gilroy CA
408-846-2844
Your licensed and well-behaved leashed dog is allowed in the store.

**Tractor Supply Company**
6881 Cameron Blvd
Gilroy CA
408-842-1594
tractorsupply.com
Some offerings of this comprehensive farm store includes agriculture, farming and ranching supplies; outdoor power equipment with all the necessities; hundreds of thousands of parts and accessories accessible for yard and garden; metal working and welding supplies; tools for auto and home; a wide range of livestock/farm feed and needs; and a variety of foods and care/play/groom items for household pets. Additionally, they provide trailer and towing supplies, vehicle maintenance accessories, clothing, work wear, foot wear, gifts, home improvement items, a lot of "know-how" and much more. Leashed, friendly dogs are welcome in the store.

**Dog-Friendly Wineries and Vineyards**
**Kirigin Cellars**
11550 Watsonville Road
Gilroy CA
408-847-8827
kirigincellars.com/
Rich in old world charm, this 1916 winery still produces wines in small hand-crafted batches. They also host

various events throughout the year, and offer their canine companions about 11 aces of fields to stretch out and play on. Dogs may be off lead if they are friendly to other dogs, animals, and people, and if they are under good voice control.

## Gorda

**Dog-Friendly Beaches**
**Kirk Creek Beach and Trailhead**
Highway 1
Gorda CA
831-385-5434
Both the Kirk Creek Beach and hiking trails allow dogs. Pets must be leashed. You can park next to the Kirk Creek Campground and either hike down to the beach or start hiking at the Kirk Creek Trailhead which leads to the Vicente Flat Trail where you can hike for miles with your dog. The beach and trailhead is part of the Los Padres National Forest and is located about 25 miles south of Big Sur.

**Sand Dollar Beach**
Highway 1
Gorda CA
805-434-1996
Walk down a path to one of the longest sandy beaches on the Big Sur Coast. This national forest managed beach is popular for surfing, fishing and walking. Dogs must be on leash and people need to clean up after their pets. There is a minimal day use fee. The dog-friendly Plaskett Creek Campground is within walking distance. This beach is part of the Los Padres National Forest and is located about 5 miles south of the Kirk Creek and about 30 miles south of Big Sur.

**Willow Creek Beach**
Highway 1
Gorda CA

831-385-5434
Dogs on leash are allowed at this day use beach and picnic area. The beach is part of the Los Padres National Forest and is located about 35 miles south of Big Sur.

## Gorman

### Dog-Friendly Hotels
**Studio 6 Gorman**
49713 Gorman Post Road
Gorman CA
661-248-6411 (877-424-6423)
The Econo Lodge is conveniently located on Interstate 5, between Bakersfield and Los Angeles.

Dogs of all sizes are allowed. Dogs are allowed for a pet fee of $10.00 per pet per night.

## Graeagle

### Dog-Friendly Parks
**Grassy Lake Trail**
County Road 519
Graeagle CA
530-836-2575
This trail is located in the Plumas National Forest and is an easy one way .8 mile trail. This trail starts at an elevation of 6,320 feet and goes past Grassy Lake. It then crosses Gray Eagle Creek to join with the Long Lake Trail. If you continue on this trail, you can hike another 3 miles one way on a moderate rated trail. Long Lake Trail gradually climbs to Long Lake. Dogs on leash or off-leash but under direct voice control are allowed. Dogs are allowed on the trails and in the water. Please clean up after your pets. The trailhead is located in the Lakes Basin Campground. The campground is located 9 miles southwest of Graeagle on County Road 519.

## Greenbrae

### Pet-Friendly Stores
**Woodlands Pet Food & Treats**
296 Bon Air Center
Greenbrae CA
415-461-PETS (7387)
woodlandspet.com
In addition to offering high quality supplies and accessories, healthy food choices, and tasty doggy treats, this pet store also offers low-cost vaccinations clinics, adoption clinics, dog training classes, and a self service dog wash. Leashed, friendly dogs are welcome.

## Gualala

### Dog-Friendly Beaches
**Gualala Point Regional Park Beach**
42401 Coast Highway 1
Gualala CA
707-565-2041
This county park offers sandy beaches, hiking trails, campsites, picnic tables and restrooms. Dogs are allowed on the beach, on the trails, and in the campground, but they must be on a 6 foot or less leash. People also need to clean up after their pets. There is a $3 day use fee.

## Guatay

### Pet-Friendly Stores
**Tryyn Wooden Spoon Gallery**

27540 Old Hwy 80
Guatay CA
619-473-9030
Tryyn.SanDiego411.net
Located on the road from I-8 to Julian, this shop has crafted

spoons, wine, jewelry, and other items. Your well-behaved, potty trained dog is allowed inside on leash.

### Dog-Friendly Parks
**Big Laguna Trail**
Sunrise Highway
Pine Valley CA
619-445-6235
This 6.7 mile easy rated trail is located in the Cleveland National Forest. The trail elevation changes from 5,400 to 5,960 feet. It is a popular trail for hiking, horseback riding and mountain biking. The trail is open year round except during winter storms. Pets on leash are allowed and please clean up after them. To reach the upper end, take Sunrise Highway from I-8 (near Pine Valley) and drive north 13.5 miles to just past the second cattle guard on the highway. Vehicles should park on either side of the highway on the paved turnouts. The access to the Big Laguna trail is via the Nobel Canyon trail that departs the western turnout and is marked by a small sign. Follow the Nobel Canyon trail about 100 yards to reach the Big Laguna trail junction. The other end of the Big Laguna trail makes a junction with the Pacific Crest Trail about .25 miles northeast of the Laguna Station (the Forest Service fire station).

## Hanford

### Dog-Friendly Hotels
**Americas Best Value Inn Hanford**
918 East Lacey Boulevard
Hanford CA
559-582-1736 (800-800-8000)
Dogs of all sizes are allowed. Dogs are allowed for a pet fee of $20.00 per pet per stay.

## Outdoor Restaurants

**Jamba Juice**
186 N 12th Avenue, Suite 113
Hanford CA
559-587-2710
jambajuice.com
All natural and organic ingredients, no high-fructose corn syrup, 0 grams trans fat, no artificial preservatives, a healthy helping of antioxidants, vitamins, and minerals, and fresh whole fruit and fruit juices set the base for these tasty and healthy beverages. Their organic Hot Blends provides a new spin on coffee, green or chai tea, and hot chocolate;plus they offer probiotic fruit and yogurt Blends. Additionally, they feature all natural salads, wraps, sandwiches, and grab n go specialties. They also offer healthy community support through fundraisers, special sales, and school lunch programs. Leashed, well mannered dogs are allowed at their outside dining area.

## Pet-Friendly Stores

**PetSmart Pet Store**
288 N 12th Ave
Hanford CA
559-587-0286
Your licensed and well-behaved leashed dog is allowed in the store.

## Harmony

## Dog-Friendly Wineries and Vineyards

**Harmony Cellars Winery**
3255 Harmony Valley Road
Harmony CA
805-927-1625
harmonycellars.com
Harmony Cellars Winery offers gardens, a tasting room, and picnic areas to kick back and relax. They allow pets if they are friendly and on leash at all times.

## Hawaiian Gardens

## Dog-Friendly Hotels

**La Quinta Inn & Suites Ne Long Beach/cypress**
12441 Carson Street
Hawaiian Gardens CA
562-860-2500 (800-531-5900)
Dogs of all sizes are allowed. Dogs may not be left alone in the room.

## Herald

## Dog-Friendly Wineries and Vineyards

**Blue Gum Winery**
13637 Borden Road
Herald CA
209-748-5669
This winery welcomes people with canine companions. Dogs must be friendly though, as they also have a dog who likes to greet visitors. Dogs can check out the grounds, but they are not allowed in the buildings. Dogs must be well behaved, leashed, and cleaned up after.

## Hollywood - West LA

## Dog-Friendly Hotels

**The Beverly Hilton**
9876 Wilshire Boulevard
Beverly Hills CA
310-274-7777
Set in the heart of the entertainment capitol of the world, this upscale hotel offers numerous amenities and a convenient location to a variety of world class dining, shopping, and entertainment venues. Dogs up to 25 pounds are allowed for an additional fee of $25 per pet.

**Los Angeles Marriott Burbank Airport**
2500 North Hollywood Way
Burbank CA
818-843-6000
Dogs up to 25 pounds are allowed. There is a $75 one time pet fee.

**Safari Inn A Coast Hotel**
1911 West Olive Avenue
Burbank CA
818-845-8586
A pool a restaurant and an airport shuttle service are people-pleasing perks at the Safari Inn a Coast Hotel. The boutique Safari Inn offers 55 retro-style rooms complete with cable TV coffeemakers mini-fridges free local calls and multi-line phones with voicemail. Take 10 in the fitness room or outdoor pool with deck featuring a vintage neon sign. The inn which has appeared in several movies and TV shows also offers a guest laundry and valet laundry services room service and express check-out. The Safari Inn is centrally located within four blocks of several restaurants and a 13-minute walk from Walt Disney Studios. Warner Brothers Studio is a five-minute drive. Griffith Park home to the Los Angeles Zoo Greek Theater and Griffith Observatory is less than three miles away. Universal Studios Hollywood is less than five miles away and Burbank Bob Hope Airport is less than four miles away.

**Four Points By Sheraton Los Angeles Westside**
5990 Green Valley Circle
Culver City CA
310-641-7740 (888-625-5144)
Setting only 3 miles from the airport, this upscale hotel offers numerous on site amenities for business and leisure travelers, plus a convenient location to shopping, dining, recreation areas, and the beach. Dogs are allowed for an additional fee of $25 per night per pet;there is a pet policy to sign at check in.

**Chateau Marmont**
8221 Sunset Boulevard
Hollywood CA
323-656-1010
chateaumarmont.com/
An iconic castle in the heart of Hollywood with lush secluded gardens and an intimate restaurant the Chateau Marmont offers a swanky retreat for our guests. Modeled after an infamous French royal residence this hotel offers 63 soundproof rooms cottages and bungalows with period furniture 42-inch flat-panel TVs signature bedding with cashmere throws iPod docks CD and DVD players and free Wi-Fi. Most accommodations have kitchenettes and some have garden patios. Let the staff unpack your suitcases while you enjoy a soothing massage. Show off your bikini by the outdoor pool before heading for an al fresco lunch at the scrumptious restaurant also open for breakfast and dinner. Let your pet also get the pampering it deserves for a fee. Parking is available for an extra charge. Get your own piece of Hollywood glamour at the boutiques on Rodeo Drive about three miles away or attend a premier at Grauman's Chinese Theater two miles east. Visit the studios in Universal City six miles north or explore the art collections at the Getty Center about a 15-minute drive. Downtown Los Angeles and Santa Monica beaches are about 20 minutes away. Bob Hope Airport is 10 miles north and Los Angeles International Airport is 14 miles south.

**Hilton Los Angeles/universal City**
555 Universal Terrace Parkway
Universal City CA
818-506-2500
Located in the heart of the city's entertainment capital, this luxury resort hotel features more than 6 landscaped acres, floor to ceiling windows in guest rooms and suites, and numerous onsite amenities for all level of

travelers. Dogs up to 75 pounds are allowed for an additional one time fee of $50 per pet.

**Sheraton Universal**
333 Universal Hollywood Drive
Universal City CA
818-980-1212 (888-625-5144)
The hotel welcomes one pet weighing up to 40 pounds. Guests must sign a waiver at check-in and pay a 75 USD non-refundable cleaning fee.

**Kimpton La Peer Hotel**
627 N La Peer Dr
West Hollywood CA
800-546-7866
This artisan hotel is located on a tree-lined side street in West Hollywood's Design District. It offers an on-site restaurant and a pool for guest relaxation. Guest bathrobes are provided in each room. Moca Pacific Design Center is 9 minutes walk away. The property offers a complimentary wine hour from 17:00-18:00 every day. Rooms at Kimpton La Peer Hotel include a flat-screen TV an iPod docking station and a minibar. The en suite bathrooms provide free toiletries a bathrobe and a hairdryer. Evening turndown service is offered for all rooms. Viale Dei Romani restaurant offers Italian hospitality with a focus on sustainable seafood. The property hosts a champagne & cocktail hour every evening and a complimentary coffee cart every morning. There is also a 24-hour fitness centre on the property with a resident trainer. The Grove LA shopping center is 12 minutes drive away from Kimpton La Peer Hotel. The Hollywood Palladium is 6.5 km away.

**Le Montrose Suite Hotel**
900 Hammond Street
West Hollywood CA
310-855-1115 (800- 776-0666)
A rooftop tennis court and swimming pool and rooms with up-to-date amenities like Wi-Fi combine to make the non-

smoking Le Montrose Suite Hotel a smart choice for our guests staying in West Hollywood. Things are looking up at the mid-rise Le Montrose Suite Hotel up to the roof where you'll find a lighted tennis court and an outdoor saltwater pool with 360-degree views of West Hollywood. Catch some rays on the sun deck or pamper yourself with an in-room massage. Spacious seating areas with LCD TVs and iPod docks distinguish the 133 accommodations all of which include unexpected touches like crackling fireplaces. There's Wi-Fi throughout the hotel and laptop-sized safes in every room. The fitness center has it all: free weights cardio machines and strength-training equipment. The restaurant with its tapered columns and white leather furnishings has an open-air terrace for al fresco dining and room service is an option around the clock. Parking is available for a fee. On a quiet street in West Hollywood Le Montrose is a five-minute stroll from the bustling Sunset Strip. There are dozens of eateries and nightspots within easy walking distance. The Los Angeles County Museum of Art is three miles southeast while the Getty Center is a 20-minute drive west. Burbank's Bob Hope Airport is 11 miles north and Los Angeles International Airport is 16 miles south.

## Pet-Friendly Extended Stay Hotels

**Extended Stay America - Los Angeles - Burbank Airport**
2200 Empire Ave
Burbank CA
818-567-0952 (800-804-3724)
One dog is allowed per suite. There is a $25 per night additional pet fee up to $150 for an entire stay.

**Residence Inn Los Angeles Burbank/downtown**
321 Ikea Way

Burbank CA
818-260-8787
Dogs of all sizes are allowed.
There is a $100 one time
additional pet fee.

## Dog-Friendly Attractions
### Hollywood Star's Homes
Self-Guided Walking Tour
Beverly Hills CA

Want to check out the Star's
homes in Beverly Hills with your
dog? How about a self-guided
walking tour of the Star's
homes? All you need is a map
and a good starting point. Maps
can be purchased at many of
the tourist shops on Hollywood
Blvd. A good place to begin is at
the Will Rogers Memorial Park
in Beverly Hills (between Sunset
Blvd, Beverly Dr and Canon
Drive). It's a small park but still a
good place for both of you to
stretch your legs before
beginning the walk. You can
certainly plot out your own tour,
but we have a few samples
tours that will help you get
started. TOUR 1 (approx 1
mile): From the park and Canon
Street, turn left (heading west)
onto Sunset Blvd. Turn right on
Roxbury. Cross Benedict
Canyon Rd and the road
becomes Hartford Way. Take
Hartford Way back to the park.
TOUR 2 (approx 3 miles): From
the park, head north on Beverly
Drive and cross Sunset Blvd.
Turn right on Rexford Drive.
Turn right on Lomitas Ave and
then left onto Crescent Drive.
Make a right at Elevado Ave,
walk for about 5 blocks and turn
right onto Bedford Dr. Then turn
left on Lomitas Ave, right on
Whittier Dr and left on Greeway.
Then turn right on Sunset Blvd
and head back to the park.

### Los Angeles Equestrian Center
480 Riverside Drive
Burbank CA
818-840-9066
la-equestriancenter.com/
This is a nice diversion for those
pups that enjoy being around

horses. Southern California's
largest Equestrian Center has
a covered arena where many
top-rated horse shows are held
throughout the year. Your dog
is welcome to watch the horse
shows if he or she doesn't bark
and distract the horses. To see
their upcoming events list,
check out the official website at
http://www.la-
equestriancenter.com or call
818-840-9066. When there are
no shows, you can still walk
around on the grounds. There
is a horse trail to the right of
the main entrance where you
can walk your dog. Or if you
want to do some shopping,
your dog is welcome in 1 of the
2 equestrian stores (which also
has some dog treats and toys).
The dog-friendly store is called
Dominion Saddlery and is
located behind the store that is
next to the parking lot. They
even have water bowls in the
store for your pup.

### Will Rogers State Hist. Park
1501 Will Rogers State Park
Rd.
Pacific Palisades CA
310-454-8212
This park was Will Roger's
personal home and ranch. Mr.
Rogers was famous for his
horse and rope tricks. He
performed on Broadway and
then moved on to Hollywood to
star in many movies. The ranch
was made into a state historic
park in 1944 after the death of
Mrs. Rogers and it reflects Will
Rogers avid horsemanship. On
the ranch there is a large polo
field, which is the only outdoor
polo field in Los Angeles
county and the only field that is
regulation size. The polo field
has been featured in many
movies and TV shows. The
ranch buildings and grounds
have been maintained to show
how the Rogers' family lived
back in the late 1920s and
1930s. Today, the grounds are
also a working ranch with a
variety of western equestrian
activities. Leashed dogs are
allowed on the property, in the
horse barn, and on the

Inspiration Point Trail. They are
not allowed inside the ranch
house. Dogs, along with people
and children, should not touch
the horses. The ranch staff
enforces the leash law and will
fine violators $82. The entrance
fee to the park is $6 per car and
$1 per dog.

### Universal Studios Kennel
Hollywood Frwy (Hwy 101)
Universal City CA
818-508-9600
This isn't really an attraction for
your pup, but will allow humans
to spend several hours in the
world's largest film and TV
studio. Universal Studios has a
day kennel located at the main
entrance. There is no full time
attendant, but the kennels are
locked. Simply stop at one of
the information booths and ask
for assistance. There is no fee
for this service. At Universal
Studios, you can learn how
movies are made, visit set and
sound stages, and enjoy a
variety of special effect rides.

## Outdoor Restaurants
### Baja Fresh Mexican Grill
475 N. Beverly Drive
Beverly Hills CA
310-858-6690
bajafresh.com
This Mexican restaurant is open
for lunch and dinner. They use
fresh ingredients and making
their salsa and beans daily.
Some of the items on their
menu include Enchiladas,
Burritos, Tacos Salads,
Quesadillas, Nachos, Chicken,
Steak and more. Well-behaved
leashed dogs are allowed at the
outdoor tables.

### Chipotle
1077 Broxton Avenue
Beverly Hills CA
310-824-4180
chipotle.com
Specializing in organic, natural
and unprocessed food, this
Mexican Eatery offers fajita
burritos, tacos, salads, and
salsas. Dogs are allowed at the
outdoor tables but you will need

to order your food inside the restaurant and dogs must remain outside.

**Chipotle**
244 South Beverly Drive
Beverly Hills CA
310-273-8265
chipotle.com
Specializing in organic, natural and unprocessed food, this Mexican Eatery offers fajita burritos, tacos, salads, and salsas. Dogs are allowed at the outdoor tables but you will need to order your food inside the restaurant and dogs must remain outside.

**Coffee Bean & Tea Leaf**
445 N Beverly Drive
Beverly Hills CA
310-278-1865
coffeebean.com
The coffee here is sourced globally from family coffee farms to procure only the top of 1% of Arabica beans. They offer 30+ varieties of coffee;the beans are roasted in small batches daily for freshness, and they also offer 20 varieties of teas that are hand-blended by their tea master. Additionally, they offer a variety of tasty sweets, powders, extracts, sauces, gifts, and cards. Leashed, well mannered dogs are allowed at their outside dining area.

**Coffee Bean & Tea Leaf**
8328 Wilshire Blvd
Beverly Hills CA
323-852-9988
coffeebean.com
The coffee here is sourced globally from family coffee farms to procure only the top of 1% of Arabica beans. They offer 30+ varieties of coffee;the beans are roasted in small batches daily for freshness, and they also offer 20 varieties of teas that are hand-blended by their tea master. Additionally, they offer a variety of tasty sweets, powders, extracts, sauces, gifts, and cards. Leashed, well mannered dogs are allowed at their outside dining area.

**Coffee Bean & Tea Leaf**

233 S. Beverly Drive
Beverly Hills CA
310-274-7801
coffeebean.com
The coffee here is sourced globally from family coffee farms to procure only the top of 1% of Arabica beans. They offer 30+ varieties of coffee;the beans are roasted in small batches daily for freshness, and they also offer 20 varieties of teas that are hand-blended by their tea master. Additionally, they offer a variety of tasty sweets, powders, extracts, sauces, gifts, and cards. Leashed, well mannered dogs are allowed at their outside dining area.

**Joan's on 3rd**
8350 W Third Street
Beverly Hills CA
323-655-2285
joansonthird.com/
This take-out cafe serves gourmet deli-type food. Leashed dogs are allowed at their outdoor tables.

**Kings Road Expresso Cafe**
8361 Beverly Blvd
Beverly Hills CA
323-655-9044
joansonthird.com/
This cafe serves coffee and sandwiches. Leashed dogs are allowed at the outdoor tables. Water is provided for your pet.

**The Lazy Daisy**
9010 Wilshire Blvd
Beverly Hills CA
310-859-1111
Dogs are allowed at the outdoor tables.

**Urth Cafe**
267 S Beverly Dr
Beverly Hills CA
310-205-9311
urthcaffe.com/
This cafe serves organic coffee and sandwiches. Leashed dogs are allowed at the outdoor tables.

**San Gennaro Cafe**
140 Barrington Place
Brentwood CA
310-476-9696

sangennarocafe.com/
Serving up genuine New York Italian cuisine, this gathering place also offers a good wine list, alfresco dining, To Go orders, and catering services. Leashed, well mannered dogs are allowed at their outer tables.

**Baja Fresh Mexican Grill**
877 N. San Fernando Blvd.
Burbank CA
818-841-4649
bajafresh.com
This Mexican restaurant is open for lunch and dinner. They use fresh ingredients and making their salsa and beans daily. Some of the items on their menu include Enchiladas, Burritos, Tacos Salads, Quesadillas, Nachos, Chicken, Steak and more. Well-behaved leashed dogs are allowed at the outdoor tables.

**Chipotle**
135 E Palm Avenue
Burbank CA
818-842-0622
chipotle.com
Specializing in organic, natural and unprocessed food, this Mexican Eatery offers fajita burritos, tacos, salads, and salsas. Dogs are allowed at the outdoor tables but you will need to order your food inside the restaurant and dogs must remain outside.

**Coffee Bean & Tea Leaf**
340 N San Fernando Blvd
Burbank CA
818-842-2394
coffeebean.com
The coffee here is sourced globally from family coffee farms to procure only the top of 1% of Arabica beans. They offer 30+ varieties of coffee;the beans are roasted in small batches daily for freshness, and they also offer 20 varieties of teas that are hand-blended by their tea master. Additionally, they offer a variety of tasty sweets, powders, extracts, sauces, gifts, and cards. Leashed, well mannered dogs are allowed at their outside dining area.

**Priscilla's Coffee and Tea**
4150 W Riverside Street, Suite A
Burbank CA
818-843-5707
Dogs are allowed at the outside tables.

**The Coffee Bean & Tea Leaf**
2000 Avenue of the Stars #100
Century City CA
310-286-2273
coffeebean.com
The coffee here is sourced globally from family coffee farms to procure only the top of 1% of Arabica beans. They offer 30+ varieties of coffee;the beans are roasted in small batches daily for freshness, and they also offer 20 varieties of teas that are hand-blended by their tea master. Additionally, they offer a variety of tasty sweets, powders, extracts, sauces, gifts, and cards. Leashed, well mannered dogs are allowed at their outside dining area.

**Baja Fresh Mexican Grill**
10768 Venice Blvd
Culver City CA
310-280-0644
bajafresh.com
This Mexican restaurant is open for lunch and dinner. They use fresh ingredients and making their salsa and beans daily. Some of the items on their menu include Enchiladas, Burritos, Tacos Salads, Quesadillas, Nachos, Chicken, Steak and more. Well-behaved leashed dogs are allowed at the outdoor tables.

**Birds Cafe-Bar**
5925 Franklin Avenue
Hollywood CA
323-465-0175
birdshollywood.com
This eatery serves up a tasty variety of starters, soups, fresh salads, burgers, wraps, hearty entrees, and their specialty - slow-roasted marinated rotisserie chicken. Well mannered, leashed dogs are welcome at their outside dining area.

**In-N-Out Burgers**
7009 Sunset Blvd.
Hollywood CA
800-786-1000
in-n-out.com/
We decided to mention this specific In-N-Out Burgers because it's very close to the Hollywood Blvd. Walk of Fame. It's a few blocks south of Hollywood Blvd (Walk of Fame). Head south on Orange Drive which is near the Mann's Chinese Theater. Leashed dogs are allowed at their outside dining area.

**Johnny Rockets**
6801 Hollywood Blvd
Hollywood CA
323-465-4456
johnnyrockets.com/
All the American favorites can be found here: A fun retro, all-American decor and atmosphere, juicy burgers, specialty sandwiches, crispy fries, hand-dipped malts and shakes (dark chocolate ones too), fresh baked apple pies, tasty vegetarian choices, and something for all ages. Leashed, friendly dogs are allowed at their outside dining area.

**La Poubelle Bistro and Bar**
5907 Franklin Avenue
Hollywood CA
323-465-0807
lapoubellebistro.com
This bistro and bar also offers alfresco dining. Leashed, well mannered dogs are allowed at their outside dining area.

**The Cat and Fiddle**
6530 Sunset Blvd
Hollywood CA
323-468-3800
thecatandfiddle.com/
Homemade foods, an eclectic beverage menu, weekday happy hours, weekly entertainment, sports viewing, a venue for special events, and patio dining are just some of the offerings of this pub and restaurant. Leashed, well mannered dogs are welcome at their outside tables.

**The Coffee Bean & Tea Leaf**
6922 Hollywood Blvd, #103
Hollywood CA
323-467-7785
coffeebean.com
The coffee here is sourced globally from family coffee farms to procure only the top of 1% of Arabica beans. They offer 30+ varieties of coffee;the beans are roasted in small batches daily for freshness, and they also offer 20 varieties of teas that are hand-blended by their tea master. Additionally, they offer a variety of tasty sweets, powders, extracts, sauces, gifts, and cards. Leashed, well mannered dogs are allowed at their outside dining area.

**The Coffee Bean & Tea Leaf**
15278 Antioch Street
Pacific Palisades CA
310-230-2587
coffeebean.com
The coffee here is sourced globally from family coffee farms to procure only the top of 1% of Arabica beans. They offer 30+ varieties of coffee;the beans are roasted in small batches daily for freshness, and they also offer 20 varieties of teas that are hand-blended by their tea master. Additionally, they offer a variety of tasty sweets, powders, extracts, sauces, gifts, and cards. Leashed, well mannered dogs are allowed at their outside dining area.

**The Coffee Bean & Tea Leaf**
13020 Pacific Promenade, Suite 9
Playa Vista CA
310-862-5725
coffeebean.com
The coffee here is sourced globally from family coffee farms to procure only the top of 1% of Arabica beans. They offer 30+ varieties of coffee;the beans are roasted in small batches daily for freshness, and they also offer 20 varieties of teas that are hand-blended by their tea master. Additionally, they offer a variety of tasty sweets, powders, extracts, sauces, gifts, and cards. Leashed, well mannered dogs are allowed at their outside

dining area.

## Argyle Terrace at The Sunset Tower Hotel
8358 Sunset Blvd
West Hollywood CA
323-654-7100
sunsettowerhotel.com
Featuring a wonderful poolside patio, this eatery offers breakfast, brunch, and lunch with an afternoon tea time from 3 pm until 6 pm--reservations are required for tea. There is an old world Hollywood ambiance here and great views of the city. Leashed, well mannered dogs are welcome at their outside tables.

## Basix Cafe
8333 Santa Monica Blvd.
West Hollywood CA
323-848-2460
basixcafe.com/
This cafe offers flavor-infused, health-conscious cuisine using the freshest ingredients. Here you can enjoy specialties like fresh-baked breads, pastas, sandwiches, wood-fired pizzas. They also serve breakfast including items like eggs, omelettes, and pancakes.

## Burger Lounge
8539 W Sunset Blvd
West Hollywood CA
310-289-9250
burgerlounge.com/
With a strong commitment to sustainable and organic, this eatery features a variety of burgers with freshly made organic lounge buns and 100% forage/grass-fed, free-range all natural beef. They also offer free-range turkey burgers, organic cheeses, quinoa veggie burgers, a variety of beverages, and a kid's menu. Leashed, well mannered dogs are allowed at their outside dining area.

## Eveleigh
8752 Sunset Blvd
West Hollywood CA
424-239-1630
theeveleigh.com
Skillfully and healthfully prepared farm-to-table cuisine and cocktails are the specialty

here. They are open every evening for dinner and also offer a weekend brunch and alfresco dining. Leashed, friendly dogs are allowed on the patio in the front garden dining area.

## Jamba Juice
7100 Santa Monica Blvd
West Hollywood CA
323-512-0552
jambajuice.com
All natural and organic ingredients, no high-fructose corn syrup, 0 grams trans fat, no artificial preservatives, a healthy helping of antioxidants, vitamins, and minerals, and fresh whole fruit and fruit juices set the base for these tasty and healthy beverages. Their organic Hot Blends provides a new spin on coffee, green or chai tea, and hot chocolate;plus they offer probiotic fruit and yogurt Blends. Additionally, they feature organic steel-cut oatmeal prepared fresh every morning, all natural salads, wraps, sandwiches, and grab n' go specialties. They also offer healthy community support through fundraisers, special sales, and school lunch programs. Leashed, well mannered dogs are allowed at their outside dining area.

## Joey's Cafe
8301 Santa Monica Blvd/H 2
West Hollywood CA
323-822-0671
joeyscafeweho.com/
Some offerings from this popular café include a full days menu that include healthy entrees, protein and fitness specialties, fresh made soups and salads, signature dishes, organic gourmet coffee, and alfresco dining. Leashed, well mannered dogs are welcome at their outside dining area.

## Le Pain Quotidien
8607 Melrose Avenue
West Hollywood CA
310-854-3700
lepainquotidien.us/
Placing an emphasis on local

farm fresh produce, herbs, artisanal cheeses, and handcrafted organic breads, this eatery features an extensive menu of bakery items, breakfasts, soups and sides, tartines, salads, seasonal and house specialties, and desserts. Leashed well mannered dogs are welcome at their outside tables.

## Marix West Hollywood
1108 N. Flores Street
West Hollywood CA
323-656-8800
This Tex-Mex restaurant allows well-behaved leashed dogs at their outdoor tables. They are open 11am to 11pm seven days a week.

## The Coffee Bean & Tea Leaf
8793 Beverly Blvd
West Hollywood CA
310-659-4592
coffeebean.com
The coffee here is sourced globally from family coffee farms to procure only the top of 1% of Arabica beans. They offer 30+ varieties of coffee;the beans are roasted in small batches daily for freshness, and they also offer 20 varieties of teas that are hand-blended by their tea master. Additionally, they offer a variety of tasty sweets, powders, extracts, sauces, gifts, and cards. Leashed, well mannered dogs are allowed at their outside dining area.

## The Coffee Bean & Tea Leaf
8735 Santa Monica Blvd/H 2
West Hollywood CA
310-659-8207
coffeebean.com
The coffee here is sourced globally from family coffee farms to procure only the top of 1% of Arabica beans. They offer 30+ varieties of coffee;the beans are roasted in small batches daily for freshness, and they also offer 20 varieties of teas that are hand-blended by their tea master. Additionally, they offer a variety of tasty sweets, powders, extracts, sauces, gifts, and cards. Leashed, well mannered dogs are allowed at their outside

dining area.

**The Coffee Bean & Tea Leaf**
8789 Sunset Blvd
West Hollywood CA
310-659-1890
coffeebean.com
The coffee here is sourced globally from family coffee farms to procure only the top of 1% of Arabica beans. They offer 30+ varieties of coffee;the beans are roasted in small batches daily for freshness, and they also offer 20 varieties of teas that are hand-blended by their tea master. Additionally, they offer a variety of tasty sweets, powders, extracts, sauces, gifts, and cards. Leashed, well mannered dogs are allowed at their outside dining area.

**Urth Cafe**
8565 Melrose Ave
West Hollywood CA
310-659-0628
urthcaffe.com/
This cafe serves organic coffee and deli-type food. Leashed dogs are allowed at the outdoor tables.

**Z Pizza**
8869 Santa Monica Blvd/H 2
West Hollywood CA
310-360-1414
zpizza.com
Specializing in organically and international inspired pizzas, this pizzeria cooks their pizzas on hot bricks in a fire baked oven. They feature a 100% certified organic gluten free wheat crust, homemade organic sauces and ingredients, fresh produce, and additive-free meats. They also offer gourmet salads, sandwiches, and catering services. Leashed, well mannered dogs are allowed at their outside tables.

**The Coffee Bean & Tea Leaf**
950 Westwood Blvd
Westwood CA
310-208-8018
coffeebean.com
The coffee here is sourced globally from family coffee farms to procure only the top of 1% of Arabica beans. They offer 30+ varieties of coffee;the beans are roasted in small batches daily for freshness, and they also offer 20 varieties of teas that are hand-blended by their tea master. Additionally, they offer a variety of tasty sweets, powders, extracts, sauces, gifts, and cards. Leashed, well mannered dogs are allowed at their outside dining area.

## Pet-Friendly Shopping Centers
**Beverly Hills Rodeo Drive Shopping District**
Rodeo Drive
Beverly Hills CA

Rodeo Drive, located in Beverly Hills, is one of the most prestigious and expensive shopping streets in the world. This is the street where the movie "Pretty Woman" starring Julia Roberts was filmed. Some actors and actresses shop along this street. Dogs are welcome to window shop with you. Tiffany & Company is one store we know of which allows dogs inside, at least pooches up to about 50 pounds. Just off of Rodeo Drive is Beverly Drive which is host to many dog-friendly stores such as Anthropologie, Banana Republic, Crate and Barrel, The Gap, Pottery Barn, and Williams-Sonoma. All of these stores allow well-behaved leashed dogs. Find more details about these stores, including addresses, under our Stores section. When you visit this shopping district, please note that it is often very crowded and it can be tough to find a parking spot.

**Sunset Plaza**
8600 - 8700 Sunset Boulevard (at Sunset Plaza Drive),
West Hollywood CA
310-652-2622
This sidewalk mall sits on both sides of the Sunset Strip, between La Cienega and San Vicente Boulevards and feature a number of fashionable boutiques, outdoor cafés, and trendy bistros. Also, don't be surprised to see a celebrity or two. Well mannered dogs are welcome to walk the sidewalk mall area, and some establishments may also allow them. Dogs must be under their owner's control, and leashed and cleaned up after at all times.

## Pet-Friendly Stores
**Anthropologie**
211 S Beverly Drive
Beverly Hills CA
310-385-7390
Items of distinction can be found for all ages and in all departments of this unique shop. Carefully selected to add to the enjoyment of the shopping experience, they carry fine clothing, amazing accessories, jewelry, hobby and leisure items, and a full line of bright and useful items for the home, garden, and office. Leashed, well behaved dogs are allowed in the store.

**Anthropologie**
320 North Beverly Dr.
Beverly Hills CA
310-385-7390
anthropologie.com/
Thanks to one of our readers who writes "They have always been especially lovely when Hector and I go in!"

**Banana Republic**
357 N Beverly Drive
Beverly Hills CA
310-858-7900
bananarepublic.com
This apparel store offers both mens and womens clothing as well as home collection, shoes, accessories and more. Well-behaved leashed dogs are allowed in the store.

**Centinela Feed and Supplies**
331 N Robertson Blvd
Beverly Hills CA
310-246-0367
centinelafeed.com/
Specializing in natural, holistic,

and raw pet foods, this pet supply store also provides healthy treats, quality supplements, pet care supplies, low-cost vaccination clinics, frequent in-store events, and a knowledgeable staff. Leashed pets are welcome.

**Crate and Barrel**
438 N. Beverly Drive
Beverly Hills CA
310-247-1700
crateandbarrel.com
This store offers fine products from around the world for in and around the home that include items for outdoor living, indoor furnishings and decorating, dining and entertaining, kitchen and food service, and gourmet food and beverages. They also have accessories for pets, bed and bath items, and organizing and storage units. Leashed, friendly dogs are welcome in the store; they must be under their owner's control at all times.

**Crate and Barrel**
438 N. Beverly Drive
Beverly Hills CA
310-247-1700
crateandbarrel.com/
Home furnishings are the focus of this store. Well-behaved leashed dogs are allowed in the store.

**Pottery Barn**
300 N Beverly Drive
Beverly Hills CA
310-860-9506
potterybarn.com
This store offers stylish and quality home furnishings. Well-behaved leashed dogs are allowed in the store.

**The Gap**
420 N Beverly Drive
Beverly Hills CA
310-274-0461
gap.com
This store offers clothing for men, women and children. Well-behaved leashed dogs are allowed in the store.

**Tiffany & Co.**
210 N Rodeo Drive
Beverly Hills CA

310-273-8880
tiffany.com/
This store offers a selection of jewelry, gifts and accessories. Well-behaved leashed dogs up to about 50 pounds are allowed in this store.

**Williams Sonoma**
339 N. Beverly Drive
Beverly Hills CA
310-274-9127
williamssonoma.com
This store offers cookware, cutlrey, electronics, food and more. Well-behaved leashed dogs are allowed in the store.

**Petco Pet Store - Brentwood**
5481 Lone Tree Way
Brentwood CA
925-308-7307
Your licensed and well-behaved leashed dog is allowed in the store.

**Petco Pet Store - Burbank**
3525 West Victory Blvd
Burbank CA
818-566-8528
Your licensed and well-behaved leashed dog is allowed in the store.

**Urban Outfitters**
330 N. San Fernando Blvd
Burbank CA
818-842-7053
In addition to a large inventory of indoor and outdoor apparel for men and women, this major department store also carries vintage wear, designer brands, and a variety of accessories for all types of active lifestyles. They also carry shoes, furnishings, home decor, cameras, electronics, novelty items and more. Leashed, well mannered dogs are allowed in the store.

**Centinela Feed and Supplies**
5299 Sepulveda Blvd
Culver City CA
310-572-6107
centinelafeed.com
Specializing in natural, holistic, and raw pet foods, this pet supply store also provides healthy treats, quality supplements, pet care

supplies, low-cost vaccination clinics, frequent in-store events, and a knowledgeable staff. Leashed pets are welcome.

**PetSmart Pet Store**
10900 W Jefferson Blvd
Culver City CA
310-390-5120
Your licensed and well-behaved leashed dog is allowed in the store.

**Petco Pet Store - Culver City**
5347 South Sepulveda Blvd
Culver City CA
310-390-7255
Your licensed and well-behaved leashed dog is allowed in the store.

**Amoeba Music**
6400 Sunset Blvd
Hollywood CA
323-245-6400
amoeba.com
Amoeba Hollywood is the largest music store in the country. For all of your music needs, this is the one stop shop. They welcome well-behaved, leashed, or carried dogs.

**Amoeba Music Store**
6400 Sunset Blvd
Hollywood CA
323-245-6400
amoebamusic.com/
This music store has the pet friendly sign right at their door, so you know that you and your canine companion are welcome. Dogs must be well behaved, leashed, and under the owner's control at all times.

**Jackalope**
10726 Burbank Blvd
North Hollywood CA
818-761-4022
jackalope.com/losangeles.htm
Specializing in International and domestic handcrafted pottery, garden decor, handmade furniture, rugs, fountains, folk art, holiday ornaments and more, this shopping destination is impressive enough to land it on the Los Angeles Magazine's 101 Best of Los Angeles list. Additionally, the store features numerous discounts/sales, a

plant nursery, and special events. Leashed dogs are welcome.

## Petco Pet Store - West Hollywood
508 North Doheny Dr.
West Hollywood CA
310-275-6012
Your licensed and well-behaved leashed dog is allowed in the store.

## Sherman McNulty Custom Framing
320 La Cienega Blvd
West Hollywood CA
310-652-6960
shermanmcnulty.com
Well-behaved, leashed dogs are allowed. One of our readers says "Dogs are definitely allowed. They have the best selection of custom frames and the best pricing I have found as of yet."

## Video West
805 Larrabee Street
West Hollywood CA
310-659-5762
Very dog friendly video store. Dogs always welcome and usually they have dog biscuits. The owner is a dog lover and is active in dog rescue. The store is open 10am-midnight, 7 days a week.

## Off-Leash Dog Parks
### Culver City Off-Leash Dog Park
Duquesne Ave near Jefferson Blvd
Culver City CA
310-390-9114
This new dog park opened in April, 2006. Known as the Boneyard to the locals, this one acre park has a large dog and a small dog area. There are benches, trees, shade and water fountains. The park is located near Jefferson Blvd on Duquesne Ave in Culver City Park. It is about 3/4 miles east of Overland.

### Whitnall Off-Leash Dog Park

5801 1/2 Whitnall Highway
North Hollywood CA
818-756-8190
laparks.org/dogpark/whitnall
Whitnall Off-Leash Dog Park is located one block west of Cahuenga Blvd on Whitnall. The park has a 50,000 square foot fenced area for large dogs and a 22,000 square foot fenced area for small dogs. The park is open during daylight hours.

## Dog-Friendly Parks
### Roxbury Park
471 S. Roxbury Dr.
Beverly Hills CA
310-285-2537
This city park offers gently rolling green hills and shady areas. The park has large children's playgrounds, tennis courts and other sports courts. Dogs are allowed but must be on a 6 foot or less leash and people are required to clean up after their pets.

### Temescal Gateway Park
15601 Sunset Blvd.
Pacific Palisades CA
310-454-1395
There are several trails at this park. Dogs are allowed but must be on a 6 foot or less leash and people need to clean up after their pets. The Sunset Trail is almost a half mile trail that begins at the lower parking lot by Sunset Blvd. It parallels Temescal Creek. Dogs are not allowed in the attached Temescal State Park. The park is located at the intersection of Temescal Canyon Road and Sunset Blvd. This park is part of the Santa Monica Recreation Area.

## Airports
### Burbank Bob Hope Airport (BUR)

Burbank CA

burbankairport.com/
A pet relief area is located

outside between the terminals A and B.

## Emergency Veterinarians
### Affordable Emergency Clinic
5558 Sepulveda Blvd
Culver City CA
310-397-4883
9:30 am - 12 midnight 7 days a week

## Other Organizations
### Friends of the Culver City Dog Park
P O Box 4129
Culver City CA
310-390-9114
culvercitydogpark.org
A 501(c)(3) non profit organization dedicated to bringing an off-leash dog park to Culver City, CA. The organization is working to raise the money to build the park which will be located at The Boneyard in Culver City Park, Duquesne & Jefferson. Goal date for opening is by the end of 2004. Park will be paid for with grants and fundraising by the Friends and not with any city funds.

## Hopland

## Dog-Friendly Attractions
### Brutocao Cellars and Vineyards
13500 H 101
Hopland CA
707-744-1664
brutocaocellars.com/
This scenic vineyard offers outside dining at their restaurant, The Crushed Grape, and a variety of great wines, but they also offer a membership program so that you can produce your own label. From the start to the finish with a custom-designed label bearing your name, you get to learn, and be involved as much as you

would like, in the winemaking process. Dogs are welcome. They must be leashed and cleaned up after. Dogs are not allowed in the tasting room, but they can sit with you at the outside dining tables.

# Huntington Park

## Dog-Friendly Hotels
**Rodeway Inn Near La Live**
6340 Sante Fe Ave
Huntington Park CA
323-589-5971 (877-424-6423)
This 100% smoke-free hotel located at the edge of the Wholesale District Los Angeles and less than 4 miles.

Dogs up to 20 pounds are allowed. Dogs are allowed for a pet fee of $10.00 per pet per night.

# Idyllwild

## Dog-Friendly Hotels
**Fireside Inn**
54540 North Circle Drive
Idyllwild CA
877-797-FIRE (3473)
thefireside-inn.com/
Set 7 km from San Jacinto Mountain Fireside Inn offers accommodation and free WiFi in Idyllwild.
The accommodation comes with a fully equipped kitchenette with a microwave a TV and a private bathroom with a bath or shower. A terrace with mountain views is offered in each unit.
The property has a hot tub. Fishing and hiking can be enjoyed nearby.
The nearest airport is Palm Springs International Airport 20 km from the holiday home.

## Accommodations

**Tahquitz Inn**
25840 Highway 243
Idyllwild CA
909-659-4554 (877-659-4554)
tahquitzinn.com
This inn is located in the heart of Idyllwild and allows all well-behaved dogs. They offer one and two bedroom suites with a separate bedroom, kitchen and porches. The inn has also been a location for several Hollywood film shoots. All of their rooms accommodate dogs and there is a $10 per day pet charge.

## Dog-Friendly Attractions
**Annual Plein Air Festival**
North Circle Drive
Idyllwild CA
866-439-5278
artinidyllwild.com/
Idyllwild is rated as one of the 100 Best Small Art Towns in America. Once a year there is a festival, usually held on a Saturday in the beginning of September, where artists create original works of art in the streets of the Idyllwild. Leashed dogs are welcome to accompany you at this outdoor event. For more details, please contact the Art Alliance of Idyllwild at 866-439-5278.

## Outdoor Restaurants
**Cafe Aroma**
54750 North Circle Drive
Idyllwild CA
951-659-5212
cafearoma.org/
More than just an eatery, this bistro is also a gallery of fine local art and a gathering place to enjoy a variety of musical guests - and sometimes even the staff will serve up an impromptu performance. The fare is Italian with Asian, French, and Nuevo Latino cuisines. Leashed dogs are allowed at their outside tables.

**Joanne's Restaurant and Bar**

25875 N Village Drive

Idyllwild CA
951-659-0295
Well-behaved, leashed dogs are allowed at the outdoor tables. They are open Sunday to Thursday from 7 am unil 9 pm;on Friday from 7 am until about 10 pm, and on Saturday from 7 am until about 11 pm.

## Dog-Friendly Parks
**Humber Park**
Fern Valley Road
Idyllwild CA
909-659-2117
The Devil's Slide Trail begins at this park. It is rated as a moderately difficult trail. The trail goes for about 6 miles and there is about a 3,000 foot elevation gain. Day passes are required. To get there, take Highway 243 to North Circle Drive. Turn right onto South Circle Drive, and then left to Fern Valley Road. Follow the signs to Humber Park.

**Idyllwild Park**
54000 Riverside County Playground Road
Idyllwild CA
951-659-2656
In addition to being only a short walk to town where there is a variety of shopping, dining, and entertainment venues, this recreation destination features 202 acres of mature forest, lots of open spaces, 5 breathtaking trails, an amphitheater, and a really nice nature center. Dogs are allowed throughout the park, on the trails, and in the campground for an additional fee of $1 per day per pet. Dogs must be kept on no more than a 6 foot leash, not be left unattended, cleaned up after promptly, and under their owner's control at all times.

**Idyllwild Park Nature Center**
Highway 243
Idyllwild CA
909-659-3850
This park offers 5 1/2 miles of hiking trails. Most of the trails are rated as easy, with the exception of one steep trail.

Dogs are allowed, but need to be leashed. Your dog will also need to have a current rabies identification tag. The day use fees are $2 per person, $2 per dog and $1 per child. The park is located on Highway 243, about one mile northwest of Idyllwild.

## Independence

### Dog-Friendly Parks
**Manzanar National Historic Site**
P.O. Box 426
Independence CA
760-878-2932
nps.gov/manz/
This site was one of ten camps where Japanese and Japanese American citizens were interned during World War II. It is located at the base of the Sierra Nevada mountains and has been identified as the best preserved camp. Dogs are allowed at the site, on the self-guided walking tour which takes about 1-2 hours, and on the 3.2 mile self-guided auto tour. A tour description and map is available at the camp entrance. Pets must be on leash and please clean up after them. The park is open all year and there is no parking fee. It is located off Highway 395, 12 miles north of Lone Pine and 5 miles south of Independence.

## Jackson - Gold Country Central

### Dog-Friendly Hotels
**The Jackson Lodge**
850 North State Highway 49
Jackson CA
209-223-0486
jacksongoldlodge.com/
Nestled in the Sierra Nevada foothills this Jackson California

lodge features an outdoor pool and a free continental breakfast daily. Free Wi-Fi is offered in all rooms.
Select cottages feature a full kitchen and a living area. Each room provides cable TV a coffee machine a desk and an en suite bathroom at The Jackson Lodge. A seating area is also offered.
Featuring a fireplace the 24-hour reception welcomes guests to Lodge Jackson. A launderette and a daily maid service are also offered. Jackson Rancheria Casino is less than 10 minutes walk away. Sutter Creek is 6 km away from The Jackson Lodge.

**Days Inn Sutter Creek**
271 Hanford Street
Sutter Creek CA
209-267-9177 (800-329-7466)
Dogs of all sizes are allowed. Dogs are allowed for a nightly pet fee.

### Dog-Friendly Attractions
**Indian Grinding Rock State Historic Park**
14881 Pine Grove - Volcano Road
Pine Grove CA
209-296-7488
This park preserves a great outcropping of marbleized limestone with 1185 mortar holes, the largest collection of bedrock mortars anywhere in North America. Visitors can find many petroglyphs here. Dogs on leash are allowed at the historic site, but not on any trails. The park is located off Highway 88.

**Deaver Vineyards**
12455 Steiner Road
Plymouth CA
209-245-4099
deavervineyard.com/index.html

Family owned/operated, and in production for more than 100 years, they offer award winning wines (some from vines more than 120 years old), a gift shop

and a picnic area. Dogs are allowed around the grounds and at the picnic area, but not in the tasting room. Dogs must be well behaved, and leashed and cleaned up after at all times. They did state there may be a few friendly neighborhood dogs that also like to check out the picnic area when they think food is available.

**Sutter Creek**
Highway 49
Sutter Creek CA
209-267-5647
suttercreek.org/
Sutter Creek, named for John Sutter of Gold Rush fame, is a well preserved 1850's western town in California's Gold Country. There is a half mile long downtown along Highway 49 with staired sidewalks and a variety of shops including wine tasting, and ice cream. There are also other stores that may allow your dog inside if you ask and some cafes with outdoor seats.

**Sutter Creek Wine Tasting**
85 Main Street
Sutter Creek CA
209-267-5838
Dogs may sit with you at the outdoor picnic bench or the two small tables in the front while you sample the wines from a local group of growers.

### Outdoor Restaurants
**Mel & Faye's Drive In**
205 N. State Hwy 49
Jackson CA
209-223-0853
melandfayesdiner.com/
This diner is open for breakfast, lunch and dinner. They have several outdoor covered picnic tables and benches where you and your pup can enjoy the American-style food. As there is no outside service, just go inside and get take-out. Also if it gets too chilly, they have an outdoor heater. The diner is located on Hwy 49

**88 Burgers**

19845 State Highway 88
Pine Grove CA
209-296-7277
Leashed dogs are allowed at the outdoor tables. They are open Sunday to Thursday from 11 am until 5 pm and on Friday and Saturday they stay open until 9 pm.

## Cafe at the Park
18265 Hwy 49
Plymouth CA
209-245-6981
49ervillage.com/
This cafe serves sandwiches, pastries, and ice cream. They are located at the entrance of the 49er RV Park in Plymouth. The dog-friendly outdoor seating is located behind the cafe. They are open weekdays from 7am to 8pm and weekends from 7am to 10pm.

## Marlene and Glen's Diner
18726 Highway 49
Plymouth CA
209-245-5778
Dogs are allowed at the outdoor seats. They are open for winter hours Wednesday thru Sunday from 7 am until 2:30 pm.

# Pet-Friendly Stores
## Paws and Claws
30 Main Street
Jackson CA
209-223-3970
In addition to a selection of gifts you will also find decorator pet collars & leashes at this store. Your pet is welcome on leash or you can carry them in. They are open 10 am to 5 pm 7 days a week.

## Petco Pet Store - Martell
12050 Industry Blvd
Jackson CA
209-257-0478
Your licensed and well-behaved leashed dog is allowed in the store.

# Dog-Friendly Wineries and Vineyards

## Drytown Cellars
16030 Highway 49
Drytown CA
209-245-3500
drytowncellars.com/
This winery is dedicated to producing high quality, well balanced, intensely flavored California wines that are affordable, and good for every day consumption. Dogs are welcome here, and there are a couple of vineyard dogs to welcome your canine companion. Dogs are allowed on the grounds and even in the tasting room. Dogs must be leashed and cleaned up after at all times.

## French Hill Winery
8032 S Main Street
Mokelumne Hill CA
209-728-0638
frenchhill.com/
French Hill specializes in Cal-Italia varietals and ultra-premium wines, which has resulted in numerous awards. Friendly dogs are welcome to explore the winery and the tasting room. Dogs must be leashed and cleaned up after at all times.

## Convergence Vineyards
14650 H 124
Plymouth CA
209-245-3600
Located where 3 creeks converge together into one running river, this winery features hand-crafted wines made in small batches that are sold directly from their vineyard. Dogs are welcome at the winery, around the grounds, and on the covered patio; they are not allowed in the tasting room. Dogs must be friendly and well behaved as there are other pets in residence. Please keep your dog leashed and clean up after your pet.

## Montevina Wines
20680 Shenandoah School Road
Plymouth CA
209-245-6942
Dogs are allowed at the outdoor tables in their patio.

The hours are 11 - 4 daily.

## Nine Gables Vineyard & Winery
10778 Shenandoah Road
Plymouth CA
209-245-3949
9gables.com/
Small batch fermentation with a hands-on approach is this winery's formula for maximum extraction of flavors, colors, and aromas. Dogs must be very friendly as there are other dogs on site that are anxious to meet new visitors. Dogs are allowed around the grounds and in the tasting room. Dogs must be leashed and cleaned up after at all times.

## Renwood Winery
12225 Steiner Road
Plymouth CA
209-245-6979
renwood.com/
Using old-world and hand crafted winemaking techniques, this vineyard showcases wines that come from some of the world's oldest and most renowned vineyards in the Shenandoah Valley. Complimentary and reserve tasting is available daily from 10:30 am to 4:30 pm. Dogs are allowed on the grounds and will probably like a roll on the grassy lawn, but they are not allowed in the tasting room. Dogs must be leashed, and please bring supplies to clean up after your pet.

## Sobon Winery
14430 Shenandoah Rd
Plymouth CA
209-245-6554
sobonwine.com/
This Shenandoah Valley winery serves and sells red and white wines made entirely from organic fruits. Wine Tasting is offered 7 days a week in the tasting room and there is a little museum on the premises. Well-behaved leashed dogs are allowed at the outdoor picnic tables at the winery.

## Dog-Friendly Parks
**Detert Park**
Hwy 49
Jackson CA

This is a small but nice city park that allows leashed dogs. It has some picnic tables and a children's playground. It is located on Hwy 49, between the Jackson Gold Lodge and historic downtown Jackson.

## Johnsondale

## Dog-Friendly Parks
**Trail of a Hundred Giants**
off Mountain Road 50
Johnsondale CA
559-539-2607
This trail is located in the Giant National Sequoia Monument which is part of the Sequoia National Forest. The universally accessible trail meanders through over 125 giant sequoias in the Long Meadow Grove. The estimated age of the trees here are estimated between 500 and 1,500 years old. Pets must be leashed and attended at all times. Please clean up after your pet. The trail is located about 45 miles northwest of Kernville. From Kernville, take State Mountain Road 99 north to Johnsondale. Go west on 50 to the Western Divide Highway turnoff. Go 2 miles to the Redwood Meadow Campground. The trail is located across the road from the campground.

## Joshua Tree National Park

## Pet-Friendly Stores
**Pets Plus**
57598 29 Palms H/H 62
Yucca Valley CA
760-228-0209

petsplususa.com/dogs.htm
Some of the products offered at this pet supply store include quality, all natural pet foods, bones and treats, healthcare items, pet care supplies, toys, collars/leashes, crates/carriers, bedding, apparel, obedience supplies, and books. Leashed dogs are welcome.

## Dog-Friendly Parks
**Joshua Tree National Park**
74485 National Park Drive
Twentynine Palms CA
760-367-5500
nps.gov/jotr
Dogs are not allowed on the trails, cannot be left unattended, and must be on leash. However, they are allowed on dirt and paved roads including the Geology Tour Road. This is actually a driving tour, but you'll be able to see the park's most fascinating landscapes from this road. It is an 18 mile tour with 16 stops. The park recommends taking about 2 hours for the round trip. At stop #9, about 5 miles out, there is room to turnaround if you do not want to complete the whole tour.

## Julian

## Dog-Friendly Hotels
**Apple Tree Inn**
4360 Highway 78
Julian CA
800-410-8683
julianappletreeinn.com
Less than 5 minutes walk from the Julian Mining Company this inn offers a swimming pool. Guest rooms feature a TV and a seating area.
A private entrance is available in all rooms at the Apple Tree Inn. Free toiletries are provided. Rooms offer mountain views.
Downtown Julian is 3.5 miles

from the Inn Apple Tree. The San Diego Zoo Safari Park is 45 minutes drive away. The San Diego Airport is 1 hour and 30 minutes drive from the property.

## Dog-Friendly Attractions
**Country Carriages**
Washington and Main St
Julian CA
760-765-1471
Reservations are recommended on the weekends. Your dog is welcome. The carriage rides go a mile out of town and back. The driver points out historic sites on the way.

**Julian Downtown and Walking Tour**
Main Street
Julian CA
760-765-1857
You and your pooch can take a self-guided tour of Julian's historical buildings which highlight history from the Gold Rush era to the 1920s. Follow the tour through Main, Second, Third, B, C, and Washington Streets. A map is available at the Julian Chamber of Commerce located on Main and Washington Streets inside the Town Hall. There are also a number of pet-friendly outdoor restaurants and a horse and carriage ride as well as shopping.

## Outdoor Restaurants
**Apple Alley Bakery**
2122 Main Street
Julian CA
760-765-2532
Dogs are allowed at the outdoor tables in the year-round patio. The bakery is open for breakfast and lunch, seven days a week. They offer apple pies made from fresh apples, pastries, cookies and more.

**Buffalo Bills**
2603 B Street
Julian CA
760-765-1560
This restaurant specializes in

buffalo burgers and apple pie. Dogs of all sizes are allowed on the patio. Dogs must be leashed and cleaned up after. They are open weekdays: 7:30 a.m. to 2 p.m. and weekends: 7:30 a.m. 5 p.m.

**Julian Pie Company**
2225 Main Street
Julian CA
760-765-2449
julianpie.com/
This pie company welcomes visitors with door handles that say, 'Begin Smelling', and their pies are popular for their variety and freshness. Pets are welcome to come into the store with their owners. Dogs must be friendly and leashed.

**The Bailey Wood Pit Barbecue**

Main and A Streets
Julian CA
760-765-3757
baileybbq.com/
Dogs are allowed at the outdoor tables. Tables are seasonal.

**The Julian Grille**
2224 Main Street
Julian CA
760-765-0173
This eatery sets in a restored cottage, and features steaks, seafood, prime rib, and outdoor dining. They are open daily for lunch and from Tuesday through Sunday for diner. Your pet is welcome to join you at the outside tables. Dogs must be well behaved, attended to at all times, and leashed.

**The Rongbranch Restaurant**
2722 Washington St
Julian CA
760-765-2265
rongbranchrestaurant.com
The Rongbranch Restaurant offers barbecue, steaks, seafood, burgers and home cooked country meals. Dogs are allowed on the outdoor patio, but must be well behaved and on leash.

**Wynola Pizza Express**
4355 H 78/79
Julian CA

760-765-1004
This eatery offers wood-fired gourmet pizza and live music on Saturday nights. They offer outside dining where your pet is welcome to join you. Dogs must be well behaved, attended to at all times, and leashed.

# Dog-Friendly Wineries and Vineyards
**Blue Door Winery**
1255 Julian Orchards Drive
Julian CA
858-278-1640
lovebluedoor.com/
In addition to offering a variety of fine wines, this winery also offers a wonderful setting for picnicking and enjoying the views of the countryside. Leashed friendly dogs are welcome.

**J. Jenkins Winery**
12555 Julian Orchards Drive
Julian CA
760-765-3267
jenkinswinery.com/
This winery set out with a goal to produce beautiful unique wines, and now they offer them in their tasting room that is open Saturdays and Sundays from 11am to 5 pm or by appointment. There is outside seating available, and dogs are allowed on the grounds, but not usually in the buildings. Dogs must be friendly, and leashed and cleaned up after at all times.

**Menghini Winery**
1150 Julian Orchards Drive
Julian CA
760-765-2072
This winery produces a variety of premium wines. The tasting room is open daily from 10 am to 4 pm, and they also have a nice picnic area. Dogs are allowed around the grounds, but not in the tasting room. Dogs must be well behaved, and leashed and cleaned up after at all times.

# Dog-Friendly Parks
**Cuyamaca Rancho State Park**
12551 Highway 79
Descanso CA
760-765-0755
parks.ca.gov/667
Leashed dogs are allowed on the paved Cuyamaca Peak Fire Road and the Los Caballos/Stonewall Mine Road trails. Bicycles and horseback riders are also allowed on these trails. Dogs are not allowed on any other trails in the park. The Cuyamaca Peak Fire Road is approximately 3.5 miles and goes all the way to the top of the park. The Cuyamaca Peak Fire Road begins at Hwy 79 about 1/4 mi south of the Paso Picacho Campground (the road is also accessible from the campground).

**William Heise County Park**
4945 Heise Park Road
Julian CA
760-765-0650 (877-565-3600)
Set among a forest of oak and pine trees at about 4,200 feet, this beautiful recreation destination offers miles of multi-use scenic trails, plenty of wildlife and birds, camping and more. Dogs of all sizes are allowed for an additional $1 per night per pet, and they must have current tags, rabies, and shot records. Dogs may not be left unattended at any time, and they must be on no more than a 6 foot leash and cleaned up after. Dogs are allowed on the trails and throughout the park.

## June Lake

# Dog-Friendly Hotels
**Double Eagle Resort And Spa**
5587 Highway 158
June Lake CA
760-648-7004
doubleeagle.com
Located 12 miles from the eastern entrance of Yosemite

National Park this June Lake resort offers free Wi-Fi an indoor swimming pool a restaurant and a spa.
Featuring a fireplace all rooms and cottages also offer free toiletries in the en suite bathroom. Select rooms provide a balcony at Double Eagle Resort and Spa. The two-bedroom cottages offer a fully equipped kitchen and terrace. The Eagle's Landing Restaurant offers breakfast lunch and dinner daily. The on-site bar Eagle's Nest Saloon offers a variety of wines and aperitifs. After a day outdoors guests can enjoy a hot tub and fitness centre onsite. A variety of spa services are available onsite. Cross country ski trails are within walking distance of Double Eagle Resort and Spa. June Mountain Ski Area is less than half a mile from the Double Eagle Resort. Mammoth Mountain ski area and Mammoth Lakes are within just 25 miles of Double Eagle Resort and Spa.

## Dog-Friendly Parks
**June Lake Area of Inyo National Forest**
Highway 158 (June Lake Loop)
June Lake CA
760-647-3044
This popular resort area is known for skiing in winter (both downhill and cross-country) and hiking and enjoying the four lakes along the June Lake Loop in the summer. These lakes are June Lake, Gulf Lake, Sliver Lake, and Grant Lake. There are a number of marinas at the lakes which may allow your dog on some of their boat rentals. This entire area is within the Inyo National Forest, which allows dogs throughout the forest on leash. Dogs are not supposed to swim in any of the lakes but they are allowed on leash up to them and on boats in the lakes. There are many hiking trails in the area, however, if you are planning a long hike make sure that you

keep your dog out of land in Yosemite National Park, where dogs are not allowed. They need to stay in the National Forest.

## Kernville

### Dog-Friendly Parks
**Lake Isabella**
Highways 155 and 178
Lake Isabella CA
661-868-7000
This lake is set at an elevation of over 2,500 feet and with a surface area of 11,200 acres it is Kern County's largest body of year round water. The lake is a popular spot for fishing and boating. Dogs are allowed at the lake and in the lake but must be on leash. Please clean up after your pets. There are nearby dog-friendly Sequoia National Forest trails within driving distance, including the Trail of a Hundred Giants. See our listing for this trail or call the Greenhorn Rangers District at 760-379-5646 for details.

## King City

### Dog-Friendly Parks
**San Lorenzo Regional Park**
1160 Broadway
King City CA
831-385-5964
This park is located in the foothills of the Santa Lucia Mountains and along the Salinas River. Amenities include a walking trail along the river, picnic areas, playgrounds, volleyball courts, softball areas and camping. Dogs are allowed but must be leashed. Please clean up after your pets.

## Kingsburg

### Dog-Friendly Hotels
**Motel 6 Kingsburg**
401 Sierra Street
Kingsburg CA
559-897-1022 (877-424-6423)
Located just off Hwy 99, near to State and National Parks. Free daily continental breakfast, outdoor pool and spa. Pet friendly hotel.

Dogs of all sizes are allowed. Dogs are allowed for a pet fee of $15.00 per pet per night.

## Kirkwood

### Dog-Friendly Parks
**Meiss Lake Trail**
Highway 88
Kirkwood CA
530-622-5061
This 4 mile moderate rated trail is used by both hikers and equestrians. Bicycling is prohibited. Take the Pacific Crest Trail one mile to the ridge, which offers great views and a wildflower display around mid-summer. Hike another three miles to Meiss Lake. The trailhead is located on the north side of Highway 88, immediately west of the Carson Pass Information Center. There is a parking fee. Pets must be leashed and please clean up after them.

## Klamath National Forest

### Dog-Friendly Parks
**Kelsey Trail**
Scott River Road
Fort Jones CA
530-468-5351
The historic Kelsey Trail offers

excellent opportunities for scenic day hikes or longer trips into the Marble Mountain Wilderness. The trail is located in the Klamath National Forest and begins at the Bridge Flat Campground. The campground is located on the Scott River approximately 17 miles from Fort Jones towards the town of Scott Bar, at a 2,000 foot elevation. Dogs should be on leash.

## LA Beach Area

## Dog-Friendly Hotels
**Aloft El Segundo - Los Angeles Airport**
475 North Sepulveda Boulevard
El Segundo CA
424-290-5555
Dogs up to 40 pounds are allowed. There is no additional pet fee.

**Westdrift Manhattan Beach Autograph Collection**
1400 Parkview Avenue
Manhattan Beach CA
810-546-7511
Dogs of all sizes are allowed. There is a $250 one time pet fee.

**Hotel Mdr Marina Del Rey- A Doubletree By Hilton**
13480 Maxella Avenue
Marina Del Rey CA

Free Wi-FI and an outdoor pool have our guests taking a close look at the non-smoking Hotel MDR Marina Del Rey- a DoubleTree by Hilton.The five-story property has 277 non-smoking rooms decorated in stylish fabrics and bold patterns. Modern conveniences include free Wi-Fi mini-fridges and flat-panel TVs. Don't fret if you're without a laptop  you can always use the computer in the business center. The hotel also sports a new exercise room a real bonus for folks who want to maintain their fitness regimen

while traveling. And this being sunny California there's also a heated outdoor pool plus a hot tub for a relaxing soak. Breakfast dinner and cocktails are served in the restaurant and the convenience store sells snacks to satisfy your cravings for late-night munchies. Additional amenities include a coin laundry and meeting space. The Hotel MDR Marina Del Rey is just a mile from Venice Beach and four miles from the Santa Monica Pier. It's 20 minutes by car to Beverly Hills and 30 minutes to Hollywood Boulevard's Walk of Fame. Los Angeles International Airport is five miles away.

**Hotel Mdr Marina Del Rey- A Doubletree By Hilton**
13480 Maxella Avenue
Marina Del Rey CA

Free Wi-FI and an outdoor pool have our guests taking a close look at the non-smoking Hotel MDR Marina Del Rey- a DoubleTree by Hilton. The five-story property has 277 non-smoking rooms decorated in stylish fabrics and bold patterns. Modern conveniences include free Wi-Fi mini-fridges and flat-panel TVs. Don't fret if you're without a laptop  you can always use the computer in the business center. The hotel also sports a new exercise room a real bonus for folks who want to maintain their fitness regimen while traveling. And this being sunny California there's also a heated outdoor pool plus a hot tub for a relaxing soak. Breakfast dinner and cocktails are served in the restaurant and the convenience store sells snacks to satisfy your cravings for late-night munchies. Additional amenities include a coin laundry and meeting space. The Hotel MDR Marina Del Rey is just a mile from Venice Beach and four miles from the Santa Monica Pier. It's 20 minutes by car to Beverly Hills and 30 minutes to Hollywood Boulevard's Walk of

Fame. Los Angeles International Airport is five miles away.

**Fairmont Miramar Hotel & Bungalows**
101 Wilshire Boulevard
Santa Monica CA
310-576-7777 (800-257-7544)
fairmont.com/santamonica/
Nestled atop the scenic bluffs of Santa Monica beach, this hotel features historic elegance with all the modern-day conveniences and services. Some of the features/amenities include 302 stylish guest rooms, 32 secluded garden bungalows, casual elegant indoor and outdoor dining, and 24 hour room service. There can be up to 3 dogs in one room if they are all small, otherwise there are only 2 dogs allowed per room. There are no additional pet fees and there is a pet policy to sign at check in. Dogs may not be left alone in the room at any time.

**Jw Marriott Santa Monica Le Merigot**
1740 Ocean Ave
Santa Monica CA
877-637-4468
Dogs up to 25 pounds are allowed. There is a $100 one time pet fee plus a $150 refundable pet deposit.

**Le Meridien Delfina Santa Monica**
530 Pico Boulevard
Santa Monica CA
310-399-9344 (800-325-3535)
There are many features in-house to please both business and leisure travelers at this upscale hotel;plus they offer a close location to the beach and many of the area's star attractions, business districts, and dining and shopping venues. One dog up to 50 pounds is allowed for an additional one time fee of $75.

**Loews Santa Monica Beach Hotel**
1700 Ocean Avenue
Santa Monica CA
310-458-6700 (888-332-0160)
This beachfront resort, luxury

hotel offers a convenient location and numerous amenities for both business and leisure travelers. They are within walking distance to the Santa Monica Pier;plus they also feature live music events and a restaurant and lounge with a focus on local, sustainable, and farm and sea fresh cuisine and beverages. Dogs are allowed for an additional one time pet fee of $100 per room. They also offer a VIP Pet Program for their canine visitors that include a gourmet room service menu, specialized bedding, dinnerware, a toy, treats, pet food, waste disposal bags, and info for local dog friendly venues. Pet walking and pet sitting services can be arranged by the hotel.

**Viceroy Santa Monica**
1819 Ocean Avenue
Santa Monica CA
310-260-7500
Beautifully decorated rooms two outdoor plunge pools holistic spa services and stellar dining add up to the non-smoking Viceroy Santa Monica one block from the beach. Guests receive a champagne welcome at this eight-story hotel with 162 rooms that feature separate sitting areas with ocean palm or pool views dreamy beds with pillowtop mattresses Egyptian cotton linens and feather duvets as well as fully stocked minibars. Bathrooms feature spa products and bathrobes for lounging. Of course you'll find flat-panel HDTVs iPod docking stations and media-hub technology systems in the room too. Wi-Fi is available for an additional fee. There is a business center with computer access for those who travel with theirs. Fitness buffs will appreciate the well-appointed gym featuring cardio and weight training equipment; more laid-back folks have a variety of in-room spa services to choose from. Two outdoor pools are doubly tempting made all the more so with private cabana rentals. Cast restaurant located

on-site offers a New American organic farm to table cuisine. The lounge just off the lobby and extending into the pool area is all about glamour and sophistication. There is mandatory resort fee charged that covers a variety of amenities and parking is available for an extra charge. Located one block from the ocean the Viceroy is less than one-half mile from the Santa Monica Pier and about one mile from Third Street Promenade. From the hotel it's less than three miles to Venice Beach. It's four miles to the Hammer Museum of Art; five miles to the Getty Villa. Downtown LA is 16 miles from the Viceroy. Los Angeles International Airport is nine miles.

**Days Inn Torrance Redondo Beach**
4111 Pacific Coast Highway
Torrance CA
310-378-8511 (800-329-7466)
Dogs of all sizes are allowed. Dogs are allowed for a pet fee of $10 per pet per night.

**Holiday Inn Torrance**
19800 S Vermont
Torrance CA
310-781-9100 (877-270-6405)
Dogs of all sizes are allowed. Dogs are allowed for a pet fee of $50.00 per pet per stay.

# Pet-Friendly Extended Stay Hotels
**Extended Stay America Los Angeles - Lax Airport - El Segundo**
1910 E Mariposa Ave
El Segundo CA
310-607-4000 (800-804-3724)
One dog is allowed per suite. There is a $25 per night additional pet fee up to $150 for an entire stay.

**Residence Inn By Marriott El Segundo**
2135 East El Segundo Blvd
El Segundo CA

310-333-0888
Dogs of all sizes are allowed. There is a $100 one time additional pet fee.

**Candlewood Suites Lax Hawthorne**
11410 Hawthorne Blvd.
Hawthorne CA
310-973-3331 (877-270-6405)
Dogs up to 40 pounds are allowed. Pets allowed with an additional pet fee. Up to $75 for 1-6 nights and up to $150 for 7+ nights. A pet agreement must be signed at check-in.

**Towneplace Suites By Marriott Lax Manhattan Beach**
14400 Aviation Blvd
Hawthorne CA
310-725-9696
Dogs of all sizes are allowed. There is a $100 one time pet fee.

**Residence Inn Los Angeles Lax/manhattan Beach**
1700 North Sepulveda Boulevard
Manhattan Beach CA
310-421-3100
Dogs of all sizes are allowed. There is a $100 one time additional pet fee.

**Extended Stay America - Los Angeles - Torrance - Del Amo Circle**
3995 Carson St
Torrance CA
310-543-0048 (800-804-3724)
One dog is allowed per suite. There is a $25 per night additional pet fee up to $150 for an entire stay.

**Extended Stay America - Los Angeles - Torrance Blvd.**
3525 Torrance Blvd
Torrance CA
310-540-5442 (800-804-3724)
One dog is allowed per suite. There is a $25 per night additional pet fee up to $150 for an entire stay.

**Extended Stay America - Los Angeles - Torrance Harbor Gateway**

19200 Harbor Gtwy
Torrance CA
310-328-6000 (800-804-3724)
One dog is allowed per suite.
There is a $25 per night
additional pet fee up to $150 for
an entire stay.

**Residence Inn By Marriott
Torrance Redondo Beach**
3701 Torrance Blvd
Torrance CA
310-543-4566
Dogs of all sizes are allowed.
There is a $100 one time
additional pet fee.

**Staybridge Suites Torrance**
19901 Prairie Ave
Torrance CA
310-371-8525 (877-270-6405)
Dogs up to 80 pounds are
allowed. Pets allowed with an
additional pet fee. Up to $75 for
1-6 nights and up to $150 for 7+
nights. A pet agreement must
be signed at check-in.

# Dog-Friendly Attractions
**Catalina Ferries**
13763 Fiji Way , C2 Terminal
Building
Marina del Rey CA
310-305-7250
catalinaferries.com/
This ferry provides
transportation from Marina Del
Rey to Avalon or Two Harbors
on Catalina Island and back.
You are welcome to take your
dog for no additional fee, but he
must be muzzled and checked
in at the office.

# Outdoor Restaurants
**Chipotle**
307 N Sepulveda Blvd
El Segundo CA
310-426-1437
chipotle.com
Specializing in organic, natural
and unprocessed food, this
Mexican Eatery offers fajita
burritos, tacos, salads, and
salsas. Dogs are allowed at the
outdoor tables but you will need
to order your food inside the
restaurant and dogs must

remain outside.

**Johnny Rockets**
1550 Rosecrans Ave.
Manhattan Beach CA
310-536-9464
Dogs are allowed at the front
outdoor tables at this Johnny
Rockets.

**The Coffee Bean & Tea Leaf**
3008 Sepulveda Blvd/H 1
Manhattan Beach CA
310-546-3359
coffeebean.com
The coffee here is sourced
globally from family coffee
farms to procure only the top of
1% of Arabica beans. They
offer 30+ varieties of coffee;the
beans are roasted in small
batches daily for freshness,
and they also offer 20 varieties
of teas that are hand-blended
by their tea master.
Additionally, they offer a variety
of tasty sweets, powders,
extracts, sauces, gifts, and
cards. Leashed, well mannered
dogs are allowed at their
outside dining area.

**The Coffee Bean & Tea Leaf**
1133 Artesia Blvd
Manhattan Beach CA
310-374-9396
coffeebean.com
The coffee here is sourced
globally from family coffee
farms to procure only the top of
1% of Arabica beans. They
offer 30+ varieties of coffee;the
beans are roasted in small
batches daily for freshness,
and they also offer 20 varieties
of teas that are hand-blended
by their tea master.
Additionally, they offer a variety
of tasty sweets, powders,
extracts, sauces, gifts, and
cards. Leashed, well mannered
dogs are allowed at their
outside dining area.

**Baja Fresh Mexican Grill**
13424 Maxella Avenue
Marina Del Rey CA
310-578-2252
bajafresh.com
This Mexican restaurant is
open for lunch and dinner.
They use fresh ingredients and

making their salsa and beans
daily. Some of the items on their
menu include Enchiladas,
Burritos, Tacos Salads,
Quesadillas, Nachos, Chicken,
Steak and more. Well-behaved
leashed dogs are allowed at the
outdoor tables.

**Coffee Bean & Tea Leaf**
13420 Maxella, Suite C20
Marina Del Rey CA
310-823-0858
coffeebean.com
The coffee here is sourced
globally from family coffee farms
to procure only the top of 1% of
Arabica beans. They offer 30+
varieties of coffee;the beans are
roasted in small batches daily
for freshness, and they also
offer 20 varieties of teas that are
hand-blended by their tea
master. Additionally, they offer a
variety of tasty sweets, powders,
extracts, sauces, gifts, and
cards. Leashed, well mannered
dogs are allowed at their outside
dining area.

**The Coffee Bean & Tea Leaf**
4020 S Lincoln Blvd, Space D/H
1
Marina Del Rey CA
310-821-1068
coffeebean.com
The coffee here is sourced
globally from family coffee farms
to procure only the top of 1% of
Arabica beans. They offer 30+
varieties of coffee;the beans are
roasted in small batches daily
for freshness, and they also
offer 20 varieties of teas that are
hand-blended by their tea
master. Additionally, they offer a
variety of tasty sweets, powders,
extracts, sauces, gifts, and
cards. Leashed, well mannered
dogs are allowed at their outside
dining area.

**Chipotle**
4718 Admiralty Way
Marina del Rey CA
310-821-0059
chipotle.com
Specializing in organic, natural
and unprocessed food, this
Mexican Eatery offers fajita
burritos, tacos, salads, and
salsas. Dogs are allowed at the

outdoor tables but you will need to order your food inside the restaurant and dogs must remain outside.

**The Coffee Bean & Tea Leaf**
1617 Pacific Coast H, #103/H 1
Redondo Beach CA
310-316-2416
coffeebean.com
The coffee here is sourced globally from family coffee farms to procure only the top of 1% of Arabica beans. They offer 30+ varieties of coffee;the beans are roasted in small batches daily for freshness, and they also offer 20 varieties of teas that are hand-blended by their tea master. Additionally, they offer a variety of tasty sweets, powders, extracts, sauces, gifts, and cards. Leashed, well mannered dogs are allowed at their outside dining area.

**Whole Foods Market**
405 N. Pacific Coast Hwy.
Redondo Beach CA
310-376-6931
wholefoods.com/
This natural food supermarket offers natural and organic foods. Order some food from their deli without your dog and bring it to an outdoor table where your well-behaved leashed dog is welcome.

**Babalu**
1002 Montana Avenue
Santa Monica CA
310-395-2500
babalu.info/
Serving lunch, dinner, and Saturday and Sunday brunches, this diner offers American cuisine with international influences, a variety of handcrafted desserts, holiday meals to-go, and alfresco dining. Leashed dogs are allowed at their outside tables.

**Baja Fresh Mexican Grill**
720 Wilshire Blvd.
Santa Monica CA
310-393-9313
bajafresh.com
This Mexican restaurant is open for lunch and dinner. They use fresh ingredients and making

their salsa and beans daily. Some of the items on their menu include Enchiladas, Burritos, Tacos Salads, Quesadillas, Nachos, Chicken, Steak and more. Well-behaved leashed dogs are allowed at the outdoor tables.

**Blue Plate**
1415 Montana Avenue
Santa Monica CA
310-260-8877
blueplatesantamonica.com
Open daily from 8 am until 9 pm, this restaurant offers a seasonally inspired menu plus a wine/beer and an extensive daily menu. Additionally, they offer family style meals, take-out and special care packages. Leashed dogs are allowed at their outside tables.

**Cezanne**
1740 Ocean Avenue
Santa Monica CA
310-395-9700
lemerigothotel.com/cuisine.htm

This restaurant presents a seasonally inspired, modern presentation of classic French cuisine in an elegant setting with an emphasis on sourcing the freshest local ingredients available. Organics are used whenever possible and they also offer vegetarian options. Leashed, well mannered dogs are allowed at their outside dining area.

**Coffee Bean & Tea Leaf**
200 Santa Monica Blvd
Santa Monica CA
310-260-0044
coffeebean.com
The coffee here is sourced globally from family coffee farms to procure only the top of 1% of Arabica beans. They offer 30+ varieties of coffee;the beans are roasted in small batches daily for freshness, and they also offer 20 varieties of teas that are hand-blended by their tea master. Additionally, they offer a variety of tasty sweets, powders, extracts, sauces, gifts, and cards. Leashed, well mannered

dogs are allowed at their outside dining area.

**Jinky's**
1447 2nd Street
Santa Monica CA
310-917-3311
jinkys.com
This gathering place offers a tasty blending of International, Southwestern, and American cuisine, a full coffee bar, a fun animime decor, and alfresco dining. Leashed dogs are allowed at their outer tables.

**The Coffee Bean & Tea Leaf**
829 Wilshire Blvd
Santa Monica CA
829 Wilshire Blvd
coffeebean.com
The coffee here is sourced globally from family coffee farms to procure only the top of 1% of Arabica beans. They offer 30+ varieties of coffee;the beans are roasted in small batches daily for freshness, and they also offer 20 varieties of teas that are hand-blended by their tea master. Additionally, they offer a variety of tasty sweets, powders, extracts, sauces, gifts, and cards. Leashed, well mannered dogs are allowed at their outside dining area.

**The Coffee Bean & Tea Leaf**
1312 Third Street Promenade
Santa Monica CA
310-394-9737
coffeebean.com
The coffee here is sourced globally from family coffee farms to procure only the top of 1% of Arabica beans. They offer 30+ varieties of coffee;the beans are roasted in small batches daily for freshness, and they also offer 20 varieties of teas that are hand-blended by their tea master. Additionally, they offer a variety of tasty sweets, powders, extracts, sauces, gifts, and cards. Leashed, well mannered dogs are allowed at their outside dining area.

**The Coffee Bean & Tea Leaf**
3150 Ocean Park Blvd
Santa Monica CA
310-396-6706

coffeebean.com
The coffee here is sourced globally from family coffee farms to procure only the top of 1% of Arabica beans. They offer 30+ varieties of coffee;the beans are roasted in small batches daily for freshness, and they also offer 20 varieties of teas that are hand-blended by their tea master. Additionally, they offer a variety of tasty sweets, powders, extracts, sauces, gifts, and cards. Leashed, well mannered dogs are allowed at their outside dining area.

**The Coffee Bean & Tea Leaf**
2901 Main Street
Santa Monica CA
310-392-1406
coffeebean.com
The coffee here is sourced globally from family coffee farms to procure only the top of 1% of Arabica beans. They offer 30+ varieties of coffee;the beans are roasted in small batches daily for freshness, and they also offer 20 varieties of teas that are hand-blended by their tea master. Additionally, they offer a variety of tasty sweets, powders, extracts, sauces, gifts, and cards. Leashed, well mannered dogs are allowed at their outside dining area.

**The Coffee Bean & Tea Leaf**
1804 Lincoln Blvd
Santa Monica CA
310-581-7991
coffeebean.com
The coffee here is sourced globally from family coffee farms to procure only the top of 1% of Arabica beans. They offer 30+ varieties of coffee;the beans are roasted in small batches daily for freshness, and they also offer 20 varieties of teas that are hand-blended by their tea master. Additionally, they offer a variety of tasty sweets, powders, extracts, sauces, gifts, and cards. Leashed, well mannered dogs are allowed at their outside dining area.

**True Food Kitchen**
395 Santa Monica Place, Suite 172

Santa Monica CA
310-593-8300
truefoodkitchen.com
With an emphasis on sourcing and developing relations with sustainable, local, and organic growers and providers, this restaurant serves up a full menu of freshly prepared and globally inspired cuisine. Certified organic coffee, all natural beverages, organic desserts, fine wines and cocktails, weekend brunches, and vegan, vegetarian, and gluten free options are also offered. Leashed, well mannered dogs are allowed at their outside dining area.

**Chipotle**
24631 Crenshaw Blvd Unit A
Torrance CA
310-530-0690
chipotle.com
Specializing in organic, natural and unprocessed food, this Mexican Eatery offers fajita burritos, tacos, salads, and salsas. Dogs are allowed at the outdoor tables but you will need to order your food inside the restaurant and dogs must remain outside.

**Johnny Rockets**
3525 Carson Street, Suite 75
Torrance CA
310-214-4051
johnnyrockets.com/
All the American favorites can be found here: A fun retro, all-American decor and atmosphere, juicy burgers, specialty sandwiches, crispy fries, hand-dipped malts and shakes (dark chocolate ones too), fresh baked apple pies, tasty vegetarian choices, and something for all ages. Leashed, friendly dogs are allowed at their outside dining area.

**Lazy Dog Restaurant & Bar**
3525 West Carson Street
Torrance CA
310-921-6080
lazydogrestaurants.com/dogs/info
Known for it's dog-friendly patio, the Lazy Dog offers your

dog a complimentary bowl of water, and a menu consisting of grilled hamburger patty, chicken breast or brown rice. They just ask that you respect their common sense rules while your dog is dining there. This is as dog-friendly as dining gets. For the humans in your party there is hamburger, steak, salads and some great desserts.

**The Coffee Bean & Tea Leaf**
21300 B Hawthorne Blvd/H 107
Torrance CA
310-792-8630
coffeebean.com
The coffee here is sourced globally from family coffee farms to procure only the top of 1% of Arabica beans. They offer 30+ varieties of coffee;the beans are roasted in small batches daily for freshness, and they also offer 20 varieties of teas that are hand-blended by their tea master. Additionally, they offer a variety of tasty sweets, powders, extracts, sauces, gifts, and cards. Leashed, well mannered dogs are allowed at their outside dining area.

**The Coffee Bean & Tea Leaf**
25345 Crenshaw Blvd, Suite B
Torrance CA
310-530-5443
coffeebean.com
The coffee here is sourced globally from family coffee farms to procure only the top of 1% of Arabica beans. They offer 30+ varieties of coffee;the beans are roasted in small batches daily for freshness, and they also offer 20 varieties of teas that are hand-blended by their tea master. Additionally, they offer a variety of tasty sweets, powders, extracts, sauces, gifts, and cards. Leashed, well mannered dogs are allowed at their outside dining area.

**Whole Foods Market**
2655 Pacific Coast Highway
Torrance CA
310-257-8700
wholefoods.com/
This natural food supermarket offers natural and organic foods. Order some food from their deli

without your dog and bring it to an outdoor table where your well-behaved leashed dog is welcome.

## Baja Fresh Mexican Grill
245 Main Street
Venice CA
310-392-3452
bajafresh.com
This Mexican restaurant is open for lunch and dinner. They use fresh ingredients and making their salsa and beans daily. Some of the items on their menu include Enchiladas, Burritos, Tacos Salads, Quesadillas, Nachos, Chicken, Steak and more. Well-behaved leashed dogs are allowed at the outdoor tables.

## The Terrace
7 Washington Blvd
Venice CA
310-578-1530
theterracecafe.com/
A full service, ocean front restaurant and bar, they offer an extensive menu of California-American cuisine, sports viewing on flat screens in the bar, a venue for special events, and heated patio dining. Leashed, well mannered dogs are welcome at their outside tables. Water and treats are provided for your pet.

## Pet-Friendly Stores
### Anthropologie
800 S. Sepulveda Blvd
El Segundo CA
310-414-0066
Items of distinction can be found for all ages and in all departments of this unique shop. Carefully selected to add to the enjoyment of the shopping experience, they carry fine clothing, amazing accessories, jewelry, hobby and leisure items, and a full line of bright and useful items for the home, garden, and office. Leashed, well behaved dogs are allowed in the store.

### Centinela Feed and Supplies
413 N Pacific Coast H/H 1

Redondo Beach CA
310-318-2653
centinelafeed.com
Specializing in natural, holistic, and raw pet foods, this pet supply store also provides healthy treats, quality supplements, pet care supplies, low-cost vaccination clinics, frequent in-store events, and a knowledgeable staff. Leashed pets are welcome.

### Petco Pet Store - Redondo Beach - North
3901 Inglewood Ave. Ste G
Redondo Beach CA
310-355-1370
Your licensed and well-behaved leashed dog is allowed in the store.

### Petco Pet Store - Redondo Beach - South
537 North Pacific Coast Hwy
Redondo Beach CA
310-374-7969
Your licensed and well-behaved leashed dog is allowed in the store.

### Petco Pet Store - Rolling Hills Estates
51-A Peninsula Center
Rolling Hills Estates CA
310-377-5560
Your licensed and well-behaved leashed dog is allowed in the store.

### Animal Wellness Center
2803 Main Street
Santa Monica CA
310-450-PETS (7387)
animalwellnesscenters.com
Modern technology meets traditional Chinese veterinary medicine at this wellness center for pets creating a revolutionary approach in pet health. Some of their products and services include organic and prescription diets, wholesome vitamins and supplements, pet care products, exercise equipment, behavior classes, collars/leashes, an on-site pharmacy, and dog walking. They also offer house-call veterinarian services.

### Anthropologie
1402 Third St. Promenade
Santa Monica CA
310-393-4763
Items of distinction can be found for all ages and in all departments of this unique shop. Carefully selected to add to the enjoyment of the shopping experience, they carry fine clothing, amazing accessories, jewelry, hobby and leisure items, and a full line of bright and useful items for the home, garden, and office. Leashed, well behaved dogs are allowed in the store.

### Barnes and Noble Bookstore
1201 3rd Street
Santa Monica CA
310-260-9110
barnesandnoble.com/
Your well-behaved leashed dog is allowed inside this store. One of our readers writes "They (dogs) are totally welcome there!"

### Bloomingdale's
315 Colorado Avenue
Santa Monica CA
310-985-6400
Some of the offerings of this major shopping destination include designer merchandise, indoor and outdoor wear for the entire family, jewelry and accessories, shoes and handbags, personal beauty aids, child care products, and home decor. They also offer a wide variety of shopping services; various fashion, beauty, and home events, and a philanthropy program that raises funds and awareness for worthy causes. Leashed, well mannered dogs are welcome in the store; they must be under their owner's control at all times.

### Centinela Feed and Supplies
1448 Lincoln Blvd
Santa Monica CA
310-451-7140
centinelafeed.com
Specializing in natural, holistic, and raw pet foods, this pet supply store also provides

healthy treats, quality
supplements, pet care supplies,
low-cost vaccination clinics,
frequent in-store events, and a
knowledgeable staff. Leashed
pets are welcome.

**Petco Pet Store - Santa
Monica**
2910 Wilshire Blvd
Santa Monica CA
310-586-1963
Your licensed and well-behaved
leashed dog is allowed in the
store.

**The Wagging Tail**
1123 Montana Avenue
Santa Monica CA
310-656-9663
wagwagwag.com/
This upscale pet boutique
carries a unique array of fine
apparel, hound and human
matching ensembles,
accessories, perfume, doggy
furnishings, flavored gourmet
waters, pet-care items, and
many other items for your
pooch. Leashed dogs are
welcome.

**Urban Outfitters**
1440 Third Street Promenade
Santa Monica CA
310-394-1404
In addition to a large inventory
of indoor and outdoor apparel
for men and women, this major
department store also carries
vintage wear, designer brands,
and a variety of accessories for
all types of active lifestyles.
They also carry shoes,
furnishings, home decor,
cameras, electronics, novelty
items and more. Leashed, well
mannered dogs are allowed in
the store.

**Wagging Tail**
1123 Montana Avenue
Santa Monica CA
310-656-9663
wagwagwag.com/
This upscale boutique has
dedicated itself to offering
unique and one of a kind items
for your pooch. They carry paw
wear, fresh bakery items, fine
art and doggie furniture, jewelry,
and even French perfume. They

are open from 10 am to 6 pm
Monday through Saturday, and
Noon to 5 pm on Sunday. Your
dog is welcome to explore this
store with their owner, and if
they are well behaved they may
be off lead.

**Anthropologie**
3525 W. Carson Street, #157
Torrance CA
310-370-9709
Items of distinction can be
found for all ages and in all
departments of this unique
shop. Carefully selected to add
to the enjoyment of the
shopping experience, they
carry fine clothing, amazing
accessories, jewelry, hobby
and leisure items, and a full
line of bright and useful items
for the home, garden, and
office. Leashed, well behaved
dogs are allowed in the store.

**Centinela Feed and Supplies**
22840 Hawthorne Blvd/H 107
Torrance CA
310-373-4437
centinelafeed.com
Specializing in natural, holistic,
and raw pet foods, this pet
supply store also provides
healthy treats, quality
supplements, pet care
supplies, low-cost vaccination
clinics, frequent in-store
events, and a knowledgeable
staff. Leashed pets are
welcome.

**Crate and Barrel**
21710 Hawthorne Blvd/H 107
Torrance CA
310-371-4804
crateandbarrel.com
This store offers fine products
from around the world for in
and around the home that
include items for outdoor living,
indoor furnishings and
decorating, dining and
entertaining, kitchen and food
service, and gourmet food and
beverages. They also have
accessories for pets, bed and
bath items, and organizing and
storage units. Leashed, friendly
dogs are welcome in the store;
they must be under their
owner's control at all times.

**PetSmart Pet Store**
3855-59 Sepulveda Blvd
Torrance CA
310-316-9047
Your licensed and well-behaved
leashed dog is allowed in the
store.

**Petco Pet Store - Torrance**
24413 Crenshaw Blvd, Ste 8
Torrance CA
310-530-5945
Your licensed and well-behaved
leashed dog is allowed in the
store.

**Urban Outfitters**
3525 W. Carson Street, #72
Torrance CA
310-370-9167
In addition to a large inventory
of indoor and outdoor apparel
for men and women, this major
department store also carries
vintage wear, designer brands,
and a variety of accessories for
all types of active lifestyles.
They also carry shoes,
furnishings, home decor,
cameras, electronics, novelty
items and more. Leashed, well
mannered dogs are allowed in
the store.

## Off-Leash Dog Parks
**Redondo Beach Dog Park**
Flagler Lane and 190th
Redondo Beach CA
310-376-9263
rbdogpark.com/
This dog park is located next to
Dominguez Park. Local dogs
and vacationing dogs are
welcome at the dog park. There
is a separate section for small
dogs and big dogs. It is
completely fenced and has
pooper scooper bags available.
From the PCH take Herondo
Street east which will become
190th Street.

**Airport Dog Park**
3201 Airport Avenue
Santa Monica CA
310-458-8411
There is almost an acre of
doggy play area at this park with
2 sections for large and small

dogs. There are waste disposal stations and water on site. Non-residents will need to get a permit to use the park, and it can be obtained at the animal shelter at 1640 9th Street just off Olympic Blvd. Dogs must be sociable, current on all vaccinations and license, and under their owner's control at all times. Dogs must be leashed when not in designated off-lead areas.

**Joslyn Park Dog Park**
633 Kensington Road
Santa Monica CA
310-458-8974
The fenced Joslyn Park dog park includes two areas. One is for small dogs and the other for large dogs.

**Memorial Park**
1401 Olympic Blvd
Santa Monica CA
310-450-1121
There is an off-leash dog run located in this park.

**Pacific Street Dog Park**
Main and Pacific Street
Santa Monica CA
310-450-6179
This off lead area offers almost an acre for playful pooches. It is open weekdays from 7:30 am until 8:30 pm and on weekends from 8:30 am until 8:30 pm. Dogs must be sociable, current on all vaccinations and license and under their owner's control at all times. Dogs must be leashed when not in designated off-lead areas.

**Westminster Dog Park**
1234 Pacific Ave
Venice CA
310-392-5566
The Westminster Dog Park is 0.8 acres in size and it is open daily from 6 am to 10 pm. There is a smaller fenced area for small dogs. The park is located one block south of Venice Blvd near Centinela Avenue.

**Dog-Friendly Parks**
**El Segundo Recreation Park**

Grande Ave at Eucalyptus Dr
El Segundo CA

This park allows dogs during all hours that the park is open, but they must be on leash at all times. Please clean up after your dogs, so the city continues to allow their presence. This park is bounded by the following streets: North by E. Pine St, South by Grande Ave, West by Eucalyptus Dr. and East by Penn St. Thanks to one of our readers for recommending this park.

## Rescue Organizations
**Rover Rescue**
402-B. North Gertruda
Redondo Beach CA
310-379-0154
roverrescue.com
Rover Rescue is a non-profit, 501(c)3 organization dedicated to rescuing and placing homeless dogs from Los Angeles area animal shelters. Rover Rescue all breeds and sizes of dogs, including sick and/or injured dogs. We are also committed to educating the public about responsible pet ownership, specifically in the areas of care, adoption, and spay/neuter. Rover Rescue runs a very successful Spay/Neuter voucher program for low income families - providing low or no cost altering surgeries to those who could not otherwise afford them.

## Other Organizations
**The PetCare Company**
1630 Pacific Coast Highway
Hermosa Beach CA
310 320 7727
petcarecompany.net
We own a pet store that has dedicated a large portion of our 7,500 to the adoption of rescues. Ken-Mar Rescue provides the orphans after they have been vet checked, vaccinated, microchipped and spayed or neutered. Before

coming to the store, they stay at Ken or Martie's house (Ken-Mar) for a few days, in order to notate any behavioral issues and make the transition less stressful. Orphans (we refer to them as guests because they are only visiting until loving committed homes can be found) are housed in large custom made dens and socialized in our day care. Once a good parent has been found, the orphan is hand delivered to their new home and a thorough home inspection is performed before the final decision is made. At this point, the New Parent packet is provided, including free bag of food and treats, free grooming, free day care, DVD on how to train a rescue, free personalized id tag and life long registration with a national lost and found registry and other important information.

**Friends of the Redondo Beach Dog Park**
200 Flagler Lane
Redondo Beach CA
(310) 376-9263
rbdogpark.com/
The Redondo Beach Dog Park is part of Dominguez Park and is on land leased from the Edison Company. "Friends of the Redondo Beach Dog Park, Inc." is a not for profit California corporation comprised of a board of directors with elected officers, all volunteers.

## Lake Arrowhead

## Dog-Friendly Attractions
**Arrowhead Queen Boat Tours**
28200 H 189 Building C100
Lake Arrowhead CA
909-336-6992
This enclosed paddlewheel boat is a great way to view beautiful Lake Arrowhead Lake and to learn about the area from their knowledgeable guides. Dogs are welcome aboard for no additional fee. They suggest that

visitors with pets tour during the off-season, or weekdays during the busy summer season. Dogs must be friendly, and under their owner's control/responsibility at all times.

## Lake Arrowhead Village
28200 Highway 189
Lake Arrowhead CA
909-337-2533
lakearrowheadvillage.com/
This outdoor shopping resort features unique specialty and factory outlet stores. While dogs are not allowed in the stores (with the exception of the Big Dogs store), it is a nice place to walk with your pup. During the summer there are usually outdoor events next to the lake. Dogs must be leashed and you must clean up after your dog.

## Children's Forest
Keller Peak Road
Sky Forest CA
909-338-5156
sbnfa.org/childrens_forest.htm
In 1993, San Bernardino National Forest set aside a 3,400-acre site within the forest to create the first Children's Forest in the United States. Forty children and teenagers from around the country were selected and brought to work with key Forest Service staff and other experts to design a trail and interpretive exhibits that teach young people about the Forest. Dogs are not allowed on the guided tour, but you and your pooch can take a self-guided tour on the 1/2 mile paved interpretive trail. Children's Forest is located off Highway 18 at Keller Peak Road, east of Running Springs in the San Bernardino Mountains.

## Pet-Friendly Stores
### Big Dogs Sportswear
28200 Hwy 189
Lake Arrowhead CA
909-336-1998
bigdogs.com
This retail store sells sportswear for people and allows well-

behaved dogs inside. It is located in the Lake Arrowhead Village.

## Coach Factory Store
28200 Highway 189
Lake Arrowhead CA
909-337-2678
Well-behaved leashed dogs are allowed inside this store.

## Jockey International
28200 Highway 189
Lake Arrowhead CA
909-337-8813
Well-behaved leashed dogs are allowed inside this store.

## Photo Express
28200 Highway 189
Lake Arrowhead CA
909-337-3224
Well-behaved leashed dogs up to about 75 pounds are allowed inside this store. They can take a photo of you, any other people with you and your dog between 10am and 3pm daily. Photos are ready the same day at 4pm.

## Three Dog Bakery
28200 Highway 189, Suite #T240
Lake Arrowhead CA
909-337-3157
Three Dog Bakery provides cookies and snacks for your dog as well as some boutique items. You well-behaved, leashed dog is welcome.

## Wildflowers
28200 Highway 189
Lake Arrowhead CA
909-337-8248
Well-behaved leashed dogs are allowed inside this store.

## Dog-Friendly Parks
### Metate Trail
Highway 173
Lake Arrowhead CA
909-337-2444
This .5 mile easy walk is located in the San Bernardino National Forest. The trail takes you to large stone slabs that were used by the Serrano Indians to grind acorns into

flour. Pets on leash are allowed and please clean up after them. To get there take Highway 173 north to the Rock Camp Station. This trail used to be called the Indian Rock Trail.

## North Shore - National Recreation Trail
Torrey Road
Lake Arrowhead CA
909-337-2444
This 1.7 mile moderate rated trail is located in the San Bernardino National Forest. The trail descends to Little Bear Creek and then goes to Forest Road 2N26Y. Pets on leash are allowed and please clean up after them. To get there from the Lake Arrowhead Marina, go east on Torrey Road. At the first left, take the dirt road to Forest Road 2N25 to the trailhead.

## Humane Society or SPCAs

### Mountains' Humane Society
P.O. Box 452
Lake Arrowhead CA
909-337-6422
mountainshumanesociety.com
We provide adoptions, foster homes, emergency medical help for 12 local mountain community animals. We have 2 major fundraisers, Strut your Mutt and a Benefit Dinner. We have rescued dogs with pups in the snow to neglected or abuse animals. If you require more information I can send you something in the mail.

## Lake Elsinore

## Outdoor Restaurants
### Coffee Bean & Tea Leaf
29263 Central Avenue, Suite P6

Lake Elsinore CA
951-245-4374
coffeebean.com
The coffee here is sourced globally from family coffee farms

to procure only the top of 1% of Arabica beans. They offer 30+ varieties of coffee;the beans are roasted in small batches daily for freshness, and they also offer 20 varieties of teas that are hand-blended by their tea master. Additionally, they offer a variety of tasty sweets, powders, extracts, sauces, gifts, and cards. Leashed, well mannered dogs are allowed at their outside dining area.

## Pet-Friendly Stores
**PetSmart Pet Store**
29227 Central Ave
Lake Elsinore CA
951-245-0267
Your licensed and well-behaved leashed dog is allowed in the store.

**Petco Pet Store - Lake Elsinore**
18290 Collier Ave.
Lake Elsinore CA
951-245-7538
Your licensed and well-behaved leashed dog is allowed in the store.

## Off-Leash Dog Parks
**Canyon Hills Community Park**

34360 Canyon Hills Road
Lake Elsinore CA
951-674-3124
The Canyon Hill Community Park is a expansive 18-acre park in Lake Elsinore, California. There are a lot of things to do, including an off-leash dog park with separate areas for small dogs and large dogs. For a complete list of rules and regulations, please contact the City.

**Rosetta Canyon Community Park**
39423 Ardenwood Way
Lake Elsinore CA
951-674-3124
The Rosetta Canyon Community Park offers a 1.25 acre dog park divided into two sections for small dogs(up to 30

pounds) and large dogs. For a complete list of rules and regulations, please go to their web site.

## Lake Shasta

## Dog-Friendly Attractions
**Self Guided Audio Cassette Tour**
204 West Alma St
Lake Shasta CA
530-926-4511
This free audio cassette tour is available when you travel the Upper Sacramento River Canyon on Interstate 5, between Mt. Shasta and Anderson in scenic Northern California. The tape and its original sound track are keyed to I-5 exit signs traveling at 65 mph. The tapes tell a colorful story filled with details of more than a century of traveling and recreating in the canyon. Pick up and drop off the free "Sacramento Canyon Auto Tour" audio cassette tape. If you are traveling south on I-5, you can pick up a tape at the Mt. Shasta Ranger Station located at 204 West Alma St. in Mt. Shasta. You can drop off your southbound tape at either the Shasta Lake Ranger Station on the east side of I-5 at the Mountain Gate exit or the California Welcome Center in Anderson, located at 1699 Highway 273, adjacent to I-5. Going north, you can pick up a tape at the California Welcome Center in Anderson and drop it off at the Mt. Shasta Ranger Station. There is even an after hours drop box in Mt. Shasta.

## Dog-Friendly Parks
**Castle Crags State Park**
Castle Creek Road
Lakehead CA
530-235-2684 (800-444-7275)
Named for 6,000-feet tall glacier-polished crags, this

park features a variety of land and water recreation, activities, and interpretive and campfire programs are offered in summer. Dogs are allowed for no additional fee. They must be under their owners control at all times, be on no more than a 6 foot leash, and cleaned up after. Dogs are not permitted on the trails, except for the campground/river trail to the picnic area, or in park buildings, and they must be inside a vehicle or tent at night.

**Shasta Lake**

Redding CA
530-365-7500
Dogs on leash are allowed on the trails and in the lake. There are miles of trails near this beautiful lake. The easiest trail to reach from Interstate 5 is the Bailey Cove Trail. For a map of all trails, stop at the Visitors Center and Ranger's Station located just south of the lake on Interstate 5 at the Wonderland Blvd exit in Mountain Gate. The Visitor's Center is about 8 miles north of Redding.

**Hirz Bay Trail**
Gilman Road
Shasta Lake CA
530-275-1587
This 1.6 mile easy rated trail is located in the Shasta-Trinity National Forest. The trail follows the shoreline and crosses several cool, shady creeks. It also provides scenic vistas of the lake. The trailhead is located at Hirz Bay Campground which is 10 miles from Interstate 5 on Gilman Road. Dogs are allowed in the lake, but not at the designated swimming beaches. Pets must be leashed and please clean up after them.

## Lake Tahoe

## Dog-Friendly Hotels
### The Beach Retreat & Lodge At Tahoe
3411 Lake Tahoe Boulevard
Lake Tahoe CA
530-541-6722
Dogs up to 80 pounds are allowed. There is a $20 per day pet fee up to $100 for the week. Up to two dogs are allowed per room.

### Heavenly Valley Lodge Bed & Breakfast
1261 Ski Run Boulevard
South Lake Tahoe CA
530-544-4244 (800-692-2246)
innatheavenly.com/
Offering 4 outdoor patios this Lake Tahoe B&B features a fire-pit and ski-to-door access. Heavenly Mountain Resort is 2 minutes drive. Free WiFi is available in all rooms.
A fireplace is provided at Heavenly Valley Lodge Bed & Breakfast. Plush bathrobes a flat-screen TV and free toiletries in the en suite bathroom are provided.
Guests are offered a different delicious hot home-cooked breakfast each morning at Heavenly Valley Lodge. Additionally this B&B serves bagels muffins pastries cereals yogurt fresh fruit coffee and a variety of teas and juices. Breakfast is served from 08:00 to 10:00. Guests can also enjoy a free daily happy hour at this B&B.
A library of 500+ DVDs is offered at reception. A sun terrace with barbecue facilities is provided at Heavenly Valley Lodge B&B.
Reno-Tahoe International Airport is 1 hours drive away. Lake Tahoe is 15 minutes walk away from Heavenly Valley Lodge Bed & Breakfast.

### Rodeway Inn Casino Center
4127 Pine Boulevard
South Lake Tahoe CA
530-541-7150 (877-424-6423)
Enjoy walkable approach to casinos, watersports, boat rentals, scenic gondola and Heavenly Ski Resort.

Dogs of all sizes are allowed. Dogs are allowed for a pet fee of $15.00 per pet per stay. Two dogs are allowed per room.

## Accommodations
### Alder Inn
1072 Ski Run Blvd
South Lake Tahoe CA
530-544-4485 (800-544-0056)
alderinntahoe.com
Minutes from Heavenly Valley Ski Resort and the casinos. All rooms have a small refrigerator and microwave. There is a $10.00 per night pet fee.

### Colony Inn at South Lake Tahoe
3794 Montreal Road
South Lake Tahoe CA
530-544-6481
gototahoe.com/rooms/colony.html
The Colony Inn at South Lake Tahoe is located just 1.5 blocks from Harrah's and the other casinos and just down the street from Heavenly Ski Resort. Want to experience the beautiful outdoors? The Colony Inn's backyard is National Forest Land, featuring dog-friendly hiking, mountain biking, and peace and quiet. There is a $25 refundable pet deposit, and pets cannot be left unattended in the rooms.

### Holiday House
7276 North Lake Blvd
Tahoe Vista CA
530-546-2369 (800-294-6378)
tahoeholidayhouse.com
This lodge in North Tahoe welcomes you and your dog. The hotel is located 1 mile west of the Hwy 267/Hwy 28 intersection near restaurants and activities.

### Tahoma Meadows Bed and Breakfast
6821 W. Lake Blvd.
Tahoma CA
530-525-1553
tahomameadows.com/
A well-behaved dog is allowed only if you let them know in

advance that you are bringing your dog. Pets are allowed in one of their cabins, the Mountain Hideaway (previously known as Dogwood). There is an extra $25 one time pet charge per stay, plus a security deposit.

## Pet Sitters
### All Tuckered Out Pet Sitting
Call To Arrange
South Lake Tahoe CA
530-318-8749
alltuckeredoutpetsitting.com
This South Lake Tahoe pet sitter will come to your hotel, campground or other rental and watch your dog when you are not able to take your pup with you. Call to make reservations.

## Dog-Friendly Attractions
### Mountain High Weddings
PO Box 294
Homewood CA
530-525-9320
mountainhighweddings.com/
Want to get married AND have your pooch with you to enjoy that special moment? Mountain High Weddings performs ceremonies on the North and West Shores of Lake Tahoe and they invite you to bring your dog. They have performed many ceremonies where rings were taken off the collars of special canine ring bearers. Couples have been married on skis on top of a mountain, under the full moon on the lake, or at a small intimate dinner party in the middle of a meadow. The weddings can be as traditional or unique as you desire. So if you are getting ready to tie the knot, now you can include your pooch in the wedding party.

### Hope Valley Outdoor Center
Intersection of H 88 and H 89
Hope Valley CA
530-694-2266
hopevalleyoutdoors.com/
There are more than 60 miles of trails offered at Hope Valley; in winter there are about 20 miles

of groomed trails and 40 miles of skier and snowshoe packed trails. They operate from a solar energy operated Yurt at the highway intersections where some of their most popular trails begin. Dogs are allowed on the specially marked trails. Dogs are not allowed on the trail run by the sled dogs and they must be leashed whenever in that area. Additionally, they offer lessons and guided tours.

**Squaw Valley USA-Gondola**
1910 Squaw Valley Rd
Olympic Valley CA
530-583-5585 (888 SNOW 3-2-1)
squaw.com
This is a summer only attraction. Dogs are allowed in the Gondola/Cable Car, but make sure your best friend is not claustrophobic. You can take the cable car from the parking lot (6,200 ft elevation) to High Camp (8,200 ft elevation). Once at the top, your well-behaved leashed pooch is welcome inside the lobby and the gift shop. Want some exercise? From High Camp, hike down the mountain along the ski path. Want a more strenuous hike? Try hiking up to High Camp. Squaw Valley is located off Hwy 89 on the northwest shore of Lake Tahoe. Dogs are not allowed on the cable car on the 4th of July weekend because of the crowds and fireworks. Squaw Valley does have special events during the summer, like Full Moon Hikes and Stargazing at High Camp. Dogs are welcome at both events.

**Tahoe Keys Boat Rentals**
2435 Venice Drive E.
South Lake Tahoe CA
530-544-8888
Rent a boat and cruise around on beautiful Lake Tahoe with your pup. Dogs are allowed as long as you clean up any 'accidents' your pup may do on the boat. Boat rentals can be seasonal, so please call ahead. It's located in Tahoe Keys. To get there from Hwy 89 north, take Hwy 50 east. Turn left onto Tahoe Keys Blvd and then right at Venice Drive East. Park at the end of Venice Drive and follow the signs to the rental office.

**Tahoe Sport Fishing**
900 Ski Run Boulevard
South Lake Tahoe CA
530-541-5448
tahoesportfishing.com
This company offers sport fishing charters in the morning or afternoon and your pooch can go with you. Travel from the south shore up to the north shore of Lake Tahoe and back. They have six fishing boats ranging from 30 to 45 foot boats. They will clean and bag the fish (trout) you catch. They can even suggest local restaurants that will cook your fresh catch for you. Call ahead to make a reservation. Rates for the morning charter are $80 per person and for the afternoon charter are $70 per person.

**Tallac Historic Site**
Highway 89
South Lake Tahoe CA

r5.fs.fed.us/heritage/047.HTM
Three of Lake Tahoe's most luxurious playgrounds of the rich and famous were here on its south shore, including the Pope Estate. The Pope Estate is used as the interpretive center for the Tallac Historic Site; it features historic tours, exhibits, and living history programs. Dogs are allowed at the trails and outside of the historic buildings. The grounds are open year-round, though most of the buildings are open only during summer. From the intersection of highways 50 and 89 in South Lake Tahoe, travel 3.5 miles west on Highway 89. The entrance and parking areas are on the lake side of the highway.

**Reel Deal Sport Fishing & Lake Tours**
P.O. Box 1173
Tahoe City CA
530-318-6272

This dog-friendly fishing charter runs year-round. After your fishing trip, they will clean the fish for you. They also offer lake tours during the summer months. Rates are $75 per person during the winter and $80 per person during the summer. Dogs are allowed on both the fishing tour and the lake tours.

**Truckee River Raft Rentals**
185 River Road
Tahoe City CA
530-581-0123
truckeeriverraft.com
Your pooch is welcome to join you on a self-guided river rafting adventure. They just ask that your dog doesn't keep going in and out of the raft constantly because their nails can damage the raft. Enjoy a 2-3 hour leisurely, self guided, 5-mile float on the Truckee River from Tahoe City to the River Ranch Bar, Restaurant & Hotel. From there you can catch a free shuttle bus back to your car any time until 6 p.m. daily.

## Outdoor Restaurants
**Old Post Office Coffee Shop**
5245 North Lake Blvd
Carnelian Bay CA
530-546-3205
This restaurant is open for breakfast and lunch. They welcome well-behaved dogs at their outdoor seats. Dogs need to be leashed while sitting at the table with you.

**Brockway Bakery**
8710 North Lake Blvd
Kings Beach CA
530-546-2431
brockwaybakery.com/
Grab one of the several outdoor tables at this bakery and enjoy. It's located on Hwy 28 in Kings Beach. Leashed dogs are allowed at their outside dining area.

**Char-Pit**
8732 N Lake Blvd
Kings Beach CA
530-546-3171

char-pit.com
This restaurant serves barbecue. Dogs are allowed at the outdoor tables. The restaurant has outdoor tables only in the summer.

### Jamba Juice
4000 Lake Tahoe Blvd. #33
Lake Tahoe CA
530-544-8890
jambajuice.com
All natural and organic ingredients, no high-fructose corn syrup, 0 grams trans fat, no artificial preservatives, a healthy helping of antioxidants, vitamins, and minerals, and fresh whole fruit and fruit juices set the base for these tasty and healthy beverages. Their organic Hot Blends provides a new spin on coffee, green or chai tea, and hot chocolate;plus they offer probiotic fruit and yogurt Blends. Additionally, they feature organic steel-cut oatmeal prepared fresh every morning, all natural salads, wraps, sandwiches, and grab n' go specialties. They also offer healthy community support through fundraisers, special sales, and school lunch programs. Leashed, well mannered dogs are allowed at their outside dining area.

### Auld Dubliner
The Village at Squaw Valley
Olympic Valley CA
530-584-6041
aulddubliner.com
Auld Dubliner is an authentic Irish Pub was actually built in Ireland, dismantled, shipped to Olympic Valley and reassembled. Enjoy Irish cuisine at the outdoor patio with your dog.

### Big Daddy's Burgers
3490 Lake Tahoe Blvd/H 50
South Lake Tahoe CA
530-541-3465
This eatery specializes in hamburgers and other American type fare. During the summer season they offer outside dining. Your leashed, well mannered pet is welcome to join you at the outdoor tables.

### Izzy's Burger Spa
2591 Highway 50
South Lake Tahoe CA
530-544-5030
izzysburgerspa.com/
This burgers and barbecue eatery welcomes at their outdoor tables.

### Meyer's Downtown Cafe
3200 Highway 50
South Lake Tahoe CA
530-573-0228
This dog-friendly cafe is off Highway 50 in Meyers, before entering South Lake Tahoe. They are open Tuesday thru Saturday from 6 am until 2 pm.

### Nikkis Restaurant
3469 Lake Tahoe Blvd
South Lake Tahoe CA
530-541-3354
nikkischaatcafe.com/
Dogs are allowed at the outdoor tables. This café specializes in E. Indian and American cuisine and is located near the shoreline of Lake Tahoe.

### Sno-Flake Drive In
3059 Harrison
South Lake Tahoe CA
530-544-6377
This is a great place for a burger or chicken sandwich. You can walk up to the outside order window and then sit on the small patio and enjoy your lunch or dinner. To get there from the intersection of Highways 50 and 89, take Hwy 50 south. It will be on y

### Sprouts Health Foods
3125 Harrison Avenue
South Lake Tahoe CA
530-541-6969
Dogs are allowed at the outdoor tables when weather permits. They are open daily from 8 am until 9 pm.

### Rosie's Cafe
571 North Lake Blvd
Tahoe City CA
530-583-8504
rosiescafe.com/
Enjoy a delicious breakfast, lunch or dinner on the porch at this cafe. It's located in Tahoe City off Hwy 28 which is located on the northwest shore of Lake Tahoe. Leashed dogs are allowed at their outside dining area.

### Tahoe House Bakery and Gourmet Store
625 W Lake Blvd
Tahoe City CA
530-583-1377
tahoe-house.com/
They offer fresh baked breads, pastries, coffee drinks, cookies, European style tortes, deli lunches fully prepared meals to go with gourmet cheeses, meats and more. Dogs are allowed at the outdoor tables.

### The Blue Agave
425 N Lake Blvd
Tahoe City CA
530-583-8113
tahoeblueagave.com/contact.htm
This Mexican eatery has seasonal outdoor seating and service. Leashed, well mannered dogs are allowed at the bar's outside tables. Just place your food and drink orders with the bartender.

### The Squeeze In
10060 Donner Pass Road
Truckee CA
530-587-9814
squeezein.com
This award-winning restaurant features a variety of specialty omelets, homemade soups, large fresh salads, signature sandwiches, burritos, and much more. They are open from 7 am until 2 pm. Leashed dogs are allowed at their outside dining area.

## Pet-Friendly Stores
### Scraps Dog Bakery
8675 N Lake Blvd/H 28
Kings Beach CA
530-546-2725
This doggy bakery and boutique offers healthy baked treats, quality foods, toys, and a variety of pet care products. Leashed dogs are welcome.

## Bone Jour-Gift Store
521 North Lake Blvd.
Tahoe City CA
530-581-2304
bone-jour.com
Dogs are welcome inside this specialty gift store for dogs, cats and people. They also have a selection of dog treats and toys. It is on the second story near Fiamma Restaurant. Bone Jour is located in Tahoe City on Hwy 28 which is on the northwest shore of Lake Tahoe.

## Scraps Dog Bakery
10344 Donner Pass Road,
Truckee, CA
Truckee CA
530-582-5044
This doggy bakery and boutique offers healthy baked treats, quality foods, toys, and a variety of pet care products. Leashed dogs are welcome.

## Dog-Friendly Beaches
### Coon Street Beach
Coon Street
Kings Beach CA

northtahoeparks.com/beaches
Located at the end of Coon Street, on the east side of Kings Beach is a small but popular dog beach. There are also picnic tables, barbecues and restrooms at this beach.

### Kiva Beach
Hwy 89
South Lake Tahoe CA
530-573-2600
tahoeactivities.com/kiva-beach/
This small but lovely beach is a perfect place for your pup to take a dip in Lake Tahoe. Dogs must be on leash. To get there from the intersection of Hwys 89 and 50, take Hwy 89 north approx 2-3 miles to the entrance on your right. Follow the road and towards the end, bear left to the parking lot. Then follow the path to the beach.

### Pebble Beach/Dog Beach
Hwy 89
Tahoe City CA

This beach is not officially called "pebble beach" but it is an accurate description. It is actually Elizabech Williams Beach. No sand at this beach, but your water-loving dog won't mind. The water is crisp and clear and perfect for a little swimming. It's not a large area, but it is very popular with many dogs. There is also a paved bike trail that is parallel to the beach. There was no official name posted for this beach, but it's located about 1-2 miles south of Tahoe City on Hwy 89. From Tahoe City, the beach and parking will be on your left. Dogs should be on leash on the beach.

## Off-Leash Dog Parks
### Bijou Dog Park
1201 Al Tahoe Blvd
S Lake Tahoe CA

Located at the Bijou Community Park, this doggy play area features separate fenced areas for small and large dogs, large grassy fields, natural areas, beautiful trees, pet sanitary stations, water, and benches. The park is closed Thursday mornings from 8 am until 10 am for upkeep. Dogs must be sociable, current on all vaccinations and license, and under their owner's control at all times. Dogs must be leashed when not in designated off-lead areas.

## Dog-Friendly Parks
### North Tahoe Regional Park
National Avenue
Kings Beach CA

In the summer this park is used for hiking and during the winter, it's used by cross-country skiers. There are about 3-4 miles of wooded trails at this park. Want to go for a longer hike? There is a National Forest that borders up to this

regional park and dogs are allowed on those trails as well. To get there, take Hwy 28 by Kings Beach to Gun Club Road (north). Turn left on Donner Road and then right on National Avenue. There is a large parking lot at the end. Dogs must be on a leash in the park.

### Squaw Valley USA
1960 Squaw Valley Rd
Olympic Valley CA
530-583-6985 (888 SNOW 3-2-1)
squaw.com
In the summer (non-snow season) you and your pup can hike on the trails at this ski resort. Both of you will feel very welcome at Squaw. You can take your dog into the lobby to purchase the tickets for the dog-friendly Cable Car ride and/or snacks. As for the trails, there are many miles of hiking trails. One of the main hikes is from High Camp to the main parking lot or visa versa. It's the trail designed for night skiing (follow the light posts). During the summer, Squaw Valley has several dog-friendly events like the Star Gazing and Full Moon Hikes where dogs are welcome. Dogs must be leashed at all times.

### Cove East
Venice Drive East
South Lake Tahoe CA

This short but nice path is located near the boat rentals and Tahoe Keys Resort. It's approximately 1-2 miles and will give your pup a chance to take care of business before hopping on board your rental boat. To get there from Hwy 89 north, take Hwy 50 east. Turn left onto Tahoe Keys Blvd and then right at Venice Drive East. Dogs must be leashed.

### Desolation Wilderness
Fall Leaf Lake Road
South Lake Tahoe CA
530-644-2349
This wilderness area is located in the Eldorado National Forest and has many access points.

One of the trailheads is located at Fallen Leaf Lake. See our Fallen Leaf Lake listing in South Lake Tahoe for more details. Dogs need to be leashed and please clean up after them.

## Eagle Falls
Hwy 89
South Lake Tahoe CA

This beautiful moderate to strenuous hiking trail in the Desolation Wilderness starts at Hwy 89 and goes up to Eagle Lake. This trail is pretty popular because it's about a 1 mile hike from the road to the lake. If you want a longer hike, you can go another 4-5 miles where there are 3 other lakes. Dogs must be leashed. To get there from the intersection of Hwys 50 and 89, take Hwy 89 north and go approximately 8 miles. The Eagle Falls Picnic Area and parking are on the left. Day and Camping Wilderness Permits are required. Go here early because it is extremely popular and parking spots fill up fast. There is a minimal fee for parking. Dogs must be on leash on the trail.

## Echo Lakes Trail
off Johnson Pass Road
South Lake Tahoe CA

See a variety of alpine lakes on this moderate rated trail. Take Highway 50 to Echo Summit and turn onto Johnson Pass Road. Stay left and the road will lead you to the parking area by Lower Echo Lake. For a short hike, go to the far end of Upper Echo Lake. A longer hike leads you to one of the many lakes further down the trail. Day hikers, pick up your permit at the self serve area just to the left of the Echo Lake Chalet. Dogs should always be on leash.

## Fallen Leaf Lake
Fallen Leaf Lake Rd off Hwy 89
South Lake Tahoe CA

There are some nice walking trails on the north shore of

Fallen Leaf Lake and the surrounding areas. To get there from the intersection of Hwys 89 and 50, take Hwy 89 north approximately 2.5 to 3 miles to Fallen Leaf Lake Rd. Turn left and in about 1/2 mile there will be parking on the right. The Fallen Leaf Lake Trail begins here. For a longer hike, there are two other options. For the first option, instead of taking the trailhead on the right, take the trail on the left side of Fallen Leaf Lake Rd. This trail is also known as the Tahoe Mountain Bike Trail. Option number two is to take Fallen Leaf Lake Rd further to the south side of Fallen Leaf Lake. Park at the Glen Alpine trailhead which offers about 3-4 miles of trails (parking is across from Lily Lake). There is also a trail here that heads off to the Desolation Wilderness which has miles and miles of trails. Dogs should be leashed.

## Truckee River Bike Path
Hwy 89
Tahoe City CA

This paved path starts at Tahoe City and heads towards Squaw Valley, paralleling Highway 89. It's about 5 miles each way with spots for your water dog to take a dip in the Truckee River (just be careful of any quick moving currents.) To get there, the path starts near the intersection of Hwys 89 and 28 in Tahoe City. You can also join the path 1/2 - 1 mile out of town by heading north on Hwy 89 and then there are 1 or 2 parking areas on the left side which are adjacent to the path. Dogs must be on leash.

## D. L. Bliss State Park
H 89/South Lake Tahoe
Tahoma CA
530-525-7277 (800-444-7275)
Donated by the D. L. Bliss family in 1929, this park of 744 acres displays the grandeur of the mountain building processes of Mother Earth and offers visitors spectacular

views of the surrounding area and deep into the lake. Dogs of all sizes are only allowed in developed areas, picnic grounds, and on paved roads. They are not allowed on the trails, beaches, or in the Vikingsholm area, and they must be inside a tent or vehicle from the hours of 10 pm to 6 am. Dogs must be under their owners control at all times, be on no more than a 6 foot leash, and be cleaned up after.

## Emerald Bay State Park
H 89/South Lake Tahoe
Tahoma CA
530-541-3030 (800-444-7275)
A National Natural Landmark, this beautiful state park is rich in its natural beauty, history, and geology, and features Vikingsholm, one of the best examples of Scandinavian architecture in the western hemisphere. The park is also home to Lake Tahoe's only island, Fannette Island, and there are a variety of recreational opportunities to pursue. Dogs of all sizes are allowed in developed areas, picnic grounds, and on paved roads. They are not allowed on the trails, beaches, or in the Vikingsholm area, and they must be inside a tent or vehicle from the hours of 10 pm to 6 am. Dogs must be under their owners control at all times, be on no more than a 6 foot leash, and be cleaned up after.

## Commemorative Overland Emigrant Trail
Alder Creek Road
Truckee CA
530-587-3558
This 15 mile moderate rated trail is located in the Tahoe National Forest. While the trail is open from May to November, it is most heavily used in the spring. The trail is popular with both hikers and mountain bikers. Pets must be either leashed or off-leash but under direct voice control. To get there from Interstate 80, take the Highway 89 North exit and go 2.3 miles to Alder Creek Road. Turn left and

go 3 miles. The trail starts on the south side of the road.

## Donner Memorial State Park
Highway 80
Truckee CA
530-582-7892
While dogs are not allowed at the China Cove Beach Area and the nature trail behind the museum, they are allowed on the rest of the trails at this park. Dogs are also allowed in the lake. Pets must be on leash at all times and please clean up after them. The park has campgrounds but they are undergoing renovation from 2003 to 2004. It is located off Highway 80 in Truckee.

## Glacier Meadow Loop Trail
Castle Peak
Truckee CA
530-587-3558
This .5 mile easy loop trail is located in the Tahoe National Forest and is used for hiking only. It is a very popular trail from June to October. Pets must be either leashed or off-leash but under direct voice control. To get there from I-80, exit Castle Peak, on the south side of I-80, turn left. The trailhead is on the east side of the parking lot.

## Sandridge Lake Trail
Castle Peak
Truckee CA
530-587-3558
This 6 miles one way moderate rated trail is located in the Tahoe National Forest. From June to October, it is heavily used for hiking and horseback riding. Pets must be either leashed or off-leash but under direct voice control. To get there from I-80, exit Castle Peak, on the south side of I-80, turn left. The trailhead is on the east side of the parking lot.

## Summit Lake Trail
Castle Peak
Truckee CA
530-587-3558
This 2 mile easy rate trail is located in the Tahoe National Forest and is popular for hiking,

mountain biking and horseback riding. The trail is most frequently used from June to October. Pets must be either leashed or off-leash but under direct voice control. To get there from Interstate 80, exit Castle Peak, on the south side of I-80, turn left. The trailhead is on the east side of the parking lot.

## Events
### The Bark Festival
The Village at Squaw Valley
Olympic Valley CA
530-583-WAGS (9247)
tailsbythebay.stores.yahoo.net/
This unique arts and wine festival for pets is an annual September event. Activities consist of live music, fine wines and foods, animal themed art, pet contests, fashion shows, massages and more. The event is held in the Village at Squaw Valley and is brought to you by Tails by the Lake. Friendly dogs of all sizes are welcome. They must be leashed, cleaned up after, and have currant vaccinations and tags.

## Veterinarians
### Avalanche Natural Health Office for Pets and Kennel
964 Rubicon Trail
South Lake Tahoe CA
530-541-3551
This veterinary hospital specializes in alternative medicine. If you need some doggy day care, they also offer a kennel that is open all year, including Sundays. They are very flexible with all aspects of the boarding kennel including hours and accommodating special needs pets usually with no extra charge.

### The Doctors Office for Pets
10939A Industrial Way Suite #101
Truckee CA
530-587-5144

thedoctorsofficeforpets.com/
In addition to a full list of services for the care of your pet, they also have their own pharmacy and carry a number of health and dental care products, flea and tick control products, toys, first aid supplies, lean and hypoallergenic treats, and custom home care. They are open Monday to Friday from 8 am until 5 pm.

## Emergency Veterinarians
### Carson Tahoe Veterinary Hospital
3389 S. Carson Street
Carson City CA
775-883-8238
Weekdays 7:30 am - 6 pm. Emergencys will be seen 24 hours with an additional $60 emergency fee.

## Humane Society or SPCAs
### Humane Society of Truckee-Tahoe
P.O. Box 9041
Truckee CA
530.587.5948
hstt.org
The Humane Society of Truckee-Tahoe is dedicated to saving and improving the lives of pets through adoptions, community spay/neuter services, and humane education programs. We are a volunteer-run organization and welcome new volunteers!

## Lancaster

## Pet-Friendly Extended Stay Hotels
### Homewood Suites Lancaster
2320 Double Play Way
Lancaster CA
661-723-8040
This upscale all suite hotel offers large, comfortable suites

for longer stays and/or temporary housing needs;plus numerous on site amenities for all level of travelers and a convenient location to local sites of interest. Dogs are allowed for an additional one time fee of $100 per pet.

## Outdoor Restaurants
### Camille's Sidewalk Cafe
43901 15th Street W
Lancaster CA
661-940-5878
A vision of healthier, tastier foods inspired the idea for the freshly made salads, gourmet wraps and sandwiches, drinks, desserts, and coffees that are offered at all of Camille's Cafes. Dogs are allowed to sit with you at your outdoor table. Dogs must be attended to at all times, well behaved, and leashed.

### Giovanni's Italian Deli & Delights
42035 10th Street W
Lancaster CA
661-729-1300
giovannisitaliandeli.com/
This eatery features a variety of fine Italian cuisine. Leashed, well mannered dogs are welcome at their outside dining area.

## Pet-Friendly Stores
### PetSmart Pet Store
44551 Valley Central Way
Lancaster CA
661-942-7330
Your licensed and well-behaved leashed dog is allowed in the store.

## Off-Leash Dog Parks
### Hull Park Dog Park
30th Street W
Lancaster CA
661-723-6000
There is a fenced 1 acre, grassy site for pooches at this park with picnic tables, benches, and doggy drinking fountains. Dogs

must be healthy, sociable, current on all vaccinations and license with tags on collar, and under their owner's control at all times. Dogs must be leashed when not in designated off-lead areas.

## Lassen Volcanic Area

## Dog-Friendly Hotels
### River Inn
1710 Main Street
Susanville CA
530-257-6051
This pet-friendly Susanville motel is 18 km away from the Bizz Johnson National Recreation Trail. It offers guest rooms with free Wi-Fi and serves a daily continental breakfast.
A cable TV and a seating area are provided in each air-conditioned room at River. Complete with a microwave the dining area also has a refrigerator. Featuring a bath or shower private bathrooms feature a hairdryer and free toiletries.
A vending machine featuring cold beverages is located at River Inn Susanville. Coffee tea and hot chocolate are available each morning.
An array of activities can be enjoyed on site or in the surroundings including hiking. The property offers free parking.
Eagle Lake is 42 km away from this motel. Lassen Volcanic National Park is 106 km away.

### Super 8 Motel - Susanville
2975 Johnstonville Rd.
Susanville CA
530-257-2782 (800-800-8000)
Dogs are welcome at this hotel.

## Dog-Friendly Attractions
### Volcanic Legacy Byway

P. O. Box 832
Mount Shasta CA
866-722-9929
volcaniclegacybyway.org
This 500 mile journey of volcanic discovery includes regions of Crater Lake; Upper Klamath Lake and Klamath Falls; the Klamath Basin, Tulelake and Lava Beds; Butte Valley Region; Mt Shasta Region; the Waterfalls Region - McCloud and Burney; Hat Creek Rim; Mt Lassen Region, and the Lake Almanor Region. From features like active geothermal features and majestic mountains to underground magma conduits, this scenic byway also shares a wide variety of other scenic wonders, historical facts and figures, educational opportunities, an amazing diversity of wildlife, and recreational activities. The website gives detailed information on Visitor Centers, points of interests, maps, and more. Dogs are allowed to accompany their owners on the byway; they must be kept leashed and signage should be in place if dogs are not allowed in certain areas.

### Spatter Cones Trail
Highway89
Old Station CA
530-257-2151
Located in the Lassen National Forest, this self-guided interpretive trails runs about 1.5 miles and it details the volcanic activities here and how life adapted to it; 3 of the 4 types of volcanoes in the world are seen along this trail. The trail is open and in the summer is quite hot; it's important to bring water for hound and human, and maybe even some paw protectors for the pooch. The trailhead parking lot is located at the Sanitary Dump Station on Highway 89 in Old Station. Dogs must be kept leashed unless under strict voice control.

## Outdoor Restaurants
### Higher Ground Coffee

28526 Highway44
Shingletown CA
530-474-1913
This coffee shop offers organic coffee and teas;plus freshly made salads, specialty sandwiches, breakfast items, pastries, and more. They are open Monday thru Friday from 6 am until 5 pm and on Saturday from 7 am until 2 pm. Leashed dogs are welcome at their outside tables.

**Frosty Mill**
605 Ash Street
Susanville CA
530-257-5894
This hamburger and ice cream joint makes to order and can take a while but the food is pretty good. Dogs can join you at the picnic tables in the front patio of the building. They are open daily from 11 am until 8:30 pm most of the year and they close at 8 pm for winter hours.

# Pet-Friendly Stores
**Trading Post & Merchantile**
28555 Highway44
Shingletown CA
530-474-4577
This trading post store will allowed well mannered, leashed dog to explore the store with their owners. The store is open Monday thru Saturday from 10 am until 6 pm.

**Margie's Book Nook**
722 Main Street
Susanville CA
530-257-2392
margiesbooknook.net
Margie's Book Nook has a mix of new and used books. They may welcome your well-behaved, leashed dog into the store to shop with you.

**Treats Dog Company**
707 Main Street
Susanville CA
530-257-3161
Looking for pet supplies, leashes, food, toys or other essentials for your dog? This store on Main Street welcomes you and your dog to shop.

# Dog-Friendly Parks
**Lassen Volcanic National Park**
Highway36
Mineral CA
530-595-4480 (877-444-6777)
nps.gov/lavo/index.htm
This park has the distinction of being home to all 4 types of volcanoes found in the world. It is also home to the Lassen Smelowskia Flower that blooms no where else on earth. Much can be seen from their seasonal 29 mile auto-tour (Highway89) that offers turn-outs for some great views of the park including Lassen Peak, Brokeoff Mountain, the Devastated Area, and more. Dogs are allowed in the park in developed areas, campgrounds, picnic areas, established roadways, and scenic pull-outs. There are no additional pet fees for camping, and they must be kept on a leash no longer than 6 feet, be cleaned up after promptly, and be current on vaccinations. Dogs may not be left unattended outside or left in a vehicle that may be a hazard to the pet without proper cooling, food, and water. Dogs are not allowed in buildings, in any body of water, in the backcountry, or on any trails or boardwalks. For those who would like to hike with their pets, this park is surrounded by great hiking places such as the Caribou Wilderness to the East, the Thousand Lakes Wilderness to the North, or the Spencer Meadows and Mill Creek Trails just outside the park off of Highway 36.

**Lassen Volcanic National Park**
PO Box 100
Mineral CA
530-595-4444
nps.gov/lavo/
This national park does not really have much to see or do if you bring your pooch, except for staying overnight at the

campgrounds. However, the dog-friendly Lassen National Forest surrounds the national park. At the national forest you will be able to find dog-friendly hiking, sightseeing and camping. Pets must be leashed and attended at all times. Please clean up after your pet.

**Biz-Johnson Trail**
2950 Riverside Drive
Susanville CA
530-257-0456
blm.gov/visit/bizz-johnson
This 25 mile trail follows the old Fernley and Lassen Branch Line of the Southern Pacific Railroad. It begins in Susanville at 4,200 feet and climbs 1,300 feet to a high point of 5,500 feet. Following the Susan River, the trail crosses over the river many times and passes through a former railroad tunnel. During the winter the trail's upper segment, located west of Highway 36, is used for cross-country skiing. Dogs on leash are allowed. Please clean up after your dog. To check on current trail conditions, call the Eagle Lake BLM Field Office at 530-257-0456. To get there from Alturas, take Highway 36 to Susanville. Follow Main Street to the stop light at the bottom of the hill by historic Uptown Susanville. Turn left on Weatherlow Street which becomes Richmond Road. Follow Richmond Road .5 miles across Susan River to Susanville Railroad Depot Trailhead and Visitor Center.

**Lassen National Forest**
Highways 44 and 89
Susanville CA
530-257-4188
fs.usda.gov/lassen
Within this forest watch prong-horn antelope, drive four-wheel trails into high granite country or discover spring wildflowers on foot. Dogs are allowed on leash in the park other than in the Subway Cave. In the past, dogs were allowed in the Subway Cave but they are not anymore. If you want to check out the lava tube take a self-guided tour of

the Subway Cave. Someone will need to stay outside the cave entrance with the dog. There are a number of hiking trails around the cave area. Be sure to bring a flashlight, as there are no other sources of light underground. Subway Cave is located near the town of Old Station, 1/4 mile north of the junction of Highway 44 & 89 across from Cave Campground. The temperature inside the cave remains a cool 46 degrees F. year around. The cave is open late May through October and closed during the winter months. Or try a hike instead. Try the Spattercone Trail which explores the volcanic landscape and how life adapts to it. Three of the four kinds of volcanoes in the world can be seen along the Spattercone Trail. The trailhead and parking area are located at the Sanitary Dump Station across the highway form Hat Creek Campground on Highway 89 in Old Station. The trail has a round-trip distance of 1.5 miles. This trail is not shaded, so during the summer, try an early morning or late afternoon walk. For information about other miles of trails throughout this beautiful National Forest, stop by any National Forest Offices in Susanville including the Eagle Lake Ranger District Office located at 477-050 Eagle Lake Road in Susanville.

## Lathrop

### Dog-Friendly Hotels
**Days Inn Lathrop**
14750 S. Harlan Road
Lathrop CA
209-982-1959 (800-329-7466)
Dogs are welcome at this hotel.

**Holiday Inn Express Lathrop - South Stockton**
15688 South Harlan Road
Lathrop CA
209-373-2700 (877-270-6405)
Dogs of all sizes are allowed.

Dogs are allowed for a pet fee of $200.00 per pet per stay.

**Quality Inn & Suites Lathrop**
16855 Harlan Road
Lathrop CA
209-858-1234 (877-424-6423)
The Quality Inn and Suites is newly renovated hotel that offers guests spacious rooms with complimentary high speed internet access.

Dogs up to 30 pounds are allowed. Dogs are allowed for a pet fee of $20.00 per pet per night.

## Lava Beds Area

### Dog-Friendly Attractions
**Medicine Lake Highlands**
Forest Road 49
Tulelake CA
530-233-5811
Medicine Lake is an area of moderately sloping to steep mountains. It was formed by a volcano and is one of North America's most unique geological areas. One feature is that it has no known outlets but yet its water remains clean and clear. It lies within the volcanic caldera of the largest shield volcano in North America. Obsidian and pumice are common in the highlands. For thousands of years Native Americans have used these substances to make tools and other objects. More recently astronauts prepared in the pumice fields for their first landing on the moon. To get there from the town of Tulelake, take Highway 139 south and follow the signs to the Tulelake National Wildlife Refuge. Then go south through the Lava Beds National Monument. Follow the signs along Forest Road 49 to Medicine Lake. This route is part of the Modoc Volcanic Scenic Byway.

**Volcanic Historic Loop**
State Route 139
Tulelake CA
530-233-5811
This self-guided auto tour takes you through an area of "rocks that float and mountains of glass" and into one of the most unique geological regions in North America. The tour begins in the town of Tulelake and heads south on State Route 139. At CR97 head west and go into the town of Tionesta. Head another 12 miles west and you will come to Glass Mountain. The glass flow is from glassy dacite and rhyolitic obsidian that flowed from the same vent simultaneously without mixing. At nearby Medicine Lake you can camp, sightsee, swim, fish or take photos. Medicine Lake was once the center of a volcano. Native Americans believed that the lake had special healing powers. About 4.5 miles southeast of the lake is the Burnt Lava Flow. It is estimated to be about 200 years old which makes it the youngest lava flow in the area. The tour continues, but goes into the Lava Beds National Monument which only allows dogs in parking lots and along roads. In the national forest, which is the majority of this tour, dogs on leash are allowed on trails and in lake waters. Please clean up after your pets. For more information including maps, contact the Modoc National Forest office at 800 West 12th Street, Alturas, CA 96101, 530-233-5811.

### Dog-Friendly Parks
**Lava Beds National Monument**
1 Indian Well
Tulelake CA
530-667-2282
nps.gov/labe/
This national park does not really have much to see or do if you bring your pooch, except for staying overnight at the Indian Well Campground. However, the dog-friendly Modoc National

Forest surrounds the national park. At the national forest you will be able to find dog-friendly hiking, sightseeing and camping. See our Modoc National Forest listing in this region for more details. Pets must be leashed and attended at all times. Please clean up after your pet.

## Medicine Lake Campground
County Road 49
Tulelake CA
530-667-2246
Located in the Modoc National Forest at 6,700 feet, this camp area gives everyone a view of the 640 acre tree-lined lake, and the fascinating surrounding landscape created from ancient volcanic activity. There is a variety of land and water recreational activities available and close access to other points of interest. Dogs of all sizes are allowed for no additional fee. Dogs must be on no more than a 6 foot leash at all times, and be leashed and cleaned up after. Dogs are allowed throughout the park and on the trails except in the picnic areas and the designated swimming area.

## Lebec

### Dog-Friendly Hotels
**Holiday Inn Express Hotel Frazier Park**
612 Wainwright Court
Lebec CA
661-248-1600 (877-270-6405)
Dogs of all sizes are allowed. Dogs are allowed for a pet fee of $20.00 per pet per night.

### Ramada Limited Lebec
9000 Countryside Ct
Lebec CA
661-248-1530
Dogs of all sizes are allowed. There is a pet fee of $10 per pet per night.

## Dog-Friendly Parks
### Fort Tejon State Historic Park

Interstate 5
Lebec CA
661-248-6692
Fort Tejon State Historical Park is a nice stop on the Grapevine about 77 miles north of LA. Dogs on leash can roam the grounds, the historical cabins and the small museum.

## Leggett

### Dog-Friendly Attractions
**Leggett Drive Thru Tree**
Hwy 1 and Hwy 101
Leggett CA

Want to drive your car through a tunnel built into a redwood tree? If your car isn't too wide you can do this at the Leggett Drive Thru Tree. From 101 take the turn-off at Hwy 1 towards Ft Bragg and immediately turn left onto Drive-Thru-Tree Road. The entrance is on your right in about 1/4 mile. There is a $5 fee to enter per vehicle. There is also a gift shop and picnic tables at the site.

### Dog-Friendly Parks
**Standish-Hickey State Recreation Area**
69350 Highway 101
Leggett CA
707-925-6482
While dogs are not allowed on the trails, they are allowed on a few fire roads. The fire roads are not passable during the winter because of the river, but are fine during the summer months. The fire roads are located near the campground and near the main swimming hole. Dogs are also allowed in the water. Pets must be on leash and please clean up after them. The park is located 1.5 miles north of Leggett on Highway 101.

## Lemoore

### Dog-Friendly Hotels
**Travelodge Lemoore**
877 East D Street
Lemoore CA
559-924-1261 (800-329-7466)
Dogs of all sizes are allowed. Dogs are allowed for a pet fee of $25.00 per pet per night.

## Lincoln

### Dog-Friendly Hotels
**Holiday Inn Express Hotel & Suites Lincoln-roseville Area**
155 Ferrari Ranch Road
Lincoln CA
916-644-3440 (877-270-6405)
Dogs up to 40 pounds are allowed. Dogs are allowed for a nightly pet fee.

### Off-Leash Dog Parks
**Auburn Ravine Dog Park**
1300 Green Ravine Dr
Lincoln CA
916-624-6808
The amenities at this dog park include 2.5 fenced acres for dogs to run off-leash, potable water, handicap accessible, parking, and limited seating. The park is open from dawn to dusk and is closed Wednesdays until 12pm.

## Lindsay

### Dog-Friendly Hotels
**Super 8 Lindsay Olive Tree**
390 N. Highway 65
Lindsay CA
559-562-5188 (800-800-8000)
Dogs up to 35 pounds are

allowed. Dogs are allowed for a pet fee of $10 per pet per stay.

## Little River

### Outdoor Restaurants
**Wild Fish Restaurant**
7750 N Highway 1
Little River CA
949-720-9925
wild-fish.com
The Wild Fish Restaurant, located at 7750 N Highway 1 in Little River, CA, is open Tuesday through Saturday for lunch & dinner. They have a changing menu with American, European and Asian flavors like hot and sour seafood soup, clam chowder, halibut, steelhead and black cod. And as wines, being near to Anderson Valley wine country, they offer a large selection of local wines - the varietals famous in their region like Pinot Noir, Pinot Gris, Gewurztraminer and many more. They also have award-winning local micro-brewery beer and a great list of imports. Well-behaved, leashed dogs are allowed at the outdoor seats.

## Lompoc

### Dog-Friendly Hotels
**O'cairns Inn And Suites**
940 East Ocean Avenue
Lompoc CA
805-735-7731
Not Found.

### Dog-Friendly Attractions
**La Purisima Mission State Historic Park**
2295 Purisima Road
Lompoc CA
805-733-3713
lapurisimamission.org/
Number 11 of the 21 Spanish

missions of California, this historic 1787 site passes along a long and rich cultural and natural history, and guided tours as well as self-guided tours are available. Additionally, they have Living History Days and a variety of special events. They are open daily from 9 am until 5 pm except Thanksgiving, Christmas and New Year's Day. Leashed dogs are allowed.

### Pet-Friendly Stores
**Petco Pet Store - Lompoc**
717 North H St.
Lompoc CA
805-735-6436
Your licensed and well-behaved leashed dog is allowed in the store.

### Dog-Friendly Wineries and Vineyards
**Foley Estates Vineyard & Winery**
6121 E H 246
Lompoc CA
805-737-6222
foleywines.com
Open daily from 10am until 5pm - with the exception of select holidays, this beautiful winery produces a variety of world class Pinot Noir and Chardonnay wines available for tasting in their 3,500 square-foot tasting room and event center. Leashed, hound and human friendly dogs are welcome on the grounds and in the tasting room.

### Dog-Friendly Parks
**La Purisima Mission State Historic Park**
2295 Purisima Road
Lompoc CA
805-733-3713
lapurisimamission.org/
This mission was founded in 1787 and is one of the most completely resorted Spanish

missions in California. While dogs are not allowed in the buildings, they are allowed on the grounds and on miles of trails. Pets must be on a 6 foot or less leash and please clean up after them. The park is located about 2 miles northeast of Lompoc.

## Lone Pine

### Dog-Friendly Hotels
**Best Western Plus Frontier Motel**
1008 South Main Street
Lone Pine CA
760-876-5571 (800-780-7234)
Dogs up to 80 pounds are allowed. Up to two dogs are allowed per room.

**Comfort Inn Lone Pine**
1920 South Main Street
Lone Pine CA
760-876-8700 (877-424-6423)
Located at the base of the Eastern Sierra Nevada Mountains and home to Mt Whitney, Lone Pine is your gateway to

Dogs of all sizes are allowed. Dogs are allowed for a pet fee of $20.00 per pet per night. Two dogs are allowed per room.

### Dog-Friendly Attractions
**Alabama Hills**
Movie Road
Lone Pine CA
760-876-6222
lonepinechamber.org
Located west of the town of Long Pine, there is an area called Alabama Hills which features unusual rock formations. Since 1920 this area has been a favorite location for television and movie filmmakers. Over 250 movies, TV episodes and commercials have been filmed in this area. Movies like Gunga Din and Maverick were filmed here. A

partial list of stars who have been filmed at Alabama Hills includes Hopalong Cassidy, Roy Rogers, Humphrey Bogard, Susan Hayward, Spencer Tracy, Natalie Wood, Clint Eastwood, Kirk Douglas, John Wayne, Steve McQueen, Shelly Winters, Luci and Desi Arnaz, Willie Nelson and Mel Gibson. You can take yourself and your pooch on a self-guided auto tour of this area. Go 2.5 miles west of Lone Pine and turn north at Movie Road. At the corner of Movie and Whitney Portal Roads, you will find the Movie Plaque which commemorates the many movies filmed in the nearby hills. Go north .25 miles to the Roy Rogers Movie Flats, an area were hundreds of westerns and other movies were filmed. Go north .25 miles and turn east to Lone Ranger Canyon. This spot is another popular filming area and was where some scenes of the Lone Ranger was filmed. Go 2.25 miles to the southern loop to find Moonscape Views. Turn south on Horseshoe Meadow Road and go 1 mile to Gunga Din Canyon. The classic 1939 movie used locations in the first canyon to the east for filming. Go south for 3 miles to the Tuttle Creek Campground. It used for camping and as a fishing spot. Go 2 miles southeast to view The Needles Formation. It is a sharp spine of rocks north of the housing area. Then take Tuttle Creek Canyon Road down the canyon and back to Lone Pine. Pets on leash are allowed to walk around the view points. Please clean up after your pets. For more information, stop by the InterAgency Visitor Center at the intersection of Highways 395 and 136 in Lone Pine. The center is open daily from 8am to 4:30pm.

## Outdoor Restaurants
**Pizza Factory**
301 S Main Street/H 395
Lone Pine CA

760-876-4707
pizzafactory.com/locations.html

In addition to freshly handcrafted pizzas with fresh ingredients and their signature dough, this eatery also offers a variety of wraps, pastas, calzones, subs, and salads. Dogs are allowed at their outer tables;they must be leashed and well mannered.

## Dog-Friendly Parks
**Mt. Whitney Trail**
Whitney Portal Road
Lone Pine CA
760-876-6200
Dogs are allowed on the first eight miles of the main Mt. Whitney Trail in the Inyo National Forest, but not on the last three miles of the trail leading to the summit which is located in Sequoia/Kings Canyon National Park. Dogs must be leashed on this trail and please clean up after them. The national forest advises that people should be aware of the high elevation affect on dogs. There is no shade or cover available and the heat of the sun at higher elevations can be intense for pets. The trail is located 13 miles west of Lone Pine on Whitney Portal Road.

## Long Barn

## Dog-Friendly Parks
**Lyons Reservoir (Sugar Pine Railroad Grade) Trail**
Fraser Flat Road
Long Barn CA
209-586-3234
This 3 mile easy rated trail parallels the South Fork of the Stanislaus River and overlays the historic Sugar Pine Railroad System. Pets on leash are allowed and please clean up after them. This trail is located in the Stanislaus

National Forest. One access point to this trail is the Fraser Flat Campground. To get there, drive 3 miles north of Highway 108 at Spring Gap turnoff (Fraser Flat Road).

## Long Beach Area

### Dog-Friendly Hotels
**Hilton Long Beach & Executive Meeting Center Hotel**
701 West Ocean Boulevard
Long Beach CA
562-983-3400
This luxury hotel offers a number of on site amenities for business and leisure travelers, plus a convenient location to the World Trade Center, LAX and the Long Beach Airport, and it is located only 1 mile from the beach. Dogs up to 75 pounds are allowed for an additional fee of $20 per day per pet with a maximum fee of $75 per pet.

**Hotel Current**
5325 E Pacific Coast Highway
Long Beach CA
562-597-1341
With uber-modern design cabanas by the pool and a local shuttle the Hotel Current is a great place to relax while seeing the sights; this isn't a cookie cutter hotel. Constructed with eco-friendly materials each of the hotel's 143 rooms on two floors feature custom-designed contemporary furniture a flat-panel TV refrigerator microwave high-end linens modern art and free Wi-Fi. Some rooms have jetted tubs. Check your e-mail in the business center. Lounge in a cabana by the heated outdoor pool and keep your swimsuit dry with laundry on site. A free shuttle service will take you within a five mile radius of the hotel including a nearby fitness center where guests get free passes. Across the street from Recreation Park Golf Course Hotel Current is located one

mile from California State University's Long Beach campus with its Japanese Gardens. Head two miles east to tour the adobe homes at the historic Rancho Los Alamitos. The paved path along the shoreline is two-and-a-half miles south while the Museum of Latin American Art and eclectic shops in the East Village Arts District are three-and-a-half miles west. Attractions downtown including the Aquarium of the Pacific and the convention center with its performance venues are 15 minutes west. The Long Beach Airport is three miles north.

**The Westin Long Beach**
333 East Ocean Boulevard
Long Beach CA
562-436-3000 (888-625-5144)
This upscale hotel offers numerous on site amenities for business and leisure travelers, plus a convenient location to LAX, the Aquarium of the Pacific, and to many shopping, dining, and entertainment areas. One dog up to 40 pounds is allowed for no additional fee;there is a pet waiver to sign at check in.

# Pet-Friendly Extended Stay Hotels
**Extended Stay America - Los Angeles - Long Beach Airport**
4105 E. Willow St.
Long Beach CA
562-989-4601 (800-804-3724)
One dog is allowed per suite. There is a $25 per night additional pet fee up to $150 for an entire stay.

**Residence Inn By Marriott Long Beach**
4111 East Willow Street
Long Beach CA
562-595-0909
Dogs of all sizes are allowed. There is a $100 one time additional pet fee.

**Residence Inn Long Beach Downtown**
600 Queensway Drive

Long Beach CA
562-495-0700
Dogs of all sizes are allowed. There is a $100 one time additional pet fee.

# Dog-Friendly Attractions
**Catalina Explorer Ferry**
100 Aquarium Way, Pine Avenue Pier
Long Beach CA
877-432-6276
catalinaferry.com
Dogs are allowed to go on this ferry that provides service from the greater Los Angeles area to Catalina Island. There is no additional pet fee. Dogs must be leashed and muzzled, or crated. One pet per person is allowed, depending on space. Reservations are suggested. Hours of operation and tour schedules alter with the seasons.

**Catalina Express**
320 Golden Shore
Long Beach CA
800-360-1212
catalinaexpress.com/
Dogs are allowed on the boats to the Catalina Island at no additional fee. Dogs must be leashed and muzzled or crated while aboard. There is a limit of one pet per person. Reservations are recommended.

**Catalina Classic Cruises**
Berth 95
San Pedro CA
800-641-1004
Dogs are allowed on the boats to the Catalina Island at no additional fee. This boat only run seasonally, and reservations are recommended. Dogs must be leashed and muzzled or crated while aboard. There is a limit of one pet per person.

# Outdoor Restaurants
**Coffee Bean & Tea Leaf**
4925 E Second Street
Belmont Shore CA

562-930-0246
coffeebean.com
The coffee here is sourced globally from family coffee farms to procure only the top of 1% of Arabica beans. They offer 30+ varieties of coffee;the beans are roasted in small batches daily for freshness, and they also offer 20 varieties of teas that are hand-blended by their tea master. Additionally, they offer a variety of tasty sweets, powders, extracts, sauces, gifts, and cards. Leashed, well mannered dogs are allowed at their outside dining area.

**Chipotle**
5310 Lakewood Blvd/H 19
Lakewood CA
562-790-8786
chipotle.com
Specializing in organic, natural and unprocessed food, this Mexican Eatery offers fajita burritos, tacos, salads, and salsas. Dogs are allowed at the outdoor tables but you will need to order your food inside the restaurant and dogs must remain outside.

**Chipotle**
1800 Ximeno Avenue
Long Beach CA
562-597-0469
chipotle.com
Specializing in organic, natural and unprocessed food, this Mexican Eatery offers fajita burritos, tacos, salads, and salsas. Dogs are allowed at the outdoor tables but you will need to order your food inside the restaurant and dogs must remain outside.

**Coffee Bean & Tea Leaf**
6471 E Pacific Coast H/H 1
Long Beach CA
562-598-2198
coffeebean.com
The coffee here is sourced globally from family coffee farms to procure only the top of 1% of Arabica beans. They offer 30+ varieties of coffee;the beans are roasted in small batches daily for freshness, and they also offer 20 varieties of teas that are hand-blended by their tea

master. Additionally, they offer a variety of tasty sweets, powders, extracts, sauces, gifts, and cards. Leashed, well mannered dogs are allowed at their outside dining area.

**Coffee Bean & Tea Leaf**
4105 S Atlantic Avenue, Suite A

Long Beach CA
562-492-9020
coffeebean.com
The coffee here is sourced globally from family coffee farms to procure only the top of 1% of Arabica beans. They offer 30+ varieties of coffee;the beans are roasted in small batches daily for freshness, and they also offer 20 varieties of teas that are hand-blended by their tea master. Additionally, they offer a variety of tasty sweets, powders, extracts, sauces, gifts, and cards. Leashed, well mannered dogs are allowed at their outside dining area.

**Coffee Bean & Tea Leaf**
6344 Spring Street, Suite 1
Long Beach CA
562-429-4139
coffeebean.com
The coffee here is sourced globally from family coffee farms to procure only the top of 1% of Arabica beans. They offer 30+ varieties of coffee;the beans are roasted in small batches daily for freshness, and they also offer 20 varieties of teas that are hand-blended by their tea master. Additionally, they offer a variety of tasty sweets, powders, extracts, sauces, gifts, and cards. Leashed, well mannered dogs are allowed at their outside dining area.

**Coffee Bean & Tea Leaf**
1996 Ximeno Avenue, Space 101
Long Beach CA
562-494-3514
coffeebean.com
The coffee here is sourced globally from family coffee farms to procure only the top of 1% of Arabica beans. They offer 30+ varieties of coffee;the beans are roasted in small batches daily

for freshness, and they also offer 20 varieties of teas that are hand-blended by their tea master. Additionally, they offer a variety of tasty sweets, powders, extracts, sauces, gifts, and cards. Leashed, well mannered dogs are allowed at their outside dining area.

**Coffee Bean & Tea Leaf**
1212 Bellflower Blvd
Long Beach CA
562-985-3477
coffeebean.com
The coffee here is sourced globally from family coffee farms to procure only the top of 1% of Arabica beans. They offer 30+ varieties of coffee;the beans are roasted in small batches daily for freshness, and they also offer 20 varieties of teas that are hand-blended by their tea master. Additionally, they offer a variety of tasty sweets, powders, extracts, sauces, gifts, and cards. Leashed, well mannered dogs are allowed at their outside dining area.

**Johnny Rockets**
245 Pine Avenue
Long Beach CA
562-983-1332
johnnyrockets.com/
All the American favorites can be found here: A fun retro, all-American decor and atmosphere, juicy burgers, specialty sandwiches, crispy fries, hand-dipped malts and shakes (dark chocolate ones too), fresh baked apple pies, tasty vegetarian choices, and something for all ages. Leashed, friendly dogs are allowed at their outside dining area.

**Kafe Neo**
2800 E. 4th St.
Long Beach CA
562-987-1210
kafeneolb.com
Kafe Neo offers greek food, including drinks, pita sandwiches, appetizers, salads, and more! Well-behaved, leashed dogs are welcome on the outdoor patio.

**Omelette Inn**
108 W 3rd Street
Long Beach CA
562-437-5625
omeletteinn.com
Breakfast and lunch specialties beginning with quality ingredients and made from scratch foods are the offerings here. Leashed, friendly dogs are allowed at their outside dining area.

**Roots Gourmet**
6473 E. Pacific Coast H/H 1
Long Beach CA
562-795-7668 (ROOT)
rootsgourmet.com
Creating an experience in Pan-Latin dining, this eco-friendly and health conscious eatery draws upon several generations of recipes and prepares their foods from scratch with the freshest natural ingredients available. Local and sustainable is the focus;they offer vegetarian/vegan and gluten free items;they serve 100% organic Fair Trade coffee/tea and fresh juices;specialty cakes and other bakery treats are prepared in-house, and then there is "Thank Dog it's Friday" where your canine companion gets a free hot meal with a purchase of an entree. Dogs must be friendly and leashed.

**Royal Cup Cafe**
194 Marina Drive #101
Long Beach CA
562-363-6069
royalcupcafe.com/
Some of the offerings of this cafe include a wide variety of beverages, all natural fresh fruit smoothies, gourmet Panini sandwiches, fresh baked goods, catering services, an artistic and musical venue, and a full calendar of events. Leashed, friendly dogs are allowed at their outside dining area.

**Royal Cup Cafe**
994 Redondo Avenue
Long Beach CA
562-987-1027
royalcupcafe.com/
Some of the offerings of this

116

cafe include a wide variety of beverages, all natural fresh fruit smoothies, gourmet Panini sandwiches, fresh baked goods, catering services, an artistic and musical venue, and a full calendar of events. Leashed, friendly dogs are allowed at their outside dining area.

## Royal Cup Cafe
994 Redondo Avenue
Long Beach CA
562-987-1027
royalcupcafe.com
Royal Cup Cafe in Long Beach, California offers gourmet coffee and teas. Smoothies, soups, sandwiches, and salads are also avaliable. Your pet is welcome to join you on the outside patio.

## Stefano's
429-C Shoreline Village Drive
Long Beach CA
562-437-2880
stefanoslongbeach.com
This Italian eatery offers selection of pizzas, calzones, salads, sandwiches, desserts, and happy hour specials Monday to Friday. Leashed, friendly dogs are allowed at their back patio dining area, and all pups get a free doggy treat and water.

## The Small Cafe
5656 E 2nd st
Long Beach CA
562-434-0226
thesmallcafe.com
The Small Cafe serves breakfast, lunch, and dinner omelets, scrambles, burgers, and more. There are three outdoor seats, which well-behaved, leashed dogs are allowed at. No alcohol at the outdoor seats.

## Whole Foods Market
6550 E. Pacific Coast Highway
Long Beach CA
562-598-8687
wholefoods.com/
This full service natural food market offers both natural and organic food. You can get food from the deli and bring it to an outdoor table where your well-behaved leashed dog is

welcome.

## Z Pizza
4612 E 2nd Street
Long Beach CA
562-987-4500
zpizza.com
Specializing in organically and internationally inspired pizzas, this pizzeria cooks their pizzas on hot bricks in a fire baked oven. They feature a 100% certified organic gluten free wheat crust, homemade organic sauces and ingredients, fresh produce, and additive-free meats. They also offer gourmet salads, sandwiches, and catering services. Leashed, well mannered dogs are allowed at their outside tables.

## Z Pizza
5718 E 7th Street
Long Beach CA
562-498-0778
zpizza.com
Specializing in organically and internationally inspired pizzas, this pizzeria cooks their pizzas on hot bricks in a fire baked oven. They feature a 100% certified organic gluten free wheat crust, homemade organic sauces and ingredients, fresh produce, and additive-free meats. They also offer gourmet salads, sandwiches, and catering services. Leashed, well mannered dogs are allowed at their outside tables.

## The Lighthouse Deli
508 W 39th Street
San Pedro CA
310-548-3354
Hearty breakfasts and lunches, a large and diverse menu, alfresco dining, and light ocean breezes are just some of the offerings of this restaurant/deli. They are open daily from 7 am until 9 pm. Leashed, friendly dogs are allowed at their outside dining area.

## Pet-Friendly Stores
## Petco Pet Store - Lakewood

5215 Lakewood Blvd
Lakewood CA
562-630-2888
Your licensed and well-behaved leashed dog is allowed in the store.

## Ace Billings Paint and Hardware
5004 E 2nd Street
Long Beach CA
562-439-2113
This hardware store knows how to treat their four-legged customers too; they can expect doggy treats. Dogs must be friendly, well behaved, under their owner's control at all times, leashed, and cleaned up after.

## Centinela Feed and Supplies
4700 Pacific Coast H/H 1
Long Beach CA
562-494-1660
centinelafeed.com
Specializing in natural, holistic, and raw pet foods, this pet supply store also provides healthy treats, quality supplements, pet care supplies, low-cost vaccination clinics, frequent in-store events, and a knowledgeable staff. Leashed pets are welcome.

## Cosmopawlitan Boutique
4107 Viking Way
Long Beach CA
562-354-6040.
cosmopawlitanboutique.com/
From the treats and quality foods to the toys, to the comfy beds, blankets, fashions, and trendy accessories, this doggy boutique carries a wide range of care items and what they don't have they will special order. They also offer dog massage, portrait painting, photography, weekly events, and support groups. Leashed, friendly dogs are welcome in the store.

## Holly's Hallmark Shop
5012 E 2nd Street
Long Beach CA
562-434-5291
rubios.com/
Friendly, well-behaved dogs are welcome at this card, stationary, and gift shop. Dogs must be under their owner's control and

leashed at all times.

## PetSmart Pet Store
7631 Carson
Long Beach CA
562-938-8056
Your licensed and well-behaved leashed dog is allowed in the store.

## Petco Pet Store - Long Beach
6500 Pacific Coast Hwy
Long Beach CA
562-493-6083
Your licensed and well-behaved leashed dog is allowed in the store.

## Pussy & Pooch Pethouse and Pawbar
4818 E. 2nd Street
Long Beach CA
562-434-7700
pussyandpooch.com
Pussy & Pooch's Long Beach location offers a "Pawbar", where pets can sit and enjoy freshly made treats and meals to order. The pet boutique and retail store sells a variety of organic, raw, dehydrated, and traditional pet food and treats, organic pet grooming and spa products, pet beds, carriers, and pet fashion and accessories. They also have pet grooming, and "mutt mingles" every month.

## Runner's High
5375 E Second Street
Long Beach CA
562-430-7833
This store is an outfitter for running, walking, and triathlon needs. Well behaved dogs are welcome to come into the store with you. Dogs must be trained, under owners control at all times, and leashed.

## Wiskers Pet Beastro and Bowteek
4818 East 2nd Street
Long Beach CA
562-433-0707
wiskers.com/Belmont.html
This specialty retailer hosts special events throughout the year in addition to offering a variety of collars,leads, toys, gifts/games for their owners,

treats, pet necessities, and they also offer a pet hand painted portrait service. Pets are welcome and treats are always accessible for pets on their best behavior. Dogs must be housetrained, leashed, and picked up after.

## Petco Pet Store - San Pedro
852 North Western Ave.
San Pedro CA
310-521-8131
Your licensed and well-behaved leashed dog is allowed in the store.

## PetSmart Pet Store
2550 Cherry Ave
Signal Hill CA
562-988-0832
Your licensed and well-behaved leashed dog is allowed in the store.

# Dog-Friendly Beaches
## Rosie's Dog Beach
between Roycroft and Argonne Avenues
Long Beach CA
562-570-3100
hautedogs.org/beach.html
This 3 acre off-leash unfenced dog beach is the only off-leash dog beach in Los Angeles County. It is open daily from 6am until 8pm. It opened on August 1, 2003. The "zone" is 235 yards along the water and 60 yards deep. There is a fresh water fountain called the "Fountain of Woof" which is located near the restrooms at the end of Granada Avenue, near the Dog Zone. Only one dog is allowed per adult and dog owners are entirely responsible for their dog's actions. The beach is located between Roycroft and Argonne avenues in Belmont Shore, Long Beach. It is a few blocks east of the Belmont Pier and Olympic pool. From Ocean Blvd, enter at Bennett Avenue for the beachfront metered parking lot. The cost is 25 cents for each 15 minutes from 8am until 6pm daily. Parking is free after 5pm in the beachfront

lot at the end of Granada Avenue. You can check with the website http://www.hautedogs.org for updates and additional rules about the Long Beach Dog Beach Zone.

# Off-Leash Dog Parks
## Recreation Park Dog Park
7th St & Federation Dr
Long Beach CA
562-570-3100
Licensed dogs over four months are allowed to run leash-free in this area by the casting pond. As usual with all dog parks, owners are responsible for their dogs and must supervise them at all times. The Recreation Park Dog Park is located off 7th Street and Federation Drive behind the Casting Pond. It is open daily until 10 p.m. Thanks to one of our readers for recommending this park.

## Knoll Hill Off-Leash Dog Park
200 Knoll Drive
San Pedro CA
310-514-0338
This 2.5 acre off-leash dog park is open during daylight hours. This park is located at the south end of the 110 Freeway. Exit 110 at Highway 47 east and exit quickly at N. Front St/Harbor Blvd. Go north on N. Front St to Knoll Drive on the left. The dog park is managed by Peninsula Dog Parks, Inc.

# Events
## Haute Dog Easter Parade and Pet Adobtion Fair
4900 E Livingston Drive
Long Beach CA
562-439-3316
hautedogs.org/
For a $10 pre-entry fee per dog ($15 on the day of the event) you can take part in this popular annual Easter Parade sponsored by Haute Dogs, where hundreds of costumed canines present their very best for the judges and thousands of spectators in this 12-block

sidewalk pooch parade. The parade begins and ends at Livingston Park, and is just the beginning of a wide variety of contests and events with various prize categories, vendors, an adoption fair, doggie demonstrations, and more. Dogs (no puppies) must have their rabies and vaccinations current, wear ID tags, and be leashed and cleaned up after at all times. No aggressive dogs or dogs in heat are allowed.

## Haute Dog Howl'oween Parade
4900 E Livingston Drive
Long Beach CA
562-439-3316
hautedogs.org/
For a $10 entry fee per dog you can take part in this popular annual Howl'oween event sponsored by the Community Action Team and Haute Dogs. Hundreds of dogs present their very best costumes for the judges and thousands of spectators in this 12-block sidewalk pooch parade. The parade begins and ends at Livingston Park, and is just the beginning of a wide variety of contests and events with various prize categories, vendors, an adoption fair, a kids' costume contest, doggie demonstrations, and more. Dogs (no puppies) must have their rabies and vaccinations current, wear ID tags, and be leashed and cleaned up after at all times. No aggressive dogs or dogs in heat are allowed.

## Airports
### Long Beach Airport (LGB)

Long Beach CA

lgb.org/
There is an outside pet relief area north of the baggage claim area.

## Emergency Veterinarians
### Evening Pet Clinic

6803 Cherry Ave
Long Beach CA
562-422-1223
Mon - Fri 8 am - 9 pm with certain lunch and dinner breaks, Sat - Sun 12 - 6 pm.

## Rescue Organizations
### Sunny Saints, California Saint Bernard Rescue
P.O. Box 870
Bellflower CA
562.619.2059
sunnysaints.org
Sunny Saints Saint Bernard Rescue is a 501(c)3 non-profit, all-volunteer organization dedicated to rescuing and rehoming adoptable lost, abandoned, or surrendered Saint Bernards.

## Other Organizations
### BARK (Beach Animals Reading with Kids)
P O Box 91478
Long Beach CA
562-235-8835
BARK is a volunteer program that encourages children to increase their reading skills and self-confidence by reading aloud to certified therapy dogs. We visit over 100 libraries and schools in LA and Orange Counties. Contact us to have your dog evaluated and to join BARK. We find the locations, provide supplies, and make it easy for you to volunteer with your dog!

### BARK (Beach Animals Reading with Kids)
2294 Roswell Avenue, Rear Unit
Long Beach CA
562-235-8835
bark.web.officelive.com
BARK is a volunteer program that encourages children to increase their reading skills and self-confidence by reading aloud to certified therapy dogs. Contact us to have your dog certified as a therapy dog or to join BARK. We find the locations, provide supplies, and

make it easy for you to volunteer with your dog!

### Friends of El Dorado Dog Park
P.O. Box 8620
Long Beach CA
562-212-8396
eldoradodogparkfriends.org
While our immediate goal is to raise funds to create, maintain andimprove a spacious off-leash dog park in El Dorado Regional Park, wehope, in addition, to make this park more than just a field of fencedgrass and trees.El Dorado Dog Park will not only provide off-leash playtime for dogs and their owners, but will also be a place to encourage responsible pet ownership and to build community awareness of animal welfare issues through classes and special events.

### Haute Dogs
5209 E. The Toledo #1
Long Beach CA
562-439-3316
HauteDogs.org
The Haute Dog organization (pronounced HOT) is a diverse and growing network of dog owners, lovers, educators, rescuers and supporters. Our common bond has resulted in a unique and lively community of folks who share some qualities of our favorite dogs: devotion, spirit and tenacity.

## Los Angeles

### Dog-Friendly Hotels
### Best Western Plus Dragon Gate Inn
818 N. Hill St.
Los Angeles CA
213-617-3077 (800-780-7234)
Dogs up to 80 pounds are allowed. There is a $20 per day pet fee up to $100 for the week. Up to two dogs are allowed per room.

### Four Points By Sheraton Los Angeles International Airport

9750 Airport Blvd
Los Angeles CA
310-645-4600 (888-625-5144)
This upscale hotel offers
numerous on site amenities for
business and leisure travelers,
plus a convenient location to
shopping, dining, beaches, and
entertainment areas. Dogs up to
40 pounds are allowed for an
additional fee of $35 per night
per pet;there is a pet policy to
sign at check in and dogs may
not be left alone in the room.
Capacity for the rooms is 4 -
including the pets.

**Hilton Checkers Los Angeles**
535 South Grand Avenue
Los Angeles CA
213-624-0000
Located in the heart of the city's
financial and business district,
this European-style boutique
hotel offers an ideal destination
for the business traveler with
amenities for all level of
travelers. Dogs up to 75 pounds
are allowed for an additional one
time fee of $75 per pet.

**Intercontinental Los Angeles
Century City**
2151 Avenue Of The Stars
Los Angeles CA
310-284-6500 (877-698-9593)
Dogs up to 25 pounds are
allowed. Dogs are allowed for a
pet fee of $200.00 per pet per
stay.

**Kimpton Everly Hotel**
1800 Argyle Avenue
Los Angeles CA
213-279-3532
Rooms exude a relaxed
sophisticated feel and offer
views of the Hollywood Hills at
the non-smoking Kimpton Everly
Hotel which features a rooftop
pool and an on-site restaurant.
Walls of windows surround the
light-filled lobby at the non-
smoking Kimpton a high-rise
property that boasts 216 rooms
all with elegant neutral decor
and contemporary touches. Wi-
Fi and flat-panel TVs keep
guests connected while minibars
robes and hairdryers are
practical conveniences. The
restaurant serves casual locally

sourced fare all day and the
bar provides a space to mingle
over snacks. After refueling
guests check out the views
from the rooftop pool which is
bordered by loungers and
private cabanas. The concierge
and 24-hour front desk are
happy to help out with local
tips. Other services on the
property include a business
center a fitness room and free
bicycle rentals. Pets are
welcome at no extra charge
and can borrow pet beds and
bowls. Valet parking is
available. A couple of blocks
off the Hollywood Freeway the
Kimpton is within a mile of the
TCL Chinese Theater Capitol
Records and the Hollywood
Walk of Fame. You'll find
shops and restaurants within a
few blocks and high-end
perusing a 15-minute drive
away on Rodeo Drive in
Beverly Hills. Family-friendly
attractions include Universal
Studios Hollywood the Griffith
Observatory and Dodger
Stadium each within 20
minutes of the hotel. Don't miss
gazing at the Pacific Ocean in
Venice Beach or at the Santa
Monica Pier each a half-hour
drive. Guests reach Los
Angeles International Airport in
24 miles and Bob Hope Airport
in eight miles.

**Kimpton Hotel Palomar Los
Angeles Beverly Hills**
10740 Wilshire Boulevard
Los Angeles CA
310-475-8711 (800-472-8556)
Offerings of this luxury resort
hotel include an Arts in Motion
decor, a sophisticated
ambiance, more than 40 earth
friendly practices throughout
the hotel, and fresh local,
sustainable, and seasonally
inspired food and beverages.
Pets of all sizes are welcome
here for no additional fee;the
pet registration form is
available on line. Pets need to
be declared at the time of
registration and there is a pet
form to fill out at the time of
arrival. Canine guests are also
greeted with their own leash,

bed and dinnerware to use
during their stay, gourmet treats,
and various other amenities
available through their specialty
pet packages. Pet walking and
pet sitting services can be
arranged by the hotel.

**Kimpton Hotel Wilshire**
6317 Wilshire Boulevard
Los Angeles CA
323-852-6000
The non-smoking Kimpton Hotel
Wilshire is a contemporary
boutique property offering a
rooftop pool on-site dining and
stylish rooms. The seven-story
non-smoking Kimpton Hotel
Wilshire features 74 rooms and
suites where you can relax on a
chaise lounge mix a drink from
the minibar and enjoy beautiful
city views. In-room amenities
include flat-panel HDTVs media
ports for Wi-Fi and TV
connectivity for your personal
electronics as well as cozy
robes and gourmet
coffeemakers. On the
landscaped rooftop patio you
can refresh in the heated pool
lounge in a private cabana or
chat with colleagues over
cocktails and dinner with views
of the Hollywood Hills. Room
service is also an option. The
business center is open 24
hours a day and Wi-Fi and valet
parking are available for an
extra charge. The hotel is in the
heart of the Miracle Mile/Mid-
Wilshire Corridor less than 10
minutes from shopping and
entertainment in Beverly Hills
and West Hollywood. Downtown
Los Angeles Century City and
the beaches of Santa Monica
and Venice are all within a 20-
minute drive. Los Angeles
International Airport is 15 miles
away.

**La Quinta Inn & Suites Lax**
5249 West Century Boulevard
Los Angeles CA
310-645-2200 (800-531-5900)
Dogs of all sizes are allowed.
There are no additional pet fees,
but they request to meet your
pet, and to know that you have a
pet so as to inform
housekeeping. Dogs must be

leashed and cleaned up after.

**Sheraton Gateway Los Angeles**
6101 West Century Boulevard
Los Angeles CA
310-642-1111 (888-625-5144)
This upscale hotel offers numerous on site amenities for business and leisure travelers, plus a convenient location to shopping, dining, beaches, and entertainment areas. Dogs up to 40 pounds are allowed for an additional 1 time $50 pet fee;there is a pet policy to sign at check in.

**Sheraton Grand Los Angeles**
711 South Hope Street
Los Angeles CA
213-488-3500 (888-625-5144)
Located central to many of the areas star attractions, activities and sports venues, this upscale hotel also sits in the heart of the financial district offering many features for both leisure and business travelers. Dogs up to 85 pounds are allowed for an additional $25 one time fee per pet, and there is a pet policy to sign at check in. Dogs may not be left alone in the rooms.

**Sls Hotel A Luxury Collection Hotel Beverly Hills**
465 South La Cienega Boulevard
Los Angeles CA
310-247-0400 (800-325-3535)
This sophisticated upscale hotel offers amenities for all level of travelers - including on site entertainment, a stunning rooftop pool, 24/7 concierges services, and a restaurant offering modern, seasonally influenced, organic cuisine. Dogs up to 40 pounds (larger dogs at hotel's discretion) are allowed for an additional one time pet fee of $125 per room. There is a pet waiver to sign at check in and their canine guests receive a welcome package with bedding, a bowl and mat, turndown treats, waste bags, doggy toys, and a list of pet related places to visit.

**Sls Hotel A Luxury Collection**

**Hotel Beverly Hills**
465 South La Cienega Boulevard
Los Angeles CA
310-247-0400
You'll feel like a high roller with super swank suites a full spa a rooftop pool and Beverly Hills just around the corner at the SLS Hotel a Luxury Collection Hotel. Innovative decor and custom-designed furnishings give this seven-story luxury hotel an edge. All 61 suites feature free Wi-Fi flat-panel TVs iPod docks pillowtop mattresses and monogrammed linens; select suites even include their own fitness equipment. An upscale restaurant and bar serve three meals a day or you can order in with 24-hour room service. You can work around the clock in the business center or get that chiseled L.A. look in the 24-hour ultramodern health club. Reward yourself with a decadent treatment in the full-service spa which features a couples' room designed by Philippe Starck. Palm a cocktail by the rooftop pool where valets fulfill your every wish. Or for an added fee reserve a private cabana complete with minibar TV and DVD player. Valet parking is available for an added fee. Located between Beverly Hills and La Brea the hotel is a five-minute walk from the Beverly Center Mall. Or you can shop until you drop on Rodeo Drive two miles west. The Los Angeles County Museum of Art Craft and Folk Art Museum and La Brea Tar Pits are two miles east. People watch at The Grove an outdoor shopping mall two miles away or head to Grauman's Chinese Theater 15 minutes north. The Staples Center L.A. Live entertainment complex and convention center are 20 minutes east and Santa Monica Pier is 15 minutes west. Los Angeles International Airport is 12 miles south.

**Sofitel Los Angeles At Beverly Hills**

8555 Beverly Boulevard
Los Angeles CA
310-278-5444
With a to-die-for location and stunning decor Sofitel Los Angeles at Beverly Hills is a luxury escape for our guests.This 295-room high-rise offers exciting decor in its public rooms and elegant simplicity in its rooms which have flat-panel HDTVs Wi-Fi internet access iPod docking stations floor-to-ceiling windows that frame fantastic nighttime city views work desks rainfall showers and lots of little touches to make you feel special like a free newspaper waiting for you every weekday morning. Non-smoking accommodations can be requested. The hotel has a new restaurant Esterel which serves contemporary French cuisine. The lounge offers signature cocktails either inside or outside on the terrace. The business center keeps you in touch but if you need a break try the heated outdoor pool gym and full-service spa with a long menu of hair and skin treatments. Pets are welcome at Sofitel with some restrictions. Parking is available for an extra fee. Sofitel Los Angeles is located five minutes from West Hollywood and Sunset Boulevard. The hotel is across the street from Beverly Center shopping center. Both downtown Los Angeles and Santa Monica Pier can be reached in 20 minutes and Los Angeles International Airport is 12 miles away.

**Super 8 Motel - Los Angeles/alhambra**
5350 S. Huntington Dr.
Los Angeles CA
323-225-2310 (800-800-8000)
Dogs of all sizes are allowed. Dogs are allowed for a pet fee of $20 per pet per night.

**The Westin Bonaventure Hotel & Suites Los Angeles**
404 South Figueroa Street
Los Angeles CA
213-624-1000 (888-625-5144)
Dogs up to 40 pounds are allowed. There is no additional

pet fee.

## The Westin Los Angeles Airport
5400 West Century Blvd
Los Angeles CA
310-216-5858 (888-625-5144)
A stylish upscale hotel, guests can enjoy a number of on site amenities for all level of travelers;plus they offer a convenient location to major business, shopping, dining, and entertainment areas. One dog up to 40 pounds is allowed for no additional fee;there is a pet policy to sign at check in.

## Travelodge Hotel At Lax Airport
5547 W. Century Blvd
Los Angeles CA
310-649-4000
Dogs of all sizes are allowed. There is a pet fee of $20 for the first pet and $5 for each additional pet.

## W Los Angeles - West Beverly Hills
930 Hilgard Avenue
Los Angeles CA
310-208-8765 (877-946-8357)
Located between world class beaches and world class shopping venues, this hotel also offers on-site amenities that include farm-fresh seasonal dining and a lush botanical setting. Dogs up to 40 pounds are allowed for an additional fee of $125 for the 1st night per pet, then $25 per night per pet thereafter. There is a pet policy to sign at check in. Canine guests are greeted with a welcome amenity package that includes a custom pet bed, food/water bowls with a mat, a Pet-in-Room sign, and special turndown treats.

## Pet-Friendly Extended Stay Hotels
### Extended Stay America - Los Angeles - Lax Airport
6531 S Sepulveda Blvd
Los Angeles CA
310-568-9337 (800-804-3724)

One dog is allowed per suite. There is a $25 per night additional pet fee up to $150 for an entire stay.

### Residence Inn Beverly Hills
1177 South Beverly Drive
Los Angeles CA
310-228-4100
Dogs of all sizes are allowed. There is a $100 one time additional pet fee.

## Dog Businesses
### K9 Loft
2170 W Sunset Blvd
Los Angeles CA
213-484-6006
k9loft.com/echopark/
In addition to offering a wide variety of pet food, treats, grooming supplies, toys, and various pet supplies, K9 Loft also offers daycare, boarding, grooming, dental cleaning, training, shuttles, and adoption services. Dogs are welcome to come in and check out all the treats and fun stuff. K9 Loft

## Dog-Friendly Attractions
### Griffith Observatory
2800 East Observatory Road
Los Angeles CA
323-664-1181
griffithobs.org/
This observatory has been a major Los Angeles landmark since 1935. Star-gazing dogs are not allowed inside the observatory but may be on the lawns. Located across the parking lot from the Observatory is the Griffith Park snack shop and the Mt. Hollywood Trail (about 6 miles of dog-friendly trails). To get to there, take Hwy 5 to the Los Feliz Blvd exit and head west. Turn right on Hillhurst or Vermont Ave (they merge later). Go past the Bird Sanctuary and Greek Theater. Stay on Vermont Ave and you'll come to the Griffith Observatory.

### Hollywood Walk of Fame

6100-6900 Hollywood Blvd.
Los Angeles CA
323-469-8311
Want to see the star that was dedicated to your favorite actor or actress? Then come to the famous Hollywood Walk of Fame on Hollywood Blvd. You'll find about 10-15 blocks of Hollywood stars placed in the sidewalks of Hollywood Blvd. Don't forget to look at the famous Footprints located at the Mann's Chinese Theater on Hollywood Blvd between Orange Drive and Orchid Ave. Want to see an actor or actress receive their honorary Star? This takes place throughout the year in front of the Hollywood Galaxy General Cinemas on Hollywood Blvd. It may be too crowded for your pup to stand directly in front of the Cinemas, but you can see plenty from across the street. Just make sure your dog is comfortable with crowds yelling and cheering as this will happen when the actor/actress arrives. Our pup was able to see Nicolas Cage receive his Hollywood Star. To find out the schedule of when the next actor/actress will receive their star, look at the Hollywood Chamber of Commerce website at http://www.hollywoodchamber.net or call 323-469-8311. To get to the Hollywood Walk of Fame, take Hwy 101 North past Sunset Blvd. Take the next exit which is Hollywood Blvd and turn left (west). The Hollywood Stars are located on 6100-6900 Hollywood Blvd. between Gower Street and Sycamore Avenue.

### Travel Town Museum
5200 Zoo Drive
Los Angeles CA
323-662-5874
Dogs are allowed on leash throughout the Travel Town Museum in Griffith Park in LA. Here you can see many trains, cars and lots more.

## Outdoor Restaurants
### Lazy Dog Restaurant & Bar

122

8800 Apollo Way
Downey CA
562-354-4910
lazydogrestaurants.com/dogs/info
Known for it's dog-friendly patio, the Lazy Dog offers your dog a complimentary bowl of water, and a menu consisting of grilled hamburger patty, chicken breast or brown rice. They just ask that you respect their common sense rules while your dog is dining there. This is as dog-friendly as dining gets. For the humans in your party there is hamburger, steak, salads and some great desserts.

**The Coffee Bean & Tea Leaf**
8550 Firestone Blvd
Downey CA
562-904-7016
coffeebean.com
The coffee here is sourced globally from family coffee farms to procure only the top of 1% of Arabica beans. They offer 30+ varieties of coffee;the beans are roasted in small batches daily for freshness, and they also offer 20 varieties of teas that are hand-blended by their tea master. Additionally, they offer a variety of tasty sweets, powders, extracts, sauces, gifts, and cards. Leashed, well mannered dogs are allowed at their outside dining area.

**Alcove**
1929 Hillhurst Avenue
Los Angeles CA
323-644-0100
alcovecafe.com/
Set among garden patios and terraces, this cafe and bakery sources many fresh local vendors to offer their customers hand-roasted coffee/espresso, daily baked goodies, fine wines from around the world, and a full menu of hearty dishes. Leashed, well mannered dogs are allowed at their outside tables.

**Baja Fresh Mexican Grill**
7919 Sunset Blvd.
Los Angeles CA
323-436-3844
bajafresh.com

This Mexican restaurant is open for lunch and dinner. They use fresh ingredients and making their salsa and beans daily. Some of the items on their menu include Enchiladas, Burritos, Tacos Salads, Quesadillas, Nachos, Chicken, Steak and more. Well-behaved leashed dogs are allowed at the outdoor tables.

**Baja Fresh Mexican Grill**
5757 Wilshire Blvd.
Los Angeles CA
323-549-9080
bajafresh.com
This Mexican restaurant is open for lunch and dinner. They use fresh ingredients and making their salsa and beans daily. Some of the items on their menu include Enchiladas, Burritos, Tacos Salads, Quesadillas, Nachos, Chicken, Steak and more. Well-behaved leashed dogs are allowed at the outdoor tables.

**Chipotle**
3748 S Figueroa Street
Los Angeles CA
213-765-9068
chipotle.com
Specializing in organic, natural and unprocessed food, this Mexican Eatery offers fajita burritos, tacos, salads, and salsas. Dogs are allowed at the outdoor tables but you will need to order your food inside the restaurant and dogs must remain outside.

**Chipotle**
110 S Fairfax Avenue
Los Angeles CA
323-857-0608
chipotle.com
Specializing in organic, natural and unprocessed food, this Mexican Eatery offers fajita burritos, tacos, salads, and salsas. Dogs are allowed at the outdoor tables but you will need to order your food inside the restaurant and dogs must remain outside.

**Coffee Bean & Tea Leaf**
3183 Wilshire Blvd #115A
Los Angeles CA

213-381-6853
coffeebean.com
The coffee here is sourced globally from family coffee farms to procure only the top of 1% of Arabica beans. They offer 30+ varieties of coffee;the beans are roasted in small batches daily for freshness, and they also offer 20 varieties of teas that are hand-blended by their tea master. Additionally, they offer a variety of tasty sweets, powders, extracts, sauces, gifts, and cards. Leashed, well mannered dogs are allowed at their outside dining area.

**Coffee Bean & Tea Leaf**
3810 Wilshire Blvd Suite 110C
Los Angeles CA
213-388-9763
coffeebean.com
The coffee here is sourced globally from family coffee farms to procure only the top of 1% of Arabica beans. They offer 30+ varieties of coffee;the beans are roasted in small batches daily for freshness, and they also offer 20 varieties of teas that are hand-blended by their tea master. Additionally, they offer a variety of tasty sweets, powders, extracts, sauces, gifts, and cards. Leashed, well mannered dogs are allowed at their outside dining area.

**Coffee Bean & Tea Leaf**
801 W 7th Street
Los Angeles CA
213-622-9748
coffeebean.com
The coffee here is sourced globally from family coffee farms to procure only the top of 1% of Arabica beans. They offer 30+ varieties of coffee;the beans are roasted in small batches daily for freshness, and they also offer 20 varieties of teas that are hand-blended by their tea master. Additionally, they offer a variety of tasty sweets, powders, extracts, sauces, gifts, and cards. Leashed, well mannered dogs are allowed at their outside dining area.

**Coffee Bean & Tea Leaf**
210 E Olympic Blvd, #102

123

Los Angeles CA
213-749-5746
coffeebean.com
The coffee here is sourced globally from family coffee farms to procure only the top of 1% of Arabica beans. They offer 30+ varieties of coffee;the beans are roasted in small batches daily for freshness, and they also offer 20 varieties of teas that are hand-blended by their tea master. Additionally, they offer a variety of tasty sweets, powders, extracts, sauces, gifts, and cards. Leashed, well mannered dogs are allowed at their outside dining area.

**Coffee Bean & Tea Leaf**
10401 Santa Monica Blvd
Los Angeles CA
310-234-8411
coffeebean.com
The coffee here is sourced globally from family coffee farms to procure only the top of 1% of Arabica beans. They offer 30+ varieties of coffee;the beans are roasted in small batches daily for freshness, and they also offer 20 varieties of teas that are hand-blended by their tea master. Additionally, they offer a variety of tasty sweets, powders, extracts, sauces, gifts, and cards. Leashed, well mannered dogs are allowed at their outside dining area.

**Coffee Bean & Tea Leaf**
6255 W Sunset Blvd, Suite 170
Los Angeles CA
323-962-7078
coffeebean.com
The coffee here is sourced globally from family coffee farms to procure only the top of 1% of Arabica beans. They offer 30+ varieties of coffee;the beans are roasted in small batches daily for freshness, and they also offer 20 varieties of teas that are hand-blended by their tea master. Additionally, they offer a variety of tasty sweets, powders, extracts, sauces, gifts, and cards. Leashed, well mannered dogs are allowed at their outside dining area.

**Coffee Bean & Tea Leaf**

9541 W Pico Blvd
Los Angeles CA
310-282-9907
coffeebean.com
The coffee here is sourced globally from family coffee farms to procure only the top of 1% of Arabica beans. They offer 30+ varieties of coffee;the beans are roasted in small batches daily for freshness, and they also offer 20 varieties of teas that are hand-blended by their tea master. Additionally, they offer a variety of tasty sweets, powders, extracts, sauces, gifts, and cards. Leashed, well mannered dogs are allowed at their outside dining area.

**Coffee Bean & Tea Leaf**
11698 San Vicente Blvd
Los Angeles CA
310-442-1019
coffeebean.com
The coffee here is sourced globally from family coffee farms to procure only the top of 1% of Arabica beans. They offer 30+ varieties of coffee;the beans are roasted in small batches daily for freshness, and they also offer 20 varieties of teas that are hand-blended by their tea master. Additionally, they offer a variety of tasty sweets, powders, extracts, sauces, gifts, and cards. Leashed, well mannered dogs are allowed at their outside dining area.

**Coffee Bean & Tea Leaf**
11913 W Olympic Blvd
Los Angeles CA
310-914-9564
coffeebean.com
The coffee here is sourced globally from family coffee farms to procure only the top of 1% of Arabica beans. They offer 30+ varieties of coffee;the beans are roasted in small batches daily for freshness, and they also offer 20 varieties of teas that are hand-blended by their tea master. Additionally, they offer a variety of tasty sweets, powders, extracts, sauces, gifts, and cards. Leashed, well mannered

dogs are allowed at their outside dining area.

**Fred's 62**
1850 N Vermont Ave
Los Angeles CA
323-667-0062
fred62.com/
This retro-kitsch diner will allow friendly, leashed dogs at the outdoor tables.

**Golden Road Brewing**
5410 W San Fernando Road
Los Angeles CA
213-373-HOPS (4677)
goldenroad.la/
With a focus and commitment to producing sustainably created craft beers, this brewery features a variety of Anytime Beers, Custom IPA, and Limited Release beers. They serve up fresh locally sourced food to compliment their craft brews, and they also offer daily specials, 20 revolving beers on tap, growlers, weekly specials, and various special events. Leashed, well mannered dogs are allowed at their outside dining area.

**Good Microbrew and Grill**
922 Lucille Avenue
Los Angeles CA
323-660-3645
Dogs are allowed at the outdoor tables. They will also provide a bowl of water for your dog.

**Griffith Park snack stand**
Vermont Ave
Los Angeles CA

This is a basic snack stand but what makes it nice is the fact that it's in Griffith Park between the Griffith Observatory and the Mt. Hollywood Trail. Your pup can't go in the Observatory, but can walk up the outside stairs to the roof and check out the

**Hollywood Blvd restaurants**
Hollywood Blvd.
Los Angeles CA

While you are looking at the Stars on the Hollywood Walk of Fame at Hollywood Blvd., you can take a lunch or snack break

124

at one of the many outdoor cafes that line this popular street. Many of them only have a few tables, but you should be able to find one.

## Home
2500 Riverside Drive
Los Angeles CA
323-669-0211
homelosfeliz.com
Home serves a variety of soups, salads, burgers, seafood, and more. They offer Breakfast, Lunch, and Dinner. They allow pets on their patio. One of our readers says "A great courtyard patio area. Covered booths keep the sun at bay as well as light sprinkles in the winter. On the weekends There will usually be 6+ tables with dogs at any given time. Good service and good food (and a pretty good happy hour too)"

## Il Capriccio on Vermont
1757 N Vermont Avenue
Los Angeles CA
323-662-5900
This fine Italian restaurant offers indoor and outdoor dining service. Dogs are allowed at the outdoor tables. They must be well behaved, under owner's control at all times and leashed.

## Jamba Juice
11911 San Vincente Blvd, #100
Los Angeles CA
310-476-5823
jambajuice.com
All natural and organic ingredients, no high-fructose corn syrup, 0 grams trans fat, no artificial preservatives, a healthy helping of antioxidants, vitamins, and minerals, and fresh whole fruit and fruit juices set the base for these tasty and healthy beverages. Their organic Hot Blends provides a new spin on coffee, green or chai tea, and hot chocolate;plus they offer probiotic fruit and yogurt Blends. Additionally, they feature organic steel-cut oatmeal prepared fresh every morning, all natural salads, wraps, sandwiches, and grab n' go specialties. They also offer healthy community support

through fundraisers, special sales, and school lunch programs. Leashed, well mannered dogs are allowed at their outside dining area.

## Johnnie's New York Pizza
10251 Santa Monica Blvd
Los Angeles CA
310-553-1188
johnniesnypizza.com/
This restaurant serves Italian/American food. Leashed dogs are allowed at the outdoor tables on the sidewalk part.

## Johnny Rockets
131 S Central Avenue
Los Angeles CA
213-687-8206
johnnyrockets.com/
All the American favorites can be found here: A fun retro, all-American decor and atmosphere, juicy burgers, specialty sandwiches, crispy fries, hand-dipped malts and shakes (dark chocolate ones too), fresh baked apple pies, tasty vegetarian choices, and something for all ages. Leashed, friendly dogs are allowed at their outside dining area.

## Lala's Argentine Grill
7229 Melrose Avenue
Los Angeles CA
323-934-6838
lalasgrill.com/
Argentinean favorites with an infusion of fine California cuisine are the specialty of this eatery. They also offer a full list of wines, specialty cocktails, and brews. Leashed dogs are allowed at their outside dining area.

## Le Figaro Bistro
1802 N Vermont Avenue
Los Angeles CA
323-662-1587
figarobistrot.com/
A Bistro, boulangerie, and lounge, this authentic French restaurant and deli offers an in-house bakery, a standard bistro menu, a full bar with daily happy hours, a warm Parisian ambiance, and alfresco dining. Leashed, well mannered dogs

are allowed at their outside tables.

## Leaf Organics
11938 W Washington Blvd
Los Angeles CA
310-397-0700
leaforganics.com
This 100% raw, vegan, and organic eatery features fresh healthy cuisine that includes smoothies, soups, salads, wraps, signature dishes, desserts, and more. They also offer Sunday brunches, catering services, and a variety of classes. Leashed, well mannered dogs are welcome at their outside dining area.

## Lulu's Cafe
7149 Beverly Blvd
Los Angeles CA
323-938-6095
luluscafelosangeles.com/
Lulu's Cafe offers a variety of sandwiches, pasta, soups, salads, pancakes, and more. Well-behaved, leashed dogs are allowed on the patio outside the cafe. One of our readers says "Excellent sidewalk cafe. They always bring your dog a bowl of water without having to ask."

## Mel's Drive-In
8585 Sunset Blvd.
Los Angeles CA
310-854-7200
melsdrive-in.com/
This 24 hour West Hollywood restaurant serves you and your pup breakfast, lunch or dinner outside.

## Millie's Restaurant
3524 W Sunset Blvd
Los Angeles CA
323-664-0404
This eatery has been serving up comfort foods with a healthy twist since the mid-1920s. Foods are prepared from scratch using the freshest, local ingredients available;the coffee is freshly ground for each pot, and breads are baked fresh every day. Leashed dogs are allowed at their outside tables.

## The Coffee Bean & Tea Leaf
135 N Larchmont

Los Angeles CA
323-469-4684
coffeebean.com
The coffee here is sourced globally from family coffee farms to procure only the top of 1% of Arabica beans. They offer 30+ varieties of coffee;the beans are roasted in small batches daily for freshness, and they also offer 20 varieties of teas that are hand-blended by their tea master. Additionally, they offer a variety of tasty sweets, powders, extracts, sauces, gifts, and cards. Leashed, well mannered dogs are allowed at their outside dining area.

**The Coffee Bean & Tea Leaf**
3726 S. Figueroa Street
Los Angeles CA
213-745-4963
coffeebean.com
The coffee here is sourced globally from family coffee farms to procure only the top of 1% of Arabica beans. They offer 30+ varieties of coffee;the beans are roasted in small batches daily for freshness, and they also offer 20 varieties of teas that are hand-blended by their tea master. Additionally, they offer a variety of tasty sweets, powders, extracts, sauces, gifts, and cards. Leashed, well mannered dogs are allowed at their outside dining area.

**The Coffee Bean & Tea Leaf**
645 W 9th Street, #108
Los Angeles CA
213-627-3816
coffeebean.com
The coffee here is sourced globally from family coffee farms to procure only the top of 1% of Arabica beans. They offer 30+ varieties of coffee;the beans are roasted in small batches daily for freshness, and they also offer 20 varieties of teas that are hand-blended by their tea master. Additionally, they offer a variety of tasty sweets, powders, extracts, sauces, gifts, and cards. Leashed, well mannered dogs are allowed at their outside dining area.

**The Coffee Bean & Tea Leaf**

209 S Mednik Avenue
Los Angeles CA
323-263-9317
coffeebean.com
The coffee here is sourced globally from family coffee farms to procure only the top of 1% of Arabica beans. They offer 30+ varieties of coffee;the beans are roasted in small batches daily for freshness, and they also offer 20 varieties of teas that are hand-blended by their tea master. Additionally, they offer a variety of tasty sweets, powders, extracts, sauces, gifts, and cards. Leashed, well mannered dogs are allowed at their outside dining area.

**The Coffee Bean & Tea Leaf**
1500 Westwood Blvd
Los Angeles CA
310-470-4226
coffeebean.com
The coffee here is sourced globally from family coffee farms to procure only the top of 1% of Arabica beans. They offer 30+ varieties of coffee;the beans are roasted in small batches daily for freshness, and they also offer 20 varieties of teas that are hand-blended by their tea master. Additionally, they offer a variety of tasty sweets, powders, extracts, sauces, gifts, and cards. Leashed, well mannered dogs are allowed at their outside dining area.

**The Coffee Bean & Tea Leaf**
11049 Santa Monica Blvd
Los Angeles CA
310-473-6618
coffeebean.com
The coffee here is sourced globally from family coffee farms to procure only the top of 1% of Arabica beans. They offer 30+ varieties of coffee;the beans are roasted in small batches daily for freshness, and they also offer 20 varieties of teas that are hand-blended by their tea master. Additionally, they offer a variety of tasty sweets, powders, extracts, sauces, gifts, and cards. Leashed, well mannered

dogs are allowed at their outside dining area.

**The Coffee Bean & Tea Leaf**
2081 Hillhurst Avenue
Los Angeles CA
323-913-3457
coffeebean.com
The coffee here is sourced globally from family coffee farms to procure only the top of 1% of Arabica beans. They offer 30+ varieties of coffee;the beans are roasted in small batches daily for freshness, and they also offer 20 varieties of teas that are hand-blended by their tea master. Additionally, they offer a variety of tasty sweets, powders, extracts, sauces, gifts, and cards. Leashed, well mannered dogs are allowed at their outside dining area.

**The Coffee Bean & Tea Leaf**
3470 S Sepulveda Blvd
Los Angeles CA
310-313-0259
coffeebean.com
The coffee here is sourced globally from family coffee farms to procure only the top of 1% of Arabica beans. They offer 30+ varieties of coffee;the beans are roasted in small batches daily for freshness, and they also offer 20 varieties of teas that are hand-blended by their tea master. Additionally, they offer a variety of tasty sweets, powders, extracts, sauces, gifts, and cards. Leashed, well mannered dogs are allowed at their outside dining area.

**The Coffee Bean & Tea Leaf**
10401 Venice BlvdH 187
Los Angeles CA
310-842-9330
coffeebean.com
The coffee here is sourced globally from family coffee farms to procure only the top of 1% of Arabica beans. They offer 30+ varieties of coffee;the beans are roasted in small batches daily for freshness, and they also offer 20 varieties of teas that are hand-blended by their tea master. Additionally, they offer a variety of tasty sweets, powders, extracts, sauces, gifts, and

cards. Leashed, well mannered dogs are allowed at their outside dining area.

## The Coffee Bean & Tea Leaf
1845 S La Cienega Blvd
Los Angeles CA
310-815-1255
coffeebean.com
The coffee here is sourced globally from family coffee farms to procure only the top of 1% of Arabica beans. They offer 30+ varieties of coffee;the beans are roasted in small batches daily for freshness, and they also offer 20 varieties of teas that are hand-blended by their tea master. Additionally, they offer a variety of tasty sweets, powders, extracts, sauces, gifts, and cards. Leashed, well mannered dogs are allowed at their outside dining area.

## The Coffee Bean & Tea Leaf
6333 W 3rd Street, E-11
Los Angeles CA
323-857-0461
coffeebean.com
The coffee here is sourced globally from family coffee farms to procure only the top of 1% of Arabica beans. They offer 30+ varieties of coffee;the beans are roasted in small batches daily for freshness, and they also offer 20 varieties of teas that are hand-blended by their tea master. Additionally, they offer a variety of tasty sweets, powders, extracts, sauces, gifts, and cards. Leashed, well mannered dogs are allowed at their outside dining area.

## The Coffee Bean & Tea Leaf
7235 Beverly Blvd
Los Angeles CA
323-934-1449
coffeebean.com
The coffee here is sourced globally from family coffee farms to procure only the top of 1% of Arabica beans. They offer 30+ varieties of coffee;the beans are roasted in small batches daily for freshness, and they also offer 20 varieties of teas that are hand-blended by their tea master. Additionally, they offer a variety of tasty sweets, powders,

extracts, sauces, gifts, and cards. Leashed, well mannered dogs are allowed at their outside dining area.

## The Coffee Bean & Tea Leaf
5979 W Third Street
Los Angeles CA
323-934-7277
coffeebean.com
The coffee here is sourced globally from family coffee farms to procure only the top of 1% of Arabica beans. They offer 30+ varieties of coffee;the beans are roasted in small batches daily for freshness, and they also offer 20 varieties of teas that are hand-blended by their tea master. Additionally, they offer a variety of tasty sweets, powders, extracts, sauces, gifts, and cards. Leashed, well mannered dogs are allowed at their outside dining area.

## The Coffee Bean & Tea Leaf
8601 S Lincoln Blvd, Suite 140/H 1
Los Angeles CA
310-665-9814
coffeebean.com
The coffee here is sourced globally from family coffee farms to procure only the top of 1% of Arabica beans. They offer 30+ varieties of coffee;the beans are roasted in small batches daily for freshness, and they also offer 20 varieties of teas that are hand-blended by their tea master. Additionally, they offer a variety of tasty sweets, powders, extracts, sauces, gifts, and cards. Leashed, well mannered dogs are allowed at their outside dining area.

## The Coffee Bean & Tea Leaf
7915 Sunset Blvd
Los Angeles CA
323-851-8392
coffeebean.com
The coffee here is sourced globally from family coffee farms to procure only the top of 1% of Arabica beans. They offer 30+ varieties of coffee;the beans are roasted in small batches daily for freshness,

and they also offer 20 varieties of teas that are hand-blended by their tea master. Additionally, they offer a variety of tasty sweets, powders, extracts, sauces, gifts, and cards. Leashed, well mannered dogs are allowed at their outside dining area.

## The Coffee Bean & Tea Leaf
10897 Pico Blvd
Los Angeles CA
310-441-1705
coffeebean.com
The coffee here is sourced globally from family coffee farms to procure only the top of 1% of Arabica beans. They offer 30+ varieties of coffee;the beans are roasted in small batches daily for freshness, and they also offer 20 varieties of teas that are hand-blended by their tea master. Additionally, they offer a variety of tasty sweets, powders, extracts, sauces, gifts, and cards. Leashed, well mannered dogs are allowed at their outside dining area.

## The Coffee Bean & Tea Leaf
601 W 5th Street, #R1
Los Angeles CA
213-689-8087
coffeebean.com
The coffee here is sourced globally from family coffee farms to procure only the top of 1% of Arabica beans. They offer 30+ varieties of coffee;the beans are roasted in small batches daily for freshness, and they also offer 20 varieties of teas that are hand-blended by their tea master. Additionally, they offer a variety of tasty sweets, powders, extracts, sauces, gifts, and cards. Leashed, well mannered dogs are allowed at their outside dining area.

## The Coffee Bean & Tea Leaf
909 Sepulveda Blvd, Suite 135/H1
Los Angeles CA
310-535-5596
coffeebean.com
The coffee here is sourced globally from family coffee farms to procure only the top of 1% of Arabica beans. They offer 30+

varieties of coffee;the beans are roasted in small batches daily for freshness, and they also offer 20 varieties of teas that are hand-blended by their tea master. Additionally, they offer a variety of tasty sweets, powders, extracts, sauces, gifts, and cards. Leashed, well mannered dogs are allowed at their outside dining area.

**Tiago Coffee Bar and Kitchen**
7080 Hollywood
Los Angeles CA
323-466-5600
tiagocoffee.com/
In addition to quality coffees, this café also serves breakfasts, daily soups, salads, wraps, and sandwiches. Leashed, well mannered dogs are welcome at their outside tables.

**Toast Bakery Cafe Inc**
8221 W 3rd St
Los Angeles CA
323-655-5018
toastbakerycafe.net/
A hip LA bakery cafe that has bee Zagat rated every year, customers can enjoy a full day's menu of handcrafted comfort cuisine, fresh bakery items, and specialty beverages. Leashed, well mannered dogs are welcome at their outside tables.

**Whole Foods Market**
1050 S. Gayley
Los Angeles CA
310-824-0858
wholefoods.com/
This natural food supermarket offers natural and organic foods. Order some food from their deli without your dog and bring it to an outdoor table where your well-behaved leashed dog is welcome. Dogs are not allowed in the store including the deli at any t

**Whole Foods Market**
6350 West 3rd Street
Los Angeles CA
323-964-6800
wholefoods.com/
This natural food supermarket offers natural and organic foods. Order some food from their deli without your dog and bring it to

an outdoor table where your well-behaved leashed dog is welcome.

**Whole Foods Market**
7871 West Santa Monica Blvd.
Los Angeles CA
323-848-4200
wholefoods.com/
This natural food supermarket offers natural and organic foods. Order some food from their deli without your dog and bring it to an outdoor table where your well-behaved leashed dog is welcome. Dogs are not allowed on any of the furnishings.

**Whole Foods Market**
11737 San Vicente Blvd.
Los Angeles CA
310-826-4433
wholefoods.com/
This natural food supermarket offers natural and organic foods. Order some food from their deli without your dog and bring it to an outdoor table where your well-behaved leashed dog is welcome.

**Whole Foods Market**
11666 National Boulevard
Los Angeles CA
310-996-8840
wholefoods.com/
This natural food supermarket offers natural and organic foods. Order some food from their deli without your dog and bring it to an outdoor table where your well-behaved leashed dog is welcome.

**Wirtshaus**
345 N La Brea Ave
Los Angeles CA
323-931-9291
wirtshausla.com/home.html
Wirtshaus is a traditional German restaurant and pub, specializing in authentic German food and freshly tapped beer. They are open 7 days a week, from 5pm-12am Monday-Thursday and 11am-12am Friday-Sunday. Well-behaved, leashed dogs are welcome on the outdoor patio.

**Home**

1760 Hillhurst Avenue
Los Feliz CA
323-665-HOME (4663)
homelosfeliz.com
This eatery offers a full menu of all American comfort foods, daily happy hours, specialty cocktails, a large martini menu, 3 large LCD TVs, a venue for special events, catering, and delivery services. Their unique natural setting is also a popular feature. Leashed, well mannered dogs are welcome at their outside tables.

## Pet-Friendly Shopping Centers

**Century City Shopping Center**
10250 Santa Monica Blvd
Los Angeles CA
310-277-3898
This dog-friendly outdoor shopping center, located just one mile from Rodeo Drive in Beverly Hills, is popular with many Hollywood actors and actresses. Your well-behaved dog is allowed inside many of the stores. For a list of dog-friendly stores, please look at our stores category. Your dog is also welcome to join you at the outdoor cafe tables in the food court area.

**The Grove Shopping Center**
189 The Grove Drive
Los Angeles CA
323-900-8080
thegrovela.com/
Offering an eclectic array of shops, casual to fine dining, and entertainment, this shopping Mecca will allow dogs in the common areas, and some of the stores are also pet friendly. Dogs must be leashed and under their owner's control at all times.

**Westfield Century City**
10250 Santa Monica Blvd/H 2
Los Angeles CA
310-277-3898
westfield.com/centurycity/
This open-air shopping center offers a variety of shopping, dining, and entertainment

venues in addition to offering Apps for the mall, free movies on the terrace during the summer, games with prizes, and a number of special events throughout the year. Dogs are allowed in the common areas of the mall; it is up to individual stores whether they allow a dog inside. There is also a dog park on the side of the mall for small dogs. Dogs must be well behaved, leashed, and under their owner's control at all times. They are not allowed in the food court.

## Pet-Friendly Stores

**Petco Pet Store - Puente Hills**
17585 Colima Road
City of Industry CA
626-964-1666
Your licensed and well-behaved leashed dog is allowed in the store.

**PetSmart Pet Store**
12126 Lakewood Blvd
Downey CA
562-803-1607
Your licensed and well-behaved leashed dog is allowed in the store.

**Petco Pet Store - Downey**
8580 Firestone Blvd
Downey CA
562-861-2093
Your licensed and well-behaved leashed dog is allowed in the store.

**American Apparel**
4665 Hollywood Blvd
Los Angeles CA
323-661-1407
americanapparel.net/
This major apparel store carries fine clothing for the whole family for all types of activities with accessories to compliment an amazing choice of items. They are open Sunday to Wednesday from 11 am until 8 pm and Thursday to Saturday from 11 am until 9 pm. Leashed, friendly dogs are welcome in the store.

**Anthropologie**
6301 W 3rd Street,#J

Los Angeles CA
323-934-8433
Items of distinction can be found for all ages and in all departments of this unique shop. Carefully selected to add to the enjoyment of the shopping experience, they carry fine clothing, amazing accessories, jewelry, hobby and leisure items, and a full line of bright and useful items for the home, garden, and office. Leashed, well behaved dogs are allowed in the store.

**Bloomingdale's**
8500 Beverly Blvd
Los Angeles CA
310-360-2700
Some of the offerings of this major shopping destination include designer merchandise, indoor and outdoor wear for the entire family, jewelry and accessories, shoes and handbags, personal beauty aids, child care products, and home decor. They also offer a wide variety of shopping services; various fashion, beauty, and home events, and a philanthropy program that raises funds and awareness for worthy causes. Leashed, well mannered dogs are welcome in the store; they must be under their owner's control at all times.

**Bloomingdale's**
10250 Santa Monica Blvd/H 2
Los Angeles CA
310-772-2100
Some of the offerings of this major shopping destination include designer merchandise, indoor and outdoor wear for the entire family, jewelry and accessories, shoes and handbags, personal beauty aids, child care products, and home decor. They also offer a wide variety of shopping services; various fashion, beauty, and home events, and a philanthropy program that raises funds and awareness for worthy causes. Leashed, well mannered dogs are welcome in the store; they must be under their owner's control at all

times.

**Brentano's Books**
Century City Shopping Center
Los Angeles CA
310-785-0204
Your well-behaved leashed dog is allowed inside this store.

**Centinela Feed and Supplies**
3860 Centinela Avenue
Los Angeles CA
310-398-2134
centinelafeed.com
Specializing in natural, holistic, and raw pet foods, this pet supply store also provides healthy treats, quality supplements, pet care supplies, low-cost vaccination clinics, frequent in-store events, and a knowledgeable staff. Leashed pets are welcome.

**Crate and Barrel**
189 The Grove Drive
Los Angeles CA
323-297-0370
crateandbarrel.com
This store offers fine products from around the world for in and around the home that include items for outdoor living, indoor furnishings and decorating, dining and entertaining, kitchen and food service, and gourmet food and beverages. They also have accessories for pets, bed and bath items, and organizing and storage units. Leashed, friendly dogs are welcome in the store; they must be under their owner's control at all times.

**Dutton's Brentwood Bookstore**
11975 San Vicente Blvd
Los Angeles CA
310-476-6263
duttonsbrentwood.com/
More than a bookstore, they also card cards and CD's, are host to a monthly reading series, special events, and more, and they have also been known to greet their canine visitors with a doggy biscuit. Friendly, well behaved dogs are welcome in the bookstore. They must be house trained, leashed, and under their owner's control/responsibility at all times.

**Foot Locker**
Century City Shopping Center
Los Angeles CA
310-556-1498
footlocker.com/
Your well-behaved leashed dog is allowed inside this store.

**Gap**
Century City Shopping Center
Los Angeles CA
310-556-1080
gap.com/
Your well-behaved leashed dog is allowed inside this store.

**Illiterature**
452 S La Brea Ave
Los Angeles CA
323-937-3505
Dogs are allowed but they must be leashed.

**Laura Ashley**
Century City Shopping Center
Los Angeles CA
310-553-0807
laura-ashley.com/
Your well-behaved leashed dog is allowed inside this store.

**Le Pet Boutique**
189 The Grove Drive
Los Angeles CA
323-935-9195
This pet gift store is located in an outdoor mall, so your pooch can join you in checking out all the toys, treats, collars, leads, and a lot more. They are open from 10 am to 9 pm Monday through Friday; from 10 am to 10 pm Friday and Saturday, and from 11 am to 8 pm on Sunday. Dogs must be well behaved and on leash.

**Origins**
Century City Shopping Center
Los Angeles CA
310-772-0272
origins.com/
Your well-behaved leashed dog is allowed inside this store.

**Petco Pet Store - La Brea**
200 South La Brea Ave Ste C
Los Angeles CA
323-934-8444
Your licensed and well-behaved leashed dog is allowed in the store.

**Petco Pet Store - Robertson**
1475 South Robertson Blvd
Los Angeles CA
310-282-8166
Your licensed and well-behaved leashed dog is allowed in the store.

**Petco Pet Store - Westchester**
8801 South Sepulveda Blvd
Los Angeles CA
310-645-7198
Your licensed and well-behaved leashed dog is allowed in the store.

**Petco Pet Store - Westwood**
1873 Westwood Blvd
Los Angeles CA
310-441-2073
Your licensed and well-behaved leashed dog is allowed in the store.

**Pottery Barn**
Century City Shopping Center
Los Angeles CA
310-552-0170
potterybarn.com/
Your well-behaved leashed dog is allowed inside this store.

**Pussy & Pooch Pethouse and Pawbar**
564 South Main Street
Los Angeles CA
213-438-0900
pussyandpooch.com/
Pussy & Pooch's Los Angeles location offers a "Pawbar", where pets can sit and enjoy freshly made treats and meals to order. The pet boutique and retail store sells a variety of organic, raw, dehydrated, and traditional pet food and treats, organic pet grooming and spa products, pet beds, carriers, and pet fashion and accessories. They also have pet grooming, and "mutt mingles" every month.

**Restoration Hardware**
Century City Shopping Center
Los Angeles CA
310-551-4995
restorationhardware.com/

Your well-behaved leashed dog is allowed inside this store.

**Rocket Video**
726 N La Brea Ave
Los Angeles CA
323-965-1100
rocketvideo.com/
Well-behaved leashed dogs are welcome in this store which is Los Angeles' premier independent video store.

**The Urban Pet**
7515 Beverly Blvd
Los Angeles CA
323-933-2100
theurbanpet.net
This comprehensive pet store offers a good variety of holistic and raw pet foods, healthy treats, leashes/collars, toys, pet care supplies, bedding, apparel, a knowledgeable staff and competitive pricing. A few nice extras of this store include a tranquil Koi pond and a Green Zone of all earth-friendly products. In addition to the store, they also offer private training, group classes, a vaccination clinic, pet teeth cleaning and consultation services.

**Three Dog Bakery**
The Grove, 6333 West 3rd Street, #710
Los Angeles CA
323-935-7512
threedog.com
Three Dog Bakery provides cookies and snacks for your dog as well as some boutique items. You well-behaved, leashed dog is welcome.

**Urban Outfitters**
7650 Melrose Avenue
Los Angeles CA
323-653-3231
In addition to a large inventory of indoor and outdoor apparel for men and women, this major department store also carries vintage wear, designer brands, and a variety of accessories for all types of active lifestyles. They also carry shoes, furnishings, home decor, cameras, electronics, novelty items and more. Leashed, well

mannered dogs are allowed in the store.

**Urban Outfitters**
1100 Westwood Blvd
Los Angeles CA
310-443-9765
In addition to a large inventory of indoor and outdoor apparel for men and women, this major department store also carries vintage wear, designer brands, and a variety of accessories for all types of active lifestyles. They also carry shoes, furnishings, home decor, cameras, electronics, novelty items and more. Leashed, well mannered dogs are allowed in the store.

**Urban Outfitters**
1520 N. Cahuenga Blvd, Suite 1

Los Angeles CA
323-465-1893
In addition to a large inventory of indoor and outdoor apparel for men and women, this major department store also carries vintage wear, designer brands, and a variety of accessories for all types of active lifestyles. They also carry shoes, furnishings, home decor, cameras, electronics, novelty items and more. Leashed, well mannered dogs are allowed in the store.

**Petco Pet Store - Montebello**
1425 North Montebello Blvd
Montebello CA
323-724-3194
Your licensed and well-behaved leashed dog is allowed in the store.

**Petco Pet Store - Walnut Park**
7308 South Alameda St.
Walnut Park CA
323-826-9607
Your licensed and well-behaved leashed dog is allowed in the store.

# Off-Leash Dog Parks
**Barrington Dog Park**
333 South Barrington Avenue
Los Angeles CA

310-476-4866
Barrington Dog Park is located just west of the 405 Freeway at Sunset Blvd. Exit the 405 at Sunset, head west, and then south onto Barrington. This fenced 1 1/2 acre dog park is open during daylight hours.

**Griffith Park Dog Park**
North Zoo Drive
Los Angeles CA
323-913-4688
laparks.org/dogpark/griffith
This dog park is located 1/2 mile west of the 134 Fwy at the John Ferraro Soccer Field, next to the Autry Museum and across from the main zoo parking. There are two separate fenced areas, one for larger dogs and the other for small or timid dogs. There is a portable restroom for people.

**Herman Park Dog Park**
5566 Via Marisol
Los Angeles CA
323-255-0370
hermondogpark.org/
Herman Park in the Arroyo Seco Dog Park is a 1 1/3 acre fenced dog park with separate areas for large and small dogs. The park is open during daylight hours. The park is located off of the 110 Freeway east on Via Marisol.

**Laurel Canyon Park**
8260 Mulholland Dr.
Los Angeles CA

This nice dog park is located in the hills of Studio City. It is completely fenced with water and even a hot dog stand. To get there, take Laurel Canyon Blvd and go west on Mulholland Blvd. Go about a 1/4 mile and turn left. There is a parking lot below.

**Runyon Canyon Park**
Mulholland Hwy
Los Angeles CA
323-666-5046
laparks.org/park/runyon-canyon

From this popular hiking trail and excellent off-leash area you can see views of

Hollywood, the Wilshire District, and the skyscrapers of downtown L.A. This park has mostly off-leash and some on-leash hiking trails. It is about a 2 mile round-trip from end to end in the park. The top of the trail is located off Mulholland Hwy (about 2 miles east of Laurel Canyon Blvd) at Desmond Street in the Hollywood Hills. The bottom part of the trail is located at the end of Fuller Ave. Parking is available on the street. The trailhead might be kind of tricky to find from Fuller, but you'll probably see other people going to or coming from the trail.

**Silverlake Dog Park**
2000 West Silverlake Blvd.
Los Angeles CA

laparks.org/dogpark/silverlake
This is one of the best dog parks in the Los Angeles area and it usually averages 30-40 dogs. It is located at approximately 2000 West Silverlake Blvd. It's on the south side of the reservoir in Silverlake, which is between Hollywood and downtown L.A. between Sunset Blvd. and the 5 Freeway. The easiest way to get there is to take the 101 Freeway to Silverlake Blvd. and go east. Be careful about street parking because they ticket in some areas. Thanks to one of our readers for recommending this dog park.

# Dog-Friendly Parks
**Elysian Park**
929 Academy Road
Los Angeles CA
805-584-4400
laparks.org/park/elysian
At 600 acres, this is the 2nd largest city park in Los Angeles, and much of the landscape of natural chaparral is crisscrossed with hiking trails. There are barbecue pits, a small man-made lake, restrooms, and a children's play area at the central picnic area.

**Griffith Park**
Los Feliz Blvd.
Los Angeles CA

laparks.org/griffithpark
This park has the Griffith Observatory, the famous Hollywood sign and plenty of hiking trails. The Mt. Hollywood Trail is about a 6 mile round trip and can get very hot in the summer season, so head out early or later in the evening during those hot days. There is also a more shaded trail that begins by the Bird Sanctuary. Be careful not to go into the Sanctuary because dogs are not allowed there. Instead go to the trail to the left of the Sanctuary entrance. That trail should go around the perimeter of the Bird Sanctuary. For more trail info, pick up a map at one of the Ranger stations (main Ranger's station is at Crystal Springs/Griffith Park Drive near Los Feliz Blvd). To get to there, take Hwy 5 to the Los Feliz Blvd exit and head west. Turn right on Hillhurst or Vermont Ave (they merge later). The trail by the Bird Sanctuary will be on the right, past the Greek Theater. To get to the Mt. Hollywood Trail, continue until you come to the Griffith Observatory. Park here and the trail is across the parking lot from the Observatory (near the outdoor cafe). Please note that no one is allowed to actually hike to the famous Hollywood sign - it is very well guarded. But from some of the trails in this park, you can get a long distance view of the sign. Dogs must be leashed in the park.

**Kenneth Hahn State Rec Area**
4100 S La Cienega
Los Angeles CA
323-298-3660
In 1932 this area hosted the 10th Olympiad, and again in 1984 Los Angeles hosted the Olympics with athletes from 140 nations, so as a reminder, 140 trees were planted here to commemorate this event. Other park features/amenities include large landscaped areas, picnic sites, barbecues, playgrounds, a fishing lake, lotus pond/Japanese Garden, gaming fields/courts, and several miles of hiking trails. Dogs are allowed throughout the park and on the trails. Dogs of all sizes are allowed for no additional fee. Dogs must be well behaved, leashed, and cleaned up after.

**Transportation Systems**
**Metro Transit Authority**
1 Gateway Plaza
Los Angeles CA
213-580-7500
metro.net
Small dogs in an enclosed carrier are allowed on the light rail and buses for no additional fee.

**Airports**

Los Angeles CA

LAX has five animal relief stations conveniently located around the central terminal area of the airport. All stations are located outside on the lower level. The relief stations are conveniently located at:

**Emergency Veterinarians**
**Animal Emergency Clinic**
1736 S Sepulveda Blvd #A
Los Angeles CA
310-473-1561
Monday - Friday 6 pm - 8 am. 24 hours weekends and holidays.

**Eagle Rock Emergency Pet Clinic**
4252 Eagle Rock Blvd
Los Angeles CA
323-254-7382
Monday - Friday 6 pm - 8 am. Saturday 12 noon - Monday 8 am.

**Other Organizations**
**Busy Beagles**

Los Angeles CA
(310) 450-9493
busybeagles.com
Busy Beagles is an informal social group of beagles and their people guardians. We get together the first Saturday of each month at 9:00am at the Barrington small dog park in Brentwood. All beagles, beagle-mixes, and their small dog siblings are welcome. We also encourage prospective beagle guardians to join us so they can find out all about beagle companionship. Our get togethers require no fee or commitment, just a dog-friendly spirit!

**Found Animals Foundation**

Los Angeles CA

foundanimals.org
Found Animals Foundation is a private operating foundation with a singular focus: to reduce the number of pets euthanized every day due to pet overpopulation. Working with local communities and animal care professionals, they deliver innovative community-based adoption, spay & neuter and pet ID programs, while offering a wealth of trusted educational resources. In addition, they fund research annually that is dedicated to solving critical animal welfare challenges. This includes the international Michelson Prize & Grants offering a $25 million prize to the individual or organization who can create a single dose, non surgical, sterilant for dogs and cats.

## Los Banos

**Dog-Friendly Hotels**
**Best Western Executive Inn**
301 W. Pacheco Boulevard

Los Banos CA
209-827-0954 (800-780-7234)
Dogs up to 50 pounds are
allowed. There is a $20 per pet
per night pet fee. Up to two dogs
are allowed per room.

**Red Roof Inn Los Banos**
2169 East Pacheco Boulevard
Los Banos CA
209-826-9690 (800-329-7466)
Dogs of all sizes are allowed.
Dogs are allowed for a pet fee of
$10.00 per pet per night.

**Sun Star Inn**
839 West Pacheco Boulevard
Los Banos CA
209-826-3805
Guests enjoy well-equipped
rooms with free Wi-Fi at the
budget-friendly Sun Star Inn in
Los Banos California. At the
low-rise Sun Star Inn 42
exterior-access rooms boast
handy microwaves mini-fridges
coffeemakers and cable TVs
with HBO. Wi-Fi is provided for
free. Non-smoking rooms can
be requested and pets are
allowed for an additional fee.
The Sun Star Inn is off Highway
152/33 and convenient to I-5 in
the heart of Los Banos midway
between Gilroy and Chowchilla.
The San Luis Reservoir State
Recreation Area is less than 20
minutes away. Los Banos
Municipal Airport is less than a
mile away. Fresno Yosemite
International Airport is 75 miles
southeast.

**Pet-Friendly Stores**
**Tractor Supply Company**
1131 W Pacheco Blvd/H 33/152

Los Banos CA
209-827-0283
tractorsupply.com
Some offerings of this
comprehensive farm store
includes agriculture, farming and
ranching supplies; outdoor
power equipment with all the
necessities; hundreds of
thousands of parts and
accessories accessible for yard
and garden; metal working and
welding supplies; tools for auto

and home; a wide range of
livestock/farm feed and needs;
and a variety of foods and
care/play/groom items for
household pets. Additionally,
they provide trailer and towing
supplies, vehicle maintenance
accessories, clothing, work
wear, foot wear, gifts, home
improvement items, a lot of
"know-how" and much more.
Leashed, friendly dogs are
welcome in the store.

## Lost Hills

### Dog-Friendly Hotels
**Days Inn Lost Hills**
14684 Aloma Street
Lost Hills CA
661-797-2371 (800-329-7466)
Dogs of all sizes are allowed.
Dogs are allowed for a pet fee
of $10 per pet per night.

## Madera

### Dog-Friendly Hotels
**Gateway Inn**
2095 West Kennedy Street
Madera CA
559-674-8817 (800-329-7466)
Dogs are welcome at this hotel.

**Knights Inn Madera**
1855 West Cleveland Avenue
Madera CA
559-661-1131 (800-800-8000)
Dogs of all sizes are allowed.
Dogs are allowed for a pet fee.

### Dog-Friendly Attractions
**Mariposa Wine Company**
20146 Road 21
Madera CA
559-673-6372
mariposawine.com/index.html
The combining of four
distinctive wineries under one
company has made for a wide

variety of wines for tasting and
purchase. Dogs are allowed on
the grounds and on the deck
where seating is also available.
Dogs must be well behaved,
leashed, and cleaned up after.

### Outdoor Restaurants
**IHOP Restaurant**
2201 W Cleveland Avenue
Madera CA
559-675-5179
ihop.com/
Besides being known for their
great pancakes, this restaurant
offers a full menu with a wide
variety of choices and seasonal
alfresco dining. Leashed, well
mannered dogs are allowed to
dine at their outside tables;enter
through the private patio
entrance.

## Malibu

### Outdoor Restaurants
**Malibu Cafe**
327 South Latigo Canyon
Malibu CA
818-540-2400
themalibucafe.com
The Malibu Cafe serves brunch,
lunch, and dinner with
vegetarian options available.
Well-behaved, leashed dogs are
allowed on the outdoor patio.

**The Coffee Bean & Tea Leaf**
3835 Cross Creek Road #7
Malibu CA
310-456-5771
coffeebean.com
The coffee here is sourced
globally from family coffee farms
to procure only the top of 1% of
Arabica beans. They offer 30+
varieties of coffee;the beans are
roasted in small batches daily
for freshness, and they also
offer 20 varieties of teas that are
hand-blended by their tea
master. Additionally, they offer a
variety of tasty sweets, powders,
extracts, sauces, gifts, and
cards. Leashed, well mannered

dogs are allowed at their outside dining area.

## Dog-Friendly Beaches
### Leo Carrillo State Beach
Hwy 1
Malibu CA
818-880-0350
This beach is one of the very few dog-friendly beaches in the Los Angeles area. In a press release dated November 27, 2002, the California State Parks clarified the rules for dogs at Leo Carrillo State Beach. We thank the State Parks for this clear announcement of the regulations. Dogs are allowed on a maximum 6 foot leash when accompanied by a person capable of controlling the dog on all beach WEST (up coast) of lifeguard tower 3 at Leo Carrillo State Park, Staircase Beach, County Line Beach, and all Beaches within Point Mugu State Park. Dogs are NOT allowed EAST of lifeguard tower 3 at Leo Carrillo State Beach at any time. And please note that dogs are not allowed in the tide pools at Leo Carrillo. There should be signs posted. A small general store is located on the mountain side of the freeway. Here you can grab some snacks and other items. The park is located on Hwy 1, approximately 30 miles northwest of Santa Monica. We ask that all dog people closely obey these regulations so that the beach continues to be dog-friendly.

## Dog-Friendly Parks
### Circle X Ranch
Yerba Buena Road
Malibu CA
805-370-2301
There are both easy and strenuous trails at this park. The Backbone Trail is a strenuous 3 mile round trip hike which starts at an elevation of 2,050 feet. This trail offers views of the Conejo and San Fernando Valleys and the Pacific Coast. This trail continues to Point

Mugu State Park but dogs are not allowed on those trails. The Grotto Trail is a 3.5 mile round trip trail rated moderate to strenuous. The trail is all downhill from the starting point which means you will be hiking uphill when you return. The Canyon View Trail is almost 2 miles and is rated easy to moderate. There are many access points to this trail, but one is located .3 miles east of the Ranger Station on Yerba Buena Road. Dogs are allowed but must be leashed and people need to clean up after their pets. To get there go about 5.4 miles north on Yerba Buena Road from Highway 1. This park is part of the Santa Monica Recreation Area.

### Escondido Canyon Park
Winding Way
Malibu CA
805-370-2301
The Escondido Falls trail is a little over 4 miles long. The trailhead is reached by a one mile walk up the road from the parking lot. The trail will cross the creek several times before opening up to grassland. You will see the waterfall about one mile from the trailhead. Hiking, horseback riding, and mountain bicycling are popular activities at the park. Dogs on a 6 foot or less leash are allowed and people need to clean up after their pets. The park is located in Malibu, about one mile from the Pacific Coast Highway on Winding Way. This park is part of the Santa Monica Recreation Area.

### Santa Clarita Woodlands Park
5750 Ramiraz Canyon Road
Malibu CA
310-589-3200
A very important park with concern to the wildlife habitat corridor that it provides, it also supplies 4000 acres of recreational land. Some of the features/amenities include globally unique combinations of tree species, lush greenery and spring wildflowers, abundant

bird and wildlife, year round streams, a nature center, hiking and multi-use trails, and picnic areas. Dogs are allowed throughout the park and on the trails. Dogs must be under their owner's immediate control, leashed, and cleaned up after at all times.

### Solstice Canyon Park
Corral Canyon Road
Malibu CA
805-370-2301
This park is a wooded, narrow coastal canyon which offers five trails, ranging from easy to moderate hikes. One of the trails is called the Solstice Canyon Trail. This is an easy 2.1 mile round trip walk which passes by the Keller House which is believed to be the oldest existing stone building in Malibu. Dogs are allowed on the trails but must be leashed and people need to clean up after their pets. To get there from the Pacific Coast Highway 1, go through Malibu and turn inland onto Corral Canyon Road. In about .25 miles the entrance will be on your left at a hairpin curve in the road. This park is part of the Santa Monica Recreation Area.

## Mammoth Lakes

## Dog-Friendly Hotels
### Convict Lake Resort
2000 Convict Lake Road
Mammoth Lakes CA
760-934-3800 (800-992-2260)
convictlake.com/index.php
Featuring a restaurant this Convict Lake Resort offers cottages with exposed wood ceilings and a mountain view. A free airport shuttle service free parking and free WiFi is provided. Mammoth Lakes Ski Area is 20 km away.
Offering mountain views Convict Lake Resort comes with a fully equipped kitchen in each accommodation with barbecue

facilities. A flat-screen satellite TV and other modern amenities are also provided. Free toiletries are included in the bathrooms. barbecue facilities a gift shop and a mini-market are also provided. Canoeing and fishing opportunities are nearby Mammoth Lakes Convict Lake Resort.
Adjacent to the 170 acre Convict Lake this resort is just 45 minutes drive away from Yosemite National Park. Mammoth Yosemite Airport is 8 km away.

## Rodeway Inn Wildwood Inn
3626 Main Street
Mammoth Lakes CA
760-934-6855 (877-424-6423)
Skiing, mountain biking, fishing, golf. Yosemite National Park 45 miles. Seasonal access to Devil's Postpile Monument

Dogs of all sizes are allowed.

## Shilo Inn Mammoth Lakes
2963 Main Street
Mammoth Lakes CA
760-934-4500 (800-222-2244)
Close to the slopes and right in the village the non-smoking Shilo Inn Mammoth Lakes offers free continental breakfast and cozy accommodations. All 70 rooms at the non-smoking Shiloh Inn are spread across three floors and come with mini-fridges microwaves coffeemakers and free local calls. Wi-Fi is available. The lobby's stone fireplace and sofas invite lingering and relaxation. Mornings start with free newspapers. After skiing guests can stow their gear in the free storage area. You'll also find a fitness center and laundry facility on-site. Covered parking is free. Dogs are welcome for a fee and with restrictions. The Shilo Inn is on Main Street two blocks from the Mammoth Lakes Visitors Bureau. It's within easy walking distance of shops and restaurants. Five miles from the hotel you'll find the 11000-foot Mammoth Mountain California's largest ski area. In the warmer months Mammoth

hosts zip lining climbing hiking gondola rides and mountain biking. Yosemite National Park is 45 minutes away and Mammoth Yosemite Airport is seven miles from the hotel. Oakland International Airport is 242 miles away. Sacramento International Airport is 251 miles away.

## Sierra Lodge
3540 Main Street
Mammoth Lakes CA
760-934-8881
Free Wi-Fi free continental breakfast and an outdoor terrace with hot tub are some of the high points for our guests at the non-smoking Sierra Lodge. This three-story hotel has 35 rooms with kitchenettes including microwaves refrigerators cookware and tableware. You can stay connected with your Facebook friends thanks to free Wi-Fi. Rooms include premium cable TVs and hairdryers. Partake of pastries and munch on muffins at the free continental breakfast. our guests grill up some goodness with the barbecue grills before soaking in the large outdoor hot tub. You can knock out some paperwork in the on-site business center. Hitch a ride to the mountain for skiing or pop over to the airport with available shuttle services. Local calls and parking are free. Sierra Lodge is three miles from Highway 395 and eight miles from Mammoth Yosemite Airport. You can make a run for it at Mammoth Mountain Ski Area five miles away. Exercise your credit cards at the Village at Mammoth one-and-a-half miles from the hotel. Golfers swing over to Sierra Star Golf Course one mile away.

## The Mammoth Creek Inn
663 Old Mammoth Road
Mammoth Lakes CA
760-934-6162
Freebies including breakfast Wi-Fi and shuttle service to the ski slopes are among the

amenities at the Mammoth Creek Inn. At the Alpine-style Mammoth Creek Inn 26 rooms on two levels feature plush beds with down comforters coffeemakers mini-fridges and flat-panel HDTVs. Suites with kitchenettes and sofa beds are also available as are non-smoking rooms. Pet-friendly accommodations can be requested for an additional fee. Check your emails with free Wi-Fi and fuel up on free breakfast before hopping on the shuttle to the slopes or airport. After a day in the great outdoors return to warm your toes near the lobby's stone fireplace or relax in the hot tub and sauna. There's also a fitness room free ski storage and free parking. The Mammoth Creek Inn is in the village of Mammoth Lakes accessible from Highway 395 and six miles from Mammoth Mountain. The inn is within walking distance of many shops and restaurants and less than an hour's drive from Yosemite National Park. Mammoth Yosemite Airport is eight miles away.

## The Westin Monache Resort Mammoth
50 Hillside Drive
Mammoth Lakes CA
760-934-0400 (888-625-5144)
A year around recreational destination, this resort offers all the comforts and equipment needed to enjoy the mountain and to relax after a day of fun. Dogs are allowed for no additional pet fee;there is a pet waiver to sign at check in. Canine guests are greeted with a welcome amenity package that includes a custom pet bed, and food and water bowls with a mat.

## Travelodge Mammoth Lakes
54 Sierra Boulevard
Mammoth Lakes CA
760-934-8892
Dogs up to 50 pounds are allowed. There is a pet fee of $10 per pet per night.

## Dog-Friendly Attractions

### Hot Creek Geologic Site
Hot Creek Hatchery Road
Mammoth Lakes CA
760-924-5500
Considered a geologic wonder complete with hot springs, fumaroles, craters, and the ever-changing earth of the area, it is also a natural sanctuary for many kinds of birds and wildlife. Because of the high concentrations of chemicals in the water and the potential danger of scalding water, swimming is not recommended, and visitors must remain on walkways and boardwalks. There is a hatchery here, and long rearing ponds (called raceways) where visitors may view the fish. Dogs are allowed at the site, but are to be kept away from the water. Dogs must be on no more than a 6 foot leash, under their owner's control at all times, and be cleaned up after.

### Mammoth Mountain-Gondola
#1 Minaret Road
Mammoth Lakes CA
760-934-0745 (800-MAMMOTH)

mammothmountain.com/
Want some awesome views of Mammoth Mountain and the surrounding areas? During the summer, you and your dog can hop on the Gondola (Cable Car) ride. You'll climb about 2,000 feet to the top of the mountain. Once there, you can enjoy a nice 1 1/2 - 2 hour hike down or take the Gondola back down the mountain. Dogs should be leashed.

## Outdoor Restaurants

### Base Camp Cafe
3325 Main Street
Mammoth Lakes CA
760-934-3900
basecampcafe.com/
Dogs are welcome at this cafe! They have a water bowl outside for your pooch.

### Looney Bean Roasting Company
26 Old Mammoth Rd
Mammoth Lakes CA
760-934-1345
looneybean.com/mammoth-lakes-ca
A great spot to start your day of hiking or skiing, the Looney Bean offers coffee in elegent surroundings. Coffee offerings include standard to exotic brands, as well as organic coffee. There are pastries and other food items as well. Your dog can join you at the outdoor tables.

### Paul Schat's Bakery
3305 Main Street
Mammoth Lakes CA
760-934-6055
This bakery offers baked goods, pastries and sandwiches. They also have fresh squeezed orange juice. There are a lot of bakery items to choose from. Leashed, well-behaved dogs are allowed to accompany you to the outdoor tables.

### Roberto's Mexican Cafe
271 Old Mammoth Road
Mammoth Lakes CA
760-934-3667
robertoscafe.com
This Mexican Restaurant & Bar has been serving locals and visitors alike in Mammoth Lakes since 1985. They serve all kinds of Mexican dishes, including Tacos, Fajitas, and even soups. The restaurant hosts a beautiful garden patio which is dog-friendly. Your well-behaved, leashed dog can join you for food on the garden patio.

### Side Door Cafe
1000 Canyon Blvd #229
Mammoth Lakes CA
760-934-5200
sidedoormammoth.com/
This European style establishment serves items from an organic martini to crepes, panini, coffee and wine. Or the Swiss Fondue and a collection of salads. Whatever your food choice, you can enjoy it on the outside patio with your four-legged travel partner. Well-behaved, leashed dogs are welcome at the outdoor tables.

## Pet-Friendly Shopping Centers

### The Village at Mammoth

Mammoth Lakes CA

villageatmammoth.com
The Village at Mammoth is a European Alps style mountain village with shops, restaurants, activities and events and more. Located next to the pet-friendly Westin and near Mammoth Mountain, dogs are welcome in the open areas of the village. They are also welcome at a number of patio restaurants and in many of the stores. There are often events at the village such as craft shows, movie nights, shows and other activities. You can find out about these activities on the website. The entire village is very pet-friendly.

## Pet-Friendly Stores

### Mammoth Sporting Goods
425 Old Mammoth Road
Mammoth Lakes CA
760-934-3239
mammothsportinggoods.com/
This sports shop specializes in skiing, biking, hiking, snowboarding, and fishing supplies and your well behaved dogs is welcome to join you in the store. Dogs must be friendly, under their owner's control at all times and leashed.

### Tailwaggers Dog Bakery & Boutique
452 Old Mammoth Rd
Mammoth Lakes CA
760-924-3400
This dog bakery and boutique is the perfect place to find a gift for your pup and anyone who loves dogs.

# Dog-Friendly Parks

## Ansel Adams Wilderness
off Highway 203
Mammoth Lakes CA
760-934-2289
The wilderness can be accessed at many points, including the John Muir Trail. See our listing for this trail under the city of Mammoth Lakes. There are miles of on or off-leash hiking opportunities.

## Devil's Postpile National Monument
Minaret Rd.
Mammoth Lakes CA
760-934-2289
nps.gov/depo/index.htm
During the summer only, take a bus ride/shuttle to the Devil's Postpile National Monument with your pup. The shuttle is the only way to drive to this National Monument unless you have a camping permit or have a vehicle with 11 people or more. The shuttle begins at the Mammoth Mountain Inn off Hwy 203 and takes you and your dog on a scenic ride along the San Joaquin River to the National Monument. The travel time is about 45 minutes to Reds Meadow (past the Monument), but there are 10 stops along the way to get out and stretch or hike. Once at the Monument, there is a short 1/2 mile walk. The Monument is a series of basalt columns, 40 to 60 feet high, that resembles a giant pipe organ. It was made by hot lava that cooled and cracked 900,000 years ago. The John Muir Trail crosses the monument, so for a longer hike, join up with nearby trails that are in the dog-friendly Inyo National Forest. Dogs should be on a leash.

## Devils Postpile National Monument
Minaret Road/H 203
Mammoth Lakes CA
760-934-2289
nps.gov/depo/
Located in the heart of California's Eastern Sierra, this National Monument usually

opens in mid-June, and depending on weather conditions they close mid to late October. The park offers a unique blending of cultural, historical, ecological, recreational and educational opportunities. Shuttle busses to the Monument are available during the summer only. Dogs are allowed on the shuttle at the discretion of the bus driver and all dogs must be muzzled during the trip. Dogs are allowed throughout the park, in the campground for no additional fee, and on the trails; they must be kept leashed at all times while in the monument and cleaned up after promptly. Mutt Mitt ? disposable plastic bags are available at the monument trailhead. Dogs may not be left unattended except for very short periods and they may not be left in vehicles when temperatures reach 70 degrees.

## Horseshoe Lake
4500 Lake Mary Rd
Mammoth Lakes CA

The area around Horseshoe Lake serves as the de facto "dog park" for Mammoth Lakes. There are usually a number of off-leash and leashed dogs in the area. There are also a number of easy hiking trails in the area.

## Inyo National Forest

Mammoth Lakes CA
760-873-2400
fs.usda.gov/inyo
Dogs are allowed on all trails in Inyo National Forest except if restricted due to a sheep habitat area. But they are allowed on the vast majority of trails. Up to two dogs are allowed to stay in each campground site in the forest. Dogs should be on a six foot leash in the forest.

## John Muir Trail
off Highway 203
Mammoth Lakes CA
760-934-2289

This trail crosses the dog-friendly Devil's Postpile National Monument. The John Muir Trail offers miles of hiking trails. Dogs must be on leash at the monument but can be off leash under direct voice control in the Inyo National Forest and Ansel Adams Wilderness. The trailhead is located near the ranger's station at the monument. To get there, you can drive directly to the monument and trailhead ONLY if you have a camping permit or a vehicle with 11 people or more. All day visitors must ride a shuttle bus from the Mammoth Mountain Ski Area at the end of Highway 203. Well-behaved leashed dogs are allowed on the bus. From Highway 395, drive 10 miles west on Highway 203 to Minaret Summit. Then drive 7 miles on a paved, narrow mountain road. Or take the shuttle bus at the end of Highway 203. The bus ride takes about 45 minutes to the monument with several stops along the way.

## Lake George
Lake George Rd.
Mammoth Lakes CA

At Lake George, you can find the trailheads for the Crystal Lake and Mammoth Crest trails. You'll be hiking among the beautiful pine trees and snow covered peaks. The trails start at the north side of Lake George. The hike to Crystal Lake is about a 3 mile round trip. If you want a longer hike, you'll have the option on your way to Crystal Lake. The Mammoth Crest trail is the trail that branches to the right. The Mammoth trail is about a 6 mile round trip and it's a more strenuous trail. To get there from the intersection of Main Street and Hwy 203, take Lake Mary Road to the left. Go past Twin Lakes. You'll see a road that goes off to the left (Lake Mary Loop Rd.). Go past this road, you'll want the other end of the loop. When you come to another road that also says

Lake Mary Loop Rd, turn left. Then turn right onto Lake George Rd. Follow this road almost to the end and you should see signs for the Crystal Lake Trail. Dogs should be leashed.

**Lake Mary**
Lake Mary Loop Rd.
Mammoth Lakes CA

Here's another lake and hiking trail to enjoy up in the high country. Lake Mary is known as one of the best fishing spots in the Eastern Sierra, regularly producing trophy size trout. After your water dog is done playing in the lake, head to the southeast side of the lake to go for a hike on the Emerald Lake Trail. The trail starts at the Cold Water trailhead next to the Cold Water campgrounds. Take the trail to the right towards Emerald Lake and Sky Meadows. The trail to Emerald Lake is about 1 1/2 miles round trip (out and back). If you continue on to Sky Meadows, then your hike is about 4 miles round trip. To get there from the intersection of Main Street and Hwy 203, take Lake Mary Road to the left. Pass Twin Lakes and then you'll come to Lake Mary. Turn left onto Lake Mary Loop Road and the trailhead is located on the southeast side of the lake. Dogs should be on a leash.

**Mammoth Mountain**
Minaret Rd.
Mammoth Lakes CA
760-934-2571 (800-MAMMOTH)

mammothmountain.com/
You can hike with your dog on "The" Mammoth Mountain in three ways. One way is to take the Gondola ride with your pup (summer only) up to the top of the mountain and then hike down. The second is to hike up the mountain from the parking lot by the Mammoth Mountain Inn and the Gondola. The third option is to start on the backside of the mountain and hike up and then of course down. For the third option, you can start at

Twin Lakes (off Lake Mary Rd). The Dragon's Back Trail is on the west side of the lakes (by the campgrounds). Dogs must be leashed.

**Shady Rest Park and Trail**
Sawmill Cutoff Rd.
Mammoth Lakes CA
760-934-8983
This park serves as a multi-use recreation park. During the winter it's popular with cross country skiers - yes dogs are allowed. In the summer, you can go for a hike on the 5-6 miles of single track and fire road trails. It's also used by 4x4 off road vehicles too, so just be aware. To get there from the Mammoth Visitor's Center, take Hwy 203 towards town. The first street on your right will be Sawmill Cutoff Road. Turn right and Shady Rest Park is at the end of the road. There are restrooms at this park which can come in handy for the humans before starting out on the trails. Dogs must be leashed.

**Tamarack Cross Country Ski Center**
Lake Mary Road
Mammoth Lakes CA
760- 934-2442
tamaracklodge.com/xc-ski-center
During the summer and fall (until first snowfall), dogs are allowed at Tamarack. They offer watercraft rentals, fishing, easy to strenuous hiking trails, an eatery, a lodge that allows dogs, and great scenery. Dogs are welcome on the deck of the restaurant. Dogs must be under their owner's control at all times, and be leashed and cleaned up after.

**Emergency Veterinarians**
**Alpen Veterinary Hospital**
217 Sierra Manor Rd
Mammoth Lakes CA
760-934-2291
Monday - Friday 9:30 am - 5:30 pm. Closed Weekends. Vet available in Emergency other

hours.

**High Country Veterinary Hospital**
148 Mountain Blvd
Mammoth Lakes CA
760-934-3775
Monday - Friday 9 am - 12 noon, 2 pm - 5 pm. Closed weekends.

## Manton

### Dog-Friendly Wineries and Vineyards
**Alger Vineyards**
31636 Forward Road
Manton CA
530-474-WINE (9463)
algervineyards.com/
Rich volcanic soils, arid slopes, cool nights, and a 'hands-on' approach help to produce a variety of fine wines at this vineyard. Leashed dogs are allowed on site; they are not allowed in the tasting room.

**Ringtail Vineyards**
32055 Forward Road
Manton CA
530-474-5350
Some of the most recent wines provided by this vineyard include Gewurztraminer, Petite Sirah, Petite Sirah Dessert Wine, Chardonnay Viognier, and a Late Harvest Chardonnay. Small yield and hands-on production as well as a rich growing area have also benefited the wines grown here. Leashed dogs are allowed on the grounds; they are not allowed in the tasting room or by food service areas. They also request that when you arrive with a dog that you go into the tasting room and let them know so they can put their little pooch away.

## Marin - North Bay

## Dog-Friendly Hotels
### Inn Marin And Suites An Ascend Hotel Collection Member
250 Entrada Drive
Novato CA
415-883-5952 (800-652-6565)
A charming resort-style ambiance is offered along with free breakfast at the non-smoking Inn Marin a boutique hotel in Novato. The family-owned Inn Marin's 70 rooms and suites combine modern amenities and Mission-style furnishings. All feature coffeemakers rainfall showerheads and flat-panel HDTVs with HBO. Wake up to the California sunshine and free breakfast off the lobby which features original terracotta tiles and a massive stone fireplace. The five-acre property boasts mature oaks magnolias and orange trees that lend welcome shade. There's also an on-site restaurant and bar with live jazz on the weekends. If you need to get some work done take advantage of the available Wi-Fi access ample desk space and business center with fax and copy services. The Inn Marin has free parking and shuttle service to local shopping destinations. Handicap-accessible rooms are available and pets are welcome for an additional fee. The Inn Marin is off Highways 101 and 37 10 minutes from the shops and cafes in Old Town Novato and the Vintage Oaks Shopping Center. The major corporate office centers of Novato and San Rafael are within a 15-minute drive and San Francisco is 30 minutes away. Guests will find it hard to choose from the variety of area attractions within 30 miles of the hotel including the Infineon Raceway Six Flags Marine World the Point Reyes National Seashore and Muir Woods. The Inn Marin is 38 miles from San Francisco International Airport and 39 miles from Oakland International Airport.

### San Francisco-days Inn Novato
8141 Redwood Boulevard
Novato CA
415-897-7111 (800-329-7466)
Dogs are welcome at this hotel.

### Best Western Petaluma Inn
200 S. Mcdowell Blvd
Petaluma CA
707-763-0994 (800-780-7234)
Dogs are allowed. There is a $20 per day pet fee. Dogs can stay up to three nights. Up to two dogs are allowed per room.

### Quality Inn Petaluma
5100 Montero Way
Petaluma CA
707-664-1155 (877-424-6423)
45 minutes north of Golden Gate Bridge. Central location to Sonoma Wine Country, Pacific Coast, and Redwoods.

Dogs of all sizes are allowed. Dogs are allowed for a pet fee of $15.00 per pet per night. Two dogs are allowed per room.

### Sheraton Sonoma County Petaluma
745 Baywood Drive
Petaluma CA
707-283-2888 (888-625-5144)
Located on the Petaluma Marina near the wetlands and Shollenberger Park's walking trails, this hotel also offers a number of on-site amenities, seasonally inspired farm-to-table cuisine, and a great location for exploring all the area has to offer. Dogs up to 180 pounds are allowed for no additional fee;there is a pet waiver to sign at check in. For the convenience of travelers with pets dogs are allowed on the 1st floor rooms only.

## Dog-Friendly Attractions
### Petaluma Adobe State Historic Park
3325 Adobe Road
Petaluma CA
707-762-4871
This old adobe ranch building, the largest private hacienda in California between 1834 and 1846, was the center of activity on one of the most prosperous private estates established during the Mexican period. The park offers shaded picnic areas with views of farmland and oak-studded hills. Leashed dogs are allowed at the park, but not inside the buildings. Once a year, usually in May, is Living History Day at this park. Volunteers dress up in authentic clothing. You will find Mexican vaqueros, musicians, blacksmiths, carpenters and more. Try brick-making, basketry, corn-grinding, candlemaking and more. The park is located a twenty minute drive from Sonoma. It is at the east edge of Petaluma, off Highway 116 and Adobe Road.

### Petaluma Self-Guided Film Walking Tour
Keller St. and Western Ave.
Petaluma CA
707-769-0429
Commercial and feature film producers love to step back in time to Petaluma's town charm. Petaluma's iron front buildings are frequently the backdrop for film sets. The Film Tour will lead you through the streets to locations of films like American Grafitti, Peggy Sue Got Married, Heroes,Howard the Duck,Shadow of A Doubt, and Basic Instinct. To begin the tour, park in the city garage at the corner of Keller Street and Western Avenue. The Riverfront at the foot of Western Avenue was where the police car was hurled into the water in Howard the Duck. This was also a film site for Explorers. Nearby, 120 Petaluma Blvd. North (Bluestone Main Building) was the site of Bodell's Appliances in Peggy Sue Got Married where Charlie worked for his father. The Mystic Theater, 23 Petaluma Blvd. North near B St. starred as the State Movie Theater in American Graffiti. Walk down Petaluma Blvd.

South to H Street. The end of H Street at the Petaluma River was Lovers Lane for Peggy Sue and her boyfriend. Head back to D Street, turning Left on D and head west to 920 D Street. The upstairs bedroom was used in Explorers, and a 20 foot tree was imported from Los Angeles for the boyfriend to climb to the girl's bedroom. Commercials for General Electric, Levi's, and catalog stills for the local Biobottoms company were shot here. At Brown Court off D Street, is an area that has a look that is a favorite with commercial producers, including Orville Redenbacher Popcorn. At 1006 D Street was Charlie's house in Peggy Sue Got Married. Backtrack down D Street to Sixth Street and go north towards town. St. Vincent's Church and neighborhood at Howard/Sixth and Liberty Streets were used for scenes in the TV remake of Shadow of a Doubt with Mark Harmon and Basic Instinct with Michael Douglas and Sharon Stone. The big white house at 226 Liberty Street, on the east side of Liberty near Washington Street was Peggy Sue's house in Peggy Sue Got Married. For more information, please visit the Petaluma Visitor Center at 800 Baywood Drive, Suite #1 in Petaluma or call 707-769-0429. The Visitor Center is located a the northwest corner of Highway 116 (Lakeville Hwy.) and Baywood Drive next to the Petaluma Marina. Take the Lakeville Hwy 116 exit off Hwy 101.

**River Walk**
Near D St. bridge and Washington St.
Petaluma CA
707-769-0429
You and your pooch can take an almost 2.5 mile stroll on the River Walk. This walk will take you around the riverfront which was once a bustling river port, and is now a favorite weekend yachting destination. There are numerous species of birds that inhabit this area. For more

details of the walk, pick up a brochure at the Petaluma Visitor Center at 800 Baywood Drive, Suite #1 in Petaluma or call 707-769-0429. The Visitor Center is located a the northwest corner of Highway 116 (Lakeville Hwy) and Baywood Drive next to the Petaluma Marina. Take the Lakeville Hwy 116 exit off Hwy 101.

# Outdoor Restaurants
**Coast Cafe**
46 Wharf Road
Bolinas CA
415-868-2298
bolinascafe.com/
This eatery offers Northern California cuisine specializing in organic and fresh local products with casual indoor or outdoor dining service. Dogs are allowed at the outdoor tables in the front of the cafe. They must be well behaved and leashed.

**A.G. Ferrari Foods**
107 Corte Madera Town Ctr
Corte Madera CA
415-927-4347
agferrari.com/
Dogs are allowed at the outdoor tables. The restaurant is at the Corte Madera Town Center Shopping Center.

**Baja Fresh Mexican Grill**
100 Corte Madera Town Center

Corte Madera CA
415-924-8522
bajafresh.com
This Mexican restaurant is open for lunch and dinner. They use fresh ingredients and making their salsa and beans daily. Some of the items on their menu include Enchiladas, Burritos, Tacos Salads, Quesadillas, Nachos, Chicken, Steak and more. Well-behaved leashed dogs are allowed at the outdoor tables.

**Book Passage Bookstore and Cafe**
51 Tamal Vista

Corte Madera CA
415-927-1503
bookpassage.com/
Dogs are allowed at the outdoor tables.

**Fairfax Scoop**
63 Broadway Blvd
Fairfax CA
415-453-3130
Organic ice cream can't get much better than this. There is a bench out front that you can sit there with your pooch and enjoy a treat. Dogs must be leashed, and please clean up after your pet.

**Iron Springs Pub and Brewery**

765 Center Blvd
Fairfax CA
415-485-1005
ironspringspub.com/pgholder.ht ml
Offering handcrafted beers and tavern fare, this restaurant also has various events throughout the year and alfresco dining. Dogs are allowed at the outer tables;they must be leashed and under their owner's control at all times.

**Jamba Juice**
301 Bon Air Shopping Center
Greenbrae CA
415-925-8470
jambajuice.com
All natural and organic ingredients, no high-fructose corn syrup, 0 grams trans fat, no artificial preservatives, a healthy helping of antioxidants, vitamins, and minerals, and fresh whole fruit and fruit juices set the base for these tasty and healthy beverages. Their organic Hot Blends provides a new spin on coffee, green or chai tea, and hot chocolate;plus they offer probiotic fruit and yogurt Blends. Additionally, they feature all natural salads, wraps, sandwiches, and grab n go specialties. They also offer healthy community support through fundraisers, special sales, and school lunch programs. Leashed, well mannered dogs are allowed at their outside dining area.

**Vladimir's Czechoslovakian Restaurant**
12785 Sir Francis Drake Blvd.
Inverness CA
415-669-1021
This restaurant is located in downtown Inverness and dogs are allowed at the outdoor tables. The restaurant has a well covered patio with heaters. They are open Tuesday thru Sunday from 12 pm until 9 pm.

**Left Bank**
507 Magnolia Avenue
Larkspur CA
415-927-3331
leftbank.com
An authentic French brasserie, guests can enjoy their Parisian casual setting with not so casual food;they offer lunch, dinner, weekend brunch, and children's menus;plus a full service bar with signature cocktails and alfresco dining. Leashed, well mannered dogs are welcome at their outside dining area.

**Baja Fresh Mexican Grill**
924 Diablo Ave.
Novato CA
415-897-4122
bajafresh.com
This Mexican restaurant is open for lunch and dinner. They use fresh ingredients and making their salsa and beans daily. Some of the items on their menu include Enchiladas, Burritos, Tacos Salads, Quesadillas, Nachos, Chicken, Steak and more. Well-behaved leashed dogs are allowed at the outdoor tables.

**La Pinata**
940 7th Street
Novato CA
415-892-1471
lapinatanovato.com/
Authentic handmade Mexican cuisine, Old-World ambiance, a spacious patio, and a full bar, can all be found at this restaurant. Dogs are allowed at the outer tables;they must be leashed and under their owner's control at all times.

**Moylans Brewing Company**

15 Rowland Way
Novato CA
415-898-4677
moylans.com
Signature beers, a full and diverse menu of tasty pub food, sports viewing, a variety of special events, and more are offered at this lively gathering spot. Leashed, friendly dogs are allowed at their outside dining area.

**Apple Box**
224 B Street
Petaluma CA
707-762-5222
facebook.com/appleboxcafe
Dogs are allowed at the outdoor seats on the patio. It overlooks the Petaluma River near the Riverwalk. They are open daily from 7 am until 5 pm.

**Della Fattoria**
141 Petaluma Blvd N
Petaluma CA
707-763-0161
dellafattoria.com
In addition to a menu of healthy and tasty cuisine, this bakery and cafe also features high quality breads with organic flours and the highest quality ingredients available. They also specialize in awesome cakes. Leashed dogs are welcome at their outside tables.

**Cowgirl Creamery**
80 Fourth Street
Point Reyes Station CA
415-663-9335
cowgirlcreamery.com/
This creamery offers award winning organic farmstead cheeses in a wide variety of flavors and styles from the local area, and from other corners of North America and Europe. They also offer some of the region's finest natural foods and other products. Leashed, well mannered dogs are welcome here.

**Java Hub Cafe**
60 Greenfield Avenue
San Anselmo CA
415-451-4928
Besides having a large pet-

friendly patio, this cafe also has a drive-thru window, a catering service, good coffee, and a variety of tasty foods with international influences. Leashed, well mannered dogs are allowed at their outer tables.

**Jamba Juice**
266 Northgate One
San Rafael CA
415-491-7700
jambajuice.com
All natural and organic ingredients, no high-fructose corn syrup, 0 grams trans fat, no artificial preservatives, a healthy helping of antioxidants, vitamins, and minerals, and fresh whole fruit and fruit juices set the base for these tasty and healthy beverages. Their organic Hot Blends provides a new spin on coffee, green or chai tea, and hot chocolate;plus they offer probiotic fruit and yogurt Blends. Additionally, they feature all natural salads, wraps, sandwiches, and grab n go specialties. They also offer healthy community support through fundraisers, special sales, and school lunch programs. Leashed, well mannered dogs are allowed at their outside dining area.

**Ristorante La Toscana**
3751 Redwood Hwy.
San Rafael CA
415-492-9100
ristorantelatoscana.com/
Dogs are allowed at the outdoor tables. This Italian restaurant features pasta, veal, seafood, rabbit and a full bar.

**The Lighthouse Diner**
1016 Court Street
San Rafael CA
415-721-7700
Located in the Rafael Town Center, this restaurant has gained its popularity for its all-American classics, Scandinavian classics brought from the home country by the proprietors, and a great alfresco dining area. Dogs are allowed at the outer tables;they must be leashed and well mannered.

## Anchorage 5
475 Gate 5 Road
Sausalito CA
415-331-8329
Open for breakfast and lunch, this café serves up all American favorites, specialty omelets, and offer alfresco dining-weather permitting. They are open Monday to Saturday from 7 am until 3 pm and on Sunday from 8 am until 3 pm. Dogs are allowed at the outer tables;they must be under their owner's control at all times.

## Poggio Trattoria
777 Bridgeway
Sausalito CA
415-332-7771
poggiotrattoria.com
This classic trattoria features a fusion of northern Italian cuisine and hospitality combined with a seasonally inspired menu created from the freshest local ingredients available. Plus, a wide variety of organic herbs and vegetables come from their own organic garden. Leashed, well mannered dogs are welcome at their outside tables.

## Scoma's
588 Bridgeway
Sausalito CA
415-332-9551
scomassausalito.com/
Dogs are allowed at the outdoor tables. This restaurant is located on the waterfront and offers a great view of the San Francisco Bay. Seafood is their specialty. Reservations are highly recommended.

## Taste of Rome
1000 Bridgeway
Sausalito CA
415-332-7660
taste-of-rome.com/
This Italian restaurant will allow your well mannered and leashed dogs at the outside dining area.

## Parkside Cafe
43 Arenal Avenue
Stinson Beach CA
415-868-1272
parksidecafe.com/
This eatery serves American favorites, pizza, barbecue, and gourmet dishes with service for both indoor and outdoor dining (weather permitting). Dogs are permitted at the outdoor tables. Dogs must be well behaved, under owner's control, and leashed.

## Sand Dollar Restaurant
3458 Shoreline Highway
Stinson Beach CA
415-868-0434
stinsonbeachrestaurant.com/
In operation since 1921, this eatery is open 7 days a week, and features classic American cuisine and seafood. They have a separate porch area with benches for visitors with pets;just order and pick-up inside. Dogs must be well behaved and leashed.

## Three Degrees Restaurant at The Lodge at Tiburon
1651 Tiburon Blvd/H 131
Tiburon CA
415-435-3133
Featuring a full bar and seasonally inspired California comfort cuisine prepared from the finest fresh, local ingredients available, this gathering place is deemed the place to meet, greet, and eat. They also offer daily happy hours, delicious weekend brunches, and alfresco dining. Leashed, well mannered dogs are welcome at their outside tables.

## Tomales Bakery
27000 Highway One
Tomales CA
707-878-2429
This bakery offers a variety of breads and pastries plus calzones and more. They have a few outdoor tables and dogs are allowed at the outdoor tables.

# Pet-Friendly Shopping Centers
## The Village at Corte Madera
1618 Redwood H
Corte Madera CA
415-924-8557
villageatcortemadera.com/
This shopping center features more than 55 shops and services. Dogs are allowed in the common areas of the mall, and some of the stores will have a "pet friendly" sticker in the window if pets are allowed. Dogs must be leashed and under their owner's control at all times.

## Petaluma Village Premium Outlets
2200 Petaluma Blvd N.
Petaluma CA
707-778-9300
Dogs are allowed on leash in the shopping center. Whether they are allowed in the stores or not is up to the individual stores. Dogs may sit with you at the outdoor tables while you eat at some of the food places.

# Pet-Friendly Stores
## Anthropologie
1848 Redwood H, The Village #B-001
Corte Madera CA
415-924-4197
Items of distinction can be found for all ages and in all departments of this unique shop. Carefully selected to add to the enjoyment of the shopping experience, they carry fine clothing, amazing accessories, jewelry, hobby and leisure items, and a full line of bright and useful items for the home, garden, and office. Leashed, well behaved dogs are allowed in the store.

## Pet Club
508 Tamalpais Drive
Corte Madera CA
415-927-2862
petclubstores.com
In addition to warehouse pricing with no membership fees, this comprehensive pet supply store offers weekly specials, and more than 11,000 pet products ranging from wellness items, bedding, dinnerware, a wide choice of quality foods, treats, leashes, toys, apparel, travel

supplies, and much more. Leashed, friendly dogs are always welcome in the store.

### The Container Store
219 Corte Madera Town Center
Corte Madera CA
415-945-9755
containerstore.com/welcome.htm
This store carries hundreds of items to help people get organized. Well mannered dogs are allowed in the store; they must be leashed and under their owner's control at all times.

### Urban Outfitters
#332 Town Center
Corte Madera CA
415-927-1844
In addition to a large inventory of indoor and outdoor apparel for men and women, this major department store also carries vintage wear, designer brands, and a variety of accessories for all types of active lifestyles. They also carry shoes, furnishings, home decor, cameras, electronics, novelty items and more. Leashed, well mannered dogs are allowed in the store.

### Woodlands Pet Food & Treats

701 Strawberry Village
Mill Valley CA
415-388-PETS (7387)
woodlandspet.com
In addition to offering high quality supplies and accessories, healthy food choices, and tasty doggy treats, this pet store also offers low-cost vaccinations clinics, adoption clinics, dog training classes, and a self service dog wash. Leashed, friendly dogs are welcome.

### Pet Food Express
912 Diablo Avenue
Novato CA
415-878-0111
One of the country's leading pet retailers, this comprehensive pet store offers a number of other stores, quality foods/treats, a wide variety of pet supplies, breed-specific items, pet care

products, apparel, health items, hound and human accessories, and much more. Some of the services they offer include working with local SPCAs and rescue groups helping tens of thousands of homeless pets find new homes (they do not sell animals as pets), providing low cost vaccination clinics, dog training classes, and self-service pet washes. All leashed, friendly pets are welcome.

### Pet Food Express
5800 Nave Drive
Novato CA
415-883-1111
One of the country's leading pet retailers, this comprehensive pet store offers a number of other stores, quality foods/treats, a wide variety of pet supplies, breed-specific items, pet care products, apparel, health items, hound and human accessories, and much more. Some of the services they offer include working with local SPCAs and rescue groups helping tens of thousands of homeless pets find new homes (they do not sell animals as pets), providing low cost vaccination clinics, dog training classes, and self-service pet washes. All leashed, friendly pets are welcome.

### Petco Pet Store - Novato
208 Vintage Way
Novato CA
415-898-9416
Your licensed and well-behaved leashed dog is allowed in the store.

### Pet Food Express
383 S McDowell Blvd
Petaluma CA
707-781-3333
One of the country's leading pet retailers, this comprehensive pet store offers a number of other stores, quality foods/treats, a wide variety of pet supplies, breed-specific items, pet care products, apparel, health items, hound and human accessories,

and much more. Some of the services they offer include working with local SPCAs and rescue groups helping tens of thousands of homeless pets find new homes (they do not sell animals as pets), providing low cost vaccination clinics, dog training classes, and self-service pet washes. All leashed, friendly pets are welcome.

### Petco Pet Store - Petaluma
165 North McDowell Blvd
Petaluma CA
707-775-3149
Your licensed and well-behaved leashed dog is allowed in the store.

### Point Reyes Books
11315 State Route 1
Point Reyes Station CA
415-663-1542
ptreyesbooks.com
Well behaved, leashed dogs are allowed to accompany you to this new and used book store on Highway 1. They have dog treats at the counter. The store is open on Monday, Wednesday, Thursday and Sunday from 10 to 6 and on Friday and Saturday from 10 - 9. The store is closed on Tuesday.

### Pet Food Express
280 Northgate One
San Rafael CA
415-492-9992
One of the country's leading pet retailers, this comprehensive pet store offers a number of other stores, quality foods/treats, a wide variety of pet supplies, breed-specific items, pet care products, apparel, health items, hound and human accessories, and much more. Some of the services they offer include working with local SPCAs and rescue groups helping tens of thousands of homeless pets find new homes (they do not sell animals as pets), providing low cost vaccination clinics, dog training classes, and self-service pet washes. All leashed, friendly pets are welcome.

### Petco Pet Store - San Rafael
375 Third St.

San Rafael CA
415-457-5262
Your licensed and well-behaved leashed dog is allowed in the store.

## Dog-Friendly Beaches

**Doran Regional Park**
201 Doran Beach Road
Bodega Bay CA
707-875-3540
This park offers 2 miles of sandy beach. It is a popular place to picnic, walk, surf, fish and fly kites. Dogs are allowed but must be on a 6 foot or less leash and proof of a rabies vaccination is required. There is a minimal parking fee. The park is located south of Bodega Bay.

**Agate Beach**
Elm Road
Bolinas CA
415-499-6387
During low tide, this 6 acre park provides access to almost 2 miles of shoreline. Leashed dogs are allowed.

**Muir Beach**
Hwy 1
Muir Beach CA

Dogs on leash are allowed on Muir Beach with you. Please clean up after your dog on the beach. To get to Muir Beach from Hwy 101 take Hwy 1 North from the north side of the Golden Gate Bridge.

**Point Reyes National Seashore**

Olema CA
415-464-5100
nps.gov/pore/
Leashed dogs (on a 6 foot or less leash) are allowed on four beaches. The dog-friendly beaches are the Limantour Beach, Kehoe Beach, North Beach and South Beach. Dogs are not allowed on the hiking trails. However, they are allowed on some hiking trails that are adjacent to Point Reyes. For a map of dog-friendly hiking trails, please stop by the Visitor

Center. Point Reyes is located about an hour north of San Francisco. From Highway 101, exit at Sir Francis Drake Highway, and continue west on Sir Francis Drake to Olema. To find the Visitor Center, turn right in Olema onto Route 1 and then make a left onto Bear Valley Road. The Visitor Center will be on the left.

**Upton Beach**
Highway 1
Stinson Beach CA
415-499-6387
Dogs not allowed on the National Park section of Stinson Beach but are allowed at Upton Beach which is under Marin County's jurisdiction. This beach is located north of the National Park. Dogs must be leashed on the beach.

## Off-Leash Dog Parks

**Canine Commons**
Doherty, East of Magnolia
Larkspur CA
415-927-5110
ci.larkspur.ca.us/591/Dog-Park
This fenced dog park is located in Piper Park. The park is run by the Larkspur Park and Recreation Department.

**Mill Valley Dog Park**
Sycamore Ave At Camino Alto
Mill Valley CA

This large, 2 acre fenced dog park in Bayfront Park in Mill Valley even has drains installed. It is located on Sycamore, east of Camino Alto.

**Dogbone Meadow at O'Hair Park**
Novato Blvd at Sutro
Novato CA

This no-frills fenced dog park is located in the Neil Ohair Park in Novato. The park has been organized by the D.O.G.B.O.N.E. Dog Park Group which is looking to improve the park.

**Rocky Memorial Dog Park**
W. Casa Grande Road
Petaluma CA
707-778-4380
Your dog can run leash-free in this 9 acre fenced dog park. To get there, take Lakeville Hwy. (Hwy 116) east, and turn west on Casa Grande Rd.

**Redhill Community Dog Park**
Shaw Drive or Sunny Hills Drive
San Anselmo CA

There is a large fenced area for dogs at this off leash play area with more amenities being planned such as benches, tables, water, trees, etc. It is located at the Red Hill Community Park of Sir Francis Drake Blvd. Dogs must be healthy, sociable, current on all vaccinations and license with tags on collar, and under their owner's control at all times. Dogs must be leashed when not in designated off-lead areas.

**Field of Dogs**
Civic Center Drive behind the Marin County Civic Center
San Rafael CA

The Field Of Dogs off-leash dog park is located behind the Marin County Civic Center. To get there from 101, take the N. San Pedro Road exit east. Turn left onto Civic Center Drive and the dog park is on the right. The park is open during daylight hours, is fenced and is 2/3 acres in size.

**Sausalito Dog Park**
Bridgeway and Ebbtide Avenues

Sausalito CA

sausalitodogpark.org/
This fenced dog park is 1.3 acres complete with lighting, picnic tables, benches, a dog drinking water area, and a scooper cleaning station. On some days, this very popular park has over 300 dogs per day.

144

## Dog-Friendly Parks
**Westside Regional Park**
2400 Westshore Road
Bodega Bay CA
707-565-2041
Located on Bodega Bay, this park is a popular spot for fishing. Dogs are allowed but must be on a 6 foot or less leash and proof of a rabies vaccination is required. To get there from Highway 1, take Eastshore Road.

**Deer Park**
Porteous Avenue
Fairfax CA
415-499-6387
Leashed dogs are allowed at this park including the nature trails. The 54 acre park is located in a wooded setting.

**Mill Valley-Sausalito Path**
Almonte Blvd.
Mill Valley CA

This multi-purpose path is used by walkers, runners, bicyclists and equestrians. Dogs on leash are allowed. The path is located in the Bothin Marsh Open Space Preserve.

**Mount Tamalpais State Park**
801 Panoramic Highway
Mill Valley CA
415-388-2070
While dogs are not allowed on most of the trails, they are allowed on the Old Stage Road. This path is about .5 to .75 miles and leads to the Marin Municipal Water District Land which allows dogs on their trails. Dogs must be leashed on both the state park and the water district lands. Please clean up after your pets. To get there, take Highway 101 north of San Francisco's Golden Gate Bridge. Then take Highway 1 to the Stinson Beach exit and follow the signs up the mountain.

**Bolinas Ridge Trail**
Drake Blvd
Olema CA

Dogs on leash may accompany you on the Bolinas Ridge Trail.

The trailhead is about 1 mile from the Pt Reyes National Seashore Visitor Center in Olema. Dogs are not allowed on trails in Pt Reyes (see Point Reyes National Seashore) so this is the closest trail available. The trailhead is one mile up Drake Blvd from Olema on the right. Parking is at the side of the road.

**Civic Center Lagoon Park**
Civic Center Drive
San Rafael CA
415-499-6387
This 20 acre park has an 11 acre lagoon which is used for fishing and non-motorized boating. The park also has picnic areas and a children's playground. Leashed dogs are allowed.

**John F. McInnis Park**
Smith Ranch Road
San Rafael CA
415-499-6387
This 440 acre parks offers nature trails, sports fields, and a golf course. Dogs are allowed not allowed on the golf course. Pets are allowed off leash but must be under immediate verbal control at all times. Owners must also carry a leash and pick up after their pets.

**Samuel P. Taylor State Park**
Sir Francis Drake Blvd.
San Rafael CA

While dogs are not allowed on the hiking trails, they are allowed on the bike trail that runs about six miles through the park. The path is nearly level and follows the Northwest Pacific Railroad right-of-way. The trail is both paved and dirt and it starts near the park entrance. Dogs are also allowed in the developed areas like the campgrounds. Pets must be leashed and please clean up after your pet. The park is located north of San Francisco, 15 miles west of San Rafael on Sir Francis Drake Blvd.

## Emergency Veterinarians
**Pet Emergency & Specialty**
901 Francisco Blvd E
San Rafael CA
415-456-7372
Monday - Friday 5:30 pm to 8 am, 24 hours on weekends.

## Humane Society or SPCAs

**Marin Humane Society**
171 Bel Marin Keys Blvd
Novato CA
415 883 4621
marinhumanesociety.org
Founded in 1907, The Marin Humane Society is a progressive, award-winning animal shelter, offering refuge and rehabilitation to nearly 8,000 animals each year through myriad community services, including adoptions, foster care, behavior and training, humane education, lost-and-found pet services, low-cost clinics, and more.

## Marysville

## Dog-Friendly Hotels
**Comfort Suites Beale Air Force Base Area**
1034 North Beale Road
Marysville CA
530-742-9200 (877-424-6423)
Shops and restaurants within walking distance. Indoor heated pool, exercise room, meeting rooms.

## McGee Creek

## Dog-Friendly Parks
**McGee Creek Trailhead**
McGee Creek Road
McGee Creek CA
760-873-2500

This trail is rated moderate to strenuous. It is located in the Inyo National Forest. From the trailhead you can hike to several lakes including Steelhead Lake. Pets must either be leashed or off-leash but under direct voice control. Please clean up after your pets. To get there from Highway 395, take the first exit after Crowley Lake. Go 4 miles heading south on McGee Creek Road to the trailhead.

# Mendocino

## Dog-Friendly Hotels
### Holiday Inn Express Ft Bragg
250 West Highway 20
Fort Bragg CA
707-964-1100 (877-270-6405)
Dogs of all sizes are allowed. Dogs are allowed for a pet fee of $20 per pet per night.

### Motel 6 Fort Bragg
400 South Main Street
Fort Bragg CA
707-964-4761 (877-424-6423)
Located 6 blocks form the center of town. One mile north or south to the closest beach. Walking distance to many shops,

Dogs of all sizes are allowed. Dogs are allowed for a pet fee of $10.00 per pet per night.

### Super 8 Fort Bragg
888 South Main Street
Fort Bragg CA
707-964-4003 (800-800-8000)
Dogs are welcome at this hotel.

### Blackberry Inn
44951 Larkin Rd
Mendocino CA
707-937-5281 (800-950-7806)
blackberryinn.biz/
Blackberry Inn offers pet-friendly accommodation in Mendocino. Free WiFi is available throughout the property and free private parking is available on site.
Every room has a TV with cable

channels. Enjoy a cup of coffee while looking out at the sea or garden. Every room is equipped with a private bathroom. Select rooms offer a fireplace.
Blackberry Inn is within 2 km of Friendship Park Agate Beach and Kelley House Museum.

## Accommodations
### Cottages at Little River Cove
7533 N. Highway 1
Mendocino CA
707-937-5339
cottagesatlittlerivercove.com
These nine stand alone cottages welcome your pet with pet beds, treats, water bowls and a pet package.

### Inn at Schoolhouse Creek
7051 N. Highway 1
Mendocino CA
707-937-5525 (800-731-5525)
schoolhousecreek.com
With 8+ acres of ocean view gardens, meadows, forest, hiking trails and a secluded beach cove you and your pets will truly feel like you've gotten away from it all. To help your pets get in the vacation mood they will be welcomed with their own pet basket that includes a bed, towel, blanket and a treat. At the end of your day, relax in the ocean view hot tub.

TOP 200 PLACE **Stanford Inn by the Sea and Spa**
44850 Comptche Ukiah Rd and Highway One
Mendocino CA
707-937-5615 (800-331-8884)
stanfordinn.com
This resort is specially designed to accommodate travelers with pets. The inn is rustic and elegant. Amenities include feather beds, wood burning fireplaces, antiques, sofas, televisions with VCRs and DVDs. The resort offers complimentary breakfast featuring a choice from organic selections of omelets, waffles, burritos, and more. A large pool, sauna and Jacuzzi are

protected from the fog by a solarium. Massage in the Forest provides massage and body work and yoga. The Inn's Catch A Canoe & Bicycles, too! offers kayaking and canoeing on Big River Estuary as well as mountain biking and. Special canoes are set-up to provide secure footing for your dog as well as a bowl of fresh water (Big River is tidal and for eight miles and therefore salty). The Ravens vegetarian/vegan restaurant serves organic cuisine. Well behaved pets may join you at breakfast or dinner in a dining area created especially for them. Feed and water dishes, covers to protect bedding and furniture, sleeping beds and treats are provided in the rooms. There is a $25 pet fee per stay.

## Dog-Friendly Vacation Home Rentals
### Sweetwater Inn And Spa
44840 Main Street
Mendocino CA
707-937-4076 (800-300-4140)
sweetwaterspa.com/
Located in Mendocino Sweetwater Inn and Spa offers massage services. Guests can relax in the clothing optional hot tub and sauna. Free WiFi is included in all guest rooms. Select rooms offer ocean views. A fireplace is featured in each room at Sweetwater Inn and Spa Mendocino. A flat-screen TV offers in-room entertainment. Guests can relax in the provided bathrobe and enjoy a cup of organic coffee or tea.
A variety of activities including kayaking and whale watching can be enjoyed in the nearby surroundings. Free parking is available on site. Private hot tubs and saunas are available for an additional fee.
Offering year-round whale watching and charter fishing Noyo Fishing Center is 15 minutes drive from this property. Guests can take a stroll through Mendocino Coast Botanical Gardens just 12.2 km away.

## Dog-Friendly Attractions

### All Aboard Adventures

32400 N Harbor Drive, Noyo Harbor
Fort Bragg CA
707-964-1881
allaboardadventures.com/
This 45 foot charter boat offers deep sea fishing, whale watching, or cruises of the bay and harbor. Dogs are allowed on all the tours except for the Salmon fishing tours. There is no additional pet fee. They suggest you bring your own dogs life jacket, and any supplies you may need for the care or clean-up of your pet. Dogs must be well behaved and leashed at all times.

### Anchor Charter Boats and the Lady Irma II

780 N Harbor Drive
Fort Bragg CA
707-964-4550
A licensed, experienced owner and crew offer a variety of ocean faring activities and fishing trips, and they will usually take about 20 people out at a time. A dog 50 pounds or under is welcome on the boat as long as it is not full or nearly full. Dogs must be very well behaved, crated or leashed at all times, and cleaned up after. There is no additional pet fee.

### Mendocino Coast Botanical Gardens

18220 N. Highway 1
Fort Bragg CA
707-964-4352
gardenbythesea.org/
This botanical garden is the only public garden in the continental United States fronting directly on the ocean. Well-behaved, leashed dogs are welcome. The gardens offer everything from colorful displays to thunderous waves. The mild maritime climate makes it a garden for all seasons, attracting gardeners and nature lovers alike. You are welcome to bring a picnic lunch to enjoy on the grounds.

### Catch a Canoe Rentals

44850 Comptche-Ukiah Rd
Mendocino CA
707-937-5615
catchacanoe.com
This canoe rental shop is located on the grounds of the dog-friendly Stanford Inn by the Sea. Feel free to walk into the shop with your pooch. If you are staying at the inn, it's a five minute walk to the shop. If you are staying at another hotel, there is ample parking. If your pup is over 50 pounds., he or she is more than welcome, but the folks at the shop will warn you that if your dog is a land-lover or decides to make a quick turn in the canoe, the whole party may become very wet. However, this dog-friendly rental shop has even modified a Mad River Winooski to create an incredibly stable canoe especially designed for dogs. Interior carpet, water bowl and a dog biscuit is included. The river you will be canoeing on is close to the ocean and it does contain alot of salt water, so make sure you bring separate water for you and your dog. Check with the shop for water conditions, but in general this is a calm river - no white water rafting here.

## Outdoor Restaurants

### Home Style Cafe

790 S. Main Street
Fort Bragg CA
707-964-6106
homestylecafe.com/
This cafe has two outdoor picnic tables and well-behaved leashed dogs are allowed during the day.

### Laurel Deli

401 N Main Street
Fort Bragg CA
707-964-7812
laurel-deli-and-desserts.com/
Well-behaved leashed dogs are allowed at the outdoor seating area.

### Mendocino Cookie Company

303 N Main St
Fort Bragg CA
707-964-0282
The Mendocino Cookie Company, serving gourmet cookies, delicious pastries, muffins, scones, Organic coffee & espresso, and lots more, is located at 303 N Main St in Fort Bragg, California. They are open daily, and well-behaved & leashed dogs are allowed at the outdoor seating.

### Piaci Pub and Pizzeria

120 W. Redwood Avenue
Fort Bragg CA
707-961-1133
piacipizza.com/
Alcohol drinks are not allowed outside but you are welcome to dine at the outdoor tables with your well-behaved leashed dog.

### Silver's at the Wharf

32260 N Harbor Dr
Fort Bragg CA
707-964-4283
wharf-restaurant.com
Silver's at the Wharf, located at 32260 N Harbor Dr in Fort Bragg, California, is open daily from 11am-10pm. They offer oysters on the half shell, prize winning crab cakes, calamari, cioppino, salmon, halibut, lobster tails, steaks, lamb shanks and games hens. Lighter Fare choices, such as fish tacos, burgers, crab melts, quesadillas and chimichangas are also available. Well-behaved, leashed dogs are welcome on the pet friendly patio.

### The Chief Smokehouse

44400 N Hwy 101
Laytonville CA
707-984-6770
The Chief's Smokehouse is a barbecue restaurant in Laytonville, California, serving all kinds of barbecue meats, and even a few vegan & vegetarian options. They also offer shakes & desserts, and well-behaved dogs are allowed in the spacious outdoor patio area.

### Frankie's Mendocino

44951 Ukiah Street
Mendocino CA

707-937-2436
frankiesmendocino.com
Serving organic & fresh pizzas, sandwiches, greens, beverages, and more, Frankie's Pizza in Mendocino, California, "offers locals and visitors a place to kick back and be themselves while feasting on yummy eats and treats." The pizzeria prides themselves on using local products and the highest quality organic ingredients in their menu. Well-behaved, leashed dogs are allowed at the outdoor seats.

## Mendo Burgers
10483 Lansing Street
Mendocino CA
707-937-1111
Look carefully or you might miss it. This place is located behind the Mendocino Bakery and Cafe. This very dog-friendly place usually has a water bucket for dogs next to the front door. If they don't, ask them and they'll be happy to bring your pooch some.

## Mendocino Cafe
10451 Lansing St
Mendocino CA
707-937-2422
mendocinocafe.com
Serving local & organic foods in Mendocino, California since 1987, the Mendocino Cafe is open daily for lunch & dinner. They serve a variety of cuisines, from Thai Noodles to Mexican dishes, using local & organic ingredients. Well-behaved, leashed dogs are welcome on the large patio.

## Pet-Friendly Shopping Centers
### Mendocino Village
Main Street at Lansing Street
Mendocino CA

This quaint village is filled with interesting shops, outdoor cafes and beautiful walks along the Mendocino coast in the Mendocino Highlands. There are also a number of dog-friendly

B&Bs in town.

## Dog-Friendly Beaches
### Caspar Beach
14441 Point Cabrillo Drive
Caspar CA
707-937-5804
Dogs on leash are allowed at this sandy beach across from the Caspar Beach RV Park. The beach is located about 4 miles north of Mendocino. Please clean up after your dog.

### MacKerricher State Park
Highway 1
Fort Bragg CA
707-964-9112
Dogs are allowed on the beach, but not on any park trails. Pets must be leashed and people need to clean up after their pets. Picnic areas, restrooms and campsites (including an ADA restroom and campsites), are available at this park. The park is located three miles north of Fort Bragg on Highway 1, near the town of Cleone.

### Noyo Beach Off-Leash Dog Beach
North Harbor Drive
Fort Bragg CA

The dog beach is located at the north side of where the Noyo River enters the Pacific Ocean. To get to the dog beach, turn EAST (away from the ocean) on N. Harbor Drive from Highway 1. N. Harbor will go down to the river and circle under Highway 1 to the beach. The beach was organized by MCDOG (Mendocino Coast Dog Owners Group) which is now working on an off-leash dog park for the Mendocino area.

### Big River Beach
N. Big River Road
Mendocino CA
707-937-5804
This small beach is located just south of downtown Mendocino. There are two ways to get

there. One way is to head south of town on Hwy 1 and turn left on N. Big River Rd. The beach will be on the right. The second way is to take Hwy 1 and exit Main Street/Jackson heading towards the coastline. In about 1/4-1/2 mile there will be a Chevron Gas Station and a historic church on the left. Park and then walk behind the church to the trailhead. Follow the trail, bearing left when appropriate, and there will be a wooden staircase that goes down to Big River Beach. Dogs must be on leash.

### Van Damme State Beach
Highway 1
Mendocino CA

This small beach is located in the town of Little River which is approximately 2 miles south of Mendocino. It is part of Van Damme State Park which is located across Highway 1. Most California State Parks, including this one, do not allow dogs on the hiking trails. Fortunately this one allows dogs on the beach. There is no parking fee at the beach and dogs must be on leash.

## Dog-Friendly Parks
### Mendocino Headlands State Park
off Hesser Drive
Mendocino CA

This trail (1-2 miles each way) is located next to the village of Mendocino and it follows the Mendocino peninsula and coastline on bluffs above the beach. The trail is part of the Mendocino Headlands State Park. To get there, take Hwy 1, exit Main Street/Jackson toward the coastline. When Main Street ends, turn right onto Hesser Drive. Go 4 blocks and turn left to continue on Hesser Drive. There are many trailheads or starting points along Hesser Drive, but in the summer, watch out for foxtails.

148

## Humane Society or SPCAs

**Mendocino Coast Humane Society**
19691 Summers Lane
Fort Bragg CA
707-964-7729
mendocinohumane.org
No-kill Shelter serving the
Mendocino Coast, assisting lost
& homeless pets. We offer low
cost spay/neuter in out Shelter.

## Mendota

**Dog-Friendly Hotels**
**Best Western Apricot Inn**
46290 West Panoche Road
Mendota CA
559-659-1444 (800-780-7234)
Dogs up to 80 pounds are
allowed. There is a $20 per day
pet fee up to $100 for the week.
Up to two dogs are allowed per
room.

## Merced

**Dog-Friendly Hotels**
**Merced Inn & Suites**
2010 East Childs Avenue
Merced CA
209-723-3121
Dogs of all sizes are allowed.
There is a pet fee of $30 per
pet.

**Motel 6 Merced**
1983 East Childs Avenue
Merced CA
209-384-1303 (800-800-8000)
Dogs of all sizes are allowed.
Dogs are allowed for a pet fee.

**Travelodge Merced Yosemite**
1260 Yosemite Parkway
Merced CA
209-722-6224
Dogs of all sizes are allowed.
There is a pet fee of $10 per pet

per night.

## Middletown

**Outdoor Restaurants**
**Mountain High Coffee and Books**
16295 H 175
Middletown CA
707-928-0461
This coffee/snack shop in the
mountains offers organic Fair
Trade Coffee and Teas,
organic dairy, fresh baked
pastries and breads, breakfast
and lunch burritos, and
breakfast sandwiches. They
also have a nice indoor seating
area surrounded by slightly
used books and outdoor
seating. Leashed, well
mannered dogs are allowed at
their outside seating area.

## Modesto

**Dog-Friendly Hotels**
**Baymont Inn & Suites Modesto Salida**
4100 Salida Blvd
Modesto CA
209-543-9000 (800-800-8000)
Dogs of all sizes are allowed.
Dogs are allowed for a pet fee.

**Clarion Inn Conference Center**
1612 Sisk Road
Modesto CA
209-521-1612 (877-424-6423)
Central Valleys only indoor
pool and atrium area complete
with arcade and fitness facility.
Only minutes from Vintage Fair
mall.

Dogs up to 40 pounds are
allowed. One dog is allowed
per room.

**Days Inn Modesto**
1312 Mchenry Avenue
Modesto CA

209-527-1010 (800-329-7466)
Dogs are welcome at this hotel.

**Doubletree By Hilton Modesto**
1150 9th Street
Modesto CA
209-526-6000 (800-222-TREE (8733))
Located in the heart of the city,
this upscale hotel has a number
of on site amenities for all level
of travelersncluding their
signature chocolate chip
cookies at check in, plus a
convenient location to shopping,
dining, entertainment and
cultural venues. Dogs up to 40
pounds are allowed for a $50
refundable deposit, plus an
additional fee of $25 per night
per pet.

**Quality Inn**
500 Kansas Ave
Modesto CA
209-578-5400 (877-424-6423)
Walking distance to shops and
restaurants. Close to downtown.

**Outdoor Restaurants**
**Baja Fresh Mexican Grill**
3801 Pelandale Ave
Modesto CA
209-545-4111
bajafresh.com
This Mexican restaurant is open
for lunch and dinner. They use
fresh ingredients and making
their salsa and beans daily.
Some of the items on their
menu include Enchiladas,
Burritos, Tacos Salads,
Quesadillas, Nachos, Chicken,
Steak and more. Well-behaved
leashed dogs are allowed at the
outdoor tables.

**Baja Fresh Mexican Grill**
801 Oakdale Road Ste
Modesto CA
209-238-0222
bajafresh.com
This Mexican restaurant is open
for lunch and dinner. They use
fresh ingredients and making
their salsa and beans daily.
Some of the items on their
menu include Enchiladas,

149

Burritos, Tacos Salads, Quesadillas, Nachos, Chicken, Steak and more. Well-behaved leashed dogs are allowed at the outdoor tables.

**Barkin' Dog Grill**
940 11th Street
Modesto CA
209-572-2341
barkindoggrill.org
All natural 100% organic hamburgers, farm fresh poultry, seasonal local produce, and a really fun atmosphere with a full monthly calendar of live entertainment have made this a popular gathering place. They also validate parking for the 11th Street parking garage. Leashed, well mannered dogs are allowed at their outside tables.

**Pet-Friendly Stores**
**PetSmart Pet Store**
2100 Mc Henry Ave
Modesto CA
209-574-0441
Your licensed and well-behaved leashed dog is allowed in the store.

**Petco Pet Store - Modesto**
2021 Evergreen Ave.
Modesto CA
209-571-0488
Your licensed and well-behaved leashed dog is allowed in the store.

**Petco Pet Store - Riverbank**
2341 Claribel Road
Riverbank CA
209-863-1384
Your licensed and well-behaved leashed dog is allowed in the store.

**Emergency Veterinarians**
**Veterinary Medical Clinic**
1800 Prescott Rd
Modesto CA
209-527-8844
Monday - Thursday 6 pm - 8 am. Friday 6 pm - Monday 8 am. 24 hours holidays.

## Modesto Ceres

**Dog-Friendly Hotels**
**Microtel Inn & Suites By Wyndham Modesto Ceres**
1760 Herndon Road
Modesto Ceres CA
209-538-6466
Dogs of all sizes are allowed. There is no pet fee.

## Mojave

**Dog-Friendly Hotels**
**Motel 6 Mojave - Airport**
16100 Sierra Highway
Mojave CA
661-824-2421 (800-329-7466)
Dogs of all sizes are allowed. Dogs are allowed for a nightly pet fee.

## Mono Lake

**Dog-Friendly Attractions**
**Mono Basin National Forest Scenic Area**
Hwy 395, 1/2 mile North of Lee Vining
Lee Vining CA
760-647-3044
Mono is the westernmost basin of the Basin and Range province, which stretches across western North America between the Rocky Mountains and Sierra Nevada. In the heart of the Basin lies the majestic Mono Lake, a quiet inland sea nestled amidst the Sierra Mountains. Estimated between one million and three million years of age, Mono Lake is one of the oldest continuous lakes in North America. It is a "terminal" lake, which means that it has no outlet water flow. Thus fresh water flows in and can only leave through evaporation. For this reason

the lake has a high content of salt. It is nearly three times saltier than the Pacific Ocean and 1,000 more alkaline than fresh water. A chemical twin of Mono Lake exists nowhere in the world; the closest kin would be found no closer than equatorial Africa. There are many trails here. The Lee Vining Creek Nature Trail is about 1 mile long and is located next to the Mono Basin National Forest Scenic Area Visitor Center. You can also get information about other hikes and trails at the visitor's center.

## Monterey

**Dog-Friendly Hotels**
**Bay Park Hotel**
1425 Munras Avenue
Monterey CA
831-649-1020
Modern amenities an on-site restaurant and lounge and a convenient location are just half the story at the Bay Park Hotel. This non-smoking three-story hotel offers convenience and full-service amenities. All 80 rooms are furnished with refrigerators and 32-inch flat-panel TVs with DVD players. Free Wi-Fi is in all rooms. The hotel's full-service restaurant Crazy Horse boasts a salad bar buffet and is open for breakfast lunch and dinner. The Safari Lounge is a happening spot to unwind after a day of touring as is the outdoor seasonal pool and hot tub. Guests have the opportunity to work out in the exercise room outfitted with both cardio and weight equipment. Well-behaved pets are welcome here for an additional charge. The Bay Park Hotel is just over four miles from the Monterey Peninsula Airport. Cannery Row is a ten- minute drive from the hotel as is the Carmel Mission. It's about three miles to the Monterey Bay Aquarium and to Monterey State Historic Park

which honors old Monterey California's capital under Spanish and Mexican rule. The park's buildings and sites include restored homes with period furnishings as well as fountains gardens and arbors.

## Best Western Plus Victorian Inn
487 Foam Street
Monterey CA
831-373-8000 (800-780-7234)
Dogs are allowed. There is a $30 per pet per night pet fee. Up to two dogs are allowed per room.

## Comfort Inn Monterey
2050 North Fremont Street
Monterey CA
831-373-3081 (877-424-6423)
Centerally located in Beach resort town of Monterey. Within minutes to Monterey Bay Aquarium,Fishermans Wharf.

Dogs up to 40 pounds are allowed.

## Comfort Inn Monterey By The Sea
1252 Munras Avenue
Monterey CA
831-372-8088 (877-424-6423)
Affordable and inviting accommodation in a beautiful Seaside community. Breathtaking sunsets and white sandy beaches.

Dogs up to 40 pounds are allowed. Dogs are allowed for a pet fee of $25.00 per pet per night.

## Inn By The Bay Monterey
936 Munras Avenue
Monterey CA
831-372-5409
Free Wi-fi complimentary parking and easy access downtown Monterey and the waterfront help the El Adobe Inn appeal to budget-conscious guests. The two-story El Adobe features 26 rooms that all come with free Wi-Fi refrigerators coffeemakers and work desks. Expanded cable TV and traditional furnishings complete the picture. Non-smoking rooms

can be requested. Each morning the inn provides a continental breakfast of coffee pastries and fruit. Business facilities are available on-site and parking is free. Pets are welcome with some restrictions. El Adobe is a 10-minute walk from downtown Monterey. The inn is across from Monterey State Historic Park and a mile from Fisherman's Wharf. Del Monte Golf Course and the Monterey Bay Aquarium are both two miles from the inn. San Jose International Airport is 75 miles away.

## Monterey Bay Travelodge
2030 North Fremont Street
Monterey CA

The non-smoking Monterey Bay Travelodge is a home-away-from-home for our guests exploring the area's many attractions. The two-story hotel is an entirely non-smoking property with 100 rooms in a variety of types to accommodate every need. Each room is stocked with conveniences like a mini-fridge a microwave a hairdryer a coffeemaker ironing equipment premium cable with HBO and free high-speed internet access. The hotel also has an exercise room and a coin laundry not to mention a restaurant and plenty of free parking. Up to two pets each weighing no more than 50 pounds are welcome in select rooms for an additional fee. Monterey Bay Travelodge is one mile from the Monterey Peninsula Airport and about two-and-one-half miles from the Monterey Bay Aquarium. Cannery Row is a 10-minute drive from the hotel; the Monterey Museum of Art at Pacific Street is just five minutes away by car.

## Monterey Tides
2600 Sand Dunes Dr.
Monterey CA
831-394-3321
Dogs are allowed. There is a

$30 per pet per night pet fee.

## Andril Fireplace Cottages
569 Asilomar Blvd
Pacific Grove CA
831-375-0994
Andril Fireplace Cottages offers accommodation in Pacific Grove and is situated on 2 acres of land. Barbecue facilities are available on site as well as outdoor seating areas. Each room features a fireplace a TV and a telephone as well as board games and DVDs for children. Each room includes an en suite bathroom. Andril Fireplace Cottages offers a 24-hour front desk a safety deposit box at the front desk free newspapers in the lobby and a fitness centre. Monterey Bay Aquarium is 4 km away. Mineta San José International Airport is 130 km away.

## Lighthouse Lodge And Cottages
1150 & 1249 Lighthouse Avenue
Pacific Grove CA
831-655-2111
Three blocks from the ocean the non-smoking Lighthouse Lodge and Suites offers a quiet getaway with an outdoor pool free breakfast beautiful grounds and easy access to Monterey Aquarium dining and shopping. Think wood ceiling beams crystal chandeliers and lots of light when you picture this two-story hotel. Its 95 rooms come with flat-panel TVs coffeemakers microwaves and mini-fridges. Some rooms have jetted tubs and gas fireplaces. Wi-Fi is available for a fee. Wake up to a hot breakfast and spend a lazy afternoon by the outdoor pool open year round. Pets are welcome for a fee. Parking is free. Three blocks from the beach this hotel makes it easy to go on hikes along the coast; or to ride a bike to Point Pinos Lighthouse and along the waterfront 17 Mile Drive. Get close to marine life at the Monterey Aquarium or dive into shopping and dining action at

Cannery Row both about two-and-a-half miles away. Several golf courses are within a 10-mile radius. Monterey Peninsula Airport is seven miles away.

## Dog-Friendly Attractions
### Ag Venture Tours & Consulting
P. O. Box 2634
Monterey CA
831-761-8463
agventuretours.com/
This touring company will allow dogs on the van tours for no additional fee. The tours specialize in sightseeing, wine tasting, and agricultural education and cover such regions as Carmel Valley, the Santa Cruz Mountains, Monterey Bay, and Salinas Valley. Dogs must be well mannered, leashed, and under their owner's control at all times. Please bring supplies to clean up after your pet.

### La Mirada House and Gardens

720 Via Mirada
Monterey CA
831-372-3689
Radiating an ambiance of early California, these magnificent gardens are surrounded by the warmly inviting adobe walls of an elegant home that has been exquisitely furnished to be reminiscent of its early years. Visitors will also enjoy spectacular views of the Monterey Bay. Although dogs are not allowed in the home, they are allowed to stroll through the gardens. Dogs must be well mannered, leashed, and cleaned up after at all times. They are closed on Monday and Tuesday.

### Monterey Bay Whale Watch Boat Tours
Fisherman's Wharf
Monterey CA
831-375-4658
montereybaywhalewatch.com/
Monterey Bay Whale Watch offers year-round whale watching trips to observe whales

and dolphins in Monterey Bay. Tours are 3 - 6 hours. Well-behaved dogs on leash are allowed. The tours are located at Sam's Fishing Fleet on Fisherman's Wharf in Monterey.

### Princess Monterey Whale Watch
96 Fishermans Wharf
Monterey CA
800-200-2203
This whale watching cruiser offers 2 ½ to 3 hour fully narrated tours by a marine biologist. With one of the largest and most comfortable boats in the bay, they offer plenty of seating in a warm cabin for cold days, a snack bar, and spacious restrooms. Dogs of all sizes are welcome to come aboard when they are not real busy. During the week and the slow part of the season are good times to plan a trip. There is no additional fee for dogs. Dogs must be friendly, boat wise, and they must be leashed at all times and cleaned up after. Please bring your own clean up supplies. Dogs are not allowed to loiter on the wharf by the shops.

### Randy's Fishing Trips
66 Old Fisherman's Wharf #1
Monterey CA
800-251-7440
randysfishingtrips.com/
This fishing and whale viewing cruiser offers fully narrated tours of this region that is as rich in marine life as it is in its history. Dogs of all sizes are welcome to come aboard when they are not busy. During the week and the slow part of the season are good times to plan a trip. There is no additional fee for dogs. Dogs must be friendly, boat wise, and they must be leashed at all times and cleaned up after. Please bring your own clean up supplies. Dogs are not allowed to loiter on the wharf by the shops.

### Sea Life Tours
90 Fishermans Wharf

Monterey CA
831-372-7150
sealifetours.com/
This boat allows leashed dogs on its 45 minute tours of the Monterey bay where you can view sea lions and sometimes whales and other sea life.

## Outdoor Restaurants
### Abalonetti Seafood Trattoria
57 Fishermans Wharf
Monterey CA
831-373-1851
abalonettimonterey.com
The Abalonetti Seafood Trattoria, located on Fisherman's Wharf in Monterey, California, is open daily from 11am-9pm. They serve a large variety of fresh seafood, and specialize in Calamari, serving 12 varieties, including their special Buffalo Calamari. Well-behaved, leashed dogs are welcome on the outdoor patio, and they even offer a few doggy menu options for your pooch-grilled chicken breast or a plain hamburger patty, served on a frisbee for your dog to bring home. Water for your pooch is complimentary.

### Ambrosia India Bistro
565 Abrego Street
Monterey CA
831-641-0610
Offering a large and diverse menu of fresh and authentic Indian food with many vegetarian choices, this restaurant also provides, a full bar, an eclectic wine list, some Indian beers, catering, a venue for special events, and a courtyard garden. Friendly, well mannered dogs are allowed at their outside tables.

### Archie's Hamburgers & Breakfast
125 Ocean View Blvd.
Monterey CA
831-375-6939
Enjoy a hamburger or chicken sandwich for lunch and dinner or come early and have some breakfast at this restaurant that overlooks the ocean. The

Monterey Recreation Trail is directly across the street. Leashed dogs are welcome at their outside dining area.

**Bubba Gump Shrimp Co.**
720 Cannery Row
Monterey CA
831-373-1884
For those who would like to re-experience the story of Forrest Gump - this is the place with recreated scenes from the movie inside the restaurant, and lots of shrimp choices in addition to burgers, steaks, ribs, and specialty drinks. Leashed, well mannered dogs are welcome at their outside dining area.

**Cafe Fina**
47 Fishermans Wharf #1
Monterey CA
831-372-5200
cafefina.com/doggie-menu.htm
Cafe Fina, located on Fisherman's Wharf in Monterey, California, is open daily 11am-9:30pm, with lunch starting at 11am, and dinner starting at 4pm. They specialize in Italian food, and serve pastas, raviolis, pizzas, and a large assortment of fresh seafood. Well-behaved, leashed dogs are welcome on the outdoor patio, and the cafe even has a doggy menu, with options like a 14oz grilled & sliced N.Y. steak, a 4oz grilled chicken breast, and a 1/2 burger patty.

**Domenico's on the Wharf**
50 Fishermans Wharf #1
Monterey CA
831-372-3655
Domenico's on the Wharf, located on Fisherman's Wharf in Monterey California, is open daily from 11am to 10pm. The restaurant serves a variety of fresh seafood, salads, soups, sandwiches, Italian cuisine, including pasta and ravioli, and more. Domenico's welcomes well-behaved, leashed dogs on the outdoor patio, and even offers a doggie menu, with items like the "Chicken a La Pooch", a 4oz chicken breast grilled & slices, "Hound Dog Heaven", a

14oz grilled & sliced NY steak, and more!

**East Village Coffee Lounge**
498 Washington St
Monterey CA
831-373-5601
eastvillagecoffeelounge.com/
This coffee lounge has a large number of outdoor seats in the Old Monterey area.

**Ghiradelli Ice Cream**
660 Cannery Row
Monterey CA
831-373-0997
ghiradelli.com/
Come here for some of the best tasting ice cream. While there, you have a choice of outdoor seating. They have nice patio seating shaded by a large tree or ocean view seating that is covered. Afterwards you and your pup can enjoy the small beach below.

**Indian Summer**
220 Olivier Street
Monterey CA
831-372-4744
indiansummermonterey.com/
Offerings at this eatery include the cuisine of India, a full bar, a Hookah Lounge, an extensive patio with 3 fireplaces, and entertainment on the weekends. Leashed, well mannered dogs are welcome at their outside tables.

**Louie Linguini's**
660 Cannery Row
Monterey CA
831-648-8500
louielinguinis.com
The specialties of the house here include a good variety of fresh seafood, innovative pasta creations, and trademark individual pizzas. They also offer fresh salads, soups, sandwiches, and a kid's menu. Leashed, friendly dogs are allowed at their outside tables.

**Paluca Trattoria**
6 Fishermans Wharf #1
Monterey CA
831-373-5559
palucatrattoria.com/

This restaurant has outdoor seating on Fisherman's Wharf in Monterey.

**Parker-Lusseau Pastries**
539 Hartnell Street
Monterey CA
831-641-9188
parker-lusseaupastries.com/
Although they specialize in wedding cakes, this pastry shop also features a tasty array of French pastries, Danishes, croissants, artisan chocolates, quiches, and - of course some good coffee drinks to go with them. Leashed, well mannered dogs are welcome at their outside tables.

**Peter B's Brewpub**
2 Portola Plaza
Monterey CA
831-649-4511
This restaurant is located in the Portola Hotel and Spal just east of Fisherman's Wharf and near the Monterey State Historic Park. They do not always offer the outdoor dining so call ahead. If they are serving outside you can order a good lunch and great handcrafted beer. Leashed dogs are allowed at their outside dining area.

**Pino's Italian Cafe & Ice Cream**
211 Alvarado St
Monterey CA
831-649-1930
This Italian cafe & ice cream/gelato shop has a few outdoor seats and is located between Fisherman's Wharf and the Portola Hotel and Spa near the Monterey State Historic Park. Leashed dogs are welcome at their outside tables.

**Tarpy's Road House**
2999 Monterey Salinas Hwy #1
Monterey CA
831-647-1444
tarpys.com/
This 1800's looking complex is an interesting atmosphere for dining with your dog. There is a courtyard with a large number of outdoor tables. The restaurant is about 5 miles out of town on the Salinas highway.

**Whole Foods Market**
800 Del Monte Center
Monterey CA
831-333-1600
wholefoods.com/
This natural food supermarket offers natural and organic foods. Order some food from their deli without your dog and bring it to an outdoor table where your well-behaved leashed dog is welcome.

**Bagel Bakery**
1132 Forest Ave
Pacific Grove CA
831-649-6272
thebagelbakery.com/
Dogs are allowed at the outdoor tables.

**First Awakenings**
125 Ocean View Blvd #105
Pacific Grove CA
831-372-1125
firstawakenings.net/
A healthy selection of breakfast and lunch items with several specialties of the house are offered at this café. Leashed dogs are allowed at their outside tables.

**Toasties Cafe**
702 Lighthouse Ave
Pacific Grove CA
831-373-7543
Toasties Cafe has a large number of outdoor tables for you and your dog. They are open Monday to Saturday from 6:30 am until 3 pm and on Sunday from 7 am until 2 pm.

**Jamba Juice**
2160 California Ave
Seaside CA
831-583-9696
jambajuice.com/
Dogs are allowed at the outdoor tables.

## Pet-Friendly Shopping Centers

**Del Monte Center**
1410 Del Monte Center
Monterey CA

delmontecenter.com/
A city landmark, this large and diverse shopping complex offers visitors a variety of dining, shopping, entertainment, and socializing opportunities. Dogs are allowed in the common areas of the mall; it is up to individual stores whether they allow a dog inside. Dogs must be well behaved, leashed, and under their owner's control at all times.

## Pet-Friendly Stores

**Petco Pet Store - Monterey**
960 Del Monte Center
Monterey CA
831-373-1310
Your licensed and well-behaved leashed dog is allowed in the store.

**Best Friends Pet Wash**
167 Central Ave # A
Pacific Grove CA
831-375-2477
After a day at the beach with your pup you may want to wash the sand away here at a self serve pet wash.

**PetSmart Pet Store**
2020 California Ave
Sand City CA
831-392-0150
Your licensed and well-behaved leashed dog is allowed in the store.

## Dog-Friendly Wineries and Vineyards

**Ventana Vineyards**
2999 Monterey-Salinas Highway, #10
Monterey CA
831-372-7415
ventanawines.com/
This award-winning winery has certain wines that are unique to Ventana and Meador Estates, such as Beaugravier, Magnus, "Due Amici", and Dry Rosado, in addition to an impressive list of other classics. The old stone house tasting room was built in

1919 and is surrounded now by lush greenery and splashes of color and fragrance from all the potted flowers. There are tables and bench seating on the patio that also has an open-top fireplace, and is a great place for a picnic. Dogs are not allowed in the building, but they are allowed on the patio and around the grounds. Dogs must be friendly, leashed, and cleaned up after.

## Dog-Friendly Beaches

**Monterey Recreation Trail**
various (see comments)
Monterey CA

Take a walk on the Monterey Recreation Trail and experience the beautiful scenery that makes Monterey so famous. This paved trail extends for miles, starting at Fisherman's Wharf and ending in the city of Pacific Grove. Dogs must be leashed. Along the path there are a few small beaches that allow dogs such as the one south of Fisherman's Wharf and another beach behind Ghirardelli Ice Cream on Cannery Row. Along the path you'll find a few more outdoor places to eat near Cannery Row and by the Monterey Bay Aquarium. Look at the Restaurants section for more info.

**Monterey State Beach**
various (see comments)
Monterey CA
831-649-2836
Take your water loving and beach loving dog to this awesome beach in Monterey. There are various starting points, but it basically stretches from Hwy 1 and the Del Rey Oaks Exit down to Fisherman's Wharf. Various beaches make up this 2 mile (each way) stretch of beach, but leashed dogs are allowed on all of them . If you want to extend your walk, you can continue on the paved Monterey Recreation Trail which goes all the way to Pacific Grove. There are a few smaller

dog-friendly beaches along the paved trail.

**Asilomar State Beach**
Along Sunset Drive
Pacific Grove CA
831-372-4076
Dogs are permitted on leash on the beach and the scenic walking trails. If you walk south along the beach and go across the stream that leads into the ocean, you can take your dog off-leash, but he or she must be under strict voice control and within your sight at all times.

**Dog-Friendly Parks**
**El Estero Park**
Camino El Estero & Fremont St
Monterey CA
831-646-3860
This is a city park with a lake, trails around the lake, a children's play area and many places to walk your dog. It's located on the east side of town.

**Jacks Peak County Park**
25020 Jacks Peak Park Road
Monterey CA
831-755-4895
This wooded park offers great views of the Monterey Bay area. You and your dog can enjoy almost 8.5 miles of hiking trails which wind through forests to ridge top vistas. Park amenities include picnic areas and restrooms. There is a $2 vehicle entrance fee during the week and a $3 fee on weekends and holidays. Dogs need to be leashed and please clean up after them.

**Emergency Veterinarians**
**Monterey Peninsula - Salinas Emergency Vet**
2 Harris Court Suite A1
Monterey CA
831-373-7374
Monday - Thursday 5:30 pm to 8 am. Friday 5:30 pm to Monday 8 am.

## Montgomery

**Outdoor Restaurants**
**Bubba Gump Shrimp Company Restaurant**
720 Cannery Row
Montgomery CA
831-373-1884
For those who would like to re-experience the story of Forrest Gump-this is the place with recreated scenes from the movie inside the restaurant, and lots of shrimp choices in addition to burgers, steaks, ribs, and specialty drinks. Leashed, well mannered dogs are allowed at their outside dining area.

## Morgan Hill

**Pet-Friendly Extended Stay Hotels**
**Extended Stay America - San Jose - Morgan Hill**
605 Jarvis Drive
Morgan Hill CA
408-779-9660 (800-804-3724)
One dog is allowed per suite. There is a $25 per night additional pet fee up to $150 for an entire stay.

**Residence Inn San Jose South Morgan Hill**
18620 Madrone Parkway
Morgan Hill CA
408-782-8311
Dogs of all sizes are allowed. There is a $100 one time additional pet fee.

**Outdoor Restaurants**
**Chipotle**
775 Cochrane Road, Bldg C
Morgan Hill CA
408-776-8505
chipotle.com
Specializing in organic, natural and unprocessed food, this Mexican Eatery offers fajita burritos, tacos, salads, and salsas. Dogs are allowed at the outdoor tables but you will need to order your food inside the restaurant and dogs must remain outside.

**Jamba Juice**
317 Vineyard Town Center Way
Morgan Hill CA
408-465-2456
jambajuice.com
All natural and organic ingredients, no high-fructose corn syrup, 0 grams trans fat, no artificial preservatives, a healthy helping of antioxidants, vitamins, and minerals, and fresh whole fruit and fruit juices set the base for these tasty and healthy beverages. Their organic Hot Blends provides a new spin on coffee, green or chai tea, and hot chocolate;plus they offer probiotic fruit and yogurt Blends. Additionally, they feature all natural salads, wraps, sandwiches, and grab n go specialties. They also offer healthy community support through fundraisers, special sales, and school lunch programs. Leashed, well mannered dogs are allowed at their outside dining area.

**Rosy's at the Beach**
17320 Monterey Road
Morgan Hill CA
408-778-0551
rosysatthebeach.com
Rosy's At The Beach serves Lunch, Dinner, Dessert, and has a kids menu. Well-behaved, leashed dogs are welcome at the outdoor seats.

**Pet-Friendly Stores**
**Petco Pet Store - Morgan Hill**
1019 Cochrane Rd
Morgan Hill CA
408-778-2465
Your licensed and well-behaved leashed dog is allowed in the store.

**Camping World**
13575 Sycamore Avenue
San Martin CA
408-683-2807

campingworld.com/
This comprehensive RV and outdoor store carries a wide variety of RV, boat, bike, and outdoor cooking accessories; all kinds of camping gear; RV screens, shades, and patio decorations; racing/tailgating gear, and all items for RV maintenance. They also carry RV towing supplies, electronics, and interior decorating items as well as pet supplies, RV directories/books, and games. Plus, they offer a tips and advice service, RV sales, rentals, and RV technicians to take care of any installations and repairs. They also welcome your canine companion in the store; they must be friendly and leashed.

## Off-Leash Dog Parks
### Morgan Hill Off-Leash Dog Park
Edumundson Avenue
Morgan Hill CA
408-779-3451
facebook.com/MorganHillDogPark/
This two acre off-leash dog park opened in January 2007 in Morgan Hill. It is managed by the Morgan Hill Dog Owner's Group. There is a separate area for small dogs and both areas have water faucets. Dogs must be licensed, vaccinated and not aggresive. The dog park is located in Community Park and is open during daylight hours.

## Mount Shasta

## Dog-Friendly Hotels
### Dunsmuir Lodge
6604 Dunsmuir Avenue
Dunsmuir CA
530-235-2884 (877-235-2884)
dunsmuirlodge.net/
Dunsmuir Lodge is located in Dunsmuir. Free WiFi access is available in this lodge. All rooms are pet-friendly air-conditioned

have a seating area as well as a refrigerator.
At Dunsmuir Lodge you will find a garden and barbecue facilities. Other facilities offered at the property include a vending machine. An array of activities can be enjoyed on site or in the surroundings including fishing and hiking. The property offers free parking.
Dunsmuir Lodge rooms come complete with a dining area and a coffee machine. The private bathroom also includes a shower.
Mt Shasta Ski Park is 25 minutes' drive from Dunsmuir Lodge.

### Comfort Inn Mount Shasta Area
1844 Shastina Dr
Weed CA
530-938-1982 (877-424-6423)
Championship Golf 5 miles. Mt. Shasta Ski Park 15 miles. Lake Siskiyou 8 miles. Airport 5 miles. Mt. Shasta 8 miles.

### Quality Inn & Suites Weed
1830 Black Butte Drive
Weed CA
530-938-1308 (877-424-6423)
Located in the Historic Lumber town of Weed in south Siskiyou County, we are a haven for the outdoor recreation enthusiatst...

Dogs of all sizes are allowed. Dogs are allowed for a pet fee of $15.00 per pet per night. Two dogs are allowed per room.

## Dog-Friendly Attractions
### Volcanic Legacy Byway
P. O. Box 832
Mount Shasta CA
866-722-9929
volcaniclegacybyway.org
This 500 mile journey of volcanic discovery includes regions of Crater Lake; Upper Klamath Lake and Klamath Falls; the Klamath Basin, Tulelake and Lava Beds; Butte Valley Region; Mt Shasta

Region; the Waterfalls Region - McCloud and Burney; Hat Creek Rim; Mt Lassen Region, and the Lake Almanor Region. From features like active geothermal features and majestic mountains to underground magma conduits, this scenic byway also shares a wide variety of other scenic wonders, historical facts and figures, educational opportunities, an amazing diversity of wildlife, and recreational activities. The website gives detailed information on Visitor Centers, points of interests, maps, and more. Dogs are allowed to accompany their owners on the byway; they must be kept leashed and signage should be in place if dogs are not allowed in certain areas.

## Outdoor Restaurants
### Cafe Maddalena
5801 Sacramento Avenue
Dunsmuir CA
530-235-2725
cafemaddalena.com/
Medium to small dogs are allowed at the outdoor seating area with prior reservations. Dogs must be well mannered and leashed.

### Cornerstone Bakery & Cafe
5759 Dunsmuir Avenue
Dunsmuir CA
530-235-4677
facebook.com/cornerstonedunsmuir
Well-behaved leashed dogs are allowed at the outdoor seating area during the day.

### Lalo's Mexican Restaurant
520 N Mount Shasta Blvd
Mount Shasta CA
530-926-5123
lalos.com/
This Mexican eatery offers seasonal outdoor patio seating. Leashed, well mannered dogs are allowed at the outdoor tables.

## Mountain Center

### Dog-Friendly Parks
**Hurkey Creek Park**
56375 H 74
Mountain Center CA
951-659-2050
Nestled in the San Jacinto
Mountains surrounded by pine
trees, this recreational
destination features a seasonal
creek, striking mountain views,
picnicking areas, extensive
hiking/biking trails, and a 10
mile bike course. Fishing is also
available at the nearby Lake
Hemet. Dogs are allowed
throughout the park, on the
trails, and in the campground for
an additional fee of $1 per day
per pet. Dogs must be kept on
no more than a 6 foot leash, not
be left unattended, cleaned up
after promptly, and under their
owner's control at all times.

**McCall Equestrian
Campground**
28500 McCall Park Road
Mountain Center CA
951-659-2311
A favorite among local
equestrian groups and devoted
riders, this park features 88
acres of open space, several
miles of multi-use trails, roomy
troughs, picnicking areas with
barbecues, and a location for
special events. Dogs are
allowed throughout the park, on
the trails, and in the
campground for an additional
fee of $1 per day per pet. Dogs
must be kept on no more than a
6 foot leash, not be left
unattended, cleaned up after
promptly, and under their
owner's control at all times.

## Murrieta

### Pet-Friendly Stores
**PetSmart Pet Store**
25290 Madison Ave
Murrieta CA

951-696-9847
Your licensed and well-
behaved leashed dog is
allowed in the store.

**Petco Pet Store - Murrieta**
24480 Village Walk Place
Murrieta CA
951-691-5063
Your licensed and well-
behaved leashed dog is
allowed in the store.

### Rescue Organizations
**Pet Haven Rescue**
40485 M.H.S. Rd #153
Murrieta CA
951-698-0940
PetHavenRescue.petfinder.com

**West Coast Mastiff and Large
Breed Rescue**
39252 Winchester Rd #107-
253
Murrieta CA

wcmastiffrescue.com
The mission of West Coast
Mastiff and Large Breed
Rescue, Inc. is to provide
shelter, food, supplies, services
and medical care for homeless
large breed Dogs and to place
them with appropriate adoptive
families.

## Napa Valley

### Dog-Friendly Hotels
**Embassy Suites Hotel Napa
Valley**
1075 California Boulevard
Napa CA
707-253-9540
A full service, atrium-style
hotel, they offer a number of on
site amenities for business and
leisure travelers, plus a
convenient location to
business, shopping, dining, and
recreation areas. They also
offer a complimentary cooked-
to-order breakfast and a

Manager's reception each
evening. Dogs up to 50 pounds
are allowed for an additional one
time pet fee of $50 per room.

**Napa River Inn**
500 Main Street
Napa CA
707-251-8500
napariverinn.com/
With free Wi-Fi complimentary
in-room breakfasts and more
than a passing nod to Napa's
past the Napa River Inn
immerses guests in the history
of this verdant valley. The Napa
River Inn's 66 non-smoking
rooms are housed in three
buildings including the historic
riverfront Napa Mill. All of the
buildings feature a combination
of exposed brick industrial metal
and upholstered finery that
evokes the spirit of Napa as it
moved into the industrial age.
Room furnishings are eclectic
mixing antiques and modern
amenities. All rooms come with
free Wi-Fi flat-panel TVs
refrigerators and coffeemakers.
Most rooms have iPod docking
stations and some have claw-
footed tubs and fireplaces. The
lobby sitting room is a great
place to meet fellow travelers.
Breakfast is delivered to guests'
rooms each morning and
evening wine tastings are
offered. Additional amenities
include an on-site wine market
bike rentals a complimentary
area shuttle and free parking.
Pets are welcome with
restrictions.The Napa River Inn
sits in downtown Napa within
walking distance of the Uptown
Theater and the Napa Opera
House. You'll also find several
dining and nighttime
destinations reachable on foot.
The Napa Valley Wine Train is a
half-mile away. More than 100
wineries are within a half-hour
radius. San Francisco is an hour
away San Francisco
International Airport is 59 miles
away and Napa County Airport
is six miles from the inn.

**The Westin Verasa Napa**
1314 Mckinstry Street
Napa CA

707-257-1800 (888-625-5144) Offering a great location for exploring all this unique area has to offer, this upscale hotel also offers a number of in-house amenities for all level of guests. They also sit within 5 miles of the Queen of the Valley Medical Center and within walking distance to downtown. Dogs are allowed for no additional fee;there is a pet waiver to sign at check in.

### Harvest Inn By Charlie Palmer

One Main Street
St Helena CA
707-963-9463 (800-950-8466)
Full of charm and offering complimentary breakfast wine and Wi-Fi the European-style Harvest Inn By Charlie Palmer sports sophisticated rooms an on-site spa a heated outdoor pool and stunning gardens. The 74 rooms of the single-story Harvest Inn are spread across eight acres of landscaped gardens featuring conifer trees flowers and walking paths surrounded by vineyards. Upscale and spacious rooms provide comfort with 400-thread-count linens plush bathrobes high-end green bath products free Wi-Fi flat-panel TVs and mini-fridges with complimentary wine. Some rooms feature stone fireplaces and private terraces. Non-smoking rooms are available. All guests can enjoy a complimentary European-style breakfast. Additional amenities include a concierge a business center a gym an outdoor heated pool and hot tub a spa that offers in-room spa services and free parking. For an additional fee pets are welcomed with a bed of their own custom pet bowls doggy bags and doggie treats. Along Highway 29 in Napa Valley's glamorous Saint Helena the Harvest Inn is hugged by wineries and is less than a mile from many of Napa Valley's exciting restaurants. Prager Port Works is next door and the shops of Saint Helena are a mile away. Calistoga is 10 miles from the property and

downtown Napa is 16 miles away. It's 68 miles to Oakland International Airport.

## Dog-Friendly Attractions
### Chateau Montelena
1429 Tubbs Lane
Calistoga CA
707-942-5105
montelena.com/
This award winning vineyard offers a variety of wines. Dogs are allowed on the grounds, by the water fountain, and there is a nice walk down to the lake that pooches really seem to like. Dogs are not allowed in the buildings. Dogs must be well mannered, under their owner's control, and be leashed and cleaned up after at all times.

### Old Faithful Geyser
1299 Tubbs Lane
Calistoga CA
707-942-6463
oldfaithfulgeyser.com
Your well-behaved dog is welcome to accompany you to this natural phenomena. Just keep him or her away from the hot water. This geyser is one of only three Old Faithful geysers in the world, erupting about every 40 minutes on a yearly average. The water is 350 degrees hot and shoots about 60 feet into the air for about three to four minutes, then recedes. To see the geyser, you and your pup will need to walk through the main entrance and gift shop. Purchase the tickets at the gift shop and then walk to the geyser area to watch Old Faithful erupt. There is also a snack bar and picnic areas onsite. The admission price is $10 per adult, $7 per senior, $3 per children 6-12 and FREE for dogs. Prices are subject to change.

### Petrified Forest
4100 Petrified Forest Rd.
Calistoga CA
707-942-6667
petrifiedforest.org
Geologists call this petrified

forest, "one of the finest examples of a pliocene fossil forest in the world." The petrified forest was created from a long ago volcanic eruption, followed by torrential rains which brought giant mudflows of volcanic ash from the eruption site to entomb the felled giants/trees. The 1/2 mile round trip meadow tour shows some of the petrified trees. Your leashed dog is welcome. Admission prices are $5 for adults, less for seniors and children, and FREE for dogs. Prices are subject to change.

### Small Lot Wine Tours
Various
Napa CA
707-294-2232
This touring company offers a unique customized wine tour in that they drive (or ride in) your car through the back roads and hidden places in wine country for some great finds and a fair price. They focus on visiting small production wineries and tailor-making your tour to the Napa and Sonoma Counties. Your canine companions are very welcome to come along.

### Beringer Vineyards
2000 Main Street
St Helena CA
707-963-4812
beringer.com/beringer/index.jsp
This busy vineyard specializes in offering a large selection of wines for every occasion and every budget, feature daily historic tours and educational seminars, and hold food and wines events often throughout the year. Dogs are welcome around the grounds, at outdoor seating areas, and at the one outside tasting room area; they are not allowed in buildings. Dogs must be well mannered, under their owner's control at all times, leashed, and cleaned up after.

## Outdoor Restaurants
### Buster's barbecue
1207 Foothills Blvd

Calistoga CA
707-942-5605
busterssouthernbbq.com/
This American-style barbecue eatery specializes in slow cooked links, ribs, steaks, and home baked items. They have an outdoor seating area, just go inside to order. Your pet is welcome to join you at the outdoor tables. Dogs must be well behaved and leashed.

**Home Plate Cafe**
2448 Foothill Blvd
Calistoga CA
707-942-5646
maryshomeplate.com/
You and your pup can enjoy hamburgers or chicken sandwiches at this cafe. The restaurant is located near the Old Faithful Geyser.

**Angele**
540 Main Street
Napa CA
707-252-8115
angelerestaurant.com
This restaurant and bar features rich French comfort cuisine, a variety of fine wines, a warm ambiance inside and outside on the terrace overlooking the Napa River, and a venue for private events. Leashed, well mannered dogs are allowed at the outside dining tables.

**Bistro Don Giovanni**
4110 Howard Street
Napa CA
707-224-3300
bistrodongiovanni.com/
A traditional wood burning fireplace, romantic outdoor terraces, an Italian and Country French menu influenced by the local region, gardens, and a showpiece water fountain surrounded by manicured lawns, bring a touch of the Tuscan Valley ambiance to this gathering place. Leashed, well mannered dogs are allowed at their outside seating area.

**Napa General Store Restaurant**
540 Main Street
Napa CA
707-259-0762

napageneralstore.com/
This store and restaurant offers a unique shopping experience, and great outdoor dining along the Napa River featuring Asian and American cuisine. Your leashed, well behaved dog is welcome to join you at the outdoor tables.

**Sweetie Pies**
520 Main Street
Napa CA
707-257-7280
sweetiepies.com
In addition to a delicious variety of bakery items, this shop also serves up tasty choices for lunch - served Monday through Saturday from 11 am until 2 pm. This bakery also provides for other distributors and retail stores;plus they offer support within the community thru a variety of venues. Leashed, well mannered dogs are welcome at their outside tables.

**Rutherford Grill**
1180 Rutherford Road
Rutherford CA
707-963-1792
This is definitely a dog-friendly restaurant. They usually bring out treats for your dog while you dine at the lovely outdoor patio. The food is great. Rutherford is north of Napa, just beyond Oakville and just south of St. Helena.

**Ristorante Tra Vigne**
1050 Charter Oak Avenue
St Helena CA
707-963-4444
travignerestaurant.com
Innovative and seasonally inspired cuisine, as beautiful garden patio, a welcoming ambiance, and a venue for special events are just some of the offerings of this fine dining establishment. Leashed, well mannered dogs are allowed in the seasonal courtyard dining area.

**Tra Vigne Cantinetta**
1050 Charter Oak Avenue
St Helena CA
707-963-4444

travignerestaurant.com/index.ht
m
This Italian wine bar features more than 50 wines by the glass and is known for having wines for retail sale that are considered impossible to find. The Italian fare can be paired with its compliment wine, and they offer outdoor courtyard seating. Leashed or crated and well mannered dogs are welcome at their outside patios, but they must be able to be carried thru the restaurant.

**Bistro Jeanty**
6510 Washington Street
Yountville CA
707-944-0103
bistrojeanty.com
This classic French bistro features regional home-style cuisine with a seasonally driven menu. They also offer daily specials, a venue for special events, and alfresco dining. Leashed, well mannered dogs are allowed at the outside dining area.

**Hurley's Restaurant**
6518 Washington Street
Yountville CA
707-944-2345
hurleysrestaurant.com/
Serving fresh seasonal wine country cuisine with a Mediterranean flair, this eatery is also popular for their 'wild game' dishes and wonderful wine and food pairings. They feature a full bar with a large open patio for outside dining, weather permitting. Leashed, well mannered dogs are allowed at their outside dining area.

## Pet-Friendly Stores
**Pet Food Express**
3916 Bel Aire Plaza
Napa CA
707-265-8888
One of the country's leading pet retailers, this comprehensive pet store offers a number of other stores, quality foods/treats, a wide variety of pet supplies, breed-specific items, pet care products, apparel, health items,

hound and human accessories, and much more. Some of the services they offer include working with local SPCAs and rescue groups helping tens of thousands of homeless pets find new homes (they do not sell animals as pets), providing low cost vaccination clinics, dog training classes, and self-service pet washes. All leashed, friendly pets are welcome.

**Petco Pet Store - Napa**
3284 Jefferson St.
Napa CA
707-224-7662
Your licensed and well-behaved leashed dog is allowed in the store.

**Fideaux**
1312 Main Street
St Helena CA
707-967-9935
Well-behaved leashed dogs are welcome to accompany you into Fideaux. The store boasts dog specialty items and gifts. It is located in the center of St. Helena.

# Dog-Friendly Wineries and Vineyards

**Cuvaison Winery**
4550 Silverado Trail
Calistoga CA
707-942-6266
Well-behaved leashed dogs are allowed in the tasting room and at the outdoor picnic areas.

**Dutch Henry Winery**
4300 Silverado Trail
Calistoga CA
707-942-5771
dutchhenry.com/
Although a small family-owned and operated winery, they specialize in artisan Bordeaux varietals in very limited releases, and are known for their Napa Valley Estate Cabernet Sauvignon. Your well behaved canine companion is welcome on the grounds and will most likely be greeted by the winery's four-legged companions. There are picnic areas and places for

dogs to play; they are not allowed inside the winery. Dogs must be leashed and cleaned up after.

**Graeser Winery**
255 Petrified Forest Road
Calistoga CA
707-942-4437
graeserwinery.com
Canine visitors to this winery may be met by the resident great dane, Jack. The winery welcomes visiting dogs as long as they are friendly towards other dogs and people. There are picnic tables on the front patio and a table on top of the hill.

**Clos Du Val Winery**
5330 Silverado Trail
Napa CA
800-993-9463
closduval.com
Dogs on leash are allowed in the tasting room and on the property. The hours are 10am-5pm Monday-Sunday.

**Hess Collection Winery**
4411 Redwood Road
Napa CA
707-255-1144
hesscollection.com/
This winery specializes in wines that embody the unique distinctive growing factors of Mount Veeder. Dogs are allowed on the grounds and bench areas; they are not allowed in the tasting room. Dogs must be well mannered, and leashed and cleaned up after at all times.

**Pine Ridge Winery**
5901 Silverado Trail
Napa CA
707-252-9777
pineridgewinery.com/
This winery specializes in wines that embody the unique distinctiveness of the Napa Valley region. Dogs are allowed on the grounds and bench areas; they are not allowed in the tasting room. Dogs must be well mannered, and leashed and cleaned up after at all times.

**Starmont Winery**
1451 Stanly Ln
Napa CA
707-252-8001
starmontwinery.com/
The Starmont Winery offers a bucolic barn tasting room in the Carneros district. Guests sip wine in an open-air courtyard, overlooking one of the vineyards. Dogs are welcome leashed, but are welcome and are treated to doggy biscuits, Frisbees or tennis balls while owners sip wine.

**Frogs Leap Winery**
8815 Conn Creek Road
Rutherford CA
707-963-4704
frogsleap.com
Utilizing organically grown grapes and traditional winemaking techniques, this award winning winery strives to produce wines that reflect the unique characteristics of the Napa Valley. Dogs are allowed on the grounds and gardens, but not in buildings. Dogs must be very well mannered, and leashed and cleaned up after.

**Mumm Napa Winery**
8445 Silverado Trail
Rutherford CA
800-686-6272
mummnapa.com/
This winery offers outside table service on their terrace (weather permitting), spectacular views, a knowledgeable staff, an art gallery, annual events, and a gift store. Your well behaved dog is welcome to explore the grounds with you or join you on the terrace. They usually have doggy treats available and are happy to get a bowl of water for your pooch. Dogs must be leashed and cleaned up after at all times.

**Sullivan Vineyards**
1090 Galleron Rd
Rutherford CA
707-963-9646
Well-behaved leashed dogs are allowed in the tasting room and at the picnic table. They have three dogs on the premises.

**Casa Nuestra Winery**
3451 Silverado Trail North
St Helena CA
866-844-WINE
Dogs are welcome in the picnic area. The winery has five dogs that "work" here as greeters, but they all work different days.

**Rustridge**
2910 Lower Chiles Valley Rd
St Helena CA
707-965-2871
Well-behaved leashed dogs are allowed in the tasting room and in the picnic area. The owner also has four dogs on the premises.

**V. Sattui Winery**
1111 White Lane
St Helena CA
707-963-7774
vsattui.com/
Established in 1885, this family owned, award-winning winery sits in the heart of the Napa Valley, and their wines can only be purchased by mail order or by a visit to the estate. Also on site are a cheese shop and deli, and 2 1/2 acres of tree-shaded picnic grounds. Dogs are allowed around the grounds and at the picnic area; they may only be in buildings if they are being carried in a carrier. Dogs must be well behaved, under their owner's control at all times, leashed, and cleaned up after.

**V. Sattui Winery**
1111 White Lane
St Helena CA
707-963-7774
Dogs are welcome in the picnic area. This winery also has an onsite deli. This winery has lawn picnic benches and a shaded area.

**Domain Chandon**
One California Drive
Yountville CA
707-944-2280
chandon.com/
This secluded winery offers a variety of sparkling and varietal wines, regular events, and beautifully landscaped grounds. Dogs are allowed on the grounds and the terrace, but not in buildings. Dogs must be well mannered, and leashed and cleaned up after.

**Hill Family Estate**
6512 Washington Street
Yountville CA
707-944-9580
hillfamilyestate.com
Now producing wines from 11 unique vineyards, this winery offers a wide range of fine estate wines as well as producing grapes for other wineries. Leashed dogs are allowed on the grounds.

## Off-Leash Dog Parks
**Canine Commons Dog Park**
Dry Creek Rd at Redwood Rd
Napa CA
707-257-9529
This fenced 3 acre dog park has water, benches, and pooper scoopers. The dog park is located in Alston Park which has about 100 acres of dog-friendly on-leash trails and some off-leash trails. To get there from Napa, take Hwy 29 North and exit Redwood Rd. Turn left on Redwood Rd and then right on Dry Creek Rd. The park will be on the left.

**Shurtleff Park Dog Park**
Shetler Avenue
Napa CA
707-257-9529
This park offers an off-leash exercise area. Dogs must be under voice control at all times. The park is located on Shetler Avenue, east of Shurtleff Avenue.

## Needles

## Dog-Friendly Hotels
**Best Western Colorado River Inn**
2371 West Broadway
Needles CA
760-326-4552 (800-780-7234)
Pets may be accepted. Please contact the hotel directly for full details.

**Rodeway Inn Needles**
1195 3rd Street
Needles CA
760-326-4900
Rodeway Inn Needles easily accessible from I-40 and one block from historic Route 66 welcomes our guests with free high-speed internet access and a heated outdoor pool. Spanning three floors the hotel features 116 rooms accessed by exterior corridors and furnished with free high-speed internet microwaves and mini-fridges. Non-smoking rooms are available. Take a dip in the heated outdoor pool open seasonally and keep your wardrobe fresh with guest laundry facilities. Pets are permitted with an additional fee and parking is free. This Rodeway Inn is just off I-40 a block from the iconic Route 66 and within two miles of fishing and outdoor recreation on the Colorado River. The historic mining town of Oatman Arizona is a 45-minute drive away and McCarran International Airport is 108 miles from the hotel.

## Outdoor Restaurants
**Juicy's River Cafe**
2411 W Broadway St
Needles CA
760-326-2233
juicysrivercafe.com
Juicy's River Cafe serves breakfast, lunch, and dinner, including wraps, melts, sandwiches, omelets, " Juicy's Burgers", and a variety of dinner entrees. Well-behaved, leashed dogs are welcome at the outdoor tables.

## Dog-Friendly Parks
**Havasu National Wildlife Refuge**
Box 3009 (Mojave County Road 227)
Needles CA
760-326-3853

This refuge is one of more than 500 managed by the Fish and Wildlife Service, and is dedicated to conserving our wildlife heritage. Various habitats provide for a wide variety of plant, bird, and animal species. The refuge office hours are 8am-4pm Monday through Friday, and they suggest you come in there first for brochures and any updates on the area. Dogs of all sizes are allowed. Dogs must be kept on lead at all times and cleaned up after. Dogs are allowed throughout the park, but may not chase or disturb the wildlife in any way.

## New Cuyama

### Dog-Friendly Parks
**Caliente Mountain Access Trail**
Highway 166
New Cuyama CA
661-391-6000
This trail is popular with hikers and mountain bikers. It is also used by hunters who take the trail to get access to adjacent public lands. This open space has a nice display of wildflowers in the Spring. The trailhead is located about 14 miles west of New Cuyama. The trail starts on the north side of the highway after crossing a bridge over the Cuyama River. Dogs are allowed on the trail.

## New Smyrna Beach

### Pet-Friendly Stores
**Silly Willie's Pet Boutique**
218 Flagler Ave
New Smyrna Beach CA
386-427-0196
silly-willies.com
A unique pet boutique providing you a large selection of hard to find pet products. Silly Willies, located New Smyrna Beach, FL.

They carry a variety of high quality food and pet treats from makers as The Real Meat Company, Nutri Source, Plato, Snook's, Life's Abundance and many other brands. They also sell toys, dishes, beds, leashes, and much more. Pets are always welcome at Silly Willie's, as long as they are on a leash.

## Newbury Park

### Outdoor Restaurants
**Baja Fresh Mexican Grill**
1015 Broadbeck Dr.
Newbury Park CA
805-376-0808
bajafresh.com
This Mexican restaurant is open for lunch and dinner. They use fresh ingredients and making their salsa and beans daily. Some of the items on their menu include Enchiladas, Burritos, Tacos Salads, Quesadillas, Nachos, Chicken, Steak and more. Well-behaved leashed dogs are allowed at the outdoor tables.

**The Natural Cafe**
1714 Newbury Road, Suite R
Newbury Park CA
805-498-0493
thenaturalcafe.com
With a focus on sourcing the freshest, naturally produced and locally grown produce and products available, this eatery offers a full menu of healthy foods and beverages. Foods are also made fresh daily with many vegan and vegetarian choices. Leashed, well mannered dogs are allowed at their outside tables.

## Oak Park

### Off-Leash Dog Parks
**Oak Canyon Dog Park**

5600 Hollytree Drive
Oak Park CA

Open daily from 7 am until around dusk daily with the exception of Friday mornings from 7 am until 10 am for maintenance, this off leash site features 2 separate sections for large and small dogs, water for dogs, a shaded area, and newly planted trees. Seasonal hours are posted at the park which is located behind Oak Canyon Community Park (use entrance for the park and continue to the end of the road and park). Although parking is about 200 feet from the entrance, there are 2 handicap parking spots right at the dog park entrance. Dogs must be healthy, sociable, current on all vaccinations and license with tags on collar, and under their owner's control at all times. Owners must clean up after their pets, and keep them leashed when not in designated off-lead areas.

## Oakdale

### Pet-Friendly Stores
**Tractor Supply Company**
1580 E F Street/H 120/108
Oakdale CA
209-845-2402
tractorsupply.com
Some offerings of this comprehensive farm store includes agriculture, farming and ranching supplies; outdoor power equipment with all the necessities; hundreds of thousands of parts and accessories accessible for yard and garden; metal working and welding supplies; tools for auto and home; a wide range of livestock/farm feed and needs; and a variety of foods and care/play/groom items for household pets. Additionally, they provide trailer and towing supplies, vehicle maintenance accessories, clothing, work wear, foot wear, gifts, home

improvement items, a lot of "know-how" and much more. Leashed, friendly dogs are welcome in the store.

## Oakland - East Bay

## Dog-Friendly Hotels
**Ramada Antioch**
2436 Mahogany Way
Antioch CA
925-754-6600
Dogs of all sizes are allowed. There is a $50 one time pet fee.

**Best Western Plus Heritage Inn**
1955 East Second Street
Benicia CA
707-746-0401 (800-780-7234)
Dogs up to 80 pounds are allowed. There is a $20 per day pet fee up to $100 for the week. Up to two dogs are allowed per room.

**Americas Best Value Inn - Berkeley San Francisco**
1620 San Pablo Ave
Berkeley CA
510-525-6770
A location two miles from University of California - Berkeley Americas Best Value Inn offers our guests a cozy crash pad with Wi-Fi and a Japanese restaurant on-site. A nod to Spanish architecture this low-rise property has 40 brightly decorated rooms with cable TV microwaves mini-fridges coffeemakers seating areas Wi-Fi and local calls. Guests can dig into Japanese flavors at the on-site restaurant and catch up on work at the business center. Parking is on the house and pets are welcome for an additional fee. Americas Best Value Inn is located about three miles from Edwards Stadium on the campus of University of California - Berkeley. Guests can spend an afternoon on the water at Cesar Chavez Park two-and-a-half miles away or get their adrenaline pumping at

Golden Gate Fields Race Track a little over one mile. Downtown San Francisco is a half-hour drive from the hotel. North Berkeley BART is two blocks and Oakland International Airport is 17 miles.

**Doubletree By Hilton Berkeley Marina**
200 Marina Boulevard
Berkeley CA
510-548-7920 (800-222-TREE (8733))
Overlooking the San Francisco Bay, this resort style, luxury hotel offers a number of on site amenities for business or leisure travelers, plus a convenient location to all this vibrant city and surrounding areas have to offer. Dogs up to 50 pounds are allowed for an additional one time pet fee of $100 per room.

**La Quinta Inn Berkeley**
920 University Avenue
Berkeley CA
510-849-1121 (800-531-5900)
Dogs up to 25 pounds are allowed for a $100 refundable deposit. Quiet dogs only may be left alone in the room.

**Comfort Inn Castro Valley**
2532 Castro Valley Blvd
Castro Valley CA
510-538-9501 (877-424-6423)
Welcome to Quality Inn Castro Valley. We are centrally located at the crossroads of the east side of San Francisco Bay Area.

Dogs up to 25 pounds are allowed. Dogs are allowed for a pet fee of $10.00 per pet per night. Three or more dogs may be allowed.

**Crowne Plaza Concord/walnut Creek**
45 John Glenn Drive
Concord CA
925-825-7700 (877-270-6405)
Dogs up to 35 pounds are allowed. Dogs are allowed for a pet fee.

**Hilton Concord**

1970 Diamond Boulevard
Concord CA
925-827-2000
This upscale hotel offers numerous on site amenities for business and leisure travelers, plus a convenient location to airports, and financial, shopping, dining, and entertainment areas. Dogs up to 75 pounds are allowed for an additional one time pet fee of $50 per room.

**Best Western Danville Sycamore Inn**
803 Camino Ramon
Danville CA
925-855-8888 (800-780-7234)
Dogs up to 80 pounds are allowed. There is a $15 per day pet fee up to $100 for the week. Up to two dogs are allowed per room.

**Holiday Inn Dublin - Pleasanton**
6680 Regional Street
Dublin CA
925-828-7750 (877-270-6405)
Dogs of all sizes are allowed. Dogs are allowed for a pet fee of $35.00 per pet per stay.

**La Quinta Inn And Suites Dublin Pleasanton**
6275 Dublin Blvd.
Dublin CA
925-828-9393 (800-531-5900)
Dogs up to 20 pounds are allowed for no additional pet fee; there is a pet policy to sign at check-in. Pet rooms are on the 1st floor, and dogs may not be left alone in the room.

**Hyatt House Emeryville/san Francisco Bay Area**
5800 Shellmound Street
Emeryville CA
510-601-5880
COMMENTS

**Best Western Plus Garden Court Inn**
5400 Mowry Avenue
Fremont CA
510-792-4300 (800-780-7234)
Dogs up to 80 pounds are allowed. There is a $20 per day pet fee up to $100 for the week. Up to two dogs are allowed per

room.

## La Quinta Inn & Suites Fremont / Silicon Valley
46200 Landing Parkway
Fremont CA
510-445-0808 (800-531-5900)
Dogs of all sizes are allowed.
There are no additional pet fees.
Dogs must be quiet, well
behaved, leashed and cleaned
up after.

## La Quinta Inn & Suites Hayward Oakland Airport
20777 Hesperian Boulevard
Hayward CA
510-732-6300 (800-531-5900)
A dog up to 50 pounds is
allowed. There is a $50
refundable pet deposit, and
there is pet waiver to sign at
check in. Dogs may not be left
unattended, and they must be
leashed and cleaned up after.

## Holiday Inn Express Hotel & Suites Livermore
3000 Constitution Drive
Livermore CA
925-961-9600 (877-270-6405)
Dogs up to 30 pounds are
allowed. Dogs are allowed for a
pet fee of $30.00 per pet per
night.

## La Quinta Inn Livermore
7700 Southfront Rd
Livermore CA
925-373-9600 (800-531-5900)
Dogs of all sizes are allowed for
no additional pet fee; there is a
pet policy to sign at check-in.
The Do Not Disturb sign must
be on the door when there is a
pet alone in the room.

## Best Western John Muir Inn
445 Muir Station Road
Martinez CA
925-229-1010 (800-780-7234)
Dogs are allowed. There is a
$50 per pet per stay pet fee. Up
to two dogs are allowed per
room.

## Aloft Silicon Valley
8200 Gateway Boulevard
Newark CA
510-494-8800 (877-946-8357)
Some of the offerings of this

upscale hotel include all-suite
accommodations,
Whatever/Whenever services,
an outdoor pool, a restaurant
and lounge, and a central
location to 3 major airports.
Dogs up to 45 pounds are
allowed for an additional $100
one time fee per room;there is
a pet waiver to sign at check in.
Canine guests are also
welcomed with a pet bed, toys,
and a turn-down treat.

## Chase Suites Hotel In Newark
39150 Cedar Boulevard
Newark CA
510-795-1200
COMMENTS

## Doubletree By Hilton Newark - Fremont
39900 Balentine Drive
Newark CA
510-490-8390
Located in the energetic East
Bay Silicon Valley, this upscale
hotel offers numerous
amenities and sits central to
several universities, shopping
and dining venues, and some
of the area's best attractions.
One dog up to 75 pounds is
allowed for an additional one
time pet fee of $50.

## Hilton Oakland Airport
1 Hegenberger Road
Oakland CA
510-635-5000
This upscale hotel offers a
number of on site amenities for
business and leisure travelers,
plus a convenient location to
the Oakland International
Airport and the Bart transit
system for easy access to all
the attractions of the big city.
Dogs up to 75 pounds are
allowed for an additional one
time pet fee of $50 per room.

## La Quinta Inn Oakland Airport
8465 Enterprise Way
Oakland CA
510-632-8900 (800-531-5900)
Dogs of all sizes are allowed.
There are no additional pet
fees. Dogs must be leashed
and cleaned up after.

## Quality Inn Oakland
8471 Enterprise Way
Oakland CA
510-562-4888 (877-424-6423)
Hotel parking is available for
length of stay only.

Dogs up to 20 pounds are
allowed. Dogs are allowed for a
pet fee of $10 per pet per night.

## Best Western Plus Pleasanton Inn
5375 Owens Court
Pleasanton CA
925-463-1300 (800-780-7234)
Dogs are allowed. There is a
$35 per pet per night pet fee. Up
to two dogs are allowed per
room.

## Pleasanton Marriott
11950 Dublin Canyon Blvd
Pleasanton CA
925-847-6000
Dogs up to 15 pounds are
allowed. There is a $75 one time
pet fee.

## Sheraton Pleasanton
5990 Stoneridge Mall Road
Pleasanton CA
925-463-3330 (888-625-5144)
This luxury hotel offers
numerous on site amenities for
discerning business and leisure
travelers, plus a convenient
location to shopping, dining, and
recreation areas as well as
cultural events, financial
districts, and entertainment
areas. Dogs are allowed for no
additional fee;there is a pet
waiver to sign at check in.

## Marriott San Ramon
2600 Bishop Drive
San Ramon CA
925-867-9200
Dogs up to 100 pounds are
allowed. There is a $100 one
time pet fee.

## Holiday Inn Express Walnut Creek
2730 N Main St
Walnut Creek CA
925-932-3332 (877-270-6405)
Dogs up to 20 pounds are
allowed. Dogs are allowed for a
pet fee of $20.00 per pet per

night.

## Pet-Friendly Extended Stay Hotels

**Extended Stay America - Oakland - Alameda**
1350 Marina Village Pkwy
Alameda CA
510-864-1333 (800-804-3724)
One dog is allowed per suite.
There is a $25 per night
additional pet fee up to $150 for
an entire stay.

**Extended Stay America - Dublin - Hacienda Dr.**
4500 Dublin Blvd
Dublin CA
925-875-9556 (800-804-3724)
One dog is allowed per suite.
There is a $25 per night
additional pet fee up to $150 for
an entire stay.

**Extended Stay America - Fairfield - Napa Valley**
1019 Oliver Rd
Fairfield CA
707-438-0932 (800-804-3724)
One dog is allowed per suite.
There is a $25 per night
additional pet fee up to $150 for
an entire stay.

**Homewood Suites By Hilton Fairfield**
4755 Business Center Drive
Fairfield CA
707-863-0300
This upscale all suite hotel
offers large, comfortable suites
for longer stays and/or
temporary housing needs;plus
numerous on site amenities for
all level of travelers and a
convenient location to local sites
of interest. Dogs up to 50
pounds are allowed for an
additional one time pet fee of
$75 per room.

**Staybridge Suites Fairfield Napa Valley Area**
4775 Business Center Drive
Fairfield CA
707-863-0900 (877-270-6405)
Dogs up to 40 pounds are
allowed. Pets allowed with an
additional pet fee. Up to $75 for

1-6 nights and up to $150 for
7+ nights. A pet agreement
must be signed at check-in.

**Extended Stay America - Fremont - Warm Springs**
46312 Mission Blvd
Fremont CA
510-979-1222 (800-804-3724)
One dog is allowed per suite.
There is a $25 per night
additional pet fee up to $150
for an entire stay.

**Extended Stay America Fremont - Fremont Blvd. South**
46080 Fremont Blvd
Fremont CA
510-353-1664 (800-804-3724)
One dog is allowed per suite.
There is a $25 per night
additional pet fee up to $150
for an entire stay.

**Residence Inn Fremont Silicon Valley**
5400 Farwell Place
Fremont CA
510-794-5900
Dogs of all sizes are allowed.
There is a $100 one time
additional pet fee.

**Extended Stay America - Livermore - Airway Blvd.**
2380 Nissen Dr
Livermore CA
925-373-1700 (800-804-3724)
One dog is allowed per suite.
There is a $25 per night
additional pet fee up to $150
for an entire stay.

**Residence Inn Livermore Pleasanton**
1000 Air Way Boulevard
Livermore CA
925-373-1800
Dogs of all sizes are allowed.
There is a $75 one time
additional pet fee.

**Homewood Suites By Hilton Newark/fremont Ca**
39270 Cedar Blvd
Newark CA
510-791-7700
This upscale all suite hotel
offers large, comfortable suites
for longer stays and/or

temporary housing needs;plus
numerous on site amenities for
all level of travelers and a
convenient location to local sites
of interest. Dogs up to 50
pounds are allowed for an
additional one time pet fee of
$75 per room.

**Residence Inn By Marriott Newark Silicon Valley**
35466 Dumbarton Court
Newark CA
510-739-6000
Dogs of all sizes are allowed.
There is a $100 one time
additional pet fee.

**Towneplace Suites By Marriott Newark Silicon Valley**

39802 Cedar Blvd
Newark CA
510-657-4600
Dogs up to 25 pounds are
allowed. There is a $100 one
time pet fee.

**Extended Stay America - Oakland - Emeryville**
3650 Mandela Pkwy
Oakland CA
510-923-1481 (800-804-3724)
One dog is allowed per suite.
There is a $25 per night
additional pet fee up to $150 for
an entire stay.

**Homewood Suites By Hilton Oakland-waterfront**
1103 Embarcadero
Oakland CA
510-663-2700
This upscale all suite hotel
offers large, comfortable suites
for longer stays and/or
temporary housing needs;plus
numerous on site amenities for
all level of travelers and a
convenient location to local sites
of interest. Dogs up to 50
pounds are allowed for an
additional one time pet fee of
$75 per room.

**Extended Stay America - Pleasant Hill - Buskirk Ave.**
3220 Buskirk Ave
Pleasant Hill CA
925-945-6788 (800-804-3724)
One dog is allowed per suite.

There is a $25 per night additional pet fee up to $150 for an entire stay.

**Residence Inn By Marriott Pleasant Hill Concord**
700 Ellinwood Way
Pleasant Hill CA
925-689-1010
Dogs of all sizes are allowed. There is a $100 one time additional pet fee.

**Residence Inn By Marriott Pleasanton**
11920 Dublin Canyon Road
Pleasanton CA
925-227-0500
Dogs of all sizes are allowed. There is a $100 one time additional pet fee.

**Extended Stay America - Richmond - Hilltop Mall**
3170 Garrity Way
Richmond CA
510-222-7383 (800-804-3724)
One dog is allowed per suite. There is a $25 per night additional pet fee up to $150 for an entire stay.

**Extended Stay America - San Ramon - Bishop Ranch - East**
2100 Camino Ramon
San Ramon CA
925-242-0991 (800-804-3724)
One dog is allowed per suite. There is a $25 per night additional pet fee up to $150 for an entire stay.

**Extended Stay America San Ramon - Bishop Ranch - West**

18000 San Ramon Valley Blvd
San Ramon CA
925-277-0833 (800-804-3724)
One dog is allowed per suite. There is a $25 per night additional pet fee up to $150 for an entire stay.

**Extended Stay America - Union City - Dyer St.**
31950 Dyer St
Union City CA
510-441-9616 (800-804-3724)
One dog is allowed per suite. There is a $25 per night additional pet fee up to $150 for

an entire stay.

# Dog-Friendly Attractions
**Redwood Valley Railway**
Tilden Park
Berkeley CA
510-548-6100
Dogs on leash are allowed to ride the miniature train for free. They do warn it is a noisy ride.

**Telegraph Ave**
Telegraph Ave
Berkeley CA

Telegraph Avenue in Berkeley is a colorful multi-cultural center. There are numerous boutiques, street vendors, artists and street performers set up along the sidewalks of Telegraph Avenue between Bancroft Way and Dwight Way. It can be quite busy here, so make sure your pup is okay in crowds. Thanks to one of our readers for the following information: "There is an ordinance prohibiting more than two 'stationary' dogs within ten feet of each other on a certain part of Telegraph Avenue. This ordinance is aimed at the homeless, and I've never personally seen it enforced in the two or so years of existence... The most likely consequence of violating the ordinance is being asked to move your dog. A more serious concern to me would be bringing a not-yet-fully immunized young puppy to the area, where it might me more likely to get parvo, etc/ from a dog that has not received much if any veterinary care." To get there from Hwy 880 heading north, take the Hwy 980 exit towards Hwy 24/Walnut Creek. Then take the Hwy 24 exit on the left towards Berkeley/Walnut Creek. Exit at Claremont Ave and turn left onto Claremont Ave. Make a slight left onto College Ave. Turn left onto Dwight Way. Then turn right onto Telegraph Ave. Parking can be very difficult except maybe during

the summer and University holidays.

**Eugene O'Neill National Historic Site**
PO Box 280
Danville CA
925-838-0249
nps.gov/euon/index.htm
Dogs must be on leash and must be cleaned up after on the grounds. Dogs are not allowed in any buildings. Home of America's only Nobel Prize winning playwright.

**Marina Boat Rentals**
Del Valle Road
Livermore CA
925-373-0332
ebparks.org/parks/delval.htm
Rent a patio boat with your dog and explore Lake Del Valle. Each patio boat holds up to 6 people. There is a 10 mph speed limit on the lake. It costs about $70 for 2 hours or less. All day rentals are available for $100. They do require a $100 refundable deposit (credit card okay). Prices are subject to change. The rentals are available from 6am-5pm, seven days a week, weather permitting. This lake is about 5 miles long and is located in Del Valle Regional Park, about 10 miles south of Livermore. To get there from Hwy 580 heading east, exit S. Vasco Road. Turn right onto Vasco and head south. When Vasco ends, turn right onto Tesla Rd. Then turn left onto Mines Rd. Turn right onto Del Valle Road. Follow Del Valle Rd to the park entrance.

**BART: Bay Area Regional Transit**
P.O. Box 12688
Oakland CA
510-465-2278
bart.gov/guide/pets.aspx
BART will allow dogs aboard that can be transported in a hand carried secure container that is manufactured specifically for pet transport only. There is no additional pet fee.

**Juan Bautista de Anza National Historic Trail**

1111 Jackson Street #700
Oakland CA
510-817-1438
nps.gov/juba/index.htm
Dogs on leash are allowed on most of the trails. You must respect state park rules and private property rules within California and Arizona. The trail features touring trail by car, bicycle, or foot depending on area. This trail commemorates the route followed by Juan Bautista de Anza, a Spanish commander, in 1775-76 when he led a contingent of 30 soldiers and their families to the San Francisco Bay.

## Outdoor Restaurants

### Jamba Juice
2306 S Shore Center
Alameda CA
510-521-1112
jambajuice.com
All natural and organic ingredients, no high-fructose corn syrup, 0 grams trans fat, no artificial preservatives, a healthy helping of antioxidants, vitamins, and minerals, and fresh whole fruit and fruit juices set the base for these tasty and healthy beverages. Their organic Hot Blends provides a new spin on coffee, green or chai tea, and hot chocolate;plus they offer probiotic fruit and yogurt Blends. Additionally, they feature all natural salads, wraps, sandwiches, and grab n go specialties. They also offer healthy community support through fundraisers, special sales, and school lunch programs. Leashed, well mannered dogs are allowed at their outside dining area.

### Tucker's Super-Creamed Ice Cream
1349 Park Street
Alameda CA
510-522-4960
tuckersicecream.com/#
This ice creamery usually has an outdoor table by the front door where you and your pooch can enjoy an ice cream. Dogs must be attended to at all times,

well behaved, and leashed.

### Cugini Restaurant
1556 Solano Ave
Albany CA
510-558-9000
cuginirestaurant.com/
Your dog is welcome to join you for dinner at this restaurant. They serve a variety of wood-fired pizzas. It is located on Solano Ave, which is a shopping area.

### Schmidts Pub
1492 Solano Avenue
Albany CA
510-525-1900
A cozy neighborhood ambiance makes this traditional English-style pub a popular gathering place. Leashed, well mannered dogs are welcome at their outside tables.

### Jamba Juice
804-A Southampton Road
Benicia CA
707-748-1203
jambajuice.com
All natural and organic ingredients, no high-fructose corn syrup, 0 grams trans fat, no artificial preservatives, a healthy helping of antioxidants, vitamins, and minerals, and fresh whole fruit and fruit juices set the base for these tasty and healthy beverages. Their organic Hot Blends provides a new spin on coffee, green or chai tea, and hot chocolate;plus they offer probiotic fruit and yogurt Blends. Additionally, they feature all natural salads, wraps, and grab n go specialties. They also offer healthy community support through fundraisers, special sales, and school lunch programs. Leashed, well mannered dogs are allowed at their outside dining area.

### Cafe Trieste
2500 San Pablo Ave
Berkeley CA
510-548-5198
caffetrieste.com/
Dogs are allowed at the outside dining area of this Italian

influenced café.

### Chipotle
1050 Gilman Street
Berkeley CA
510-526-6047
chipotle.com
Specializing in organic, natural and unprocessed food, this Mexican Eatery offers fajita burritos, tacos, salads, and salsas. Dogs are allowed at the outdoor tables but you will need to order your food inside the restaurant and dogs must remain outside.

### Chipotle
2311 Telegraph Ave.
Berkeley CA
510-548-0340
chipotle.com
Specializing in organic, natural and unprocessed food, this Mexican Eatery offers fajita burritos, tacos, salads, and salsas. Dogs are allowed at the outdoor tables but you will need to order your food inside the restaurant and dogs must remain outside.

### Crepevine
1600 Shattuck Avenue
Berkeley CA
510-705-1836
crepevine.com
With a focus on local and organic, this eatery specializes in a variety of sweet and savory crepes and offers 100% all natural beef, ocean raised Canadian salmon, organic Fair-Trade coffee, all natural fed cage free eggs, and farm fresh produce. In addition to breakfast items they offer salads, sandwiches, pastas, and a kid's menu. Leashed, friendly dogs are allowed at their outside dining area.

### Espresso Roma Café at the French Hotel
1538 Shattuck Ave
Berkeley CA
510-548-9930
french-hotel-berkeley.com/
You and your dog are welcome at the outdoor tables. The cafe is located northwest of the UC Berkeley campus.

**Gather**
2200 Oxford Street
Berkeley CA
510-809-0400
gatherrestaurant.com/
Featuring farm-to-table American cuisine showcasing the regions best ingredients, this restaurant and bar offers a made-from-scratch kitchen with about 50% vegetarian and 50% meats and fish on the menu. They also serve up a variety of innovative organic cocktails, organic spirits, and biodynamic wines. They are open weekdays for lunch from 11:30 am until 2 pm;dinner nightly from 5 pm until 10 pm, and weekend brunches are from 10 am until 2:30 pm. Reservations are recommended - especially for the weekends reservations may need to be at least a week in advance. Leashed, friendly dogs are allowed at their outside dining area.

**Homemade Cafe**
2454 Sacramento St
Berkeley CA
510-845-1940
homemade-cafe.com/
A full menu of freshly prepared American foods are offered at this eatery. Leashed dogs are allowed at the outdoor tables.

**La Mediterranee**
2936 College Avenue
Berkeley CA
510-540-7773
Mediterranean cuisine is the specialty of this house;plus they also offer catering services, take out, box lunches, and alfresco dining. Leashed, well mannered dogs are allowed at their outside dining area;they must be able to be placed under the table.

**Pasta Shop**
1786 4th Street
Berkeley CA
510-528-1786
Specialty salads and sandwiches, unique grocery items, and gift baskets are just some of the offerings at this restaurant. Leashed, well mannered dogs are welcome at

their outside tables.

**Riva Cucina**
800 Heinz Avenue
Berkeley CA
510-841-RIVA (7482)
rivacucina.com
A certified Bay Area Green Business, this Italian eatery sources a wide selection of local all natural and organic produce and products as well as some select favorites direct from Italy. In addition to lunch, dinner, and wine menus, they also have a children's menu. Leashed, well mannered dogs are allowed at their outside tables.

**Tacubaya**
1788 4th Street
Berkeley CA
510-525-5160
tacubaya.net/
This restaurant serves Mexican food. Leashed dogs are allowed at the outdoor tables.

**Whole Foods Market**
3000 Telegraph Ave.
Berkeley CA
510-649-1333
wholefoods.com/
This natural food supermarket offers natural and organic foods. Order some food from their deli without your dog and bring it to an outdoor table where your well-behaved leashed dog is welcome. Dogs are not allowed in the store including the deli at any time. There is also a water bowl for thirsty pups.

**Chipotle**
3369 Castro Valley Blvd
Castro Valley CA
510-582-8643
chipotle.com
Specializing in organic, natural and unprocessed food, this Mexican Eatery offers fajita burritos, tacos, salads, and salsas. Dogs are allowed at the outdoor tables but you will need to order your food inside the restaurant and dogs must remain outside.

**Skipolini's Pizza**

1033 Diablo St
Clayton CA
925-672-1111
skipolinispizza.com/
Pizza and pasta are the specialties of this eatery. Leashed dogs are allowed at the outdoor tables.

**Lazy Dog Restaurant & Bar**
1961 Diamond Blvd
Concord CA
925-849-1221
lazydogrestaurants.com/dogs/info
Known for it's dog-friendly patio, the Lazy Dog offers your dog a complimentary bowl of water, and a menu consisting of grilled hamburger patty, chicken breast or brown rice. They just ask that you respect their common sense rules while your dog is dining there. This is as dog-friendly as dining gets. For the humans in your party there is hamburger, steak, salads and some great desserts.

**Baja Fresh Mexican Grill**
4550 Tassajara Rd.
Dublin CA
925-556-9199
bajafresh.com
This Mexican restaurant is open for lunch and dinner. They use fresh ingredients and making their salsa and beans daily. Some of the items on their menu include Enchiladas, Burritos, Tacos Salads, Quesadillas, Nachos, Chicken, Steak and more. Well-behaved leashed dogs are allowed at the outdoor tables.

**Chipotle**
7020 Amador Plaza Road
Dublin CA
925-828-4361
chipotle.com
Specializing in organic, natural and unprocessed food, this Mexican Eatery offers fajita burritos, tacos, salads, and salsas. Dogs are allowed at the outdoor tables but you will need to order your food inside the restaurant and dogs must remain outside.

**Lazy Dog Restaurant & Bar**

4805 Hacienda Dr
Dublin CA
925-361-3690
lazydogrestaurants.com/dogs/info
Known for it's dog-friendly patio, the Lazy Dog offers your dog a complimentary bowl of water, and a menu consisting of grilled hamburger patty, chicken breast or brown rice. They just ask that you respect their common sense rules while your dog is dining there. This is as dog-friendly as dining gets. For the humans in your party there is hamburger, steak, salads and some great desserts.

**Jamba Juice**
5761 Christie Avenue
Emeryville CA
415-288-9980
jambajuice.com
All natural and organic ingredients, no high-fructose corn syrup, 0 grams trans fat, no artificial preservatives, a healthy helping of antioxidants, vitamins, and minerals, and fresh whole fruit and fruit juices set the base for these tasty and healthy beverages. Their organic Hot Blends provides a new spin on coffee, green or chai tea, and hot chocolate;plus they offer probiotic fruit and yogurt Blends. Additionally, they feature all natural salads, wraps, sandwiches, and grab n go specialties. They also offer healthy community support through fundraisers, special sales, and school lunch programs. Leashed, well mannered dogs are allowed at their outside dining area.

**Baja Fresh Mexican Grill**
1450 Travis Blvd
Fairfield CA
707-432-0460
bajafresh.com
This Mexican restaurant is open for lunch and dinner. They use fresh ingredients and making their salsa and beans daily. Some of the items on their menu include Enchiladas, Burritos, Tacos Salads, Quesadillas, Nachos, Chicken, Steak and more. Well-behaved

leashed dogs are allowed at the outdoor tables.

**Chipotle**
5565 Auto Mall Parkway
Fremont CA
510-979-9397
chipotle.com
Specializing in organic, natural and unprocessed food, this Mexican Eatery offers fajita burritos, tacos, salads, and salsas. Dogs are allowed at the outdoor tables but you will need to order your food inside the restaurant and dogs must remain outside.

**Baja Fresh Mexican Grill**
3596 Mt. Diablo Blvd.
Lafayette CA
925-283-8740
bajafresh.com
This Mexican restaurant is open for lunch and dinner. They use fresh ingredients and making their salsa and beans daily. Some of the items on their menu include Enchiladas, Burritos, Tacos Salads, Quesadillas, Nachos, Chicken, Steak and more. Well-behaved leashed dogs are allowed at the outdoor tables.

**Chow Restaurant**
53 Lafayette Circle
Lafayette CA
925-962-2469
chowfoodbar.com/
In addition to supporting and developing relations with local and organic farms and ranchers, this eatery offers all natural and organic beef and pork, free range poultry, pressed to order juices, daily handcrafted desserts, and a market with prepared meals to-go. Leashed, well mannered dogs are welcome at their outside tables.

**Uncle Yu's Szechuan**
999 Oak Hill Rd
Lafayette CA
925-283-1688
uncleyu.stores.yahoo.net/
Traditional and contemporary Chinese cuisine and a notable wine list are offered at this restaurant. Leashed, well

mannered dogs are welcome at their outside tables.

**Baja Fresh Mexican Grill**
2298 Las Positas
Livermore CA
925-245-9888
bajafresh.com
This Mexican restaurant is open for lunch and dinner. They use fresh ingredients and making their salsa and beans daily. Some of the items on their menu include Enchiladas, Burritos, Tacos Salads, Quesadillas, Nachos, Chicken, Steak and more. Well-behaved leashed dogs are allowed at the outdoor tables.

**First Street Ale House**
2086 1st Street
Livermore CA
925-371-6588
firststreetalehouse.com/
This popular ale house features 20 beers on tap, a variety of appetizers, burgers and sandwiches, a fun relaxed ambiance, and front and back patios. Leashed, well mannered dogs are welcome at their outer tables.

**Manpuku**
4363 First Street
Livermore CA
925-371-9038
Well-behaved leashed dogs are allowed at the outdoor seating area. This restaurant serves Oriental cuisine. They are open Monday to Saturday from 5 pm until 9:30 pm and on Sunday from 4 pm until 8:30 pm.

**Olive Tree Café and Catering**
7633 Southfront Road
Livermore CA
925-960-0636
altamontpasscafe.com
Well-behaved leashed dogs are allowed at the outdoor seating area. They offer specialty coffee drinks, health-conscious dining, and corporate catering.

**Panama Red Coffee Co.**
2115 First Street
Livermore CA
925-245-1700
Well-behaved leashed dogs are

allowed at the outdoor seating area.

## Chipotle
34883 Newark Blvd
Newark CA
510-742-8010
chipotle.com
Specializing in organic, natural and unprocessed food, this Mexican Eatery offers fajita burritos, tacos, salads, and salsas. Dogs are allowed at the outdoor tables but you will need to order your food inside the restaurant and dogs must remain outside.

## Crepevine
5600 College Avenue
Oakland CA
510-658-2026
crepevine.com
With a focus on local and organic, this eatery specializes in a variety of sweet and savory crepes and offers 100% all natural beef, ocean raised Canadian salmon, organic Fair-Trade coffee, all natural fed cage free eggs, and farm fresh produce. In addition to a breakfast items they offer salads, sandwiches, pastas, and a kid's menu. Leashed, friendly dogs are allowed at their sidewalk tables only.

## Fentons Creamery & Restaurant
4226 Piedmont Avenue
Oakland CA
510-658-7000
Although famous for their fresh hand-made ice cream and classic soda fountain, they also feature classic American fare. They also offer a venue for special events and catering services. Leashed, friendly dogs are allowed at their outside tables.

## Filippo's
5400 College
Oakland CA
510-601-8646
filippos.biz/
This Italian restaurant features freshly made foods, a variety of wines, and alfresco dining. Dogs are allowed at the outer

tables;they must be leashed and under their owner's control at all times.

## Heinolds First & Last Chance
56 Jack London Sq
Oakland CA
510-839-6761
Dogs are welcome at the outdoor tables of this bar. The saloon serves beer, wine and cocktails. Heinold's First and Last Chance Saloon is where the famous author, Jack London, borrowed his entrance fee for college from the proprietor. This bar is the

## Italian Colors Ristorante
2220 Mountain Boulevard
Oakland CA
510-482-8094
italiancolorsrestaurant.com/
Specializing in Italian and California inspired Italian cuisine, this restaurant also provides a live guitarist Wednesday thru Saturday evenings. Dogs are allowed at the outdoor tables.

## Posh Bagel
4037 Piedmont Avenue
Oakland CA
510-597-0381
This bagel shop also provides outside dining when the weather permits. Dogs are allowed at the outer tables;they must be under their owner's control at all times.

## Urban Legend Cellars
621 4th Street
Oakland CA
510-545-4356
ulcellars.com/
This winery features a variety of fine wines and a focus on traditional wines as well as organic and sustainable. Dogs are allowed on the grounds of the winery and in the tasting room. Also be sure to check their calendar for special events and wine pairing dinners. The tasting room is open Friday thru Sunday from 1 pm until 6 pm. Dogs must be leashed and under their owner's control at all times.

## Shelby's
2 Theater Square
Orinda CA
925-254-9687
shelbyseatbetter.com/
French-California bistro cuisine that is skillfully blended with globally influenced culinary traditions is the specialty of this gathering place. Leashed, well mannered dogs are welcome at their outside tables.

## Jamba Juice
2794 Pinole Valley Road
Pinole CA
510-669-1321
jambajuice.com
All natural and organic ingredients, no high-fructose corn syrup, 0 grams trans fat, no artificial preservatives, a healthy helping of antioxidants, vitamins, and minerals, and fresh whole fruit and fruit juices set the base for these tasty and healthy beverages. Their organic Hot Blends provides a new spin on coffee, green or chai tea, and hot chocolate;plus they offer probiotic fruit and yogurt Blends. Additionally, they feature all natural salads, wraps, sandwiches, and grab n go specialties. They also offer healthy community support through fundraisers, special sales, and school lunch programs. Leashed, well mannered dogs are allowed at their outside dining area.

## Chipotle
4418 Century Blvd
Pittsburg CA
925-754-3270
chipotle.com
Specializing in organic, natural and unprocessed food, this Mexican Eatery offers fajita burritos, tacos, salads, and salsas. Dogs are allowed at the outdoor tables but you will need to order your food inside the restaurant and dogs must remain outside.

## Chipotle
60 Crescent Drive
Pleasant Hill CA
925-674-0615

chipotle.com
Specializing in organic, natural and unprocessed food, this Mexican Eatery offers fajita burritos, tacos, salads, and salsas. Dogs are allowed at the outdoor tables but you will need to order your food inside the restaurant and dogs must remain outside.

## Baci Restaurant
500 Main Street
Pleasanton CA
925-600-0600
bacibistroandbar.com/
Well-behaved leashed dogs are allowed at the outdoor seating area.

## Baja Fresh Mexican Grill
2457 Stoneridge Mall Ste.
Pleasanton CA
925-251-1500
bajafresh.com
This Mexican restaurant is open for lunch and dinner. They use fresh ingredients and making their salsa and beans daily. Some of the items on their menu include Enchiladas, Burritos, Tacos Salads, Quesadillas, Nachos, Chicken, Steak and more. Well-behaved leashed dogs are allowed at the outdoor tables.

## Bob's House
5321 Hopyard Road
Pleasanton CA
925-847-1700
mixandeatbobshouse.com/
Well-behaved leashed dogs are allowed at the outdoor seating area. They specialize in Korean rice bowls and New York style pizza.

## Erik's Deli
4247 Rosewood Drive
Pleasanton CA
925-847-9755
eriksdelicafe.com/
Well-behaved leashed dogs are allowed at the outdoor seating area.

## Handles
855 Main Street
Pleasanton CA
925-399-6690
handlesgastropub.com/

This gastro pub offers a seasonally influenced menu with a focus on farm to table dining, 16 wines and 30 craft brews on tap, a full bar, various special food/drink/fun events, live entertainment, and alfresco dining. Leashed, well mannered dogs are welcome at their outside tables.

## Baja Fresh Mexican Grill
132 Sunset Drive
San Ramon CA
925-866-6667
bajafresh.com
Your dog is welcome here! This Mexican restaurant is open for lunch and dinner. They use fresh ingredients and making their salsa and beans daily. Some of the items on their menu include Enchiladas, Burritos, Tacos Salads, Quesadillas, Nachos, Chicken, Steak and more. Well-behaved leashed dogs are allowed at the outdoor tables.

## Whole Foods Market
100 Sunset Drive
San Ramon CA
925-355-9000
wholefoods.com/
This natural food supermarket offers natural and organic foods. Order some food from their deli without your dog and bring it to an outdoor table where your well-behaved leashed dog is welcome.

## Z Pizza
3141-D Crow Canyon Place
San Ramon CA
925-328-0525
zpizza.com
Specializing in organically and international inspired pizzas, this pizzeria cooks their pizzas on hot bricks in a fire baked oven. They feature a 100% certified organic gluten free wheat crust, homemade organic sauces and ingredients, fresh produce, and additive-free meats. They also offer gourmet salads, sandwiches, and catering services. Leashed, well mannered dogs are allowed at their outside tables.

## Baja Fresh Mexican Grill
1271-1273 S. California Blvd.
Walnut Creek CA
925-947-0588
bajafresh.com
This Mexican restaurant is open for lunch and dinner. They use fresh ingredients and making their salsa and beans daily. Some of the items on their menu include Enchiladas, Burritos, Tacos Salads, Quesadillas, Nachos, Chicken, Steak and more. Well-behaved leashed dogs are allowed at the outdoor tables.

## Chipotle
1158 Locust Street
Walnut Creek CA
925-935-9307
chipotle.com
Specializing in organic, natural and unprocessed food, this Mexican Eatery offers fajita burritos, tacos, salads, and salsas. Dogs are allowed at the outdoor tables but you will need to order your food inside the restaurant and dogs must remain outside.

## Pacific Bay Coffee Co and Micro-Roastry
1495 Newell Ave
Walnut Creek CA
925-935-1709
pacificbaycoffee.com/
This cafe serves coffee,smoothies and pastries. Dogs are allowed at the outdoor tables.

# Pet-Friendly Shopping Centers
## Jack London Square
Broadway & Embarcadero
Oakland CA
510-814-6000
jacklondonsquare.com
Historic Jack London Square was named after the famous author, who spent his early years in Oakland. In the 1800's, this waterfront was one of Oakland's main shipping ports. Today it is a shopping village with shops, restaurants,

entertainment and more. While at the village, you and your dog can take a self-guided history walk by following the distinctive bronze wolf tracks in the walkway. The walk begins at Heinold's First and Last Chance Saloon. At the village you will also find musical entertainment Sunday afternoons in the courtyard. Be aware that on Sundays, from 10am-2pm, there is a Farmer's Market in the main walkway (center and north end of the village). Dogs are not allowed in the market and the security attendants will remind you. The market pretty much fills up the main walkway, so it is tough to walk around it. There are some dog-friendly outdoor restaurants located at the village. To get there from Hwy 880 heading north, exit Broadway. Turn left onto Broadway. Follow Broadway into Jack London Square.

**Broadway Plaza Shopping Center**
1275 Broadway Plaza
Walnut Creek CA
925-939-7600
broadwayplaza.com/
This open-air regional shopping complex features a variety of 95 shopping, dining, entertainment, and socializing venues. The center is especially noted for its European inspired exterior with beautiful water fountain, sculptures and more. Dogs are allowed in the common areas of the mall; it is up to individual stores whether they allow a dog inside. Many stores have water bowls outside for their visiting canine guests. Dogs must be well behaved, leashed, and under their owner's control at all times.

**Pet-Friendly Stores**
**Alameda Pet Food Express**
2661 Blanding Avenue Suite. 9F

Alameda CA
510-864-2222
One of the country's leading pet retailers, this comprehensive pet

store offers a number of other stores, quality foods/treats, a wide variety of pet supplies, breed-specific items, pet care products, apparel, health items, hound and human accessories, and much more. Some of the services they offer include working with local SPCAs and rescue groups helping tens of thousands of homeless pets find new homes (they do not sell animals as pets), providing low cost vaccination clinics, dog training classes, and self-service pet washes. All leashed, friendly pets are welcome.

**Petco Pet Store - Alameda**
2310 South Shore Center
Alameda CA
510-864-1844
Your licensed and well-behaved leashed dog is allowed in the store.

**PetSmart Pet Store**
1001 Eastshore Hwy
Albany CA
510-524-1518
Your licensed and well-behaved leashed dog is allowed in the store.

**Pet Food Express**
3448 Deer Valley Road
Antioch CA
925-978-7777
One of the country's leading pet retailers, this comprehensive pet store offers a number of other stores, quality foods/treats, a wide variety of pet supplies, breed-specific items, pet care products, apparel, health items, hound and human accessories, and much more. Some of the services they offer include working with local SPCAs and rescue groups helping tens of thousands of homeless pets find new homes (they do not sell animals as pets), providing low cost vaccination clinics, dog training classes, and self-service pet washes. All leashed, friendly pets are welcome.

**Pet Food Express**

5829 Lone Tree Way
Antioch CA
925-778-9999
One of the country's leading pet retailers, this comprehensive pet store offers a number of other stores, quality foods/treats, a wide variety of pet supplies, breed-specific items, pet care products, apparel, health items, hound and human accessories, and much more. Some of the services they offer include working with local SPCAs and rescue groups helping tens of thousands of homeless pets find new homes (they do not sell animals as pets), providing low cost vaccination clinics, dog training classes, and self-service pet washes. All leashed, friendly pets are welcome.

**PetSmart Pet Store**
5879 Lone Tree Way
Antioch CA
925-755-8504
Your licensed and well-behaved leashed dog is allowed in the store.

**Pet Food Express**
838 Southampton Road
Benicia CA
707-748-4477
One of the country's leading pet retailers, this comprehensive pet store offers a number of other stores, quality foods/treats, a wide variety of pet supplies, breed-specific items, pet care products, apparel, health items, hound and human accessories, and much more. Some of the services they offer include working with local SPCAs and rescue groups helping tens of thousands of homeless pets find new homes (they do not sell animals as pets), providing low cost vaccination clinics, dog training classes, and self-service pet washes. All leashed, friendly pets are welcome.

**Anthropologie**
750 Hearst Avenue
Berkeley CA
510-486-0705
Items of distinction can be found for all ages and in all departments of this unique

shop. Carefully selected to add to the enjoyment of the shopping experience, they carry fine clothing, amazing accessories, jewelry, hobby and leisure items, and a full line of bright and useful items for the home, garden, and office. Leashed, well behaved dogs are allowed in the store.

### Avenue Books
2904 College Avenue
Berkeley CA
510-549-3532
Thanks to one of our readers who writes "So dog-friendly, they offer doggie biscuits!" They are located in the Elmwood district and are open 7 days a week.

### Crate and Barrel
1785 4th Street
Berkeley CA
510-528-5500
crateandbarrel.com
This store offers fine products from around the world for in and around the home that include items for outdoor living, indoor furnishings and decorating, dining and entertaining, kitchen and food service, and gourmet food and beverages. They also have accessories for pets, bed and bath items, and organizing and storage units. Leashed, friendly dogs are welcome in the store; they must be under their owner's control at all times.

### Half Price Books, Records, Magazines
2036 Shattuck Avenue
Berkeley CA
510-526-6080
halfpricebooks.com
In addition to a unique and diverse selection of 1000s of new and used books, this shop also offers an extensive collection of LPs, cassettes, CDs, videos, DVDs and games. They also buy used books; there is always new stock added daily; most everything is priced at the publisher's price or less; and they offer additional discounting options. Additionally, 1000s of books are donated to hospitals through their Half Pint Library

program each year. Leashed, friendly dogs are welcome in the store.

### Pet Food Express
1101 University Avenue
Berkeley CA
510-540-7777
One of the country's leading pet retailers, this comprehensive pet store offers a number of other stores, quality foods/treats, a wide variety of pet supplies, breed-specific items, pet care products, apparel, health items, hound and human accessories, and much more. Some of the services they offer include working with local SPCAs and rescue groups helping tens of thousands of homeless pets find new homes (they do not sell animals as pets), providing low cost vaccination clinics, dog training classes, and self-service pet washes. All leashed, friendly pets are welcome.

### Restoration Hardware
1733 Fourth Street
Berkeley CA
510-526-6424
restorationhardware.com/

### Urban Outfitters
2590 Bancroft Way
Berkeley CA
510-486-1300
In addition to a large inventory of indoor and outdoor apparel for men and women, this major department store also carries vintage wear, designer brands, and a variety of accessories for all types of active lifestyles. They also carry shoes, furnishings, home decor, cameras, electronics, novelty items and more. Leashed, well mannered dogs are allowed in the store.

### Pet Food Express
3385 Castro Valley Blvd
Castro Valley CA
510-728-7788
One of the country's leading pet retailers, this comprehensive pet store offers

a number of other stores, quality foods/treats, a wide variety of pet supplies, breed-specific items, pet care products, apparel, health items, hound and human accessories, and much more. Some of the services they offer include working with local SPCAs and rescue groups helping tens of thousands of homeless pets find new homes (they do not sell animals as pets), providing low cost vaccination clinics, dog training classes, and self-service pet washes. All leashed, friendly pets are welcome.

### Petco Pet Store - Castro Valley
3735 East Castro Valley Blvd
Castro Valley CA
510-886-4466
Your licensed and well-behaved leashed dog is allowed in the store.

### Half Price Books, Records, Magazines
1935 Mt. Diablo
Concord CA
925-288-9060
halfpricebooks.com
In addition to a unique and diverse selection of 1000s of new and used books, this shop also offers an extensive collection of LPs, cassettes, CDs, videos, DVDs and games. They also buy used books; there is always new stock added daily; most everything is priced at the publisher's price or less; and they offer additional discounting options. Additionally, 1000s of books are donated to hospitals through their Half Pint Library program each year. Leashed, friendly dogs are welcome in the store.

### Pet Food Express
5404 Ygnacio Valley Road
Concord CA
925-673-8888
One of the country's leading pet retailers, this comprehensive pet store offers a number of other stores, quality foods/treats, a wide variety of pet supplies, breed-specific items, pet care products, apparel, health items,

hound and human accessories, and much more. Some of the services they offer include working with local SPCAs and rescue groups helping tens of thousands of homeless pets find new homes (they do not sell animals as pets), providing low cost vaccination clinics, dog training classes, and self-service pet washes. All leashed, friendly pets are welcome.

**PetSmart Pet Store**
1700 Willow Pass Rd
Concord CA
925-687-7199
Your licensed and well-behaved leashed dog is allowed in the store.

**Petco Pet Store - Concord**
1825 Salvio St.
Concord CA
925-827-3338
Your licensed and well-behaved leashed dog is allowed in the store.

**Anthropologie**
3380 Blackhawk Plaza Circle, #118
Danville CA
925-648-4991
Items of distinction can be found for all ages and in all departments of this unique shop. Carefully selected to add to the enjoyment of the shopping experience, they carry fine clothing, amazing accessories, jewelry, hobby and leisure items, and a full line of bright and useful items for the home, garden, and office. Leashed, well behaved dogs are allowed in the store.

**Pet Food Express**
609 San Ramon Valley Blvd
Danville CA
925-837-1777
One of the country's leading pet retailers, this comprehensive pet store offers a number of other stores, quality foods/treats, a wide variety of pet supplies, breed-specific items, pet care products, apparel, health items, hound and human accessories, and much more. Some of the services they offer include

working with local SPCAs and rescue groups helping tens of thousands of homeless pets find new homes (they do not sell animals as pets), providing low cost vaccination clinics, dog training classes, and self-service pet washes. All leashed, friendly pets are welcome.

**Pet Food Express**
4460 Tassajara Road
Dublin CA
925-556-1111
One of the country's leading pet retailers, this comprehensive pet store offers a number of other stores, quality foods/treats, a wide variety of pet supplies, breed-specific items, pet care products, apparel, health items, hound and human accessories, and much more. Some of the services they offer include working with local SPCAs and rescue groups helping tens of thousands of homeless pets find new homes (they do not sell animals as pets), providing low cost vaccination clinics, dog training classes, and self-service pet washes. All leashed, friendly pets are welcome.

**PetSmart Pet Store**
6960 Amador Plaza Rd
Dublin CA
925-803-8370
Your licensed and well-behaved leashed dog is allowed in the store.

**Petco Pet Store - Dublin**
11976 Dublin Blvd
Dublin CA
925-803-4045
Your licensed and well-behaved leashed dog is allowed in the store.

**Petco Pet Store - El Cerrito**
420 El Cerrito Plaza
El Cerrito CA
510-528-7919
Your licensed and well-behaved leashed dog is allowed in the store.

**Pet Club**

3535 Hollis Street
Emeryville CA
510-595-7955
petclubstores.com
In addition to warehouse pricing with no membership fees, this comprehensive pet supply store offers weekly specials and more than 11,000 pet products ranging from wellness items, bedding, dinnerware, a wide choice of quality foods, treats, leashes, toys, apparel, travel supplies, and much more. Leashed, friendly dogs are always welcome in the store.

**Pet Club**
5125 Business Center Drive
Fairfield CA
707-864-9688
petclubstores.com
In addition to warehouse pricing with no membership fees, this comprehensive pet supply store offers weekly specials and more than 11,000 pet products ranging from wellness items, bedding, dinnerware, a wide choice of quality foods, treats, leashes, toys, apparel, travel supplies, and much more. Leashed, friendly dogs are always welcome in the store.

**Petco Pet Store - Fairfield**
1370 Holiday Lane Ste A
Fairfield CA
707-427-8162
Your licensed and well-behaved leashed dog is allowed in the store.

**Half Price Books, Records, Magazines**
43473 Boscell Road
Fremont CA
510-744-0333
halfpricebooks.com
In addition to a unique and diverse selection of 1000s of new and used books, this shop also offers an extensive collection of LPs, cassettes, CDs, videos, DVDs and games. They also buy used books; there is always new stock added daily; most everything is priced at the publisher's price or less; and they offer additional discounting options. Additionally, 1000s of books are donated to hospitals

through their Half Pint Library program each year. Leashed, friendly dogs are welcome in the store.

## Pet Food Express
39010 Paseo Padre Parkway
Fremont CA
510-713-9999
One of the country's leading pet retailers, this comprehensive pet store offers a number of other stores, quality foods/treats, a wide variety of pet supplies, breed-specific items, pet care products, apparel, health items, hound and human accessories, and much more. Some of the services they offer include working with local SPCAs and rescue groups helping tens of thousands of homeless pets find new homes (they do not sell animals as pets), providing low cost vaccination clinics, dog training classes, and self-service pet washes. All leashed, friendly pets are welcome.

## PetSmart Pet Store
39410 Argonaut Way
Fremont CA
510-790-1459
Your licensed and well-behaved leashed dog is allowed in the store.

## Petco Pet Store - Fremont
3780 Mowry Ave.
Fremont CA
510-742-0573
Your licensed and well-behaved leashed dog is allowed in the store.

## Pet Club
27451 Hesperian Blvd
Hayward CA
510-887-0898
petclubstores.com
In addition to warehouse pricing with no membership fees, this comprehensive pet supply store offers weekly specials and more than 11,000 pet products ranging from wellness items, bedding, dinnerware, a wide choice of quality foods, treats, leashes, toys, apparel, travel supplies, and much more. Leashed, friendly dogs are always welcome in the store.

## Pet Food Express
3610 Mt Diablo Blvd
Lafayette CA
925-962-0000
One of the country's leading pet retailers, this comprehensive pet store offers a number of other stores, quality foods/treats, a wide variety of pet supplies, breed-specific items, pet care products, apparel, health items, hound and human accessories, and much more. Some of the services they offer include working with local SPCAs and rescue groups helping tens of thousands of homeless pets find new homes (they do not sell animals as pets), providing low cost vaccination clinics, dog training classes, and self-service pet washes. All leashed, friendly pets are welcome.

## Pet Food Express
1436 1st Street
Livermore CA
925-447-7777
One of the country's leading pet retailers, this comprehensive pet store offers a number of other stores, quality foods/treats, a wide variety of pet supplies, breed-specific items, pet care products, apparel, health items, hound and human accessories, and much more. Some of the services they offer include working with local SPCAs and rescue groups helping tens of thousands of homeless pets find new homes (they do not sell animals as pets), providing low cost vaccination clinics, dog training classes, and self-service pet washes. All leashed, friendly pets are welcome.

## Petco Pet Store - Martinez
1170 Arnold Dr. #115
Martinez CA
925-370-6060
Your licensed and well-behaved leashed dog is allowed in the store.

## Pet Food Express

2220 Mountain Blvd #170
Oakland CA
510-530-5300
One of the country's leading pet retailers, this comprehensive pet store offers a number of other stores, quality foods/treats, a wide variety of pet supplies, breed-specific items, pet care products, apparel, health items, hound and human accessories, and much more. Some of the services they offer include working with local SPCAs and rescue groups helping tens of thousands of homeless pets find new homes (they do not sell animals as pets), providing low cost vaccination clinics, dog training classes, and self-service pet washes. All leashed, friendly pets are welcome.

## Pet Food Express
6398 Telegraph Avenue
Oakland CA
510-923-9500
One of the country's leading pet retailers, this comprehensive pet store offers a number of other stores, quality foods/treats, a wide variety of pet supplies, breed-specific items, pet care products, apparel, health items, hound and human accessories, and much more. Some of the services they offer include working with local SPCAs and rescue groups helping tens of thousands of homeless pets find new homes (they do not sell animals as pets), providing low cost vaccination clinics, dog training classes, and self-service pet washes. All leashed, friendly pets are welcome.

## Pet Food Express
5144 Broadway
Oakland CA
510-654-8888
One of the country's leading pet retailers, this comprehensive pet store offers a number of other stores, quality foods/treats, a wide variety of pet supplies, breed-specific items, pet care products, apparel, health items, hound and human accessories, and much more. Some of the services they offer include working with local SPCAs and

rescue groups helping tens of thousands of homeless pets find new homes (they do not sell animals as pets), providing low cost vaccination clinics, dog training classes, and self-service pet washes. All leashed, friendly pets are welcome.

**Pet Food Express**
1430 Fitzgerald Drive
Pinole CA
510-758-7779
One of the country's leading pet retailers, this comprehensive pet store offers a number of other stores, quality foods/treats, a wide variety of pet supplies, breed-specific items, pet care products, apparel, health items, hound and human accessories, and much more. Some of the services they offer include working with local SPCAs and rescue groups helping tens of thousands of homeless pets find new homes (they do not sell animals as pets), providing low cost vaccination clinics, dog training classes, and self-service pet washes. All leashed, friendly pets are welcome.

**PetSmart Pet Store**
4655 Century Blvd
Pittsburg CA
925-706-9975
Your licensed and well-behaved leashed dog is allowed in the store.

**Pet Food Express**
2158 Contra Costa Blvd
Pleasant Hill CA
925-603-8888
One of the country's leading pet retailers, this comprehensive pet store offers a number of other stores, quality foods/treats, a wide variety of pet supplies, breed-specific items, pet care products, apparel, health items, hound and human accessories, and much more. Some of the services they offer include working with local SPCAs and rescue groups helping tens of thousands of homeless pets find new homes (they do not sell animals as pets), providing low cost vaccination clinics, dog training classes, and self-

service pet washes. All leashed, friendly pets are welcome.

**Dogtopia of Tri-Valley (Pleasanton)**
7132 Johnson Drive
Pleasanton CA
925-22K-9DOG
dogdaycare.com/trivalley
With a stated mission of providing the highest quality dog care in the country, this company offers well trained staff for all their services. Services include doggy day care, overnight accommodations, positive reinforcement training classes, a self serve dog wash, professional grooming, and a doggy boutique with quality foods/treats, pet care supplies, toys, and much more. They also offer support in the community through a variety of venues.

**Dogtopia of Tri-Valley (Pleasanton)**
7132 Johnson Drive
Pleasanton CA
925-22K-9DOG (225-9364)
dogdaycare.com/trivalley/
With a stated mission of providing the highest quality dog care in the country, this company offers well trained staff for all their services. Services include doggy day care, overnight accommodations, positive reinforcement training classes, a self serve dog wash, professional grooming, and a doggy boutique with quality foods/treats, pet care supplies, toys, and much more. They also offer support in the community through a variety of venues.

**PetSmart Pet Store**
3700 Klose Way Bldg 4
Richmond CA
510-758-8990
Your licensed and well-behaved leashed dog is allowed in the store.

**PetSmart Pet Store**
15555 E 14th St

San Leandro CA
510-317-1880
Your licensed and well-behaved leashed dog is allowed in the store.

**Petco Pet Store - San Ramon**
2005 Crow Canyon Place
San Ramon CA
925-275-2111
Your licensed and well-behaved leashed dog is allowed in the store.

**Petco Pet Store - Union City**
31090 Dyer St.
Union City CA
510-477-9235
Your licensed and well-behaved leashed dog is allowed in the store.

**Crate and Barrel**
1115 Broadway Plaza
Walnut Creek CA
925-947-3500
crateandbarrel.com
This store offers fine products from around the world for in and around the home that include items for outdoor living, indoor furnishings and decorating, dining and entertaining, kitchen and food service, and gourmet food and beverages. They also have accessories for pets, bed and bath items, and organizing and storage units. Leashed, friendly dogs are welcome in the store; they must be under their owner's control at all times.

**Petco Pet Store - Walnut Creek**
1301 South California St.
Walnut Creek CA
925-988-9370
Your licensed and well-behaved leashed dog is allowed in the store.

**Restoration Hardware**
1460 Mt Diablo Blvd
Walnut Creek CA
925-906-9230
restorationhardware.com/
Your well-behaved leashed dog is allowed inside this store. They love having dogs in the store!

**Urban Outfitters**
1530 Olympic Blvd

Walnut Creek CA
925-932-5046
In addition to a large inventory of indoor and outdoor apparel for men and women, this major department store also carries vintage wear, designer brands, and a variety of accessories for all types of active lifestyles. They also carry shoes, furnishings, home decor, cameras, electronics, novelty items and more. Leashed, well mannered dogs are allowed in the store.

## Dog-Friendly Wineries and Vineyards

### Rosenblum Cellars
2900 Main Street
Alameda CA
510-865-7007
rosenblumcellars.com/
Well-behaved dogs are allowed at the outdoor tables. The tasting room hours are 12pm-5pm daily.

## Off-Leash Dog Parks

### Cesar Chavez Park Off-Leash Dog Area
11 Spinnaker Way
Berkeley CA
510-981-6700
There is an off-leash dog area in the north side of the park. Your dog must be leashed while walking to and from this area, and dogs must be cleaned up after. Bags are available at the park. To get to the park from Berkeley go over I-80 on University Ave. From I-80 exit University Avenue and go west towards the bay. However, you will have to turn around on University Avenue if coming from the south.

### Ohlone Dog Park
Hearst Avenue
Berkeley CA

ohlonedogpark.org/
This is a relatively small dog park. At certain times, there can be lots of dogs here. The hours

are 6am-10pm on weekdays and 9am-10pm on weekends. The park is located at Hearst Ave, just west of Martin Luther King Jr. Way. There is limited street parking.

### Earl Warren Dog Park
4660 Crow Canyon
Castro Valley CA
510-881-6700
The Castro Valley Dog Run has two fenced areas, one for larger dogs and one for small dogs. There are two parking lots, rest rooms, an open lawn area and picnic tables. The park is open during daylight hours daily. The dog park is located in Earl Warren Park. Exit I 580 at Crow Canyon and head north.

### Newhall Community Park Paw Patch
Turtle Creek Road
Concord CA
925-671-3329
Offering 126 acres along Galindo Creek, this park is mostly wide open spaces with picnic areas, gaming courts/fields, more than 2 miles of multi-use trails, a Vietnam War Memorial, great views, and an off leash, fenced doggy play area. Dogs must be sociable, current on all vaccinations and license, and under their owner's control at all times. Dogs must be leashed when not in designated off-lead areas.

### Paw Patch in Newhall Community Park
Clayton Rd & Newhall Pkwy
Concord CA
925-671-3329
This fenced dog park is located in Newhall Community Park in Concord. To get to the park from Clayton Road or Turtle Creek Road head south on Newhall Parkway. Local dog groups frequently meet at the dog park.

### Dougherty Hills Dog Park
Stagecoach Road and Amador Valley Blvd
Dublin CA

925-833-6600
There are separate areas for small and large dogs, an agility course, drinking fountains for hounds and humans, benches, and fun public art. Dogs must be sociable, current on all vaccinations and license, and under their owner's control at all times. Dogs must be leashed when not in designated off-lead areas.

### Central Park Dog Park
1110 Stevenson Blvd
Fremont CA
510-494-4800
Thanks to one of our readers who writes: "Fenced, fresh water on demand, plenty of free parking, easy to find, all grass." Pet waste disposal bags are available at the park. The dog park is open from sunrise to 10 pm. The park is located on one acre, is adjacent to the Central Park Softball Complex with access off of Stevenson Blvd. To get there from I 680 head north on Mission Blvd and turn left on Stevenson Blvd. The park is on the left. From I 880 take Stevenson Blvd east to the park on the right.

### Del Valle Dog Run
Del Valle Road
Livermore CA
510-562-PARK
ebparks.org/parks/del_valle
This dog run is located in Del Valle Regional Park. Here your dog can walk leash free along the trail with you. Del Valle Regional Park is over 3,997 acres of land and it includes a five mile long lake. To get there from Hwy 580 heading east, exit S. Vasco Road. Turn right onto Vasco and head south. When Vasco ends, turn right onto Tesla Rd. Then turn left onto Mines Rd. Turn right onto Del Valle Road. Follow Del Valle Rd to the park entrance. The dog run is to the right of the marina.

### Livermore Canine Parks
Murdell Lane
Livermore CA

larpd.org/parks/dogparks.html

This dog park is located in Max Baer Park. There are also six more dog parks nearby. It has several trees and a lawn. To get there from downtown Livermore, head west on Stanely Blvd. Turn left on Isabel Ave. Then turn left onto Concannon Blvd (if you reach Alden Ln, you've passed Concannon). Turn left on Murdell Lane and the park will be on the right.

**Rancho Laguna Park**
2101 Camino Pablo
Moraga CA
925-888-7045
lamorindadogs.org/rancholagun
a
This beautiful multi-use park offers special times for well socialized pooches to run leash free too - from April 1st to September 30th after 6 pm until the park closes, and from October 1st until March 31st after 4 pm until the park closes. They are also allowed every morning before 9 am. Dogs must be well mannered, under firm voice control, and cleaned up after promptly at all times. Please bring your own disposal bags.

**Hardy Dog Park**
491 Hardy Street
Oakland CA
510-238-PARK
This 2 acre dog park in fully fenced. Dogs must be on-leash outside of the park. The park is located on Hardy Street at Claremont Avenue in the Rockridge District. It is just under the 24 Freeway.

**Pinole Dog Park**
3790 Pinole Valley Road
Pinole CA
510-741-2999
Located behind the playing fields at Pinole Valley Park, this off-lead area has 2 sections for large and small dogs, water, lots of green grass, benches, and shade. There is closer parking to this area just before the fire

**Oakley**

**Dog-Friendly Hotels**
**Best Western Plus Delta Hotel**
5549 Bridgehead Road
Oakley CA
925-755-1222 (800-780-7234)
100% non smoking suites, Free extended continental breakfast buffet, Fitness Center, pool, and spa

**Ojai**

**Dog-Friendly Hotels**
**Oakridge Inn**
780 North Ventura Avenue
Oak View CA
805-649-4018
oakridgeinn.com/
An outdoor pool free Wi-Fi and free breakfast make for a comfortable stop at the pet-friendly Oakridge Inn. This low-rise hotel has 33 rooms with free Wi-Fi cable TV microwaves mini-fridges and coffeemakers. Kick-start your day with a free continental breakfast and go for a dip in the outdoor pool or hot tub. Pets are allowed for a fee. Parking is free. This hotel is surrounded by restaurants for every taste and is about three miles from Lake Las Casitas. Drive five miles to the colorful Ojai downtown and find your new favorite vintage at the Ojai Vineyard or enjoy a concert at the Libbey Bowl. Outdoor enthusiasts will appreciate local biking trails and the vast wilderness of the Los Padres National Forest. Santa Barbara Municipal Airport is 45 miles west.

**Blue Iguana Inn**
11794 North Ventura Avenue
Ojai CA
805-646-5277
blueiguanainn.com/
A lush retreat with beautiful gardens an outdoor pool and free breakfast are on offer at the non-smoking Blue Iguana Inn. Gaudi meets Southwest at

this tranquil yet full-of-character boutique hotel. Its adobe buildings are surrounded by greenery and flowers and secluded paths meander towards a fountain with a mosaic iguana and outdoor pool. The 20 rooms sport hardwood floors rustic furniture and rugs and range from single-bedroom to bungalows with full kitchens. Each comes with free Wi-Fi a flat-panel TV coffeemaker hairdryer plush bathrobes and luxury toiletries. Pastries juice and coffee are served in the morning. Pets are allowed for a fee. Parking is free. Dive into the vibrant art scene in downtown Ojai two miles away and savor locally sourced flavors at the many area restaurants. Take a cooking class at the Ojai Culinary Studio three miles away or find your new favorite vintage at the local tasting rooms. Soule Park Golf Course beckons with its greens three miles away. Los Padres National Forest six miles north and Lake Casitas five miles west let you unwind and bond with nature. Santa Barbara Municipal Airport is 40 miles away.

**Ojai Valley Inn And Spa**
905 Country Club Road
Ojai CA
805-646-2420 (888-697-8780)
ojairesort.com/
A historic jewel set against picturesque mountains the non-smoking Ojai Valley Inn and Spa offers a relaxing retreat with a full spa championship golf course and dining fit for Hollywood royalty. This historic resort is still full of Spanish Colonial charm yet chock-full of modern conveniences. Its 308 rooms feature free Wi-Fi flat-panel TVs Egyptian satin sheets iPod docks Turkish bathrobes and bath products created at the on-site apothecary. Some rooms also have patios or balconies. Challenge your partners to a game of golf on the adjacent course or spend a relaxing afternoon at the

Moroccan-inspired spa. Show off your serve at the tennis courts or find your muse at the Artist Cottage. Wrap up the night with a fresh margarita and locally grown fare at one of the on-site restaurants. Pets are allowed for a fee and they'll also get the royal treatment. Parking is free. Hop on a trolley that stops by the hotel and explore Ojai's eclectic shopping wine tasting rooms and farm-to-table restaurants. Sample local vintages at the Ojai Wine Festival held every year at Lake Casitas seven miles away or go on a picturesque bike ride down to Ventura 22 miles south. Los Padres National Forest offers a perfect playground for horseback riding and hiking. Santa Barbara Municipal Airport is 42 miles west.

## Dog-Friendly Attractions
### Casitas Boat Rentals
11311 Santa Ana Road
Oak View CA
805-649-2043
lakecasitas.info/boatrental.html
You, your family and your dog can go for a boat adventure on Lake Casitas. Pontoon and row boat rentals are available and your dog is welcome to accompany you. Boating on the lake is only permitted during daylight hours. There are four floating restrooms for people on the lake. Lake Casitas is a drinking water reservoir and does not allow swimming by people or dogs. Dogs must be on-leash throughout the Lake Casitas Rec Area and may not go within 50 feet of the lake.

## Outdoor Restaurants
### Agave Maria's
106 S Montgomery St
Ojai CA
805-646-6353
agavemarias.com/
Notable appetizers, an impressive tequila and beer selection, and freshly prepared Mexican cuisine is offered at this

eatery. Leashed dogs are allowed at the outdoor tables.

### Deer Lodge Tavern
2261 Maricopa Hwy
Ojai CA
805-646-4256
ojaideerlodge.net/
Dogs are allowed at the outdoor tables.

### Full of Beans
11534 N Ventura Avenue/H 33
Ojai CA
805-640-8500
fullofbeanscoffeehouse.net/
A large comfortable patio with plenty of lush foliage and large shade trees, good coffee - made any number of ways, freshly baked pastries, and free WiFi are just some of the popularities of this coffee house. Leashed dogs are welcomed at the outside patio tables.

### Jim & Rob's Fresh Grill
535 E Ojai Ave
Ojai CA
805-640-1301
jimandrobsojai.com/
Dogs are allowed at the outdoor tables.

### Rainbow Bridge Natural Foods Market
211 East Matilija Street
Ojai CA
805-646-4017
rainbowbridgeojai.com
This natural food market has outdoor tables where you may sit with your dog. You will need to get the food yourself as your dog may not enter the store.

### Sea Fresh Seafood
533 E. Ojai Avenue/H 150
Ojai CA
805-646-7747
seafreshseafood.com
This fresh fish market, eatery, and sushi and oyster bar will allowed friendly, leashed dogs at their outside dining area. They are open Sunday to Thursday from 11 am until 9 pm and on Friday and Saturday from 11 am until 10 pm.

## Pet-Friendly Shopping Centers
### Downtown Ojai
E Ojai Ave at S Montgomery St
Ojai CA
805-646-8126
ci.ojai.ca.us
Ojai is a quaint artist town with a number of art studios, boutique shopping and restaurants, many of which have outdoor dining where your dog is welcome. Ask at the stores if your dog may join you. The downtown district is about ten blocks long and stretches along Ojai Avenue in both directions from Libbey Park, which is home to a number of annual outdoor music festivals during the summer months.

## Off-Leash Dog Parks
### Soule Dog Park
310 Soule Park Drive
Ojai CA
805-654-3951
Although dogs are not allowed in Soule Park proper, they are now allowed in the newly opened 2008 off leash dog area. There are sections for large and small dogs (under 20 pounds), waste disposal stations, and benches in the shade. General admission is $2 weekdays, $4 weekends, and annual passes are $55 ($25 for seniors).

## Dog-Friendly Parks
### Lake Casitas Rec Area
11311 Santa Ana Road
Oak View CA
805-649-2233
Lake Casitas was created as a drinking water reservoir by the creation of the Casitas Dam. It is well known as one of the top bass fishing lakes in America. Hiking, camping and boating are available in the Recreation Area. Dogs must be on a six foot leash at all times. They must be under control and are not allowed within 50 feet of the lake

or streams or inside the Water Adventure area. Dogs are allowed in boats on the lake including the rental boats. There is an $8.00 automobile fee to enter the Rec Area and a $1.50 pet fee per pet per day to use the Rec Area. There is camping in the Rec Area for RVs with lots priced from $19 to $50 per night. Full hookups are available.

**Cozy Dell Trail**
Highway 33
Ojai CA

This trail offers great panoramic views of the Ojai Valley. It is about a 4 mile round trip trail and can take a couple of hours to walk. It is rated an easy to moderate trail. The trail might be a little overgrown during certain times of the year. To get there, take Highway 33 north and go about 3.3 miles north of Ojai. The trail begins near the Friends Ranch Packing House. Park on the left side of the highway. Dogs need to be leashed.

**Libbey Park**
Ojai Ave at Signal Street
Ojai CA
805-646-5581
This city park that is home to many events is located in the heart of picturesque Ojai. Dogs must be on leash at all times. The park boasts a music amphitheater, playground and a well-cut grass area. There are clean up bags for dogs located in the park.

**Ojai Valley Trail**
Hwy 33 at Casitas Vista Rd
Ojai CA
805-654-3951
This 9.5 mile trail has a paved pedestrian path and a wood-chip bridle path. Dogs are allowed but must always be on leash. The trail parallels Highway 33 from Foster Park, just outside Ventura to Fox Street, in Ojai.

## Olympic Valley

## Dog-Friendly Attractions
**Ann Poole Weddings, Nature's Chapel**
P.O. Box 3768
Olympic Valley CA
530-412-5436
tahoeminister.com
This business offers Lake Tahoe and Bay Area Weddings. Make it a special day by bringing your dog along with you. Here is an excerpt from the Wedding Minister: "You are planning to marry the Love of Your Life... so naturally, you will bring your 'best friend' to your wedding, won't you? Dogs do great at weddings... they are excellent ring bearers or proudly stand up with you, with flowers around their collars. They seem to simply KNOW that this is a Special Day for you and that they have an important part in it." They have many Wedding locations to choose from. You can choose your own unique location or have your wedding in a wedding chapel, nestled in the woods, or at one of their favorite locations like on a cliff overlooking beautiful Lake Tahoe, surrounded by tall pine trees.

**The Village At Squaw Valley**
Squaw Valley
Olympic Valley CA
530-584-6267
thevillageatsquaw.com
This European style village is very dog-friendly. You can ride the Gondola in the summer with your dog, take in a pet boutique store Tails by the Lake, enjoy numerous outdoor restaurants with your pup and browse the various stores with your leashed dog. There is a miniature golf course sprinkled throughout the walkways where kids and adults can play mini-golf with your dog along for the fun. And throughout the summer there are events such as music festivals and outdoor movies on a large screen where you and your dog are welcome for most events.

Check out their website at http://www.thevillageatsquaw.com for more information and event schedules. The village is located at Squaw Valley USA just off Highway 89 between Tahoe City and Truckee in the north Tahoe area.

## Onyx

## Dog-Friendly Parks
**Pacific Crest Trail-Owens Peak Segment**
Highway 178
Onyx CA
661-391-6000
The Owens Peak Segment of the Pacific Crest Trail is managed by the Bureau of Land Management. This section begins at Walker Pass in Kern County and goes 41 miles north to the Sequoia National Forest at Rockhouse Basin. Elevations on this portion range from 5,245 feet at Walker Pass to 7,900 feet on Bear Mountain. The trail offers great views of the surrounding mountains and valleys. Dogs are allowed on the Owen's Peak Segment of the Pacific Crest Trail. Trail conditions can change due to fires, storms and landslides. To confirm current conditions, contact the Bakersfield BLM Office at 661-391-6000. There are many trailheads, but one of the more popular staging areas is at Walker Pass. From Ridgecrest go 27 miles west on Highway 178 to Walker Pass.

## Orange County Beaches

## Dog-Friendly Hotels
**Avenue Of The Arts Costa Mesa A Tribute Portfolio Hotel**

3350 Avenue Of The Arts
Costa Mesa CA
714-751-5100

Dogs of all sizes are allowed. There is a $50 per day pet cleaning fee. Some rooms are pet-friendly. There is also a $60 cleaning fee on departure.

## Hilton Orange County-costa Mesa

3050 Bristol St.
Costa Mesa CA
714-540-7000

This upscale hotel offers a number of on site amenities for business and leisure travelers, plus a convenient location to business, shopping, dining, and entertainment areas. Dogs up to 25 pounds are allowed for an additional one time fee of $50 per pet.

## La Quinta Inn John Wayne Orange County Airport

1515 South Coast Drive
Costa Mesa CA
714-957-5841 (800-531-5900)

Dogs up to 25 pounds are allowed. There are no additional pet fees. Dogs must be leashed and cleaned up after.

## The Westin South Coast Plaza Costa Mesa

686 Anton Boulevard
Costa Mesa CA
714-540-2500 (888-625-5144)

Dogs up to 40 pounds are allowed. There is no additional pet fee.

## Kimpton Shorebreak Hotel

500 Pacific Coast Highway
Huntington Beach CA
714-861-4470

A location across from the beach and a block from the pier amenity-filled accommodations a fitness room and on-site restaurant welcome our guests at the non-smoking Kimpton Shorebreak Hotel. The Kimpton Shorebreak Hotel has 157 rooms overlooking the ocean right across the street. All accommodations feature extra-thick mattresses covered with 300-thread-count linens 42-inch flat-panel TVs with premium cable channels iPod docking stations and work desks. Wi-Fi access is available for an additional fee. The hotel has a fitness room with yoga studio open courtyard with several romantic fire pits business center on-site restaurant and bike rentals for further convenience. Underground parking is available for an additional fee. The Shorebreak is on the world-famous Pacific Coast Highway one block from the Huntington Beach Pier. The International Surfing Museum is three blocks away and Disneyland is about 17 miles. John Wayne Airport is 12 miles from the hotel and Long Beach Airport is 15 miles.

## The Waterfront Beach Resort A Hilton Hotel

21100 Pacific Coast Highway
Huntington Beach CA
714-845-8000

A tropical terrace overlooking the ocean glorious freeform pool and ultra-modern touches make the non-smoking Waterfront Beach Resort a Hilton Hotel one of Huntington Beach's most popular hotels among our guests. Rising 12 stories above Huntington Beach the Waterfront Beach Resort has unmatched ocean views from most of its 290 non-smoking rooms. Creature comforts start with pillowtop mattresses dressed with silky-soft linens. High-definition TVs iPod docking stations and free high-speed internet access are among the top-of-the-line amenities. Grab a beverage from your mini-fridge and head out to your private balcony to enjoy the sea breezes. This is a pet-friendly lodging so you can bring along yours for an extra charge. The heated pool and hot tub are set on a palm-shaded ocean-facing terrace that might remind you of Hawaii. If you're feeling active try the tennis and volleyball courts or the fitness room with free weights cardio machines and strength-training equipment. Two elegant restaurants serve breakfast lunch and dinner and room service is available. Parking is available for a fee. A three-minute walk to Huntington Beach the Waterfront Beach Resort sits on the Pacific Coast Highway. The location gives you easy access to some of the area's most popular beaches. Beautiful Balboa Island is seven miles down the coast. Disneyland is a 30-minute drive from the hotel. John Wayne Airport is 11 miles northeast and Long Beach Airport is 16 miles northwest.

## Renaissance Newport Beach Hotel

4500 Mcarthur Boulevard
Newport Beach CA
949-476-2001 (800-257-7544)

A $32 million renovation was undergone at this hotel to ensure visitors a true luxury hotel experience with all the conveniences and services. Some of the features/amenities include 440 elegant guest rooms and 54 suites, a restaurant and lounge with 24 hour room service, a state of the art business center, a heated sky pool and deck, and tennis courts. Dogs up to 40 pounds are allowed for an additional one time pet fee of $25 per pet, and there is a pet policy to sign at check in. Dogs must be leashed, cleaned up after, and the Do Not Disturb sign put on the door if they are in the room alone.

# Pet-Friendly Extended Stay Hotels

## Residence Inn Costa Mesa

881 West Baker Street
Costa Mesa CA
714-241-8800

Dogs of all sizes are allowed. There is a $100 one time additional pet fee.

## Residence Inn Huntington Beach Fountain Valley

9930 Slater Ave
Fountain Valley CA
714-965-8000

Dogs of all sizes are allowed. There is a $100 one time additional pet fee.

### Extended Stay America - Orange County - Huntington Beach

5050 Skylab West Circle
Huntington Beach CA
714-799-4887 (800-804-3724)
One dog is allowed per suite.
There is a $25 per night
additional pet fee up to $150 for
an entire stay.

### Extended Stay America Orange County - John Wayne Airport

4881 Birch St.
Newport Beach CA
949-851-2711 (800-804-3724)
One dog is allowed per suite.
There is a $25 per night
additional pet fee up to $150 for
an entire stay.

## Dog Camps
### Your Animals Best Friend

15392 Assembly Ln
Huntington Beach CA
949-375-1832
youranimalsbestfriend.com/
Your Animals Best Friend offers
a variety of services to assist
you with your animal. They offer
customized services for your
pets such as overnight pet
sitting at your house or theirs or
multiple visits to your home.
They also have long term and
short term options for day and
overnight care for dogs at their
new center for dogs which is a
non cage home like
environment. They also offer
dog walks custom to your
needs. Custom errand services
and project help is also
available.

## Dog Businesses
### Doggietown Usa

7466 Edinger Ave
Huntington Beach CA
714-841-3330
doggietownusa.com/
Doggietown USA is an over
5,000 square foot facility located
in Huntington Beach, California
and dedicated to the health,

happiness and well-being of
man's best friend. Dogs play in
a safe cage-free, leash free,
supervised environment while
you work. They have indoor
potty areas complete with real
grass and a fire hydrant, and
also are a great place to
socialize puppies.

## Dog-Friendly Attractions
### Boat Rentals of America

510 E Edgewater
Newport Beach CA
949-673-7200
boats4rent.com/
There are a total of 3 boat
rental locations in the Southern
California area where they offer
a variety of safe, reliable
watercraft and many
recreational boating options.
Dogs are welcome aboard the
harbor power boat rentals for
no additional pet fee as long as
the boat is left clean. Dogs
must be under their owner's
control, and leashed and
cleaned up after at all times.

### Fun Zone Boat Tours

6000 Edgewater Place
Newport Beach CA
949-673-0240
newportbeach.com/funzoneboa
ts
The people here are very dog-
friendly and welcome your pup
on several of their boat tours.
The narrated trips range in
length from 45 to 90 minutes
and can include a harbor, sea
lion and Lido Island tour. The
prices range from $6.00 to
$9.00 and less for children.
Prices are subject to change.
Boat tours depart every half
hour seven days a week. They
do have a summer and winter
schedule, so please call ahead
for the hours. Whale watching
tours are also available from
January through March. (see
Attractions). The Fun Zone
Boat Co. is located at the end
of Palm Street next to the
Ferris Wheel.

### Fun Zone Boat-Whale Watching Tours

600 Edgewater Place
Newport Beach CA
949-673-0240
newportbeach.com/funzoneboat
s
These nice folks allow dogs on
their whale watching boat tours.
The tour guide has a golden
retriever that rides with him. He
asks that your dog be friendly
around other dogs and remain
leashed while on the boat. He
might also limit the number of
dogs on the tour depending on
how all the pups get along with
each other. The whale watching
tours are seasonal and last from
January through the end of
March. Tours are $12 per
person for 2 hours. The boat
departs for the tour twice per
day, so please call ahead for
hours. Fun Zone Boat Co. is
located off Balboa Blvd. in
Balboa (near Newport Beach).
It's next to the Balboa Fun Zone
and Ferris Wheel.

### Marina Water Sports-Boat Rentals

600 E Bay Ave
Newport Beach CA
949-673-3372
Want to drive your own rental
boat on Newport Bay? This
company allows dogs on their
pontoon boats. These are flat
bottom boats usually with
canopies on top which are great
for dogs. Rental rates start at
$45-50 per hour. They are
located on Bay Ave next to the
Balboa Fun Zone/Ferris Wheel
near Washington Ave and Palm
St.

## Outdoor Restaurants
### Baja Fresh Mexican Grill

3050 E. Coast Hwy
Corona Del Mar CA
949-760-8000
bajafresh.com
This Mexican restaurant is open
for lunch and dinner. They use
fresh ingredients and making
their salsa and beans daily.
Some of the items on their
menu include Enchiladas,
Burritos, Tacos Salads,
Quesadillas, Nachos, Chicken,

Steak and more. Well-behaved leashed dogs are allowed at the outdoor tables.

### Coffee Bean & Tea Leaf
2933 Coast H E, Space 3A/H 1
Corona Del Mar CA
949-673-7062
coffeebean.com
The coffee here is sourced globally from family coffee farms to procure only the top of 1% of Arabica beans. They offer 30+ varieties of coffee;the beans are roasted in small batches daily for freshness, and they also offer 20 varieties of teas that are hand-blended by their tea master. Additionally, they offer a variety of tasty sweets, powders, extracts, sauces, gifts, and cards. Leashed, well mannered dogs are allowed at their outside dining area.

### Baja Fresh Mexican Grill
3030 Harbor Blvd
Costa Mesa CA
949-675-2252
bajafresh.com
This Mexican restaurant is open for lunch and dinner. They use fresh ingredients and making their salsa and beans daily. Some of the items on their menu include Enchiladas, Burritos, Tacos Salads, Quesadillas, Nachos, Chicken, Steak and more. Well-behaved leashed dogs are allowed at the outdoor tables.

### Chipotle
2300 Harbor Blvd
Costa Mesa CA
949-646-1288 (949-646-1288)
chipotle.com
Specializing in organic, natural and unprocessed food, this Mexican Eatery offers fajita burritos, tacos, salads, and salsas. Dogs are allowed at the outdoor tables but you will need to order your food inside the restaurant and dogs must remain outside.

### Side Street Cafe
1799 Newport Blvd Ste A105
Costa Mesa CA
949-650-1986
This restaurant serves American

food. Dogs are allowed at the outdoor tables. Water is provided for your pet.

### The Coffee Bean & Tea Leaf
1835 Newport Blvd. # B122
Costa Mesa CA
949-722-9673
coffeebean.com
The coffee here is sourced globally from family coffee farms to procure only the top of 1% of Arabica beans. They offer 30+ varieties of coffee;the beans are roasted in small batches daily for freshness, and they also offer 20 varieties of teas that are hand-blended by their tea master. Additionally, they offer a variety of tasty sweets, powders, extracts, sauces, gifts, and cards. Leashed, well mannered dogs are allowed at their outside dining area.

### Chipotle
18951 Brookhurst
Fountain Valley CA
951-817-0447
chipotle.com
Specializing in organic, natural and unprocessed food, this Mexican Eatery offers fajita burritos, tacos, salads, and salsas. Dogs are allowed at the outdoor tables but you will need to order your food inside the restaurant and dogs must remain outside.

### The Coffee Bean & Tea Leaf
18011 Newhope Street, Suite G
Fountain Valley CA
714-438-0138
coffeebean.com
The coffee here is sourced globally from family coffee farms to procure only the top of 1% of Arabica beans. They offer 30+ varieties of coffee;the beans are roasted in small batches daily for freshness, and they also offer 20 varieties of teas that are hand-blended by their tea master. Additionally, they offer a variety of tasty sweets, powders, extracts, sauces, gifts, and cards. Leashed, well mannered dogs are allowed at their

outside dining area.

### Corner Bakery Cafe
7621 Edinger Ave Ste 110
Huntington Beach CA
714-891-8400
cornerbakerycafe.com
Corner Bakery Cafe offers breakfast, salad, soups & chili, signature sandwiches, pastas, a kid's menu, beverages, and more. Well behaved, leashed dogs are allowed on the outdoor patio.

### Johnny Rockets
7801 Edinger Avenue
Huntington Beach CA
714-901-1100
johnnyrockets.com/
All the American favorites can be found here: A fun retro, all-American decor and atmosphere, juicy burgers, specialty sandwiches, crispy fries, hand-dipped malts and shakes (dark chocolate ones too), fresh baked apple pies, tasty vegetarian choices, and something for all ages. Leashed, friendly dogs are allowed at their outside dining area.

### Kahoots Pet Store
18681 Main St
Huntington Beach CA
714-842-1841
The Kahoots Pet Store in Huntington Beach, California is a family pet store not offering just dog supplies, but also horse, livestock, cats, small pets, and more.

### Slaters
8082 Adams Ave
Huntington Beach CA
714-594-5730
https://slaters5050.com
Dogs are no only welcome but they have a dog menu consisting of 50/50 burger patty, turkey patty, beef, bacon and chicken strips. With over 50 beers, lots of burgers and food options and gluten-free options there is a lot to choose.

### Spark Woodfire Grill
300 Pacific Coast H
Huntington Beach CA

714-960-0996
sparkwoodfiregrill.com/index.php
For ocean front, casual dining, this award-wining steak and seafood, dinner-only house, is the place. They feature a large terrace with an open fire pit, contemporary American cuisine specializing in wood-fire grilling and slow roasting, a full bar with a variety of some 50+ martinis, and an extensive wine list. Leashed, well mannered dogs are welcome at their outside dining area.

**The Coffee Bean & Tea Leaf**
17969 Beach Blvd
Huntington Beach CA
714-375-9274
coffeebean.com
The coffee here is sourced globally from family coffee farms to procure only the top of 1% of Arabica beans. They offer 30+ varieties of coffee;the beans are roasted in small batches daily for freshness, and they also offer 20 varieties of teas that are hand-blended by their tea master. Additionally, they offer a variety of tasty sweets, powders, extracts, sauces, gifts, and cards. Leashed, well mannered dogs are allowed at their outside dining area.

**The Coffee Bean & Tea Leaf**
200 Main Street, Suite 109
Huntington Beach CA
714-960-1582
coffeebean.com
The coffee here is sourced globally from family coffee farms to procure only the top of 1% of Arabica beans. They offer 30+ varieties of coffee;the beans are roasted in small batches daily for freshness, and they also offer 20 varieties of teas that are hand-blended by their tea master. Additionally, they offer a variety of tasty sweets, powders, extracts, sauces, gifts, and cards. Leashed, well mannered dogs are allowed at their outside dining area.

**The Park Bench Cafe**
17732 Goldenwest Street
Huntington Beach CA

714-842-0775
parkbenchcafe.com/
This is one of the most dog-friendly restaurants that we have found in our travels. Your dog will absolutely feel welcome here. They even have a separate Doggie Dining Area. And if these tables are full as they often are, the nice folks will try to accommodate.

**Z Pizza**
10035 Adams Avenue
Huntington Beach CA
714-968-8844
zpizza.com
Specializing in organically and internationally inspired pizzas, this pizzeria cooks their pizzas on hot bricks in a fire baked oven. They feature a 100% certified organic gluten free wheat crust, homemade organic sauces and ingredients, fresh produce, and additive-free meats. They also offer gourmet salads, sandwiches, and catering services. Leashed, well mannered dogs are allowed at their outside tables.

**Z Pizza**
19035 Golden West Avenue,
Huntington Beach, CA - (
Huntington Beach CA
714-536-3444
zpizza.com
Specializing in organically and internationally inspired pizzas, this pizzeria cooks their pizzas on hot bricks in a fire baked oven. They feature a 100% certified organic gluten free wheat crust, homemade organic sauces and ingredients, fresh produce, and additive-free meats. They also offer gourmet salads, sandwiches, and catering services. Leashed, well mannered dogs are allowed at their outside tables.

**Baja Fresh Mexican Grill**
1324 Bison Avenue
Newport Beach CA
949-759-0010
bajafresh.com
This Mexican restaurant is open for lunch and dinner.

They use fresh ingredients and making their salsa and beans daily. Some of the items on their menu include Enchiladas, Burritos, Tacos Salads, Quesadillas, Nachos, Chicken, Steak and more. Well-behaved leashed dogs are allowed at the outdoor tables.

**Cafe Beau Soleil**
953 Newport Center Drive
Newport Beach CA
949-640-4402
cafebeausoleil.net
The Cafe Beau Soleil is a French Cafe that serves breakfast, lunch, dinner, dessert, and crepes. Well-behaved, leashed dogs are welcome at the outdoor seats.

**Charlie's Chili**
102 McFadden Place
Newport Beach CA
949-675-7991
charlieschili-newportbeach.com/

Breakfasts, signature chili, starters, salads, sandwiches, seafood, Baja specials, a kid's menu, specialty cocktails/beer and wines, happy hours, and patio dining are some of the offerings at this eatery. Leashed, well mannered dogs are welcome at their outside tables.

**Jamba Juice**
4341 MacArthur Blvd, #A
Newport Beach CA
949-852-6500
jambajuice.com
All natural and organic ingredients, no high-fructose corn syrup, 0 grams trans fat, no artificial preservatives, a healthy helping of antioxidants, vitamins, and minerals, and fresh whole fruit and fruit juices set the base for these tasty and healthy beverages. Their organic Hot Blends provides a new spin on coffee, green or chai tea, and hot chocolate;plus they offer probiotic fruit and yogurt Blends. Additionally, they feature organic steel-cut oatmeal prepared fresh every morning, all natural salads, wraps, sandwiches, and grab n' go

specialties. They also offer healthy community support through fundraisers, special sales, and school lunch programs. Leashed, well mannered dogs are allowed at their outside dining area.

**Park Avenue Cafe**
501 Park Avenue
Newport Beach CA
949-673-3830
Dogs are allowed at the outdoor tables. Thanks to one of our readers for recommending this cafe. They are open Monday to Friday from 8 am until 9 pm and on Saturday and Sunday from 7 am until 9 pm.

**The Coffee Bean & Tea Leaf**
1316 Bison Avenue
Newport Beach CA
949-719-0524
coffeebean.com
The coffee here is sourced globally from family coffee farms to procure only the top of 1% of Arabica beans. They offer 30+ varieties of coffee;the beans are roasted in small batches daily for freshness, and they also offer 20 varieties of teas that are hand-blended by their tea master. Additionally, they offer a variety of tasty sweets, powders, extracts, sauces, gifts, and cards. Leashed, well mannered dogs are allowed at their outside dining area.

**Top Dog Barkery**
924 Avocado Ave
Newport Beach CA
949-759-3647
topdogbarkery.net
The Top Dog Barkery, located at 924 Avocado Ave in Newport Beach, California, is a pet bakery, baking and serving many freshly made dog treats daily, including their made-to-order cakes and treats. The "barkery" also sells dog treats, including a "made in America" line, and offers feline treats and equipment as well.

**Wilma's Patio**
203 Marine Avenue
Newport Beach CA
949-675-5542

wilmaspatio.com/index.htm
A casual, family dining eatery, they offer fresh, homemade favorites of American and Mexican cuisine with a wide selection of dishes for breakfast, lunch, and diner. Dogs are allowed at the outdoor tables. They must be well behaved, under owner's control/care, and leashed.

**Z Pizza**
7956 E Pacific Coast H/H 1
Newport Beach CA
949-715-1117
zpizza.com
Specializing in organically and internationally inspired pizzas, this pizzeria cooks their pizzas on hot bricks in a fire baked oven. They feature a 100% certified organic gluten free wheat crust, homemade organic sauces and ingredients, fresh produce, and additive-free meats. They also offer gourmet salads, sandwiches, and catering services. Leashed, well mannered dogs are allowed at their outside tables.

**Z Pizza**
2549 Eastbluff Drive
Newport Beach CA
949-760-3100
zpizza.com
Specializing in organically and internationally inspired pizzas, this pizzeria cooks their pizzas on hot bricks in a fire baked oven. They feature a 100% certified organic gluten free wheat crust, homemade organic sauces and ingredients, fresh produce, and additive-free meats. They also offer gourmet salads, sandwiches, and catering services. Leashed, well mannered dogs are allowed at their outside tables.

**Z Pizza**
1616 San Miguel Drive-
Newport Beach CA
949-219-9939
zpizza.com
Specializing in organically and internationally inspired pizzas, this pizzeria cooks their pizzas

on hot bricks in a fire baked oven. They feature a 100% certified organic gluten free wheat crust, homemade organic sauces and ingredients, fresh produce, and additive-free meats. They also offer gourmet salads, sandwiches, and catering services. Leashed, well mannered dogs are allowed at their outside tables.

**Z Pizza**
3423 Via Lido
Newport Beach CA
949-723-0707
zpizza.com
Specializing in organically and internationally inspired pizzas, this pizzeria cooks their pizzas on hot bricks in a fire baked oven. They feature a 100% certified organic gluten free wheat crust, homemade organic sauces and ingredients, fresh produce, and additive-free meats. They also offer gourmet salads, sandwiches, and catering services. Leashed, well mannered dogs are allowed at their outside tables.

**River's End Cafe**
15 1st Street
Seal Beach CA
562-431-5558
riversendcafe.com/
This eatery offers a great location on a tropical beach, a tasty selection of Central American, Southern Caribbean, and American cuisine, outstanding views of the ocean, and patio dining. Leashed, well mannered dogs are allowed at the outer tables.

**The Coffee Bean & Tea Leaf**
347 Main Street, Suite A
Seal Beach CA
562-596-4006
coffeebean.com
The coffee here is sourced globally from family coffee farms to procure only the top of 1% of Arabica beans. They offer 30+ varieties of coffee;the beans are roasted in small batches daily for freshness, and they also offer 20 varieties of teas that are hand-blended by their tea master. Additionally, they offer a

variety of tasty sweets, powders, extracts, sauces, gifts, and cards. Leashed, well mannered dogs are allowed at their outside dining area.

**Z Pizza**
12430 Seal Beach Blvd
Seal Beach CA
562-493-3440
zpizza.com
Specializing in organically and international inspired pizzas, this pizzeria cooks their pizzas on hot bricks in a fire baked oven. They feature a 100% certified organic gluten free wheat crust, homemade organic sauces and ingredients, fresh produce, and additive-free meats. They also offer gourmet salads, sandwiches, and catering services. Leashed, well mannered dogs are allowed at their outside tables.

# Pet-Friendly Shopping Centers
## Fashion Island Mall
1133 Newport Center Dr
Newport Beach CA
800-495-4753
Fashion Island Mall is known as Southern California's premier open-air shopping center. And they allow dogs. Some of the stores allow your well-behaved dog inside. Please always ask the store clerk before bringing your dog inside, just in case policies have changed. For a list of dog-friendly stores, please look at our stores category. You can also shop at the numerous outdoor retail kiosks located throughout the mall. Work up an appetite after walking around? Try dining at the fast food court located upstairs which has many outdoor seats complete with heaters.

# Pet-Friendly Stores
## Bloomingdale's
3333 S Bristol Street
Costa Mesa CA
714-824-4600

Some of the offerings of this major shopping destination include designer merchandise, indoor and outdoor wear for the entire family, jewelry and accessories, shoes and handbags, personal beauty aids, child care products, and home decor. They also offer a wide variety of shopping services; various fashion, beauty, and home events, and a philanthropy program that raises funds and awareness for worthy causes. Leashed, well mannered dogs are welcome in the store; they must be under their owner's control at all times.

**Centinela Feed and Supplies**
2320 Harbor Blvd
Costa Mesa CA
714-540-4036
centinelafeed.com/
Specializing in natural, holistic, and raw pet foods, this pet supply store also provides healthy treats, quality supplements, pet care supplies, low-cost vaccination clinics, frequent in-store events, and a knowledgeable staff. Leashed pets are welcome.

**PetSmart Pet Store**
620 West 17th St
Costa Mesa CA
949-764-9277
Your licensed and well-behaved leashed dog is allowed in the store.

**Petco Pet Store - Costa Mesa**
1815 Newport Blvd
Costa Mesa CA
949-722-6316
Your licensed and well-behaved leashed dog is allowed in the store.

**Urban Outfitters**
2930 Bristol Street
Costa Mesa CA
714-966-1666
In addition to a large inventory of indoor and outdoor apparel for men and women, this major department store also carries vintage wear, designer brands,

and a variety of accessories for all types of active lifestyles. They also carry shoes, furnishings, home decor, cameras, electronics, novelty items and more. Leashed, well mannered dogs are allowed in the store.

**PetSmart Pet Store**
17940 Newhope St
Fountain Valley CA
714-241-0317
Your licensed and well-behaved leashed dog is allowed in the store.

**Petco Pet Store - Fountain Valley**
16055 Brookhurst St.
Fountain Valley CA
714-839-2544
Your licensed and well-behaved leashed dog is allowed in the store.

**Kahoots Pet Store**
18681 Main St
Huntington Beach CA
714-842-1841
The Kahoots Pet Store in Huntington Beach, California, offers products for every animal from hamster to horse, cat to cow,backyard to barn. Need some food for your fish, a toy for your terrier, or hay for your horse? Check out Kahoots. Other services at the Huntington Beach location include dog training, pet vaccinations, and teeth cleaning.

**PetSmart Pet Store**
7600 Edinger Ave
Huntington Beach CA
714-842-5253
Your licensed and well-behaved leashed dog is allowed in the store.

**Petco Pet Store - Huntington Beach**
8909 Adams Ave.
Huntington Beach CA
714-964-4717
Your licensed and well-behaved leashed dog is allowed in the store.

**Petco Pet Store - Huntington**

## Beach
5961 Warner Ave.
Huntington Beach CA
714-846-7331
Your licensed and well-behaved
leashed dog is allowed in the
store.

## Anthropologie
823 Newport Center Drive
Newport Beach CA
949-720-9946
Items of distinction can be found
for all ages and in all
departments of this unique
shop. Carefully selected to add
to the enjoyment of the
shopping experience, they carry
fine clothing, amazing
accessories, jewelry, hobby and
leisure items, and a full line of
bright and useful items for the
home, garden, and office.
Leashed, well behaved dogs are
allowed in the store.

## Anthropologie
Fashion Island Mall
Newport Beach CA
949-720-9946
anthropologie.com/
Your well-behaved leashed dog
is allowed inside this store.

## Barnes and Noble
Fashion Island Mall
Newport Beach CA
949-759-0982
barnesandnoble.com/
Your well-behaved leashed dog
is allowed inside this store.

## Bebe
Fashion Island Mall
Newport Beach CA
949-640-2429
bebe.com/
Your well-behaved leashed dog
is allowed inside this store.

## Bloomingdale's
701 Newport Center Drive
Newport Beach CA
949-729-6600
Some of the offerings of this
major shopping destination
include designer merchandise,
indoor and outdoor wear for the
entire family, jewelry and
accessories, shoes and
handbags, personal beauty aids,
child care products, and home
decor. They also offer a wide
variety of shopping services;
various fashion, beauty, and
home events, and a
philanthropy program that
raises funds and awareness for
worthy causes. Leashed, well
mannered dogs are welcome in
the store; they must be under
their owner's control at all
times.

## Bloomingdale's
Fashion Island Mall
Newport Beach CA
949-729-6600
bloomingdales.com/
Your well-behaved leashed dog
is allowed inside this store.

## Georgiou
Fashion Island Mall
Newport Beach CA
949-760-2558
Your well-behaved leashed dog
is allowed inside this store.
They told us on the phone that
"We always welcome dogs!".

## Neiman Marcus
601 Newport Center Drive
Newport Beach CA
949-759-1900
neimanmarcus.com
This famous department store,
which sells everything from
clothing to home furnishings,
allows your well-behaved
leashed dog to shop with you.
It is located in Fashion Island
Shopping Center, which is very
dog-friendly.

## Petco Pet Store - Newport
1280 Bison Ave.
Newport Beach CA
949-759-9520
Your licensed and well-
behaved leashed dog is
allowed in the store.

## Pottery Barn
Fashion Island Mall
Newport Beach CA
949-644-2406
potterybarn.com/
Your well-behaved leashed dog
is allowed inside this store.

## Restoration Hardware
Fashion Island Mall
Newport Beach CA
949-760-9232
restorationhardware.com/
Your well-behaved leashed dog
is allowed inside this store.

## Robinsons-May
Fashion Island Mall
Newport Beach CA
949-644-2800
mayco.com/
Your well-behaved leashed dog
is allowed inside this store.

## Sharper Image
Fashion Island Mall
Newport Beach CA
949-640-8800
sharperimage.com/
Your well-behaved leashed dog
is allowed inside this store.

## St. Croix
Fashion Island Mall
Newport Beach CA
949-760-8191
stcroixshop.com/
Your well-behaved leashed dog
is allowed inside this store.

## The Limited
Fashion Island Mall
Newport Beach CA
949-720-9891
Your well-behaved leashed dog
is allowed inside this store.

## Urban Outfitters
857 Newport Center Drive
Newport Beach CA
949-760-0267
In addition to a large inventory
of indoor and outdoor apparel
for men and women, this major
department store also carries
vintage wear, designer brands,
and a variety of accessories for
all types of active lifestyles.
They also carry shoes,
furnishings, home decor,
cameras, electronics, novelty
items and more. Leashed, well
mannered dogs are allowed in
the store.

## Victoria's Secret
Fashion Island Mall
Newport Beach CA
949-721-9606
victoriassecret.com/
Your well-behaved leashed dog
is allowed inside this store.

## Dog-Friendly Beaches

### Corona Del Mar State Beach
Iris Street and Ocean Blvd.
Corona Del Mar CA
949-644-3151
This is a popular beach for swimming, surfing and diving. The sandy beach is about a half mile long. Dogs are allowed on this beach during certain hours. They are allowed before 9am and after 5pm, year round. Pets must be on a 6 foot or less leash. Tickets will be issued if your dog is off leash.

### Huntington Dog Beach
Pacific Coast Hwy (Hwy 1)
Huntington Beach CA
714-841-8644
dogbeach.org
This beautiful beach is about a mile long and allows dogs from 5 am to 10 pm. Dogs must be under control but may be off leash and owners must pick up after them. Dogs are only allowed on the beach between Golden West Street and Seapoint Ave. Please adhere to these rules as there are only a couple of dog-friendly beaches left in the entire Los Angeles area. The beach is located off the Pacific Coast Hwy (Hwy 1) at Golden West Street. Please remember to pick up after your dog... the city wanted to prohibit dogs in 1997 because of the dog waste left on the beach. But thanks to The Preservation Society of Huntington Dog Beach (http://www.dogbeach.org), it continues to be dog-friendly. City ordinances require owners to pick up after their dogs. It is suggested that you bring plenty of quarters in order to feed the parking meters near the beach.

### Newport and Balboa Beaches
Balboa Blvd.
Newport Beach CA
949-644-3211
There are several smaller beaches which run along Balboa Blvd. Dogs are only allowed before 9am and after 5pm, year round. Pets must be on a 6 foot or less leash and people are required to clean up after their pets. Tickets will be issued if your dog is off leash. The beaches are located along Balboa Blvd and ample parking is located near the Balboa and Newport Piers.

## Off-Leash Dog Parks

### Bark Park Dog Park
Arlington Dr
Costa Mesa CA
949-73-4101
costamesabarkpark.com/
Located in TeWinkle Park, this two acre dog park is fully fenced. It is open from 7am until dusk every day except for Tuesday, which is clean-up day. The park is located near the Orange County Fairgrounds on Arlington Drive, between Junipero Drive and Newport Blvd.

### Huntington Beach Central Park
18000 Goldenwest St
Huntington Beach CA
714-536-5486
The Huntington Beach Central Park, located at 18000 Goldenwest St in Huntington Beach, California is open weekdays from 9:00 am to 7:00 pm, and weekends 10:00 am to 7:00 pm. The park has two separate fenced areas for dogs, one for small dogs/puppies and one for larger dogs. The park also offers a dog "hall of fame", snacks, and benches.

### Huntington Beach Dog Park
Edwards Street
Huntington Beach CA
949-536-5672
This dog park has a small dog run for pups under 25 pounds and a separate dog run for the larger pooches. It's been open since 1995 and donations are always welcome. They have a coin meter at the entrance. The money is used to keep the park maintained and for doggie waste bags. If you want to go for a walk with your leashed pup afterwards, there many walking trails at the adjacent Huntington Central Park.

### Arbor Dog Park
Lampson Avenue at Heather St.

Seal Beach CA
562-799-9660
This entirely fenced dog park is 2 1/2 acres in size. It has a number of large shade trees. There is water for people and dogs. The dog park is open during all daylight hours weather permitting except that it is closed on Thursdays from 8 am until noon for maintenance. To get to the dog park, take Valley View Street from the 22 or 405 Freeways north. Turn left on Lampson Avenue. You will have to turn right to the dog park which is directly behind the building at 4665 Lampson Avenue.

## Dog-Friendly Parks

### Talbert Nature Preserve
Victoria Street
Costa Mesa CA
949-923-2250
ocparks.com/parks/talbert
This 180 acre park offers hiking trails. Dogs on a 6 foot or less leash are allowed and please clean up after them.

### Huntington Central Park
Golden West Street
Huntington Beach CA
949-960-8847
This city park is over 350 acres with six miles of trails. There are expansive lawns, lots of trees and two lakes. Huntington Lake is by Inlet Drive between Golden West and Edwards Streets and next to Alice's Breakfast in the Park Restaurant. Talbert Lake is off Golden West near Slater Ave and Gothard St. The Huntington Dog Park is located within this park.

### Upper Newport Bay Nature Preserve
University Dr & Irvine Ave
Newport Beach CA
949-640-1751

ocparks.com/parks/newport/
This regional park borders the
Newport Back Bay and consists
of approximately 140 acres of
open space. This coastal
wetland is renowned as one of
the finest bird watching sites in
North America. During winter
migration, there can be tens of
thousands of birds at one time.
It is also home to six rare or
endangered bird species. The
park has a 2-3 mile one-way
paved path that is used by
walkers, joggers and bicyclists.
Additional dirt trails run along
the hills. You can park at a
variety of points along the road,
but many people park at Irvine
Ave and University Dr. Dogs
must be leashed in the park.

## Humane Society or SPCAs

### Orange County Society for the Prevention of Cruelty to Animals
9582 Hamilton Avenue #164
Huntington Beach CA
(714) 596-7387
orangecountyspca.org
The organization's programs
include cruelty prevention;
veterinary care for sick and
injured animals; subsidized
spay/neuter, feral cat rescue;
humane education in the
classroom; refuge for pets of
domestic violence victims; and
pet-assisted therapy. We are a
non-profit, tax-exempt charity.

### Orange County Society for the Prevention of Cruelty to Animals
PO Box 6507
Huntington Beach CA
714/374-7738
orangecountyspca.org

## Rescue Organizations
### Westie Rescue of Orange County & Beyond
9151 Atlanta Avenue #5006
Huntington Beach CA
(805) 208-4322

WestieRescueOC.com
Westie Rescue of Orange
County (WROC) is a 100%
nonprofit organization
dedicated to saving the lives of
forgotten West Highland White
Terriers. WROC is run entirely
by volunteers, rescuing stray
animals from shelters that have
not been adopted, reclaimed by
their owners, or abandoned.
Our rescues are cared for in
private homes where they
receive medical care and
rehabilitation.

### Westie Rescue of Orange County & Beyond
9151 Atlanta Ave #5006
Huntington Beach CA
(805) 208-4322
westierescueoc.com
Westie Rescue of Orange
County & Beyond is a 501(c)(3)
non-profit corporation
dedicated to saving the lives of
forgotten West Highland White
Terriers. WROC is run entirely
by volunteers, rescuing stray
animals from shelters that have
not been adopted, reclaimed by
their owners, or abandoned.
Our rescues are cared for in
private homes where they
receive medical care and
rehabilitation. We specialize in
Westie skin issues, work with a
behaviorist for special needs
dogs, and senior Westies have
a special place in our hearts.

## Other Organizations
### Surf City Animal Response Team
18685-A Main Street PMB 458
Huntington Beach CA

surfcityanimalresponseteam.or
g
SCART is a non-profit
organization and was founded
to respond to pet needs and
assist other agencies during a
local or national disaster or
crisis. We educate the public
on how to prepare for a
disaster and care for their pets
before, during, and after an
emergency. We also assist
local and national agencies by

responding with trained
volunteers, which can include
search and rescue and/or
sheltering management teams.
We are an all-volunteer
organization and rely on
fundraisers and donations to
support our team and their
efforts. Please feel free to
browse our website
(www.surfcityanimalresponsetea
m.org)where you can learn more
about us and review our
upcoming events and training
sessions.

## Orange County North

## Dog-Friendly Hotels
### Chase Suites
3100 E. Imperial Highway
Brea CA
714-579-3200
Roomy suites and freebies
including Wi-Fi breakfast and a
local shuttle make the non-
smoking Chase Suites a smart
choice for business and leisure
travelers alike. Travel-weary folk
appreciate homey touches of
the 88 suites at this two-story
non-smoking hotel. Each
includes a full kitchen or
kitchenette living room with sofa
bed and work area. Free Wi-Fi
and free newspaper delivery
help corporate guests stay on
track while cable TVs and
pillowtop mattresses ensure a
quick wind-down when the work
is done. Guests take advantage
of the hotel's generosity by
partaking in the complimentary
hot breakfast buffet each
morning. Additional amenities
include a heated outdoor pool
hot tub and sun deck business
center free local shuttle within
five miles and laundry services.
Parking is available. Pets are
welcome for a fee. The hotel is
centrally located in North
Orange County. Numerous
corporate headquarters are
close at hand including
American Suzuki across the

street. Nearby attractions
include Disneyland 12 miles
away and Knott's Berry Farm 14
miles away. John Wayne Airport
is 21 miles away.

## Pet-Friendly Extended Stay Hotels

### Residence Inn By Marriott Anaheim Hills Yorba Linda
125 South Festival Drive
Anaheim Hills CA
714-974-8880
Dogs of all sizes are allowed.
There is a $75 one time
additional pet fee.

### Extended Stay America - Orange County - Brea
3050 E. Imperial Highway
Brea CA
714-528-2500 (800-804-3724)
One dog is allowed per suite.
There is a $25 per night
additional pet fee up to $150 for
an entire stay.

### Extended Stay America - Los Angeles - La Mirada
14775 Firestone Blvd
La Mirada CA
714-670-8579 (800-804-3724)
One dog is allowed per suite.
There is a $25 per night
additional pet fee up to $150 for
an entire stay.

### Residence Inn By Marriott La Mirada-buena Park
14419 Firestone Blvd
La Mirada CA
714-523-2800
Dogs of all sizes are allowed.
There is a $100 one time
additional pet fee.

### Residence Inn Placentia Fullerton
700 West Kimberly Avenue
Placentia CA
714-996-0555
Dogs of all sizes are allowed.
There is a $100 one time
additional pet fee.

### Extended Stay America - Orange County - Yorba Linda
22711 Oakcrest Circle
Yorba Linda CA

714-998-9060 (800-804-3724)
One dog is allowed per suite.
There is a $25 per night
additional pet fee up to $150
for an entire stay.

## Outdoor Restaurants

### Baja Fresh Mexican Grill
5781 E. Santa Ana Canyon Rd.

Anaheim Hills CA
714-685-9386
bajafresh.com
This Mexican restaurant is
open for lunch and dinner.
They use fresh ingredients and
making their salsa and beans
daily. Some of the items on
their menu include Enchiladas,
Burritos, Tacos Salads,
Quesadillas, Nachos, Chicken,
Steak and more. Well-behaved
leashed dogs are allowed at
the outdoor tables.

### Z Pizza
5745 E Santa Ana Canyon
Road
Anaheim Hills CA
714-998-4171
zpizza.com
Specializing in organically and
internationally inspired pizzas,
this pizzeria cooks their pizzas
on hot bricks in a fire baked
oven. They feature a 100%
certified organic gluten free
wheat crust, homemade
organic sauces and
ingredients, fresh produce, and
additive-free meats. They also
offer gourmet salads,
sandwiches, and catering
services. Leashed, well
mannered dogs are allowed at
their outside tables.

### Baja Fresh Mexican Grill
2445 Imperial Hwy. Suite H
Brea CA
714-671-9992
bajafresh.com
This Mexican restaurant is
open for lunch and dinner.
They use fresh ingredients and
making their salsa and beans
daily. Some of the items on
their menu include Enchiladas,
Burritos, Tacos Salads,
Quesadillas, Nachos, Chicken,

Steak and more. Well-behaved
leashed dogs are allowed at the
outdoor tables.

### Coffee Bean & Tea Leaf
1080 E. Imperial H/H 90, #E-2
Brea CA
714-255-8026
coffeebean.com
The coffee here is sourced
globally from family coffee farms
to procure only the top of 1% of
Arabica beans. They offer 30+
varieties of coffee;the beans are
roasted in small batches daily
for freshness, and they also
offer 20 varieties of teas that are
hand-blended by their tea
master. Additionally, they offer a
variety of tasty sweets, powders,
extracts, sauces, gifts, and
cards. Leashed, well mannered
dogs are allowed at their outside
dining area.

### Lazy Dog Restaurant & Bar
240 S State College Blvd
Brea CA
714-529-9300
lazydogrestaurants.com/dogs/info
Known for it's dog-friendly patio,
the Lazy Dog offers your dog a
complimentary bowl of water,
and a menu consisting of grilled
hamburger patty, chicken breast
or brown rice. They just ask that
you respect their common
sense rules while your dog is
dining there. This is as dog-
friendly as dining gets. For the
humans in your party there is
hamburger, steak, salads and
some great desserts.

### Schlotzsky's Deli
2500 E. Imperial Hwy #196
Brea CA
714-256-1100
schlotzskys.com/brea/1715/home
Dogs are allowed at the outdoor
tables.

### Chipotle
1202 S Idaho Street, Unit A
La Habra CA
714-526-0800
chipotle.com
Specializing in organic, natural
and unprocessed food, this
Mexican Eatery offers fajita

burritos, tacos, salads, and salsas. Dogs are allowed at the outdoor tables but you will need to order your food inside the restaurant and dogs must remain outside.

**The Coffee Bean & Tea Leaf**
18503 Yorba Linda Blvd, #A
Yorba Linda CA
202-483-3000
coffeebean.com
The coffee here is sourced globally from family coffee farms to procure only the top of 1% of Arabica beans. They offer 30+ varieties of coffee;the beans are roasted in small batches daily for freshness, and they also offer 20 varieties of teas that are hand-blended by their tea master. Additionally, they offer a variety of tasty sweets, powders, extracts, sauces, gifts, and cards. Leashed, well mannered dogs are allowed at their outside dining area.

**Pet-Friendly Stores**
**PetSmart Pet Store**
2465 E Imperial Hwy
Brea CA
714-256-0205
Your licensed and well-behaved leashed dog is allowed in the store.

**Petco Pet Store - Brea**
2500 Imperial Hwy Ste 114
Brea CA
714-255-8162
Your licensed and well-behaved leashed dog is allowed in the store.

**Urban Outfitters**
Brea Mall #2011
Brea CA
714-672-1275
In addition to a large inventory of indoor and outdoor apparel for men and women, this major department store also carries vintage wear, designer brands, and a variety of accessories for all types of active lifestyles. They also carry shoes, furnishings, home decor, cameras, electronics, novelty items and more. Leashed, well

mannered dogs are allowed in the store.

**Petco Pet Store - La Habra**
1201 West Whittier Blvd
La Habra CA
562-690-0410
Your licensed and well-behaved leashed dog is allowed in the store.

**Camping World**
14900 S. Firestone Blvd
La Mirada CA
714-522-8400
campingworld.com/
This comprehensive RV and outdoor store carries a wide variety of RV, boat, bike, and outdoor cooking accessories; all kinds of camping gear; RV screens, shades, and patio decorations; racing/tailgating gear, and all items for RV maintenance. They also carry RV towing supplies, electronics, and interior decorating items as well as pet supplies, RV directories/books, and games. Plus, they offer a tips and advice service, RV sales, rentals, and RV technicians to take care of any installations and repairs. They also welcome your canine companion in the store; they must be friendly and leashed.

**PetSmart Pet Store**
5521 Mirage St
Yorba Linda CA
714-637-8088
Your licensed and well-behaved leashed dog is allowed in the store.

**Day Kennels**
**PetsHotel by PetsMart Day Kennel**
2465 E. Imperial Highway
Brea CA
714-256-0396
petsmart.com/PETsHOTEL/
This PetSmart pet store offers day care, day camp and overnight care. You can drop your dog off and pick up your dog between the hours of 7 am - 9 pm M-F, Sunday 8 am - 6 pm. Dogs are required to have

proof of current rabies, DPP and Bordatella vaccinations.

**Orange County South**

**Dog-Friendly Hotels**
**Best Western Plus Marina Shores Hotel**
34280 Pacific Coast Highway
Dana Point CA
949-248-1000 (800-780-7234)
Dogs of all sizes are allowed. Dogs are allowed for a pet fee of $75.00 per pet per night.

**Doubletree Suites By Hilton Doheny Beach - Dana Point**
34402 Pacific Coast Highway
Dana Point CA
949-661-1100 (800-222-TREE (8733))
Only steps from the beach but still close to the big city, this upscale hotel offers a number of on site amenities for business or leisure travelers, plus a convenient location to business, shopping, dining, and recreation areas. Dogs are allowed for an additional fee of $30 per night per pet.

**Monarch Beach Resort**
One Monarch Beach Resort
Dana Point CA
949-234-3200 (877-787-3477)
This award-winning destination resort features a fantastic setting overlooking the ocean with access to their private beach via a nature trail, immaculately kept grounds, championship golf, 8 dining and beverage venues, and a kid's club. Dogs up to 30 pounds are allowed for an additional 1 time fee of $150 per room;there is a pet policy to sign at check in.

**Hilton Irvine/orange County Airport**
18800 Macarthur Blvd
Irvine CA
949-833-9999
Located in the heart of the city, this upscale, downtown hotel offers a number of on site

amenities for business and leisure travelers, plus a convenient location to business, shopping, dining, and entertainment districts. Dogs are allowed for an additional one time pet fee of $50 per room.

### Hilton Irvine/orange County Airport
18800 Macarthur Blvd
Irvine CA
949-833-9999 (800-HILTONS (445-8667))
Offering sophisticated style and a sleek outdoor pool the non-smoking Hilton Irvine/Orange County Airport has an array of amenities and services that make it popular with our guests. The 306-room Hilton boasts a contemporary So-Cal attitude starting in its modern lobby with curved lounge seating. Guests can enjoy a meal or cocktails at the hotel's casual indoor/outdoor restaurant or order room service. There's no need to miss a workout thanks to the fitness room and the seasonal outdoor pool and hot tub. Road warriors will appreciate the well-equipped business center. Rooms feature 42-inch flat-panel HDTVs with premium cable alarm clock/radios with mp3 docks and premium bedding. Wi-Fi is accessible with an extra fee. Pets are welcome and self- and valet parking are available all for a nightly charge. There's also free area shuttle service. The hotel is less than three miles from John Wayne Airport in Orange County almost halfway between Los Angeles and San Diego. It's within 10 minutes of Fortune 500 companies like Rockwell Collins Cisco Systems and Broadcom and within a 15-minute drive of area beaches golf courses shopping and restaurants. University of California-Irvine is eight minutes away and Disneyland is 12 miles from the hotel.

### La Quinta Inn & Suites Irvine Spectrum
14972 Sand Canyon Avenue
Irvine CA
949-551-0909 (800-531-5900)

Dogs up to 25 pounds are allowed. There are no additional pet fees. Dogs may not be left unattended, and they must be leashed and cleaned up after.

### Holiday Inn Laguna Beach
696 South Coast Highway
Laguna Beach CA
949-494-1001 (877-270-6405)
Dogs up to 20 pounds are allowed. Dogs are allowed for a pet fee of $75.00 per pet per stay.

### Quality Inn & Suites Irvine Spectrum
23702 Rockfield Boulevard
Lake Forest CA
949-458-1900 (877-424-6423)
Quality Inn & Suites Lake Forest is conveniently located in central Orange County, with easy access to I-5, I-405, SR-241.

Dogs of all sizes are allowed. Dogs are allowed for a pet fee of $25, per pet per night.

### Best Western Plus Casablanca Inn
1601 North El Camino Real
San Clemente CA
949-361-1644 (800-780-7234)
Dogs are allowed. There is a $20 per pet per night pet fee. Up to two dogs are allowed per room.

## Pet-Friendly Extended Stay Hotels

### Candlewood Suites Orange County/irvine Spectrum
16150 Sand Canyon Avenue
Irvine CA
949-788-0500 (877-270-6405)
Dogs up to 80 pounds are allowed. Pets allowed with an additional pet fee. Up to $75 for 1-6 nights and up to $150 for 7+ nights. A pet agreement must be signed at check-in.

### Extended Stay America - Orange County - Irvine Spectrum
30 Technology Dr

Irvine CA
949-727-4228 (800-804-3724)
One dog is allowed per suite. There is a $25 per night additional pet fee up to $150 for an entire stay.

### Residence Inn Irvine John Wayne Airport
2855 Main Street
Irvine CA
949-261-2020
Dogs of all sizes are allowed. There is a $100 one time additional pet fee.

### Residence Inn Irvine Spectrum
10 Morgan Street
Irvine CA
949-380-3000
Dogs of all sizes are allowed. There is a $100 one time additional pet fee.

### Candlewood Suites Irvine East
3 South Pointe Drive
Lake Forest CA
949-598-9105 (877-270-6405)
Dogs up to 80 pounds are allowed. Pets allowed with an additional pet fee. Up to $75 for 1-6 nights and up to $150 for 7+ nights. A pet agreement must be signed at check-in.

### Extended Stay America - Orange County - Lake Forest
20251 Lake Forest Dr
Lake Forest CA
949-598-1898 (800-804-3724)
One dog is allowed per suite. There is a $25 per night additional pet fee up to $150 for an entire stay.

### Staybridge Suites Irvine East/lake Forest
2 Orchard
Lake Forest CA
949-462-9500 (877-270-6405)
Dogs up to 80 pounds are allowed. Pets allowed with an additional pet fee. Up to $75 for 1-6 nights and up to $150 for 7+ nights. A pet agreement must be signed at check-in.

## Dog-Friendly Attractions

### Catalina Express
34675 Golden Lantern
Dana Point CA
800-360-1212
catalinaexpress.com/
Dogs are allowed on the boats to the Catalina Island at no additional fee. Dogs must be leashed and muzzled or crated while aboard. There is a limit of one pet per person.

### Orange County Great Park
6990 Marine Way
Irvine CA
866-829-3829
ocgp.org
Although a gradual conversion from the former Marine Corps Air Station El Toro into a 1,300+ acre recreation site will be a while before completion, there is still some interesting activities at this future playground. The visible big orange in the sky is actually a large helium-filled ball with a basket big enough to hold 25 people. It is permanently tethered, flies 4 days a week, and rises 400 feet giving outstanding views up to 40 miles away and of the interesting sites below. Lasting about 8 to 10 minutes, the rides run from10:30 am until 3 pm and from 7 pm until 10 pm on Thursdays and Fridays, and from 9 am until 3 pm and from 7 pm until 10 pm on Saturdays and Sundays (wind and weather permitting). There are also free carousel rides. Leashed, well mannered dogs are allowed at the site and on the "Great Orange in the Sky" ride; there is no additional fee for hounds or humans.

## Outdoor Restaurants

### Z Pizza
26921 Aliso Creek Road
Aliso Viejo CA
949-425-0102
zpizza.com
Specializing in organically and internationally inspired pizzas, this pizzeria cooks their pizzas on hot bricks in a fire baked oven. They feature a 100% certified organic gluten free wheat crust, homemade organic sauces and ingredients, fresh produce, and additive-free meats. They also offer gourmet salads, sandwiches, and catering services. Leashed, well mannered dogs are allowed at their outside tables.

### Luxe Restaurant & Martini Bar
24582 Del Prado # A/H 1
Dana Point CA
949-276-4990
luxedanapoint.com
Featuring an eclectic fusion menu, this eatery and bar provides guests with a sophisticated ambiance, vegetarian choices, fresh fruit martinis, alfresco dining, and more. Leashed, friendly dogs are allowed at their outside dining area.

### Wind and Sea
34699 Golden Lantern
Dana Point CA
949-496-6500
windandsearestaurants.com
Surrounded by water on 3 sides, this restaurant offers indoor and deck dining of fine Pacific Rim Fusion cuisine, up to 10 fresh-catch selections each day, all-you-can-eat breakfast buffets every Sunday, and a full bar. Leashed, friendly dogs are allowed at their outside dining area.

### Baja Fresh Mexican Grill
13248 Jamboree Rd.
Irvine CA
714-508-7777
bajafresh.com
This Mexican restaurant is open for lunch and dinner. They use fresh ingredients and making their salsa and beans daily. Some of the items on their menu include Enchiladas, Burritos, Tacos Salads, Quesadillas, Nachos, Chicken, Steak and more. Well-behaved leashed dogs are allowed at the outdoor tables.

### Chipotle
81 Fortune Drive Suite 107
Irvine CA
949-753-0554
chipotle.com
Specializing in organic, natural and unprocessed food, this Mexican Eatery offers fajita burritos, tacos, salads, and salsas. Dogs are allowed at the outdoor tables but you will need to order your food inside the restaurant and dogs must remain outside.

### Chipotle
3955 Irvine Blvd
Irvine CA
714-508-2463
chipotle.com
Specializing in organic, natural and unprocessed food, this Mexican Eatery offers fajita burritos, tacos, salads, and salsas. Dogs are allowed at the outdoor tables but you will need to order your food inside the restaurant and dogs must remain outside.

### Coffee Bean & Tea Leaf
13786-B Jamboree Road
Irvine CA
714-505-0498
coffeebean.com
The coffee here is sourced globally from family coffee farms to procure only the top of 1% of Arabica beans. They offer 30+ varieties of coffee;the beans are roasted in small batches daily for freshness, and they also offer 20 varieties of teas that are hand-blended by their tea master. Additionally, they offer a variety of tasty sweets, powders, extracts, sauces, gifts, and cards. Leashed, well mannered dogs are allowed at their outside dining area.

### Coffee Bean & Tea Leaf
5653 Alton Parkway
Irvine CA
949-651-9903
coffeebean.com
The coffee here is sourced globally from family coffee farms to procure only the top of 1% of Arabica beans. They offer 30+ varieties of coffee;the beans are roasted in small batches daily for freshness, and they also

offer 20 varieties of teas that are hand-blended by their tea master. Additionally, they offer a variety of tasty sweets, powders, extracts, sauces, gifts, and cards. Leashed, well mannered dogs are allowed at their outside dining area.

**Corner Bakery Cafe**
13786 Jamboree Rd
Irvine CA
714-734-8270
cornerbakerycafe.com/home.as px
Dogs are allowed at the outdoor seats.

**Johnny Rockets**
73 Fortune Drive
Irvine CA
949-753-8144
johnnyrockets.com/
All the American favorites can be found here: A fun retro, all-American decor and atmosphere, juicy burgers, specialty sandwiches, crispy fries, hand-dipped malts and shakes (dark chocolate ones too), fresh baked apple pies, tasty vegetarian choices, and something for all ages. Leashed, friendly dogs are allowed at their outside dining area.

**Lazy Dog Restaurant & Bar**
13290 Jamboree Rd
Irvine CA
714-731-9700
lazydogrestaurants.com/dogs/inf o
Known for it's dog-friendly patio, the Lazy Dog offers your dog a complimentary bowl of water, and a menu consisting of grilled hamburger patty, chicken breast or brown rice. They just ask that you respect their common sense rules while your dog is dining there. This is as dog-friendly as dining gets. For the humans in your party there is hamburger, steak, salads and some great desserts.

**Mother's Market & Kitchen**
2963 Michelson Drive
Irvine CA
949-752-6667
mothersmarket.com/

This natural food market offers natural and organic food plus a kitchen where you can order a smoothie, sandwiches and more. Just order your food to go and they offer outside table seating. Well-behaved leashed dogs are allowed at their outdoor tables.

**Philly's Best**
4250 Barranca Parkway #R
Irvine CA
949-857-2448
eatphillysbest.com/
This authentic Philadelphia Cheesesteak and Hoagie sandwich shop is open Monday to Saturday from 11 am to 9 pm and on Sunday from 11 am to 7: 30 pm. Dogs are allowed at their outer tables;they must be leashed and under their owner's control at all times.

**The Coffee Bean & Tea Leaf**
17595 Harvard Avenue, #B
Irvine CA
949-660-1332
coffeebean.com
The coffee here is sourced globally from family coffee farms to procure only the top of 1% of Arabica beans. They offer 30+ varieties of coffee;the beans are roasted in small batches daily for freshness, and they also offer 20 varieties of teas that are hand-blended by their tea master. Additionally, they offer a variety of tasty sweets, powders, extracts, sauces, gifts, and cards. Leashed, well mannered dogs are allowed at their outside dining area.

**The Coffee Bean & Tea Leaf**
71 Fortune Drive, #844
Irvine CA
949-453-1815
coffeebean.com
The coffee here is sourced globally from family coffee farms to procure only the top of 1% of Arabica beans. They offer 30+ varieties of coffee;the beans are roasted in small batches daily for freshness, and they also offer 20 varieties of teas that are hand-blended by their tea master.

Additionally, they offer a variety of tasty sweets, powders, extracts, sauces, gifts, and cards. Leashed, well mannered dogs are allowed at their outside dining area.

**Z Pizza**
25672 Crown Valley Parkway
Ladera Ranch CA
949-347-8999
zpizza.com
Specializing in organically and internationally inspired pizzas, this pizzeria cooks their pizzas on hot bricks in a fire baked oven. They feature a 100% certified organic gluten free wheat crust, homemade organic sauces and ingredients, fresh produce, and additive-free meats. They also offer gourmet salads, sandwiches, and catering services. Leashed, well mannered dogs are allowed at their outside tables.

**Food Village**
211-217 Broadway St
Laguna Beach CA
949-464-0060
The Food Village consists of several different restaurants like Gina's Pizza, El Pollo Loco and more. All of these restaurants share the same 8-10 tables. Just order food inside and grab one of the tables outside. It's located on Broadway St at Pacific.

**Madison Squar and Garden Cafe**
320 N Coast Hwy
Laguna Beach CA
949-494-0137
madisonsquare.com/
This restaurant serves breakfast and deli-type food;plus they feature an amazing garden setting. Leashed dogs are allowed at the outdoor tables.

**Zinc Cafe and Market**
350 Ocean Avenue
Laguna Beach CA
949-494-6302
zinccafe.com/
A sophisticated eatery with an extensive breakfast, lunch, and dinner menu, they also offer a market with a large variety of to-

go salads, entrees, breads, desserts, grocery items, as well as carefully selected items to compliment the home kitchen and pantry. Leashed, well mannered dogs are welcome at their outside seating area.

**Baja Fresh Mexican Grill**
26548 Moulton Park Way
Laguna Hills CA
949-360-4222
bajafresh.com
This Mexican restaurant is open for lunch and dinner. They use fresh ingredients and making their salsa and beans daily. Some of the items on their menu include Enchiladas, Burritos, Tacos Salads, Quesadillas, Nachos, Chicken, Steak and more. Well-behaved leashed dogs are allowed at the outdoor tables.

**Coffee Bean & Tea Leaf**
24155 Laguna Hills Mall #1635
Laguna Hills CA
949-583-9216
coffeebean.com
The coffee here is sourced globally from family coffee farms to procure only the top of 1% of Arabica beans. They offer 30+ varieties of coffee;the beans are roasted in small batches daily for freshness, and they also offer 20 varieties of teas that are hand-blended by their tea master. Additionally, they offer a variety of tasty sweets, powders, extracts, sauces, gifts, and cards. Leashed, well mannered dogs are allowed at their outside dining area.

**Lulu's Creperie Cafe**
24781 Alicia Parkway, Suite E
Laguna Hills CA
949-855-2222
lulus-cafe.com
Lulu's Creperie Cafe is a French cafe that serves french and american dishes. Well-behaved, leashed dogs are welcome at the outdoor patio.

**Z Pizza**
32371 Golden Lantern Street
Laguna Niguel CA
949-481-3948
zpizza.com

Specializing in organically and internationally inspired pizzas, this pizzeria cooks their pizzas on hot bricks in a fire baked oven. They feature a 100% certified organic gluten free wheat crust, homemade organic sauces and ingredients, fresh produce, and additive-free meats. They also offer gourmet salads, sandwiches, and catering services. Leashed, well mannered dogs are allowed at their outside tables.

**Chipotle**
22379 El Toro Road
Lake Forest CA
949-830-9091
chipotle.com
Specializing in organic, natural and unprocessed food, this Mexican Eatery offers fajita burritos, tacos, salads, and salsas. Dogs are allowed at the outdoor tables but you will need to order your food inside the restaurant and dogs must remain outside.

**Chipotle**
23645 El Toro Road
Lake Forest CA
949-587-1550
chipotle.com
Specializing in organic, natural and unprocessed food, this Mexican Eatery offers fajita burritos, tacos, salads, and salsas. Dogs are allowed at the outdoor tables but you will need to order your food inside the restaurant and dogs must remain outside.

**Jamba Juice**
23628 El Toro Road
Lake Forest CA
949-587-9891
jambajuice.com
All natural and organic ingredients, no high-fructose corn syrup, 0 grams trans fat, no artificial preservatives, a healthy helping of antioxidants, vitamins, and minerals, and fresh whole fruit and fruit juices set the base for these tasty and healthy beverages. Their organic Hot Blends provides a new spin on coffee, green or

chai tea, and hot chocolate;plus they offer probiotic fruit and yogurt Blends. Additionally, they feature organic steel-cut oatmeal prepared fresh every morning, all natural salads, wraps, sandwiches, and grab n' go specialties. They also offer healthy community support through fundraisers, special sales, and school lunch programs. Leashed, well mannered dogs are allowed at their outside dining area.

**The Coffee Bean & Tea Leaf**
23647 El Toro Road, Suite E
Lake Forest CA
949-458-1907
coffeebean.com
The coffee here is sourced globally from family coffee farms to procure only the top of 1% of Arabica beans. They offer 30+ varieties of coffee;the beans are roasted in small batches daily for freshness, and they also offer 20 varieties of teas that are hand-blended by their tea master. Additionally, they offer a variety of tasty sweets, powders, extracts, sauces, gifts, and cards. Leashed, well mannered dogs are allowed at their outside dining area.

**Baja Fresh Mexican Grill**
27620 Marguerite Pkwy Ste C
Mission Viejo CA
949-347-9033
bajafresh.com
This Mexican restaurant is open for lunch and dinner. They use fresh ingredients and making their salsa and beans daily. Some of the items on their menu include Enchiladas, Burritos, Tacos Salads, Quesadillas, Nachos, Chicken, Steak and more. Well-behaved leashed dogs are allowed at the outdoor tables.

**Skimmer's Panini Cafe**
25290 Marguerite Parkway
Mission Viejo CA
949-855-8500
Although Panini-style sandwiches are the specialty of the house, they also feature a full menu of fresh foods that are skillfully prepared and artfully

presented. Leashed, well behaved dogs are allowed at their outside seating area.

## Taco Mesa
27702 Crown Valley Parkway
Mission Viejo CA
949-364-1957
tacomesa.com/
With a focus on local, organic, all natural and wild caught fish, this restaurant features authentic Mexican cuisine with vegetarian and gluten free options, all natural meats, organic greens, and healthy cooking techniques. Leashed, well mannered dogs are welcome at their outside tables.

## Baja Fresh Mexican Grill
979 Avenida Pico
San Clemente CA
949-361-4667
bajafresh.com
This Mexican restaurant is open for lunch and dinner. They use fresh ingredients and making their salsa and beans daily. Some of the items on their menu include Enchiladas, Burritos, Tacos Salads, Quesadillas, Nachos, Chicken, Steak and more. Well-behaved leashed dogs are allowed at the outdoor tables.

## Italian Cravings
105 S Ola Vis
San Clemente CA
949-492-2777
italiancravings.com
This Italian eatery also features a number of homemade specialty and signature dishes, a brunch buffet every Sunday from 10:30 am until 3 pm, and alfresco dining. Leashed, friendly dogs are allowed at their outside dining area.

## The Cellar
156 Avenida Del Mar
San Clemente CA
949-492-3663
thecellarsite.com/
The menu at this gathering place offers freshly prepared gourmet cuisine with many vegetarian items, hand-crafted desserts, weekly specials, and "wine down hour" Tuesday thru

Sunday from 4 to 6 pm. And, in addition to a wide variety of carefully selected international and domestic artisanal cheeses, they also feature an impressive global list of wines by the glass, flight or bottle;an extensive selection of domestic and European brews, and a premium sake selection. Some of the wines/beers offered are grown biodynamic, organic, or by sustainable practices. Leashed, friendly dogs are allowed at their outside dining area.

## Z Pizza
1021 Avenida Pico
San Clemente CA
949-498-3505
zpizza.com
Specializing in organically and international inspired pizzas, this pizzeria cooks their pizzas on hot bricks in a fire baked oven. They feature a 100% certified organic gluten free wheat crust, homemade organic sauces and ingredients, fresh produce, and additive-free meats. They also offer gourmet salads, sandwiches, and catering services. Leashed, well mannered dogs are allowed at their outside tables.

## L'Hirondelle Restaurant
31631 Camino Capistrano
San Juan Capistrano CA
949-661-0425
lhirondellesjc.com
Some of the offerings of this fine dining restaurant include a full menu of gourmet regional and international choices, Sunday Champagne Brunches, a variety of fine wines, handcrafted desserts, and alfresco dining. Leashed, friendly dogs are allowed at their outside dining area.

## Z Pizza
32341 Camino Capistrano
San Juan Capistrano CA
949-429-8888
zpizza.com
Specializing in organically and international inspired pizzas, this pizzeria cooks their pizzas

on hot bricks in a fire baked oven. They feature a 100% certified organic gluten free wheat crust, homemade organic sauces and ingredients, fresh produce, and additive-free meats. They also offer gourmet salads, sandwiches, and catering services. Leashed, well mannered dogs are allowed at their outside tables.

## Pet-Friendly Shopping Centers
### Irvine Spectrum Center
71 Fortune Drive
Irvine CA
877-ISC-4FUN
shopirvinespectrumcenter.com
Dogs on leash are allowed to walk through the shopping areas. They are allowed at many of the outdoor restaurants if they are well-behaved. Some stores may allow dogs inside if you ask as it is up to the individual stores.

## Pet-Friendly Stores
### PetSmart Pet Store
26761 Aliso Creek Rd
Aliso Viejo CA
949-643-2285
Your licensed and well-behaved leashed dog is allowed in the store.

### Anthropologie
99 Fortune Drive, #707
Irvine CA
949-341-0104
Items of distinction can be found for all ages and in all departments of this unique shop. Carefully selected to add to the enjoyment of the shopping experience, they carry fine clothing, amazing accessories, jewelry, hobby and leisure items, and a full line of bright and useful items for the home, garden, and office. Leashed, well behaved dogs are allowed in the store.

### PetSmart Pet Store
3775 Alton Pkwy

Irvine CA
949-252-9027
Your licensed and well-behaved leashed dog is allowed in the store.

**Petco Pet Store - Irvine**
15333 Culver Plaza
Irvine CA
949-262-1400
Your licensed and well-behaved leashed dog is allowed in the store.

**Urban Outfitters**
81 Fortune Drive, #119
Irvine CA
949-727-0951
In addition to a large inventory of indoor and outdoor apparel for men and women, this major department store also carries vintage wear, designer brands, and a variety of accessories for all types of active lifestyles. They also carry shoes, furnishings, home decor, cameras, electronics, novelty items and more. Leashed, well mannered dogs are allowed in the store.

**PetSmart Pet Store**
23602 El Toro Rd
Lake Forest CA
949-768-6373
Your licensed and well-behaved leashed dog is allowed in the store.

**Petco Pet Store - Lake Forest**
24332 Rockfield Blvd
Lake Forest CA
949-859-6590
Your licensed and well-behaved leashed dog is allowed in the store.

**Petco Pet Store - Mission Viejo**
25592 El Paseo
Mission Viejo CA
949-348-2310
Your licensed and well-behaved leashed dog is allowed in the store.

**PetSmart Pet Store**
30515 Avenida De Las Flores
Rancho Santa Margarita CA
949-766-7746
Your licensed and well-behaved

leashed dog is allowed in the store.

**Petco Pet Store - Rancho Santa Margarita**
30682 Santa Margarita Pkwy
Rancho Santa Margarita CA
949-888-0478
Your licensed and well-behaved leashed dog is allowed in the store.

**Three Dog Bakery**
174 Avenida Del Mar
San Clemente CA
949-218-3364
Three Dog Bakery provides cookies and snacks for your dog as well as some boutique items. You well-behaved, leashed dog is welcome.

**PetSmart Pet Store**
33963 Doheny Park Rd
San Juan Capistrano CA
949-443-5336
Your licensed and well-behaved leashed dog is allowed in the store.

**Petco Pet Store - San Juan Capistrano**
32391 Camino Capistrano Ste A
San Juan Capistrano CA
949-240-9388
Your licensed and well-behaved leashed dog is allowed in the store.

# Dog-Friendly Beaches
**Main Beach**
Pacific Hwy (Hwy 1)
Laguna Beach CA
949-497-3311
Dogs are allowed on this beach between 6pm and 8am, June 1 to September 16. The rest of the year, they are allowed on the beach from dawn until dusk. Dogs must be on a leash at all times.

# Off-Leash Dog Parks
**Central Bark**
6405 Oak Canyon
Irvine CA

949-724-7740
Thanks to one of our readers who writes: "Irvine's dog park is open daily from 6:30 am to 9 pm, closed Wednesdays." The dog park is located next to the Irvine Animal Care Center and is a 2.8 acre fenced dog park. There is a separate area for small dogs and water for your dog.

**Irvine Central Bark Dog Park**
6405 Oak Canyon
Irvine CA
949-724-6833
Opened in 2000, the Irvine Central Bark Dog Park features almost three acres of open field for off-leash play. It offers many features, including a watering facility for dogs, a main yard with a separate fenced area for small or frail dogs, covered seating, handicap accessible, and lighting. The park is open 6:30 a.m.-10 p.m. daily, but is closed Wednesday for maintenance.

**Laguna Beach Dog Park**
20672 Laguna Canyon Road
Laguna Beach CA

The Laguna Beach Dog Park is located about one-mile south of the intersection of Laguna Canyon and El Toro Roads, or if you are heading north, from the beach, the park is about three miles inland from the Pacific Coast Highway. The park is open Dawn to Dusk, Thursdays through Tuesdays. The park is closed on Wednesdays for maintenance, and also closes during and after rainy days.

**Laguna Beach Dog Park**
Laguna Canyon Rd at El Toro Rd
Laguna Beach CA

lagunabeachdogpark.com/
This dog park, known by the locals as Bark Park, is open six days a week and closed on Wednesdays for clean-up. The park is open from dawn to dusk. The park will be closed during and after heavy rains.

## Laguna Niguel Pooch Park
Golden Latern
Laguna Niguel CA

This fully enclosed dog park is located in the city of Laguna Niguel, which is between Laguna Beach and Dana Point. The park is operated by the City of Laguna Niguel's Parks and Recreation Department. It is located on Golden Latern, next to fire station 49. From the Pacific Coast Highway in Dana Point, go up Goldern Latern about 2 miles. Thanks to one of our readers for this information.

## Baron Von Willard Dog Park
301 Avenida La Pata
San Clemente CA

Baron Von Willard Dog Park has two fenced areas, one for large dogs and one for small dogs. The park has benches and water for dogs.

## Dog-Friendly Parks
### Holy Jim Historic Trail
Trabuco Canyon Road
Mission Viejo CA
909-736-1811
This trail is part of the Cleveland National Forest. It is about a 4.5 mile hike on a combination of fire roads and single track trails. You can see a small waterfall on this trail which is best viewed in early spring. This trail is used by both hikers and mountain bikers. Pets on leash are allowed and please clean up after them. To get there from Highway 5, exit El Toro Road and head north (away from the coast). Take Live Oak Canyon Road to the right, then turn left onto Trabuco Canyon Road.

### O'Neill Regional Park
30892 Trabuco Canyon Road
Trabuco Canyon CA
949-923-2260
ocparks.com/parks/oneill/
This heavily wooded park offers hiking trails. Dogs on a 6 foot or less leash are allowed and please clean up after them.

## Day Kennels
### PetsHotel by PetsMart Day Kennel
26761 Aliso Creek Rd.
Aliso Viejo CA
949-643-3056
petsmart.com/PETsHOTEL/
This PetSmart pet store offers day care, day camp and overnight care. You may drop off and pick up your dog during the hours the store is open seven days a week. Dogs must have proof of current rabies, DPP and Bordatella vaccinations.

## Emergency Veterinarians
### Animal Urgent Care Clinic
28085 Hillcrest
Mission Viejo CA
949-364-6228
Monday - Friday 6pm to 8am, Noon Saturday to 8 am Monday.

## Rescue Organizations
### Ask Ariel Your Pet Nutrtionist
P.O. Box 723
Dana Point CA
949-499-9380
askariel.com
Ariel Ask Ariel provides education about holistic pet care and the treatment of cats and dogs using nutrition, diet, vitamins and supplements. It is a completely library of information about pet health, pet nutrition and common pet diseases, particularly those that affect newly rescued shelter animals. It features photos of many rescued animals that would have otherwise been euthanized. Ask Ariel is the fundraising arm for Ariel Rescue, our non-profit charity that saves the lives of shelter dogs in impoverished communities.

## Other Organizations
### AHF Pet Partners of Southern California
22365 El Toro Road, #240
Lake Forest CA
949.614.0204
sharingpaws.info
Pet Partners of Orange County is an organization which supports and promotes the Delta Society Pet Partners Program goals in Orange County and throughout Southern California. Our registered pet partner teams do visits in settings such as hospitals, nursing homes, senior long-term and day-care centers, childrens shelters, etc. We conduct workshops and evaluations, mentor new members in Orange County, set up additional facilities to visit and have booths at dog walks and other major events. Potential pet partner teams must complete an 8 hour Team Training Course and observational visit prior to being evaluated.

## Orcutt

## Off-Leash Dog Parks
### Orcutt Community Park Dog Park
5800 S. Bradley
Orcutt CA
805-934-6211
Open daily from 8 am until sunset, this 2.5 acre doggy play area features separate sections for small and large dogs, dog water fountains, and benches. Dogs must be healthy, sociable, current on all vaccinations and license with tags on collar, and under their owner's control at all times. Owners must clean up after their pets, and keep them leashed when not in designated off-lead areas.

## Orland

## Dog-Friendly Parks
**Black Butte Lake Recreation Area**
19225 Newville Road
Orland CA
530-865-4781 (877-444-6777)
Located on Stony Creek, this popular recreation area features a 4,460 surface acre lake with 40 miles of shoreline, and during the spring nature puts on a wonderful display of wildflowers. Some of the features/amenities include 3 self-guided nature trails, interpretive programs, well maintained picnic facilities, a playground, and a variety of land and water recreational activities. Dogs of all sizes are allowed for no additional fee. Dogs must be under their owners control at all times, and be leashed and cleaned up after. Dogs are not allowed at the beach.

## Orleans

## Dog-Friendly Wineries and Vineyards
**Coates Family Vineyards**
3255 Red Cap Road
Orleans CA
530-627-3369
The CCOF (California Certified Organic Farmers) have only certified a few wineries as organic and this winery is one of them. The grapes are aged in oak barrels the traditional way in small lots, sulfite free, unfiltered, unrefined, and with perfect growing conditions. Tours are available by reservation by phone or at norman@coatesvineyards.com. Dogs are welcome; they just need to be social and friendly as there are also 5 other happy dogs on site. Dogs must be well behaved, leashed, and cleaned up after.

## Oroville

## Dog-Friendly Hotels
**Days Inn Oroville**
1745 Feather River Boulevard
Oroville CA
530-533-3297 (800-329-7466)
Dogs of all sizes are allowed. Dogs are allowed for a pet fee of $10 per pet per night.

**Super 8 Oroville**
1470 Feather River Boulevard
Oroville CA
530-533-9673 (800-800-8000)
Beautifully appointed guest rooms and suites. Surrounded by breathtaking scenery and various recreational activities.

Dogs of all sizes are allowed. Dogs are allowed for a pet fee of $10.00 per pet per night. Two dogs are allowed per room.

## Dog-Friendly Parks
**Oroville State Wildlife Area**
945 Oroville Dam Blvd West
Oroville CA
530-538-2236
Just outside the city limits sits this wildlife area of almost 12,000 acres of riparian forest bordered by 12 miles of river channels. The area is popular for fishing, birding, and hiking. Dogs of all sizes are allowed for no additional fee. Dogs must be under their owners control, and leashed and cleaned up after at all times.

**Spenceville Wildlife and Recreation Area**
Larkin Road
Oroville CA
530-538-2236
Fishing and birding are popular at this 11,448 acre park of mostly foothill oak trees and grasslands with creeks and springs found throughout. Dogs of all sizes are allowed for no additional fee. They must be under their owners control at all times, and be leashed and

cleaned up after.

## Palm Springs

## Dog-Friendly Hotels
**Cathedral City Travelodge**
67495 East Palm Canyon Drive
Cathedral City CA
760-328-2616
Dogs up to 35 pounds are allowed. There is a pet fee of $10 per pet per night.

**Doubletree By Hilton Golf Resort Palm Springs**
67967 Vista Chino
Cathedral City CA
760-322-7000 (888-FUN-IN-PS (386-4677))
Enchanting views of the San Jacinto mountains a championship golf course and a desert setting delight guests at the non-smoking DoubleTree by Hilton Golf Resort Palm Springs. The non-smoking DoubleTree by Hilton Golf Resort Palm is a four-story desert oasis in the desert. All 285 rooms have free Wi-Fi 49-inch cable TVs work desks mini-fridges coffeemakers free local calling and little touches like complimentary morning newspapers. Each room also has a balcony or a patio. The hotel's restaurants offer three meals a day including Baja-inspired cuisine. Fax services are available for the road warrior. When it's time to relax head for the 27 holes of championship golf or the sparkling Olympic-size outdoor pool with sun deck. More recreation can be found on the tennis courts racquetball basketball and squash courts the driving range and the putting green. There's also a gift shop and a convenience store. Make time for the full-service spa with massage services and stop in the hotel bar for signature cocktails and local craft beers. Parking is free and pets weighing 50 pounds or less are

welcome for a fee. DoubleTree by Hilton Golf Resort Palm is easily accessible from I-10. The Palm Springs Aerial Tramway is five miles west and Knott's Soak City is five miles south. The Moorten Botanical Gardens is seven miles southwest. Shopping in downtown Palm Springs is 10 minutes away and it's five miles to Palm Springs International Airport.

**Red Lion Inn & Suites - Cathedral City - Palm Springs**
69151 East Palm Canyon Drive
Cathedral City CA
760-324-5939 (877-424-6423)
The Palm Springs Aerial Tramway, Big League Dreams Sports Park are all nearby. Many casinos and golf courses in the area.

Dogs of all sizes are allowed. Dogs are allowed for a pet fee of $12.00 per pet per night.

**Best Western Date Tree Hotel**
81909 Indio Boulevard
Indio CA
760-347-3421 (800-780-7234)
Dogs up to 80 pounds are allowed. There is a $15 per day pet fee up to $100 for the week. Up to two dogs are allowed per room.

**Days Inn Indio**
43505 Monroe St
Indio CA
760-347-4044 (800-329-7466)
Two miles to Indio's financial and judicial districts. Minutes to golf and event locations. Pet Friendly, free continental brkfst.

Dogs up to 30 pounds are allowed. Dogs are allowed for a pet fee of $10.00/ per pet per night.

**Royal Plaza Inn**
82347 Highway 111
Indio CA
760-347-0911 (800-228-9559)
A central location free Wi-Fi outdoor pool full-service restaurant and reasonable rates are featured at the pet-friendly Royal Plaza Inn. A desk free Wi-Fi and voicemail in all 99 rooms

of this two-story property help keep business travelers on track. Also standard in all rooms some non-smoking are a seating area and cable TV. Many rooms have balconies overlooking the pool and hot tub which sit in a courtyard surrounded by a large sundeck. The restaurant specializes in steaks and seafood for lunch and dinner; a coffee shop serves breakfast lunch and dinner; and a sports bar is also on-site. Laundry service is available. Parking is free. Pets are welcome for a fee. The hotel is on Highway 111 one block from the Indio Fashion Mall and within walking distance of drugstores groceries and restaurants. The Indio Municipal Golf Course and Fantasy Springs Casino are both less than three miles away. Joshua Tree National Park is a 30-minute drive on I-10. Palm Springs is about 35 minutes the opposite direction. Palm Springs International Airport is 22 miles away.

**Super 8 Indio**
81-753 Highway 111
Indio CA
760-342-0264 (800-800-8000)
Dogs of all sizes are allowed. Dogs are allowed for a pet fee of $15.00 per pet per night.

**La Quinta Resort & Club A Waldorf Astoria Resort**
49-499 Eisenhower Drive
La Quinta CA
760-564-4111 (800-WALDORF (800-925-3673))
Casually luxurious and pet-friendly with world-class golf a pampering spa and more than 40 outdoor pools are among the perks at the non-smoking La Quinta Resort & Club A Waldorf Astoria Resort. Built in 1926 as a desert oasis for Hollywood luminaries the sprawling La Quinta Resort includes 796 red tile-roofed vintage non-smoking casitas suites and spa villas set amidst lushly landscaped paths. Inside guests find Mediterranean-inspired dÃ©cor with plush

linens glowing fireplaces and French doors leading to private patios or balconies overlooking fragrant gardens. Free Wi-Fi flat-panel TVs and mini-fridges are standard amenities and select accommodations also include kitchenettes and private pools with hot tubs. Guests can tee off on any of five legendary courses play a set on the resort's tournament-style center court soak in a garden bath at the award-winning spa or relax beside one of more than 40 pools and 50 hot tubs. Dine on freshly prepared locally sourced cuisine in one of six onsite restaurants and lounges. The resort makes pets feel especially welcome with gifts treats and services including special doggie massages. The resort also features a business center. La Quinta Resort is less than a mile from charming shops and restaurants in Old Town La Quinta and 22 miles from Palm Springs. Joshua Tree National Park is within an hour's drive and Palm Springs International Airport is 20 miles away.

**Best Western Plus Palm Desert Resort**
74695 Highway 111
Palm Desert CA
760-340-4441 (800-780-7234)
Dogs up to 80 pounds are allowed. There is a $10 per day pet fee up to $100 for the week. Up to two dogs are allowed per room.

**Comfort Suites Palm Desert**
39585 Washington Street
Palm Desert CA
760-360-3337 (877-424-6423)
Comfort Suites is conveniently located near I-10 and Sun City Shadow Hills, Del Webbs newest community.

Dogs up to 40 pounds are allowed. Dogs are allowed for a pet fee of $20.00 per pet per night. Two dogs are allowed per room.

**Holiday Inn Express Palm Desert**

74675 Highway 111
Palm Desert CA
760-340-4303 (877-270-6405)
Dogs up to 80 pounds are allowed. Dogs are allowed for a pet fee.

**The Inn At Deep Canyon**
74470 Abronia Trail
Palm Desert CA
760-346-8061 (800-253-0004)
An intimate hotel offering free breakfast and free Wi-Fi an outdoor pool and a pet-friendly policy the Inn at Deep Canyon features spacious rooms and suites within minutes of Palm Desert attractions. This hotel has two floors and 32 rooms some of which are designated for smokers. Each room provides a microwave refrigerator coffeemaker and cable TV. From a large king room to a duplex with a private pool the rooms have various configurations and features. Most rooms have views of the outdoor pool or garden. During their stay guests can enjoy a free continental breakfast including pastries bagels and beverages and use the hotel's barbecue facilities for other meals. Free Wi-Fi is available. A business center with computer and fax is on hand for guest use and parking is free. Small pets are welcome. The Inn at Deep Canyon is located one mile from the College of the Desert. El Paseo shopping district is also just one mile from the hotel. The Palm Springs Aerial Tramway is 17 miles away. Palm Springs International Airport is 13 miles away.

**Ace Hotel And Swim Club**
701 East Palm Canyon Drive
Palm Springs CA
760-325-9900
Boasting Wi-Fi two outdoor pools a hot tub a fitness center and a full-service spa plus a hip restaurant that's open latethe uber-cool pet-friendly Ace Hotel and Swim Club is a solid Palm Springs choice. Opened in 2009 the Ace Hotel part of a stylish chain based in Portland Oregon is a complete overhaul of a

1960s hotel. There are 180 rooms from budget to luxe each with an mp3 player 42-inch flat-panel TV and high-end bath products. Hang out by the outdoor fireplace get a massage poolside or in the spa order up room service or join a poolside yoga class. Next door the restaurant dishes out diner food with a locavore twist which you complement with Stumptown coffee or a craft beer. The resort fee includes parking Wi-Fi bike rentals and pool/gym access. Centrally located the Ace is about two-and-a-half miles from Palm Springs International Airport and within walking distance of downtown with plenty of dining options from humble to haute plus shopping and art galleries. The Palm Springs Art Museum is two miles away.

**Best Western Inn At Palm Springs**
1633 S. Palm Canyon Drive
Palm Springs CA
760-325-9177 (800-780-7234)
Dogs up to 80 pounds are allowed. There is a $20 per day pet fee up to $100 for the week. Up to two dogs are allowed per room.

**Casa Cody**
175 South Cahuilla Rd
Palm Springs CA
760-320-9346
casacody.com
A historic hacienda engulfed in flowers Casa Cody is a charming bed and breakfast with an outdoor pool free Wi-Fi and eclectic rooms with Southwest flair. Built in the 1920s by Buffalo Bill's cousin Harriet Cody this boutique hotel features 28 ground-floor rooms with an lively mix of period and modern furniture unpainted millwork free Wi-Fi cable TV mini-fridges and beautiful bathrooms. Some rooms also have kitchens and fireplaces. Enjoy breakfast on the patio then put on your movie-star sunglasses and lounge by the outdoor pool. Pets are allowed for a fee. Parking is free. Two

miles from Palm Springs International Airport this hotel is in the heart of historic downtown Palm Springs. Plaza Theater is a block away and numerous restaurants and bars are within walking distance. Historic Tennis Club is two blocks away. Live the high life at El Paseo Shopping District about 20 minutes away or stick to a budget at the Cabazon Outlets a 25-minute drive.

**Del Marcos Hotel - Adults Only 21 & Up**
225 West Baristo Road
Palm Springs CA
800-676-1214
delmarcoshotel.com/
Palm Springs Airport is 10 minutes drive from this adults-only modern hotel. A free welcome drink is provided and guests can borrow a beach cruiser bicycle. Rooms at this completely non-smoking hotel feature free WiFi.
A flat-screen cable TV is included in each guest room at the Del Marcos Hotel. A mountain or pool view is available and a microwave small fridge and coffee-making facilities are provided.
A heated outdoor saltwater pool with poolside fire pits and cabanas with flat-screen TVs are available at Del Marcos Hotel. Full service concierge services a business center and massage are all offered on site. The Historic Tennis Club is less than 10 minutes walk from the hotel. Whitewater Country Club is less than 15 minutes drive away. Downtown Palm Springs is 1 block away. Complimentary Palm Springs Art Museum Passes and Discounted Tram Tickets are available as is a continental breakfast and parking with no resort fees.

**Hilton Palm Springs Resort**
400 East Tahquitz Canyon Way
Palm Springs CA
760-320-6868
Sitting on seven lushly landscaped acres, this upscale hotel offers a number of on site

amenities for business and leisure travelers, plus a convenient location to business, shopping, dining, and entertainment areas. Dogs up to 75 pounds are allowed for an additional one time pet fee of $85 per room.

### Ivy Palm Resort And Spa
2000 North Palm Canyon Drive
Palm Springs CA
760-320-0555
Dogs up to 20 pounds are allowed. There is a $25 per night pet. No cats.

### Kimpton Rowan Palm Springs Hotel
100 W. Tahquitz Canyon Way
Palm Springs CA
760-904-5015
A rooftop bar year-round pool and central location within a couple of blocks of the city's fabulous restaurants and shops make the Kimpton Rowan Palm Springs Hotel a perfect choice for guests visiting Palm Springs. The Kimpton's seven-story geometric exterior is reminiscent of the 1950s and mid-century elements blend with contemporary flair inside as well. All 153 non-smoking rooms are outfitted with Wi-Fi minibars and flat-panel TVs. High-end toiletries and plush robes adorn the sleek bathrooms some of which boast soaking tubs. Guests savor meals at four different venues ranging from the stunning rooftop bar to the breakfast cafe. After working out at the gym guests swim in the all-season outdoor pool or relax on the deck's cushioned loungers. Practical perks include laundry service a 24-hour front desk a business center and valet parking. Pets are welcome for no additional charge. In downtown Palm Springs the Kimpton is within a short stroll of several restaurants and shops. It's within a couple of blocks of the Palm Springs Art Museum and the Palm Springs Walk of Stars. A five-minute walk from the hotel lands guests at the Skyline Trail and its spectacular views. Adventures within a half-

hour include the Palm Springs Aerial Tramway Coachella Valley Preserve and Moorten Botanical Garden. Guests reach Palm Springs International Airport in two miles.

### Musicland Hotel
1342 South Palm Canyon Drive

Palm Springs CA
760-325-1326
An outdoor pool and rooms with free Wi-Fi and microwaves come at budget rates at the pet-friendly Musicland Hotel. This two-story hotel offers 42 rooms with free Wi-Fi cable TV microwaves and refrigerators. Some also have kitchenettes and separate sitting areas. Guests enjoy quality pool time with a view of the mountains and can relax in the outdoor hot tub. Pets are welcome for a fee and parking is free. About a mile from the historic Palm Springs downtown this hotel is within walking distance of several restaurants and nightclubs. Test out your fortune at the craps table at Spa Resort Casino one-and-a-half miles north or go hiking and horseback riding in the Indian Canyons two miles south. The Cabazon Outlets are a 20-minute drive. Palm Springs International Airport is four miles away.

### Parker Palm Springs
4200 East Palm Canyon Drive
Palm Springs CA
760-770-5000 (800-543-4300)
Some offerings of this desert resort include amenity filled accommodations, a noted 16,500 square foot spa with indoor pools, beautifully landscaped grounds, and a restaurant and lounge. Dogs are allowed for an additional fee of $150 per night per pet, and there is a pet waiver to sign at check in.

### Quality Inn Palm Springs
1269 E Palm Canyon Dr
Palm Springs CA
760-323-2775 (877-424-6423)

Quality Inn is conveniently located close to downtown Palm Springs, home to the Fabulous Palm Springs Follies at the Plaza Theater.

### Renaissance Palm Springs Hotel
888 Tahquitz Canyon Way
Palm Springs CA
760-322-6000
Dogs up to 50 pounds allowed. There is a $50 one time pet fee per pet.

### The Riviera Palm Springs A Tribute Portfolio Resort
1600 North Indian Canyon Drive

Palm Springs CA
760-327-8311
The hotel allows a maximum of two dogs up to 50 pounds per room. Guests are required to sign a liability waiver at check-in. An additional fee of $100 per room per stay will apply.

### The Riviera Palm Springs A Tribute Portfolio Resort
1600 North Indian Canyon Drive

Palm Springs CA
760-327-8311
Newly renovated the pet-friendly Riviera Palm Springs offers copious comforts both in rooms (signature bedding flat-panel TVs private patios/balconies) and on grounds (restaurant immense spa). Set on 24 acres the legendary Riviera Palm Springs became a celebrity stomping ground on its 1959 opening the Rat Pack and Elvis swung here. Its 400 up-to-date rooms feature 37-inch flat-panel TVs 300-thread-count sheets down duvets and pillows and electronics docking stations. Sip a cocktail at your pick of four watering holes sample a steak at the on-site restaurant try a Thai treatment in the 11000-square-foot spa or get work done in the business center. There's also a children's club. =Self- and valet parking are available for an additional fee. The hotel charges a resort fee that includes access to the fitness and business centers

and tennis courts in-room coffee and tea service Wi-Fi access daily newspapers and local calls. The Riviera is less than three miles from Palm Springs International Airport and five miles from various golf courses. The Palm Springs Aerial Tramway is one mile away.

### Westin Mission Hills Golf Resort & Spa

71333 Dinah Shore Drive
Rancho Mirage CA
760-328-5955 (888-625-5144)
An oasis destination resort for all ages, this 360 acre resort and spa offers 2 world class golf courses, a wide variety of recreational activities, amenities for business travelers, and fresh seasonally and locally inspired dining. One dog up to 40 pounds is allowed at the hotel for no additional fee;they are not allowed in the villas and there is a pet waiver to sign at check in.

### Motel 6 Thousand Palms

72215 Varner Road
Thousand Palms CA
760-343-1381 (800-RED-ROOF)

One well-behaved family pet per room. Guest must notify front desk upon arrival. Guest is liable for any damages. In consideration of all guests, pets must never be left unattended in the guest rooms.

## Accommodations
### Sunset Ranch Oasis

69-520 South Lincoln
Mecca CA
626-705-3273
sunsetranchoasis.com
Dogs are allowed at this vacation ranch.

### Palm Springs Hotels Caliente Tropics Resort

411 E. Palm Canyon Drive
Palm Springs CA
800-658-5975
calientetropics.com
Well-behaved dogs up to 60 pounds are allowed. Leashed pets are allowed in the lawn and pool areas. Pets may not be left

alone in the rooms. There is no smoking indoors at the Caliente Tropics Resort.

## Pet-Friendly Extended Stay Hotels
### Homewood Suites By Hilton Palm Desert

36999 Cook Street
Palm Desert CA
760-568-1600
This upscale all suite hotel offers large, comfortable suites for longer stays and/or temporary housing needs;plus numerous on site amenities for all level of travelers and a convenient location to local sites of interest. One dog between 25 and 75 pounds is allowed for an additional one time pet fee of $75;one dog up to 25 pounds is allowed for an additional one time pet fee of $45.

### Residence Inn By Marriott Palm Desert

38-305 Cook Street
Palm Desert CA
760-776-0050
Dogs of all sizes are allowed. There is a $75 one time additional pet fee.

### Extended Stay America - Palm Springs - Airport

1400 E. Tahquitz Canyon Way
Palm Springs CA
760-416-0084 (800-804-3724)
One dog is allowed per suite. There is a $25 per night additional pet fee up to $150 for an entire stay.

## Dog-Friendly Attractions
### Oasis Date Gardens

59111 Hwy 111
Indio CA
800-827-8017
You and your dog are welcome to walk through the date gardens at Oasis. They also have picnic tables outside where you can enjoy the dates and a variety of date products. Dogs must be leashed.

### Moorten Botanical Garden

1701 S Palm Drive
Palm Springs CA
760-327-6555
moortengarden.com
Although a small private garden, there are over 3000 desert plants from around the world; some not found anywhere else. There is also a petrified tree, dinosaur fossils, a green house, and a dog that lives on site that looks forward to friendly four-legged visitors. Dogs must be well mannered, and leashed and cleaned up after at all times.

### Palm Canyon Drive/Star Walk

Palm Canyon Drive
Palm Springs CA

palmsprings.com/stars/
Take a stroll down historic Palm Canyon Drive (between Tahquitz and Ramon) with your dog. The street is lined with beautiful palm trees and all kinds of restaurants and specialty shops including the Cold Nose, Warm Heart store (see Attractions). If you want to see some stars, Hollywood-style stars, this is the place to be. The Palm Springs Walk of Stars is dedicated to honoring many Hollywood celebrities that have come to Palm Springs. Come see if your favorite actor or actress has a dedicated star in the sidewalk of Palm Canyon Drive. If you want to watch a celebrity receive his/her star, look at the Star Walk website (http://www.palmsprings.com/stars/) or call 760-322-1563 for a current list of upcoming star dedications (date, time and address included.)

## Outdoor Restaurants
### Michael's Cafe

35955 Date Palm Drive
Cathedral City CA
760-321-7197
michaelscafecc.com/
This breakfast and lunch eatery also offers a full bar and outside dining. Dogs are allowed at the outer tables;they must be under

their owner's control at all times.

**Chipotle**
79-174 H 111, Suite 101
La Quinta CA
760-564-3079
chipotle.com
Specializing in organic, natural and unprocessed food, this Mexican Eatery offers fajita burritos, tacos, salads, and salsas. Dogs are allowed at the outdoor tables but you will need to order your food inside the restaurant and dogs must remain outside.

**The Coffee Bean & Tea Leaf**
79-024 H 111, Suite 101
La Quinta CA
760-771-8012
coffeebean.com
The coffee here is sourced globally from family coffee farms to procure only the top of 1% of Arabica beans. They offer 30+ varieties of coffee;the beans are roasted in small batches daily for freshness, and they also offer 20 varieties of teas that are hand-blended by their tea master. Additionally, they offer a variety of tasty sweets, powders, extracts, sauces, gifts, and cards. Leashed, well mannered dogs are allowed at their outside dining area.

**The Coffee Bean & Tea Leaf**
73400 El Paseo Drive #9
Palm Desert CA
760-674-9056
coffeebean.com
The coffee here is sourced globally from family coffee farms to procure only the top of 1% of Arabica beans. They offer 30+ varieties of coffee;the beans are roasted in small batches daily for freshness, and they also offer 20 varieties of teas that are hand-blended by their tea master. Additionally, they offer a variety of tasty sweets, powders, extracts, sauces, gifts, and cards. Leashed, well mannered dogs are allowed at their outside dining area.

**Chipotle**
2465 East Palm Canyon Drive,

Bldg. 11, Ste. 1110
Palm Springs CA
760-325-0346
chipotle.com
Specializing in organic, natural and unprocessed food, this Mexican Eatery offers fajita burritos, tacos, salads, and salsas. Dogs are allowed at the outdoor tables but you will need to order your food inside the restaurant and dogs must remain outside.

**Coffee Bean & Tea Leaf**
100 N Palm Canyon Drive/H 111
Palm Springs CA
760-325-9402
coffeebean.com
The coffee here is sourced globally from family coffee farms to procure only the top of 1% of Arabica beans. They offer 30+ varieties of coffee;the beans are roasted in small batches daily for freshness, and they also offer 20 varieties of teas that are hand-blended by their tea master. Additionally, they offer a variety of tasty sweets, powders, extracts, sauces, gifts, and cards. Leashed, well mannered dogs are allowed at their outside dining area.

**Hair of the Dog English Pub**
238 N Palm Canyon Dr
Palm Springs CA
760-323-9890
thehairofthedog.net/
This English Pub has a couple of outdoor tables which are pretty close together, but your dog is welcome.

**Native Foods**
1775 E. Palm Canyon Drive
Palm Springs CA
760-416-0070
nativefoods.com/
This restaurant serves organic vegetarian dishes. Dogs are welcome at the outdoor seats. The hours are 11:30 am to 9:30 pm except Sunday when the restaurant is closed.

**Nature's Health Food and Café**
555 South Sunrise Way

Palm Springs CA
760-323-9487
natureshealthfoodcafe.com/
A vegan / vegetarian café with organic tendencies;they offer an extensive globally and seasonally influenced menu of all organic and freshly prepared foods and beverages. Leashed, well mannered dogs are welcome at their outside tables.

**New York Pizza Delivery**
260 N. Palm Canyon Drive
Palm Springs CA
760-778-6973
nypd-pizza.com/links.asp
This pizza restaurant allows well-behaved leashed dogs at their outdoor tables.

**Peabody's Coffee Bar**
134 S Palm Canyon Dr
Palm Springs CA
760-322-1877
peabodyscafepalmsprings.com/
Bring yourself and your dog for breakfast, lunch or dinner at this restaurant and coffee bar.

**Pomme Frite**
256 S. Palm Canyon Drive
Palm Springs CA
760-778-3727
pomme-frite.com/
This bistro features Belgian and French food. They are open six days a week for dinner and both lunch and dinner is served on the weekends. The restaurant is closed on Tuesdays. Well-behaved leashed dogs are allowed at the outdoor tables.

**Shermans Deli and Bakery**
401 Tahquitz Canyon Way
Palm Springs CA
760-325-1199
shermansdeli.com/
Enjoy bagels and bakery treats or choose from their selection of hot or cold sandwiches. Dogs are welcome at their outside dining area with cool water and a few doggie biscuits.

**Spencer's Restaurant**
701 West Baristo Road
Palm Springs CA
760-327-3446
spencersrestaurant.com/
This restaurant features

California Continental Cuisine. Well-behaved leashed dogs are allowed at the outdoor tables. The restaurant is located four blocks west of Palm Canyon Drive on Baristo. Thanks to one of our readers for recommending this restaurant

### Starbucks
682 S. Palm Canyon Drive
Palm Springs CA
760-323-8023
starbucks.com
This coffee shop allows well-behaved leashed dogs at their outdoor tables.

### Baja Fresh Mexican Grill
71-800 Highway 111, Ste A-116
Rancho Mirage CA
760-674-9380
bajafresh.com
This Mexican restaurant is open for lunch and dinner. They use fresh ingredients and making their salsa and beans daily. Some of the items on their menu include Enchiladas, Burritos, Tacos Salads, Quesadillas, Nachos, Chicken, Steak and more. Well-behaved leashed dogs are allowed at the outdoor tables.

## Pet-Friendly Shopping Centers
### El Paseo Shopping District
El Paseo Drive
Palm Desert CA

World famous as the Rodeo Drive of the Desert, the El Paseo Shopping District is a beautifully maintained picture-postcard floral and statue-filled mile with over 300 world class shops, award-winning restaurants, boutiques, galleries, jewelers, and more. It is up to individual stores whether pets are allowed to enter their store. Your well mannered pooch is welcome to join you exploring this wonderful area. Dogs must be leashed, and please clean up after your pet at all times.

### Palm Canyon Shopping

### District
Palm Canyon Drive/H 111
Palm Springs CA

The historic Palm Canyon Drive runs between the 300 block and the 1,400 block of S Canyon Drive and it is considered a cultural artery of the city. The area features an abundance of shops, restaurants, pubs, art galleries, and boutiques. It is up to individual stores whether pets are allowed to enter. Also, on both sides of the Palm Canyon Drive and on adjacent streets visitors can view the 250 sidewalk stars of some of the world's greatest entertainment personalities. Your well mannered pooch is welcome to join you exploring this great area. Dogs must be leashed, and please clean up after your pet at all times.

## Pet-Friendly Stores
### PetSmart Pet Store
79375 Hwy 111
La Quinta CA
760-771-4058
Your licensed and well-behaved leashed dog is allowed in the store.

### Petco Pet Store - La Quinta
78720 Hwy 111
La Quinta CA
760-564-3869
Your licensed and well-behaved leashed dog is allowed in the store.

### Anthropologie
73-595 El Paseo, #B-1204
Gardens
Palm Desert CA
760-346-3537
Items of distinction can be found for all ages and in all departments of this unique shop. Carefully selected to add to the enjoyment of the shopping experience, they carry fine clothing, amazing accessories, jewelry, hobby and leisure items, and a full line of bright and useful items for the home, garden, and

office. Leashed, well behaved dogs are allowed in the store.

### PetSmart Pet Store
72-630 Dinah Shore Dr
Palm Desert CA
760-328-4630
Your licensed and well-behaved leashed dog is allowed in the store.

### Petco Pet Store - Palm Desert
72453 Hwy 111
Palm Desert CA
760-341-3541
Your licensed and well-behaved leashed dog is allowed in the store.

### Cold Nose, Warm Heart-Gift Store
187 S. Palm Canyon Drive
Palm Springs CA
760-327-7747 (877-327-7747)
doggoneit.net
Enjoy browsing inside this specialty gift store with your pup. (The previous name of the store was "Dog Gone It.") They have all kinds of gifts for dog lovers. And your dog is welcome on leash in the store. This store is located at the main shopping area (Palm Canyon Drive) in downtown Palm Springs. They are open daily from 10am until 6pm.

### PetSmart Pet Store
5601 Ramon Rd E
Palm Springs CA
760-325-9711
Your licensed and well-behaved leashed dog is allowed in the store.

## Off-Leash Dog Parks
### Civic Center Dog Park
73-510 Fred Waring Dr
Palm Desert CA
760-346-0611
The Civic Center Dog Park is open from Dawn to 11 pm and is lighted at night. It is about 3/4 acres in size and has two separate fenced areas for large and small dogs. The dog park is located in Civic Center Park on Fred Waring Drive between Monterey Avenue and Portola

Ave.

## Joe Mann Dog Park
California Drive
Palm Desert CA
888-636-7387
This off lead area is only a short distance from the Palm Desert Civic Center Park and offers 1/3 of an acre for pups to run and play. Dogs must be sociable, current on all vaccinations, and under their owner's control at all times. Dogs must be leashed when not in designated off-lead areas.

## Palm Desert Civic Center Park

Fred Waring
Palm Desert CA
888-636-7387
Located at the 70 acre Palm Desert Civic Center Park is a ¾ acre section fenced as an off-leash area, and when the pups are through playing, there is a pathway around the park with artwork and a small lake. Dogs must be sociable, current on all vaccinations, and under their owner's control at all times. Dogs must be leashed when not in designated off-lead areas.

## Palm Springs Dog Park
222 Civic Drive N
Palm Springs CA
888-636-7387
This green pooch oasis is open 24 hours and provides a smaller fenced area for little dogs, 11 antique-style fire hydrants, dual drinking fountains, benches, and pooper scoopers. Dogs must be sociable, current on all vaccinations, and under their owner's control at all times. Dogs must be leashed when not in designated off-lead areas.

## Dog-Friendly Parks
### Lake Cahuilla Recreation Area

Avenue 58
Indio CA
760-564-4712
Come here to sit by the lake, walk around it or on one of the many trails at this 710 acre

park. There are also 50 campsites at the park. The park is located in Indio, 4 miles southeast of La Quinta. To get there, take Interstate 10 to Washington St., south on Washington 3 miles to Highway 111, east on 111, 2 miles to Jefferson Street, south on Jefferson, 3 miles to Avenue 54, east on Avenue 54 one mile to Madison Street, south on Madison 2 miles to Avenue 58, west on Avenue 58 one mile to the park. There is a day use fee. Dogs must be leashed.

## Magnesia Park
Palm Desert Comm. Park
Palm Desert CA
760-347-3484
Enjoy walking through this shaded park or having lunch at one of the many picnic tables. It's located in the city of Palm Desert at Magnesia Falls Drive and Portola Avenue. Dogs must be leashed.

## Lykken Trail
Ramon Road
Palm Springs CA

When you begin this hike, there is a choice of two trails (one is pretty steep) which eventually join together up the mountain. The hike is a total of 6 miles round trip and includes a 1,000 foot elevation gain. This trail provides excellent views. It is located at the west end of Ramon Road. Dogs must be leashed. There are many rattlesnakes in the area.

## Emergency Veterinarians
### Animal Emergency Clinic
72374 Ramon Rd
Thousand Palms CA
760-343-3438
Monday - Friday 5 pm to 8 am, Saturday noon - Monday 8 am.

## Palmdale

## Dog-Friendly Hotels
### Red Roof Inn Palmdale - Lancaster
200 West Palmdale Boulevard
Palmdale CA
661-273-8000 (800-800-8000)
Dogs of all sizes are allowed.
Dogs are allowed for a pet fee.

## Pet-Friendly Extended Stay Hotels
### Residence Inn Palmdale
514 West Rancho Vista Boulevard (avenue P)
Palmdale CA
661-947-4204
Dogs of all sizes are allowed. There is a $100 one time additional pet fee.

## Outdoor Restaurants
### Baja Fresh Mexican Grill
39332 10th St. W.
Palmdale CA
661-947-1682
bajafresh.com
This Mexican restaurant is open for lunch and dinner. They use fresh ingredients and making their salsa and beans daily. Some of the items on their menu include Enchiladas, Burritos, Tacos Salads, Quesadillas, Nachos, Chicken, Steak and more. Well-behaved leashed dogs are allowed at the outdoor tables.

### Chipotle
1125 Rancho Vista
Palmdale CA
661-266-0944
chipotle.com
Specializing in organic, natural and unprocessed food, this Mexican Eatery offers fajita burritos, tacos, salads, and salsas. Dogs are allowed at the outdoor tables but you will need to order your food inside the restaurant and dogs must remain outside.

### The Coffee Bean & Tea Leaf
39605 10th Street W, Unit D

Palmdale CA
661-273-7441
coffeebean.com
The coffee here is sourced
globally from family coffee farms
to procure only the top of 1% of
Arabica beans. They offer 30+
varieties of coffee;the beans are
roasted in small batches daily
for freshness, and they also
offer 20 varieties of teas that are
hand-blended by their tea
master. Additionally, they offer a
variety of tasty sweets, powders,
extracts, sauces, gifts, and
cards. Leashed, well mannered
dogs are allowed at their outside
dining area.

## Pet-Friendly Stores
**PetSmart Pet Store**
39523 S 10th St West
Palmdale CA
661-947-8900
Your licensed and well-behaved
leashed dog is allowed in the
store.

**Petco Pet Store - Palmdale**
39522 10th St. West Ste A
Palmdale CA
661-267-2447
Your licensed and well-behaved
leashed dog is allowed in the
store.

## Events
**Rattlesnake Avoidance Clinic**
P. O. Box 3174
Quartz Hill CA

This annual Spring Rattlesnake
Avoidance clinic in the Palmdale
area is sponsored by Jin-Sohl
Jindo Dog Rescue. It offers a
pro-active training method for
keeping dogs safe from
rattlesnakes, which are common
on hiking trails throughout
Southern California and most of
the U.S. The fee is $70 per dog
and proceeds go to the rescue
and placement of Jindo dogs.
Pre-registration is required.
Email snakeclinic@hotmail.com
for more information. Dogs must
be leashed and under owner's
control and care at all times.

## Emergency Veterinarians
**Animal Emergency Clinic**
1055 W Avenue M #101
Lancaster CA
661-723-3959
Monday - Friday 6 pm to 8 am,
Saturday noon - Monday 8 am.

## Palo Alto - Peninsula

## Dog-Friendly Hotels
**Crowne Plaza San Francisco Airport**
1177 Airport Boulevard
Burlingame CA
650-342-9200 (877-270-6405)
Dogs of all sizes are allowed.
Dogs are allowed for a pet fee
of $25.00 per pet per night.

**Doubletree Hotel San Francisco Airport**
835 Airport Boulevard
Burlingame CA
650-344-5500 (800-222-TREE (8733))
Overlooking the beautiful San
Francisco Bay, this upscale
hotel offers numerous on site
amenities, plus they are only 2
miles to the SF Airport, and
their location gives a
convenient starting point to
explore an amazing choice of
world class attractions, dining,
and shopping arenas. Dogs are
allowed for an additional one
time fee of $40 per pet.

**Embassy Suites By Hilton San Francisco Airport Waterfront**
150 Anza Boulevard
Burlingame CA
650-342-4600
Only minutes from downtown
and one of the city's largest
hotels, they offer full service,
upscale accommodations, and
a number of on site amenities
for business and leisure
travelers, plus a convenient
location to business, shopping,

and dining scenes, and an
amazing amount of tourist
attractions. They also offer a
complimentary cooked-to-order
breakfast and a Manager's
reception each evening. Dogs
up to 75 pounds are allowed for
an additional one time fee of
$50 per pet.

**Hilton San Francisco Airport Bayfront**
600 Airport Blvd
Burlingame CA
650-340-8500
Offering panoramic views of the
San Francisco Bay, this resort
style hotel offers numerous on
site amenities for business and
leisure travelers, plus a
convenient location to the
airport, historic, shopping,
dining, and entertainment areas.
Dogs up to 35 pounds are
allowed for an additional one
time pet fee of $75 per room.

**Red Roof Plus+ San Francisco Airport**
777 Airport Boulevard
Burlingame CA
650-342-7772 (800-RED-ROOF)

One well-behaved family pet per
room. Guest must notify front
desk upon arrival. Guest is liable
for any damages. In
consideration of all guests, pets
must never be left unattended in
the guest rooms.

**San Francisco Airport Marriott Waterfront**
1800 Old Bayshore Hwy
Burlingame CA
650-692-9100
Dogs up to 50 pound sare
allowed. There is a $75 one time
pet fee.

**Aloft San Francisco Airport**
401 East Millbrae Avenue
Millbrae CA
650-692-6363 (877-424-6423)
Hotel is located on the San
Francisco Peninsula and is very
close to the San Francisco
International Airport.

**La Quinta Inn & Suites San Francisco Airport West**

1390 El Camino Real
Millbrae CA
650-952-3200 (800-531-5900)
Dogs of all sizes are allowed.
Dogs may not be left alone in
the room.

**Westin San Francisco Airport**
1 Old Bayshore Highway
Millbrae CA
650-692-3500 (888-625-5144)
This upscale hotel offers
numerous on site amenities for
business and leisure travelers
including extra quiet rooms,
ocean views, and airport shuttle
service to San Francisco's
International Airport. They also
offer a convenient location to the
downtown area, and world class
shopping, dining, recreation,
and entertainment venues. Dogs
are allowed for no additional
fee;there is a pet waiver to sign
at check in.

**Global Luxury Suites At
Downtown Mountain View**
1720 El Camino Real
Mountain View CA
650-961-0220
Showcasing an outdoor pool
and sun terrace Global Luxury
Suites at Downtown Mountain
View is situated in Mountain
View California. Shoreline
Amphitheater is 4.1 km away.
Free private parking is available
on site.
Some units are air conditioned
and include a seating area with
a flat-screen TV. Some units
also have a kitchen equipped
with a dishwasher and
microwave. Global Luxury
Suites at Downtown Mountain
View features free WiFi
throughout the property.
Global Luxury Suites at
Downtown Mountain View also
includes a hot tub.
The Computer History Museum
is 3 km from Global Luxury
Suites at Downtown Mountain
View. Mineta San Jose
International Airport is 15 km
from the property.

**Comfort Inn Palo Alto**
3945 El Camino Real
Palo Alto CA
650-493-3141 (877-424-6423)

Close to Stanford University.
Walking distance to
restaurants.

Dogs of all sizes are allowed.
Dogs are allowed for a pet fee
of $20.00 per pet per night.
Two dogs are allowed per
room.

**Crowne Plaza Cabana Palo
Alto**
4290 El Camino Real
Palo Alto CA
650-857-0787 (877-270-6405)
Dogs of all sizes are allowed.
Dogs are allowed for a pet fee.

**Garden Court Hotel**
520 Cowper Street
Palo Alto CA
650-322-9000 (800-824-9028)
In the centre of Palo Alto
California near attractions such
as Stanford University and
Silicon Valley Garden Court
Hotel offers contemporary
guestrooms with GLink iPhone
and Android docking stations
and thoughtful services.
The guestrooms at the Garden
Court Hotel offer twice daily
housekeeping services with
nightly turndown. Guests will
also enjoy the fully stocked
minibar and 24-hour ice
service. After a busy day
guests can listen to their Glink
iPhone or Android on a docking
station. A private balcony is
offered in all rooms.
Garden Court features coffee
tea and breakfast pastry
service in the lobby each
morning. Guests will also
appreciate evening afternoon
sweets and evening port
services. Guests can also dine
at Il Fornaio the italian
restaurant located within the
hotel.
Visitors can take advantage of
the hotel's fitness center with
cardiovascular equipment then
arrange an in-room massage
through the concierge service.
The concierge can also
arrange restaurant reservations
and private car service.

**Sheraton Palo Alto Hotel**
625 El Camino Real

Palo Alto CA
650-328-2800 (888-625-5144)
Featuring a resort like setting,
this upscale hotel offers a
number of onsite amenities for
all level of travelers, plus a
central location to many of the
area's best boutiques, galleries,
restaurants, and more. Dogs up
to 40 pounds are allowed for no
additional pet fee;there is a pet
waiver to sign at check in.

**The Nest Hotel**
3901 El Camino Real
Palo Alto CA
650-493-2760 (877-424-6423)
Beautifully decorated executive
rooms walking distance to
shops and restaurants, 2 miles
from Stanford University,

Dogs of all sizes are allowed.
Dogs are allowed for a pet fee of
$20.00 per pet per night. Two
dogs are allowed per room.

**Westin Palo Alto**
675 El Camino Real
Palo Alto CA
650-321-4422 (888-625-5144)
Located adjacent to the Stanford
University, this upscale hotel
also features amenities for
business and leisure travelers, 5
Mediterranean style courtyards,
and a location within walking
distance of some of the area's
best shopping, dining, and
nightlife venues. Dogs up to 40
pounds are allowed for no
additional fee;there is a pet
waiver to sign at check in.

**Pullman San Francisco Bay**
223 Twin Dolphin Drive
Redwood City CA
650-598-9000
The Pullman San Francisco Bay
offers lagoon views outdoor
swimming upscale dining and
freebies like airport shuttle
service and Wi-Fi all close to
Silicon Valley's thriving tech
scene. The 421 rooms of the
high-rise Pullman San Francisco
Bay feature European touches
like complimentary mineral
water and fresh flowers by your
bed. The rooms have an
upscale design and offer free
Wi-Fi work desks and high-end

bath products. Non-smoking rooms are available. The hotel's signature restaurant Bay 223 offers vistas of the lagoon and indulgent French cuisine. The adjacent Baybar provides views of the pool a light menu and innovative cocktails. Room service is available. Additional amenities include an outdoor pool gym jogging course free airport shuttle concierge and parking. Pets are allowed for an additional fee. Off Highway 101 in Redwood City this hotel is less than a mile from businesses like Electronic Arts. Perched along a lagoon that feeds into the San Francisco Bay the hotel is four miles from historic downtown Redwood City. It's 11 miles from Stanford University and 16 miles from Mountain View. Downtown San Francisco is 25 miles from the hotel and San Francisco International Airport is 13 miles away.

**Embassy Suites Hotel San Francisco-airport South San Fran.**
250 Gateway Blvd
South San Francisco CA
650-589-3400
This upscale hotel offers a number of on site amenities for business and leisure travelers, plus a convenient location to business, shopping, dining, and entertainment districts. They also offer a complimentary cooked-to-order breakfast and a Manager's reception each evening. Dogs up to 25 pounds are allowed for an additional one time pet fee of $50 per room.

## Pet-Friendly Extended Stay Hotels
**Extended Stay America - San Francisco - Belmont**
120 Sem Lane
Belmont CA
650-654-0344 (800-804-3724)
One dog is allowed per suite. There is a $25 per night additional pet fee up to $150 for an entire stay.

**Extended Stay America San Jose-mountain View**
190 East El Camino Real
Mountain View CA
650-962-1500 (800-804-3724)
One dog is allowed per suite. There is a $25 per night additional pet fee up to $150 for an entire stay.

**Residence Inn By Marriott Palo Alto Mountain View**
1854 El Camino Real West
Mountain View CA
650-940-1300
Dogs of all sizes are allowed. There is a $75 one time additional pet fee.

**Towneplace Suites Redwood City Redwood Shores**
1000 Twin Dolphin Drive
Redwood City CA
650-593-4100
Dogs of all sizes are allowed. There is a $75 one time pet fee.

**Extended Stay America San Francisco - San Carlos**
3 Circle Star Way
San Carlos CA
650-368-2600 (800-804-3724)
One dog is allowed per suite. There is a $25 per night additional pet fee up to $150 for an entire stay.

**Extended Stay America San Francisco - San Mateo - Sfo**
1830 Gateway Drive
San Mateo CA
650-574-1744 (800-804-3724)
One dog is allowed per suite. There is a $25 per night additional pet fee up to $150 for an entire stay.

**Residence Inn San Mateo**
2000 Winward Way
San Mateo CA
650-574-4700
Dogs of all sizes are allowed. There is a $75 one time additional pet fee.

**Residence Inn San Francisco Airport Oyster Point Waterfront**
1350 Veterns Boulevard

South San Francisco CA
650-837-9000
Dogs of all sizes are allowed. There is a $100 one time additional pet fee.

## Dog-Friendly Attractions
**Santa's Tree Farm**
78 Pilarcitos Creek Road
Half Moon Bay CA
650-726-2246
members.aol.com/DSare/index.htm
Well-behaved leashed dogs are allowed at this farm, but please note that the owners and/or employees reserve the right to request that your dog wait in the car if your pup misbehaves. Be watchful of others, especially children who may be frightened of dogs. They are open year-round. Santa's Tree Farm offers complimentary candy canes, hot apple cider, and of course, a great selection of Christmas trees. To get there from Hwy 280, take Hwy 92 West towards Half Moon Bay. Hwy 92 becomes Half Moon Bay Road. Go approximately 4 miles and then make a right turn onto Pilarcitos Creek Road.

**Hewlett-Packard Garage**
367 Addison Ave
Palo Alto CA

The HP Garage is known as the birthplace of Silicon Valley. You and your pup can see where William Hewlett and David Packard started HP. Please note that the house is now a private residence, so you'll need to view it from the sidewalk only.

## Outdoor Restaurants
**Coyote Cafe**
1003 Alameda de las Pulgas
Belmont CA
650-595-1422
This restaurant serves Mexican food. Dogs are allowed at the outdoor tables. Water is provided for your pet.

**Copenhagen Bakery and Cafe**
1216 Burlingame Ave
Burlingame CA
650-342-1357
copenhagenbakery.com/
In addition to numerous
signature bakery specialties,
this café also serves up a full
days menu for breakfast, lunch,
and dinner. Dogs are allowed at
their outside tables.

**Crepevine**
1310 Burlingame Avenue
Burlingame CA
650-344-1310
crepevine.com
With a focus on local and
organic, this restaurant
specializes in a variety of sweet
and savory crepes and offers
100% all natural beef, ocean
raised Canadian salmon,
organic Fair-Trade coffee, all
natural fed cage free eggs, and
farm fresh produce. In addition
to a breakfast items they offer
salads, sandwiches, pastas, and
a kid's menu. Leashed, friendly
dogs are allowed at their
sidewalk tables.

**Urban Bistro**
270 Lorton Avenue
Burlingame CA
650-347-7687
With an emphasis on
sustainable, local, and organic
this eatery features
contemporary comfort food with
a daily line-up of made-from-
scratch vegetarian, lowfat, spicy,
dairy free, low carb, gluten-free,
and limited quantity soups. They
also offer sandwiches,
flatbreads, salads, a kids menu,
desserts, and specialty coffee
drinks. They are open daily from
11 am until 9 pm. Leashed,
friendly dogs are allowed at their
outside dining area.

**Baja Fresh Mexican Grill**
1031 East Hillsdale Blvd.
Foster City CA
650-358-8632
bajafresh.com
This Mexican restaurant is open
for lunch and dinner. They use
fresh ingredients and making
their salsa and beans daily.
Some of the items on their

menu include Enchiladas,
Burritos, Tacos Salads,
Quesadillas, Nachos, Chicken,
Steak and more. Well-behaved
leashed dogs are allowed at
the outdoor tables.

**El Torito Mexican Restaurant
and Cantina**
388 Vintage Park Drive
Foster City CA
650-574-6844
This eatery serves up authentic
Mexican food. Your pet is
welcome to join you at the
outside tables. Dogs must be
well behaved, attended to at all
times, and leashed.

**Half Moon Bay Brewery**
390 Capistrano Road
Half Moon Bay CA
650-728-2739
hmbbrewingco.com/
Fresh, local and seasonal
coastal cuisine is the specialty
here. Offerings include
homemade soups, salads,
burgers and sandwiches,
entrées, desserts, and a kid's
menu. Leashed, well mannered
dogs are welcome at their
outside tables.

**Half Moon Bay Coffee
Company**
20 Stone Pine Rd #A
Half Moon Bay CA
650-726-3664
This café will allow leashed
dogs at their outside tables.
They are open Monday to
Thursday from 6 am until 6 pm,
and on Friday thru Sunday
from 6 am until 8 pm with the
kitchen closing at 7 pm.

**It's Italia Pizzeria**
401 Main Street
Half Moon Bay CA
650-726-4444
itsitaliarestaurant.com/
This Italian restaurant sources
the freshest and organic
produce, products, meats, and
seafood available offering tasty
and nutritious meals with a
California coastal influence. In
addition to their gourmet pizzas
and skillfully crafted entrees,
they also offer weekend
brunches, live entertainment,

and courtyard dining. Leashed,
friendly dogs are welcome at
their outside dining area.

**Three-Zero Cafe**
9850 Cabrillo Hwy N
Half Moon Bay CA
650-728-1411
3-zero.com/toppage11.htm
Eight years in a row this
restaurant won 'Best Breakfast
on the Coast'. They offer indoor
and outdoor dining-weather
permitting. Dogs are allowed at
the outdoor tables. Dogs must
be under owner's control/care at
all times and leashed.

**Left Bank**
635 Santa Cruz Avenue
Menlo Park CA
650-473-6543
leftbank.com
An authentic French brasserie,
guests can enjoy their Parisian
casual setting with not so casual
food;they offer lunch, dinner,
weekend brunch, and children's
menus;plus a full service bar
with signature cocktails and
alfresco dining. Leashed, well
mannered dogs are welcome at
their outside dining area.

**Chipotle**
135 S El Camino Real
Millbrae CA
650-259-9301
chipotle.com
Specializing in organic, natural
and unprocessed food, this
Mexican Eatery offers fajita
burritos, tacos, salads, and
salsas. Dogs are allowed at the
outdoor tables but you will need
to order your food inside the
restaurant and dogs must
remain outside.

**Moss Beach Distillery**
140 Beach Way @ Ocean Blvd
Moss Beach CA
650-728-5595
mossbeachdistillery.com/
Fine dining in an elegant,
romantic setting on the
oceanfront is the specialty here.
Their menu is seasonally
inspired, and they source
organic produce (when
available), naturally raised
poultry and meats, and wild-

caught seafood. There is no service at the outside tables, so order from the bartender and they will give out a beeper for when the order is done. Leashed, well mannered dogs are allowed at the outside tables.

## Amici's East Coast Pizza
790 Castro Street
Mountain View CA
650-961-6666
amicis.com/default.asp
This pizzeria features pizzas with an East coast Italian flare. Dogs are allowed at their outside tables.

## Cafe Baklava
341 Castro Street
Mountain View CA
650-969-3835
cafebaklava.com/cuisine.php
A casual cafe atmosphere, freshly prepared Turkish foods, a good selection of fine wines, and a comfortable patio are just some of the offerings of this restaurant. Leashed, well mannered dogs are welcome at their outside tables.

## Chipotle
2400 Charleston Road
Mountain View CA
650-969-6528
chipotle.com
Specializing in organic, natural and unprocessed food, this Mexican Eatery offers fajita burritos, tacos, salads, and salsas. Dogs are allowed at the outdoor tables but you will need to order your food inside the restaurant and dogs must remain outside.

## Clarkes Charcoal Broiler
615 W El Camino Real
Mountain View CA
650-967-0851
waiter.com/restaurants/clarkes#
Enjoy their hamburgers, steak or chicken sandwiches.

## Hobee's
2312 Central Expressway
Mountain View CA
650-968-6050
hobees.com/
Popular for their distinctive

California cuisine at modest prices, this eatery also provides outside dining options. Dogs are allowed at the outer tables;they must be under their owner's control at all times.

## La Salsa Restaurant
660 San Antonio Rd
Mountain View CA
650-917-8290
lasalsa.com/
This restaurant has several kinds of tacos and burritos to choose from. Leashed dogs are allowed at the outside tables.

## Le Boulanger
650 Castro St #160
Mountain View CA
650-961-1787
leboulanger.com/
This family owned bakery features daily baked breads from the finest ingredients available. They also serve up made-from-scratch soups, salads, gourmet pizzas, sandwiches, and a full service espresso bar. Leashed dogs are welcome at their outside tables.

## Posh Bagel
444 Castro Street #120
Mountain View CA
650-968-5308
This bagel shop allows friendly, leashed dogs at their outside tables.

## Steak Out
383 Castro Street
Mountain View CA
650-209-0383
steakout.us
This burger restaurant and Beer Garden serves 18 beers including a gluten free beer. It serves locally grown, 100% grass-fed beef. The restaurant is open 7 days a week from 11 am to 9 pm or later on Thursday, Friday and Saturday. There is a large outdoor patio where dogs are allowed. They even have a restaurant dog named Stout which visits the restaurant on Monday, Wednesday and Friday from 5:30 to 6:30.

## Baja Fresh Mexican Grill
3990 El Camino Real
Palo Alto CA
650-424-8599
bajafresh.com
This Mexican restaurant is open for lunch and dinner. They use fresh ingredients and making their salsa and beans daily. Some of the items on their menu include Enchiladas, Burritos, Tacos Salads, Quesadillas, Nachos, Chicken, Steak and more. Well-behaved leashed dogs are allowed at the outdoor tables.

## Coupa Cafe
538 Ramona Street
Palo Alto CA
650-322-6872
Certified organic, Fair Trade coffee is the specialty here: From seeking out and helping to reestablish coffee production in what is considered 1 of the world's best coffee growing areas, this company now has direct working relations with almost 20 Venezuelan single estate plantations. Their extensive, globally conscience menu features full breakfasts, breakfast and French pastries, arepas, salads, paninis, Venezuelan specialties, crepes, pastas, pizza, and beer and wine. They also offer daily Happy Hours. Leashed, well mannered dogs are allowed at their outside dining area.

## Crepevine
367 University Avenue
Palo Alto CA
650-323-3900
crepevine.com
With a focus on local and organic, this eatery specializes in a variety of sweet and savory crepes and offers 100% all natural beef, ocean raised Canadian salmon, organic Fair-Trade coffee, all natural fed cage free eggs, and farm fresh produce. In addition to breakfast items they offer salads, sandwiches, pastas, and a kid's menu. Leashed, friendly dogs are allowed at their outside dining area.

**Izzy's Brooklyn Bagels**
477 S California Ave
Palo Alto CA
650-329-0700
izzysbrooklynbagels.com/
This bagel shop has a wide variety of bagels and pastries. Leashed dogs are allowed at their outside tables.

**Joanie's Cafe**
447 S California Ave
Palo Alto CA
650-326-6505
joaniescafepaloalto.com/
If you come here for breakfast, you can order a variety of dishes like Belgium waffles, pancakes and more. They also serve sandwiches for lunch. Leashed dogs are allowed at their outside dining area.

**Spalti Ristorante**
417 S California Ave
Palo Alto CA
650-327-9390
spalti.com/
This nice Italian restaurant has outdoor heaters to keep you and your pup warm. Sidewalk and patio seating are available. They are open for lunch and dinner.

**St. Michael's Alley**
140 Homer Avenue
Palo Alto CA
650-326-2530
stmikes.com
This restaurant has dog-friendly outdoor seating and they love dogs. The owners also have two dogs. They serve brunch, lunch and dinner. For brunch they offer omelets, french toast, pancakes and more. The lunch menu has a wide variety of appetizers,

**Whole Foods Market**
774 Emerson Street
Palo Alto CA
650-326-8676
wholefoods.com/
This natural food supermarket offers natural and organic foods. Order some food from their deli without your dog and bring it to an outdoor table where your well-behaved leashed dog is welcome.

**Half Moon Bay Brewing Company**
390 Capistrano Rd
Princeton CA
650-728-BREW (2739)
hmbbrewingco.com/
Thanks to one of our readers who writes: A great setting south of San Francisco to spend the day walking your dog on the beautiful San Mateo Coastal Beaches. You can enjoy an open air meal with your furry friend sitting beside you in a fun and relaxed environment.

**Cafe La Tartine**
830 Middlefield Road
Redwood City CA
650-474-2233
This cafe offers an upscale yet casual ambiance, a bakery with specialty desserts, burgers, sandwiches, and alfresco dining. They are open Sunday to Thursday from 8 am until 9 pm, and on Friday and Saturday from 8 am until 11 pm. Leashed, friendly dogs are allowed at their outside dining area.

**Chipotle**
861 Middlefield Road
Redwood City CA
650-216-9325
chipotle.com
Specializing in organic, natural and unprocessed food, this Mexican Eatery offers fajita burritos, tacos, salads, and salsas. Dogs are allowed at the outdoor tables but you will need to order your food inside the restaurant and dogs must remain outside.

**City Pub**
2620 Broadway
Redwood City CA
650-363-2620
city-pub.com/
Dogs are allowed at the outside tables. They will bring your dog a bowl of water as well. They serve burgers, other food and many beers.

**Talk of Broadway**
2096 Broadway Street

Redwood City CA
650-368-3295
This diner serves up a good variety of American comfort cuisine with indoor and outdoor seating options. Leashed, well mannered dogs are allowed at their outside dining area.

**The Sandwich Spot**
2420 Broadway Street
Redwood City CA
650-299-1300
Burgers, beer, and a sandwich hot spot are just a few of the offerings here. They also offer courtyard dining. The restaurant is open Monday to Thursday from 10 am until 5 pm;Friday from 10 am until 7 pm, and on Saturday and Sunday from 10 am until 5 pm. Leashed, friendly dogs are allowed at their outside dining area.

**Whole Foods Market**
1250 Jefferson Avenue
Redwood City CA
650-367-1400
wholefoods.com/
This natural food supermarket offers natural and organic foods. Order some food from their deli without your dog and bring it to an outdoor table where your well-behaved leashed dog is welcome.

**Chipotle**
1135 Industrial Road, Suite C
San Carlos CA
650-598-0847
chipotle.com
Specializing in organic, natural and unprocessed food, this Mexican Eatery offers fajita burritos, tacos, salads, and salsas. Dogs are allowed at the outdoor tables but you will need to order your food inside the restaurant and dogs must remain outside.

**Santorini**
753 Laurel Street
San Carlos CA
650-637-8283
santorinisancarlos.com/
Featuring authentic Greek and Mediterranean cuisine, this eatery also offers a warm ambiance, an extensive wine

list, catering services, and alfresco dining. Leashed, well mannered dogs are welcome at their outer tables.

### Chipotle
1062 Foster City Blvd
San Mateo CA
650-627-9245
chipotle.com
Specializing in organic, natural and unprocessed food, this Mexican Eatery offers fajita burritos, tacos, salads, and salsas. Dogs are allowed at the outdoor tables but you will need to order your food inside the restaurant and dogs must remain outside.

### Whole Foods Market
1010 Park Place
San Mateo CA
650-358-6900
wholefoods.com/
This natural food supermarket offers natural and organic foods. Order some food from their deli without your dog and bring it to an outdoor table where your well-behaved leashed dog is welcome. Dogs are not allowed on any of the furnishings.

## Pet-Friendly Shopping Centers
### Downtown Palo Alto
University Ave
Palo Alto CA

Downtown Palo Alto is a nice area to walk with your leashed dog. There are many shops and outdoor restaurants that line University Ave. Some of the stores allow dogs inside, like Restoration Hardware. However, please ask the store clerk before bringing your dog inside each store just in case their policies have changed. Enjoy lunch or dinner at one of the many nearby outdoor cafes (see Restaurants).

### Stanford Shopping Center
680 Stanford Shopping Center
Palo Alto CA
650-617-8585 (800-772-9332)
stanfordshop.com/
Stanford Shopping Center is the Bay Area's premier open-air shopping center. This dog-friendly mall has a beautiful outdoor garden environment. Thirty-five varieties of trees are represented by 1,300 specimens throughout the mall. There are hundreds of hanging baskets and flower-filled planters located in four microclimates. We have found that many of the stores do allow well-behaved dogs inside. For a list of dog-friendly stores, please look at our stores category. However, please ask the store clerk before bringing your dog inside each store just in case their policies have changed. Depending on the season, there will be many outdoor tables adjacent to the food stands and cafes. Here you can order the food inside and then enjoy it with your pup at one of the outside tables.

## Pet-Friendly Stores
### Anthropologie
220 Primrose Road
Burlingame CA
650-685-6637
Items of distinction can be found for all ages and in all departments of this unique shop. Carefully selected to add to the enjoyment of the shopping experience, they carry fine clothing, amazing accessories, jewelry, hobby and leisure items, and a full line of bright and useful items for the home, garden, and office. Leashed, well behaved dogs are allowed in the store.

### Pet Club
1010 Rengstorff Avenue
Mountain View CA
650-988-1316
petclubstores.com
In addition to warehouse pricing with no membership fees, this comprehensive pet supply store offers weekly specials and more than 11,000 pet products ranging from wellness items, bedding, dinnerware, a wide choice of quality foods, treats, leashes, toys, apparel, travel supplies, and much more. Leashed, friendly dogs are always welcome in the store.

### Petco Pet Store - Mountain View
1919 El Camino Real
Mountain View CA
650-966-1233
Your licensed and well-behaved leashed dog is allowed in the store.

### Anthropologie
999 Alma Street
Palo Alto CA
650-322-0435
Items of distinction can be found for all ages and in all departments of this unique shop. Carefully selected to add to the enjoyment of the shopping experience, they carry fine clothing, amazing accessories, jewelry, hobby and leisure items, and a full line of bright and useful items for the home, garden, and office. Leashed, well behaved dogs are allowed in the store.

### Bang & Olufsen
Stanford Shopping Center
Palo Alto CA
650-322-2264
bang-olufsen.com/
Your well-behaved leashed dog is allowed inside this store.

### Bloomingdale's
1 Stanford Shopping Center
Palo Alto CA
650-463-2000
Some of the offerings of this major shopping destination include designer merchandise, indoor and outdoor wear for the entire family, jewelry and accessories, shoes and handbags, personal beauty aids, child care products, and home decor. They also offer a wide variety of shopping services; various fashion, beauty, and home events, and a philanthropy program that raises funds and awareness for worthy causes. Leashed, well mannered dogs are welcome in

the store; they must be under their owner's control at all times.

**Bloomingdale's**
Stanford Shopping Center
Palo Alto CA
650-463-2000
bloomindales.com/
Your well-behaved leashed dog is allowed inside this store.

**Books Inc.**
Stanford Shopping Center
Palo Alto CA
650-321-0600
Your well-behaved leashed dog is allowed inside this store.

**Crate & Barrel**
530 Stanford Shopping Center
Palo Alto CA
650-321-7800
crateandbarrel.com
Fine products for the home to be found at this store include items for outdoor living, indoor furnishings, dining and entertaining, kitchen, decorating, bed and bath, organizing and storage, and much more. Leashed, friendly dogs are welcome in the store.

**Giants Dugout**
Stanford Shopping Center
Palo Alto CA
650-323-9790
Your well-behaved leashed dog is allowed inside this store.

**Going in Style Travel Accessories**
Stanford Shopping Center
Palo Alto CA
650-326-2066
goinginstyle.com/
Your well-behaved leashed dog is allowed inside this store.

**Hear Music**
Stanford Shopping Center
Palo Alto CA
650-473-9142
hearmusic.com/
Your well-behaved leashed dog is allowed inside this store.

**Kenneth Cole Mens & Womens Shoes & More**
Stanford Shopping Center

Palo Alto CA
650-853-8365
kennethcole.com/
Your well-behaved leashed dog is allowed inside this store.

**Lady Foot Locker**
Stanford Shopping Center
Palo Alto CA
650-325-2301
ladyfootlocker.com/
Your well-behaved leashed dog is allowed inside this store.

**Macy's and Macy's Mens Store**
Stanford Shopping Center
Palo Alto CA
650-326-3333
macys.com/
Your well-behaved leashed dog is allowed inside this store.

**Neiman Marcus**
400 Stanford Shopping Center
Palo Alto CA
650-329-3300
neimanmarcus.com
This famous department store, which sells everything from clothing to home furnishings, allows your well-behaved leashed dog to shop with you. It is located in Stanford Shopping Center, which is very dog-friendly.

**Nordstrom**
Stanford Shopping Center
Palo Alto CA
650-323-5111
nordstrom.com/
Your well-behaved leashed dog is allowed inside this store.

**Pet Food Express**
3910 Middlefield Road
Palo Alto CA
650-856-6666
One of the country's leading pet retailers, this comprehensive pet store offers a number of other stores, quality foods/treats, a wide variety of pet supplies, breed-specific items, pet care products, apparel, health items, hound and human accessories, and much more. Some of the services they offer include working with local SPCAs and rescue groups helping tens of

thousands of homeless pets find new homes (they do not sell animals as pets), providing low cost vaccination clinics, dog training classes, and self-service pet washes. All leashed, friendly pets are welcome.

**Postal Annex**
Stanford Shopping Center
Palo Alto CA
650-324-8082
postalannex.com/
Your well-behaved leashed dog is allowed inside this store.

**Pottery Barn**
Stanford Shopping Center
Palo Alto CA
650-473-0449
potterybarn.com/
Your well-behaved leashed dog is allowed inside this store.

**Restoration Hardware**
281 University Avenue
Palo Alto CA
650-328-4004
restorationhardware.com/
They love having dogs in the store!

**Summer Winds Nursery**
725 San Antonio Rd
Palo Alto CA
650-493-5136
summerwindsnursery.com
Summer Winds Nursery welcomes well-behaved, leashed dogs.

**The Discovery Channel Store**
Stanford Shopping Center
Palo Alto CA
650-321-9833
shopping.discovery.com/
Your well-behaved leashed dog is allowed inside this store.

**The Sharper Image**
Stanford Shopping Center
Palo Alto CA
650-322-5488
sharperimage.com/
Your well-behaved leashed dog is allowed inside this store.

**Pet Food Express**
372 Woodside Plaza
Redwood City CA
650-298-9999
One of the country's leading pet

retailers, this comprehensive pet store offers a number of other stores, quality foods/treats, a wide variety of pet supplies, breed-specific items, pet care products, apparel, health items, hound and human accessories, and much more. Some of the services they offer include working with local SPCAs and rescue groups helping tens of thousands of homeless pets find new homes (they do not sell animals as pets), providing low cost vaccination clinics, dog training classes, and self-service pet washes. All leashed, friendly pets are welcome.

**Petco Pet Store - Redwood City**
520 Woodside Road
Redwood City CA
650-364-6077
Your licensed and well-behaved leashed dog is allowed in the store.

**Petco Pet Store - San Bruno**
1150 El Camino Real #167
San Bruno CA
650-589-3757
Your licensed and well-behaved leashed dog is allowed in the store.

**Pet Food Express**
1129 Old County Road
San Carlos CA
650-591-5555
One of the country's leading pet retailers, this comprehensive pet store offers a number of other stores, quality foods/treats, a wide variety of pet supplies, breed-specific items, pet care products, apparel, health items, hound and human accessories, and much more. Some of the services they offer include working with local SPCAs and rescue groups helping tens of thousands of homeless pets find new homes (they do not sell animals as pets), providing low cost vaccination clinics, dog training classes, and self-service pet washes. All leashed, friendly pets are welcome.

**Pet Club**
1850 Norfolk Street

San Mateo CA
650-358-0347
petclubstores.com
In addition to warehouse pricing with no membership fees, this comprehensive pet supply store offers weekly specials, and more than 11,000 pet products ranging from wellness items, bedding, dinnerware, a wide choice of quality foods, treats, leashes, toys, apparel, travel supplies, and much more. Leashed, friendly dogs are always welcome in the store.

**PetSmart Pet Store**
3520 S El Camino Real
San Mateo CA
650-577-9010
Your licensed and well-behaved leashed dog is allowed in the store.

**Petco Pet Store - San Mateo**
3012 Bridgepointe Pkwy
San Mateo CA
650-357-9480
Your licensed and well-behaved leashed dog is allowed in the store.

**Pet Club**
2256 W Borough Blvd
South San Francisco CA
650-583-2186
petclubstores.com
In addition to warehouse pricing with no membership fees, this comprehensive pet supply store offers weekly specials and more than 11,000 pet products ranging from wellness items, bedding, dinnerware, a wide choice of quality foods, treats, leashes, toys, apparel, travel supplies, and much more. Leashed, friendly dogs are always welcome in the store.

## Dog-Friendly Beaches
**Blufftop Coastal Park**
Poplar Street
Half Moon Bay CA
650-726-8297
Leashed dogs are allowed at this beach. The beach is located on the west end of

Poplar Street, off Highway 1.

**Montara State Beach**
Highway 1
Half Moon Bay CA
650-726-8819
Dogs on leash are allowed at this beach. Please clean up after your pets. The beach is located 8 miles north of Half Moon Bay on Highway 1. There are two beach access points. The first access point is across from Second Street, immediately south of the Outrigger Restaurant. The second access point is about a 1/2 mile north on the ocean side of Highway 1. Both access points have steep paths down to the beach.

**Surfer's Beach**
Highway 1
Half Moon Bay CA
650-726-8297
Dogs on leash are allowed on the beach. It is located at Highway 1 and Coronado Street.

**Esplanade Beach**
Esplanade
Pacifica CA
650-738-7381
This beach offers an off-leash area for dogs. To get to the beach, take the stairs at the end of Esplanade. Esplanade is just north of Manor Drive, off Highway 1.

**Bean Hollow State Beach**
Highway 1
Pescadero CA
650-879-2170
This is a very rocky beach with not much sand. Dogs are allowed but must be on a 6 foot or less leash. Please clean up after your pets. The beach is located 3 miles south of Pescadero on Highway 1.

## Off-Leash Dog Parks
**Cipriani Dog Park**
2525 Buena Vista Avenue
Belmont CA
650-365-3524
This dog park is located at the

Cipriani Elementary School.

**Bayside Park Dog Park**
1125 South Airport Blvd
Burlingame CA
650-558-7300
This dog park is over 570 feet long. It is in the back of the parking area and then you have to walk about 1/8 mile down a path to the off-leash dog park.

**Foster City Dog Park**
Foster City Blvd at Bounty
Foster City CA

There is a separate dog area for small dogs and large dogs at this off leash dog park. The parks are about 1/2 an acre in size. There are tables and benches. The dog park is located in Boat Park at the corner of Bounty Drive and Foster City Blvd.

**Half Moon Bay Dog Park**
Wavecrest Rd
Half Moon Bay CA
650-560-9822
halfmoonbaydogpark.weebly.co
m/
The Half Moon Bay Dog Park, located at Wavecrest Road in Half Moon Bay, California, is a off-leash dog park that advertises a good time for both dogs and their owners. The dog park is open from sunrise to sunset. For a complete list of rules, visit
http://dogpark.tripod.com/id1.ht
ml

**Half Moon Bay Dog Park**
Wavecrest Road
Half Moon Bay CA
650-726-8297
halfmoonbaydogpark.weebly.co
m/
This fenced, public off-leash dog park is supported by citizen volunteers. The dog park is located at Smith Field, at the western end of Wavecrest Road. The organization that runs the park would appreciate a $20 annual membership from locals that use the park regularly but it is not mandatory.

**Mountain View Dog Park**

Shoreline Blvd at North Rd
Mountain View CA

This fenced, off leash dog park is located across from Shoreline Amphitheater at the entrance to Shoreline Park. Dogs are not allowed in Shoreline Park itself.

**Greer Dog Park**
1098 Amarillo Avenue
Palo Alto CA
650-329-2261
This is a fenced off leash dog exercise park. Dogs on leash are allowed in the rest of the park.

**Hoover Park**
2901 Cowper St
Palo Alto CA
650-329-2261
This is a small off leash dog exercise area. Dogs on leash are allowed in the rest of the park.

**Mitchell Park/Dog Run**
3800 Middlefield Rd
Palo Alto CA
650-329-2261
Located in Mitchell Park at 3800 Middlefield Rd (between E. Charleston and E. Meadow) Note: It can be tough to find at first. The dog run is closer to E. Charleston by the baseball fields and over a small hill.

**Shores Dog Park**
Radio Road
Redwood City CA

This dog park (opened Nov/Dec 98) was funded by Redwood City residents. To get there from Hwy 101, take Holly/Redwood Shores Parkway Exit. Go east (Redwood Shore Parkway). Turn right on Radio Road (this is almost at the end of the street). The park will be on the right. Thanks to one of our readers for this information.

**San Bruno Dog Park**
Commodore Lane and Cherry Ave
San Bruno CA
650-877-8868

San Bruno moved its dog park to this new location. The dog park has two fenced areas for large and small dogs, water for dogs and people, benches, bags to clean up and shade. If your dog doesn't like loud noises, beware of the large jets taking off from San Francisco Airport less than 2 miles away. The dog park is located in Commodore Park the intersection of I-280 and I-380. Take the 280 San Bruno Avenue exit east and turn left on Cherry Avenue to the park.

**Heather Dog Exercise Area**
2757 Melendy Drive
San Carlos CA
650-802-4382
This 1.5 acre park offers a small area where dogs can run off-leash as well as an on-leash hiking trail. Access the park through the Heather School parking lot.

**Pulgas Ridge Off-Leash Dog Area**
Edmonds Road and Crestview Drive
San Carlos CA
650-691-1200
Most of Pulgas Ridge Open Space Preserve allows dogs on leash. There is a large, seventeen acre area in the center of the preserve that allows dogs off-leash under voice control. Please check the signs for the appropriate boundaries of the off-leash area. To get to the preserve, take I-280 to Edgewood Rd. Head east on Edgewood and turn left on Crestview. Immediately after that turn, turn left onto Edmonds to the entrance to the preserve.

# Dog-Friendly Parks
**Pacifica State Beach**
Highway 1
Pacifica CA
650-738-7381
This wide crescent shaped beach is located off Highway 1 in downtown Pacifica. Dogs on leash are allowed and please clean up after them.

## Palo Alto Baylands Preserve

San Antonio Road
Palo Alto CA
650-329-2506
The Palo Alto Baylands Preserve is a flat mostly unpaved 5 mile loop trail. Leashed dogs are allowed, unless posted in special bird nesting areas. There are several entrance points. One of the main starting points is from Hwy 101 heading north, exit San Antonio Road and turn right. San Antonio Road will bring you directly into the start of the Preserve. Please note that there is an adjacent park on the right which is a City of Mountain View park that does not allow dogs. However, no need to worry, the dog-friendly Palo Alto side has plenty of trails for you and your pooch to walk or run.

## Stanford University

Palm Drive
Palo Alto CA
408-225-0225
stanford.edu/
Stanford University has miles of tree covered sidewalks and paths that wind through the campus. There is also a park at the end of Palm Drive which is a small but popular hang out for locals and their leashed dogs on warm days . To get there from downtown Palo Alto, take University Ave west toward the hills. University Ave turns into Palm Drive. There are tree lined walking paths along this street. The park is at the end of Palm. Ample parking is available.

## Butano State Park

Highway 1
Pescadero CA
650-879-2040
This 2,200 acre park is located in a secluded redwood-filled canyon. While dogs are not allowed on the trails, they are allowed in the campground and on miles of fire roads. Mountain biking is also allowed on the fire roads. Pets must be on a 6 foot or less leash. Please clean up after them. The park is located on the San Mateo Coast off

Highway 1. To get there go 4.5 miles southeast of Pescadero via Pescadero and Cloverdale Roads.

## Windy Hill Preserve

Hwys 84 and 35
Portola Valley CA
650-691-1200
openspace.org/WINDY.html
At this park there are views of the Santa Clara Valley, San Francisco and the ocean. This preserve features grassy meadows and redwood, fir, and oak trees. Leashed dogs are allowed on designated trails. Directions: From Hwy 280, take Hwy 84 west (La Honda Rd). Go about 2.3 miles to Hwy 35 (Skyline Blvd). The main parking is at the intersection of Hwys 84 and 35. Another starting option is to park at the Portola Valley Town Hall and begin there.

## Pulgas Ridge Open Space Preserve

Edmonds Road
Redwood City CA
650-691-1200
This park has about 293 acres and some great trails. There are are about 3 miles of trails that will provide moderate to strenuous exercise. Leashed dogs are allowed on the trails. The park offers some nice shade on warm days. To get there from Interstate 280, take the Edgewood Road exit. Travel 0.75 miles northeast on Edgewood Road toward San Carlos and Redwood City. Turn left (north) on Crestview Drive, and then immediately turn left on Edmonds Road. Limited roadside parking is available along Crestview Drive and Edmonds Road.

## Day Kennels

### PetsHotel by PetsMart Day Kennel

2440 E. Charleston Rd.
Mountain View CA

petsmart.com/PETsHOTEL/
This PetsMart pet store offers

day care, day camp, and overnight care. Dogs may be dropped off and picked up during the hours of 7 am - 7 pm M-S, Sunday 9 am - 6 pm. Dogs must have proof of current rabies, DPP and bordatella vaccinations.

## Emergency Veterinarians

### Emergency Veterinary Clinic

3045 Middlefield Rd
Palo Alto CA
650-494-1461
Monday - Thursday 6 pm to 8 am, Friday 6 pm - Monday 8 am.

## Pasadena - East LA

## Dog-Friendly Hotels

### Sheraton Cerritos

12725 Center Court Drive
Cerritos CA
562-809-1500 (888-625-5144)
In addition to being located within walking distance to the Cerritos Center for the Performing Arts, this upscale hotel also offers a convenient location for exploring some of the greatest attractions in Southern California. Dogs up to 50 pounds are allowed for an additional pet fee of $25 per night per room and there is a pet waiver to sign at check in. Dogs may not be left alone in the room.

### Hilton Los Angeles North/glendale And Executive Meeting Ctr

100 West Glenoaks Blvd
Glendale CA
818-956-5466
Located in the upscale business district, this hotel and meeting center features a number of amenities for all level of travelers and a convenient location to many of the area's world class attractions and activities. Dogs are allowed for an additional one time pet fee of

$75 per room.

## Hotel Le Reve Pasadena
3321 East Colorado Boulevard
Pasadena CA
626-796-9291 (877-424-6423)
Quietly nestled in the foothills of
the majestic San Gabriel
Mountains.

Dogs of all sizes are allowed.
Dogs are allowed for a pet fee of
$20/ per pet per night.

## Sheraton Pasadena Hotel
303 Cordova Street
Pasadena CA
626-449-4000 (888-625-5144)
Beside a number of amenities
for all level of travelers, this
upscale hotel is located central
to many of the area's star
attractions and sits within
walking distance of Old Town
Pasadena where there are many
shopping, dining, and
entertainment venues. Dogs up
to 45 pounds are allowed for no
additional fee;there is a pet
waiver to sign at check in.

## Super 8 Pasadena/la Area
2863 East Colorado Boulevard
Pasadena CA
626-449-3020 (800-800-8000)
Small dogs are allowed.

## Westin Pasadena
191 North Los Robles
Pasadena CA
626-792-2727 (888-625-5144)
In addition to a number of
amenities for all level of
travelers, this upscale hotel is
located central to many of the
area's star attractions, including
the Pasadena Conference
Center and Old Town Pasadena
where there are many shopping,
dining, and entertainment
venues. Dogs up to 40 pounds
are allowed for no additional
fee;there is a pet waiver to sign
at check in.

## Hilton Los Angeles - San Gabriel
225 West Valley Boulevard
San Gabriel CA
626-270-2700
This luxury hotel offers a
number of on site amenities for

business and leisure travelers,
plus a convenient location to
historical, business, shopping,
dining, and entertainment
areas. One dog up to 50
pounds is allowed for an
additional one time pet fee of
$50.

## Pet-Friendly Extended Stay Hotels
**Extended Stay America - Los Angeles - Arcadia**
401 E Santa Clara St
Arcadia CA
626-446-6422 (800-804-3724)
One dog is allowed per suite.
There is a $25 per night
additional pet fee up to $150
for an entire stay.

## Residence Inn Arcadia
321 East Hungtington Drive
Arcadia CA
626-446-6500
Dogs of all sizes are allowed.
There is a $100 one time
additional pet fee.

**Extended Stay America - Los Angeles - Glendale**
1377 W Glenoaks Blvd
Glendale CA
818-956-6665 (800-804-3724)
One dog is allowed per suite.
There is a $25 per night
additional pet fee up to $150
for an entire stay.

**Extended Stay America - Los Angeles-monrovia**
930 S Fifth Ave
Monrovia CA
626-256-6999 (800-804-3724)
One dog is allowed per suite.
There is a $25 per night
additional pet fee up to $150
for an entire stay.

## Dog Businesses
**K9 Loft**
495 S Arroyo Parkway
Pasadena CA
626-795-6060
k9loft.com/pasadena/
In addition to offering a wide
variety of pet food, treats,

grooming supplies, toys, and
various pet supplies, K9 Loft
also offers daycare, boarding,
grooming, dental cleaning,
training, shuttles, and adoption
services. Dogs are welcome to
come in and check out all the
treats and fun stuff.

## Dog-Friendly Attractions
**Frisbee Golf Course**
Oak Grove Drive
Pasadena CA

members.aol.com/throwgolf
This disc golf course in
Pasadena is the world's first
disc golf course. It is an
extremely popular course, with
over 100 golfers playing daily
during the week and twice that
on the weekends. If you are a
beginner, this might not be the
right course for you, but you can
watch some of the pros at work.
Disc golf is similar to golf with
clubs and balls, but the main
difference is the equipment.
Discs are shot into elevated
baskets/holes. Your dog is
allowed to go with you on this
course, just watch out for flying
discs. Dogs must be leashed
and poop bags/scoopers are
necessary. During the summer
months, there can be
rattlesnakes, so make sure your
dog stays leashed. You'll also
want to keep your pup away
from the ground squirrels (they
can potentially be rabid). This
course is located in
Hahamongna Watershed Park
(formerly Oak Grove Park). If
you don't have any discs, you
can purchase them online at
http://www.gottagogottathrow.co
m. The prices range from $8-12.
Directions to the course are on
their website. The park is off
Hwy 210 near Altadena.

## Outdoor Restaurants
**Diner on Main**
201 W Main Street
Alhambra CA
626-281-3488
dineronmainrestaurant.net

This is the place for a true 50's 'diner' encounter with classic American and signature fare, homemade desserts, live entertainment, a full bar, and 3 big screen TVs for sports viewing. Leashed dogs are welcome at the outside dining area.

**Matt Denny's Ale House**
145 E Huntington Dr
Arcadia CA
626-462-0250
Cuisine influenced by early California, the Pacific Northwest, Mexico, and the Caribbean, and quality handcrafted ales are offered at this ale house. Leashed, well mannered dogs are welcome at their outside tables.

**Jamba Juice**
832 E Alosta Avenue
Azusa CA
626-334-1268
jambajuice.com
All natural and organic ingredients, no high-fructose corn syrup, 0 grams trans fat, no artificial preservatives, a healthy helping of antioxidants, vitamins, and minerals, and fresh whole fruit and fruit juices set the base for these tasty and healthy beverages. Their organic Hot Blends provides a new spin on coffee, green or chai tea, and hot chocolate;plus they offer probiotic fruit and yogurt Blends. Additionally, they feature organic steel-cut oatmeal prepared fresh every morning, all natural salads, wraps, sandwiches, and grab n' go specialties. They also offer healthy community support through fundraisers, special sales, and school lunch programs. Leashed, well mannered dogs are allowed at their outside dining area.

**Lazy Dog Restaurant & Bar**
278 Los Cerritos Center
Cerritos CA
562-402-6644
lazydogrestaurants.com/dogs/info
Known for it's dog-friendly patio, the Lazy Dog offers your dog a

complimentary bowl of water, and a menu consisting of grilled hamburger patty, chicken breast or brown rice. They just ask that you respect their common sense rules while your dog is dining there. This is as dog-friendly as dining gets. For the humans in your party there is hamburger, steak, salads and some great desserts.

**The Coffee Bean & Tea Leaf**
12550 Artesia Blvd
Cerritos CA
562-865-9713
coffeebean.com
The coffee here is sourced globally from family coffee farms to procure only the top of 1% of Arabica beans. They offer 30+ varieties of coffee;the beans are roasted in small batches daily for freshness, and they also offer 20 varieties of teas that are hand-blended by their tea master. Additionally, they offer a variety of tasty sweets, powders, extracts, sauces, gifts, and cards. Leashed, well mannered dogs are allowed at their outside dining area.

**The Coffee Bean & Tea Leaf**
300A N Glendale Avenue
Glendale CA
818-242-4074
coffeebean.com
The coffee here is sourced globally from family coffee farms to procure only the top of 1% of Arabica beans. They offer 30+ varieties of coffee;the beans are roasted in small batches daily for freshness, and they also offer 20 varieties of teas that are hand-blended by their tea master. Additionally, they offer a variety of tasty sweets, powders, extracts, sauces, gifts, and cards. Leashed, well mannered dogs are allowed at their outside dining area.

**The Coffee Bean & Tea Leaf**
1500 Canada Blvd, Unit C
Glendale CA
818-956-8303
coffeebean.com

The coffee here is sourced globally from family coffee farms to procure only the top of 1% of Arabica beans. They offer 30+ varieties of coffee;the beans are roasted in small batches daily for freshness, and they also offer 20 varieties of teas that are hand-blended by their tea master. Additionally, they offer a variety of tasty sweets, powders, extracts, sauces, gifts, and cards. Leashed, well mannered dogs are allowed at their outside dining area.

**The Coffee Bean & Tea Leaf**
763 Americana Way
Glendale CA
818-242-6123
coffeebean.com
The coffee here is sourced globally from family coffee farms to procure only the top of 1% of Arabica beans. They offer 30+ varieties of coffee;the beans are roasted in small batches daily for freshness, and they also offer 20 varieties of teas that are hand-blended by their tea master. Additionally, they offer a variety of tasty sweets, powders, extracts, sauces, gifts, and cards. Leashed, well mannered dogs are allowed at their outside dining area.

**Picasso's Cafe Bakery and Catering Co**
6070 N. Irwindale Ave.
Irwindale CA
626-969-6100
picassoscafe.com
The owners of this restaurant are very dog-friendly. This restaurant was one of the sponsors in the spcaLA's 1999 Petelethon. Your pup is welcome to dine with you at the outdoor tables. They serve a full breakfast and lunch. Also enjoy some great desserts.

**Pinkberry**
712 Foothill Blvd
La Canada CA
818-952-0128
Guilt free, healthy frozen yogurt is the specialty of this shop;it's active and live cultures have earned it the seal of approval from the National Yogurt

Association, and many of the toppings are also all natural and organic. Additionally, they provide a venue for fundraising events. Leashed, friendly dogs are allowed at their outside dining area.

**Baja Fresh Mexican Grill**
2637 Foothill Blvd
La Crescenta CA
818-541-0568
bajafresh.com
This Mexican restaurant is open for lunch and dinner. They use fresh ingredients and making their salsa and beans daily. Some of the items on their menu include Enchiladas, Burritos, Tacos Salads, Quesadillas, Nachos, Chicken, Steak and more. Well-behaved leashed dogs are allowed at the outdoor tables.

**Jeremy's**
3009 Honolulu Avenue
La Crescenta CA
818-248-7772
This breakfast and lunch eatery offers a side of value along with a variety of all American favorites. They are open Monday to Friday from 6 am until 8 pm;Saturday from 6 am until 2 pm, and on Sunday from 7 am until 2 pm. (The last orders are taken a 1/2 hour before closing.) Friendly, leashed dogs are allowed at their outside dining area and water and a doggy biscuit await them.

**Peach Cafe**
141 E Colorado Blvd
Monrovia CA
626-599-9092
thepeachcafe.com/
Freshly prepared foods with quality ingredients, espressos and smoothies, homemade pastries, and a unique artsy ambiance are some of the offerings of this cafe and coffee bar. Leashed, well mannered dogs are welcome at their outer tables.

**The Coffee Bean & Tea Leaf**
102 S Myrtle Avenue
Monrovia CA
626-301-0317

coffeebean.com
The coffee here is sourced globally from family coffee farms to procure only the top of 1% of Arabica beans. They offer 30+ varieties of coffee;the beans are roasted in small batches daily for freshness, and they also offer 20 varieties of teas that are hand-blended by their tea master. Additionally, they offer a variety of tasty sweets, powders, extracts, sauces, gifts, and cards. Leashed, well mannered dogs are allowed at their outside dining area.

**The Coffee Bean & Tea Leaf**
702 E Huntington Drive
Monrovia CA
626-657-1404
coffeebean.com
The coffee here is sourced globally from family coffee farms to procure only the top of 1% of Arabica beans. They offer 30+ varieties of coffee;the beans are roasted in small batches daily for freshness, and they also offer 20 varieties of teas that are hand-blended by their tea master. Additionally, they offer a variety of tasty sweets, powders, extracts, sauces, gifts, and cards. Leashed, well mannered dogs are allowed at their outside dining area.

**All India Cafe**
39 S Fair Oaks Ave
Pasadena CA
626-440-0309
allindiacafe.com/
An eclectic selection of authentic sub-continent cuisine, home-cooked with natural ingredients is the specialty at this eatery. Leashed dogs are allowed at their outside dining area.

**Baja Fresh Mexican Grill**
899 E. Del Mar
Pasadena CA
626-792-0446
bajafresh.com
This Mexican restaurant is open for lunch and dinner. They use fresh ingredients and making their salsa and beans

daily. Some of the items on their menu include Enchiladas, Burritos, Tacos Salads, Quesadillas, Nachos, Chicken, Steak and more. Well-behaved leashed dogs are allowed at the outdoor tables.

**Chipotle**
246 S Lake Avenue
Pasadena CA
626-229-9173
chipotle.com
Specializing in organic, natural and unprocessed food, this Mexican Eatery offers fajita burritos, tacos, salads, and salsas. Dogs are allowed at the outdoor tables but you will need to order your food inside the restaurant and dogs must remain outside.

**Chipotle**
3409 E Foothill Blvd
Pasadena CA
626-351-6017
chipotle.com
Specializing in organic, natural and unprocessed food, this Mexican Eatery offers fajita burritos, tacos, salads, and salsas. Dogs are allowed at the outdoor tables but you will need to order your food inside the restaurant and dogs must remain outside.

**Coffee Bean & Tea Leaf**
18 S Fair Oaks
Pasadena CA
626-449-5499
coffeebean.com
The coffee here is sourced globally from family coffee farms to procure only the top of 1% of Arabica beans. They offer 30+ varieties of coffee;the beans are roasted in small batches daily for freshness, and they also offer 20 varieties of teas that are hand-blended by their tea master. Additionally, they offer a variety of tasty sweets, powders, extracts, sauces, gifts, and cards. Leashed, well mannered dogs are allowed at their outside dining area.

**Il Fornaio**
24 W Union
Pasadena CA

626-683-9797
This Italian restaurant features fine dining, wines to compliment your meal from local wineries, and a bakery counter showcasing award-winning baked goods and branded products. Leashed, well mannered dogs are welcome at their outside dining area.

## Jones Coffee Roasters
693 S Raymond Avenue
Pasadena CA
626-564-9291
thebestcoffee.com/
This cafe serves coffee and pastries. Leashed dogs are allowed at the outdoor tables.

## Kabuki Japanese Restaurant
88 W. Colorado Blvd.
Pasadena CA
626-568-9310
kabukirestaurants.com/home.as
p
You are welcome to dine with your dog at the outdoor tables.

## Lucky Baldwins Trappiste
1770 E Colorado Blvd
Pasadena CA
626-844-0447
luckybaldwins.com/
In addition to 63 crafted beers on tap, this pub also features a unique variety of brews in their tap and bottled beers. They also feature a full day's menu of traditional British food, a family friendly atmosphere, and a number of special events throughout the year. Leashed, well mannered dogs are allowed at their outside dining area.

## Mi Piace
25 E Colorado Blvd
Pasadena CA
626-795-3131
mipiace.com/
Some of the offerings here include a variety of appetizers, salads, pastas, seafood, pizzas, exotic weekly specials, a martini lounge, and alfresco dining. Leashed, well mannered dogs are welcome at their outside tables.

## The Coffee Bean & Tea Leaf
415 S Lake Avenue, Suite 108

Pasadena CA
626-744-9370
coffeebean.com
The coffee here is sourced globally from family coffee farms to procure only the top of 1% of Arabica beans. They offer 30+ varieties of coffee;the beans are roasted in small batches daily for freshness, and they also offer 20 varieties of teas that are hand-blended by their tea master. Additionally, they offer a variety of tasty sweets, powders, extracts, sauces, gifts, and cards. Leashed, well mannered dogs are allowed at their outside dining area.

## Fair Oaks Pharmacy and Soda Fountain
1526 Mission St
South Pasadena CA
626-799-1414
fairoakspharmacy.net/index2.ht
ml
Stop in for a nostalgia fix and some sandwiches, tasty treats or beverages at this old fashioned soda fountain. Leashed, well mannered dogs are welcome at their outside tables.

## The Coffee Bean & Tea Leaf
700 S Fair Oaks, #A
South Pasadena CA
626-403-2141
coffeebean.com
The coffee here is sourced globally from family coffee farms to procure only the top of 1% of Arabica beans. They offer 30+ varieties of coffee;the beans are roasted in small batches daily for freshness, and they also offer 20 varieties of teas that are hand-blended by their tea master. Additionally, they offer a variety of tasty sweets, powders, extracts, sauces, gifts, and cards. Leashed, well mannered dogs are allowed at their outside dining area.

## Chipolte
143 N Barranca # A
West Covina CA
626-967-6680
chipotle.com

Specializing in organic, natural and unprocessed food, this Mexican Eatery offers fajita burritos, tacos, salads, and salsas. Dogs are allowed at the outdoor tables but you will need to order your food inside the restaurant and dogs must remain outside.

## Lazy Dog Restaurant & Bar
1440 Plaza Drive
West Covina CA
626-480-8603
lazydogrestaurants.com/dogs/inf
o
Known for it's dog-friendly patio, the Lazy Dog offers your dog a complimentary bowl of water, and a menu consisting of grilled hamburger patty, chicken breast or brown rice. They just ask that you respect their common sense rules while your dog is dining there. This is as dog-friendly as dining gets. For the humans in your party there is hamburger, steak, salads and some great desserts.

## Baja Fresh Mexican Grill
13582 Whittier Blvd
Whittier CA
562-464-5900
bajafresh.com
This Mexican restaurant is open for lunch and dinner. They use fresh ingredients and making their salsa and beans daily. Some of the items on their menu include Enchiladas, Burritos, Tacos Salads, Quesadillas, Nachos, Chicken, Steak and more. Well-behaved leashed dogs are allowed at the outdoor tables.

## The Coffee Bean & Tea Leaf
7201 Greenleaf Avenue
Whittier CA
562-696-8452
coffeebean.com
The coffee here is sourced globally from family coffee farms to procure only the top of 1% of Arabica beans. They offer 30+ varieties of coffee;the beans are roasted in small batches daily for freshness, and they also offer 20 varieties of teas that are hand-blended by their tea master. Additionally, they offer a

variety of tasty sweets, powders, extracts, sauces, gifts, and cards. Leashed, well mannered dogs are allowed at their outside dining area.

## Pet-Friendly Shopping Centers
### The Americana at Brand
889 Americana Way
Glendale CA
877-897-2097
americanaatbrand.com/
In addition to numerous shops and services, this mall also offers summer concerts under the stars. Dogs are allowed in the common areas of the mall; they must be leashed and under their owner's control at all times. Dogs are not allowed on the grassy areas by they playground or the fountain in the middle of the mall.

### Old Town Pasadena
100W-100E Colorado Blvd.
Pasadena CA

oldpasadena.com/oldpas/
Old Town Pasadena is Pasadena's premier shopping and dining district. This area is a nice place to walk around with your pup. While dogs are not allowed inside the stores, they can sit at one of the many dog-friendly outdoor cafes and dine with you (see our restaurant listings). A major portion of the popular annual Rose Parade takes place on this part of Colorado Boulevard. The shopping area is the 100 West to 100 East blocks of Colorado Blvd., and between Marengo & Pasadena Avenues.

## Pet-Friendly Stores
### PetSmart Pet Store
2568 W Commonwealth Ave
Alhambra CA
626-284-3390
Your licensed and well-behaved leashed dog is allowed in the store.

### Petco Pet Store - Cerritos
12601 Towne Center Dr.
Cerritos CA
562-924-3018
Your licensed and well-behaved leashed dog is allowed in the store.

### Anthropologie
519 Americana Way
Glendale CA
818-502-2058
Items of distinction can be found for all ages and in all departments of this unique shop. Carefully selected to add to the enjoyment of the shopping experience, they carry fine clothing, amazing accessories, jewelry, hobby and leisure items, and a full line of bright and useful items for the home, garden, and office. Leashed, well behaved dogs are allowed in the store.

### Petco Pet Store - Glendale
231 North Glendale Ave.
Glendale CA
818-548-0411
Your licensed and well-behaved leashed dog is allowed in the store.

### Urban Outfitters
260 Americana Way
Glendale CA
818-545-9208
In addition to a large inventory of indoor and outdoor apparel for men and women, this major department store also carries vintage wear, designer brands, and a variety of accessories for all types of active lifestyles. They also carry shoes, furnishings, home decor, cameras, electronics, novelty items and more. Leashed, well mannered dogs are allowed in the store.

### Petco Pet Store - La Canada
475 Foothill Blvd
La Canada CA
818-790-3165
Your licensed and well-behaved leashed dog is allowed in the store.

### Anthropologie
340 S. Lake Avenue

Pasadena CA
626-796-5120
Items of distinction can be found for all ages and in all departments of this unique shop. Carefully selected to add to the enjoyment of the shopping experience, they carry fine clothing, amazing accessories, jewelry, hobby and leisure items, and a full line of bright and useful items for the home, garden, and office. Leashed, well behaved dogs are allowed in the store.

### Centinela Feed and Supplies
3120 E Colorado Blvd
Pasadena CA
626-795-9858
centinelafeed.com
Specializing in natural, holistic, and raw pet foods, this pet supply store also provides healthy treats, quality supplements, pet care supplies, low-cost vaccination clinics, frequent in-store events, and a knowledgeable staff. Leashed pets are welcome.

### Century Books of Pasadena
1039 East Green Street
Pasadena CA
626-796-1703
facebook.com/centurybookshop
Well-behaved, leashed dogs are allowed in this cozy bookstore!

### Crate and Barrel
75 W. Colorado Blvd
Pasadena CA
626-683-8000
crateandbarrel.com
This store offers fine products from around the world for in and around the home that include items for outdoor living, indoor furnishings and decorating, dining and entertaining, kitchen and food service, and gourmet food and beverages. They also have accessories for pets, bed and bath items, and organizing and storage units. Leashed, friendly dogs are welcome in the store; they must be under their owner's control at all times.

### Orvis Company Store
345 S Lake Avenue, Suite #102
Pasadena CA

626-356-8000
orvis.com
This comprehensive outfitters store offers a wide array of sporting goods and services, clothing and accessories for all types of active lifestyles, quality products for home and pets, gifts and travel items, and much more. Well mannered dogs are welcome in the store; they must be leashed and under their owner's control at all times.

**PetSmart Pet Store**
3347 E Foothill Blvd
Pasadena CA
626-351-8434
Your licensed and well-behaved leashed dog is allowed in the store.

**Petco Pet Store - Pasadena - South**
845 South Arroyo Pkwy
Pasadena CA
626-577-2600
Your licensed and well-behaved leashed dog is allowed in the store.

**Three Dog Bakery**
36 W Colorado Blvd #3
Pasadena CA
626-440-0443
threedogla.com
Three Dog Bakery provides cookies and snacks for your dog as well as some boutique items. You well-behaved, leashed dog is welcome.

**Urban Outfitters**
139 W Colorado Blvd
Pasadena CA
626-449-1818
In addition to a large inventory of indoor and outdoor apparel for men and women, this major department store also carries vintage wear, designer brands, and a variety of accessories for all types of active lifestyles. They also carry shoes, furnishings, home decor, cameras, electronics, novelty items and more. Leashed, well mannered dogs are allowed in the store.

**Petco Pet Store - San Gabriel**
7262 North Rosemead Blvd

San Gabriel CA
626-287-9847
Your licensed and well-behaved leashed dog is allowed in the store.

**Petco Pet Store - West Covina**
1050 West Covina Pkwy
West Covina CA
626-813-9040
Your licensed and well-behaved leashed dog is allowed in the store.

**Petco Pet Store - Whittier**
13420 Whittier Blvd
Whittier CA
562-907-2300
Your licensed and well-behaved leashed dog is allowed in the store.

## Off-Leash Dog Parks
**Arcadia Dog Park**
Second Avenue and Colorado Blvd
Arcadia CA
626-574-5400
The fenced dog park is located in Eisenhower Park in Arcadia. The park is open from 7 am to 10 pm daily. On even numbered days the park is reserved for small dogs. On odd numbered days it is open to large dogs. The park is near I-210 at the Santa Anita Ave exit. Go north on Santa Anita, turn right on E Foothill and go right on 2nd Ave to the park.

**La Crescenta Dog Park**
3901 Dunsmore Avenue
La Crescenta CA
818-249-5940
Open daily from 7 am until sunset, this 1 acre doggy play area is located in the Crescenta Valley Park and offers benches, drinking water, and shade trees. Dogs must be healthy, sociable, current on all vaccinations and license with tags on collar, and under their owner's control at all times. Owners must clean up after their pets, and keep them leashed when not in designated off-lead areas.

**Alice Frost Kennedy Off-Leash Dog Area**
3026 East Orange Grove Blvd
Pasadena CA
626-744-4321
The dog park is located in Vina Vieja Park. It is open during daylight hours and is 2.5 acres and fenced. There is a large dog area and a small dog area. The dog park has a grass surface with no herbicides used. The park is maintained by the City of Pasadena and capital improvements are done by POOCH, a dog group in Pasadena. To get to the dog park from I-210 exit at Sierra Madre Blvd and head east. Turn right onto Orange Grove Blvd to the dog park.

## Dog-Friendly Parks
**Angeles National Forest**
701 N Santa Anita Ave
Arcadia CA
626-574-1613
fs.usda.gov/angeles
This national forest covers over 650,000 acres and is known as the backyard playground to the metropolitan area of Los Angeles. Elevations range from 1,200 to 10,064 feet. Please see our listings in this region for dog-friendly hikes and/or campgrounds.

**Deukemjian Wilderness Park**
5142 Dunsmore Avenue
Glendale CA
818-548-2000
Sitting on 700 acres of chaparral-covered slopes at the northernmost part of the city, this park has a variety of multi-use trails available for first time and experienced hikers, a year round stream, and great views. Dogs are allowed throughout the park and on the trails. Dogs must be under their owner's immediate control, leashed, and cleaned up after at all times.

**Santa Fe Dam Recreation Area**
15501 E. Arrow Highway
Irwindale CA

626-334-1065
This 836 acre park has a 70 acre lake which popular for sailing and fishing. The lake is stocked with bass, trout and catfish. Other park amenities include picnic areas and hiking and biking trails. Dogs are allowed on the hiking trails, but not in the lake. Pets must be leashed and people need to clean up after their pet.

**Brookside Park**
360 N Arroyo Blvd
Pasadena CA
626-744-4386
A 61.1 acre park, and the city's largest fully maintained park, is located just south of the Rose Bowl Stadium, and offers a variety of recreational opportunities. Some of the park's features/amenities include lighted gaming fields, picnic areas-most with barbecue pits, drinking fountains, playground areas, and restrooms. Dogs of all sizes are allowed. They must be well mannered, and leashed and cleaned up after at all times.

**Eaton Canyon Nature Center**
1750 N Altadena Drive
Pasadena CA
626-398-5420
ecnca.org/
This 190 acre day-use park is considered to be a zoological, botanical, and geological wonderland, and there are also a variety of recreational opportunities available. Some of the features/amenities include a nature center/gift shop, hiking trails, and restrooms. Dogs of all sizes are allowed for no additional fee. Dogs must be under their owner's control at all times, and be leashed and cleaned up after.

**Hahamongna Watershed**
Oak Grove Drive
Pasadena CA

The Hahamongna Watershed Park (formerly Oak Grove Park) allows leashed dogs on the trails and on the world's first disc golf course. During the summer

months, there can be rattlesnakes here, so make sure your dog stays leashed. You'll also want to keep your pup away from the ground squirrels. Some squirrels in this mountain range have been known to carry rabies. Aside from being a very popular disc golf course, this park is also very popular with bird watchers. To get there from Hwy 210, take the Berkshire Ave. exit and head east. Turn left onto Oak Grove Drive and the park will be on the right. To get to one of the trails, follow the signs to the disc golf course. After going downhill, turn right and the trail begins.

**Whittier Narrows Nature Center**
1000 N. Durfee Ave.
South El Monte CA
626-575-5523
This park has over 200 acres of natural woodland and includes four lakes which offer a winter sanctuary for migrating waterfowl. Dogs are allowed on the trails, but not in the water. Pets must be leashed and please clean up after them.

**Whittier Narrows Recreation Area**
823 Lexinton-Gallatin Road
South El Monte CA
310-589-3200
This 1,400 acre day use park offers a wide variety of land and water recreational opportunities, in addition to hosting carnivals, festivals, and dog shows. Some of the features/amenities include fishing lakes, comfort stations, gaming courts/fields, playgrounds, picnicking areas, and hiking and multi-use trails. Dogs are allowed throughout the park and on the trails. Dogs must be under their owner's immediate control, leashed, and cleaned up after at all times.

**Day Kennels**
**PetsHotel by PetsMart Day**

Kennel
3347 E. Foothill Blvd.
Pasadena CA
626-351-8434
petsmart.com/PETsHOTEL/
This PetSmart pet store offers doggy day camp only. You may drop off and pick up your dog during the hours the store is open seven days a week. Dogs must have proof of current rabies, DPP and Bordatella vaccinations.

**PetsHotel by PetsMart Day Kennel**
15618 Whittwood Lane
Whittier CA
562-902-1394
petsmart.com/PETsHOTEL/
This PetSmart pet store offers day camp, day care and overnight care. You can drop off and pick up your dog during the hours of 7 am - 7 pm M-S, Sunday 7 am - 6 pm. Dogs are required to have current proof of rabies, DPP and bordatella vaccinations.

**Emergency Veterinarians**
**Emergency Pet Clinic**
3254 Santa Anita Ave
El Monte CA
626-579-4550
Monday - Friday 6 pm to 8 am, Noon Saturday to 8 am Monday.

**Animal Emergency Clinic**
831 Milford St
Glendale CA
818-247-3973
Mon - Tues 8 am - 7 pm. Wed - Fri 8 am - 6 pm, Sat 8 am - 12 noon, Closed Sunday.

**Crossroads Animal Emergency Hospital**
11057 Rosecrans Ave
Norwalk CA
562-863-2522
Monday - Thursday 6 pm to 8 am, Friday 6 pm to 8 am Monday.

**Animal Emergency Clinic**
2121 E Foothill Blvd
Pasadena CA

626-564-0704
Monday - Friday 6 pm - 8 am.
Saturday 12 noon - Monday 8
am.

## Rescue Organizations
**Basset Hound Rescue
Southern California**
P.O. Box 88
Whittier CA
805-524-9353
bhrsc.info
To offer sanctuary, healing and placement into a new family to distressed, abandoned, injured or homeless Hounds. We work to raise funds to save as many Hounds as possible and constantly strive to grow our network of volunteers and foster homes.

## Pearblossom

## Dog-Friendly Parks
**Devil's Punchbowl Natural Area**
28000 Devil's Punchbowl Road
Pearblossom CA
661-944-2743
devils-punchbowl.com/
This 1,310 acre nature park offers unusual rock formations and is just one mile away from the famous San Andreas fault. The park elevation starts at 4,200 feet and climbs up to 6,500 feet. There are miles of trails rated easy to strenuous. The visitor center is open daily from 9am to 4pm. There is no charge for parking. Dogs must be on leash and please clean up after them.

## Perris

## Dog-Friendly Hotels
**Best Western Plus Diamond Valley Inn**
3510 West Florida Avenue

Hemet CA
951-658-2281 (800-780-7234)
Dogs are welcome at this hotel.

**Quality Inn Hemet**
1201 West Florida Avenue
Hemet CA
951-766-1902 (877-424-6423)
Hotel is located in the heart of beautiful downtown Hemet between San Diego and Palm Springs.

Dogs up to 20 pounds are allowed. Dogs are allowed for a pet fee of $20.00 per pet per night.

**Red Lion Inn & Suites Perris**
480 South Redlands Avenue
Perris CA
951-943-5577 (877-698-9593)
Dogs of all sizes are allowed. Dogs are allowed for a nightly pet fee.

## Dog-Friendly Attractions
**Orange Empire Railway Museum**
2201 South A Street
Perris CA
951-657-2605
oerm.org/
Home to the West's largest collection of railway locomotives, streetcars, freight/passenger cars, interurban electric cars, buildings, and other objects dating from the 1870's, this museum also educates the public of the rail history and offers a variety of interactive programs. You can ride or drive a locomotive, have a special caboose birthday party, visit the museum store, picnic, or take self-guided or guided tours. Dogs of all sizes are welcome. Dogs are allowed throughout the grounds; they are not allowed in the gift shop. Dogs must be well mannered, leashed, and cleaned up after.

## Pet-Friendly Stores
**PetSmart Pet Store**

2771 Florida Ave W
Hemet CA
951-925-8400
Your licensed and well-behaved leashed dog is allowed in the store.

**Petco Pet Store - Hemet**
2545 West Florida Ave.
Hemet CA
951-652-3437
Your licensed and well-behaved leashed dog is allowed in the store.

## Dog-Friendly Parks
**Lake Perris State Recreation Area**
off Cajalco Expressway
Lakeview CA
909-657-0676
While dogs are not allowed in the lake or within 100 feet of the water, they are allowed on miles of trails including the bike trail that loops around the lake. Pets must be leashed and please clean up after them. Pets are also allowed in the campgrounds. The park is located 11 miles south of Riverside via Highway 60 or Interstate 215.

**Harford Springs Reserve**
Gavilan Road
Perris CA
909-684-7032
This 325 acre park offer hiking and equestrian trails. The park is located about 7 miles west of Perris, 2 miles south of Cajalco Road on Gavilan Road. Dogs must be leashed and please clean up after them.

## Philo

## Dog-Friendly Wineries and Vineyards
**Christine Woods Vineyards**
3155 H 128
Philo CA
707-895-2115
Specializing in Pinot Noir, this

225

winery is one of the few that grow their own grapes and make all their wines on site from their own grapes. Dogs are allowed on the grounds but not in the tasting room. Dogs must be well behaved, leashed, and cleaned up after at all times.

**Esterlina Vineyards**
1200 Holmes Ranch Road
Philo CA
707-895-2920
esterlinavineyards.com./
This family owned boutique winery features a variety of fine handcrafted wines. Tastings are by appointment only. Dogs are allowed on the grounds; they are not allowed in the tasting room. Dogs must be leashed and under their owner's control at all times.

**Handley Cellars**
3151 H 128
Philo CA
707-895-3876
This winery specializes in Pinot Noir, Chardonnay, and Gewurztraminer wines, and feature a beautiful fenced garden courtyard by their tasting room for those who also might like to picnic. Dogs are welcome around the grounds and in the courtyard where they are even met with water and treats. Dogs must be friendly, well mannered, and leashed and cleaned up after at all times.

**Husch Vineyards**
4400 H 128
Philo CA
1-800-55-HUSCH (555-8724)
huschvineyards.com/
This small, family owned and operated winery produces 18 different wines plus some specialty wines. The converted 1800's pony barn works well for the tasting room, and they offer a picnic area on the deck or at a table under one of the many grape arbors. Dogs are welcome on the grounds and picnic areas, just not in the buildings. Dogs must be well behaved, leashed, and cleaned up after.

**Navarro Vineyards**
5601 H 128
Philo CA
800-537-9463
navarrowine.com/main.php
This small family owned and operated winery specializes in a variety of fine wines and non-alcoholic grape juices, and most of their products are sold directly. Well mannered hound and human-friendly leashed dogs are allowed on the grounds and in the tasting room - where happy pooches will find a bowl of water and treats. There are also picnic tables on the grounds and a fenced-in doggy play area.

**Toulouse Vineyards**
800 H 128
Philo CA
707-895-2828
toulousevineyards.com
Although specializing in Pinots, this winery also produces a Gewrztraminer and a Riesling. The vineyard is set in the heart of the Anderson Valley only 12 miles from the Ocean. Leashed dogs are allowed on the grounds, and "polite" dogs are even allowed in the tasting room. Dogs must be hound and human friendly.

## Pioneertown

### Dog-Friendly Attractions
**Pioneertown**
Pioneertown Road
Pioneertown CA
760-964-6549
pioneertown.com/f-index.htm
Because the town was also built as a movie set to be a complete old west town, numerous Western stars and movie star greats of the past spent a lot of time here. The movie sets that were used in filming also provided homes for the actors and crew and with an emphasis placed on experiencing the old west, this place is like stepping back to

the 1800's. The town has its own pioneer posse, and offers seasonal old west reenactments, dozens of shops and exhibits to explore, western cooking, a motel that accepts dogs, and a lot more. Dogs are welcome all around town, and they may even end up with their picture on the website. They are not allowed in buildings. Dogs must be leashed at all times and cleaned up after. Please carry supplies.

## Piru

### Dog-Friendly Attractions
**Lake Piru Marina**
4780 Piru Canyon Road
Piru CA
805-521-1231
lake-piru.org/
While dogs are not allowed in the water at Lake Piru, they are allowed on a boat on the water. This marina rents pontoon boats starting at $65 for 4 hours. Well-behaved dogs are allowed on the boats.

## Placerville - Highway 50 Corridor

### Dog-Friendly Hotels
**Quality Inn & Suites Cameron Park**
3361 Coach Lane
Cameron Park CA
530-677-2203 (877-424-6423)
Located just off Hwy 50 in Cameron Park, close to all North Central California attractions.

Dogs up to 100 pounds are allowed. Dogs are allowed for a pet fee of $15.00 per pet per night. Three or more dogs may be allowed.

**Best Western Plus Placerville**

**Inn**
6850 Greenleaf Drive
Placerville CA
530-622-9100 (800-780-7234)
Dogs up to 80 pounds are
allowed. There is a $20 per day
pet fee up to $100 for the week.
Up to two dogs are allowed per
room.

**Best Western Stagecoach Inn**
5940 Pony Express Trail
Pollock Pines CA
530-644-2029 (800-780-7234)
Small dogs up to 20 pounds are
allowed. There is a $10 per pet
per night pet fee. Up to one dog
is allowed per room.

## Accommodations
**Fleming Jones Homestead
B&B**
3170 Newtown Road
Placerville CA
530-344-0943
robinsnestranch.com
This historic homestead is a
B&B at a working miniature
horse ranch. It is located 5
minutes from Placerville and
near the Apple Hill farms that
are open to the public each fall.
Well-behaved dogs are
welcome in the Woodshed and
Bunkhouse rooms of the B&B.
There is a $10 per day per dog.
Dogs may not be left unattended
and guests are responsible for
any damages caused by their
pets.

## Dog-Friendly Attractions
**Argyres Orchard**
4220 N. Canyon Rd.
Camino CA
530-644-3862
Located in Apple Hill, this ranch
is open mid-September through
October. Leashed dogs are
allowed outside. You can pick
your own apples and grapes at
this ranch.

**Bodhaine Ranch**
2315 Cable Road
Camino CA
530-644-1686
bodhaineranch.com/

This apple hill farm is a
California Certified Organic
Grower, and their bake shop
offers a variety of tasty baked
treats, hearty meals, and
gourmet coffees. There are
picnic tables on the grounds
and on the terrace for outside
dining. They also host an
organic farmer's market every
weekend from June to
Christmas, and feature arts
and crafts from local artisans.
Dogs of all sizes are welcome.
They must be leashed and
cleaned up after at all times.

**Bolster's Hilltop Ranch**
2000 Larsen Drive
Camino CA
530-644-2230
bolsters.net
Located in Apple Hill, this
ranch is open daily June
through the beginning of
December. Leashed dogs are
allowed outside. This ranch
offers u-pick blueberries from
June through August including
a Blueberry Festival in June
(blueberry plants available), u-
pick apples on the weekends
from September to November,
outdoor arts & crafts booths,
barbecue, picnic area,
pumpkins, Christmas trees and
more.

**Celtic Gardens Organic Farm**

4221 North Canyon Road
Camino CA
530-647-0689
This organic farm sells mostly
wholesale (produce only-no pie
shop) and are open only a
short time to the public before
they usually sell out of product.
Table grapes become available
sometime in August when they
partially open; then by
September they are open for
about a month before they
close until the next season.
Your well behaved, leashed
dog is allowed to explore the
farm with you. Dogs must be
cleaned up after at all times.

**Denver Dan's**
4344 Bumblebee Ln.
Camino CA

530-644-6881
Located in Apple Hill, this ranch
is open during the fall season,
September through mid-
December. They are closed on
Tuesdays and only open Friday,
Saturday and Sunday from late
November through December.
Leashed dogs are allowed
outside. This ranch offers a
bake shop, candy & caramel
apples, gift shop, picnic area
and u-pick apples.

**Grandpa's Cellar**
2360 Cable Rd.
Camino CA
530-644-2153
Located in Apple Hill, this ranch
is open daily during the fall
season, September through
mid-December. Leashed dogs
are allowed outside. The owners
have an old black lab on the
premises. This ranch offers a
bake shop, country store, nature
trail, and on the weekends only,
an outdoor craft fair and
barbecue.

**Honey Bear Ranch**
2826 Barkley Rd.
Camino CA
530-644-3934
Located in Apple Hill, this ranch
is open during the fall season,
September through December.
Open daily September through
October, and weekends only
November through mid-
December). Leashed dogs are
allowed outside and you need to
clean up after them. This ranch
offers a restaurant with outdoor
dining, bake shop, fudge
kitchen, general store with
antiques & crafts, and a picnic
area with outdoor arts & crafts
booths and live music.

**Kids, Inc.**
3245 N. Canyon Rd.
Camino CA
530-622-0084
kidsincapples.com
Located in Apple Hill, this ranch
is open during the fall season.
Open all week during
September and October and
open weekends only in
November through mid-
December. Leashed dogs are

allowed outside. This ranch offers a bake shop, gift shop, antiques, grassy picnic area, farm animals, nature trail, family activities, apples, pumpkins and Christmas trees.

**Mother Lode Orchards**
4341 N. Canyon Rd.
Camino CA
530-644-5101
motherlodeorchards.com/
Located in Apple Hill, this ranch is open during the fall season, September through December. Open weekends only in November through mid-December. Leashed dogs are allowed outside including at the picnic tables. This ranch offers over 30 varieties of fruit and vegetables, pumpkins and Christmas trees. The owner also has a dog on the premises.

**O'Hallorans Apple Trail Ranch**

2261 Cable Rd.
Camino CA
530-644-3389
Located in Apple Hill, this ranch is open during the fall season (September through mid-December). Leashed dogs are allowed outside. This ranch offers a fruit store, handmade crafts, nature trail, picnic area, u-pick pumpkin patch, and cut & choose Christmas trees.

**Plubell's Family Orchard**
1800 Larsen Dr.
Camino CA
530-647-0613
Located in Apple Hill, this ranch is open during the fall season, September through mid-November. Leashed dogs are allowed outside. This ranch offers fresh produce, a grassy picnic area, nature walk, pumpkin patch and on weekends a barbecue, miniature horse & wagon rides and more.

**Summerfield Berry Farm**
4455 Pony Express Trail
Camino CA
530-647-2833
jps.net/mountain/sumrorder.htm
Located in Apple Hill, this ranch is open mid-June through mid-

November on Fridays, Saturdays and Sundays. Leashed dogs are allowed in the u-pick fruit area and picnic area. You can pick fresh raspberries and blackberries.

**Gold Country Carriages**
Hwy 49
Coloma CA
530-622-6111
windjammer.net/coloma/concar.htm
Dogs and families are welcome on this horse and carriage ride located at Marshall Gold Discovery State Park in Coloma on Hwy 49 (see Attractions for more information about the park). They offer tours of historic Coloma. Dogs need to stay on the floor of the carriage, not on the seat.

**Marshall Gold Discovery State Park**
Hwy 49
Coloma CA
530-622-3470
windjammer.net/coloma/
This is the place where James W. Marshall found some shining flecks of gold in the tailrace of a sawmill he was building for himself and John Sutter in 1848. This began the famous Gold Rush era. The park has a replica of the sawmill and a number of historic buildings. Gold Country Carriage operates frequently on Hwy 49 at this park and dogs are welcome to join their family on this horse and carriage ride (see Attractions). Dogs on leash are welcome at several trails near the river. They are allowed in the picnic areas, but not allowed in the hiking trails across the street from the river side. Throughout the year the park has many special events, and dogs are welcome at most of the outdoor events. The park is located in Coloma on Highway 49 between Placerville and Auburn. It is open year round from 8am to sunset. There is a minimal fee for parking and for dogs.

**Abel's Apple Acres**

2345 Carson Rd.
Placerville CA
530-626-0138
Located in Apple Hill, this ranch is open daily, September through Christmas Eve. Leashed dogs are allowed outside. This ranch offers a bake shop, fudge, homemade caramel, barbecue, fresh apples, gift store, outdoor arts & crafts booths, pony & horse rides, duck pond, picnic area, hay maze & hay rides, and pumpkin patch.

**Apple Creek Ranch**
2979 Carson Rd.
Placerville CA
530-644-5073
Located in Apple Hill, this ranch is open during apple season, usually mid-September through October. Leashed dogs are allowed outside. This ranch offer fresh apples.

**Boa Vista Orchards**
2952 Carson Rd.
Placerville CA
530-622-5522
boavista.com/
This ranch is open year round (closed on Christmas Day). Dogs are not allowed in the store, but are allowed at the picnic tables. Dogs must be leashed. At the tables, you and your pooch can enjoy goodies from their bakery, like a fresh apple pie with ice cream or try their barbecue sandwiches on the weekends. They also have outdoor arts and crafts booths during the fall, on the weekends.

**High Hill Ranch**
2901 High Hill Rd.
Placerville CA
530-644-1973
Located in Apple Hill, this ranch is open daily during the fall season (September through December). Leashed dogs are allowed outside. They offer a bake shop (with lunch on the weekends), a cider mill, wine tasting, outdoor arts & crafts booths, a picnic area overlooking the Sierra Nevada mountains, trout fishing, pony

rides (weekends only), a fudge shop and a farm shop including fresh apples and produce, apple butter, dried fruits, gift packs and more.

### Hooverville Orchards
1100 Wallace Rd.
Placerville CA
530-622-2155
Open daily year-round, this orchard offers peaches, nectarines, plums, apricots, cherries, apples, avocados, pumpkins, vegetables and more. They also have a bake shop and a picnic area. Leashed dogs are allowed at the picnic area.

### Harris Tree Farm
2640 Blair Road
Pollock Pines CA
530-644-2194
applehill.com/harris.htm
Harris Tree Farm features 30 acres of Christmas trees and fruit orchard, plus a variety of fruits and home-made goodies. Come for a nature walk, picnic in the orchard, fruit pies or choose and cut your Christmas Tree. Your leashed dog is welcome here. They are open every year from August through December 24. During these months, the farm is open daily from 8:30am to 4-4:30pm. To get there, take Hwy 50 approximately 1 hour east of Sacramento to the town of Pollock Pines. Take the first Pollock Pines exit which is the Cedar Grove Exit and turn left on this street. At the Pony Express Trail Road turn right. Then turn left onto Blair Rd. Go approximately 1 mile and the Harris Tree Farm will be on the left.

## Outdoor Restaurants
### Mountain Mike's Pizza
3600 Carson Rd #C
Camino CA
530-644-6000
mountainmikespizza.com/
This pizzeria will allow dogs at their outside seating area.

### Argonaut Cafe
Hwy 49
Coloma CA
530-626-7345
Thanks to one of our readers who writes: Located in the Marshall Gold Discovery State Historic Park, The Argonaut serves up sandwiches, sodas, candy, pie, ice cream, coffee and more. They are open Wednesday to Saturday from 10 am until 4 pm and on Sunday they are open from 11 am until 4 pm. In spring and early summer they may also be open on Tuesdays. Leashed dogs are allowed at their outside tables.

### Sutter Center Market
378 Highway 49
Coloma CA
530-626-0849
In addition to selling gifts and food items, this market also has a deli where you can order pastries, sandwiches, burritos, ice cream and more. It is located near the dog-friendly Marshall Gold Discovery State Park (see Parks). Dogs are allowed at the outside tables.

### Bella Bru Coffee Company
3941 Park Drive #50
El Dorado Hills CA
916-933-5454
Dogs are allowed at the outdoor tables.

### Juice It Up
4355 Town Center Blvd, #113
El Dorado Hills CA
916-941-7140
Dogs are allowed at the outdoor tables.

### Mama Ann's Deli & Bakery
4359 Town Center Blvd #111
El Dorado Hills CA
916-939-1700
Dogs are allowed at the outdoor tables.

### Steve's Place Pizza & Pasta
3941 Park Drive, #100
El Dorado Hills CA
916-939-2100
Dogs are allowed at the outdoor tables.

### Jamba Juice
3987 Missouri Flat Road, Suite 300
Placerville CA
530-344-1675
jambajuice.com
All natural and organic ingredients, no high-fructose corn syrup, 0 grams trans fat, no artificial preservatives, a healthy helping of antioxidants, vitamins, and minerals, and fresh whole fruit and fruit juices set the base for these tasty and healthy beverages. Their organic Hot Blends provides a new spin on coffee, green or chai tea, and hot chocolate;plus they offer probiotic fruit and yogurt Blends. Additionally, they feature all natural salads, wraps, sandwiches, and grab n go specialties. They also offer healthy community support through fundraisers, special sales, and school lunch programs. Leashed, well mannered dogs are allowed at their outside dining area.

### Noah's Ark
535 Placerville Drive
Placerville CA
530-621-3663
This natural food market has outdoor tables where your well-behaved leashed dog is welcome. During the week they usually have pre-made vegan sandwiches and hot slices of organic veggie pizza. You will need to pick up your food inside and bring it to your outside table.

### Pizza Factory
4570 Pleasant Valley Road
Placerville CA
530-644-6043
pizzafactory.com/
This restaurant serves a variety of pizzas, pasta and salad. Well-behaved leashed dogs are allowed at the outdoor tables.

### Quiznos Sub
3967 Missouri Flat Road
Placerville CA
530-622-7878
Dogs are allowed at the outdoor tables.

## Teriyaki Junction
1216 Broadway
Placerville CA
530-295-1413
This Japanese restaurant serves bento dishes, teriyaki, and sushi. There are 5-6 tables outside where you can enjoy lunch or dinner. The tables are also shared by Baskin Robbins. To get there from Hwy 50 heading east, take the Broadway exit and turn left. Leashed dogs are allowed at the outdoor tables.

## The Cellar at Smith Flat House

2021 Smith Flat Road
Placerville CA
530-621-1003
The Cellar Restaurant offers Brick Oven pizza, steak and many other menu items. It has a large, dog-friendly patio during the summer, spring and fall. On some evenings they have live music as well.

## Burger Barn & Cafe
6404 Pony Express Trail
Pollock Pines CA
530-344-7167
burgerbarn.co/
This restaurant makes delicious burgers - plain, cheese, mushroom, bacon or more. They are also known for their milkshakes. Leashed dogs are allowed on the outside deck.

## Pet-Friendly Shopping Centers
### Placerville Downtown Area
Main Street & Hwy 49
Placerville CA

Placerville is a historic gold rush town that was established in the late 1840's. The town got its name from the placer gold deposits found in its hills and river beds. Today, Placerville serves as a hub for activities in the gold country including the Marshall Gold Discovery State Historic Park, Apple Hill farms, white water rafting on the American River, and the nearby wine country. You can still see this town's historic charm when you visit downtown Placerville. There you will find many shops, some of which may allow well-behaved dogs inside. You can also stroll down the sidewalks and see a number of buildings that were build over a hundred years ago. There are outdoor events held in historic downtown Placerville throughout the year and many of these events allow well-behaved leashed dogs.

## Pet-Friendly Stores
### Act 1 Video & Music
1345 Broadway
Placerville CA
530-621-1919
Your leashed, well-behaved dog is allowed inside the store. Here you can rent your favorite video or browse through their selection of music CDs. The store is located across the street from the Mountain Democrat Newspaper building.

### Mosquito Creek Outfitters
3000 Mosquito Road
Placerville CA
530-621-4500
mosquitocreekoutfitter.com/
This comprehensive outdoorsman store offers 1000's of sporting goods, apparel, and accessories for all ages and all types of active lifestyles. Leashed, friendly dogs are allowed in the store.

## Dog-Friendly Wineries and Vineyards
### Crystal Basin Cellars
3550 Carson Road
Camino CA
530 647-1767
crystalbasin.com
Located in the Sierra Nevada foothills, this winery offers a variety of fine wines as well as special wine events, release parties, and fun activities. Dogs are allowed on the grounds of the winery; they are not allowed in the tasting room. Dogs must be friendly with other pets (on site), leashed, and under their owner's control at all times.

### Stone's Throw Vineyard & Winery
3541 North Canyon Rd.
Camino CA
530-622-5100
Leashed dogs are allowed at the picnic area. The owners also have their own dogs on the premises. Their wine tasting is open Thursday through Sunday year-round (except major holidays).

### Venezio Winery & Vineyard
5821 Highway 49
Coloma CA
530-885-WINE
venezio.com/
Leashed and well-behaved dogs are allowed in the picnic area. This vineyard is nestled in the lovely Coloma Valley, 3.5 miles from the dog-friendly Marshall Gold Discovery State Park. From Placerville, take Hwy 49 north. Go past the town of Coloma, and the winery will be on the right.

### Charles B. Mitchell Vineyards
8221 Stoney Creek Road
Fair Play CA
800-704-WINE
charlesbmitchell.com/
Leashed dogs are allowed in the picnic area. The owners have an older dog that resides on the premises. From E-16, take Fair Play Rd. east. Turn right on Stoney Creek Rd. The winery will be on the left.

### Oakstone Winery
6440 Slug Gulch Rd.
Fair Play CA
530-620-5303
oakstone-winery.com/
Well-behaved, leashed dogs are allowed in both of their picnic areas. From E-16, turn onto Fair Play Rd. Turn right on Slug Gulch Rd.

### Perry Creek Vineyards
7400 Perry Creek Rd.
Fair Play CA
530-620-5175

perrycreek.com/
Well-behaved, leashed dogs are allowed at the picnic area. Their tasting room opens to the spacious outdoor verandah picnic area. From E-16, turn onto Fair Play Rd. Turn left onto Perry Creek Rd. Winery will be on the left.

**Latcham Vineyards**
2860 Omo Ranch Road
Mount Aukum CA
530-620-6642
latcham.com
Leashed dogs are allowed at the picnic tables. The winery is located on the north slope of a valley in Mt. Aukum. From E-16, take Omo Ranch Rd east. The winery will be on the right.

**Auriga Wine Cellars**
4520 Pleasant Valley Road
Placerville CA
530-621-0700
aurigawines.com/
A variety of fine wines made from grapes of the Sierra Foothills are featured at this vineyard. They are open on Friday, Saturday, and Sunday from 11 am until 5 pm (or until the last customer wants to leave). They are also dog friendly; your dog may be unleashed if they are other animal and human friendly and is well mannered. Water bowls and biscuits are available for their canine visitors.

**Boeger Winery**
1709 Carson Road
Placerville CA
530-622-8094
boegerwinery.com/
Well-behaved leashed dogs are allowed at the picnic tables at this winery. People can bring some of the wine to the picnic tables to taste. The winery is one of the oldest family owned and operated wineries in the Sierra Foothills of Northern California. They are open 10a.m.-5p.m. daily.

**Gold Hill Vineyard**
5660 Vineyard Lane
Placerville CA
530-626-6522

goldhillvineyard.com/
Dogs are allowed at the picnic tables near the tasting room. They allow well-behaved and leashed dogs outside. From Hwy 50, take Cold Springs Rd. north (towards Coloma). Turn right on Vineyard Lane.

**Lava Cap Winery**
2221 Fruitridge Road
Placerville CA
530-621-0175
lavacap.com/
Well-behaved, leashed dogs are allowed at the tables on their deck. Relax on the deck with a picnic and savor the scenic view of their vineyard. They are located just 5 minutes from Hwy 50. From Placerville, exit Schnell School Rd. (at the exit, head north by turning left at stop sign), turn right onto Carson Rd, turn left on Union Ridge, then veer right on Hassler Rd, then left on Fruitridge Rd.

**Sierra Vista Winery & Vineyard**
4560 Cabernet Way
Placerville CA
530-622-7841
sierravistawinery.com
Leashed and well-behaved dogs are allowed in the picnic area. The picnic grounds offer a beautiful view of The Sierra Nevada mountains. From Pleasant Valley Road, turn right onto Leisure Lane. The winery is at the end of Leisure Lane.

# Dog-Friendly Parks
**Dave Moore Nature Area**
Highway 49
Coloma CA
916-985-4474
This nature area features a one mile loop and about half of the trail is wheelchair, walker and stroller accessible. It starts at the parking lot and goes down to the South Fork of the American River and back, passing through several types of habitat. Located in the heart of the historic Gold Rush area,

the trail is lined with remnants from about 150 years ago when Chinese laborers channeled the creek water by hand with a pick and shovel to find gold. Leashed dogs are welcome. Please clean up after your dog. To get there from Sacramento, take Highway 50 east towards Placerville. In Shingle Springs, take the Ponderosa Road exit and go over the freeway bridge to the stop sign (located just north of Highway 50). Turn right onto North Shingles Road and go 3 miles. Turn left at the Y in the road onto Lotus Road. Continue for 5 miles heading north. At Highway 49 turn left and cross the bridge at the river. Continue for about 1 mile along Highway 49. Turn left at the cobblestone wall. There are no park fees, but donations are accepted.

**El Dorado Trail**
Mosquito Rd.
Placerville CA

eldoradotrail.com/trail-map/
This part of the El Dorado Trail is a nice paved path that is popular with runners and walkers. Leashed dogs are allowed. The trail was originally 2 miles each way for a total of 4 miles, but the trail has been expanded a few extra miles. Most of the path is wide enough that there is a dirt trail paralleling the paved trail. It is located near historic downtown Placerville. To get there from Hwy 50 heading east, exit Broadway and turn right. When Broadway ends, turn right onto Mosquito Rd and go back under the freeway. At the second street, turn left. If you go too far, you'll end up going back onto Hwy 50. The trail will be on the right. Park along the street.

**Eldorado National Forest**
100 Forni Road
Placerville CA
530-622-5061
fs.usda.gov/eldorado/
This national forest covers over 590,000 acres of land which ranges in elevation from 1,000 feet in the foothills to more than

10,000 feet along the Sierras. Please see the listings in our Sierra Nevada region for dog-friendly hikes and/or campgrounds.

## Gold Bug Park
2635 Gold Bug Lane
Placerville CA
530-642-5207
goldbugpark.org/
Gold Bug Park is a 60 acre park that was once the home of many gold mines. Your leashed dog is allowed at the picnic areas and on the trails, but is not allowed into the mine.

## Cedar Park Trail
Sly Park Road
Pollock Pines CA
530-644-2349
This easy paved trail, set amongst pine and conifer trees, has two small paved loops which total 1.2 miles in length. The elevation ranges from about 3,640 to 3,700 feet. Pets must be leashed and please clean up after them. The trail is located in the Eldorado National Forest. From Highway 50 in Pollock Pines, take Sly Park Road south (away from the Safeway). Drive about 6 miles to the parking area and trailhead on the left side of the road. There is ample parking.

## Sly Park/Jenkinson Lake
4771 Sly Park Road
Pollock Pines CA
530-644-2545
This beautiful wooded recreation area is at an elevation of 3500 feet. There is an 8 mile loop trail that circles Jenkinson Lake. It is a popular park for hiking, horseback riding, fishing and camping. Leashed dogs are allowed on the trails and in the campgrounds. The west side of the park (next to the campgrounds) offers wide fire road trails, while the east side has single track trails. Be sure to check your pup for ticks after walking here. The park is open from sunrise to sunset. It is located about 30 minutes from Placerville. To get there from Hwy 50, take the Sly Park Rd

exit and turn right. Drive about 5-10 minutes and the park will be on the left.

## Emergency Veterinarians
**Mother Lode Pet Emergency Clinic**
4050 Durock Rd
Shingle Springs CA
530-676-9044
Monday - Thursday 6 pm to 8 am, Friday 6 pm to 8 am Monday.

## Pleasant Grove

## Dog Businesses
**Performance Dogs In Action**
7089 Pleasant Grove Road
Pleasant Grove CA
916-655-1558
Performance Dogs in action offers a wide variety of classes and events for dogs, including agility lessons, obedience lessons, herding lessons (With ducks, geese, and sheep), daycare, dock jumping, workshops, clinics, seminars, and trials. They are located about 15 minutes from Sacramento.

## Plumas National Forest - Quincy

## Outdoor Restaurants
**Neighbors Bar-B-Que**
58421 H 70
Cromberg CA
530-836-1365
neighborsbarbecue.com/
In addition to their specialty barbecue dishes, this eatery also offers a variety of bottled and draft beers, local brews, wines, grab-n-go sandwiches, a full bar with sports viewing, and alfresco dining. They are closed on Tuesdays. Leashed,

friendly dogs are allowed at their outside dining area.

## Sweet Lorraine's
384 W Main Street/H 70
Quincy CA
530-283-5300
Fine food and wines are the specialty here, and they also offer alfresco dining on their spacious patio-weather permitting. They are open during the summer Tuesday to Friday for lunch from 11:30 am until 2:30 pm and for dinner Tuesday to Saturday from 5:30 pm until 8:30 pm. Dogs are allowed at the outer tables;they must be under their owner's control/care at all times.

## Dog-Friendly Parks
**Yellow Creek Trail**
Highway 70
Belden CA
530-283-0555
This trail is located in the Plumas National Forest and is an easy one way 1.4 mile trail. This day hike ends in a box canyon. Dogs on leash or off-leash but under direct voice control are allowed. Please clean up after your pets. The trailhead is location about 25 miles west of Quincy on Highway 70. It is to the right of the Ely Stamp Mill rest area, across from Belden.

**Bald Rock Trail**
Road #57
Berry Creek CA
530-534-6500
berrycreekca.org/recreation.html

This trail is located in the Plumas National Forest and is a short one way .5 mile hike through the forest to impressive rock formations. The elevation ranges from 3100 feet to 3270 feet. Big Bald Rock provides great views of Oroville Lake and the Sacramento Valley. The trail is usually open for hiking from February to December, weather permitting. Dogs on leash or off-leash but under direct voice control are allowed. Please clean up after your pets. To get there from Oroville, take Highway 162 east. Drive for about 17-18 miles and turn right onto Bald Rock Road. Drive for about 5.8 on the gravel road. Then turn left at the Big Bald Rock turn-off and go .1 miles.

**Plumas-Eureka State Park**
Johnsonville Road
Blairsden CA
530-836-2380
Dogs are allowed on one trail which is called the Grass Lake Trail. This 3.8 mile trail climbs steadily to the Pacific Crest Trail passing several lakes. Pets must be on leash and please clean up after them. The trailhead is at the Jamison Mine. To get there take Johnsonville Road (County Road A14) off Highway 89 in Graeagle. Go about 4.5 miles to the unimproved Jamison Mine Road. There should be a sign on the left for the Jamison Mine/Grass Lake Trail. Continue another 1.5 miles to the parking area.

**Lakeshore Trail**
off La Porte Road
Brownsville CA

This trail is located in the Plumas National Forest and is an easy but long 13.5 mile hike around the Little Grass Valley Reservoir. The trail is at a 5,100 foot elevation and is heavily used by hikers. In some areas the trail becomes a walk along the beach. Dogs on leash are allowed on the trail and in the water. The trail is usually open for hiking from early June to early September, weather permitting. Please clean up after your pets. To get there from Oroville, take Highway 162 east. Drive for about 7 miles and then turn right onto Forbestown Road (Challenge Cut-Off). Drive 16.6 miles and then turn left on La Porte Road. Go 27.4 miles and then make a right at Road #57 (South Fork Rec Area).

**Gold Lake Trail**
Forest Road 24N29X

Bucks Lake CA
530-283-0555
This trail is located in the Plumas National Forest and is an easy one way 1.5 mile trail. This trail provides access to the Bucks Lake Wilderness and the Pacific Crest Trail. At Bucks Lake swimming and fishing are popular activities. Dogs on leash or off-leash but under direct voice control are allowed. Dogs are allowed on the trails and in the water. Please clean up after your pets. To get there from Quincy, go west 9.2 miles on Bucks Lake Road. Turn right on a gravel road, 24N29X (Silver Lake sign). Go 6.4 miles to the lake and the Silver Lake Campground. The trail begins at the campground.

**Chambers Creek Trail**
Highway 70
Pulga CA
530-283-0555
This trail is located in the Plumas National Forest and is a moderate one way 4.2 mile trail. There are some great waterfalls at the bridge. It takes about 2 to 3 hours to reach the bridge and a total of 6 hours to the top of the trail. Dogs on leash or off-leash but under direct voice control are allowed. Please clean up after your pets. The trailhead is location about 40 miles west of Quincy on Highway 70, or about 40 miles from Oroville.

**Buck's Lake Recreation Area**
Bucks Lake Road
Quincy CA
530-283-0555 (877-444-6777)
This recreation area of 1,827 acres sits at an elevation of over 5,100 feet and provides a wide variety of year round land and water recreational activities. There are several businesses surrounding the 103,000 acre-feet Buck's Lake, with an assortment of services available. The park also offers 4 boat launch areas and access to the Pacific Crest Trail. Dogs of all sizes are allowed for no additional fee.

Dogs must be leashed and cleaned up after. They are not allowed in the public swim areas; they are allowed on the trails.

**Plumas National Forest**
159 Lawrence Street
Quincy CA
530-283-2050
fs.usda.gov/plumas
This national forest covers over 1.1 million acres of land which ranges in elevation from around 2,000 to over 7,000 feet. Please see our listings in this region for dog-friendly hikes and/or campgrounds.

## Pomona - Ontario

### Dog-Friendly Hotels
**Best Western Plus Innsuites Ontario Airport E Hotel & Suites**
3400 Shelby Street
Ontario CA
909-466-9600 (800-780-7234)
Dogs up to 80 pounds are allowed. There is a $20 per stay pet fee. Up to two dogs are allowed per room.

**Doubletree Hotel Ontario Airport**
222 North Vineyard
Ontario CA
909-937-0900 (800-222-TREE (8733))
Located adjacent to the Ontario Convention Center and only 3 minutes away from the international airport, this upscale hotel offers a number of on site amenities for business and leisure travelers, plus a convenient location to shopping, dining, and recreation areas. Dogs are allowed for an additional one time fee of $50 per pet.

**Econo Lodge Ontario**
1655 East 4th Street
Ontario CA
909-986-7000 (877-424-6423)
Near Ontario Airport, Ontario

Mills Mall. Walking distance to shopping & restaurants. Located just off I-10.

Dogs up to 70 pounds are allowed. Dogs are allowed for a pet fee of $25.00 per pet per night.

### Knights Inn Ontario
1120 East Holt Blvd
Ontario CA
909-984-9655 (800-843-5644)
Dogs are welcome at this hotel.

### La Quinta Inn & Suites Ontario Airport
3555 Inland Empire Boulevard
Ontario CA
909-476-1112 (800-531-5900)
Dogs of all sizes are allowed. There are no additional pet fees, but a credit card must be on file. Dogs must be crated if left alone in the room, and be leashed and cleaned up after.

### Motel 6 Ontario California
231 North Vineyard Avenue
Ontario CA
909-937-6000
Dogs of all sizes are allowed for no additional pet fee. Some rooms have full kitchens and wireless high-speed Internet access. There is an outdoor pool and a fitness center.

### Ontario Airport Hotel
700 North Haven Avenue
Ontario CA
909-980-0400
This upscale hotel offers a number of on site amenities for business and leisure travelers, plus a convenient location to business, shopping, dining, and entertainment areas. Dogs up to 75 pounds are allowed for an additional one time fee of $75 per pet.

### Red Roof Inn Ontario Airport
1818 East Holt Blvd
Ontario CA
909-988-8466 (800-RED-ROOF)

One well-behaved family pet per room. Guest must notify front desk upon arrival. Guest is liable for any damages. In consideration of all guests, pets

must never be left unattended in the guest rooms.

### Rodeway Inn Ontario Mills Mall
4075 East Guasti Road
Ontario CA
909-390-8886 (877-424-6423)
Conveniently located just off I-10 Freeway only 2 miles from Ontario International Airport, Convention Center.

Dogs up to 25 pounds are allowed. Dogs are allowed for a pet fee of $10, per pet per night. Two dogs are allowed per room.

### Sheraton Ontario Airport
429 North Vineyard Avenue
Ontario CA
909-937-8000 (888-625-5144)
Only a short distance from the airport and offering amenities for business and leisure travelers, this hotel also offers a walking distance location to local shopping, dining, and attractions. Dogs up to 40 pounds are allowed for no additional fee. Dogs must be declared at check in and there is a pet waiver to sign at check in.

### La Quinta Inn & Suites Pomona
3200 W Temple Ave
Pomona CA
909-598-0073 (800-222-2244)
shiloinns.com
Just off Highway 57 and adjacent to the convention center the non-smoking La Quinta Inn & Suites Pomona offers beautiful views an outdoor pool and complimentary in-room coffee. The four-story La Quinta Inn & Suites features a Spanish-style exterior and 161 non-smoking rooms with cable TVs coffeemakers microwaves and work desks. Internet access is available for an additional charge. The on-site restaurant serves breakfast and dinner and there's a fitness room a 24-hour front desk a 24-hour business center and a conference center. The outdoor

pool and hot tub provide a mellow place to relax in the sun. Pets are permitted and parking is free. The hotel is off Highway 57 close to many restaurants and a mile from I-10. The hotel is two miles from California State Polytechnic University. Disneyland is 21 miles from the property and Knott's Berry Farm is 24 miles away. Ontario International Airport is 16 miles away.

### Sheraton Fairplex Hotel & Conference Center
601 W Mckinley Avenue
Pomona CA
909-622-2220 (888-625-5144)
Located on the 543-acre Fairplex Exposition Complex where they also hold the county fair, this upscale hotel offers numerous on site amenities for business and leisure travelers, plus a convenient location to shopping, dining, nightlife, and entertainment areas. Dogs are allowed for no additional fee;there is a pet waiver to sign at check in. Dogs may not be left alone in the rooms.

### Red Roof Inn San Dimas
204 North Village Court
San Dimas CA
909-599-2362 (800-RED-ROOF)

One well-behaved family pet per room. Guest must notify front desk upon arrival. Guest is liable for any damages. In consideration of all guests, pets must never be left unattended in the guest rooms.

### Quality Inn & Suites Walnut
1170 Fairway Drive
Walnut CA
(877-424-6423)
Quiet and relaxing Spanish 2-story building at freeway off-ramp location. Easy access, garden/courtyard style,

## Pet-Friendly Extended Stay Hotels
### Extended Stay America - Los Angeles - Chino Valley

4325 Corporate Center Ave
Chino CA
909-597-8675 (800-804-3724)
One dog is allowed per suite.
There is a $25 per night
additional pet fee up to $150 for
an entire stay.

**Extended Stay America - Los
Angeles - Ontario Airport**
3990 East Inland Empire Blvd.
Ontario CA
909-944-8900 (800-804-3724)
One dog is allowed per suite.
There is a $25 per night
additional pet fee up to $150 for
an entire stay.

**Residence Inn Ontario**
2025 Convention Center Way
Ontario CA
909-937-6788
Dogs of all sizes are allowed.
There is a $100 one time
additional pet fee.

**Extended Stay America - Los
Angeles - San Dimas**
601 W. Bonita Ave
San Dimas CA
909-394-1022 (800-804-3724)
One dog is allowed per suite.
There is a $25 per night
additional pet fee up to $150 for
an entire stay.

## Outdoor Restaurants
**Blue Fire Grill**
5670 Schaefer Avenue
Chino CA
909-591-8783
bluefirebbq.com/
Open for lunch and dinner, this
grill offers an extensive lunch
and dinner menu, a number of
house specialties, a full bar with
Happy Hour specials, a venue
for special events, and alfresco
dining. Leashed, well mannered
dogs are allowed at their outside
dining area.

**Chipotle**
13920 City Center Drive, Suite
4005
Chino Hills CA
909-548-3721
chipotle.com
Specializing in organic, natural
and unprocessed food, this

Mexican Eatery offers fajita
burritos, tacos, salads, and
salsas. Dogs are allowed at the
outdoor tables but you will
need to order your food inside
the restaurant and dogs must
remain outside.

**Jamba Juice**
3660 Grand Avenue, Suite F
Chino Hills CA
909-591-8019
jambajuice.com
All natural and organic
ingredients, no high-fructose
corn syrup, 0 grams trans fat,
no artificial preservatives, a
healthy helping of antioxidants,
vitamins, and minerals, and
fresh whole fruit and fruit juices
set the base for these tasty and
healthy beverages. Their
organic Hot Blends provides a
new spin on coffee, green or
chai tea, and hot
chocolate;plus they offer
probiotic fruit and yogurt
Blends. Additionally, they
feature organic steel-cut
oatmeal prepared fresh every
morning, all natural salads,
wraps, sandwiches, and grab n'
go specialties. They also offer
healthy community support
through fundraisers, special
sales, and school lunch
programs. Leashed, well
mannered dogs are allowed at
their outside dining area.

**Aruffo's Italian Cuisine**
126 Yale Ave
Claremont CA
909-624-9624
aruffositaliancuisine.com/
Dogs are allowed at the
outdoor tables.

**Espiau's Restaurant**
109 Yale Ave
Claremont CA
909-621-1818
espiaus.com/
Food and drink specials, happy
hours Monday to Thursday, live
music most nights, a large all
weather patio, a sports
atmosphere with 19 flat screen
TVs inside and out, and fresh
Mexican cuisine are offered at
this restaurant and cantina.
Leashed, well mannered dogs

are welcome at their outside
dining area.

**Some Crust Bakery**
119 Yale Avenue
Claremont CA
909-621-9772
somecrust.com/
Dogs are allowed at the outdoor
tables, and don't forget to grab
your pub one of their
complimentary doggie buscuits.

**The Coffee Bean & Tea Leaf**
101 N. Indian Hill, # 105
Claremont CA
909-624-2147
coffeebean.com
The coffee here is sourced
globally from family coffee farms
to procure only the top of 1% of
Arabica beans. They offer 30+
varieties of coffee;the beans are
roasted in small batches daily
for freshness, and they also
offer 20 varieties of teas that are
hand-blended by their tea
master. Additionally, they offer a
variety of tasty sweets, powders,
extracts, sauces, gifts, and
cards. Leashed, well mannered
dogs are allowed at their outside
dining area.

**The Loving Hut**
175 N Indian Hill Blvd, Building
A 102
Claremont CA
909-621-1668
lovinghut.us/claremont_01/
A quick-service 100% vegan
eatery, guests will find a full
menu of affordable, freshly
prepared gourmet cuisine made
with the finest and freshest
quality ingredients available.
They offer organic coffee and
tea, specialize in traditional,
regional, and Chinese vegan
cuisines, and in providing foods
that are gluten free with no
GMOs, milk or eggs. Services
include dine-in, take-out, frozen
and dried food sales, and
catering. Leashed, well
mannered dogs are allowed at
their outside dining area.

**Village Grill**
148 Yale Ave
Claremont CA
909-626-8813

villagegrille50sdiner.com/
Dogs are allowed at the outdoor tables.

**Johnny Rockets**
7800 Kew Avenue
Etiwanda CA
909-463-2800
johnnyrockets.com/index2.php
All the American favorites can be found here: juicy burgers, specialty sandwiches, hand-dipped shakes and malts, crispy fries and onion rings, and fresh baked pies, plus they even have vegetarian options and a doggy menu. Dogs are allowed at their outside tables;they must be leashed and under their owner's control/care.

**Chipolte**
1365 E Gladstone Street, Suite 700
Glendora CA
909-595-7063
chipotle.com
Specializing in organic, natural and unprocessed food, this Mexican Eatery offers fajita burritos, tacos, salads, and salsas. Dogs are allowed at the outdoor tables but you will need to order your food inside the restaurant and dogs must remain outside.

**Z Pizza**
1365 E Gladstone Street
Glendora CA
909-599-4500
zpizza.com
Specializing in organically and internationally inspired pizzas, this pizzeria cooks their pizzas on hot bricks in a fire baked oven. They feature a 100% certified organic gluten free wheat crust, homemade organic sauces and ingredients, fresh produce, and additive-free meats. They also offer gourmet salads, sandwiches, and catering services. Leashed, well mannered dogs are allowed at their outside tables.

**Aoki Japanese Restaurant**
2307 D Street
La Verne CA
909-593-2239
aokirestaurant.com/

Dogs are allowed at the outdoor tables.

**Cafe Allegro**
2124 3rd Street
La Verne CA
909-593-0788
caffe-allegro.com/
Dogs are allowed at the outdoor tables.

**Jamba Juice**
1614 Foothill Blvd/H 66
La Verne CA
909-392-4927
jambajuice.com
All natural and organic ingredients, no high-fructose corn syrup, 0 grams trans fat, no artificial preservatives, a healthy helping of antioxidants, vitamins, and minerals, and fresh whole fruit and fruit juices set the base for these tasty and healthy beverages. Their organic Hot Blends provides a new spin on coffee, green or chai tea, and hot chocolate;plus they offer probiotic fruit and yogurt Blends. Additionally, they feature organic steel-cut oatmeal prepared fresh every morning, all natural salads, wraps, sandwiches, and grab n' go specialties. They also offer healthy community support through fundraisers, special sales, and school lunch programs. Leashed, well mannered dogs are allowed at their outside dining area.

**Baja Fresh Mexican Grill**
929 N. Milliken Ave Ste C
Ontario CA
909-484-6200
bajafresh.com
This Mexican restaurant is open for lunch and dinner. They use fresh ingredients and making their salsa and beans daily. Some of the items on their menu include Enchiladas, Burritos, Tacos Salads, Quesadillas, Nachos, Chicken, Steak and more. Well-behaved leashed dogs are allowed at the outdoor tables.

**In-N-Out Burger**
1891 E. G Street

Ontario CA
800-786-1000
in-n-out.com/
This In-N-Out Burger has an outside window where you can place an order with your pup.

**Jamba Juice**
990 Ontario Mills Drive
Ontario CA
909-476-8008
jambajuice.com
All natural and organic ingredients, no high-fructose corn syrup, 0 grams trans fat, no artificial preservatives, a healthy helping of antioxidants, vitamins, and minerals, and fresh whole fruit and fruit juices set the base for these tasty and healthy beverages. Their organic Hot Blends provides a new spin on coffee, green or chai tea, and hot chocolate;plus they offer probiotic fruit and yogurt Blends. Additionally, they feature organic steel-cut oatmeal prepared fresh every morning, all natural salads, wraps, sandwiches, and grab n' go specialties. They also offer healthy community support through fundraisers, special sales, and school lunch programs. Leashed, well mannered dogs are allowed at their outside dining area.

**Roady's Restaurant**
160 W. Bonita Ave
San Dimas CA
909-592-0980
Dogs are allowed at the outdoor tables. They are open Monday to Saturday from 8 am until 8 pm and on Sunday from 7 am until 7 pm.

**Chipotle**
1092 North Mountain Avenue
Upland CA
909-579-0999
chipotle.com
Specializing in organic, natural and unprocessed food, this Mexican Eatery offers fajita burritos, tacos, salads, and salsas. Dogs are allowed at the outdoor tables but you will need to order your food inside the restaurant and dogs must remain outside.

**Molly's Souper**
388 N 1st Avenue
Upland CA
909-982-1114
This breakfast and lunch shop is open daily from 6 am until 2 pm. Leashed dogs are allowed at their outside dining area.

**Molly's Souper**
220 E A Street
Upland CA
909-982-1114"";
Home cooked meals, homemade bread, an inviting ambiance, a doggy menu, and patio dining are just some of the offerings of this eatery. Leashed, friendly dogs are welcome at the outside dining area.

**Molly's Souper**
388 N 1st Ave
Upland CA
909-982-1114
Molly's Souper, located in Upland, California, is open 7 days a week, from 6am-2pm daily. They serve a variety of breakfast and lunch dishes, especially their soups, hence their name. They have a large, shaded outdoor patio which well-behaved, leashed dogs are welcome. They even offer a doggie menu.

**Qdoba Mexican Grill**
1902 N Campus Avenue
Upland CA
909-932-0090
qdoba.com
Touting original flavors not found anywhere else, this Mexican eatery serves up a variety of unique flavors prepared in innovative ways to order, and artfully prepared in front of patrons. They source the freshest produce and products available;plus they offer box lunches, catering and delivery services, and many vegetarian choices. Leashed, well mannered dogs are allowed at their outside tables.

**Z Pizza**
1943-C N Campus Avenue
Upland CA
909-949-1939
zpizza.com
Specializing in organically and international inspired pizzas, this pizzeria cooks their pizzas on hot bricks in a fire baked oven. They feature a 100% certified organic gluten free wheat crust, homemade organic sauces and ingredients, fresh produce, and additive-free meats. They also offer gourmet salads, sandwiches, and catering services. Leashed, well mannered dogs are allowed at their outside tables.

**Chipolte**
21710-A Valley Blvd
Walnut CA
909-595-1502
chipotle.com
Specializing in organic, natural and unprocessed food, this Mexican Eatery offers fajita burritos, tacos, salads, and salsas. Dogs are allowed at the outdoor tables but you will need to order your food inside the restaurant and dogs must remain outside.

## Pet-Friendly Stores

**Petco Pet Store - Rancho Cucamonga**
7221 Haven Ave.
Alta Loma CA
909-945-5881
Your licensed and well-behaved leashed dog is allowed in the store.

**PetSmart Pet Store**
11945 Central Ave
Chino CA
909-628-6665
Your licensed and well-behaved leashed dog is allowed in the store.

**Petco Pet Store - Chino**
3820 Grand Ave.
Chino CA
909-364-9807
Your licensed and well-behaved leashed dog is allowed in the store.

**PetSmart Pet Store**
13001 Peyton Dr
Chino Hills CA
909-627-4849
Your licensed and well-behaved leashed dog is allowed in the store.

**PetSmart Pet Store**
1314 N Azusa Ave
Covina CA
626-967-6099
Your licensed and well-behaved leashed dog is allowed in the store.

**PetSmart Pet Store**
21050 Golden Springs
Diamond Bar CA
909-595-0097
Your licensed and well-behaved leashed dog is allowed in the store.

**PetSmart Pet Store**
12483 Limonite Ave
Mira Loma CA
951-685-1927
Your licensed and well-behaved leashed dog is allowed in the store.

**Petco Pet Store - Mira Loma**
6301 Pat's Ranch Road
Mira Loma CA
951-817-9535
Your licensed and well-behaved leashed dog is allowed in the store.

**Petco Pet Store - Montclair**
9137 Central Ave.
Montclair CA
909-621-3618
Your licensed and well-behaved leashed dog is allowed in the store.

**Petco Pet Store - San Dimas**
822 West Arrow Hwy
San Dimas CA
909-394-2037
Your licensed and well-behaved leashed dog is allowed in the store.

**PetSmart Pet Store**
1935 N Campus Ave
Upland CA
909-981-4139
Your licensed and well-behaved leashed dog is allowed in the store.

## Off-Leash Dog Parks
**Pooch Park**
100 S. College Avenue
Claremont CA

This park has lots of grass and trees and a ravine for the dogs to climb up and down. There is a 3 foot fence around the park. The Pooch Park is located in College Park, just south of the Metrolink tracks on S. College Avenue.

**San Dimas Dog Park**
301 Horsethief Canyon Rd
San Dimas CA
909-394-6230
sandimasdogpark.org/
The fenced dog park is open during daylight hours. The park is closed on Wednesday afternoons for cleaning. The dog park is located in the Horsethief Canyon Park which is one mile north of the 210 Freeway.

**Baldy View Dog Park**
11th Street at Mountain Ave.
Upland CA
909-931-4280
The 1.3 acre Baldy View Dog Park has two fenced areas for large and small dogs. To get to the dog park, which is in Baldy View Park, take the I-10 to Mountain Ave. Head north on Mountain Ave and turn right on 11th Street. The park will be on your left.

## Dog-Friendly Parks
**Cucamonga-Guasti Park**
800 N. Archibald Ave.
Ontario CA
909-945-4321
This regional park allows leashed dogs. There is a nice path that winds along the lake which is a popular fishing spot. There is a minimal day use fee.

**Ganesha Park**
McKinley Ave
Pomona CA

It is not a large park, but is a

nice place to walk with your dog. The park also has several playground and picnic areas. Dogs must be leashed.

**Schabarum Regional Park**
17250 E. Colima Road
Rowland Heights CA
626-854-5560
This 640 acre wilderness park offers open space, picturesque canyons and rolling hills. Popular activities at the park including hiking, biking and horseback riding. Park amenities include an 18 station fitness trail, picnic areas, equestrian center, playgrounds and sports fields. There is a parking fee on weekends, holidays and during special events. Dogs are allowed at the park and on the hiking trails. Pets must be leashed and people need to clean up after their pet.

**Frank Bonelli Park**
120 Via Verde Road
San Dimas CA
909-599-8411
bonellipark.org/
This 1,980 acre park has a 250 acre lake for swimming, water skiing, wind surfing, sailing and fishing. The lake is stocked with trout, bluegill, catfish, and largemouth bass. Park amenities include hiking trails, playgrounds and food stands. There is a parking fee on weekends, holidays and during special events. Dogs are allowed at the park and on the hiking trails, but not in the water or at the beach area. Pets must be leashed and people need to clean up after their pet.

**San Dimas Canyon Nature Center**
1628 N. Sycamore Canyon Road
San Dimas CA
909-599-7512
sandimascanyonnaturecenter.com/
This 1,000 plus acre park offers a variety of nature trails. There is a minimal parking fee. Dogs are allowed on the trails,

but must be leashed. Please clean up after your dog.

## Events
**Inland Valley Humane Society Dog Walk**
120 Via Verde, Bonelli Park
San Dimas CA
909-623977
This pledge walk is an annual event where you and your pet (or even those without pets) walk a scenic 1, 2, or 3 mile route through Bonelli Park to benefit the animals of the IVHS and S.P.C.A. Thousands attend this event, usually held in May, because in addition to the cause, there are prizes, games and activities for dogs and their owners, a pancake breakfast, live music, a variety of vendors, and a lot more. Dogs must be well mannered, leashed, and cleaned up after at all times.

## Airports
**Ontario International Airport (ONT)**

Ontario CA

ONT's pet relief areas are located at the west ends of both Terminals 2 and 4. The area is approximately 12' X 12', with a few trees, sand, fire hydrant, dog house (not usable), and baggies available for dog waste. In using the pet areas, please remember that your pet must be on a leash at all times.

## Emergency Veterinarians
**East Valley Emergency Pet Clinic**
938 N Diamond Bar Blvd
Diamond Bar CA
909-861-5737
Monday - Friday 6 pm to 8 am, Saturday 12 noon to 8 am Monday.

**Emergency Pet Clinic of Pomona**

8980 Benson Ave
Montclair CA
909-981-1051
Monday - Friday 6 pm to 8 am,
Noon Saturday to 8 am Monday.

## Porterville

### Dog-Friendly Hotels
**Best Western Porterville Inn**
350 West Montgomery Avenue
Porterville CA
559-781-7411 (800-780-7234)
Dogs are allowed. There is a
$35 per pet per stay pet fee. Up
to two dogs are allowed per
room.

### Outdoor Restaurants
**Jamba Juice**
1395 W Henderson Avenue
Porterville CA
559-784-0196
jambajuice.com
All natural and organic
ingredients, no high-fructose
corn syrup, 0 grams trans fat, no
artificial preservatives, a healthy
helping of antioxidants, vitamins,
and minerals, and fresh whole
fruit and fruit juices set the base
for these tasty and healthy
beverages. Their organic Hot
Blends provides a new spin on
coffee, green or chai tea, and
hot chocolate;plus they offer
probiotic fruit and yogurt Blends.
Additionally, they feature all
natural salads, wraps,
sandwiches, and grab n go
specialties. They also offer
healthy community support
through fundraisers, special
sales, and school lunch
programs. Leashed, well
mannered dogs are allowed at
their outside dining area.

### Dog-Friendly Parks
**Sequoia National Forest**
1839 South Newcomb Street
Porterville CA

559-784-1500 (877-444-6777)
fs.usda.gov/sequoia/
Named for the world's largest
tree, this forest is home to 38
groves of the giant sequoias,
as well as impressive granite
monoliths, glacier torn
canyons, lush meadows, and
rushing rivers. There are also
several features/attractions
here, some of which include; a
50 mile auto route (Kings
Canyon Scenic Byway) that
descends into one of North
America's deepest canyons;
several lookout stations-
including the highest lookout
(Bald Mountain) in the southern
Sierra Nevadans; there are 3
National Recreation Trails, 45
miles of the Pacific Crest
National Scenic Trail, and more
than 800 miles of maintained
roads/over a 1,000 miles of
trails. There is a wide variety of
year round land and water
recreational opportunities. Your
dog is welcome here at
Sequoia National Forest (not to
be confused with the less than
dog-friendly Sequoia National
Park). Dogs must be friendly,
well behaved, on no more than
a 6 foot leash, cleaned up
after, and inside an enclosed
vehicle or tent at night. Dogs
may go on all the trails and
throughout the park; they are
not allowed on developed
swimming beaches or in park
buildings.

## Potter Valley

### Dog-Friendly Parks
**Milk Ranch Loop**

Potter Valley CA
530-934-3316
This trail is 9.5 miles long and
is rated moderate. Located in
the Mendocino National Forest
at an elevation of 5,200 feet,
this trail is one of the most
popular loops on Snow
Mountain. The route offers
dense red fir forests, meadows

and a barren peak. The Milk
Ranch meadow is private
property, but the landowner
allows horse and foot travelers
to pass through on the trail.
They just request that no camps
be set up within the posted
portion of the meadow. Pets are
allowed on the trail. They must
be leashed in the campground,
but are allowed off-leash under
voice control on the trail. Please
clean up after your pets. The
loop can be started at the
Summit Springs Trailhead. To
get there from Ukiah, take
Highway 101 North then take
Highway 20 East towards Upper
Lake/Williams. Go about 5 miles
and turn left onto Potter Valley
Road towards Potter Valley.
Turn right on Forest Service
Road M8 towards Lake
Pillsbury. The road towards the
lake is not paved. The trail starts
near the lake at the Summit
Springs Trailhead. Dogs are
also allowed at the lake but
should be leashed.

## Ragged Point

### Outdoor Restaurants
**Ragged Point Restaurant**
19019 H 1
Ragged Point CA
805-927-5708
Innovative, seasonally inspired
California cuisine with an
emphasis on fresh caught
seafood, and local and all
natural produce and products is
the specialty of this ocean-side
eatery. They also feature fine
California wines, catering
services, and alfresco dining in
a lush garden setting. Leashed,
friendly dogs are allowed at their
outside dining area.

## Rancho Cucmonga

### Pet-Friendly Stores

**Bass Pro Shops**
7777 Victoria Gardens Lane
Rancho Cucmonga CA
909-922-5500
Well-behaved, leashed dogs are allowed in the store. Dogs are not allowed in the shopping carts.

**Pet-Friendly Stores**
**Centinela Feed and Supplies**
28901 Western Avenue/H 213
Rancho Palos Verdes CA
310-547-3008
centinelafeed.com
Specializing in natural, holistic, and raw pet foods, this pet supply store also provides healthy treats, quality supplements, pet care supplies, low-cost vaccination clinics, frequent in-store events, and a knowledgeable staff. Leashed pets are welcome.

**Red Bluff**

**Dog-Friendly Hotels**
**Best Western Antelope Inn**
203 Antelope Boulevard
Red Bluff CA
530-527-8882 (800-780-7234)
Dogs up to 80 pounds are allowed. There is a $20 per day pet fee up to $100 for the week. Up to two dogs are allowed per room.

**Comfort Inn Red Bluff**
90 Sale Lane
Red Bluff CA
530-529-7060 (877-424-6423)
Beautifully appointed guest rooms and suites. Near restaurants and historic downtown Red Bluff.

Dogs of all sizes are allowed. Dogs are allowed for a pet fee of

$15.00/ per pet per night.

**Days Inn Red Bluff**
5 Sutter Street
Red Bluff CA
530-527-6130 (800-329-7466)
Dogs are welcome at this hotel.

**Super 8 Red Bluff**
30 Gilmore Road
Red Bluff CA
530-529-2028 (800-800-8000)
Dogs of all sizes are allowed. Dogs are allowed for a pet fee.

**Travelodge Red Bluff**
38 Antelope Boulevard
Red Bluff CA
530-527-6020
Dogs up to 50 pounds are allowed. There is a pet fee of $8 per pet per night.

**Dog-Friendly Parks**
**Red Bluff Recreation Area**
825 North Humboldt Avenue
Red Bluff CA
530-934-3316
The popular Red Bluff Recreation Area is part of the Mendocino National Forest. The recreation area includes the Lake Red Bluff Trail (1.5 mi.), which is accessible and paved. The trail travels along the Sacramento River and through a wildlife viewing area. Popular activities at the lake include boating, water skiing, swimming, camping and fishing. The facilities include accessible restrooms with showers, a boat ramp and campground. Dogs are allowed including on the trails and in the water but pets should be leashed. The park is located just east of the city of Red Bluff in the Sacramento Valley. If you are heading North on I-5, take the Highway 36 East exit towards Central Red Bluff/Chico. Continue of Antelope Blvd for less than 1/2 mile and turn right on Sale Lane. The park is open year round unless there is flooding or high winds.

**Samuel Ayer/Dog Island Park**
1360 Main Street
Red Bluff CA
530-527-2605
This day-use park offers multi-use trails, fishing on the Sacramento River, a large group barbecue area, horseshoe pits, picnic areas with fire pits, and restrooms. Dogs of all sizes are allowed; they must be leashed and cleaned up after at all times.

**Redding**

**Dog-Friendly Hotels**
**Best Western Plus Twin View Inn & Suites**
1080 Twin View Boulevard
Redding CA
530-241-5500 (800-780-7234)
Dogs up to 80 pounds are allowed. There is a $20 per day pet fee up to $100 for the week. Up to two dogs are allowed per room.

**Bridge Bay Resort**
10300 Bridge Bay Road
Redding CA
530-275-3021 (800-752-9669)
Featuring an outdoor pool and an a la carte restaurant Bridge Bay Resort is located in Shasta Lake California.
All rooms and studios at this resort offer dining areas coffee machines cable TVs and air conditioning. Some rooms have panoramic lake views.
Guests at Bridge Bay Resort are provided 24-hour front desk assistance and free parking. The property has barbecue facilities and a vending machine. Ski equipment can be rented on site.
An array of activities can be enjoyed on site or in the surroundings including skiing and hiking.
Bridge Bay Resort is a 5-minute drive from several dining options and convenience stores in the area.

## Comfort Inn Redding
850 Mistletoe Lane
Redding CA
530-221-4472 (877-424-6423)
The Comfort Inn lies in the shadows of beautiful Mount Shasta, surrounded by stunning mountains in a pristine recreational area.

Dogs up to 20 pounds are allowed. Dogs are allowed for a pet fee of $10.00 per pet per night.

## La Quinta Inn & Suites Redding
2180 Hilltop Drive
Redding CA
530-221-8200 (800-531-5900)
Dogs of all sizes are allowed. There are no additional pet fees. Dogs may not be left unattended at any time, and they must be leashed and cleaned up after.

## Quality Inn Redding
2059 Hilltop Dr.
Redding CA
530-221-6530 (877-424-6423)
Located in the main hotel/motel area of Redding. Shopping, restaurants, golf, lake and airport within easy access.

Dogs up to 25 pounds are allowed. Dogs are allowed for a pet fee of $15.00 per pet per stay. Two dogs are allowed per room.

## Ramada Limited Redding
1286 Twin View Boulevard
Redding CA
530-246-2222
Dogs of all sizes are allowed. There is a pet fee of $20 per pet per night.

## Red Lion Redding
1830 Hilltop Dr
Redding CA
530-221-8700
There is a $20 per night per pet additional fee. There is a $15 pet fee for R&R members, and the R&R program is free to sign up.

# Dog-Friendly Attractions

## Kent's Meat and Grocery and Kathy's Deli
8080 Airport Road
Redding CA
530-365-4322
kentsmeats.com/
Some of the items available at this market include fresh organic produce, a full service meat department with a variety of all natural beef, pork, buffalo, elk, deer, goat, and poultry, local and international cheeses, and wholesome groceries. Additionally, they smoke their own ham and bacon as well as various sausages and bratwurst, and offers a 'parking lot' barbecue on Fridays with all the fixings. Their deli serves up homemade soups, salads, hearty sandwiches, fresh baked breads, handcrafted desserts, and full gourmet meals to go. Leashed dogs are allowed at their outside dining area.

# Outdoor Restaurants

## Bartel's Giant Burger
75 Lake Blvd E/ H 299
Redding CA
530-243-7313
This hamburger specialty eatery welcome friendly leashed dogs at their outside dining area. They are open Monday to Saturday from 10 am until 9 pm and on Sunday from 11:30 am until 9 pm.

## Burrito Bandito
8938 Airport Road
Redding CA
530-222-6640
juanmeanburrito.com/
Well-behaved leashed dogs are allowed at the outdoor seating area.

## Chipotle
961 Dana Drive
Redding CA
530-223-9292
chipotle.com
Specializing in organic, natural and unprocessed food, this Mexican Eatery offers fajita burritos, tacos, salads, and salsas. Dogs are allowed at the outdoor tables but you will need to order your food inside the restaurant and dogs must remain outside.

## In-n-Out
1275 Dana Dr
Redding CA
800-786-1000
in-n-out.com/
Burgers, fries, and shakes are offered at this fast food eatery. Leashed dogs are allowed at the outdoor tables.

## Jamba Juice
3455 Placer Street, Unit B
Redding CA
530-243-1736
jambajuice.com
All natural and organic ingredients, no high-fructose corn syrup, 0 grams trans fat, no artificial preservatives, a healthy helping of antioxidants, vitamins, and minerals, and fresh whole fruit and fruit juices set the base for these tasty and healthy beverages. Their organic Hot Blends provides a new spin on coffee, green or chai tea, and hot chocolate;plus they offer probiotic fruit and yogurt Blends. Additionally, they feature organic steel-cut oatmeal prepared fresh every morning, all natural salads, wraps, sandwiches, and grab n' go specialties. They also offer healthy community support through fundraisers, special sales, and school lunch programs. Leashed, well mannered dogs are allowed at their outside dining area.

## Manhattan Bagel
913 Dana Drive
Redding CA
530-222-2221
manhattanbagel.com/
Well-behaved leashed dogs are allowed at the outdoor seating area.

## Sandwichery
1341 Tehama Street
Redding CA
530-246-2020
thesandwichery.net/about-us
Well-behaved leashed dogs are allowed at the outdoor seating

area. Homemade soups, fresh salads, and made to order sandwiches are the specialties here. They are open Monday to Friday from 8:30 am until 2:30 pm.

**Togos**
1030 East Cypress Avenue Ste B
Redding CA
530-222-9212
togos.com/
This restaurant serves deli-type food with sub-sandwiches their specialty. Leashed dogs are allowed at the outdoor tables.

## Pet-Friendly Stores
**Petco Pet Store - Redding**
1603 East Hilltop Dr.
Redding CA
530-226-1200
Your licensed and well-behaved leashed dog is allowed in the store.

## Off-Leash Dog Parks
**Benton Dog Park**
1700 Airpark Drive
Redding CA
530-941-8200
visitredding.com/benton-dog-park
This fenced off-lead dog park is located on 2.30 acres. Dogs of all sizes are welcome, they must be leashed when out of the off-lead area, and please clean up after your pet.

**Benton Dog Park**
1700 Airpark Drive
Redding CA
530-941-8200
visitredding.com/benton-dog-park
This fenced off-lead dog park is located on 2.30 acres with separate sections for large and small dogs, lots of grassy and shaded areas, a watering station, benches, and waste disposal stations. The park is open daily from 6 am until 10 pm. Dogs must be healthy, sociable, current on all vaccinations and license with

tags on collar, and under their owner's control at all times. Owners must clean up after their pets, and keep them leashed when not in designated off-lead areas.

## Dog-Friendly Parks
**Sacramento River Trail**
North Market Street
Redding CA
530-224-6100
This trail attracts people of all ages, from the walkers and joggers to bicyclists and fisherman looking for an ideal angling spot. The complete trail, round-trip, is approximately 6 miles and can easily be walked in a couple of hours. It is located along the Sacramento River from the North Market Street bridge to Keswick Dam. There are also several access points to the paved trail in Caldwell Park.

**Shasta-Trinity National Forest**
3644 Avtech Pkwy
Redding CA
530-226-2500
fs.usda.gov/stnf
This national forest covers over 2 million acres of land which ranges in elevation from 1,000 to 14,162 feet. Please see our listings in this region for dog-friendly hikes and/or campgrounds.

**Turtle Bay Exploration Park**
840 Auditorium Drive
Redding CA
800-TURTLEBAY (887-8532)
turtlebay.org/
This amazing exploration park is 300 acres of educational and entertaining activities with a focus on relationships between humans and nature through the telling of the region and its peoples. It is home to the translucent Sundial Bridge, a free-standing, technical marvel spanning the Sacramento River that connects the north and south campuses of the park. There is also a historical railroad exhibit, an arboretum

that extends over 200 acres, a series of climate display gardens, a medicinal garden, children's garden, a variety of several other gardens, and much more. Dogs are allowed throughout most of the park, in the gardens, the bridge, and on the hiking trails. They are not allowed at Paul Bunyan's Forest Camp or in the museum. Dogs must be leashed and cleaned up after at all times. There are doggy clean-up supplies on site.

## Other Organizations
**Benton Dog Park**
1700 Airpark Drive
Redding CA
530.941.8200
bentondogpark.com
We are a non profit off leash dog park. Where your dog can socialize and exercise in a safe environment. You do need to be present and watch your dog. It is a 2 acre fully enclosed area. Come join us!

## Redwood National and State Parks

## Dog-Friendly Attractions
**Trees of Mystery**
15500 Highway 101 N.
Klamath CA
800-638-3389
treesofmystery.net
Located in the center of the Redwood National and State Parks, this attraction allows leashed dogs everywhere people are welcome. They have an 8/10ths of a mile groomed interpretive trail through the awe-inspiring Redwoods of California. Also located here is a world-class Native American Museum and a gondola which takes you and your pooch on an aerial ride through the redwood forest canopy. They are located along Highway 101 in Klamath. Klamath is 36 miles south of the

Oregon border and 260 miles north of Santa Rosa.

## Dog-Friendly Beaches
### Crescent Beach - Del Norte SP

Enderts Beach Rd
Crescent Beach CA
707-464-6101
Dogs are allowed on the ocean beach at Crescent Beach in the Del Norte Coast Redwoods State Park. They are not allowed on any trails within the Redwood National or State Parks. Pets are also allowed at road accessible picnic areas and campgrounds. Dogs must be on a 6 foot or less leash and people need to pick up after their pets. To get to the beach take Enderts Beach Road South from Highway 101 just south of Crescent City.

### Freshwater Lagoon Beach - Redwood NP
Highway 101 south end of Redwood National Park
Orick CA
707-464-6101
nps.gov/redw
Dogs are allowed on the ocean beaches around Freshwater Lagoon, but not on any trails within Redwood National Park. Picnic tables are available at the beach. Pets are also allowed at road accessible picnic areas and campgrounds. Dogs must be on a 6 foot or less leash and people need to pick up after their pets. The beach is located off Highway 101 behind the Redwood Information Center at the south end of the Redwood National Park. The parking area for the beach is about 2 miles south of Orick. Some portions of this beach are rather rocky but there are also sandy portions as well.

### Gold Bluffs Beach - Redwood NP
Davison Road
Orick CA
707-464-6101
nps.gov/redw
Dogs are allowed on this beach,

but not on any trails within this park. Picnic tables and campgrounds are available at the beach. Pets are also allowed at road accessible picnic areas and campgrounds. Dogs must be on a 6 foot or less leash and people need to pick up after their pets. The beach is located off Highway 101. Take Highway 101 heading north. Pass Orick and drive about 3-4 miles, then exit Davison Rd. Head towards the coast on an unpaved road (trailers are not allowed on the unpaved road).

## Dog-Friendly Parks
### Redwood National and State Parks
1111 Second Street
Crescent City CA
707-464-6101
nps.gov/redw/
The National and State Parks do not allow dogs on any trails but some of the beaches and campgrounds welcome dogs. Pets are allowed on Crescent Beach, Gold Bluffs Beach and the Freshwater Spit Lagoon. The campgrounds that allow pets include Jedediah Smith Redwoods State Park campground, Prairie Creek Redwoods State Park campground and Gold Bluffs Beach campground. One way to see a number of redwood groves with dogs is to take the Newton B. Drury Scenic Bypass off of Highway 101. You may see large elk grazing near the parking lots as you drive through the park. Dogs are also allowed to walk along some gravel roads. Two roads that can be walked along with dog include Cal Barrel Road (3 miles long) and Howland Hill Rd (6 miles long). These roads will usually not be too crowded with cars except at the busiest times. Old growth Redwood groves line these gravel roads. Pets must be leashed and attended at all times and please clean up after them.

### Patrick's Point State Park
4150 Patrick's Point Drive
Trinidad CA
707-677-3570
Located in the heart of the coastal redwood country, this park is a mix of dense forests and wildflower filled meadows. They feature a recreated Yurok Village, a Native American Plant Garden, fully developed picnic areas with barbecues and restrooms, and interpretive programs in the summer. Dogs are allowed for no additional fee. They are allowed at the lagoons, and in developed and paved areas only; they are not allowed on the trails or the beaches. Dogs must be inside an enclosed vehicle or tent at night, be on no more than a 6 foot leash, and cleaned up after.

## Redwood Valley

## Dog-Friendly Attractions
### Elizabeth Vineyards
8591 Colony Drive
Redwood Valley CA
707-485-9009
elizabethvineyards.com/
Redwood Valley is blessed with excellent soil and a favorable climate, giving the grapes the unique flavor and character of the region. The vineyard is open by appointment only, and during harvest they are almost too busy for visitors. They suggest also checking out the other events in which they participate on their website. Dogs are welcome on the grounds when you do visit the vineyard, but they are not allowed in the tasting room. Dogs must be leashed and cleaned up after at all times.

## Dog-Friendly Wineries and Vineyards
### Gabrielli Winery
10950 West Road
Redwood Valley CA
707-485-1221

This winery is not usually open during harvest time, but they reopen the first of the year, so they suggest to be sure and call before coming out to make sure they are open. Usually they are open from 10 am to 4 pm Monday through Friday, and all other times by appointment. Well behaved dogs are welcome on the grounds, but not in the tasting room. Dogs must be leashed and cleaned up after at all times.

## Reedley

### Outdoor Restaurants
**Jamba Juice**
765 N Reed Avenue
Reedley CA
559-637-1496
jambajuice.com
All natural and organic ingredients, no high-fructose corn syrup, 0 grams trans fat, no artificial preservatives, a healthy helping of antioxidants, vitamins, and minerals, and fresh whole fruit and fruit juices set the base for these tasty and healthy beverages. Their organic Hot Blends provides a new spin on coffee, green or chai tea, and hot chocolate;plus they offer probiotic fruit and yogurt Blends. Additionally, they feature all natural salads, wraps, sandwiches, and grab n go specialties. They also offer healthy community support through fundraisers, special sales, and school lunch programs. Leashed, well mannered dogs are allowed at their outside dining area.

## Ridgecrest

### Dog-Friendly Hotels
**Best Western China Lake Inn**
400 S China Lake Blvd
Ridgecrest CA

760-371-2300 (800-780-7234)
Dogs up to 80 pounds are allowed. There is a $25 per day pet fee up to $100 for the week. Up to two dogs are allowed per room.

**Econo Lodge Inn & Suites Ridgecrest**
201 West Inyokern Road
Ridgecrest CA
760-446-2551 (877-424-6423)
Next to China Lake NWC. On the route from Death Valley to Sequoia.

**Quality Inn Near China Lake Naval Station**
507 S. China Lake Blvd.
Ridgecrest CA
760-375-9732 (877-424-6423)
Located off US 398 at Ridgecrest Exit or SR 178 west at China Lake Blvd.Exit.

Dogs up to 30 pounds are allowed. Dogs are allowed for a pet fee of $25.00 per pet per night.

**Travel Inn Ridgecrest**
131 West Upjohn Avenue
Ridgecrest CA
760-384-3575 (877-424-6423)
The Rodeway Inn is your home away from home, centrally located in the heart of Ridgecrest and only minutes away

Dogs of all sizes are allowed.

## Rio Linda

### Other Organizations
**Rio Linda Elverta Park District**
810 Oak Lane
Rio Linda CA
916-991-7521
riolindaelvertaparks.org
We are a park district that is having a grand opening for our dog park on May 5th at 10am. 6601 West 2nd street, rio linda, 95673. dog games, doggy parade, doggy biscuits, doggie

paws, doggie kissing booth. vendors welcome.

## Ripon

### Dog-Friendly Hotels
**La Quinta Inn & Suites Manteca Ripon**
1524 Colony Road
Ripon CA
209-599-8999 (800-531-5900)
Dogs of all sizes are allowed. There are no additional pet fees. Dogs must be leashed and cleaned up after.

### Pet-Friendly Stores
**Swier Tire/Napa Auto parts**
121 W. Main St
Ripon CA
209-599-7512
napaonline.com
The Sweir Tires/Napa Auto Parts store in Ripon, CA welcomes dogs in the store, and their employees often bring their dogs into work. They offer a large selection of auto parts and more.

**Tractor Supply Company**
860 N Jack Tone Road
Ripon CA
209-599-1150
tractorsupply.com
Some offerings of this comprehensive farm store includes agriculture, farming and ranching supplies; outdoor power equipment with all the necessities; hundreds of thousands of parts and accessories accessible for yard and garden; metal working and welding supplies; tools for auto and home; a wide range of livestock/farm feed and needs; and a variety of foods and care/play/groom items for household pets. Additionally, they provide trailer and towing supplies, vehicle maintenance accessories, clothing, work wear, foot wear, gifts, home improvement items, a lot of

"know-how" and much more. Leashed, friendly dogs are welcome in the store.

## Riverside

### Dog-Friendly Hotels
**Comfort Inn Moreno Valley**
23330 Sunnymead Blvd.
Moreno Valley CA
951-242-0699 (877-424-6423)
In between Los Angeles and Palm Springs, Near beaches, Mts, Desert, Casino. Deluxe Continental Breakfast, outdoor

Dogs up to 50 pounds are allowed. Dogs are allowed for a pet fee of $10.00 per pet per night. Two dogs are allowed per room.

**Econo Lodge Moreno Valley**
24412 Sunnymead Boulevard
Moreno Valley CA
951-247-6699 (877-424-6423)
California Speedway 18 miles. Moreno Ranch Golf only 5 miles. Parris Auto Speedway 9 miles. Pool/Spa.

Dogs up to 25 pounds are allowed. Dogs are allowed for a pet fee of $10.00/pet, per pet per night.

**La Quinta Inn Suites Moreno Valley**
23090 Sunnymead Blvd
Moreno Valley CA
951-486-9000 (800-531-5900)
Dogs of all sizes are allowed. Dogs may not be left alone in the room.

**Riverside Inn & Suites**
10705 Magnolia
Riverside CA
951-351-2424 (877-424-6423)
Directly across the street from Kaiser Permanente Hospital. Wireless high-speed Internet access in all rooms.

Dogs of all sizes are allowed. Dogs are allowed for a pet fee of $10.00 per pet per night.

**Rodeway Inn Riverside**
10518 Magnolia Avenue
Riverside CA
951-359-0770 (877-424-6423)
Walking distance to Tyler Mall, restaurants, Castle Park and ice rink. Largest swimming pool in the area. Free Continental breakfast.

Dogs up to 60 pounds are allowed. Dogs are allowed for a pet fee of $20.00 per pet per night. Two dogs are allowed per room.

### Pet-Friendly Extended Stay Hotels
**Residence Inn By Marriott Corona Riverside**
1015 Montecito Drive
Corona CA
951-371-0107
Dogs of all sizes are allowed. There is a $75 one time additional pet fee.

### Dog-Friendly Attractions
**Citrus State Historic Park**
Van Buren Blvd.
Riverside CA
909-780-6222
This 400-acre historic park recognizes the importance of the citrus industry in southern California. In the early 1900s, "Citrus was King" and there was a "second Gold Rush" which brought potential citrus barons to California. The park, which is reminiscent of a 1900s city park, has demonstration groves, an interpretive structure and picnic areas. Today it is also a working citrus grove and continues to produce high-quality fruits. Dogs are not allowed in the buildings, but are welcome to walk leashed on the grounds, including several trails around the groves. The park is located in Riverside, one mile east of Highway 91. It at the corner of Van Buren Blvd. and Dufferin Ave.

### Outdoor Restaurants
**Jamba Juice**
2620 Tuscany Street, Suite 106
Corona CA
951-371-9450
jambajuice.com
All natural and organic ingredients, no high-fructose corn syrup, 0 grams trans fat, no artificial preservatives, a healthy helping of antioxidants, vitamins, and minerals, and fresh whole fruit and fruit juices set the base for these tasty and healthy beverages. Their organic Hot Blends provides a new spin on coffee, green or chai tea, and hot chocolate;plus they offer probiotic fruit and yogurt Blends. Additionally, they feature organic steel-cut oatmeal prepared fresh every morning, all natural salads, wraps, sandwiches, and grab n' go specialties. They also offer healthy community support through fundraisers, special sales, and school lunch programs. Leashed, well mannered dogs are allowed at their outside dining area.

**Jamba Juice**
12430 Day Street, Suite C-4
Moreno Valley CA
951-697-8880
jambajuice.com
All natural and organic ingredients, no high-fructose corn syrup, 0 grams trans fat, no artificial preservatives, a healthy helping of antioxidants, vitamins, and minerals, and fresh whole fruit and fruit juices set the base for these tasty and healthy beverages. Their organic Hot Blends provides a new spin on coffee, green or chai tea, and hot chocolate;plus they offer probiotic fruit and yogurt Blends. Additionally, they feature organic steel-cut oatmeal prepared fresh every morning, all natural salads, wraps, sandwiches, and grab n' go specialties. They also offer healthy community support through fundraisers, special sales, and school lunch programs. Leashed, well

mannered dogs are allowed at their outside dining area.

### Rubio's Baja Grill
110 Hidden Valley Pkwy
Norco CA
951-898-3591
rubios.com/
Dogs are allowed at the outdoor tables.

### Antonious Pizza
3737 Main Street
Riverside CA
951-682-9100
antoniouspizzariverside.com/
This pizza place, which has dog-friendly outdoor seating, is located in downtown Riverside.

### The Coffee Bean & Tea Leaf
3712 Mission Inn Avenue, Suite N-4
Riverside CA
951-684-3803
coffeebean.com
The coffee here is sourced globally from family coffee farms to procure only the top of 1% of Arabica beans. They offer 30+ varieties of coffee;the beans are roasted in small batches daily for freshness, and they also offer 20 varieties of teas that are hand-blended by their tea master. Additionally, they offer a variety of tasty sweets, powders, extracts, sauces, gifts, and cards. Leashed, well mannered dogs are allowed at their outside dining area.

## Pet-Friendly Shopping Centers
### The Promenade Shops at Dos Lagos
2780 Cabot Drive
Corona CA
921-277-7601
This premier shopping Mecca offers an eclectic array of stores, entertainment, and eateries. Dogs are allowed throughout the common areas; it is up to individual stores whether a pet may enter. Dogs must be under their owner's control, leashed, and cleaned up after at all times.

## Pet-Friendly Stores
### Anthropologie
2785 Cabot Drive, #170
Corona CA
951-277-0866
Items of distinction can be found for all ages and in all departments of this unique shop. Carefully selected to add to the enjoyment of the shopping experience, they carry fine clothing, amazing accessories, jewelry, hobby and leisure items, and a full line of bright and useful items for the home, garden, and office. Leashed, well behaved dogs are allowed in the store.

### PetSmart Pet Store
573 Mckinley St
Corona CA
951-340-0501
Your licensed and well-behaved leashed dog is allowed in the store.

### Petco Pet Store - South Corona
3485 Grand Oaks
Corona CA
951-808-4765
Your licensed and well-behaved leashed dog is allowed in the store.

### PetSmart Pet Store
2828 Campus Pkwy
Riverside CA
951-653-8482
Your licensed and well-behaved leashed dog is allowed in the store.

### Petco Pet Store - Moreno Valley
2630 Canyon Springs Pkwy
Riverside CA
951-697-8060
Your licensed and well-behaved leashed dog is allowed in the store.

### Petco Pet Store - Riverside
3384 Tyler St.
Riverside CA
951-688-8886
Your licensed and well-

behaved leashed dog is allowed in the store.

### Petco Pet Store - Riverside - East
8974 Trautwein Road
Riverside CA
951-697-4024
Your licensed and well-behaved leashed dog is allowed in the store.

## Off-Leash Dog Parks
### Butterfield Park Dog Park
1886 Butterfield Drive
Corona CA
909-736-2241
This .8 acre fenced off-leash dog area is located in Butterfield Park. The dog park is well-shaded with benches, a picnic table and a doggie drinking fountain. From the 91 Freeway, take the Maple Street exit and go north. Maple will dead end at Smith Street. Go left on Smith Street about .5 miles to Butterfield Drive. Then turn left to Butterfield Park just across the street from the airport. Thanks to one of our readers for recommending this dog park.

### Corona Dog Park
Butterfield Drive and Smith Avenue
Corona CA
888-636-7387
incorona.com/dogparks.asp
This park is almost an acre of off leash doggy fun; there is a drinking fountain for pups and their owners. Dogs must be sociable, current on all vaccinations, and under their owner's control at all times. Dogs must be leashed when not in designated off-lead areas.

### Harada Heritage Dogs Park
13100 65th Street
Corona CA
888-636-7387
One of the county's newest off lead areas, and it is located in the unincorporated town of Eastvale just north of Corona. Dogs must be sociable, current on all vaccinations, and under their owner's control at all times.

Dogs must be leashed when not in designated off-lead areas.

## Carlson Dog Park
At the foot of Mt. Rubidoux
Riverside CA
888-636-7387
In addition to providing 2 sections; one for large dogs, and one for the small pooches, this off leash area is also a good starting point to take a walk along the Santa Ana River trail or hike the paved trail up Mt. Rubidoux. Dogs must be sociable, current on all vaccinations, and under their owner's control at all times. Dogs must be leashed when not in designated off-lead areas.

## Pat Merritt Dog Park
Limonite Frontage Road
Riverside CA
888-636-7387
This doggy free run area offers great views of the Santa Ana River and offer 2 sections; one for large dogs, and one for the small pooches. Dogs must be sociable, current on all vaccinations, and under their owner's control at all times. Dogs must be leashed when not in designated off-lead areas.

## Riverwalk Dog Park
Pierce Street and Collett Avenue
Riverside CA
951-358- 7387
dogpark.com/riverwalk-dog-park/
Riverwalk Dog Park is divided into two areas for large and small dogs. The park has water, cleanup bags and benches. There is not much shade in the park yet as the trees that have been planted there are still small. To get to the dog park from the 91 Freeway exit at Magnolia and head north on Pierce. Pierce will turn into Esplanade but Pierce will head off to the left. Follow Pierce by turning left to the dog park.

## Dog-Friendly Parks
**Box Springs Mountain**

**Reserve**
Pigeon Pass Road
Riverside CA
909-684-7032
This 1,155 acre park offers hiking and equestrian trails. The park is located 5 miles east of Riverside off Highway 60 and Pigeon Pass Road. Dogs must be leashed and please clean up after them.

## Hidden Valley Wildlife Area
Arlington Avenue
Riverside CA
909-785-6362
Dogs on leash are allowed at this wildlife reserve. It is a popular spot for birdwatching and walking. There is a minimal fee for day use. This reserve is part of the Santa Ana River Regional Park. To get there from the 91 Fwy, go east to the city of Riverside. Exit on La Sierra Ave. and turn left (north). La Sierra dead-ends into Arlington. Bear left at the signal. Drive past the hills until you come to the sign that says "Hidden Valley." Take the first dirt road to the right.

## Mount Rubidoux Park
Mt. Rubidoux Drive
Riverside CA

This park is the highest point in downtown Riverside. It is a popular hiking trail which offers a spectacular 360 degree view of Riverside. Dogs on leash are allowed on the trails. To get there from downtown Riverside, take Mission Inn Avenue northeast (towards the Santa Ana River). Turn left (west) onto Redwood Street. Continue straight to stay on Redwood (otherwise you will go onto University Ave). Turn right on 9th Street and follow it to the park.

## Rancho Jurupa Park
Crestmore Road
Riverside CA
909-684-7032
This 350 acre park is part of the Santa Ana Regional Park and has more than 10 miles of hiking and equestrian trails.

There are also horseshoe pits and picnic areas. To get there from downtown Riverside, take Mission Inn Ave northwest (towards the Santa Ana River). Go over the river and turn left at Crestmore Road. Follow this road to the park entrance. There is a minimal fee for parking and for dogs. Dogs must be leashed.

## Emergency Veterinarians
**Animal Emergency Clinic**
12022 La Crosse Ave
Grand Terrace CA
909-783-1300
Monday - Friday 6 pm to 8 am, 24 hours on weekends and holidays.

## Rescue Organizations
**Alleys Rescued Angels
Siberian Husky Rescue**
PO Box 79246
Corona CA
951 532 0491
alleysrescuedangels.org
We are a 501(c)(3) non-profit animal rescue organization dedicated to saving the lives of abandoned Siberian Huskies throughout Los Angeles, Southern California and beyond. In the last year alone we have saved over 300 dogs from euthanasia and placed them in loving homes. All donations are tax deductible.

## Riverton

## Dog-Friendly Parks
**Ice House Bike Trail**
Ice House Road
Riverton CA
530-644-2349
This 3.1 mile dirt trail winds along the ridge tops and shaded slopes, through old and new forest growths. The trail, located in the Eldorado National Forest at about 5,400 feet, is rated

easy and offers great views of the Ice House Reservoir. Both hikers and mountain bikers use this trail. Dogs should be on leash and are allowed on the trail and in the water. To get there from Placerville, take Highway 50 east for 21 miles to Ice House Road turnoff. Turn left and go 11 miles north to the campground turnoff. Then go one mile to the campgrounds. The trail can be accessed from any of the Ice House Reservoir campgrounds or at the intersection of Road 12N06 and Ice House Road which is located about 200 yards north of the turnoff to Big Hill Lookout.

**Union Valley Bike Trail**
Ice House Road
Riverton CA
530-644-2349
This 4.8 mile two-lane paved trail is located in the Eldorado National Forest. Elevations range from 4,860 to 5,160 feet. The trail connects all the campgrounds on the east side of Union Valley Reservoir, from Jones Fork to Wench Creek Campgrounds. Parking is available at the campgrounds except for Lone Rock and Azalea Cove. Views and interpretive signs complement this high country trail. Dogs should be on leash and are allowed on the trail and in the water. To get there from Placerville, take Highway 50 east and go 21 miles to Riverton. Turn left on Ice House Road. Go about 19 miles north to the reservoir.

## S. San Francisco

### Dog-Friendly Hotels
**La Quinta Inn & Suites San Francisco Airport North**
20 Airport Boulevard
S. San Francisco CA
650-583-2223 (800-531-5900)
Dogs of all sizes are allowed. There are no additional pet fees.

Dogs must be leashed and cleaned up after. Be sure to inform the front desk you have a pet, and put the Do Not Disturb sign on the door if the dog is alone in the room.

## Sacramento

### Dog-Friendly Hotels
**Fairfield Inn & Suites By Marriott Sacramento Elk Grove**
8058 Orchard Loop Lane
Elk Grove CA
916-681-5400
Dogs of all sizes are allowed. There is a pet fee of $35 per night up to $150. You may have two large dogs or three small dogs.

**Holiday Inn Express & Suites Elk Grove - Sacramento**
2460 Maritime Drive
Elk Grove CA
916-478-4000 (877-270-6405)
Dogs of all sizes are allowed. Dogs are allowed for a pet fee of $35.00 per pet per stay.

**Holiday Inn Express Hotel & Suites Elk Grove**
9175 W. Stockton Blvd.
Elk Grove CA
916-478-9000 (877-270-6405)
Dogs up to 50 pounds are allowed. Dogs are allowed for a pet fee of $35.00 per pet per stay.

**Lake Natoma Inn**
702 Gold Lake Drive
Folsom CA
916-351-1500
An outdoor pool and hot tub on-site restaurant and a scenic waterside setting are a few of our guests' favorite things at the non-smoking Lake Natoma Inn. The mid-rise Lake Natoma Inn has 138 non-smoking rooms with pillowtop mattresses free Wi-Fi and flat-panel cable TVs with premium channels. Some rooms offer fireplaces jetted tubs

microwaves mini-fridges and desks with ergonomic chairs. Enjoy on-site dining at the hotel's bar and grill and save some time to re-energize and relax in the 24-hour fitness room and seasonal outdoor pool hot tub and sauna. The hotel provides a business center valet laundry/dry cleaning room service and free parking. Pets are welcome for an additional fee. The hotel is on the American River Bike Trail and is a five-minute walk from historic downtown Folsom where the Folsom History Museum and other Sutter Street landmarks recall the Gold Rush era. Folsom Powerhouse Historic State Park is two blocks away. The museum at Folsom Prison made famous in song is less than two miles from the hotel. Folsom Premium Outlets and the Willow Creek Recreation Area are within three miles. The hotel is 29 miles from Sacramento International Airport.

**Comfort Inn & Suites Near Folsom Lake Rancho Cordova**

12249 Folsom Boulevard
Rancho Cordova CA
916-351-1213 (877-424-6423)
Conveniently located just two blocks from the heart of the heart of Highway 50 Commerce Corridor, let the newly -renovated Comfort Inn

**Comfort Inn & Suites Near Folsom Lake Rancho Cordova**

12249 Folsom Boulevard
Rancho Cordova CA
916-351-1213 (877-424-6423)
Free breakfasts and Wi-Fi and in-room mini-fridges are among the perks at Comfort Inn & Suites Near Folsom Lake. The three-story Spanish-style hotel has 118 rooms well-equipped with flat-panel TVs with premium cable as well as free Wi-Fi hairdryers coffeemakers microwaves and mini-fridges. Non-smoking rooms can be requested. Come morning set yourself up with the hotel's free

hot breakfast buffet served daily. There's a seasonal outdoor pool to enjoy if time allows and a coin laundry and meeting room should those needs arise. Just two blocks from Highway 50 the Comfort Inn is one mile from the Sacramento State Aquatic Center and Lake Natoma which has 11 miles of paved bicycle trails and year-round bank or boat fishing. It's seven miles to the Folsom Historic District and eight miles to Folsom Lake. The Sacramento Convention Center Complex is 14 miles from the hotel. Sacramento International Airport is 20 miles away.

**Fairfield Inn And Suites By Marriott Sacramento Rancho Cordova**
10745 Gold Center Drive
Rancho Cordova CA
916-858-8680
Dogs of all sizes are allowed. There is a $75 one time pet fee.

**La Quinta Inn & Suites Rancho Cordova Sacramento**
11131 Folsom Boulevard
Rancho Cordova CA
916-638-1111 (800-531-5900)
Dogs up to 65 pounds are allowed for no additional pet fee; there is a pet policy to sign at check-in. Dogs may not be left alone in the room.

**Red Roof Inn Rancho Cordova**
10800 Olson Drive
Rancho Cordova CA
916-638-2500 (800-RED-ROOF)

One well-behaved family pet per room. Guest must notify front desk upon arrival. Guest is liable for any damages. In consideration of all guests, pets must never be left unattended in the guest rooms.

**Best Western Roseville Inn**
220 Harding Boulevard
Roseville CA
916-782-4434 (800-780-7234)
Dogs up to 80 pounds are allowed. There is a $10 per day pet fee up to $100 for the week. Up to two dogs are allowed per room.

**Best Western Sandman Motel**
236 Jibboom Street
Sacramento CA
916-443-6515 (800-780-7234)
Dogs up to 80 pounds are allowed. There is a $15 per day pet fee up to $100 for the week. Up to two dogs are allowed per room.

**Days Inn Sacramento Downtown**
228 Jibboom Street
Sacramento CA
916-443-4811 (800-329-7466)
Dogs of all sizes are allowed. Dogs are allowed for a pet fee of $10 per pet per night.

**Doubletree By Hilton Sacramento**
2001 Point West Way
Sacramento CA
916-929-8855 (800-222-TREE (8733))
Although conveniently located across the street from the Arden Mall Shopping Center;only 20 minutes to the Sacramento International Airport, just a couple of blocks to Cal Expo, and only minutes to the State Capitol, this full service hotel also offers a number of on site amenities for business and leisure travelers. Dogs are allowed for an additional one time pet fee of $50 per room.

**Econo Lodge Sacramento Convention Center**
711 16th St.
Sacramento CA
916-443-6631 (877-424-6423)
Walking distance to Convention Center & Capitol. 1 1/2 miles to historic Old Sacramento.

Dogs of all sizes are allowed. Dogs are allowed for a pet fee of $6.00 per pet per night.

**Holiday Inn Express Downtown Sacramento**
728 Sixteenth Street
Sacramento CA
916-444-4436 (877-270-6405)

Dogs up to 25 pounds are allowed. Dogs are allowed for a pet fee of $75 per pet per stay.

**Kimpton Sawyer Hotel**
500 J Street
Sacramento CA
877-678-6255
The awesome amenities include a year-round pool morning yoga spa services and a downtown location at the non-smoking pet-friendly Kimpton Sawyer Hotel. Yoga mats flat-panel TVs iPod docks and premium toiletries come furnished in all 250 stylish rooms at the 16-story Kimpton Sawyer Hotel. Guests mingle over munchies in the restaurant and lounge. The outdoor pool and deck offer a spot for relaxation year-round. Guests stay trim with help from morning yoga by the pool and hula-hoops medicine balls and more in the fitness room. Free bikes are provided. Spa sessions are available. Pets are allowed for no additional fee. The Kimpton Sawyer Hotel is adjacent to the Golden 1 Center and Downtown Commons in the heart of Sacramento. It's less than a 10-minute stroll west to the California State Railroad Museum and Old Sacramento Historic District bordering the Sacramento River. Explore the California State Capitol and Museum within a 15-minute walk or check out the races exhibits and performances at Cal Expo within six miles. Sacramento International Airport is 11 miles northwest.

**La Quinta Inn Sacramento Downtown**
200 Jibboom Street
Sacramento CA
916-448-8100 (800-531-5900)
Dogs of all sizes are allowed. There are no additional pet fees. Dogs must be leashed and cleaned up after.

**La Quinta Inn Sacramento North**
4604 Madison Avenue
Sacramento CA
916-348-0900 (800-531-5900)
Dogs up to 25 pounds are

allowed. There are no additional pet fees. Dogs must be leashed and cleaned up after.

**Sheraton Grand Sacramento Hotel**
1230 J Street
Sacramento CA
916-447-1700 (888-625-5144)
In addition to offering amenity-filled accommodations and on-site seasonally inspired farm-to-table cuisine, this upscale hotel also offers a great location to some of the areas best shopping, dining, historic, and business districts. Dogs up to 80 pounds are allowed for a $100 refundable deposit plus $25 per day per room;there is a pet waiver to sign at check in.

**Surestay Plus Hotel By Best Western Sacramento North**
350 Bercut Drive
Sacramento CA
916-442-6971 (800-780-7234)
Dogs of all sizes are allowed. There is a pet fee of $20 per pet per night.

**Travelodge Sacramento/rancho Cordova**
9646 Micron Avenue
Sacramento CA
916-361-3131
Dogs up to 15 pounds are allowed. There is a pet fee of $10 per pet per night.

**Westin Sacramento**
4800 Riverside Boulevard
Sacramento CA
916-443-8400 (888-625-5144)
Dogs up to 45 pounds are allowed free of charge. Guests will be asked to sign a waiver upon check-in. No other pets are permitted.

**Ramada Inn & Plaza Harbor Conference Center**
1250 Halyard Drive
West Sacramento CA
916-371-2100
Dogs up to 25 pounds are allowed. There is a pet fee of $25 per day.

**Rodeway Inn Capitol**
817 W Capitol Ave

West Sacramento CA
916-371-6983 (877-424-6423)
The Rodeway Inn hotel is walking distance from Old Sacramento, a museum, riverboat rides, shops and restaurants. Free breakfast.

Dogs up to 20 pounds are allowed. Dogs are allowed for a pet fee of $10.00 per pet per night.

## Pet-Friendly Extended Stay Hotels

**Extended Stay America - Sacramento - Elk Grove**
2201 Long Port Court
Elk Grove CA
916-683-3753 (800-804-3724)
One dog is allowed per suite. There is a $25 per night additional pet fee up to $150 for an entire stay.

**Residence Inn By Marriott Sacramento Folsom**
2555 Iron Point Road
Folsom CA
916-983-7289
Dogs of all sizes are allowed. There is a $100 one time additional pet fee.

**Extended Stay America - Sacramento - White Rock Rd.**

10721 White Rock Rd
Rancho Cordova CA
916-635-2363 (800-804-3724)
One dog is allowed per suite. There is a $25 per night additional pet fee up to $150 for an entire stay.

**Residence Inn Sacramento Rancho Cordova**
2779 Prospect Park Drive
Rancho Cordova CA
916-851-1550
Dogs of all sizes are allowed. There is a $50 one time additional pet fee.

**Staybridge Suites Rocklin**
6664 Lonetree Blvd
Rocklin CA
916-781-7500 (877-270-6405)
Dogs of all sizes are allowed.

Pets allowed with an additional pet fee. Up to $75 for 1-6 nights and up to $150 for 7+ nights. A pet agreement must be signed at check-in. Two dogs are allowed per room.

**Extended Stay America - Sacramento - Roseville**
1000 Lead Hill Blvd
Roseville CA
916-781-9001 (800-804-3724)
One dog is allowed per suite. There is a $25 per night additional pet fee up to $150 for an entire stay.

**Residence Inn Roseville**
1930 Taylor Road
Roseville CA
916-772-5500
Dogs of all sizes are allowed. There is a $100 one time additional pet fee.

**Towneplace Suites Sacramento Roseville**
10569 Fairway Drive
Roseville CA
916-782-2232
Dogs of all sizes are allowed. There is a $100 one time pet fee.

**Extended Stay America - Sacramento - Arden Way**
2100 Harvard Street
Sacramento CA
916-921-9942 (800-804-3724)
One dog is allowed per suite. There is a $25 per night additional pet fee up to $150 for an entire stay.

**Extended Stay America - Sacramento - South Natomas**
2810 Gateway Oaks Drive
Sacramento CA
916-564-7500 (800-804-3724)
One dog is allowed per suite. There is a $25 per night additional pet fee up to $150 for an entire stay.

**Residence Inn By Marriott Sacramento Downtown At Capitol Park**
1121 15th Street
Sacramento CA
916-443-0500
Dogs of all sizes are allowed.

There is a $100 one time additional pet fee.

## Residence Inn Sacramento Airport Natomas
2618 Gateway Oaks Drive
Sacramento CA
916-649-1300
Dogs of all sizes are allowed. There is a $75 one time additional pet fee.

## Residence Inn Sacramento Airport Natomas
2618 Gateway Oaks Drive
Sacramento CA
916-649-1300
Dogs of all sizes are allowed. There is a $75 one time additional pet fee.

## Residence Inn Sacramento Cal Expo
1530 Howe Ave
Sacramento CA
916-920-9111
Dogs of all sizes are allowed. There is a $100 one time additional pet fee.

## Staybridge Suites Sacramento Airport Natomas
140 Promenade Circle
Sacramento CA
916-575-7907 (877-270-6405)
Dogs up to 80 pounds are allowed. Pets allowed with an additional pet fee. Up to $75 for 1-6 nights and up to $150 for 7+ nights. A pet agreement must be signed at check-in.

## Towneplace Suites By Marriott Sacramento Cal Expo

1784 Tribute Road
Sacramento CA
916-920-5400
Dogs of all sizes are allowed. tThere is a $100 one time pet fee.

## Extended Stay America - Sacramento - West Sacramento
795 Stillwater Rd
West Sacramento CA
916-371-1270 (800-804-3724)
One dog is allowed per suite. There is a $25 per night additional pet fee up to $150 for

an entire stay.

# Dog-Friendly Attractions
## Old Towne Folsom
Sutter St & Riley St
Folsom CA

This few block area of Folsom represents the historic mid 1800's gold rush days. There are shops, restaurants, and places to explore. Some of the restaurants will allow your well-behaved, leashed dog at their outdoor tables.

## Nimbus Fish Hatchery
2001 Nimbus Rd
Rancho Cordova CA
916-358-2884
There is a free self-guided tour of the fish hatchery, where salmon eggs are hatched every year. Your well-behaved dog may accompany you leashed. The hours are daily 9 am - 3 pm.

## Capitol Park-Self-Guided Walk
10th and L Streets
Sacramento CA
916-324-0333
At this park, you can enjoy the historic nostalgia of California's State Capitol. The Capitol Building has been the home of the California Legislature since 1869. While dogs are not allowed inside the Capitol Building, you can walk up to it and around it on the 40 acres known as Capitol Park. This park is home to a variety of different trees from around the world. There is a self-guided tour that explains the origin of the trees and plants. Squirrels are also in abundance here, so be sure to hold on to the leash if your pup likes those little creatures. Capitol Park is located in downtown Sacramento at 10th and L Streets.

## Old Sacramento Historic Area
between I and L Streets
Sacramento CA

916-442-7644
oldsacramento.com/
Old Sacramento is a state historic park located in downtown Sacramento, next to the Sacramento River. This National Registered Landmark covers 28 acres and includes a variety of shops and restaurants (see Restaurants). Take the self-guided audio tour of Old Sacramento and learn about life in the 1860's. There are nine audio stations ($.50 per station) placed throughout Old Sacramento. The California State Railroad Museum is also located here. Dogs aren't allowed inside the museum, but there are several locomotives outside. You and your pup can investigate these large trains outside of the museum. Dogs are allowed on the horse and carriage rides located throughout town. Top Hand Ranch Carriage Rides will be more than happy to take you and your well-behaved pup on their carriages. (see Attractions). Old Sacramento is located in downtown Sacramento, between I and L Streets, and Hwy 5 and the Sacramento River. Parking garages are located at 3rd and J Streets or at Capitol Mall and Front Streets. There is a minimal fee for parking.

## Scribner Bend Vineyards
9051 River Road
Sacramento CA
916-744-1803
scribnerbend.com/
Located along the Delta, this award winning vineyard offers complimentary wine tasting Friday through Sunday, beautiful landscaped gardens, a courtyard and water fountain, and picnic tables/benches around the grounds. Dogs are allowed on the grounds, but not in the tasting room. Dogs must be leashed and cleaned up after.

## Top Hand Ranch Carriage Rides
Old Sacramento
Sacramento CA

916-655-3444
Top Hand Ranch offers horse and carriage rides in Old Sacramento and around the State Capitol. Your pooch is welcome in the carriage. Prices are subject to change, but when we checked it cost $10 for a 15 minute ride or $30 for a 35 minute ride around Old Sacramento. If you want to tour Sacramento in style, take the horse and carriage from Old Sacramento to the State Capitol Building and back. This ride lasts about 50 minutes and costs $50. The carriage rides are available daily in Old Sacramento. The carriages are located in several spots, but the main location is at the Old Supreme Court building near J and 2nd Streets. Old Sacramento is located in downtown Sacramento, between I and L Streets, and Hwy 5 and the Sacramento River. Parking garages are located at 3rd and J Streets or at Capitol Mall and Front Streets. There is a minimal fee for parking.

## Outdoor Restaurants

**Bella Bru Coffee Co**
5038 Fair Oaks Blvd
Carmichael CA
916-485-2883
bellabrucafe.com/carmichael.php
They allow dogs at their outdoor tables and may even have dog cookies for your pup.

**Chipotle**
5851 Sunrise Blvd
Citrus Heights CA
916-967-7881
chipotle.com
Specializing in organic, natural and unprocessed food, this Mexican Eatery offers fajita burritos, tacos, salads, and salsas. Dogs are allowed at the outdoor tables but you will need to order your food inside the restaurant and dogs must remain outside.

**Baja Fresh Mexican Grill**
7419 Laguna Blvd. Ste 220

Elk Grove CA
916-691-2252
bajafresh.com
This Mexican restaurant is open for lunch and dinner. They use fresh ingredients and making their salsa and beans daily. Some of the items on their menu include Enchiladas, Burritos, Tacos Salads, Quesadillas, Nachos, Chicken, Steak and more. Well-behaved leashed dogs are allowed at the outdoor tables.

**Chipotle**
7440 Laguna Blvd. #124
Elk Grove CA
916-478-2360
chipotle.com
Specializing in organic, natural and unprocessed food, this Mexican Eatery offers fajita burritos, tacos, salads, and salsas. Dogs are allowed at the outdoor tables but you will need to order your food inside the restaurant and dogs must remain outside.

**Dos Coyotes**
8519 Bond Road, Suite 100
Elk Grove CA
916-687-3790
doscoyotes.net/home.html
Fresh local produce, all natural cheeses, a seasonally evolving menu, freshly made guacamole, salsas and marinades, several vegetarian choices, daily specials, and alfresco dining are just some of the offerings of this Mexican eatery. No animal products are used in their foods and they also offer catering services. Leashed, friendly dogs are allowed at their outside dining area.

**Chipotle**
1001 E Bidwell Street Suite 160
Folsom CA
916-983-9374
chipotle.com
Specializing in organic, natural and unprocessed food, this Mexican Eatery offers fajita burritos, tacos, salads, and salsas. Dogs are allowed at the outdoor tables but you will

need to order your food inside the restaurant and dogs must remain outside.

**Coffee Republic**
6610 Folsom Auburn Rd
Folsom CA
916-987-8001
This coffee bar will allow your pet at the outside tables. They are open Monday to Friday from 5:30 am until 8 pm and on Saturday and Sunday from 6:30 am until 6 pm.

**Jamba Juice**
13389 Folsom Blvd. #400
Folsom CA
916-985-0164
jambajuice.com
All natural and organic ingredients, no high-fructose corn syrup, 0 grams trans fat, no artificial preservatives, a healthy helping of antioxidants, vitamins, and minerals, and fresh whole fruit and fruit juices set the base for these tasty and healthy beverages. Their organic Hot Blends provides a new spin on coffee, green or chai tea, and hot chocolate;plus they offer probiotic fruit and yogurt Blends. Additionally, they feature all natural salads, wraps, sandwiches, and grab n go specialties. They also offer healthy community support through fundraisers, special sales, and school lunch programs. Leashed, well mannered dogs are allowed at their outside dining area.

**Panera Bread**
380 Palladio Parkway, #301
Folsom CA
916-984-4953
panerabread.com/en-us/home.html
The Folsom Panera Bread, located at 380 Palladio Parkway, #301 in Folsom, CA, serves a large variety of Bagels, breakfast sandwiches & favorites, sandwiches, pastas & soups, paninis, salads, breads, freshly baked pastries & sweets, and so much more! Well-behaved, leashed dogs are welcome at the outdoor seating.

**Pinkberry**
280 Palladio Pkwy #933
Folsom CA
916-983-3550
pinkberry.com/palladio
The Folsom Pinkberry is located at 280 Palladio Pkwy #933 in Folsom, California. The nationwide chain serves handcrafted yogurts, including greek yogurt, frozen yogurts, yogurt smoothies, toppings, and lots more. Well-behaved, leashed dogs are welcome at the outdoor seating.

**Pizzeria Classico**
702 Sutter St
Folsom CA
916-351-1430
Outdoor seating is available during the summer months only.

**Rubio's Baja Grill**
2776 E Bidwell Street
Folsom CA
916-983-0645
Dogs are allowed at the outdoor tables.

**Snook's Candies and Ice Cream**
731 Sutter Street
Folsom CA
916-985-0620
snookscandies.com/
There are benches outside but no tables. Dogs are welcome to join you at these benches.

**La Bou**
4110 Douglas Blvd
Granite Bay CA
916-791-2142
labou.com/
This café and bakery specializes in gourmet made from scratch soup, pastries, and breakfast items. Leashed dogs are allowed at their outside seating area.

**Jamba Juice**
4981 Watt Avenue
North Highlands CA
916-344-4108
jambajuice.com
All natural and organic ingredients, no high-fructose corn syrup, 0 grams trans fat, no artificial preservatives, a healthy helping of antioxidants, vitamins, and minerals, and fresh whole fruit and fruit juices set the base for these tasty and healthy beverages. Their organic Hot Blends provides a new spin on coffee, green or chai tea, and hot chocolate;plus they offer probiotic fruit and yogurt Blends. Additionally, they feature all natural salads, wraps, sandwiches, and grab n go specialties. They also offer healthy community support through fundraisers, special sales, and school lunch programs. Leashed, well mannered dogs are allowed at their outside dining area.

**Baja Fresh Mexican Grill**
2210 Sunset Blvd.
Rocklin CA
916-772-1600
bajafresh.com
This Mexican restaurant is open for lunch and dinner. They use fresh ingredients and making their salsa and beans daily. Some of the items on their menu include Enchiladas, Burritos, Tacos Salads, Quesadillas, Nachos, Chicken, Steak and more. Well-behaved leashed dogs are allowed at the outdoor tables.

**Baja Fresh Mexican Grill**
1850 Douglas Blvd
Roseville CA
916-773-2252
bajafresh.com
This Mexican restaurant is open for lunch and dinner. They use fresh ingredients and making their salsa and beans daily. Some of the items on their menu include Enchiladas, Burritos, Tacos Salads, Quesadillas, Nachos, Chicken, Steak and more. Well-behaved leashed dogs are allowed at the outdoor tables.

**Cafe Elletti**
2240 Douglas Blvd
Roseville CA
916-774-6704
This café and deli offers outside seating service. They are open Monday through Friday from 7:30 am to 3:30 pm. Your pet is welcome to join you on the patio. Dogs must be attended to at all times, well behaved, and leashed.

**Chipotle**
3988 Douglas Blvd
Roseville CA
916-786-9218
chipotle.com
Specializing in organic, natural and unprocessed food, this Mexican Eatery offers fajita burritos, tacos, and salsas. Dogs are allowed at the outdoor tables but you will need to order your food inside the restaurant and dogs must remain outside.

**Chipotle**
781 Pleasant Grove Blvd
Roseville CA
916-788-8282
chipotle.com
Specializing in organic, natural and unprocessed food, this Mexican Eatery offers fajita burritos, tacos, salads, and salsas. Dogs are allowed at the outdoor tables but you will need to order your food inside the restaurant and dogs must remain outside.

**Chipotle**
1136 Galleria Blvd
Roseville CA
916-783-8841
chipotle.com
Specializing in organic, natural and unprocessed food, this Mexican Eatery offers fajita burritos, tacos, salads, and salsas. Dogs are allowed at the outdoor tables but you will need to order your food inside the restaurant and dogs must remain outside.

**Dos Coyotes**
2030 Douglas Blvd Suite 4
Roseville CA
916-772-0775
doscoyotes.net/index.html
Fresh local produce, all natural cheeses, a seasonally evolving menu, freshly made guacamole, salsas and marinades, several vegetarian choices, daily specials, and alfresco dining are

just some of the offerings of this Mexican eatery. No animal products are used in their foods. Leashed, friendly dogs are welcome at their outside tables.

### Mas Mexican Food
1563 Eureka Roa
Roseville CA
916-773-3778
This Mexican style restaurant offers inside and outside dining service. Your pet is welcome to join you on the patio. Dogs must be attended to at all times, well behaved, and leashed.

### Quizno's Classic Subs
1228 Galleria Blvd #130
Roseville CA
916-787-1940
quiznos.com/home.aspx
Dogs are allowed at the outdoor tables.

### Togo's Eatery
1825 Douglas Blvd
Roseville CA
916-782-4546
togos.com/
This is a fast food sandwich place. It is within walking distance of Marco Dog Park (see Sacramento Parks). To get there, take Hwy 80 and exit Douglas Blvd. east (towards Folsom). Turn left at the third street which is Sierra Gardens Drive. Leashed dogs are allowed at their outside tables.

### Z Pizza
3984 Douglas Blvd
Roseville CA
916-786-9797
zpizza.com
Specializing in organically and internationally inspired pizzas, this pizzeria cooks their pizzas on hot bricks in a fire baked oven. They feature a 100% certified organic gluten free wheat crust, homemade organic sauces and ingredients, fresh produce, and additive-free meats. They also offer gourmet salads, sandwiches, and catering services. Leashed, well mannered dogs are allowed at their outside tables.

### Ambrosia Cafe & Catering

1030 K Street
Sacramento CA
916-444-8129
ambrosiacafesacramento.com
In addition to a strong commitment to sustainable business practices and sourcing other like local companies, this cafe offers 'California Fresh' cuisine with a daily changing menu based on the freshest market fare. Some other offerings include freshly baked breads/pastries, homemade desserts, organic coffee, and a venue for special events. Leashed, well mannered dogs are allowed at their outside dining area.

### Annabelle's Pizza-Pasta
200 J Street
Sacramento CA
916-448-6239
Located in Old Sacramento, this restaurant allows dogs at the outdoor seating area in the back of the restaurant. There you will find several picnic tables.

### Baja Fresh Mexican Grill
2100 Arden Way
Sacramento CA
916-564-2252
bajafresh.com
This Mexican restaurant is open for lunch and dinner. They use fresh ingredients and making their salsa and beans daily. Some of the items on their menu include Enchiladas, Burritos, Tacos Salads, Quesadillas, Nachos, Chicken, Steak and more. Well-behaved leashed dogs are allowed at the outdoor tables.

### Baja Fresh Mexican Grill
2600 Gateway Oaks Dr.
Sacramento CA
916-920-5201
bajafresh.com
This Mexican restaurant is open for lunch and dinner. They use fresh ingredients and making their salsa and beans daily. Some of the items on their menu include Enchiladas, Burritos, Tacos Salads, Quesadillas, Nachos, Chicken, Steak and more. Well-behaved

leashed dogs are allowed at the outdoor tables.

### Bella Bru Cafe and Catering
4680 Natomas Blvd
Sacramento CA
916-928-1770
This café offers American food, a full service bar, and full-service indoor and outdoor dining. Dogs are allowed to join you on the patio. Dogs must be attended to at all times, well behaved, and leashed.

### Cafe Bernardo
2726 Capitol Avenue
Sacramento CA
916-443-1180
Dogs are allowed at the outdoor tables. This restaurant serves California Cuisine. This popular restaurant's outdoor seating areas can be packed during nice weather for lunch and on weekends.

### Cafe Bernardo / R15
1431 R Street
Sacramento CA
916-930-9191
With the ambiance of a traditional European cafe, this gathering place puts an emphasis on sustainable and locally sourced ingredients. The menu changes seasonally;breads are made fresh every day;they offer a full bar, and their foods are all prepared in their certified green kitchen. Some of their offerings include sandwiches, pizzettas, burgers, fresh caught fish, and steaks. Leashed, well mannered dogs are welcome at their outside tables.

### Cafe Bernardo Midtown / Monkey Bar
2726 Capitol Avenue
Sacramento CA
916-443-1180
With the ambiance of a traditional European cafe, this gathering place puts an emphasis on sustainable and locally sourced ingredients. The menu changes seasonally;breads are made fresh every day;they offer a full bar, and their foods are all

prepared in their certified green kitchen. Some of their offerings include sandwiches, pizzettas, burgers, fresh caught fish, and steaks. Leashed, well mannered dogs are welcome at their outside tables.

## Chipotle
2878 Zinfandel Drive
Sacramento CA
916-861-0620
chipotle.com
Specializing in organic, natural and unprocessed food, this Mexican Eatery offers fajita burritos, tacos, salads, and salsas. Dogs are allowed at the outdoor tables but you will need to order your food inside the restaurant and dogs must remain outside.

## Chipotle
1831 Capitol Avenue
Sacramento CA
916-444-8940
chipotle.com
Specializing in organic, natural and unprocessed food, this Mexican Eatery offers fajita burritos, tacos, salads, and salsas. Dogs are allowed at the outdoor tables but you will need to order your food inside the restaurant and dogs must remain outside.

## Chipotle
3328 El Camino Avenue
Sacramento CA
916-485-6305
chipotle.com
Specializing in organic, natural and unprocessed food, this Mexican Eatery offers fajita burritos, tacos, salads, and salsas. Dogs are allowed at the outdoor tables but you will need to order your food inside the restaurant and dogs must remain outside.

## Chipotle
1729 Howe Avenue
Sacramento CA
916-646-4571
chipotle.com
Specializing in organic, natural and unprocessed food, this Mexican Eatery offers fajita burritos, tacos, salads, and

salsas. Dogs are allowed at the outdoor tables but you will need to order your food inside the restaurant and dogs must remain outside.

## Chipotle
2517 Fair Oaks Blvd
Sacramento CA
916-487-1125
chipotle.com
Specializing in organic, natural and unprocessed food, this Mexican Eatery offers fajita burritos, tacos, salads, and salsas. Dogs are allowed at the outdoor tables but you will need to order your food inside the restaurant and dogs must remain outside.

## Chipotle
5040 Auburn Blvd
Sacramento CA
916-334-5200
chipotle.com
Specializing in organic, natural and unprocessed food, this Mexican Eatery offers fajita burritos, tacos, salads, and salsas. Dogs are allowed at the outdoor tables but you will need to order your food inside the restaurant and dogs must remain outside.

## Danielle's Creperie
3535 B Fair Oaks Blvd
Sacramento CA
916-972-1911
daniellescreperie.com/
The outdoor tables here are seasonal. Well-behaved dogs on leash are permitted at the outdoor tables.

## Dos Coyotes
6450 Folsom Blvd #110
Sacramento CA
916-452-5696
doscoyotes.net/home.html
Fresh local produce, all natural cheeses, a seasonally evolving menu, freshly made guacamole, salsas and marinades, several vegetarian choices, daily specials, and alfresco dining are just some of the offerings of this Mexican eatery. No animal products are used in their foods and they also offer catering services.

Leashed, friendly dogs are allowed at their outside dining area.

## Jamba Juice
2600 Gateway Oaks, #300
Sacramento CA
916-927-2051
jambajuice.com
All natural and organic ingredients, no high-fructose corn syrup, 0 grams trans fat, no artificial preservatives, a healthy helping of antioxidants, vitamins, and minerals, and fresh whole fruit and fruit juices set the base for these tasty and healthy beverages. Their organic Hot Blends provides a new spin on coffee, green or chai tea, and hot chocolate;plus they offer probiotic fruit and yogurt Blends. Additionally, they feature all natural salads, wraps, sandwiches, and grab n go specialties. They also offer healthy community support through fundraisers, special sales, and school lunch programs. Leashed, well mannered dogs are allowed at their outside dining area.

## Jamba Juice
4640 Natomas Blvd, #120
Sacramento CA
916-419-6092
jambajuice.com
All natural and organic ingredients, no high-fructose corn syrup, 0 grams trans fat, no artificial preservatives, a healthy helping of antioxidants, vitamins, and minerals, and fresh whole fruit and fruit juices set the base for these tasty and healthy beverages. Their organic Hot Blends provides a new spin on coffee, green or chai tea, and hot chocolate;plus they offer probiotic fruit and yogurt Blends. Additionally, they feature all natural salads, wraps, sandwiches, and grab n go specialties. They also offer healthy community support through fundraisers, special sales, and school lunch programs. Leashed, well mannered dogs are allowed at their outside dining area.

## La Bou
10395 Rockingham Dr
Sacramento CA
916-369-7824
labou.com/
This café and bakery specializes in gourmet made from scratch soup, pastries, and breakfast items. Leashed dogs are allowed at their outside seating area.

## Magpie Cafe & Catering
1409 R Street Suite 102
Sacramento CA
916-452-7594
magpiecaterers.com
With an emphasis on sustainable, local, and organic, this cafe and caterer features a seasonally-driven menu of skillfully handcrafted central and northern California cuisine using organic and all-natural ingredients. Leashed, well mannered dogs are welcome at their outside dining area.

## Original Pete's Pizza, Pasta and Grill
2001 J Street
Sacramento CA
916-442-6770
Dogs are allowed at the outdoor tables.

## Pyramid Alehouse
1029 K Street
Sacramento CA
916-498-9800
Offering a menu of classic brew house cuisine, guests will also find at this alehouse an eclectic selection of household specialty brews, seasonal offerings, and year around brews on draft. Leashed, friendly dogs are allowed at their outside dining area.

## River City Brewing Company
545 Downtown Plaza Ste 1115
Sacramento CA
916-447-2739
rivercitybrewing.net/
Some of the offerings at this brewing company include more than 22 ales and lagers created throughout the year, signature cuisine, a full bar, a venue for special events, and alfresco dining. Leashed, well mannered

dogs are welcome at their outside tables.

## Rubicon Brewing Company
2004 Capitol Avenue
Sacramento CA
916-448-7032
Dogs are allowed at the outdoor tables.

## Sacramento Natural Foods Cooperative
1900 Alhambra Blvd.
Sacramento CA
916-455-2667
sacfoodcoop.com
Dogs are allowed at the outdoor tables. You will need to go inside without your dog to get your food.

## Spataro Restaurant and Bar
1415 L Street
Sacramento CA
916-440-8888
This eatery, located at lobby level in the Meridian Plaza building, offers authentic fine Italian cuisine with local, seasonal and organic infusions. They have an open kitchen, house-made breads and cured meats, freshly made pastas, an extensive wine selection, and a full bar. Leashed, well mannered dogs are welcome at their outside tables.

## Streets of London Pub
1804 J Street
Sacramento CA
916-498-1388
streetsoflondon.net
Dogs are allowed at the outdoor tables.

## Ten 22
1022 Second Street
Sacramento CA
916-441-2211
info@ten22oldsac.com
Innovative, handcrafted farm-to-table American cuisine showcasing regional ingredients is the specialty of this dining destination. Food and drink specials, craft beers on tap, special events, and live music every Friday and Saturday from 7 pm until 10 pm are also offered. The restaurant is open daily from 11:30 am

until 10 pm. Leashed, friendly dogs are allowed at their front outside dining area.

## The Bread Store
1716 J Street
Sacramento CA
916-557-1600
thebreadstoresacramento.com/
This sandwich shoppe allows dogs at the outdoor patio. The patio is covered.

## Whole Foods Market
4315 Arden Way
Sacramento CA
916-488-2800
wholefoods.com/
This natural food supermarket offers natural and organic foods. Order some food from their deli without your dog and bring it to an outdoor table where your well-behaved leashed dog is welcome.

# Pet-Friendly Shopping Centers
## Palladio
East Bidwell Rd & Iron Point Rd
Folsom CA
916-983-9793
gopalladio.com
This European style open air shopping center is located just off Highway 50 at East Bidwell Rd. Dogs are allowed in the common areas of the shopping center and it is up to the individual stores if dogs are allowed inside. Dogs are allowed at a number of the patio restaurants, including Pinkberry and San Francisco Sourdough Eatery.

## Downtown Plaza
547 L Street
Sacramento CA
915-442-4000
westfield.com/downtownplaza/
This open air mall has great outdoor views and 120 stores in various categories. They also offer a concierge center, a 7 theater cinema complex, a kid's playground, a great imported carousel, several well-known eateries, and is home to

Sacramento's only outdoor skating rink. Dogs are allowed to walk through the area, and it is up to the individual stores whether or not they are allowed inside. Dogs must be well mannered at all times, and be leashed and cleaned up after.

## Pet-Friendly Stores

**PetSmart Pet Store**
6434 Sunrise Blvd
Citrus Heights CA
916-729-2866
Your licensed and well-behaved leashed dog is allowed in the store.

**Petco Pet Store - Citrus Heights**
6067 Greenback Lane
Citrus Heights CA
916-725-2556
Your licensed and well-behaved leashed dog is allowed in the store.

**Pet Club**
8515 Bond Road
Elk Grove CA
916-686-7808
petclubstores.com
In addition to warehouse pricing with no membership fees, this comprehensive pet supply store offers weekly specials and more than 11,000 pet products ranging from wellness items, bedding, dinnerware, a wide choice of quality foods, treats, leashes, toys, apparel, travel supplies, and much more. Leashed, friendly dogs are always welcome in the store.

**PetSmart Pet Store**
8215 Laguna Blvd
Elk Grove CA
916-691-3700
Your licensed and well-behaved leashed dog is allowed in the store.

**Petco Pet Store - Elk Grove**
7715 Laguna Blvd
Elk Grove CA
916-683-5155
Your licensed and well-behaved leashed dog is allowed in the store.

**Petco Pet Store - Fair Oaks**
8840 Madison Ave.
Fair Oaks CA
916-863-7387
Your licensed and well-behaved leashed dog is allowed in the store.

**PetSmart Pet Store**
2705 E Bidwell St
Folsom CA
916-984-4748
Your licensed and well-behaved leashed dog is allowed in the store.

**Petco Pet Store - Folsom**
855 East Bidwell St.
Folsom CA
916-984-6141
Your licensed and well-behaved leashed dog is allowed in the store.

**PetSmart Pet Store**
10830 Olson Dr
Rancho Cordova CA
916-851-1813
Your licensed and well-behaved leashed dog is allowed in the store.

**Camping World**
4435 Granite Drive
Rocklin CA
916-632-1023
campingworld.com/
This comprehensive RV and outdoor store carries a wide variety of RV, boat, bike, and outdoor cooking accessories; all kinds of camping gear; RV screens, shades, and patio decorations; racing/tailgating gear, and all items for RV maintenance. They also carry RV towing supplies, electronics, and interior decorating items as well as pet supplies, RV directories/books, and games. Plus, they offer a tips and advice service, RV sales, rentals, and RV technicians to take care of any installations and repairs. They also welcome your canine companion in the store; they must be friendly and leashed.

**Petco Pet Store - Rocklin**
6672 Lonetree Blvd
Rocklin CA
916-786-6030
Your licensed and well-behaved leashed dog is allowed in the store.

**Anthropologie**
1182 Roseville Parkway, #150
Roseville CA
916-789-9100
Items of distinction can be found for all ages and in all departments of this unique shop. Carefully selected to add to the enjoyment of the shopping experience, they carry fine clothing, amazing accessories, jewelry, hobby and leisure items, and a full line of bright and useful items for the home, garden, and office. Leashed, well behaved dogs are allowed in the store.

**Camping World**
1039 Orlando Avenue
Roseville CA
916-772-1155
campingworld.com/
This comprehensive RV and outdoor store carries a wide variety of RV, boat, bike, and outdoor cooking accessories; all kinds of camping gear; RV screens, shades, and patio decorations; racing/tailgating gear, and all items for RV maintenance. They also carry RV towing supplies, electronics, and interior decorating items as well as pet supplies, RV directories/books, and games. Plus, they offer a tips and advice service, RV sales, rentals, and RV technicians to take care of any installations and repairs. They also welcome your canine companion in the store; they must be friendly and leashed.

**Crate and Barrel**
1151 Galleria Blvd
Roseville CA
916-784-9100
crateandbarrel.com
This store offers fine products from around the world that include items for outdoor living, indoor furnishings and decorating, dining and entertaining, kitchen

and food service, and gourmet food and beverages. They also have accessories for pets, bed and bath items, and organizing and storage units. Leashed, friendly dogs are welcome in the store; they must be under their owner's control at all times.

### Orvis Company Store
1009 Galleria Blvd
Roseville CA
916-783-9400
orvis.com
This comprehensive outfitters store offers a wide array of sporting goods and services, clothing and accessories for all types of active lifestyles, quality products for home and pets, gifts and travel items, and much more. Well mannered dogs are welcome in the store; they must be leashed and under their owner's control at all times.

### PetSmart Pet Store
318 N Sunrise Blvd
Roseville CA
916-786-5512
Your licensed and well-behaved leashed dog is allowed in the store.

### PetSmart Pet Store
10363 Fairway Dr
Roseville CA
916-774-8205
Your licensed and well-behaved leashed dog is allowed in the store.

### Petco Pet Store - Roseville
1917 Douglas Blvd
Roseville CA
916-786-8655
Your licensed and well-behaved leashed dog is allowed in the store.

### Chez Pooche
900 2nd Street
Sacramento CA
916-446-1213
chezpoocheinc.com/
A variety of fun activities year round, a great selection of designer clothes, all natural gourmet treats, pet strollers, grooming and health supplies, jewelry, pet sitting, and lots more have made this a popular

stop for pet lovers and pets. It is located in the popular Old Sacramento area. They will validate your parking ticket with any purchase, and pooches will get a free gourmet treat. Dogs must be under their owner's control at all times.

### PetSmart Pet Store
1738 Watt Ave
Sacramento CA
916-973-8391
Your licensed and well-behaved leashed dog is allowed in the store.

### PetSmart Pet Store
7923 E Stockton Blvd
Sacramento CA
916-689-3000
Your licensed and well-behaved leashed dog is allowed in the store.

### PetSmart Pet Store
3641 Truxel Rd
Sacramento CA
916-928-0314
Your licensed and well-behaved leashed dog is allowed in the store.

### Petco Pet Store - Sacramento - Arden
1878 Arden Way
Sacramento CA
916-923-1082
Your licensed and well-behaved leashed dog is allowed in the store.

### Urban Outfitters
1703 Arden Way
Sacramento CA
916-565-0638
In addition to a large inventory of indoor and outdoor apparel for men and women, this major department store also carries vintage wear, designer brands, and a variety of accessories for all types of active lifestyles. They also carry shoes, furnishings, home decor, cameras, electronics, novelty items and more. Leashed, well mannered dogs are allowed in the store.

## Off-Leash Dog Parks
### Carmichael Park and Dog Park
Fair Oaks Blvd & Grant Ave
Carmichael CA
916-485-5322
This is a one acre off leash dog park. It is located in Carmichael Park which can be accessed from Fair Oaks Blvd in Carmichael. The rest of the park is nice for picnics and other activities. Dogs must be leashed when not inside the dog park.

### C-Bar-C Dog Park
Oak Avenue east of Fair Oaks
Citrus Heights CA
916-725-1585
facebook.com/cbarcpark/
The dog park is located in C-Bar-C Park on Oak Ave. east of Fair Oaks and West of Wachtel. The dog park is over 2 acres in size and fenced. Benches are available and there is shade in the park. There is drinking water for dogs and people. For your water loving pups there are hoses and small wading pools in the park. The park is host to a number of dog events annually.

### Elk Grove Dog Park
9950 Elk Grove Florin Rd
Elk Grove CA
916-405-5600
yourcsd.com/315/Dog-Parks
The fenced dog park is best accessed from the East Stockton Blvd side of Elk Grove Park.From 99 take Grant Line Rd east and go left on East Stockton. The Elk Grove dog parks are monitored and maintained by the Park department and W.O.O.F. (We Offer Off-leash Fun), a dog owners organization in Elk Grove.

### Laguna Dog Park
9014 Bruceville Rd
Elk Grove CA
916-405-5600
yourcsd.com/315/Dog-Parks
The fenced Laguna Community Dog Park is located on the west side of Laguna Community Park. The small Laguna Community Park is located

south of Big Horn Blvd and west of Brucevill Rd. The Elk Grove dog parks are monitored and maintained by the Park department and W.O.O.F. (We Offer Off-leash Fun), a dog owners organization in Elk Grove.

### Phoenix Dog Park
9050 Sunset Ave
Fair Oaks CA
916-966-1036
The Phoenix Dog Park is located in Phoenix Park in Fair Oaks. It is just under 2 acres in size and has three separate fenced areas. There is one area for large dogs, one area for small dogs and an area for shy dogs. There are shade structures, benches and a washoff pad just outside of the dog park. The park is sponsored by FORDOG which stands for Fair Oaks Responsible Dog Owners Group. The park is located on Sunset Avenue east of Hazel. To get to the dog park from Highway 50, take Hazel north to Sunset and turn right. The dog park will be on your right.

### FIDO Field Dog Park
1780 Creekside Drive
Folsom CA
916-355-7283
Located at the Cummings Family Park, this off lead doggy play area offers lots of room, benches, shaded areas, and waste disposal stations. Call 916-817-2767 if concerned that the park may be closed due to inclement weather. Dogs must be healthy, sociable, current on all vaccinations and license with tags on collar, and under their owner's control at all times. Dogs must be leashed when not in designated off-lead areas.

### Westside Dog Park
810 Oak Lane
Rio Linda CA
916) 991-5929
rleparks.com/westside-park1
This one acre fenced dog park is located in Westside Park at 810 Oak Lane in Rio Linda.

### Marco Dog Park
1800 Sierra Gardens Drive
Roseville CA
916-774-5950
RDOG (Roseville Dog Owners Group) helped to establish this 2 acre dog park which is Roseville's first off-leash dog park. This park was named Marco Dog Park in memory of a Roseville Police Department canine named Marco who was killed in the line of duty. The park has a large grassy area with a few trees and doggie fire hydrants. It is closed on Wednesdays from dawn until 3:30pm for weekly maintenance. Like other dog parks, it may also be closed some days during the winter due to mud. To get there from Hwy 80, exit Douglas Blvd. heading east. Go about 1/2 mile and turn left on Sierra Gardens Drive. Marco Dog Park will be on the right.

### Bannon Creek Dog Park
Bannon Creek Drive near West El Camino
Sacramento CA
916-264-5200
This off leash dog park is in Bannon Creek Park. Its hours are 5am to 10 pm daily. The park is 0.6 acres in size.

### Bradshaw Dog Park
3839 Bradshaw Road
Sacramento CA
916-368-7387
The Bark Park is located in front of the new Sacramento County Animal Shelter and features 2 acres with sections for larges and small dogs as well as water for dogs. The park is open daily from 8 am until dusk. Dogs must be healthy, sociable, current on all vaccinations and license with tags on collar, and under their owner's control at all times. Owners must clean up after their pets, and keep them leashed when not in designated off-lead areas.

### Glenbrook Dog Park
8500 La Riviera Drive
Sacramento CA

Offerings of this doggy play park include mature shade trees, a long run turf area, a drinking fountain for dogs, and a shaded seating area and picnic tables for pet owners. Dogs must be healthy, sociable, current on all vaccinations and license with tags on collar, and under their owner's control at all times. Owners must clean up after their pets, and keep them leashed when not in designated off-lead areas.

### Granite Park Dog Park
Ramona Avenue near Power Inn Rd
Sacramento CA
916-264-5200
This dog park is in Granite Regional Park. Its hours are 5 am to 10 pm daily. It is 2 acres in size.

### Howe Dog Park
2201 Cottage Way
Sacramento CA
916-927-3802
Howe Dog Park is completely fenced and located in Howe Park. It has grass and several trees. To get there, take Business Route 80 and exit El Camino Ave. Head east on El Camino Ave. Turn right on Howe Ave. Howe Park will be on the left. Turn left onto Cottage Way and park in the lot. From the parking lot, the dog park is located to the right of the tennis courts.

### North Natomas Regional Park Dog Park
2501 New Market Drive
Sacramento CA

A separate half acre has been set aside for small or timid dogs under 25 pounds at this 2.5 acre off leash site. Dogs must be healthy, sociable, current on all vaccinations and license with tags on collar, and under their owner's control at all times. Owners must clean up after their pets, and keep them leashed when not in designated off-lead areas.

### Partner Park Dog Park
5699 South Land Park Drive
Sacramento CA
916-264-5200
This dog park is located behind
the Bell Cooledge Community
Center. The park is 2.5 acres
and its hours are 5 am to 10 pm
daily. There are lights at the
park.

### Regency Community Park Dog Park
5500 Honor Parkway
Sacramento CA

This 2 acre off leash area has
turf and decomposed granite
areas, a water fountain for dogs,
shade trees, an obstacle course
for dogs and benches. Dogs
must be healthy, sociable,
current on all vaccinations and
license with tags on collar, and
under their owner's control at all
times. Owners must clean up
after their pets, and keep them
leashed when not in designated
off-lead areas.

### Sutter's Landing Dog Park
20 28th Street
Sacramento CA
916-875-6961
There are 2 separate areas for
large and small dogs at this 2
acre doggy park, as well as
drinking fountains, benches, and
shade umbrellas. Dogs must be
healthy, sociable, current on all
vaccinations and license with
tags on collar, and under their
owner's control at all times.
Dogs must be leashed when not
in designated off-lead areas.

### Tanzanite Community Park Dog Park
Tanzanite Dr at Innovator Dr
Sacramento CA
916-808-5200
Tanzanite Community Park Dog
Park is located in the Tanzanite
Community Park in North
Natomas. This new two acre
fenced dog park is scheduled to
open by the Fall of 2006. The
park is located east of Airport
Road in the Tanzanite
Community Park.

### Sam Combs Dog Park

205 Stone Blvd
West Sacramento CA
916-617-4620
This fenced off-leash dog park
opened in early 2006. There is
a separate area for large dogs
and small dogs. Take Jefferson
Blvd south from the I-80
Freeway, left on Stone Blvd to
the park on the left.

# Dog-Friendly Parks
### Rusch Community Park and Gardens
Antelope Road & Auburn Blvd
Citrus Heights CA

This is a nice city park with
walkways, bridges and views
plus a botanical garden to
explore. The botanical garden
is accessed from Antelope Rd
and Rosswood. Dogs must be
on leash at all times.

### Folsom Lake State Recreation Area
various (see comments)
Folsom CA
916-988-0205
This popular lake and
recreation area is located in the
Sierra Foothills. The Folsom
Lake State Rec Area is
approximately 18,000 acres, of
which, 45% is land. Leashed
dogs are allowed almost
everywhere in this park except
on the main beaches (there will
be signs posted). But there are
many other non-main beaches
all around Folsom Lake where
your dog is welcome. There are
about 80 miles of dog-friendly
trails in this park. This park is
also adjacent to the American
River Parkway, a 32 mile
paved and dirt path, which
stretches from Folsom Lake to
downtown Sacramento. Folsom
Lake has various entry points
and can be reached via Hwy 80
or Hwy 50. It is located about
25 miles east of Sacramento.
From Hwy 80, exit Douglas
Blvd in Roseville and head
east. From Hwy 50, exit
Folsom Blvd. and head north.
There is a minimal day use fee.

### Gibson Ranch Park
Elverta Rd West of Watt Ave
North Highlands CA
916-875-6961
gibsonranchpark.com
This park allows dogs on leash.
There are a lot of dirt walking or
jogging trails which must be
shared with horses as this is
predominantly an equestrian
park. There is a lake in the
center with picnic areas and
fishing available.

### Orangevale Community Park
Oak Ave & Filbert Ave
Orangevale CA
916-988-4373
ovparks.com/
Dogs must be on leash at this
city park.

### Maidu Park
Rocky Ridge Rd & Maidu Dr
Roseville CA
916-774-5969
Dogs must be on leash in this
new 152 acre park in Roseville.

### American River Parkway
various (see comments)
Sacramento CA
916-875-6672
The American River Parkway is
a very popular recreation trail for
locals and visitors. There are
over 32 miles of paved and dirt
paths that stretch from Folsom
Lake in the Sierra Foothills to
Old Sacramento in downtown
Sacramento. It is enjoyed by
hikers, wildlife viewers, boaters,
equestrians and bicyclists. And
of course, by dogs. Dogs must
be on leash. There are various
starting points, like the Folsom
Lake State Recreation Area in
Folsom or just north of
downtown Sacramento. To start
just north of downtown, take
Hwy 5 north of downtown and
exit Richards Blvd. Turn left onto
Richards Blvd. Then turn right
on Jibboom Street. Take
Jibboom St to the parking lot.

### William Land Park
4000 S Land Park Drive
Sacramento CA
916-808-5200
With just over 166 developed

acres, this park offers a variety of recreational opportunities and amenities, some of which include family and group picnic areas, gaming courts, playing fields, an adventure play area, an amphitheater, rock garden, and a jogging path. They are also home to the Sacramento Zoo, Fairytale town, Funderland, and a golf course. Dogs are allowed throughout the park unless otherwise noted. They must be leashed and cleaned up after at all times.

## Events
**Doggy Dash**
915 I St
Sacramento CA
916-383-7387
sspca.org/Events.html
This annual summer event at William Land Park, sponsored by the Sacramento SPCA, offers a full day of activities for canines and their human companions. It includes a scenic run/walk, specialty vendors, contests, demonstrations, agility shows, and more. Dogs must be leashed and cleaned up after at all times.

## Transportation Systems
**RT (Rapid Transit)**
Regional
Sacramento CA
916-321-2877
sacrt.com
Small dogs in carriers are allowed on the buses and light rail. The carrier must fit on the person's lap.

## Airports
**Sacramento International Airport (SMF)**

Sacramento CA

sacramento.aero/smf/about/faq/
Sacramento International Airport has two pet relief areas. The Terminal A Pet Relief Area is located immediately behind the

Southwest Airlines curbside check-in area. The Terminal B Pet Relief Area is located in the grass patio area on the south end of the terminal on the first level.

## Emergency Veterinarians
**Greenback Veterinary Hospital**
8311 Greenback Lane
Fair Oaks CA
916-725-1541
There is also an on site kennel - Greenback Pet Resort. This is a 24 hour emergency veterinarian.

**Pet Emergency Center**
1100 Atlantic St
Roseville CA
916-783-4655
The vet is open 24 hours for emergencies.

**Emergency Animal Clinic**
9700 Business Park Dr #404
Sacramento CA
916-362-3146
Monday - Saturday 9 am - 6 pm, Emergencies handled 24 hours.

**Sacramento Emergency Vet Clinic**
2201 El Camino Ave
Sacramento CA
916-922-3425
Monday - Friday 6 pm to 8 am, 24 hours on the weekend.

## Vets and Kennels
**Kenar Pet Resort**
3633 Garfield Ave
Carmichael CA
916-487-5221
Monday - Saturday 7 am - 6 pm, Sunday 3 pm - 6 pm pickup with extra day fee.

**Greenback Pet Resort**
8311 Greenback Lane
Fair Oaks CA
916-726-3400
This kennel is attached to a veterinary clinic. The kennel hours are Monday - Friday 8am

to 6 pm, Saturday 8am - 5pm, Sunday 10am - 5pm.

**Wag Pet Hotel**
1759 Enterprise Blvd
West Sacramento CA
916-373-0300
This new pet kennel is notable for its 24 hour pick up and drop off - making it ideal for Sacramento Visitors who need to drop there dog off for a while if they are unable to take their dog with them. It also features play areas and webcams to check on your pet.

## Humane Society or SPCAs

**Sacramento SPCA**
6201 Florin Perkins Road
Sacramento CA
916 383 7387 x 9102
sspca.org
The Sacramento Society for the Prevention of Cruelty to Animals (SSPCA) was established 1894 and is dedicated to ensuring the humane treatment of all animals in the Sacramento area. We provide a safe and nurturing environment for unwanted, abandoned and mistreated pets until they can be placed into loving homes. Through proactive intervention, public education and community outreach, the Sacramento SPCA seeks to promote respect for all life by breaking the cycle of abuse, neglect and pet overpopulation in our communities.

## Rescue Organizations
**Homeward Bound Golden Retriever Rescue and Sanctuary**
7495 Natomas Road
Elverta CA
916-655-1410
hbgrr.org
Homeward Bound Golden Retriever Rescue & Sanctuary, Inc. is a local non-profit, all volunteer rescue organization dedicated to securing safe,

loving homes for displaced or homeless Golden Retrievers. The organization receives Golden Retrievers from owners who can no longer care for them because of changing circumstances in their lives. We also maintain close working relationships with animal shelters to ensure that Goldens are relinquished to us instead of being euthanized at the shelter. We also rescue Golden Retrievers found wandering the streets or reported to us by concerned neighbors. Homeward Bound rescues Goldens of all ages and medical conditions.

## Other Organizations
**Toy Dog Meetup**
7100 Fair Oaks Blvd
Carmichael CA
916-722-7277
ToyDog.Meetup.com/3
We are a toy dog meet up group that gets together for playdates to help socialize our dogs. We meet three times a month, the second Friday, third Saturday and last Sunday of each month. There is no fee to join the group or attend the meetings/playdates. We meet at Carmichael Park in the small dog area of the Canine Corral. Dogs must be up to date on their shots to use the park. This is an informal get together and we just have fun with our dogs.

**POOCH (Pet Owners Organization of Citrus Heights**

P.O. Box 962
Citrus Heights CA
916-725-4297
poochdogpark.com
POOCH IS A 501C (C3)non-profit organization dedicated to improving the lives of dogs and their owners through recreational facilities, rescue efforts, humane training and responsible ownership. Operates a 3 acre dogpark at C-Bar-C PARK, located on Oak Ave. between Kenneth and Fair Oaks Blvd, in Citrus Heights, Ca

95610. Offers grassy, wooded area for dogs to run.

**W.O.O.F. "We Offer Off-leash Fun"**
8820 Elk Grove Blvd
Elk Grove CA
916-714-3696
We are the Elk Grove Dog Park Advisory Committee, called W.O.O.F. which stands for We Offer Off-leash Fun. Our committee is through the Elk Grove Community Services District, Parks and Rec. We meet on a regular basis to discuss issues with the two Elk Grove dog parks, make suggestions for improvements, we are actively at the dog parks on a regular basis educating and monitoring the dog park conditions, we also hold fundraising events to raise money to improve the dog parks and hope to get more dog parks approved in additional parks in Elk Grove. We are always looking for new members and welcome any feedback and involvement.

## Saint Helena

### Dog-Friendly Wineries and Vineyards
**Frenchie Winery (at Raymond Vineyards)**
849 Zinfandel Lane
Saint Helena CA
707-963-3141
frenchiewinery.com/
Frenchie's Winery is the Napa Valley's first dog winery. It was created from the belief that all creatures deserve a tasting room in the Napa Valley. The winery offers outdoor, shady "dog suites" complete with wine barrel beds for your dog to relax in while owners taste wine inside.

## Salida

### Dog-Friendly Hotels
**La Quinta Inn & Suites Salida/modesto**
4909 Sisk Road
Salida CA
209-579-8723 (800-531-5900)
Dogs of all sizes are allowed for no additional pet fee; there is a pet policy to sign at check-in. Dogs may not be left alone in the room.

## Salinas

### Pet-Friendly Extended Stay Hotels
**Residence Inn By Marriott Salinas Monterey**
17215 El Rancho Way
Salinas CA
831-775-0410
Dogs of all sizes are allowed. There is a $100 one time additional pet fee.

### Outdoor Restaurants
**Jamba Juice**
1552-A N Main Street
Salinas CA
831-449-3200
jambajuice.com
All natural and organic ingredients, no high-fructose corn syrup, zero grams trans fat, no artificial preservatives, a healthy helping of antioxidants, vitamins, and minerals, and fresh whole fruit and fruit juices set the base for these tasty and healthy beverages. Their organic Hot Blends provides a new spin on coffee, green or chai tea, and hot chocolate;plus they offer probiotic fruit and yogurt Blends. Additionally, they feature all natural salads, wraps, sandwiches, and grab n go specialties. They also offer healthy community support through fundraisers, special sales, and school lunch programs. Leashed, well mannered dogs are allowed at

their outside dining area.

## Pet-Friendly Stores
### Collier Feed & Pet Supply
101 W Laurel Dr
Salinas CA
831-443-6161
The Collier Feed & Pet Supply in Salinas, California, is a feed & supply store not only carrying dogs and cat products, but also ranges in farm animal supplies. Well-behaved, leashed dogs are allowed in the store.

### Jurassic Pets
925 S Main St
Salinas CA
831-759-8841
Jurassic Pets is a pet supply store offering pet food, supplies, toys, beds, doggy clothing, and more. They also sell natural, high-quality dog and cat food brands. They specialize in unique animals, also selling reptiles, chicks, and more. Well-behaved, leashed dogs are allowed in the store.

### Pet Fun at Harden Ranch Plaza
1780 N. Main St.
Salinas CA
831-443-1873
petfunsalinas.com
The Pet Fun at Harden Ranch Plaza pet supply store offers a large selection of quality pet foods and supplies, discounted prices, premium pet foods, and lots more. They offer everything you need for your dog, cat, fish, bird, reptile or small animal, from dog clothing & leashes to beds, carriers, and premium dog food.

### PetSmart Pet Store
1265 N Davis Rd
Salinas CA
831-775-0318
Your licensed and well-behaved leashed dog is allowed in the store.

## Dog-Friendly Parks
### Toro County Park
501 Monterey-Salinas Highway 68
Salinas CA
831-755-4895
This 4,756 acre park offers over 20 miles of hiking, biking and horseback riding trails. Other park amenities include playgrounds, picnic sites, volleyball courts and an equestrian staging area. There is a $3 vehicle entrance fee during the week and a $5 fee on weekends and holidays. This park is located 6 miles from downtown Salinas and 13 miles from the Monterey Peninsula. Dogs need to be leashed and please clean up after them.

## Veterinarians
### Animal Health Center
1261 B. S. Main St
Salinas CA
831-422-7387
animalhealthcentersalinas.com/
Animal Health Center is a full service animal hospital and will handle emergency cases as well as less urgent medical, surgical, and dental issues. They are open Monday & Tuesday 8am-5:30pm, Wednesday 8am-1:30pm, Thursday 8am-6:30pm, Friday 8am-5:30pm, and every other Sunday 10am-3pm.

# San Bernardino

## Dog-Friendly Hotels
### Aloft Ontario-rancho Cucamonga
10480 Fourth Street
Rancho Cucamonga CA
909-484-2018 (877-GO-ALOFT (462-5638))
Offering a contemporary ambiance and amenities for all level of travelers, this upscale hotel also provides a central location to some of the area's best attractions, world class shopping, and sports activities. Dogs up to 40 pounds are allowed for no additional fee;there is a pet waiver to sign at check in. Canine guests are welcomed with a dog bed, dinnerware, toys, and treats.

### Four Points By Sheraton Ontario-rancho Cucamonga
11960 Foothill Boulevard
Rancho Cucamonga CA
909-204-6100 (888-625-5144)
This luxury hotel offers numerous on site amenities for discerning business and leisure travelers, plus a convenient location to world-class shopping, dining, recreation, attractions, and entertainment areas. Dogs are allowed for an additional one time $75 pet fee per room and there is a pet waiver to sign at check in.

### Best Western Hospitality Lane
294 East Hospitality Lane
San Bernardino CA
909-381-1681 (800-780-7234)
Dogs up to 80 pounds are allowed. There is a $10 per day pet fee up to $100 for the week. Up to two dogs are allowed per room.

### Doubletree By Hilton San Bernardino
285 East Hospitality Lane
San Bernardino CA
909-889-0133
Located in the heart of the city, this upscale hotel offers numerous on site amenities for business and leisure travelers, plus a convenient location to an international airport, business, shopping, dining, and entertainment areas. Dogs up to 75 pounds are allowed for an additional one time pet fee of $50 per room.

### Quality Inn San Bernardino
1750 South Waterman Avenue
San Bernardino CA
909-888-4827 (877-424-6423)
From beautiful mountain views to our deluxe continental breakfast, from richly designed guest rooms to our

Dogs of all sizes are allowed. Dogs are allowed for a pet fee of $$50.00 per pet per stay.

## Pet-Friendly Extended Stay Hotels

### Homewood Suites By Hilton Ontario-rancho Cucamonga Ca

11433 Mission Vista Drive
Rancho Cucamonga CA
909-481-6480
This upscale all suite hotel offers large, comfortable suites for longer stays and/or temporary housing needs;plus numerous on site amenities for all level of travelers and a convenient location to local sites of interest. Dogs up to 50 pounds are allowed for an additional one time pet fee of $75 per room.

### Towneplace Suites By Marriott Ontario Airport

9625 Milliken Avenue
Rancho Cucamonga CA
909-466-2200
Dogs of all sizes are allowed. There is a $100 one time pet fee.

### Residence Inn San Bernardino

1040 East Harriman Place
San Bernardino CA
909-382-4564
Dogs of all sizes are allowed. There is a $75 one time additional pet fee.

## Outdoor Restaurants

### Coffee Bean & Tea Leaf

16215 Sierra Lakes Parkway
Fontana CA
909-349-0811
coffeebean.com
The coffee here is sourced globally from family coffee farms to procure only the top of 1% of Arabica beans. They offer 30+ varieties of coffee;the beans are roasted in small batches daily for freshness, and they also offer 20 varieties of teas that are hand-blended by their tea master. Additionally, they offer a variety of tasty sweets, powders, extracts, sauces, gifts, and cards. Leashed, well mannered dogs are allowed at their outside dining area.

### Jamba Juice

16635 Sierra Lakes Parkway, Suite 100
Fontana CA
909-823-6303
jambajuice.com
All natural and organic ingredients, no high-fructose corn syrup, 0 grams trans fat, no artificial preservatives, a healthy helping of antioxidants, vitamins, and minerals, and fresh whole fruit and fruit juices set the base for these tasty and healthy beverages. Their organic Hot Blends provides a new spin on coffee, green or chai tea, and hot chocolate;plus they offer probiotic fruit and yogurt Blends. Additionally, they feature organic steel-cut oatmeal prepared fresh every morning, all natural salads, wraps, sandwiches, and grab n' go specialties. They also offer healthy community support through fundraisers, special sales, and school lunch programs. Leashed, well mannered dogs are allowed at their outside dining area.

### Chipotle

10811 Foothill Blvd/Historic H 66
Rancho Cucamonga CA
909-476-8424
chipotle.com
Specializing in organic, natural and unprocessed food, this Mexican Eatery offers fajita burritos, tacos, salads, and salsas. Dogs are allowed at the outdoor tables but you will need to order your food inside the restaurant and dogs must remain outside.

### Chipotle

11334 4th Street
Rancho Cucamonga CA
909-476-7863
chipotle.com
Specializing in organic, natural and unprocessed food, this Mexican Eatery offers fajita burritos, tacos, salads, and salsas. Dogs are allowed at the outdoor tables but you will need to order your food inside the restaurant and dogs must remain outside.

### Coffee Bean & Tea Leaf

8140 Haven Avenue, Suite 100
Rancho Cucamonga CA
909-483-2544
coffeebean.com
The coffee here is sourced globally from family coffee farms to procure only the top of 1% of Arabica beans. They offer 30+ varieties of coffee;the beans are roasted in small batches daily for freshness, and they also offer 20 varieties of teas that are hand-blended by their tea master. Additionally, they offer a variety of tasty sweets, powders, extracts, sauces, gifts, and cards. Leashed, well mannered dogs are allowed at their outside dining area.

### Corner Bakery Cafe

12375 N Main Street
Rancho Cucamonga CA
909-803-2600
cornerbakerycafe.com/home.as px
Located in the Victoria Gardens Shopping Center, diners will find a full line of daily fresh baked goodies for all tastes, breakfast specialties, salads, homemade soups and chili, signature sandwiches, pastas, and hand-roasted coffees at this bakery/café. Leashed, well mannered dogs are allowed at their outside tables.

### Johnny Rockets

7800 Kew Avenue
Rancho Cucamonga CA
909-463-2800
johnnyrockets.com/
All the American favorites can be found here: A fun retro, all-American decor and atmosphere, juicy burgers, specialty sandwiches, crispy fries, hand-dipped malts and shakes (dark chocolate ones too), fresh baked apple pies, tasty vegetarian choices, and

something for all ages. Leashed, friendly dogs are allowed at their outside dining area.

**Lazy Dog Restaurant & Bar**
11560 4th Street
Rancho Cucamonga CA
909-987-4131
lazydogrestaurants.com/dogs/info
Known for it's dog-friendly patio, the Lazy Dog offers your dog a complimentary bowl of water, and a menu consisting of grilled hamburger patty, chicken breast or brown rice. They just ask that you respect their common sense rules while your dog is dining there. This is as dog-friendly as dining gets. For the humans in your party there is hamburger, steak, salads and some great desserts.

**Panera Bread**
8055 Haven Avenue
Rancho Cucamonga CA
909-919-7999
panerabread.com/
This cafe specializes in freshly baked bread sandwiches for all meals;plus they offer soups, salads, homemade cookies, free WiFi, and alfresco dining. Dogs are allowed at the outer tables;they must be under their owner's control and leashed at all times

**Chipolte**
625 Orange Street
Redlands CA
909-307-8424
chipotle.com
Specializing in organic, natural and unprocessed food, this Mexican Eatery offers fajita burritos, tacos, salads, and salsas. Dogs are allowed at the outdoor tables but you will need to order your food inside the restaurant and dogs must remain outside.

**Jamba Juice**
27510 Lugonia Avenue, Suite F
Redlands CA
909-792-0900
jambajuice.com
All natural and organic ingredients, no high-fructose corn syrup, 0 grams trans fat, no artificial preservatives, a healthy helping of antioxidants, vitamins, and minerals, and fresh whole fruit and fruit juices set the base for these tasty and healthy beverages. Their organic Hot Blends provides a new spin on coffee, green or chai tea, and hot chocolate;plus they offer probiotic fruit and yogurt Blends. Additionally, they feature organic steel-cut oatmeal prepared fresh every morning, all natural salads, wraps, sandwiches, and grab n' go specialties. They also offer healthy community support through fundraisers, special sales, and school lunch programs. Leashed, well mannered dogs are allowed at their outside dining area.

**The Coffee Bean & Tea Leaf**
528 Orange Street
Redlands CA
909-798-0454
coffeebean.com
The coffee here is sourced globally from family coffee farms to procure only the top of 1% of Arabica beans. They offer 30+ varieties of coffee;the beans are roasted in small batches daily for freshness, and they also offer 20 varieties of teas that are hand-blended by their tea master. Additionally, they offer a variety of tasty sweets, powders, extracts, sauces, gifts, and cards. Leashed, well mannered dogs are allowed at their outside dining area.

**Baja Fresh Mexican Grill**
745 E. Hospitality Lane Ste C
San Bernardino CA
909-890-1854
bajafresh.com
This Mexican restaurant is open for lunch and dinner. They use fresh ingredients and making their salsa and beans daily. Some of the items on their menu include Enchiladas, Burritos, Tacos Salads, Quesadillas, Nachos, Chicken, Steak and more. Well-behaved leashed dogs are allowed at

the outdoor tables.

**Chipotle**
1092 Hospitality Lane, Suite B
San Bernardino CA
909-799-9420
chipotle.com
Specializing in organic, natural and unprocessed food, this Mexican Eatery offers fajita burritos, tacos, salads, and salsas. Dogs are allowed at the outdoor tables but you will need to order your food inside the restaurant and dogs must remain outside.

**Jamba Juice**
1078 E Hospitality Lane, Suite F
San Bernardino CA
909-796-6012
jambajuice.com
All natural and organic ingredients, no high-fructose corn syrup, 0 grams trans fat, no artificial preservatives, a healthy helping of antioxidants, vitamins, and minerals, and fresh whole fruit and fruit juices set the base for these tasty and healthy beverages. Their organic Hot Blends provides a new spin on coffee, green or chai tea, and hot chocolate;plus they offer probiotic fruit and yogurt Blends. Additionally, they feature organic steel-cut oatmeal prepared fresh every morning, all natural salads, wraps, sandwiches, and grab n' go specialties. They also offer healthy community support through fundraisers, special sales, and school lunch programs. Leashed, well mannered dogs are allowed at their outside dining area.

# Pet-Friendly Shopping Centers
**Victoria Gardens**
12505 North Mainstreet
Rancho Cucamonga CA
909-463-2830
victoriagardensie.com/
This one destination offer guests a variety of dining, shopping, and entertainment

opportunities. Dogs are allowed in the common areas of the mall; it is up to individual stores whether they allow a dog inside. Dogs must be well behaved, leashed, and under their owner's control at all times.

## Pet-Friendly Stores

**PetSmart Pet Store**
15042 Summit Ave
Fontana CA
909-463-2900
Your licensed and well-behaved leashed dog is allowed in the store.

**Petco Pet Store - North Fontana**
16639 Sierra Lakes Pkwy
Fontana CA
909-349-1830
Your licensed and well-behaved leashed dog is allowed in the store.

**Anthropologie**
7812 Monet Avenue, #3020
Rancho Cucamonga CA
909-899-0201
Items of distinction can be found for all ages and in all departments of this unique shop. Carefully selected to add to the enjoyment of the shopping experience, they carry fine clothing, amazing accessories, jewelry, hobby and leisure items, and a full line of bright and useful items for the home, garden, and office. Leashed, well behaved dogs are allowed in the store.

**Crate and Barrel**
12367 N. Mainstreet
Rancho Cucamonga CA
909-646-8668
crateandbarrel.com
This store offers fine products from around the world for in and around the home that include items for outdoor living, indoor furnishings and decorating, dining and entertaining, kitchen and food service, and gourmet food and beverages. They also have accessories for pets, bed and bath items, and organizing and storage units. Leashed,

friendly dogs are welcome in the store; they must be under their owner's control at all times.

**PetSmart Pet Store**
10940 Foothill Blvd
Rancho Cucamonga CA
909-481-8700
Your licensed and well-behaved leashed dog is allowed in the store.

**Urban Outfitters**
12587 N. Main Street, #5040
Rancho Cucamonga CA
909-803-2099
In addition to a large inventory of indoor and outdoor apparel for men and women, this major department store also carries vintage wear, designer brands, and a variety of accessories for all types of active lifestyles. They also carry shoes, furnishings, home decor, cameras, electronics, novelty items and more. Leashed, well mannered dogs are allowed in the store.

**Petco Pet Store - Redlands**
27580 West Lugonia Ave.
Redlands CA
909-335-0842
Your licensed and well-behaved leashed dog is allowed in the store.

**Camping World**
151 E Redlands Blvd
San Bernardino CA
909-370-4580
campingworld.com/
This comprehensive RV and outdoor store carries a wide variety of RV, boat, bike, and outdoor cooking accessories; all kinds of camping gear; RV screens, shades, and patio decorations; racing/tailgating gear, and all items for RV maintenance. They also carry RV towing supplies, electronics, and interior decorating items as well as pet supplies, RV directories/books, and games. Plus, they offer a tips and advice service, RV sales, rentals, and RV technicians to take care of any installations and repairs. They

also welcome your canine companion in the store; they must be friendly and leashed.

**PetSmart Pet Store**
595 E Hospitality Lane
San Bernardino CA
909-383-1055
Your licensed and well-behaved leashed dog is allowed in the store.

## Off-Leash Dog Parks

**Aurantia Dog Park**
Greenspot Road
Highland CA
909-864-6861
Plans are in the works to add to this fairly new fenced doggy play area. At present there are waste disposal sites, benches, and only one fenced area for all sizes dogs. Dogs must be sociable, current on all vaccinations and license, and under their owner's control at all times. Dogs must be leashed when not in designated off-lead areas.

**Loma Linda Dog Park**
Beaumont Ave and Mountain View Ave.
Loma Linda CA

facebook.com/lomalindadogs/
There are two fenced areas at this dog park. One is for large dogs and one is for small dogs. The dog park is open during daylight hours. The dog park is on the side of a hill so it can get slick after rain. From I-10 take Mountain View south to Beaumont. Turn left on Beaumont and the park is on the right.

**Etiwanda Creek Dog Park**
5939 East Avenue
Rancho Cucamonga CA

This off-leash, fenced dog park is located at the Etiwanda Creek Community Park near the intersections of East Avenue and Banyon. Dogs must be sociable, current on all vaccinations and license, and under their owner's control at all times. Dogs must be leashed when not in designated off-lead areas.

## Wildwood Dog Park
536 E. 40th St
San Bernardino CA

cityofwildwood.com/542/Dog-Park
Thanks to one of our readers who writes: "We have 3.5 acres divided into 2 large areas & 1 smaller area just for little and older dogs. The larger areas are rotated to help reduce wear & tear on the turf. Amenities include: Fencing, Benches, Handicapped Access, Lighting, Parking, Poop Bags, Restrooms, Shelter, Trash Cans, Water Available. Current Shots & License Required. We are also double-gated for Safety."

## Dog-Friendly Parks
### Prospect Park
Cajon Street
Redlands CA
909-798-7572
Prospect Park is a 11.4 acre natural park with trails and picnic facilities. Dogs on leash are allowed.

### San Bernardino National Forest
1824 S. Commercenter Circle
San Bernardino CA
909-382-2600
fs.usda.gov/sbnf
This national forest covers over 600,000 acres of land which ranges in elevation from 2,000 to 11,502 feet. Please see our listings in this region for dog-friendly hikes and/or campgrounds.

## San Diego

## Dog-Friendly Hotels
### La Quinta Inn San Diego Chula Vista
150 Bonita Road

Chula Vista CA
619-691-1211 (800-531-5900)
Dogs up to 25 pounds are allowed. There are no additional pet fees. Dogs must be attended to or crated for housekeeping. Dogs must be leashed and cleaned up after.

### Crown City Inn Coronado
520 Orange Avenue
Coronado CA
619-435-3116
crowncityinn.com/
Situated on Coronado Island 8 miles from San Diego International Airport this inn boasts an outdoor pool has an on-site restaurant and features pet-friendly guest rooms with free Wi-Fi. It offers free on-site guest parking.
Rooms at Crown City Inn Coronado are decorated in soft pastels and include a cable TV with HBO film channels. All guest rooms are equipped with a microwave a fridge and tea and coffee-making facilities. Select rooms offer kitchenettes.
Serving breakfast lunch and dinner Crown Bistro is located on-site at Coronado Crown City Inn. The restaurant specializes in gourmet French and American cuisine and offers a wide selection of California and European wines.
Guests of Crown City Inn are offered afternoon refreshments which include homemade biscuits coffee and tea. The inn provides free use of bicycles. Children's beach toys are also available.
Within 1 mile from this motel guests will find Coronado beaches the Coronado Municipal Golf Course and the Hotel del Coronado. The San Diego Zoo is 15 minutes drive away.

### Loews Coronado Bay Resort
4000 Coronado Bay Road
Coronado CA
619-424-4000 (800-815-6397)
Offerings at this hotel include a fabulous oceanfront setting, luxury - amenity filled accommodations for all level of

travelers, and a restaurant specializing in farm-to-table sustainable dining with many items sourced from their onsite 3,800 square-foot organic herb garden. Dogs up to 40 pounds are allowed for an additional one time pet fee of $100 per room, and they must be declared at the time of reservations. They also offer a VIP Pet Program for their canine visitors that include a gourmet room service menu, specialized bedding, dinnerware, a toy, treats, pet food, waste disposal bags, and info for local dog friendly venues. Pet walking and pet sitting services can be arranged by the hotel.

### Travelodge El Cajon
425 West Main Street
El Cajon CA
619-441-8250
Dogs of all sizes are allowed. There is a pet fee of $11 per pet per night.

### Holiday Inn Express & Suites
### La Jolla - Beach Area
6705 La Jolla Boulevard
La Jolla CA
858-454-7101 (877-270-6405)
Dogs up to 10 pounds are allowed. Dogs are allowed for a pet fee of $75.00 per pet per stay.

### La Valencia Hotel
1132 Prospect Street
La Jolla CA
858-454-0771 (800-451-0772)
lavalencia.com/
Panoramic ocean views blend with Old World charm and impeccable service at La Jolla's renowned La Valencia Hotel. An iconic getaway for Hollywood celebrities since 1926 La Valencia known as "The Pink Lady" for its distinctive rosy exterior evokes the Mediterranean with Spanish mosaics hand-painted murals and lush courtyards. Guests can choose from 112 rooms suites and villas with ocean or garden views and amenities including down comforters and high-thread-count sheets plush robes and slippers well-stocked mini-

bars and flat-panel plasma TVs. Select accommodations include fireplaces jetted tubs and petite balconies for enjoying the views. Non-smoking options are available. Your daily newspaper is complimentary and in-room dining is available around the clock. Soothe body and soul with a therapeutic treatment in the inviting spa. As the sun sets you can sip a cocktail in the lounge as you savor the ocean views from oversize bay windows. Three distinctive restaurants feature Mediterranean and California cuisine and a thousand-label wine list. The hotel also has a health club business center and concierge. La Valencia is located in the village of La Jolla in San Diego directly across from the two-mile beach boardwalk where surfing sailing and swimming await. Local attractions including SeaWorld the San Diego Zoo and the San Diego-La Jolla Underwater Park are all within a 20-minute drive while the Torrey Pines Golf Course is 15 minutes away. The University of California-San Diego is four miles from the hotel and San Diego International is 13 miles away.

**Sheraton La Jolla**
3299 Holiday Court
La Jolla CA
858-453-5550 (888-625-5144)
Set in a 7 acre lush tropical setting, this resort hotel offers many features for leisure and business travelers as well as a central location to medical institutes, business districts, shopping and dining venues, recreation, and world class entertainments. Dogs are allowed for an additional one time fee of $100 per room plus $25 per night per pet, and there is a pet policy to sign at check in.

**Best Western Plus Marina Gateway**
800 Bay Marina Drive
National City CA
619-259-2800 (800-780-7234)
Dogs up to 80 pounds are allowed. There is a $20 per day pet fee up to $100 for the week. Up to two dogs are allowed per room.

**Baymont Inn & Suites San Diego Downtown**
719 Ash Street
San Diego CA
619-232-2525 (877-424-6423)
Located off of Interstate 163 exit Ash Street West. Only a mile and a half from the San Diego Zoo.

Dogs up to 35 pounds are allowed. One dog is allowed per room.

**Best Western Lamplighter Inn & Suites At Sdsu**
6474 El Cajon Boulevard
San Diego CA
619-582-3088 (800-780-7234)
Dogs up to 50 pounds are allowed. There is a $15 per pet per night pet fee. Up to two dogs are allowed per room.

**Best Western Plus Hacienda Suites-old Town**
4041 Harney Street
San Diego CA
619-298-4707 (800-780-7234)
Dogs up to 80 pounds are allowed. There is a $20 per day pet fee up to $100 for the week. Up to two dogs are allowed per room.

**Crowne Plaza Hotel San Diego - Mission Valley**
2270 Hotel Circle North
San Diego CA
619-297-1101 (877-270-6405)
Dogs of all sizes are allowed. Dogs are allowed for a pet fee of $75.00 per pet per night.

**Doubletree Hotel San Diego/del Mar**
11915 El Camino Real
San Diego CA
858-481-5900 (800-222-TREE (8733))
Sitting central to world class beaches, tourist/animal attractions, championship golf courses, and outstanding dining and shopping areas, this resort style hotel also offers a

number of on site amenities for all level of travelers. Dogs up to 50 pounds are allowed for an additional one time pet fee of $50 per room.

**Hampton Inn San Diego/del Mar**
11920 El Camino Real
San Diego CA
858-792-5557
Dogs of all sizes are allowed. There is a $50 one time pet fee.

**Heritage Inn San Diego**
3333 Channel Way
San Diego CA
619-223-9500 (877-300-9126)
Complimentary coffee and pastries free Wi-Fi an outdoor pool and SeaWorld one mile away are the highlights our guests find at the Heritage Inn San Diego. All 119 rooms at the three-floor Heritage Inn come complete with coffeemakers mini-fridges free Wi-Fi and premium cable TV. A microwave is available in the vending room. Before you fly out the door in the morning grab some free coffee and pastries. Don't mind that splashing it's just The Negotiator fooling around in the heated outdoor pool. The hotel also has a hot tub laundry facility and on-site parking (for a fee). The Heritage Inn is right off I-8 two blocks from Valley View Casino and one mile south of SeaWorld. The San Diego Zoo is seven miles southeast. If you're driving from San Diego International Airport the hotel is four miles north.

**Hilton San Diego Airport/harbor Island**
1960 Harbor Island Drive
San Diego CA
619-291-6700
Featuring a central location to some of the area's best attractions, downtown, and the San Diego International Airport this scenic resort-style waterfront hotel also offers luxury accommodations and several in-house amenities. Dogs up to 75 pounds are allowed for an additional one time fee of $75 per pet.

**Hilton San Diego Bayfront**
1 Park Boulevard
San Diego CA
619-564-3333
Featuring a dramatic oceanfront location with great views, this 30 story, upscale hotel has much to offer in amenities;plus a great location for exploring all the best sights and activities of the area. Dogs up to 75 pounds are allowed for an additional one time pet fee of $75 per room.

**Hilton San Diego Gaslamp Quarter**
401 K Street
San Diego CA
619-231-4040
Located in the historic Gaslamp Quarter and sitting central to numerous world class dining, night life, shopping, and entertainment areas, this luxury hotel also features a number of onsite amenities for all level of travelers. Dogs up to 75 pounds are allowed for an additional one time pet fee of $75 per room.

**Hilton San Diego Mission Valley**
901 Camino Del Rio South
San Diego CA
619-543-9000
Located in the heart of the city, this upscale hotel offers numerous on site amenities for business and leisure travelers, plus a convenient location to business, shopping, dining, historical, and entertainment areas. Dogs are allowed for an additional one time fee of $50 per pet.

**Hilton San Diego Resort**
1775 East Mission Bay Drive
San Diego CA
619-276-4010
Thanks to its huge lagoon-style pool private beach marina and Mission Bay location the non-smoking Hilton San Diego Resort is a true crowd-pleaser among our guests. The sprawling non-smoking Hilton San Diego Resort is set on 18 acres featuring lush gardens palm trees rolling lawns and a sandy beach on Mission Bay.

Each of the 325 Mediterranean-style rooms has a balcony or a patio some with bay views 42-inch LCD TV a coffeemaker and a comfy signature bed with a down duvet and 250-thread-count sheets. It's magic on Mission Bay outside: a lagoon-style pool poolside bar hot tubs a children's wading pool Kids Kamp private beach with marina watercraft rentals lighted tennis courts bayfront fire pits concerts on the bay and much more. When hunger hits visit any of the resorts several restaurants. For pampering don't miss in in-house day spa. Parking and Wi-Fi are available for a fee. The property charges a service fee that includes local and toll-free calls access to the business center the tennis courts and the steam room a fitness center locker and a variety of discounts on resort activities. The Hilton is right on Mission Bay off I-5 just one mile north of SeaWorld. If you're driving from San Diego International Airport the hotel is five miles north.

**Hotel Indigo San Diego Gaslamp Quarter**
509 9th Avenue
San Diego CA
619-727-4000 (877-698-9593)
Dogs of all sizes are allowed.

**Hotel Republic San Diego Autograph Collection**
421 West B Street
San Diego CA
619-398-3100 (877-946-8357)
Some of the amenities offered at this upscale downtown hotel include a convenient location to the area's star attractions, shopping, dining, corporate districts, and entertainment areas;their Whatever/Whenever Service;a rooftop Beach Bar, and transportation services. Dogs are allowed for an additional $100 one time fee per room plus $25 per night per pet;there is pet waiver to sign at check in. There are also pampering

and partying amenities for canine guests.

**Kimpton Hotel Palomar San Diego**
1047 5th Avenue
San Diego CA
619-515-3000 (888-288-6601)
Located in the heart of downtown, this luxury resort hotel's offerings include a convenient central location and numerous services and amenities for all level of travelers, dozens of earth friendly practices throughout the hotel, and fresh local, sustainable, and seasonally inspired food and beverages. Pets of all sizes are welcome here for no additional fee;the pet registration form is available on line. Pets need to be declared at the time of registration and there is a pet form to fill out at the time of arrival. Canine guests are also greeted with their own leash, bed and dinnerware to use during their stay, gourmet treats, and various other amenities available through their specialty pet packages. Pet sitting and grooming is available through the hotel.

**Kimpton Solamar Hotel**
435 6th Avenue
San Diego CA
619-531-8740 (877-230-0300)
hotelsolamar.com/index.html
Located in the heart of the Gaslight District, this luxury resort hotel's offers include amenities, services and a great location convenient for business or leisure travelers;dozens of earth friendly practices throughout the hotel, and fresh local, sustainable, and seasonally inspired food and beverages at the adjacent Jsix's and the LOUNGE six Rooftop pool bar. Pets of all sizes are welcome here for no additional fee;the pet registration form is available on line. Pets need to be declared at the time of registration and there is a pet form to fill out at the time of arrival. Canine guests are also greeted with their own leash, bed and dinnerware to use

during their stay, gourmet treats, and various other amenities available through their specialty pet packages. Pet walking and pet sitting services can be arranged by the hotel.

### Kona Kai Resort & Marina A Noble House Resort

1551 Shelter Island Drive
San Diego CA
619-221-8000 (800-566-2524)
Our guests can sun themselves on the private beach get a massage in the full-service spa or relax on cushy mattresses at the Kona Kai Resort & Marina a Noble House Resort. The resort has three floors and 129 rooms with tropical island decor. Kick back on plush bedding and watch cable TV. Enjoy the marina or garden views from your choice of private balcony or patio. Google up a game plan with free Wi-Fi. Rooms also feature mini-fridges coffeemakers and Nintendo game systems. Dine on American and Polynesian cuisine in the on-site restaurant. Sun worshippers can soak up some rays on the private beach or splash in the outdoor pool. Soak in the soothing hot tub after some volleyball action on the sandy beach. Parking is available for a fee and pets are permitted. Kona Kai Resort is on Shelter Island about four miles from San Diego International Airport. Visit lush Balboa Park and meet wild animals up close at the San Diego Zoo a 20-minute drive. Guests can kick off some fun at Qualcomm Stadium home of the San Diego Chargers football team a 23-minute drive. The San Diego Opera is an 18-minute drive.

### La Quinta Inn & Suites San Diego Mission Bay

4610 De Soto Street
San Diego CA
858-483-9800 (800-531-5900)
Dogs of all sizes are allowed. Dogs may not be left alone in the room.

### La Quinta Inn San Diego Old Town

2380 Moore Street
San Diego CA
619-291-9100 (800-531-5900)
Dogs of all sizes are allowed for no additional pet fee; there is a pet policy to sign at check-in. Dogs may not be left alone in the room.

### La Quinta Inn San Diego Scripps Poway

10185 Paseo Montril
San Diego CA
858-484-8800 (800-531-5900)
Dogs up to 60 pounds are allowed. There are no additional pet fees, but a credit card must be on file. Dogs must be crated when left alone in the room or place the Do Not Disturb sign on the door. Dogs must be leashed and cleaned up after.

### La Quinta Inn San Diego Seaworld/zoo Area

641 Camino Del Rio South
San Diego CA
619-295-6886 (800-531-5900)
Dogs of all sizes are allowed for no additional pet fee; there is a pet policy to sign at check-in. Dogs may not be left alone in the room.

### Old Town Inn

4444 Pacific Highway
San Diego CA
619-260-8024 (800-643-3025)
oldtown-inn.com/oldtown.htm
Surrounded by lush landscaping the Old Town Inn offers our guests complimentary Wi-Fi daily breakfasts and a heated outdoor pool. Guests find free Wi-Fi cable TV (HBO included) DVD players and coffeemakers in all 73 rooms at the two-story hotel. Non-smoking rooms are available and guests have access to a microwave in the inn's lobby. Mornings here start with an expanded continental breakfast. When recreation time hits take a dip in the heated outdoor pool. Additional amenities include a 24-hour front desk guest laundry and a game room. Parking is free. The charming inn is less than one mile from the Old Town

San Diego State Historic Park and Presidio Hills Golf Course. The University of San Diego is two miles SeaWorld San Diego is three miles and the San Diego Zoo is six miles away. San Diego International Airport is four miles from the inn.

### Pacific Inn And Suites-convention Center-gaslamp-seaworld

1655 Pacific Highway
San Diego CA
619-232-6391
Wi-Fi plus a terrific location for getting around make Pacific Inn Hotel And Suites a winner with our guests. The two-story 34-room hotel has a bevy of amenities in store for guests. Rooms feature pillowtop beds microwaves mini-fridges and coffeemakers. Wi-Fi is available. This hotel is family-friendly and pets are allowed. The hotel is in downtown San Diego's Little Italy with ethnic shopping and tasty traditional treats everywhere. It's a stone's throw to the bay and Maritime Museum of San Diego and about a mile to Balboa Park which warrants many an hour of enjoyable wandering with 13 museums plus the San Diego Zoo. It's a five-minute drive to Westfield Horton Plaza for open-air shopping galore and just two miles to San Diego International Airport.

### Premier Inns San Diego

2484 Hotel Circle Place
San Diego CA
619-291-8252
premierinns.com
This hotel offers an outdoor pool and hot tub. Cable TV with free movie channels is featured in all guest rooms. San Diego Convention Center is 10 minutes drive away.
Simply furnished each air-conditioned room at Premier Inns San Diego is equipped with a desk. A fridge is provided for added convenience.
A 24-hour reception is offered at San Diego Premier Inns. A business center complete with fax and photocopying services is

available. A launderette and vending machines are located on site.
This hotel is conveniently located near several major attractions including the San Diego Zoo just 4.8 km away. San Diego International Airport is 8.5 km from this hotel.

### Quality Inn San Diego Miramar
9350 Kearny Mesa Road
San Diego CA
858-578-4350 (877-424-6423)
We are conveniently located in the general vicinity of all major San Diego tourist attractions and are the closest hotel to the Marine

Dogs up to 100 pounds are allowed. Dogs are allowed for a pet fee of $USD per pet per stay. Two dogs are allowed per room.

### San Diego Marriott Del Mar
11966 El Camino Real
San Diego CA
858-523-1700
Dogs up to 50 pounds are allowed. There is a $75 one time pet fee.

### Sheraton Mission Valley San Diego Hotel
1433 Camino Del Rio S
San Diego CA
619-260-0111 (888-625-5144)
This upscale hotel offers on site amenities for all level of travelers;plus, a great location to world-class attractions, entertainment sites, and shopping, dining, and recreation destinations. One dog up to 30 pounds is allowed for no additional fee and there is a pet waiver to sign at check in.

### Sheraton San Diego Hotel And Marina
1380 Harbor Island Drive
San Diego CA
619-291-2900 (888-625-5144)
In addition to featuring a number of on-site recreational activities and amenities, this upscale hotel also offers a great waterside setting with views of the bay and in-house

restaurants and lounges. Dogs up to 40 pounds are allowed for no additional fee;there is a pet waiver to sign at check in.

### The Atwood Hotel San Diego - Seaworld/zoo
1201 Hotel Circle South
San Diego CA
619-297-2271
Dogs of all sizes are allowed. There is a pet fee of $10 per pet per night.

### The Us Grant A Luxury Collection Hotel San Diego
326 Broadway
San Diego CA
619-232-3121 (800-325-3589)
Located in the historic Gaslamp Quarter among almost 20 blocks of world class shopping, dining, historic, and entertainment venues, this elegant hotel also features amenity-filled accommodations and on site farm-fresh and seasonally inspired dining. Dogs up to 40 pounds are allowed for an additional $150 one time pet fee per room;there is a pet waiver to sign at check in. A couple of breeds are not allowed.

### The Us Grant A Luxury Collection Hotel San Diego
326 Broadway
San Diego CA
619-232-3121 (800-237-5029)
The luxurious style and superb location of The US Grant a Luxury Collection Hotel San Diego make it a favorite among our guests in the city. The 11-story 270-room hotel is housed in an iconic 1910 building a holdover from the "Grande Dame" era of hotels. Its style is a fusion of classic and contemporary with elaborate chandeliers and deco touches alongside modern artwork. The rooms are swanky with Empire-inspired furnishings modern-art headboards and mini-fridge. There is an Art Deco-designed lounge plus a restaurant for elegant dining and 24-hour room service for languid in-room meals. There is a fitness center to keep your workout in

gear and a business center for staying up-to-date with the office. The lobby offers free Wi-Fi. The US Grant is located in the heart of downtown San Diego four blocks from the historic Gaslamp Quarter home to nightlife dining and entertainment. Just around the corner is Westfield Horton Plaza a premier outdoor shopping mall and the trolley at the hotel's front door will take you to Old Town the historic mission village where San Diego got its start. The airport is a quick three-mile drive away.

### The Westin San Diego
400 West Broadway
San Diego CA
619-239-4500 (888-625-5144)
This beautiful atrium-style downtown hotel offers many on site amenities for business and leisure travelers. The hotel offer great views of the bay, and it sits within walking distance to the convention center, major attractions, and to many historic, shopping, dining, and entertainment areas. One dog up to 40 pounds is allowed for no additional fee;there is a pet waiver to sign at check in.

### The Westin San Diego Gaslamp Quarter
910 Broadway Circle
San Diego CA
619-937-8461 (888-625-5144)
Located in the historic Gaslamp Quarter among almost 20 blocks of world class shopping, dining, entertainment and nightlife venues, this upscale hotel also features amenity-filled accommodations for all level of travelers. Dogs up to 50 pounds are allowed for no additional pet fee;there is a pet waiver to sign at check in.

### Wyndham San Diego Bayside
1355 North Harbor Drive
San Diego CA
619-232-3861 (877-698-9593)
Dogs of all sizes are allowed. Dogs are allowed for a pet fee of $25.00 per pet per night. Two dogs are allowed per room.

## Accommodations

**Ocean Villa Inn**
5142 West Point Loma Blvd
San Diego CA
619-224-3481 (800-759-0012)
oceanvillainn.com
Ocean Villa Inn is in the Ocean Beach district near the Dog Beach. They allow pets in all of their downstairs rooms with a $100.00 refundable deposit and a one time per stay fee of $25.00.

**Town and Country San Diego**
500 Hotel Circle North
San Diego CA
619-291-7131 (800-772-8527)
Dogs are welcome at the Town and Country Hotel.

## Pet-Friendly Extended Stay Hotels

**Residence Inn La Jolla**
8901 Gilman Drive
La Jolla CA
858-587-1770
Dogs of all sizes are allowed. There is a $100 one time additional pet fee.

**Extended Stay America - San Diego - Fashion Valley**
7444 Mission Valley Road
San Diego CA
619-299-2292 (800-804-3724)
One dog is allowed per suite. There is a $25 per night additional pet fee up to $150 for an entire stay.

**Extended Stay America - San Diego - Fashion Valley**
7444 Mission Valley Road
San Diego CA
619-299-2292
Free continental breakfast and Wi-Fi full kitchens and a pet-friendly policy make our guests feel comfortable at Extended Stay America - San Diego - Fashion Valley. The three-story hotel has 107 rooms with satellite TV free local phone calls and full kitchens with refrigerators microwaves and stovetops as well as dishes and cooking utensils. Wi-Fi is free. Non-smoking rooms are available. The hotel provides an on-site guest laundromat business services and discounts to a nearby fitness facility. Pets are allowed and parking is available both for an additional fee. Located one mile off I-8 in Mission Valley the hotel is less than two miles from shopping at Fashion Valley and Mission Valley Center. The San Diego Zoo and Old Town San Diego State Historic Park are both four miles from the hotel and Balboa Park SeaWorld and the Gaslamp Quarter are within a five-mile drive. Catch a Padres game at Petco Park brush up your swing at Mission Bay Public Golf Course or do some beachcombing about 10 minutes from the hotel. San Diego International Airport is seven miles away.

**Extended Stay America - San Diego - Hotel Circle**
2087 Hotel Circle South
San Diego CA
619-296-5570 (800-804-3724)
One dog is allowed per suite. There is a $25 per night additional pet fee up to $150 for an entire stay.

**Extended Stay America - San Diego - Mission Valley - Stadium**
3860 Murphy Canyon Road
San Diego CA
858-292-8927 (800-804-3724)
One dog is allowed per suite. There is a $25 per night additional pet fee up to $150 for an entire stay.

**Extended Stay America - San Diego - Sorrento Mesa**
9880 Pacific Heights Blvd
San Diego CA
858-623-0100 (800-804-3724)
One dog is allowed per suite. There is a $25 per night additional pet fee up to $150 for an entire stay.

**Residence Inn By Marriott Rancho Bernardo / Scripps Poway**
12011 Scripps Highland Drive
San Diego CA
858-635-5724
Dogs of all sizes are allowed. There is a $75 one time additional pet fee.

**Residence Inn By Marriott San Diego Downtown**
1747 Pacific Highway
San Diego CA
619-338-8200
Dogs of all sizes are allowed. There is a $100 one time additional pet fee.

**Residence Inn By Marriott San Diego Downtown/gaslamp Quarter**
356 6th Avenue
San Diego CA
619-487-1200
Dogs of all sizes are allowed. There is a $100 one time additional pet fee.

**Residence Inn Rancho Bernardo Carmel Mountain**
11002 Rancho Carmel Drive
San Diego CA
858-673-1900
Dogs of all sizes are allowed. There is a $100 one time additional pet fee.

**Residence Inn San Diego Mission Valley**
1865 Hotel Circle South
San Diego CA
619-881-3600
Dogs of all sizes are allowed. There is a $100 one time additional pet fee.

**Residence Inn San Diego Sorrento Mesa/sorrento Valley**
5995 Pacific Mesa Court
San Diego CA
858-552-9100
Dogs of all sizes are allowed. There is a $100 one time additional pet fee.

**Staybridge Suites San Diego Rancho Bernardo Area**
11855 Avenue Of Industry
San Diego CA
858-487-0900 (877-270-6405)
Dogs up to 80 pounds are

allowed. Pets allowed with an additional pet fee. Up to $75 for 1-6 nights and up to $150 for 7+ nights. A pet agreement must be signed at check-in.

### Staybridge Suites Sorrento Mesa
6639 Mira Mesa Blvd
San Diego CA
858-453-5343 (877-270-6405)
Dogs of all sizes are allowed. Pets allowed with an additional pet fee. Up to $75 for 1-6 nights and up to $150 for 7+ nights. A pet agreement must be signed at check-in.

# Dog-Friendly Attractions
### Action Sport Rentals
1775 Mission Bay
San Diego CA
619-275-8945
actionsportrentals.com/
This sports rental company offers a wide variety of watercraft for rent, fishing charters and equipment, and also bicycles and skate rentals. The marina has a bait and tackle shop, and a deli and market. Dogs of all sizes are welcome on the boat rentals for no additional fee; they must have their own doggie life jackets. Dogs must be friendly, well behaved, under their owner's control at all times, and leashed and cleaned up after.

### Aqua Adventures Kayak Center
1548 Quivira Way
San Diego CA
619-523-9577
aqua-adventures.com
Aqua Adventures Kayak Center offers retail sales, lessons, local tours, rentals, and multi-day adventures. Dogs are allowed. Please contact Aqua Adventures for complete list of rules. Doggie life jackets are also sold in the store.

### Cinderella Carriage Rides

San Diego CA
619-239-8080
You and your dog can enjoy a carriage ride throughout downtown San Diego. The horse and carriages are located in the Gaslamp Quarter at 5th and F Streets, or call ahead and get a carriage to pick you up from your downtown hotel. The rides are from 6pm-11pm. Rates start at $15 for about a 10 minute ride and go up to $95 for 60 minutes. Prices are subject to change. The carriages hold 3-4 people plus a dog. They accept cash or credit card.

### Family Kayak Adventure Center
4217 Swift Avenue
San Diego CA
619-282-3520
familykayak.com
This company offers guided kayaking adventure tours to people of all ages and abilities. For beginners they offer paddles on flat water in stable tandem kayaks that hold one to four people. All equipment and instruction is provided for an enjoyable first outing. Well-behaved dogs are also welcome. There is even a "Dog Paddles" tour which is an evening tour on Mission Bay that includes quality time on the water and on Fiesta Island's leash free area.

### Gaslamp Quarter Guided Walking Tour
410 Island Avenue
San Diego CA
619-233-4692
gaslampquarter.org/
The historical focal point of this 16 1/2 block district is the William Heath Davis Historic House Museum, where visitors can get information on the walking tours, the museum, and self-guided maps. The foundation began as a way promote and preserve the history and culture of the Gaslamp Quarter. Dogs are welcome on the guided walking tours for no additional fee as long as other guests don't mind, and so far that has never been a problem. They just ask that dogs be friendly and that

you call ahead if you have a pet. Dogs are welcome for no additional fee. Dogs must be under their owner's control, and leashed and cleaned up after at all times.

### Old Town State Historic Park
San Diego Ave & Twiggs St
San Diego CA
619-220-5422
Old Town demonstrates life in the Mexican and early American periods of 1821 to 1872 (including 5 original adobe buildings). There are shops, several outdoor cafes and live music. Since pups are not allowed inside the buildings, you can shop at the many outdoor retail kiosks throughout the town. There are several food concessions where you can order the food and then take it to an outdoor table. After walking around, relax with your best friend by listening to a variety of live music. If your dog wants to see more trees and green grass, take a quick drive over to Presidio Park which is close to Old Town (see Parks).

### SeaWorld of California-Kennels
1720 South Shore Rd.
San Diego CA
619-226-3901
This may not be your dog's idea of an attraction, but it is nice to know that SeaWorld has day kennels at the main entrance of their Adventure Park. The kennels are attended at all times and you can visit your dog throughout the day when you need a break from the attractions. The day boarding is open the same hours as the park and cost only $5 for the whole day. Kennels range in size from small to large. Thanks to one of our San Diego readers for telling us about this.

### Seaforth Boat Rentals
1641 Quivira Road
San Diego CA
619-223-1681
seaforthboatrental.com/
This boat rental/adventure tour company feature over 200

watercraft rentals available at 3 locations. They offer a wide variety of adventure packages, including manned or unmanned rentals, sailing lessons, fishing excursions/tournaments, remote or on-site picnicking, whale watching, and they will even organize beach parties. Dogs of all sizes are welcome on the boat rentals for no additional fee. Dogs must be friendly, well behaved, under their owner's control at all times, and leashed and cleaned up after.

## Outdoor Restaurants

### Jamba Juice
555 Broadway, Suite 135
Chula Vista CA
619-409-9840
jambajuice.com
All natural and organic ingredients, no high-fructose corn syrup, 0 grams trans fat, no artificial preservatives, a healthy helping of antioxidants, vitamins, and minerals, and fresh whole fruit and fruit juices set the base for these tasty and healthy beverages. Their organic Hot Blends provides a new spin on coffee, green or chai tea, and hot chocolate;plus they offer probiotic fruit and yogurt Blends. Additionally, they feature organic steel-cut oatmeal prepared fresh every morning, all natural salads, wraps, sandwiches, and grab n' go specialties. They also offer healthy community support through fundraisers, special sales, and school lunch programs. Leashed, well mannered dogs are allowed at their outside dining area.

### Jamba Juice
2275 Otay Lakes Road, #117
Chula Vista CA
619-656-5030
jambajuice.com
All natural and organic ingredients, no high-fructose corn syrup, 0 grams trans fat, no artificial preservatives, a healthy helping of antioxidants, vitamins, and minerals, and fresh whole fruit and fruit juices set the base

for these tasty and healthy beverages. Their organic Hot Blends provides a new spin on coffee, green or chai tea, and hot chocolate;plus they offer probiotic fruit and yogurt Blends. Additionally, they feature organic steel-cut oatmeal prepared fresh every morning, all natural salads, wraps, sandwiches, and grab n' go specialties. They also offer healthy community support through fundraisers, special sales, and school lunch programs. Leashed, well mannered dogs are allowed at their outside dining area.

### Cucina Italiana
4705-A Clairemont Drive
Clairemont CA
858-274-9732
This eatery features authentic Italian cuisine from many regions, house-made breads, freshly prepared foods, and a heated patio. They are located at the Clairemont Square Shopping Center near the movie multiplex, and weekends can be quite busy. Your pet is welcome to join you at the outside tables. Dogs must be attended to at all times, well behaved, and leashed.

### Burger Lounge
922 Orange Avenue/H 75
Coronado CA
619-435-6835
burgerlounge.com/
With a strong commitment to sustainable and organic, this eatery features a variety of burgers with freshly made organic lounge buns and 100% forage/grass-fed, free-range all natural beef. They also offer free-range turkey burgers, organic cheeses, quinoa veggie burgers, a variety of beverages, and a kid's menu. Leashed, well mannered dogs are allowed at their outside dining area.

### Cafe 1134
1134 Orange Ave
Coronado CA
619-437-1134
cafe1134.net/

Cafe 1134 offers coffee and a full bistro menu. Dogs are allowed at the outdoor tables.

### McP's Irish Pub and Grill
1107 Orange Avenue
Coronado CA
619-435-5280
mcpspub.com/
This authentic Irish pub serves up popular Irish dishes and beer and offers live entertainment nightly. They offer service on the patio, and when it is cold they turn on the patio heaters. Your friendly pet is welcome to join you at the outside tables. Dogs must be attended to at all times, well behaved, and leashed

### Spiro's Gyros
1201 First Street
Coronado CA
619-435-1225
This restaurant offers casual dining with a view and classic Greek food. There is patio seating, but go inside to order and pick up your meal. Dogs must be quiet, well behaved, under owners control at all times, and leashed.

### Katy's Cafe
704 Seacoast Drive
Imperial Beach CA
619-863-5524
katyscafeib.com
This cafe serves up a fun atmosphere along with a fun menu of freshly made specialty sandwiches and beverages. Leashed, friendly dogs are allowed at their patio dining area.

### Burger Lounge
1101 Wall Street
La Jolla CA
858-456-0196
burgerlounge.com/
With a strong commitment to sustainable and organic, this eatery features a variety of burgers with freshly made organic lounge buns and 100% forage/grass-fed, free-range all natural beef. They also offer free-range turkey burgers, organic cheeses, quinoa veggie burgers, a variety of beverages, and a kid's menu. Leashed, well

mannered dogs are allowed at their outside dining area.

### Cass Street Café and Bakery
5550 La Jolla Blvd
La Jolla CA
858-454-9094
In addition to featuring delicious fresh bakery treats, they also serve breakfast, lunch, and dinners offering fresh, homemade food, and patio dining. Your pet is welcome to join you at the outside tables. Dogs must be attended to at all times, well behaved, and leashed.

### Chipotle
8657 Villa La Jolla
La Jolla CA
858-554-1866
chipotle.com
Specializing in organic, natural and unprocessed food, this Mexican Eatery offers fajita burritos, tacos, salads, and salsas. Dogs are allowed at the outdoor tables but you will need to order your food inside the restaurant and dogs must remain outside.

### Girard Gourmet
7837 Girard Avenue
La Jolla CA
858-454-3321
girardgourmet.com/
This award winning gourmet eatery offers a wide variety of freshly prepared baked goods (their specialty being custom made cookies for all occasions), a seasonally influenced menu, homemade soups/quiches/deserts, and great comfort food. Leashed, well mannered dogs are allowed at their outside dining area.

### Harry's Coffee Shop
7545 Girard Avenue
La Jolla CA
858-454-7381
harryscoffeeshop.com/
This breakfast and lunch restaurant serves up old-fashioned American food as well as espresso and fountain drinks. They are open daily from 6 am to 3 pm, and they also offer patio seating. Your pet is

welcome to join you at the outside tables. Dogs must be attended to at all times, well behaved, and leashed.

### Rubio's
8855 Villa La Jolla Drive
La Jolla CA
858-546-9377
rubios.com/
Sustainable and innovatively prepared seafood is the specialty of this eatery. They also offer a full day's menu and many made-from-scratch foods highlighting Mexican and Southern California cuisines. They are open Monday to Saturday from 10 am until 11 pm and on Sunday from 10 am until 10 pm. Leashed, well mannered dogs are allowed at their outside dining area.

### The 910 Restaurant and Bar
910 Prospect St
La Jolla CA
858-454-2181
nine-ten.com/home.php
Located in the Grand Colonial Inn, Putnam's serves breakfast, lunch, dinner and Sunday brunch. They offer contemporary world cuisine by an award-winning chef. Dogs are allowed at the outdoor tables.

### Whole Foods Market
8825 Villa La Jolla Drive
La Jolla CA
858-642-6700
wholefoods.com/
This natural food supermarket offers natural and organic foods. Order some food from their deli without your dog and bring it to an outdoor table where your well-behaved leashed dog is welcome.

### Yummy Maki Yummy Box
3211 Holiday Ct # 101A
La Jolla CA
858-587-9848
This eatery specializes in oriental cuisine and offer indoor and outdoor dining service. They are open Monday to Saturday from 11 am until 9:30 pm. Dogs are allowed at the outer tables. They must be

under owner's control at all times, be well behaved, and leashed.

### Zenbu Sushi Bar & Restaurant
7660 Fay Avenue
La Jolla CA
858-454-4540
rimelsrestaurants.com/
This eatery has been called the hot spot for all things fresh and Asian. They offer indoor and outdoor dining, weather permitting. Dogs are welcome at the outer tables. Dogs must be well behaved, attended to at all times, and leashed.

### Chipotle
8005 Fletcher Parkway
La Mesa CA
619-589-2258
chipotle.com
Specializing in organic, natural and unprocessed food, this Mexican Eatery offers fajita burritos, tacos, salads, and salsas. Dogs are allowed at the outdoor tables but you will need to order your food inside the restaurant and dogs must remain outside.

### Bar-B-Que House
5025 Newport Avenue
Ocean Beach CA
619-222-4311
barbquehouse.com/
Located in the heart of Ocean Beach just up the street from the water, this award- winning barbecue restaurant offers slow cooked recipes made from scratch. Your pet is welcome to join you at the outside tables. Place and pick up your order inside. Dogs must be attended to at all times, well behaved, and leashed.

### Tower Two Beach Cafe
5083 Santa Monica Avenue # 1B
Ocean Beach CA
619-223-4059
towertwocafe.com/
A great view of the ocean, a large open patio, and a full menu has helped to popularize this café, plus they welcome canine companions on their

deck with fresh bowls of water. Dogs must be leashed and under their owner's control.

**Acapulco Restaurant**
2467 Juan Street
San Diego CA
619-260-8124
haciendahotel-oldtown.com/
Located at the Hacienda Hotel, this restaurant and bar offers California style Mexican food, signature dishes and cocktails, a Sunday Champagne Brunch, Happy Hours Monday to Friday, beautiful views of the bay, and a large outdoor patio. Leashed, friendly dogs are allowed at their outside dining area.

**Baja Fresh Mexican Grill**
3369 Rosecrans
San Diego CA
619-222-3399
bajafresh.com
This Mexican restaurant is open for lunch and dinner. They use fresh ingredients and making their salsa and beans daily. Some of the items on their menu include Enchiladas, Burritos, Tacos Salads, Quesadillas, Nachos, Chicken, Steak and more. Well-behaved leashed dogs are allowed at the outdoor tables.

**Baja Fresh Mexican Grill**
3737 Murphy Cyn Rd
San Diego CA
858-277-5700
bajafresh.com
This Mexican restaurant is open for lunch and dinner. They use fresh ingredients and making their salsa and beans daily. Some of the items on their menu include Enchiladas, Burritos, Tacos Salads, Quesadillas, Nachos, Chicken, Steak and more. Well-behaved leashed dogs are allowed at the outdoor tables.

**Baja Fresh Mexican Grill**
845 Camino De La Reina
San Diego CA
619-295-1122
bajafresh.com
This Mexican restaurant is open for lunch and dinner. They use fresh ingredients and making

their salsa and beans daily. Some of the items on their menu include Enchiladas, Burritos, Tacos Salads, Quesadillas, Nachos, Chicken, Steak and more. Well-behaved leashed dogs are allowed at the outdoor tables.

**Bare Back Grill**
4640 Mission Blvd
San Diego CA
858-274-7117
barebackgrill.com/
Voted 'Best Burger' in San Diego for 2006, 2007, 2008, and 2009;this grill has paved its way by sourcing local, organic produce, using all natural poultry and lamb, and their beef is 100% organic that is ground fresh daily on-site. They also have a good line-up of wines and beers, a venue for special events, and alfresco dining. Leashed, well mannered dogs are allowed at their outside tables.

**Bull's Smokin' barbecue**
1127 W Morena Blvd
San Diego CA
619-276-2855
bullssmokinbbq.com
barbecue is the specialty at this eatery;plus brews, wines, and alfresco dining are offered. There is also a daily happy hour from 3 pm to 6 pm. Leashed dogs are allowed at the outside tables.

**Burger Lounge**
1608 India Street
San Diego CA
619-237-7878
burgerlounge.com/
With a strong commitment to sustainable and organic, this eatery features a variety of burgers with freshly made organic lounge buns and 100% forage/grass-fed, free-range all natural beef. They also offer free-range turkey burgers, organic cheeses, quinoa veggie burgers, a variety of beverages, and a kid's menu. Leashed, well mannered dogs are allowed at their outside dining area.

**Burger Lounge**
528 5th Avenue
San Diego CA
619-955-5727
burgerlounge.com/
With a strong commitment to sustainable and organic, this eatery features a variety of burgers with freshly made organic lounge buns and 100% forage/grass-fed, free-range all natural beef. They also offer free-range turkey burgers, organic cheeses, quinoa veggie burgers, a variety of beverages, and a kid's menu. Leashed, well mannered dogs are allowed at their front patio dining area.

**Burger Lounge**
406 University Avenue
San Diego CA
619-487-1183
burgerlounge.com/
With a strong commitment to sustainable and organic, this eatery features a variety of burgers with freshly made organic lounge buns and 100% forage/grass-fed, free-range all natural beef. They also offer free-range turkey burgers, organic cheeses, quinoa veggie burgers, a variety of beverages, and a kid's menu. Leashed, well mannered dogs are allowed at their outside dining area.

**Burger Lounge**
4116 Adams Avenue
San Diego CA
619-584-2929
burgerlounge.com/
With a strong commitment to sustainable and organic, this eatery features a variety of burgers with freshly made organic lounge buns and 100% forage/grass-fed, free-range all natural beef. They also offer free-range turkey burgers, organic cheeses, quinoa veggie burgers, a variety of beverages, and a kid's menu. Leashed, well mannered dogs are allowed at their outside dining area.

**Champagne French Bakery Cafe**
12955 El Camino Real
San Diego CA
858-792-2222

champagnebakery.com
Located in the Del Mar Highlands Town Center, this restaurant allows well-behaved leashed dogs at the outdoor tables. Thanks to one of our readers for recommending this cafe.

**Chipotle**
734 University Avenue Suite C
San Diego CA
619-209-3688
chipotle.com
Specializing in organic, natural and unprocessed food, this Mexican Eatery offers fajita burritos, tacos, salads, and salsas. Dogs are allowed at the outdoor tables but you will need to order your food inside the restaurant and dogs must remain outside.

**Chipotle**
1025 Camino De La Reina, Suite 2
San Diego CA
619-491-0481
chipotle.com
Specializing in organic, natural and unprocessed food, this Mexican Eatery offers fajita burritos, tacos, salads, and salsas. Dogs are allowed at the outdoor tables but you will need to order your food inside the restaurant and dogs must remain outside.

**Chipotle**
1504 Garnet Avenue
San Diego CA
858-274-3093
chipotle.com
Specializing in organic, natural and unprocessed food, this Mexican Eatery offers fajita burritos, tacos, salads, and salsas. Dogs are allowed at the outdoor tables but you will need to order your food inside the restaurant and dogs must remain outside.

**Chipotle**
3680 Rosecrans Street
San Diego CA
619-222-0508
chipotle.com
Specializing in organic, natural and unprocessed food, this

Mexican Eatery offers fajita burritos, tacos, salads, and salsas. Dogs are allowed at the outdoor tables but you will need to order your food inside the restaurant and dogs must remain outside.

**Chipotle**
8250 Mira Mesa Blvd, Suite G
San Diego CA
858-586-2147
chipotle.com
Specializing in organic, natural and unprocessed food, this Mexican Eatery offers fajita burritos, tacos, salads, and salsas. Dogs are allowed at the outdoor tables but you will need to order your food inside the restaurant and dogs must remain outside.

**Chipotle SDSU**
5842 Hardy Avenue
San Diego CA
619-265-2778
chipotle.com
Specializing in organic, natural and unprocessed food, this Mexican Eatery offers fajita burritos, tacos, salads, and salsas. Dogs are allowed at the outdoor tables but you will need to order your food inside the restaurant and dogs must remain outside.

**Coffee Bean & Tea Leaf**
5657 Balboa Avenue
San Diego CA
858-715-0278
coffeebean.com
The coffee here is sourced globally from family coffee farms to procure only the top of 1% of Arabica beans. They offer 30+ varieties of coffee;the beans are roasted in small batches daily for freshness, and they also offer 20 varieties of teas that are hand-blended by their tea master. Additionally, they offer a variety of tasty sweets, powders, extracts, sauces, gifts, and cards. Leashed, well mannered dogs are allowed at their outside dining area.

**Coffee Bean & Tea Leaf**
9343 Clairemont Mesa Blvd

San Diego CA
858-505-9909
coffeebean.com
The coffee here is sourced globally from family coffee farms to procure only the top of 1% of Arabica beans. They offer 30+ varieties of coffee;the beans are roasted in small batches daily for freshness, and they also offer 20 varieties of teas that are hand-blended by their tea master. Additionally, they offer a variety of tasty sweets, powders, extracts, sauces, gifts, and cards. Leashed, well mannered dogs are allowed at their outside dining area.

**El Indio**
3695 India Street
San Diego CA
619-299-0333
el-indio.com/
This Mexican eatery has been family owned and operating since 1940, and they offer a wide variety of dishes, including vegetarian choices. Dogs are allowed on the side patio or at the tables across the street. Orders are placed and picked up inside. Dogs must be leashed and under owner's control/care.

**Elephant & Castle Pub**
1355 N Harbor Drive
San Diego CA
619-234-9977
elephantcastle.com
This eatery and pub serves up seasonally-generated, made from scratch, British classic and North American cuisine, and a good selection of wines, beers, and scotches for some great food pairings. They also have 2 large screen TVs and host various special events. Leashed, well mannered dogs are welcome at their outside tables.

**Fig Tree Cafe Restaurant & Catering**
5119 Cass Street
San Diego CA
858-274-2233
figtreecafepb.com/
Offering a fusion of traditional Italian and innovative California

cuisine, this eatery serves up a variety of tasty dishes coupled with a side of value. Leashed, friendly dogs are welcome at their outside garden dining area.

**Fred's Mexican Cafe**
2470 San Diego Avenue
San Diego CA
619-858-TACO (8226)
Beside a full menu of freshly prepared Mexican cuisine, some highlights of this eatery include their Taco-Licious Tuesdays, Happy Hour food and drink specials Monday thru Friday from 4pm until 7pm, patio dining, and every Monday nights 'Doggie Date Nights' at which a free doggy dinner is offered with purchase of an entree (6 pm until midnight). Leashed, friendly dogs are allowed at their outside dining area.

**Indigo Grill**
1536 India Street
San Diego CA
619-234-6802
Located in the hip Little Italy district;this grill welcomes well-behaved, leashed dogs at their outside tables. They open nightly for dinner at 5 pm and they are open for Sunday brunch from 9:30 am until 1:30 pm.

**Jamba Juice**
1774 Garnet Avenue #D
San Diego CA
858-490-5177
jambajuice.com
All natural and organic ingredients, no high-fructose corn syrup, 0 grams trans fat, no artificial preservatives, a healthy helping of antioxidants, vitamins, and minerals, and fresh whole fruit and fruit juices set the base for these tasty and healthy beverages. Their organic Hot Blends provides a new spin on coffee, green or chai tea, and hot chocolate;plus they offer probiotic fruit and yogurt Blends. Additionally, they feature organic steel-cut oatmeal prepared fresh every morning, all natural salads, wraps, sandwiches, and grab n' go

specialties. They also offer healthy community support through fundraisers, special sales, and school lunch programs. Leashed, well mannered dogs are allowed at their outside dining area.

**Jamba Juice**
11738 Carmel Mountain Road, #178
San Diego CA
858-487-1500
jambajuice.com
All natural and organic ingredients, no high-fructose corn syrup, 0 grams trans fat, no artificial preservatives, a healthy helping of antioxidants, vitamins, and minerals, and fresh whole fruit and fruit juices set the base for these tasty and healthy beverages. Their organic Hot Blends provides a new spin on coffee, green or chai tea, and hot chocolate; plus they offer probiotic fruit and yogurt Blends. Additionally, they feature organic steel-cut oatmeal prepared fresh every morning, all natural salads, wraps, sandwiches, and grab n' go specialties. They also offer healthy community support through fundraisers, special sales, and school lunch programs. Leashed, well mannered dogs are allowed at their outside dining area.

**King's Fish House**
825 Camino de la Reina
San Diego CA
619-574-1230
kingsfishhouse.com/
Specializing in seafood at is best, steaks, freshly prepared salads, desserts, and a daily and seasonally changing menu, this restaurant also offers a full bar and outdoor patio service. Your pet is welcome to join you at the outside tables. Dogs must be attended to at all times, well behaved, and leashed.

**Korky's Ice Cream and Coffee**
2371 San Diego Avenue
San Diego CA
619-297-3080

korkys.biz/
Home to world famous Niederfranks handmade ice cream, this old-fashioned ice cream parlor comes with the modern comforts of a neighborhood coffee house, and for a quick bite they also offer sandwiches, salads, and pastries. Your pet is welcome to join you at the outside tables. Dogs must be attended to at all times, well behaved, and leashed.

**Lazy Dog Restaurant & Bar**
1202 Camino Del Rio N
San Diego CA
619-481-6191
lazydogrestaurants.com/dogs/info
Known for it's dog-friendly patio, the Lazy Dog offers your dog a complimentary bowl of water, and a menu consisting of grilled hamburger patty, chicken breast or brown rice. They just ask that you respect their common sense rules while your dog is dining there. This is as dog-friendly as dining gets. For the humans in your party there is hamburger, steak, salads and some great desserts.

**Mitch's Seafood**
1403 Scott Street
San Diego CA
619-222-8787
mitchsseafood.com/
Featuring a great location on the waterfront, this seafood eatery also places an importance on fresh local and sustainably caught seafood as well as in sourcing from the local farmers, ranchers, and beer and wine crafters. Leashed, well mannered dogs are welcome at their outside tables.

**Oggi's Pizza**
2245 Fenton Parkway
San Diego CA
619-640-1072
oggis.com/
A family-friendly pizzeria and brewing company;they serves up quality pizzas, jumbo wings, burgers, salads, pastas, micro-brewed beers on tap, guest beers, and a sports atmosphere.

Leashed, well mannered dogs are welcome at their outside tables.

**Pampas Argentine Grill**
8690 Aero Drive Suite 105
San Diego CA
858-278-5971
pampasrestaurant.com/
This Argentinean grill features authentic regional dishes with an emphasis on using naturally raised beef, free range poultry, and the freshest of goods in all their preparations. They also provide 'happy hours', live music Wednesday to Sunday evenings, catering, and alfresco dining. Leashed, well behaved dogs are welcome at their outside tables.

**Panera Bread**
12156 Carmel Mountain Road
San Diego CA
858-385-9066
panerabread.com/
This cafe specializes in freshly baked bread sandwiches for all meals;plus they offer soups, salads, homemade cookies, free WiFi, and alfresco dining. Dogs are allowed at the outer tables;they must be under their owner's control and leashed at all times.

**Peace Pies**
4230 Voltaire Street
San Diego CA
619-223-2880
peacepies.com/
With an emphasis on sourcing and developing relations with sustainable, local, and organic providers, this eatery features a seasonally changing menu of starters, salads, sandwiches, wraps, pizzas, desserts, and beverages. Their innovative cuisine of sweet or savory foods are always raw, gluten/soy-free, vegan, and healthily prepared;they also practice a zero waste policy. There is one table outside for alfresco dining. A leashed, well mannered dog is welcome at the outside table.

**Saffron Thai Grilled Chicken**
3137 India Street
San Diego CA

619-574-0177
sumeiyu.com/rest.htm
This eatery specializes in traditional Thai grilled chicken in the style of the northeastern region of Thailand in addition to many other tasty items. They offer indoor and outdoor dining service. Dogs are allowed at the outer tables. Dogs must be well mannered and leashed.

**Sally's Seafood on the Water**
1 Market Place
San Diego CA
619-358-6740
sallyssandiego.com/
Some of the features at this fine dining seafood restaurant include an exhibition kitchen, specialty drinks as well as wines and meal pairing, a wonderful waterside patio, and a venue for special events. Leashed, well mannered dogs are welcome at their outside table seating. They will bring your dog water and biscuits.

**Slaters**
2750 Dewey Rd #193
San Diego CA
619-398-2600
https://slaters5050.com
Dogs are no only welcome but they have a dog menu consisting of 50/50 burger patty, turkey patty, beef, bacon and chicken strips. With over 50 beers, lots of burgers and food options and gluten-free options there is a lot to choose.

**The Coffee Bean & Tea Leaf**
120 W Washington, Suite B
San Diego CA
619-574-7588
coffeebean.com
The coffee here is sourced globally from family coffee farms to procure only the top of 1% of Arabica beans. They offer 30+ varieties of coffee;the beans are roasted in small batches daily for freshness, and they also offer 20 varieties of teas that are hand-blended by their tea master. Additionally, they offer a variety of tasty sweets, powders, extracts, sauces, gifts, and

cards. Leashed, well mannered dogs are allowed at their outside dining area.

**The Coffee Bean & Tea Leaf**
160 W Broadway
San Diego CA
619-238-8047
coffeebean.com
The coffee here is sourced globally from family coffee farms to procure only the top of 1% of Arabica beans. They offer 30+ varieties of coffee;the beans are roasted in small batches daily for freshness, and they also offer 20 varieties of teas that are hand-blended by their tea master. Additionally, they offer a variety of tasty sweets, powders, extracts, sauces, gifts, and cards. Leashed, well mannered dogs are allowed at their outside dining area.

**The Coffee Bean & Tea Leaf**
925 C Camino De La Reina
San Diego CA
619-299-5072
coffeebean.com
The coffee here is sourced globally from family coffee farms to procure only the top of 1% of Arabica beans. They offer 30+ varieties of coffee;the beans are roasted in small batches daily for freshness, and they also offer 20 varieties of teas that are hand-blended by their tea master. Additionally, they offer a variety of tasty sweets, powders, extracts, sauces, gifts, and cards. Leashed, well mannered dogs are allowed at their outside dining area.

**The Coffee Bean & Tea Leaf**
10550 Craftsman Way, Suite #187
San Diego CA
858-385-7895
coffeebean.com
The coffee here is sourced globally from family coffee farms to procure only the top of 1% of Arabica beans. They offer 30+ varieties of coffee;the beans are roasted in small batches daily for freshness, and they also offer 20 varieties of teas that are hand-blended by their tea master. Additionally, they offer a

variety of tasty sweets, powders, extracts, sauces, gifts, and cards. Leashed, well mannered dogs are allowed at their outside dining area.

**The Coffee Bean & Tea Leaf**
12070 Caramel Mountain Road, Suite 296
San Diego CA
858-592-7348
coffeebean.com
The coffee here is sourced globally from family coffee farms to procure only the top of 1% of Arabica beans. They offer 30+ varieties of coffee;the beans are roasted in small batches daily for freshness, and they also offer 20 varieties of teas that are hand-blended by their tea master. Additionally, they offer a variety of tasty sweets, powders, extracts, sauces, gifts, and cards. Leashed, well mannered dogs are allowed at their outside dining area.

**The Coffee Bean & Tea Leaf**
12730 Carmel Country Road
San Diego CA
858-350-9673
coffeebean.com
The coffee here is sourced globally from family coffee farms to procure only the top of 1% of Arabica beans. They offer 30+ varieties of coffee;the beans are roasted in small batches daily for freshness, and they also offer 20 varieties of teas that are hand-blended by their tea master. Additionally, they offer a variety of tasty sweets, powders, extracts, sauces, gifts, and cards. Leashed, well mannered dogs are allowed at their outside dining area.

**The Patio on Lamont Street**
4445 Lamont Street
San Diego CA
858-412-4648
thepatioonlamont.com
The Patio on Lamont Street features locally-crafted beer, fresh dishes, and more. They offer a "Pups On The Patio" Happy Hour daily from 3pm-6pm, where dogs can enjoy "dawg grog" and homemade dog biscuits. Pets are welcome

at the outdoorpatio.

**The Wine Pub**
2907 Shelter Island Dr. #108
San Diego CA
619-758-9325
thewinepubsd.com
In addition to 25 new world and domestic wines by the glass, this 21 and older only wine bar and lounge also features handcrafted beers on drought and a restaurant offering 'grown-up comfort food', cheese boards, handcrafted desserts, daily specials, and live music on select nights. They will also donated 10% of your dining bill for guests dining with their dog on Wednesdays. Leashed, friendly dogs are allowed at their outside dining area.

**Trattoria Fantastica**
1735 India Street
San Diego CA
619-234-1735
Dogs are allowed at the tables on the front patio.

**Twisted Vine Bistro**
7845 Highland Village Place
San Diego CA
858-780-2501
thetwistedvinebistro.com/
Farm to fork cuisine with international inspirations, a wine bar to compliment all their meals, locally crafted beer, and an artistic décor of local and domestic artists are just some of the offerings of this gathering places. Leashed, friendly dogs are welcome at their outside tables.

**Whole Foods Market**
711 University Avenue
San Diego CA
619-294-2800
wholefoods.com/
This natural food supermarket offers natural and organic foods. Order some food from their deli without your dog and bring it to an outdoor table where your well-behaved leashed dog is welcome.

**Zia's**
1845 India Street

San Diego CA
619-234-1344
ziasbistro.com/
This steak and seafood restaurant also offers a full bar and alfresco dining. Dogs are allowed at the outer tables;they must be under their owner's control at all times.

# Pet-Friendly Shopping Centers
**Otay Ranch Town Center**
Eastlake Pkwy At Olympic Pkwy

Chula Vista CA
619-656-9100
otayranchtowncenter.com
This upscale outdoor mall opened in October, 2006. It was the first new mall opened in the San Diego area in 20 years. It is pet-friendly and it even has a dog park on the premises next to the Macy's. Many stores allow dogs inside but you will need to ask first. There are poop bags available at the mall and many stores have water dishes for dogs. There is also a vet located at the mall. To get to the mall and dog park from San Diego go south on the 805 Freeway to the Orange Avenue Exit. Head east on Orange Avenue which will become Olympic Parkway. Go 4 miles east to the mall.

**Horton Plaza Shopping Center**

324 Horton Plaza
San Diego CA
619-239-8180
westfield.com/hortonplaza/
This outdoor shopping center features 196 stores, a variety of dining options and entertainment, annual activities, concierge services, and more. Dogs are allowed to walk the mall. Dogs must be well behaved, under their owner's control at all times, and leashed and cleaned up after.

**Westfield UTC Mall**
4545 La Jolla Village Drive, Suite E-25
San Diego CA

858-546-8858
westfield.com/utc
This outdoor mall in San Diego offers over 100 stores, a variety of dining options, a dog park, and more. Banana Republic, American Eagle, and many more stores allow well-behaved, leashed dogs. Dogs must be well-behaved and on leash at all times while in the mall.

## Pet-Friendly Stores

**Anthropologie**
2015 Birch Road., #1017
Chula Vista CA
619-421-1497
Items of distinction can be found for all ages and in all departments of this unique shop. Carefully selected to add to the enjoyment of the shopping experience, they carry fine clothing, amazing accessories, jewelry, hobby and leisure items, and a full line of bright and useful items for the home, garden, and office. Leashed, well behaved dogs are allowed in the store.

**PetSmart Pet Store**
820 Paseo Del Rey
Chula Vista CA
619-656-0071
Your licensed and well-behaved leashed dog is allowed in the store.

**PetSmart Pet Store**
1840 Main Ct
Chula Vista CA
619-397-0605
Your licensed and well-behaved leashed dog is allowed in the store.

**Petco Pet Store - Chula Vista**
1142 Broadway
Chula Vista CA
619-476-8064
Your licensed and well-behaved leashed dog is allowed in the store.

**Petco Pet Store - Chula Vista - Eastlake**
878 Eastlake Pkwy
Chula Vista CA
619-397-6809

Your licensed and well-behaved leashed dog is allowed in the store.

**Petco Pet Store - Coronado**
925 Orange Ave.
Coronado CA
619-437-6557
Your licensed and well-behaved leashed dog is allowed in the store.

**PetSmart Pet Store**
865 Jackman St
El Cajon CA
619-442-0600
Your licensed and well-behaved leashed dog is allowed in the store.

**Petco Pet Store - El Cajon**
540 North 2nd St.
El Cajon CA
619-441-5200
Your licensed and well-behaved leashed dog is allowed in the store.

**Petco Pet Store - Rancho San Diego**
2510 Jamacha Road
El Cajon CA
619-670-9688
Your licensed and well-behaved leashed dog is allowed in the store.

**PetSmart Pet Store**
8657 Villa La Jolla Dr
La Jolla CA
858-535-9175
Your licensed and well-behaved leashed dog is allowed in the store.

**Pharmaca Integrative Pharmacy**
7650 Girard Avenue
La Jolla CA
858-454-1337
pharmaca.com/stores/ca/la-jolla
In addition to the pharmacy, this store also carries a full line of integrative medicines and alternative remedies; plus, they offer a Healthy Living Lecture Series coving a variety of subjects. Leashed, well mannered dogs are allowed in the store.

**Restoration Hardware**
4405 La Jolla Village Drive
La Jolla CA
858-784-0575
restorationhardware.com/
Your well-behaved leashed dog is allowed inside this store.

**Petco Pet Store - La Mesa**
8501 Fletcher Pkwy
La Mesa CA
619-337-0701
Your licensed and well-behaved leashed dog is allowed in the store.

**American Eagle Outfitters**
4353 La Jolla Village Dr
San Diego CA
858-552-8006
ae.com/web/index.jsp
American Eagle Outfitters allows well-behaved, leashed dogs in the store. They are located in Westfield UTC Mall, which is also pet friendly.

**Anthropologie**
4525 La Jolla Village Drive, #D-11 UTC
San Diego CA
858-962-5461
Items of distinction can be found for all ages and in all departments of this unique shop. Carefully selected to add to the enjoyment of the shopping experience, they carry fine clothing, amazing accessories, jewelry, hobby and leisure items, and a full line of bright and useful items for the home, garden, and office. Leashed, well behaved dogs are allowed in the store.

**Anthropologie**
7007 Friars Road, #870-A
San Diego CA
619-291-2891
Items of distinction can be found for all ages and in all departments of this unique shop. Carefully selected to add to the enjoyment of the shopping experience, they carr

## San Diego County North

## Dog-Friendly Hotels

### La Quinta Inn San Diego-carlsbad
760 Macadamia Drive
Carlsbad CA
760-438-2828 (800-531-5900)
Dogs up to 40 pounds are allowed. There are no additional pet fees. Dogs must be leashed and cleaned up after.

### Ramada Carlsbad
751 Macadamia Drive
Carlsbad CA
760-438-2285
Dogs up to 50 pounds are allowed. There is no pet fee.

### Sheraton Carlsbad Resort & Spa
5480 Grand Pacific Drive
Carlsbad CA
760-827-2400 (888-625-5144)
Besides offering a number of in-house amenities for all level of travelers, this luxury hotel also provides a convenient location to corporate, shopping, dining, and entertainment areas. One dog up to 80 pounds is allowed for an additional pet fee of $35 per night;there is a pet waiver to sign at check in.

### Hilton San Diego/del Mar
15575 Jimmy Durante Boulevard
Del Mar CA
858-792-5200
Located in the heart of the city, this upscale hotel offers numerous on site amenities for business and leisure travelers, plus a convenient location to beaches, business districts, shopping, dining, historical, and entertainment areas. Dogs are allowed for an additional one time pet fee of $50 per room.

### Les Artistes Inn
944 Camino Del Mar
Del Mar CA
858-755-4646
A 15-minute walk to Del Mar City Beach this California boutique hotel features a courtyard complete with an outdoor fireplace. Offering ocean and garden views all guest rooms include free Wi-Fi.

Boasting 12 art inspired rooms accommodations at Les Artistes Inn provide cable TV. All vibrant rooms include a microwave and comfortable seating area. Surrounded by unique architecture Les Artistes Inn features outdoor seating areas complete with barbecue facilities and fireplaces. Guests can stroll among the gardens featuring lush greenery and a stone walkway. Serving Peruvian cuisine CafÃ© Secret is a short walk from the hotel. San Diego is 26 minutes drive away.

### Best Western Encinitas Inn & Suites At Moonlight Beach
85 Encinitas Blvd
Encinitas CA
760-942-7455 (800-780-7234)
Dogs up to 80 pounds are allowed. There is a $20 per day pet fee up to $100 for the week. Up to two dogs are allowed per room.

### Econo Lodge Encinitas Moonlight Beach
410 N. Coast Hwy 101
Encinitas CA
760-436-4999 (877-424-6423)
100 percent non-smoking hotel.

Dogs up to 40 pounds are allowed. Dogs are allowed for a pet fee of $25.00 per pet per night.

### Quality Inn Encinitas Near Legoland
607 Leucadia Boulevard
Encinitas CA
760-944-3800 (877-424-6423)
Dogs of all sizes are allowed. There is a pet fee of $25 per night to a maximum of $75.

### La Quinta Inn San Diego Oceanside
937 North Coast Highway
Oceanside CA
760-450-0730 (800-531-5900)
Dogs of all sizes are allowed. There are no additional pet fees. Dogs may not be left unattended, and they must be leashed and cleaned up after.

### Ramada Oceanside
1440 Mission Avenue
Oceanside CA
760-967-4100
Dogs up to 50 pounds are allowed. There is no pet fee.

### Best Western Poway/san Diego Hotel
13845 Poway Road
Poway CA
858-748-6320 (800-780-7234)
Dogs up to 80 pounds are allowed. There is a $10 per day pet fee up to $100 for the week. Up to two dogs are allowed per room.

### Ramada Poway
12448 Poway Road
Poway CA
858-748-7311
Dogs of all sizes are allowed. There is a pet fee of $15 per pet per night and a $50 refundable deposit.

### La Quinta Inn San Diego Vista
630 Sycamore Avenue
Vista CA
760-727-8180 (800-531-5900)
Dogs of all sizes are allowed. There are no additional pet fees. Dogs may not be left unattended, and they must be leashed and cleaned up after.

## Pet-Friendly Extended Stay Hotels

### Extended Stay America - San Diego - Carlsbad Village By The Sea
1050 Grand Avenue
Carlsbad CA
760-729-9380 (800-804-3724)
One dog is allowed per suite. There is a $25 per night additional pet fee up to $150 for an entire stay.

### Homewood Suites By Hilton Carlsbad-north San Diego County
2223 Palomar Airport Road
Carlsbad CA
760-431-2266
This upscale all suite hotel

offers large, comfortable suites for longer stays and/or temporary housing needs;plus numerous on site amenities for all level of travelers and a convenient location to local sites of interest. Dogs up to 50 pounds are allowed for an additional one time pet fee of $75 per room.

**Residence Inn By Marriott Carlsbad**
2000 Faraday Avenue
Carlsbad CA
760-431-9999
Dogs of all sizes are allowed. There is a $75 one time additional pet fee.

**Extended Stay America - San Diego - Oceanside**
3190 Vista Way
Oceanside CA
760-439-1499 (800-804-3724)
One dog is allowed per suite. There is a $25 per night additional pet fee up to $150 for an entire stay.

**Residence Inn By Marriott San Diego Oceanside**
3603 Ocean Ranch Blvd.
Oceanside CA
760-722-9600
Dogs of all sizes are allowed. There is a $100 one time additional pet fee.

**Towneplace Suites By Marriott San Diego Carlsbad-vista**
2201 South Melrose Drive
Vista CA
760-216-6010
Dogs of all sizes are allowed. There is a $100 one time pet fee.

# Dog Camps
**Bark Avenue Resort & Kamp**
655 Benet Road
Oceanside CA
760-433-3763
barkforpets.com/index.html
Bark Avenue Resort & Kamp is a Pet Hotel and Doggie Day camp, located in Oceanside, California. When you check into

the pet resort, your pet is pampered with luxury accommodations, the suites providing a bed, glass doors, water, "room service", satellite radio, even color TVs. Dogs are escorted to the enclosed dog park at least four times each day for potty breaks. There is also a doggie day camp, where there are no breed, age or size restrictions. The camp hours are: Monday - Friday: 7am - 6pm and Saturday - Sunday: 8am - 3pm. Bark Avenue Resport & Kamp also offers a beautifully designed dog park. Five separate enclosed areas, within the park, allow dogs the best experience. Whether it be a game of fetch or tug of war, a run thru the obstacle course and over the exercise ramp or just a dip in the pool.

# Dog-Friendly Attractions
**Carlsbad Village**
Carlsbad Village Drive
Carlsbad CA

Carlsbad Village has a number of shops and restaurants that are dog-friendly. Its about 4 blocks long and 2 blocks wide.

**Legoland Kennel**
One Legoland Drive
Carlsbad CA
760-918-5346
legoland.com/California.htm
This amusement park offers a trilling variety of rides, shows and attractions. Although dogs are not allowed in the park they are allowed in the kennels that are provided out front. Individual kennels are provided, and there is a $15 refundable deposit for the key. Water and dishes are provided; they request that you bring food, blankets, and whatever comfort toys along for your pet.

**California Surf Museum**
223 N Coast H
Oceanside CA
760-721-6876

surfmuseum.org/
This interesting museum is a resource and educational center to gather, preserve, and document the art, culture and heritage of this lifestyle sport for generations to come. Well mannered dogs are welcome at this small museum; they must be leashed and under their owner's control at all times.

# Outdoor Restaurants
**Johnny Rockets**
15103 Mainside Center
Camp Pendleton CA
760-829-1258
johnnyrockets.com/
All the American favorites can be found here: A fun retro, all-American decor and atmosphere, juicy burgers, specialty sandwiches, crispy fries, hand-dipped malts and shakes (dark chocolate ones too), fresh baked apple pies, tasty vegetarian choices, and something for all ages. Leashed, friendly dogs are allowed at their outside dining area.

**Cafe Elysa**
3076 Carlsbad Blvd
Carlsbad CA
760-434-4100
facebook.com/cafeelysa
Cuisine with a French flair is offered for breakfast and brunch at this eatery. Leashed dogs are allowed at their outside tables.

**Coffee Bean & Tea Leaf**
2508 El Camino Real Suite F
Carlsbad CA
760-720-1381
coffeebean.com
The coffee here is sourced globally from family coffee farms to procure only the top of 1% of Arabica beans. They offer 30+ varieties of coffee;the beans are roasted in small batches daily for freshness, and they also offer 20 varieties of teas that are hand-blended by their tea master. Additionally, they offer a variety of tasty sweets, powders, extracts, sauces, gifts, and cards. Leashed, well mannered

dogs are allowed at their outside dining area.

### Coffee Bean & Tea Leaf
1935 Calle Barcelona, #176
Carlsbad CA
760-634-3268
coffeebean.com
The coffee here is sourced globally from family coffee farms to procure only the top of 1% of Arabica beans. They offer 30+ varieties of coffee;the beans are roasted in small batches daily for freshness, and they also offer 20 varieties of teas that are hand-blended by their tea master. Additionally, they offer a variety of tasty sweets, powders, extracts, sauces, gifts, and cards. Leashed, well mannered dogs are allowed at their outside dining area.

### Gregorio's Restaurant
300 Carlsbad Village Dr #208
Carlsbad CA
760-720-1132
gregoriosrestaurant.com/
This Italian and Pizza restaurant allows dogs at the outdoor seats.

### Mas Fina Cantina
2780 State Street
Carlsbad CA
760-434-3497
masfinacantina.com/menu_3.ht
ml
Some of the popularities of this restaurant include a variety of Mexican and all American favorites, a full service bar, live entertainment select nights, happy hours Monday to Friday and late night Sundays, daily and weekly specials, and a patio dining area. Leashed dogs are allowed at their outside tables;they must be under their owner's control/care at all times.

### O'Sullivan's Irish Pub and Restaurant
640 Grand Ave
Carlsbad CA
760-729-7234
osullivanscarlsbad.com/
In addition to traditional Irish fare, this restaurant and bar also offers a variety of salads,

burgers, seafood, steaks, chicken, a sports atmosphere, and one of the largest assortment of Irish and Scotch whiskey in the area. Leashed, well mannered dogs are welcome at their outside tables.

### Vigilucci's Cucina Italiana
2943 State Street
Carlsbad CA
760-434-2500
Besides offering a full menu of tasty Italian foods reminiscent of the cuisine from the Milano region of Italy, this eatery also features a variety of red and white wines, a full bar, alfresco dining, and catering services. Leashed, well mannered dogs are welcome at their outside tables.

### Vinaka Cafe
300 Carlsbad Village Dr #211
Carlsbad CA
760-720-7890
Specialty beverages and espressos, breakfasts, alfresco dining, and more is offered at this café. Leashed dogs are allowed at their outside tables.

### Tom Giblin's Irish Pub
640 Grand Avenue
Carlsbad Village CA
760-729-7234
tomgiblins.com/
This authentic Irish pub offers a variety of American and Irish foods, indoor/outdoor service, premium draft beers with many specialty drinks, and live traditional and contemporary Irish music. Your pet is welcome to join you at the outside tables. Dogs must be attended to at all times, well behaved, and leashed.

### Americana
1454 Camino Del Mar
Del Mar CA
858-794-6838
americanarestaurant.com/
With a farm to table approach this restaurant features a full's days menu of handcrafted American cuisine with global flavors, a notable dessert list, signature cocktails, fine wines-

many chosen to compliment their foods, and a global selection of beers. Leashed, well mannered dogs are allowed at their outside dining area.

### Del Mar Rendezvous
1555 Camino Del Mar Suite # 102
Del Mar CA
858-755-2669
delmarrendezvous.com
Del Mar Rendezvous serves Chinese food. Well-behaved, leashed dogs are welcome on the outdoor patio.

### En Fuego Cantina & Grill
1342 Camino del Mar
Del Mar CA
858-792-6551
enfuegocantina.com/
Enjoy dining with your dog at the tables in the nicely designed patio. Thanks to one of our readers for recommending this restaurant.

### Pacifica Breeze Cafe
1555 Camino Del Mar #209
Del Mar CA
858-509-9147
pacificadelmar.com/
Seafood is the specialty of this fine dining restaurant. Leashed dogs are allowed at their outside dining area.

### Smashburger
1555 Camino Del Mar
Del Mar CA
858-461-4105
smashburger.com/
Smashburger, believes that "smashing is better". Their handcrafted burgers are smashed, seared and seasoned to order, using fresh, never frozen 100% Certified Angus Beef. Offering many dishes like their Classic Smashburger, Smashfries hand-tossed with garlic, rosemary and olive oil, hand-breaded haystack onions and fried pickles, grilled or crispy chicken sandwiches, split and grilled hot dogs, crisp entree salads and black bean veggie burgers, and more. Well-behaved, leashed dogs are allowed at the outdoor seats at the Del Mar, California location.

**Stratford Court Cafe**
1307 Stratford Court
Del Mar CA
858-792-7433
stratfordcourtcafe.com/
Thanks to one of our readers who writes: This is THE dog-friendly restaurant in Del Mar. All seating outdoor and you and your dog can order at a walk-up counter. They even offer home-made dog biscuits and have a stack of water bowls.

**The Coffee Bean & Tea Leaf**
2689 Via de la Valle, Suite E
Del Mar CA
858-481-6229
coffeebean.com
The coffee here is sourced globally from family coffee farms to procure only the top of 1% of Arabica beans. They offer 30+ varieties of coffee;the beans are roasted in small batches daily for freshness, and they also offer 20 varieties of teas that are hand-blended by their tea master. Additionally, they offer a variety of tasty sweets, powders, extracts, sauces, gifts, and cards. Leashed, well mannered dogs are allowed at their outside dining area.

**Baja Fresh Mexican Grill**
194 El Camino Real Blvd
Encinitas CA
760-633-2262
bajafresh.com
This Mexican restaurant is open for lunch and dinner. They use fresh ingredients and making their salsa and beans daily. Some of the items on their menu include Enchiladas, Burritos, Tacos Salads, Quesadillas, Nachos, Chicken, Steak and more. Well-behaved leashed dogs are allowed at the outdoor tables.

**Beachside Bar & Grill**
806 S Coast Highway101
Encinitas CA
760-942-0738
beachsidebarandgrill.com
This neighborhood bar and grill serves up freshly prepared burgers and sandwiches, signature paninis, pasta and

pizzas, beers (12 on tap), cocktails, and more. They also offer nightly chef specials, a family friendly atmosphere, weekday happy hours, and live music. Leashed, well mannered dogs are allowed at their outside tables.

**Bentley's Steak and Chop House**
162 S Rancho Santa Fe Rd
Encinitas CA
760-632-9333
bentleyssteak.com
Bentley's Steak and Chop House offers lunch, dinner, and Sunday brunch. Well-behaved, leashed dogs are allowed if they don't bark.

**Chipotle**
268 North El Camino Real
Encinitas CA
760-635-3863
chipotle.com
Specializing in organic, natural and unprocessed food, this Mexican Eatery offers fajita burritos, tacos, salads, and salsas. Dogs are allowed at the outdoor tables but you will need to order your food inside the restaurant and dogs must remain outside.

**Encinitas Cafe**
531 S Coast Hwy 101
Encinitas CA
760-632-0919
encinitascafe.com/
Freshly prepared American and regional favorites are offered for breakfast, lunch, and dinner at this cafe. They also offer weekly and web only specials. Leashed, well mannered dogs are welcome at their outside tables.

**Firenze Trattoria**
162 S Rancho Santa Fe Road
Encinitas CA
760-944-9000
firenzetrattoria.com/
This upscale restaurant features the finest in Italian cuisine, an extensive wine list, and a flower adorned patio. Service is provided on the patio where your pet is welcome to join you. Dogs must be well

behaved, attended to at all times, and leashed.

**Jamba Juice**
272-A N El Camino Real
Encinitas CA
760-943-9751
jambajuice.com
All natural and organic ingredients, no high-fructose corn syrup, 0 grams trans fat, no artificial preservatives, a healthy helping of antioxidants, vitamins, and minerals, and fresh whole fruit and fruit juices set the base for these tasty and healthy beverages. Their organic Hot Blends provides a new spin on coffee, green or chai tea, and hot chocolate;plus they offer probiotic fruit and yogurt Blends. Additionally, they feature organic steel-cut oatmeal prepared fresh every morning, all natural salads, wraps, sandwiches, and grab n' go specialties. They also offer healthy community support through fundraisers, special sales, and school lunch programs. Leashed, well mannered dogs are allowed at their outside dining area.

**Mr. Peabody's**
136 Encinitas Blvd
Encinitas CA
760-753-7192
PeabodysRocks.com
Southern California cuisine, a from-scratch kitchen, signature specialties, weekday happy hours, daily drink and food specials, and numerous music and special events are just a few of the offerings of this gathering spot. Leashed, friendly dogs are allowed at their outside dining area.

**Peace Pies**
133 Daphne Street
Encinitas CA
760-479-0996
peacepies.com/
With an emphasis on sourcing and developing relations with sustainable, local, and organic providers, this eatery features a seasonally changing menu of starters, salads, sandwiches, wraps, pizzas, desserts, and

beverages. Their innovative cuisine of sweet or savory foods are always raw, gluten/soy-free, vegan, and healthily prepared;they also practice a zero waste policy. Leashed, well mannered dogs are allowed at their outside tables.

**Chipotle**
2611 Vista Way
Oceanside CA
760-721-6904
chipotle.com
Specializing in organic, natural and unprocessed food, this Mexican Eatery offers fajita burritos, tacos, salads, and salsas. Dogs are allowed at the outdoor tables but you will need to order your food inside the restaurant and dogs must remain outside.

**Don's Country Kitchen**
1938 Coast Highway
Oceanside CA
760-722-7337
donscountrykitchen.com/
This restaurant serves American food. Leashed dogs are allowed at the outdoor tables.

**Hill Street Coffee House**
524 S Coast Hwy
Oceanside CA
760-966-0985
hillst.org/
A Certified GREEN restaurant, they offer a full day's menu of handcrafted cuisine sourced from local and organic farms, a full espresso bar, and fine wine and beer. Leashed, well mannered dogs are welcome at their outside tables.

**Jamba Juice**
2619 Vista Way, Suite B-2
Oceanside CA
760-433-6719
jambajuice.com
All natural and organic ingredients, no high-fructose corn syrup, 0 grams trans fat, no artificial preservatives, a healthy helping of antioxidants, vitamins, and minerals, and fresh whole fruit and fruit juices set the base for these tasty and healthy beverages. Their organic Hot Blends provides a new spin on

coffee, green or chai tea, and hot chocolate;plus they offer probiotic fruit and yogurt Blends. Additionally, they feature organic steel-cut oatmeal prepared fresh every morning, all natural salads, wraps, sandwiches, and grab n' go specialties. They also offer healthy community support through fundraisers, special sales, and school lunch programs. Leashed, well mannered dogs are allowed at their outside dining area.

**Chipotle**
13495 Poway Road
Poway CA
858-748-9200
chipotle.com
Specializing in organic, natural and unprocessed food, this Mexican Eatery offers fajita burritos, tacos, salads, and salsas. Dogs are allowed at the outdoor tables but you will need to order your food inside the restaurant and dogs must remain outside.

**Cafe 56**
13211 Black Mountain Rd
Rancho Penasquitos CA
858-484-5789&8206
Specializing in American comfort foods with international inspirations, this eatery sources the freshest local produce and products available to provide a wide menu of freshly prepared signature homemade dishes. They also offer weekly specials and alfresco dining. Leashed, well mannered dogs are welcome at their outside dining area.

**Beach Grass Cafe**
159 S H 101
Solana Beach CA
858-509-0632
beachgrasscafe.com/
A casual ambiance, fresh/premium ingredients, daily handcrafted foods, a Jasmine garden, a European-style patio, micro brews, and boutique wines backed with music drifting throughout can all be found at this eatery. Leashed, well mannered dogs

are allowed at their outside dining area.

**Jamba Juice**
689-D Lomas Santa Fe Drive
Solana Beach CA
858-755-2056
jambajuice.com
All natural and organic ingredients, no high-fructose corn syrup, 0 grams trans fat, no artificial preservatives, a healthy helping of antioxidants, vitamins, and minerals, and fresh whole fruit and fruit juices set the base for these tasty and healthy beverages. Their organic Hot Blends provides a new spin on coffee, green or chai tea, and hot chocolate;plus they offer probiotic fruit and yogurt Blends. Additionally, they feature organic steel-cut oatmeal prepared fresh every morning, all natural salads, wraps, sandwiches, and grab n' go specialties. They also offer healthy community support through fundraisers, special sales, and school lunch programs. Leashed, well mannered dogs are allowed at their outside dining area.

**Baja Fresh Mexican Grill**
620 Hacienda Dr.
Vista CA
760-643-0110
bajafresh.com
This Mexican restaurant is open for lunch and dinner. They use fresh ingredients and making their salsa and beans daily. Some of the items on their menu include Enchiladas, Burritos, Tacos Salads, Quesadillas, Nachos, Chicken, Steak and more. Well-behaved leashed dogs are allowed at the outdoor tables.

**Chipotle**
30 Main Street
Vista CA
760-639-0529
chipotle.com
Specializing in organic, natural and unprocessed food, this Mexican Eatery offers fajita burritos, tacos, salads, and salsas. Dogs are allowed at the outdoor tables but you will need

to order your food inside the restaurant and dogs must remain outside.

## Jamba Juice
1661-A S Melrose Drive
Vista CA
760-599-0215
jambajuice.com
All natural and organic ingredients, no high-fructose corn syrup, 0 grams trans fat, no artificial preservatives, a healthy helping of antioxidants, vitamins, and minerals, and fresh whole fruit and fruit juices set the base for these tasty and healthy beverages. Their organic Hot Blends provides a new spin on coffee, green or chai tea, and hot chocolate;plus they offer probiotic fruit and yogurt Blends. Additionally, they feature organic steel-cut oatmeal prepared fresh every morning, all natural salads, wraps, sandwiches, and grab n' go specialties. They also offer healthy community support through fundraisers, special sales, and school lunch programs. Leashed, well mannered dogs are allowed at their outside dining area.

## Pet-Friendly Stores
### Anthropologie
1911 Calle Barcelona, #4-158
Carlsbad CA
760-436-9110
Items of distinction can be found for all ages and in all departments of this unique shop. Carefully selected to add to the enjoyment of the shopping experience, they carry fine clothing, amazing accessories, jewelry, hobby and leisure items, and a full line of bright and useful items for the home, garden, and office. Leashed, well behaved dogs are allowed in the store.

### Crate and Barrel
5600 Paseo Del Norte
Carlsbad CA
760-692-2100
crateandbarrel.com
This store offers fine products from around the world for in and around the home that include items for outdoor living, indoor furnishings and decorating, dining and entertaining, kitchen and food service, and gourmet food and beverages. They also have accessories for pets, bed and bath items, and organizing and storage units. Leashed, friendly dogs are welcome in the store; they must be under their owner's control at all times.

### Petco Pet Store - La Costa
3239 Camino De Los Coches
Carlsbad CA
760-753-0814
Your licensed and well-behaved leashed dog is allowed in the store.

### Dexter's Deli
1229 Camino Del Mar
Del Mar CA
858-792-3707
dextersdeli.com/
Specializing in natural food diets, fresh baked treats and cakes and a selection of dog and cat toys and gifts.

### Petco Pet Store - Del Mar
2749 Via De La Valle
Del Mar CA
858-259-0110
Your licensed and well-behaved leashed dog is allowed in the store.

### Three Dog Bakery
2670 Via De La Valle, Suite #A160/A170
Del Mar CA
858-793-0755
threedogsd.com/
Three Dog Bakery provides cookies and snacks for your dog as well as some boutique items. You well-behaved, leashed dog is welcome.

### PetSmart Pet Store
1034 N El Camino Real
Encinitas CA
760-436-1220
Your licensed and well-behaved leashed dog is allowed in the store.

### Petco Pet Store - Encinitas
154 Encinitas Blvd
Encinitas CA
760-632-6600
Your licensed and well-behaved leashed dog is allowed in the store.

### PetSmart Pet Store
3420 Marron
Oceanside CA
760-729-4546
Your licensed and well-behaved leashed dog is allowed in the store.

### Petco Pet Store - Oceanside
2445 West Vista Way
Oceanside CA
760-967-7387
Your licensed and well-behaved leashed dog is allowed in the store.

### Petco Pet Store - Oceanside - North
3875 Mission Ave.
Oceanside CA
760-754-1400
Your licensed and well-behaved leashed dog is allowed in the store.

### Petco Pet Store - Poway
13375 Poway Road
Poway CA
858-679-2020
Your licensed and well-behaved leashed dog is allowed in the store.

### PetSmart Pet Store
1740 University Dr
Vista CA
760-630-3544
Your licensed and well-behaved leashed dog is allowed in the store.

### Petco Pet Store - Vista
520 Hacienda Dr.
Vista CA
760-631-5770
Your licensed and well-behaved leashed dog is allowed in the store.

## Dog-Friendly Wineries and Vineyards
### Witch Creek Winery

2906 Carlsbad Blvd/H 101
Carlsbad CA
760-720-7499
This winery focuses on
handcrafted wines that are rich,
full bodied, and well balanced.
They have two tasting rooms;
one in Carlsbad and the other
one in Julian, California. They
consider themselves dog-
friendly, and your pet is
welcome to go wherever you
can go, including the tasting
room in Carlsbad. Dogs must be
well behaved, and leashed and
cleaned up after at all times.

## Dog-Friendly Beaches
### Cardiff State Beach
Old Highway 101
Cardiff CA
760-753-5091
This is a gently sloping sandy
beach with warm water. Popular
activities include swimming,
surfing and beachcombing.
Dogs on leash are allowed and
please clean up after your pets.
The beach is located on Old
Highway 101, one mile south of
Cardiff.

### Del Mar Beach
Seventeenth Street
Del Mar CA
858-755-1556
Dogs are allowed on the beach
as follows. South of 17th Street,
dogs are allowed on a 6 foot
leash year-round. Between 17th
Street and 29th Street, dogs are
allowed on a 6 foot leash from
October through May (from June
through September, dogs are
not allowed at all). Between 29th
Street and northern city limits,
dogs are allowed without a
leash, but must be under voice
control from October through
May (from June through
September, dogs must be on a
6 foot leash). Owners must
clean up after their dogs.

### Dog Beach Del Mar
3006 Sandy Ln
Del Mar CA
858-755-9313
The Dog Beach in Del Mar is a
off-leash dog beach September

through May. During the
summer your pooch must be
on a leash. Dogs must be well
behaved and multiple poop bag
stations and trash cans are
located on the beach for your
convenience.

### Rivermouth Beach
Highway 101
Del Mar CA

This beach allows voice
controlled dogs to run leash
free from September 15
through June 15 (no specified
hours). Leashes are required
during mid-summer tourist
season from mid June to mid
Sept. Fans of this beach are
trying to convince the Del Mar
City council to extend the
leash-free period to year round.
The beach is located on
Highway 101 just south of
Border Avenue at the north end
of the City of Del Mar. Thanks
to one of our readers for
recommending this beach.

## Off-Leash Dog Parks
### Ann D. L'Heureaux Memorial Dog Park
Carlsbad Village Drive
Carlsbad CA
760-434-2825
This memorial dog park offers
over 13,000 square feet of
fenced off lead area with shade
trees, benches, a doggy
sanitary station, and a pet
drinking fountain. Dogs must
be sociable, current on all
vaccinations and license, and
under their owner's control at
all times. Dogs must be
leashed when not in
designated off-lead areas.

### Encinitas Park
D Street
Encinitas CA

Thanks to one of our readers
who recommends the following
two dog parks in Encinitas
Park. Encinitas Viewpoint Park,
on "D" Street at Cornish Drive,
off-leash dogs permitted 6:00-
7:30 AM and 4:00-6:00 PM on

MWF only. Other days of the
week, dogs must be on leash.
Orpheus Park, on Orpheus
Avenue at Union Street, off-
leash dogs permitted 6:00-7:30
AM and 4:00-6:00 PM on MWF
only. Other days of the week,
dogs must be on leash.

### Oceanside Dog Park
2905 San Luis Rey Rd
Oceanside CA
760-757-4357
The first off-leash dog park in
Oceanside is located next to the
North County Humane Society
buiding. The fenced park is
open from 7 am to 7 pm except
for Wednesday when it is closed
for maintenance.

### San Diego Humane Society and SPCA Dog Park
2905 San Luis Rey Road
Oceanside CA
760-757-4357
Located at the north campus of
the San Diego Humane Society,
this doggie play area is open to
the public daily from 7 am until 7
pm. Exceptions include closures
for muddy conditions, inclement
weather, and upkeep. The
hotline number to check
conditions of the park is also
760-757-4357. Dogs must be
healthy, sociable, current on all
vaccinations and license with
tags on collar, and under their
owner's control at all times.
Dogs must be leashed when not
in designated off-lead areas.

### Poway Dog Park
13094 Civic Center Drive
Poway CA

poway.org/324/Dog-Park
This 1 3/4 acre dog park is open
from sunrise to 9:30 pm. The
park is lighted at night. There
are three separate fenced
areas. From the I-15 freeway
take Poway Rd east 3.9 miles.
Turn right on Bowron and park
at the lot at the end of the road.

### The Poway Dog Park
13094 Civic Center Drive
Poway CA
858-668-4673
poway.org/324/Dog-Park

Located at the Poway Community Park, this off-leash, fenced park is open daily from dawn to 9:30 pm and features lighted fields, 3 large separately fenced areas, water for thirsty pups, and picnic benches. Dogs must be sociable, current on all vaccinations and license, and under their owner's control at all times. Dogs must be leashed when not in designated off-lead areas.

## Dog-Friendly Parks
**Guajome Regional Park**
3000 Guajome Lake Road
Oceanside CA
858-565-3600
Rich in natural and cultural history, this historic 557 acre park features a wide diversity of plant, bird, and wildlife, spring-fed lakes, scenic picnic areas, trails, a gazebo and an enclosed pavilion that overlooks the lake. There is a variety of land and water recreational opportunities to explore. Dogs of all sizes are allowed for an additional fee of $1 per pet. Dogs must have current tags or shot records, be on no more than a 6 foot leash, and be cleaned up after. Dogs must remain in developed and paved areas; they are not allowed on the trails.

## Veterinarians
**All Creatures Hospital Inc**
3665 Via De La Valle
Del Mar CA
858-481-7992
allcreatureshospital.com/
The All Creatures Veterinary Hospital has been serving the North County Coastal Area for close to 30 years. They are a family-owned business and strive to provide a friendly and compassionate environment for pet parents and their animal companions. Services they offer include Preventative Medicine Programs, Puppy and Kitten Health Care Packages, Immunizations, Spay and neuter surgeries, Mature/Senior Pet

Programs, HomeAgain Microchips, Surgical Services, Annual Wellness Exams, and Dental Health Care.

## Humane Society or SPCAs
**San Diego Humane Society and SPCA North Campus**
2905 San Luis Rey Road
Oceanside CA
760-757-4357
sdhumane.org
A private nonprofit organization that receives no government grant funding, the San Diego Humane Society and SPCA is supported solely by contributions, grants, bequests, investments, proceeds from it retail outlets and some fees for service.

Our Vision is to Inspire and Engage the Community to End Animal Suffering.

Our Mission is too promote the humane treatment of animals, to prevent cruelty to animals,and provide education to enhance the human-animal bond.

The following services may be provided at either the North Campus and/or Gaines Campus:

Comprehensive Medical & Behavioral Services for Humane Society Animals
On-Site and Mobile Adoptions (All come with spay/neuter, microchips, shots, health & behavioral tested, etc.)
Intake of Owner-Relinquished Pets & Pets from other Shelters
Litter Abatement Program (Spaying/Neutering parent animals of relinquished litters.)
Foster Care Program
Owner Requested Euthanasia (For terminally ill or suffering animals.)
Pet Loss Support Group
Pet-Assisted Therapy
Animal Cruelty and Neglect Investigations

Animal Rescue Reserve
Behavior Helpline & Private Behavioral Consultations
Behavior & Training Classes
Educational Programs for Youth & Adults
Scout Programs
Campus Tours
Pet PALS Kid's Club
Animal Adventure Camp

## Other Organizations
**Sage Canyon Animal Sanctuary**
44444 Sage Road
Aguanga CA
909-767-3200
sagecanyon.org
S.C.A.S. is a privately owned and runned non-profit no kill sanctuary that is located in Riverside County California. We are dependent on charitable donations. The health and happiness of all of our dogs is our number one priority. We offer adoption and volunteer opportunities for anyone who qualifies.

**jewel in lotus**
1619 MAPLELEAF CT.
Encinitas CA
760-633-4544
We are a Buddhist group that offers: healing prayers; private consults by appointment. We will be in varius cafes that are doggy friendly in the Encinitas area. Call Chris 760 633-4544 or Donna 760-305-3792 donations needed. Oh mani Padme ohm

## San Diego I-15 Corridor

## Dog-Friendly Hotels
**Best Western Escondido Hotel**
1700 Seven Oakes Road
Escondido CA
760-740-1700 (800-780-7234)
Dogs are allowed up to 35 pounds. There is a $25 per pet one time fee. Up to two dogs are

allowed per room.

## Rodeway Inn Escondido
250 West El Norte Parkway
Escondido CA
760-746-0441 (877-424-6423)
If you love one-on-one, people-to-people service, you'll love the Rodeway Inn, Escondido.

Dogs up to 50 pounds are allowed. Dogs are allowed for a pet fee of $30.00 per pet per night. Two dogs are allowed per room.

## Tuscany Hills Retreat
29850 Circle R Way
Escondido CA
760-751-8800 (800-253-5341)
Our guests enjoy free parking and Wi-Fi at Tuscany Hills Retreat & Inn. Golfers and tennis players can sharpen their games soothe sore muscles in the four outdoor hot tubs and book a massage at the spa. The low-rise lodge-style Tuscany Hills Resort sits next to an 18-hole golf course. The 30 non-smoking suites all have cable TVs private balconies or patios overlooking the golf course or well-landscaped courtyard. Guests can store and fix snacks using the convenient in-room microwaves coffeemakers and mini-fridges. After dining at the patio restaurant guests can burn some calories at the fitness center in the outdoor pool and on the walking trails. About 12 miles from downtown Escondido's shops and restaurants Tuscany Hills Resort is less than five minutes from I-15 on a lush 18-hole golf course. San Diego International Airport is 44 miles away and McClellan-Palomar Airport is a 21-mile drive.

## Pala Mesa Golf Resort
2001 Old Highway 395
Fallbrook CA
760-728-5881 (800-722-4700)
palamesa.com/
Golfers populate the non-smoking Pala Mesa Golf Resort soaking up the rays on the greens or in the pool and hot tub and then retreating to the posh

rooms to take advantage of the free Wi-Fi. Spread across 205 acres of landscaped greens the 133 non-smoking rooms of the low-rise Pala Mesa Golf Resort cater to discerning travelers. Rooms include fine linens atop comfortable beds flat-panel cable TVs video games and refrigerators. Gaze upon the greens as you surf the web on the free Wi-Fi. The resort's onsite AquaTerra Restaurant & Seafood Bar serves California cuisine with golf-course views. The Sandwedge Snack Bar features sandwiches and beers. The hotel also offers an 18-hole golf course with free use of clubs. Other amenities include a pool and hot tub business center fitness center and free parking. Pets are allowed for an extra fee. Off I-15 in the foothills of Temecula the Pala Mesa Golf Resort is surrounded by trees hiking trails and a golf course. The Temecula Wine Region is a 16-mile drive from the resort. The San Diego Wild Animal Park is 26 miles away. Oceanside's beaches are 21 miles from the resort. San Diego International Airport is 50 miles from the hotel.

## Days Inn San Marcos
517 West San Marcos Boulevard
San Marcos CA
760-471-2800 (800-329-7466)
Dogs of all sizes are allowed. There is a pet fee of $25 per pet.

## Pet-Friendly Extended Stay Hotels
### Residence Inn By Marriott San Diego North/san Marcos
1245 Los Vallecitos Boulevard
San Marcos CA
760-591-9828
Dogs of all sizes are allowed. There is a $50 one time additional pet fee.

## Dog-Friendly Attractions
### Palomar Observatory
County Road S-6
Palomar Mountain CA
760-742-2100
The observatory is located within the Cleveland National Forest on Palomar Mountain at an elevation of 5000 feet. Dogs on leash may accompany you on the self-guided tour and on the grounds including the gallery to view the 200 inch telescope. To reach Palomar exit Interstate 15 at Highway 76 east. Take S-6 to the left in 25 miles up the mountain to Palomar. The hours are 9 am - 4 pm daily except Christmas and Christmas eve. The gift shop is only open on weekends except in July and August.

## Outdoor Restaurants
### Baja Fresh Mexican Grill
890 W Valley Parkway
Escondido CA
760-480-9997
bajafresh.com
This Mexican restaurant is open for lunch and dinner. They use fresh ingredients and making their salsa and beans daily. Some of the items on their menu include Enchiladas, Burritos, Tacos Salads, Quesadillas, Nachos, Chicken, Steak and more. Well-behaved leashed dogs are allowed at the outdoor tables.

### Centre City Cafe
2680 S Escondido Blvd
Escondido CA
760-489-6011
Specializing in American comfort foods with international inspirations, this eatery sources the freshest local produce and products available to provide a wide menu of freshly prepared signature homemade dishes. They also offer weekly specials and alfresco dining. Leashed, well mannered dogs are welcome at their outside dining area.

### Charlie's Family Restaurant

210 N Ivy Street
Escondido CA
760-738-1545
This eatery serves up all American comfort cuisine in a family friendly atmosphere. Leashed, well mannered dogs are allowed at the outer tables.

**Chipotle**
1282 Auto Park Way
Escondido CA
760-740-9043
chipotle.com
Specializing in organic, natural and unprocessed food, this Mexican Eatery offers fajita burritos, tacos, salads, and salsas. Dogs are allowed at the outdoor tables but you will need to order your food inside the restaurant and dogs must remain outside.

**Baja Fresh Mexican Grill**
11980-11976 Bernardo Plaza Dr.
Rancho Bernardo CA
858-592-7788
bajafresh.com
This Mexican restaurant is open for lunch and dinner. They use fresh ingredients and making their salsa and beans daily. Some of the items on their menu include Enchiladas, Burritos, Tacos Salads, Quesadillas, Nachos, Chicken, Steak and more. Well-behaved leashed dogs are allowed at the outdoor tables.

**Jamba Juice**
591 Grand Avenue, Suite 100
San Marcos CA
760-471-9404
jambajuice.com
All natural and organic ingredients, no high-fructose corn syrup, 0 grams trans fat, no artificial preservatives, a healthy helping of antioxidants, vitamins, and minerals, and fresh whole fruit and fruit juices set the base for these tasty and healthy beverages. Their organic Hot Blends provides a new spin on coffee, green or chai tea, and hot chocolate;plus they offer probiotic fruit and yogurt Blends. Additionally, they feature organic steel-cut oatmeal

prepared fresh every morning, all natural salads, wraps, sandwiches, and grab n' go specialties. They also offer healthy community support through fundraisers, special sales, and school lunch programs. Leashed, well mannered dogs are allowed at their outside dining area.

**Old California Coffee House**
1080 W. San Marcos Blvd #176
San Marcos CA
760-744-2112
oldcalcoffee.com/
In addition to their specialty and espresso beverages, this café also offers breakfast and lunch items that include gluten-free and vegetarian choices. Leashed dogs are allowed at their outside dining area.

**Pet-Friendly Stores**
**Petco Pet Store - Escondido**
1000 West Valley Pkwy
Escondido CA
760-781-1600
Your licensed and well-behaved leashed dog is allowed in the store.

**Camping World**
200 Travelers Way
San Marcos CA
760-471-0645
campingworld.com/
This comprehensive RV and outdoor store carries a wide variety of RV, boat, bike, and outdoor cooking accessories; all kinds of camping gear; RV screens, shades, and patio decorations; racing/tailgating gear, and all items for RV maintenance. They also carry RV towing supplies, electronics, and interior decorating items as well as pet supplies, RV directories/books, and games. Plus, they offer a tips and advice service, RV sales, rentals, and RV technicians to take care of any installations and repairs. They also welcome your canine companion in the store; they must be friendly and leashed.

**Dogtopia of San Marcos**
925 W San Marcos Blvd/H 12
San Marcos CA
760-471-MUTT (6888)
dogdaycare.com/sanmarcos
With a stated mission of providing the highest quality dog care in the country, this company offers well trained staff for all their services. Services include doggy day care, overnight accommodations, positive reinforcement training classes, a self serve dog wash, professional grooming, and a doggy boutique with quality foods/treats, pet care supplies, toys, and much more. They also offer support in the community through a variety of venues.

**Dogtopia of San Marcos**
925 W San Marcos Blvd/H 12
San Marcos CA
760-471-MUTT (6888)
dogdaycare.com/sanmarcos/
With a stated mission of providing the highest quality dog care in the country, this company offers well trained staff for all their services. Services include doggy day care, overnight accommodations, positive reinforcement training classes, a self serve dog wash, professional grooming, and a doggy boutique with quality foods/treats, pet care supplies, toys, and much more. They also offer support in the community through a variety of venues.

**Petco Pet Store - San Marcos**
141 South Las Posas Road
San Marcos CA
760-471-1501
Your licensed and well-behaved leashed dog is allowed in the store.

**Dog-Friendly Wineries and Vineyards**
**Belle Marie Winery and Chateau Dragoo**
26312 Mesa Rock Road
Escondido CA
760-796-7557
bellemarie.com/contact/index.ht

m
In addition to their tasting room, this winery offers a globally inspired demonstration vineyard, special venue areas, and picnic grounds with outstanding views. Dogs are allowed throughout the grounds. Dogs must be leashed and under their owner's control at all times.

### Orfila Vineyards
13455 San Pasqual Road
Escondido CA
760-738-6500
orfila.com/
With about 900 Medals since 1994, this award winning winery also offers caterers, event staff, manicured lawns, flowering gardens, picnic areas, a gift shop and tasting room, all with a view of the mountains and cascading vineyards. Dogs are allowed around the grounds, but not in the tasting room or grape growing areas. Dogs must be well behaved, and leashed and cleaned up after at all times.

## Off-Leash Dog Parks
### Mayflower Dog Park
3420 Valley Center Road
Escondido CA

Mayflower Dog Park is a 1.5 acre fenced area for off-leash dog play.

### Hollandia Off Leash Dog Park
12 Mission Hills Court
San Marcos CA
760-744-900
In addition to a number of fun amenities, this beautiful park also has a fenced off leash doggy play area. Dogs must be healthy, sociable, current on all vaccinations and license with tags on collar, and under their owner's control at all times. Dogs must be leashed when not in designated off-lead areas.

### Montiel Off Leash Dog Park
2290 Montiel Road
San Marcos CA
760-744-1050
In addition to a number of fun amenities, this beautiful park

also has a fenced off leash doggy play area. Dogs must be healthy, sociable, current on all vaccinations and license with tags on collar, and under their owner's control at all times. Dogs must be leashed when not in designated off-lead areas.

### San Elijo Hills Community Bark Park
Elfin Forest Road
San Marcos CA
760-798-1765
One of the many amenities of this popular 19 acre neighborhood park include the off leash doggy play area. This fenced area offers 2 sections for large and small pets, and is located in the center of the park. Dogs must be sociable, current on all vaccinations and license, and under their owner's control at all times. Dogs must be leashed when not in designated off-lead areas.

### San Elijo Off Leash Dog Park

1105 Elfin Forest Road
San Marcos CA
760-744-1050
In addition to a number of fun amenities, this beautiful park also has a fenced off leash doggy play area. Dogs must be healthy, sociable, current on all vaccinations and license with tags on collar, and under their owner's control at all times. Dogs must be leashed when not in designated off-lead areas.

### Sunset Off Leash Dog Park
909 Puesta Del Sol- East Entrance
San Marcos CA
760-744-9000
In addition to a number of fun amenities, this beautiful park also has a fenced off leash doggy play area. The West entrance is at 3337 La Mirada Drive. Dogs must be healthy, sociable, current on all vaccinations and license with tags on collar, and under their owner's control at all times.

Dogs must be leashed when not in designated off-lead areas.

## Dog-Friendly Parks
### San Pasqual Battlefield State Historical Park
15808 San Pasqual Valley Road
Escondido CA
760-737-2201
This historic park honors the soldiers who fought here and stands as a reminder of the passions that can drive countries to bloodshed, and not as a monument to the Mexican-American war. There are interpretive exhibits/programs, nature and hiking trails, picnic areas, restrooms, and a visitor center. The park is only open on Saturday and Sunday, but during the week you can park on the street and walk into the park. Dogs of all sizes are allowed. Dogs must be on no more than a 6 foot leash, and leashed and cleaned up after at all times. Dogs are allowed throughout the park and on the trails.

### Observatory Trail - Cleveland National Forest
Observatory Campground
Palomar Mountain CA
760-788-0250
This trail is located in the dog-friendly Cleveland National Forest. The 2. 2 mile trail offers a pleasant hike to the Palomar Observatory site. It meanders through pine and oak woodlands and offers some great views of the Mendenhall and French Valleys. There is a 200 foot elevation gain, with a starting elevation of 4800 feet. Dogs are allowed on leash. From San Diego, drive north on I-15 to Highway 76 (Oceanside-Pala exit) Head east on Hwy 76 to S6 and drive north toward Palomar Mountain. Follow S6 to Observatory Campground. Trailhead parking is near the amphitheater inside the campground (follow the signs). The trailhead is adjacent to the amphitheater. Vehicles must display a Forest Adventure

Pass. The pass can be purchased from local vendors and from the Forest Service Offices. Call (760) 788-0250 for a list of forest offices.

## Emergency Veterinarians
**Animal Urgent Care**
2430-A S. Escondido Blvd
Escondido CA
760-738-9600
animalurgentcare.com
Monday - Friday 6 pm to 8 am,
Friday 6pm - Monday 8 am.

## Rescue Organizations
**German Shorthaired Pointer Rescue of De Luz Mountain Empire**
PO Box 974
Bonsall CA
760-726-4813
GSP-Rescue.org
We are a breed-specific Rescue specializing in German Shorthaired Pointers. As a not-for-profit organization, we operate through volunteers and networking to assure proper placement and lifetime assistance for each dog and enjoyment by adopting families.

## San Fernando Valley

### Dog-Friendly Hotels
**Sheraton Agoura Hills Hotel**
30100 Agoura Road
Agoura Hills CA
818-707-1220 (888-625-5144)
This resort style hotel offers the ambiance of a boutique hotel with a number of amenities for leisure and business travelers and a central location to many of the areas major attractions and corporation districts. Dogs up to 50 pounds are allowed for no additional fee;there is a pet waiver to sign at check in and they must be declared at the time of check-in.

**Ramada Inn Chatsworth**
21340 Devonshire Street
Chatsworth CA
818-998-5289
Dogs up to 15 pounds are allowed. There is a pet fee of $10 per pet per night.

**Best Western Plus Carriage Inn**
5525 Sepulveda Boulevard
Van Nuys CA
818-787-2300 (800-780-7234)
Not Found

**Hilton Woodland Hills**
6360 Canoga Ave
Woodland Hills CA
818-595-1000
This upscale hotel offers numerous on site amenities for business and leisure travelers, plus a convenient location to business, shopping, dining, and entertainment areas. Dogs up to 75 pounds are allowed for an additional one time pet fee of $50 per room.

## Pet-Friendly Extended Stay Hotels
**Staybridge Suites Chatsworth**
21902 Lassen St
Chatsworth CA
818-773-0707 (877-270-6405)
Dogs up to 50 pounds are allowed. Pets allowed with an additional pet fee. Up to $75 for 1-6 nights and up to $150 for 7+ nights. A pet agreement must be signed at check-in. Two dogs are allowed per room.

**Extended Stay America - Los Angeles - Northridge**
19325 Londelius St.
Northridge CA
818-734-1787 (800-804-3724)
One dog is allowed per suite. There is a $25 per night additional pet fee up to $150 for an entire stay.

**Extended Stay America - Los Angeles - Simi Valley**
2498 Stearns St.
Simi Valley CA

805-584-8880 (800-804-3724)
One dog is allowed per suite. There is a $25 per night additional pet fee up to $150 for an entire stay.

**Residence Inn Los Angeles Westlake Village**
30950 Russell Ranch Road
Westlake Village CA
818-707-4411
Dogs of all sizes are allowed. There is a $100 one time additional pet fee.

**Extended Stay America - Los Angeles - Woodland Hills**
20205 Ventura Blvd.
Woodland Hills CA
818-710-1170 (800-804-3724)
One dog is allowed per suite. There is a $25 per night additional pet fee up to $150 for an entire stay.

## Dog Businesses
**K9 Loft**
14257 Ventura Blvd
Sherman Oaks CA
818-905-6006
k9loft.com/shermanoaks/
In addition to offering a wide variety of pet food, treats, grooming supplies, toys, and various pet supplies, K9 Loft also offers daycare, boarding, grooming, dental cleaning, training, shuttles, and adoption services. Dogs are welcome to come in and check out all the treats and fun.

## Dog-Friendly Attractions
**Paramount Ranch**
Cornell Road
Agoura Hills CA
805-370-2301
Part of the Santa Monica National Recreation Area, Paramount Ranch is a Western Town movie set that has been used in hundreds of televisions shows and movies. Most recently the set was used to film the television show, Dr. Quinn, Medicine Woman from 1991 to 1998. You and your leashed pooch can walk around the set

and explore the Western Town. Just remember the town is a movie set only so walk carefully on the boardwalks and do not lean or climb on the buildings. There are also a few trails located in this 700 acre park. The Coyote Canyon Trail is an easy .5 mile round trip which follows a small chaparral-covered canyon and climbs to a small knoll overlooking the valley. It is located on the west side of the Western Town. The Medea Creek Trail is an easy . 75 mile round trip which loops through the streamside and oak woodlands. From this trail you an reach the Overlook Trail which is another .5 mile one way moderate climb. The Medea Creek Trail starts at the southern end of the parking area. To get to the park take the Ventura Freeway/101 to the Kanan exit and head south for . 75 miles. Turn left onto Cornell Way and continue south for 2.5 miles to the main entrances on the right side.

### Los Encinos State Historic Park
16756 Moorpark Street
Encino CA
818-784-4849
lahacal.org/losencinos.html
This park covers 5 acres and includes several historic buildings. The park contains exhibits on early California ranch life. The springs at this site attracted Native Americans for centuries. The spot later became a stagecoach stopover and a Basque sheepherder's home before construction of the rancho buildings. While dogs are not allowed inside the buildings, they are allowed to walk (leashed) on the grounds. The park is closed on Monday and Tuesday. The rest of the week, the park is open from 10am-5pm.

### The Dogs Gallery
31139 Via Colinas, Suite 204
Westlake Village CA
818-707-8070
thedogsgallery.com/
This fine art gallery offers 2,000

square feet of contemporary paintings, sculptures and photographs of dogs and other animals. North American artists are featured. Well-behaved leashed dogs are welcome at the art gallery. There are a couple of dogs on the premises but they are usually put in the office when there are dog visitors.

## Outdoor Restaurants
### Baja Fresh Mexican Grill
16542 Ventura Blvd
Encino CA
818-907-9998
bajafresh.com
This Mexican restaurant is open for lunch and dinner. They use fresh ingredients and making their salsa and beans daily. Some of the items on their menu include Enchiladas, Burritos, Tacos Salads, Quesadillas, Nachos, Chicken, Steak and more. Well-behaved leashed dogs are allowed at the outdoor tables.

### Coffee Bean & Tea Leaf
16101 Ventura Blvd. Suite 180
Encino CA
818-386-0935
coffeebean.com
The coffee here is sourced globally from family coffee farms to procure only the top of 1% of Arabica beans. They offer 30+ varieties of coffee;the beans are roasted in small batches daily for freshness, and they also offer 20 varieties of teas that are hand-blended by their tea master. Additionally, they offer a variety of tasty sweets, powders, extracts, sauces, gifts, and cards. Leashed, well mannered dogs are allowed at their outside dining area.

### Johnny Rockets
16901 Ventura Blvd
Encino CA
818-981-5900
johnnyrockets.com/
All the American favorites can be found here: A fun retro, all-American decor and

atmosphere, juicy burgers, specialty sandwiches, crispy fries, hand-dipped malts and shakes (dark chocolate ones too), fresh baked apple pies, tasty vegetarian choices, and something for all ages. Leashed, friendly dogs are allowed at their outside dining area.

### The Coffee Bean & Tea Leaf
17301-1 Ventura Blvd
Encino CA
818-906-9551
coffeebean.com
The coffee here is sourced globally from family coffee farms to procure only the top of 1% of Arabica beans. They offer 30+ varieties of coffee;the beans are roasted in small batches daily for freshness, and they also offer 20 varieties of teas that are hand-blended by their tea master. Additionally, they offer a variety of tasty sweets, powders, extracts, sauces, gifts, and cards. Leashed, well mannered dogs are allowed at their outside dining area.

### The Coffee Bean & Tea Leaf
3701 Ocean View Blvd
Montrose CA
818-249-7848
coffeebean.com
The coffee here is sourced globally from family coffee farms to procure only the top of 1% of Arabica beans. They offer 30+ varieties of coffee;the beans are roasted in small batches daily for freshness, and they also offer 20 varieties of teas that are hand-blended by their tea master. Additionally, they offer a variety of tasty sweets, powders, extracts, sauces, gifts, and cards. Leashed, well mannered dogs are allowed at their outside dining area.

### Zeke's Smokehouse Restaurant
2209 Honolulu Avenue
Montrose CA
818-957-7045
zekessmokehouse.com/
This is the place to go for contemporary American comfort food and great tasting barbecue.

They offer service for their outdoor dining customers, and will even bring out a bowl of water for your canine companion. Your leashed pet is allowed to join you at the outside tables.

**Jamba Juice**
2944 Tapo Canyon Road, #H
Moorpark CA
805-529-7381
jambajuice.com
All natural and organic ingredients, no high-fructose corn syrup, 0 grams trans fat, no artificial preservatives, a healthy helping of antioxidants, vitamins, and minerals, and fresh whole fruit and fruit juices set the base for these tasty and healthy beverages. Their organic Hot Blends provides a new spin on coffee, green or chai tea, and hot chocolate;plus they offer probiotic fruit and yogurt Blends. Additionally, they feature all natural salads, wraps, sandwiches, and grab n go specialties. They also offer healthy community support through fundraisers, special sales, and school lunch programs. Leashed, well mannered dogs are allowed at their outside dining area.

**The Natural Cafe**
840 New Los Angeles Avenue #A-2/H 23/118
Moorpark CA
805-523-2016
thenaturalcafe.com
With a focus on sourcing the freshest, naturally produced and locally grown produce, this eatery offers a full menu of healthy foods and beverages. Foods are also made fresh daily with many vegan and vegetarian choices. Leashed, well mannered dogs are allowed at their outside tables.

**Jamba Juice**
9012 Balboa Blvd
Northridge CA
818-893-1256
jambajuice.com
All natural and organic ingredients, no high-fructose

corn syrup, 0 grams trans fat, no artificial preservatives, a healthy helping of antioxidants, vitamins, and minerals, and fresh whole fruit and fruit juices set the base for these tasty and healthy beverages. Their organic Hot Blends provides a new spin on coffee, green or chai tea, and hot chocolate;plus they offer probiotic fruit and yogurt Blends. Additionally, they feature all natural salads, wraps, sandwiches, and grab n go specialties. They also offer healthy community support through fundraisers, special sales, and school lunch programs. Leashed, well mannered dogs are allowed at their outside dining area.

**The Coffee Bean & Tea Leaf**
18705 Devonshire Street
Northridge CA
818-360-8299
coffeebean.com
The coffee here is sourced globally from family coffee farms to procure only the top of 1% of Arabica beans. They offer 30+ varieties of coffee;the beans are roasted in small batches daily for freshness, and they also offer 20 varieties of teas that are hand-blended by their tea master. Additionally, they offer a variety of tasty sweets, powders, extracts, sauces, gifts, and cards. Leashed, well mannered dogs are allowed at their outside dining area.

**Whole Foods Market**
19340 Rinaldi
Northridge CA
818-363-3933
wholefoods.com/
This natural food supermarket offers natural and organic foods. Order some food from their deli without your dog and bring it to an outdoor table where your well-behaved leashed dog is welcome.

**Baja Fresh Mexican Grill**
19701 Rinaldi St.
Porter Ranch CA
818-831-3100

bajafresh.com
This Mexican restaurant is open for lunch and dinner. They use fresh ingredients and making their salsa and beans daily. Some of the items on their menu include Enchiladas, Burritos, Tacos Salads, Quesadillas, Nachos, Chicken, Steak and more. Well-behaved leashed dogs are allowed at the outdoor tables.

**Z Pizza**
19300 Rinaldi Street
Porter Ranch CA
818-363-2600
zpizza.com
Specializing in organically and internationally inspired pizzas, this pizzeria cooks their pizzas on hot bricks in a fire baked oven. They feature a 100% certified organic gluten free wheat crust, homemade organic sauces and ingredients, fresh produce, and additive-free meats. They also offer gourmet salads, sandwiches, and catering services. Leashed, well mannered dogs are allowed at their outside tables.

**Baja Fresh Mexican Grill**
14622 Ventura Blvd.
Sherman Oaks CA
818-789-0602
bajafresh.com
This Mexican restaurant is open for lunch and dinner. They use fresh ingredients and making their salsa and beans daily. Some of the items on their menu include Enchiladas, Burritos, Tacos Salads, Quesadillas, Nachos, Chicken, Steak and more. Well-behaved leashed dogs are allowed at the outdoor tables.

**Whole Foods Market**
4520 Sepulveda Boulevard
Sherman Oaks CA
818-382-3700
wholefoods.com/
This natural food supermarket offers natural and organic foods. Order some food from their deli without your dog and bring it to an outdoor table where your well-behaved leashed dog is welcome.

**Whole Foods Market**
12905 Riverside Drive
Sherman Oaks CA
818-762-5548
wholefoods.com/
This natural food supermarket offers natural and organic foods. Order some food from their deli without your dog and bring it to an outdoor table where your well-behaved leashed dog is welcome.

**Baja Fresh Mexican Grill**
2679 Tapo Cyn Rd
Simi Valley CA
805-581-6001
bajafresh.com
This Mexican restaurant is open for lunch and dinner. They use fresh ingredients and making their salsa and beans daily. Some of the items on their menu include Enchiladas, Burritos, Tacos Salads, Quesadillas, Nachos, Chicken, Steak and more. Well-behaved leashed dogs are allowed at the outdoor tables.

**Chipotle**
1263 Simi Town Center Way
Simi Valley CA
805-584-0514
chipotle.com
Specializing in organic, natural and unprocessed food, this Mexican Eatery offers fajita burritos, tacos, salads, and salsas. Dogs are allowed at the outdoor tables but you will need to order your food inside the restaurant and dogs must remain outside.

**Jamba Juice**
2944 Tapo Canyon Road, #H
Simi Valley CA
805-522-1055
jambajuice.com
All natural and organic ingredients, no high-fructose corn syrup, 0 grams trans fat, no artificial preservatives, a healthy helping of antioxidants, vitamins, and minerals, and fresh whole fruit and fruit juices set the base for these tasty and healthy beverages. Their organic Hot Blends provides a new spin on coffee, green or chai tea, and hot chocolate;plus they offer probiotic fruit and yogurt Blends. Additionally, they feature all natural salads, wraps, sandwiches, and grab n go specialties. They also offer healthy community support through fundraisers, special sales, and school lunch programs. Leashed, well mannered dogs are allowed at their outside dining area.

**The Coffee Bean & Tea Leaf**
2944-G Tapo Canyon Road
Simi Valley CA
805-582-0566
coffeebean.com
The coffee here is sourced globally from family coffee farms to procure only the top of 1% of Arabica beans. They offer 30+ varieties of coffee;the beans are roasted in small batches daily for freshness, and they also offer 20 varieties of teas that are hand-blended by their tea master. Additionally, they offer a variety of tasty sweets, powders, extracts, sauces, gifts, and cards. Leashed, well mannered dogs are allowed at their outside dining area.

**The Natural Cafe**
2667 Tapo Canyon Road, Unit G
Simi Valley CA
805-527-2272
thenaturalcafe.com
With a focus on sourcing the freshest, naturally produced and locally grown produce and products available, this eatery offers a full menu of healthy foods and beverages. Foods are also made fresh daily with many vegan and vegetarian choices. Leashed, well mannered dogs are allowed at their outside tables.

**Topper's Pizza**
2408 Erringer Rd
Simi Valley CA
805-385-4444
topperspizzaplace.com/index.php
Topper's Pizza offers oven-baked sandwiches, pizzas, build your own pizzas, and more! Well-behaved, leashed dogs are welcome at the outdoor patio.

**Jamba Juice**
10955 Ventura Blvd
Studio City CA
818-769-6705
jambajuice.com
All natural and organic ingredients, no high-fructose corn syrup, 0 grams trans fat, no artificial preservatives, a healthy helping of antioxidants, vitamins, and minerals, and fresh whole fruit and fruit juices set the base for these tasty and healthy beverages. Their organic Hot Blends provides a new spin on coffee, green or chai tea, and hot chocolate;plus they offer probiotic fruit and yogurt Blends. Additionally, they feature organic steel-cut oatmeal prepared fresh every morning, all natural salads, wraps, sandwiches, and grab n' go specialties. They also offer healthy community support through fundraisers, special sales, and school lunch programs. Leashed, well mannered dogs are allowed at their outside dining area.

**Le Pain Quotidien**
13045 Ventura Blvd
Studio City CA
818-986-1929
lepainquotidien.com/
Their bread, the specialty here-made 'old world' style, and their communal table are some of the popularities of this eatery. Dogs are allowed at their outer tables;they must be leashed and under their owner's control.

**The Coffee Bean & Tea Leaf**
12050 Ventura Blvd, C-104
Studio City CA
818-506-4620
coffeebean.com
The coffee here is sourced globally from family coffee farms to procure only the top of 1% of Arabica beans. They offer 30+ varieties of coffee;the beans are roasted in small batches daily for freshness, and they also offer 20 varieties of teas that are hand-blended by their tea

master. Additionally, they offer a variety of tasty sweets, powders, extracts, sauces, gifts, and cards. Leashed, well mannered dogs are allowed at their outside dining area.

### The Coffee Bean & Tea Leaf
12930 Ventura Blvd, #122
Studio City CA
818-783-8068
coffeebean.com
The coffee here is sourced globally from family coffee farms to procure only the top of 1% of Arabica beans. They offer 30+ varieties of coffee;the beans are roasted in small batches daily for freshness, and they also offer 20 varieties of teas that are hand-blended by their tea master. Additionally, they offer a variety of tasty sweets, powders, extracts, sauces, gifts, and cards. Leashed, well mannered dogs are allowed at their outside dining area.

### The Coffee Bean & Tea Leaf
12501 W Ventura Blvd
Studio City CA
818-763-7271
coffeebean.com
The coffee here is sourced globally from family coffee farms to procure only the top of 1% of Arabica beans. They offer 30+ varieties of coffee;the beans are roasted in small batches daily for freshness, and they also offer 20 varieties of teas that are hand-blended by their tea master. Additionally, they offer a variety of tasty sweets, powders, extracts, sauces, gifts, and cards. Leashed, well mannered dogs are allowed at their outside dining area.

### Big Jim's
8950 Laurel Canyon Blvd
Sun Valley CA
818-768-0213
bigjimsinc.com/index.html
Thanks to one of our readers who writes: Outdoor patio is shady with plants and a fountain. Steaks, Mexican, Sunday Champagne Brunch. Leashed dogs are allowed at their outside tables.

### The Coffee Bean & Tea Leaf
18505 Ventura Blvd
Tarzana CA
818-776-1178
coffeebean.com
The coffee here is sourced globally from family coffee farms to procure only the top of 1% of Arabica beans. They offer 30+ varieties of coffee;the beans are roasted in small batches daily for freshness, and they also offer 20 varieties of teas that are hand-blended by their tea master. Additionally, they offer a variety of tasty sweets, powders, extracts, sauces, gifts, and cards. Leashed, well mannered dogs are allowed at their outside dining area.

### The Coffee Bean & Tea Leaf
31938 Temecula Parkway, Suite D/H 79
Tarzana CA
951-694-0723
coffeebean.com
The coffee here is sourced globally from family coffee farms to procure only the top of 1% of Arabica beans. They offer 30+ varieties of coffee;the beans are roasted in small batches daily for freshness, and they also offer 20 varieties of teas that are hand-blended by their tea master. Additionally, they offer a variety of tasty sweets, powders, extracts, sauces, gifts, and cards. Leashed, well mannered dogs are allowed at their outside dining area.

### Baja Fresh Mexican Grill
10760 Riverside Drive
Toluca Lake CA
818-762-7326
bajafresh.com
This Mexican restaurant is open for lunch and dinner. They use fresh ingredients and making their salsa and beans daily. Some of the items on their menu include Enchiladas, Burritos, Tacos Salads, Quesadillas, Nachos, Chicken, Steak and more. Well-behaved leashed dogs are allowed at the outdoor tables.

### Priscilla's Gourmet Cafe
4150 Riverside Dr
Toluca Lake CA
818-843-5707
priscillascoffee.com/
This cafe serves deli-type food and gourmet teas and coffees. Leashed dogs are allowed at the outdoor tables. There is a walk up window available so that pets don't have to be left alone.

### The Coffee Bean & Tea Leaf
10121 Riverside Drive
Toluca Lake CA
818-763-4815
coffeebean.com
The coffee here is sourced globally from family coffee farms to procure only the top of 1% of Arabica beans. They offer 30+ varieties of coffee;the beans are roasted in small batches daily for freshness, and they also offer 20 varieties of teas that are hand-blended by their tea master. Additionally, they offer a variety of tasty sweets, powders, extracts, sauces, gifts, and cards. Leashed, well mannered dogs are allowed at their outside dining area.

### The Coffee Bean & Tea Leaf
4444 Lankershim Blvd. #114
Toluca Lake CA
818-763-3387
coffeebean.com
The coffee here is sourced globally from family coffee farms to procure only the top of 1% of Arabica beans. They offer 30+ varieties of coffee;the beans are roasted in small batches daily for freshness, and they also offer 20 varieties of teas that are hand-blended by their tea master. Additionally, they offer a variety of tasty sweets, powders, extracts, sauces, gifts, and cards. Leashed, well mannered dogs are allowed at their outside dining area.

### Springboc Bar and Grill
16153 Victory Blvd
Van Nuys CA
818-988-9786
springbokbar.com
This rugby bar offers a great sports atmosphere with an eclectic menu featuring a

culturally diverse selection of Southern hemispheric foods. Leashed, well mannered dogs are welcome at their outside tables.

**Baja Fresh Mexican Grill**
30861 Thousand Oaks Blvd.
Westlake Village CA
818-889-1347
bajafresh.com
This Mexican restaurant is open for lunch and dinner. They use fresh ingredients and making their salsa and beans daily. Some of the items on their menu include Enchiladas, Burritos, Tacos Salads, Quesadillas, Nachos, Chicken, Steak and more. Well-behaved leashed dogs are allowed at the outdoor tables.

**Jamba Juice**
2749 Agoura Road
Westlake Village CA
805-778-0854
jambajuice.com
All natural and organic ingredients, no high-fructose corn syrup, 0 grams trans fat, no artificial preservatives, a healthy helping of antioxidants, vitamins, and minerals, and fresh whole fruit and fruit juices set the base for these tasty and healthy beverages. Their organic Hot Blends provides a new spin on coffee, green or chai tea, and hot chocolate;plus they offer probiotic fruit and yogurt Blends. Additionally, they feature all natural salads, wraps, sandwiches, and grab n go specialties. They also offer healthy community support through fundraisers, special sales, and school lunch programs. Leashed, well mannered dogs are allowed at their outside dining area.

**The Coffee Bean & Tea Leaf**
968 S Westlake Blvd, Suite 6
Westlake Village CA
805-497-1256
coffeebean.com
The coffee here is sourced globally from family coffee farms to procure only the top of 1% of Arabica beans. They offer 30+ varieties of coffee;the beans are

roasted in small batches daily for freshness, and they also offer 20 varieties of teas that are hand-blended by their tea master. Additionally, they offer a variety of tasty sweets, powders, extracts, sauces, gifts, and cards. Leashed, well mannered dogs are allowed at their outside dining area.

**Baja Fresh Mexican Grill**
19960 Ventura Blvd.
Woodland Hills CA
818-888-3976
bajafresh.com
This Mexican restaurant is open for lunch and dinner. They use fresh ingredients and making their salsa and beans daily. Some of the items on their menu include Enchiladas, Burritos, Tacos Salads, Quesadillas, Nachos, Chicken, Steak and more. Well-behaved leashed dogs are allowed at the outdoor tables.

**Baja Fresh Mexican Grill**
5780 Canoga Avenue
Woodland Hills CA
818-347-9033
bajafresh.com
This Mexican restaurant is open for lunch and dinner. They use fresh ingredients and making their salsa and beans daily. Some of the items on their menu include Enchiladas, Burritos, Tacos Salads, Quesadillas, Nachos, Chicken, Steak and more. Well-behaved leashed dogs are allowed at the outdoor tables.

**Chipotle**
5430 Topanga Canyon Blvd
Woodland Hills CA
818-710-0466
chipotle.com
Specializing in organic, natural and unprocessed food, this Mexican Eatery offers fajita burritos, tacos, salads, and salsas. Dogs are allowed at the outdoor tables but you will need to order your food inside the restaurant and dogs must remain outside.

**Jamba Juice**
22815 Victory Blvd, #B

Woodland Hills CA
818-340-5770
jambajuice.com
All natural and organic ingredients, no high-fructose corn syrup, 0 grams trans fat, no artificial preservatives, a healthy helping of antioxidants, vitamins, and minerals, and fresh whole fruit and fruit juices set the base for these tasty and healthy beverages. Their organic Hot Blends provides a new spin on coffee, green or chai tea, and hot chocolate;plus they offer probiotic fruit and yogurt Blends. Additionally, they feature all natural salads, wraps, sandwiches, and grab n go specialties. They also offer healthy community support through fundraisers, special sales, and school lunch programs. Leashed, well mannered dogs are allowed at their outside dining area.

**Pickwick's Pub**
21010 Ventura Blvd
Woodland Hills CA
818-340-9673
This English pub will allow dogs at their outside dining area.

**The Coffee Bean & Tea Leaf**
21851 Ventura Blvd
Woodland Hills CA
818-716-7981
coffeebean.com
The coffee here is sourced globally from family coffee farms to procure only the top of 1% of Arabica beans. They offer 30+ varieties of coffee;the beans are roasted in small batches daily for freshness, and they also offer 20 varieties of teas that are hand-blended by their tea master. Additionally, they offer a variety of tasty sweets, powders, extracts, sauces, gifts, and cards. Leashed, well mannered dogs are allowed at their outside dining area.

**The Coffee Bean & Tea Leaf**
19732 Ventura Blvd
Woodland Hills CA
818-346-4863
coffeebean.com
The coffee here is sourced globally from family coffee farms

to procure only the top of 1% of Arabica beans. They offer 30+ varieties of coffee;the beans are roasted in small batches daily for freshness, and they also offer 20 varieties of teas that are hand-blended by their tea master. Additionally, they offer a variety of tasty sweets, powders, extracts, sauces, gifts, and cards. Leashed, well mannered dogs are allowed at their outside dining area.

**The Coffee Bean & Tea Leaf**
5780 Canoga Avenue, Suite F
Woodland Hills CA
818-348-2609
coffeebean.com
The coffee here is sourced globally from family coffee farms to procure only the top of 1% of Arabica beans. They offer 30+ varieties of coffee;the beans are roasted in small batches daily for freshness, and they also offer 20 varieties of teas that are hand-blended by their tea master. Additionally, they offer a variety of tasty sweets, powders, extracts, sauces, gifts, and cards. Leashed, well mannered dogs are allowed at their outside dining area.

## Pet-Friendly Shopping Centers
**Simi Valley Town Center Mall**
1555 Simi Town Center Way
Simi Valley CA
805-581-1430
simivalleytc.com/
Offering an eclectic array of shops, casual to fine dining, and entertainment, this shopping Mecca will allow dogs in the common areas, and some of the stores are also pet friendly. Dogs must be leashed and under their owner's control at all times.

## Pet-Friendly Stores
**Petco Pet Store - Canoga Park**

6615 Fallbrook Ave.
Canoga Park CA

818-883-0210
Your licensed and well-behaved leashed dog is allowed in the store.

**Urban Outfitters**
6600 Topanga Canyon Blvd/H 27
Canoga Park CA
818-703-6715
In addition to a large inventory of indoor and outdoor apparel for men and women, this major department store also carries vintage wear, designer brands, and a variety of accessories for all types of active lifestyles. They also carry shoes, furnishings, home decor, cameras, electronics, novelty items and more. Leashed, well mannered dogs are allowed in the store.

**Petco Pet Store - Encino**
17919 Ventura Blvd
Encino CA
818-343-1124
Your licensed and well-behaved leashed dog is allowed in the store.

**Petco Pet Store - Moorpark**
742 New Los Angeles Ave. Ste A
Moorpark CA
805-552-0370
Your licensed and well-behaved leashed dog is allowed in the store.

**Petco Pet Store - Northridge**
8800 Tampa Ave.
Northridge CA
818-993-1871
Your licensed and well-behaved leashed dog is allowed in the store.

**Petco Pet Store - Porter Ranch**
19869 Rinaldi St.
Porter Ranch CA
818-368-3062
Your licensed and well-behaved leashed dog is allowed in the store.

**Three Dog Bakery**
14545 Ventura Blvd
Sherman Oaks CA
818-304-0440

threedog.com
Three Dog Bakery provides cookies and snacks for your dog as well as some boutique items. You well-behaved, leashed dog is welcome.

**Anthropologie**
1555 Simi Town Center Way, #505
Simi Valley CA
805-306-0342
Items of distinction can be found for all ages and in all departments of this unique shop. Carefully selected to add to the enjoyment of the shopping experience, they carry fine clothing, amazing accessories, jewelry, hobby and leisure items, and a full line of bright and useful items for the home, garden, and office. Leashed, well behaved dogs are allowed in the store.

**PetSmart Pet Store**
455 E Cochran St
Simi Valley CA
805-306-1912
Your licensed and well-behaved leashed dog is allowed in the store.

**Urban Outfitters**
1555 Simi Town Center Way, #230
Simi Valley CA
805-581-8031
In addition to a large inventory of indoor and outdoor apparel for men and women, this major department store also carries vintage wear, designer brands, and a variety of accessories for all types of active lifestyles. They also carry shoes, furnishings, home decor, cameras, electronics, novelty items and more. Leashed, well mannered dogs are allowed in the store.

**Petco Pet Store - Studio City**
12800 Ventura Blvd
Studio City CA
818-506-6416
Your licensed and well-behaved leashed dog is allowed in the store.

**Urban Outfitters**

12110 Ventura Blvd
Studio City CA
818-761-0104
In addition to a large inventory of indoor and outdoor apparel for men and women, this major department store also carries vintage wear, designer brands, and a variety of accessories for all types of active lifestyles. They also carry shoes, furnishings, home decor, cameras, electronics, novelty items and more. Leashed, well mannered dogs are allowed in the store.

**Petco Pet Store - Van Nuys**
5850 Sepulveda Blvd
Van Nuys CA
818-997-4009
Your licensed and well-behaved leashed dog is allowed in the store.

**PetSmart Pet Store**
5766 Lindero Canyon Rd
Westlake Village CA
818-865-8626
Your licensed and well-behaved leashed dog is allowed in the store.

**PetSmart Pet Store**
22914 Victory Blvd
Woodland Hills CA
818-340-2816
Your licensed and well-behaved leashed dog is allowed in the store.

**Petco Pet Store - Woodland Hills**
21943-21947 Ventura Blvd
Woodland Hills CA
818-346-9397
Your licensed and well-behaved leashed dog is allowed in the store.

## Off-Leash Dog Parks
**Sepulveda Basin Dog Park**
17550 Victory Blvd.
Encino CA
818-756-7667
laparks.org/dogpark/sepulveda
Sepulveda Basin Dog Park is located near the Sepulved Dam Rec Area. It consists of 5 acres of legal off-leash roaming that is

fully fenced. There is a smaller area for small dogs that is about half an acre. The dog park is near the junction of I 405 with Highway 101. It is at the corner of White Oak Ave and Victory Blvd. There is parking for about 100 cars at the location.

**Simi Dog Park**
2151 Lost Canyons Drive
Simi Valley CA

Open daily from 7 am until around dusk daily with the exception of Thursday mornings from 7 am until 10 am for maintenance, this off leash site features 2 separate sections for large and small dogs, water, picnic tables, and new trees planted for shade. Seasonal hours are posted at the park which is located behind Big Sky Park (use entrance for Big Sky and go to the back of the property). Dogs must be healthy, sociable, current on all vaccinations and license with tags on collar, and under their owner's control at all times. Owners must clean up after their pets, and keep them leashed when not in designated off-lead areas.

## Dog-Friendly Parks
**Peter Strauss Ranch**
Mulholland Highway
Agoura Hills CA
805-370-2301
The Peter Strauss Trail is an easy .6 mile round trip trail which traverses through chaparral and oak trees. Dogs are allowed on the trail but must be leashed and people need to clean up after their pets. From the Ventura Freeway/101, take the Kanan exit and head south for 2.8 miles to Troutdale Rd. Turn left onto Troutdale Rd and then left on Mulholland Highway. This park is part of the Santa Monica Recreation Area.

**Rocky Oaks Park**
Mulholland Highway

Agoura Hills CA
805-370-2301
This park offers an open grassland area with oak groves and small rock outcroppings. There are four trails ranging from 100 yards to just over one mile and are rated easy to moderate. Dogs are allowed on the trails but must be leashed and people need to clean up after their pets. To get there take the Ventura Freeway/101 to Kanan Road. Head south on Kanan and then turn right on Mulholland Highway. Then make a right into the parking lot. This park is part of the Santa Monica Recreation Area.

**Beilenson Park Lake Balboa**
6300 Balboa Blvd
Encino CA
818-756-9743
laparks.org/aquatic/balboa
This park consists of large grass fields, sports fields and a nice lake. There is an approximate 1 mile walk around the lake perimeter. You and your leashed pup are welcome to explore this 70+ acre park. To get there, take the Balboa Blvd exit from Hwy 101. Head north on Balboa.

**San Vicente Mountain Park**
17500 Mulholland Drive
Encino CA
310-589-3200
This 10.2 acre park is a historical military site, complete with a radar tower that features 360 degree spectacular views, making it a great place for sunsets. There are self-guided interpretive displays, restrooms, drinking water, picnic tables, and a large network of multi-use trails. The park is located about a 10 minute walk along a dirt road from the parking area. Dogs are allowed at this park; they must be leashed, under their owner's immediate control, and cleaned up after at all times.

**O'Melveny Park**
Orozco Street
Granada Hills CA

laparks.org/park/omelveny
This 600+ acre park has a nice variety of single track and fire road hiking trails. The park is popular with bird watchers, mountain bikers, hikers and leashed dogs. The best way to get there is from Hwy 118. Take the Balboa Blvd. exit and head north. Go about 1.5 to 2 miles and turn left onto Orozco. Take this road to the park.

**Hansen Dam**
11770 Foothill Blvd.
Lakeview Terrace CA
818-756-8190
This 1,437-acre basin has lots of hills and grassy meadows. There are several large picnic areas and firepits, and a children's play area. There wasn't much water in the lake but your leashed pup will have lots of land to roam. To get there, take Hwy 210 and exit Foothill Blvd south. The park will be on your left.

**Angeles National Forest**
Little Tujunga Canyon Rd.
San Fernando CA
626-574-1613
fs.usda.gov/angeles
This forest is over 690,000 acres and covers one-fourth of the land in Los Angeles County. We have selected a couple of trails near San Fernando Valley ranging from 2.5 to 3 miles. Dogs are allowed on leash or leash free but under voice control. Both of the trails are single-track, foot trails. The first trail is called Gold Creek Trail. It is about 2.5 miles long. The second trail is called Oaks Springs Trail and it is about 3 miles long. To get there from Hwy 215, take the Foothill Blvd. exit and head north towards the mountains. Turn left onto Little Tujunga Canyon Rd. You will see the Little Tujunga Forest Station on the left. After you pass the station, continue on Little Tujunga Canyon Rd. Go about 1-1.5 miles and then turn right onto Gold Creek Rd. Go about 1 mile and on the right you will see the trailhead for Oak Springs Trail. If you

continue to the end of Gold Creek Rd, you will see the trailhead for Gold Creek Trail. There should be parking along the road.

**Van Nuys/Sherman Oaks Park**
14201 Huston St
Sherman Oaks CA
818-783-5121
This park has an approximate 1.5 mile walking and jogging path that winds through and around the sports fields. There are also many picnic tables near the Recreation Center. To get there from Hwy 101, take the Van Nuys exit and head north.

**Corriganville Park**
7001 Smith Road
Simi Valley CA
805-584-4400
Once owned by a cowboy actor and used as a western setting for hundreds of movies and TV shows in the 1940's and 50's, this 190 acre day use park now offers visitors several recreational activities, hiking trails, picnic areas, park benches, restrooms, and drinking fountains. Dogs are allowed throughout the park and on the trails. Dogs must be under their owner's immediate control, leashed, and cleaned up after at all times.

**Emergency Veterinarians**
**Affordable Animal Emergency Clinic**
16907 San Fernando Mission
Granada Hills CA
818-363-8143
Monday - Friday 6 pm - Midnight for appointments, Midnight to 8 am for emergencies. Saturday 1:30 pm - Monday 8 am. You must call ahead during emergency hours after midnight.

**Emergency Animal Clinic**
14302 Ventura Blvd
Sherman Oaks CA
818-788-7860
24 hours everyday.

**Animal Emergency Center**
11730 Ventura Blvd
Studio City CA
818-760-3882
Monday - Friday 6 pm to Monday 8 am. Holidays 24 hours.

**Rescue Organizations**
**Hearts for Hounds**
15142 Hartsook Street
Sherman Oaks CA
818 788-5840
heartsforhounds.com
We resue dogs from shelters and move them into a home environment where they receive full medical care. We work from our website to find the perfect match in a loving home. We are a non-profit organization. We need business events for an adoption opportunity.

**Animal Rescue Volunteers**
1464 Madera Rd #N350
Simi Valley CA
805-579-8047
arvsimi.org
Animal Rescue Volunteers, Inc. is a non-profit organization that began in 1994. We are all non paid volunteers who love animals and wish to make a difference by helping end the pet over population problem and rescuing abandoned animals. We are a well respected, long-standing organization that fosters pets in our homes and adopt them to the Ventura and Los Angeles county communities. We feed, house, spay/neuter, microchip and provide medical care, behavior evaluation and behavior modification for animals that have been rescued from animal shelters, or from a natural disaster. We hold weekly adoptions at PetSmart in Simi Valley to find the very best home for each animal.

**Animal Rescue Volunteers**
1464 Madera Rd., #N350
Simi Valley CA
(805) 579-8047
arvsimi.org

Our mission is to make a difference to the pet over population problem by rescuing and re-homing abandoned animals in the Simi Valley Community as well as the greater Ventura and Los Angeles County areas. In working with local animal shelters, veterinarians, and other rescue groups, we locate animals most in need of care. While in our foster care, we ensure animals are properly fed and exercised, spay/neutered, microchipped and have high quality medical attention. Animal Rescue Volunteers (ARV), Inc. is a non-profit organization which began in 1994. We are all volunteers who love animals and wish to make a difference. We welcome all who wish to volunteer in whatever capacity they can! Please contact us today if you'd like to volunteer or are interested in adopting one of our fantastic animals!

**Rescue Me Incorporated**
P.O. Box 385
Woodland Hills CA
818-999-2400
rescuemeinc.org
To empower and educate our community, to end the cycle of violence in the lives of our k-9 companions. We also serve the community by rescue, rehabilitation and re-homing the animals in our care. We are the rescues rescue. We focus a great deal of our attention on assisting other rescue organizations, as well as the general public. Our hope is that no rescue organization will ever be forced to turn down an animal in need due to a health problem, or high medical bills. We at Rescue Me, Incorporated believe that the high cost of a medical procedure should not determine if an animal should live or die. We are also involved heavily in animal rescue, rehabilitation and placement. We are very careful in the placement of our animals. It is our job and responsibility to see that our animals go to the perfect life-long, loving home.

We have a very extensive and careful screening process to insure that our animals find the perfect forever home. One of our goals is to help cut the euthanasia rate by educating the public on the importance of animal rescue and spay/neuter programs.

## San Francisco

## Dog-Friendly Hotels
**Americania Hotel**
121 7th Street
San Francisco CA
415-626-0200
Dogs are allowed. There is a $25 per stay pet fee.

**Argonaut Hotel**
495 Jefferson Street
San Francisco CA
415-563-0800 (800-790-1415)
argonauthotel.com/index.html
Offerings of this historic, 1907 waterfront hotel include fantastic waterfront views, a rich nautical decor, all the modern amenities and luxuries, dozens of earth friendly practices throughout the hotel, and fresh local, sustainable, and seasonally inspired cuisine and beverages. Pets of all sizes are welcome here for no additional fee;the pet registration form is available on line. Pets need to be declared at the time of registration and there is a pet form to fill out at the time of arrival. Canine guests are also greeted with their own leash, bed and dinnerware to use during their stay, gourmet treats, and various other amenities available through their specialty pet packages. Pet walking and pet sitting services can be arranged by the hotel.

**Beresford Arms**
701 Post Street
San Francisco CA
415-673-2600 (800-533-6533)
beresford.com/arms/default.ht

m
they must be declared at the time of reservations. Dogs may not be left alone in the room, and they must be leashed and cleaned up after at all times.

**Harbor Court Hotel**
165 Steuart St
San Francisco CA
415-882-1300 (866-792-6283)
harborcourthotel.com/
A premier waterfront boutique hotel offering a great location for business or leisure travelers, amenity filled accommodations, dozens of earth friendly practices throughout the hotel, and fresh local, sustainable, and seasonally inspired cuisine and beverages. Pets of all sizes are welcome here for no additional fee;the pet registration form is available on line. Pets need to be declared at the time of registration and there is a pet form to fill out at the time of arrival. Canine guests are also greeted with their own leash, bed and dinnerware to use during their stay, gourmet treats, and various other amenities available through their specialty pet packages. Pet walking and pet sitting services can be arranged by the hotel.

**Hilton San Francisco**
333 Ofarrell Street
San Francisco CA
415-771-1400
Located in the heart of the city, this upscale hotel offers numerous on site amenities for business and leisure travelers, plus a convenient location to numerous beaches, business districts, shopping, dining, historical, and entertainment areas. Dogs up to 70 pounds are allowed for an additional one time fee of $50 per pet.

**Hilton San Francisco Financial District**
750 Kearny Street
San Francisco CA
415-433-6600
In addition to spectacular views of this very diverse, bustling city, this 27 floor hotel also offers a convenient location to the

Financial District, Chinatown, and a number of other sites of interest and recreational areas. Dogs up to 75 pounds are allowed for an additional one time fee of $50 per pet.

### Holiday Inn Civic Center
50 Eighth Street
San Francisco CA
415-626-6103 (877-270-6405)
Dogs up to 20 pounds are allowed. Dogs are allowed for a pet fee of $75 per pet per stay.

### Hotel Diva San Francisco
440 Geary Street
San Francisco CA
800-553-1900
hoteldiva.com/
Designer internet lounges stylish rooms and free Wi-Fi heighten the hip factor for our guests at the non-smoking Hotel Diva - A Personality Hotel. Freshly recast the pet-friendly six-story hotel has 114 rooms with comfy beds cobalt blue carpeting flat-panel TVs and free Wi-Fi (available throughout the building). Leave the laptop and head down to the designer internet lounge for Googling galore. Guests can work out in the fitness center or work on a last-minute project in the 24-hour business center. Located on Geary Street just one block from Union Square the hotel is 14 miles from San Francisco International Airport (SFO) and 20 miles northwest of Oakland International Airport. Guests can stroll across the street to The Curran Theater and catch a live play or discover the next acting sensation at the American Conservatory Theater. Union Square lies a block east of the hotel and is lined with several designer boutiques and department stores.

### Hotel Triton
342 Grant Ave
San Francisco CA
415-394-0500 (800-800-1299)
hoteltriton.com/
Literally in the heart of some of the city's star attractions, cultural neighborhoods, and world class shopping, dining, and entertainment venues, this boutique hotel also offers numerous amenities for all level of travelers and dozens of earth friendly practices throughout the hotel. Pets of all sizes are welcome here for no additional fee;the pet registration form is available on line. Pets need to be declared at the time of registration and there is a pet form to fill out at the time of arrival. Canine guests are also greeted with their own leash, bed and dinnerware to use during their stay, gourmet treats, and various other amenities available through their specialty pet packages. Pet walking and pet sitting services can be arranged by the hotel.

### Hotel Union Square San Francisco
114 Powell Street
San Francisco CA
800-553-1900
hotelunionsquare.com/
A convenient location and free Wi-Fi the historic Hotel Union Square - A Personality Hotel a prize for our guests who appreciate its stylish decor and cozy accommodations. The 1913 Hotel Union Square has 131 rooms spread across six floors. Rooms feature flat-panel cable TVs iPod docking stations 600-thread-count luxury bedding and deluxe bath products. The hotel has retained its Art Deco style while also offering modern amenities such as a business center restaurant and lounge. Guests can get active at a fitness center found two blocks away at the Hotel Union Square's sister property Diva. In the morning they can enjoy complimentary coffee or tea. In the afternoon there is a free wine reception as well. Those who rolled into town with their own set of wheels will appreciate the on-site parking (for a fee). The Hotel Union Square is located less than 14 miles from San Francisco International Airport and is situated in the Union Square area an area known for excellent shopping restaurants art galleries and entertainment. Guests can also check out other popular city attractions including the San Francisco Museum of Modern Art and Moscone Convention Center found three blocks away. Those wishing to take advantage of public transportation can catch the BART (Bay Area Rapid Transit) less than two blocks from the hotel or San Francisco's famous cable car line right out front.

### Hotel Zelos San Francisco
12 Fourth Street
San Francisco CA
415-348-1111 (866-373-4941)
Offerings of this upscale boutique hotel include a convenient downtown location, amenity-filled accommodations, dozens of earth friendly practices throughout the hotel, and fresh local, sustainable, and seasonally inspired cuisine and beverages. Pets of all sizes are welcome here for no additional fee;the pet registration form is available on line. Pets need to be declared at the time of registration and there is a pet form to fill out at the time of arrival. Canine guests are also greeted with their own leash, bed and dinnerware to use during their stay, gourmet treats, and various other amenities available through their specialty pet packages. Pet walking and pet sitting services can be arranged by the hotel.

### Hotel Zeppelin San Francisco
545 Post Street
San Francisco CA
415-563-0303 (866-271-3632)
prescotthotel.com/index.html
This luxury, boutique hotel offers numerous amenities for all level of travelers, a convenient location near Union Square and the cable car lines, dozens of earth friendly practices throughout the hotel, and fresh local, sustainable, and seasonally inspired cuisine and beverages. Pets of all sizes are welcome here for no additional fee;the pet registration form is available on line. Pets need to

be declared at the time of registration and there is a pet form to fill out at the time of arrival. Canine guests are also greeted with their own leash, bed and dinnerware to use during their stay, gourmet treats, and various other amenities available through their specialty pet packages. Pet walking and pet sitting services can be arranged by the hotel.

### Hotel Zoe Fishermans Wharf: A Noble House Hotel

425 North Point Street
San Francisco CA
415-561-1100
Dogs are allowed at this hotel.

### Hotel Zoe Fishermans Wharf: A Noble House Hotel

425 North Point Street
San Francisco CA
415-561-1100 (800-648-4626)
tuscaninn.com/
Some of the offerings of this luxury hotel include a central location in Fisherman's Wharf near the Mason Street Cable Car turnaround, the ambiance of an Italian countryside villa, dozens of earth friendly practices throughout the hotel, and fresh local, sustainable, and seasonally inspired cuisine and beverages. Pets of all sizes are welcome here for no additional fee;the pet registration form is available on line. Pets need to be declared at the time of registration and there is a pet form to fill out at the time of arrival. Canine guests are also greeted with their own leash, bed and dinnerware to use during their stay, gourmet treats, and various other amenities available through their specialty pet packages. Pet walking and pet sitting services can be arranged by the hotel.

### Intercontinental San Francisco

888 Howard Street
San Francisco CA
415-616-6500 (877-698-9593)
Dogs of all sizes are allowed. Dogs are allowed for a nightly pet fee.

### Kensington Park Hotel

450 Post Street
San Francisco CA
800-553-9100
kensingtonparkhotel.com/
Free Wi-Fi complimentary tea and sherry service and a central location get the royal wave from our guests at the non-smoking pet-friendly Kensington Park Hotel - A Personality Hotel. The 12-story hotel has 92 rooms with mahogany writing desks armoires and cable TV. Power up the iPad because Wi-Fi is free in the rooms lobby and meeting areas. Guests enjoy free access to a nearby fitness center and preferred seating at a noted nearby restaurant. Burn the midnight oil in the 24-hour business center or relax with complimentary tea and sherry in the lobby. Located on Post Street right on the cable car line the Kensington Park Hotel is 14 miles north of San Francisco International Airport and 20 miles northwest of Oakland International Airport. The BART transit system brings guests from SFO to the Powell Street Station a six-minute walk from the hotel. Take the cable car north 20 minutes to Fisherman's Wharf and enjoy bowls of clam chowder and mounds of ice-cold Dungeness crab. Alcatraz Island the infamous inescapable prison is accessible by ferry at Pier 33. Rent a bike and ride across the Golden Gate Bridge; it's only a 13-minute cab ride northwest.

### Kimpton Buchanan Hotel

1800 Sutter Street
San Francisco CA
415-921-4000
Located in the heart of San Francisco's Japantown the Kimpton Buchanan Hotel has rooms with high-tech amenities on-site dining and a 24-hour front desk. The eight-story Kimpton Buchanan has 131 rooms with flat-panel TVs mini-fridges and video-game systems; Wi-Fi is available for an additional fee but is free in

public areas. The popular on-site Japanese restaurant also offers room service and the staffed business center helps you keep on top of work. There's a well-equipped gym and a front desk that's staffed 24/7. Valet parking only is available for an additional fee. The residential neighborhood of Pacific Heights with its amazing views of the city and San Francisco Bay is a 15-minute walk from the Kimpton Buchanan Hotel. Japantown has Japanese theaters Japan Peace Plaza the shops at Japan Center and movies at the nearby Sundance Kabuki Cinema. Haight-Ashbury and Golden Gate Park are within three miles. The hotel is 15 miles from San Francisco International Airport and 22 miles from Oakland International Airport.

### Kimpton Sir Francis Drake Hotel

450 Powell Street
San Francisco CA
415-392-7755 (800-795-7129)
sirfrancisdrake.com/
A regal ambiance sets the tone for this luxury hotel grandly restored with an Italian Renaissance theme. Offerings include a convenient downtown location and numerous amenities for either business or leisure travelers, dozens of earth friendly practices throughout the hotel, and fresh local, sustainable, and seasonally inspired cuisine and beverages. Pets of all sizes are welcome here for no additional fee;the pet registration form is available on line. Pets need to be declared at the time of registration and there is a pet form to fill out at the time of arrival. Canine guests are also greeted with their own leash, bed and dinnerware to use during their stay, gourmet treats, and various other amenities available through their specialty pet packages. Pet walking and pet sitting services can be arranged by the hotel.

### Laurel Inn A Joie De Vivre

**Hotel**
444 Presidio Ave
San Francisco CA
415-567-8467
Cable TVs with DVD/CD players and a great location are among the perks our guests find at the non-smoking Laurel Inn a Joie de Vivre Hotel. All 49 non-smoking rooms in this three-floor hotel are designed like studio apartments and furnished in mid-century style with rich colors. All have flat-panel TVs with premium cable DVD/CD players and dual-line phones with voicemail and work desks; some also have kitchenettes. The hotel offers covered parking (for an additional fee) a CD/DVD lending library and same-day laundry and dry-cleaning services. A bar/lounge is located next door and complete tour assistance and concierge services are available on-site to assist with recommendations and reservations. Located in the Pacific Heights neighborhood the Laurel Inn is a three-minute walk from UCSF and a 10-minute scenic drive from the Golden Gate Bridge the Presidio and Golden Gate Park. Sacramento Street with trendy boutiques and restaurants is within a couple of blocks. The hotel is 15 miles from San Francisco International Airport.

**Le Meridien San Francisco**
333 Battery Street
San Francisco CA
415-296-2900 (800-543-4300)
Great views of the bay and city;amenity-filled accommodations;connection by bridge to the Federal Reserve Building and the shopping, dining, and entertainment offerings of the Embarcadero Center, and much more are offered at this upscale hotel. Dogs are allowed for no additional pet fee;there is a pet waiver to sign at check in. Dogs may not be left alone in the rooms.

**Loews Regency San Francisco Hotel**
222 Sansome Street

San Francisco CA
415-276-9888
Spa sessions free Wi-Fi and a super Financial District location attract guests to the Loews Regency San Francisco Hotel. Premium bedding and toiletries free Wi-Fi iPod docks and 47-inch flat-panel TVs are featured within all 155 stylish rooms located on the top 11 floors at this 48-story Loews Regency. Stay in shape with a workout in the 24-hour fitness room and there's also a business center. The hotel restaurant satisfies the pickiest of palates during breakfast lunch and dinner and room service is offered 24 hours a day. The hotel allows pets for a fee. The Loews Regency is centered in San Francisco's Financial District three blocks west of the Embarcadero BART stop and within a 15-minute walk of Union Square. It's a half-mile walk to Chinatown's Dragon's Gate or grab the kiddos hop on the trolley a couple of blocks away and make your way to the Aquarium of the Bay a 20-minute ride or mile-and-a-half jaunt north. San Francisco International Airport is 15 miles south.

**Mark Hopkins Intercontinental**
Number One Nob Hill
San Francisco CA
415-392-3434 (877-698-9593)
Dogs up to 25 pounds are allowed. Dogs are allowed for a nightly pet fee.

**Palace Hotel A Luxury Collection Hotel San Francisco**
2 New Montgomery Street
San Francisco CA
415-512-1111 (800-325-3589)
This landmark grand hotel presents an elegant, sophisticated ambiance and offers amenity-filled accommodations for all level of travelers;plus it is located only short distances from the financial district, Chinatown, the Moscone Convention Center, and Union Square.

One dog up to 40 pounds is allowed for an additional $100 one time fee;there is a pet waiver to sign at check in.

**Park Central San Francisco Union Square A Starwood Hotel**
50 Third Street
San Francisco CA
415-974-6400 (800-937-8461)
Located in the South of Market district surrounded by world class dining, shopping, and entertainment venues, this hotel also features floor-to-ceiling windows for great views and a number of amenities for business and leisure travelers. One dog up to 40 pounds is allowed for no additional fee, and there is a pet waiver to sign at check in.

**San Francisco At The Presidio Travelodge**
2755 Lombard Street
San Francisco CA
415-931-8581
Dogs up to 40 pounds are allowed. There is a pet fee of $20 per pet per night.

**San Francisco Marriott Fisherman's Wharf**
1250 Columbus Avenue
San Francisco CA
415-775-7555
Dogs up to 50 pounds are allowed. There is a $100 one time pet fee. You must sign an agreement at check in.

**Serrano Hotel**
405 Taylor Street
San Francisco CA
415-885-2500 (866-289-6561)
Located in the downtown Theater District, this luxury boutique hotel offers a number of sophisticated amenities, dozens of earth friendly practices throughout the hotel, and fresh local, sustainable, and seasonally inspired cuisine and beverages. Pets of all sizes are welcome here for no additional fee;the pet registration form is available on line. Pets need to be declared at the time of registration and there is a pet form to fill out at the time of

arrival. Canine guests are also greeted with their own leash, bed and dinnerware to use during their stay, gourmet treats, and various other amenities available through their specialty pet packages. Pet walking and pet sitting services can be arranged by the hotel.

**Sheraton Fishermans Wharf**
2500 Mason Street
San Francisco CA
415-362-5500 (888-625-5144)
Located in one of the most famous districts in the country with an abundance of activities to pursue, this upscale hotel also provides a bright, colorful ambiance and amenities for all level of travelers. One dog up to 40 pounds is allowed for no additional fee;there is a pet waiver to sign at check in.

**St. Regis Hotel San Francisco**
125 3rd Street
San Francisco CA
415-284-4000 (877-787-3447)
Adjoining the San Francisco Museum of Modern Art, this upscale contemporary hotel offers bright amenity-filled accommodations and eateries showcasing New American cuisine and local seasonal ingredients. Dogs up to 30 pounds are allowed for an additional $150 one time pet fee per room, and there is a pet waiver to sign at check in.

**Stanford Court San Francisco**
905 California Street
San Francisco CA
415-989-3500
Dogs up to 25 pounds are allowed. There is a $25 one time pet fee.

**Taj Campton Place**
340 Stockton Street
San Francisco CA
415-781-5555
Luxurious furnishings combine with a 24-hour rooftop fitness center and an award-winning restaurant at the highly rated Taj Campton Place. The 15-story Taj Campton Place is an upscale choice with 110 plush rooms each with limestone

baths and deep-soaking tubs. Sink into slumber on feather beds topped with Egyptian cotton linens cinnamon-colored throw blankets and goose-down pillows. Cable TVs and high-speed internet access are also available (the latter for a fee). Ascend to the cool 24-hour rooftop fitness center for your work then indulge in specialty cocktails wines burgers and dessert at the bar and bistro. Enjoy breakfast lunch or dinner in the award-winning French restaurant. Overnight shoeshine service and a 24-hour concierge desk are further convenient features. Located on Stockton Street one block from the high-end shopping and boutiques of Union Square Taj Campton Place is 14 miles north of San Francisco International Airport (SFO) and 20 miles northwest of Oakland International Airport. The BART transit system brings guests from SFO to the Powell Street Station a six-minute walk from the hotel. Take a historic cable car near the hotel north to Fisherman's Wharf.

**The Marker San Francisco A Joie De Vivre Hotel**
501 Geary Street
San Francisco CA
415-292-0100 (866-373-4941)
Some of the offerings of this hip luxury hotel include a number of services and amenities for discerning business and leisure travelers;a central location to world class shopping, dining, nightlife, and business venues;dozens of earth friendly practices throughout the hotel, and fresh local, sustainable, and seasonally inspired cuisine and beverages. Pets of all sizes are welcome here for no additional fee;the pet registration form is available on line. Pets need to be declared at the time of registration and there is a pet form to fill out at the time of arrival. Canine guests are also greeted with their own leash, bed and

dinnerware to use during their stay, gourmet treats, and various other amenities available through their specialty pet packages. Pet walking and pet sitting services can be arranged by the hotel.

**The Ritz-carlton San Francisco**
600 Stockton Street At California Street
San Francisco CA
415-296-7465
Large luxurious rooms exceptional service and spectacular views are the hallmarks of The Ritz-Carlton San Francisco set in a prime Nob Hill location. This palatial hotel sits on Nob Hill commanding spectacular views of Coit Tower San Francisco Bay and Chinatown. The 336 rooms are sumptuous located off massive hallways hung with crystal chandeliers. They are outfitted with high-end linens Wi-Fi (for a fee) and bathrooms with designer toiletries and plush robes and slippers. Mini-fridges complimentary shoe shines 24-hour room service and twice-a-day housekeeping are further features. Other highlights include a full-service spa a highly rated restaurant a lobby lounge that serves afternoon tea and a clubby bar. Pets up to 30 pounds are permitted. The Ritz-Carlton San Francisco is in Nob Hill putting many attractions including Chinatown and Fisherman's Wharf within easy reach. It's a 10-minute walk to Union Square and the Financial District. San Francisco International Airport is 14 miles away and it's 19 miles from Oakland International Airport.

**The Westin St. Francis San Francisco On Union Square**
335 Powell Street
San Francisco CA
415-397-7000 (888-625-5144)
Featuring a long rich history with all the modern luxuries and amenities, this landmark 1904 hotel also offers a great location for the needs of business and

leisure travelers. Additionally they offer an on-site restaurant showcasing contemporary cuisine with a focus on local, organic, fresh caught seafood, and all natural meats. One dog up to 40 pounds is allowed for no additional fee;there is a pet waiver to sign at check in.

## W San Francisco
181 Third Street
San Francisco CA
415-777-5300 (877-946-8357)
Besides a location near the San Francisco Museum of Modern Art, the financial district, waterfront, and Union Square, this upscale hotel offers a number of on-site amenities - including a restaurant with a focus on sustainable, local, and organic cuisine. One dog up to 40 pounds is allowed for no additional fee;there is a pet waiver to sign at check in. Dogs may not be left alone in the rooms.

## Dog-Friendly Attractions
### Barbary Coast Trail

San Francisco CA
415-775-1111
barbarycoasttrail.com/
The Barbary Coast Trail is a 3.8-mile walk through historic San Francisco. Bronze medallions and arrows in the sidewalk mark the trail and guide you to 20 of the City's most important historic sites. It was created by the San Francisco Historical Society. Begin the self-guided walking tour at the Old U.S. Mint building on the corner of Mission and 5th Street. Along the trail you will find historic Union Square, the oldest Chinatown in North America, Plymouth Square, the Pony Express site and more.

## Coit Tower
1 Telegraph Hill Blvd
San Francisco CA
415-362-0808
Sitting atop Telegraph Hill is this beautiful monument believed to be in remembrance for the fire

fighters who fought the 1906 earthquake fire. The beautiful grounds overlook the Bay Bridge, Golden Gate Bridge, Pier 39, Fisherman's Wharf, and it also gives an impressive view of the city at night. Inside the tower are a history museum, murals, and a greater view of the city. Dogs are allowed on the grounds and around the walking areas; they are not allowed inside the tower. Dogs must be under their owner's control at all times, and be leashed and cleaned up after.

## Extranominal Tours
690 Fifth Street (cross street Townsend)
San Francisco CA
866-231-3752
This private (and public) tour company features a number of fun and interesting tours in the bay and surrounding area. Dogs are allowed for private tours for no additional fee; tours vary in price depending on hours and destination. Dogs must be leashed and under their owner's control at all times.

## Fisherman's Wharf Shopping

Jefferson Street
San Francisco CA

Fisherman's Wharf is a classic tourist attraction. The walkways follow the bayshore and are complete with all types of street vendors and performers. It's a great dog-friendly place to walk your dog as long as your pup doesn't mind crowds. You can start at Ghirardelli Square and walk along the bayshore to Jefferson Street. Some of the piers don't allow dogs, but there are plenty of things to see and do on Jefferson Street.

## Fort Point National Historic Site
Fort Mason, Building 201
San Francisco CA
415-556-1693
nps.gov/fopo/index.htm
Dogs on leash are allowed on

the property of Fort Point. They are not allowed in any buildings. The park area is open sunrise to sunset.

## Pac Bell Park
24 Willie Mays Plaza
San Francisco CA
415-972-2000
There is a viewing deck along the water where you can view a few minutes of the game from way out in right field without entering the ballpark. You may take a leashed and well-behaved dog here. Also, one game a year the bleachers are open to you and your well-behaved pup. It is usually in August and is known as Dog Days of Summer. Get tickets early.

## Vampire Tour of San Francisco
Nob Hill, Corner of California and Tayor Streets
San Francisco CA
866-4-BITTEN (424-8836)
sfvampiretour.com/
This self-proclaimed vampire hostess leads guests on about a 2 hour unique journey of history and entertainment of the Vampires of the city. Although the tour is open all year, it is a good idea to check ahead if there is inclement weather. This has become a popular attraction, especially around Halloween, so reservations are also suggested. Well mannered dogs are welcome to join this tour because the only building they enter is the Fairmont Hotel, and they are pet friendly. There is no additional fee; dogs must be under their owner's control at all times, be leashed, and please carry supplies to clean up after your pet.

## Outdoor Restaurants
### Chipotle
213 Westlake Center
Daly City CA
650-757-4587
chipotle.com
Specializing in organic, natural and unprocessed food, this

Mexican Eatery offers fajita burritos, tacos, salads, and salsas. Dogs are allowed at the outdoor tables but you will need to order your food inside the restaurant and dogs must remain outside.

**Jamba Juice**
127 Serramonte Center
Daly City CA
650-992-2610
jambajuice.com
All natural and organic ingredients, no high-fructose corn syrup, 0 grams trans fat, no artificial preservatives, a healthy helping of antioxidants, vitamins, and minerals, and fresh whole fruit and fruit juices set the base for these tasty and healthy beverages. Their organic Hot Blends provides a new spin on coffee, green or chai tea, and hot chocolate;plus they offer probiotic fruit and yogurt Blends. Additionally, they feature all natural salads, wraps, sandwiches, and grab n go specialties. They also offer healthy community support through fundraisers, special sales, and school lunch programs. Leashed, well mannered dogs are allowed at their outside dining area.

**Absinthe Brasserie and Bar**
398 Hayes Street
San Francisco CA
415-551-1590
absinthe.com/
With an emphasis on sourcing sustainable, local, and organic, this fine dining restaurant and bar features a full menu of handcrafted gourmet and healthy food and beverage choices. They also offer private dinners, various special events, and food To-Go. Leashed, well mannered dogs are welcome at their outside tables.

**Alaturca Restaurant**
869 Geary Street
San Francisco CA
415-345-1011
alaturcasf.com/
This is the place for an authentic Turkish dining experience;they prepare their foods using

traditional methods, and they also offer Turkish beers and wines, and seasonal alfresco dining. Leashed, well mannered dogs are welcome at their outer tables.

**B44 Bistro**
44 Belden Place
San Francisco CA
415-986-6287
b44.citysearch.com/
This restaurant specializes in Spanish dishes and serves seafood, chicken and steak entrees as well as a vegetarian sandwich. They are open for lunch Monday through Friday from 11:30am until 2 :30pm. They serve dinner Monday through Saturday from 5:30pm. Leashed, well mannered dogs are welcome at their outside dining area.

**Baja Fresh Mexican Grill**
30 Fremont St
San Francisco CA
415-369-9760
bajafresh.com
This Mexican restaurant is open for lunch and dinner. They use fresh ingredients and making their salsa and beans daily. Some of the items on their menu include Enchiladas, Burritos, Tacos Salads, Quesadillas, Nachos, Chicken, Steak and more. Well-behaved leashed dogs are allowed at the outdoor tables.

**Beach Chalet Brewery & Restaurant**
1000 Great Highway @ Ocean Beach
San Francisco CA
415-386-8439
beachchalet.com/
Spectacular ocean and garden views, live entertainment many evenings, handcrafted brews, a full bar, alfresco dining, and California cuisine are the offerings of these gathering places. There are actually 2 eateries here--Park Chalet and the Beach Chalet;dogs are allowed at the Park Chalet outside seating area. Dogs must be leashed and under owner's control/care.

**Blissful Bites**
397 Arguello Blvd
San Francisco CA
415-750-9460
Leashed dogs are allowed at the outside tables of this coffee house. They are open from 7 am until 10 pm daily.

**Blue Danube Coffee House**
306 Clement St
San Francisco CA
415-221-9041
There is an outside counter where you can sit with your dog.

**Cafe De La Presse**
352 Grant Ave
San Francisco CA
415-398-2680
cafedelapresse.com/
It is located next to the Hotel Triton and Chinatown. This cafe also serves beer. Dogs are allowed at the outdoor tables.

**Calzone's**
430 Columbus Ave
San Francisco CA
415-397-3600
calzonesf.com/
Located in North Beach, this Euro bistro features pasta, pizza and much more. Well-behaved, leashed dogs are allowed at the outdoor tables. The restaurant is open everyday from 9am-1am.

**Chipotle**
525 Market Street
San Francisco CA
415-278-0461
chipotle.com
Specializing in organic, natural and unprocessed food, this Mexican Eatery offers fajita burritos, tacos, salads, and salsas. Dogs are allowed at the outdoor tables but you will need to order your food inside the restaurant and dogs must remain outside.

**Chipotle**
126 New Montgomery Street
San Francisco CA
415-512-8113
chipotle.com
Specializing in organic, natural and unprocessed food, this

Mexican Eatery offers fajita burritos, tacos, salads, and salsas. Dogs are allowed at the outdoor tables but you will need to order your food inside the restaurant and dogs must remain outside.

## Cioppino's
400 Jefferson Street
San Francisco CA
415-775-9311
facebook.com/Cioppinos
Cioppino's offers soups, salads, pastas, pizzas, entrees with fish, meat and chicken, and of course Cioppino. Well-behaved leashed dogs are allowed at the outdoor tables. The restaurant is located in the Fisherman's Wharf area, on the corner of Jeffers.

## Coffee Bean and Tea Leaf
2201 Fillmore St
San Francisco CA
415-447-9733
This coffee shop is very popular with the dogs. Dogs are allowed at the outdoor tables.

## Coffee Roastery
2191 Union Street
San Francisco CA
415-922-9559
Leashed dogs are welcome at the outside seating of this roastery and café.

## Crepevine
216 Church Street
San Francisco CA
415-431-4646
crepevine.com
With a focus on local and organic, this eatery specializes in a variety of sweet and savory crepes and offers 100% all natural beef, ocean raised Canadian salmon, organic Fair-Trade coffee, all natural fed cage free eggs, and farm fresh produce. In addition to a breakfast items they offer salads, sandwiches, pastas, and a kid's menu. Leashed, friendly dogs are allowed at their outside dining area.

## Crepevine
624 Irving Street
San Francisco CA

415-681-5858
crepevine.com
With a focus on local and organic, this restaurant specializes in a variety of sweet and savory crepes and offers 100% all natural beef, ocean raised Canadian salmon, organic Fair-Trade coffee, all natural fed cage free eggs, and farm fresh produce. In addition to a breakfast items they offer salads, sandwiches, pastas, and a kid's menu. Leashed, friendly dogs are allowed at their outside dining area.

## Dolores Park Cafe
18th and Dolores
San Francisco CA
415-621-2936
doloresparkcafe.com/
Dogs are allowed at the outdoor tables.

## Farley's
1315-18th Street
San Francisco CA
415-648-1545
farleyscoffee.com/potrero.html
Paninis, soups, salads and more are offered in addition to a choice selection of coffees at this shop. They also offer a fairly large magazine selection and souvenir items. Leashed, well mannered dogs are welcome at their outside tables.

## Flippers
482 Hayes Street
San Francisco CA
415-552-8880
All American favorites are the specialty at this eatery. Dogs are allowed at their outside tables.

## Ghirardelli Ice Cream Fountain
Ghirardelli Square/900 N Point Street
San Francisco CA
415-771-4903
Come here to taste some of the best ice cream around. It's in Ghirardelli Square by the Clock Tower on the first floor (by Larkin Street). This place is almost always crowded, but there are several outdoor

tables. You'll need to order inside and bring out to the tables. Leashed dogs are allowed at the outside tables.

## Jamba Juice
2300 16th Street, #245
San Francisco CA
415-864-7105
jambajuice.com
All natural and organic ingredients, no high-fructose corn syrup, 0 grams trans fat, no artificial preservatives, a healthy helping of antioxidants, vitamins, and minerals, and fresh whole fruit and fruit juices set the base for these tasty and healthy beverages. Their organic Hot Blends provides a new spin on coffee, green or chai tea, and hot chocolate;plus they offer probiotic fruit and yogurt Blends. Additionally, they feature all natural salads, wraps, sandwiches, and grab n go specialties. They also offer healthy community support through fundraisers, special sales, and school lunch programs. Leashed, well mannered dogs are allowed at their outside dining area.

## Jamba Juice
152 Kearny Street
San Francisco CA
415-616-9949
jambajuice.com
All natural and organic ingredients, no high-fructose corn syrup, 0 grams trans fat, no artificial preservatives, a healthy helping of antioxidants, vitamins, and minerals, and fresh whole fruit and fruit juices set the base for these tasty and healthy beverages. Their organic Hot Blends provides a new spin on coffee, green or chai tea, and hot chocolate;plus they offer probiotic fruit and yogurt Blends. Additionally, they feature all natural salads, wraps, sandwiches, and grab n go specialties. They also offer healthy community support through fundraisers, special sales, and school lunch programs. Leashed, well mannered dogs are allowed at their outside dining area.

**Jamba Juice**
2014 Market Street
San Francisco CA
415-703-6011
jambajuice.com
All natural and organic ingredients, no high-fructose corn syrup, 0 grams trans fat, no artificial preservatives, a healthy helping of antioxidants, vitamins, and minerals, and fresh whole fruit and fruit juices set the base for these tasty and healthy beverages. Their organic Hot Blends provides a new spin on coffee, green or chai tea, and hot chocolate;plus they offer probiotic fruit and yogurt Blends. Additionally, they feature all natural salads, wraps, sandwiches, and grab n go specialties. They also offer healthy community support through fundraisers, special sales, and school lunch programs. Leashed, well mannered dogs are allowed at their outside dining area.

**La Mediterranee**
288 Noe Street
San Francisco CA
415-431-7210
cafelamed.com
Dogs are allowed at the outdoor tables.

**Lou's Pier 47 Restaurant**
300 Jefferson St
San Francisco CA
415-771-5687
This cajun seafood restaurant opens daily at 11am. Lou's is located in the Fisherman's Wharf area on Jefferson by Jones Street. They have live bands seven days a week and you might be able to hear the music from outside. Well-behaved leashed dogs are allowed at the outdoor tables on the front deck.

**Martha & Brothers Coffee Company**
1551 Church Street
San Francisco CA
415-648-1166
marthabros.com/
Leashed dogs are allowed at the outside tables of this coffee house.

**Panta Rei**
431 Columbus
San Francisco CA
415-591-0900
pantareirestaurant.com/
Truly authentic Italian cuisine is created at this restaurant;they also feature an extensive wine list to compliment their foods, a daily changing menu, and alfresco dining. Leashed, well mannered dogs are welcome at their outside tables.

**Park Chow**
1240 9th Avenue
San Francisco CA
415-665-9912
With an emphasis on local organic produce and ingredients, free range and organic poultry and beef, and wild caught seafood, this restaurant also features fresh organic beverages, fine wines, draft/bottled beers, organic desserts, and a kid's menu. Leashed, friendly dogs are welcome at their outside dining area.

**Peet's Coffee and Tea**
2197 Fillmore St
San Francisco CA
415-563-9930
peets.com/
This coffee shop is very popular with pups and their people.

**Plant Organic Cafe;Downtown Cafe**
101 California Street
San Francisco CA
415-693-9730
theplantcafe.com
With a emphasis on sustainable, organic, and artisan quality ingredients, this wholesome cafe offers freshly prepared juices, soups, a build your own salad menu, sandwiches, entrees, and desserts. They also offer vegetarian choices, a Grab & Go case, and catering services. Leashed, well mannered dogs are allowed at their outside dining area.

**Plant Organic Cafe;Marina**
3352 Steiner Street
San Francisco CA
415-931-2777
theplantcafe.com
With a emphasis on sustainable, organic, and artisan quality ingredients, this wholesome cafe offers freshly prepared juices, soups, a build your own salad menu, sandwiches, entrees, and desserts. They also offer vegetarian choices, a Grab & Go case, and catering services. Leashed, well mannered dogs are allowed at their outside dining area.

**Plant Organic Cafe;Pier 3**
Pier 3, Suite 108, The Embarcadero
San Francisco CA
415-984-0437
theplantcafe.com/
With a emphasis on sustainable, organic, and artisan quality ingredients, this wholesome cafe offers freshly prepared juices, soups, a build your own salad menu, sandwiches, entrees, and desserts. They also offer vegetarian choices, a Grab & Go case, and catering services. Leashed, well mannered dogs are allowed at their outside dining area.

**Plouf**
40 Belden Place
San Francisco CA
415-986-6491
plouf.citysearch.com/
This French seafood bistro specializes in mussels, unique appetizers, salads, seafood entrees and grilled meats. They are open Monday through Wednesday for lunch from 11:30am to 3pm and for dinner from 5:30pm to 10pm. Well mannered, leashed dogs are allowed at their outside tables.

**Pluto's Fresh Food**
3258 Scott St
San Francisco CA
415-775-8867
plutosfreshfood.com/
Fresh produce delivered daily, breads and goodies baked every

morning, vegetarian options, all made to order, and more are offered at this eatery. Leashed dogs are allowed at their outside dining area.

### Pompei's Grotto
340 Jefferson St
San Francisco CA
415-776-9265
pompeisgrotto.com/
This restaurant specializes in seafood but also serves meat and chicken entrees. Pompei's Grotto is located in the Fisherman's Wharf area on Jefferson Street by Jones Street. Well-behaved leashed dogs are allowed at the outdoor tables.

### Public House
24 Willie Mays Plaza
San Francisco CA
415-644-0240
publichousesf.com
This modern sports pub has one of the largest draft beer and cask ale selections in the city, and offers a casual public house ambiance, 22 giant TVs, south-of-the-boarder handcrafted cuisine, Happy Hours from 4 pm until 6 pm, and a dog-friendly heated patio. Dogs must be friendly, leashed, and under their owner's care at all times.

### Rogue Ales Public House
673 Union
San Francisco CA
415-362-7880
A family friendly pub, they offer a kid's menu and game place, gastro-pub fare, a full service multi-tap bar, a choice variety of fine handcrafted brews, and a dog friendly patio with a doggy menu and free water. Dogs must be leashed and well mannered

### The Curbside Cafe
2417 California St
San Francisco CA
415-929-9030
sfcurbside.com
French and California cuisine is the specialty of this cafe. Leashed dogs are allowed at the outdoor tables.

## Pet-Friendly Shopping Centers
### Ghirardelli Square Shopping Center
900 North Point Street
San Francisco CA
415-775-5500
ghirardellisq.com/
Back in 1893, the famous Ghirardelli chocolate factory occupied these buildings. Today, it is a popular shopping center with numerous shops including the dog-friendly Beastro By the Bay (your dog is welcome inside this unique animal motif gift store). At Ghirardelli Square, you and your pup can take the self-guided outside walking tour and learn about the area's history. Just pick up a free map at the information booth at the west end of Fountain Plaza.

### Westfield San Francisco Center
865 Market Street
San Francisco CA
415-512-6776
westfield.com/sanfrancisco
This one destination offers guests a variety of dining, shopping, and entertainment opportunities. Dogs are allowed in the common areas of the mall; it is up to individual stores whether they allow a dog inside. Dogs must be well behaved, in a carrier, and under their owner's control at all times.

## Pet-Friendly Stores
### Petco Pet Store - Colma
5075 Junipero Serra Blvd
Colma CA
650-755-1153
Your licensed and well-behaved leashed dog is allowed in the store.

### Pet Food Express
6925 Mission Street/H 82
Daly City CA
650-997-3333
One of the country's leading

pet retailers, this comprehensive pet store offers a number of other stores, quality foods/treats, a wide variety of pet supplies, breed-specific items, pet care products, apparel, health items, hound and human accessories, and much more. Some of the services they offer include working with local SPCAs and rescue groups helping tens of thousands of homeless pets find new homes (they do not sell animals as pets), providing low cost vaccination clinics, dog training classes, and self-service pet washes. All leashed, friendly pets are welcome.

### PetSmart Pet Store
315 Gellert Blvd
Daly City CA
650-997-0395
Your licensed and well-behaved leashed dog is allowed in the store.

### Anthropologie
880 Market Street
San Francisco CA
510-486-0705
Items of distinction can be found for all ages and in all departments of this unique shop. Carefully selected to add to the enjoyment of the shopping experience, they carry fine clothing, amazing accessories, jewelry, hobby and leisure items, and a full line of bright and useful items for the home, garden, and office. Leashed, well behaved dogs are allowed in the store.

### Bloomingdale's
845 Market Street
San Francisco CA
415-856-5300
Some of the offerings of this major shopping destination include designer merchandise, indoor and outdoor wear for the entire family, jewelry and accessories, shoes and handbags, personal beauty aids, child care products, and home decor. They also offer a wide variety of shopping services; various fashion, beauty, and home events, and a

philanthropy program that raises funds and awareness for worthy causes. Leashed, well mannered dogs are welcome in the store; they must be under their owner's control at all times.

**Circle Bank, Noe Valley Branch**
3938 24th Street
San Francisco CA
415-285-7600
circlebank.com/
In addition to being open 7 days a week, this community-centered bank offers a wide number of services; plus free WiFi, a stroller corral, a media center, and they are pet friendly. They are open Monday thru Thursday from 9 am until 6:30 pm; Friday from 9 am until 7 pm, and on Saturday and Sunday from 9 am until 2 pm.

**Le Video**
1231 and 1239 9th Avenue
San Francisco CA
415-566-3606
levideo.com/
Your well-behaved leashed dog is allowed inside this store.

**Macy's**
170 O'Farrell Street
San Francisco CA
415-397-3333
macys.com
This Macy's store offers clothing, housewares, electronics and much more. Well-behaved leashed dogs are allowed in the store. It is located on O'Farrell between Powell and Stockton Streets at Union Square.

**Neiman Marcus**
150 Stockton Street
San Francisco CA
877-634-6264
neimanmarcus.com
This famous department store, which sells everything from clothing to home furnishings, allows your well-behaved leashed dog to shop with you.

**Orvis Company Store**
248 Sutter Street
San Francisco CA

415-392-1600
orvis.com
This comprehensive outfitters store offers a wide array of sporting goods and services, clothing and accessories for all types of active lifestyles, quality products for home and pets, gifts and travel items, and much more. Well mannered dogs are welcome in the store; they must be leashed and under their owner's control at all times.

**Pawtrero Hill Bathhouse and Feed Store and Dog Bath**
199 Mississippi Street
San Francisco CA
415-863-7297
pawtrero.com/
This store offers natural and specialized foods, toys, gifts, grooming supplies, natural and homeopathic supplements, collars and leashes, and they have 2 state of the art bathing stations. They are open from 11 am to 7 pm Monday through Friday; from 11 am to 6 pm on Saturday, and from Noon to 5 pm on Sunday. Your well behaved pet is welcome to explore the store with you, and if they respond to voice command, they can be off lead.

**Pet Food Express**
1975 Market Street
San Francisco CA
415-431-4567
One of the country's leading pet retailers, this comprehensive pet store offers a number of other stores, quality foods/treats, a wide variety of pet supplies, breed-specific items, pet care products, apparel, health items, hound and human accessories, and much more. Some of the services they offer include working with local SPCAs and rescue groups helping tens of thousands of homeless pets find new homes (they do not sell animals as pets), providing low cost vaccination clinics, dog training classes, and self-service pet washes. All leashed, friendly pets are

welcome.

**Pet Food Express**
3160 20th Avenue
San Francisco CA
415-759-7777
One of the country's leading pet retailers, this comprehensive pet store offers a number of other stores, quality foods/treats, a wide variety of pet supplies, breed-specific items, pet care products, apparel, health items, hound and human accessories, and much more. Some of the services they offer include working with local SPCAs and rescue groups helping tens of thousands of homeless pets find new homes (they do not sell animals as pets), providing low cost vaccination clinics, dog training classes, and self-service pet washes. All leashed, friendly pets are welcome.

**Petco Pet Store - San Francisco - Potrero**
1685 Bryant St.
San Francisco CA
415-863-1840
Your licensed and well-behaved leashed dog is allowed in the store.

**Petco Pet Store - Sloat**
1591 Sloat Blvd
San Francisco CA
415-665-3700
Your licensed and well-behaved leashed dog is allowed in the store.

**Saks Fifth Avenue**
384 Post Street
San Francisco CA
415-986-4300
saksfifthavenue.com
This upscale department store at Union Square allows well-behaved dogs, but they need to be kept on a short leash.

**South Paw Bathhouse and Feed Store and Dog Bath**
199 Brannan Street
San Francisco CA
415-882-7297
pawtrero.com/
This store offers natural and specialized foods, toys, gifts, grooming supplies, natural and

homeopathic supplements, collars and leashes, and they have 2 state of the art bathing stations. They are open from 11 am to 7 pm Monday through Friday; from 11 am to 6 pm on Saturday, and from Noon to 5 pm on Sunday. Your well behaved pet is welcome to explore the store with you, and if they respond to voice command, they can be off lead.

## The Container Store
26 4th Street
San Francisco CA
415-777-9755
containerstore.com/welcome.ht
m
This store carries hundreds of items to help people get organized. Well mannered dogs are allowed in the store; they must be leashed and under their owner's control at all times.

## Urban Outfitters
80 Powell Street
San Francisco CA
415-989-1515
In addition to a large inventory of indoor and outdoor apparel for men and women, this major department store also carries vintage wear, designer brands, and a variety of accessories for all types of active lifestyles. They also carry shoes, furnishings, home decor, cameras, electronics, novelty items and more. Leashed, well mannered dogs are allowed in the store.

## Urban Outfitters
3322 Fillmore Street
San Francisco CA
415-409-6497
In addition to a large inventory of indoor and outdoor apparel for men and women, this major department store also carries vintage wear, designer brands, and a variety of accessories for all types of active lifestyles. They also carry shoes, furnishings, home decor, cameras, electronics, novelty items and more. Leashed, well mannered dogs are allowed in the store.

## Williams-Sonoma
340 Post Street
San Francisco CA
415-362-9450
williamssonoma.com
Located at Union Square, this store offers cookware, cutlrey, electronics, food and more. Well-behaved leashed dogs are allowed in the store.

# Dog-Friendly Beaches
## Baker Beach
Lincoln Blvd and Bowley St/Golden Gate Nat'l Rec Area
San Francisco CA
415-561-4700
This dog-friendly beach in the Golden Gate National Recreation Area has a great view of the Golden Gate Bridge. Dogs are permitted off leash under voice control on Baker Beach North of Lobos Creek; they must be leashed South of Lobos Creek. The beach is located approx. 1.5 to 2 miles south of the Golden Gate Bridge. From Lincoln Avenue, turn onto Bowley Street and head towards the ocean. There is a parking lot next to the beach. This is a clothing optional beach, so there may be the occasional sunbather.

## Fort Funston/Burton Beach
Skyline Blvd./Hwy 35
San Francisco CA

This is a very popular dog-friendly park and beach. Dogs are allowed off leash here with the exception of the 12 acre enclosure in the northwest section. In the past, dogs have been allowed off-leash. However, currently all dogs must be on leash. Fort Funston is part of the Golden Gate National Recreation Area. There are trails that run through the dunes & ice plant from the parking lot above with good access to the beach below. It overlooks the southern end of Ocean Beach, with a large parking area accessible from Skyline

Boulevard. There is also a water faucet and trough at the parking lot for thirsty pups. It's located off Skyline Blvd. (also known Hwy 35) by John Muir Drive. It is south of Ocean Beach. Thanks to one of our readers for this info. Expect to see lots and lots of dogs having a great time. But not to worry, there is plenty of room for everyone.

## Lands End Off Leash Dog Area
El Camino Del Mar
San Francisco CA
415-561-4700
Owned and operated by the Golden Gate National Recreation Area, Lands End is everything west of and including the Coast Trail, and is an extraordinary combination of parkland, natural areas, and dramatic coastal cliffs. It offers great hiking, ocean and city views, a museum, the ruins of the Sutro Baths, and includes the Sutro Heights Park (dogs must be on lead in this area). This area can be accessed at Merrie Way for the cliffside paths, and at this entrance or the large lot at the end of El Camino Del Mar off Point Lobos for the Coast Trail and beaches. Dogs must be on leash on the Coast Trail, under firm voice control when in off leash areas, and they must be cleaned up after.

## Ocean Beach
Great Hwy
San Francisco CA
415-556-8642
You'll get a chance to stretch your legs at this beach which has about 4 miles of sand. The beach runs parallel to the Great Highway (north of Fort Funston). There are several access points including Sloat Blvd., Fulton Street or Lincoln Way. This beach has a mix of off-leash and leash required areas. Thanks to the San Francisco Dog Owners Group (SFDOG) for providing the following information: Dogs must be on leash on Ocean Beach between Sloat Blvd and Stairwell #21 (roughly at Fulton).

North of Fulton to the Cliff House and South of Sloat for several miles are still okay for off-leash dogs, however parts of these areas may be impassible at high tide. The Golden Gate National Rec Area (GGNRA) strictly enforces the on-leash area between Sloat and Fulton. They usually give no warning tickets ($50 fine). As with all other leash required areas, we encourage dog owners to comply with the rules.

## Off-Leash Dog Parks
### Alamo Square Off Leash Dog Park
Scott Street, between Hayes and Fulton Streets
San Francisco CA
415-831-2084
sfdogparks.com/Alamo_Square.html
Dogs may be off leash under voice control in the Western half of this 5 1/2 acre multi-use park; it is not fenced in. The Eastern half of the park is on-leash. This park offers beautiful panoramic views and rolling hills, and is the second largest legal off-leash area in San Francisco.

### Alta Plaza Off Leash Dog Park

Steiner and Clay Street
San Francisco CA
415-831-2084
This many tiered, Pacific Heights park takes up one square block, and from the top of the park you can enjoy panoramic views of the city. It is bordered by Jackson, Clay, Steiner and Scott streets, and is across from the tennis courts. The first Sunday of every month is Pug Day at this park. It's a casual meeting of pug owners which takes place at the north end of park, usually between 3:30 - 5:00, weather permitting. At the gathering, there can be 20-50 pugs. The legal off-leash area is well marked with paint on the pathways. Dogs should be leashed when not in this area, and they must be cleaned up after at all times.

### Bernal Heights Dog Play Area

Bernal Heights and Esmerelda
San Francisco CA
415-831-2084
This popular park is the largest official DPA/off-leash area in San Francisco. It is on a rocky steep hill, and is accessible via narrow, single track trails. They are situated such that you can walk for up to an hour without retracing any steps. There are also paved trails, an abundance of nature to enjoy, and great views of the city. You can enter either at the parking lot located at Folsom Street at Bernal Heights Ave or at the end of Bernal Heights Ave where the street dead-ends (on the South side of the hill). Dogs must be cleaned up after at all times.

### Buena Vista Dog Play Area
Buena Vista West at Central Avenue
San Francisco CA
415-831-2084
This is the city's oldest park and is basically a giant one acre hill offering expansive views at the top. It is a popular destination location because of its size and safety/isolation from traffic, for the most part. The legal off-leash area is hardly used by dog walkers because it is not safe being so close to the road and most would prefer the enjoyment of the fantastic trail experience Buena Vista offers. You can enter the park at the intersection of Buena Vista Ave. and Central St. or at any of the other park entrances along Buena Vista Ave. The off-leash area is located in a lower area, along the Western side of the park near Central Ave. Dogs must be leashed in the off leash areas, and please clean up after your pet.

### Corona Heights
16th and Roosevelt
San Francisco CA
415-831-2084
This park is for those who

enjoy the climb as much as the view. To get there, go almost to the top of 17th Street and take a right on Roosevelt and follow it around to another right on Levant. It is located adjacent to the Field Museum. There is a green area used by local dog-walkers and pet owners in addition to the fenced-in area to allow the dogs to socialize and run off-leash. Extended walking is required and be prepared for dirt/off road and steep walks at this park. Dogs must be on leash when not in the off lead area, and always please clean up after your pet.

### Crocker Amazon Dog Play Area
At Geneva Avenue and Moscow Street
San Francisco CA
415-831-2084
This 1.8 acre park is located in the northern part of the park, adjacent to the community garden. This is an unfenced area so dogs must be under firm voice control, and please clean up after your pet.

### Delores Park South Dog Play Area
19th Street and Delores Street
San Francisco CA
415-831-2700
This area is a large, grassy, gently sloping and sometimes hilly, mixed use park, with gorgeous views of the city from the top half. There are 6 tennis courts, a basketball court, 2 soccer fields, a playground, and a club house with public restrooms. As a popular relaxation/recreation area, it does tend to be quite crowed on weekends. Also, since there is no fenced in off-lead area, it is a good idea to stay away from the streets, and please clean up after your pet.

### Eureka Valley Dog Play Area
100 Collingwood Street
San Francisco CA
415-831-6810
This small neighborhood recreation park of 2 acres is known for its gymnasium,

playground structure, athletic field, and excellent recreational programs. The fenced in off lead area is East of the baseball diamond and adjacent to the tennis courts. Dogs must be cleaned up after, and leashed when out of the fenced area.

### Fort Miley Off Lead Dog Area
Point Lobos and 48th Avenues
San Francisco CA
415-561-4700
Owned and operated by the Golden Gate National Recreation Area, this area is actually a combination of 3 parks entities, which are Land's End, Lincoln Park, and Fort Miley. There is a large parking and viewing area at the end of El Camino Del Mar off Point Lobos Avenue, and this is where you can take one of the paths to the above. An easier access from the Veteran's Administration Hospital parking lot is also available. Fort Miley is home to the historical ruins of a fully recessed military armament. A large open lawn encloses a recessed bunker that is sunny and has great views over the Ocean Beach and Richmond area. It is a nice place to picnic and is one of the only multi-use open field areas here. There are plenty of areas to explore, and your pet may be off lead, except where marked. Please be sure to clean up after your pet.

### Glen Canyon Park Off Leash Dog Area
400 O'Shaughnessy Blvd
San Francisco CA
415-337-4705
sfdogparks.com/Glen_Canyon.html
This large, natural canyon area is a well used neighborhood park with wonderful trails throughout where there are edible berries to find and a variety of naturescapes to enjoy. Although not an official DPA yet is a great place to walk your dog. They request that you keep the dogs out of the newly planted areas and the seasonal "creek". Enter the park at

Bosworth and O'Shaughnessy Blvd. Please clean up after your pet.

### Golden Gate Park Off Leash Dog Areas
Sloat & Great Highway
San Francisco CA
415-751-8987
Listed among the world's greatest urban parks at over 1,000 acres, there are grassy meadows, wooded trails, secluded lakes, open groves, gardens, museums, and four official, legal off leash dog areas. (1) The Southeast area is located in a wooded strip of land bounded by 3rd Ave., 7th Ave., North of Lincoln Way, and South of Martin Luther King Blvd. It is small, not well marked, with lots of traffic and foxtails in the spring, so the Big Rec locale is the de facto mixed-use off-leash area. Enter Lincoln Way at 7th or 9th Avenue, and the area used is located above/behind the athletic fields. This area is preferred because it is safer and easier to use. (2) The Northeast section is at Fulton and Willard in a Natural Area of 0 .2 acres. This park is near the intersection of Stanyan & Fulton Streets, and is a small, little used area with no fences and prone to heavy traffic. (3) The Southcentral area is bounded by Martin Luther King Drive, Middle Drive and 34th and 38th Avenues; 4.4 acres. This dog friendly knoll has become the last immediate off leash area for people in the outer district. (4) The Northcentral area near 38th Ave. and Fulton (Fenced, training area; 1.4 acres) is the bay areas largest, fenced, exclusive-use off-leash area. It is located behind the Bison pens and West of Spreckles Lake. You can walk in near 39th Avenue and Fulton, or drive in from 38th Ave. The area is surrounded by a low fence that larger dogs could jump and they suggest that this play area may be more suitable for dogs that are in training or

not under voice control. Dogs under 4 months old are not allowed, and females in heat should be leashed, and they are not allowed in the single use areas. Dogs must be under control and cleaned up after at all times.

### Head & Brotherhood Dog Park

Head St & Brotherhood Way
San Francisco CA
415-831-2700
This small park is located on Public Works property along Brotherhood Way at Head Street, and covers about an 1/8 of an acre. Dogs can run off leash in the designated dog park. Please clean up after your pet.

### Jefferson Square Off Lead Dog Park
Eddy and Laguna Streets
San Francisco CA
415-831-2084
The legal off-leash area is a gently sloping grassy park located on the Northwest side of Jefferson Square Park at the corner of Eddy and Laguna. Dogs must be cleaned up after at all times.

### Lafayette Park Dog Play Area
Washington/Clay/Laguna
San Francisco CA
415-831-2084
The legal off-leash area at this park is quite small and located on a slope adjacent to a busy street, so dogs must be under firm voice control. It is near Sacramento Street between Octavia and Gough Streets, and offers beautiful views of downtown. It is suggested to use caution by the steep slope that leads down to heavy traffic on Sacramento Street. This large city park has lots of trees, hills, and is a great place for walking. Dogs must be leashed when not in the off-leash area, and they must be cleaned up after at all times.

### McLaren Park Geneva Dog Play Area
1600 Geneva Avenue

San Francisco CA
415-831-2084
This park of about 60 acres has two locations for off lead. The top section at the North end of the park is bounded by Shelly Drive with a fence at the roadway, trails, an open area, a natural area, and a reservoir. Dogs are not allowed at the group picnic or children's play area, and leash restrictions apply during performances at the Amphitheater. The South entrance is accessible via the 1600 block of Geneva or Sunnydale. Dogs are not allowed in sensitive habitat areas, they must be leashed when not in the off leash areas, and cleaned up after at all times.

**Mountain Lake Dog Play Area**
12th Avenue and Lake Street
San Francisco CA
415-666-7005
Although small, this popular park has a strong local dog community. The off-leash area is at the Eastern corner of the park on the opposite end of the lake area. You can enter at 8th Avenue and Lake Street, but for wheelchair access and the doggy water fountain, enter one block west at 9th Avenue. Dogs must be leashed when not in the off-leash area, and they must be cleaned up after at all times.

**Pine Lake Dog Play Area - Stern Grove Trail**
Between H 1(Stern Grove) and Wawona (Pine Lake)
San Francisco CA
415-252-6252
This off leash trail runs west from the Pine Lake Meadow DPA to the Stern Grove DPA. Dogs must be cleaned up after.

**Pine Lake Park Dog Play Area**
Sloat Boulevard & Vale Street
San Francisco CA
415-831-2700
This park's lake is one of only 3 natural lakes left in San Francisco. The off leash area is on the second terrace of the park, west, and shares a boundary with Stern Grove Park,

which also has an off leash area. There is a 1/5 mile trail from the Pine Lake DPA to the Stern Grove DPA. Dogs must be on leash when not in off lead areas, and they must be cleaned up after at all times.

**Portrero Hill Mini Park Dog Play Area**
22nd Street and Arkansas
San Francisco CA
415-695-5009
This .04 acre park is located on 22nd Street between Arkansas and Connecticut Streets and offers a great view of the bay. The area is unfenced so dogs must be under firm voice control. Dogs must be leashed when not in the off leash area, and be cleaned up after at all times.

**St Mary's Off Leash Dog Park**

95 Justin Drive
San Francisco CA
415-695-5006
This 3 tiered multi-use park offers a fenced-in dog park with grassy and paved areas on the lower level (below the playground), benches, and canine and human water fountains. It is frequently closed (locked shut) during rain or wet seasons. Dogs must be on leash when not in off lead areas, and they must be cleaned up after at all times.

**Stern Grove Dog Play Area**
19th Avenue and Wawona Avenue
San Francisco CA
415-252-6252
Stern Grove is said to be one of the most peaceful getaways in the c

## San Jose

## Dog-Friendly Hotels
**Aloft Cupertino**
10165 North De Anza Boulevard
Cupertino CA
408-766-7000
Dogs up to 40 pounds are

allowed. There is no additional pet fee. The hotel offers a special bed, bowl, and a doggie bag of treats and toys.

**Best Western Plus Brookside Inn**
400 Valley Way
Milpitas CA
408-263-5566 (800-780-7234)
Dogs up to 80 pounds are allowed. There is a $20 per day pet fee up to $100 for the week. Up to two dogs are allowed per room.

**Crowne Plaza Hotel San Jose-silicon Valley**
777 Bellew Drive
Milpitas CA
408-321-9500 (877-270-6405)
Dogs up to 50 pounds are allowed. Dogs are allowed for a pet fee of $25.00 per pet per night.

**Sheraton San Jose Hotel**
1801 Barber Lane
Milpitas CA
408-943-0600 (888-625-5144)
Beside a number of on-site amenities for all level of travelers at this upscale hotel, they are also located only a mile from the Great Mall of the Bay Area and just 4 miles to the airport. Dogs are allowed for no additional pet fee;there is a pet waiver to sign at check in.

**Doubletree By Hilton San Jose**
2050 Gateway Place
San Jose CA
408-453-4000 (800-222-TREE (8733))
This upscale hotel has a number of on site amenities for all level of travelers - including their signature chocolate chip cookies at check in, plus a convenient location to business, shopping, dining, historical, and entertainment areas. Dogs are allowed for an additional one time fee of $50 per pet. Dogs must be crated when left alone in the room.

**Hilton San Jose**
300 Almaden Boulevard
San Jose CA

408-287-2100
Located in the heart of Silicon Valley and only 3 miles to an international airport, this upscale hotel also offers a convenient location to shopping, dining, and entertainment areas. Dogs are allowed for no additional pet fee.

**La Quinta Inn San Jose Airport**
2585 Seaboard Avenue
San Jose CA
408-435-8800 (800-531-5900)
Dogs of all sizes are allowed for no additional pet fee; there is a pet policy to sign at check-in.

**San Jose Marriott**
301 South Market Street
San Jose CA
408-280-1300
Dogs up to 50 pounds are allowed. There is a $75 one time pet fee.

**The Fairmont San Jose**
170 South Market Street
San Jose CA
408-998-1900 (800-257-7544)
This luxury hotel offers 731 beautifully appointed guest rooms and 74 suites, and being set in the high-tech Silicon Valley, they are fully equipped for the business traveler. Vacationers can enjoy the historic grandeur of the inn and its close proximity to several recreational activities. Some of the features include several dining options, a lounge, pool and spa, and many in room amenities. Dogs up to 70 pounds are allowed for an additional one time fee of $75 per pet. Dogs may not be left alone in the room at any time, and they must be leashed and cleaned up after.

**The Westin San Jose**
302 South Market Street
San Jose CA
408-295-2000 (888-625-5144)
One dog per room, up to 40 pounds is permitted.

**Hilton Santa Clara**
4949 Great America Parkway
Santa Clara CA

408-330-0001
Located in the heart of Silicon Valley, this upscale hotel offers numerous on site amenities for business and leisure travelers, plus a convenient location to business, shopping, dining, and entertainment areas. Dogs up to 45 pounds are allowed for an additional one time pet fee of $50 per room.

**Hotel E Real**
3580 El Camino Real
Santa Clara CA
408-241-0771
Free Wi-Fi in-room microwaves and a complimentary breakfast near shopping and dining make for a hassle-free stay at Hotel E Real. The two-story Hotel E Real boasts 70 rooms with free Wi-Fi microwaves mini-fridges pillowtop mattresses premium cable channels and free local calls. The outdoor pool is a great place to relax and soak in the sun. Keep your duds looking fresh with on-site laundry facilities and enjoy a meal in the restaurant. Pets are welcome for an extra charge and parking is free. The hotel charges a daily service fee. Located on the west side of Santa Clara on bustling El Camino Real the Hotel E Real is across the street from the Lawrence Square Shopping Center. You're two miles from the International Swim Center in Central Park. The Triton Museum of Art is three miles away and the Intel headquarters and Santa Clara University are four miles away. Head 10 minutes north to check out the rides and slides at California's Great America theme park or the restaurants and nightlife in the Mercado Santa Clara. Spooky tours of the Winchester Mystery House and upscale shopping on Santana Row are 10 minutes southeast. San Jose International Airport is seven miles away.

**Aloft Sunnyvale**
170 South Sunnyvale Avenue
Sunnyvale CA

408-736-0300
Dogs up to 40 pounds are allowed. There is no additional pet fee.

**Quality Inn Santa Clara Convention Center**
1280 Persian Drive
Sunnyvale CA
408-744-1100 (877-424-6423)
The Quality Inn is located at the triangle of Tasman Drive, Lawrence Expressway and Highway 237.

Dogs of all sizes are allowed. Dogs are allowed for a pet fee of $15.00/pet per pet per night.

**Sheraton Sunnyvale Hotel**
1100 North Mathilda Ave
Sunnyvale CA
408-745-6000 (888-625-5144)
This resort style hotel offers guests a tranquil ambiance amid gardens, oversized rooms, an Olympic-sized pool, a comfy lounge, and a bi-level restaurant with garden views. Dogs up to 15 pounds are allowed for no additional fee;there is a pet waiver to sign at check in.

## Pet-Friendly Extended Stay Hotels

**Residence Inn San Jose Campbell**
2761 South Bascom Avenue
Campbell CA
408-559-1551
Dogs of all sizes are allowed. There is a $100 one time additional pet fee.

**Towneplace Suites San Jose Campbell**
700 East Campbell Avenue
Campbell CA
408-370-4510
Dogs of all sizes are allowed. There is a $75 one time pet fee.

**Residence Inn By Marriott Palo Alto**
4460 El Camino Real
Los Altos CA
650-559-7890
Dogs of all sizes are allowed. There is a $100 one time

additional pet fee.

## Extended Stay America - San Jose - Milpitas
1000 Hillview Court
Milpitas CA
408-941-9977 (800-804-3724)
One dog is allowed per suite.
There is a $25 per night
additional pet fee up to $150 for
an entire stay.

## Extended Stay America San Jose - Milpitas - Mccarthy Ranch
330 Cypress Drive
Milpitas CA
408-433-9700 (800-804-3724)
One dog is allowed per suite.
There is a $25 per night
additional pet fee up to $150 for
an entire stay.

## Residence Inn Milpitas Silicon Valley
1501 California Circle
Milpitas CA
408-941-9222
Dogs of all sizes are allowed.
There is a $100 one time
additional pet fee.

## Staybridge Suites Silicon Valley-milpitas
321 Cypress Drive
Milpitas CA
408-383-9500 (877-270-6405)
Dogs up to 80 pounds are
allowed. Pets allowed with an
additional pet fee. Up to $75 for
1-6 nights and up to $150 for 7+
nights. A pet agreement must
be signed at check-in.

## Towneplace Suites By Marriott Milpitas
1428 Falcon Drive
Milpitas CA
408-719-1959
Dogs of all sizes are allowed.
There is a $100 one time pet
fee.

## Extended Stay America - San Jose - Edenvale - North
6199 San Ignacio Avenue
San Jose CA
408-226-4499 (800-804-3724)
One dog is allowed per suite.
There is a $25 per night
additional pet fee up to $150 for

an entire stay.

## Extended Stay America - San Jose - Santa Clara
2131 Gold Street
San Jose CA
408-262-0401 (800-804-3724)
One dog is allowed per suite.
There is a $25 per night
additional pet fee up to $150
for an entire stay.

## Extended Stay America San Jose-downtown
1560 North First Street
San Jose CA
408-573-0648 (800-804-3724)
One dog is allowed per suite.
There is a $25 per night
additional pet fee up to $150
for an entire stay.

## Homewood Suites By Hilton San Jose Airport-silicon Valley
10 West Trimble Road
San Jose CA
408-428-9900
This upscale all suite hotel
offers large, comfortable suites
for longer stays and/or
temporary housing needs;plus
numerous on site amenities for
all level of travelers and a
convenient location to local
sites of interest. One dog up to
50 pounds is allowed for no
additional fee;there is a pet
policy to sign at check in.

## Homewood Suites By Hilton San Jose Airport-silicon Valley
10 West Trimble Road
San Jose CA
408-428-9900
With modern interiors 37-inch
flat-panel TVs free buffet
breakfast a complimentary
shuttle an attractive outdoor
pool with hot tub and lush
landscaping you'll feel like
you're staying in an upscale
condo during your visit at
Homewood Suites By Hilton
San Jose Airport-Silicon Valley.
This appealing extended-stay
hotel offers the comforts of
home in a resort-style setting.
Suites have fully equipped
kitchens with granite counters

attractive living rooms with sofa
beds and separate bedrooms.
Some suites even have
fireplaces. Homewood Suites
also has an ample fitness room
and a basketball court where
you can wind down at the end of
the day. With 140 suites on two
or three floors depending on the
building this facility provides free
Wi-Fi throughout and rooms
also have complimentary wired
internet access. Pets are not
permitted except for service
animals. Note: For guests within
a 2-hour driving radius a
refundable deposit is required
which will be returned upon
check-out. Set in the heart of
Silicon Valley four miles north of
downtown San Jose the
Homewood Suites is just a half-
mile from the San Jose
International Airport. There's a
free hotel shuttle service to the
airport plus any location within a
five-mile radius. Intel Corp is a
three-mile drive and many other
major employers are nearby.
Santa Clara University is three
miles from the hotel.

## Residence Inn By Marriott San Jose South
6111 San Ignacio Avenue
San Jose CA
408-226-7676
Dogs of all sizes are allowed.
There is a $100 one time
additional pet fee.

## Staybridge Suites San Jose
1602 Crane Court
San Jose CA
408-436-1600 (877-270-6405)
Dogs up to 40 pounds are
allowed. Pets allowed with an
additional pet fee. Up to $75 for
1-6 nights and up to $150 for 7+
nights. A pet agreement must
be signed at check-in.

## Towneplace Suites San Jose Cupertino
440 Saratoga Avenue
San Jose CA
408-984-5903
Dogs up to 25 pounds are
allowed. There is a $100 one
time pet fee.

## Candlewood Suites Silicon

## Valley San Jose
481 El Camino Real
Santa Clara CA
408-241-9305 (877-270-6405)
Dogs up to 80 pounds are allowed. Pets allowed with an additional pet fee. Up to $75 for 1-6 nights and up to $150 for 7+ nights. A pet agreement must be signed at check-in.

## Extended Stay America San Jose-sunnyvale
1255 Orleans Drive
Sunnyvale CA
408-734-3431 (800-804-3724)
One dog is allowed per suite. There is a $25 per night additional pet fee up to $150 for an entire stay.

## Residence Inn Silicon Valley I
750 Lakeway Drive
Sunnyvale CA
408-720-1000
Dogs of all sizes are allowed. There is a $100 one time additional pet fee.

## Residence Inn Silicon Valley Ii

1080 Stewart Drive
Sunnyvale CA
408-720-8893
Dogs of all sizes are allowed. There is a $100 one time additional pet fee.

## Staybridge Suites Sunnyvale
900 Hamlin Court
Sunnyvale CA
408-745-1515 (877-270-6405)
Dogs up to 80 pounds are allowed. Pets allowed with an additional pet fee. Up to $75 for 1-6 nights and up to $150 for 7+ nights. A pet agreement must be signed at check-in.

## Towneplace Suites By Marriott Sunnyvale Mountain View
606 South Bernardo Avenue
Sunnyvale CA
408-733-4200
Dogs up to 75 pounds are allowed. There is a $75 one time pet fee.

# Dog-Friendly Attractions
## Ron's Tours / Pedicab Service
Call to Arrange.
San Jose CA
408-859-8961
Providing pedicab taxi and tour services for the downtown area of San Jose. The pedicab can also be hired for weddings and other special events. Dogs ride free.

# Outdoor Restaurants
## Aqui Cal-Mex
201 East Campbell Ave
Campbell CA
408-374-2784
aquicalmex.com
This restaurant serves many choices from lighter small plates to Tortill Rollups with crab cakes. The food is generally Mexican food with a California style to it. There is plentiful outdoor seating and your well-behaved leashed dog is allowed.

## Baja Fresh Mexican Grill
1976 S. Bascom Ave
Campbell CA
408-377-2600
bajafresh.com
This Mexican restaurant is open for lunch and dinner. They use fresh ingredients and making their salsa and beans daily. Some of the items on their menu include Enchiladas, Burritos, Tacos Salads, Quesadillas, Nachos, Chicken, Steak and more. Well-behaved leashed dogs are allowed at the outdoor tables.

## Chipotle
1815 S Bascom Avenue
Campbell CA
408-371-5284
chipotle.com
Specializing in organic, natural and unprocessed food, this Mexican Eatery offers fajita burritos, tacos, salads, and salsas. Dogs are allowed at the outdoor tables but you will need to order your food inside the restaurant and dogs must remain outside.

## Rock Bottom Restaurant & Brewery
1875 S Bascom Ave
Campbell CA
408-377-0707
rockbottom.com/campbell
This dog-friendly restaurant is located in the Pruneyard Shopping Center. The Campbell-Los Gatos path is within walking distance. Water is provided for your pet. There is a nice outdoor seating area with heaters.

## Stacks
139 E Campbell Ave
Campbell CA
408-376-3516
stacksbreakfast.com/
Sourcing sustainable fresh ingredients, this restaurant features healthy and tasty breakfasts and lunches, daily Chef's Specials, and a commitment to implementing GREEN, eco-friendly initiatives. Leashed, well mannered dogs are welcome at their outside tables.

## Yiassoo
2180 S Bascom Ave
Campbell CA
408-559-0312
yiassoo.com/campbell/
Delicious Greek food.

## Baja Fresh Mexican Grill
20735 Stevens Creek Blvd
Cupertino CA
408-257-6141
bajafresh.com
This Mexican restaurant is open for lunch and dinner. They use fresh ingredients and making their salsa and beans daily. Some of the items on their menu include Enchiladas, Burritos, Tacos Salads, Quesadillas, Nachos, Chicken, Steak and more. Well-behaved leashed dogs are allowed at the outdoor tables.

## Cafe Society
21265 Stevens Creek Blvd #202

Cupertino CA
408-725-8091

coffeesociety.com/
This coffee shop serves coffee and pastries. Leashed dogs are allowed at the outdoor tables.

### Lazy Dog Restaurant & Bar
19359 Stevens Creek Blvd
Cupertino CA
408-359-4690
lazydogrestaurants.com/dogs/info
Known for it's dog-friendly patio, the Lazy Dog offers your dog a complimentary bowl of water, and a menu consisting of grilled hamburger patty, chicken breast or brown rice. They just ask that you respect their common sense rules while your dog is dining there. This is as dog-friendly as dining gets. For the humans in your party there is hamburger, steak, salads and some great desserts.

### Whole Foods Market
20830 Stevens Creek Blvd.
Cupertino CA
408-257-7000
wholefoods.com/
This natural food supermarket offers natural and organic foods. Order some food from their deli without your dog and bring it to an outdoor table where your well-behaved leashed dog is welcome. Dogs are not allowed in the store including the deli at any time.

### Happy Hound
15899 Los Gatos Blvd
Los Gatos CA
408-358-2444
Happy Hound serves burgers, hot dogs, milkshakes, and more. Well-behaved, leashed dogs are allowed at the outdoor seats.

### Whole Foods Market
15980 Los Gatos Blvd.
Los Gatos CA
408-358-4434
wholefoods.com/
This natural food supermarket offers natural and organic foods. Order some food from their deli without your dog and bring it to an outdoor table where your well-behaved leashed dog is welcome.

### Willow Street Pizza
20 S. Santa Cruz Ave
Los Gatos CA
408-354-5566
willowstreet.com/
There is a large outdoor seating area with heat lamps. The hours are 11:30 am to 10 pm, 11 pm on Friday and Saturday.

### Bento Xpress
23 N. Milpitas Blvd
Milpitas CA
408-262-7544
bentoxpress.com/
This restaurant offers quick Japanese cuisine. Dogs are allowed at the outdoor tables.

### Amato Pizzeria
6081 Meridian Avenue #A
San Jose CA
408-997-7727
amatopizzeria.com/index.html
This pizzeria has some nice tables and chairs out front where you can sit with your pet and enjoy the fair. Dogs must be well behaved, leashed, and please clean up after your pet.

### Aqui Cal-Mex
5679 Snell Avenue
San Jose CA
408-362-3456
aquicalmex.com
This restaurant serves many choices from lighter small plates to Tortill Rollups with crab cakes. The food is generally Mexican food with a California style to it. There is plentiful outdoor seating and your well-behaved leashed dog is allowed.

### Baja Fresh Mexican Grill
1708 Oakland Road
San Jose CA
408-436-5000
bajafresh.com/
This Mexican restaurant is open for lunch and dinner. They use fresh ingredients and making their salsa and beans daily. Some of the items on their menu include Enchiladas, Burritos, Tacos Salads, Quesadillas, Nachos, Chicken, Steak and more. Well-behaved leashed dogs are allowed at

the outdoor tables.

### Bill's Cafe
1115 Willow Street
San Jose CA
408-294-1125
billscafe.com/
Bill's cafe has outdoor seating for you and your dog. Dogs sometimes get biscuits and water.

### Britannia Arms
173 W Santa Clara Street
San Jose CA
408-278-1400
Dogs are allowed at the outdoor tables.

### Camille's Sidewalk Cafe
90 Skyport Drive
San Jose CA
408-436-5333
A vision of healthier, tastier foods inspired the idea for the freshly made salads, gourmet wraps and sandwiches, drinks, desserts, and coffees that are offered at all of Camille's Cafes. Dogs are allowed to sit with you at your outdoor table. Dogs must be attended to at all times, well behaved, and leashed.

### Casa Vicky's Catering and Cafe
792 E Julian St
San Jose CA
408-995-5488
casavicky.com/
This restaurant serves Mexican food. Leashed dogs are allowed at the outdoor tables.

### Chipotle
975 The Alameda/H 82, Suite 10
San Jose CA
408-288-9172
chipotle.com
Specializing in organic, natural and unprocessed food, this Mexican Eatery offers fajita burritos, tacos, salads, and salsas. Dogs are allowed at the outdoor tables but you will need to order your food inside the restaurant and dogs must remain outside.

### Chipotle
1751 N First Street

San Jose CA
408-453-6115
chipotle.com
Specializing in organic, natural and unprocessed food, this Mexican Eatery offers fajita burritos, tacos, salads, and salsas. Dogs are allowed at the outdoor tables but you will need to order your food inside the restaurant and dogs must remain outside.

### Chipotle
2007 Camden Avenue, #50
San Jose CA
408-369-8163
chipotle.com
Specializing in organic, natural and unprocessed food, this Mexican Eatery offers fajita burritos, tacos, salads, and salsas. Dogs are allowed at the outdoor tables but you will need to order your food inside the restaurant and dogs must remain outside.

### Fu Kee Chinese Restaurant
121 Bernal Road
San Jose CA
408-225-3218
fukeerestaurant.com/
This eatery specializes in Asian Fusion, Chinese, Thai, and Vietnamese cuisine. Guests order and pick-up at the counter, and leashed, friendly dogs are welcome at their outdoor tables.

### Grande Pizzeria
150 E San Carlos Street
San Jose CA
408-292-2840
This pizzeria also offers a variety of Italian dishes, happy hours, and alfresco dining. Leashed, well mannered dogs are allowed at the outside dining area.

### Johnny Rockets
150 S First Street, # 115
San Jose CA
408-977-1414
johnnyrockets.com/
All the American favorites can be found here: A fun retro, all-American decor and atmosphere, juicy burgers, specialty sandwiches, crispy fries, hand-dipped malts and shakes (dark chocolate ones too), fresh baked apple pies, tasty vegetarian choices, and something for all ages. Leashed, friendly dogs are allowed at their outside dining area.

### Johnny Rockets
840 Blossom Hill
San Jose CA
408-229-1414
johnnyrockets.com/
All the American favorites can be found here: A fun retro, all-American decor and atmosphere, juicy burgers, specialty sandwiches, crispy fries, hand-dipped malts and shakes (dark chocolate ones too), fresh baked apple pies, tasty vegetarian choices, and something for all ages. Leashed, friendly dogs are allowed at their outside dining area.

### Left Bank
377 Santana Row, Suite 1100
San Jose CA
408-984-3500
leftbank.com
An authentic French brasserie, guests can enjoy their Parisian casual setting with not so casual food;they offer lunch, dinner, weekend brunch, and children's menus;plus a full service bar with signature cocktails and alfresco dining. Leashed, well mannered dogs are welcome at their outside dining area.

### Noah's Bagels
1578 S Bascom Ave
San Jose CA
408-371-8321
Dogs are allowed at the outdoor seats.

### Pasta Pomodoro
378 Santana Row #1130
San Jose CA
408-241-2200
pastapomodoro.com/
Sourcing the local area's best organic farmers and artisan purveyors, this eatery presents a full menu of made-from scratch and innovatively prepared classic Italian cuisine.

They offer a seasonally generated menu and vegetarian and gluten free options as well. Leashed, well mannered dogs are welcome at their outside dining area.

### Pizza Antica
334 Santana Row #1065
San Jose CA
408-557-8373
pizzaantica.com/
Sourcing fresh seasonal ingredients from local and organic artisans, this eatery features a full menu of Italian dishes, signature pizzas, a fresh daily soup, a global selection of fine wines, and a mostly made-from-scratch kitchen. Leashed, well mannered dogs are welcome at their outside dining area.

### Poor House Bistro
91 S Autumn Street/H 82
San Jose CA
408-292-5837
poorhousebistro.com/
Offering the favorites of New Orleans dining, this Cajun bistro also serves up live music every Friday and Saturday night, and there is also a nice outdoor patio. Dogs are allowed at the outer tables;they must be under their owner's control at all times.

### Sam's barbecue
1110 S Bascom Avenue
San Jose CA
408-297-9151
samsbbq.com/
Authentic Kansas City style baby back ribs, perfectly seasoned Carolina pulled pork, moist Southwestern chicken, hand-cut steaks, tasty barbecue sandwiches, and much more are offered at this eatery. They also slow-cook their specialties over oak wood;offer a children's menu, and there is live music on Tuesday and Wednesday evenings. Leashed, friendly dogs are allowed at their outside dining area.

### Siena Bistro
1359 Lincoln Avenue
San Jose CA

408-271-0837
sienabistro.com/
This Mediterranean eatery allows dogs on the patio on Thursday nights year around. Dogs must be leashed and under their owner's control at all times.

**Straits**
333 Santana Row
San Jose CA
408-246-6320
Singaporean cuisine with Southeast Asia influences are featured at this restaurant and lounge. Leashed, well mannered dogs are welcome at their outside dining area.

**The Loft Bar and Bistro**
90 S Second Street
San Jose CA
408-291-0677
sanjose.com/loft-bar-and-bistro/
This American restaurant with a Mediterranean twist offers a variety of dining areas and 2 bar areas. They offer service at the street level patio where dogs are allowed. Dogs must be attended to at all times, well behaved, and leashed.

**Willow Street Wood Fired Pizza**
1072 Willow St
San Jose CA
408-971-7080
willowstreet.com/
This restaurant serves Italian food and signature wood-fired pizzas.Leashed, well mannered dogs are allowed at the outdoor tables.

**Baja Fresh Mexican Grill**
3950 Rivermark Plaza
Santa Clara CA
408-588-4060
bajafresh.com
This Mexican restaurant is open for lunch and dinner. They use fresh ingredients and making their salsa and beans daily. Some of the items on their menu include Enchiladas, Burritos, Tacos Salads, Quesadillas, Nachos, Chicken, Steak and more. Well-behaved leashed dogs are allowed at the outdoor tables.

**Pizz'a Chicago**
1576 Halford Ave
Santa Clara CA
408-244-2246
pizzachicagoonline.com/
They have delicious deep dish style pizza. They only have 3 outdoor tables, so try to arrive before the lunch or dinner rush. Once there, you and your pup can enjoy being served pizza at the covered tables. This is a good place to go even if it's raining.

**Red Robin Gourmet Burgers**
3906 Rivermark Plaza
Santa Clara CA
408-855-0630
redrobin.com/
Artfully created appetizers, soups, salads, gourmet burgers, signature sandwiches, wraps, and specialty desserts are just some of the offerings of this restaurant. They also offer a gluten-free menu, a children's menu, wine/beer and cocktails, and alfresco dining. Leashed, friendly dogs are allowed at their outside dining area.

**Tony & Alba's Pizza & Pasta**
3137 Stevens Creek Blvd
Santa Clara CA
408-246-4605
tonyandalbaspizza.com/
Great food and nice outdoor seating. They have warm outdoor heat lamps. If for some reason they don't have them turned on, just ask one of the folks working there and they'll be happy to turn them on. They will also bring water for your pooch if requested.

**La Fondue**
14550 Big Basin Way
Saratoga CA
408-867-3332
lafondue.com/
Guests can expect a unique dining experience at this eatery that offers more than 50 different fondues. A dog friendly, upscale restaurant, the LaFondue has 2 patios with doggy tie downs and complimentary filet mignon for

all their canine guests. Dogs must be kept under owner's control and leashed.

**Chipotle**
324 W El Camino Real/H 82
Sunnyvale CA
408-773-1304
chipotle.com
Specializing in organic, natural and unprocessed food, this Mexican Eatery offers fajita burritos, tacos, salads, and salsas. Dogs are allowed at the outdoor tables but you will need to order your food inside the restaurant and dogs must remain outside.

## Pet-Friendly Shopping Centers
**Santana Row**
368 Santana Row
San Jose CA
408-551-4611
santanarow.com
This European style community with nearly 100 shops beneath condos is dog-friendly. There are clean up bags located at various spots for your dog throughout Santana Row. There are a number of dog-friendly stores and outdoor restaurants and sidewalk cafes in Santana Row. Please ask each individual store if you may bring your dog in. Santana Row is located in the heart of Silicon Valley on Stevens Creek Blvd just west of I-880.

## Pet-Friendly Stores
**Pet Food Express**
1902 S Bascom Avenue
Campbell CA
408-371-5555
One of the country's leading pet retailers, this comprehensive pet store offers a number of other stores, quality foods/treats, a wide variety of pet supplies, breed-specific items, pet care products, apparel, health items, hound and human accessories, and much more. Some of the services they offer include

working with local SPCAs and rescue groups helping tens of thousands of homeless pets find new homes (they do not sell animals as pets), providing low cost vaccination clinics, dog training classes, and self-service pet washes. All leashed, friendly pets are welcome.

**PetSmart Pet Store**
850 W Hamilton Ave
Campbell CA
408-374-9321
Your licensed and well-behaved leashed dog is allowed in the store.

**PetSmart Pet Store**
20558 Stevens Creek Blvd
Cupertino CA
408-725-9530
Your licensed and well-behaved leashed dog is allowed in the store.

**Pet Food Express**
15466 Los Gatos Blvd
Los Gatos CA
408-356-7600
One of the country's leading pet retailers, this comprehensive pet store offers a number of other stores, quality foods/treats, a wide variety of pet supplies, breed-specific items, pet care products, apparel, health items, hound and human accessories, and much more. Some of the services they offer include working with local SPCAs and rescue groups helping tens of thousands of homeless pets find new homes (they do not sell animals as pets), providing low cost vaccination clinics, dog training classes, and self-service pet washes. All leashed, friendly pets are welcome.

**Petco Pet Store - Los Gatos**
444 North Santa Cruz Ave.
Los Gatos CA
408-395-7074
Your licensed and well-behaved leashed dog is allowed in the store.

**PetSmart Pet Store**
175 Ranch Dr
Milpitas CA
408-956-1044

Your licensed and well-behaved leashed dog is allowed in the store.

**Anthropologie**
356 Santana Row - S. 1000
San Jose CA
408-249-0436
Items of distinction can be found for all ages and in all departments of this unique shop. Carefully selected to add to the enjoyment of the shopping experience, they carry fine clothing, amazing accessories, jewelry, hobby and leisure items, and a full line of bright and useful items for the home, garden, and office. Leashed, well behaved dogs are allowed in the store.

**Crate & Barrel**
301 Santana Row
San Jose CA
408-247-0600
crateandbarrel.com
Fine products for the home to be found at this store include items for outdoor living, indoor furnishings, dining and entertaining, kitchen, decorating, bed and bath, organizing and storage, and much more. Leashed, friendly dogs are welcome in the store.

**Gussied Up Dog Boutique**
1310 Lincoln Avenue
San Jose CA
408-279-2544
This is a rather large store a wide variety of gifts, treats, and supplies. Your leashed (or carried), well behaved pet is allowed to explore the store with you. They are open 7 days a week from 10 am to 7 pm.

**Hahn's Lighting Store**
260 E Virginia St
San Jose CA
408-295-1755
Your well-behaved leashed dog is allowed inside this store.

**Happy Go Lucky Dog Boutique**
925 Blossom Hill Road
San Jose CA
408-360-0508
happygoluckydogs.com/

Located in the Oakridge Mall, there is an outer door so your pet can join you to explore this pet friendly store. They offer designer dog collars, dog carriers, dog beds, fun toys, hip doggie clothes, healthy snacks and more at competitive prices. Dogs must be leashed, but if they are well behaved and will respond to voice control, they may be off lead in the store. They are open from 10 am to 9:30 pm Monday to Friday; 10 am to 9 pm on Saturday, and from 11 am to 7 pm on Sunday.

**Orvis Company Store**
377 Santana Row
San Jose CA
408-961-6450
orvis.com
This comprehensive outfitters store offers a wide array of sporting goods and services, clothing and accessories for all types of active lifestyles, quality products for home and pets, gifts and travel items, and much more. Well mannered dogs are welcome in the store; they must be leashed and under their owner's control at all times.

**Pet Club**
5625 Snell Avenue
San Jose CA
408-363-6068
petclubstores.com
In addition to warehouse pricing with no membership fees, this comprehensive pet supply store offers weekly specials, and more than 11,000 pet products ranging from wellness items, bedding, dinnerware, a wide choice of quality foods, treats, leashes, toys, apparel, travel supplies, and much more. Leashed, friendly dogs are always welcome in the store.

**Pet Food Express**
1787 E Capitol Expressway
San Jose CA
408-239-7777
One of the country's leading pet retailers, this comprehensive pet store offers a number of other stores, quality foods/treats, a wide variety of pet supplies, breed-specific items, pet care

products, apparel, health items, hound and human accessories, and much more. Some of the services they offer include working with local SPCAs and rescue groups helping tens of thousands of homeless pets find new homes (they do not sell animals as pets), providing low cost vaccination clinics, dog training classes, and self-service pet washes. All leashed, friendly pets are welcome.

**Pet Food Express**
5148 Stevens Creek Blvd
San Jose CA
408-247-0077
One of the country's leading pet retailers, this comprehensive pet store offers a number of other stores, quality foods/treats, a wide variety of pet supplies, breed-specific items, pet care products, apparel, health items, hound and human accessories, and much more. Some of the services they offer include working with local SPCAs and rescue groups helping tens of thousands of homeless pets find new homes (they do not sell animals as pets), providing low cost vaccination clinics, dog training classes, and self-service pet washes. All leashed, friendly pets are welcome.

**PetSmart Pet Store**
607 Coleman Ave
San Jose CA
408-920-0316
Your licensed and well-behaved leashed dog is allowed in the store.

**Petco Pet Store - San Jose - Meridian**
4698 Meridian Ave.
San Jose CA
408-269-2481
Your licensed and well-behaved leashed dog is allowed in the store.

**Petco Pet Store - San Jose - Saratoga**
500 El Paseo De Saratoga
San Jose CA
408-866-7387
Your licensed and well-behaved leashed dog is allowed in the

store.

**Petco Pet Store - San Jose - Tully**
1960 Tully Road
San Jose CA
408-532-9030
Your licensed and well-behaved leashed dog is allowed in the store.

**Petco Pet Store - San Jose-Blossom Hill**
886 Blossom Hill Rd
San Jose CA
408-365-5760
Your licensed and well-behaved leashed dog is allowed in the store.

**Summer Winds Nursery**
4606 Almaden Expy
San Jose CA
408-266-4440
summerwindsnursery.com
Summer Winds Nursery welcomes well-behaved, leashed dogs.

**The Tileshop**
480 E Brokaw Road
San Jose CA
408-436-8877
tile-shop.com/
This full service Tile specialty store welcomes leashed, friendly dogs in the store. They are open Monday to Friday from 8 am until 4:30 pm and on Saturday from 9 am until 5 pm.

**Tileshop**
480 E Brokaw Road
San Jose CA
408-436-8877
tile-shop.com/
Just some of the tile styles offered here include porcelain, ceramic, eco-friendly "Green", glass mosaics, metal decoratives, Italian, cross-cut wood, and stone. They are a full service shop with all the "trimmings" for any tile creations. Leashed, friendly dogs are welcome in the store.

**Urban Outfitters**
355 Santana Row, #1050
San Jose CA
408-244-3329
In addition to a large inventory

of indoor and outdoor apparel for men and women, this major department store also carries vintage wear, designer brands, and a variety of accessories for all types of active lifestyles. They also carry shoes, furnishings, home decor, cameras, electronics, novelty items and more. Leashed, well mannered dogs are allowed in the store.

**Willow Glen Ace Hardware**
2253 Lincoln Avenue
San Jose CA
408-267-0223
willowglenace.com/
This hardware store will allow well mannered, leashed dogs in the store, and they have been known to give out doggie treats too.

**Wilson Motor Sports**
1980 Kingman Avenue
San Jose CA
408-371-9199
Your well-behaved leashed dog is allowed inside this store. We are a dog-friendly environment and welcome all animal owners.

**Happy Go Lucky Dog Boutique**
2855 Stevens Creek Blvd., Suite.1066
Santa Clara CA
408-204-9339
happygoluckydogs.com/
This doggy boutique offers designer dog collars/leads, carriers, bedding, fun toys, hip doggie clothes, pet care items, travel gear, costumes, healthy snacks, and gift items for hounds and humans. Dogs must be leashed and under owners control.

**Petco Pet Store - Santa Clara**
2775 El Camino Real
Santa Clara CA
408-423-9110
Your licensed and well-behaved leashed dog is allowed in the store.

**PetSmart Pet Store**
770 E El Camino Real
Sunnyvale CA
408-773-0215

Your licensed and well-behaved leashed dog is allowed in the store.

## Petco Pet Store - Sunnyvale
160 East El Camino Real
Sunnyvale CA
408-774-0171
Your licensed and well-behaved leashed dog is allowed in the store.

## Off-Leash Dog Parks
### Los Gatos Creek County Dog Park
1250 Dell Avenue
Campbell CA
408-866-2105
The dog park offers separate fenced off-leash areas for large and small dogs. Water for dogs, benches for people, and pooper scoopers are at the park. The dog park is located in Los Gatos Creek Park. If you park at the Dell Avenue parking area to access the park there is a $5 parking fee. Alternatively, you can walk in from Dell Avenue or by a pedestrian bridge over the 17 freeway. The location of the dog park is between the ponds and San Tomas Expressway, just east of 17.

### Dog Park at Ed Levin
3100 Calveras Blvd.
Milpitas CA
408-262-6980
This dog park has separate sections for small and large dogs. The dog park is run by the City of Milpitas, but it is located at Ed Levin County Park. The dog park is located off Calaveras Blvd. Turn onto Downing Road and head toward Sandy Wool Lake. Go uphill by the lake until you come to the dog park.

### Humane Society Silicon Valley

901 Ames Avenue
Milpitas CA
408-262-2133 x164
This regularly maintained member's only dog park offers separate play areas for large and small dogs, play pools,

fresh drinking water for pooches, multiple double entry gates, and exclusive doggy events; clean-up stations and covered seating are coming soon. Dogs must be sociable, current on all vaccinations and license, and under their owner's control at all times. Dogs must be leashed when not in designated off-lead areas.

### Delmas Dog Park
Park Avenue and Delmas Avenue
San Jose CA
408-535-3570
Delmas Dog Park opened in February, 2006. It is completely fenced and nearly 1/2 an acre in size. The dog park is a joint venture between the City of San Jose and the Santa Clara Valley Transportation Authority. The dog park is located just under Highway 87 one block south of San Carlos Street on Dalmas Avenue just south of downtown.

### Fontana Dog Park
Golden Oak Way at Castello Drive
San Jose CA
408-535-3570
Fontana Dog Park is a fenced dog park with two sections. It is closed on Tuesdays and some Fridays for maintainence. There are benches and bags provided to clean up after your dog.

### Hellyer Park/Dog Run
Hellyer Ave
San Jose CA
408-225-0225
This two acre dog park has a nice lawn and is completely fenced. It is closed Wednesdays for maintenance. The dog park is located at the northeast end of Hellyer Park, near the Shadowbluff group area. There is a minimal fee for parking. To get there, take Hwy 101 to Hellyer Ave. Exit and head west on Hellyer. Continue straight, pay at the booth and drive to the parking lot where the dog park is located.

### Miyuki Dog Park
Santa Teresa Boulevard
San Jose CA
408-277-4573
This dog park is almost one half acre. There is a rack where dog owners can leave spare toys for other pups to use. All dogs that use this off-leash park must wear a current dog license and proof of the rabies vaccine. The park is open from sunrise to one hour after sunset.

### Roy M. Butcher Dog Park
Camden Avenue at Lancaster Drive
San Jose CA
408-277-2757
This entirely fenced and double gated off-leash dog park has benches, grass and water fountains for dogs. There is a separate area for small dogs as well.

### Ryland Dog Park
First Street at Bassett Street
San Jose CA
408-535-3570
This dog park is located in Ryland Park which is a few blocks north of Julian Street on North First Street. The dog park is on the west side of Ryland Park and is under the Coleman Avenue overpass. This gives it shade and protection from rain. It has a gravel surface.

### Saratoga Creek Dog Park
Graves Avenue
San Jose CA
650-499-6387
There is a fenced off leash area at the west end of the Saratoga Creek Park where Graves Avenue dead-ends at the Lawrence Expressway. It includes a drinking fountain, artificial turf, benches, and trees. The park is open daily from dawn to dusk. Dogs must be healthy, sociable, current on all vaccinations and license with tags on collar, and under their owner's control at all times. Owners must clean up after their pets, and keep them leashed when not in designated off-lead areas.

**Watson Park Dog Park**
Jackson Avenue & 22nd St
San Jose CA

Watson Park in East San Jose has a fenced off-leash dog park. There are two separate fenced areas, one for larger dogs and one for smaller dogs. There are benches at the dog park for people to sit on. Some of the rules are that a person may only bring up to 2 dogs to the park at a time and dogs must have licenses and legal vaccinations.

**Raymond G. Gamma Dog Park**

888 Reed Street
Santa Clara CA
408-615-3140
Thanks to one of our readers for letting us know about this new dog park which replaces the Brookdale Dog Park which is now closed. The Reed Street Dog Park is 1 1/2 acres in size and has two separate fenced areas for larger and smaller dogs. The park is open during daylight hours except that it is closed on Thursdays for maintenance. The dog park is located about 4 blocks north of El Camino Real on Lafayette at Reed.

**Santa Clara Dog Park**
3450 Brookdale Drive
Santa Clara CA
408-615-3144
The Raymond G. Gamma Dog Park was originally located on Lochnivar Ave. but has moved to a new location at 3450 Brookdale Drive right across the park from the original location. This park is completely fenced. Weekday hours are from 7am to a 1/2 hour after sunset and weekend hours are from 9am to a 1/2 hour after sunset.

**Las Palmas Park - Dog Park**
850 Russett Drive
Sunnyvale CA
408-730-7506
After your pup finishes playing with other dogs at this dog park, you can both relax by the pond at one of the many picnic tables.

It's located at 850 Russett Drive (by Remington Avenue and Saratoga-Sunnyvale Rd).

# Dog-Friendly Parks
**Los Gatos Creek Park**
Dell Avenue
Campbell CA
408-356-2729
This 80 acre park has a small lake, a couple of ponds, picnic benches, barbecues and restroom facilities. The Campbell-Los Gatos Creek Trail runs through the park which goes to the Los Gatos Vasona Park and downtown Los Gatos. Leashed dogs are welcome at this park and on the Creek Trail.

**Los Gatos Creek Trail**
various-see comments
Campbell CA
408-356-2729
The Los Gatos Creek Trail is about 7 miles long each way. Most of it is paved until you enter the path at downtown Los Gatos heading towards the Lexington Reservoir County Park. You can gain access to the trail at numerous points. Some of the popular starting sites are at the Campbell Park in Campbell (Campbell Ave & Gilman Ave), Los Gatos Park in Campbell (Dell Ave & Hacienda Ave), Vasona Lake Park in Los Gatos (Blossom Hill Rd between Highway 17 & University Ave), and downtown Los Gatos (Main Street & Maple Ln-near Hwy 17).

**Fremont Older Preserve**
Prospect Road
Cupertino CA
650-691-1200
This preserve offers excellent views of the Santa Clara Valley. There are about 9 miles of trails. Dogs must be leashed. One of the popular hikes starts at Prospect Road, goes to Hunter's Point and then continues to Seven Springs Loop. On a hot day, you may want to bring some water with you. Here are directions to the

park: From Hwy 280, take DeAnza Blvd south towards Saratoga. After crossing Hwy 85, you will soon come to Prospect Road. Turn right onto Prospect. Go about 1.5 miles on Prospect. Before Prospect Road ends, turn left onto a one lane road (should be signs to Fremont Older). There is parking for approximately 15 cars.

**Lexington Reservoir Trail**
University Avenue
Los Gatos CA
408-356-2729
This is a popular hike with about 5-7 miles of trails. There is a nice combination of fire roads and single track trails with streams. A loop trail begins at University Ave (by Hwy 17). The fire road trail parallels Hwy 17 for a while until you reach the Lexington Reservoir. Across the street from the parking lot (the one w/the portable restrooms) by the Reservoir, the trail continues. You'll hike uphill to the top and then back towards the bottom where you started. There are several forks in the trail. Always stay to the left and you'll be back where you started.

**Vasona Lake Park**
Blossom Hill Rd
Los Gatos CA
408-356-2729
Your dog is welcome at this 151 acre park. This is a very popular park during the summer because of the nice lake, green landscape, walking trails and picnic tables. There are six miles of paved trails that wind through the park. The paved trails join the Los Gatos Creek Park to the south and the Los Gatos Creek Trail to the north. In the summer, there is usually a hot dog stand by the childen's playground. Your pup can also get his or her paws wet in the lake. The easiest spot is near the playground. The park is located on Blossom Hill Road between University Ave and Hwy 17 (no Hwy exit here). From southbound Hwy 17, take

the Saratoga-Los Gatos (Hwy 9) exit and head east/right. At University Avenue, turn right. Turn right again at Blossom Hill and the park will be on the left. There is a fee for parking.

## Dixon Landing Park
Milmont Drive
Milpitas CA

Dixon Landing Park is a relatively small park, but has much to offer. There are numerous picnic tables, a children's playground, tennis courts and a basketball court. You can grab food to go at one of the restaurants near Dixon Landing Rd and Milmont Drive, then bring it back to enjoy at the picnic tables. This park is a few blocks away (heading west) from the Levee Path. To get there from Hwy 880 heading north, exit Dixon Landing Rd. At the light, turn left then make a right onto Dixon Landing Rd. Turn right onto Milmont Dr/California Circle. The park will be on the right.

## Ed Levin County Park
3100 Calveras Blvd.
Milpitas CA
408-262-6980
Dogs are allowed on the Bay Area Ridge Trail from Sandy Wool Lake to Mission Peak. They are not allowed on any other trails in the park. Dogs must be leashed, except when in the off-leash dog park.

## Anderson Lake/Park
Cochrane Rd.
Morgan Hill CA
408-779-3634
The 2,365 acre Anderson Lake/Park also features the Coyote Creek Parkway's multiple use trails. Dogs on a 6 foot leash are allowed. Anderson Lake and the picnic areas along the Coyote Creek are located off of Cochrane Road in Morgan Hill, east of Highway 101.

## Almaden Quicksilver
McAbee Ave.
San Jose CA

408-268-8220
This park encompasses over 3900 acres. Dogs are allowed on a 6 foot leash. During early spring the park offers a wildflower display. Remnants of the mining era also offer a look at the mining operations of the 1800's. The park may be accessed from two areas. The Mockingbird Hill entrance is accessed off Mockingbird Hill Lane. This entrance is accessible to pedestrians and equestrians only. From Highway 85, take the Almaden Expressway exit south 4.5 miles to Almaden Road. Proceed .5 miles on Almaden Road to Mockingbird Hill Lane, turn right and continue .4 miles to the parking entrance is accessible to all users, including bicyclists. From Almaden Expressway, proceed 3 miles along Almaden Road through the town of New Almaden to the unpaved staging area on the right.

## Coyote Creek Parkway
various-see comments
San Jose CA
408-225-0225
The Coyote Creek Trail is approximately 13 miles each way. The north end is paved and popular with bicyclists, rollerbladers and hikers. The sound end (south of Metcalf Rd) has an equestrian dirt trail that parallels the paved trail. Leashed dogs are allowed on both the paved and dirt trails. You can gain access to the trail at numerous points. The south trail access has parking off Burnett Ave. From Hwy 101 South, exit Cochrane Rd. Turn right on Cochrane. Then turn right on Monterey Hwy (Hwy 82). Right on Burnett Ave and the parking will be at the end of Burnett. The north trail access has parking at Hellyer Park. From Hwy 101, exit Hellyer Ave and head west. Continue straight, pay at the booth and then park. There is also parking at Silver Creek Valley Blvd for north trail access. Take Hwy 101 and exit Silver Creek

Valley Blvd. Head east (toward the hills). Parking will be on the right.

## Guadalupe River Park & Gardens
715 Spring Street
San Jose CA
408-298-7657
grpg.org/river-park-gardens/
The river park is a 3-mile section of land that runs along the banks of the Guadalupe River in the heart of downtown, and adjacent to the park are the gardens, together providing 150 acres open to the public. The Heritage Rose Garden has over 3,700 varieties of roses, and has been further developed to include 2.6 miles of trails, over 15,000 trees, 9,000 shrubs, and 60,000 ground cover plants, and is also beneficial in providing the town with 100 year flood protection. Dogs of all sizes are welcome. Dogs must be on lead at all times, cleaned up after, and all must stay on the paths.

## Santa Teresa County Park
San Vicente Avenue
San Jose CA
408-268-3883
Dogs are allowed on a 6 foot leash. This diverse 1,688 acre park, located ten miles south of downtown San Jose, is rich in history and offers spectacular views from its trails located above the Almaden and Santa Clara Valleys. The secluded upland valleys of the park provide a quiet place for exploring the natural environment minutes away from the surrounding developed areas. From San Jose, follow Almaden Expressway until it ends. Turn right onto Harry Road, then turn left onto McKean Road. Travel approximately 1.3 miles to Fortini Road. Turn left onto Fortini Road toward the Santa Teresa Hills. At the end of Fortini Road, turn left onto San Vicente Avenue. A ten car parking area is located on the right about 500 feet from Fortini Road.

## Events

**Bark in the Park**
William and South 16th Streets
San Jose CA
408-793-5125
barksanjose.org/
This huge annual September fundraising event at William Street Park is sponsored by the Naglee Park neighborhood's Campus Community Association in central San Jose. Thousands of people and dogs attend this event, which may be the largest pet event in the west each year. A $5 donation per registered dog is requested. Festivities include doggy demonstrations, contests, performances, live music, specialty and food vendors, and much more. Dogs must be leashed and cleaned up after at all times.

## Airports

**San Jose International Airport (SJC)**

San Jose CA
Outside, North of Ticketing Area

## Day Kennels

**PetsHotel by PetsMart Day Kennel**
607 Coleman Ave.
San Jose CA
408-920-0472
petsmart.com/PETsHOTEL/
This PetSmart pet store offers day camp only. You can drop off and pick up your dog between the hours of 7 am - 7 pm, M-S, Sunday 9 am - 5 pm. Dogs are required to have proof of current rabies, DPP and bordatella vaccinations.

**PetsHotel by PetsMart Day Kennel**
770 Camino Real
Sunnyvale CA
408-773-0215
petsmart.com/PETsHOTEL/
This PetSmart pet store offers day camp only. You may drop off and pick up your dog during the hours the store is open seven days a week. Dogs must have proof of current rabies, DPP and Bordatella vaccinations.

## Emergency Veterinarians

**United Emergency Animal Clinic**
911 Dell Avenue
Campbell CA
408-371-6252
emergencyanimalclinic.com
Monday - Friday 6 pm to 8 am, 24 hours on weekends.

**Emergency Animal Clinic**
5440 Thornwood Dr.
San Jose CA
408-578-5622
Monday - Friday 6 pm to 8 am, 24 hours on weekends.

## Rescue Organizations

**GPA-NORCAL/Greyhound Adoption California**
1582 Wright Avenue
Sunnyvale CA
408-749-0899
greyhoundadoptioncalifornia.com
We rescue retired racing Greyhounds from the track and find good homes for them. Our Greyhounds are spayed/neutered, teeth cleaned, given a complete vet check, shots and blood work. They are then placed in foster homes for a minimum of two weeks to socialize them. After going through our adoption process, we then match the appropriate Greyhound to the adopter.

## Service Dog Organizations

**Lincoln Hound Society**
1346 The Alameda, Suite 7-306
San Jose CA
(408) 244-2535
Lincoln Hound Society is a group of conscientious dog owners who are seeking to promote responsible dog ownership, community involvement and the formation of city sanctified Dog Parks within the City of San Jose, the County of Santa Clara, California and surrounding areas.

## Other Organizations

**Friends o fthe Silicon Valley Animal Control Authority**
PO Box 132
Santa Clara CA
408-423-8600
friendsofsvaca.org
Our mission is to raise funds for the Silicon Valley Animal Control Authority (SVACA), increase awareness of its programs and services, and to work to reduce the companion animal overpopulation problem. Our goal is to ensure the well-being of animals through education, outreach, and fund raising. We also aim to establish programs which will support SVACA and benefit the animals in its care.We are a nonprofit 501(c)3 formed in 2008. We have no paid officers or staff and are a completely volunteer organization. We have 5 volunteer Board Members; Caryn Linn - President, Eva Schmitz - Treasurer, Reina Remigio - Secretary, Jamie-Sue West - Member at Large. We also have a few volunteers that help us in a variety of ways. Our vision is to help SVACA find loving families for every adoptable companion animal, assist with financial support for ill and injured animals, and work to reduce the companion animal overpopulation problem in our area.

## San Juan Bautista

## Outdoor Restaurants
**JJ's Homemade Burgers**

100 The Alameda
San Juan Bautista CA
831-623-1748
This restaurant offers a variety
of hamburgers and all the
fixings. They offer outside dining
service, and your pet is
welcome to join you. Dogs must
be attended to at all times, well
behaved, and leashed.

## San Luis Obispo

## Dog-Friendly Hotels
### Best Western Casa Grande Inn
850 Oak Park Boulevard
Arroyo Grande CA
805-481-7398 (800-780-7234)
Dogs up to 80 pounds are
allowed. There is a $20 per day
pet fee up to $100 for the week.
Up to two dogs are allowed per
room.

### Cayucos Beach Inn
333 South Ocean Avenue
Cayucos CA
805-995-2828
Located just one block from the
beach Cayucos Beach Inn offers
convenience and location for our
guests. This 36-room motel on
two exterior-access floors
provides free Wi-Fi in all rooms
along with cable TVs
microwaves and refrigerators.
Non-smoking rooms can be
requested. There are business
services such as fax and copy
facilities for the road warrior and
there's even an on-site laundry
facility to keep you looking
sharp. Outside barbecue
facilities come in handy. Parking
is free and pets are welcome
with some restrictions. Cayucos
Beach Inn is one block from
Cayucos State Beach and two
miles from Estero Bluffs. Morro
Bay is 10 minutes away. The
Hearst Castle is 45 minutes
from the motel. The state
Elephant Seal Rookery is 30
minutes. Piedras Blancas Light
Station is 40 minutes and the
San Luis Obispo Regional

Airport is 23 miles southeast.

### Shoreline Inn...on The Beach
1 North Ocean Avenue
Cayucos CA
805-995-3681 (800-549-2244)
centralcoast.com/shorelineinn
Located on the beach this hotel
offers a daily continental
breakfast and afternoon
biscuits. Rooms include cable
TV. Hearst Castle is 40
minutes drive away.
A small fridge and coffee-
making facilities are included in
all rooms at Shoreline Innâ?¦
on the beach. Most rooms
feature sweeping ocean views
and either offer a private patio
or a balcony.
Picnic and barbecue areas are
available at the Shoreline Inn.
A beach shower is also on site.
Guests can use the in-lobby
internet station at their
convenience.
Big Sur is 1 hours drive from
the hotel. Various local
wineries are within 20 miles of
the property.

### The Dolphin Inn
399 South Ocean Avenue
Cayucos CA
805-995-3810
A half-mile from Cayucos State
Beach the Dolphin Inn provides
rooms with full kitchens and a
laid-back atmosphere for a
good price. This 19-room
ground-level motel offers
rooms with Wi-Fi microwaves
refrigerators dining areas cable
TV with HBO and jetted
bathtubs. Non-smoking units
can be requested. The motel
serves a continental breakfast
each morning and there's an
on-site fitness room and
laundry facility. Parking is free
and pets are welcome with
certain restrictions. The
Dolphin Inn is five minutes from
Cayucos State Beach. San
Simeon home of the Hearst
Castle is 45 minutes away.
Piedras Blancas Light Station
is 40 minutes and the Central
California Elephant Seal
Rookery is 30 minutes from the
motel. Morro Bay State Park is
15 minutes away. The San Luis

Obispo airport is 23 miles
southeast.

### Bayfront Inn
1150 Embarcadero
Morro Bay CA
805-772-5607
bayfront-inn.com
Splendid views of Morro Rock
and Estero Bay come with
complimentary internet and free
breakfast at the budget-friendly
non-smoking Bayfront Inn. The
Bayfront Inn's 16 rooms are
housed on two floors and
feature free Wi-Fi cable TV with
HBO mini-fridges and
coffeemakers. Each morning
guests are treated to a
complimentary continental
breakfast that includes oatmeal
and waffles. The on-site
restaurant is also open for
lunch. Business services such
as faxing and copying are
available. Parking is free and
pets are welcome with some
restrictions. The entire property
is non-smoking. The Bayfront
Inn is next to the harbor and
embarcadero at Morro Bay.
Morro Estuary Nature Preserve
an 800-acre wetland
showcasing the natural wonders
of this area is a mile from the
inn. You'll find golf and tennis
within two miles of the property
and bicycles can be rented
nearby. McChesney Field
Airport in San Luis Obispo is 17
miles away.

### Harbor House Inn
1095 Main Street
Morro Bay CA
805-772-2711 (800-329-7466)
Dogs of all sizes are allowed.
Dogs are allowed for a nightly
pet fee.

### Morro Bay Sandpiper Inn
540 Main Street
Morro Bay CA
805-772-7503 (877-424-6423)
Morro Bay's best kept secret!
Spectacular views! Beach,
shops, restaurants, fishing and
kayaking 2 blocks.

Dogs up to 60 pounds are
allowed. Dogs are allowed for a
pet fee of $25.00 per pet per

night. Two dogs are allowed per room.

## Pleasant Inn
235 Harbor Street
Morro Bay CA
805-772-8521
pleasantinnmotel.com/
Located 3.2 km from Morro Bay State Park and a golf course Pleasant Inn features free WiFi. Sub Sea Tours and Kayaks is 5 minutes walk away.
Each room offers a flat-screen TV with cable and premium movie channels. Quality coastal theme furnishings are featured throughout. A seating area microwave and a refrigerator are included in all guest rooms. Cal Poly and San Luis Obsipo are 15 minutes' drive away. Sea Pines Golf Resort is 15 minutes drive away. Wine country Hearst Castle and Piedras Blancas Elephant Seal Rookery are within 34 miles of Pleasant Inn.

## Bestway Inn
2701 Spring Street
Paso Robles CA

An outdoor pool plus freebies such as breakfast parking and high-speed internet access welcome our guests at Paso Robles Travelodge. This low-rise property houses 31 spacious rooms with coffeemakers satellite TVs with premium cable channels mini-fridges and free high-speed internet access. Breakfast is free at this hotel and includes a continental spread of bagels pastries cereal oatmeal fresh fruit coffee and juice each morning. Guests may sunbathe and swim in the large outdoor pool. Vending machines and picnic areas are on-site for further convenience. Parking including space for trucks and RVs is complimentary. Pets are welcome for an additional fee. Paso Robles Travelodge is one mile west of US-101 at 24th Street about three miles from downtown Paso Robles. The hotel is one mile north of Paso Robles Event Center and Pioneer Museum. Several local

wineries and Ravine Water Park are all within a 10-minute drive. Hearst Castle is one hour away. Paso Robles Airport is five miles.

## Holiday Inn Express Hotel & Suites - Paso Robles
2455 Riverside Avenue
Paso Robles CA
805-238-6500 (877-270-6405)
Dogs of all sizes are allowed. Dogs are allowed for a pet fee of $35.00 per pet per night.

## La Quinta Inn & Suites Paso Robles
2615 Buena Vista Drive
Paso Robles CA
805-239-3004 (800-531-5900)
Dogs of all sizes are allowed for no additional pet fee. Dogs may only be left alone in the room if they can be quiet, and they must be crated when alone unless they are well trained.

## Oxford Suites Pismo Beach
651 Five Cities Drive
Pismo Beach CA
805-773-3773 (800-982-SUITE)
oxfordsuites.com
Ideally located in the Pismo Marsh area Oxford Suites Pismo Beach promises a relaxing and wonderful visit. The property offers a high standard of service and amenities to suit the individual needs of all travelers. Service-minded staff will welcome and guide you at Oxford Suites Pismo Beach. Comfortable guestrooms ensure a good night's sleep with some rooms featuring facilities such as air conditioning heating balcony/terrace alarm clock telephone. The property offers various recreational opportunities. A welcoming atmosphere and excellent service are what you can expect during your stay at Oxford Suites Pismo Beach.

## Best Western Plus Royal Oak Hotel
214 Madonna Road
San Luis Obispo CA

805-544-4410 (800-780-7234)
Dogs up to 80 pounds are allowed. There is a $15 per day pet fee up to $100 for the week. Up to two dogs are allowed per room.

## Sands Inn & Suites
1930 Monterey Street
San Luis Obispo CA
805-544-0500 (800-441-4657)
sandssuites.com/
Hot breakfast free Wi-Fi an outdoor pool and the Cal Poly campus less than a mile away make Sands Inn & Suites a sweet spot for our guests who also appreciate the location near U.S.-101 and downtown San Luis Obispo. The Sands Inn has 70 rooms in a two-story building with exterior corridors and no elevator. Rooms feature coffeemakers microwaves mini-fridges free Wi-Fi cable TV and DVD players. Non-smoking rooms are available. Start your day at the Sands with the breakfast with a rotating menu of eggs potatoes fresh waffles cereal coffee juice and more. The hotel also has an outdoor heated pool hot tub laundry facility lobby computer free parking and collection of watches and famous guns from the Wild West. Pets are allowed (fee). The Sands Inn is just off U.S.-101 less than a mile south of California Polytechnic State University. The San Luis Obispo downtown core and Old Mission San Luis Obispo de Tolosa are about one mile southwest. The ocean is about 10 miles southwest. If you're driving from San Luis Obispo County Regional Airport the hotel is four miles north.

## Super 8 Motel - San Luis Obispo
1951 Monterey Street
San Luis Obispo CA
805-544-6888 (800-800-8000)
Dogs of all sizes are allowed. Dogs are allowed for a pet fee.

## Vagabond Inn San Luis Obispo
210 Madonna Road
San Luis Obispo CA

805-544-4710 (800-522-1555)
Free breakfast on-the-house Wi-Fi and a heated outdoor pool all make for a pleasant stay at the Vagabond Inn San Luis Obispo. At the two-story Vagabond Inn all 61 rooms feature coffeemakers cable TV with premium channels free Wi-Fi microwaves and refrigerators. Start the day with a complimentary continental breakfast accompanied by a free newspaper. Swim year-round in the heated pool and hot tub. There's a Denny's restaurant on site. Located just off US-101 the Vagabond Inn is less than three miles from downtown San Luis Obispo and California Polytechnic State University. The Pacific Ocean is 10 miles away. Avila Beach Pismo Beach and Morro Bay are all a 20-minute drive. Five miles away you'll find Tolosa Solar Sustainable Central Coast Winery. San Luis Obispo County Airport is less than five miles from the hotel. Santa Barbara Municipal Airport is an hour-and-45-minute drive.

**Cavalier Oceanfront Resort**
9415 Hearst Dr.
San Simeon CA
805-927-4688
Dogs up to 80 pounds are allowed. Up to two dogs are allowed per room.

# Accommodations

TOP 200 PLACE **Cambria Shores Inn**
6276 Moonstone Beach Drive
Cambria CA
805-927-8644 (800-433-9179)
cambriashores.com
Dogs are allowed for a $10.00 per night per dog fee. Pets must be leashed and never left alone. The inn offers local pet sitting services and provide treats for dogs.

**La Serena Inn**
990 Morro Ave
Morro Bay CA
805-772-5665 (800-248-1511)

laserenainn.com
Up to 3 dogs are allowed. There is a $25 nightly pet fee for one pet and $15 for each additional pet.

# Dog-Friendly Attractions
**Lake Lopez Boat Rentals**
6820 Lopez Drive
Arroyo Grande CA
805-489-1006
Rent a motor boat or pontoon boat on Lake Lopez and take your dog along with you. Boat rentals start at about $35 for 2 hours and there is a $10 one time per rental pet fee. The rentals are available year-round.

**Canterbury Tails Dog Resort**
6970 Benton Rd
Paso Robles CA
805-467-0021
canterburytailsdogresort.com
Canterbury Tails Dog Resort is located minutes from the historic downtown Paso Robles, California. They advertise having spacious temperature controlled suites, large patio and custom bed's with real mattresses and fresh linens for their canine guests, and separate play yards for small dogs and large play yards for high energy dogs.

**Paso Robles Pet Boarding**
2940 Union Rd
Paso Robles CA
805-238-4340
pasoroblespetboarding.com
The staff of Paso Robles Pet Boarding pledges to "care for your pooch as we do our own, and make it a habit to give lots of pats, hugs and ear scratches to our guest." They offer a variety of services, including dog walking, dog socialization (two yards for socialization with other pooches), anesthesia free teeth cleaning, dog bathing, and lots more.

**San Luis Obispo Botanical Garden**
Post Office Box 4957
San Luis Obispo CA

805-546-3501
slobg.org/
This dog-friendly botanical garden is devoted to the display and study of the plants and ecosystems of the five Mediterranean-climate zones of the world: parts of California, Chile, Australia, South Africa and the countries surrounding the Mediterranean Sea. Dogs on leash are allowed. Please pick up after them. The garden is located on Highway 1 in El Chorro Regional Park, between San Luis Obispo and Morro Bay. The garden is open during daylight hours and admission is free. On the weekends, there is a dog fee for entering the regional park. There is also an off leash area for your dog to run, just up the street from the garden.

# Outdoor Restaurants
**Baja Fresh Mexican Grill**
929 Rancho Pkwy
Arroyo Grande CA
805-474-8900
bajafresh.com
This Mexican restaurant is open for lunch and dinner. They use fresh ingredients and making their salsa and beans daily. Some of the items on their menu include Enchiladas, Burritos, Tacos Salads, Quesadillas, Nachos, Chicken, Steak and more. Well-behaved leashed dogs are allowed at the outdoor tables.

**Jamba Juice**
926 Rancho Parkway
Arroyo Grande CA
805-481-8930
jambajuice.com
All natural and organic ingredients, no high-fructose corn syrup, 0 grams trans fat, no artificial preservatives, a healthy helping of antioxidants, vitamins, and minerals, and fresh whole fruit and fruit juices set the base for these tasty and healthy beverages. Their organic Hot Blends provides a new spin on coffee, green or chai tea, and hot chocolate;plus they offer

probiotic fruit and yogurt Blends. Additionally, they feature all natural salads, wraps, sandwiches, and grab n go specialties. They also offer healthy community support through fundraisers, special sales, and school lunch programs. Leashed, well mannered dogs are allowed at their outside dining area.

**Old Village Grill**
101 E. Branch St
Arroyo Grande CA
805-489-4915
This restaurant has several outdoor dog-friendly tables.

**Las Cambritas**
2336 Main Street
Cambria CA
805-927-0175
This eatery serves up a wide variety of Mexican cuisine, and also offers a nice outdoor patio dining area. Leashed, well mannered dogs are allowed at their outer tables.

**Madeline's**
788 Main St
Cambria CA
805-927-4175
madelinescambria.com/
This restaurant serves American/French influenced, gourmet style food. Leashed dogs are allowed at the outdoor tables. Reservations are required for the two patio tables outside.

**Dorn's Original Breakers Cafe**
801 Market Ave
Morro Bay CA
805-772-4415
dornscafe.com/
American cuisine with seafood a specialty, this restaurant and bar also serves up made-from-scratch desserts, signature cocktails, and deck dining with great views. Leashed, well mannered dogs are welcome at their outside tables.

**Big Bubba's barbecue**
1125 24th Street
Paso Robles CA
805-238-6272
Oak-wood fired barbecueing is

"king of the house" at this lively restaurant, but they also offer their signature savory flavors and a full menu of tasty choices. Leashed, well mannered dogs are welcome at their outside tables.

**Big Bubba's Bad barbecue**
1125 24th St
Paso Robles CA
805-238-6272
bigbubbasbadbbq.com
Big Bubba's Bad barbecue, located at 1125 24th St in Paso Robles serves oak-wood fired barbecue tri-tip, ribs, burgers and other barbecue specialties. The barbecue advertises to be the "home of the best Bad to the Bone barbecue you've ever tasted." Along with their barbecue, they have a vegetarian menu, which includes savory veggie burgers, super salads and avocado tacos. Well-behaved, leashed dogs are welcome at the outdoor seating.

**Chubby Chandler's**
1304 Railroad St.
Paso Robles CA
805-239-2141
chubbychandlerspizza.com/
You and your pup can order some pizza from the outdoor window and then enjoy it at one of their outdoor picnic tables.

**Good Ol' Burgers**
1145 24th St
Paso Robles CA
805-238-0655
goodolburgers.com
Famous for their sizzling, flame grilled hamburgers, Good Ol' Burgers also offers other popular menu items. There's the Good Ol' Burgers Garden Burger, Western Steak Sandwich, Corn Dog, or Spicy Chicken or Chicken Cobb wraps. There are also tater tots, salads, milkshakes, and lots more! Well-behaved, leashed dogs are allowed at the outdoor seating.

**Good Ol' Burgers**
1145 24th Street
Paso Robles CA

805-238-0655
goodolburgers.com/
Dogs are allowed at the outdoor tables on the grass and at the side of the building. Your pup will help you enjoy the burgers or the delicious steak sandwich. There is also a little tree house next to the tables for kids to enjoy.

**Jamba Juice**
96 Niblick Road
Paso Robles CA
805-227-0826
jambajuice.com
All natural and organic ingredients, no high-fructose corn syrup, 0 grams trans fat, no artificial preservatives, a healthy helping of antioxidants, vitamins, and minerals, and fresh whole fruit and fruit juices set the base for these tasty and healthy beverages. Their organic Hot Blends provides a new spin on coffee, green or chai tea, and hot chocolate;plus they offer probiotic fruit and yogurt Blends. Additionally, they feature all natural salads, wraps, sandwiches, and grab n go specialties. They also offer healthy community support through fundraisers, special sales, and school lunch programs. Leashed, well mannered dogs are allowed at their outside dining area.

**Odyssey World Café**
1214 Pine St
Paso Robles CA
805-237-7516
Odyssey World Café offers American favorites plus many interesting dishes from around the world. Their atmosphere is described as 'reminiscent of a European Café, Pub, Taverna or Trattoria'. The cafe is open 7 days a week from 11 am until 9:00 pm. Well-behaved, leashed dogs are allowed on the outdoor patio.

**Panolivo Family Bistro**
1344 Park Street
Paso Robles CA
805-239-3366
panolivo.com
Panolivo caters to locals and

wine country visitors looking for a fresh and tasty dining experience in a warm and inviting, casual atmosphere. Breakfast, lunch & dinner is served everyday, and Panolivo's in-house bakery offers desserts and French pastries, while the wine list features reasonably priced French and local wines. Well-behaved, leashed pooches are welcome at the outdoor seating.

**Pappy McGregor's Irish Pub**
1122 Pine Street
Paso Robles CA
805-238-7070
pappymcgregors.com
Sourcing their seafood, produce, meats and bread from local fishermen, farmers, ranchers and bakers on the Central Coast, Pappy McGregor's Irish Pub offers gastro-pub dining in a traditional and relaxed Irish pub atmosphere. Well-behaved, leashed dogs are allowed at the outdoor seating.

**Thomas Hill Organics Bistro & Wine Lounge**
1305 Park St
Paso Robles CA
805-226-5888
thomashillorganics.com
The Thomas Hill Organics Bistro & Wine Lounge staff believe in the significance of organic, regionally-produced food, and work with local purveyors for their poultry, fish and grass-fed beef, lamb and exotic meats, while local farmers grow all their fruits & vegetables. They serve brunch, lunch, and dinner Sunday through Monday. Well-behaved, leashed dogs are allowed on the outdoor patio.

**Mo's Smokehouse barbecue**
221 Pomeroy Ave
Pismo Beach CA
805-773-6193
smokinmosbbq.com/
Authentic hickory barbecue is the specialty at this smokehouse. Leashed, well mannered dogs are welcome at their outside tables.

**Seaside Cafe and Bakery**

1327 Shell Beach Road
Pismo Beach CA
805-773-4360
This cafe offers freshly made foods, daily made bakery items, and outside dining. Leashed, well mannered dogs are allowed at their outside tables.

**The Coffee Bean & Tea Leaf**
354 Five Cities Drive
Pismo Beach CA
805-773-6420
coffeebean.com
The coffee here is sourced globally from family coffee farms to procure only the top of 1% of Arabica beans. They offer 30+ varieties of coffee;the beans are roasted in small batches daily for freshness, and they also offer 20 varieties of teas that are hand-blended by their tea master. Additionally, they offer a variety of tasty sweets, powders, extracts, sauces, gifts, and cards. Leashed, well mannered dogs are allowed at their outside dining area.

**Baja Fresh Mexican Grill**
1085 Higuera Street
San Luis Obispo CA
805-544-5450
bajafresh.com
This Mexican restaurant is open for lunch and dinner. They use fresh ingredients and making their salsa and beans daily. Some of the items on their menu include Enchiladas, Burritos, Tacos Salads, Quesadillas, Nachos, Chicken, Steak and more. Well-behaved leashed dogs are allowed at the outdoor tables.

**Jamba Juice**
890 Marsh Street
San Luis Obispo CA
805-549-0733
jambajuice.com
All natural and organic ingredients, no high-fructose corn syrup, 0 grams trans fat, no artificial preservatives, a healthy helping of antioxidants, vitamins, and minerals, and fresh whole fruit and fruit juices set the base for these tasty and

healthy beverages. Their organic Hot Blends provides a new spin on coffee, green or chai tea, and hot chocolate;plus they offer probiotic fruit and yogurt Blends. Additionally, they feature all natural salads, wraps, sandwiches, and grab n go specialties. They also offer healthy community support through fundraisers, special sales, and school lunch programs. Leashed, well mannered dogs are allowed at their outside dining area.

**Novo Restaurant**
726 Higuera Street
San Luis Obispo CA
805-543-3986
novorestaurant.com
This restaurant in downtown San Luis Obispo offers creekside dining on its patio. Well-behaved, leashed dogs are allowed on the outside patio. The restaurant serves Brazilian, Mediterranean and Asian foods.

**Splash Cafe**
1491 Monterey Street
San Luis Obispo CA
805-544-7567
splashbakery.com/
Featuring daily hand-crafted specials, fresh baked goods, designer chocolates, and a bright, cheerful environment, this eatery offers indoor or outdoor dining options. Your well behaved dog is welcome to join you at the outer tables. Dogs must be well mannered and leashed.

**San Simeon Restaurant**
9520 Castillo Dr.
San Simeon CA
805-927-4604
sansimeonrestaurant.com/
Dogs are allowed at the outdoor tables at this restaurant.

**Zorro's Cafe and Cantina**
927 Shell Beach Road
Shell Beach CA
805-773-ZORO (9676)
This Mexican café also offers a shady patio for outside dining. Dogs are allowed at the outer tables;they must be under their owner's control at all times.

## Pet-Friendly Shopping Centers

### Cambria Historic Downtown
1880-2580 Main Street
Cambria CA

Cambria was settled in the early 1860s. In the 1880s it was the second largest town in the county, with an active center of shipping, mining, dairy farming, logging, and ranching. The isolation of Cambria occurred in 1894, when railroad lines were extended into San Luis Obispo from the south, resulting in the decline of coastal shipping. The town's main industry today is tourism. Cambria's Historic Downtown includes 22 historic sites which can be viewed on a self-guided walking tour with your dog. A list of the historic sites can be found at their website (http://new.cambria-online.com/historic/index.asp). There are a few outdoor cafes in downtown Cambria where you and your pup can grab some lunch or dinner.

### Pismo Beach Premium Outlets
333 Five Cities Drive, Suite 100
Pismo Beach CA
805-773-4661
Visitors will find some 40 designer and name brand stores and more at this outlet mall. Dogs are allowed in the common areas of the mall; it is up to individual stores whether they allow a dog inside. There is a Paw Print on businesses that welcome pets. Also be sure to take a stop at the welcome center in the eastern courtyard for doggie biscuits. Dogs must be well behaved, leashed, and under their owner's control at all times.

## Pet-Friendly Stores

### Reigning Cats and Dogs
816 Main Street, Suite B
Cambria CA

805-927-0857
thelittledoglaughed.com/
Located on the Central Coast of California, near San Luis Obispo, this store specializes in gifts, collectibles, and unique pet gifts and merchandise for both common and uncommon dog breeds. They are usually open seven days a week.

### Teresa Belle Gallery
766 Main Street (H 1)
Cambria CA
805-927-4556
teresabelle.com/
This store, only a few blocks from Moonstone Beach on California's Central Coast, features a unique collection of handmade jewelry and contemporary crafts. Dogs of all sizes are welcome to explore the shope with their owners, and their shop dog looks forward to visitors. Dogs must be well behaved and leashed. The store is open daily from 10 am to 6pm.

### Best Bike Zone
712 Paso Robles Street
Paso Robles CA
805-237-2453
bestbikezone.com
Best Bike Zone not only offers a selection of biking accessories & bikes, but they also rent out bikes for reasonable prices. Their bike mechanic is also on hand to quickly fix & repair your bike. Well-behaved, leashed dogs are welcome in the store.

### Firefly Gallery
839 12th St
Paso Robles CA
805-237-9265
Firefly is a unique store located in downtown Paso Robles, CA, where you'll find everything from clothing & jewelry, locally handmade furniture, candles & soaps, and more to household items. Well-behaved, leashed dogs are allowed in the store.

### Jayde Boutique
823 12th St
Paso Robles CA
8050238-3337

jaydeboutique.com
Located across from the park in historic downtown Paso Robles, California, Jayde is a boutique designed for women of any age and specializing in a warm and friendly atmosphere. A few of the many brands they carry include Jag, Worn, Tribal, Plastic, Mavi, Kersh, and Teezhers, also having one of the largest selections of Brighton in Paso Robles which includes, Brighton shoes, Brighton handbags, Brighton luggage, Brighton sunglasses, Brighton watches, Brighton home accessories, Brighton key fobs, Brighton wallets, and the Brighton Charms and jewelry. Well-behaved, leashed pooches are allowed in the store.

### Petco Pet Store - Paso Robles

2051 Theater Dr.
Paso Robles CA
805-238-5857
Your licensed and well-behaved leashed dog is allowed in the store.

### Petco Pet Store - San Luis Obispo
271 Madonna Road
San Luis Obispo CA
805-596-0836
Your licensed and well-behaved leashed dog is allowed in the store.

### Urban Outfitters
962 Monterey Street
San Luis Obispo CA
805-549-9402
In addition to a large inventory of indoor and outdoor apparel for men and women, this major department store also carries vintage wear, designer brands, and a variety of accessories for all types of active lifestyles. They also carry shoes, furnishings, home decor, cameras, electronics, novelty items and more. Leashed, well mannered dogs are allowed in the store.

### Vintage House Thrift
532 Higuera St
San Luis Obispo CA

805-593-0255
Vintage House Thrift sells
houseware, clothing (Men's,
Women's, and kids), shoes,
misc items, and more. Well-
behaved, leashed dogs are
allowed in the store.

## Dog-Friendly Wineries and Vineyards
### Changala Winery
3770 Willow Creek Road
Paso Robles CA
805-226-9060
changalawinery.com/
Changala features a variety of
fine quality red and white wines
from the appellation of
California's Central Coast. Dogs
are allowed on the grounds and
creek of the winery; they are not
allowed in the tasting room.
Dogs must be friendly with other
pets (on site), leashed, and
under their owner's control at all
times.

### Chumeia Vineyards
8331 H 46E
Paso Robles CA
805-226-0102
Guests are invited to experience
the "true joy of alchemy" at this
winery; they feature a variety of
fine wines, vintage wines, gift
and logo items, and ongoing
special events throughout the
year - including several
fundraising events for animals.
Pups will enjoy the large grassy
picnic area and playing with the
other on-site dogs and cats;
they must be friendly, leashed,
and under their owner's control
at all times.

### Tablas Creek Vineyard
9339 Adelaida Rd
Paso Robles CA
805-237-1231
tablascreek.com
Dogs are allowed on and off-
leash at the outdoor tables and
property. There are several
other dogs on the premises so
the dogs will have to be able to
get along. You must have your
dog under complete control. The
hours are 10am-5pm Monday-

Sunday.

## Dog-Friendly Beaches
### Cayucos State Beach
Cayucos Drive
Cayucos CA
805-781-5200
This state beach allows
leashed dogs. The beach is
located in the small town of
Cayucos. To get to the beach
from Hwy 1, exit Cayucos Drive
and head west. There is a
parking lot and parking along
the street.

### Oceano Dunes State Vehicular Recreation Area
Highway 1
Oceano CA
805-473-7220
This 3,600 acre off road area
offers 5 1/2 miles of beach
which is open for vehicle use.
Pets on leash are allowed too.
Swimming, surfing, horseback
riding and bird watching are all
popular activities at the beach.
The park is located three miles
south of Pismo Beach off
Highway 1.

### Lake Nacimento Resort Day Use Area
10625 Nacimiento Lake Drive
Paso Robles CA
805-238-3256
In addition to the campgrounds
and RV area, this resort also
offers day use of the lake.
Dogs can swim in the water,
but be very careful of boats, as
this is a popular lake for water-
skiing. Day use fees vary by
season and location, but in
general rates are about $5 to
$8 per person. Senior
discounts are available. Dogs
are an extra $5 per day. Proof
of your dog's rabies vaccination
is required.

### Pismo State Beach
Grand Ave.
Pismo Beach CA
805-489-2684
Leashed dogs are allowed on
this state beach. This beach is
popular for walking,
sunbathing, swimming and the

annual winter migration of
millions of monarch butterflies
(the park has the largest over-
wintering colony of monarch
butterflies in the U.S.). To get
there from Hwy 101, exit 4th
Street and head south. In about
a mile, turn right onto Grand
Ave. You can park along the
road.

### Coastal Access
off Hearst Drive
San Simeon CA

There is parking just north of the
Best Western Hotel, next to the
"Coastal Access" sign. Dogs
must be on leash.

## Off-Leash Dog Parks
### Elm Street Dog Park
380 Elm Street
Arroyo Grande CA

facebook.com/Elmstreetdogpark
/
The Elm Street Dog Park,
located in Arroyo Grande,
California, is open from 8am-
dusk. The park features
numerous benches as well as a
'staging' area, and fenced areas
for your dog. Dogs must be
collared, licensed, vaccinated
and parasite free. For a
complete list of rules and
policies, go here:
http://www.fivecitiesdogpark.org/
rules.php

### Heilmann Dog Park

Atascadero CA

heilmanndogpark.com/
The Heilmann Dog Park is
almost one acre in size, fenced,
and has restrooms for people.
From Highway 101 take the
Santa Rosa Avenue exit east,
turn right (south) on El Camino
Real, and left (east) on El Bordo
Avenue.

### Cambria Dog Park
Main Street and Santa Rosa
Creek Rd
Cambria CA

The fenced Cambria Dog Park is located south of the town center on Main Street. From Highway 1 North or South take Main Street to the dog park.

**Jodi Giannini Family Dog Park at Del Mar Park**
Ironwood Avenue
Morro Bay CA

There is lots of green space, shade trees, and sections for small and large dogs are this off leash play area. As this is a new park, upgrades are planned. Dogs must be healthy, sociable, current on all vaccinations and license with tags on collar, and under their owner's control at all times. Dogs must be leashed when not in designated off-lead areas.

**Sherwood Dog Park of Paso Robles**
290 Scott Street
Paso Robles CA
805-239-9326
facebook.com/SherwoodDogPark/
Sherwood Dog Park opened in April 2012 due to the efforts of a hard-working group of volunteers and local businesses, and is 1.25 acres in size, cross fenced for separate big dog and small dog play areas. The park is open from sunrise to sunset. For complete list of park rules, visit http://www.parks4pups.org/sites/default/files/imce_image_uploads/SDPtrifold.pdf

**El Chorro Regional Park and Dog Park**
Hwy 1
San Luis Obispo CA
805-781-5930
elchorrodogpark.org/
This regional park offers hiking trails, a botanical garden, volleyball courts, softball fields, campground and a designated off-leash dog park. The hiking trails offer scenic views on Eagle Rock and a cool creek walk along Dairy Creek. The Eagle Rock trail is about .7 miles and is rated strenuous. There are two other trails

including Dairy Creek that are about 1 to 2 miles long and rated easy. Dogs must be on leash at all times, except in the dog park. To get to the park from Highway 101, head south and then take the Santa Rosa St. exit. Turn left on Santa Rosa which will turn into Highway 1 after Highland Drive. Continue about 5 miles and the park will be on your left, across from Cuesta College.

**Laguna Lake Dog Park**
504 Madonna Road
San Luis Obispo CA
805-781-7300
Located at the 375 acre Laguna Lake Park, this doggy play area is open from dawn to dusk. The off leash area is comprised of a 500 foot radius section by the restrooms located at the end of Dalidio Road. Dogs must be healthy, sociable, current on all vaccinations and license with tags on collar, and under their owner's control at all times. Owners must clean up after their pets, and keep them leashed when not in designated off-lead areas.

**Nipomo Park Off-Leash Area**
W. Tefft St and Pomery Rd
San Luis Obispo CA
805-781-5930
This off-leash area in Nipoma Park is fully fenced and is open during daylight hours. There are two separate enclosed areas for large dogs and small dogs. The park is located 3/4 miles west of 101 on W. Tefft St.

# Dog-Friendly Parks
**Lake Lopez Recreation Area**
6820 Lopez Drive
Arroyo Grande CA
805-781-5930
This lake has 22 miles of shoreline and is a popular place for fishing, camping, boating, sailing, water skiing, canoeing, birdwatching and hiking. There are miles of hiking trails, ranging from easy

to strenuous. The marina allows dogs on their boat rentals for an extra $10 fee. Dogs must be leashed at all times and people need to clean up after their pets.

**Heilmann Regional Park**
Cortez Avenue
Atascadero CA
805-781-5930
This park offers hiking trails, tennis courts and a disc golf course. The Blue Oak trail is 1.3 miles and is an easy multi-use trail. The Jim Green trail is 1.7 miles multi-use trail that is rated moderate. Dogs must be leashed at all times and people need to clean up after their pets.

**Lake San Antonio**
2610 San Antonio Road
Bradley CA
805-472-2311
This park offers a variety of activities including boating, swimming, fishing and miles of hiking trails. Dogs are allowed on the trails and in the water. This park also offers dog-friendly campgrounds. Pets need to be leashed and please clean up after them. There is a $6 day use fee per vehicle.

**Lake Nacimiento**
Lake Nacimiento Drive
Paso Robles CA
805-238-3256
nacimientoresort.com/dayuse.htm
There are approximately 170 miles of tree lined shoreline at this lake. This is a popular lake for boating and fishing. It is the only lake in California that is stocked with White Bass fish. There is also a good population of largemouth and smallmouth bass. The lake offers over 400 campsites and RV sites have both full or partial hook ups. Dogs are allowed around and in the lake. They must be on leash and attended at all times. There is a $5 per day charge for dogs. The lake is located west of Hwy 101, seventeen miles north of Paso Robles. Take the 24th Street (G-14 West) exit in Paso

Robles and proceed west on G-14 to the lake.

**Santa Margarita Lake Regional Park**
off Pozo Road
Santa Margarita CA
805-781-5930
This lake is popular for fishing, boating and hiking. Swimming is not allowed at the lake because it is a reservoir which is used for city drinking water. There is a seasonal swimming pool at the park. Hiking can be enjoyed at this park which offers miles of trails, ranging from easy to strenuous. Dogs must be leashed at all times and people need to clean up after their pets.

**Emergency Veterinarians**
**Central Coast Pet Emergency Clinic**
1558 W Branch St
Arroyo Grande CA
805-489-6573
Monday - Friday 6 pm to 8 am, 24 hours on weekends.

**Other Organizations**
**Five Cities Dog Park Association**
P.O. Box 61
Pismo Beach CA
805-473-0323
fivecitiesdogpark.org
The Five Cities Dog Park Association was created to locate and create a suitable area for Five Cites residents to run their dogs off-leash. The association is committed to facilitating and maintaining an off-leash park through volunteering and donations from the community. The association is a non-profit organization.

## San Miguel

## Dog-Friendly Attractions

**The Rios-Caledonia Adobe**
700 S. Mission Street
San Miguel CA
805-467-3357
The century-old inn and stage stop is located on the old mission trail between San Francisco and Los Angeles and is found eight miles north of Paso Robles and adjacent to the San Miguel Mission. Preserved buildings, beautifully landscaped grounds, picnic sites, a gift shop and restrooms are found at the Rios-Caledonia Adobe. Well-behaved, leashed dogs are allowed on the property.

## Santa

**Pet-Friendly Stores**
**Summer Winds Nursery**
2931 El Camino Real
Santa CA
408-423-8445
Summer Winds Nursery allows well-behaved, leashed dogs in the nursery.

## Santa Barbara

**Dog-Friendly Hotels**
**Holiday Inn Express Hotel & Suites Carpinteria**
5606 Carpinteria Avenue
Carpinteria CA
805-566-9499 (877-270-6405)
Dogs of all sizes are allowed. Dogs are allowed for a pet fee of $10 per pet per night.

**Kimpton Goodland**
5650 Calle Real
Goleta CA
805-964-6241
Welcoming our guests with free Wi-Fi and an outdoor pool Kimpton Goodland also features a garden courtyard with a fire pit and an al fresco bar. The hotel's two stories house 158 rooms all equipped

with cable TVs work desks and hairdryers. Non-smoking rooms are available. Wi-Fi is also available for an additional fee. The hotel charges a resort fee that includes daily fitness classes self-parking complimentary coffee and tea and live music events. Enjoy a meal at the on-site restaurant or sip on a cool cocktail at the patio bar near the cozy fire pit. The hotel also has a pool and a business center. The hotel is eight miles from the Santa Barbara Mission and nine miles from the Santa Barbara Zoo. It's three miles from the beach and 50 minutes from Channel Islands National Park. Santa Barbara Municipal Airport is two miles from the hotel and Los Angeles International Airport is 105 miles away.

**Best Western Beachside Inn**
336 West Cabrillo Boulevard
Santa Barbara CA
805 965-6556 (800-780-7234)
Dogs up to 80 pounds are allowed. There is a $20 per day pet fee up to $100 for the week. Up to two dogs are allowed per room.

**Casa Del Mar Inn - Bed And Breakfast**
18 Bath Street
Santa Barbara CA
805-963-4418 (800-433-3097)
casadelmar.com
Free Wi-Fi and breakfast in a location that's a stone's throw from West Beach and the Harbor give the Casa del Mar Inn an edge.
The two-story Mediterranean-style Csa del Mar Inn has a terracotta roof and 21 rooms with free Wi-Fi flat-panel TVs with cable and private baths; most rooms have kitchenettes and some include a gas fireplace. Free buffet breakfast and evening wine and cheese are provided daily. In-room spa treatments are available for a charge and parking is free. NOTE: Front desk hours vary. Guests planning to arrive before or after the designated check-in time must contact the property

prior to arrival for special instructions. Guests can contact the property using the number on the reservations confirmation received after booking. Just off Cabrillo Boulevard the Casa Del Mar Inn is one-and-a-half blocks from West Beach and the Santa Barbara Harbor. Stroll five minutes to the Dolphin Fountain or to the shops and restaurants along Stearn's Wharf. Walk 10 minutes to Ledbetter Beach and Park the Santa Barbara Maritime Museum or Santa Barbara City College. State Street attractions in the heart of downtown including the Santa Barbara Museum of Art and the Granada Theater are less than two miles away. Two golf courses are within a 10-minute drive. Santa Barbara Municipal Airport is 10 miles west and Los Angeles International Airport is 100 miles southeast.

**Kimpton Canary Hotel**
31 West Carrillo Street
Santa Barbara CA
805-884-0300
In the heart of downtown fashion and dining action Kimpton Canary Hotel offers a Spanish-style oasis with elegant suites a California fusion restaurant spa services and a rooftop pool. Think hand-painted tiles wrought-iron accents and crisp colors when you picture this five-story mansion. Its 97 contemporary rooms feature four-poster beds flat-panel TVs down comforters iHome docks and plush bathrobes. Enjoy local flavors at two on-site restaurants and sample local vintages and cheeses during hosted wine hour. Work on your tan by the rooftop pool or order a soothing massage in your room. Event space is available. Pets are allowed and parking is extra. The hotel is one block from State Street this hotel plunges you into shopping nirvana at Paseo Nuevo the historic Lobero Theater and numerous galleries and cafes. Follow the Urban Wine Trail to discover new vintages at several nearby tasting rooms. Go for a walk

along the ocean about one mile away or hit the greens at Sandpiper Golf Course about a 15-minute drive away. Santa Barbara Municipal Airport is nine miles west of the property.

**La Quinta Inn & Suites Santa Barbara Downtown**
1601 State Street
Santa Barbara CA
805-966-0807 (800-531-5900)
Dogs of all sizes are allowed. Dogs may not be left alone in the room.

## Pet-Friendly Extended Stay Hotels
**Extended Stay America - Santa Barbara - Calle Real**
4870 Calle Real
Santa Barbara CA
805-692-1882 (800-804-3724)
One dog is allowed per suite. There is a $25 per night additional pet fee up to $150 for an entire stay.

## Dog Businesses
**Dioji K-9 Resort and Athletic Club**
7340 Hollister Avenue
Goleta CA
805-685-6068
dioji.com
An exclusive canine resort and athletic center, this 10,000 square foot, cage free doggy oasis comes complete with a large bone shaped pool, luxury overnight pet accommodations for when you must be away, a 6-week puppy play school, a signature spa, and a hands-on training course. They also offer a boutique full of hand-chosen pet supplies, human grade organic dog foods and treats, and all natural grooming products. Socialized dogs and puppies are welcome to come and enjoy the lap of luxury.

**Camp Canine**
803 E Montecito Street
Santa Barbara CA

805-962-4790
campcanineinc.com
Services offered at this canine resort and spa include overnight lodging for your pet on elevated sheepskin bedding, a retreat that features several personal care amenities, a doggy day camp, a spa doggy day with all natural products and a HydroSurge bath, and a variety of training programs. Puppies must have completed at least 2 rounds of puppy vaccinations, and dogs over 5 months must have current vaccination proof of Bordatella, DHLPP, and rabies.

**Dioji K-9 Resort and Athletic Club**
822 E Yanonali Street
Santa Barbara CA
805-845-0500
dioji.com
An exclusive canine resort and athletic center, this 10,000 square foot, cage free doggy oasis comes complete with a large bone shaped pool, luxury overnight pet accommodations for when you must be away, a 6-week puppy play school, a signature spa, and a hands-on training course. They also offer a boutique full of hand-chosen pet supplies, human grade organic dog foods and treats, and all natural grooming products. Socialized dogs and puppies are welcome to come and enjoy the lap of luxury.

## Dog-Friendly Attractions
**Chumash Painted Cave State Historic Park**
Painted Caves Road
Goleta CA
805-733-3713
The drawings in this cave are from Chumash Native Americans and coastal fishermen that date back to the 1600s. Dogs are allowed but need to be leashed. Please clean up after your pets. The cave is located in a steep canyon above Santa Barbara. The site is located three miles south of the San Marcos Pass.

To get there, take Highway 154 out of Santa Barbara and turn right on Painted Caves Road. The cave is on the left, about two miles up a steep narrow road. There is parking for only one or two vehicles. Trailers and RVs are not advised.

### Santa Barbara Botanical Garden
1212 Mission Canyon Road
Santa Barbara CA
805-682-4726
santabarbarabotanicgarden.org/
This beautiful botanical garden is located on 65 acres in historic Mission Canyon and they allow dogs in the garden and on the trails. This garden features over 1,000 species of rare and indigenous California plants. There are five and a half miles of scenic trails that take you through meadows and canyons, across historic Mission Dam, and along ridge-tops that offer sweeping views of the California Islands. The garden is about a 15-20 minute drive from downtown Santa Barbara.

### Stearns Wharf
Cabrillo Blvd
Santa Barbara CA
805-897-1961
stearnswharf.org/
This is the state's oldest working wharf, and it is still offering a fun and exciting place to go. Although dogs are not allowed down on the sandy areas, they are allowed to check out the sights and smells all along the Wharf. Dogs must be well mannered, leashed, and under their owner's control at all times.

### TJ Paws Pet Wash
2601 De La Vina Street
Santa Barbara CA
805-687-8772
tjpaws.com/
This self-serve pet wash can come in very handy after your pup has played around on some dirt trails or in the ocean and sand. Dogs can ruff it during the day and come back to the hotel nice and clean. At TJ Paws, you'll wash and groom your pet

yourself, using their supplies and equipment. The staff at TJs will be there if any assistance is required.

## Outdoor Restaurants
### Crushcakes & Cafe
4945 Carpinteria Avenue
Carpinteria CA
805-684-4300
crushcakes.com/
With a focus on sustainable, local and organic, this cafe and bakery features a made-from-scratch kitchen, organic eggs, hormone-free meats, a seasonally influenced menu, and signature dishes, beverages, and desserts. They also offer healthy support in the community through a variety of venues. Leashed, well mannered dogs are allowed at their outside dining area.

### The Coffee Bean & Tea Leaf
4991 Carpinteria Avenue
Carpinteria CA
805-745-5861
coffeebean.com
The coffee here is sourced globally from family coffee farms to procure only the top of 1% of Arabica beans. They offer 30+ varieties of coffee;the beans are roasted in small batches daily for freshness, and they also offer 20 varieties of teas that are hand-blended by their tea master. Additionally, they offer a variety of tasty sweets, powders, extracts, sauces, gifts, and cards. Leashed, well mannered dogs are allowed at their outside dining area.

### Baja Fresh Mexican Grill
7127 Hollister Ave.
Goleta CA
805-685-9988
bajafresh.com
This Mexican restaurant is open for lunch and dinner. They use fresh ingredients and making their salsa and beans daily. Some of the items on their menu include Enchiladas, Burritos, Tacos Salads, Quesadillas, Nachos, Chicken,

Steak and more. Well-behaved leashed dogs are allowed at the outdoor tables.

### Hollister Brewing Company
6980 Market Place Drive
Goleta CA
805-968-2810
hollisterbrewco.com/index.html
With an emphasis on sourcing and developing relations with sustainable, local, and artisan providers, this brewing company offers up to 15 unique handcrafted beers on tap, seasonally influenced food and beverage menus, daily specials, and a full bar. They also feature special NFL breakfasts beginning in September. Leashed, well mannered dogs are allowed at their outside dining area.

### The Coffee Bean & Tea Leaf
5745 Calle Real
Goleta CA
805-696-6845
coffeebean.com
The coffee here is sourced globally from family coffee farms to procure only the top of 1% of Arabica beans. They offer 30+ varieties of coffee;the beans are roasted in small batches daily for freshness, and they also offer 20 varieties of teas that are hand-blended by their tea master. Additionally, they offer a variety of tasty sweets, powders, extracts, sauces, gifts, and cards. Leashed, well mannered dogs are allowed at their outside dining area.

### The Natural Cafe
5892 Hollister Avenue
Goleta CA
805-692-2363
thenaturalcafe.com
With a focus on sourcing the freshest, naturally produced and locally grown produce and products available, this eatery offers a full menu of healthy foods and beverages. Foods are also made fresh daily with many vegan and vegetarian choices. Leashed, well mannered dogs are allowed at their outside tables.

**Pierre Lafond Montecito Deli**
516 San Ysidro Road
Montecito CA
805-565-1504
pierrelafond.com/
This full-service deli provides seasonally inspired breakfast and lunches sourcing the freshest organic and local produce and free range and naturally grown fowl and meats available. They also offer a number of vegetarian choices. Leashed, well mannered dogs are welcome at their outside tables.

**Baja Fresh Mexican Grill**
3851 State Street
Santa Barbara CA
805-687-9966
bajafresh.com
This Mexican restaurant is open for lunch and dinner. They use fresh ingredients and making their salsa and beans daily. Some of the items on their menu include Enchiladas, Burritos, Tacos Salads, Quesadillas, Nachos, Chicken, Steak and more. Well-behaved leashed dogs are allowed at the outdoor tables.

**Chipotle**
723 State Street
Santa Barbara CA
805-730-9195
chipotle.com
Specializing in organic, natural and unprocessed food, this Mexican Eatery offers fajita burritos, tacos, salads, and salsas. Dogs are allowed at the outdoor tables but you will need to order your food inside the restaurant and dogs must remain outside.

**Coffee Bean & Tea Leaf**
3052 De La Vina
Santa Barbara CA
805-565-7559
coffeebean.com/
The coffee here is sourced globally from family coffee farms to procure only the top of 1% of Arabica beans. They offer 30+ varieties of coffee;the beans are roasted in small batches daily for freshness, and they also offer 20 varieties of teas that are

hand-blended by their tea master. Additionally, they offer a variety of tasty sweets, powders, extracts, sauces, gifts, and cards. Leashed, well mannered dogs are allowed at their outside dining area.

**Crushcakes & Cafe**
1315 Anacapa Street
Santa Barbara CA
805-963-9353
crushcakes.com/
With a focus on sustainable, local and organic, this cafe and bakery features a made-from-scratch kitchen, organic eggs, hormone-free meats, a seasonally influenced menu, and signature dishes, beverages, and desserts. They also offer healthy support in the community through a variety of venues. Leashed, well mannered dogs are allowed at their outside dining area.

**Dargan's Irish Pub**
18 E. Ortega Street
Santa Barbara CA
805-568-0702
darganssb.com/
Dogs are allowed on the outdoor patio. The pub serves food and drinks. It's hours are 4 pm to 2 am Monday to Friday and 11:30 am to 2 am on Saturday and Sunday.

**Emilio's Restaurant**
324 W Cabrillo Blvd
Santa Barbara CA
805-966-4426
emilios-restaurant.com/
This quaint Italian eatery is located along the waterfront and offers indoor and outdoor dining. Dogs are allowed at the outdoor tables. They must be well behaved, under owner's control/care at all times and leashed.

**Fresco Cafe**
3987 State Street, #B
Santa Barbara CA
805-967-6037
frescosb.com/
Some of the offerings of this cafe include freshly prepared foods with an emphasis on all natural and organic ingredients,

daily specials, signature dishes, and a seasonally influenced eclectic menu of fresh salads, homemade soups, pizza, burgers, wraps, custom made sandwiches, and handcrafted desserts. Spring and winter hours vary. Leashed, well mannered dogs are allowed at their outside dining area.

**Intermezzo**
813 Anacapa Street
Santa Barbara CA
805-966-9463
winecask.com/restaurants.cfm
Seasonally influenced menus, a wide variety of wine choices, an elegant setting, and alfresco dining are some of the pluses of this restaurant. Leashed and well mannered dogs up to about 25 pounds are allowed at the outer tables, and they must be able to be under the table-not in the aisles.

**Java Station**
4447 Hollister Avenue
Santa Barbara CA
805-681-0202
This java stop offers a variety of specialty beverages and a variety of foods. Leashed well mannered dogs are allowed at their outside seating area.

**Le Cafe Stella**
3302 McCaw Avenue
Santa Barbara CA
805-569-7698
lecafestella.com
This French-American cafe features an eclectic extensive menu, a full bar, happy hours, a venue for special events, and a dog friendly patio. They are open daily from 9 am until 10 pm. Dogs must be well mannered and leashed.

**Mesa Cafe**
1972 Cliff Drive/H 225
Santa Barbara CA
805-966-5303
mesacafesb.com
Some of the offerings of this cafe include fresh salads, appetizers, daily specials, sandwiches, seafood, pastas, steaks, and handcrafted desserts. Leashed, well

mannered dogs are allowed at their outside dining area.

### Pascucci's Restaurant
729 State Street
Santa Barbara CA
805-963-8123
pascuccirestaurant.com/
Sourcing all the best local and organic products, as well as produce, seafood, and all natural meats that are delivered daily, this eatery serves up their own homemade dressings, made-to-order pasta, house specialties, sandwiches, and gourmet pizzas. Leashed, friendly dogs are allowed at their outside tables.

### Pizza Mizza
140 S Hope Avenue, Suite 102A

Santa Barbara CA
805-564-3900
pizzamizza.com/
In addition to a wide variety of pizzas, this eatery also offers pastas, sandwiches, salads, and more, plus they have an outdoor seating area. Dogs are allowed at the outer tables;they must be under their owner's control at all times.

### Renaud's Patisserie & Bistro
1324 State Street
Santa Barbara CA
805-892-2800
renaudsbakery.com
Signature French style cake creations and pastries made from the finest ingredients available are the specialties at this patisserie. Their bistro features a contemporary French atmosphere, and an impressive breakfast and lunch menu reflecting the chef's personal favorites and the cuisine from the Provence region of France. They also offer fresh organic greens, free-range grain fed poultry, and homemade jams and breads. They are open daily from 7 am until 3 pm. Leashed, well mannered dogs are allowed at their outside dining area.

### Renaud's Patisserie & Bistro
3315 State Street
Santa Barbara CA

805-569-2400
renaudsbakery.com
Signature French style cake creations and pastries are the specialty at this patisserie. Their bistro features a contemporary French atmosphere, and an impressive breakfast and lunch menu reflecting the chef's personal favorites and the cuisine from the Provence region of France. They also offer fresh organic greens, free-range grain fed poultry, and homemade jams and breads. They are open from 7 am until 5 pm Monday to Saturday and from 7 am until 3 pm on Sunday. Leashed, well mannered dogs are allowed at their outside dining area.

### Santa Barbara Shellfish Company
230 Stearns Wharf
Santa Barbara CA
805-966-6676
sbfishhouse.com/shellfish-co/
This seafood restaurant offers a full menu of seafood delights such as their homemade clam chowder and seasonal bisques, their tasty Small Bites, Fresh from the Sea choices, specialties of the house, pastas, wine and bottled and draft beers. Leashed, well mannered dogs are allowed at their outside dining area.

### The Brewhouse
229 W Montecito Street
Santa Barbara CA
805-884-4664
brewhousesb.com
Offerings at this popular gathering spot include handcrafted brews made fresh on the premises, daily happy hours, a full menu of fine comfort foods, Saturday and Sunday buffets, live music Wednesday thru Saturday, a local artistic decor, a great doggy menu, and a calendar of various events. Leashed, well mannered dogs are allowed at their outside dining area.

### The Coffee Bean & Tea Leaf
1209 Coast Village Road
Santa Barbara CA

310-260-0044
coffeebean.com
The coffee here is sourced globally from family coffee farms to procure only the top of 1% of Arabica beans. They offer 30+ varieties of coffee;the beans are roasted in small batches daily for freshness, and they also offer 20 varieties of teas that are hand-blended by their tea master. Additionally, they offer a variety of tasty sweets, powders, extracts, sauces, gifts, and cards. Leashed, well mannered dogs are allowed at their outside dining area.

### The Coffee Bean & Tea Leaf
811 State Street
Santa Barbara CA
805-966-2442
coffeebean.com
The coffee here is sourced globally from family coffee farms to procure only the top of 1% of Arabica beans. They offer 30+ varieties of coffee;the beans are roasted in small batches daily for freshness, and they also offer 20 varieties of teas that are hand-blended by their tea master. Additionally, they offer a variety of tasty sweets, powders, extracts, sauces, gifts, and cards. Leashed, well mannered dogs are allowed at their outside dining area.

### The Coffee Bean & Tea Leaf
3052 De La Vina
Santa Barbara CA
805-569-1809
coffeebean.com
The coffee here is sourced globally from family coffee farms to procure only the top of 1% of Arabica beans. They offer 30+ varieties of coffee;the beans are roasted in small batches daily for freshness, and they also offer 20 varieties of teas that are hand-blended by their tea master. Additionally, they offer a variety of tasty sweets, powders, extracts, sauces, gifts, and cards. Leashed, well mannered dogs are allowed at their outside dining area.

### The Natural Cafe
508 State Street

Santa Barbara CA
805-962-9494
thenaturalcafe.com/
With a focus on sourcing the
freshest, naturally produced and
locally grown produce and
products available, this eatery
offers a full menu of healthy
foods and beverages. Foods are
also made fresh daily with many
vegan and vegetarian choices.
Leashed, well mannered dogs
are allowed at their outside
tables.

**The Natural Cafe**
361 Hitchcock Way
Santa Barbara CA
805-563-1163
thenaturalcafe.com
With a focus on sourcing the
freshest, naturally produced and
locally grown produce and
products available, this eatery
offers a full menu of healthy
foods and beverages. Foods are
also made fresh daily with many
vegan and vegetarian choices.
Leashed, well mannered dogs
are allowed at their outside
tables.

**Tupelo Junction Cafe**
1218 State Street
Santa Barbara CA
805-899-3100
tupelojunction.com
Offering a fusion of Southern,
home style cooking with fresh
local produce, this eatery offers
a number of signature
specialties throughout their
menus, a mostly made-from-
scratch kitchen, happy hours
Tuesday to Saturday, and
alfresco dining. Leashed, well
mannered dogs are allowed at
their outside dining area.

**Vices & Spices**
3558 State Street
Santa Barbara CA
805-687-7196
vicesnspices.com/
This coffee, tea, spice, and gift
store is family owned and
features an eclectic and unique
selection of gifts, cards, fresh
baked breakfast desserts,
locally baked pastries, and a
choice selection of organic
coffee, teas, and spices.

Leashed, well mannered dogs
are allowed at their front
outside dining area on the
sidewalk just off the short wood
deck next to your table.

**The Summerland Beach Cafe**

2294 Lillie Avenue
Summerland CA
805-969-1019
summerlandbeachcafe.com
Set in a beautiful Victorian
house by the Pacific Ocean,
this breakfast and lunch cafe
offers hearty portions of home-
style cooking featuring many
specialties of the house as well
as regional and American
favorites. Leashed, friendly
dogs are allowed at their
outside dining area.

# Pet-Friendly Shopping Centers
**La Cumbre Plaza**
120 South Hope Avenue
Santa Barbara CA
805-687-3500
shoplacumbre.com/
Offering more than 50 shops
and services, this center also
allows well mannered dogs in
the common areas of the mall
and some of the stores are
also dog friendly. There are
water bowls at Guest Services
as well at some of the stores,
and the security officer has
been known to carry doggy
treats. Dogs must be leashed
and under their owner's control
at all times.

**State Street Shopping Area**
100-700 State Street
Santa Barbara CA
805-963-2202
In downtown Santa Barbara
there are several popular
shopping areas. One shopping
area is on State Street. Two
dog-friendly stores, Big Dog
Sportswear and The Territory
Ahead, allows dogs inside the
store. Another area, an outdoor
mall adjacent to State Street, is
called the Paseo Nuevo
Shopping Center. Here there

are several outdoor retail kiosks.
State Street shopping is
between the 100 and 700 block
of State Street between Cabrillo
Boulevard and Carrillo Street.
Paseo Nuevo is around the 700
block of State Street, between
Ortega Street and Canon
Perdido Street.

## Pet-Friendly Stores
**Lemos Feed and Pet Supply**
4945 Carpinteria Avenue
Carpinteria CA
805-566-9700
lemospet.com/
Products carried at this pet
specialty store include a wide
variety of high quality pet foods,
treats, toys, medicinal items,
and grooming supplies. Friendly,
leashed dogs are welcome.

**Lemos Feed and Pet Supply**
320-A S Kellogg
Goleta CA
805-692-8566
lemospet.com/
Products carried at this pet
specialty store include a wide
variety of high quality pet foods,
treats, toys, medicinal items,
and grooming supplies. Friendly,
leashed dogs are welcome.

**Anthropologie**
1123 State Street
Santa Barbara CA
805-962-5461
Items of distinction can be found
for all ages and in all
departments of this unique
shop. Carefully selected to add
to the enjoyment of the
shopping experience, they carry
fine clothing, amazing
accessories, jewelry, hobby and
leisure items, and a full line of
bright and useful items for the
home, garden, and office.
Leashed, well behaved dogs are
allowed in the store.

**Big 5 Sporting Goods**
3935 State Street
Santa Barbara CA
805-964-4749
big5sportinggoods.com/
This comprehensive sporting
goods store will allow your

leashed canine companion to accompany you inside.

## Big Dog Sportswear Store
6 E. Yanonali Street
Santa Barbara CA
805-963-8728
bigdogs.com/
This factory outlet store allows dogs inside. Big Dogs Sportswear is a Santa Barbara-based company and produces high quality, reasonably priced activewear and accessories for men, women, and children of all ages. No clothes for the pup, but the human clothes have the cool "Big Dog" logo. The store is located at the corner of State Street and Yanonali Street, across from the Amtrak station.

## Coach
3825 State Street
Santa Barbara CA
805-682-0647
coach.com/default.aspx
Coach, a leading designer and producer of fine leather products, markets a number of luxury accessories and gifts, some of which include business cases, travel accessories, footwear, outerwear, handbags, fragrances, and even some pet accessories. Well mannered, leashed pooches are welcome in the store.

## Coach Factory Store
808 State Street
Santa Barbara CA
805-884-1161
coach.com/default.aspx
This is a factory store for Coach, a leading designer and producer of fine leather products that markets a number of luxury accessories and gifts, some of which include business cases, travel accessories, footwear, outerwear, handbags, fragrances, and even some pet accessories. Well mannered, leashed pooches are welcome in the store.

## Healthy Pet
3018 State Street
Santa Barbara CA
805-687-2804
This store provides a variety of

high quality pet foods, a full line of hard-to-find frozen raw foods, and a number of pet supply products. They open daily at 10 am and close at 7 pm Monday to Friday, at 6 pm on Saturday, and a 5 pm on Sunday. Leashed, friendly dogs are welcome.

## Lemos Feed and Pet Supply
330 E. Gutierrez Street
Santa Barbara CA
805-882-2336
lemospet.com/
Products carried at this pet specialty store include a wide variety of high quality pet foods, treats, toys, medicinal items, and grooming supplies. Friendly, leashed dogs are welcome.

## Macy's Paseo Nuevo
701 State Street
Santa Barbara CA
805-730-3242
macys.com/
This major department store carries a vast variety of items for everyone in the family and for the home. Friendly dogs are welcome in the store; they must be leashed or in a carrier and under their owner's control at all times.

## Nordstrom
17 W Canon Perdido Street
Santa Barbara CA
805-564-8770
This major department store will allow well mannered pooches to browse with their owners; they must be leashed (or carried) and under their owner's control at all times.

## Office Max
219 E. Gutierrez Street
Santa Barbara CA
805-899-4983
officemax.com/
This comprehensive office supply store will allow your leashed canine companion to accompany you inside. Dogs must be well mannered and under their owner's control.

## Petco Pet Store - Santa Barbara - Central

3985 State St.
Santa Barbara CA
805-964-2868
Your licensed and well-behaved leashed dog is allowed in the store.

## Petco Pet Store - Santa Barbara - East
19 South Milpas St.
Santa Barbara CA
805-966-7292
Your licensed and well-behaved leashed dog is allowed in the store.

## The Gap
615 Paseo Nuevo
Santa Barbara CA
805-965-6336
gap.com/
Contemporary, chic clothing and accessories for the whole family are the specialty of this clothing store. Leashed, well mannered dogs are welcome in the store; they must be under owner's care at all times.

## The Territory Ahead
515 State Street
Santa Barbara CA
805-962-5558
territoryahead.com/
A nature influenced clothier, they focus on comfortable but outdoors and internationally inspired clothing and accessories. The store is open Monday through Saturday from 10 am until 7 pm, and on Sunday from 11 am until 6 pm. This is their flagship store and they also have an outlet store at 400 State Street. The outlet is open Monday through Saturday from 10 am until 6 pm, and on Sunday from 11 am until 6 pm. Friendly, leashed dogs are welcome in the store.

## The Territory Ahead Store
515 State Street
Santa Barbara CA
805-962-5558 x181
territoryahead.com/
The Territory Ahead was founded in 1988 and set out to create a new kind of clothing catalog that offered personality through special fabrics, distinguishing details, and easy,

wearable designs. All the men's and women's clothing, as well as many of the accessory and gift items are designed in-house, to offer a collection of merchandise that can't be found anywhere else. The Territory Ahead allows well-behaved dogs inside their flagship store on State Street.

**Urban Outfitters**
624 State Street
Santa Barbara CA
805-966-7416
In addition to a large inventory of indoor and outdoor apparel for men and women, this major department store also carries vintage wear, designer brands, and a variety of accessories for all types of active lifestyles. They also carry shoes, furnishings, home decor, cameras, electronics, novelty items and more. Leashed, well mannered dogs are allowed in the store.

# Dog-Friendly Wineries and Vineyards

**Municipal Winemakers**
28 Anacapa Street
Santa Barbara CA
805-931 MUNI (6864)
municipalwinemakers.com
Years of combined travel, experience, and education led to this winery's creation. They specialize in globally influenced, high quality wines handmade in small lots using traditional techniques - with an insertion of modern styles. Dogs are allowed on the grounds; they are not allowed in the tasting room. Dogs must be leashed and under their owner's control at all times.

**Oreana Winery**
205 Anacapa Street
Santa Barbara CA
805-962-5857
oreanawinery.com/
In addition to the production of a wide selection of fine red, white, and sparkling wines, this winery also offers a great venue for

special events and live music on the patio on the weekends. This is a dog friendly winery; dogs must be friendly too and leashed.

**Stearns Wharf Vinters**
217-G Stearns Wharf
Santa Barbara CA
805-966-6624
Located on California's oldest working wharf, visitors can enjoy the fresh ocean breeze and watch the comings and goings on the waterfront while savoring fine wines from the Santa Ynez Winery. They also offer a variety of cheese plates, fondues, gourmet sandwiches, picnic items, fondues, and coffee and espresso drinks. Dogs are allowed at the outdoor tables. They must be well behaved, under their owner's control at all times, leashed, and cleaned up after.

# Dog-Friendly Beaches

**Goleta Beach County Park**
5990 Sandspit Road
Goleta CA
805-568-2460
Leashed dogs are allowed at this county beach. The beach and park are about 1/2 mile long. There are picnic tables and a children's playground at the park. It's located near the Santa Barbara Municipal Airport in Goleta, just north of Santa Barbara. To get there, take Hwy 101 to Hwy 217 and head west. Before you reach UC Santa Barbara, there will be an exit for Goleta Beach.

**Arroyo Burro Beach County Park**
2981 Cliff Drive
Santa Barbara CA
805-967-1300
Leashed dogs are allowed at this county beach and park. The beach is about 1/2 mile long and it is adjacent to a palm-lined grassy area with picnic tables. To get to the beach from Hwy 101, exit Las Positas Rd/Hwy 225. Head south (towards the ocean).

When the street ends, turn right onto Cliff Drive. The beach will be on the left.

**Arroyo Burro Off-Leash Beach**

Cliff Drive
Santa Barbara CA

countyofsb.org/parks/dog.sbc
While dogs are not allowed off-leash at the Arroyo Burro Beach County Park (both the beach and grass area), they are allowed to run leash free on the adjacent beach. The dog beach starts east of the slough at Arroyo Burro and stretches almost to the stairs at Mesa Lane. To get to the off-leash area, walk your leashed dog from the parking lot to the beach, turn left and cross the slough. At this point you can remove your dog's leash.

**Rincon Park and Beach**
Bates Road
Santa Barbara CA

This beach is at Rincon Point which has some of the best surfing waves in the world. In the winter, it is very popular with surfers. In the summer, it is a popular swimming beach. Year-round, leashed dogs are welcome. The beach is about 1/2-1 mile long. Next to the parking lot there are picnic tables, phones and restrooms. The beach is in Santa Barbara County, about 15-20 minutes south of Santa Barbara. To get there from Santa Barbara, take Hwy 101 south and go past Carpinteria. Take the Bates Rd exit towards the ocean. When the road ends, turn right into the Rincon Park and Beach parking lot.

# Off-Leash Dog Parks
**Douglas Family Preserve**
Linda Street
Santa Barbara CA
805-564-5418
Once planned to support a major housing development, this beautiful, undeveloped stretch of

property was rescued to be enjoyed by all. Features include spectacular ocean and beach views and a great walking path along the bluffs. Dogs are allowed throughout the park and on the trails. Dogs must be under their owner's immediate control at all times, and cleaned up after.

## Santa Barbara Off-Leash Areas

Various
Santa Barbara CA
805-564-5418
countyofsb.org/parks/dog.sbc
Unlike almost all larger California cities, Santa Barbara does not have any fenced off-leash dog parks nor any off-leash unfenced dog runs that are available throughout the day. However, they do have five unfenced park areas with very limited off-leash hours. Please check the signs to find the off-leash areas and the hours as they may change. The five parks are Toro Canyon Park Meadow, daily (8 am to 10 am, 4 pm - sunset), Patterson Open Space, M - F (8 am to 10 am), Tucker's Grove, M - F (8 am - 10 am, 4 pm - sunset), Tabano Hollow, daily (4 pm to sunset) and Isla Vista Park, M - F (8 am - 10 am, 4 pm - sunset). Please keep in mind that in winter there is not much time between 4 pm and sunset.

## Dog-Friendly Parks

### Beach Walkway

Cabrillo Blvd.
Santa Barbara CA

We couldn't find the official name of this paved path (it might be part of Chase Palm Park), so we are labeling it the "Beach Walkway". This path parallels the beach. While dogs are not allowed on this beach, they can walk along the paved path which has grass and lots of palm trees. There are also many public restrooms along the path. The path is about 1.5 miles long each way.

### Chase Palm Park

323 E. Cabrillo Boulevard
Santa Barbara CA
805-564-5433
This beautiful waterfront city park opened in May 1998. It is about a mile long and has many sections including a carousel, plaza, pavilion, shipwreck playground, the wilds, fountain gateway and casa las palmas. It is on Cabrillo Blvd. between Garden Street and Calle Cesar Chavez Street.

### Plaza Del Mar

129 Castillo Street
Santa Barbara CA

This city park is about 4 blocks long and is close to several hotels and restaurants. The park is home to the Old Spanish Days Carriage Museum. While dogs are not allowed inside the museum, you can see many of the carriages from the outside.

### Shoreline Park

1200 Shoreline Drive
Santa Barbara CA

This 1/2 mile paved path winds along the headlands and provides scenic overlooks of Santa Barbara and the ocean. It is located northwest of Leadbetter Beach and Santa Barbara City College.

## Events

### Wags n Whiskers Festival

7050 Phelps Road
Goleta CA
805-683-3368
C.A.R.E.4Paws will be hosting its 3rd annual Wags n Whiskers Festival at Girsh Park in August 2012. In addition to a number of agility presentations, dog training demos, animal wellness information, a Pawsitive Thinking Kids Corner, a police dog demonstrations, and lots of prizes, this activity is also the county's largest adoption

festival featuring adoptable pets from 20 local shelters and animal groups. Pets must be kept leashed and under their owner's control at all times. This event should be repeated annually so check the date for the current year.

### Big Dog Parade and Canine Festival

121 Gray Ave
Santa Barbara CA
805-963-8727, Ext:1398
bigdogs.com/
This is the largest dog parade in the country (with proceeds benefiting our canine companions), and thousands from all over the west come to watch, participate, or compete in this fun event sponsored by the Big Dog Foundation. It is held annually (usually in early June) with the parade beginning at State and De La Guerra Streets with a regalia of costumed canines strutting for the judges and spectators. It ends at the Canine Festival in Old Chase Palm Park where there awaits vendors, activities, celebrities, food, music, and more. Dogs must be well mannered, leashed, and cleaned up after.

### The French Festival Poodle Parade

Junipero and Alamar Streets at Oak Park
Santa Barbara CA
805-564-PARIS (7274)
frenchfestival.com/
This event is held every Bastille Day, July 14. It is sponsored by the Santa Barbara French Festival, and is the largest French celebration in the Western U.S. with all the sights, sounds, art, foods, wines, and exuberance of France. There is even a model Eiffel Tower. There is a menagerie of free entertainment, but the "Poodle Parade" where every dog can strut their stuff (and their most impressive costumes) is one of the biggest and most fun draws. Dogs must be well mannered, leashed, and cleaned up after. Your dog doesn't have to be a poodle to attend.

## Veterinarians

**Rolling Pet Vet**
315 Meigs Road, Suite A254
Santa Barbara CA
855-838-8663
rollingpetvet.com/home
This professional and caring staff provides a number of curbside services for your pets including examinations, complete dental care, a variety of surgeries, laboratory work/testing, pain management, and hospice care. They also offer behavior management, alternative medicines, nutritional counseling, supplements, and a full service pharmacy. They service the greater Santa Barbara area.

## Emergency Veterinarians

**CARE Hospital**
301 E. Haley St.
Santa Barbara CA
805-899-2273
This 24 hour veterinary has a state-of-the-art veterinary center which offers advanced medical and surgical procedures for pets. They have a veterinarian on the premises at all times and a surgeon on call for emergency surgeries.

## Santa Clarita

## Dog-Friendly Hotels

**Fairfield Inn By Marriott Santa Clarita Valencia**
25340 The Old Road
Santa Clarita CA
661-290-2828
Dogs of all sizes are allowed. There is $75 one time pet fee.

**La Quinta Inn & Suites Stevenson Ranch**
25201 The Old Road
Stevenson Ranch CA
661-286-1111 (800-531-5900)
Dogs up to 100 pounds are allowed for no additional pet fee; there is a pet policy to sign at check-in.

## Pet-Friendly Extended Stay Hotels

**Residence Inn By Marriott Santa Clarita Valencia**
25320 The Old Road
Santa Clarita CA
661-290-2800
Dogs of all sizes are allowed. There is a $75 one time additional pet fee.

**Extended Stay America - Los Angeles - Valencia**
24940 Pico Canyon Rd
Stevenson Ranch CA
661-255-1044 (800-804-3724)
One dog is allowed per suite. There is a $25 per night additional pet fee up to $150 for an entire stay.

## Outdoor Restaurants

**Jamba Juice**
27061 McBean Parkway
Santa Clarita CA
661-284-6347
jambajuice.com
All natural and organic ingredients, no high-fructose corn syrup, 0 grams trans fat, no artificial preservatives, a healthy helping of antioxidants, vitamins, and minerals, and fresh whole fruit and fruit juices set the base for these tasty and healthy beverages. Their organic Hot Blends provides a new spin on coffee, green or chai tea, and hot chocolate;plus they offer probiotic fruit and yogurt Blends. Additionally, they feature all natural salads, wraps, sandwiches, and grab n go specialties. They also offer healthy community support through fundraisers, special sales, and school lunch programs. Leashed, well mannered dogs are allowed at their outside dining area.

**The Big Oaks**
33101 Bouquet Canyon Road
Santa Clarita CA
661-296-5656
cavibigoaks.com
Located in a 1920's lodge in the Angeles National Forest, this eatery offers a wonderful ambiance and menu items include salads, pasta, pizza, steaks, salmon, and weekend barbecues. Leashed, well mannered dogs are welcome on their large dining patio.

## Pet-Friendly Stores

**Camping World**
24901 W Pico Canyon Road
Newhall CA
661-255-9220
campingworld.com/
This comprehensive RV and outdoor store carries a wide variety of RV, boat, bike, and outdoor cooking accessories; all kinds of camping gear; RV screens, shades, and patio decorations; racing/tailgating gear, and all items for RV maintenance. They also carry RV towing supplies, electronics, and interior decorating items as well as pet supplies, RV directories/books, and games. Plus, they offer a tips and advice service, RV sales, rentals, and RV technicians to take care of any installations and repairs. They also welcome your canine companion in the store; they must be friendly and leashed.

**PetSmart Pet Store**
24965 Pico Canyon Rd
Stevenson Ranch CA
661-260-3990
Your licensed and well-behaved leashed dog is allowed in the store.

**Starpups Depot**
25818 Hemingway Avenue
Stevenson Ranch CA
661-255-2208
starpupsdepot.com/
This is an upscale dog boutique that caters to discerning dogs and their people, and they offer a large selection of gifts, toys, treats, and even birthday cakes.

They are open from 10 am to 7 pm Tuesday through Friday; 10 am to 6 pm on Saturday; 11 am to 5 pm on Sunday, and closed Mondays. Well behaved, leashed dogs are allowed to explore the store with their owners.

## Dog-Friendly Parks
### Placerita Canyon Nature Center
19152 Placerita Canyon Road
Newhall CA
661-259-7721
placerita.org/
This 350 acre nature park is one of the first places where gold was discovered in California. An early frontier cabin called Walker's Cabin is located at this park. Hiking trails are accessible for wheelchairs and strollers. The paved trail is about .3 miles. Dogs must be on leash and please clean up after them.

### William S. Hart Regional Park
24151 N. San Fernando Road
Newhall CA
661-259-0855
This 265 acre ranch was donated to the public by William S. Hart, also known as "Two Gun Bill". He was a popular cowboy actor during the silent film era. The park includes a western art museum and barnyard animals including wild buffalo. Dogs are allowed at the park and on trails, but not inside any buildings. Pets must be leashed and please clean up after them.

## Rescue Organizations
### Jin-Sohl Jindo Dog Rescue
P.O. Box 1364
Santa Clarita CA

jindo-dog-rescue.org
Jin-Sohl Jindo Dog Rescue is an organization dedicated to educating the public about Jindo dogs, to providing support and guidance to Jindo owners, and to rescuing Jindos from Southern California shelters

when possible.

## Santa Cruz

## Dog-Friendly Hotels
### Hilton Santa Cruz / Scotts Valley
6001 La Madrona Dr.
Santa Cruz CA
831-440-1000
Centrally located between Silicon Valley and Monterey Bay, this upscale hotel offers numerous on site amenities for business and leisure travelers, plus a convenient location to business districts, beaches, shopping, dining, and entertainment areas. Dogs up to 75 pounds are allowed for an additional one time pet fee of $50 per room.

### Pacific Inn Santa Cruz
330 Ocean Street
Santa Cruz CA
831-425-3722
A stellar location near the beach plus cozy accommodations make our guests applaud the Pacific Inn Santa Cruz which also has a hot tub and sauna. The two-floor Mediterranean-style Pacific Inn Santa Cruz has 36 rooms all with coffee/tea makers microwaves mini-fridges and premium cable TV. Select accommodations have jetted tubs. There's a hot tub and sauna on-site and hotel offers free newspapers and a laundry facility. The Pacific Inn Santa Cruz is located on Ocean Street within walking distance of the Santa Cruz Beach about a 15-minute stroll away. It's six blocks east across the San Lorenzo River from downtown Santa Cruz. If you're driving from San Jose International Airport the hotel is 31 miles south.

### Best Western Plus Inn Scotts Valley
6020 Scotts Valley Drive

Scotts Valley CA
831-438-6666 (800-780-7234)
Dogs up to 80 pounds are allowed. There is a $15 per day pet fee up to $100 for the week. Up to two dogs are allowed per room.

## Dog-Friendly Attractions
### Roaring Camp & Big Trees RR

P.O.Box G-1
Felton CA
831-335-4484
roaringcamprr.com/
As of the summer of 1999, dogs are required to wear muzzles on this train ride but not on the grounds. They provide free muzzles you can borrow. At Roaring Camp you will find daily musical entertainment (Old Western style) and a couple of outdoor cafes that serve burgers, chicken sandwiches and more. They also hold many seasonal events here like a Harvest Fair and Steam Festival. The train ride takes you into the beautiful Santa Cruz Mountains. This is America's last steam-powered passenger railroad with year-round passenger service. They operate daily from 11am to 5pm. To get there, take Hwy 17 to the Scotts Valley Mount Hermon Road exit. Stay on Mount Hermon Road until it ends. Turn left onto Graham Hill Road. Roaring Camp is 1/4 mile ahead on the right.

### De Laveaga Park Disc Golf
Branciforte
Santa Cruz CA

Santa Cruz is quickly gaining recognition for being home to one of disc golf's premier courses. Disc golf is similar to golf with clubs and balls, but the main difference is the equipment. Discs are shot into elevated baskets/holes. Your leashed dog is allowed to go with you on this course (pick up after your pooch). Rangers patrol the park frequently and will fine any dog owner that doesn't have their dog on a leash or doesn't clean up after their pup. This course has 27 baskets and is part of an over 1200 acre park which allows dogs. If you do not have any discs, you can purchase them at various locations in the Santa Cruz area. You can purchase discs at Play it Again Sports in Soquel, on Soquel Ave right past Capitola Ave. Another place that sells discs is Johnny's Sports in downtown Santa Cruz. New discs cost about $8.00 to $12.00 depending on the make and model. To get to the park, take Hwy 17 south to Santa Cruz and exit Hwy 1 south (towards Watsonville). Take the first exit, Morrissey Blvd (the exit has a sharp 90 degree turn). Turn right at the stop sign, and then go to the end of the street where it dead ends at Branciforte. Turn right. Go over Hwy 1, stop at the stop sign, and continue straight up the hill. Follow the signs to the De Laveaga Golf Course. Go approx. 1/4 mile past the club house and the disc golf parking will be on the right. The first hole is across the road in the Oak Grove. Maps should be available.

**Harbor Water Taxis**
Lake Avenue
Santa Cruz CA
831-475-6161
The water taxis run inside the Santa Cruz Harbor only. The taxis are small barges (flat-bottomed boats). They have several very short hops across and around the harbor. It's something fun to do while walking around the harbor. If you are on the east side of the harbor by Lake Ave., you and your dog can take the taxi across the harbor to dine at Aldo's Restaurant (see Restaurants). There is more parking by Lake Ave than by Aldos. The taxi's are seasonal, usually running from May through October. There are several spots around the harbor where you can catch the water taxis and there is a minimal fee

for the taxi. To get there from Hwy 17 heading south, take the Ocean Street exit on the left towards the beaches. Turn left onto East Cliff Drive. Go straight to go onto Murray Street. Turn right on Lake Avenue (East Santa Cruz Harbor). Take Lake Ave until it ends near Shamrock Charters. There is a minimal fee for parking.

**Lighthouse Point Surfer's Museum**
W. Cliff Dr
Santa Cruz CA
831-420-6289
This lighthouse is home to California's first surfing museum. Well-behaved, leashed dogs are allowed inside. It is open from noon to 6pm daily, except it is closed on Tuesdays. The museum is located on West Cliff Drive, about a 5-10 minute drive north of the Santa Cruz Boardwalk.

**Santa Cruz Harley Davidson Motorcyles**
1148 Soquel Ave
Santa Cruz CA
831-421-9600
santacruzharley.com/
Well-behaved, leashed dogs are allowed in the store and the museum. They have dogs come into the store all the time. The museum, located inside the store, features vintage motorcycles, memorabilia, photos and more. Located at the corner of Soquel and Seabright.

# Outdoor Restaurants
**Bittersweet Bistro**
787 Rio Del Mar Blvd
Aptos CA
831-662-9899
bittersweetbistro.com/
With a focus on sourcing the finest natural high quality ingredients, this fine dining establishment offers freshly prepared American Bistro cuisine with Mediterranean inspirations, an exceptional dessert menu, a notable wine

list, daily happy hours, and a wonderful garden patio. Leashed, well mannered dogs are allowed at their outside dining area.

**Cole's Bar-B-Q**
8059 Aptos Street
Aptos CA
831-662-1721
This award winning barbecue establishment has one table outside for customers who bring their canine companions with them. Dogs must be attended to at all times, well behaved, and leashed.

**Spanky's**
9520 H 9
Ben Lomond CA
831-336-8949
This breakfast and lunch restaurant is decorated with Spanky and The Gang, and also has outdoor dining. Your dog is allowed to sit with you outside. Dogs must be attended to at all times, well behaved, and leashed.

**Gayle's Bakery and Rosticceria**
504 Bay Avenue
Capitola CA
831-462-1200
gaylesbakery.com/
This bakery features more than 500 cakes, cookies, pastries, and breads made with the all the best organic and natural ingredients available;plus, their Italian-style deli features a wood-burning rotisserie for some delectable tastes as well. Leashed, well mannered dogs are allowed at their outside tables.

**Rocky's Cafe**
6560 H 9
Felton CA
831-335-4637
Located in a beautiful old house set among the trees, this breakfast and lunch restaurant also has outdoor service on the veranda. Your pet is welcome, and dogs must be attended to at all times, well behaved, and leashed.

348

**Aldo's Harbor Restaurant**
616 Atlantic Avenue
Santa Cruz CA
831-426-3736
aldos-cruz.com/
Aldo's outdoor dining area overlooks the Santa Cruz Harbor. They are open for breakfast and lunch. After dining here, you can go for a walk around the harbor. To get there from Hwy 17 south, exit Ocean Street on the left towards the beaches. Leashed dogs are allowed at their outside tables.

**Black China Cafe and Bakery**
1121 Soquel Avenue
Santa Cruz CA
831-460-1600
This outdoor café/bakery is combined with a furnishings, accessories, and gift store that sits in front of the café. They specialize in vegetarian food and bakery items. Visitors with dogs can use the back entry to the café by the alley. Dogs must be well behaved, leashed, and cleaned up after at all times.

**Cafe Limelight**
1016 Cedar St
Santa Cruz CA
831-425-7873
Cafe Limelight, located in Santa Cruz, California, is open Tuesday throughout Friday 11:30am-2:30pm for lunch, and 5:30-8:30pm for dinner, and Saturdays noon-3pm for lunch, and 6pm-8:30pm for dinner. They serve a large variety of Panini sandwiches, fresh soups, and garden salads . Well behaved, leashed dogs are always welcome on the shaded outdoor patio, and they even offer a doggy menu, with options like roasted pig ears, fresh roasted turkey, milk bones, and more.

**Cole's Bar-B-Q**
2590 Portola Drive
Santa Cruz CA
831-476-4424
This award winning barbecue establishment allows your dog to join you at their outdoor tables. They must be attended to at all times, well behaved,

and leashed.

**Engfer's Pizza**
537 Seabright Avenue
Santa Cruz CA
831-429-1856
engferpizzaworks.com
Offerings from this pizzeria include fresh quality ingredients, authentic wood-fired pizzas from fresh handcrafted dough with original sauce recipes, vegan pies, organic salads, homemade soups and desserts, wine and beer on tap, and a fun atmosphere. They are open Tuesday to Sunday from 4 pm until about 9:30. Leashed, friendly dogs are allowed at their outside dining area.

**Firefly Coffee House**
131 A Front Street
Santa Cruz CA
801-598-3937
myspace.com/fireflycoffeehouse
Gourmet and organic coffees, a variety of freshly prepared foods, and a fun atmosphere are the specialties at this gathering place. There are all kinds of music played or being played, movie and television nights, and an exchange library. Leashed, well mannered dogs are welcome at their outside tables and get treated with a doggy biscuit too.

**Harbor Bay**
535 7th Avenue
Santa Cruz CA
831-475-4948
harborcafesantacruz.com/
This breakfast and lunch diner also has outside dining. Friendly, leashed dogs are welcome at the outer tables.

**Joe's Pizza and Subs**
841 N Branciforte Avenue
Santa Cruz CA
831-426-5955
joespizzaandsubs.net/
In addition to specialty pizzas and subs, this pizzeria also serves up burgers, falafel, pastas, shawarma, grilled chicken, sandwiches, salads,

wine, and a good selection of beers on tap. They are open daily from 11 am until 9:30 pm. Leashed, well mannered dogs are allowed at their outside dining area.

**Kelly's French Bakery**
402 Ingalls Street, Santa Cruz, Ca 95060:
Santa Cruz CA
831-423-9059
kellysfrenchbakery.com/
This traditional French Provencal bakery offers more than their skillfully crafted breads, pastries and desserts;they also offer breakfast, lunch, and dinner with organic produce and products sourced from the local farmers' market. Leashed, well mannered dogs are allowed at their outside dining area.

**Las Palmas Taco Bar**
55 Front Street
Santa Cruz CA
831-429-1220
This taco bar allows dogs to sit at their outside tables. Dogs must be well behaved, leashed, and cleaned up after.

**Mamma Lucia Cafe Bar Pizzeria**
1618 Mission Street
Santa Cruz CA
831-458-2222
Mamma Lucia Cafe Bar Pizzeria mainly serves pizza and pasta, 7 days a week from 11am-9pm. They welcome well-behaved, leashed dogs on their outdoor patio.

**Pleasure Pizza**
4000 Portola Drive
Santa Cruz CA
831-475-4999
pleasurepizzasc.com/
This pizza place serves slices and whole pizzas. It is located near the East Cliff Coastal Access Points/Beaches (see Parks). To get there from Hwy 17 south, exit Hwy 1 south towards Watsonville. Take the 41st Avenue exit. Turn right onto 41st Avenue. Leashed dogs are allowed at their outside dining area.

**River Cafe**
415 River Street, Suite K
Santa Cruz CA
831-420-1280
rivercafesantacruz.com/
A focus on local and organic, this eatery features a seasonally generated menu, mostly made-from-scratch foods, fresh baked goods, Mediterranean platters, specialty paninis, small plates, tapas, and a beer and wine bar. Happy Hours are from 5:30 pm until 7 pm daily. They are open Monday to Saturday from 6:30 am until 6 pm;Sundays from 10 am until 3 pm for brunch, and from 5:30 pm until 10 pm on Thursdays and Fridays for dinner. Leashed, friendly dogs are allowed at their outside dining area.

**Woodstock's Pizza**
710 Front Street
Santa Cruz CA
831-427-4444
woodstockscruz.com
Some of the offerings of this fun gathering spot include a variety of appetizers, salads, pizzas, sandwiches, desserts, and brews, lots of themed events/specials, various entertainment, TVs for sports viewing, and a venue for special events.

**Michael's on Main**
2591 Main Street
Soquel CA
831-479-9777
Known for their back to basics cutting edge comfort cuisine in a friendly, casual setting, this restaurant allows dogs on their patio. Dogs must be well behaved, leashed, and cleaned up after.

**Pet-Friendly Stores**
**Marshalls**
1664 Commercial Way
Santa Cruz CA
831-462-2168
marshallsonline.com/
Designer apparel for all sizes, accessories, shoes, household items, designer labels, travel equipment, tech supplies, and much more are offered at this department store. Leashed, well mannered dogs are welcome in the store; they must be under their owner's care at all times.

**PetSmart Pet Store**
490 River St
Santa Cruz CA
831-429-2780
Your licensed and well-behaved leashed dog is allowed in the store.

**Urban Outfitters**
1401 Pacific Avenue
Santa Cruz CA
831-423-9357
In addition to a large inventory of indoor and outdoor apparel for men and women, this major department store also carries vintage wear, designer brands, and a variety of accessories for all types of active lifestyles. They also carry shoes, furnishings, home decor, cameras, electronics, novelty items and more. Leashed, well mannered dogs are allowed in the store.

**Pet Pals**
3660 Soquel Drive
Soquel CA
831-464-8775
epetpals.com/
This family owned pet supply store carries a variety of dog and puppy foods, grooming supplies, bedding, dinnerware, health care products, and more. Leashed dogs are welcome in the store.

**Dog-Friendly Beaches**
**Rio Del Mar Beach**
Rio Del Mar
Aptos CA
831-685-6500
Dogs on leash are allowed at this beach which offers a wide strip of sand. From Highway 1, take the Rio Del Mar exit.

**Davenport Landing Beach**
Hwy 1
Davenport CA
831-462-8333
This beautiful beach is surrounded by high bluffs and cliff trails. Leashes are required. To get to the beach from Santa Cruz, head north on Hwy 1 for about 10 miles.

**Manresa State Beach**
San Andreas Road
Manresa CA
831-761-1795
Surfing and surf fishing are both popular activities at this beach. Dogs are allowed on the beach, but must be leashed. To get there from Aptos, head south on Highway 1. Take San Andreas Road southwest for several miles until you reach Manresa. Upon reaching the coast, you will find the first beach access point.

**East Cliff Coast Access Points**

East Cliff Drive
Santa Cruz CA
831-454-7900
There are many small dog-friendly beaches and coastal access points that stretch along East Cliff Drive between 12th Avenue to 41st Avenue. This is not one long beach because the water comes up to cliffs in certain areas and breaks it up into many smaller beaches. Dogs are allowed on leash. Parking is on city streets along East Cliff or the numbered avenues. To get there from Hwy 17 south, take the Hwy 1 exit south towards Watsonville. Take the exit towards Soquel Drive. Turn left onto Soquel Avenue. Turn right onto 17th Avenue. Continue straight until you reach East Cliff Drive. From here, you can head north or south on East Cliff Drive and park anywhere between 12th and 41st street to access the beaches.

**Its Beach**
West Cliff Drive
Santa Cruz CA
831-429-3777
This is not a large beach, but it is big enough for your water loving dog to take a dip in the water and get lots of sand

between his or her paws. Dogs must be on leash at all times. The beach is located on West Cliff Drive, just north of the Lighthouse, and south of Columbia Street.

## Mitchell's Cove Beach
West Cliff Drive at Almar
Santa Cruz CA
831-420-5270
Dogs are allowed off-leash on Mitchell's Cove Beach between sunrise and 10 am and from 4 pm to sunset. They must be on-leash during other hours. The beach is along West Cliff Drive between Woodward and Almar. While off-leash dogs must be under voice control.

## Seabright Beach
Seabright Ave
Santa Cruz CA
831-429-2850
This beach is located south of the Santa Cruz Beach Boardwalk and north of the Santa Cruz Harbor. Dogs are allowed on leash. Fire rings are available for beach bonfires. It is open from sunrise to sunset. To get there from Hwy 17 south, exit Ocean Street on the left towards the beaches. Merge onto Ocean Street. Turn left onto East Cliff Drive and stay straight to go onto Murray Street. Then turn right onto Seabright Ave. Seabright Ave will take you to the beach (near the corner of East Cliff Drive and Seabright).

## Twin Lakes State Beach
East Cliff Drive
Santa Cruz CA
831-429-2850
This beach is one of the area's warmest beaches, due to its location at the entrance of Schwann Lagoon. Dogs are allowed on leash. The beach is located just south of the Santa Cruz Harbor where Aldo's Restaurant is located. Fire rings for beach bonfires, outdoor showers and restrooms are available. It is open from sunrise to sunset. To get there from Hwy 17 south, exit Ocean Street on the left towards the beaches.

Merge onto Ocean Street. Turn left onto East Cliff Drive and stay straight to go onto Murray Street. Murray Street becomes Eaton Street. Turn right onto 7th Avenue.

# Off-Leash Dog Parks
## Polo Grounds Dog Park
2255 Huntington Avenue
Aptos CA
831-454-7900
This one acre off leash dog park is fenced and includes water and benches. The park is open during daylight hours. To get there, take Highway 1 and exit at Rio Del Mar. Go left over the freeway and turn right onto Monroe Avenue (second stop light). After Monroe turns into Wallace Avenue, look for Huntington Drive on the left. Turn left on Huntington and the park entrance will be on the left.

## Frederick Street Park Dog Park
168 Frederick Street (Frederick at Broadway)
Santa Cruz CA
831-420-5270
Located at Frederick Street Park, this off leash area is open from sunrise to sunset and is marked by signs and a split rail fence. Dogs must be healthy, sociable, current on all vaccinations and license with tags on collar, and under their owner's control at all times. Owners must clean up after their pets, and keep them leashed when not in designated off-lead areas.

## Grant Park Dog Park
180 Grant Street
Santa Cruz CA
831-420-5270
There is clear signage for the off leash area at this park; it is open from sunrise to sunset. Dogs must be healthy, sociable, current on all vaccinations and license with tags on collar, and under their owner's control at all times. Owners must clean up after

their pets, and keep them leashed when not in designated off-lead areas.

## Ocean View Park
102 Ocean View Avenue
Santa Cruz CA
831-420-5270
The off leash area at this doggy playground has clearly marked off with signs and it is open from sunrise to sunset. Dogs must be healthy, sociable, current on all vaccinations and license with tags on collar, and under their owner's control at all times. Owners must clean up after their pets, and keep them leashed when not in designated off-lead areas.

## Pacheco Dog Park
Pacheco Avenue and Prospect Heights
Santa Cruz CA
831-420-5270
This completely fenced off leash doggy play area is open from sunrise to sunset. Dogs must be healthy, sociable, current on all vaccinations and license with tags on collar, and under their owner's control at all times. Owners must clean up after their pets, and keep them leashed when not in designated off-lead areas.

## University Terrace Dog Run
Meder Street and Nobel Drive
Santa Cruz CA
831-420-5270
Dogs are allowed off leash in University Terrace from sunrise to 10 am and from 4 pm to sunset. They are allowed on-leash from 10 am to 4 pm. The park is on the corner of Meder Street and Noble Drive. Please check the signs for the off-leash area in the park.

## University Terrace Park
Nobel Drive and Meder Street
Santa Cruz CA
831-420-5270
This fenced-off pooch playground is located at the 2nd entrance at Nobel Drive and Meder Street and is open from sunrise to sunset. Dogs must be healthy, sociable, current on all

vaccinations and license with tags on collar, and under their owner's control at all times. Owners must clean up after their pets, and keep them leashed when not in designated off-lead areas.

## Scotts Valley Dog Park
Bluebonnet Road
Scotts Valley CA
831-438-3251
This off leash dog park is located in the Skypark complex next to the soccer fields. The dog park offers 1.2 fully enclosed acres which is divided into two sections. One section is for small dogs under 25 pounds, puppies or shy dogs. The other section is for all dogs but primarily for larger and more active dogs. Other amenities include water bowls, wading pools, tennis balls, other dog toys, drinking fountains, shaded seating, plastic bags and pooper scoopers. To get there from Highway 17, take the Mt. Hermon exit and follow Mt. Hermon Road straight. Pass two stoplights and take the second right into the shopping center at the movie theater sign. Go about .1 miles and turn left on Bluebonnet Road. The dog park is on the left.

# Dog-Friendly Parks
## Forest of Nisene Marks
Aptos Creek Road
Aptos CA
831-763-7062
Dogs on leash are allowed in part of this park. They are allowed on a beautiful wooded trail that parallels the gravel Aptos Creek Road (on the left or west side of the road only). A good starting point is at the park entrance booth. Park after paying the minimal day use fee and then join the trail next to the parking lot. On this trail, head into the park (north). Dogs are allowed on the dirt trail up to the Steel Bridge (about 1 mile each way). You can continue on Aptos Creek Rd to the Porter Family Picnic Area, but dogs

need to stay on the road (cars also allowed). The dirt trail up to the bridge is usually the best hiking trail that allows dogs and it includes several trails that divert towards the creek. Here your pup can enjoy playing in the water. To get there from Hwy 17, exit Hwy 1 south towards Watsonville. Drive through Santa Cruz and Capitola on Hwy 1 and then exit at the Seacliff Beach/Aptos exit. Turn left onto State Park Drive. Then turn right on Soquel Avenue. After going under the train bridge, you'll soon turn left onto Aptos Creek Rd. It's a small street, so be careful not to miss it. Drive up this road until you reach the park entrance booth.

## Henry Cowell Redwoods State Park
Highway 9
Felton CA
831-335-4598
Dogs are allowed in the picnic area, the campground, and on Pipeline Road, Graham Hill Trail, and Meadow Trail. They are not allowed on any other trails or interior roads. Dogs must be leashed. The park is near Felton on Highway 9 in the Santa Cruz Mountains. Traveling from San Jose to the main entrance: Take Highway 17 towards Santa Cruz. After you go over the mountains, turn right on Mt. Hermon Road. Follow Mt. Hermon road until it ends at Graham Hill Road. Turn right, and go to the next stop light (Highway 9). Turn left on Highway 9 and go through downtown Felton. The park entrance will be a half mile down on your left. You can park outside and walk a half mile into the park, or you can drive in and pay a fee.

## Lighthouse Field
West Cliff Drive
Santa Cruz CA
831-429-3777
Leashes are required at all times now at Lighthouse Field. It used to have off-leash hours but this was discontinued. This

field is not fenced and there are several busy streets nearby, so if your dog runs off-leash, make sure he or she is very well trained. It is located on West Cliff Drive, just north of the Lighthouse, and south of Columbia Street. It is also across from the West Lighthouse Beach. To get there, head south on Hwy 17. Take the Hwy 1 North exit, heading towards Half Moon Bay and Hwy 9. Merge onto Mission Street (Hwy 1). Turn left onto Swift Street. Then turn left on West Cliff Drive. Limited parking will be on the right or on other sides of the field.

## West Cliff Drive Walkway
West Cliff Drive
Santa Cruz CA
831-429-3777
This is a popular paved walking path that follows the beautiful Santa Cruz coastline. It is about 2 miles long each way and is frequented by walkers, runners, bicyclists and of course, dogs. It is located on West Cliff Drive, north of the Santa Cruz Beach Boardwalk and south of Natural Bridges State Beach. While dogs are not allowed on either the Boardwalk or the State Beach, there is a dog beach along this path called West Lighthouse Beach. There are several areas where you can park near the path. The easiest is by the north end of the path: Heading south on Hwy 17, take the Hwy 1 North exit towards Half Moon Bay and Hwy 9. Merge onto Mission Street (Hwy 1). Turn left onto Swift Street. Then turn right on West Cliff Drive. Turn right onto Swanton Blvd. Parking is available on Swanton Blvd. If you prefer to park closer to the Boardwalk, follow these directions: From Hwy 17 heading south, take the Hwy 1 North exit towards Half Moon Bay and Hwy 9. Merge onto Chestnut Street. Turn left onto Laurel Street, then right onto Center Street. Make a slight left onto Washington Street and Washington will become Pacific Avenue. Then

turn right onto Beach Street. There is limited metered parked available near the Municipal Wharf.

## Emergency Veterinarians
**Santa Cruz Veterinary**
2585 Soquel Dr
Santa Cruz CA
831-475-5400
24 hours for emergencys. 8 - 5 pm for routine visits.

## Humane Society or SPCAs

**Santa CRUZ SPCA**
2685 Chanticleer Ave.
Santa Cruz CA
(831) 465-5000
santacruzspca.org/
Established in 1938, the purpose of the Santa Cruz SPCA is to ensure the best possible quality of life for animals and to promote respect and reverence for all. We do not receive any federal, state, or local government funding. We are a no-kill shelter that adopts out close to 150 animals a month to kind and loving homes.

We offer:
Adoptions
Volunteer Opportunities
Free Food Bank
Licensing
Shelter to Shelter Transfer

## Other Organizations
**C-DOG (Coastal Dog Owners Group)**
500 Oak Drive
Capitola CA
831-427-0350
coastaldogs.com
Coastal Dog Owners Group is a volunteer run 501(c)3 non-profit organization. Our mission is to:- Provide education on sensible dog ownership and off-leash exercise options- Make good news about dogs in the community- Support for local pet non-profit organizations-

Support humane, dog friendly positive training methods - Having fun while being with our dogs!"Making the community richer through sensible dog ownership"

**Santa Cruz Pugs**
Events at various dog parks around Santa Cruz
Santa Cruz CA
831.359.8071
santacruzpugs.org
We are a free pug play group, open to all. No cost to attend, and attendance is not restricted to pugs. All dogs welcome. We hold events on the 2nd and 4th Sunday's of every month, as well as Wednesday evenings in the summer, and holiday parties. See our events calendar for more info, which can be found on our website.

**Woofers & Walkers**
121 First Avenue
Santa Cruz CA
831.427.0350
woofersandwalkers.com
Woofers & Walkers is a collective of responsible dog owners that enjoy having fun, getting exercise and sharing a meal alongside their pooches. Some of our walks are docent-led and informative, like the Capitola History Dog Walk that talks about the dog history of Capitola Village. Every Sunday, we go for an hour and a half walk with our dogs, then have Yappy Hour at a dog-friendly restaurant. The walks are free. During summer months, we also have Doggie Drive-in (a free movie with your dog) and Cafe Canine (free live acoustic music with your dog).Occasionally, we also have other events.

## Santa Maria

## Dog-Friendly Hotels
**Best Western Plus Big America**

1725 North Broadway
Santa Maria CA
805-922-5200 (800-780-7234)
Dogs up to 80 pounds are allowed. Up to two dogs are allowed per room.

**Holiday Inn Hotel & Suites Santa Maria**
2100 North Broadway
Santa Maria CA
805-928-6000 (877-270-6405)
Dogs of all sizes are allowed. Dogs are allowed for a pet fee of $25.00 per pet per night.

## Pet-Friendly Extended Stay Hotels
**Candlewood Suites Santa Maria**
2079 N. Roemer Court
Santa Maria CA
805-928-4155 (877-270-6405)
Dogs up to 80 pounds are allowed. Pets allowed with an additional pet fee. Up to $75 for 1-6 nights and up to $150 for 7+ nights. A pet agreement must be signed at check-in. Two dogs are allowed per room.

## Outdoor Restaurants
**Jamba Juice**
530 E Betteravia Road, Suite A-3
Santa Maria CA
805-922-3240
jambajuice.com
All natural and organic ingredients, no high-fructose corn syrup, 0 grams trans fat, no artificial preservatives, a healthy helping of antioxidants, vitamins, and minerals, and fresh whole fruit and fruit juices set the base for these tasty and healthy beverages. Their organic Hot Blends provides a new spin on coffee, green or chai tea, and hot chocolate;plus they offer probiotic fruit and yogurt Blends. Additionally, they feature all natural salads, wraps, sandwiches, and grab n go specialties. They also offer healthy community support through fundraisers, special

sales, and school lunch programs. Leashed, well mannered dogs are allowed at their outside dining area.

### The Natural Cafe
2407 S Broadway/H 135
Santa Maria CA
805-937-2735
thenaturalcafe.com
With a focus on sourcing the freshest, naturally produced and locally grown produce and products available, this eatery offers a full menu of healthy foods and beverages. Foods are also made fresh daily with many vegan and vegetarian choices. Leashed, well mannered dogs are allowed at their outside tables.

## Pet-Friendly Stores
### PetSmart Pet Store
2306 S Bradley Rd
Santa Maria CA
805-348-1075
Your licensed and well-behaved leashed dog is allowed in the store.

## Off-Leash Dog Parks
### Woof-Pac Park
300 Goodwin Rd
Santa Maria CA
805-896-2344
countyofsb.org/parks/dog.sbc
This three acre fenced dog park opened in 2006 in Waller Park. It is located next to the Hagerman Softball Complex. Its hours are dawn to dusk. From 101 take Betteravia Rd west and turn left onto Orcutt Expy. Turn right into Waller Park.

## Other Organizations
### WOOF! Winners Of Off-leash Recreation
221 Town Center East #100
Santa Maria CA
(805) 929-7406
woofpac.org
Winners Of Off-leash Freedom (WOOF) is a non-profit

organization formed in 2001 to advocate for off-leash recreational areas in the Santa Maria Valley. WOOF celebrated the opening of WOOF Pac Park on Feb. 24, 2002. Called the "Pick of the Litter" by the "Dog Lovers Companion to California," the park provides ample space in separate small and big dog areas for dogs and their people to socialize with their peers.

### Winners Of -Offleash Freedom, Inc. (WOOF!)
221 Town Center West, #100
Santa Maria CA
8059297406
woofpac.org
We are a 501(3)(c) non profit corp dedicated to helping to create off-leash recreation areas for dogs and their owners. We have an annual event at the first off-leash dog park that we helped create, (Woof Pac Park in Waller Park in Santa Maria) the last Saturday of each June.

## Santa Nella

## Dog-Friendly Hotels
### Quality Inn Santa Nella
28976 West Plaza Drive
Santa Nella CA
209-826-8282 (877-424-6423)
Dogs of all sizes are allowed. Dogs are allowed for a pet fee of $10.00 per pet per night.

## Santa Ysabel

## Outdoor Restaurants
### Dudley's Bakery
30218 H 78
Santa Ysabel CA
760-765-0488
dudleysbakery.com/
Offering tasty treats warm from the oven and a nice picnic table in a grassy area, makes this a

favorite for visitors with canine companions. Well behaved, leashed dogs are welcome to enter the store with their owner. Dogs must be under owner's control/care and leashed.

### Jeremy's on the Hill
4354 California 78
Santa Ysabel CA
760-765-1587
jeremysonthehill.com
Jeremy's On The Hill serves lunch and dinner, including burgers, appetizers, sandwiches, steak, and more! Well-behaved, leashed dogs are welcome at the outdoor patio.

## Santee

## Dog-Friendly Hotels
### Best Western Santee Lodge
10726 Woodside Avenue
Santee CA
619-449-2626 (800-780-7234)
Dogs up to 80 pounds are allowed. There is a $10 per day pet fee up to $100 for the week. Up to two dogs are allowed per room.

## Outdoor Restaurants
### Jamba Juice
9828 Mission Gorge Road
Santee CA
619-448-2746
jambajuice.com
All natural and organic ingredients, no high-fructose corn syrup, 0 grams trans fat, no artificial preservatives, a healthy helping of antioxidants, vitamins, and minerals, and fresh whole fruit and fruit juices set the base for these tasty and healthy beverages. Their organic Hot Blends provides a new spin on coffee, green or chai tea, and hot chocolate;plus they offer probiotic fruit and yogurt Blends. Additionally, they feature organic steel-cut oatmeal prepared fresh every morning, all natural salads, wraps,

sandwiches, and grab n' go specialties. They also offer healthy community support through fundraisers, special sales, and school lunch programs. Leashed, well mannered dogs are allowed at their outside dining area.

## Pet-Friendly Stores
**PetSmart Pet Store**
9896 Mission Gorge Rd
Santee CA
619-448-1921
Your licensed and well-behaved leashed dog is allowed in the store.

**Petco Pet Store - Santee**
9745 Mission Gorge Road
Santee CA
619-449-1668
Your licensed and well-behaved leashed dog is allowed in the store.

## Other Organizations
**Labrador Harbor, Inc.**
P.O. Box 712552
Santee CA
619-892-0049
labradorharbor.org
Labrador Harbor is a non-profit, 501(c)(3) corporation that provides funding for privately owned Labs, and Labs in Rescue in California who need medical intervention and/or training intervention to enhance their quality of life. It is our goal to eliminate euthanasia that occurs due to lack of financial resources of owners and rescue organizations. Please see our website for additional information, including eligibility criteria and application process.

## Sea Ranch

## Dog-Friendly Hotels
**Sea Ranch Lodge**
60 Sea Walk Drive

Sea Ranch CA
707-785-2371 (800-SEA-RANCH (732-7262))
searanchlodge.com/
Situated in Sea Ranch in the California region Sea Ranch Lodge offers accommodation with free WiFi.
A fridge and kettle are also provided.
Guests can enjoy a meal at the on-site restaurant which specializes in local cuisine.
A bicycle rental service is available at this property.
Healdsburg is 49 km from the lodge while Gualala is 13 km away.

## Seaside

## Veterinarians
**Animal Health Center**
1760 Fremont Blvd Suite 2B
Seaside CA
831-394-7387
Animal Health Center is a full service animal hospital and will handle emergency cases as well as less urgent medical, surgical, and dental issues. They are open Monday & Tuesday 8am-5:30pm, Wednesday 8am-1:30pm, Thursday 8am-6:30pm, Friday 8am-5:30pm, and every other Sunday 10am-3pm.

## Selma

## Dog-Friendly Hotels
**Super 8 Selma/fresno Area**
3142 S Highland Ave
Selma CA
559-896-2800 (800-800-8000)
Dogs are welcome at this hotel.

## Sequoia National Park

## Dog-Friendly Hotels
**Comfort Inn At Sequoia National Park**
40820 Sierra Drive
Three Rivers CA
559-561-9000 (877-424-6423)
Hotel offers free high-speed Internet access, fitness room with sauna, seasonal outdoor pool/hot tub, and picnic area.

Dogs up to 20 pounds are allowed. Dogs are allowed for a pet fee of $35.00 per pet per stay. Two dogs are allowed per room.

## Dog-Friendly Parks
**Sequoia and Kings Canyon National Park**
47050 General Highway
Three Rivers CA
559-565-3341
nps.gov/seki/
This national park does not really have much to see or do if you bring your pooch, except for driving through a giant redwood forest in your car and staying overnight at the campgrounds. However, located to the west and south of this national park is the dog-friendly Giant National Sequoia Monument. There you will be able to find dog-friendly hiking, sightseeing and camping. Pets must be leashed and attended at all times. Please clean up after your pet.

## Shasta

## Dog-Friendly Attractions
**Shasta State Historic Park**
15312 H 299 W
Shasta CA
530-243-8194
This historic park pays tribute to the "Queen City of the Northern

Mines"; a main shipping area for supplies and gold from the 1849 rush, and includes the old brick remains of the buildings. There are exhibits, interpretive programs, picnic areas, and an unparalleled collection of historic California artwork on display. Dogs of all sizes are allowed throughout the park, at the picnic areas, and on the trails; they are not allowed in the museum. Dogs must be well mannered, leashed, and cleaned up after at all times.

## Shasta - Trinity National Forest

### Dog-Friendly Attractions
**Trinity Alps Marina**
Fairview Marina Rd.
Lewiston CA
530-286-2282
trinityalpsmarina.com
Rent a houseboat on Lake Trinity with your well-behaved dog. There is a $75 one time pet fee.

### Dog-Friendly Parks
**Trinity Lakeshore Trail**
Highway 3
Trinity Center CA
530-623-2121
This easy to moderate hike follows the western shore of Trinity Lake. The four mile trail runs from Clark Springs Campground to a private resort. There are a few short, steep stretches along the route. The trail offers shade and goes through an old-growth forest. Please stay on the trail when walking through private facilities. The majority of this trail is in the Shasta-Trinity National Forest. The trailhead at the Clark Springs Campground which is located 18 miles north of Weaverville off Highway 3. Pets should be leashed and please clean up after them.

**Whiskeytown National Recreation Area**
P.O. Box 188
Whiskeytown CA
530-246-1225
nps.gov/whis/
The main highlight of this park is Whiskeytown Lake. Popular activities include swimming, sailing, water-skiing, scuba diving and fishing. The land surrounding the lake offers ample opportunities for hiking, mountain biking and horseback riding. Dogs are allowed on the trails, in the campgrounds and in the water at non-swim beaches which are beaches without sand. Pets are not allowed on the sandy swimming beaches or inside any buildings. Dogs must be leashed and attended at all times. Please clean up after your pet. This recreation area is located on Highway 299 near Highway 5.

## Sierra City

### Outdoor Restaurants
**Herrington's Sierra Pines Resort Restaurant**
104 Main Street/H 49
Sierra City CA
530-862-1151
herringtonssierrapines.com/
Offering a number of specialties of the house, this resort restaurant serves up breakfasts and dinners with fresh baked items, homemade soups, fresh caught trout, a variety of fine wines, regional specialties, and a full service bar. The restaurant is open from mid-May until mid-October. Dogs are allowed at the outside picnic tables. When the restaurant is not busy they may service the picnic table;however, when they are busy patrons will need to order to-go. Dogs are also allowed at the resort for overnight accommodations.

## Sierra Madre

### Off-Leash Dog Parks
**Sierra Madre Dog Park**
611 E. Sierra Madre Blvd
Sierra Madre CA
626-355-5278
Located at the Sierra Vista Park, this off leash area is open from dawn to dusk and offers a separately fenced section for small dogs. There is a $5 daily fee that can be obtained at City Hall at 232 W Sierra Madre Blvd. Dogs must be healthy, sociable, current on all vaccinations and license with tags on collar, and under their owner's control at all times. Owners must clean up after their pets, and keep them leashed when not in designated off-lead areas.

## Six Rivers National Forest

### Dog-Friendly Parks
**Ruth Lake Community Services District**
Lower Mad River Rd, south of Hwy 36
Mad River CA
800-500-0285
ruthlakecsd.org/
Dogs on leash are allowed on the trails and in the lake. RV and camp sites are available with reservations.

## Solvang

### Dog-Friendly Hotels
**Quality Inn Santa Ynez Valley**
630 Avenue Of The Flags
Buellton CA
805-688-0022 (877-424-6423)
The Quality Inn is located on the central coast in the Santa Ynez Valley.

**Quality Inn Santa Ynez Valley**
630 Avenue Of The Flags
Buellton CA
805-688-0022 (877-424-6423)
Free breakfast free internet and
a pet-friendly attitude impress
our guests at Quality Inn Santa
Ynez Valley. This 60-room
motel on three floors offers
rooms with free high-speed
internet access cable TVs free
local calling work desks and
plenty of space to stretch out
and get comfortable. Non-
smoking rooms can be
requested as can rooms with
microwaves and mini-fridges.
The motel's free deluxe
continental breakfast will get
your day off on the right foot.
Fax services are available for
the business traveler. There's
an on-site laundry for guests
and even a free newspaper
waiting for you every weekday
morning. Parking is available
and pets are welcome with
some restrictions. Quality Inn is
off Highway 101. The quaint
Danish town of Solvang a
favorite with tourists is four
miles away. Cachuma Lake
Recreation Area is 20 minutes
away and the valley's 80
wineries provide days of wine-
country touring. Santa Barbara
Airport is 37 miles east and Los
Angeles International Airport is
142 miles southeast.

**Santa Ynez Valley Marriott**
555 Mcmurray Road
Buellton CA
805-688-1000
Dogs up to 50 pounds are
allowed.There is a $75 one time
pet fee.

**Royal Copenhagen Inn**
1579 Mission Drive
Solvang CA
800-624-6604
Featuring free WiFi and an
outdoor pool the Royal
Copenhagen Inn offers
accommodation in the heart of
downtown Solvang 45 km from
Santa Barbara.
The rooms are decorated in
Danish tradition and include a
private bathroom. A flat-screen
TV is also included. All rooms
come with air-conditioning and
coffee makers.
This Danish-themed Inn is
surrounded by downtown's
shops restaurants and
bakeries. Guests can enjoy a
complimentary fresh Danish
pastry and coffee each morning
and complimentary wine tasting
at a nearby tasting room.
Santa Maria is 48 km from
Royal Copenhagen Inn while
Santa Ynez is 6 km away. The
closest airport Los Angeles
International is 3.5 hours' drive
away.

## Dog-Friendly Attractions

**Solvang Horsedrawn**
**Streetcars**
P.O. Box 531
Solvang CA

solvangstreetcar.com
When this streetcar is not too
crowed, your well-behaved dog
is welcome. They offer a twenty
minute guided tour of the
beautiful Danish village of
Solvang. The tour costs less
than $5 per person. Prices are
subject to change. The tour
starts on Copenhagen Drive,
opposite the Blue Windmill.

**Solvang Village**
1500-2000 Mission Drive
Solvang CA
800-468-6765
solvang.org/
As the Solvang Visitor's Bureau
states, "Visiting Danes have
described Solvang as 'more
like Denmark than Denmark' -
a remarkable tribute to the
town's passion for Danish
architecture, cuisine and
customs." Solvang is a quaint
shopping village and a great
place to walk with your dog.
Several stores along Mission
Drive are dog-friendly like The
Book Loft and Lemo's Feed &
Pet Supply (please always
verify that stores are dog-
friendly by asking the clerk
before entering). There are
also many dog-friendly
restaurants in town including
bakeries that have mouth
watering goodies. Sunset
Magazine recently voted
Solvang as one of the '10 Most
Beautiful Small Towns' in the
Western United States.

## Outdoor Restaurants

**Bit O'Denmark**
473 Alisal Road
Solvang CA
805-688-5426
bitodenmark.com/
This restaurant allows 1 dog per
table (maybe 2, depending on
how many other dogs are there).
They are open from 9:30am until
9pm.

**Cali Love Wine**
1651 Copenhagen Drive
Solvang CA
805-688-1678
calilovewine.com
Cali Love is a spot for the
combination of music and wine.
They have a tasting room and
wine bar for their private label
wines. There is live
entertainment periodically.
Leashed and well-behaved dogs
are allowed.

**Fresco Valley Cafe**
442 Atterdag Road
Solvang CA
805-688-8857
frescosb.com/
Some of the offerings of this
cafe include freshly prepared
foods with an emphasis on all
natural and organic ingredients,
daily specials, signature dishes,
and a seasonally influenced
eclectic menu of fresh salads,
homemade soups, pizza,
burgers, wraps, custom made
sandwiches, and handcrafted
desserts. Spring and winter
hours vary. Leashed, well
mannered dogs are allowed at
their outside dining area.

**Giovanni's Italian Restaurant**
1988 Old Mission Drive
Solvang CA
805-688-1888
This pizza place is located about
one mile outside of the village.
To get there, head east on

Mission Drive/Hwy 246 and it will be on the left. They are open from 11am until 9:30pm. On Friday and Saturday, they are open until 10:30pm. Leashed dogs are allowed at their outside tables.

**Olsen's Danish Village Bakery**

1529 Mission Drive
Solvang CA
805-688-6314
The bakery is open from 7:30am until 6 pm. A 4th generation Danish Master Baker offers up a delicious variety of baked goods at this bakery. Leashed dogs are allowed at their outside tables.

**Panino**
475 First Street
Solvang CA
805-688-0608
paninorestaurants.com/
One well-behaved dog is okay at the outdoor tables.

**River Grill at The Alisal**
150 Alisal Rd
Solvang CA
805-688-7784
The River Grille has a nice outdoor patio for you and your well-behaved pup to watch the golf course. But beware of stray golf balls.

**Subway**
1641 Mission Dr
Solvang CA
805-688-7650
This eatery specializes in made-to-order fresh, baked bread sandwiches with a variety of accompaniments to round out your meals. They also provide a kid's menu and catering services. Leashed dogs are allowed at the outer tables.

**The Belgian Cafe**
1671 Copenhagen Drive
Solvang CA
805-688-6630
They only have 1 table outside, so many people with dogs sit at this outdoor table. The table seats up to 4-5 people. The hours are from 7am until 3pm.

**The Big Bopper**
1510 Mission Drive
Solvang CA
805-688-6018
You and your pup can order food from the outside window. They are open from 11am until 8:30pm.

**The Mustard Seed Restaurant**
1655 Mission Drive/H 246
Solvang CA
805-688-1318
This eatery serves up a full menu of choices featuring salads, burgers, specialty sandwiches, steaks, seafood, ethnic dishes, and more. Leashed dogs are welcome at their outside tables.

**The Solvang Brew Company**
1547 Mission Street/H 246
Solvang CA
805-688-2337
solvangbrewingcompany.com
Some of the offerings at this brewing company include several fresh brews on tap, handcrafted soups, sandwiches, burgers, entrees, house made desserts, and various events. Leashed, friendly dogs are allowed at their outside dining area.

**The Touch**
1635 Mission Drive
Solvang CA
805-686-0222
mandarintouch.net/
This dog-friendly restaurant serves American style breakfast and lunch. They serve Chinese food for dinner. The owner of this restaurant is a dog lover and has several dogs.

**Tower Pizza**
436 Alisal Rd, Units C + D
Solvang CA
805-688-3036
towerpizzasolvang.com/
Dogs are welcome at the outside tables here with doggie biscuits

**Viking Garden Restaurant**
446C Alisal Rd

Solvang CA
805-688-1250
vikinggardenrestaurant.com/
Danish cuisine and the largest selection of draft beer in town is offered at this eatery and pub. Leashed dogs are welcome at the outdoor tables.

**Wandering Dog Wine Bar**
1539 C Mission Drive/H 246
Solvang CA
805-686-9126
wanderingdogwinebar.com
Featuring an eclectic, and sometimes hard to find, selection of the finest wines from around the world and the Central Coast, this wine bar also offers a full calendar of special events, samplings, wine soires, and food/wine pairings. Leashed, friendly dogs are welcome at their outside tables.

## Pet-Friendly Stores
**Big Dog**
485 Alisal Rd #D1-2
Solvang CA
805-693-0899
Your well-behaved, leashed dog may shop with you at this Big Dog shop.

**Book Loft**
1680 Mission Drive
Solvang CA
805-688-6010
Your leashed, well-behaved dog can browse this bookstore with you and sit with you at the outdoor seats of the attached Kaffe Hus.

**Lemo's Feed and Pet Supply**
1511 Mission Dr
Solvang CA
805-693-8180
This feed and pet store in Solvang has some nice treats for your dog, as well as regular dog supplies.

## Dog-Friendly Wineries and Vineyards
**LinCourt Vineyards**
343 North Refugio Rd

Santa Ynez CA
805-688-8381
Dogs are allowed at the outdoor picnic tables.

**Buttonwood Farm Winery**
1500 Alamo Pintado Rd
Solvang CA
805-688-3032

**D'Alfonso-Curran Wines**
1557 Mission Drive/H 246
Solvang CA
805-693-8864
d-cwines.com
This winery features a variety of fine wines produced from fruit grown in the valleys and on the mesas of the Santa Rita Hills as well as from the Santa Ynez Valley AVA's. Dogs are allowed on the grounds of the winery; they are not allowed in the tasting room. Dogs must be leashed and under their owner's control at all times.

**Lucas and Lewellen Winery**
1645 Copenhagen Drive
Solvang CA
805-686-9336
Located along the coastal mountains of the Pacific Ocean, this beautiful winery specializes in a variety of red and white wines. Dogs are allowed on the grounds, and this pet friendly place even allows their canine visitors in the tasting room. Dogs must be well mannered, leashed, and under their owner's control at all times.

**Mandolina Wines**
1665 Copenhagen Drive
Solvang CA
888-777-6663
Located along the coastal mountains of the Pacific Ocean, this beautiful winery specializes in California and Italian grape varieties of red and white wines. Dogs are allowed on the grounds, and this pet friendly place even allows their canine visitors in the tasting room. Dogs must be well mannered, leashed, and under their owner's control at all times.

**Dog-Friendly Parks**
**Santa Ynez Recreation Area**
Paradise Road
Santa Ynez CA
805-967-3481
Dogs on leash are allowed on the nature trails and hikes. There are miles of trails at this park. Other activities include swimming and fishing. This recreation area is actually part of the Los Padres National Forest. From Highway l0l at west end of Santa Barbara, turn north on Highway l54 (San Marcos Pass Road) for about10- l2 miles, then go east on Paradise Road to the Santa Ynez Recreation Area.

**Hans Christian Andersen Park**
Atterdag Road
Solvang CA

You and your leashed pup can enjoy a 1.3 mile round trip hike along meadows lined with majestic oak trees. This park's 50 acres also has picnic facilities, a playground for kids and tennis courts. It is open daily from 8 a.m. to dusk. The park is located within walking distance of the village. It on Atterdag Road, just 3 blocks north of Mission Drive and the village of Solvang.

**Nojoqui Falls Park**
Alisal Road
Solvang CA

Nojoqui Falls is a 160+ foot waterfall which towers over the park grounds. It is best viewed after a rainy period. You and your leashed pup can view the waterfall by embarking on an easy 10 minute hike through a wooded canyon. This park also has a sports playing field, playgrounds for kids, and a picnic area. The park is open every day from dawn to dusk. It is located on Alisal Road, just 7 miles south of Solvang on a country road.

**Solvang Park**

Mission Drive
Solvang CA

This small city park is located in the middle of the Solvang village. It is a nice spot to rest after walking around town. It is located on Mission Drive at the corner of First Street.

**Emergency Veterinarians**
**Valley Pet Emergency Clinic**
914 W Highway 246
Buellton CA
805-688-2334
Monday - Friday 8 am - 5:30 pm, Saturday 8 am - 5 pm, Closed Sunday.

**Sonoma Coast**

**Dog-Friendly Beaches**
**Stillwater Cove Regional Park**
22455 Highway 1
Jenner CA
707-565-2041
This 210 acre park includes a small beach, campground, picnic tables, and restrooms. The park offers a great view of the Pacific Ocean from Stillwater Cove. Dogs are allowed on the beach, and in the campground, but they must be on a 6 foot or less leash. People also need to clean up after their pets. There is a $3 day use fee. The park is located off Highway 1, about 16 miles north of Jenner.

**Sonoma Coast State Beach**
Highway 1
Salmon Creek CA
707-875-3483
Dogs on leash are allowed at some of the beaches in this state park. Dogs are allowed at Shell Beach, Portuguese Beach and Schoolhouse Beach. They are not allowed at Goat Rock or Salmon Creek Beach due to the protected seals and snowy plovers. Please clean up after your pets. While dogs are

allowed on some of the beaches and campgrounds, they are not allowed on any hiking trails at this park.

## Dog-Friendly Parks
### Salt Point State Park
25050 Hwy 1
Jenner CA
707-847-3221
Enjoy panoramic views and the dramatic sounds of the surf at this park that offers a variety of sights and recreational activities. This park is also home to one of the first underwater parks in California. Dogs of all sizes are allowed at the campgrounds and in any of the developed areas. Dogs are not allowed on the trails or on the beaches, and they must be inside at night. There is no additional pet fee. Dogs must be leashed and cleaned up after at all times.

## Sonoma Wine Country

## Dog-Friendly Hotels
### Cottages On River Road
14880 River Road
Guerneville CA
888-342-2624
rivervillageresort.com
Private balconies or patios are provided in every cottage and studio at Cottages On River Road. It features a seasonal outdoor pool opened from Memorial Day through Labor Day and offers evening campfire and s'mores weather permitting. Free WiFi is available throughout the common areas and all guest rooms. All room types offer a refrigerator a microwave a coffee machine a flat screen TV with cable channels a heather and an en suite bathroom.
Guests of Cottages On River Road are offered a daily complimentary continental breakfast. Complimentary coffee

and fruit is available in the lobby.
Activities such as hiking are available nearby. Board games are available at the property. Free parking is available onsite. Cottages On River Road is located off Highway 116. Northwood Golf Club is 7 km away and 5.3 km from Armstrong Redwoods State Preserve.

### Best Western Dry Creek Inn
198 Dry Creek Road
Healdsburg CA
707-433-0300 (800-780-7234)
Dogs are allowed. There is a $30 per pet per night pet fee. Up to three dogs are allowed per room. Dogs are allowed in one out of two buildings.

### Hotel Healdsburg
25 Matheson Street
Healdsburg CA
707-431-2800
Guests are treated to free breakfasts and free Wi-Fi at the non-smoking Hotel Healdsburg an oasis in the center of town that features a gorgeous spa an outdoor pool and an on-site gourmet restaurant. The three-story non-smoking Hotel Healdsburg houses 55 airy rooms all adorned with an understated elegance and local artwork. Wi-Fi is free and rooms supply guests with HDTVs Bluetooth audio systems and coffeemakers with snacks. The luxurious bathrooms feature glass showers bathrobes and high-end toiletries with some boasting soaking tubs. The hotel offers a complimentary breakfast buffet and has a concierge to help plan adventures. Guests can check out a bicycle at the 24-hour front desk or burn calories in the fitness center and for those who need to stay in touch with the office there are business services. Guests can soothe sore muscles with a massage at the spa then savor a swim in the 60-foot outdoor pool or soak in the hot tub amidst the hotel's gardens. There is a

pool-side bar with plenty of loungers and guests won't want to miss the menu at the two on-site restaurants one featuring wood-fired pizzas and the other boasting an upscale menu. Valet parking is free and pets are allowed for a fee. In northern Sonoma County the Hotel Healdsburg sits on a corner lot surrounded by blocks of galleries shops and cafes in downtown Healdsburg. Santa Rosa offers more commercial stores 15 minutes south and more than 100 wineries await tasting within a half-hour of the hotel. Nature lovers can get outdoors on the Armstrong Redwoods Trail or explore Lake Sonoma each within a half-hour's drive. The closest airport is Charles M. Schulz-Sonoma County Airport eight miles south and San Francisco International Airport is an 82-mile trip.

### Inn At Occidental
3657 Church Street
Occidental CA
707-874-1047 (800-522-6324)
innatoccidental.com/
Nestled beneath redwoods and centrally located to wine country the Sonoma Coast and the Russian River the non-smoking Inn at Occidental welcomes our guests with a secluded setting and wine and cheese gatherings. Comprised of 16 rooms and a cottage the Inn at Occidental offers in-room amenities such as private bathrooms Wi-Fi access hairdryers bathrobes upscale bath amenities sitting areas and fireplaces. Mingle with other guests at the afternoon wine and cheese receptions. Relax on the veranda or amble amongst the inn's antiques and artwork. Pets are welcome for an additional fee. Tucked within the redwood forests of Sonoma Wine Country the Inn at Occidental is situated in the quaint bohemian town of Occidental. The property is located within minutes of art galleries shops and fine restaurants and within 10 minutes of historic Bohemian

Grove. It's within a 20-minute drive of Bodega Bay and a one-hour drive from all four Sonoma wine valleys. Oakland International Airport is 77 miles away.

**Occidental Hotel**
3610 Bohemian Highway
Occidental CA
707-874-3623
Featuring a pool and sun terrace Occidental Hotel is located within 5 minutes' walk of shops and cafes. Over 200 Sonoma County wineries are within 30 minutes' drive of this hotel. Marble counters a separate vanity sink and a separate dressing area is featured in the en suite bathroom of all rooms. A flat-screen TV and tea and coffee-making facilities are also featured in rooms at Hotel Occidental.
Bodega Bay is 12 km from Occidental Hotel while Santa Rosa is 21 km from the property. Downtown Santa Rosa and the Charles M. Schultz Museum is 20 minutes' drive away.

**Best Western Inn Rohnert Park**
6500 Redwood Drive
Rohnert Park CA
707-584-7435 (800-780-7234)
Dogs up to 80 pounds are allowed. There is a $20 per day pet fee up to $100 for the week. Up to two dogs are allowed per room.

**Doubletree Hotel Sonoma Wine Country**
One Doubletree Drive
Rohnert Park CA
707-584-5466 (800-222-TREE (8733))
Located in the heart of the state's central wine country, this luxury hotel offers a number of on site amenities for all level of travelers - including their signature chocolate chip cookies at check in, plus a convenient location to hundreds of wineries, and shopping, dining, and recreation areas. Dogs up to about 50 pounds (exceptions may be made for

show dogs) are allowed for an additional pet fee of $35 per night per room.

**Rodeway Inn Wine Country**
6288 Redwood Drive
Rohnert Park CA
707-584-1600 (877-424-6423)
Located in heart of Somona County, this Rohnert Park hotel is within 30 minutes of all wine country attractions.

Dogs up to 20 pounds are allowed. Dogs are allowed for a pet fee of $15.00 per pet per night.

**Best Western Garden Inn**
1500 Santa Rosa Avenue
Santa Rosa CA
707-546-4031 (800-780-7234)
Dogs up to 80 pounds are allowed. There is a $15 per day pet fee up to $100 for the week. Up to two dogs are allowed per room.

**Best Western Plus Wine Country Inn & Suites**
870 Hopper Avenue
Santa Rosa CA
707-545-9000 (800-780-7234)
Dogs up to 80 pounds are allowed. There is a $20 per day pet fee up to $100 for the week. Up to two dogs are allowed per room.

**Hotel Santa Rosa**
2632 Cleveland Ave
Santa Rosa CA
707-542-5544 (877-424-6423)
Sonoma County Fair Grounds 4 miles. San Francisco 1 hour south.

Dogs of all sizes are allowed. Dogs are allowed for a pet fee of $15.00 per pet per night.

**Quality Inn & Suites Santa Rosa**
3000 Santa Rosa Avenue
Santa Rosa CA
707-521-2100 (877-424-6423)
The Quality Inn is located in the heart of wine country, and walking distance to major shops.

Dogs of all sizes are allowed.

Dogs are allowed for a pet fee of $15.00 per pet per night.

**Travelodge Santa Rosa**
1815 Santa Rosa Avenue
Santa Rosa CA
707-542-3472
Dogs of all sizes are allowed. There is a pet fee of $10 per pet per night.

**Best Western Sonoma Valley Inn & Krug Event Center**
550 Second Street West
Sonoma CA
707-938-9200 (800-780-7234)
Dogs up to 80 pounds are allowed. There is a $20 per day pet fee up to $100 for the week. Up to two dogs are allowed per room.

**The Lodge At Sonoma Renaissance Resort & Spa**
1325 Broadway
Sonoma CA
707-935-6600
Dogs of all sizes are allowed. There is a $75 one time pet fee.

# Pet-Friendly Extended Stay Hotels
**Extended Stay America - Santa Rosa - North**
100 Fountain Grove Pkwy
Santa Rosa CA
707-541-0959 (800-804-3724)
One dog is allowed per suite. There is a $25 per night additional pet fee up to $150 for an entire stay.

**Extended Stay America - Santa Rosa - South**
2600 Corby Ave
Santa Rosa CA
707-546-4808 (800-804-3724)
One dog is allowed per suite. There is a $25 per night additional pet fee up to $150 for an entire stay.

# Dog-Friendly Attractions
**Jack London State Historic Park**
2400 London Ranch Road
Glen Ellen CA

707-938-5216
This park is a memorial to adventurer/writer Jack London, and is home to various personal artifacts and the cottage residence where he lived and tended various agriculture projects while producing a variety of famous writings. They offer a variety of trails, exhibits, programs, and tours. There are two first come first served picnic areas and one group picnic area. Dogs are allowed at the picnic areas, and on the trails to the Wolf House ruins and Beauty Ranch as far as the silos. Dogs must be under their owner's control at all times, and leashed and cleaned up after.

**Dry Creek Vineyard**
3770 Lambert Bridge Road
Healdsburg CA
707-433-1000
drycreekvineyard.com/
This award winning vineyard produces an impressive list of wines using the "small batch" method, and they are known for producing some of California's best Fume Blancs and Zinfandels. There are benches outside for visitors to sit and enjoy the lush surroundings of the vineyard. Dogs are welcome on the grounds; they must be well behaved, leashed, and cleaned up after. Dogs are not allowed in the tasting room.

**Small Lot Wine Tours**
Various
Sonoma CA
707-294-2232
This touring company offers a unique customized wine tour in that they drive (or ride in) your car through the back roads and hidden places in wine country for some great finds and a fair price. They focus on visiting small production wineries and tailor-making your tour to the Napa and Sonoma Counties. Your canine companions are very welcome to come along.

**Attractions**
TOP 200 PLACE **Russian**

**River Adventures Canoe Rentals**
20 Healdsburg Ave
Healdsburg CA
707-433-5599 (800-280-7627 (SOAR))
Take a self-guided eco-adventure with your pooch. Rent an inflatable canoe and adventure along the Russian River. The SOAR 16 is the largest model and is great for taking children and dogs. There are many refreshing swimming holes along the way. Dogs and families of all ages are welcome. Be sure to call ahead as reservations are required.

**Outdoor Restaurants**
**Redwood Cafe**
8240 Old Redwood Highway
Cotati CA
707-795-7868
redwoodcafe.com/
A popular neighborhood café, offerings include organic Fair Trade coffee, a full days menu, a Bohemian chic ambiance, fine wine and beer, live music and dancing, and alfresco dining. Leashed, well mannered dogs are welcome at their outside tables.

**Russian River Pub**
11829 River Road
Forestville CA
707-887-7932
russianriverpub.com/default.aspx
This family style pub has new owners but still serve their famous chicken wings and the Ultimate Pub Burger. They provide service at their outdoor patio where your pet is welcome to join you. Dogs must be friendly, attended to at all times, and leashed.

**Russian River Vineyards and the Corks Restaurant**
5700 Gravenstein H N/H 116
Forestville CA
707-887-3344
russianrivervineyards.com
In addition to featuring a variety of fine distinctive wines, this vineyard also has the

distinction of being the only winery in the Russian River Valley with a cafe. The cafe presents a seasonally changing menu with fresh locally sourced produce, brunch/lunch and dinner menus with vegetarian options, and cuisine tailored to compliment their wines. Leashed, well mannered dogs are welcome at their outside tables.

**Garden Court Cafe & Bakery**
13875 Sonoma Highway 12
Glen Ellen CA
707-935-1565
gardencourtcafe.com/bleu.html
Well-behaved, leashed dogs may accompany owners at the outside dining area. They have a special dog menu as well. Their hours are 8:30 am to 2 pm Monday to Friday (except closed on Tuesday), and from 8 am until 2 pm on Saturday and Sunday.

**Main Street Station Ristorante, Cabaret & Pizzeria,**
16280 Main Street
Guerneville CA
707-869-0501
mainststation.com/
This restaurant offers fun and food with an Italian flair. Your pet is welcome to sit with you at the outdoor tables. They must be attended to at all times, well behaved, and leashed.

**Roadhouse Restaurant at Dawn Ranch Lodge**
16467 River Road
Guerneville CA
707-869-0656
This restaurant offers a variety of wines from the Russian River area, a full bar and contemporary California cuisine. They offer outside dining on their deck, and your pet is welcome to join you. Dogs must be attended to at all times, well behaved, and leashed.

**Barndiva**
231 Center Street
Healdsburg CA
707-431-0100
barndiva.com

With an emphasis on sourcing and supporting sustainable ranchers, farmers, fishmongers, and small batch purveyors, this restaurant and lounge features a diverse menu of skillfully created cuisine and beverages. Additionally, they offer fine dining specials and specialty cocktails. Leashed, well mannered dogs are welcome at their outside tables.

**Dry Creek General Store**
3495 Dry Creek Rd
Healdsburg CA
707-433-4171
drycreekgeneralstore1881.com/
Enjoy a breakfast sandwich or a variety of sandwiches for lunch including turkey, roast beef, ham and veggie. Dogs are welcome at the outdoor tables.

**Giorgio's Pizzeria**
25 Grant Avenue
Healdsburg CA
707-433-1106
Dogs are allowed at the outdoor tables. The outdoor tables are on a covered deck.

**Howard's Cafe**
3811 Bohemian H
Occidental CA
707-874-2838
In addition to a menu with organic choices throughout, this eatery also features an organic bakery with vegan options, and organic juice, smoothie, and coffee bars. They are open Monday to Friday from 7 am until 2:30 pm and on Saturday and Sunday from 7 am until 3 pm. Leashed, friendly dogs are allowed at their outside dining area.

**Baja Fresh Mexican Grill**
451 Rohnert Pk. Expressway West
Rohnert Park CA
707-585-2252
bajafresh.com
This Mexican restaurant is open for lunch and dinner. They use fresh ingredients and making their salsa and beans daily. Some of the items on their menu include Enchiladas, Burritos, Tacos Salads,

Quesadillas, Nachos, Chicken, Steak and more. Well-behaved leashed dogs are allowed at the outdoor tables.

**Golden B Cafe**
101 Golf Course Drive
Rohnert Park CA
707-585-6185
Dogs are allowed at the outdoor tables. They are open Monday to Friday from 7 am until 3 pm and on Saturday and Sunday from 9 am until 1 pm.

**Flying Goat Coffee**
10 4th Street
Santa Rosa CA
707-575-1202
flyinggoatcoffee.com/
Dogs are allowed at the outdoor seats. The coffee shop is in Railroad Square in Santa Rosa, next to the train station.

**Jamba Juice**
2360 Mendocino Avenue
Santa Rosa CA
707-527-5501
jambajuice.com
All natural and organic ingredients, no high-fructose corn syrup, 0 grams trans fat, no artificial preservatives, a healthy helping of antioxidants, vitamins, and minerals, and fresh whole fruit and fruit juices set the base for these tasty and healthy beverages. Their organic Hot Blends provides a new spin on coffee, green or chai tea, and hot chocolate;plus they offer probiotic fruit and yogurt Blends. Additionally, they feature organic steel-cut oatmeal prepared fresh every morning, all natural salads, wraps, sandwiches, and grab n' go specialties. They also offer healthy community support through fundraisers, special sales, and school lunch programs. Leashed, well mannered dogs are allowed at their outside dining area.

**Lita's Cafe**
1973 Mendocino Avenue
Santa Rosa CA
707-575-1628
litasrestaurant.com/

This cafe features a full day's menu of all American favorites, seafood and Mexican specialties. They also offer specials for every day of the week. Leashed, well mannered dogs are allowed at their outside dining area.

**Sunnyside Tokyo**
3800 Sebastopol Road
Santa Rosa CA
707-526-2652
sunnysidetokyo.com/default.aspx
A Japanese, boutique-fusion restaurant, they serve up healthy portions family style with a full menu of choices, including fresh sushi. They are open Monday to Saturday from 11 am until 9 pm;happy hour is from 3 to 6 pm. Leashed, well mannered dogs are allowed at their outside tables.

**Sweet Spot Pub & Lounge**
619 Fourth Street
Santa Rosa CA
707-528-7566
sweetspotpub.com/index.htm
This lively pub serves up a variety of specialty beers as well as traditional pub brews, conventional pub cuisine with Belizean influences, seasonal specialties with tastings each month, and happy hours Monday to Saturday from 4 pm until 6 pm. They also have a big screen TV with several flat screens for sports viewing and a full calendar of special events. Leashed, friendly dogs are allowed at their outside dining area.

**Whole Foods Market**
1181 Yulupa Ave.
Santa Rosa CA
707-575-7915
wholefoods.com/
This natural food supermarket offers natural and organic foods. Order some food from their deli without your dog and bring it to an outdoor table where your well-behaved leashed dog is welcome.

**Whole Foods Market**
6910 McKinley St.

Sebastopol CA
707-829-9801
wholefoods.com/
This natural food supermarket offers natural and organic foods. Order some food from their deli without your dog and bring it to one of their benches outside where your well-behaved leashed dog is welcome.

**Centre Du Vin**
480 First Street East
Sonoma CA
707-996-9779
ledsonhotel.com/dining.html
This French bistro restaurant and wine bar is located at the elegant Ledson Hotel. You can dine at their outside sidewalk tables where they offer service, a heated patio, and live music drifting throughout. Leashed, well mannered dogs are welcome at their outside dining area.

**La Casa**
121 E Spain Street
Sonoma CA
707-996-3406
lacasarestaurant.com/
This Mexican restaurant offers a generous made-from-scratch menu with traditional favorites and regional specialties, and a full bar. Leashed, well behaved dogs are welcome at the bar patio, and table service is offered.

**Pet-Friendly Stores**
**PetSmart Pet Store**
575 Rohnert Park Expry.
Rohnert Park CA
707-586-1891
Your licensed and well-behaved leashed dog is allowed in the store.

**Pet Club**
1935 Santa Rosa Avenue
Santa Rosa CA
707-523-3083
petclubstores.com
In addition to warehouse pricing with no membership fees, this comprehensive pet supply store offers weekly specials and more than 11,000 pet products

ranging from wellness items, bedding, dinnerware, a wide choice of quality foods, treats, leashes, toys, apparel, travel supplies, and much more. Leashed, friendly dogs are always welcome in the store.

**Petco Pet Store - Santa Rosa**
2765 Santa Rosa Ave.
Santa Rosa CA
707-566-7900
Your licensed and well-behaved leashed dog is allowed in the store.

**Three Dog Bakery**
526 Broadway
Sonoma CA
707-933-9780
threedog.com
Three Dog Bakery provides cookies and snacks for your dog as well as some boutique items. You well-behaved, leashed dog is welcome.

**Three Dog Bakery**
526 Broadway
Sonoma CA
707-933-9780
Three Dog Bakery provides cookies and snacks for your dog as well as some boutique items. You well-behaved, leashed dog is welcome.

**Dog-Friendly Wineries and Vineyards**
**Sebastiani Vineyards and Winery**
389 Fourth Street
East Sonoma CA
800-888-5532
sebastiani.com/home.asp
Dogs of all sizes are welcome to explore the vineyard and enjoy the picnic area with their owners. Small dogs that can be carried are allowed in the tasting room. They provide water bowls outside all the time, and anchored leash extensions. They are open daily from 10 am to 5 pm. Dogs must be well behaved, leashed at all times, and please clean up after your pet.

**Joseph Swan Vineyards**
2916 Laguna Road
Forestville CA
707-573-3747
swanwinery.com/
A small family-owned winery, they specialize in old vine zinfandel and pinot noir wines with Rhone style wines, chardonnay, and pinot gris also added. They also offer various events during the year and welcome canine visitors throughout the vineyard and tasting room as well. Friendly, leashed dogs will usually find water and treats available too.

**Topolos Vineyards**
5700 Gravenstein Hwy N.
Forestville CA
707-887-1575
topolos.com/
Dogs are allowed in the tasting room. The tasting room is open 11 am to 5:30 pm daily.

**Benziger Family Winery**
1883 London Ranch Road
Glen Ellen CA
707-935-3000
benziger.com/
This 85 acre winery specializes in organic and Biodynamic winegrowing practices producing wines with an accent on more flavor, intensity, and site-specific vineyard traits. A deck with tables and chairs allows a nice area to rest. Dogs are welcome on the grounds and on the deck. Dogs must be well mannered, leashed, and cleaned up after. They are not allowed in the tasting room.

**F. Korbel and Brothers Champagne Cellars**
13250 River Road
Guerneville CA
707-824-7000
Well-behaved leashed dogs are allowed at the outdoor picnic area.

**Foppiano Vineyards**
12707 Old Redwood Highway
Healdsburg CA
707-433-7272
lfoppiano.com.
Dogs are allowed at the picnic area and on the self-guided

vineyard tour.

**Lambert Bridge Winery**
4085 W. Dry Creek Rd
Healdsburg CA
800-975-0555
lambertbridge.com/
Dogs are allowed in the wine tasting room and the large picnic grounds. The winery is open daily from 10:30 am to 4:30 pm.

**Porter Creek Vineyard and Winery**
8735 Westside Road
Healdsburg CA
707-433-6321
The wines here impart flavors indigenous to the Russian River Valley, and they specializing in organic, hillside grown grapes from the Burgundy and Rhone varieties. Dogs are allowed throughout the grounds; they are not allowed in the tasting room. Dogs must be friendly with other pets (on site), leashed, and under their owner's control at all times.

**Porter Creek Vineyard and Winery**
8735 Westside Road
Healdsburg CA
707-433-6321
Nestled among the hills of the Russian River Valley, this estate specializes in hillside, organically grown grape varietals of the Rhone and Burgundian variety. Leashed, well mannered dogs are allowed on the grounds. They are not allowed in the tasting room.

**Quivira Vineyards**
4900 W Dry Creek Road
Healdsburg CA
707-431-8333
quivirawine.com/
This small, family owned winery believes in crafting wines that capture and accentuate the delicious, lively fruit flavors that is characteristic of their wines, and they were recently certified for using Biodynamic agricultural growing methods. There are benches for those wanting to sit outside and picnic tables. Dogs are allowed on the grounds and

the picnic area; they are not allowed in the tasting room. Dogs must be well mannered, leashed, and cleaned up after.

**Rodney Strong Vineyards**
11455 Old Redwood H
Healdsburg CA
707-433-6511
rodneystrong.com/
This award winning winery is committed to crafting exceptional wines sourced from 12 unique vineyards and four of Sonoma County's distinct growing appellations. There is a lawn and picnic area for visitors to enjoy that is surrounded by acres of beautiful vineyards. Dogs must be well behaved, leashed, and cleaned up after. Dogs are allowed on the lawn and at the picnic area, but they are not allowed in buildings.

**Deerfield Ranch Winery and Tasting Room**
10200 Sonoma H/H 12
Kenwood CA
707-833-5215
deerfieldranch.com
Traveling canines will enjoy the tasting room atmosphere at this winery - it's located in a cave that stays at about 60 degrees all year. They offer a variety of fine white and red wines' several award winning. The tasting room is open daily from 10:30 am until 4:30 pm. Leashed, friendly dogs are allowed, and please clean up after your pet.

**Deloach Vineyards**
1791 Olivet Road
Santa Rosa CA
707-526-9111
deloachvineyards.com.
Dogs are allowed at the picnic area.

**Hanna Winery**
5353 Occidental Road
Santa Rosa CA
707-575-3371
Well-behaved, leashed dogs are allowed in the tasting room and in the picnic area.

**Martini and Prati Wines**

2191 Laguna Road
Santa Rosa CA
707-823-2404
Well-behaved, leashed dogs area allowed at the picnic area.

**Matanzas Creek Winery**
6097 Bennet Valley Road
Santa Rosa CA
707-528-6464
matanzascreek.com/
This scenic winery is dedicated to offering exceptionally crafted wines sourced from Sonoma County's finest vineyards. They also offer gardens carefully planned and planted to attractively appear as part of the native landscape, a picnic area, and a deck with benches. Well behaved dogs are allowed. Dogs must be leashed and cleaned up after at all times. Dogs are not allowed in the tasting room.

**Taft Street Winery**
2030 Barlow Lane
Sebastopol CA
707-823-2404
Dogs are allowed on the picnic deck.

**Bartholomew Park Winery**
1000 Vineyard Ln
Sonoma CA
707-935-9511
Bartholomew Park Winery allows pets to join you in visiting the vineyards. Dogs must be well-behaved and on leash at all times.

**Sebastiani Vineyards and Winery**
389 Fourth Street East
Sonoma CA
800-888-5532
sebastiani.com
Well-behaved dogs are allowed on and off-leash at the outdoor tables and on the property. Water bowls and cleanup stations are provided. They ask that dogs stay out of the fountain. This is a very dog friendly winery.

**Martinell Vineyards**
3360 River Road
Windsor CA
707-525-0570

Dogs are allowed at the picnic area.

## Mutt Lynch Winery
9050 Windsor Road
Windsor CA
707-942-6180
muttlynchwinery.com
This small one woman winery is usually open only by appointment. However, by combining humor, a love of dogs and passion for wine, this winery offers such items as the "Big Dog" wines, or their Merlot Over and Play Dead, and their annual Dog Days of Summer festival is a fun event for pet and owner with a dog art exhibit, good food, and music. They also have other related events. Dogs are welcome throughout the winery, and they must be leashed at all times and cleaned up after.

## Dog-Friendly Beaches

### Cloverdale River Park
31820 McCray Road
Cloverdale CA
707-565-2041
This park is located along the Russian River and offers seasonal fishing and river access for kayaks and canoes. There are no lifeguards at the beach area. Dogs are allowed, but must be on a 6 foot or less leash. They can wade into the water, but cannot really swim because pets must remain on leash. There is a $3 per car parking fee.

### Healdsburg Veterans Memorial Beach
13839 Old Redwood Highway
Healdsburg CA
707-565-2041
This man-made swimming beach is located on the Russian River. Dogs are allowed at this park, but must be on a 6 foot or less leash. They can wade into the water, but cannot really swim because pets must remain on leash. People are urged to swim only when lifeguards are present, which is usually between Memorial Day and

Labor Day. The beach area also offers picnic tables and a restroom. There is a $3 to $4 parking fee per day, depending on the season.

### Sea Ranch Coastal Access Trails
Highway 1
Sea Ranch CA
707-785-2377
Walk along coastal headlands or the beach in Sea Ranch. There are six trailhead parking areas which are located along Highway 1, south of the Sonoma Mendocino County Line. Access points include Black Point, Bluff Top Trail, Pebble Beach, Stengal Beach, Shell Beach and Walk on Beach. Dogs must be on a 6 foot or less leash. There is a $3 per car parking fee. RVs and vehicles with trailers are not allowed to use the parking areas.

## Off-Leash Dog Parks

### Elizabeth Anne Perrone Dog Park
13630 Sonoma H/H 12
Glen Ellen CA
707-565-2041
Located at the 162 acre Sonoma Valley Regional Park, this fenced 1 acre off leash area offers a drinking fountain for thirsty pooches, a gazebo, wooded areas and pathways. Dogs must be sociable, current on all vaccinations, and under their owner's control at all times. Dogs must be leashed on no more than a 6 foot leash when not in designated off-lead areas.

### DeTurk Round Barn Dog Park
819 Donahue Street
Santa Rosa CA
707-543-3292
This dog park is fully fenced.

### Doyle Community Park Dog Park
700 Doyle Park Drive
Santa Rosa CA

707-543-3292
This dog park is fully fenced.

### Galvin Community Park Dog Park
3330 Yulupa Avenue
Santa Rosa CA
707-543-3292
This dog park is fully fenced.

### Northwest Community Dog Park
2620 W. Steele Lane
Santa Rosa CA
707-543-3292
Thanks to one of our readers who writes "Wonderful dog park. 2 separately fenced areas (one for little dogs too... It's all grassy and some trees and right near the creek. Also a brand new childrens play area (one for big kids and one fenced for toddlers). This dog park is sponsored by the Peanut's comics creator Charles M. Schultz's estate."

### Rincon Valley Community Park Dog Park
5108 Badger Road
Santa Rosa CA
707-543-3292
This dog park is fully fenced.

### Sebastopol Dog Park
500 Ragle Rd
Sebastopol CA
707-823-7262
This off lead area is located at the 157 acre Ragle Ranch Regional recreational park that is also home to a peace garden with a sculpture by a famed artist and a nature trail leading to the Atascadero Creek. Dogs must be sociable, current on all vaccinations, and under their owner's control at all times. Dogs must be leashed on no more than a 6 foot leash when not in designated off-lead areas.

### Ernie Smith Community Park Dog Park
18776 Gilman Drive
Sonoma CA
707-539-8092
Located at the Ernest Maynard Smith Park recreational park,

this off lead area provides a pet drinking fountain and tables. Dogs must be sociable, current on all vaccinations, and under their owner's control at all times. Dogs must be leashed on no more than a 6 foot leash when not in designated off-lead areas.

## Dog-Friendly Parks
### Jack London State Historic Park
2400 London Ranch Road
Glen Ellen CA
707-938-5216
jacklondonpark.com/
This park is a memorial to the famous writer and adventurer Jack London. He lived here from 1905 until his death in 1916. Dogs on leash are allowed around the ranch and historic buildings, but not inside. Pets are also allowed on the Wolf House Trail which is a 1.2 mile round trip trail. Please clean up after your pet. The park is located about 20 minutes north of Sonoma.

### Sonoma Valley Regional Park
13630 Sonoma Highway
Glen Ellen CA
707-565-2041
This 162 acre park offers both paved and dirt trails which are used for hiking, bicycling and horseback riding. Dogs are allowed but must be on a 6 foot or less leash. The Elizabeth Anne Perrone Dog Park is also located within this park and allows dogs to run leash-free within the one acre. There is a $3 parking fee.

### Crane Creek Regional Park
5000 Pressley Road
Rohnert Park CA
707-565-2041
Located just east of Sonoma State University, this 128 acre foothills park offers hiking and bicycling trails. There are picnic tables and restrooms at the trailhead. Dogs must be kept on a 6 foot or less leash. There is a $3 per car parking fee.

### Hood Mountain Regional Park
3000 Los Alamos Road
Santa Rosa CA
707-565-2041
This 1,450 acre wilderness park offers bicycling, equestrian and rugged hiking trails for experienced hikers in good physical condition. Dogs are allowed at this park, but must be on a 6 foot or less leash. Access to the park is on Los Alamos Road which is a very narrow and winding road. There is a $3 per car parking fee.

### Spring Lake Regional Park
391 Violetti Drive
Santa Rosa CA
707-785-2377
This 320 acre park with a 72 acre lake offers miles of easy walking trails and a campground. Dogs are allowed but must be on a 6 foot or less leash and proof of a rabies vaccination is required.

### Joe Rodota Trail
Petaluma Avenue
Sebastopol CA
707-565-2041
This is a 2.8 mile paved trail that runs parallel to an abandoned railway line. There are agricultural ranches and farms along the trail. Dogs are allowed, but must be on a 6 foot or less leash. Parking is available in the town of Sebastopol, at the trailhead located off of Petaluma Avenue.

### Ragle Ranch Regional Park
500 Ragle Road
Sebastopol CA
707-565-2041
This 157 acre park offers walking trails, sports courts, picnic areas and a children's playground. Dogs are allowed, but must be on a 6 foot or less leash. There is a $3 per car parking fee.

### Maxwell Farms Regional Park
100 Verano Avenue
Sonoma CA

707-565-2041
This 85 acre park offers meadow nature trails on 40 acres, multi-use fields for soccer and softball, a children's playground and picnic areas. Dogs are allowed but must be on a 6 foot or less leash. There is a $3 parking fee.

### Foothill Regional Park
1351 Arata Lane
Windsor CA
707-565-2041
Hiking, bicycling, horseback riding and fishing are popular activities at this 211 acre park. Dogs must be kept on a 6 foot or less leash. No swimming, wading or boating is allowed on the lakes. There is a $3 per car parking fee.

## Rescue Organizations
### Wine Country Greyhound Adoption
PO Box 6266
Santa Rosa CA
1-800-WC-GREYS
winecountrygreyhounds.com
WCGA is an all-volunteer, nonprofit organization dedicated to finding caring, permanent homes for retired racing greyhounds, and to provide support and guidance for the adopted dogs and their families. We endeavor to educate the public of the plight of these wonderful dogs and demonstrate what loving companions they make.

# Sonora - Gold Country South

## Dog-Friendly Hotels
### Historic National Hotel & Restaurant
18183 Main Street
Jamestown CA
209-984-3446
national-hotel.com
A charming gem Historic National Hotel and Restaurant

welcomes guests with a 19th-century Gold Rush vibe a classy restaurant convenient access to national parks and its own friendly ghost. Originally built in 1859 this two-story mansion offers nine plush rooms featuring antique furniture free Wi-Fi cable TV and hairdryers. Ask about access to the Soaking Room featuring the 19th-century claw-foot soaking tub perfect for two. Wake up to a breakfast buffet often served on the balcony and wrap up the night at the on-site saloon known for its wine list. And be nice to Flo the resident ghost. Pets are welcome for a fee and get their own basket of goodies. Parking is free. In the heart of historic Jamestown this hotel makes it easy to explore antique shops museums and Railtown 1897 State Historic Park a mile south. Take in the spectacular sights of Yosemite National Park about half-an-hour away; or sample Zinfandels at Gianelli Vineyards less than a mile away. Sacramento International Airport is 122 miles away.

## Historic National Hotel & Restaurant

18183 Main Street
Jamestown CA
209-984-3446
national-hotel.com
A charming gem Historic National Hotel and Restaurant welcomes guests with a 19th-century Gold Rush vibe a classy restaurant convenient access to national parks and its own friendly ghost. Originally built in 1859 this two-story mansion offers nine plush rooms featuring antique furniture free Wi-Fi cable TV and hairdryers. Ask about access to the Soaking Room featuring the 19th-century claw-foot soaking tub perfect for two. Wake up to a breakfast buffet often served on the balcony and wrap up the night at the on-site saloon known for its wine list. And be nice to Flo the resident ghost. Pets are welcome for a fee and get their own basket of goodies. Parking is free. In the heart of

historic Jamestown this hotel makes it easy to explore antique shops museums and Railtown 1897 State Historic Park a mile south. Take in the spectacular sights of Yosemite National Park about half-an-hour away; or sample Zinfandels at Gianelli Vineyards less than a mile away. Sacramento International Airport is 122 miles away.

## Best Western Plus Sonora Oaks Hotel & Conference Center

19551 Hess Avenue
Sonora CA
209-533-4400 (800-780-7234)
Dogs up to 80 pounds are allowed. There is a $20 per day pet fee up to $100 for the week. Up to two dogs are allowed per room.

# Dog-Friendly Attractions

## Columbia State Historic Park

Parrotts Ferry Rd.
Columbia CA
209-532-0150
The popular Columbia State Historic Park represents a gold rush town of the 1850-1870 time period. In 1945 the State Legislature made this site a State Historic Park in order to preserve a typical Gold Rush town, an example of one of the most colorful eras in American history. The town's old Gold Rush-era business district has been preserved with many shops and restaurants. The proprietors of the shops are dressed in mid 1800s period clothing. Activities include viewing over a dozen historic structures, shopping, picnic facilities and a few hiking trails. One of the trails, The Karen Bakerville Smith Memorial Trail is a self-guided 1/2 mile loop trail which was dedicated to a teacher. The trail is located by the historic school building and there is a brochure describing the plants and surroundings. The park operates daily from 9am to 5 pm. They are closed

on Thankgiving and Christmas days. Admission is free. Your leashed dog is welcome. It is located on Parrotts Ferry Road, between Hwy 4 and Hwy 49 (near Sonora).

## Railtown 1897 State Historic Park

Highway 49
Jamestown CA
209-984-3953
This park is home to one of America's last authentic, operating railroad roundhouses. Still a popular Hollywood location site, Railtown 1897 has been called "the most photographed railroad in the world." "Petticoat Junction," "The Wild, Wild West," "High Noon," "The Virginian," and "Unforgiven" were all filmed here. Movie crews also produced the railroad sequences in "Back to the Future Part III" at Railtown. Dogs on leash are allowed in the park, and dogs are now allowed on the trains as well.

## Mark Twain Cabin

Jackass Hill Rd.
Tuttletown CA

This replica of Mark Twain's cabin has the original chimney and fireplace. During 1864-1865, young Mark Twain was a guest of the Gillis Brothers. While he stayed at this cabin, he gathered material for The Jumping Frog of Calaveras County (this book brought him fame) and for Roughing It. The cabin is located near Sonora, approximately 1 mile northwest of Tuttletown off Hwy 49. There are several parking spots next to the cabin.

# Outdoor Restaurants

## Giant Burger

846 Highway 4
Arnold CA
209-795-1594
Dogs are allowed at the outdoor tables of this .

## Historic National Hotel

18187 Main St
Jamestown CA
209-984-3446
national-hotel.com/
Freshly prepared, innovatively
created, and a focus placed on
originality best describes this
restaurant. They also feature a
notable wine list, daily fresh-
ground coffee, and a vine-
covered dog friendly patio.
Leashed, well mannered dogs
are welcome at their outside
tables;they must be cat, hound,
and human friendly.

**Pizza Plus**
18251 Main St
Jamestown CA
209-984-3700
Dogs on leash are allowed at
the outdoor seats. They are
open Monday to Saturday from
11 am until 9 pm.

**Pine Tree Restaurant**
19601 Hess Ave
Sonora CA
209-536-6065
Dogs are allowed at the outdoor
tables. They are open daily from
6 am until 9 pm.

**Pet-Friendly Stores**
**Sierra Nevada Adventure
Company (SNAC)**
2293 Highway 4
Arnold CA
209-795-9310
snacattack.com/
This store carries outdoor gear
and clothing for kayaking, rock-
climbing, hiking, cross-country
skiing and more. They always
encouraged dog owners to bring
their pets into the store to try on
dog packs, dog lifevests, and
more! It comes highly
recommended from one of our
readers and her Australian
Shepherd.

**Tractor Supply Company**
14879 Mono Way
Sonora CA
209-533-4840
tractorsupply.com
Some offerings of this
comprehensive farm store
includes agriculture, farming and

ranching supplies; outdoor
power equipment with all the
necessities; hundreds of
thousands of parts and
accessories accessible for yard
and garden; metal working and
welding supplies; tools for auto
and home; a wide range of
livestock/farm feed and needs;
and a variety of foods and
care/play/groom items for
household pets. Additionally,
they provide trailer and towing
supplies, vehicle maintenance
accessories, clothing, work
wear, foot wear, gifts, home
improvement items, a lot of
"know-how" and much more.
Leashed, friendly dogs are
welcome in the store.

**Dog-Friendly Wineries
and Vineyards**
**Black Sheep Winery**
West end of Main Street
Murphys CA
209-728-2157
blacksheepwinery.com/
This winery specializes in
zinfandel, with production also
of sauvignon, sauvignon blanc
and a second label called True
Frogs Lily Pad Red. Well
behaved dogs are welcome.
Dogs must be leashed and
cleaned up after at all times.

**Rocco's Com'e Bella Winery**
457-C Algiers
Murphys CA
209-728-9030
This scenic winery believes in
developing wines in the old
Italian way, and they specialize
in Mission, Zinfandel, Cabernet
Sauvignon, and Chardonnay.
Their Mission wine, though, is
produced from descendants of
the first vines ever planted in
California. Dogs are welcome
here and many enjoy the park
like setting and walking by the
nearby stream. There is also a
table out back for a picnic or
just a rest. Dogs must be well
behaved, and leashed and
cleaned up after at all times.

**Stevenot Winery**

2690 San Domingo Road
Murphys CA
209-728-0638
stevenotwinery.com/
This premier winery is located in
an area that has been an
esteemed wine grape growing
region since the mid 1800s, and
they offer complimentary tasting
of their world class wines. Dogs
are welcome to join you on the
grounds, the lawns, or at the
picnic area under the grape
arbor. Dogs must be well
behaved, leashed, and cleaned
up after.

**Twisted Oak Winery**
350 Main Street
Murphys CA
209-736-9080
twistedoak.com/twisted/index.js
p
This "twisted" winery is about
fun and high quality wines. Dogs
are allowed throughout the
grounds; they are not allowed in
the tasting room. Dogs must be
leashed and under their owner's
control at all times.

**Off-Leash Dog Parks**
**JD's Bark Park**
3069 Highway 49 S
Angels Camp CA
209-736-0404
angelscamprv.com/
JD's Bark Park, located in the
Angels Camp RV & Camping
Resort in Angels Camp,
California, is a fenced, off-leash
dog park that features agility
features, water, and a covered
bench seating area. JD's Bark
Park is free for all guests of the
RV park.

**Dog-Friendly Parks**
**Utica Park**
Hwy 49
Angels Camp CA
209-736-2187
Utica Park was built in 1954 on
the site of the Utica Mine after
the ground had been leveled
and shafts filled to the 60 foot
level. Today it is a great park for
having a picnic or watching the

kids have fun in the large playground area. The historic Lightner Mine at this park operated from 1896-1915. It produced over $6 million dollars in ore. The mine was filled, but you will still see some of the equipment that was used above ground. The park is located off Hwy 49, just north of downtown Angels Camp.

**Calaveras Big Trees State Park**
Highway 4
Arnold CA
209-795-2334
Just three species of redwood trees remain; the dawn redwood in central China; the coast redwood along the coast of northern California and southern Oregon; and the Sierra redwoods which grow at Calaveras Big Trees State Park and other widely scattered groves along the western slope of the Sierra Nevada. These redwood trees have evolved from the Mesozoic Era, the time when dinosaurs roamed the Earth. Dogs are not allowed on the trails, but are allowed on the dirt fire roads. There are miles of fire roads at this park. They are used by hikers, bicyclists and equestrians. Dogs must be on leash. The state park is about a 35 minute drive from Angel's Camp on Highway 4.

**Red Hills Area Hiking**
Red Hills Road
Chinese Camp CA
916-985-4474
This 7,000 acres of public land has just over 17 miles of trails with various loops. Elevations vary between 750 and 1,750 feet. This is a popular area for hunting, hiking, horseback riding and wildflower viewing. Leashed dogs are welcome. Please clean up after your dog. There are no park fees. The land is located near Highways 49 and 120. From Sonora, take Highway 49 south 15 miles to Chinese Camp. Then drive south on Red Hills Road for .5 miles.

**Stanislaus National Forest**

19777 Greenley Road
Sonora CA
209-532-3671
fs.usda.gov/stanislaus
This national forest covers almost 900,000 acres of land which ranges in elevation from 1,200 to over 10,000 feet. Please see our listings in the Sierra Nevada region for dog-friendly hikes and campgrounds.

## Service Dog Organizations
**Therapy Dogs of the Sierra**
14801 Lakeside Dr.
Sonora CA

motherlodek9.com
Therapy Dogs of the Sierra is Chapter #186 of Therapy Dogs International. We have approximately 70 dogs and handlers in the chapter, mostly in Tuolumne County. We visit most of the hospitals, rest homes, WATCH programs, ICES, Paws to Read programs at the library, and pre schools in the county bringing a little cheer to the residents. We also participate in the annual Christmas Parade, Mother Lode Parade and sponsor the annual Happy Paws Dog Walk with proceeds donated to the Humane Society of Tuolumne County and Rose Wolf Wildlife Rehab Center

## South Sacramento

## Off-Leash Dog Parks
**Jacinto Creek Park Dog Park**
8600 W Stockton Blvd
South Sacramento CA

This 2 acre off leash area has turf and decomposed granite areas, a water fountain for dogs, shade trees, an obstacle course for dogs and benches. Dogs must be healthy, sociable, current on all

vaccinations and license with tags on collar, and under their owner's control at all times. Owners must clean up after their pets, and keep them leashed when not in designated off-lead areas.

## Stockton

## Dog-Friendly Hotels
**Microtel Inn & Suites By Wyndham Lodi/north Stockton**
6428 West Banner Street
Lodi CA
209-367-9700
Dogs of all sizes are allowed. There is a pet fee of $10 per pet per night.

**Best Western Plus Executive Inn And Suites**
1415 East Yosemite Avenue
Manteca CA
209-825-1415 (800-780-7234)
Dogs up to 80 pounds are allowed. There is a $20 per night pet fee. Up to two dogs are allowed per room.

**American Inn Stockton**
550 West Charter Way
Stockton CA
209-948-0321 (800-329-7466)
Dogs are welcome at this hotel.

**Americas Best Value Inn Stockton**
3951 Budweiser Court
Stockton CA
209-931-9341 (877-424-6423)
Stockton Comfort Inn is at an ideal midpoint between the Bay Area, Sacramento, Reno and Jackson Casino.

Dogs up to 25 pounds are allowed. Dogs are allowed for a pet fee of $15:00 per pet per night.

**Clarion Inn & Suites Stockton**
4219 East Waterloo Road
Stockton CA
209-931-3131 (877-424-6423)
The Clarion Inn and Suites is

located in an industrial area within walking distance of Starbucks.

Dogs up to 10 pounds are allowed. Dogs are allowed for a pet fee of $25.00 per pet per stay.

**La Quinta Inn Stockton**
2710 West March Lane
Stockton CA
209-952-7800 (800-531-5900)
Dogs of all sizes are allowed. There are no additional pet fees. Dogs must be leashed and cleaned up after. The Do Not Disturb sign must be placed on the door if there is a pet alone in the room.

**Red Roof Inn Stockton**
1707 West Freemont St
Stockton CA
209-466-7777 (800-RED-ROOF)

One well-behaved family pet per room. Guest must notify front desk upon arrival. Guest is liable for any damages. In consideration of all guests, pets must never be left unattended in the guest rooms.

**Best Western Luxury Inn**
811 Clover Road
Tracy CA
209-832-0271 (800-780-7234)
Small dogs up to 40 pounds are allowed. There is a $10 per pet per night pet fee. Up to two dogs are allowed per room.

**Econo Lodge Tracy**
3511 North Tracy Boulevard
Tracy CA
209-835-1335 (877-424-6423)
Conveniently located 60 miles east of San Francisco just off I-205.

Dogs of all sizes are allowed. Dogs are allowed for a pet fee of $10.00 per pet per night.

**Microtel Inn & Suites By Wyndham Tracy**
861 W Clover Road
Tracy CA
209-229-1201
Dogs up to 50 pounds are allowed. There is a pet fee of

$10 per pet per night

## Pet-Friendly Extended Stay Hotels
**Extended Stay America - Stockton - March Lane**
2844 W. March Lane
Stockton CA
209-472-7588 (800-804-3724)
One dog is allowed per suite. There is a $25 per night additional pet fee up to $150 for an entire stay.

**Residence Inn By Marriott Stockton**
3240 March Lane
Stockton CA
209-472-9800
Dogs of all sizes are allowed. There is a $100 one time additional pet fee.

**Extended Stay America - Stockton - Tracy**
2526 Pavilion Pkwy
Tracy CA
209-832-4700 (800-804-3724)
One dog is allowed per suite. There is a $25 per night additional pet fee up to $150 for an entire stay.

## Dog-Friendly Attractions
**The Downtown Lodi Certified Farmers Market**
School Street between Lodi Avenue and Elm Street
Lodi CA
209-369-8052
downtownlodi.com/farmers.php

This large certified market features more than 25 certified farmers in addition to dozens of other vendors and food purveyors offering a wide selection of produce, products, and services. They also have a beer garden, an entertainment stage with live music and activities, an eclectic food court, a variety of special market events, and a kid's zone. The market is open Thursdays from the beginning of June until almost the end of

September from 5 pm until 9 pm. Well mannered dogs are allowed at the market; they must be leashed and cleaned up after promptly. Dogs are allowed on the vendor side of the market; they are not allowed on the Certified producers side of the market or by any food vendors.

**Manteca Farmers Market**
Yosemite and Manteca Avenues

Manteca CA
209-823-7229
visitmanteca.org
A variety of farmers, ranchers, artisans, and commercial vendors gather every Tuesday at Library Park from 4:30 pm until 7:30 pm to bring a variety of farm fresh produce and products, homemade foods and canned goods, handmade items, and much more to the market. The market runs from the beginning of June until the end of August. Leashed, well mannered dogs are welcome; they must be cleaned up after promptly.

## Outdoor Restaurants
**Chipotle**
1440 Hulsey Way
Manteca CA
209-823-1017
chipotle.com
Specializing in organic, natural and unprocessed food, this Mexican Eatery offers fajita burritos, tacos, salads, and salsas. Dogs are allowed at the outdoor tables but you will need to order your food inside the restaurant and dogs must remain outside.

**Baja Fresh Mexican Grill**
5350 Pacific Ave
Stockton CA
209-477-5024
bajafresh.com
This Mexican restaurant is open for lunch and dinner. They use fresh ingredients and making their salsa and beans daily. Some of the items on their menu include Enchiladas, Burritos, Tacos Salads,

Quesadillas, Nachos, Chicken, Steak and more. Well-behaved leashed dogs are allowed at the outdoor tables.

## Chipotle
4940 Pacific Avenue
Stockton CA
209-476-7217
chipotle.com
Specializing in organic, natural and unprocessed food, this Mexican Eatery offers fajita burritos, tacos, salads, and salsas. Dogs are allowed at the outdoor tables but you will need to order your food inside the restaurant and dogs must remain outside.

## Baja Fresh Mexican Grill
1855 W. 11th Street
Tracy CA
209-834-2252
bajafresh.com
This Mexican restaurant is open for lunch and dinner. They use fresh ingredients and making their salsa and beans daily. Some of the items on their menu include Enchiladas, Burritos, Tacos Salads, Quesadillas, Nachos, Chicken, Steak and more. Well-behaved leashed dogs are allowed at the outdoor tables.

## Pet-Friendly Stores
### PetSmart Pet Store
10520 Trinity Pkwy
Stockton CA
209-474-9748
Your licensed and well-behaved leashed dog is allowed in the store.

### Petco Pet Store - Stockton
5406 Pacific Ave.
Stockton CA
209-478-7726
Your licensed and well-behaved leashed dog is allowed in the store.

### PetSmart Pet Store
2477 Naglee Rd
Tracy CA
209-836-6080
Your licensed and well-behaved leashed dog is allowed in the

store.

### Petco Pet Store - Tracy
2888 West Grant Line Road
Tracy CA
209-830-4476
Your licensed and well-behaved leashed dog is allowed in the store.

## Dog-Friendly Wineries and Vineyards
### Jessie's Grove Winery
1973 W Turner Road
Lodi CA
209-368-0880
jgwinery.com/#
This winery, located along the delta in the foothills of the Sierra Nevada Mountains, specializes in wines that embody the unique distinctive growing factors of the area. They offer events and concerts throughout the year; dogs are not allowed during concerts. Dogs are allowed around the grounds of the winery; they must be friendly, well behaved, and leashed and cleaned up after.

### Phillips Farm/ Michael-David Vineyards
4580 H 12
Lodi CA
209-368-7384
lodivineyards.com/
Six generations of winegrowers have made this an award winning winery, producing some of the finest varietals in California, and they are also know for producing the very popular 7 Deadly Zins and the 6th Sense Syrah. Dogs are allowed to explore the grounds and the large farm area; dogs must be friendly towards farm and domestic animals. Dogs must be well behaved, leashed, and cleaned up after at all times. They are not allowed in the tasting room.

## Off-Leash Dog Parks
### BarkleyVille Dog Park

5505 Feather River Drive
Stockton CA
209-937-8206
There are 3 safe play areas for your pooch at this park. There is 1 area for dogs under 20 pounds, one for dogs over 20 pounds, and a separate agility and play area. The park offers benches, doggie water fountains, and waste disposal stations. Dogs must be sociable, current on all vaccinations and license, and under their owner's control at all times. Dogs must be leashed when not in designated off-lead areas.

## Emergency Veterinarians
### Associated Veterinary Emergency Hospital
3008 E Hammer Lane #115
Stockton CA
209-952-8387
Monday - Friday 6 pm to 8 am, 24 hours on weekends.

## Suisun City

## Dog-Friendly Hotels
### Hampton Inn And Suites Suisun City
2 Harbor Center
Suisun City CA
707-429-0900
Dogs up to 40 pounds are allowed. There is no pet fee.

## Summerland

## Dog-Friendly Beaches
### Summerland Beach
Evans Avenue
Summerland CA
805-568-2461
This conveniently located beach sits only a block off Highway 101, features an easy paved path to the water, and offers a mile of beach to explore. The beach also sits below Lookout

Park complete with picnic tables, barbecues, and a playground. Dogs are welcome to frolic on the beach, but they must be kept leashed and cleaned up after promptly.

## Sun City

### Veterinarians
**Menifee Valley Animal Clinic**
26900 Newport Rd # 105
Sun City CA
951-672-8077
This veterinary clinic is open during regular business hours.

**Sun City Veterinary Clinic**
27994 Bradley Rd # J
Sun City CA
951-672-1802
This veterinary clinic is open during regular business hours.

## Tehachapi

### Dog-Friendly Hotels
**Baymont Inn & Suites Tehachapi**
500 Steuber Rd
Tehachapi CA

Free breakfast with waffles free Wi-Fi and an outdoor pool make for a comfortable stay at La Quinta Inn Tehachapi. This two-story hotel offers 107 rooms with free Wi-Fi cable TV refrigerators microwaves coffeemakers hairdryers and irons with ironing boards. Some also have jetted tubs. Make your own hot waffles for breakfast and go for a dip in the outdoor pool with a hot tub. Work out in the fitness room and catch up on work at the business center. A guest laundry is available. Pets are permitted for a fee and parking is free. Located on Highway 58 two miles from Tehachapi several family and fast-food restaurants are within two miles

of La Quinta Inn. Enjoy a breathtaking view from Tehachapi Summit Pass 15 minutes away or check out the Zinfandels at Souza Winery about 20 minutes away. Edwards Air Force Base and Bakersfield are both 45-minute drives from the hotel. Bob Hope Airport in Burbank is 103 miles south.

### Dog-Friendly Parks
**Tehachapi Mountain Park**
Highway 58
Tehachapi CA
661-868-7000
This 5,000 acre park offers views of the Tehachapi Mountains, the dividing line between the San Joaquin Valley and the Los Angeles Basin. The Nuooah Nature Trail is an interesting interpretive 1/4 mile trail. The park is located between Bakersfield and Mojave. It is 8 miles southwest of the town of Tehachapi and is on the southern side of Hwy. 58. Dogs must be on leash.

## Temecula

### Dog-Friendly Hotels
**La Quinta Inn & Suites Temecula**
27330 Jefferson Avenue
Temecula CA
951-296-1003 (800-531-5900)
Dogs of all sizes are allowed for no additional pet fee; there is a pet policy to sign at check in, and pet rooms are on ground floors only. Dogs must be crated when left alone in the room, and they are not allowed in food or pool areas.

**Quality Inn Temecula Valley Wine Country**
27338 Jefferson Avenue
Temecula CA
951-296-3788 (877-424-6423)
Centrally located between San

Diego and Los Angeles with 20 local wineries and 7 golf courses minutes away. Pet-friendly hotel.

Dogs up to 40 pounds are allowed. Two dogs are allowed per room.

### Pet-Friendly Extended Stay Hotels
**Extended Stay America - Temecula - Wine Country**
27622 Jefferson Avenue
Temecula CA
951-587-8881 (800-804-3724)
One dog is allowed per suite. There is a $25 per night additional pet fee up to $150 for an entire stay.

### Dog-Friendly Attractions
**Old Town Temecula**
Front Street
Temecula CA

Old Town Temecula is a quaint historic area with wooden sidewalks where you and your leashed dog can walk. There are shops and some restaurants with outdoor seating.

**Stuart Cellars**
33515 Rancho California Road
Temecula CA
888-260-0870
stuartcellars.com/main.html
This enterprise has been the recipient of many award winning wines, and continues to incorporate the rich wine making traditions of the Old World with a bit of California flair. They also offer a nice picnic area on spacious grounds overlooking the Temecula Valley. Dogs are allowed around the grounds and the picnic area, but not in the tasting room. Dogs must be well behaved, and leashed and cleaned up after at all times.

**Wine Country Wedding Chapel**
41973 6th Steet
Temecula CA

951-760-3399
WineCountryWeddingChapel.com
This wedding cottage in historical Old Town Temecula offers a romantic, intimate setting for taking vows or for renewing them; plus they will welcome your well mannered pooch to sit in on the ceremony. Dogs must be leashed.

## Outdoor Restaurants
### Applebees
32175 H 79
Temecula CA
951-506-7852
applebees.com
Offerings at this restaurant includes a full line of appetizers, salads, specialty burgers, value meals, fresh soups and salads, healthy selections, signature entrees and main dishes, house-made desserts, a full bar, and plenty of TVs for sports viewing and special events. They also offer community support through a variety of venues. Leashed, friendly dogs are allowed at their outside dining area.

### Baja Fresh Mexican Grill
40688 Winchester Rd
Temecula CA
909-719-1570
bajafresh.com
This Mexican restaurant is open for lunch and dinner. They use fresh ingredients and making their salsa and beans daily. Some of the items on their menu include Enchiladas, Burritos, Tacos Salads, Quesadillas, Nachos, Chicken, Steak and more. Well-behaved leashed dogs are allowed at the outdoor tables.

### Bushfire Grill
40665 Winchester Rd
Temecula CA
951-296-0190
bushfiregrill.com
Bushfire Grill features free-range chicken, locally sourced vegetables, organicsides and much more. Bushfire Grill's cuisine is all natural, antibiotic and hormone-free. Many menu items are gluten-free. Well-behaved, leashed dogs are welcome at the outdoor seats.

### Cafe Daniel
28601 Old Town Front Street
Temecula CA
951-676-8408
This cafe offers a casual ambiance, and a variety of crepes, sandwiches, paninis, pastries, gelato, and coffee drinks. Leashed, well mannered dogs are welcome at their outer tables.

### Carol's Restaurant
33440 La Serena Way
Temecula CA
951-676-9243
bailywinery.com/carols.html
This restaurant is on the site of the Baily Vineyard. They offer patio dining service, and a selection of luncheon salads, sandwiches, grilled fish and steak, and pasta dishes. Dogs are allowed around the grounds, and at the outside dining area, but not in any of the buildings.

### Chili's
27645 Ynez Road
Temecula CA
951-694-0099
chilis.com/EN/Pages/home.aspx
This Mexican eatery features a full and diverse menu of signature appetizers, handcrafted soups, salads, specialty entrees, gourmet burgers, sandwiches, healthy option items, value meals, house made desserts, and a full bar known for their specialty cocktails. Leashed, friendly dogs are allowed at their outside dining area.

### Chipotle
40573 Margarita Road
Temecula CA
951-506-1734
chipotle.com
Specializing in organic, natural and unprocessed food, this Mexican Eatery offers fajita burritos, tacos, salads, and salsas. Dogs are allowed at the outdoor tables but you will need to order your food inside the restaurant and dogs must remain outside.

### Front Street Bar and Grill
28699 Old Town Front Street
Temecula CA
951-676-9567
American regional cuisine of appetizers, soups, salads, gourmet burgers, Cajun foods, barbecue, entrées and desserts are offered at this bar and grill. Leashed, well mannered dogs are welcome at their outside tables.

### Lazy Dog Restaurant & Bar
40754 Winchester Road
Temecula CA
951-719-1884
lazydogrestaurants.com/dogs/info
Known for it's dog-friendly patio, the Lazy Dog offers your dog a complimentary bowl of water, and a menu consisting of grilled hamburger patty, chicken breast or brown rice. They just ask that you respect their common sense rules while your dog is dining there. This is as dog-friendly as dining gets. For the humans in your party there is hamburger, steak, salads and some great desserts.

### Marie Callender's
29363 Rancho California Rd
Temecula CA
951-699-9339
mariecallenders.com/
Famous for their pies, this eatery also serves up a full days menu and specialty barbecue items. Dogs are allowed at their outside tables.

### Natural Pet Food Market, Dog Park Cafe and Encore Grooming & Spaw
31795 Rancho California Road
Temecula CA
951-308-4545
dogparkcafe.net/
This natural pet foods market and doggie cafe provides healthy, wholesome foods and treats that are as pesticide and additive free as possible. They also carry high-quality

supplements and top-of-the-line pet supplies. Another highlight of this store is indoor dining with your canine companion. They provide private indoor eating enclosures and deliver to your table doggylicious items from Jackboy's Bakery (like chicken pot pie, pumpkin dogsert pie, and 'mutt'wich cookies) for their canine guests, and from a natural foods market next door they provide healthy salads, sandwiches, and sushi for human guests. They also offer a full service groomer on site. They are open Monday to Friday from 9 am until 6 pm;Saturday from 9 am until 5 pm, and on Sunday from 11 am until 5 pm.

**Outback Steakhouse**
40275 Winchester Road/H 79
Temecula CA
951-719-3700
outback.com
Big, bold flavors, quality ingredients, fresh made-from-scratch soups/salads/sauces, signature appetizers, a gluten-free menu, house-made desserts, and signature cocktails with a notable list of wines and beers are the specialties of this steak house. Leashed, friendly dogs are allowed at their outside dining area.

**Scarcella's Italian Grille**
27525 Ynez Rd
Temecula CA
951-676-5450
scarcellasgrill.com/
An extensive menu of fine Italian cuisine and fine domestic and imported wines are the specialty of this restaurant. Leashed dogs are allowed at their outside dining area.

**Temecula Pizza Company**
44535 Bedford Ct # D
Temecula CA
951-694-9463
temeculapizzacompany.com/
Dogs are allowed on the front patio only.

**Texas Lil's Mesquite Grill**
28495 Old Town Front St
Temecula CA

951-699-5457
Texas Lil's Mesquite Grill, in Temecula, California, is open 7 days a week, Mon-Thu 11am-12am, Fri & Sat 11am-1:30am, and Sun 9am-10pm. They serve burgers, brunch, tex-mex, steaks, seafood, and more. Well-behaved, leashed dogs are welcome on the dog friendly patio, and complimentary water and doggie treats are available. They even offer a "K9 menu", which offers Meaty Beef Rib (served cold), Chicken Breast (grilled), 1/4 lb Burger Patty (grilled), 1/2 lb Burger Patty (grilled) and a Hot Dog (no bun).

# Pet-Friendly Stores
**Dog Park Cafe and Encore Grooming & Spaw**
31795 Rancho California Road
Temecula CA
951-308-4545
dogparkcafe.net/
This natural pet foods market and doggie cafe provides healthy, wholesome foods and treats that are as pesticide and additive free as possible. They also carry high-quality supplements and top-of-the-line pet supplies. Another highlight of this store is indoor dining with your canine companion. They provide private indoor eating enclosures and deliver to your table doggylicious items from Jackboy's Bakery (like chicken pot pie, pumpkin dogsert pie, and 'mutt'wich cookies) for their canine guests, and from a natural foods market next door they provide healthy salads, sandwiches, and sushi for human guests. They also offer a full service groomer on site. They are open Monday to Friday from 9 am until 6 pm; Saturday from 9 am until 5 pm, and on Sunday from 11 am until 5 pm.

**Dogtopia of Temecula**
27629 Commerce Center Drive

Temecula CA
951-506-1200
dogdaycare.com/temecula
With a stated mission of providing the highest quality dog care in the country, this company offers well trained staff for all their services. Services include doggy day care, overnight accommodations, positive reinforcement training classes, a self serve dog wash, professional grooming, and a doggy boutique with quality foods/treats, pet care supplies, toys, and much more. They also offer support in the community through a variety of venues.

**Dogtopia of Temecula**
27629 Commerce Center Drive
Temecula CA
951-506-1200
dogdaycare.com/temecula/
With a stated mission of providing the highest quality dog care in the country, this company offers well trained staff for all their services. Services include doggy day care, overnight accommodations, positive reinforcement training classes, a self serve dog wash, professional grooming, and a doggy boutique with quality foods/treats, pet care supplies, toys, and much more. They also offer support in the community through a variety of venues.

**PetSmart Pet Store**
32413 Hwy 79
Temecula CA
951-302-1209
Your licensed and well-behaved leashed dog is allowed in the store.

**Petco Pet Store - Temecula**
40474 Winchester Road
Temecula CA
951-296-0388
Your licensed and well-behaved leashed dog is allowed in the store.

# Dog-Friendly Wineries and Vineyards
**Baily Vineyard**

33440 La Serena Way
Temecula CA
951-676-WINE (9463)
bailywinery.com/
Grapes are brought to this winery's state-of-the-art production facility from 32 acres of grapes grown in 4 different sites in the Temecula Valley. The restaurant on site (Carol's) offers patio dining service, and a selection of luncheon salads, sandwiches, grilled fish and steak, and pasta dishes. Dogs are allowed around the grounds, and at the outside dining area, but not in the tasting room. Dogs must be well behaved, and leashed and cleaned up after at all times.

## Europa Village Winery
33475 La Serena Way
Temecula CA
888-383-8767
europavillage.com/
Offerings of this village-style winery include an Old World country atmosphere, a full menu of fine hand-crafted wines created via Old World European traditions, a membership program offering extra savings and selections, a beautiful venue for special events, and a calendar full of specials, wine-pairing dinners, and musical events. Leashed, friendly dogs are welcome at the winery; they are not allowed inside the buildings.

## Falkner Winery
40620 Calle Contento
Temecula CA
951-676-8231
falknerwinery.com/
The wines here display a similar taste of full fruit flavors with a soft, clean finish, and they offer both inside and outside wine tasting areas, a grassy tree-lined picnic area with tables, and a gift shop that offers unique gifts and foods for hungry/thirsty visitors. Dogs are allowed around the grounds, but not in the tasting room or the outside dining area of the Pinnacle Restaurant. Dogs must be well behaved, and leashed and cleaned up after at all times.

## Filsinger Vineyards and Winery
39050 De Portola Rd
Temecula CA
909-302-6363
Dogs are allowed at the outdoor picnic tables.

## Maurice Carrie Vineyard
34225 Rancho California Road
Temecula CA
951-676-1711
mauricecarriewinery.com/
This winery features award wining wines, picnic grounds where you can dine on their specialty of baked brie in Sourdough, a unique gift shop, and a new Pineapple flavored Champagne. Dogs are allowed around the grounds, but not in the tasting room. Dogs must be well behaved, and leashed and cleaned up after at all times.

## Miramonte Winery
33410 Rancho California Road
Temecula CA
951-506-5500
miramontewinery.com/
This award winning winery's wine program is maturing with a clear focus on southern Rhone varietals. They regularly host special events, and offer one of the most stunning views in the valley. Dogs must be friendly though, as they also have a dog who likes to greet visitors. Dogs can check out the grounds and the tasting room. Dogs must be well behaved, leashed, and cleaned up after.

## Oak Mountain Winery
36522 Via Verde
Temecula CA
951-699-9102
oakmountainwinery.com/
Specializing in classic Bordeaux varieties, this winery also features a number of fun events and special wine pairing meals. Additionally, this dog-friendly winery welcomes canine companions in and around the winery with doggy treats and fresh water. Dogs must be well mannered, leashed, and under their

owner's control at all times.

## Tesoro Winery
28475 Old Town Front Street
Temecula CA
951-308-0000
tesorowines.com/
Rich in the ambiance of old Italy, this winery specializes in premium Mediterranean style wines. A variety of special events are common such as their 'Evening of Music and Wine' and themed activities. Leashed, friendly dogs are welcome throughout the winery, and doggy treats have been known to be available for canine visitors.

## Van Roekel Winery
34567 Rancho California Rd
Temecula CA
909-699-6961
Dogs are allowed at the picnic area.

## Off-Leash Dog Parks
### Redhawk Dog Park
44747 Redhawk Parkway
Temecula CA
951-694-6444
Temecula's first dog park was opened in 2006 in the Redhawk Community Park. The fenced park is divided into two areas, one for large dogs and one for small dogs. To get to the dog park from Interstate 15 take Highway 79 east and turn right onto Redhawk Parkway.

## Dog-Friendly Parks
### Duck Pond
Rancho California and Ynez Rd
Temecula CA
909-836-3285
Dogs on leash are allowed in the park. Owners must pick up after their dog.

### Lake Skinner Recreation Area
Rancho California Road
Temecula CA
909-926-1541
This 6,040 acre park features a lake, hiking trails, equestrian trails and camping. Dogs are

allowed on the trails and in the campgrounds, but not in the lake or within 50 feet of the lake. Dogs must be on a 6 foot or less leash and please clean up after them. To get there, take Highway 15 to Rancho California Road and go north 10 miles. There is a minimal fee for day use of the park.

**Sam Hicks Monument Park**
Old Town Temecula
Temecula CA
909-836-3285
Dogs are allowed on leash. Owners must pick up after their pets.

**Emergency Veterinarians**
Emergency Pet Clinic
27443 Jefferson Ave
Temecula CA
909-695-5044
Monday - Friday 6 pm to 8 am, 24 hours on weekends.

## Templeton

### Dog-Friendly Wineries and Vineyards
Venteux Vineyards
1795 Las Tablas Road
Templeton CA
805-369-0127
venteuxvineyards.com/
This winery takes a hands-on approach from beginning to end to produce a variety of fine handcrafted wines - including beginning with an organically grown vineyard. They are also active in fund raising for the local Humane Society, and offer a special wine "Hospice du Bone" to help with the cause. Dogs are allowed at the vineyard. Dogs must be friendly with other pets (on site), leashed, and under their owner's control at all times.

### Off-Leash Dog Parks

**Vineyard Dog Park**
1010 Semillon Lane
Templeton CA
805-239-4437
Vineyard Dog Park opened on February 14, 2009 with construction paid for by donations from dog owners and local businesses. The fenced off-leash dog park is located on the west side of Templeton in north San Luis Obispo County with views of the surrounding hillsides. The park is about 1 acre in size and is cross-fenced for separate big dog and small dog play areas. Park amenities include water, shade trees, picnic tables, park benches, dog bag dispensers, dog toys, and wading pool (summer time only).

## Thousand Oaks

### Dog-Friendly Hotels
La Quinta Inn & Suites Thousand Oaks Newbury Park
1320 Newbury Road
Thousand Oaks CA
805-499-5910 (800-531-5900)
Dogs of all sizes are allowed for no additional pet fee; there is a pet policy to sign at check-in. The Do Not Disturb sign must be on the door if there is a pet alone in the room.

**Towneplace Suites Thousand Oaks Ventura County**
1712 Newbury Road
Thousand Oaks CA
805-499-3111
Dogs of all sizes are allowed. There is a $75 one time pet fee.

### Outdoor Restaurants
Baja Fresh Mexican Grill
23697 Calabasas Parkway
Calabasas CA
818-591-2262
bajafresh.com

This Mexican restaurant is open for lunch and dinner. They use fresh ingredients and making their salsa and beans daily. Some of the items on their menu include Enchiladas, Burritos, Tacos Salads, Quesadillas, Nachos, Chicken, Steak and more. Well-behaved leashed dogs are allowed at the outdoor tables.

**Coffee Bean & Tea Leaf**
23635 Calabasas Road
Calabasas CA
818-225-1887
coffeebean.com
The coffee here is sourced globally from family coffee farms to procure only the top of 1% of Arabica beans. They offer 30+ varieties of coffee;the beans are roasted in small batches daily for freshness, and they also offer 20 varieties of teas that are hand-blended by their tea master. Additionally, they offer a variety of tasty sweets, powders, extracts, sauces, gifts, and cards. Leashed, well mannered dogs are allowed at their outside dining area.

**Baja Fresh Mexican Grill**
595 N Moorpark Rd
Thousand Oaks CA
805-778-0877
bajafresh.com
This Mexican restaurant is open for lunch and dinner. They use fresh ingredients and making their salsa and beans daily. Some of the items on their menu include Enchiladas, Burritos, Tacos Salads, Quesadillas, Nachos, Chicken, Steak and more. Well-behaved leashed dogs are allowed at the outdoor tables.

**Chipotle**
935 Broadbeck Drive
Thousand Oaks CA
805-499-3561
chipotle.com
Specializing in organic, natural and unprocessed food, this Mexican Eatery offers fajita burritos, tacos, salads, and salsas. Dogs are allowed at the outdoor tables but you will need to order your food inside the

restaurant and dogs must remain outside.

**Johnny Rockets**
322 W Hillcrest
Thousand Oaks CA
805-778-0780
johnnyrockets.com/
All the American favorites can be found here: A fun retro, all-American decor and atmosphere, juicy burgers, specialty sandwiches, crispy fries, hand-dipped malts and shakes (dark chocolate ones too), fresh baked apple pies, tasty vegetarian choices, and something for all ages. Leashed, friendly dogs are allowed at their outside dining area.

**Lazy Dog Restaurant & Bar**
172 West Hillcrest Drive
Thousand Oaks CA
805-449-5206
lazydogrestaurants.com/dogs/info
Known for it's dog-friendly patio, the Lazy Dog offers your dog a complimentary bowl of water, and a menu consisting of grilled hamburger patty, chicken breast or brown rice. They just ask that you respect their common sense rules while your dog is dining there. This is as dog-friendly as dining gets. For the humans in your party there is hamburger, steak, salads and some great desserts.

**The Coffee Bean & Tea Leaf**
487 N Moorpark Road Unit 3
Thousand Oaks CA
805-497-7467
coffeebean.com
The coffee here is sourced globally from family coffee farms to procure only the top of 1% of Arabica beans. They offer 30+ varieties of coffee;the beans are roasted in small batches daily for freshness, and they also offer 20 varieties of teas that are hand-blended by their tea master. Additionally, they offer a variety of tasty sweets, powders, extracts, sauces, gifts, and cards. Leashed, well mannered dogs are allowed at their outside dining area.

**The Coffee Bean & Tea Leaf**
1772-A E Avenida De Los Arboles
Thousand Oaks CA
805-241-2499
coffeebean.com
The coffee here is sourced globally from family coffee farms to procure only the top of 1% of Arabica beans. They offer 30+ varieties of coffee;the beans are roasted in small batches daily for freshness, and they also offer 20 varieties of teas that are hand-blended by their tea master. Additionally, they offer a variety of tasty sweets, powders, extracts, sauces, gifts, and cards. Leashed, well mannered dogs are allowed at their outside dining area.

**Thousand Oaks Meat Locker**
2684 E Thousand Oaks Blvd
Thousand Oaks CA
805-495-3211
The Meat Locker tempts barbecue lovers with their large outdoor barbecue. Dogs are allowed at the outdoor tables.

**Topper's Pizza**
1416 N. Moorpark Rd.
Thousand Oaks CA
805-385-4444
topperspizzaplace.com/index.php
Topper's Pizza offers oven-baked sandwiches, pizzas, build your own pizzas, and more! Well-behaved, leashed dogs are welcome at the outdoor patio.

**Z Pizza**
5776 Lindero Canyon Road
Thousand Oaks CA
818-991-4999
zpizza.com
Specializing in organically and international inspired pizzas, this pizzeria cooks their pizzas on hot bricks in a fire baked oven. They feature a 100% certified organic gluten free wheat crust, homemade organic sauces and ingredients, fresh produce, and additive-free meats. They also offer gourmet salads,

sandwiches, and catering services. Leashed, well mannered dogs are allowed at their outside tables.

**Baja Fresh Mexican Grill**
22815 Victory Blvd. Ste C
West Hills CA
818-704-4267
bajafresh.com
This Mexican restaurant is open for lunch and dinner. They use fresh ingredients and making their salsa and beans daily. Some of the items on their menu include Enchiladas, Burritos, Tacos Salads, Quesadillas, Nachos, Chicken, Steak and more. Well-behaved leashed dogs are allowed at the outdoor tables.

**The Coffee Bean & Tea Leaf**
6401 Platt Avenue
West Hills CA
818-704-5867
coffeebean.com
The coffee here is sourced globally from family coffee farms to procure only the top of 1% of Arabica beans. They offer 30+ varieties of coffee;the beans are roasted in small batches daily for freshness, and they also offer 20 varieties of teas that are hand-blended by their tea master. Additionally, they offer a variety of tasty sweets, powders, extracts, sauces, gifts, and cards. Leashed, well mannered dogs are allowed at their outside dining area.

**Pet-Friendly Stores**
**Anthropologie**
502 W. Hillcrest Drive, #R 13-16

Thousand Oaks CA
805-230-2900
Items of distinction can be found for all ages and in all departments of this unique shop. Carefully selected to add to the enjoyment of the shopping experience, they carry fine clothing, amazing accessories, jewelry, hobby and leisure items, and a full line of bright and useful items for the home, garden, and office.

Leashed, well behaved dogs are allowed in the store.

**Petco Pet Store - Thousand Oaks**
140 West Hillcrest Dr. Ste 101
Thousand Oaks CA
805-777-7554
Your licensed and well-behaved leashed dog is allowed in the store.

**Urban Outfitters**
310 West Hillcrest Drive, #L-15
Thousand Oaks CA
805-494-7606
In addition to a large inventory of indoor and outdoor apparel for men and women, this major department store also carries vintage wear, designer brands, and a variety of accessories for all types of active lifestyles. They also carry shoes, furnishings, home decor, cameras, electronics, novelty items and more. Leashed, well mannered dogs are allowed in the store.

**Off-Leash Dog Parks**
**Calabasas Bark Park**
Las Virgines Road
Calabasas CA

Thanks to one of our readers for recommending this dog park. It is located on Las Virgines Road, south of the Agoura Road and Las Virgines Road intersection. This fenced dog park is open from 5 am to 9 pm daily. There is a separate fenced children's play area next to the dog park.

**Conejo Creek Dog Park**
1350 Avenida de las Flores
Thousand Oaks CA
805-495-6471
This 3.75 acre enclosed dog park has a separate section for large dogs and small dogs. Amenities include picnic tables and three drinking fountains. The dog park is located at Avenida de las Flores, at the northwest quadrant of Conejo Creek.

**Dog-Friendly Parks**
**Upper Las Virgenes Canyon Open Space Preserve**
26135 Mureau Road
Calabasas CA
818-878-4225
This park is part of the Santa Monica Mountains Conservancy and allows leashed dogs on the trails. Please clean up after your pets. No hunting is allowed in the park. In the past, some movies have been filmed at this ranch, including Gone With The Wind. The easiest access to the trails is at the north end of Las Virgenes Road. In early 2004 there are plans to having a parking area at the end of Victory Blvd. in Woodland Hills. It used to be called Ahmanson Ranch.

**Santa Monica Mountains National Recreation Area**
401 West Hillcrest Drive
Thousand Oaks CA
805-370-2301
nps.gov/samo/index.htm
Dogs on leash are allowed in the park. They must stay on trails, roads and campgrounds. They are not allowed in any buildings or undeveloped areas. This park features fishing, hiking, camping, swimming, and more.

**Wildwood Regional Park**
Ave. De Los Arboles
Thousand Oaks CA

This park has hiking trails that run along a beautiful hill and streams (the streams have water at certain times of the year). It makes for a great morning hike in the summer. Leashed dogs are allowed on the trails. There are also picnic tables at the park. During the winter (rainy season), the trails are subject to flash flooding. To get there from the 101 freeway, take the Lynn Road exit and head north. Turn left onto Avenida de los Arboles. Go until you reach Wildwood School. Park there and take

the trail to the left of the parking lot. It will take you to a large wooden "Fort". Go past or through the fort to the trails. Thanks to one of our readers for recommending this park.

**Emergency Veterinarians**
**Pet Emergency Clinic**
2967 N Moorpark Rd
Thousand Oaks CA
805-492-2436
Monday - Friday 6 pm to 8 am, 24 hours on weekends.

## Topanga

**Outdoor Restaurants**
**Abuelitas Restaurant**
137 South Topanga Canyon Blvd
Topanga CA
310-455-8788
abuelitastopanga.com/
Fine Mexican cuisine with a diverse menu, a full bar, weekend brunches, scenic patio dining, live entertainment on the weekends and more are offered at this creek-side eatery. Leashed, well mannered dogs are welcome at their outside tables.

## Tulare

**Dog-Friendly Hotels**
**Best Western Town & Country Lodge**
1051 North Blackstone
Tulare CA
559-688-7537 (800-780-7234)
Dogs up to 80 pounds are allowed. There is a $20 per day pet fee up to $100 for the week. Up to two dogs are allowed per room.

**La Quinta Inn & Suites Tulare**
1500 North Cherry Court
Tulare CA

559-685-8900 (800-531-5900)
Dogs of all sizes are allowed.
Dogs may not be left alone in
the room.

### Quality Inn Tulare
1010 East Prosperity Avenue
Tulare CA
559-686-3432 (877-424-6423)
Easy to access from Hwy 99.
Next to the discount outlet
center and theater.

Dogs of all sizes are allowed.
Dogs are allowed for a pet fee of
$15.00 per pet per night.

### Red Roof Inn Tulare -
### Downtown/fairgrounds
1183 N Blackstone Street
Tulare CA
559-686-0985 (800-329-7466)
Dogs are welcome at this hotel.

## Outdoor Restaurants
### Jamba Juice
1681 Hillman Street
Tulare CA
559-686-1857
jambajuice.com
All natural and organic
ingredients, no high-fructose
corn syrup, 0 grams trans fat, no
artificial preservatives, a healthy
helping of antioxidants, vitamins,
and minerals, and fresh whole
fruit and fruit juices set the base
for these tasty and healthy
beverages. Their organic Hot
Blends provides a new spin on
coffee, green or chai tea, and
hot chocolate;plus they offer
probiotic fruit and yogurt Blends.
Additionally, they feature all
natural salads, wraps,
sandwiches, and grab n go
specialties. They also offer
healthy community support
through fundraisers, special
sales, and school lunch
programs.

## Pet-Friendly Stores
### Tractor Supply Company
1949 E Prosperity Avenue
Tulare CA
559-688-1334
tractorsupply.com

Some offerings of this
comprehensive farm store
includes agriculture, farming
and ranching supplies; outdoor
power equipment with all the
necessities; hundreds of
thousands of parts and
accessories accessible for yard
and garden; metal working and
welding supplies; tools for auto
and home; a wide range of
livestock/farm feed and needs;
and a variety of foods and
care/play/groom items for
household pets. Additionally,
they provide trailer and towing
supplies, vehicle maintenance
accessories, clothing, work
wear, foot wear, gifts, home
improvement items, a lot of
"know-how" and much more.
Leashed, friendly dogs are
welcome in the store.

## Turlock

### Dog-Friendly Hotels
### Comfort Suites Turlock
191 North Tully Road
Turlock CA
209-667-7777 (877-424-6423)
Located at the heart of Turlock
and the Central Valley, free
wireless internet, daily
continental breakfast.

### Travelodge Turlock Ca
201 West Glenwood Avenue
Turlock CA
209-668-3400
Dogs up to 75 pounds are
allowed. There is a pet fee of
$10 per pet per night.

## Pet-Friendly Extended
## Stay Hotels
### Candlewood Suites Turlock
1000 Powers Court
Turlock CA
209-250-1501 (877-270-6405)
Dogs up to 80 pounds are
allowed. Pets allowed with an
additional pet fee. Up to $75 for
1-6 nights and up to $150 for
7+ nights. A pet agreement

must be signed at check-in.

## Outdoor Restaurants
### Chipotle
3090 Countryside Drive
Turlock CA
209-656-7647
chipotle.com
Specializing in organic, natural
and unprocessed food, this
Mexican Eatery offers fajita
burritos, tacos, salads, and
salsas. Dogs are allowed at the
outdoor tables but you will need
to order your food inside the
restaurant and dogs must
remain outside.

## Pet-Friendly Stores
### Tractor Supply Company
201 N Walnut Road
Turlock CA
209-664-0695
tractorsupply.com
Some offerings of this
comprehensive farm store
includes agriculture, farming and
ranching supplies; outdoor
power equipment with all the
necessities; hundreds of
thousands of parts and
accessories accessible for yard
and garden; metal working and
welding supplies; tools for auto
and home; a wide range of
livestock/farm feed and needs;
and a variety of foods and
care/play/groom items for
household pets. Additionally,
they provide trailer and towing
supplies, vehicle maintenance
accessories, clothing, work
wear, foot wear, gifts, home
improvement items, a lot of
"know-how" and much more.
Leashed, friendly dogs are
welcome in the store.

## Twin Bridges

### Dog-Friendly Parks
### Bryan Meadows Trail
Bryan Road

Twin Bridges CA
530-644-2545
This 4 mile moderate rated trail passes through stands of lodgepole pine and mountain hemlock. From the parking area, hike one mile up Sayles Canyon Trail along the creek to the junction of Bryan Meadows Trail. The trail continues east for about three miles. The elevation ranges from about 7,200 to 8,400 feet. Pets must be leashed and please clean up after them. This trail is located in the Eldorado National Forest. From Highway 50 go about 48 miles east of Placerville. Turn onto the Sierra-At-Tahoe Road and go 2 miles. Turn right onto Bryan Road (17E13). Go another 2.5 miles to the parking area where the trailhead is located.

### Pyramid Creek Loop Trail
Highway 50
Twin Bridges CA
530-644-2545
This 1.7 mile Eldorado National Forest trail is rated moderate to strenuous. The elevation ranges from 6,120 to 6,400 feet. At the trailhead, begin your hike by heading east and then north up to Pyramid Creek. Turn right (east) at the sign and follow the trail along the creek. The trail offers great views of the American River Canyon, Lover's Leap, Horsetail Falls and other geological interests. Follow the trail north, then loop back south on the old trail bed down to the granite slabs and return to Highway 50. Pets must be leashed and please clean up after them. The trailhead is located on the north side of Highway 50 at Twin Bridges, about .5 miles east of Strawberry.

### Ukiah

## Dog-Friendly Hotels
### Best Western Orchard Inn
555 South Orchard Avenue
Ukiah CA

707-462-1514 (800-780-7234)
Dogs up to 80 pounds are allowed. There is a $20 per day pet fee up to $100 for the week. Up to two dogs are allowed per room.

### Comfort Inn & Suites Ukiah
1220 Airport Park Blvd
Ukiah CA
707-462-3442 (877-424-6423)
New property in the heart of Mendocino County, surrounded by wineries, lakes, casinos and a growing number of businesses.

Dogs up to 30 pounds are allowed. Dogs are allowed for a pet fee of $20.00 per pet per night.

### Days Inn Ukiah/gateway To Redwoods Wine Country
950 North State Street
Ukiah CA
707-462-7584 (800-329-7466)
Dogs of all sizes are allowed. Dogs are allowed for a nightly pet fee.

### Quality Inn Ukiah
1050 South State St
Ukiah CA
707-462-2906 (877-424-6423)
Located nearby local wineries and wine country. Redwood forest and Skunk Railroad nearby.

Dogs of all sizes are allowed. Dogs are allowed for a pet fee of $10.00 per pet per night.

### Super 8 Ukiah
693 South Orchard Avenue
Ukiah CA
707-468-8181 (800-800-8000)
Dogs of all sizes are allowed. Dogs are allowed for a pet fee.

## Dog-Friendly Parks
### Cache Creek Recreation Area

2550 N State Street/Ukiah Field Office
Ukiah CA
707-468-4000
Rich in natural and cultural history, this day-use primitive

recreation area has no developed camp areas or facilities and is located along Highways 20 and 16. It is maintained and managed for wildlife habitat, rare plants, the protection of archaeological resources, and to provide primitive recreational opportunities including offering multi-use trails, wildlife viewing, river running, hunting, and fishing. Dogs of all sizes are allowed for no additional fee. Dogs must be under their owner's control at all times. They may be off lead if they are under voice command. Please clean up after your pet, especially on the trails.

### Cow Mountain Recreation Area/Ukiah Field Office
2550 North State Street
Ukiah CA
707-468-4000
blm.gov/ca/ukiah/cowmtn.html
Dogs are allowed at the North Cow Mountain portion of this recreation area off Mill Creek Road; the South area is mostly for off-road vehicles. There are a variety of recreational opportunities available, a rifle range, and 17 miles of foot trails. Dogs of all sizes are allowed for no additional fee. Dogs must be under their owners control at all times, and leashed and cleaned up after.

### Lake Mendocino Recreation Area
1160 Lake Mendocino Drive
Ukiah CA
707-462-7581 (877-444-6777)
Created by the construction of the Coyote Dam, this beautiful lake recreation area is set among rolling hills and oak groves near the headwaters of the Russian River offering plenty of hiking trails. The lake has more than 1,800 surface acres, and there is a wide variety of land and water recreational opportunities. Dogs of all sizes are allowed for no additional fee. Dogs must be on no more than a 6 foot leash and be cleaned up after. Dogs are allowed throughout the park and on the

trails.

## Vacaville

### Dog-Friendly Hotels
**Best Western Heritage Inn**
1420 E Monte Vista Ave
Vacaville CA
707-448-8453 (800-780-7234)
Not Found.

**Hampton Inn & Suites Vacaville Ca**
800 Mason Street
Vacaville CA
707-469-6200
Dogs of all sizes are allowed.
There is no pet fee.

**Quality Inn & Suites Vacaville**
1050 Orange Drive
Vacaville CA
707-446-8888 (877-424-6423)
Quality Inn and Suites Vacaville
is centrally located between
Sacramento and San Francisco.
It is also down the

**Super 8 Vacaville**
101 Allison Court
Vacaville CA
707-449-8884 (800-800-8000)
Dogs are welcome at this hotel.

### Pet-Friendly Extended Stay Hotels
**Extended Stay America - Sacramento - Vacaville**
799 Orange Drive
Vacaville CA
707-469-1371 (800-804-3724)
One dog is allowed per suite.
There is a $25 per night
additional pet fee up to $150 for
an entire stay.

**Residence Inn By Marriott Vacaville**
360 Orange Drive
Vacaville CA
707-469-0300
Dogs of all sizes are allowed.
There is a $100 one time
additional pet fee.

### Dog-Friendly Attractions
**The Nut Tree**
1681 East Monte Vista Avenue
Vacaville CA
707-447-6000
nuttreeusa.com/
This has long been a popular
site to stop for food, fun, and
shopping. Dogs are allowed in
the common walk and picnic
areas; they are not allowed in
the theme park, restaurants, or
in buildings-except for the
PetSmart. Dogs must be
leashed and under their
owner's control at all times.

### Outdoor Restaurants
**Baja Fresh Mexican Grill**
150 Nut Tree Parkway
Vacaville CA
707-446-6736
bajafresh.com
This Mexican restaurant is
open for lunch and dinner.
They use fresh ingredients and
making their salsa and beans
daily. Some of the items on
their menu include Enchiladas,
Burritos, Tacos Salads,
Quesadillas, Nachos, Chicken,
Steak and more. Well-behaved
leashed dogs are allowed at
the outdoor tables.

**Fentons Creamery & Restaurant at the Nut Tree**
E Monte Vista Avenue
Vacaville CA
707-469-7200
pigletspantry.com/
Although famous for their fresh
hand-made ice cream and
classic soda fountain, they also
feature classic American fare.
They also offer a venue for
special events and catering
services. Leashed, friendly
dogs are allowed at their
outside tables.

**Jamba Juice**
1651 E Monte Vista Avenue,
Suite 101 @ Nut Tree Village
Vacaville CA
707-455-7302
jambajuice.com
All natural and organic
ingredients, no high-fructose
corn syrup, 0 grams trans fat, no
artificial preservatives, a healthy
helping of antioxidants, vitamins,
and minerals, and fresh whole
fruit and fruit juices set the base
for these tasty and healthy
beverages. Their organic Hot
Blends provides a new spin on
coffee, green or chai tea, and
hot chocolate;plus they offer
probiotic fruit and yogurt Blends.
Additionally, they feature all
natural salads, wraps,
sandwiches, and grab n go
specialties. They also offer
healthy community support
through fundraisers, special
sales, and school lunch
programs. Leashed, well
mannered dogs are allowed at
their outside dining area.

### Pet-Friendly Stores
**Camping World**
5065 Quinn Road
Vacaville CA
707-864-2267
campingworld.com/
This comprehensive RV and
outdoor store carries a wide
variety of RV, boat, bike, and
outdoor cooking accessories; all
kinds of camping gear; RV
screens, shades, and patio
decorations; racing/tailgating
gear, and all items for RV
maintenance. They also carry
RV towing supplies, electronics,
and interior decorating items as
well as pet supplies, RV
directories/books, and games.
Plus, they offer a tips and
advice service, RV sales,
rentals, and RV technicians to
take care of any installations
and repairs. They also welcome
your canine companion in the
store; they must be friendly and
leashed.

**PetSmart Pet Store**
1621 E Monte Vista Ave Ste B
Vacaville CA
707-469-9066
Your licensed and well-behaved
leashed dog is allowed in the
store.

**Petco Pet Store - Vacaville**

210 Nut Tree Pkwy
Vacaville CA
707-448-2020
Your licensed and well-behaved leashed dog is allowed in the store.

## Valencia

## Dog-Friendly Hotels

**Best Western Valencia Inn**
27413 Wayne Mills Place
Valencia CA
661-255-0555 (800-780-7234)
Dogs up to 80 pounds are allowed. There is a $10 per day pet fee up to $100 for the week. Up to two dogs are allowed per room.

## Dog-Friendly Attractions

**Six Flags Magic Mountain**
26101 Magic Mountain Parkway
Valencia CA
661-255-4100
Although dogs are not allowed inside this major recreation and entertainment destination, they do provide a free secured dog kennel for their canine visitors. Owners are to provide their food, toys, and any comfort items. The kennel is open during park hours.

## Outdoor Restaurants

**Baja Fresh Mexican Grill**
23630 W. Valencia Blvd.
Valencia CA
661-254-6060
bajafresh.com
This Mexican restaurant is open for lunch and dinner. They use fresh ingredients and making their salsa and beans daily. Some of the items on their menu include Enchiladas, Burritos, Tacos Salads, Quesadillas, Nachos, Chicken, Steak and more. Well-behaved leashed dogs are allowed at the outdoor tables.

**Chipotle**
28102 Newhall Ranch Road
Valencia CA
916-600-9477
chipotle.com
Specializing in organic, natural and unprocessed food, this Mexican Eatery offers fajita burritos, tacos, salads, and salsas. Dogs are allowed at the outdoor tables but you will need to order your food inside the restaurant and dogs must remain outside.

**Jamba Juice**
25888 The Old Road
Valencia CA
661-222-3174
jambajuice.com
All natural and organic ingredients, no high-fructose corn syrup, 0 grams trans fat, no artificial preservatives, a healthy helping of antioxidants, vitamins, and minerals, and fresh whole fruit and fruit juices set the base for these tasty and healthy beverages. Their organic Hot Blends provides a new spin on coffee, green or chai tea, and hot chocolate;plus they offer probiotic fruit and yogurt Blends. Additionally, they feature all natural salads, wraps, sandwiches, and grab n go specialties. They also offer healthy community support through fundraisers, special sales, and school lunch programs. Leashed, well mannered dogs are allowed at their outside dining area.

**Johnny Rockets**
24425 Town Center Drive
Valencia CA
661-291-2590
johnnyrockets.com/
All the American favorites can be found here: A fun retro, all-American decor and atmosphere, juicy burgers, specialty sandwiches, crispy fries, hand-dipped malts and shakes (dark chocolate ones too), fresh baked apple pies, tasty vegetarian choices, and something for all ages. Leashed, friendly dogs are allowed at their outside dining

area.

**Lazy Dog Restaurant & Bar**
24201 Valencia Blvd
Valencia CA
661-253-9996
lazydogrestaurants.com/dogs/info
Known for it's dog-friendly patio, the Lazy Dog offers your dog a complimentary bowl of water, and a menu consisting of grilled hamburger patty, chicken breast or brown rice. They just ask that you respect their common sense rules while your dog is dining there. This is as dog-friendly as dining gets. For the humans in your party there is hamburger, steak, salads and some great desserts.

**Lucille's Smokehouse barbecue**
24201 Valencia Blvd
Valencia CA
661-255-1227
Lucille's Smokehouse barbecue in Valencia, California, is open 7 days a week, from Monday-Thursday 11am-11pm, and Friday-Sunday 11am-12am. They serve a variety of food, including barbecue, sandwiches, salads, and more.

**The Coffee Bean & Tea Leaf**
28291 Newhall Ranch Road
Valencia CA
661-702-1760
coffeebean.com
The coffee here is sourced globally from family coffee farms to procure only the top of 1% of Arabica beans. They offer 30+ varieties of coffee;the beans are roasted in small batches daily for freshness, and they also offer 20 varieties of teas that are hand-blended by their tea master. Additionally, they offer a variety of tasty sweets, powders, extracts, sauces, gifts, and cards. Leashed, well mannered dogs are allowed at their outside dining area.

**The Coffee Bean & Tea Leaf**
24201 Valencia Blvd, Space #3648
Valencia CA
661-291-1134

coffeebean.com
The coffee here is sourced globally from family coffee farms to procure only the top of 1% of Arabica beans. They offer 30+ varieties of coffee;the beans are roasted in small batches daily for freshness, and they also offer 20 varieties of teas that are hand-blended by their tea master. Additionally, they offer a variety of tasty sweets, powders, extracts, sauces, gifts, and cards. Leashed, well mannered dogs are allowed at their outside dining area.

## Pet-Friendly Stores
**Petco Pet Store - Santa Clarita**

26501 Bouquet Canyon Road
Saugus CA
661-297-6936
Your licensed and well-behaved leashed dog is allowed in the store.

## Vallejo

## Dog-Friendly Hotels
**Holiday Inn Express And Suites Napa Valley-american Canyon**
5001 Main Street
American Canyon CA
+17-075-5281 (877-270-6405)
Dogs of all sizes are allowed.
Dogs are allowed for a pet fee of $50.00 per pet per stay.

**Courtyard By Marriott Vallejo Napa Valley**
1000 Fairgrounds Drive
Vallejo CA
707-644-1200
Dogs of all sizes are allowed.
There is a $75 one time pet fee.

**Ramada Inn Vallejo / Napa Valley Area**
1000 Admiral Callaghan Lane
Vallejo CA
707-643-2700
Dogs of all sizes are allowed.
There is a $50 one time pet fee.

## Outdoor Restaurants
**Jamba Juice**
165 Plaza Drive #709
Vallejo CA
707-645-8912
jambajuice.com
All natural and organic ingredients, no high-fructose corn syrup, 0 grams trans fat, no artificial preservatives, a healthy helping of antioxidants, vitamins, and minerals, and fresh whole fruit and fruit juices set the base for these tasty and healthy beverages. Their organic Hot Blends provides a new spin on coffee, green or chai tea, and hot chocolate;plus they offer probiotic fruit and yogurt Blends. Additionally, they feature all natural salads, wraps, sandwiches, and grab n go specialties. They also offer healthy community support through fundraisers, special sales, and school lunch programs. Leashed, well mannered dogs are allowed at their outside dining area.

## Pet-Friendly Stores
**Petco Pet Store - Vallejo**
161 Plaza Dr.
Vallejo CA
707-649-8081
Your licensed and well-behaved leashed dog is allowed in the store.

## Off-Leash Dog Parks
**Wardlaw Dog Park**
Redwood Pkwy at Ascot Pkwy
Vallejo CA

Located in Blue Rock Springs Corridor Park, the dog park is 2.2 acres in size and fully fenced. There is a separate area for small, shy or older dogs. There is a 2 mile walking path in Blue Rock Springs Park where you can take your leashed dog. From I-80 take the Redwood Pkwy East exit.

Turn right on Ascot Parkway to the park.

## Valley Center

## Dog-Friendly Attractions
**Bates Nut Farm**
15954 Woods Valley Road
Valley Center CA
760-749-3333
batesnutfarm.biz
This nut farm also offers dried and glazed fruits, regular and sugar free chocolates, snacks and gift packs, and a full calendar of fun events. They have a farm zoo, picnicking areas, a pumpkin patch, holiday celebrations, art and craft festivals, farm tours, and a variety of special events for dogs. The farm is open daily from 9 am until 5 pm and the gift shop opens at 9:30 am. Leashed, friendly dogs are welcome, and please clean up after your pet.

## Events
**Doggie Costume Parade & Contest**
15954 Woods Valley Road
Valley Center CA
760-749-3333
This canine event, located at the dog-friendly Bates Nut Farm and sponsored by Armstrong Feed & Supply, promises to be a 'howling' good time for fun-loving pooches and their owners. The event takes place on Sunday, October 23, 2011 at 11 am; registration begins at 10 am. Dogs must be leashed, friendly, and cleaned up after promptly.

## Ventura - Oxnard

## Dog-Friendly Hotels
**Best Western Camarillo Inn**

295 E Daily Dr
Camarillo CA
805-987-4991 (800-780-7234)
Dogs up to 80 pounds are allowed. There is a $20 per day pet fee up to $100 for the week. Up to two dogs are allowed per room.

**Best Western Oxnard Inn**
1156 South Oxnard Blvd.
Oxnard CA
805-483-9581 (800-780-7234)
Dogs under 30 pounds are allowed. There is a $40 per pet per stay pet fee.

**Vagabond Inn Oxnard**
1245 North Oxnard Boulevard
Oxnard CA
805-983-0251
Nestled in downtown Oxnard near restaurants and the Oxnard Performing Arts and Convention Center Vagabond Inn Oxnard offers our guests complimentary breakfast free Wi-Fi and an outdoor pool. Offering two floors with exterior corridors and 70 rooms Vagabond Inn features standard in-room amenities as complimentary Wi-Fi free weekday newspapers cable TV mini-fridges microwaves and hairdryers. Non-smoking accommodations are available. Wake up to the hotel's complimentary continental breakfast and end your day with some relaxing laps in the outdoor pool. Pets are welcome at an additional fee. The downtown Oxnard Vagabond Inn puts guests within walking distance of restaurants and two miles from the Oxnard Performing Arts and Convention Center. The Carnegie Art Museum is less than two miles away while the Channel Island Harbor home to marinas slips and shops is six miles from the hotel. Los Angeles International Airport is 65 miles.

**Crowne Plaza Ventura**
450 East Harbor Boulevard
Ventura CA
805-648-2100 (877-270-6405)
Dogs of all sizes are allowed. Dogs are allowed for a pet fee of $50.00 per pet per stay.

**Four Points By Sheraton Ventura Harbor Resort**
1050 Schooner Drive
Ventura CA
805-658-1212 (888-625-5144)
This upscale resort hotel offers a number of on site amenities for business and leisure travelers, plus a convenient location to shopping, dining, and entertainment areas. Dogs are allowed for an additional one time pet fee of $75;there is a pet waiver to sign at check in.

**Holiday Inn Express Hotel & Suites Ventura Harbor**
1080 Navigator Drive
Ventura CA
805-856-9533 (877-270-6405)
Dogs of all sizes are allowed. Dogs are allowed for a pet fee of $75.00 per pet per stay.

**La Quinta Inn Ventura**
5818 Valentine Road
Ventura CA
805-658-6200 (800-531-5900)
Dogs of all sizes are allowed. There are no additional pet fees. Dogs must be leashed and cleaned up after. Dogs must be crated or attended to for housekeeping.

**Marriott Ventura Beach**
2055 East Harbor Boulevard
Ventura CA
805-643-6000
Dogs up to 15 pounds are allowed. There is a $75 one time pet fee.

**Vagabond Inn Ventura**
756 East Thompson Boulevard
Ventura CA
805-648-5371
Offering free breakfast complimentary Wi-Fi and a heated outdoor pool the pet-accommodating Vagabond Inn Ventura is a budget-friendly option for a stay near the beach. The low-rise Vagabond features 82 cozy rooms accessed by exterior corridors. Guests can surf the web thanks to free Wi-Fi access or catch a movie on the cable TV with premium channels.

Coffeemakers microwaves and mini-fridges are handy for whipping up breakfast or a midnight snack. Business-friendly features include fax and copy services and free local calling. Accessible and non-smoking rooms are available and pets are welcome for an additional fee. The hotel's sun-filled lobby is the go-to place for free coffee weekday newspapers and daily continental breakfast before heading out to the pool hot tub or nearby beach. There's also an on-site restaurant and a 24-hour front desk. The Vagabond Inn is located in downtown Ventura less than one mile from the San Buenaventura Mission and within walking distance of restaurants shops and the San Buenaventura State Beach which can be accessed by a footbridge behind the hotel. Boating and fishing enthusiasts will appreciate the close proximity to the Ventura Marina and Channel Islands National Park both within a 10-minute drive. It's 10 miles from Oxnard Airport.

## Pet-Friendly Extended Stay Hotels
**Residence Inn Camarillo**
2912 Petit Street
Camarillo CA
805-388-7997
Dogs of all sizes are allowed. There is a $100 one time additional pet fee.

**Residence Inn By Marriott Oxnard River Ridge**
2101 W Vineyard Ave
Oxnard CA
805-278-2200
Dogs of all sizes are allowed. There is a $100 one time additional pet fee.

## Dog-Friendly Attractions
**Hopper Boat Rentals**
3600 Harbor Blvd # 368
Oxnard CA

805-382-1100
This boat rental company, located at Fisherman's Wharf in Oxnard, allows well-behaved dogs on their motor skiff boats. You and your pup can cruise the Channel Islands Harbor between the hours of 10am until dusk. The boat rentals are $45 per hour. Prices are subject to change.

**Albinger Archaeological Museum**
113 East Main Street
Ventura CA
805-648-5823
Well-behaved dogs are allowed. This museum was once the home to five different cultures spanning 3,500 years of history. Learn about the Chumash Indians, Chinese immigrants and others who resided on the site, as well as the archaeological digs uncovered in 1974. The museum is on the National Register of Historic Places. It is open Wednesday through Sunday.

**Ventura Pier**
668 Harbor Blvd
Ventura CA

Ventura Pier was originally built in 1872. The wooden pier is about 2000 feet long. On the pier, the restaurant Eric Ericsson's on the Pier has dog-friendly outdoor seating and there is also a snack bar where you can get a quick bite on the pier. Dogs on leash are allowed on the pier.

## Outdoor Restaurants
**Baja Fresh Mexican Grill**
1855 Daily Drive
Camarillo CA
805-383-6884
bajafresh.com
This Mexican restaurant is open for lunch and dinner. They use fresh ingredients and making their salsa and beans daily. Some of the items on their menu include Enchiladas, Burritos, Tacos Salads, Quesadillas, Nachos, Chicken,

Steak and more. Well-behaved leashed dogs are allowed at the outdoor tables.

**Coffee Bean & Tea Leaf**
824 Arneil Road
Camarillo CA
805-383-7767
coffeebean.com
The coffee here is sourced globally from family coffee farms to procure only the top of 1% of Arabica beans. They offer 30+ varieties of coffee;the beans are roasted in small batches daily for freshness, and they also offer 20 varieties of teas that are hand-blended by their tea master. Additionally, they offer a variety of tasty sweets, powders, extracts, sauces, gifts, and cards. Leashed, well mannered dogs are allowed at their outside dining area.

**Old Town Cafe**
2050 E. Ventura Blvd
Camarillo CA
805-484-5500
All American and regional specialties top the menu at this cafe. They feature daily specials, daily made soups, house specialties, and patio dining. Leashed, friendly dogs are allowed at their outside dining area.

**Panda Express**
199 W Ventura Blvd
Camarillo CA
805-987-3368
pandaexpress.com
Gourmet Chinese cuisine to dine-in, To-Go, or to cater is the specialties of this eatery. They will also host charity events and they offer patio dining. Leashed dogs are allowed at the outside dining area.

**The Way Point Cafe**
325 Durley Avenue
Camarillo CA
805-388-2535
thewaypointcafe.com
Fly in or drive to this theme cafe;they served up home style cooked breakfasts and lunches as well as offering coffee

specialty drinks. They are open Monday to Saturday from 7 am until 4 pm and on Sunday from 8 am until 4 pm. Leashed, friendly dogs are allowed at their outside dining area.

**Topper's Pizza**
520 Arneill Rd
Camarillo CA
805-385-4444
topperspizzaplace.com/index.php
Topper's Pizza offers oven-baked sandwiches, pizzas, build your own pizzas, and more! Well-behaved, leashed dogs are welcome at the outdoor patio.

**Baja Fresh Mexican Grill**
2350 Vineyard Ave
Oxnard CA
805-988-7878
bajafresh.com
This Mexican restaurant is open for lunch and dinner. They use fresh ingredients and making their salsa and beans daily. Some of the items on their menu include Enchiladas, Burritos, Tacos Salads, Quesadillas, Nachos, Chicken, Steak and more. Well-behaved leashed dogs are allowed at the outdoor tables.

**Café Amri**
2000 Outlet Center Dr #295
Oxnard CA
805-983-3026
cafeamri.com/
This breakfast and lunch eatery will allow friendly, leashed dogs at their outside dining area.

**Lazy Dog Restaurant & Bar**
598 Town Center Drive
Oxnard CA
805-351-4888
lazydogrestaurants.com/dogs/info
Known for it's dog-friendly patio, the Lazy Dog offers your dog a complimentary bowl of water, and a menu consisting of grilled hamburger patty, chicken breast or brown rice. They just ask that you respect their common sense rules while your dog is dining there. This is as dog-friendly as dining gets. For the humans in your party there is

hamburger, steak, salads and some great desserts.

### Sea Fresh Restaurant
3550 Harbor Blvd
Oxnard CA
805-204-0974
seafreshci.com
The freshest seafood and regionally inspired cuisine is the specialty of this waterfront diner. They also have Happy Hour Monday through Friday from 2 pm until 6 pm. Leashed well mannered dogs are allowed at the patio dining area.

### The Coffee Bean & Tea Leaf
2180 N Rose Avenue
Oxnard CA
805-485-8112
coffeebean.com
The coffee here is sourced globally from family coffee farms to procure only the top of 1% of Arabica beans. They offer 30+ varieties of coffee;the beans are roasted in small batches daily for freshness, and they also offer 20 varieties of teas that are hand-blended by their tea master. Additionally, they offer a variety of tasty sweets, powders, extracts, sauces, gifts, and cards. Leashed, well mannered dogs are allowed at their outside dining area.

### The Coffee Bean & Tea Leaf
1191 S Victoria Avenue
Oxnard CA
805-984-7162
coffeebean.com
The coffee here is sourced globally from family coffee farms to procure only the top of 1% of Arabica beans. They offer 30+ varieties of coffee;the beans are roasted in small batches daily for freshness, and they also offer 20 varieties of teas that are hand-blended by their tea master. Additionally, they offer a variety of tasty sweets, powders, extracts, sauces, gifts, and cards. Leashed, well mannered dogs are allowed at their outside dining area.

### Topper's Pizza
2100 S. Saviers Rd
Oxnard CA

805-385-4444
topperspizzaplace.com
Topper's Pizza offers oven-baked sandwiches, pizzas, build your own pizzas, and more! Well-behaved, leashed dogs are welcome at the outdoor patio.

### Topper's Pizza
2701 Peninsula Rd
Oxnard CA
805-385-4444
topperspizzaplace.com
Topper's Pizza offers oven-baked sandwiches, pizzas, build your own pizzas, and more! Well-behaved, leashed dogs are welcome at the outdoor patio.

### Topper's Pizza
111 E. Gonzales Rd
Oxnard CA
805-385-4444
topperspizzaplace.com
Topper's Pizza offers oven-baked sandwiches, pizzas, build your own pizzas, and more! Well-behaved, leashed dogs are welcome at the outdoor patio.

### Chinese Dumpling House
575 W. Channel Islands Blvd.
Port Hueneme CA
805-985-4849
This restaurant is open from 11am until 9pm. Leashed dogs are welcome at their outside dining area.

### Anacapa Brewing Company
472 E Main Street
Ventura CA
805-643-BEER (2337)
anacapabrewing.com/index.asp

This is Ventura's only restaurant and brewery, or Brewpub. They are open daily at 11:30 a.m. except for Mondays when they open at 5:00 p.m. Well behaved, leashed dogs of all sizes are allowed to join you on the patio while you enjoy handcrafted food and ale.

### Baja Fresh Mexican Grill
4726-2 Telephone Road
Ventura CA

805-650-3535
bajafresh.com
This Mexican restaurant is open for lunch and dinner. They use fresh ingredients and making their salsa and beans daily. Some of the items on their menu include Enchiladas, Burritos, Tacos Salads, Quesadillas, Nachos, Chicken, Steak and more. Well-behaved leashed dogs are allowed at the outdoor tables.

### Cafe Nouveau
1497 E Thompson Blvd
Ventura CA
805-648-1422
cafenouveau.net/
Set in a 1920's Spanish bungalow, this California style restaurant features Italian cuisine, a notable wine list, and lush Mediterranean garden dining. Leashed, well mannered dogs are allowed at their outside dining area.

### Chipotle
1145 S Victoria Avenue
Ventura CA
805-650-6627
chipotle.com
Specializing in organic, natural and unprocessed food, this Mexican Eatery offers fajita burritos, tacos, salads, and salsas. Dogs are allowed at the outdoor tables but you will need to order your food inside the restaurant and dogs must remain outside.

### Chipotle
488 S Mills Road
Ventura CA
805-654-0143
chipotle.com
Specializing in organic, natural and unprocessed food, this Mexican Eatery offers fajita burritos, tacos, salads, and salsas. Dogs are allowed at the outdoor tables but you will need to order your food inside the restaurant and dogs must remain outside.

### Golden Egg Cafe
2009 East Main Street
Ventura CA
805-641-2866

Golden Egg Cafe in Ventura, California serves breakfast and brunch. Well-behaved, leashed dogs are welcome at the outdoor seats!

**Lassen Ventura Market and Deli**
4071 E Main Street
Ventura CA
805-644-6990
Although dogs are not allowed inside this 'healthy choices' store and deli, outside seating is available where you may sit with your pet while you dine or wait for someone shopping. Dogs must be well mannered, leashed, and cleaned up after quickly.

**Nature's Grill**
566 E Main Street
Ventura CA
805-643-7855
Nature's Grill welcomes all well behaved, leashed dogs to join you on their patio. They offer health-minded diners vegetarian and California cuisine. They are open from 11 am to 9 pm 7 days a week.

**RedBrick Pizza Ventura**
4990 Telephone Road
Ventura CA
805-658-2828
rbpcafe.com
Old world Italian tradition paired with contemporary recipes creates the signature fire-roasted gourmet pizzas at this specialty eatery. They feature organic red sauce and pepperoni, healthy dough and ingredient choices, Italian gelato, triple-filtered water, signature flat-bread Fhazani sandwiches, natural, pure cane sodas on tap, and all natural low carbon micro-brews. They have also implemented several GREEN initiatives throughout their establishment. Leashed, friendly dogs are allowed at their outside dining area.

**Spasso Cucina Italiana**
1140 Seaward Avenue
Ventura CA
805-643-2777
spassorestaurant.com/

This Italian eatery features their own handmade pastas, European style crepe brunches, fine Italian wines, and alfresco dining. Leashed dogs are welcome at their outside dining area, and water bowls are provided.

**The Coffee Bean & Tea Leaf**
1780 S Victoria Avenue, Suite A
Ventura CA
805-639-0795
coffeebean.com
The coffee here is sourced globally from family coffee farms to procure only the top of 1% of Arabica beans. They offer 30+ varieties of coffee;the beans are roasted in small batches daily for freshness, and they also offer 20 varieties of teas that are hand-blended by their tea master. Additionally, they offer a variety of tasty sweets, powders, extracts, sauces, gifts, and cards. Leashed, well mannered dogs are allowed at their outside dining area.

**The Coffee Bean & Tea Leaf**
4360 E Main Street, Suite 3
Ventura CA
805-644-6000
coffeebean.com
The coffee here is sourced globally from family coffee farms to procure only the top of 1% of Arabica beans. They offer 30+ varieties of coffee;the beans are roasted in small batches daily for freshness, and they also offer 20 varieties of teas that are hand-blended by their tea master. Additionally, they offer a variety of tasty sweets, powders, extracts, sauces, gifts, and cards. Leashed, well mannered dogs are allowed at their outside dining area.

**The Wharf**
980 E Front Street
Ventura CA
805-648-5035
thewharfonline.com/
This apparel superstore carries clothing for the whole family, footwear, work-wear, major

brand wear, and a comprehensive section for pet/animal foods and supplies. Leashed, well mannered dogs are allowed in the store.

**Tony's Pizzeria**
186 E Thompson Blvd
Ventura CA
805-643-8425
They welcome all dogs on a leash in the outdoor patio. People just tie their dogs right to the tables and enjoy the pizza. No dogs allowed inside but you can order from the side window. They are located one block from the beach.

**Topper's Pizza**
3940 E. Main St.
Ventura CA
805-385-4444
topperspizzaplace.com
Topper's Pizza offers oven-baked sandwiches, pizzas, build your own pizzas, and more! Well-behaved, leashed dogs are welcome at the outdoor patio.

# Pet-Friendly Shopping Centers

**Camarillo Outlet Stores**
740 E. Ventura Blvd, Camarillo, CA 93010
Camarillo CA
805-445-8520
With 160 shops and services, this outlet mall offers guests a wide variety of dining and shopping opportunities. Special sales and events are always happening here as well. Dogs are allowed in the common areas of the mall; it is up to individual stores whether they allow a dog inside. Dogs must be well behaved, leashed, and under their owner's control at all times.

**Ventura Harbor Village**
1559 Spinnaker Drive
Ventura CA
805-644-0169
venturaharborvillage.com
This nice seaside shopping village allows your leashed dog. While dogs are not allowed

inside the stores, there are several outdoor dog-friendly restaurants (see Restaurants). During the summer weekends, the village usually has outdoor art exhibits and concerts where your pup is welcome.

## Pet-Friendly Stores

### Petco Pet Store - Camarillo
177 West Ventura Blvd
Camarillo CA
805-384-5435
Your licensed and well-behaved leashed dog is allowed in the store.

### Ventura Harley-Davidson
1326 Del Norte Road
Camarillo CA
805-981-9904
venturaharley.com/
This specialty motorcycle store will allow leashed friendly dogs in the store. They also have some dog leashes, collars, toys, and apparel items. The store is open Tuesday to Friday from 9 am until 6 pm; Saturday from 9 am until 5 pm, and on Sunday from 10 am until 4 pm. Service hours are a bit longer and closed for Sunday and Monday.

### PetSmart Pet Store
2021 N Oxnard Blvd
Oxnard CA
805-981-4012
Your licensed and well-behaved leashed dog is allowed in the store.

### Petco Pet Store - Port Hueneme
545 West Channel Islands Blvd
Port Hueneme CA
805-984-3470
Your licensed and well-behaved leashed dog is allowed in the store.

### PetSmart Pet Store
4840 Telephone Rd
Ventura CA
805-650-9191
Your licensed and well-behaved leashed dog is allowed in the store.

### Petco Pet Store - Ventura
4300-A East Main St.
Ventura CA
805-639-3016
Your licensed and well-behaved leashed dog is allowed in the store.

### The Wharf
980 E Front Street
Ventura CA
805-648-5035
thewharfonline.com/
This apparel superstore carries clothing for the whole family, footwear, work-wear, major brand wear, and a comprehensive section for pet/animal foods and supplies. Leashed, well mannered dogs are allowed in the store.

### Urban Outfitters
327 E. Main Street
Ventura CA
805-652-0133
In addition to a large inventory of indoor and outdoor apparel for men and women, this major department store also carries vintage wear, designer brands, and a variety of accessories for all types of active lifestyles. They also carry shoes, furnishings, home decor, cameras, electronics, novelty items and more. Leashed, well mannered dogs are allowed in the store.

## Dog-Friendly Beaches

### Hollywood Beach
4199 Ocean Drive
Oxnard CA

This beach is located on the west side of the Channel Islands Harbor. The beach is 4 miles southwest of Oxnard. Dogs must be on leash and owners must clean up after their pets. Dogs are allowed on Hollywood Beach before 9 am and after 5 pm.

### Oxnard Beach Park
Harbor Blvd.
Oxnard CA
805-385-7946
North of 5th street is Mandalay State Beach and dogs are not allowed at all. This beach is nesting habitat for the endangered western snowy plover. Dog owners entering the beach from 5th street must go south towards the houses.

### Silver Strand Beach
various addresses
Oxnard CA

This beach is located between the Channel Islands Harbor and the U.S. Naval Construction Battalion Center. Dogs are now only allowed on the beach after 5 pm and before 8 am. The beach is 4 miles southwest of Oxnard. Dogs must be on leash and owners must clean up after their pets.

### Harbor Cove Beach
West end of Spinnaker Drive
Ventura CA
805-652-4550
This beach is considered the safest swimming area in Ventura because of the protection of the cove. Dogs of all sizes are allowed at this beach as well as on the 6 miles of Ventura City Beaches and on the long wooden pier, but they are not allowed on any of the beaches south of the Ventura Pier or on any of the State beaches. Dogs must be leashed and cleaned up after at all times.

### Promenade Park
Figueroa Street at the Promenade
Ventura CA
805-652-4550
This park is a one acre oceanfront park on the site of an old Indian village near Seaside Park. Dogs of all sizes are are allowed at this beach as well as on the 6 miles of Ventura City Beaches and on the long wooden pier, but they are not allowed on any of the beaches south of the Ventura Pier or on any of the State beaches. Dogs must be leashed and cleaned up after at all times.

### Surfers Point at Seaside Park
Figueroa Street at the

Promenade
Ventura CA
800-483-6215
This park is one of the area's
most popular surfing and
windsurfing beaches, and it
offers showers, picnic facilities
and restrooms, and is
connected with the Ventura Pier
by a scenic landscaped
Promenade walkway and the
Omer Rains Bike Trail. Dogs are
allowed on the 6 miles of
Ventura City Beaches and on
the long wooden pier, but they
are not allowed on any of the
beaches south of the Ventura
Pier or on any of the State
beaches. Dogs must be leashed
and cleaned up after at all
times.

## Off-Leash Dog Parks
**Camarillo Grove Dog Park**
off Camarillo Springs Road
East Camarillo CA
805-482-1996
This fenced dog park is about
one acre and double gated.
Amenities include a water
fountain for dogs and people,
benches, and a fire hydrant. The
dog park is located off Camarillo
Springs Road, at the base of the
Conejo Grade. Dogs are not
allowed in other parts of the
park except for the off-leash
area.

**College Park Dog Park**
3250 S Rose Avenue
Oxnard CA
805-385-7950
Offering shade, lots of grass,
and benches, this off lead area
has 2 separate areas for small
and large pets and both sides
feature obstacle courses. Dogs
must be sociable, current on all
vaccinations and license, and
under their owner's control at all
times. Dogs must be leashed
when not in designated off-lead
areas.

**College Park Dog Park**
3200 S Rose Avenue
Oxnard CA
805-385-7950
Perks of this fenced doggy

playground include a variety of
agility obstacles, half dirt/half
grass grounds, a separate
small dog area, dog waste
stations, and a coin-operated
dog bathing area. Dogs must
be healthy, sociable, current on
all vaccinations and license
with tags on collar, and under
their owner's control at all
times. Owners must clean up
after their pets, and keep them
leashed when not in
designated off-lead areas.

**Arroyo Verde Park**
Foothill and Day Road
Ventura CA
805-658-4740
This park has a designated off-
leash area for use at specific
times. There are benches and
drinking fountains for the dogs
and their people. Only well-
socialized, dogs are permitted
in the off-leash areas. All dogs
must be vaccinated for rabies
and have a current license, and
owners are expected to be
responsible for their dogs
including keeping them under
voice control and cleaning up
after them. Their hours are
Tuesday through Sunday from
6 to 9 AM, excluding holidays
and days reserved for special
events.

**Camino Real Park**
At Dean Drive and Varsity
Street
Ventura CA
805-658-4740
This park has a fenced in area
in the southwest corner of the
park for dogs and their owners
to socialize and exercise.
Hours of the dog park are from
dawn to dusk, and amenities
include drinking fountains for
the dogs and their people,
benches, and doggie-doo bags.
Double gates allow both small
and large dogs to come in and
out of the area safely. All dogs
must be vaccinated for rabies
and have a current license, and
owners are expected to be
responsible for their dogs
including keeping them under
voice control and cleaning up
after them.

## Dog-Friendly Parks
**Orchard Park**
Geranium Place
Oxnard CA

yelp.com/biz/orchard-park-
oxnard
This small city park has tennis
courts and a nice playground for
kids. It is located on the corner
of Geranium Place and Camelot
Way. Dogs must be on leash.

**Channel Islands National Park**

1901 Spinnaker Drive
Ventura CA
805-658-5730
nps.gov/chis/index.htm
Pets are not allowed on the
islands.

**Grant Park**
Brakey Road
Ventura CA

The park has a few hiking trails
and the Padre Serra Cross.
There are some great views of
the Ventura Harbor from this
park. It is located about 1/2 mile
north of Hwy 101, near
California Street. Dogs must be
on leash.

**Ojai Valley Trail**
Hwy 33 at Casitas Vista Rd
Ventura CA
805-654-3951
This 9.5 mile trail has a paved
pedestrian path and a wood-chip
bridle path. Dogs are allowed
but must always be on leash.
The trail parallels Highway 33
from Foster Park, just outside
Ventura to Fox Street, in Ojai.

**Ventura River Trail**
Old Town Ventura to Foster
Park
Ventura CA
805-658-4740
This 6.5 mile paved trail heads
from Old Town Ventura near
Main Street and Hwy 33 along
the Ventura River to Foster Park
where it hooks up with the Ojai
Valley Trail which continues to
Ojai nearly 10 miles away. Dogs

on leash may share the trail with joggers, bicycles and others.

## Events
### Pooch Parade Dog Walk and Pet Expo
10 West Harbor Blvd
Ventura CA
805-488-7533
poochparade.org/
Sponsored by the Canine Adoption and Rescue League, the Pooch Parade benefits the Project Second Chance Adoption Programs. It is an annual summer, day long event of fun-filled contests, doggy demonstrations, a pet expo, silent auction, and a beautiful 3 mile round trip Pooch Parade along the Ventura Beach Promenade. All well behaved, leashed dogs are welcome, and please clean up after your pet.

## Emergency Veterinarians
### Pet Emergency Clinic
2301 S Victoria Ave
Ventura CA
805-642-8562
Monday - Friday 6 pm to 8 am, 24 hours on weekends.

### Veterinary Medical and Surgical Group
2199 Sperry Avenue
Ventura CA
805-339-2290
vmsg.com
This emergency veterinary clinic is open for emergency services 24 hours a day.

## Service Dog Organizations

### VENTURA SHERIFF K9 FOUNDATION
800 S Victoria Av #3320
Ventura CA
805 654-5158
9k4k9.org
The Ventura Sheriff K9 Foundation was organized to support the Ventura County Sheriff's Department canine

program. Public monies pay the canine handler's salary and the cost of a basic patrol unit. Private donations pay for the cost of the dog, modifications to the patrol unit, special equipment, ongoing training for the dog and the handler, medical and food for the dog. It costs about $14,000.00 to put a trained dog in a modified unit with a trained handler.

## Victorville

### Dog-Friendly Hotels
### Americas Best Value Inn - Hesperia
12033 Oakwood Avenue
Hesperia CA
760-949-3231 (800-800-8000)
Dogs are welcome at this hotel.

### Econo Lodge Hesperia
11976 Mariposa Rd
Hesperia CA
760-949-1515 (877-424-6423)
Econo Lodge located off I-15, 35 miles from LA/Ontario Arpt, near Arrowhead Lake. Free wireless hi-speed, continental breakfast.

Dogs up to 25 pounds are allowed. Dogs are allowed for a pet fee of $10 per pet per night.

### La Quinta Inn And Suites Hesperia Victorville
12000 Mariposa Road
Hesperia CA
760-949-9900 (800-531-5900)
Dogs up to 50 pounds are allowed. There are no additional pet fees, but a credit card must be on file. Dogs may not be left unattended, and they must be leashed and cleaned up after.

### Red Roof Inn Victorville
13409 Mariposa Road
Victorville CA
760-241-1577 (800-RED-ROOF)

One well-behaved family pet per room. Guest must notify front desk upon arrival. Guest is liable for any damages. In consideration of all guests, pets must never be left unattended in the guest rooms.

### Travelodge Victorville
12175 Mariposa Road
Victorville CA
760-241-7200
Dogs of all sizes are allowed. There is a pet fee of $10 per pet per night.

### Pet-Friendly Extended Stay Hotels
### Green Tree Inn And Extended Stay Suites
14173 Green Tree Boulevard
Victorville CA
760-245-3461 (877-424-6423)
The Quality Inn and Suites is a golfer's paradise overlooking an 18-hole championship golf course.

### Pet-Friendly Stores
### PetSmart Pet Store
12624 Amargosa Rd
Victorville CA
760-955-1030
Your licensed and well-behaved leashed dog is allowed in the store.

### Petco Pet Store - Victorville
17150 Bear Valley Road
Victorville CA
760-241-8137
Your licensed and well-behaved leashed dog is allowed in the store.

## Visalia

### Dog-Friendly Hotels
### La Quinta Inn & Suites Visalia
5438 West Cypress Avenue
Visalia CA
559-739-9800 (800-531-5900)
Dogs of all sizes are allowed for

no additional pet fee; there is a pet policy to sign at check-in. Dogs may not be left alone in the room, and they may not be in the common areas of the hotel.

**Super 8 Visalia**
4801 West Noble Avenue
Visalia CA
559-627-2885 (800-800-8000)
Dogs of all sizes are allowed. Dogs are allowed for a pet fee.

**Visalia Marriott At The Convention Center**
300 South Court Street
Visalia CA
559-636-1111
Dogs up to 75 pounds are allowed. There is a $75 one time pet fee. You must sign an agreement at check in.

**Wyndham Visalia**
9000 West Airport Drive
Visalia CA
559-651-5000 (877-698-9593)
Dogs of all sizes are allowed. Dogs are allowed for a nightly pet fee.

## Outdoor Restaurants
**Jamba Juice**
2028 S Mooney M-1/H 63
Visalia CA
559-713-0704
jambajuice.com
All natural and organic ingredients, no high-fructose corn syrup, 0 grams trans fat, no artificial preservatives, a healthy helping of antioxidants, vitamins, and minerals, and fresh whole fruit and fruit juices set the base for these tasty and healthy beverages. Their organic Hot Blends provides a new spin on coffee, green or chai tea, and hot chocolate;plus they offer probiotic fruit and yogurt Blends. Additionally, they feature all natural salads, wraps, sandwiches, and grab n go specialties. They also offer healthy community support through fundraisers, special sales, and school lunch programs. Leashed, well mannered dogs are allowed at

their outside dining area.

## Pet-Friendly Stores
**PetSmart Pet Store**
4240 S Mooney Blvd
Visalia CA
559-625-0299
Your licensed and well-behaved leashed dog is allowed in the store.

**Petco Pet Store - Visalia**
3444 South Mooney Blvd
Visalia CA
559-733-5646
Your licensed and well-behaved leashed dog is allowed in the store.

## Off-Leash Dog Parks
**Cody Kelly Bark Park**
Plaza Drive and Airport Road
Visalia CA

Located in Plaza Park, this is a large, well maintained off leash area with separately fenced areas for large and small dogs, grassy and shaded areas, and water on site. Dogs must be healthy, sociable, current on all vaccinations and license with tags on collar, and under owner's control/care at all times. Owners must clean up after their pets, and keep them leashed when not in designated off-lead areas.

**Seven Oaks Bark Park**
900 S Edison Street
Visalia CA
559-713-4586
Located in Seven Oaks Park, this fenced off leash area has grassy and shaded areas and water on site. Dogs must be healthy, sociable, current on all vaccinations and license with tags on collar, and under owner's control/care at all times. Owners must clean up after their pets, and keep them leashed when not in designated off-lead areas.

## Dog-Friendly Parks
**Sunset Park**
Monte Verde and Liserdra
Visalia CA
559-713-4300
Thanks to one of our readers who writes "It is a well kept park with plenty of friendly people and dogs."

## Other Organizations
**Homemade Natural Dog Food**
6030 W. Dartmouth Ave.
Visalia CA
5597455567
homemadenaturaldogfood.com
Homemade Natural Dog Food offers recipes, advice, and information about caring for your dog. We provide articles on various dog-care topics such as healthy food choices, weight management, canine disease, and general health maintenance for all dogs.

## Walker

## Pet-Friendly Stores
**Out West Gallery**
107281 H 395
Walker CA
530-495-2415
outwestgalleries.com/
Customers will find high quality Native American handcrafted art and artifacts at this gallery and trading company. Leashed, well mannered dogs are welcome in the store.

## Warner Springs

## Dog-Friendly Parks
**Barker Valley Spur Trail**
Forest Road 9S07
Warner Springs CA
760-788-0250
This 3.4 mile moderate rated trail is located in the Cleveland

National Forest. The trail elevation changes from 4,000 to 5,100 feet. It is open from early spring through late fall. Pets on leash are allowed and please clean up after them. To get there, take Highway 79 south toward Warner Springs. At about 2 miles southeast of Sunshine Summit take Forest Road 9S07 west. In about 7 miles the trailhead sign will be found on the left side of the road. Parking is in the wide area along the road. (Vehicles must display a Forest Adventure Pass.)

## Watsonville

### Dog-Friendly Hotels
**Best Western Rose Garden Inn**
740 Freedom Boulevard
Watsonville CA
831-724-3367 (800-780-7234)
Dogs up to 80 pounds are allowed. There is a $20 per day pet fee up to $100 for the week. Up to two dogs are allowed per room.

**Comfort Inn Watsonville**
112 Airport Boulevard
Watsonville CA
831-728-2300 (877-424-6423)
The Comfort Inn is conveniently located between Santa Cruz and Monterey, close to Capitol State Beach.

Dogs up to 50 pounds are allowed. Dogs are allowed for a pet fee of $15/ per pet per night. Two dogs are allowed per room.

**Rodeway Inn Watsonville**
1620 W. Beach Street
Watsonville CA
831-740-4520 (800-RED-ROOF)

One well-behaved family pet per room. Guest must notify front desk upon arrival. Guest is liable for any damages. In consideration of all guests, pets

must never be left unattended in the guest rooms.

### Outdoor Restaurants
**El Alteno**
323 Main Street
Watsonville CA
831-768-9876
This Mexican food restaurant allows your pet to join you on the outside deck. They just request that you bring your dog when they are not real busy. Dogs must be well behaved, leashed, and cleaned up after.

### Off-Leash Dog Parks
**Pinto Lake Dog Park**
757 Green Valley Road
Watsonville CA
831-454-7900
Watsonville Dog Park is located in the Pinto Lake County Park off of Green Valley Rd at Dalton Lane. Head west on Dalton Lane until you reach the park. The fenced dog park is about 1/3 of an acre.

### Dog-Friendly Parks
**Mount Madonna**

Watsonville CA
408-842-2341
This 3,219 acre park is dominated by a redwood forest. The park offers redwood and oak forests as well as meadows. Visitors may choose from 118 drive-in and walk-in first-come, first-served campsites spread throughout four campgrounds. Each site comes equipped with a barbecue pit, food locker and picnic table. Showers (for a small fee) are also available, as well as 17 partial hook-up RV sites. Hikers have access to an extensive 20 mile trail system. Park visitors may learn about areas where Ohlone Indians hunted and harvested. A one mile self-guided nature trail winds around the ruins of cattle baron Henry Miller's

summer home. White fallow deer, descendants of a pair donated by William Randolph Hearst in 1932, can be viewed in an enclosed pen. The park is located on Highway 152 (Hecker Pass Highway), ten miles west of Gilroy.

**Royal Oaks Park**
537 Maher Road
Watsonville CA
831-755-4895
This 122 acre park offers miles of hiking trails, a playground, picnic areas, basketball, volleyball and tennis courts. There is a $3 vehicle entrance fee during the week and a $5 fee on weekends and holidays. Dogs need to be leashed and please clean up after them.

## West Los Angeles

### Pet-Friendly Stores
**Centinela Feed and Supplies**
11055 Pico Blvd
West Los Angeles CA
310-473-5099
centinelafeed.com
Specializing in natural, holistic, and raw pet foods, this pet supply store also provides healthy treats, quality supplements, pet care supplies, low-cost vaccination clinics, frequent in-store events, and a knowledgeable staff. Leashed pets are welcome.

## Westchester

### Pet-Friendly Stores
**Centinela Feed and Supplies**
7600 S Sepulveda Blvd
Westchester CA
310-216-9261
centinelafeed.com
Specializing in natural, holistic, and raw pet foods, this pet supply store also provides healthy treats, quality

supplements, pet care supplies, low-cost vaccination clinics, frequent in-store events, and a knowledgeable staff. Leashed pets are welcome.

## Westley

### Dog-Friendly Hotels
**Econo Lodge Westley**
7100 Mccracken Road
Westley CA
209-894-3900 (877-424-6423)
Diblo Grande Golf Course nearby.

Dogs up to 20 pounds are allowed. Dogs are allowed for a pet fee of $10.00 per pet per night.

**Holiday Inn Express Westley**
4525 Howard Road
Westley CA
209-894-8940 (877-270-6405)
Dogs of all sizes are allowed. Dogs are allowed for a pet fee of $20.00 per pet per stay.

## Westport

### Dog-Friendly Beaches
**Westport-Union Landing State Beach**
Highway 1
Westport CA
707-937-5804
This park offers about 2 miles of sandy beach. Dogs must be on a 6 foot or less leash at all times and people need to clean up after their pets. Picnic tables, restrooms (including an ADA restroom) and campsites are available at this park. Dogs are also allowed at the campsites, but not on any park trails. The park is located off Highway 1, about 2 miles north of Westport or 19 miles north of Fort Bragg.

## Whitehorn

### Dog-Friendly Parks
**Chemise Mountain Trail**
Chemise Mountain Road
Whitehorn CA
707-825-2300
This trail is about 1.5 miles long and involves an 800 foot climb. At the top of the trail you will see vistas of the coastline and inland mountain ranges. This trail is popular with hikers and mountain bikers. Pets are required to be leashed in the campgrounds. On the trails there is no leash requirement but your dog needs to be under direct voice control. There is a $1 day use fee. To get there, take Highway 101 to Redway. Go west on Briceland/Shelter Cove Road for 22 miles and then head south on Chemise Mountain Road for just over 1.5 miles. Trailhead parking is available at the Wailaki or Nadelos Campgrounds. Travel time from Highway 101 is about 55 minutes.

## Williams

### Dog-Friendly Hotels
**Econo Lodge Williams**
400 C Street
Williams CA
530-473-2381 (877-424-6423)
Walking distance to shops and restaurants. Close to Highway 20 going to Colusa or Clear Lake.

Dogs of all sizes are allowed. Dogs are allowed for a pet fee of $10.00 per pet per night.

**Ramada Williams**
374 Ruggeiri Way
Williams CA
530-473-5120
Dogs up to 30 pounds are allowed. There is a pet fee of $10 per pet per night.

## Willits

### Dog-Friendly Hotels
**Baechtel Creek Inn & Spa An Ascend Collection Hotel**
101 Gregory Lane
Willits CA
707-459-9063 (877-424-6423)
The Baechtel Creek Inn and Spa, an Ascend Collection hotel is located in the heart of Mendocino County.

Dogs up to 25 pounds are allowed. Dogs are allowed for a pet fee of $20.00 per pet per night. Two dogs are allowed per room.

## Willow Glen

### Outdoor Restaurants
**Aqui Cal-Mex**
1145 Lincoln Ave.
Willow Glen CA
408-995-0381
aquicalmex.com
This restaurant serves many choices from lighter small plates to Tortill Rollups with crab cakes. The food is generally Mexican food with a California style to it. There is plentiful outdoor seating and your well-behaved leashed dog is allowed.

## Willows

### Dog-Friendly Hotels
**Best Western Willows Inn**
475 North Humboldt Avenue
Willows CA
530-934-4444 (800-780-7234)
Dogs are welcome at this hotel.

**Holiday Inn Express Hotel &**

**Suites Willows**
545 Humboldt Avenue
Willows CA
530-934-8900 (877-270-6405)
Dogs of all sizes are allowed.
Dogs are allowed for a pet fee of
$20.00 per pet per stay.

**Willows Travelodge**
249 North Humboldt Avenue
Willows CA
530-934-4603
Dogs of all sizes are allowed.
There is a pet fee of $20 per
night.

## Dog-Friendly Parks
**Sacramento National Wildlife Refuge**
752 County Road 99W
Willows CA
530-934-2801
fws.gov/refuge/sacramento/
This day use park is one of the
state's premier waterfowl
refuges with hundreds of
thousands of geese and ducks
making their winter home here,
and numerous other birds and
mammals making it their home
year round. The habitat consists
of almost 11,000 acres of
seasonal marsh lands,
permanent ponds, and uplands.
There are interpretive kiosks, a
six mile auto tour, a two mile
walking trail, and benches and
restrooms outside the visitor
center. Dogs of all sizes are
allowed throughout the park and
on the trails. Dogs must be
under their owner's control at all
times, and be leashed and
cleaned up after.

## Woodland

## Dog-Friendly Hotels
**Holiday Inn Express
Sacramento Airport Woodland**

2070 Freeway Drive
Woodland CA
530-662-7750 (877-270-6405)
Dogs of all sizes are allowed.

Dogs are allowed for a nightly
pet fee. Two dogs are allowed
per room.

## Outdoor Restaurants
**Jamba Juice**
1897 E Gibson Road, Suite E
Woodland CA
530-406-0486
jambajuice.com
All natural and organic
ingredients, no high-fructose
corn syrup, 0 grams trans fat,
no artificial preservatives, a
healthy helping of antioxidants,
vitamins, and minerals, and
fresh whole fruit and fruit juices
set the base for these tasty and
healthy beverages. Their
organic Hot Blends provides a
new spin on coffee, green or
chai tea, and hot
chocolate;plus they offer
probiotic fruit and yogurt
Blends. Additionally, they
feature all natural salads,
wraps, sandwiches, and grab n
go specialties. They also offer
healthy community support
through fundraisers, special
sales, and school lunch
programs. Leashed, well
mannered dogs are allowed at
their outside dining area.

**Steve's Place Pizza Pasta**
714 Main Street
Woodland CA
530-666-2100
stevespizza.com/
This pizza pasta restaurant
offers outside dining for guests
with canine companions. Dogs
of all sizes are welcome. They
must be attended to at all
times, well behaved, and
leashed.

## Wrightwood

## Dog-Friendly Hotels
**Best Western Cajon Pass**
8317 Us Highway 138
Wrightwood CA
760-249-6777 (800-780-7234)

Not Found

## Yorkville

## Dog-Friendly Attractions
**Meyer Family Cellars**
19750 H 128
Yorkville CA
707-895-2341
meyerfamilycellars.com/
Located in the rolling oak-laden
hills of Anderson Valley, this
scenic winery produces a
popular unique solera-style,
tawny port wine. There offer
picnic areas and gardens, and
your pet is welcome to join you
on the grounds. Dogs must be
friendly, and leashed and
cleaned up after at all times.

**Yorkville Cellars**
25701 H 128
Yorkville CA
707-894-9177
YorkvilleCellars.com
This vineyard has been CCOF
certified since 1986, and they
are a recipient of prestigious
"Masters of Organics" award.
Their free tasting room is
located in the middle of the
estate vineyards, and they are
open daily from 11 am to 6 pm.
Your well behaved, leashed dog
is welcome to explore the
vineyard with you; they are
allowed in some of the buildings
and the picnic area as well.
They would also like your dog to
be cat friendly, and that you
clean up after your pet.

## Yosemite

## Dog-Friendly Hotels
**Yosemite Gold Country Lodge**

10407 Highway 49 North
Coulterville CA
209-878-3400
yosemitegoldcountrymotel.com
Located 42 km from the

Western Entrance to Yosemite National Park this Coulterville motel offers guest rooms with a microwave and compact fridge. Free Wi-Fi is included.
Boasting mountain views each air-conditioned guest room at Yosemite Gold Country Lodge features a flat-screen satellite TV. An en suite bathroom with free toiletries is also provided. A 24-hour front desk welcomes guests to Yosemite Gold Country Lodge. A garden and barbecue facilities are also available. Vending machines provide late-night snacking options.
Coulterville Park and Swimming Pool is 1 minutes drive away. Mariposa is 45 minutes drive away.

**Narrow Gauge Inn**
48571 Highway 41
Fish Camp CA
559-683-7720
narrowgaugeinn.com/
Four miles from Yosemite National Park and surrounded by conifer-dotted mountains the pet-friendly Narrow Gauge Inn offers alpine-themed non-smoking rooms with free Wi-Fi. The low-rise Narrow Gauge Inn offers 26 non-smoking rooms with forest views. Timbered walls and furnishings are livened up with colorful comforters and homey paintings. Rooms offer free Wi-Fi and cable TV. A continental breakfast is served in the morning and the seasonal Dining Hall and Buffalo Bar serves lumberjack-sized steaks in the dining room warmed by an oak and cedar fireplace. The hotel offers a seasonal outdoor pool fax and copying services and free parking. Pets are welcome for an extra fee. Four miles from the entrance to Yosemite National Park and surrounded by the stunning Sierra National Forest the Narrow Gauge Inn is six miles from the Mariposa Grove of giant sequoias 35 miles from Yosemite Valley and less than a mile from Yosemite Mountain Sugar Pine Railroad. Bass Lake is 13 miles away and Fresno

Yosemite International Airport is 60 miles from the inn.

**Hotel Charlotte**
18736 Main Street
Groveland CA
209-962-6455
Offering an on-site restaurant this Groveland California hotel is 30 minutes drive to the entrance of Yosemite National Park. Pine Mountain Lake is less 5 minutes drive away. Equipped with free WiFi all soundproofed rooms include satellite TV and an en suite bathroom at Hotel Charlotte. The Charlotte Bistro & Bar restaurant offers on-site dining. Featured are small-plates house made sauces and desserts gluten-free and vegetarian options along with local wine beer and specialty cocktails.
Pine Mountain Lake Golf Course is 5 minutes drive away. Pine Mountain Lake Airport is 10 minutes drive away from Hotel Charlotte.

**Hotel Charlotte**
18736 Main Street
Groveland CA
209-962-6455 (1-800-961-7799)
hotelcharlotte.com
Offering an on-site restaurant this Groveland California hotel is 30 minutes drive to the entrance of Yosemite National Park. Pine Mountain Lake is less 5 minutes drive away. Equipped with free WiFi all soundproofed rooms include satellite TV and an en suite bathroom at Hotel Charlotte. The Charlotte Bistro & Bar restaurant offers on-site dining. Featured are small-plates house made sauces and desserts gluten-free and vegetarian options along with local wine beer and specialty cocktails.
Pine Mountain Lake Golf Course is 5 minutes drive away. Pine Mountain Lake Airport is 10 minutes drive away from Hotel Charlotte.

**The Groveland Hotel**

18767 Main Street
Groveland CA
209-962-4000 (800-273-3314.)
groveland.com/
Free Wi-Fi antique decor and convenient access to the park make the Groveland Hotel a great home base for our guests headed to the area. All 17 rooms on two floors are non-smoking and furnished with antiques. Standard amenities include featherbeds down comforters private baths robes and coffeemakers. Most accommodations have a TV and select rooms have a jetted tub or fireplace. Breakfast is available and includes hot items such as omelets and Belgian waffles as well as baked goods. Staying in touch is easy with complimentary Wi-Fi. Pets are welcome for an added fee and parking is on the house. Note: Front desk hours vary. Guests planning to arrive before or after the designated check-in time must contact the property prior to arrival for special instructions. Guests can contact the property using the number on the reservations confirmation received after booking. Located on Highway 120 the Groveland Hotel is a half-hour west of the year-round entrance to Yosemite National Park known as Big Oak Flat. The visitors center in Yosemite Village Bridalveil Falls and El Capitan are roughly an hour east. Glacier Point is less than two hours east. The vineyards in Murphys are an hour north and the Black Oak Casino in Tuolumne is 45 minutes north. Merced Regional Airport is 60 miles south and Fresno Yosemite International Airport is 115 miles south.

**Americas Best Value Inn Mariposa Lodge**
5052 Highway 140
Mariposa CA
209-966-3607 (800-341-8000)
mariposalodge.com
An outdoor pool and free parking are set 45 minutes from the entrance to Yosemite National Park at the wallet-

friendly Americas Best Value Inn Mariposa Lodge.The one-story Americas Best is home to 45 rooms all with cable TV writing desks refrigerators ceiling fans free local calling and balconies that overlook the hotel's gardens. Wi-Fi is available in public areas. Business services such as faxing are offered. Active guests make time for the fitness center hot tub and outdoor pool. Parking is free. Pets are allowed with restrictions. Americas Best is on Highway 140 in the heart of Mariposa village. The California State Mining and Minerals Museum is less than two miles away and Yosemite National Park can be reached in 45 minutes. Merced is an hour away. Mariposa-Yosemite Airport is five miles from the hotel and Fresno-Yosemite International Airport is 75 miles.

**Best Western Plus Yosemite Gateway Inn**
40530 Highway 41
Oakhurst CA
559-683-2378 (800-780-7234)
Dogs up to 80 pounds are allowed. There is a $20 per day pet fee up to $100 for the week. Up to two dogs are allowed per room.

**Comfort Inn Yosemite Area**
40489 Highway 41
Oakhurst CA
559-683-8282 (877-424-6423)
Our hotel is in the closest town to the wonders of Yosemite National Park, just a 15-minute drive away.

Dogs of all sizes are allowed. Dogs are allowed for a pet fee of $20.00 per pet per night.

## Accommodations
**Pine Rose Inn Bed and Breakfast**
41703 Road 222
Oakhurst CA
559-642-2800 (866-642-2800)
pineroseinn.com/
The inn is located 13 miles from the south gate of Yosemite

National Park, 2 miles from Bass Lake and surrounded by the Sierra National Forest. The entire inn is non-smoking, except for outside. There is a $10 per day pet charge. Dogs and other pets are welcome.

## Dog-Friendly Attractions
**Yosemite Mountain Sugar Pine Railroad**
56001 Highway 41
Fish Camp CA
559-683-7273
ymsprr.com/
Hop aboard a four mile railroad excursion with your pooch and enjoy a narrative ride through the Sierra National Forest. One of their steam engines is the heaviest operating narrow gauge Shay locomotive in use today. Well-behaved leashed dogs are welcome. The railroad is located near Yosemite Park's south gate on Highway 41.

**Millers Landing Resort - Bass Lake**
37976 Road 222
Wishon CA
559-642-3633
millerslanding.com
Dogs on are allowed on the boat rentals. They ask that all dogs be leashed while in the public areas such as the office and parking lot areas but can be off leash on the boats if they are well-behaved.

## Outdoor Restaurants
**Pizza Factory**
40120 Highway 41 #B
Oakhurst CA
559-683-2700
pizzafactory.com/main.html
Well-behaved, leashed dogs may sit at the outside tables.

## Dog-Friendly Wineries and Vineyards
**Mount Bullion Vineyard**
6947 H 49N

Mariposa CA
209-377-8450
mtbullionvineyard.com/home.ht
m
The tasting room and tours are by appointment only, and they look forward to showing visitors around the winery. Some of the other amenities include a picnic deck shaded by oak trees, a bocce ball court, horseshoe pit, and a barbecue area. Your dog is welcome but must be very social and friendly with people and other animals as there are cats, dogs, and chickens roaming about. Dogs must be leashed and cleaned up after at all times.

## Dog-Friendly Parks
**The Way of the Mono Trail**
off Road 222
Bass Lake CA
559-877-2218
On this .5 mile trail you can see authentic Mono Indian grinding holes, plus you will get some great views of Bass Lake. The trail is located next to Bass Lake in the Sierra National Forest. Stop at the Yosemite/Sierra Visitors Bureau at 41969 Highway 41 in Oakhurst for the trail location. The office is open 7 days a week from 8:30am to 5pm.

**Shadow of the Giants Trail**
off Sky Ranch Road
Oakhurst CA
559-297-0706
This one mile each way self-guided trail is located in the Nelder Grove Giant Sequoia Preservation Area. Along the trail you will see some of the best giant sequoia trees in the state. Pets on leash are allowed and please clean up after them. The trail is located in the Nelder Grove Giant Sequoia Preservation Area. To get there from Oakhurst, go about 5 miles north on Highway 41. Turn right (east) onto Sky Ranch Road. Along Sky Ranch Road you will find Nelder Grove.

**Badger Pass Ski Area**

P.O. Box 578/Badger Pass Road
Yosemite National Park CA
209-372-1220
This popular family-friendly ski area offers great scenery, and a variety of activities, festivals, and friendly competitions throughout the season. Although dogs are not allowed on the ski slopes in winter, they are allowed to go anywhere a car can go-being paved roads and developed areas. Dogs must be under their owner's control at all times, and be leashed and cleaned up after.

**Yosemite National Park**
PO Box 577
Yosemite National Park CA
209-372-0200
nps.gov/yose
This 750,000 acre park is one of the most popular national parks in the country. Yosemite's geology is world famous for its granite cliffs, tall waterfalls and giant sequoia groves. As with most national parks, pets have limited access within the park. Pets are not allowed on unpaved or poorly paved trails, in wilderness areas including hiking trails, in park lodging (except for some campgrounds) and on shuttle buses. However, there are still several nice areas to walk with your pooch and you will be able to see the majority of sights and points of interest that most visitors see. Dogs are allowed in developed areas and on fully paved trails, include Yosemite Valley which offers about 2 miles of paved trails. From these trails you can view El Capitan, Half Dome and Yosemite Falls. You can also take the .5 mile paved trail right up to the base of Bridalveil Fall which is a 620 foot year round waterfall. The best time to view this waterfall is in the spring or early summer. The water thunders down and almost creates a nice rain at the base. Water-loving dogs will be sure to like this attraction. In general dogs are not allowed on unpaved trails, but this park does make the following

exceptions. Dogs are allowed on the Meadow Loop and Four Mile fire roads in Wawona. They are also allowed on the Carlon Road and on the Old Big Oak Flat Road between Hodgdon Meadow and Hazel Green Creek. Dogs must be on a 6 foot or less leash and attended at all times. People must also clean up after their pets. For a detailed map of Yosemite, visit their web site at http://www.nps.gov/yose/pphtml/maps.html. The green dots show the paved trails. There are four main entrances to the park and all four lead to the Yosemite Valley. The park entrance fees are as follows: $20 per vehicle, $40 annual pass or $10 per individual on foot. The pass is good for 7 days. Prices are subject to change. Yosemite Valley is open year round and may be reached via Highway 41 from Fresno, Highway 140 from Merced, Highway 120 from Manteca and in late spring through late fall via the Tioga Road (Highway 120 East) from Lee Vining. From November through March, all park roads are subject to snow chain control (including 4x4s) or temporary closure at any time due to hazardous winter driving conditions. For updated 24 hour road and weather conditions call (209) 372-0200.

## Emergency Veterinarians
**Hoof and Paw Veterinary Hospital**
41149 Highway 41
Oakhurst CA
559-683-3313
sierratel.com/hoofnpaw

**Oakhurst Veterinary Hospital**
40799 Highway 41
Oakhurst CA
559-683-2135

## Yreka

### Dog-Friendly Hotels
**Baymont Inn Yreka**
148 Moonlit Oaks Avenue
Yreka CA
530-841-1300
Dogs up to 40 pounds are allowed. There is a $10 one time pet fee.

**Best Western Miners Inn**
122 East Miner Street
Yreka CA
530-842-4355 (800-780-7234)
Pets may be accepted. Please contact the hotel directly for full details.

**Comfort Inn Yreka**
1804 B Fort Jones Rd
Yreka CA
530-842-1612 (877-424-6423)
Easy freeway off/on location with great restaurants and shops within walking distance. Outdoor pool.

Dogs of all sizes are allowed. Dogs are allowed for a pet fee of $10.00 per pet per night. Two dogs are allowed per room.

**Econo Lodge Inn & Suites**
526 South Main Street
Yreka CA
530-842-4404 (877-424-6423)
Historic shops & Victorian homes. Skiing, fishing, hiking, golf, gold panning, ride Blue Goose Steam Engine.

Dogs up to 50 pounds are allowed. Dogs are allowed for a pet fee of $10.00/ per pet per night. Two dogs are allowed per room.

**Relax Inn Yreka**
1210 South Main Street
Yreka CA
530-842-2791
Free breakfast an outdoor pool and rooms with microwaves fridges free Wi-Fi and cable TV please our guests at Relax Inn Yreka where value rates give them another reason to smile. The single-story inn has 36

rooms that come with cable TV clock radios and free Wi-Fi. Coffeemakers microwaves and mini-fridges add to the convenience. Non-smoking rooms are available. The hotel serves guests a free continental breakfast each morning. A seasonal outdoor pool and sundeck with loungers hit the spot when it's time to refresh and relax. A 24-hour front desk and free parking are provided and pets are welcome on request. Located about a half-mile off I-5 the hotel is two miles from downtown Yreka. The Siskiyou County Museum and Siskiyou Golden Fairgrounds are a mile from the motel. If you're a golfer head to Shasta Valley Golf Club 12 minutes away for a round or two. The Fort Jones Museum is a 20-minute drive. Gorgeous scenery and outdoor fun in Klamath National Forest are a half-hour away. You can take a 35-minute drive to explore Stewart Mineral Springs. Southern Oregon University and the Oregon Shakespeare Festival in Ashland are within 45 minutes. Rogue Valley International Airport - Medford is a 57-mile drive north.

**Rodeway Inn Yreka**
1235 South Main Street
Yreka CA
530-842-4412 (877-424-6423)
Conveniently located on I-5 for easy freeway off and on access. Clean comfortable rooms with in-room coffee,

Dogs of all sizes are allowed. Dogs are allowed for a pet fee of $5.00 per pet per night. Two dogs are allowed per room.

# Dog-Friendly Attractions
**Blue Goose Steam Excursion Train**
300 East Miner Street
Yreka CA
530-842-4146 (800-973-5277)
yrekawesternrr.com/
The Blue Goose excursion train rides on railroad tracks that

were built in 1888. The train travels over Butcher Hill in Yreka and then down through the scenic Shasta Valley with Mt. Shasta in the view. The train then crosses over the Shasta River and continues on to the old cattle town of Montague. The distance is about 7.5 miles one way and takes approximately 1 hour to arrive. Upon arrival in Montague, passengers disembark the train and will have about 1.5 hours for lunch and to explore the historic town of Montague. During lunchtime, the train is pushed back in preparation for the return trip to Yreka. The train returns to pick up passengers about 15 minutes before departure. The total round trip time for this ride is about 3.5 hours. Trains run from Memorial Day Weekend to the end of October on a limited schedule. Well-behaved leashed dogs that are friendly towards people and children are welcome. They ask that you please keep your pooch out of the aisles once on the train.

# Dog-Friendly Parks
**Klamath National Forest**
1312 Fairlane Road
Yreka CA
530-842-6131
fs.usda.gov/klamath
This forest has over 1,700,000 acres of land throughout Siskiyou County in California and Jackson County in Oregon. Dogs should be on leash. Hiking from East Fork Campground provides access to the lakes in the Caribou Basin, Rush Creek, and Little South Fork drainages. The campground is located 27 miles southwest of Callahan next to the East and the South Forks of the Salmon River, at a 2,600 foot elevation. From the Bridge Flat Campground, the historic Kelsey Trail offers excellent opportunities for scenic day hikes or longer trips into the Marble Mountain

Wilderness. The campground is located on the Scott River approximately 17 miles from Fort Jones, at a 2,000 foot elevation. For more details, call or visit the Salmon River Ranger District, 11263 N. Highway 3,Fort Jones, (530) 468-5351. The Klamath National Forest offers miles of other hiking trails. For maps and more information on trails throughout this forest, please contact the forest office in Yreka.

## Yuba City

# Dog-Friendly Hotels
**Days Inn - Yuba City**
700 North Palora Ave
Yuba City CA
530-674-1711 (800-329-7466)
Dogs of all sizes are allowed. Dogs are allowed for a pet fee of $10 per pet per night.

**Econo Lodge Inn & Suites**
730 Palora Ave.
Yuba City CA
530-674-1592 (877-424-6423)
Hotel is within walking distance of restaurants and shopping. They offer a free deluxe continental breakfast.

Dogs up to 60 pounds are allowed. Dogs are allowed for a pet fee of $10.00 per pet per night.

**Lexington Inn & Suites Yuba City**
4228 South Highway 99
Yuba City CA
530-674-0201 (877-424-6423)
Located within walking distance of an excellent nine hole golf course. On site restaurant and full bar.

Dogs up to 40 pounds are allowed. Dogs are allowed for a pet fee of $10.00 per pet per night. Two dogs are allowed per room.

## Outdoor Restaurants
**Chipotle**
1005 Gray Avenue
Yuba City CA
530-671-1581
chipotle.com
Specializing in organic, natural and unprocessed food, this Mexican Eatery offers fajita burritos, tacos, salads, and salsas. Dogs are allowed at the outdoor tables but you will need to order your food inside the restaurant and dogs must remain outside.

**Sonic Drive-in**
981 Grey Avenue
Yuba City CA
530-671-3736
This drive-in hamburger restaurant also offers indoor and outdoor seating. Your pet is welcome to join you at the outdoor tables. You will need to go inside to order. Dogs must be attended to at all times, well behaved, and leashed.

**The City Cafe**
667 Plumas Street
Yuba City CA
530-671-1501
Serving American and international cuisine, this café also offers outside dining on the patio. Dogs of all sizes are allowed. Dogs must be well behaved, attended to at all times, and leashed.

## Pet-Friendly Stores
**PetSmart Pet Store**
865 Colusa Ave
Yuba City CA
530-822-0623
Your licensed and well-behaved leashed dog is allowed in the store.

**Petco Pet Store - Yuba City**
1110 Harter Road
Yuba City CA
530-674-1816
Your licensed and well-behaved leashed dog is allowed in the store.

# Nevada Listings

## Austin

### Dog-Friendly Parks
**Berlin-Ichthyosaur State Park**
HC 61 Box 61200
Austin NV
775-964-2440
Once a mining area, this park sits at about 7,000 feet and came into being to protect and display North America's richest concentration and largest known Ichthyosaur fossils. It also oversees the old mining town of Berlin and the Diana Mine. There is an extensive sign/trail system that tells the history and features of this Registered Natural Landmark, a nature trail, and viewing windows at the Fossils Shelter. Dogs of all sizes are allowed for no additional fee. Dogs must be well mannered, be on no more than a 6 foot leash, and be cleaned up after. They are allowed throughout the park and on the trails; they are not allowed in park buildings.

## Baker

### Dog-Friendly Parks
**Great Basin National Park**
100 Great Basin
Baker NV
775-234-7331
nps.gov/grba
The Great Basin Park rises to over 13,000 feet and hosts the Lehman Caves and an abundant variety of wildlife, plants, and waterways. They are open year round for tent and RV camping with no hook ups. There is no additional fee for dogs, but they may not be left unattended, they must be on no more than a 6 foot leash, and be cleaned up after. Dogs are not allowed on any of the

trails.

## Battle Mountain

### Dog-Friendly Hotels
**Super 8 Battle Mountain**
825 Super 8 Dr.
Battle Mountain NV
775-635-8808 (800-800-8000)
Dogs of all sizes are allowed. Dogs are allowed for a pet fee.

## Beatty

### Dog-Friendly Attractions
**Rhyolite Ghost Town**
off Highway 374
Beatty NV
760-786-3200
nps.gov/deva/rhyolite.htm
In 1904 two prospectors found quartz all over a hill which was "full of free gold". Soon the rush was on and camps were set up in the area including the townsite called Rhyolite. The name was derived from the silica-rich volcanic rock in the area. The most prominent mine in the area was the Montgomery Shoshone mine which prompted everyone to move to Rhyolite. This boomtown once had a 3 story building, a stock exchange, board of trade, red light district, hotels, stores, a school for 250 children, an ice plant, two electric plants, foundries, machine shops and a miner's union hospital. Today you can see several remnants of Rhyolite. The 3 story building still has some walls standing and so does an old jail. A privately owned train depot was restored and so was the Bottle House. The Bottle House was made out of whiskey bottles by a miner. This house was restored in 1925 by Paramount Pictures. Rhyolite is located 35 miles from the Furnace Creek Visitor Center in Death Valley

400

National Park. Drive towards Beatty, Nevada. Before you reach Beatty, take a paved road north (left) from Highway 374. It will take you right into the ghost town. Pets are allowed but must be leashed. Please clean up after your pet. Remember to watch out for rattlesnakes.

## Blue Diamond

### Dog-Friendly Parks
**Spring Mountain Ranch State Park**
P. O. Box 124
Blue Diamond NV
702-875-4141
This luxury retreat offers a long and colorful history with such owners as Howard Hughes and Vera Krupp. In addition the park offers great scenery, a visitor's center, picnicking, historic sites, living history programs, guided tours, opportunities for nature study, and various trails. Dogs of all sizes are allowed at no additional fee. Dogs may not be left unattended, and they must be leashed and cleaned up after.

## Boulder City

### Outdoor Restaurants
**Milo's Best Cellars**
538 Nevada Way
Boulder City NV
702-293-9540
miloswinebar.com/content
Located in the historic old town of Boulder City, this sidewalk café offers sandwiches/soups/salads and more than 50 beer and wines choices by the glass. Dogs are allowed at the outside tables;they must be leashed and under their owner's control at all times.

## Caliente

### Dog-Friendly Parks
**Kershaw-Ryan State Park**
P. O. Box 985/300 Kershaw Canyon Drive
Caliente NV
775-726-3564
parks.nv.gov/parks/kershaw-ryan
This high mountain desert day park offers a spring-fed pond, scenic rugged landscapes, a picnic area, restrooms, trails, and various outdoor recreation. Dogs of all sizes are allowed at no additional fee. Dogs may not be left unattended, and they must be leashed and cleaned up after. Dogs are allowed on the trails. Hours may vary between the seasons, however winter hours are daily from 8 am to 4:30 pm, and summer hours are daily from 7 am to 8 pm.

## Carlin

### Dog-Friendly Hotels
**Carlin Inn**
1018 Fir St
Carlin NV
775-754-6110 (877-424-6423)
Beautifully appointed guest rooms. Suites available. Nearby UNR Fire Academy.

Dogs of all sizes are allowed. Dogs are allowed for a pet fee of $10.00/ per pet per night.

## Carson City

### Dog-Friendly Hotels
**Americas Best Value Inn/carson City**
2731 S. Carson St.
Carson City NV
775-882-2007

Wi-Fi access continental breakfast and on-site parking are all included in the easy-on-the-wallet rates at the Americas Best Value Inn/Carson City. With 57 spacious and comfortable rooms the two-story Americas Best Value Inn has a traditional decor and modern amenities like free Wi-Fi and TVs with premium cable channels. Enjoy a cup of java from the in-room coffeemaker or head downstairs to the free continental breakfast. Just outside is a heated pool where you can swim a few laps and a terrace where you can work on your tan. Bring along your four-legged family member as this is a pet-friendly lodging. Parking is free. Off Highway 395 the Americas Best Value Inn puts you close to downtown destinations like the Nevada State Railroad Museum less than a mile north. If you want to practice your putting the Silver Oak Golf Course is four miles away. Lake Tahoe is 30 minutes west and Washoe Lake is 20 minutes north. Reno-Tahoe International Airport is 28 miles from the hotel.

**Days Inn Carson City**
3103 North Carson Street
Carson City NV
775-883-3343 (800-329-7466)
Dogs of all sizes are allowed. Dogs are allowed for a pet fee.

**Holiday Inn Express Hotel & Suites Carson City**
4055 North Carson Street
Carson City NV
775-283-4055 (877-270-6405)
Dogs up to 80 pounds are allowed. Dogs are allowed for a pet fee of $20.00 per pet per night.

**Rodeway Inn At Nevada State Capitol**
1300 North Carson Street
Carson City NV
775-883-7300 (877-424-6423)
The hotel is located mid town in Carson City. The hotel is one half mile from the state capital buildings, casino's,

Dogs up to 100 pounds are allowed. Dogs are allowed for a pet fee of $10.00 per pet per night. Two dogs are allowed per room.

**Super 8 Carson City**
2829 South Carson Street
Carson City NV
775-883-7800 (800-800-8000)
Dogs of all sizes are allowed. Dogs are allowed for a pet fee of $10.00 per pet per night.

## Outdoor Restaurants
**Comma Coffee**
312 S. Carson Street
Carson City NV
775-883-2662
commacoffee.com/
This cafe serves breakfast and lunch, as well as fruit smoothies, juices, cappuccinos, lattes, mochas and more. Dogs are welcome at the outdoor patio tables.

**Johnny Rockets**
4600 Snyder Avenue/H 518
Carson City NV
775-883-2607
johnnyrockets.com/index2.php
A fun retro, all-American decor and atmosphere, all American comfort cuisine, and something for all ages are just a few of the offerings of this eatery. Leashed, friendly dogs are allowed at their outside dining area.

**Johnny Rockets**
4600 Snyder Avenue #B/H 518
Carson City NV
775-883-2607
johnnyrockets.com/
All the American favorites can be found here: A fun retro, all-American decor and atmosphere, juicy burgers, specialty sandwiches, crispy fries, hand-dipped malts and shakes (dark chocolate ones too), fresh baked apple pies, tasty vegetarian choices, and something for all ages. Leashed, friendly dogs are allowed at their outside dining area.

**Mom and Pops Diner**
224 S. Carson St.
Carson City NV
775-884-4411
This restaurant serves breakfast, lunch and dinner. Leashed, friendly dogs are allowed at the outdoor tables.

## Pet-Friendly Stores
**Alie's Flowers and Gifts**
1233 S Carson Street/H 50/395

Carson City NV
775-882-8490
aliesflowers.biz/
Besides offering flowers for every occasion, this shop also carries live plants, gifts, gourmet and fruit baskets, silk arrangements, and more. Leashed, well mannered dogs are welcome to come in and sniff the roses too; they must be hound (others on site) and human friendly.

**C-A-L Ranch and Home Store**

2035 N. Carson St
Carson City NV
775-461-2213
The C-A-L Ranch and Home Store in Carson City welcomes leashed dogs in their store. They have a pet products section, and some stores may also offer pet grooming services.

**PetSmart Pet Store**
250 Fairview Dr
Carson City NV
775-841-9200
Your licensed and well-behaved leashed dog is allowed in the store.

**Petco Pet Store - Carson City**

911 Topsy Lane #108
Carson City NV
775-267-2826
Your licensed and well-behaved leashed dog is allowed in the store.

## Dog-Friendly Parks

**Toiyabe National Forest**
Hwy 395
Carson City NV

fs.usda.gov/htnf
There are several dog-friendly hiking trails on the national forest land in Carson City. These are desert-like trails, so only go with your dog when the weather is cooler. If it's hot, the sand may burn your pup's paws. Visit the Carson Ranger Station for maps and trail information about the Toiyable National Forest. The station is located on Hwy 395, near S. Stewart Street. Dogs should be leashed.

**Washoe Lake State Park**
4855 East Lake Blvd.
Carson City NV
775-687-4319
parks.nv.gov/parks/washoe-lake

This park is frequently used for bird watching, hiking, horseback riding, picnicking, windsurfing, water skiing, jet skiing, fishing and during certain times of the year, hunting. There are many trails at this park for hikers, mountain bikers, and equestrians. Pets must be leashed at all times, except at the Wetlands during hunting season. The park is located off U.S. 395, 10 miles north of Carson City and 15 miles south of Reno.

## Emergency Veterinarians
**Carson Tahoe Veterinary Hospital**
3389 S. Carson Street
Carson City NV
775-883-8238
Weekdays 7:30 am - 6 pm. Emergencys will be seen 24 hours with an additional $60 emergency fee.

## Charleston

## Outdoor Restaurants

### Tropical Smoothie Cafe
6350 W. Charleston Blvd/H 159
Charleston NV
702-304-1931
tropicalsmoothie.com
Offerings from this health-minded cafe include all natural real fruit Super Fruit, Simply Indulgent, Super Charged, and Low Fat Smoothies;plus a selection of Coffee Smoothies. They also serve up freshly prepared signature wraps, flatbread and bistro sandwiches, garden fresh salads, all natural gourmet cheeses and meats, artisanal breads, vegan/vegetarian choices, and catering services. They are open for breakfast, lunch, and dinner. Leashed, well mannered dogs are allowed at their outside seating area.

## Elko

### Dog-Friendly Hotels

### Best Western Elko Inn
1930 Idaho Street
Elko NV
775-738-8787 (800-780-7234)
Dogs are allowed. There is a $20 per pet per night pet fee. Up to two dogs are allowed per room.

### Quality Inn & Suites Elko
3320 East Idaho Street
Elko NV
775-777-8000 (877-424-6423)
Walking distance to major casinos, restaurants and shops. Situated in the heart of Elko Business Loop. Gold mines

Dogs up to 50 pounds are allowed. Dogs are allowed for a pet fee of $15.00 per pet per night.

### Red Lion Hotel And Casino Elko
2065 Idaho Street
Elko NV
775-738-2111
There is a $20 one time pet fee

per room. There is a $15 pet fee for R&R members, and the R&R program is free to sign up.

### Rodeway Inn Elko
736 Idaho Street
Elko NV
775-738-7152 (877-424-6423)
Court House 1 block, Museum, Convention Center, Park 7 blocks. Airport, Shopping 1 1/2 miles. Hospital 2 miles.

Dogs of all sizes are allowed. Dogs are allowed for a pet fee of $15.00 per pet per night.

### Shilo Inn Elko
2401 Mountain City Highway
Elko NV
775-738-5522 (800-222-2244)
shiloinn.com/Nevada/elko.html
Free breakfast is a welcome perk for our guests at the non-smoking Shilo Inn Elko conveniently located across the highway from Elko Airport. This two-story property has 70 rooms all featuring coffeemakers and cable TVs. Select accommodations also have microwaves mini-fridges and kitchenettes. In the morning guests wake up to a continental breakfast served on the house. The hotel also has event space a business center and workout facility on-site. Parking is free and dogs are welcome for an additional fee. Located off I-80 Shilo Inn Elko is in the middle of shopping and dining action. Guests can try their luck at Gold Country Casino four miles away or show off their swing at Ruby View Golf Course five miles away. Lamoille Canyon is about a half-hour from the hotel. Elko Regional Airport is two miles away.

### Super 8 Elko
1755 Idaho Street
Elko NV
775-738-8488 (800-800-8000)
Dogs are welcome at this hotel.

### Travelodge Elko
1785 Idaho Street

Elko NV
775-753-7747
Dogs of all sizes are allowed. There is a pet fee of $10 per pet per night.

## Pet-Friendly Stores

### C-A-L Ranch and Home Store
2540 Idaho Street
Elko NV
775-753-7000
The C-A-L Ranch and Home Store in Elko welcomes leashed dogs in their store. They have a pet products section, and some stores may also offer pet grooming services.

## Veterinarians

### Elko Veterinary Clinic
1850 Lamoille Hwy
Elko NV
775-738-6116
elkovet.com
This veterinary clinic is open 7 am to 6 pm Monday thru Friday and on Saturday from 8 am to 4 pm. Somebody is often available on call for after hours serious emergencies.

## Ely

### Dog-Friendly Hotels

### La Quinta Inn & Suites Ely
1591 Great Basin Boulevard
Ely NV
775-289-8833 (800-531-5900)
Dogs of all sizes are allowed. Dogs may not be left alone in the room.

### Magnuson Hotel Park Vue
930 W. Aultman Street
Ely NV
775-289-4497
Dogs up to 80 pounds are allowed. There is a $20 per day pet fee up to $100 for the week. Up to two dogs are allowed per room.

### Ramada Ely

805 Great Basin Boulevard
Ely NV
775-289-4884
Dogs up to 100 pounds are
allowed. There is no pet fee.

## Veterinarians
**White Pine Veterinary Clinic**
159 MC Gill Hwy
Ely NV
775-289-3459
This veterinary clinic has regular
weekday hours.

## Fallon

### Dog-Friendly Hotels
**Best Western Fallon Inn &
Suites**
1035 West Williams Avenue
Fallon NV
775-423-6005 (800-780-7234)
Dogs are allowed. There is a
$15 per pet per night pet fee.
Dogs must be well-behaved.

**Comfort Inn Near Fallon Naval
Air Station**
1830 West Williams Avenue
Fallon NV
775-423-5554 (877-424-6423)
Free high-speed Internet access
in all rooms. Free wireless
Internet access available in
lobby. Heated indoor pool.

Dogs up to 50 pounds are
allowed. Dogs are allowed for a
pet fee of $15.00 per pet per
night. Two dogs are allowed per
room.

**Econo Lodge Fallon Naval Air
Station Area**
70 East Williams Avenue
Fallon NV
775-423-2194 (877-424-6423)
Centrally located near State
Hwy Junction of 95 and Hwy 50.

Dogs up to 20 pounds are
allowed. Dogs are allowed for a
pet fee of $10.00 per pet per
night.

**Holiday Inn Express Fallon**
55 Commercial Way
Fallon NV
775-428-2588 (877-270-6405)
Dogs of all sizes are allowed.
Dogs are allowed for a pet fee.
Two dogs are allowed per
room.

### Dog-Friendly Parks
**Walker Lake, c/o Fallon
Region Headquarters**
16799 Lahontan Dam
Fallon NV
775-867-3001
This rec area is on one of the
last remnants of an ancient
inland sea that covered the
area about 10,000 years ago.
There is a boat launch, shade
ramadas, tables and grills
along a sandy beach.
Recreation includes fishing,
boating, swimming and
picnicking. Dogs of all sizes are
allowed at no additional fee.
Dogs may not be left
unattended, and they must be
leashed and cleaned up after.

## Fernley

### Dog-Friendly Hotels
**Best Western Fernley Inn**
1405 Newlands Drive E
Fernley NV
775-575-6776 (800-780-7234)
Dogs up to 80 pounds are
allowed. There is a $20 per day
pet fee up to $100 for the
week. Up to two dogs are
allowed per room.

## Gardnerville

### Dog-Friendly Hotels
**Best Western Topaz Lake Inn**

3410 Sandy Bowers Avenue
Gardnerville NV

7752664661 (800-780-7234)
Dogs up to 60 pounds are
allowed in pet rooms only. There
is a $12 per pet per night pet
fee. Up to two dogs are allowed
per room.

**Super 8 Gardnerville/minden**
1979 Highway 395 South
Gardnerville NV
775-266-3338 (800-800-8000)
Dogs of all sizes are allowed.
Dogs are allowed for a pet fee of
$12.00 per pet per night.

## Lake Tahoe

### Dog-Friendly Attractions
**North South Lake Tahoe Boat
Rentals**

Lake Tahoe NV
888-312-1116
tahoeboatrentals.com/
This boat rental company
delivers your boat direct to you
for weekly or daily outings. They
offer a variety of value-priced
boat rentals, and a Coast Guard
approved skipper is available for
an additional fee if needed.
Friendly dogs are also welcome
on boat rentals; they must be
under their owner's control at all
times. Owners agree to accept
full responsibility for any
damage that may be incurred by
pets at the time of occurrence;
otherwise there are no additional
pet fees.

**Borges Sleigh and Carriage
Rides**
P.O. Box 5905
Stateline NV
775-588-2953
sleighride.com/
Take your pooch on a carriage
or sleigh ride in Lake Tahoe.
The carriage rides start in the
casino area between Harveys
and Horizon, and in front of
Embassy Suites. The sleigh
rides begin in the field next to
Caesars Tahoe (on the corner of
hwy 50 and Lake Parkway). The
carriages and sleighs are pulled

by their 2000 pound Blond Belgium horses or one of their rare American- Russian Baskhir Curlies which have been featured in Pasadena's Tournament of Rose Parade over the past few years. Carriage rides open noon until sunset daily, weather permitting. Prices are $15 per adult $7.50 per child under 11. Sleigh rides are given during the winter. Sleigh rides are open 10:00am to sunset (about 4:45pm). Sleigh rides are $15 per Adult $7.50 per child under 11.

## Outdoor Restaurants
**T's Rotisserie**
901 Tahoe Blvd
Incline Village NV
775-831-2832
This restaurant serves rotisserie sandwiches and more.They are open daily from 11 am until 8 pm. Your dog can sit with you at the outdoor tables.

## Dog-Friendly Beaches
### North Beach at Zephyr Cove Resort
460 Highway 50
Zephyr Cove NV
775-588-6644
Dogs are not allowed at the main beach at the Zephyr Cove Resort. They are allowed on leash, however, at the north beach at the resort. There is a $5.00 parking fee for day use. When you enter Zephyr Cover Resort head to the right (North) to the last parking area and walk the few hundred feet to the beach. The North Beach is located just into the National Forest. There usually are cleanup bags on the walkway to the beach but bring your own in case they run out. This is a nice beach that is used by a lot of people in the summer. The cabins at Zephyr Cove Resort also allow dogs.

## Dog-Friendly Parks

### Lake Tahoe State Park - Spooner Lake
Hwy 28
Glenbrook NV
775-831-0494
This hiking trail is known as the world famous "Flume Trail". This is one of the most beautiful places in the world to mountain bike. But as a hiker, you'll hardly notice the bicyclists because this trail is so long and a good portion of the path consists of nice wide fire trails. It starts at Spooner Lake and the entire loop of the Flume Trail is about 25 miles which can satisfy even the most avid hiker. For a shorter hike, try the trail that loops around Spooner Lake. For a longer 10-12 mile out and back hike, start at Spooner Lake and hike up to Marlette Lake. Although there is a rise in elevation, it's not a rock climbing path as most of this is a fire road trail. Even if you are used to hiking 10 miles, don't forget about the altitude which will make you tired quicker. Also, do not forget to bring enough water and food. To get to the start of the trail, from South Lake Tahoe, take Hwy 50 towards Nevada (north). Then turn left onto Hwy 28. Follow the signs to the Lake Tahoe State Park and Spooner Lake. Parking for Spooner Lake is on the right. There is a parking fee of approx. $5-7. This includes an extra fee for the pup - but well worth it. From South Lake Tahoe, it's about a 25-30 minute drive to Spooner Lake. Dogs must be leashed in the park.

## Las Vegas

## Dog-Friendly Hotels
**Best Western Plus Henderson Hotel**
1553 North Boulder Highway
Henderson NV
702-564-9200 (800-780-7234)
Dogs up to 80 pounds are allowed. There is a $20 per day pet fee up to $100 for the week. Up to two dogs are allowed per room.

**Hampton Inn And Suites Las Vegas - Henderson**
421 Astaire Drive
Henderson NV
702-992-9292
Dogs of all sizes are allowed. There is no pet fee.

**Holiday Inn Express Hotel & Suites Henderson**
441 Astaire Drive
Henderson NV
702-990-2323 (877-270-6405)
Dogs of all sizes are allowed. Dogs are allowed for a pet fee of $25.00 per pet per night.

**Westin Lake Las Vegas Resort & Spa**
101 Montelago Boulevard
Henderson NV
702-567-6000 (888-625-5144)
Besides being only a short distance from the entertainment capital of the world and world-class wining, dining, shopping, and around-the-clock entertainment opportunities, this Moroccan-style luxury hotel is an oasis in the desert offering something for everyone. Dogs are allowed for an additional one time $35 pet fee per room, and there is a pet waiver to sign at check in.

**Americas Best Value Inn**
167 East Tropicana Avenue
Las Vegas NV
702-795-3311
The pet-friendly Americas Best Value Inn two blocks off the Strip is just the ticket for budget-conscious our guests with reasonable rates and lots of extras like free internet. The 257 rooms at the Americas Best Value Inn are so easy on the wallet you'll have plenty of money left over for an extra hour at a nearby casino. High-speed internet access and coffee are both free. The freeform splash pool and year-round hot tub are a nice surprise for anyone in need of some fun in the sun.

Pets are welcome fees and restrictions apply. Additional amenities include a 24-hour front desk coin-operated laundry facilities and concierge services. Located two blocks off the Las Vegas Strip almost all of the city's most famous casinos entertainment and restaurants are within walking distance. The Las Vegas Monorail stops one block away so even attractions further north on the Strip are easily accessible. The University of Nevada Las Vegas is one-and-a-half miles east. McCarran International Airport is three miles from the hotel.

**Baymont Inn And Suites Airport South Las Vegas**
55 East Robindale Road
Las Vegas NV
702-273-2500
Dogs up to 60 pounds are allowed. There is a pet fee of $25 per night.

**Best Western Plus Las Vegas West**
8669 West Sahara Avenue
Las Vegas NV
702-256-3766 (800-780-7234)
Dogs up to 80 pounds are allowed. There is a $20 per day pet fee up to $100 for the week. Up to two dogs are allowed per room.

**Delano Las Vegas At Mandalay Bay**
3940 Las Vegas Blvd South
Las Vegas NV
702-632-7777 (877-632-7800)
Delano Las Vegas at Mandalay Bay with its luxurious suites marble baths and sleek style makes our guests feel like A-list celebrities. The 43-story tower connected to sister property Mandalay Bay features 1118 thoughtfully designed suites featuring pillowtop mattresses and fluffy down comforters 42-inch flat-panel TVs spacious baths with Italian marble floors and extra-large soaking tubs in-room wet bars and floor-to-ceiling views of the landscape. Larger suites feature in-ceiling speaker systems and dual plasmas. Guests have exclusive

access to the luxurious pool club and the beach club features an underwater chess board chaise lounges and signature cocktails. The hotel also offers an elegant coffee bar a clubby cocktail lounge and billiards tables. Stop by the Bathhouse Spa for a contemporary spa experience. While the hotel maintains a casino-free environment all you need to do is travel down a corridor to encounter all the energy excitement and gaming action of Mandalay Bay. Awaiting you is a one-of-a-kind pool and beach complex impressive casino Shark Aquarium and even more upscale dining.

**Element Las Vegas Summerlin**
10555 Discovery Drive
Las Vegas NV
702-589-2000 (877-ELEMENT (353-6368))
Offerings from this upscale hotel include spacious nature-influenced and amenity-filled accommodations, several eco-conscious initiatives in action with more to come, 1 and 2 bedroom suites specifically designed for the greatest use and openness of space possible, and fully stocked kitchens. They also sit only 15 minutes from the Las Vegas strip and world class shopping, dining, and around the clock entertainment venues. Dogs are allowed for no additional pet fee;there is a pet waiver to sign at check in.

**Fortune Hotel & Suites**
325 East Flamingo Road
Las Vegas NV
702-732-9100
Dogs of all sizes are allowed. There is a pet fee of $10 per pet per night. No aggressive breeds.

**Holiday Inn Express Las Vegas-nellis**
4035 North Nellis Boulevard
Las Vegas NV
702-644-5700 (877-270-6405)
Dogs of all sizes are allowed.

Dogs are allowed for a pet fee of $20.00 per pet per night.

**La Quinta Inn & Suites Las Vegas Airport North Convention Center**
3970 Paradise Road
Las Vegas NV
702-796-9000 (800-531-5900)
Dogs up to 25 pounds are allowed. There are no additional pet fees. Dogs may not be left unattended, and they must be leashed and cleaned up after.

**La Quinta Inn & Suites Las Vegas Airport South**
6560 Surrey Street
Las Vegas NV
702-492-8900 (800-531-5900)
Dogs of all sizes are allowed. Dogs may not be left alone in the room.

**La Quinta Inn & Suites Las Vegas Summerlin Tech**
7101 Cascade Valley Court
Las Vegas NV
702-360-1200 (800-531-5900)
Dogs of all sizes are allowed. There are no additional pet fees. Dogs may not be left unattended, and they must be leashed and cleaned up after. Dogs are not allowed in the lounge, pool area, or the courtyard.

**La Quinta Inn And Suites Las Vegas Red Rock / Summerlan**
9570 West Sahara Avenue
Las Vegas NV
702-243-0356 (800-531-5900)
Dogs of all sizes are allowed. There are no additional pet fees. Dogs may not be left unattended, and they must be leashed and cleaned up after.

**La Quinta Inn Las Vegas Nellis**
4288 North Nellis Boulevard
Las Vegas NV
702-632-0229 (800-531-5900)
Dogs of all sizes are allowed. There are no additional pet fees. Dogs must be crated if left alone in the room, and they must be leashed and cleaned up after.

**Red Roof Inn Las Vegas**

4350 Paradise Road
Las Vegas NV
702-938-2000 (877-424-6423)
Only one mile from the famous Las Vegas Strip. Walking distance to quality shops and restaurants.

Dogs up to 15 pounds are allowed. Dogs are allowed for a pet fee of $25.00 per pet per night.

**Shalimar Hotel Of Las Vegas**
1401 South Las Vegas Boulevard
Las Vegas NV
702-388-0301
Dogs up to 35 pounds are allowed. There is a pet fee of $30 per pet per night.

**Siegel Suites Select Convention Center**
220 Convention Center Drive
Las Vegas NV
702-735-4151 (877-424-6423)
The Rodeway Inn is conveniently located off the Las Vegas strip, only a five-minute walk from the Las Vegas Convention Center.

Dogs up to 75 pounds are allowed. Dogs are allowed for a pet fee of $10 per pet per night.

**The Platinum Hotel**
211 East Flamingo Road
Las Vegas NV
702-365-5000
theplatinumhotel.com
Set apart from the chaos and noise of Las Vegas The Platinum Hotel is an all-suite non-smoking property located just one-and-a-half blocks off the Strip. The Platinum charges a daily resort fee and the hotel's 255 one- and two-bedroom suites resemble personal sanctuaries rather than traditional hotel rooms. Gourmet kitchens with stainless steel appliances and granite countertops can be found in every room. Princess and Marquise suites have fireplaces and washers and dryers. Thoughtful extras like pillowtop mattresses 42-inch plasma TVs and mp3 docking stations make

all the difference when it's time to relax and unwind. For an extra treat try sipping a glass of wine or enjoy a steaming cup of tea on your own personal walk-out balcony. There's free internet as well. Head downstairs to the hotel's sophisticated Stir Lounge for light fare and happy hour specials. The hotel's other restaurant Kilawat is open for breakfast and lunch. Staying true to its name The Platinum is also home to an incredible spa. Enjoy a unique body treatment facial or aromatherapy massage then slip into the hotel's heated outdoor pool. Laundry facilities are available. There's a full-service concierge and both self and valet parking is free. You won't miss a beat unless of course you want to being just steps off The Strip and minutes from all the Las Vegas nightlife. World-famous restaurants and shopping can be found at the nearby Crystals mall and McCarran Airport is just minutes away.

**Travelodge Las Vegas**
2830 Las Vegas Boulevard South
Las Vegas NV
702-735-4222
Dogs up to 70 pounds are allowed. There is a pet fee of $20 per pet per night.

**Trump International Hotel Las Vegas**
2000 Fashion Show Drive
Las Vegas NV
702-982-0000 (866-939-8786)
Luxury is a word heard again and again at the non-smoking Trump International Hotel Las Vegas where a diligent staff's commitment to superior style enhances this towering landmark's elegance. The 64-story Trump International is a luxury hotel-condominium with 1282 suites that feature kitchenettes furnished with Bosh Wolfe and Sub-Zero appliances. Floor-to-ceiling windows come standard as do flat screen TVs mp3 docking

stations and 500-thread count bed linens. The hotel is designed to serve as a casino-free haven from the hustle and bustle of Las Vegas. It offers 11000-square-feet of scented pampering at The Spa and a heated outdoor pool that is open year-round. Dine at one of two on-site restaurants or take advantage of 24-hour room service. Catch the hotel's complimentary shuttle service to the Las Vegas Strip from the lobby. Parking is available and pets are welcome both for additional fees. The hotel is adjacent to the Fashion Show Mall and just steps away from Wynn Las Vegas and many of the city's best resort casinos. It's less than two miles from the Las Vegas Strip and McCarran International Airport is four miles away.

**Vdara Hotel & Spa**
2600 West Harmon Avenue
Las Vegas NV
702-590-2111
vdara.com
Suites with kitchenettes and premium amenities await at Vdara Hotel & Spa a luxury hotel without so much as a single slot machine. Designed to be both environmentally sound and visually stunning this 57-story slice of heaven attracts a discerning crowd. Each of the hotel's 1495 suites features kitchenettes luxury linens and floor-to-ceiling windows. Plush robes hang in every closet while deluxe toiletries are provided in every bathroom. Wi-Fi is free. Vice Versa Patio and Lodge offers mid-afternoon espressos or late-night martinis along with casual lunch and dinner options. Market Cafe Vdara features a gourmet coffee bar pastries paninis and a menu of freshly prepared breakfast and lunch items. The 18000 square-foot two-level spa salon and fitness center is the pride and joy of Vdara. Guests also enjoy access to the hotel's rooftop pool which accommodates private cabanas and daybeds

for an additional fee. Vdara Hotel & Spa is steps from CityCenter Las Vegas and the Bellagio allowing guests exclusive access to some of the city's most exciting resorts. A 67-acre city-within-a-city the Aria Campus is also home to Crystals and the Aria Fine Art Collection a public exhibit of featured works by acclaimed artists and sculptors.

**W Las Vegas**
2535 Las Vegas Blvd South
Las Vegas NV
702-761-8700
Dogs up to 40 pounds are allowed. There is a $125 one time additional pet fee.

**Westin Las Vegas Hotel & Spa**

160 East Flamingo Road
Las Vegas NV
702-836-5900 (888-625-5144)
Set in the entertainment capitol of the world, this upscale hotel and casino offers a number of onsite amenities and sits only a block of the strip offering guests a variety of world-class wining, dining, shopping, and around-the-clock entertainment opportunities. Dogs up to 30 pounds are allowed for a $150 refundable deposit plus an additional one time $35 pet fee per room, and there is a pet waiver to sign at check in.

**Best Western Plus North Las Vegas Inn & Suites**
4540 Donovan Way
North Las Vegas NV
702-649-3000 (800-780-7234)
Dogs up to 80 pounds are allowed. There is a $20 per day pet fee up to $100 for the week. Up to two dogs are allowed per room.

**Lucky Club Casino And Hotel**
3227 Civic Center Drive
North Las Vegas NV
702-399-3297 (877-333-9291)
luckyclublv.com/hotel.php
Large enough to accommodate both you and your pets the conveniently-located Lucky Club Casino & Hotel delights our guests with free wifi parking

nightly drink specials and well-priced dining. Located at the intersection of I-15 and Cheyenne Road Lucky Club Casino & Hotel provides easy on easy off access for those passing though the area for work or play. The hotel offers basic accommodations with the added benefit of free wifi an amenity you won't often find at the higher priced hotels along The Strip. There's an outdoor pool on-site and the hotel's restaurant Lucy's Bar and Grill serves comfort food around the clock. There is also nightly entertainment at the bar and a revolving menu of drink specials. Pets are welcome at Lucky Club and stay free with a paying owner. Additional amenities include free parking for both cars and trucks laundry facilities and an on-site dog park. The local area around the hotel offers plenty of casual and affordable dining options including many fast food favorites. Nellis Air Force Base is a few minutes away by car and if you want to travel to The Strip it won't take long at all. The closest airport is North Las Vegas Airport located about four miles west.

## Pet-Friendly Extended Stay Hotels

**Residence Inn By Marriott Las Vegas Henderson/green Valley**
2190 Olympic Avenue
Henderson NV
702-434-2700
Dogs of all sizes are allowed. There is a $100 one time additional pet fee.

**Towneplace Suites By Marriott Las Vegas Henderson**
1471 Paseo Verde Parkway
Henderson NV
702-896-2900
Dogs of all sizes are allowed. There is a $100 one time pet fee.

**Candlewood Suites Las Vegas**

4034 South Paradise Road
Las Vegas NV
702-836-3660 (877-270-6405)
Dogs of all sizes are allowed. Pets allowed with an additional pet fee. Up to $75 for 1-6 nights and up to $150 for 7+ nights. A pet agreement must be signed at check-in.

**Extended Stay America - Las Vegas - Midtown**
3045 South Maryland Parkway
Las Vegas NV
702-369-1414 (800-804-3724)
One dog is allowed per suite. There is a $25 per night additional pet fee up to $150 for an entire stay.

**Extended Stay America Las Vegas - Valley View**
4270 South Valley View Boulevard
Las Vegas NV
702-221-7600 (800-804-3724)
One dog is allowed per suite. There is a $25 per night additional pet fee up to $150 for an entire stay.

**Residence Inn By Marriott Las Vegas Convention Center**
3225 Paradise Road
Las Vegas NV
702-796-9300
Dogs of all sizes are allowed. There is a $100 one time additional pet fee.

**Residence Inn By Marriott Las Vegas Hughes Center**
370 Hughes Center Drive
Las Vegas NV
702-650-0040
Dogs of all sizes are allowed. There is a $100 one time additional pet fee.

**Residence Inn Las Vegas South**
5875 Dean Martin Drive
Las Vegas NV
702-795-7378
Dogs of all sizes are allowed. There is a $100 one time additional pet fee.

**Staybridge Suites Las Vegas**

5735 Dean Martin Drive
Las Vegas NV
702-259-2663 (877-270-6405)
Dogs up to 80 pounds are
allowed. Pets allowed with an
additional pet fee. Up to $75 for
1-6 nights and up to $150 for 7+
nights. A pet agreement must
be signed at check-in.

## Dog-Friendly Attractions
### Camp Bow Wow
5175 S Valley View Blvd
Las Vegas NV
702-255-2267
campbowwow.com/us/nv/lasveg
as/
Some of the perks of this doggy
day care center include indoor
and outdoor play yards, well-
trained staff, cams for viewing
the camp via the web, and
cushy accommodations for
pampered pups. Dogs must be
current on all vaccinations, be
spayed or neutered (four to six
months old okay without
spay/neuter), and hound and
human friendly.

### Historic Spring Mountain Ranch
State Route 159
Las Vegas NV
702-875-4141
state.nv.us/stparks/smr.htm
Previous owners of this historic
ranch include Chester Lauck of
the comedy team "Lum &
Abner," German actress Vera
Krupp, and millionaire Howard
Hughes. Guided tours through
the Ranch House and other
historic ranch buildings are
available on weekends and
holidays. The visitor center is
open Monday through Friday
and on holidays. Dogs on leash
are allowed on the grounds, but
not inside the buildings. Other
amenities at this park include a
tree-shaded picnic area and
scenic hiking trails.

### Las Vegas Strip Walking Tour
3300-3900 Las Vegas Blvd.
Las Vegas NV

This walk can now only be taken
between the hours of 5 am and

noon as the county no longer
allows dogs on the strip at
other times. Since dogs are not
allowed inside the buildings or
attractions on the Vegas strip,
we have put together an
outdoor self-guided walking
tour that you can take with your
pooch. It is kid-friendly too!
While you can take the tour
any time of day, probably the
best time is late afternoon or
early evening because of the
special effects and light shows
at some of the points of
interest. All places mentioned
can be viewed from the
sidewalk. Start the walk at the
Treasure Island Hotel at 3300
South Las Vegas Blvd. In the
front of this hotel you can view
two battle ships duke it out.
Every 90 minutes, each
evening at Buccaneer Bay,
musket and cannon fire are
exchanged in a pyrotechnic
battle between the pirate ship
Hispaniola and the British
frigate H.M.S. Britannia. This is
a popular attraction and it can
become very crowded on the
sidewalk. Next stop is the
Volcano in front of the Mirage
Hotel at 3400 South Las Vegas
Blvd. From dusk to midnight,
every 15 minutes, flames shoot
into the sky, spewing smoke
and fire 100 feet above the
water, transforming a tranquil
waterfall into streams of molten
lava. For a little musical
entertainment, walk over to the
Musical Fountains at the
Bellagio Hotel at 3600 South
Las Vegas Blvd. Here you will
find spectacular fountains that
fill a 1/4 mile long lake in front
of the hotel. Every evening
there is a water show that is
timed to music. The show
takes place every 15 minutes.
For some interesting
architecture, walk over to the
Eiffel Tower at the Paris Hotel
at 3655 South Las Vegas Blvd.
While your pooch cannot go
into the Paris Hotel or the
tower, you can view this half
size Paris replica from the
street. You can also visit the
Statue of Liberty right in Las
Vegas. Walk over to the New

York, New York Hotel at 3790
South Las Vegas Blvd. Again,
your pooch cannot go inside this
hotel, but you can view the
replica from the street. The last
stop is the Luxor Hotel at 3900
South Las Vegas Blvd. From the
sidewalk you will see the large
pyramid with hotel rooms inside
and a large sphinx in the front of
the hotel. Please note that some
of the attractions might be
closed during certain times of
the year or during bad weather,
especially when it is windy.

### Old Las Vegas Mormon Fort
500 E Washington Ave
Las Vegas NV
702-486-3511
state.nv.us/stparks/olvmf.htm
This park includes a remnant of
the original adobe fort which
housed the first permanent non-
native Mormon missionary
settlers in the Las Vegas Valley.
They successfully diverted water
from the Las Vegas Creek in
1855 for farming. There are
future plans to re-create many
more historic features at this
park. The park is open all year
and allows leashed dogs on the
outside grounds.

## Outdoor Restaurants
### Baja Fresh Mexican Grill
675 Mall Ring Circle
Henderson NV
702-450-6551
bajafresh.com
This Mexican restaurant is open
for lunch and dinner. They use
fresh ingredients and making
their salsa and beans daily.
Some of the items on their
menu include Enchiladas,
Burritos, Tacos Salads,
Quesadillas, Nachos, Chicken,
Steak and more. Well-behaved
leashed dogs are allowed at the
outdoor tables.

### Chipotle - St. Rose
10251 S Eastern Avenue
Henderson NV
702-361-6438
chipotle.com/#
Specializing in organic,
unprocessed, and naturally

raised ingredients, this 'made fresh and healthy' Mexican eatery features tasty burritos - including their famous fajita burrito;plus tacos, salads, salsas, and more. All items are made in front of the customer to their specific order. They also offer outdoor dining. Dogs are allowed at the outer tables;they must be under their owner's control and leashed at all times. Someone will need to go inside to order food without the dog and bring the food outside.

**Chipotle - Sunset Station**
1311 W Sunset Road
Henderson NV
702-436-7740
chipotle.com/#
Specializing in organic, unprocessed, and naturally raised ingredients, this 'made fresh and healthy' Mexican eatery features tasty burritos - including their famous fajita burrito;plus tacos, salads, salsas, and more. All items are made in front of the customer to their specific order. They also offer outdoor dining. Dogs are allowed at the outer tables;they must be under their owner's control and leashed at all times. Someone will need to go inside to order food without the dog and bring the food outside.

**The Brooklyn Bagel**
1500 N. Green Valley Parkway
Henderson NV
702-260-9511
Dogs are allowed at the outdoor tables. They are open Monday to Friday from 6 am until 4 pm and on Saturday and Sunday from 6 pm until 3 pm.

**The Coffee Bean & Tea Leaf**
2220 Village Walk Drive
Henderson NV
702-260-3075
coffeebean.com
The coffee here is sourced globally from family coffee farms to procure only the top of 1% of Arabica beans. They offer 30+ varieties of coffee;the beans are roasted in small batches daily for freshness, and they also offer 20 varieties of teas that are

hand-blended by their tea master. Additionally, they offer a variety of tasty sweets, powders, extracts, sauces, gifts, and cards. Leashed, well mannered dogs are allowed at their outside dining area.

**Baja Fresh Mexican Grill**
1380 E Flamingo Rd
Las Vegas NV
702-699-8920
bajafresh.com/
Dogs are allowed at the outdoor tables.

**Baja Fresh Mexican Grill**
8780 W Charleston Blvd # 100
Las Vegas NV
702-948-4043
bajafresh.com/
Dogs are allowed at the outdoor tables.

**Baja Fresh Mexican Grill**
7501 W Lake Mead Blvd # 100
Las Vegas NV
702-838-4100
bajafresh.com/
Dogs are allowed at the outdoor tables.

**Baja Fresh Mexican Grill**
9310 S Eastern Ave
Las Vegas NV
702-563-2800
bajafresh.com/
Dogs on leash are allowed at the outdoor tables.

**Chipotle**
4530 S Maryland Parkway
Las Vegas NV
702-436-9177
chipotle.com/#
Specializing in organic, unprocessed, and naturally raised ingredients, this 'made fresh and healthy' Mexican eatery features tasty burritos - including their famous fajita burrito;plus tacos, salads, salsas, and more. All items are made in front of the customer to their specific order. They also offer outdoor dining. Dogs are allowed at the outer tables;they must be under their owner's control and leashed at all times. Someone will need to go inside to order food without the dog and bring the food

outside.

**Chipotle - Belz**
7370 S Las Vegas Blvd/H 604
Las Vegas NV
702-270-1973
chipotle.com/#
Specializing in organic, unprocessed, and naturally raised ingredients, this 'made fresh and healthy' Mexican eatery features tasty burritos - including their famous fajita burrito;plus tacos, salads, salsas, and more. All items are made in front of the customer to their specific order. They also offer outdoor dining. Dogs are allowed at the outer tables;they must be under their owner's control and leashed at all times. Someone will need to go inside to order food without the dog and bring the food outside.

**Chipotle - Rock Springs**
7175 W. Lake Mead
Las Vegas NV
702-233-3199
chipotle.com/#
Specializing in organic, unprocessed, and naturally raised ingredients, this 'made fresh and healthy' Mexican eatery features tasty burritos - including their famous fajita burrito;plus tacos, salads, salsas, and more. All items are made in front of the customer to their specific order. They also offer outdoor dining. Dogs are allowed at the outer tables;they must be under their owner's control and leashed at all times. Someone will need to go inside to order food without the dog and bring the food outside.

**Chipotle - Sahara Pavilion**
2540 S Decatur Blvd
Las Vegas NV
702-252-4013
chipotle.com/#
Specializing in organic, unprocessed, and naturally raised ingredients, this 'made fresh and healthy' Mexican eatery features tasty burritos - including their famous fajita burrito;plus tacos, salads, salsas, and more. All items are made in front of the customer to

their specific order. They also offer outdoor dining. Dogs are allowed at the outer tables;they must be under their owner's control and leashed at all times. Someone will need to go inside to order food without the dog and bring the food outside.

**Chipotle - The Arroyo**
7340 Arroyo Crossing Parkway, Suite 100
Las Vegas NV
702-361-0203
chipotle.com/#
Specializing in organic, unprocessed, and naturally raised ingredients, this 'made fresh and healthy' Mexican eatery features tasty burritos - including their famous fajita burrito;plus tacos, salads, salsas, and more. All items are made in front of the customer to their specific order. They also offer outdoor dining. Dogs are allowed at the outer tables;they must be under their owner's control and leashed at all times. Someone will need to go inside to order food without the dog and bring the food outside.

**Chipotle - The Cannery**
2546 E Craig Road, Suite 100
Las Vegas NV
702-633-4463
chipotle.com/#
Specializing in organic, unprocessed, and naturally raised ingredients, this 'made fresh and healthy' Mexican eatery features tasty burritos - including their famous fajita burrito;plus tacos, salads, salsas, and more. All items are made in front of the customer to their specific order. They also offer outdoor dining. Dogs are allowed at the outer tables;they must be under their owner's control and leashed at all times. Someone will need to go inside to order food without the dog and bring the food outside.

**Einstein Brothers Bagels**
9031 W. Sahara Ave
Las Vegas NV
702-254-0919
einsteinbros.com/
Dogs are allowed at the outdoor

tables.

**Firehouse Subs**
9555 S Eastern Avenue, Suite 130
Las Vegas NV
702-893-3473
firehousesubs.com
Founded by firemen and specializing in made-to-order fresh, baked bread sandwiches, this sub-shop features a number of specialty hot and cold sub sandwiches. They also offer fresh salads, various beverages, a variety of sides, a kid's menu, catering, and alfresco dining. Leashed, friendly dogs are allowed at their outside dining area.

**Grape Vine Cafe**
7501 W Lake Mead Blvd #120
Las Vegas NV
702-228-9463
grapestreetvegas.com/
The Grape Street Cafe, located in Las Vegas, Nevada, is an italian restaurant designed to replicate a wine cellar. Bold hues, iron features and a rustic ambiance surround the restaurant. Candlelight illuminates the restaurant at night. They offer appetizers, salads, sandwiches, pastas, pizzas, and more. The cafe also offers a wine & beer list. Well-behaved, leashed dogs are allowed at the outdoor seating.

**Havana Grill**
8878 S Eastern Ave #100
Las Vegas NV
702-932-9310
havanagrillcuban.com/
The Havana Grill in Las Vegas, NV, is known for using only the freshest and natural ingredients, which create tasteful and unique Cuban cuisine. Well-behaved, leashed dogs are welcome at the outdoor seating.

**Holly's Cuppa**
9265 S Cimarron Rd #115
Las Vegas NV
702-778-7750
holleyscuppa.com
Holly's Cuppa serves coffee,

tea, and other beverages. Well-behaved, leashed dogs are welcome at the outdoor seats.

**In-N-Out Burger**
2900 W. Sahara Ave.
Las Vegas NV
800-786-1000
This fast food restaurant serves great hamburgers and fries.

**It's A Grind**
8470 W Desert Inn Rd
Las Vegas NV
702-360-4232
itsagrind.com/
In addition to providing premium coffees and espressos, this shop also offers other tasty items, various special events, and outside seating. Dogs are allowed at the outside tables;they must be leashed and under their owner's control at all times.

**Jamba Juice**
1121 S Decatur Blvd
Las Vegas NV
702-633-0097
jambajuice.com
All natural and organic ingredients, no high-fructose corn syrup, 0 grams trans fat, no artificial preservatives, a healthy helping of antioxidants, vitamins, and minerals, and fresh whole fruit and fruit juices set the base for these tasty and healthy beverages. Their organic Hot Blends provides a new spin on coffee, green or chai tea, and hot chocolate;plus they offer probiotic fruit and yogurt Blends. Additionally, they feature organic steel-cut oatmeal prepared fresh every morning, all natural salads, wraps, sandwiches, and grab n' go specialties. They also offer healthy community support through fundraisers, special sales, and school lunch programs. Leashed, well mannered dogs are allowed at their outside dining area.

**Jamba Juice**
2675 S Eastern Avenue, Suite 400
Las Vegas NV
702-457-7015

jambajuice.com
All natural and organic ingredients, no high-fructose corn syrup, 0 grams trans fat, no artificial preservatives, a healthy helping of antioxidants, vitamins, and minerals, and fresh whole fruit and fruit juices set the base for these tasty and healthy beverages. Their organic Hot Blends provides a new spin on coffee, green or chai tea, and hot chocolate;plus they offer probiotic fruit and yogurt Blends. Additionally, they feature organic steel-cut oatmeal prepared fresh every morning, all natural salads, wraps, sandwiches, and grab n' go specialties. They also offer healthy community support through fundraisers, special sales, and school lunch programs. Leashed, well mannered dogs are allowed at their outside dining area.

**Jason's Deli**
100 City Parkway
Las Vegas NV
702-366-0130
jasonsdeli.com
This health-conscious deli-style restaurant offers a diverse and extensive menu that includes vegetarian/dietary specific choices with a colored coded menu for easy recognition, USDA certified organics, naturally raised meats, and wholesome high quality ingredients. Some offerings include made-from-scratch soups, an organically-inclined fresh salad bar, organic coffee/teas and beverages, specialty sandwiches - or build-your-own, signature dishes, and a kid's menu. Their foods have 0% artificial trans fats, processed MSG, artificial colors, dyes and nitrates, or high fructose corn syrup (a few soda exceptions). Delivery and catering services are offered at most of the delis;they offer community support though a number of venues, and they have implemented programs to reduce their footprint on the environment with more GREEN initiatives planned. Leashed,

friendly dogs are allowed at their outside dining area.

**Lazy Dog Restaurant & Bar**
6509 Las Vegas Blvd. South
Las Vegas NV
702-941-1920
lazydogrestaurants.com/dogs/info
Known for it's dog-friendly patio, the Lazy Dog offers your dog a complimentary bowl of water, and a menu consisting of grilled hamburger patty, chicken breast or brown rice. They just ask that you respect their common sense rules while your dog is dining there. This is as dog-friendly as dining gets. For the humans in your party there is hamburger, steak, salads and some great desserts.

**Lazy Dog Restaurant & Bar**
1725 Festival Plaza Dr
Las Vegas NV
702-727-4784
lazydogrestaurants.com/dogs/info
Known for it's dog-friendly patio, the Lazy Dog offers your dog a complimentary bowl of water, and a menu consisting of grilled hamburger patty, chicken breast or brown rice. They just ask that you respect their common sense rules while your dog is dining there. This is as dog-friendly as dining gets. For the humans in your party there is hamburger, steak, salads and some great desserts.

**Mountain Springs Saloon**
Highway 160
Las Vegas NV
702-875-4266
Dogs are welcome at the outdoor dining area. This bar has a limited food menu and serves a variety of beer. The bar has live music Friday and Saturday nights. They are located near the Mountain Springs Summit, about 15-20 minutes west of downtown Las Vegas. The restaurant is open daily, except closed on Tuesday, from 11 am until 7 pm, and the bar is open daily

from 9 am until 10 pm.

**Rainbow's End Natural Foods**
1100 E Sahara Avenue, Suite #120
Las Vegas NV
702-737-1338
rainbowsendlv.info
This natural grocery features a variety of local produce and products, refrigerated and frozen foods;dietary specific items, wholesome packaged groceries, quality nutritional supplements, herbs and spices, Fair Trade products, and personal and household items. They also have a healthy living section and offer seminars, lectures, weekly classes, and in store demos. The deli offers a tasty and extensive menu of vegetarian and vegan cuisine. The deli is closed Sundays and closes earlier than the store. Leashed, well mannered dogs are allowed at their outside dining area.

**Starbucks**
395 Hughes Center Drive
Las Vegas NV
702-369-5537
starbucks.com
This coffee shop allows well-behaved leashed dogs at their outdoor tables.

**TGI Fridays**
4570 W Sahara Avenue/H 589
Las Vegas NV
702-889-1866
fridays.com/
Artfully created appetizers, soups, salads, steaks, seafood, barbecue dishes, burgers, sandwiches, and desserts are just some of the offerings of this lively restaurant. They also offer a children's menu, party platters, a full bar, and a large outdoor dining area. Leashed, well mannered dogs are allowed at the outside tables.

**The Coffee Bean & Tea Leaf**
9091 W Sahara Avenue
Las Vegas NV
702-998-0216
coffeebean.com
The coffee here is sourced globally from family coffee farms

to procure only the top of 1% of Arabica beans. They offer 30+ varieties of coffee;the beans are roasted in small batches daily for freshness, and they also offer 20 varieties of teas that are hand-blended by their tea master. Additionally, they offer a variety of tasty sweets, powders, extracts, sauces, gifts, and cards. Leashed, well mannered dogs are allowed at their outside dining area.

### The Coffee Bean & Tea Leaf
6115 S Rainbow Blvd, Suite 101

Las Vegas NV
702-220-6820
coffeebean.com
The coffee here is sourced globally from family coffee farms to procure only the top of 1% of Arabica beans. They offer 30+ varieties of coffee;the beans are roasted in small batches daily for freshness, and they also offer 20 varieties of teas that are hand-blended by their tea master. Additionally, they offer a variety of tasty sweets, powders, extracts, sauces, gifts, and cards. Leashed, well mannered dogs are allowed at their outside dining area.

### The Coffee Bean & Tea Leaf
4550 S Maryland Parkway, Suite A
Las Vegas NV
702-944-5029
coffeebean.com
The coffee here is sourced globally from family coffee farms to procure only the top of 1% of Arabica beans. They offer 30+ varieties of coffee;the beans are roasted in small batches daily for freshness, and they also offer 20 varieties of teas that are hand-blended by their tea master. Additionally, they offer a variety of tasty sweets, powders, extracts, sauces, gifts, and cards. Leashed, well mannered dogs are allowed at their outside dining area.

### The Coffee Bean & Tea Leaf
7291 W Lake Mead Drive
Las Vegas NV
702-944-0030

coffeebean.com
The coffee here is sourced globally from family coffee farms to procure only the top of 1% of Arabica beans. They offer 30+ varieties of coffee;the beans are roasted in small batches daily for freshness, and they also offer 20 varieties of teas that are hand-blended by their tea master. Additionally, they offer a variety of tasty sweets, powders, extracts, sauces, gifts, and cards. Leashed, well mannered dogs are allowed at their outside dining area.

### The Coffee Bean & Tea Leaf
3645 S Towncenter Drive, Suite 101
Las Vegas NV
702-785-0419
coffeebean.com
The coffee here is sourced globally from family coffee farms to procure only the top of 1% of Arabica beans. They offer 30+ varieties of coffee;the beans are roasted in small batches daily for freshness, and they also offer 20 varieties of teas that are hand-blended by their tea master. Additionally, they offer a variety of tasty sweets, powders, extracts, sauces, gifts, and cards. Leashed, well mannered dogs are allowed at their outside dining area.

### The Coffee Bean & Tea Leaf
10834 W Charleston Blvd
Las Vegas NV
702-838-5661
coffeebean.com
The coffee here is sourced globally from family coffee farms to procure only the top of 1% of Arabica beans. They offer 30+ varieties of coffee;the beans are roasted in small batches daily for freshness, and they also offer 20 varieties of teas that are hand-blended by their tea master. Additionally, they offer a variety of tasty sweets, powders, extracts, sauces, gifts, and cards. Leashed, well mannered dogs are allowed at their outside dining area.

### Triple George Grill
201 N 3rd St #120
Las Vegas NV
702-384-2761
triplegeorgegrill.com/
The Triple George Grill in Las Vegas, Nevada, is open Monday-Friday 10am-11pm and Saturdays & Sundays 4pm-10pm. They offer a great lunch or dinner in a comfortable atmosphere. Well-behaved, leashed dogs are allowed at the outdoor seats.

### Tropical Smoothie Cafe
Lowes & Kohl's Plaza
Las Vegas NV
603-509-3000
tropicalsmoothie.com
Offerings from this health-minded cafe include all natural real fruit Super Fruit, Simply Indulgent, Super Charged, and Low Fat Smoothies;plus a selection of Coffee Smoothies. They also serve up freshly prepared signature wraps, flatbread and bistro sandwiches, garden fresh salads, all natural gourmet cheeses and meats, artisanal breads, vegan/vegetarian choices, and catering services. They are open for breakfast, lunch, and dinner. Leashed, well mannered dogs are allowed at their outside seating area.

### Tropical Smoothie Cafe
10612 S. Eastern Avenue
Las Vegas NV
702-616-1931
tropicalsmoothie.com
Offerings from this health-minded cafe include all natural real fruit Super Fruit, Simply Indulgent, Super Charged, and Low Fat Smoothies;plus a selection of Coffee Smoothies. They also serve up freshly prepared signature wraps, flatbread and bistro sandwiches, garden fresh salads, all natural gourmet cheeses and meats, artisanal breads, vegan/vegetarian choices, and catering services. They are open for breakfast, lunch, and dinner. Leashed, well mannered dogs are allowed at their outside

seating area.

**Tropical Smoothie Cafe**
9440 W. Sahara Blvd
Las Vegas NV
702-207-1931
tropicalsmoothie.com
Offerings from this health-minded cafe include all natural real fruit Super Fruit, Simply Indulgent, Super Charged, and Low Fat Smoothies;plus a selection of Coffee Smoothies. They also serve up freshly prepared signature wraps, flatbread and bistro sandwiches, garden fresh salads, all natural gourmet cheeses and meats, artisanal breads, vegan/vegetarian choices, and catering services. They are open for breakfast, lunch, and dinner. Leashed, well mannered dogs are allowed at their outside seating area.

**Tropical Smoothie Cafe**
6555 S. Jones Blvd, #110
Las Vegas NV
702-247-6208
tropicalsmoothie.com
Offerings from this health-minded cafe include all natural real fruit Super Fruit, Simply Indulgent, Super Charged, and Low Fat Smoothies;plus a selection of Coffee Smoothies. They also serve up freshly prepared signature wraps, flatbread and bistro sandwiches, garden fresh salads, all natural gourmet cheeses and meats, artisanal breads, vegan/vegetarian choices, and catering services. They are open for breakfast, lunch, and dinner. Leashed, well mannered dogs are allowed at their outside seating area.

**Tropical Smoothie Cafe**
7291 S Eastern Avenue
Las Vegas NV
702-450-1931
tropicalsmoothie.com
Offerings from this health-minded cafe include all natural real fruit Super Fruit, Simply Indulgent, Super Charged, and Low Fat Smoothies;plus a selection of Coffee Smoothies. They also serve up freshly

prepared signature wraps, flatbread and bistro sandwiches, garden fresh salads, all natural gourmet cheeses and meats, artisanal breads, vegan/vegetarian choices, and catering services. They are open for breakfast, lunch, and dinner. Leashed, well mannered dogs are allowed at their outside seating area.

**Tropical Smoothie Cafe**
7580 S. Las Vegas Blvd
Las Vegas NV
702-257-1931
tropicalsmoothie.com
Offerings from this health-minded cafe include all natural real fruit Super Fruit, Simply Indulgent, Super Charged, and Low Fat Smoothies;plus a selection of Coffee Smoothies. They also serve up freshly prepared signature wraps, flatbread and bistro sandwiches, garden fresh salads, all natural gourmet cheeses and meats, artisanal breads, vegan/vegetarian choices, and catering services. They are open for breakfast, lunch, and dinner. Leashed, well mannered dogs are allowed at their outside seating area.

**Tropical Smoothie Cafe**
7660 W Cheyenne Avenue
Las Vegas NV
702-365-1931
tropicalsmoothie.com
Offerings from this health-minded cafe include all natural real fruit Super Fruit, Simply Indulgent, Super Charged, and Low Fat Smoothies;plus a selection of Coffee Smoothies. They also serve up freshly prepared signature wraps, flatbread and bistro sandwiches, garden fresh salads, all natural gourmet cheeses and meats, artisanal breads, vegan/vegetarian choices, and catering services. They are open for breakfast, lunch, and dinner. Leashed, well mannered dogs are allowed at their outside seating area.

**Tropical Smoothie Cafe**
10260 W. Charleston Blvd/H
159
Las Vegas NV
702-869-0603
tropicalsmoothie.com
Offerings from this health-minded cafe include all natural real fruit Super Fruit, Simply Indulgent, Super Charged, and Low Fat Smoothies;plus a selection of Coffee Smoothies. They also serve up freshly prepared signature wraps, flatbread and bistro sandwiches, garden fresh salads, all natural gourmet cheeses and meats, artisanal breads, vegan/vegetarian choices, and catering services. They are open for breakfast, lunch, and dinner. Leashed, well mannered dogs are allowed at their outside seating area.

**Tropical Smoothie Cafe**
4262 Blue Diamond Road, #103

Las Vegas NV
702-629-3692
tropicalsmoothie.com
Offerings from this health-minded cafe include all natural real fruit Super Fruit, Simply Indulgent, Super Charged, and Low Fat Smoothies;plus a selection of Coffee Smoothies. They also serve up freshly prepared signature wraps, flatbread and bistro sandwiches, garden fresh salads, all natural gourmet cheeses and meats, artisanal breads, vegan/vegetarian choices, and catering services. They are open for breakfast, lunch, and dinner. Leashed, well mannered dogs are allowed at their outside seating area.

**Tropical Smoothie Cafe**
4165 S. Grand Canyon Drive, #
106
Las Vegas NV
702-242-1931
tropicalsmoothie.com
Offerings from this health-minded cafe include all natural real fruit Super Fruit, Simply Indulgent, Super Charged, and Low Fat Smoothies;plus a

selection of Coffee Smoothies. They also serve up freshly prepared signature wraps, flatbread and bistro sandwiches, garden fresh salads, all natural gourmet cheeses and meats, artisanal breads, vegan/vegetarian choices, and catering services. They are open for breakfast, lunch, and dinner. Leashed, well mannered dogs are allowed at their outside seating area.

**Tropical Smoothie Cafe**
5035 S Fort Apache Road
Las Vegas NV
702-459-8000
tropicalsmoothie.com
Offerings from this health-minded cafe include all natural real fruit Super Fruit, Simply Indulgent, Super Charged, and Low Fat Smoothies;plus a selection of Coffee Smoothies. They also serve up freshly prepared signature wraps, flatbread and bistro sandwiches, garden fresh salads, all natural gourmet cheeses and meats, artisanal breads, vegan/vegetarian choices, and catering services. They are open for breakfast, lunch, and dinner. Leashed, well mannered dogs are allowed at their outside seating area.

**Whole Foods Market**
8855 West Charleston Blvd.
Las Vegas NV
702-254-8655
wholefoods.com/
This natural food supermarket offers natural and organic foods. Order some food from their deli without your dog and bring it to an outdoor table where your well-behaved leashed dog is welcome.

**Whole Foods Market**
7250 W. Lake Mead Blvd
Las Vegas NV
702-942-1500
wholefoods.com/
This full service natural food market offers both natural and organic food. You can get food from the deli and bring it to an outdoor table where your well-behaved leashed dog is

welcome.

**Jamba Juice**
1829 W Craig Road, Unit 3/H 573
North Las Vegas NV
702-633-0097
jambajuice.com
All natural and organic ingredients, no high-fructose corn syrup, 0 grams trans fat, no artificial preservatives, a healthy helping of antioxidants, vitamins, and minerals, and fresh whole fruit and fruit juices set the base for these tasty and healthy beverages. Their organic Hot Blends provides a new spin on coffee, green or chai tea, and hot chocolate;plus they offer probiotic fruit and yogurt Blends. Additionally, they feature organic steel-cut oatmeal prepared fresh every morning, all natural salads, wraps, sandwiches, and grab n' go specialties. They also offer healthy community support through fundraisers, special sales, and school lunch programs. Leashed, well mannered dogs are allowed at their outside dining area.

## Pet-Friendly Shopping Centers
**District at Green Valley Ranch**
2240 Village Walk Drive
Henderson NV
702-564-8595
thedistrictatgvr.com/
Thanks to a reader for recommending this dog-friendly shopping district in Henderson. She says "This place is all about dogs. Each store has water and dog biscuits out front." Many stores allow dogs inside but please remember to ask first.

**Tivoli Village**
440 S Rampart Blvd
Las Vegas NV
702-570-7400
tivolivillagelv.com/
The Tivoli Village, located in

Las Vegas, Nevada, showcases a unique mix of retailers ranging from luxury brands to one-of-a-kind boutiques, as well as a collection of restaurants and high-end offices. They offer a dog-friendly environment throughout the outdoor areas of the village. Owners must keep dogs on their leashes at all times and ensure their pet's waste is disposed of properly. Tivoli Village will provide pet waste bags and containers throughout the property for your convenience. They also ask that you be mindful of individual store's pet policies.

**Town Square Las Vegas**
6605 Las Vegas Blvd S
Las Vegas NV
702-269-5000
townsquarelasvegas.com/
This one destination offers guests a variety of dining, shopping, and entertainment opportunities. Dogs are allowed in the common areas of the mall; it is up to individual stores whether they allow a dog inside. Dogs must be well behaved, leashed in the common areas of the mall, in a carrier only when in the stores, and under their owner's control at all times.

## Pet-Friendly Stores
**Anthropologie**
2275 Village Walk Drive, Green Valley
Henderson NV
702-617-2247
Items of distinction can be found for all ages and in all departments of this unique shop. Carefully selected to add to the enjoyment of the shopping experience, they carry fine clothing, amazing accessories, jewelry, hobby and leisure items, and a full line of bright and useful items for the home, garden, and office. Leashed, well behaved dogs are allowed in the store.

**Camping World**
1600 S Boulder H/H 582
Henderson NV

702-565-6525
campingworld.com/
This comprehensive RV and outdoor store carries a wide variety of RV, boat, bike, and outdoor cooking accessories; all kinds of camping gear; RV screens, shades, and patio decorations; racing/tailgating gear, and all items for RV maintenance. They also carry RV towing supplies, electronics, and interior decorating items as well as pet supplies, RV directories/books, and games. Plus, they offer a tips and advice service, RV sales, rentals, and RV technicians to take care of any installations and repairs. They also welcome your canine companion in the store with a treat; they must be friendly and leashed.

**PetSmart Pet Store**
531 N Stephanie St
Henderson NV
702-898-0055
Your licensed and well-behaved leashed dog is allowed in the store.

**Petco Pet Store - Henderson - East**
631 Marks St.
Henderson NV
702-458-1435
Your licensed and well-behaved leashed dog is allowed in the store.

**The Soggy Dog**
1450 W Horizon Ridge Parkway
Henderson NV
702-452-3647
thesoggydog.com/storeinfo.htm
In addition to providing a variety of pet foods, supplements, collars and leashes, pet care products, and toys, this shop also offers a do-it-yourself doggy wash station with all the extras. Dogs must be well mannered and leashed.

**Anthropologie**
3500 Las Vegas Blvd S, #T-11
Las Vegas NV
702-650-0466
Items of distinction can be found for all ages and in all departments of this unique

shop. Carefully selected to add to the enjoyment of the shopping experience, they carry fine clothing, amazing accessories, jewelry, hobby and leisure items, and a full line of bright and useful items for the home, garden, and office. Leashed, well behaved dogs are allowed in the store.

**Bass Pro**
8200 Dean Martin Drive
Las Vegas NV
702-730-5200
This comprehensive outdoorsman store offers thousands of sporting goods, clothing, and accessories for all types of active lifestyles. Leashed, well mannered dogs are welcome in the store.

**Bloomingdale's**
3200 Las Vegas Blvd S
Las Vegas NV
702-784-5400
Some of the offerings of this major shopping destination include designer merchandise, indoor and outdoor wear for the entire family, jewelry and accessories, shoes and handbags, personal beauty aids, child care products, and home decor. They also offer a wide variety of shopping services; various fashion, beauty, and home events, and a philanthropy program that raises funds and awareness for worthy causes. Leashed, well mannered dogs are welcome in the store; they must be under their owner's control at all times.

**Bogart's Bone Appetit**
10660 Southern Highlands Pkwy
Las Vegas NV
702-435-3644
bogartspet.com/
Bogart's Bone Appetit is a fun place for you and your dog to shop. They sell products for your pets needs. Carrying the best foods, a wide variety of toys, apparel, and accessories. They offer experienced groomers, as well as having Tropicana and Fort Apache

stores with self wash executive suites, so you and your family can enjoy washing your dog in a first class environment.

**C-A-L Ranch and Home Store**
232 N. Jones Blvd
Las Vegas NV
702-430-7002
The C-A-L Ranch and Home Store in Las Vegas welcomes leashed dogs in their store. They have a pet products section, and some stores may also offer pet grooming services.

**Camping World**
13175 Las Vegas Blvd S
Las Vegas NV
877-594-3353
campingworld.com/
This comprehensive RV and outdoor store carries a wide variety of RV, boat, bike, and outdoor cooking accessories; all kinds of camping gear; RV screens, shades, and patio decorations; racing/tailgating gear, and all items for RV maintenance. They also carry RV towing supplies, electronics, and interior decorating items as well as pet supplies, RV directories/books, and games. Plus, they offer a tips and advice service, RV sales, rentals, and RV technicians to take care of any installations and repairs. They also welcome your canine companion in the store; they must be friendly and leashed.

**Harley-Davidson Store**
2605 S. Eastern Avenue
Las Vegas NV
702-431-8500
lvhd.com/
Well-behaved, leashed dogs are allowed inside this store, which is the world's largest Harley dealership. Whether you own a Harley or just wish you could own one, stop by the store and take a look around. This is a popular place for locals and tourists. The store is located about 15 minutes north of downtown Las Vegas.

**PetSmart Pet Store**

2140 N Rainbow
Las Vegas NV
702-631-8422
Your licensed and well-behaved leashed dog is allowed in the store.

**PetSmart Pet Store**
171 N Nellis Blvd
Las Vegas NV
702-438-5771
Your licensed and well-behaved leashed dog is allowed in the store.

**PetSmart Pet Store**
1261 S Decatur Blvd
Las Vegas NV
702-870-8200
Your licensed and well-behaved leashed dog is allowed in the store.

**PetSmart Pet Store**
9775 W Charleston
Las Vegas NV
702-940-5200
Your licensed and well-behaved leashed dog is allowed in the store.

**PetSmart Pet Store**
9869 S Eastern Ave
Las Vegas NV
702-951-0045
Your licensed and well-behaved leashed dog is allowed in the store.

**PetSmart Pet Store**
5160 S Fort Apache Rd
Las Vegas NV
702-253-1431
Your licensed and well-behaved leashed dog is allowed in the store.

**PetSmart Pet Store**
6650 N Durango Dr
Las Vegas NV
702-839-0479
Your licensed and well-behaved leashed dog is allowed in the store.

**Petco Pet Store - Blue Diamond**
3890 Blue Diamond Road #A
Las Vegas NV
702-616-7067
Your licensed and well-behaved leashed dog is allowed in the store.

**Petco Pet Store - Las Vegas - Lake Mead**
2091 North Rainbow Blvd
Las Vegas NV
702-648-7106
Your licensed and well-behaved leashed dog is allowed in the store.

**Petco Pet Store - Las Vegas - North**
1631 West Craig Road Ste 5-8
Las Vegas NV
702-399-5850
Your licensed and well-behaved leashed dog is allowed in the store.

**Petco Pet Store - Las Vegas - Northwest**
7731 West Tropical Pkwy
Las Vegas NV
702-395-1177
Your licensed and well-behaved leashed dog is allowed in the store.

**Petco Pet Store - Las Vegas - South**
2340 East Serene Ave.
Las Vegas NV
702-914-0500
Your licensed and well-behaved leashed dog is allowed in the store.

**Petco Pet Store - Las Vegas - Southwest**
3577 South Rainbow Blvd
Las Vegas NV
702-253-7800
Your licensed and well-behaved leashed dog is allowed in the store.

**Scraps Dog Bakery**
9310 Sun City Blvd
Las Vegas NV
702-360-1927
This dog bakery makes tasty treats for your dog. The bakery is located in North Las Vegas on the west side of the city. Your well-behaved leashed dog is welcome.

**Three Dog Bakery**
2110 N. Rampart Suite 150
Las Vegas NV

702-737-3364
threedogvegas.com/
Three Dog Bakery provides cookies and snacks for your dog as well as some boutique items. You well-behaved, leashed dog is welcome.

**Urban Outfitters**
3930 Las Vegas Blvd S
Las Vegas NV
702-650-2199
In addition to a large inventory of indoor and outdoor apparel for men and women, this major department store also carries vintage wear, designer brands, and a variety of accessories for all types of active lifestyles. They also carry shoes, furnishings, home decor, cameras, electronics, novelty items and more. Well mannered dogs that can be hand-carried are allowed in the store.

**Urban Outfitters**
3663 Las Vegas Blvd. S., #150
Las Vegas NV
702-733-0058
In addition to a large inventory of indoor and outdoor apparel for men and women, this major department store also carries vintage wear, designer brands, and a variety of accessories for all types of active lifestyles. They also carry shoes, furnishings, home decor, cameras, electronics, novelty items and more. Leashed, well mannered dogs are allowed in the store.

**PetSmart Pet Store**
1321 W Craig Rd
North Las Vegas NV
702-938-5880
Your licensed and well-behaved leashed dog is allowed in the store.

# Off-Leash Dog Parks
**Acacia Park Dog Park**
S Gibson Road and Las Palmas Entrada
Henderson NV
702-267-4000
This fenced dog park is open daily from 6 am to midnight. The

park is just south of I-215 at Gibson Rd.

## Dos Escuelas Park Dog Park
1 Golden View Street
Henderson NV
702-267-4000
This fenced dog park is open daily from 6 am to midnight. To get to the park, which is just south of I-215, take the S. Green Valley Pkwy exit and head south. Turn left onto Paseo Verde Pkwy and make a left onto Desert Shadow Trail. Turn left onto Rainbow View Street and left again onto Golden View Street. The park will be on the left.

## All American Park
121 E Sunset Road
Las Vegas NV
702-317-7777
This 45 acre community park offers a variety of recreational opportunities as well as a fenced dog run for canine visitors. Dogs must be sociable, current on all vaccinations and license, and under their owner's control at all times. Dogs must be leashed when not in designated off-lead areas.

## Barkin' Basin Park
Alexander Road and Tenaya Way
Las Vegas NV
702-229-6297
There are 7.75 acres for doggy play area at this park that sits adjacent to the W Wayne Bunker Park. It has 3 separate fenced areas with shaded seating and water fountains for hounds and humans. Dogs must be sociable, current on all vaccinations and license, and under their owner's control at all times. Dogs must be leashed when not in designated off-lead areas.

## Centennial Hills Dog Park
Buffalo Drive and Elkhorn Road
Las Vegas NV
702-229-6297
This park is a major recreation destination for the whole family - including the family dog with a fenced, 2 part, doggy play area.

Dogs must be sociable, current on all vaccinations and license, and under their owner's control at all times. Dogs must be leashed when not in designated off-lead areas.

## Children's Memorial Park
6601 W Gowan Road
Las Vegas NV
702-229-6718
There are almost 35 recreational acres at this park, and in addition to a fair balance of amenities, this park features a 2 part off lead doggy play area. Dogs must be sociable, current on all vaccinations and license, and under their owner's control at all times. Dogs must be leashed when not in designated off-lead areas.

## Desert Breeze Dog Run
8425 W. Spring Mtn. Road
Las Vegas NV

This dog park is fully enclosed with benches, trees, trash cans and water. There are three dog runs available, one for small dogs, one for middle sized dogs and one for larger dogs over 30 pounds. The park is located approximately 5 miles west of downtown Las Vegas and the Strip. From Flamingo Road/589 in downtown, head west and pass Hwy 15. Turn right on Durango Drive. Then turn right onto Spring Mountain Road. The dog park is located off Spring Mountain Rd., between the Community Center and Desert Breeze County Park.

## Desert Inn Dog Park
3570 Vista del Monte
Las Vegas NV
702-455-8200
This fenced dog park is open daily from 6 am to 11 pm. The park is located off of Boulder Highway east of the 515 freeway. From Boulder Highway take Indios Avenue east to Twain Ave. Turn right on Twain and go two blocks. Turn left on Vista Del Monte Drive to the park.

## Dog Fancier's Park
5800 E. Flamingo Rd.
Las Vegas NV
702-455-8200
Dog Fancier's Park is a 12 acre park that allows canine enthusiasts to train their dogs off leash. Owner's must still have control over their dogs and may be cited if their dogs (while off leash) interfere with other animals training at the park. This dog park has benches, poop bags and water taps.

## Justice Myron E. Leavitt Family Park (formerly known as Jaycee Park)
E St Louis Avenue and Eastern Avenue
Las Vegas NV
702-229-6718
In addition to almost 20 recreational acres, this park also offers a fenced, 3-section doggy play area. Dogs must be sociable, current on all vaccinations and license, and under their owner's control at all times. Dogs must be leashed when not in designated off-lead areas.

## Lorenzi Park
3075 W Washington Avenue
Las Vegas NV
702-229-4867
In addition to almost 60 recreational acres, this park also offers a large pond, walking paths, and a 2-section fenced, doggy play area. Dogs must be sociable, current on all vaccinations and license, and under their owner's control at all times. Dogs must be leashed when not in designated off-lead areas.

## Molasky Park Dog Run
1065 E. Twain Ave
Las Vegas NV
702-455-8200
This fenced dog park is open daily from 6 am to 11 pm. To get to the dog park from the Strip take Flamingo Rd east past Paradise. Turn left (north) on Cambridge St and east on Twain Ave. The dog park is located between Cambridge St

and Maryland Parkway on Twain.

**Police Memorial Park**
Cheyenne Avenue and Metro Academy Way
Las Vegas NV
702-229-6297
Memorials, a variety of recreation, and a fenced, 3 section doggy play area are just some of the attractions of this park. Dogs must be sociable, current on all vaccinations and license, and under their owner's control at all times. Dogs must be leashed when not in designated off-lead areas.

**Shadow Rock Dog Run**
2650 Los Feliz on Sunrise Mountain
Las Vegas NV
702-455-8200
This is a 1.5 acre dog park with benches, poop bags and water taps.

**Silverado Ranch Park Dog Park**
9855 S. Gillespie
Las Vegas NV
702-455-8200
This fenced dog park is open daily from 6 am to 11 pm. The park is south of the Strip off of Las Vegas Blvd. From the Strip head south on Las Vegas Blvd and turn left onto Silverado Ranch Blvd. Turn right onto Gillespie and the park will be on the right.

**Sunset Park Dog Run**
2601 E. Sunset Rd
Las Vegas NV
702-455-8200
Located in Sunset Park, this dog park offers about 1.5 acres of land for your pooch to play. The dog park has benches, poop bags and water taps.

**Woofter Park**
Rock Springs and Vegas Drive
Las Vegas NV
702-633-1171
Some of the amenities of this 9 acre neighborhood park include a fitness course, playground, and a fenced doggy play area. Dogs must be sociable, current

on all vaccinations and license, and under their owner's control at all times. Dogs must be leashed when not in designated off-lead areas.

## Dog-Friendly Parks
**Lake Mead National Recreation Area**
Lakeshore Rd/166
Boulder City NV
702-293-8907
nps.gov/lame/
This recreation area covers 1.5 million acres. The west side of the park is about 25 miles from downtown Las Vegas. We didn't see any designated trails, but leashed dogs are allowed on many of the trails and at the lake. To get there from Las Vegas, take Hwy 146 east to Lakeshore Rd./166. Lakeshore Rd. is the scenic drive along Lake Mead.

**Desert Breeze County Park**
8425 W. Spring Mtn. Road
Las Vegas NV

This county park has picnic tables, sports fields, a bike/walking path and a dog park. It is located approximately 5 miles east of downtown Las Vegas and the Strip. From Flamingo Road/589 in downtown, head west and pass Hwy 15. Turn right on Durango Drive. Then turn right onto Spring Mountain Road and the park will be on the corner. Dogs must be leashed, except for in the dog park.

**Floyd Lamb State Park**
9200 Tule Springs Road
Las Vegas NV
702-486-5413
This park offers tree-shaded groves alongside four small fishing lakes, allowing for nature study, and some of the amenities include picnic areas with tables and grills, restrooms, group areas, a walking/bicycle path that winds through the park, and historic sites. Dogs of all sizes are allowed at no additional fee.

Dogs may not be left unattended, and they must be leashed at all times, and cleaned up after. Times vary through the seasons, but the winter hours are from 7 am to 5 pm, and in June and July they are open from 7 am to 8 pm.

**Lorenzi Park**
3333 W. Washington Ave.
Las Vegas NV
702-229-6297
This park is about a mile west of downtown Las Vegas. Leashed dogs are allowed. Lorenzi Park features tennis courts, playgrounds, picnic tables and a five acre lake.

**Red Rock Canyon National Area**
Charleston Blvd/159
Las Vegas NV
702-363-1921
Located just 20-25 minutes west of downtown Las Vegas is the beautiful Red Rock Canyon National Conservation Area. This preserve has over 60,000 acres and includes unique geological formations. There is a popular 13 mile one-way scenic loop road that winds around the park, providing sightseeing, vistas and overlooks. Many of the hiking trails begin off this road. Leashed dogs are allowed on most of the trails. Some of the trails they are not allowed on are more like rock climbing expeditions than hiking trails. There are a variety of hiking trails ranging from easy to difficult. The visitor center is open daily and should have trail maps. On the trails, be aware of extreme heat or cold. Also watch out for flash floods, especially near creeks and streams. According to the BLM (Bureau of Land Management), violent downpours can cause flash flooding in areas untouched by rain. Do not cross low places when water is running through a stream. The park entrance fee is $5 per vehicle and $5 per dog. To get there from downtown Las Vegas, take Charleston

Blvd./159 and head west.

## Spring Mountain National Recreation Area
Echo Road
Mount Charleston NV
702-515-5400
This 316,000 acre park, part of the Toiyabe National Forest, is located about 35 miles northwest of Las Vegas. Mt. Charleston is located in this dog-friendly park and has many hiking trails. Temperatures here can average 25 to 30 degrees cooler than in Las Vegas. The Mary Jane Falls trail, located on Mt. Charleston, is one of the more popular trails. The trail passes a seasonal waterfall and several small caves. The trail is about 2.4 miles and starts at about 7840 foot elevation. To reach the trailhead, take State Route 157, travel 2 miles west of the ranger station to Echo Road. After traveling .35 mile, take the left fork off Echo Road and continue up until the road ends. Dogs must be on leash.

## Events
**Strut Your Mutt**
5800 E Flamingo/H 592
Las Vegas NV
702-455-8264
strutyourmuttlv.com/
This annual event (usually in November) is sponsored by the Clark County Parks and Recreation Department. It is an all day affair held at the Dog Fanciers Park. Th

## Laughlin

## Dog-Friendly Hotels
**Pioneer Hotel And Gambling Hall**
2200 South Casino Drive
Laughlin NV
702-298-2442 (800-634-3469)
With boat and watercraft parking and a location right on the Colorado River the Pioneer Hotel And Gambling Hall impresses our guests with low prices a 24-hour casino and Wi-

Fi. This 416-room mid-rise Pioneer Hotel And Gambling Hall sits on the banks of the river and offers complimentary Wi-Fi in public areas. Behind an Old West facade accommodations have Victorian touches and modern-day amenities such internet access cable TVs and work desks. Non-smoking options can be requested. You'll see plenty of cowboy hats in the restaurants lounges and the 24-hour casino with slots keno and card games including poker. Outside the hotel take a walk along a paved path at the river's edge. You can dock your boat or personal watercraft right outside the hotel. Fax and copy facilities are available. Pets are permitted with some restrictions. The Pioneer Hotel And Gambling Hall is located less than two hours from Las Vegas. Big Bend of the Colorado State Recreation Area is six miles away. Riverview Resort Golf Course is 15 minutes from the hotel. Laughlin/Bullhead International Airport is two miles away.

## Veterinarians
**Spirit Mountain Animal Hospital**
1670 E Lakeside Dr
Bullhead City NV
928-758-3979
This veterinary clinic has regular weekday hours.

## Mesquite

## Dog-Friendly Hotels
**Best Western Mesquite Inn**
390 N Sandhill Boulevard
Mesquite NV
702-346-7444 (800-780-7234)
Dogs up to 80 pounds are allowed. There is a $20 per day pet fee up to $100 for the week. Up to two dogs are allowed per room.

## Veterinarians
**Virgin Valley Veterinary Hospital**
660 Hardy Way Suite #44
Mesquite NV
702-346-4401
virginvalleyvets.com
This veterinary clinic is open from 8 to 6 on most days, 8 - 8 on Tuesday and 8 to 4 on Saturday.

## Minden

## Dog-Friendly Hotels
**Holiday Inn Express Hotel & Suites Minden**
1659 Hwy 88
Minden NV
775-782-7500 (877-270-6405)
Dogs of all sizes are allowed. Dogs are allowed for a pet fee of $20.00 per pet per stay.

## Overton

## Dog-Friendly Parks
**Valley of Fire State Park**
off Interstate 15, exit 75
Overton NV
702-397-2088
This park derives its name from red sandstone formations, formed from great shifting sand dunes during the age of dinosaurs, 150 million years ago. Ancient trees are represented throughout the park by areas of petrified wood. There is also a 3,000 year-old Indian petroglyph. Popular activities include camping, hiking, picnicking and photography. Sites of special interest are the Atlatl Rock, the Arch Rock, the Beehives, Elephant Rock, Seven Sisters, and more. There are many intriguing hikes available. Please inquire at the visitor

center for suggestions on day hikes of varying length and terrain. The visitor's center is open daily, 8:30am to 4:30pm. The park is open all year. Pets are welcome, but they must be kept on a leash of not more than six feet in length. They are not allowed in the visitor center. The park is located six miles from Lake Mead and 55 miles northeast of Las Vegas via Interstate 15 and on exit 75.

## Pahrump

### Dog-Friendly Hotels
**Best Western Pahrump Oasis**
1101 South Highway 160
Pahrump NV
775-727-5100 (800-780-7234)
Dogs are allowed. There is a $10 per pet per night fee.

## Panaca

### Dog-Friendly Parks
**Cathedral Gorge State Park**
P. O. Box 176
Panaca NV
775-728-4460
A geological delight, this park sits at 4,800 feet in a long, narrow valley and offers several trails to explore the cathedral spires and cave-like formations, including a 4 mile loop trail for accessing more remote areas. At Miller Point Overlook, there are excellent views of the canyon, and the visitor center offers interpretive displays and related information. Popular activities include nature study, photography, ranger programs, camping, hiking and picnicking. Dogs of all sizes are allowed for no additional fee. Dogs must be well mannered, be on no more than a 6 foot leash, and be cleaned up after. They are allowed throughout the park and on the trails; they are not

allowed in park buildings.

## Reno

### Dog-Friendly Hotels
**Baymont Inn And Suites Reno**
2050 B Market Street
Reno NV
775-786-2506
Dogs of all sizes are allowed. There is a pet fee of $10 per pet per night.

**Econo Lodge Near Reno-sparks Convention Center**
1885 South Virginia Street
Reno NV
775-329-1001 (877-424-6423)
Close to casinos and attractions. Close to Tahoe Rim trail. Year-round outdoor heated pool. Free Continental Breakfast.

Dogs up to 25 pounds are allowed. Dogs are allowed for a pet fee of $10.00 per pet per night. Two dogs are allowed per room.

**Holiday Inn Express Hotel & Suites Reno**
2375 Market Street
Reno NV
775-229-7070 (877-270-6405)
Dogs of all sizes are allowed. Dogs are allowed for a pet fee of $20.00 per pet per night.

**La Quinta Inn Reno**
4001 Market Street
Reno NV
775-348-6100 (800-531-5900)
Dogs of all sizes are allowed. There are no additional pet fees. Dogs must be leashed, cleaned up after, and crated or removed for housekeeping.

**Ramada Reno Hotel & Casino**
1000 East Sixth Street
Reno NV
775-786-5151
Dogs of all sizes are allowed. There is a pet fee of $10 per

day.

**Surestay Plus Hotel By Best Western Reno Airport**
1981 Terminal Way
Reno NV
775-348-6370 (800-780-7234)
Dogs up to 80 pounds are allowed. Up to two dogs are allowed per room.

**Vagabond Inn Reno**
3131 South Virginia Street
Reno NV
775-825-7134 (800-522-1555)
Low rates combined with a prime location between two of Reno's top casinos make the Vagabond Inn Executive Reno a good choice for budget travelers looking for some action. This two-story inn has 129 rooms featuring cable TV with HBO. Bring the whole family kids under 18 stay free with parents. In summer you'll all enjoy taking a dip in the seasonal outdoor pool. Continental breakfast and newspapers are available daily. Parking is free. Walk six minutes north and you're at the Peppermill Casino; six minutes south and you're at the Atlantis. Of course you're also within walking distance of countless restaurants and stores as well as Reno-Sparks Convention Center 15 minutes away. Reno-Tahoe International Airport is two miles from the hotel.

**Holiday Inn Reno-sparks**
55 East Nugget Avenue
Sparks NV
775-358-6900 (877-270-6405)
Dogs of all sizes are allowed. Dogs are allowed for a pet fee of $20.00 per pet per night.

**Super 8 Sparks**
1900 East Greg Street
Sparks NV
775-358-8884 (800-800-8000)
Dogs of all sizes are allowed. Dogs are allowed for a pet fee of $10 per pet per night.

**Western Village Inn And Casino**
815 Nichols Boulevard
Sparks NV
800-648-1170

westernvillagesparks.com/
A 24-hour casino four restaurants and bars free Wi-Fi and a free airport shuttle are among the impressive amenities that our guests will enjoy for rock-bottom rates at the Western Village Inn and Casino. Located in a separate building from the casino this quiet three-story hotel houses 147 smoking and non-smoking rooms with cable TV mini-fridges seating areas and coffee and tea service. For hearty meals guests choose among four restaurants: a steakhouse 24-hour cafe Mexican cantina and New York-style deli. There are also four bars to satisfy the thirsty and a festively lit casino for around-the-clock entertainment. Other amenities include a gift shop airport shuttle and free valet parking. Pets are welcome for an additional fee. The Western Village Inn is located next to the 77-acre Sparks Marina Park Lake offering boating swimming fishing and jogging paths. Downtown Sparks is a mile west of the hotel; downtown Reno is four miles further west. Reno-Tahoe International Airport is five miles away.

## Pet-Friendly Extended Stay Hotels

### Extended Stay America - Reno - South Meadows
9795 Gateway Drive
Reno NV
775-852-5611 (800-804-3724)
One dog is allowed per suite. There is a $25 per night additional pet fee up to $150 for an entire stay.

### Homewood Suites By Hilton Reno
5450 Kietzke Lane
Reno NV
775-853-7100
This upscale all suite hotel offers large, comfortable suites for longer stays and/or temporary housing needs;plus numerous on site amenities for

all level of travelers and a convenient location to local sites of interest. Dogs are allowed for an additional one time pet fee of $75 per room.

### Residence Inn Reno
9845 Gateway Drive
Reno NV
775-853-8800
Dogs of all sizes are allowed. There is a $100 one time additional pet fee.

### Staybridge Suites Reno Nevada
10559 Professional Circle
Reno NV
775-657-8999 (877-270-6405)
Dogs up to 30 pounds are allowed. Pets allowed with an additional pet fee. Up to $75 for 1-6 nights and up to $150 for 7+ nights. A pet agreement must be signed at check-in.

## Dog Camps

### Camp Winnaribbun
PO Box 50300
Reno NV
775-348-8412
campw.com/
This canine and human vacation destination, located at Lake Tahoe's south shore at Stateline, Nevada, offers summer camps amid 33 acres of pine forest and private beach. You and your pet can share, along with other campers and their dogs, dormitory style, rustic log cabin accommodations. Some of the activities include all levels of agility; lure coursing, pet and competitive obedience, craft projects with your dog, flyball, canine healing and homeopathies, tracking, herding, hiking, photo shoots, swimming, and a variety of games. There is also a costume contest, evening programs, campfire fun, and trained professionals dedicated to you and your pet having a great time. Meals, a week of lodging, and all the programs are included in the camping fee. Dogs must be healthy with

a valid Health Certificate, have proof of rabies vaccinations, and be under owner's control/care at all times.

## Dog-Friendly Attractions
### Scraps Dog Bakery at Sparks Marina
325 Harbour Cove Drive
Sparks NV
775-358-9663
myfavoritescraps.com
This Scraps dog bakery is located right along the 3 mill paved path that circles the lake at the Sparks Marina. This is a very dog friendly area. The dog bakery offers cookies and snacks for your dog as well as leashes, toys, food and other pet needs.

## Outdoor Restaurants
### 4th Street Bistro
3065 W 4th Street
Reno NV
775-323-3200
4thstbistro.com
In addition to a strong commitment to sustainable business practices and sourcing other like local companies, this market and seasonally driven eatery features a full menu of freshly prepared contemporary cuisine. Their all natural meats and organic produce are all obtained from sustainable ranches. Leashed, well mannered dogs are welcome at their outside tables.

### Archie's Grill
2195 N. Virginia St.
Reno NV
775-322-9595
archiesfamousgrill.com/
This restaurant serves breakfast, lunch and dinner. Your dog is allowed at the outdoor tables.

### Baja Fresh Mexican Grill
5140 Kietzke Ln.
Reno NV
775-826-8900
bajafresh.com
This Mexican restaurant is open

for lunch and dinner. They use fresh ingredients and making their salsa and beans daily. Some of the items on their menu include Enchiladas, Burritos, Tacos Salads, Quesadillas, Nachos, Chicken, Steak and more. Well-behaved leashed dogs are allowed at the outdoor tables.

**Jamba Juice**
5140 Kietzke Lane
Reno NV
775-828-5483
jambajuice.com
All natural and organic ingredients, no high-fructose corn syrup, 0 grams trans fat, no artificial preservatives, a healthy helping of antioxidants, vitamins, and minerals, and fresh whole fruit and fruit juices set the base for these tasty and healthy beverages. Their organic Hot Blends provides a new spin on coffee, green or chai tea, and hot chocolate;plus they offer probiotic fruit and yogurt Blends. Additionally, they feature organic steel-cut oatmeal prepared fresh every morning, all natural salads, wraps, sandwiches, and grab n' go specialties. They also offer healthy community support through fundraisers, special sales, and school lunch programs. Leashed, well mannered dogs are allowed at their outside dining area.

**Java Jungle**
246 W. 1st Street
Reno NV
775-329-4484
javajunglevino.com/
Java Jungle was voted Best Espresso and Cappuccino of Reno in the Reno Gazette-Journal reader surveys. The wide variety of their customers include lawyers and judges on their way to the Washoe County Courthouse as well as joggers and dog walkers. It

**My Favorite Muffin & Bagel Cafe**
340 California Ave.
Reno NV
775-333-1025

This cafe was voted Reno's Best Bagels. As the name of the cafe implies, they serve bagels and muffins. Your dog is allowed at the outdoor tables.

**Peg's Glorified Ham & Eggs**
420 S. Sierra St.
Reno NV
775-329-2600
eatatpegs.com/
This restaurant is located in downtown and has a few outdoor tables. Your dog is allowed at the outdoor tables.

**Riverview Café**
1 Lake Street
Reno NV
877-743-6233
sienareno.com/riverview
Located at the Siena Hotel, Spa and Casino, this café serves up breakfasts, brick oven pizzas, classic all American favorites, and a great setting overlooking the Truckee River. Leashed, well mannered dogs are allowed at their outside dining area.

**Sup Restaurant**
719 S Virginia Street
Reno NV
775-324-4787
myspace.com/stockpotinc
Gourmet, hand-crafted soups, freshly made salads and made-to order sandwiches with a focus on healthy, fresh and organic whenever possible. The Sup is open Monday thru Friday from 11 am until 4 pm for lunch and from 5 pm until 9 pm for dinner. Leashed, well mannered dogs are allowed at their outside tables.

**The Squeeze In**
5020 Las Brisas Blvd
Reno NV
775-787-2700
squeezein.com
This restaurant serves up a variety of specialty omelets, homemade soups, large fresh salads, signature sandwiches, burritos, and much more. They are open from 7 am until 2 pm. Leashed dogs are allowed at their outside dining area.

**The Stone House**
1907 S Arlington Avenue
Reno NV
775-284-3895
stonehousecafereno.com/
Set amid gardens and pines, this eatery features a full day's menu, seasonally influenced specials, freshly prepared foods, daily happy hours, and a European ambiance. Leashed, well mannered dogs are welcome at their outside tables.

**Walden's Coffee Co.**
3940 Mayberry Drive
Reno NV
775-787-3307
waldenscoffeehouse.net/
Your dog is welcome at the outdoor tables at coffee house. They have a variety of pastries and snacks available. The Scraps Dog Bakery is in the same shopping center (see Attractions.)

**Walden's Coffee House**
3940 Mayberry Drive
Reno NV
775-787-3307
waldenscoffeehouse.net/
Offerings at this coffee house include locally roasted and organic coffee, organic loose leaf teas, daily specials, seasonal offerings, in-house baked goods, vegetarian choices, and freshly prepared salads and sandwiches. They are open Monday to Thursday from 6 am until 7 pm;Friday from 6 am until 9 pm;Saturday from 7 am until 9 pm, and on Sunday from 7 am until 3 pm. Leashed, friendly dogs are allowed at their outside dining area. They are given water and usually a treat or 2 as well.

**Wild River Grille**
17 S Virginia Street, # 180/H 395
Reno NV
775-284-7455
wildrivergrille.com/
Beautifully situated on the River Walk downtown, this gathering place features a large riverside patio dining area, contemporary and innovative cuisine with

nature inspired influences, a full bar with handcrafted specialty cocktails, happy hours Monday to Friday, and special in-house events/specials. Leashed, well mannered dogs are allowed at their outside dining area.

## Z Pizza
4796 Caughlin Parkway
Reno NV
775-828-6565
zpizza.com
Specializing in organically and internationally inspired pizzas, this pizzeria cooks their pizzas on hot bricks in a fire baked oven. They feature a 100% certified organic gluten free wheat crust, homemade organic sauces and ingredients, fresh produce, and additive-free meats. They also offer gourmet salads, sandwiches, and catering services. Leashed, well mannered dogs are allowed at their outside tables.

## Zpizza
3600 Warren Way
Reno NV
775-828-6565
zpizza.com/
Specializing in organically and international inspired pizzas, this pizzeria also cooks their pizzas on hot bricks in a fire baked oven, and offering catering services. They are open Sunday through Thursday from 11 am until 9 pm, and on Friday and Saturday from 11 am until 10 pm. Leashed dogs are allowed at their outside dining area.

## Sunset Cove Coffee and Wine House
325 Harbour Cove Drive
Sparks NV
775-657-8505
This gourmet coffee and wine shop also serves up a breakfast and lunch menu of homemade, innovative comfort foods and a casual relaxed ambiance. Leashed, well mannered dogs are welcome at their outside dining area.

## Pet-Friendly Shopping

## Centers
### Legends Outlets Sparks
1310 Scheels Dr
Sparks NV
775-358-3800
experiencelegends.com
This outdoor shopping mall right next to the Sparks Marina 3 mile loop trail around the lake offers shopping and seasonal patio dining. You will need to check with each store to see which stores allow pets.

### Legends at Sparks Marina
1310 Scheels Drive
Sparks NV
775-358-3800
experiencelegends.com
Honoring the state's legends in a number of categories, this one destination gives guests a bit of history as well as a wide variety of shopping, dining, and entertainment opportunities. Dogs are allowed in the common areas of the mall; it is up to individual stores whether they allow a dog inside. Dogs must be well behaved, leashed, and under their owner's control at all times.

## Pet-Friendly Stores
### Harley Davidson of Reno
2295 Market Street
Reno NV
775-329-2913
harley-davidsonreno.com/
Well-behaved leashed dogs are allowed in this store. In addition to the motorcycles, they also sell collectibles, riding gear and accessories.

### Orvis Company Store
13945 S Virginia Street,
Summit Sierra, Suite 640
Reno NV
775-850-2272
orvis.com
This comprehensive outfitters store offers a wide array of sporting goods and services, clothing and accessories for all types of active lifestyles, quality products for home and pets, gifts and travel items, and much more. Well mannered

dogs are welcome in the store; they must be leashed and under their owner's control at all times.

### PetSmart Pet Store
6675 S Virginia St
Reno NV
775-852-8490
Your licensed and well-behaved leashed dog is allowed in the store.

### Petco Pet Store - Reno
5565 South Virginia St.
Reno NV
775-829-9200
Your licensed and well-behaved leashed dog is allowed in the store.

### Petco Pet Store - Reno - North
2970 Northtowne Lane
Reno NV
775-673-9200
Your licensed and well-behaved leashed dog is allowed in the store.

### Scraps Dog Bakery
3890 Mayberry Drive
Reno NV
775-787-3647 (888-332-DOGS)
go-reno.com/scraps/
Your dog is welcome inside this bakery which sells cookies and goodies for your pup. They also have a general store which sells other doggie items.

### Nevada Motorcycle Specialties
540 S Rock Blvd
Sparks NV
775-358-4388
nevadaktm.com/
These motorcycle specialists offer a comprehensive list of services and products for sale to keep happy bikers on the road - including trained mechanics and all the accessories needed to be on the go. They also allow friendly, leashed dogs to accompany their owners in checking out the store.

## Dog-Friendly Beaches
### Sparks Marina Dog Park and

**Beach**
300 Howard Drive
Reno NV
775-353-2376
This city park surrounding a 77 acre lake offers a wide variety of land and water activities and recreational pursuits. They also have the only fenced, off-lead dog park in the Reno area where dogs can play in the water. The off lead area is almost an acre in size on the south side of the marina and features lots of grass, 150 feet of shoreline, clean-up stations, a fire hydrant, and a doggie drinking fountain. The marina is surrounded by a walking trail almost 2 miles long that is lighted for nighttime walks with your pet. Dogs must be on leash when not in the fenced, off-lead area, and they must be cleaned up after at all times. Dogs are not allowed on any of the beaches except for the dog beach in the dog park.

**Sparks Marina Park**
300 Howard Drive
Reno NV
775-353-2376
This city park surrounding a 77 acre lake offers a wide variety of land and water activities and recreational pursuits. They also have the only fenced, off-lead dog park in the Reno area where dogs can play in the water. The off lead area is almost an acre in size on the south side of the marina and features lots of grass, 150 feet of shoreline, clean-up stations, a fire hydrant, and a doggie drinking fountain. The marina is surrounded by a walking trail almost 2 miles long that is lighted for nighttime walks with your pet. Dogs must be on leash when not in the fenced, off-lead area, and they must be cleaned up after at all times. Dogs are not allowed on any of the beaches except for the dog beach in the dog park.

**Off-Leash Dog Parks**
**Link Piazzo Dog Park**

4740 Parkway Drive
Reno NV
775-823-6501
facebook.com/LinkPiazzoDogP
ark/
Located at the Hidden Valley Regional Park, this fenced doggy play area offers double gated entry, separate areas for large and small dogs, shaded seating areas, watering stations, and walking trails. Dogs must be sociable, current on all vaccinations and license, and under their owner's control at all times. Dogs must be leashed when not in designated off-lead areas.

**Rancho San Rafael Regional Park**
1595 North Sierra Street
Reno NV
775-785-4512
Home to the annual Great Reno Balloon races, this huge park covers almost 600 acres of manicured turf, natural desert and wetlands, and has the largest off-leash space in the area. There is a pond and creek for dogs to play in with a walking path that surrounds it. Some of the amenities include benches, picnic areas, restrooms, and clean-up stations. Dogs must be on lead when not in the off leash areas, and there is signage indicating the areas in the park where pets are not allowed. Dogs must be cleaned up after at all times.

**Sparks Marina Dog Park and Beach**
300 Howard Drive
Reno NV
775-353-2376
This city park surrounding a 77 acre lake offers a wide variety of land and water activities and recreational pursuits. They also have the only fenced, off-lead dog park in the Reno area where dogs can play in the water. The off lead area is almost an acre in size on the south side of the marina and features lots of grass, 150 feet of shoreline, clean-up stations, a fire hydrant, and a doggie

drinking fountain. The marina is surrounded by a walking trail almost 2 miles long that is lighted for nighttime walks with your pet. Dogs must be on leash when not in the fenced, off-lead area, and they must be cleaned up after at all times. Dogs are not allowed on any of the beaches except for the dog beach in the dog park.

**Virginia Lake Dog Park**
Lakeside Drive
Reno NV
775-334-2099
This one acre dog park includes mitt dispensers. The park is located at Mountain View and Lakeside Drive, at the north field.

**Whitaker Dog Park**
550 University Terrace
Reno NV
775-334-2099
This fenced dog park is about .75 acres. Amenities include mitt dispensers.

**Dog-Friendly Parks**
**Donnelly Park**
Mayberry Drive
Reno NV

This is a small, but nice park to walk around with your dog. It is across the street from Scraps Dog Bakery and Walden's Coffee. Dogs must be leashed.

**Rancho San Rafael Park**
1595 N. Sierra Street
Reno NV
775-828-6642
Dogs are allowed in the undeveloped areas of this park. Dogs must be leashed with one exception. Dogs may be off-leash only at certain times at the multi-use pasture area. If there are special events or activities on the multi-use area then dogs are not allowed at all on the field. This includes when the hay is being cut and harvested. Portions of the field may be muddy when the pasture is being irrigated. Leashed dogs are allowed on a hiking and

walking path which crosses over McCarren Blvd. It is a dirt trail which narrows to a single track trail once you cross over McCarren Blvd. Just be careful when crossing over McCarren because the speed limit on the road is about 45-50mph. To get there from Hwy 80, exit Keystone Ave. Head north on Keystone. Turn right onto Coleman Drive. Take Coleman until it almost ends and turn right into the park. Park near the Coleman intersection and the trailhead will be nearby.

### Humboldt-Toiyabe National Forest
1200 Franklin Way
Sparks NV
775-331-6444
fs.usda.gov/htnf
The largest national forest in the lower 48 states, it covers 6.3 million acres and is located mostly in Nevada with a small portion in California. In addition to its spectacular scenery, it features hundreds of miles of trails and diverse ecosystems that support a large variety of flora, fauna, recreation, and educational opportunities. Due to its size and disbursement there are 10 ranger stations to oversee the park. Dogs are allowed for no additional fee; they must be leashed in all campgrounds, picnic areas and trailheads at all times. Dogs may not be left unattended.

### Pyramid Lake
Hwy 445
Sutcliffe NV
775-574-1000
pyramidlake.us/
Pyramid Lake is located in an Indian reservation, but visitors to the lake are welcomed guests of the Pyramid Lake Tribe of the Paiute Indians. Your leashed dog is also welcome. The lake is a beautiful contrast to the desert sandstone mountains which surround it. It is about 15 miles long by 11 miles wide, and among interesting rock formations. Pyramid Lake is Nevada's largest natural lake. It is popular for fishing and

photography. The north end of the lake is off-limits to visitors because it is a sacred area to the Paiutes. There is a beach area near the ranger's station in Sutcliffe. Be careful when wading into the water, as there are some ledges which drop off into deeper water. Also, do not wade in the water at the south end of the lake because the dirt acts like quick sand. The lake is about 35-40 minutes north of Reno, off Hwy 445.

### Airports
### Reno International Airport (RNO)

Reno NV

The Reno-Tahoe International Airport is proud to offer a special kind of customer service feature that caters to man?s (and woman's) best friend. We are proud to announce not one, but two dog parks to serve our four-legged passengers.

Since 2004, ?Gate K-9 Bark Park? has provided a convenient place where passengers traveling with their pets can give their dogs a restroom and water break. The Bark Park is fully fenced, with ADA accessibility, running water, mutt mitts to clean up after dogs, a fire hydrant and a canopy for inclement weather.

The original Gate K-9 Bark Park is located north of Baggage Claim. Just exit Door D by ground transportation and follow the paw prints to the Bark Park. In 2012, a second dog park opened for passengers flying out of Reno-Tahoe International with their pet. It is located south of the terminal building, just outside of the Southwest Airlines Ticket Counter.

### Emergency Veterinarians

### Animal Emergency Center
6425 S Virginia St
Reno NV
775-851-3600
Monday - Friday 6 pm to 8 am, Saturday noon - Monday 8 am.

### Other Organizations
### Shakespeare Animal Fund
P.O. Box 8201
Reno NV
775-342-7040
shakespeareanimalfund,org
To many of us a $50.00 medical bill at the vet is nothing, but for an elderly person on a fixed income, a single mother, a student, and for many others, it's an impossibility. There are many instances of elderly people doing without their own medicine or even food in order to care for their animals' medical needs. So what do you do if you love your animal but can't afford to pay the bill- Shakespeare Animal Fund, a non-profit charity was founded after the loss of a beloved Cocker Spaniel "Shakespeare". He died after a very costly illness, and in his memory this fund was founded to help others who might face financial problems while trying to save their pet. Shakespeare Animal Fund, a non-profit charity was founded after the loss of a beloved Cocker Spaniel "Shakespeare". He died after a very costly illness, and in his memory this fund was founded to help others who might face financial problems while trying to save their pet. Let Shakespeare help you!You can be a hero to people in need. Support the efforts of the Shakespeare Animal Fund with your donations of funding and of time.

## Tonopah

### Dog-Friendly Hotels
Tonopah Station Hotel And

**Casino**
1137 South Main Street
Tonopah NV
775-482-9777
Dogs of all sizes are allowed.
There is no pet fee. 2 large dogs
or 3 small dogs are allowedl

## Dog-Friendly Attractions
**Tonopah Historic Mining Park**
520 McCullough Avenue
Tonopah NV
775-482-9274
This 1900's, 110 acre mining
park is dedicated to restoring,
preserving, and educating
visitors to turn-of-the-century
mining with a comprehensive
museum that has ongoing and
changing exhibits, self-guided
paths around and into the mine
for a view down a 500 foot
stope, a visitor center/gift store
packed with books and specialty
items, and by events like the
annual Nevada State Mining
Championships. Dogs are
allowed throughout the park, in
the buildings, on all the trails,
and in the mine tunnels. Dogs
may be off lead if they are under
strict voice control and the park
or tunnels are not busy. Dogs
must be well behaved, under
their owner's control, and
cleaned up after at all times.

## Virginia City

## Dog-Friendly Attractions
**Comstock Firemen's Museum**
117 S. C St.
Virginia City NV
775-847-0717
comstockfiremuseum.com
The old fire station on the main
street of Virginia City serves as
a museum to the history of fire-
fighting in the Comstock region.
Well-behaved, leashed or
carried dogs may enter with you
to view the exhibits.

**Gold Panning Lessons**
C Street

Virginia City NV

In this alley off of main street in
Virginia City you will be given
lessons in gold panning. You
will learn how to search for gold
in streams and creeks. Just
head down the stairs to the
gold panning site. Your dog
may accompany you, although
we're not sure how useful they
will be in finding gold.

**Happy Hoofers Carriage
Service**

Virginia City NV
775-848-4421
happyhoofers.com
This carriage company features
a number of services in
addition to touring; they also
provide shuttle service,
wedding and special event
transport, use of carriages in
parades, and even hay rides.
The provide coverage for Reno,
Sparks, Carson City, Lake
Tahoe, the Sierra Mountains,
and the Virginia City area. The
will also let well mannered
dogs ride for no additional fee.
Dogs must be well mannered,
leashed, and under their
owner's control at all times.

**Masonic and Mt St Mary's
Cemeteries**
Just out of town
Virginia City NV
775-847-0281
comstockcemeteryfoundation.c
om
In these cemeteries lay some
of the founders and first
settlers of Virginia City, the
gold rush and the region. One
such celebrity is Captain
Edward Farris Storey, after
whom Storey County Nevada
was named. Captain Storey
was a casualty of the 1860
Pyramid Lake Indian War. The
cemetery is open for viewing
from dawn to dusk daily. Dogs
on leash are allowed. You must
be certain to clean up after
your dog.

**TNT Stagecoach Rides**
F Street across from the
Railroad

Virginia City NV
775-721-1496
Journey back to the old west
with one of the fastest
stagecoach rides you can find
without a time machine. These
four horses gallop around a oval
track to let you know what
transportation was truly like in
the 1800's. And your dog can go
too. The ride is bumpy, fast and
somewhat noisy so make sure
that your dog is up to the ride.
The price is $12 per adult, with
children 4 and under free. Dogs
are free.

**Virginia & Truckee Railroad
Co.**
565 S. K Street
Virginia City NV
775-847-0380
vtrailroad.com
You and your dog can ride back
in time on this steam train. The
train takes you on a leisurely 35
minute round trip to the historic
station in the city of Gold Hill.
Passengers can get off the train
at Gold Hill, visit the historic old
town and then board the next
train. The conductor gives a
narration of the many historic
sites you will view from the train.
Your dog is welcome to join you
on either the open air railcar or
the enclosed railcar. Trains
operate everyday from May
through October. The round trip
fare is about $5 for adults and
about $3 for children. Prices are
subject to change. Tickets can
be purchased at the railcar on C
Street or next to the train depot
near Washington and F Streets.
The train ride is located in
Virginia City, about 30-40
minutes south of Reno.

**Virginia City**
Hwy 341
Virginia City NV
775-847-0311
virginiacity-nv.com/
This small town was built in the
late 1800s and was a booming
mining town. The restored Old
Western town now has a variety
of shops with wooden walkways.
Dogs are allowed to window
shop with you. Dogs are also
welcome to ride the Virginia &

Truckee Steam Train with you. Virginia City is located about 30-40 minutes south of Reno.

## Virginia City Tractor Tram
C Street
Virginia City NV

This tram ride is pulled by a tractor and offers a 20 minute narrated tour of the old west town of Virginia City. Small dogs are ok on the tour and well-behaved, larger dogs may be accepted at their discretion if the tram is not packed.

## Outdoor Restaurants
### Virginia City Coffee House
North C Steet
Virginia City NV
775-847-0159
This coffee shop has an outdoor deck. Dogs may sit with you at the outdoor seats.

### Virginia City Jerky Company
204 C St
Virginia City NV
775-847-7444
This Barbecue restaurant at the end of the C Street business district in Virginia City has excellent ribs, pork and beef meals. There are a number of covered outdoor tables and your dog is welcome to accompany you at the patio seats.

## Pet-Friendly Stores
### Little City Items
145 C Street
Virginia City NV
775-847-4200
This unique Virginia City toy store has western type toys for kids of all ages. They will welcome your well-behaved, leashed dog to help you shop.

### Virginia City Mechantile
85 C Street
Virginia City NV
775-847-0184
virginiacitymercantile.com
This store specializes in things that are hard to find, nostalgic and funny. It is located on the

old west sidewalks of Virginia City. They are dog-friendly and usually have a water dish in front for dogs as well.

## Wells

## Dog-Friendly Hotels
### Super 8 Wells
Box 302 I-80 Exit 352
Wells NV
775-752-3384 (800-800-8000)
Dogs of all sizes are allowed. Dogs are allowed for a pet fee of $10.00 per pet per night.

## Winnemucca

## Dog-Friendly Hotels
### Best Western Plus Gold Country Inn
921 West Winnemucca Boulevard
Winnemucca NV
775-623-6999 (800-780-7234)
Dogs up to 80 pounds are allowed. There is a $15 per day pet fee up to $100 for the week. Up to two dogs are allowed per room.

### Country Hearth Inn Winnemucca
511 W Winnemucca Boulevard

Winnemucca NV
775-623-3661 (800-329-7466)
Dogs are welcome at this hotel.

### Super 8 Winnemucca
1157 West Winnemucca Boulevard
Winnemucca NV
775-625-1818 (800-800-8000)
Dogs are welcome at this hotel.

### Winnemucca Inn
741 West Winnemucca Boulevard
Winnemucca NV
775-623-2565

Dogs of all sizes are allowed. There is no fee with a credit card on file and there is a pet policy to sign at check in. Dogs are not allowed to be left alone in the room.

## Veterinarians
### Keystone Veterinary Hospital
1050 Grass Valley Rd
Winnemucca NV
775-623-5100
This veterinary clinic has regular weekday hours.

Chapter 3

# Dog-Friendly Highway Guides

## Guides to Highways To, From and Within California and Nevada

# Interstate 5 Accommodation Listings

## Washington Listings  (Interstate 5)

Dogs per Room

### Blaine

| | | | |
|---|---|---|---|
| Semiahmoo Resort And Spa | 360-371-2000 | 9565 Semiahmoo Parkway   Blaine WA | 1 |

### Ferndale

| | | | |
|---|---|---|---|
| Super 8 Bellingham Airport/ferndale | 360-384-8881 | Interstate 5 Exit 262 5788 Barrette Road   Ferndale WA | 1+ |

### Bellingham

| | | | |
|---|---|---|---|
| Econo Lodge Inn And Suites Bellingham | 360-671-4600 | 3750 Meridian Street   Bellingham WA | 1+ |
| Four Points By Sheraton Bellingham Hotel & Conference Center | 360-671-1011 | 714 Lakeway Drive   Bellingham WA | 1+ |
| Four Points By Sheraton Bellingham Hotel & Conference Center | 360-671-1011 | 714 Lakeway Drive   Bellingham WA | 1+ |
| Holiday Inn Express Bellingham | 360-671-4800 | 4160 Guide Meridian   Bellingham WA | 1+ |
| La Quinta Inn & Suites Bellingham | 360-738-7088 | 1063 West Bakerview Road   Bellingham WA | 1+ |
| Quality Inn Grand Suites | 360-647-8000 | 100 E. Kellogg Rd.   Bellingham WA | 1+ |
| Rodeway Inn Bellingham | 360-738-6000 | 3710 Meridian St.   Bellingham WA | 1+ |

### Mount Vernon

| | | | |
|---|---|---|---|
| Best Western College Way Inn | 360-424-4287 | 300 West College Way   Mount Vernon WA | 1+ |
| Days Inn Mt. Vernon | 360-424-4141 | 2009 Riverside Drive   Mount Vernon WA | 1+ |
| Quality Inn Mount Vernon | 360-428-7020 | 1910 Freeway Drive   Mount Vernon WA | 1+ |

### Arlington

| | | | |
|---|---|---|---|
| Quality Inn Near Seattle Premium Outlets | 360-403-7222 | 5200 172nd Street N.e.   Arlington WA | 1+ |

### Marysville

| | | | |
|---|---|---|---|
| Holiday Inn Express Hotel & Suites Marysville | 360-530-1234 | 8606 36th Ave Ne   Marysville WA | 1+ |

### Everett

| | | | |
|---|---|---|---|
| Best Western Cascadia Inn | 425-258-4141 | 2800 Pacific Avenue   Everett WA | 1+ |
| Best Western Plus Navigator Inn & Suites | 425-347-2555 | 10210 Evergreen Way   Everett WA | 1+ |
| Days Inn Everett | 425-355-1570 | 1602 Se Everett Mall Way   Everett WA | 1+ |
| Extended Stay America Seattle - Everett - North | 425-355-1923 | 8410 Broadway   Everett WA | 1+ |
| La Quinta Inn Everett | 425-347-9099 | 12619 4th Avenue West   Everett WA | 2 |

### Lynnwood

| | | | |
|---|---|---|---|
| Embassy Suites Hotel Seattle-north/lynnwood | 425-775-2500 | 20610 44th Ave West   Lynnwood WA | 1+ |
| Extended Stay America Seattle - Lynnwood | 425-670-2520 | 3021 196th Street Sw   Lynnwood WA | 1+ |
| La Quinta Inn Lynnwood | 425-775-7447 | 4300 Alderwood Mall Boulevard   Lynnwood WA | 1+ |
| Residence Inn Bellevue | 425-882-1222 | 14455 Ne 29th Place   Lynnwood WA | 1+ |

### Seattle

| | | | |
|---|---|---|---|
| Country Inn & Suites By Radisson Seattle-tacoma Airport | 206-433-8188 | 3100 South 192nd   Seattle WA | 1+ |

| | | | |
|---|---|---|---|
| Homewood Suites By Hilton Seattle-downtown | 206-281-9393 | 206 Western Avenue West   Seattle WA | 1+ |
| Kimpton Alexis Hotel | 206-624-4844 | 1007 First Avenue   Seattle WA | 3+ |
| Kimpton Hotel Monaco Seattle | 206-621-1770 | 1101 Fourth Avenue   Seattle WA | 3+ |
| Kimpton Hotel Vintage Seattle | 206-624-8000 | 1100 Fifth Avenue   Seattle WA | 3+ |
| La Quinta Inn & Suites Seattle Downtown | 206-624-6820 | 2224 8th Ave   Seattle WA | 3+ |
| La Quinta Inn Sea Tac Seattle Airport | 206-241-5211 | 2824 South 188th Street   Seattle WA | 3+ |
| Motif Seattle | 206-971-8000 | 1415 Fifth Avenue   Seattle WA | 2 |
| Pan Pacific Seattle | 206-264-8111 | 2125 Terry Avenue   Seattle WA | 1+ |
| Renaissance Seattle Hotel | 206-583-0300 | 515 Madison Street   Seattle WA | 1+ |
| Residence Inn By Marriott Spokane East Valley | 509-892-9300 | 15915 East Indiana Avenue   Seattle WA | 1+ |
| Sheraton Seattle | 206-621-9000 | 1400 Sixth Avenue   Seattle WA | 2 |
| Staypineapple At University Inn | 206-632-5055 | 4140 Roosevelt Way Northeast   Seattle WA | 2 |
| The Fairmont Olympic Hotel Seattle | 206-621-1700 | 411 University Street   Seattle WA | 1+ |
| The Westin Seattle | 206-728-1000 | 1900 Fifth Ave   Seattle WA | 1+ |
| W Seattle Hotel | 206-264-6000 | 1112 Fourth Ave   Seattle WA | 2 |
| **Fife** | | | |
| Quality Inn And Suites Fife/tacoma | 253-922-2500 | 5805 Pacific Highway East   Fife WA | 1+ |
| **Tacoma** | | | |
| La Quinta Inn & Suites Tacoma Seattle | 253-383-0146 | 1425 East 27th Street   Tacoma WA | 2 |
| **Olympia** | | | |
| Candlewood Suites Olympia - Lacey | 360-491-1698 | 4440 3rd Avenue Southeast   Lacey WA | 1+ |
| La Quinta Inn Olympia - Lacey | 360-412-1200 | 4704 Park Center Ave Northeast   Lacey WA | 3+ |
| Quality Inn & Suites Lacey | 360-493-1991 | 120 College Street Southeast   Lacey WA | 1+ |
| Best Western Plus Lacey Inn & Suites | 360-456-5655 | 8326 Quinault Drive North East   Olympia WA | 1+ |
| Best Western Tumwater Inn | 360-956-1235 | 5188 Capitol Blvd Se   Olympia WA | 1+ |
| Quality Inn Olympia | 360-943-4710 | 1211 Quince Street Southeast   Olympia WA | 1+ |
| Comfort Inn Conference Center Tumwater - Olympia | 360-352-0691 | 1620 74th Ave. Sw   Tumwater WA | 1+ |
| Extended Stay America - Olympia - Tumwater | 360-754-6063 | 1675 Mottman Road Sw   Tumwater WA | 1+ |
| **Chehalis** | | | |
| Holiday Inn Express Hotel & Suites Chehalis-centralia | 360-740-1800 | 730 Nw Liberty Plaza   Chehalis WA | 1+ |
| **Kelso** | | | |
| Best Western Aladdin Inn | 360-425-9660 | 310 Long Avenue   Kelso WA | 1+ |
| Econo Lodge Kelso | 360-636-4610 | 505 North Pacific Avenue   Kelso WA | 1+ |
| Red Lion Hotel Kelso | 360-636-4400 | 510 Kelso Drive   Kelso WA | 2 |
| Super 8 Kelso Longview Area | 360-423-8880 | 250 Kelso Drive   Kelso WA | 1+ |
| **Vancouver** | | | |
| Comfort Inn & Suites Vancouver | 360-696-0411 | 401 E 13th Street   Vancouver WA | 1+ |
| Comfort Suites Vancouver | 360-253-3100 | 4714 N E 94th Ave   Vancouver WA | 1+ |

| | | | |
|---|---|---|---|
| Days Inn & Suites Vancouver | 360-253-5000 | 9107 Ne Vancouver Mall Drive   Vancouver WA | 1+ |
| Econo Lodge Vancouver | 360-693-3668 | 601 Broadway   Vancouver WA | 1+ |
| Extended Stay America - Portland - Vancouver | 360-604-8530 | 300 Ne 115th Avenue   Vancouver WA | 1+ |
| Hilton Vancouver Washington | 360-993-4500 | 301 W 6th Street   Vancouver WA | 1+ |
| Homewood Suites By Hilton Vancouver-portland | 360-750-1100 | 701 Se Columbia Shores   Vancouver WA | 1+ |
| Howard Johnson Vancouver Wa | 360-254-0900 | 9201 Ne Vancouvermall Dr   Vancouver WA | 1+ |
| La Quinta Inn & Suites Vancouver | 360-566-1100 | 1500 Northeast 134th Street   Vancouver WA | 3+ |
| La Quinta Inn & Suites Vancouver | 360-566-1100 | 1500 Northeast 134th Street   Vancouver WA | 1+ |
| Quality Inn & Suites Vancouver | 360-696-0516 | 7001 N.e. Highway 99   Vancouver WA | 1+ |
| Quality Inn Vancouver | 360-574-6000 | 13207 North East 20th Avenue   Vancouver WA | 1+ |
| Residence Inn By Marriott Seattle Northeast-bothell | 425-485-3030 | 11920 Ne 195th Street   Vancouver WA | 1+ |
| Staybridge Suites Vancouver Portland | 360-891-8282 | 7301 Northeast 41st Street   Vancouver WA | 1+ |
| **Woodland** | | | |
| Rodeway Inn - Woodland | 360-225-6548 | 1500 Atlantic Avenue   Woodland WA | 2 |

# Oregon Listings  (Interstate 5)

Dogs per Room

| | | | |
|---|---|---|---|
| **Portland** | | | |
| Residence Inn Portland South - Lake Oswego | 503-684-2603 | 15200 Sw Bangy Road   Lake Oswego OR | 1+ |
| Courtyard By Marriott Portland City Center | 503-505-5000 | 550 Sw Oak Street   Portland OR | 1+ |
| Dossier A Provenance Hotel | 503-294-9000 | 750 Sw Alder Street   Portland OR | 3+ |
| Hilton Portland Downtown | 503-226-1611 | 921 Sw Sixth Avenue   Portland OR | 1+ |
| Kimpton Hotel Vintage Portland | 503-228-1212 | 422 Southwest Broadway   Portland OR | 3+ |
| Kimpton Riverplace Hotel | 503-288-3233 | 1510 Southwest Harbor Way   Portland OR | 3+ |
| Residence Inn By Marriott Portland Downtown/riverplace | 503-552-9500 | 2115 Sw River Parkway   Portland OR | 1+ |
| Residence Inn By Marriott Portland North | 503-285-9888 | 1250 North Anchor Way   Portland OR | 1+ |
| The Nines A Luxury Collection Hotel Portland | 877-229-9995 | 525 Southwest Morrison   Portland OR | 2 |
| La Quinta Inn Wilsonville | 503-682-3184 | 8815 South West Sun Place   Wilsonville OR | 3+ |
| **Woodburn** | | | |
| Best Western Woodburn | 503-982-6515 | 2887 Newberg Highway   Woodburn OR | 1+ |
| Super 8 Woodburn | 503-981-8881 | 821 Evergreen Rd.   Woodburn OR | 1+ |
| **Salem** | | | |
| Best Western Pacific Highway Inn | 503-390-3200 | 4646 Portland Road Northeast   Salem OR | 1+ |
| Best Western Plus Mill Creek Inn | 503-585-3332 | 3125 Ryan Drive Southeast   Salem OR | 1+ |
| Comfort Suites Airport Salem | 503-585-9705 | 630 Hawthorne Southeast   Salem OR | 1+ |
| Howard Johnson Inn Salem | 503-375-7710 | 2250 Mission St. Se   Salem OR | 1+ |
| La Quinta Inn & Suites Salem Or | 503-391-7000 | 890 Hawthorne Avenue Southeast   Salem OR | 1+ |
| Red Lion Hotel Salem | 503-370-7888 | 3301 Market Street Ne   Salem OR | 3+ |
| Residence Inn By Marriott Salem | 503-585-6500 | 640 Hawthorne Avenue Southeast   Salem OR | 1+ |
| Super 8 Salem | 503-370-8888 | 1288 Hawthorne Ne   Salem OR | 1+ |

## Albany

| | | | |
|---|---|---|---|
| Best Western Plus Prairie Inn | 541-928-5050 | 1100 Price Road South East   Albany OR | 1+ |
| Comfort Suites Linn County Fairground And Expo | 541-928-2053 | 100 Opal Court Northeast   Albany OR | 1+ |
| Holiday Inn Express Hotel And Suites Albany | 541-928-8820 | 105 Opal Court Ne   Albany OR | 1+ |
| Quality Inn & Suites Albany | 541-928-0921 | 251 Airport Road Southeast   Albany OR | 3+ |
| Rodeway Inn Albany | 541-926-0170 | 1212 Se Price Road   Albany OR | 1+ |
| Super 8 Albany | 541-928-6322 | 315 Airport Road Se   Albany OR | 1+ |

## Eugene

| | | | |
|---|---|---|---|
| Best Western Greentree Inn | 541-485-2727 | 1759 Franklin Blvd.   Eugene OR | 1+ |
| Days Inn Eugene Downtown/university | 541-342-6383 | 1859 Franklin Boulevard   Eugene OR | 1+ |
| Hilton Eugene | 541-342-2000 | 66 East Sixth Avenue   Eugene OR | 1+ |
| La Quinta Inn & Suites Eugene | 541-344-8335 | 155 Day Island Road   Eugene OR | 3+ |
| Residence Inn Eugene | 541-342-7171 | 25 Club Road   Eugene OR | 1+ |
| Valley River Inn | 541-687-0123 | 1000 Valley River Way   Eugene OR | 2 |

## Creswell

| | | | |
|---|---|---|---|
| Comfort Inn & Suites Creswell | 541-895-4025 | 247 Melton Road   Creswell OR | 1+ |
| Super 8 Creswell | 541-895-3341 | 345 East Oregon Avenue   Creswell OR | 1+ |

## Cottage Grove

| | | | |
|---|---|---|---|
| Quality Inn Cottage Grove | 541-942-9747 | 845 Gateway Boulevard   Cottage Grove OR | 1+ |

## Roseburg

| | | | |
|---|---|---|---|
| Best Western Garden Villa Inn | 541-672-1601 | 760 Northwest Garden Valley Boulevard   Roseburg OR | 1+ |
| Holiday Inn Express Roseburg | 541-673-7517 | 375 West Harvard Boulevard   Roseburg OR | 1+ |
| Quality Inn Central Roseburg | 541-673-5561 | 427 Northwest Garden Valley Boulevard   Roseburg OR | 1+ |
| Sleep Inn & Suites Roseburg | 541-464-8338 | 2855 Northwest Edenbower Boulevard   Roseburg OR | 1+ |
| Super 8 Roseburg | 541-672-8880 | 3200 North West Aviation Drive   Roseburg OR | 1+ |
| Travelodge Roseburg | 541-672-4836 | 315 West Harvard Avenue   Roseburg OR | 1+ |

## Grants Pass

| | | | |
|---|---|---|---|
| Best Western Grants Pass Inn | 541-476-1117 | 111 N.e. Agness Ave.   Grants Pass OR | 1+ |
| Holiday Inn Express Grants Pass | 541-471-6144 | 105 North East Agness Avenue   Grants Pass OR | 1+ |
| Quality Inn Grants Pass | 541-479-8301 | 1889 Ne 6th St.   Grants Pass OR | 1+ |
| Super 8 Grants Pass | 541-474-0888 | 1949 North East 7th Street   Grants Pass OR | 1+ |

## Medford

| | | | |
|---|---|---|---|
| Best Western Horizon Inn | 541-779-5085 | 1154 E Barnett Road   Medford OR | 1+ |
| Candlewood Suites Medford | 541-772-2800 | 3548 Heathrow Way   Medford OR | 1+ |
| Homewood Suites By Hilton Medford | 541-779-9800 | 2010 Hospitality Way   Medford OR | 1+ |
| Inn At The Commons | 541-779-5811 | 200 North Riverside   Medford OR | 3+ |
| Ramada Medford & Convention Center | 541-779-3141 | 2250 Biddle Road   Medford OR | 3+ |
| Ramada Medford & Convention Center | 541-779-3141 | 2250 Biddle Road   Medford OR | 1+ |
| Towneplace Suites By Marriott Medford | 541-842-5757 | 1395 Center Drive   Medford OR | 1+ |

| | | | |
|---|---|---|---|
| Travelers Inn Medford | | 954 Alba Drive   Medford OR | 1+ |

## Ashland

| | | | |
|---|---|---|---|
| Ashland Hills Hotel & Suites | 541-482-8310 | 2525 Ashland Street   Ashland OR | 2 |
| Bard's Inn | 541-482-0049 | 132 North Main Street   Ashland OR | 1+ |
| Best Western Windsor Inn | 541-488-2330 | 2520 Ashland Street   Ashland OR | 1+ |
| Comfort Inn & Suites Ashland | 541-482-6932 | 434 S. Valley View Rd   Ashland OR | 3+ |
| Econo Lodge Ashland | 541-482-4700 | 50 Lowe Road   Ashland OR | 1+ |
| Holiday Inn Express Hotel & Suites Ashland | 541-201-0202 | 565 Clover Lane   Ashland OR | 1+ |

# California Listings  (Interstate 5)

Dogs per Room

## Marysville

| | | | |
|---|---|---|---|
| Comfort Suites Beale Air Force Base Area | 530-742-9200 | 1034 North Beale Road   Marysville CA | 1+ |

## Yreka

| | | | |
|---|---|---|---|
| Baymont Inn Yreka | 530-841-1300 | 148 Moonlit Oaks Avenue   Yreka CA | 1+ |
| Best Western Miners Inn | 530-842-4355 | 122 East Miner Street   Yreka CA | 1+ |
| Comfort Inn Yreka | 530-842-1612 | 1804 B Fort Jones Rd   Yreka CA | 1+ |
| Econo Lodge Inn & Suites | 530-842-4404 | 526 South Main Street   Yreka CA | 1+ |
| Relax Inn Yreka | 530-842-2791 | 1210 South Main Street   Yreka CA | 2 |
| Rodeway Inn Yreka | 530-842-4412 | 1235 South Main Street   Yreka CA | 1+ |

## Mount Shasta

| | | | |
|---|---|---|---|
| Dunsmuir Lodge | 530-235-2884 | 6604 Dunsmuir Avenue   Dunsmuir CA | 1+ |
| Comfort Inn Mount Shasta Area | 530-938-1982 | 1844 Shastina Dr   Weed CA | 1+ |
| Quality Inn & Suites Weed | 530-938-1308 | 1830 Black Butte Drive   Weed CA | 1+ |

## Redding

| | | | |
|---|---|---|---|
| Best Western Plus Twin View Inn & Suites | 530-241-5500 | 1080 Twin View Boulevard   Redding CA | 1+ |
| Bridge Bay Resort | 530-275-3021 | 10300 Bridge Bay Road   Redding CA | 1+ |
| Comfort Inn Redding | 530-221-4472 | 850 Mistletoe Lane   Redding CA | 1+ |
| La Quinta Inn & Suites Redding | 530-221-8200 | 2180 Hilltop Drive   Redding CA | 3+ |
| Quality Inn Redding | 530-221-6530 | 2059 Hilltop Dr.   Redding CA | 1+ |
| Ramada Limited Redding | 530-246-2222 | 1286 Twin View Boulevard   Redding CA | 1+ |
| Red Lion Redding | 530-221-8700 | 1830 Hilltop Dr   Redding CA | 3+ |

## Anderson

| | | | |
|---|---|---|---|
| Baymont Inn & Suites Anderson | 530-365-6100 | 2040 Factory Outlets Drive   Anderson CA | 1+ |
| Best Western Anderson Inn | 530-365-2753 | 2688 Gateway Drive   Anderson CA | 1+ |

## Red Bluff

| | | | |
|---|---|---|---|
| Best Western Antelope Inn | 530-527-8882 | 203 Antelope Boulevard   Red Bluff CA | 1+ |
| Comfort Inn Red Bluff | 530-529-7060 | 90 Sale Lane   Red Bluff CA | 1+ |
| Days Inn Red Bluff | 530-527-6130 | 5 Sutter Street   Red Bluff CA | 1+ |
| Super 8 Red Bluff | 530-529-2028 | 30 Gilmore Road   Red Bluff CA | 1+ |
| Travelodge Red Bluff | 530-527-6020 | 38 Antelope Boulevard   Red Bluff CA | 1+ |

## Corning

| | | | |
|---|---|---|---|
| Best Western Plus Corning Inn | 530-824-5200 | 910 Highway 99 W   Corning CA | 1+ |
| Econo Lodge Inn & Suites Corning | 530-824-2000 | 3475 Highway 99 West   Corning CA | 1+ |
| Holiday Inn Express Corning | 530-824-6400 | 3350 Sunrise Way   Corning CA | 1+ |

## Willows

| | | | |
|---|---|---|---|
| Best Western Willows Inn | 530-934-4444 | 475 North Humboldt Avenue   Willows CA | 1+ |
| Holiday Inn Express Hotel & Suites Willows | 530-934-8900 | 545 Humboldt Avenue   Willows CA | 1+ |
| Willows Travelodge | 530-934-4603 | 249 North Humboldt Avenue   Willows CA | 1+ |

## Williams

| | | | |
|---|---|---|---|
| Econo Lodge Williams | 530-473-2381 | 400 C Street   Williams CA | 1+ |
| Ramada Williams | 530-473-5120 | 374 Ruggeiri Way   Williams CA | 1+ |

## Woodland

| | | | |
|---|---|---|---|
| Holiday Inn Express Sacramento Airport Woodland | 530-662-7750 | 2070 Freeway Drive   Woodland CA | 1+ |

## Sacramento

| | | | |
|---|---|---|---|
| La Quinta Inn Sacramento Downtown | 916-448-8100 | 200 Jibboom Street   Sacramento CA | 3+ |
| Residence Inn Sacramento Airport Natomas | 916-649-1300 | 2618 Gateway Oaks Drive   Sacramento CA | 1+ |
| Residence Inn Sacramento Airport Natomas | 916-649-1300 | 2618 Gateway Oaks Drive   Sacramento CA | 1+ |
| Sheraton Grand Sacramento Hotel | 916-447-1700 | 1230 J Street   Sacramento CA | 3+ |
| Surestay Plus Hotel By Best Western Sacramento North | 916-442-6971 | 350 Bercut Drive   Sacramento CA | 1+ |

## Stockton

| | | | |
|---|---|---|---|
| Microtel Inn & Suites By Wyndham Lodi/north Stockton | 209-367-9700 | 6428 West Banner Street   Lodi CA | 1+ |
| La Quinta Inn Stockton | 209-952-7800 | 2710 West March Lane   Stockton CA | 3+ |
| Residence Inn By Marriott Stockton | 209-472-9800 | 3240 March Lane   Stockton CA | 1+ |

## Lathrop

| | | | |
|---|---|---|---|
| Days Inn Lathrop | 209-982-1959 | 14750 S. Harlan Road   Lathrop CA | 1+ |
| Holiday Inn Express Lathrop - South Stockton | 209-373-2700 | 15688 South Harlan Road   Lathrop CA | 1+ |
| Quality Inn & Suites Lathrop | 209-858-1234 | 16855 Harlan Road   Lathrop CA | 1+ |

## Santa Nella

| | | | |
|---|---|---|---|
| Quality Inn Santa Nella | 209-826-8282 | 28976 West Plaza Drive   Santa Nella CA | 1+ |

## Los Banos

| | | | |
|---|---|---|---|
| Best Western Executive Inn | 209-827-0954 | 301 W. Pacheco Boulevard   Los Banos CA | 1+ |
| Red Roof Inn Los Banos | 209-826-9690 | 2169 East Pacheco Boulevard   Los Banos CA | 1+ |
| Sun Star Inn | 209-826-3805 | 839 West Pacheco Boulevard   Los Banos CA | 3+ |

## Coalinga

| | | | |
|---|---|---|---|
| Best Western Big Country Inn | 559-935-0866 | 25020 West Dorris Avenue   Coalinga CA | 1+ |
| Coalinga Travelodge | 559-935-2063 | 25278 West Dorris Avenue   Coalinga CA | 1+ |

## Lost Hills

| | | | |
|---|---|---|---|
| Days Inn Lost Hills | 661-797-2371 | 14684 Aloma Street   Lost Hills CA | 1+ |

## Buttonwillow

| | | | |
|---|---|---|---|
| Motel 6 Buttonwillow Central | 661-764-5121 | 20645 Tracy Avenue   Buttonwillow CA | 1+ |
| Rodeway Inn I-5 At Rt. 58 | 661-764-5207 | 20688 Tracy Avenue   Buttonwillow CA | 1+ |
| Super 8 Buttonwillow | 661-764-5117 | 20681 Tracy Avenue   Buttonwillow CA | 1+ |
| **Lebec** | | | |
| Holiday Inn Express Hotel Frazier Park | 661-248-1600 | 612 Wainwright Court   Lebec CA | 1+ |
| Ramada Limited Lebec | 661-248-1530 | 9000 Countryside Ct   Lebec CA | 1+ |
| **Gorman** | | | |
| Studio 6 Gorman | 661-248-6411 | 49713 Gorman Post Road   Gorman CA | 1+ |
| **Castaic** | | | |
| Rodeway Inn Magic Mountain Area | 661-295-1100 | 31558 Castaic Road   Castaic CA | 1+ |
| **Santa Clarita** | | | |
| Fairfield Inn By Marriott Santa Clarita Valencia | 661-290-2828 | 25340 The Old Road   Santa Clarita CA | 1+ |
| Residence Inn By Marriott Santa Clarita Valencia | 661-290-2800 | 25320 The Old Road   Santa Clarita CA | 1+ |
| Extended Stay America - Los Angeles - Valencia | 661-255-1044 | 24940 Pico Canyon Rd   Stevenson Ranch CA | 1+ |
| La Quinta Inn & Suites Stevenson Ranch | 661-286-1111 | 25201 The Old Road   Stevenson Ranch CA | 2 |
| **Hollywood - West LA** | | | |
| Los Angeles Marriott Burbank Airport | 818-843-6000 | 2500 North Hollywood Way   Burbank CA | 1+ |
| Residence Inn Los Angeles Burbank/downtown | 818-260-8787 | 321 Ikea Way   Burbank CA | 1+ |
| **Anaheim Resort Area** | | | |
| Residence Inn Anaheim Maingate | 714-533-3555 | 1700 South Clementine Street   Anaheim CA | 1+ |
| Sheraton Park Hotel At The Anaheim Resort | 714-750-1811 | 1855 South Harbor Boulevard   Anaheim CA | 1 |
| Towneplace Suites By Marriott Anaheim Maingate Angel Stadium | 714-939-9700 | 1730 South State College Boulevard   Anaheim CA | 1+ |
| Anaheim Marriott Suites | 714-750-1000 | 12015 Harbor Boulevard   Garden Grove CA | 1+ |
| Sheraton Garden Grove-anaheim South | 714-703-8400 | 12221 Harbor Boulevard   Garden Grove CA | 1 |
| **Orange County South** | | | |
| Doubletree Suites By Hilton Doheny Beach - Dana Point | 949-661-1100 | 34402 Pacific Coast Highway   Dana Point CA | 3+ |
| La Quinta Inn & Suites Irvine Spectrum | 949-551-0909 | 14972 Sand Canyon Avenue   Irvine CA | 3+ |
| **San Diego County North** | | | |
| Homewood Suites By Hilton Carlsbad-north San Diego County | 760-431-2266 | 2223 Palomar Airport Road   Carlsbad CA | 1+ |
| La Quinta Inn San Diego-carlsbad | 760-438-2828 | 760 Macadamia Drive   Carlsbad CA | 3+ |
| Ramada Carlsbad | 760-438-2285 | 751 Macadamia Drive   Carlsbad CA | 1+ |
| Sheraton Carlsbad Resort & Spa | 760-827-2400 | 5480 Grand Pacific Drive   Carlsbad CA | 1 |
| Hilton San Diego/del Mar | 858-792-5200 | 15575 Jimmy Durante Boulevard   Del Mar CA | 1+ |
| Quality Inn Encinitas Near Legoland | 760-944-3800 | 607 Leucadia Boulevard   Encinitas CA | 1+ |
| La Quinta Inn San Diego Oceanside | 760-450-0730 | 937 North Coast Highway   Oceanside CA | 3+ |
| Ramada Oceanside | 760-967-4100 | 1440 Mission Avenue   Oceanside CA | 1+ |
| Towneplace Suites By Marriott San Diego Carlsbad-vista | 760-216-6010 | 2201 South Melrose Drive   Vista CA | 1+ |

## San Diego

| | | | |
|---|---|---|---|
| Loews Coronado Bay Resort | 619-424-4000 | 4000 Coronado Bay Road   Coronado CA | 2 |
| La Valencia Hotel | 858-454-0771 | 1132 Prospect Street   La Jolla CA | 1+ |
| Residence Inn La Jolla | 858-587-1770 | 8901 Gilman Drive   La Jolla CA | 1+ |
| Sheraton La Jolla | 858-453-5550 | 3299 Holiday Court   La Jolla CA | 2 |
| Doubletree Hotel San Diego/del Mar | 858-481-5900 | 11915 El Camino Real   San Diego CA | 2 |
| Hampton Inn San Diego/del Mar | 858-792-5557 | 11920 El Camino Real   San Diego CA | 1+ |
| Hilton San Diego Airport/harbor Island | 619-291-6700 | 1960 Harbor Island Drive   San Diego CA | 1+ |
| Hilton San Diego Bayfront | 619-564-3333 | 1 Park Boulevard   San Diego CA | 1+ |
| Hilton San Diego Gaslamp Quarter | 619-231-4040 | 401 K Street   San Diego CA | 1+ |
| Hotel Republic San Diego Autograph Collection | 619-398-3100 | 421 West B Street   San Diego CA | 2 |
| Kimpton Hotel Palomar San Diego | 619-515-3000 | 1047 5th Avenue   San Diego CA | 3+ |
| Kimpton Solamar Hotel | 619-531-8740 | 435 6th Avenue   San Diego CA | 3+ |
| Kona Kai Resort & Marina A Noble House Resort | 619-221-8000 | 1551 Shelter Island Drive   San Diego CA | 1 |
| La Quinta Inn San Diego Old Town | 619-291-9100 | 2380 Moore Street   San Diego CA | 3+ |
| Old Town Inn | 619-260-8024 | 4444 Pacific Highway   San Diego CA | 1+ |
| San Diego Marriott Del Mar | 858-523-1700 | 11966 El Camino Real   San Diego CA | 1+ |
| Sheraton San Diego Hotel And Marina | 619-291-2900 | 1380 Harbor Island Drive   San Diego CA | 2 |
| The Us Grant A Luxury Collection Hotel San Diego | 619-232-3121 | 326 Broadway   San Diego CA | 3+ |
| The Westin San Diego | 619-239-4500 | 400 West Broadway   San Diego CA | 1 |
| The Westin San Diego Gaslamp Quarter | 619-937-8461 | 910 Broadway Circle   San Diego CA | 2 |

# Highway 101 Accommodation Listings

# Washington Listings   (Highway 101)

Dogs per Room

## Olympia

| | | | |
|---|---|---|---|
| Candlewood Suites Olympia - Lacey | 360-491-1698 | 4440 3rd Avenue Southeast   Lacey WA | 1+ |
| La Quinta Inn Olympia - Lacey | 360-412-1200 | 4704 Park Center Ave Northeast   Lacey WA | 3+ |
| Quality Inn & Suites Lacey | 360-493-1991 | 120 College Street Southeast   Lacey WA | 1+ |
| Best Western Plus Lacey Inn & Suites | 360-456-5655 | 8326 Quinault Drive North East   Olympia WA | 1+ |
| Best Western Tumwater Inn | 360-956-1235 | 5188 Capitol Blvd Se   Olympia WA | 1+ |
| Quality Inn Olympia | 360-943-4710 | 1211 Quince Street Southeast   Olympia WA | 1+ |
| Comfort Inn Conference Center Tumwater - Olympia | 360-352-0691 | 1620 74th Ave. Sw   Tumwater WA | 1+ |
| Extended Stay America - Olympia - Tumwater | 360-754-6063 | 1675 Mottman Road Sw   Tumwater WA | 1+ |

## Shelton

| | | | |
|---|---|---|---|
| Super 8 Shelton | 360-426-1654 | 2943 Northview Circle   Shelton WA | 1+ |

## Sequim

| | | | |
|---|---|---|---|
| Econo Lodge Sequim | 360-683-7113 | 801 E Washington St   Sequim WA | 1+ |

| | | | |
|---|---|---|---|
| Staypineapple At University Inn | 206-632-5055 | 4140 Roosevelt Way Northeast   Sequim WA | 1+ |
| **Port Angeles** | | | |
| Days Inn Port Angeles | 360-452-4015 | 1510 E Front St   Port Angeles WA | 1+ |
| Quality Inn Uptown | 360-457-9434 | 101 East 2nd Street   Port Angeles WA | 1+ |
| Red Lion Hotel Port Angeles | 360-452-9215 | 221 North Lincoln Street   Port Angeles WA | 2 |
| **Forks** | | | |
| Kalaloch Lodge | 360-962-2271 | 157151 Highway 101   Forks WA | 3+ |
| **Hoquiam** | | | |
| Econo Lodge Inn & Suites Hoquiam | 360-532-8161 | 910 Simpson Avenue   Hoquiam WA | 1+ |
| **Aberdeen** | | | |
| Travelodge Aberdeen | 360-532-5210 | 521 W Wishkah Street   Aberdeen WA | 3+ |

# Oregon Listings  (Highway 101)

Dogs per Room

| | | | |
|---|---|---|---|
| **Astoria** | | | |
| Best Western Lincoln Inn | 503-325-2205 | 555 Hamburg Avenue   Astoria OR | 1+ |
| Holiday Inn Express Hotel & Suites Astoria | 503-325-6222 | 204 West Marine Drive   Astoria OR | 1+ |
| **Seaside** | | | |
| Best Western Ocean View Resort | 503-738-3334 | 414 North Prom   Seaside OR | 1+ |
| Comfort Inn & Suites By Seaside Convention Center/boardwalk | 503-738-3011 | 545 Broadway Avenue   Seaside OR | 1+ |
| Holiday Inn Express Seaside-convention Center | 503-717-8000 | 34 North Holladay Drive   Seaside OR | 1+ |
| Inn At Seaside | 503-738-9581 | 441 Second Avenue   Seaside OR | 3+ |
| Sandy Cove Inn | 503-738-7473 | 241 Avenue U   Seaside OR | 2 |
| **Cannon Beach** | | | |
| Inn At Cannon Beach | 503-436-9085 | 3215 South Hemlock Street   Cannon Beach OR | 2 |
| Surfsand Resort | 503-436-2274 | 148 West Gower   Cannon Beach OR | 3+ |
| The Ocean Lodge | 503-436-2241 | 2864 South Pacific Street   Cannon Beach OR | 2 |
| **Lincoln City** | | | |
| Comfort Inn & Suites Lincoln City | 541-994-8155 | 136 Northeast Highway 101   Lincoln City OR | 1+ |
| **Newport** | | | |
| Econo Lodge Newport | 541-265-7723 | 606 Sw Coast Hwy 101   Newport OR | 1+ |
| Hallmark Resort - Newport | 541-265-2600 | 744 Sw Elizabeth Street   Newport OR | 3+ |
| Hallmark Resort - Newport | 541-265-2600 | 744 Sw Elizabeth Street   Newport OR | 3+ |
| La Quinta Inn & Suites Newport | 541-867-7727 | 45 Southeast 32nd Street   Newport OR | 2 |
| **Yachats** | | | |
| Fireside Motel | 541-547-3636 | 1881 Hwy 101 North   Yachats OR | 1+ |
| **Florence** | | | |
| Best Western Pier Point Inn | 541-997-7191 | 85625 Highway 101   Florence OR | 1+ |
| **Reedsport** | | | |
| Economy Inn | 541-271-3671 | 1593 Highway 101   Reedsport OR | 2 |
| Loon Lake Lodge and RV Resort | 541-599-2244 | 9011 Loon Lake Rd   Reedsport OR | 1+ |

## North Bend

| | | | |
|---|---|---|---|
| Quality Inn & Suites At Coos Bay | 541-756-3191 | 1503 Virginia Avenue   North Bend OR | 1+ |

## Coos Bay

| | | | |
|---|---|---|---|
| Best Western Plus Holiday Hotel | 541-269-5111 | 411 North Bayshore Drive   Coos Bay OR | 1+ |
| Red Lion Hotel Coos Bay | 541-267-4141 | 1313 North Bayshore Drive   Coos Bay OR | 2 |
| Super 8 Coos Bay/north Bend | 541-808-0704 | 1001 North Bayshore Drive   Coos Bay OR | 1+ |

# California Listings  (Highway 101)          Dogs per Room

## Crescent City

| | | | |
|---|---|---|---|
| Quality Inn & Suites Redwood Coast | 707-464-3885 | 100 Walton Street   Crescent City CA | 1+ |
| Super 8 Crescent City | 707-464-4111 | 685 Redwood Highway   Crescent City CA | 1+ |

## Arcata

| | | | |
|---|---|---|---|
| Best Western Arcata Inn | 707-826-0313 | 4827 Valley West Blvd.   Arcata CA | 1+ |
| Ramada Arcata | 707-822-0409 | 3535 Janes Road   Arcata CA | 1+ |
| Red Roof Inn Arcata | 707-822-4861 | 4975 Valley West Boulevard   Arcata CA | 1+ |
| Super 8 Arcata | 707-822-8888 | 4887 Valley West Boulevard   Arcata CA | 1+ |

## Eureka

| | | | |
|---|---|---|---|
| Carter House Inns | 707-444-8062 | 301 L Street   Eureka CA | 1+ |
| Discovery Inn - Eureka | 707-441-8442 | 2832 Broadway Street   Eureka CA | 2 |
| Laguna Inn | 707-443-8041 | 1630 4th St   Eureka CA | 1+ |
| Quality Inn Eureka | 707-443-1601 | 1209 Fourth Street   Eureka CA | 1+ |

## Fortuna

| | | | |
|---|---|---|---|
| Best Western Country Inn Fortuna | 707-725-6822 | 2025 Riverwalk Drive   Fortuna CA | 1+ |
| The Redwood Fortuna Riverwalk Hotel | 707-725-5500 | 1859 Alamar Way   Fortuna CA | 1+ |

## Ukiah

| | | | |
|---|---|---|---|
| Best Western Orchard Inn | 707-462-1514 | 555 South Orchard Avenue   Ukiah CA | 1+ |
| Comfort Inn & Suites Ukiah | 707-462-3442 | 1220 Airport Park Blvd   Ukiah CA | 1+ |
| Days Inn Ukiah/gateway To Redwoods Wine Country | 707-462-7584 | 950 North State Street   Ukiah CA | 1+ |
| Quality Inn Ukiah | 707-462-2906 | 1050 South State St   Ukiah CA | 1+ |
| Super 8 Ukiah | 707-468-8181 | 693 South Orchard Avenue   Ukiah CA | 1+ |

## Marin - North Bay

| | | | |
|---|---|---|---|
| Inn Marin And Suites An Ascend Hotel Collection Member | 415-883-5952 | 250 Entrada Drive   Novato CA | 3+ |
| Sheraton Sonoma County Petaluma | 707-283-2888 | 745 Baywood Drive   Petaluma CA | 3+ |

## San Francisco

| | | | |
|---|---|---|---|
| Argonaut Hotel | 415-563-0800 | 495 Jefferson Street   San Francisco CA | 3+ |
| Hotel Diva San Francisco | 800-553-1900 | 440 Geary Street   San Francisco CA | 1 |
| Hotel Union Square San Francisco | 800-553-1900 | 114 Powell Street   San Francisco CA | 1 |
| Hotel Zoe Fishermans Wharf: A Noble House Hotel | 415-561-1100 | 425 North Point Street   San Francisco CA | 3+ |
| San Francisco At The Presidio Travelodge | 415-931-8581 | 2755 Lombard Street   San Francisco CA | 1+ |

## Palo Alto - Peninsula

| | | | |
|---|---|---|---|
| Doubletree Hotel San Francisco Airport | 650-344-5500 | 835 Airport Boulevard  Burlingame CA | 2 |
| Embassy Suites By Hilton San Francisco Airport Waterfront | 650-342-4600 | 150 Anza Boulevard  Burlingame CA | 1+ |
| Hilton San Francisco Airport Bayfront | 650-340-8500 | 600 Airport Blvd  Burlingame CA | 1+ |
| San Francisco Airport Marriott Waterfront | 650-692-9100 | 1800 Old Bayshore Hwy  Burlingame CA | 1+ |
| Westin San Francisco Airport | 650-692-3500 | 1 Old Bayshore Highway  Millbrae CA | 3+ |
| Global Luxury Suites At Downtown Mountain View | 650-961-0220 | 1720 El Camino Real  Mountain View CA | 2 |
| Garden Court Hotel | 650-322-9000 | 520 Cowper Street  Palo Alto CA | 2 |
| Sheraton Palo Alto Hotel | 650-328-2800 | 625 El Camino Real  Palo Alto CA | 2 |
| Westin Palo Alto | 650-321-4422 | 675 El Camino Real  Palo Alto CA | 2 |
| Pullman San Francisco Bay | 650-598-9000 | 223 Twin Dolphin Drive  Redwood City CA | 2 |
| Towneplace Suites Redwood City Redwood Shores | 650-593-4100 | 1000 Twin Dolphin Drive  Redwood City CA | 1+ |
| Embassy Suites Hotel San Francisco-airport South San Fran. | 650-589-3400 | 250 Gateway Blvd  South San Francisco CA | 1+ |
| Residence Inn San Francisco Airport Oyster Point Waterfront | 650-837-9000 | 1350 Veterns Boulevard  South San Francisco CA | 1+ |

## San Jose

| | | | |
|---|---|---|---|
| Doubletree By Hilton San Jose | 408-453-4000 | 2050 Gateway Place  San Jose CA | 3+ |
| Homewood Suites By Hilton San Jose Airport-silicon Valley | 408-428-9900 | 10 West Trimble Road  San Jose CA | 1+ |
| La Quinta Inn San Jose Airport | 408-435-8800 | 2585 Seaboard Avenue  San Jose CA | 2 |
| Residence Inn By Marriott San Jose South | 408-226-7676 | 6111 San Ignacio Avenue  San Jose CA | 1+ |
| Hilton Santa Clara | 408-330-0001 | 4949 Great America Parkway  Santa Clara CA | 1+ |
| Hotel E Real | 408-241-0771 | 3580 El Camino Real  Santa Clara CA | 1+ |
| Residence Inn Silicon Valley I | 408-720-1000 | 750 Lakeway Drive  Sunnyvale CA | 1+ |
| Sheraton Sunnyvale Hotel | 408-745-6000 | 1100 North Mathilda Ave  Sunnyvale CA | 2 |

## Salinas

| | | | |
|---|---|---|---|
| Residence Inn By Marriott Salinas Monterey | 831-775-0410 | 17215 El Rancho Way  Salinas CA | 1+ |

## San Luis Obispo

| | | | |
|---|---|---|---|
| La Quinta Inn & Suites Paso Robles | 805-239-3004 | 2615 Buena Vista Drive  Paso Robles CA | 3+ |
| Oxford Suites Pismo Beach | 805-773-3773 | 651 Five Cities Drive  Pismo Beach CA | 2 |
| Sands Inn & Suites | 805-544-0500 | 1930 Monterey Street  San Luis Obispo CA | 3+ |
| Vagabond Inn San Luis Obispo | 805-544-4710 | 210 Madonna Road  San Luis Obispo CA | 3+ |

## Santa Maria

| | | | |
|---|---|---|---|
| Best Western Plus Big America | 805-922-5200 | 1725 North Broadway  Santa Maria CA | 1+ |
| Candlewood Suites Santa Maria | 805-928-4155 | 2079 N. Roemer Court  Santa Maria CA | 1+ |
| Holiday Inn Hotel & Suites Santa Maria | 805-928-6000 | 2100 North Broadway  Santa Maria CA | 1+ |

## Solvang

| | | | |
|---|---|---|---|
| Quality Inn Santa Ynez Valley | 805-688-0022 | 630 Avenue Of The Flags  Buellton CA | 1+ |
| Quality Inn Santa Ynez Valley | 805-688-0022 | 630 Avenue Of The Flags  Buellton CA | 2 |
| Santa Ynez Valley Marriott | 805-688-1000 | 555 Mcmurray Road  Buellton CA | 1+ |
| Royal Copenhagen Inn | 800-624-6604 | 1579 Mission Drive  Solvang CA | 3+ |

### Santa Barbara

| | | | |
|---|---|---|---|
| Holiday Inn Express Hotel & Suites Carpinteria | 805-566-9499 | 5606 Carpinteria Avenue   Carpinteria CA | 1+ |
| Kimpton Goodland | 805-964-6241 | 5650 Calle Real   Goleta CA | 1+ |
| Best Western Beachside Inn | 805 965-6556 | 336 West Cabrillo Boulevard   Santa Barbara CA | 1+ |
| Casa Del Mar Inn - Bed And Breakfast | 805-963-4418 | 18 Bath Street   Santa Barbara CA | 3+ |
| Extended Stay America - Santa Barbara - Calle Real | 805-692-1882 | 4870 Calle Real   Santa Barbara CA | 1+ |
| Kimpton Canary Hotel | 805-884-0300 | 31 West Carrillo Street   Santa Barbara CA | 1+ |
| La Quinta Inn & Suites Santa Barbara Downtown | 805-966-0807 | 1601 State Street   Santa Barbara CA | 1+ |

### Ventura - Oxnard

| | | | |
|---|---|---|---|
| Best Western Camarillo Inn | 805-987-4991 | 295 E Daily Dr   Camarillo CA | 1+ |
| Residence Inn Camarillo | 805-388-7997 | 2912 Petit Street   Camarillo CA | 1+ |
| Best Western Oxnard Inn | 805-483-9581 | 1156 South Oxnard Blvd.  Oxnard CA | 1+ |
| Residence Inn By Marriott Oxnard River Ridge | 805-278-2200 | 2101 W Vineyard Ave   Oxnard CA | 1+ |
| Vagabond Inn Oxnard | 805-983-0251 | 1245 North Oxnard Boulevard   Oxnard CA | 2 |
| Crowne Plaza Ventura | 805-648-2100 | 450 East Harbor Boulevard   Ventura CA | 1+ |
| Four Points By Sheraton Ventura Harbor Resort | 805-658-1212 | 1050 Schooner Drive   Ventura CA | 3+ |
| Holiday Inn Express Hotel & Suites Ventura Harbor | 805-856-9533 | 1080 Navigator Drive   Ventura CA | 1+ |
| La Quinta Inn Ventura | 805-658-6200 | 5818 Valentine Road   Ventura CA | 3+ |
| Marriott Ventura Beach | 805-643-6000 | 2055 East Harbor Boulevard   Ventura CA | 1+ |
| Vagabond Inn Ventura | 805-648-5371 | 756 East Thompson Boulevard   Ventura CA | 2 |

### Thousand Oaks

| | | | |
|---|---|---|---|
| La Quinta Inn & Suites Thousand Oaks Newbury Park | 805-499-5910 | 1320 Newbury Road   Thousand Oaks CA | 2 |
| Towneplace Suites Thousand Oaks Ventura County | 805-499-3111 | 1712 Newbury Road   Thousand Oaks CA | 1+ |

### San Fernando Valley

| | | | |
|---|---|---|---|
| Sheraton Agoura Hills Hotel | 818-707-1220 | 30100 Agoura Road   Agoura Hills CA | 3+ |
| Residence Inn Los Angeles Westlake Village | 818-707-4411 | 30950 Russell Ranch Road   Westlake Village CA | 1+ |
| Hilton Woodland Hills | 818-595-1000 | 6360 Canoga Ave   Woodland Hills CA | 1+ |

# Interstate 15 Accommodation Listings

# Montana Listings  (Interstate 15)                    Dogs per Room

### Shelby

| | | | |
|---|---|---|---|
| Comfort Inn Shelby | 406-434-2212 | 455 Mckinley   Shelby MT | 1+ |

### Conrad

| | | | |
|---|---|---|---|
| Super 8 Conrad | 406-278-7676 | 215 North Main Street   Conrad MT | 1+ |

### Great Falls

| | | | |
|---|---|---|---|
| Hampton Inn Great Falls Mt | 406-453-2675 | 2301 14th Street Sw   Great Falls MT | 1+ |
| La Quinta Inn & Suites Great Falls | 406-761-2600 | 600 River Drive South   Great Falls MT | 3+ |

| | | | |
|---|---|---|---|
| Super 8 Great Falls Mt | 406-727-7600 | 1214 13th Street South   Great Falls MT | 1+ |
| **Helena** | | | |
| Howard Johnson Helena | 406-443-2300 | 2101 East 11th Avenue   Helena MT | 1+ |
| Radisson Colonial Hotel Helena | 406-443-2100 | 2301 Colonial Drive   Helena MT | 3+ |
| Wingate By Wyndham - Helena | 406-449-3000 | 2007 North Oakes   Helena MT | 1+ |
| Wingate By Wyndham - Helena | 406-449-3000 | 2007 North Oakes   Helena MT | 1+ |
| **Dillon** | | | |
| Best Western Paradise Inn | 406-683-4214 | 650 North Montana Street   Dillon MT | 1+ |
| Comfort Inn Dillon | 406-683-6831 | 450 North Interchange   Dillon MT | 1+ |
| Super 8 Dillon | 406-683-4288 | 550 North Montana Street   Dillon MT | 1+ |

# Idaho Listings   (Interstate 15)

Dogs per Room

| | | | |
|---|---|---|---|
| **Idaho Falls** | | | |
| Rodeway Inn Idaho Falls | 208-523-8000 | 525 River Parkway   Idaho Falls ID | 2 |
| **Blackfoot** | | | |
| Best Western Blackfoot Inn | 208-785-4144 | 750 Jensen Grove Drive   Blackfoot ID | 1+ |
| Super 8 Blackfoot | 208-785-9333 | 1279 Parkway Drive   Blackfoot ID | 1+ |
| **Pocatello** | | | |
| Towneplace Suites By Marriott Pocatello | 208-478-7000 | 2376 Via Caporatti Drive   Pocatello ID | 1+ |

# Utah Listings   (Interstate 15)

Dogs per Room

| | | | |
|---|---|---|---|
| **Tremonton** | | | |
| Hampton Inn Tremonton | 435-257-6000 | 2145 West Main Street   Tremonton UT | 1+ |
| **Ogden** | | | |
| Hampton Inn Salt Lake City/layton | 801-775-8800 | 1700 N Woodland Park Dr   Layton UT | 1+ |
| La Quinta Inn & Suites Salt Lake City Layton | 801-776-6700 | 1965 North 1200 West   Layton UT | 3+ |
| Towneplace Suites Salt Lake City Layton | 801-779-2422 | 1743 Woodland Park Blvd   Layton UT | 1+ |
| Comfort Inn Ogden | 801-737-5660 | 1776 West 2550 North   Ogden UT | 1+ |
| Comfort Suites Ogden | 801-621-2545 | 2250 South 1200 West   Ogden UT | 1+ |
| Days Inn Ogden | 801-399-5671 | 3306 Washington Blvd   Ogden UT | 1+ |
| Holiday Inn Express Hotel And Suites Ogden | 801-392-5000 | 2245 South 1200 West   Ogden UT | 1+ |
| Sleep Inn Ogden | 801-731-6500 | 1155 South 1700 West   Ogden UT | 1+ |
| **Clearfield** | | | |
| Days Inn Clearfield | 801-825-8000 | 572 North Main Street   Clearfield UT | 1+ |
| **Salt Lake City** | | | |
| Ramada Inn Draper | 801-571-1122 | 12605 South Minuteman Drive   Draper UT | 1+ |
| Kimpton Hotel Monaco Salt Lake City | 877-294-9710 | 15 West 200 South   Salt Lake City UT | 3+ |
| Residence Inn By Marriott Salt Lake City Downtown | 801-355-3300 | 285 W. Broadway 300 South   Salt Lake City UT | 1+ |
| Sheraton Salt Lake City Hotel | 801-401-2000 | 150 West 500 South   Salt Lake City UT | 3+ |
| Residence Inn Salt Lake City - Sandy | 801-561-5005 | 270 West 10000 South   Sandy UT | 1+ |

| | | | | |
|---|---|---|---|---|
| Hampton Inn Salt Lake City-north | 801-296-1211 | 2393 South 800 West | Woods Cross UT | 1+ |

**Midvale**

| | | | | |
|---|---|---|---|---|
| La Quinta Inn Salt Lake City Midvale | 801-566-3291 | 7231 South Catalpa Street | Midvale UT | 3+ |

**Orem**

| | | | | |
|---|---|---|---|---|
| La Quinta Inn & Suites North Orem | 801-235-9555 | 1100 West 780 North | Orem UT | 3+ |
| La Quinta Inn & Suites Orem University Parkway | 801-226-0440 | 521 West University Parkway | Orem UT | 3+ |
| Towneplace Suites By Marriott Provo Orem | 801-225-4477 | 873 North 1200 West | Orem UT | 1+ |

**Provo**

| | | | | |
|---|---|---|---|---|
| Baymont Inn & Suites Provo River | 801-373-7044 | 2230 North University Parkway | Provo UT | 1+ |
| Days Inn Provo | 801-375-8600 | 1675 North Freedom Blvd | Provo UT | 1+ |
| Hampton Inn Provo | 801-377-6396 | 1511 South 40 East | Provo UT | 1+ |
| Ramada Provo | 801-374-9750 | 1460 South University Avenue | Provo UT | 2 |
| Sleep Inn Provo | 801-377-6597 | 1505 South 4o East | Provo UT | 1+ |
| Super 8 Motel Provo Byu Orem | 801-374-6020 | 1555 North Canyon Road | Provo UT | 1+ |

**Springville**

| | | | | |
|---|---|---|---|---|
| Best Western Mountain View Inn | 8014893641 | 1455 N 1750 W | Springville UT | 1+ |

**Scipio**

| | | | | |
|---|---|---|---|---|
| Scipio Hotel | 435-758-9188 | 230 West 400 North | Scipio UT | 1+ |

**Fillmore**

| | | | | |
|---|---|---|---|---|
| Best Western Paradise Inn And Resort | 435-743-6895 | 905 N Main Street | Fillmore UT | 1+ |
| Comfort Inn & Suites Fillmore | 435-743-4334 | 940 South Hwy 99 | Fillmore UT | 1+ |

**Nephi**

| | | | | |
|---|---|---|---|---|
| Best Western Paradise Inn Of Nephi | 435-623-0624 | 1025 S Main Street | Nephi UT | 1+ |
| Super 8 Nephi | 435-623-0888 | 1901 South Main Street | Nephi UT | 1+ |

**Beaver**

| | | | | |
|---|---|---|---|---|
| Best Western Paradise Inn | 435-438-2455 | 1451 North 300 West | Beaver UT | 1+ |

**Washington**

| | | | | |
|---|---|---|---|---|
| Holiday Inn Express Hotel & Suites Washington-north St. George | 435-986-1313 | 2450 N Town Center Drive | Washington UT | 1+ |

**St George**

| | | | | |
|---|---|---|---|---|
| Howard Johnson Inn-saint George | 435-628-8000 | 1040 South Main Street | St George UT | 1+ |
| La Quinta Inn & Suites St. George | 435-674-2664 | 91 East 2680 South | St George UT | 2 |
| Towneplace Suites By Marriott St. George | 455-986-9955 | 251 South 1470 East | St George UT | 1+ |

# Nevada Listings  (Interstate 15)    Dogs per Room

**Mesquite**

| | | | | |
|---|---|---|---|---|
| Best Western Mesquite Inn | 702-346-7444 | 390 N Sandhill Boulevard | Mesquite NV | 1+ |

**Las Vegas**

| | | | | |
|---|---|---|---|---|
| Americas Best Value Inn | 702-795-3311 | 167 East Tropicana Avenue | Las Vegas NV | 3+ |
| Baymont Inn And Suites Airport South Las Vegas | 702-273-2500 | 55 East Robindale Road | Las Vegas NV | 1+ |

| | | | |
|---|---|---|---|
| Delano Las Vegas At Mandalay Bay | 702-632-7777 | 3940 Las Vegas Blvd South   Las Vegas NV | 2 |
| Element Las Vegas Summerlin | 702-589-2000 | 10555 Discovery Drive   Las Vegas NV | 3+ |
| Fortune Hotel & Suites | 702-732-9100 | 325 East Flamingo Road   Las Vegas NV | 1+ |
| La Quinta Inn & Suites Las Vegas Airport North Convention Center | 702-796-9000 | 3970 Paradise Road   Las Vegas NV | 2 |
| La Quinta Inn Las Vegas Nellis | 702-632-0229 | 4288 North Nellis Boulevard   Las Vegas NV | 3+ |
| Residence Inn By Marriott Las Vegas Convention Center | 702-796-9300 | 3225 Paradise Road   Las Vegas NV | 1+ |
| Residence Inn By Marriott Las Vegas Hughes Center | 702-650-0040 | 370 Hughes Center Drive   Las Vegas NV | 1+ |
| Residence Inn Las Vegas South | 702-795-7378 | 5875 Dean Martin Drive   Las Vegas NV | 1+ |
| Shalimar Hotel Of Las Vegas | 702-388-0301 | 1401 South Las Vegas Boulevard   Las Vegas NV | 1+ |
| The Platinum Hotel | 702-365-5000 | 211 East Flamingo Road   Las Vegas NV | 2 |
| Travelodge Las Vegas | 702-735-4222 | 2830 Las Vegas Boulevard South   Las Vegas NV | 1+ |
| Trump International Hotel Las Vegas | 702-982-0000 | 2000 Fashion Show Drive   Las Vegas NV | 2 |
| Westin Las Vegas Hotel & Spa | 702-836-5900 | 160 East Flamingo Road   Las Vegas NV | 2 |
| Lucky Club Casino And Hotel | 702-399-3297 | 3227 Civic Center Drive   North Las Vegas NV | 2 |

# California Listings   (Interstate 15)

Dogs per Room

| Barstow | | | |
|---|---|---|---|
| Baymont Inn And Suites Barstow Historic Route 66 | 760-256-1300 | 1861 W. Main St.   Barstow CA | 1+ |
| Best Western Desert Villa Inn | 760-256-1781 | 1984 East Main Street   Barstow CA | 1+ |
| Comfort Suites Barstow | 760-253-3600 | 2571 Fisher Blvd.   Barstow CA | 1+ |
| Days Inn South Lenwood | 760-253-2121 | 2551 Commerce Parkway   Barstow CA | 1+ |
| Econo Lodge On Historic Route 66 | 760-256-2133 | 1230 E Main St   Barstow CA | 1+ |
| Hampton Inn & Suites Barstow | 760-253-2600 | 2710 Lenwood Road   Barstow CA | 1+ |
| Holiday Inn Express Hotel & Suites Barstow | 760-253-9200 | 2700 Lenwood Road   Barstow CA | 1+ |
| Quality Inn On Historic Route 66 | 760-256-6891 | 1520 E. Main St.   Barstow CA | 1+ |
| Ramada Barstow | 760-256-5673 | 1511 East Main Street   Barstow CA | 1+ |
| Super 8 Barstow | 760-256-8443 | 170 Coolwater Lane   Barstow CA | 1+ |
| Travelodge Barstow | 760-256-8931 | 1630 E Main St   Barstow CA | 1+ |
| Victorville | | | |
| Americas Best Value Inn - Hesperia | 760-949-3231 | 12033 Oakwood Avenue   Hesperia CA | 1+ |
| Econo Lodge Hesperia | 760-949-1515 | 11976 Mariposa Rd   Hesperia CA | 1+ |
| La Quinta Inn And Suites Hesperia Victorville | 760-949-9900 | 12000 Mariposa Road   Hesperia CA | 2 |
| Green Tree Inn And Extended Stay Suites | 760-245-3461 | 14173 Green Tree Boulevard   Victorville CA | 1+ |
| Red Roof Inn Victorville | 760-241-1577 | 13409 Mariposa Road   Victorville CA | 1+ |
| Travelodge Victorville | 760-241-7200 | 12175 Mariposa Road   Victorville CA | 1+ |
| Temecula | | | |
| Extended Stay America - Temecula - Wine Country | 951-587-8881 | 27622 Jefferson Avenue   Temecula CA | 1+ |
| La Quinta Inn & Suites Temecula | 951-296-1003 | 27330 Jefferson Avenue   Temecula CA | 3+ |
| Quality Inn Temecula Valley Wine Country | 951-296-3788 | 27338 Jefferson Avenue   Temecula CA | 1+ |

| San Diego I-15 Corridor | | | |
|---|---|---|---|
| Tuscany Hills Retreat | 760-751-8800 | 29850 Circle R Way   Escondido CA | 2 |
| Pala Mesa Golf Resort | 760-728-5881 | 2001 Old Highway 395   Fallbrook CA | 2 |
| **San Diego County North** | | | |
| Ramada Poway | 858-748-7311 | 12448 Poway Road   Poway CA | 1+ |
| **San Diego** | | | |
| La Quinta Inn San Diego Scripps Poway | 858-484-8800 | 10185 Paseo Montril   San Diego CA | 2 |
| Residence Inn By Marriott Rancho Bernardo / Scripps Poway | 858-635-5724 | 12011 Scripps Highland Drive   San Diego CA | 1+ |
| Residence Inn Rancho Bernardo Carmel Mountain | 858-673-1900 | 11002 Rancho Carmel Drive   San Diego CA | 1+ |

# Interstate 80 Accommodation Listings

## California Listings (Interstate 80)

Dogs per Room

| San Francisco | | | |
|---|---|---|---|
| Harbor Court Hotel | 415-882-1300 | 165 Steuart St   San Francisco CA | 3+ |
| Hilton San Francisco | 415-771-1400 | 333 Ofarrell Street   San Francisco CA | 1+ |
| Hilton San Francisco Financial District | 415-433-6600 | 750 Kearny Street   San Francisco CA | 1+ |
| Hotel Triton | 415-394-0500 | 342 Grant Ave   San Francisco CA | 3+ |
| Hotel Zelos San Francisco | 415-348-1111 | 12 Fourth Street   San Francisco CA | 3+ |
| Kensington Park Hotel | 800-553-9100 | 450 Post Street   San Francisco CA | 1 |
| Kimpton Sir Francis Drake Hotel | 415-392-7755 | 450 Powell Street   San Francisco CA | 3+ |
| Le Meridien San Francisco | 415-296-2900 | 333 Battery Street   San Francisco CA | 3+ |
| Palace Hotel A Luxury Collection Hotel San Francisco | 415-512-1111 | 2 New Montgomery Street   San Francisco CA | 1 |
| Park Central San Francisco Union Square A Starwood Hotel | 415-974-6400 | 50 Third Street   San Francisco CA | 1 |
| San Francisco Marriott Fisherman's Wharf | 415-775-7555 | 1250 Columbus Avenue   San Francisco CA | 1+ |
| Serrano Hotel | 415-885-2500 | 405 Taylor Street   San Francisco CA | 3+ |
| St. Regis Hotel San Francisco | 415-284-4000 | 125 3rd Street   San Francisco CA | 2 |
| Stanford Court San Francisco | 415-989-3500 | 905 California Street   San Francisco CA | 1+ |
| The Marker San Francisco A Joie De Vivre Hotel | 415-292-0100 | 501 Geary Street   San Francisco CA | 3+ |
| The Ritz-carlton San Francisco | 415-296-7465 | 600 Stockton Street At California Street   San Francisco CA | 2 |
| W San Francisco | 415-777-5300 | 181 Third Street   San Francisco CA | 1 |
| **Vallejo** | | | |
| Holiday Inn Express And Suites Napa Valley-american Canyon | +17-075-5281 | 5001 Main Street   American Canyon CA | 1+ |
| Courtyard By Marriott Vallejo Napa Valley | 707-644-1200 | 1000 Fairgrounds Drive   Vallejo CA | 1+ |
| Ramada Inn Vallejo / Napa Valley Area | 707-643-2700 | 1000 Admiral Callaghan Lane   Vallejo CA | 1+ |
| **Vacaville** | | | |
| Best Western Heritage Inn | 707-448-8453 | 1420 E Monte Vista Ave   Vacaville CA | 1+ |

| | | | |
|---|---|---|---|
| Extended Stay America - Sacramento - Vacaville | 707-469-1371 | 799 Orange Drive  Vacaville CA | 1+ |
| Hampton Inn & Suites Vacaville Ca | 707-469-6200 | 800 Mason Street  Vacaville CA | 1+ |
| Quality Inn & Suites Vacaville | 707-446-8888 | 1050 Orange Drive  Vacaville CA | 1+ |
| Residence Inn By Marriott Vacaville | 707-469-0300 | 360 Orange Drive  Vacaville CA | 1+ |
| Super 8 Vacaville | 707-449-8884 | 101 Allison Court  Vacaville CA | 1+ |

**Dixon**

| | | | |
|---|---|---|---|
| Best Western Plus Inn Dixon | 707-678-1400 | 1345 Commercial Way  Dixon CA | 1+ |

**Davis**

| | | | |
|---|---|---|---|
| Best Western University Lodge | 530-756-7890 | 123 B Street  Davis CA | 1+ |
| Econo Lodge Davis | 530-756-1040 | 221 D Street  Davis CA | 1+ |
| La Quinta Inn & Suites Davis | 530-758-2600 | 1771 Research Park Drive  Davis CA | 1+ |

**Sacramento**

| | | | |
|---|---|---|---|
| Residence Inn Roseville | 916-772-5500 | 1930 Taylor Road  Roseville CA | 1+ |
| Doubletree By Hilton Sacramento | 916-929-8855 | 2001 Point West Way  Sacramento CA | 2 |
| La Quinta Inn Sacramento North | 916-348-0900 | 4604 Madison Avenue  Sacramento CA | 3+ |
| Residence Inn Sacramento Cal Expo | 916-920-9111 | 1530 Howe Ave  Sacramento CA | 1+ |
| Towneplace Suites By Marriott Sacramento Cal Expo | 916-920-5400 | 1784 Tribute Road  Sacramento CA | 1+ |
| Ramada Inn & Plaza Harbor Conference Center | 916-371-2100 | 1250 Halyard Drive  West Sacramento CA | 1+ |

# Nevada Listings  (Interstate 80)   Dogs per Room

**Reno**

| | | | |
|---|---|---|---|
| Ramada Reno Hotel & Casino | 775-786-5151 | 1000 East Sixth Street  Reno NV | 1+ |
| Western Village Inn And Casino | 800-648-1170 | 815 Nichols Boulevard  Sparks NV | 2 |

**Fernley**

| | | | |
|---|---|---|---|
| Best Western Fernley Inn | 775-575-6776 | 1405 Newlands Drive E  Fernley NV | 1+ |

**Winnemucca**

| | | | |
|---|---|---|---|
| Best Western Plus Gold Country Inn | 775-623-6999 | 921 West Winnemucca Boulevard  Winnemucca NV | 1+ |
| Country Hearth Inn Winnemucca | 775-623-3661 | 511 W Winnemucca Boulevard  Winnemucca NV | 1+ |
| Super 8 Winnemucca | 775-625-1818 | 1157 West Winnemucca Boulevard  Winnemucca NV | 1+ |
| Winnemucca Inn | 775-623-2565 | 741 West Winnemucca Boulevard  Winnemucca NV | 3+ |

**Battle Mountain**

| | | | |
|---|---|---|---|
| Super 8 Battle Mountain | 775-635-8808 | 825 Super 8 Dr.  Battle Mountain NV | 1+ |

**Elko**

| | | | |
|---|---|---|---|
| Best Western Elko Inn | 775-738-8787 | 1930 Idaho Street  Elko NV | 1+ |
| Quality Inn & Suites Elko | 775-777-8000 | 3320 East Idaho Street  Elko NV | 1+ |
| Red Lion Hotel And Casino Elko | 775-738-2111 | 2065 Idaho Street  Elko NV | 2 |
| Rodeway Inn Elko | 775-738-7152 | 736 Idaho Street  Elko NV | 1+ |
| Shilo Inn Elko | 775-738-5522 | 2401 Mountain City Highway  Elko NV | 2 |
| Super 8 Elko | 775-738-8488 | 1755 Idaho Street  Elko NV | 1+ |
| Travelodge Elko | 775-753-7747 | 1785 Idaho Street  Elko NV | 1+ |

## Wells

| | | | |
|---|---|---|---|
| Super 8 Wells | 775-752-3384 | Box 302 I-80 Exit 352  Wells NV | 1+ |

# Utah Listings  (Interstate 80)                    Dogs per Room

## Wendover

| | | | |
|---|---|---|---|
| Best Western Plus Wendover Inn | 435-665-2215 | 685 East Wendover Boulevard  Wendover UT | 1+ |
| Knights Inn Wendover | 435-665-7744 | 505 East Wendover Boulevard  Wendover UT | 1+ |

## Salt Lake City

| | | | |
|---|---|---|---|
| Doubletree By Hilton Hotel Salt Lake City Airport | 801-539-1515 | 5151 Wiley Post Way  Salt Lake City UT | 1+ |
| La Quinta Inn Salt Lake City Airport | 801-366-4444 | 4905 West Wiley Post Way  Salt Lake City UT | 3+ |
| Microtel Inn & Suites By Wyndham Salt Lake City Airport | 801-236-2800 | 61 North Tommy Thompson Road  Salt Lake City UT | 1+ |
| Ramada Salt Lake City | 801-486-2400 | 2455 South State Street  Salt Lake City UT | 1+ |
| Residence Inn By Marriott Salt Lake City Airport | 801-532-4101 | 4883 West Douglas Corrigan Way  Salt Lake City UT | 1+ |
| Super 8 Motel - Salt Lake City/airport | 801-533-8878 | 223 N. Jimmy Doolittle Rd.  Salt Lake City UT | 1+ |

## Park City

| | | | |
|---|---|---|---|
| Best Western Plus Landmark Inn & Pancake House | 435-649-7300 | 6560 North Landmark Drive  Park City UT | 1+ |
| Holiday Inn Express Hotel & Suites Park City | 435-658-1600 | 1501 West Ute Boulevard  Park City UT | 1+ |
| St. Regis Deer Valley | 435-940-5700 | 2300 Deer Valley Drive East  Park City UT | 1+ |
| The Gables Hotel | 435-655-3315 | 1335 Lowell Avenue, PO Box 905  Park City UT | 1+ |

82211590R00256

Made in the USA
Middletown, DE
01 August 2018